Scott Rothkopf

Whitney Museum of American Art, New York
Distributed by Yale University Press, New Haven and London

CONTENTS

Oral Histories

Essays

FOREWORD

Twenty years ago, when I was curator of the permanent collection at the Whitney, I was approached by the forward-thinking, free-spirited, nonconformist collector Norman Dubrow, who asked if the Museum would be interested in acquiring the work of a fantastic young painter. Norman, with his rollicking and breathless enthusiasm, barraged me with a litany of facts about Laura Owens: she had attended the Rhode Island School of Design; had recently graduated from the California Institute of the Arts; and, most important, her paintings were fresh, alive, and unlike anything he had seen before. Hearing Norman's boiling-point excitement and knowing his extraordinary ability to spot new talent—unencumbered by other people's prejudices—I of course paid attention.

He sent me a photograph of *Untitled* (1994, see p. 65) and, I must say, I wasn't sure what to make of it. It seemed slight, pretty, decorative—all pejorative terms when used to describe painting. Yet I was inexplicably intrigued. What was it? It was seemingly all things, bits of painterly information both applied and inscribed in various modes. My eyes leapt from element to element in an attempt to assemble visual and contextual coherence. The atomized forms were free-floating, as suggested by the cartoonlike cloud structure barely anchored to the rainbow-striped triangle in the lower left corner. Trying to connect the disparate, seemingly random parts was futile—but pleasurable. This was a painting without substance, and yet it was a *very* substantial painting.

At the time Owens made the painting, she was beginning to use appropriation, combining imagery from works by artists as dissimilar as British painter Fiona Rae; New York School painter Philip Guston; and Color Field painter Morris Louis. (While this is good to know, the magnetic experience of actually viewing the work far surpasses visual analysis of its sources.) I remember sharing the painting with my curatorial colleagues. Like me, they were fascinated by what they saw but knew little about her, her art, or what she was pursuing. Deciding to bring this work into the Museum's collection was an act of faith.

Indeed, historically, the role of the Whitney Museum is to show faith—in artists, in the creative process, and in risk-taking, accepting the potential for failure or, worse, ignominy. This is why the Whitney exists and matters. Even before the Museum was founded in 1930, Gertrude Vanderbilt Whitney hosted exhibitions and salons in her Greenwich Village studio. She supported and nurtured artists, providing the encouragement she had needed as a young woman in her own career. She understood that finding one's voice was an unpredictable, unassured, and vulnerable endeavor. She did not believe in orthodoxy; she presented exhibitions of divergent styles and tastes, figurative and abstract art alike. She also championed women artists at a time when most were excluded from academic circles. In the pre–Whitney Museum days, she presented one-person exhibitions of then unfamiliar artists such as Stuart Davis, Edward Hopper, John Sloan, and Joseph Stella. She also hosted exhibitions by significant artists such as Glenn O. Coleman, Andrew Dasburg, Katherine Schmidt, and Dorothy Varian, artists whose accomplishments would be largely unknown to the general public. And, unsurprisingly, there were many missed opportunities that were the result of choice or neglect.

With the founding of the Museum, however, the Whitney discontinued its lauded and historically important presentations of solo exhibitions until 1948. Although a well-intentioned effort made in the hope of resisting market pressures, this was regrettable for both the Whitney and artists. (The Museum's fears about the negative effects of "branding," promotion, and marketability, though, have undeniably come true.) Since that time, the solo exhibition has become a staple not only of the Whitney but also of the museum world at large.

The Whitney's mission to discern, select, and support salient artistic visions endures with great relevance today. While the attitude toward contemporary art—and to some degree the needs of artists—has shifted since Mrs. Whitney began her crusade on behalf of living American artists, the task of identifying critical, paradigm-shifting, and often disruptive visions is more urgent than ever. And it has tremendous art historical, cultural, social, and even political ramifications. In recent years, with more than two million artists working in the United States, this goal is far more difficult and daunting to accomplish.

The Whitney has long realized that it has a responsibility to artists of all generations: younger artists who need affirmation; mid-career artists who are worthy of continued support; and senior artists, some of whom are considered masters, as well as those who, late in life, are at last being acknowledged. The Whitney has responded to these commitments throughout its history with varying degrees of focus depending on the cultural climate and its own institutional leadership and curatorial vision. It is also important to recognize that the Museum has not always been responsive to marginalized artists and artists of color.

Since the opening of the Whitney on Gansevoort Street, increased gallery space has afforded greater exhibition opportunities. We have rededicated ourselves, in the spirit of Mrs. Whitney, to presenting artists of different backgrounds, genders, and styles, so that the Museum's exhibition program—and the collection bedrock upon which it rests—look more like the United States. We have also renewed our commitment to generational diversity. Our ability to support new artists had diminished in the years before our move downtown; following the closure of the Whitney's branch museums in the early 2000s, exposure for new voices had largely been limited to the Biennial. Since 2015, though, we have exhibited about a dozen solo projects and exhibitions by emerging artists (and many more in group exhibitions) through the efforts of a curatorial working group led by Christopher Y. Lew, our Nancy and Fred Poses Associate Curator. In the last few years we have also presented solo exhibitions and installations by senior artists. Some are well-known, such as Frank Stella, Michael Heizer, and Mary Heilmann. Others—like June Leaf, Carmen Herrera, and Cecil Taylor—have sometimes been obscured from view.

While historically the Whitney is perhaps most identified with emerging artists, its record of presenting mid-career surveys, especially beginning in the late 1960s, is one of the most distinguished aspects of the Museum's program. An impressive array of artists have had major mid-career presentations at the Whitney: from Donald Judd, Helen Frankenthaler, Robert Morris, James Rosenquist, Jo Baer, Richard Tuttle, Fred Eversley, Mark Di Suvero, Robert Irwin, Jasper Johns, Cy Twombly, Nam June Paik, and Ellsworth Kelly to Cindy Sherman, Elizabeth Murray, David Salle, Terry Winters, Richard Prince, Jean-Michel Basquiat, Mike Kelley, Nan Goldin, Keith Haring, Lorna Simpson, Roni Horn, and Glenn Ligon. For many, these were the first surveys or in-depth exposures of their work and often represented the defining exhibition for the artist as well as the public. In our new home downtown, the Whitney has presented mid-career projects by Laura Poitras and Andrea Fraser. Laura Owens, however, will have the first mid-career survey in this building.

It would be redundant for me to explicate why Owens has been chosen for this signal honor. Scott Rothkopf, the Whitney's Deputy Director for Programs and Nancy and Steve Crown Family Chief Curator, has made the case well in this impressive, complex, layered, amusing, and unconventional tome, as have Owens's mentors, teachers, curators, critics, colleagues, friends, and many others. Above all, the case for Owens is made by Owens herself in her paintings, as displayed in the exhibition.

A further word about the publication itself and the role of Whitney catalogues: In the early days, the Whitney's publications, like those of most museums, were scant, simple documents enumerating the works in the exhibition, without images, descriptions, or texts. By mid-century, though, the Museum's catalogues became more lavish, sophisticated, and comprehensive. Beginning in the 1970s, often in response to the needs of artists, the Whitney's catalogues became more collaborative. Accordingly, artists today are deeply engaged in their catalogue's conception and design. Thus, this publication is the brainchild of the artist and the curator—realized with the significant contributions of many others—and must be seen as coterminous with the exhibition itself.

This project would not have been possible without the crucial support of the Andy Warhol Foundation for the Visual Arts and the Whitney's National Committee. For their tremendous generosity, I must thank Nancy and Steve Crown; Candy and Michael Barasch; the Brown Foundation, Inc., of Houston; Mariel and Jack Cayre; Marcia Dunn and Jonathan Sobel; and Erin and Peter Friedland. The support of Fotene Demoulas and Tom Coté, Allison and Warren Kanders, Ashley Leeds and Christopher Harland, and anonymous donors was also vital to this endeavor, as was additional support from Rebecca and Martin Eisenberg, Susan and Leonard Feinstein, and endowment support from Sueyun and Gene Locks and Donna Perret Rosen and Benjamin M. Rosen. I am appreciative of Rosina Lee Yue and Bert A. Lies, Jr., whose endowment funded curatorial travel and research. In addition, this expansive and beautiful catalogue would not have been realized without generous assistance from Galerie Gisela Capitain, Cologne; Gavin Brown's enterprise, New York; and Sadie Coles HQ, London. I extend my great appreciation as well to the public institutions and private individuals who have graciously parted temporarily with works from their collections so that they may be included in the exhibition. It is a pleasure to work with other institutions that share our enthusiasm and regard for Owens's work, and I am grateful to Agustín Arteaga, Eugene McDermott Director, at the Dallas Museum of Art, and Philippe Vergne, director, at the Museum of Contemporary Art, Los Angeles. We are enormously grateful to the Kaleta A. Doolin Fund for Women Artists for making the exhibition possible in Dallas.

An unparalleled publication like this, and the exhibition it accompanies, can only come to fruition through a trusted relationship between artist and curator—a trust that is personal, professional, and part of the Whitney's historic ethos of putting the artist first. With this in mind, I offer my sincere congratulations to Scott Rothkopf and my profound gratitude to Laura Owens. For Laura to meet her commitments to her artmaking and her artist space 356 Mission while working on this project cross-country has been no easy feat—and I thank her for trusting in the Whitney and in the very process of creating the exhibition and book. It is this act of faith that has made for an important result.

Adam D. Weinberg
Alice Pratt Brown Director

INTRODUCTION
SCOTT ROTHKOPF

This book could use some explaining. When Laura Owens and I embarked on planning a Whitney survey of her paintings late in 2014, I assumed the show would be accompanied by a typical museum catalogue featuring a few scholarly essays and illustrations of her work. The following year Skira Rizzoli released a lavish monograph on her art, which took the form of my imagined catalogue and the wind out of my sails. With its insightful texts and ample reproductions, the tome proved both a boon to my research and an obstacle to my thinking. Now what kind of book could we possibly make? Eventually, as months ticked by and deadlines neared, a sense of hindrance gave way to liberation.

One thing you should know about Laura is that she likes a good adventure. At an early brainstorming session she produced *The Daring Book for Girls*, pilfered from her daughter Nova's shelf. We pored over this bestselling children's title, its pages bursting with a motley assortment of obscure facts and DIY crafts, all assembled to inspire curiosity and wonder. Something about the book's energy and aim squared nicely with Laura's aspirations for her art and also with our inchoate sense that whatever we published ought to be both a chronicle and a catalyst of artistic production—a kind of instruction manual or curriculum without a prescribed objective. Soon we were devising an improbable miscellany that wouldn't so much trace the arc of Laura's art as touch on related topics, from Victorian needlework to the invention of wallpaper. We traded ideas back and forth, some of which stuck, but after a few months our approach started to feel, well, too miscellaneous. So I headed out to LA to dig into Laura's archive in search of bedrock on which to ground the project.

Another thing you should know about Laura is that she's a pack rat. One by one, we raided more than a dozen plastic trunks stuffed with preparatory drawings and research materials, as well as shipping receipts and decades-old price lists still stamped with little red dots. There was also a trove of personal effects, such as childhood notebooks, fading faxes, snapshots from openings, and scads of valentines and birthday cards tenderly inscribed by her grandmother. As we sifted through the reams of information we began to realize that the contents of this archive could tell the story of Laura's life and art—and, importantly, the crosscurrents between them. For many artists such connections could seem tangential at best and superfluous at worst. Yet Laura's work has always been open to and guided by her personal life and artistic passions, inflected with a sense of excitement and discovery as much as one of frustration and failure. I wanted this unbridled spirit to guide our book, and Laura proved willing to put literally everything on the table. It takes a certain kind of courage and confidence to lay oneself so bare.

We envisioned a narrative that stretched from Laura's childhood home in Norwalk, Ohio, right up to the very show we were making—largely told, appropriately enough, through pictures. Aided by the invaluable insights of Laura's collaborator and fellow artist Asha Schechter we assembled a timeline of key moments that might structure the story. Some, particularly in the early years, have a strong biographical tilt. The opening pages, for instance, provide a taste of Laura's suburban Midwestern roots, which can feel utterly generic on the one hand yet pointed and prophetic on the other. She played high school tennis with bangs in the 1980s, sketched the Beatles, and painted a jangly abstraction crowned with an egg sunny-side up. Sound familiar? If so, that's because one could easily imagine the same motifs and palette cropping up in one of Laura's paintings decades later, just as a local newspaper article picturing her as a teenager actually did. Fast-forward to 1999 and this echt American milieu is warmly evoked in an exchange between the artist and a German gallery assistant delicately inquiring after Laura's recipe for a mysterious homegrown delicacy commonly known as Rice Krispies Treats. Yet another vignette in this bildungsroman covers Laura's grad school years at CalArts. The period comes to life through images of paintings, diary entries, report cards, photos of fellow students, and even a touching plea to her advisor Charles Gaines for more financial support. Political commitments surface in ephemera related to the safe-sex advocacy group REACH LA and later reappear in correspondence promoting Howard Dean's failed presidential bid and deploring Donald Trump's successful one. Sometimes the paintings grow dark with the epoch.

The bulk of this book's sections delve deeply into individual exhibitions. Not all of Laura's shows are covered, but paradigmatic cases highlight different facets of the genesis and experience of her art. For example, she has long pursued an unusual form of site-specificity by making paintings that address a particular place's physical and associative qualities. These crucial traits, however, are ordinarily lost when her canvases subsequently circulate in the world. They shed both the memory of the walls they were designed to fill and their poetic resonances, with venues ranging from a Scottish botanical library to a Boston museum crammed with Old Masters. But within the pages of this book, initial exhibition sites are conjured through floor plans, installation diagrams, and documentation, along with meticulous notes and epistolary exchanges about precisely what size a painting should be in relation to precisely where it should hang. One finds a Polaroid sent by the art dealer Sadie Coles that pictures a column standing between a window and a wall in her gallery, an installation view of the painting Laura made to hang opposite the pole, and a detail of the dusky trompe l'oeil shadow she brushed onto the canvas to mimic one the column might cast. Other spreads illuminate how she often works in sets of interrelated pictures rather than in traditional series. Two canvases obliquely depict others with which they were originally displayed, while fragments of words span multiple panels that ultimately lead separate lives. One aim of this book is to reconstruct these largely forgotten histories.

Once we had assembled the broad strokes of the narrative, we often chose to burrow deep. Production notes, studies, source material, full-scale cartoons, process photographs, computer files, and detail photography reveal how Laura figures out paintings both before and while she makes them. In the beginning she performed much of this work on her own, though she has increasingly come to depend on studio assistants and collaborators who lend their own considerable ideas and expertise. Individual shows like *Pavement Karaoke* in London and the mind-bogglingly complex *Ten Paintings* in San Francisco are revivified through archival materials that reveal Laura's practice to be among the most audacious, assiduous, and technologically challenging of any contemporary painter.

The story lines and digressions within this book coalesced over countless hours in front of a computer screen. I would go out to LA and sit for days alongside Laura, Asha, and the graphic designer Tiffany Malakooti, who gave subtle structure to the sprawling contours of the project. Tiffany devised a template in which factual information like captions, plates of paintings, and even this introduction would sit on a neutral white ground, while a polyphony of voices and images piled up in the spaces above and between. Although at first glance the results might look like a casual scrapbook, each bespoke spread functions as a mini subplot amid larger ones, with connections sparked among the words, images, and pages. Taken together they constitute a sequence of authored arguments, albeit in a highly unconventional form. Intermittently, longer texts appear. Those in white letters on a dark blue ground derive from interviews we conducted with Laura and others who played key roles in shaping her journey. The more substantial of these oral histories specifically introduce vignettes that unfold on the following pages, while the shorter commentaries relate to individual works or documents illustrated nearby. Texts in black on a lighter blue background fall roughly into one of three categories. Some, such as those by bell hooks and Gil Saunders,

inspired Laura at around the point at which they sit in the book's chronology. Others, such as David Foster Wallace's reminiscence of his teenage years playing tennis in the Midwest or Francine Prose's meditation on the painter Elizabeth Murray's feminism, were chosen to refract various aspects of Laura's life and work. The remaining essays were newly commissioned for this volume from critics and curators whom Laura admires.

One more thing you should know about Laura is that she's a very social animal. This volume demonstrates how she and her art have evolved within a capacious network of friends, colleagues, teachers, students, assistants, rivals, dealers, lovers, patrons, curators, family members, and other sundry characters. Their likenesses appear in photographs, their words in emails and texts, and their recent recollections in the oral histories that trail like bread crumbs throughout the book. We sought to reveal, unvarnished, the impact these relationships have had on Laura and to suggest more universally the complicated interpersonal dynamics at play in an artist's life. The book relates, for example, the intense amalgam of desire, need, trust, and support that can exist between an artist and a dealer; the mutually enriching creative dialogues that mature between intimates over time; and even the possibility that a child might shape a mother's work. Laura's abiding knack for fostering friendship and community manifests itself through group shows she has organized and, most conspicuously, in 356 Mission, the exhibition, event, and gathering space that she cofounded with Gavin Brown and Wendy Yao near downtown LA. The personal and the professional are inextricably entwined.

This book tells Laura's story as well as many broader tales. Nearly every document and image within it was selected not only to elaborate her history but also to open onto a more general case. At least that was the criterion by which we hoped generosity and scholarship might forestall narcissism and anecdote for its own sake. How does a student find her voice in school or hustle up contact with a famous artist she admires? How does she make rent? What potent mixture of trepidation and yearning propels the preparations for a first survey show? How do such mundane trials as ordering a crate or making a child's birthday cake embroider an artist's life? As the pages and years flip by, we sense the changing contexts in which such questions are raised. Communications flow from postcard and fax to email and text; studies pass from notebook doodles to progressively sophisticated digital files; and images travel from minilab prints to pictures snapped on phones. Prices rise; rejections occur; the art world grows; new generations emerge in LA; and an artist's horizon expands from a tight-knit circle of friends to encompass the larger globe. This book is a portrait of an individual called Laura Owens and also a glimpse into how art gets made, eras take shape, and an artist's life—a person's, really—might unfold.

Carol Hendrickson: When Laura was about a year old we moved to Norwalk, Ohio, a small, rural town about an hour's drive from Cleveland. I think the population was about fifteen thousand. Laura is the oldest of my three children; she was born in 1970. She always learned and did things ahead of the time you would think that a child would do them. When she was growing up, I would often say to myself, "Oh, wow, I wouldn't think she'd be showing interest in that or doing that already."

She liked to draw. She liked to paint. I always bought presents for her that involved doing art; it was probably because I had wanted to go to art school and never could. She really liked that, and she would do artwork for the 4-H club. When she was in grade school the Huron County Department of Human Services held a drawing contest: the winning picture about children and families would be made into a poster and displayed throughout the county. Laura won the contest, and this poster was distributed everywhere. Throughout grade school she was always entering art contests. During the summertime she would do artwork and win awards at the county fair. She was very passionate and intense about everything she wanted to do. No matter what she got involved with, she always wanted to do the most, not just a little bit. I remember when she was learning to parallel park for her driving test. I went with her to the parking lot at the school. She wouldn't just practice three or four times. She must have done it at least twenty times to make sure she had it right. It was getting dark and I kept saying, "You've got it." But she still wanted to keep practicing and practicing.

Laura was very serious, always getting involved in everything. Every little school play, she would volunteer. She took ballet lessons, piano lessons, and tennis lessons. She even lettered in tennis for a couple years. She played the coronet in the school band. She was doing a lot of different things and she was always creative. She got

 Carol Hendrickson, a public health nurse and watercolor artist living in Los Angeles, is Owens's mother.

into this thing where she would make some of her own clothing. She made her prom dress and she made jean jackets that had different things on them that were indicative of her own personality. She and her sister would go to the Goodwill—this was before vintage was a cool thing—and bring home bags of clothes. She spent all her money on putting outfits together in a creative way. She was always doing something that no one else had done yet. For instance, when she was in high school she was getting ready to go to a concert and came downstairs and had jeans on with big holes cut out in the knees. And I said, "I thought you'd be dressed up." I'd never seen anyone in Norwalk with holes in their jeans. I think she may have been the first one. We'd go to New York on family vacations. We'd go to museums and into Greenwich Village and she'd spend a lot of time in the record stores. I always knew she'd want to move away to the city. There was very little diversity in our small Midwestern town. Laura went to Interlochen Center for the Arts between her junior and senior years, and after that she had an "I'm going to be an artist no matter what" attitude. I really think that was the turning point. She was with a diverse population of kids who were from all over the country, all involved in creative arts. We went to visit her at Interlochen—her grandmother and me and her sister and brother—and when we arrived a bunch of kids came up and started saying, "Did you know that I was the first Jewish person Laura ever met?" And three other kids argued, "No, I'm the first one, I'm the first one." So it was really good for her to go there at an early age.

I think Laura's dad assumed that she was going to go into math—she was extremely good at it. A lot of people of that era were like, "Art? What are you going to do with that? You're never going to make a living." But I was excited for her. I knew that she would do well, because she always did well. She graduated as a salutatorian even though she missed many days of school. I don't think she was really challenged by high school. I never realized the aspirations that she had. Personally, if I were going to achieve something, my goal would be maybe two or three steps ahead of what I was trying to do. I would think, "Okay, her goal is to go to art school and maybe find a job in art or have a show or something." I didn't think ahead to what her goals would really be, or how huge they would be. I remember one time I said, nonchalantly, in a conversation about how things were going, "What about working for American Greetings or something?" Not having any knowledge of the art world, and not knowing, in her case, what a foolish thing that was to suggest. So then I said, "Or teaching, maybe teaching art somewhere, for little children, or something." She was very upset with me, and tearful, and said, "Don't you think you'll ever see my art in a museum?" And I thought, "An art museum? Wow!" So I stopped short for a second and said, "Well, yes, of course I think that." I had never really thought that far ahead. I never thought she wouldn't be in an art museum, but I was really surprised that so soon after graduating from art school her goal was to have her artwork in museums, which of course has happened. I always wondered how she understood how to maneuver her way, because I know talent is one thing, but I now realize it's not just about being a good artist, but also about understanding and persevering.

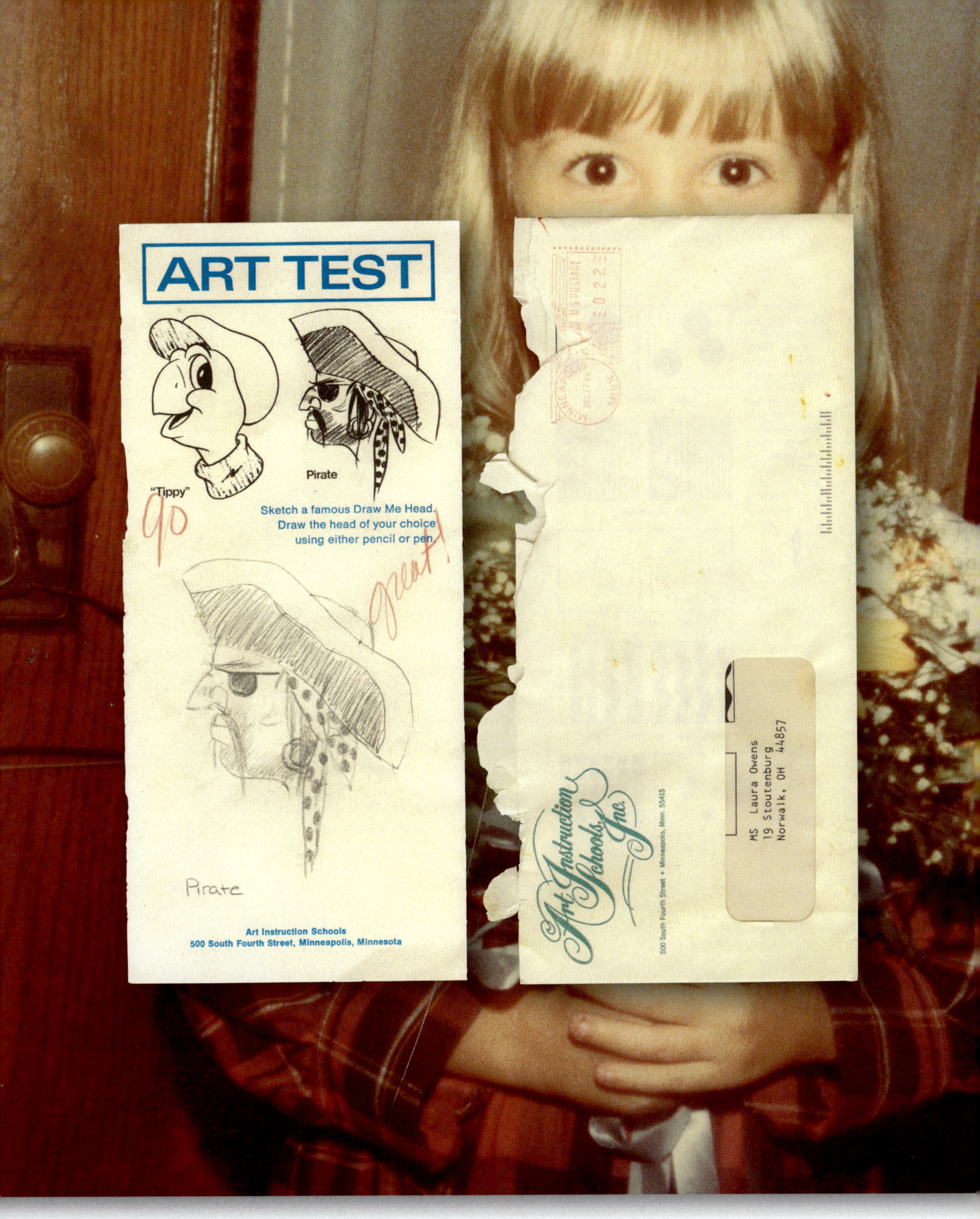

Foreground: Mail-in art test, 1985
Background: Owens, 1977

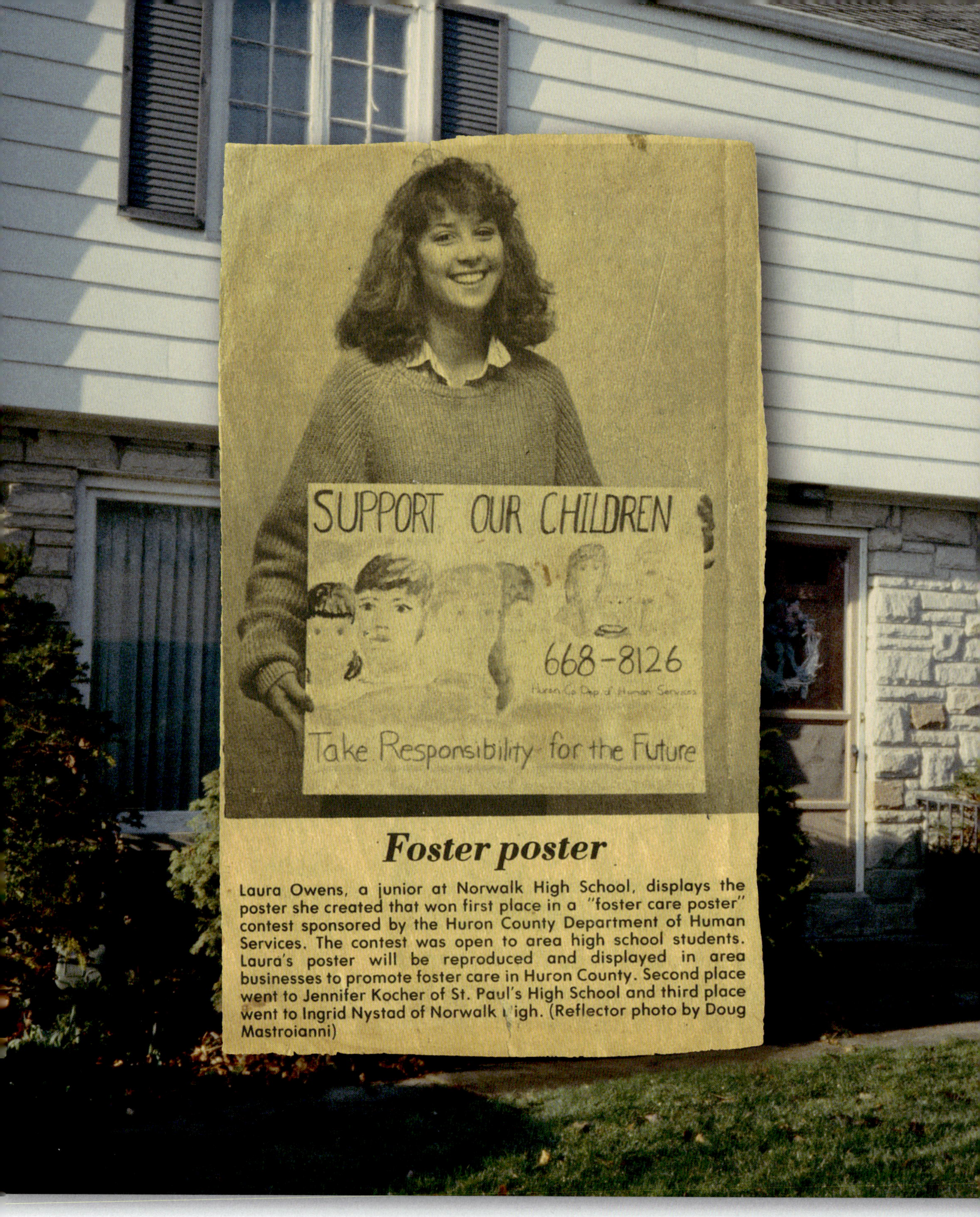

Foster poster

Laura Owens, a junior at Norwalk High School, displays the poster she created that won first place in a "foster care poster" contest sponsored by the Huron County Department of Human Services. The contest was open to area high school students. Laura's poster will be reproduced and displayed in area businesses to promote foster care in Huron County. Second place went to Jennifer Kocher of St. Paul's High School and third place went to Ingrid Nystad of Norwalk High. (Reflector photo by Doug Mastroianni)

Foreground: Owens in the *Norwalk Reflector*, 1985
Background: Childhood home, Norwalk, Ohio, 1986

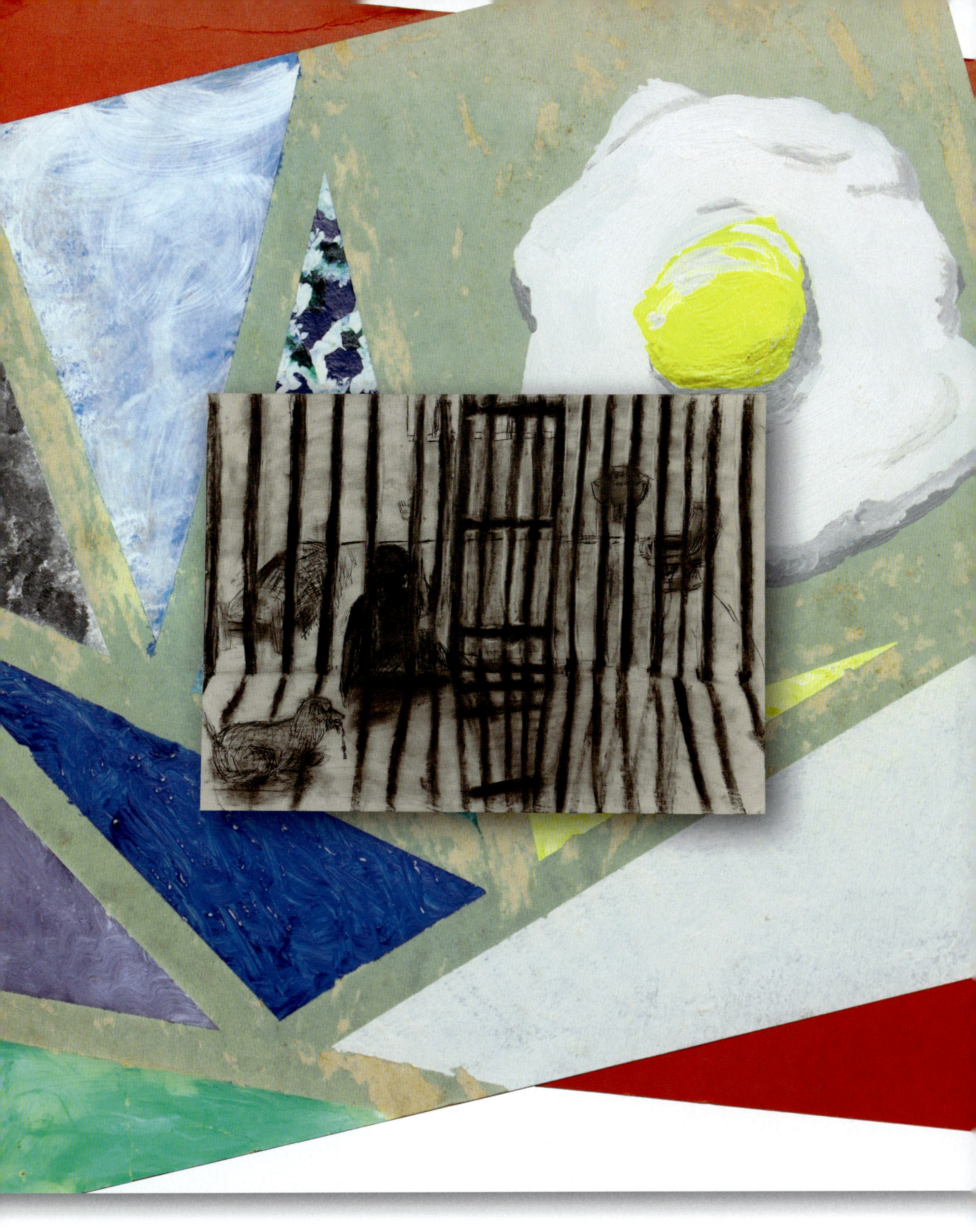

Foreground: *Untitled*, 1987, charcoal on paper, 18 × 25 in. (45.7 × 63.5 cm)
Background: Detail of *Untitled*, ca. 1986, acrylic and collaged paper on posterboard, 28 × 34 in. (71.1 × 86.4 cm)

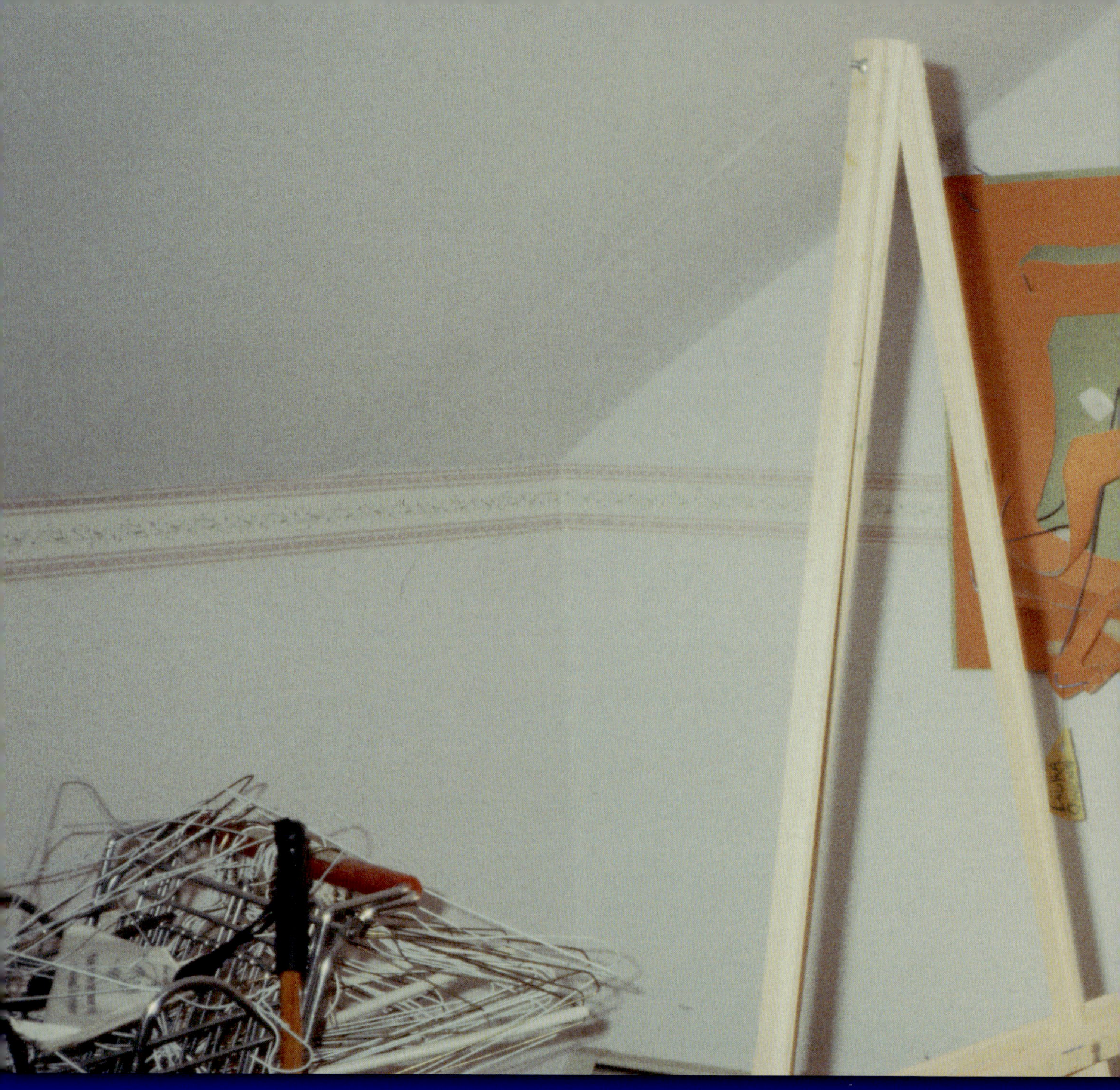

Laura Owens: When I was nine years old I moved my bedroom into the attic to get away from my brother and sister. I would sometimes paint up there and often listened to music—mixtapes from friends, or the radio. This picture is the other side of the attic. Later in high school I spent a lot of time going to thrift stores. I would also drive to Cleveland and see punk shows, or go record shopping and hang out on streets, from Huron to Coventry. Anything to get out of Norwalk—it was so boring. In my high school art class part of your grade was based on your Halloween costume. I dressed up as a flower child and my history teacher started kicking my desk and yelling at me, "We got four of you at Kent State" (meaning hippies—he was in the National Guard). I took three art classes my senior year along with calculus, French, and AP history. I was tardy forty-three times and missed a lot of those classes, but the bar was pretty low, so I still graduated second in my class. Our art teacher, Mrs. Magi, took us on field trips to the Cleveland Museum of Art and the Toledo Museum of Art. My grandpa Gutheinz made watercolors and built model ships, and my grandma Owens did needlework and sewing every night while she smoked and watched TV. I found my mom's old pastel drawings of flowers in our basement, and she told me she had wanted to be an artist.

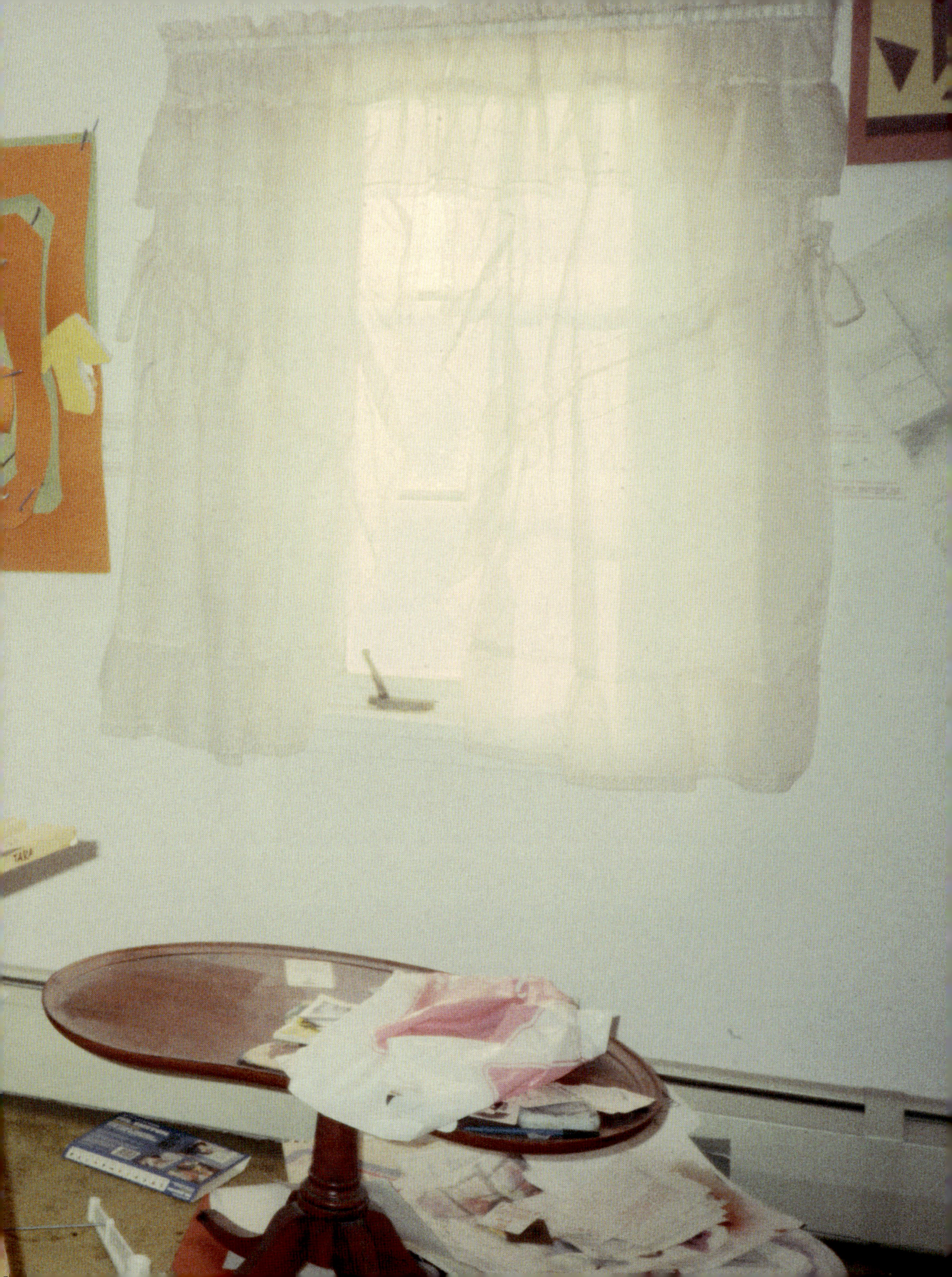

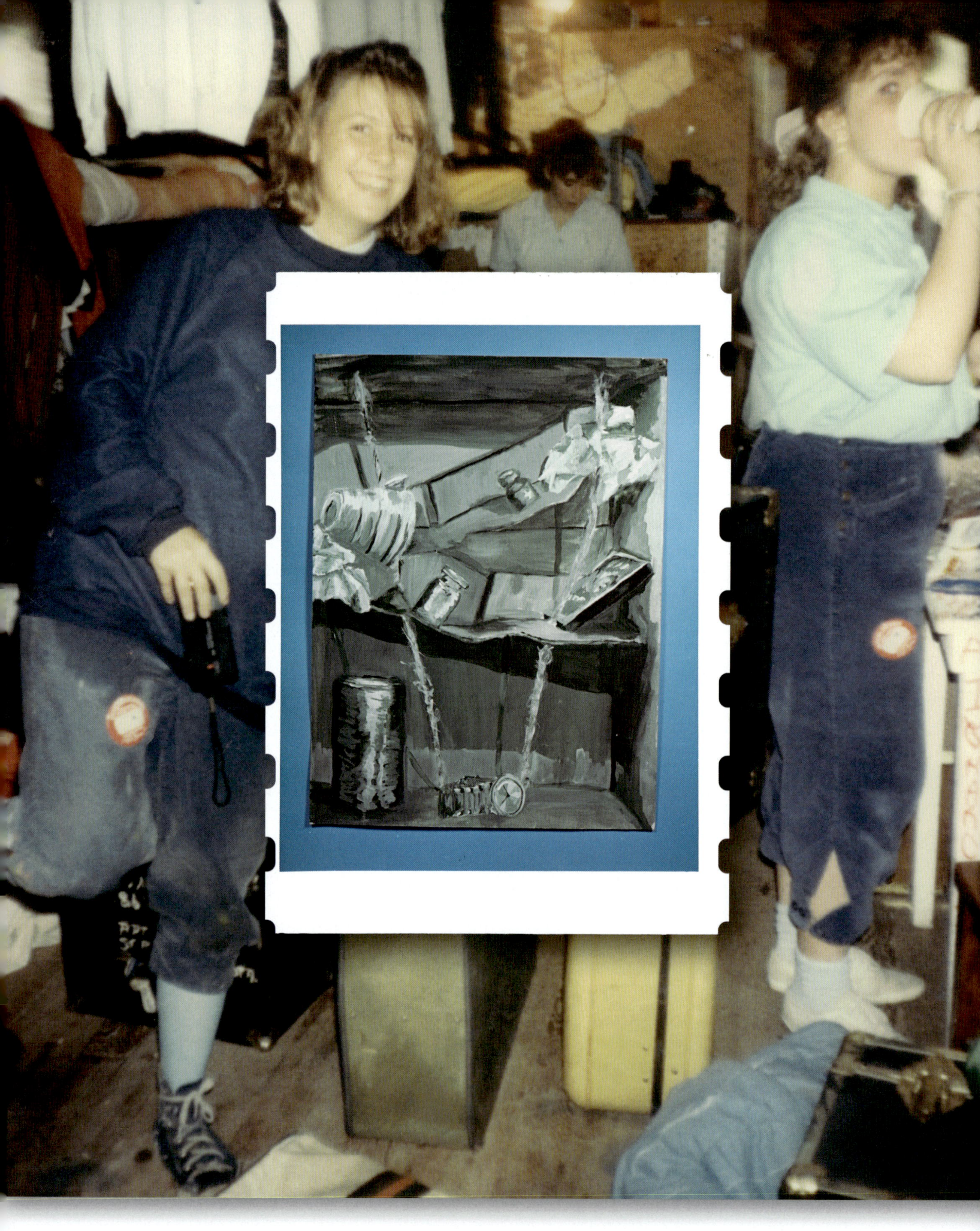

Foreground: *Untitled*, 1987, oil on canvas, 25 × 20 in. (63.5 × 50.8 cm)
Background: Owens, Interlochen Center for the Arts summer camp, Interlochen, Michigan, 1987

July 4   1988

Today → 8:30   Wake up - Cindy Called
         9:30   Went to Cindys sister
         10:-   Went to Parade → SKARUPA in it
                    so was Hilary for 'Scoopers'
                Lincoln was in the band but
                I didn't see him
                Willy Lang, Mr Aschmeer
                Kilgore Kilbane Heit Commissioners etc

           I held Adam during PARADE
                            got ready for Picnic
11:30 Went home
12:30 Left for Huron
1:- got to Matts   Dave, Dave Beckom BMatt & Chad
                went - Me & Dave drove

 2:00   got to Chris' house.
 2:30   got to Mill hollow
          had picnic Dave, Mike John
               Cathy Chris Michelle John
                  Diane Janel Amy
           'came & Pat
 4 left with John to take Pat & Mike
 home.   Picked up Eric & Nik
            on the way back

 6 30 left M. Hollow
 7:30 Got to Amy's
 9:00 → went to Homestead beach
            Swam
 11 → went to Matts
 12:30 -1:30   Sat around
 1:30 went home
 2   Ate Brownies.
 3 listen to Joni Mitchell

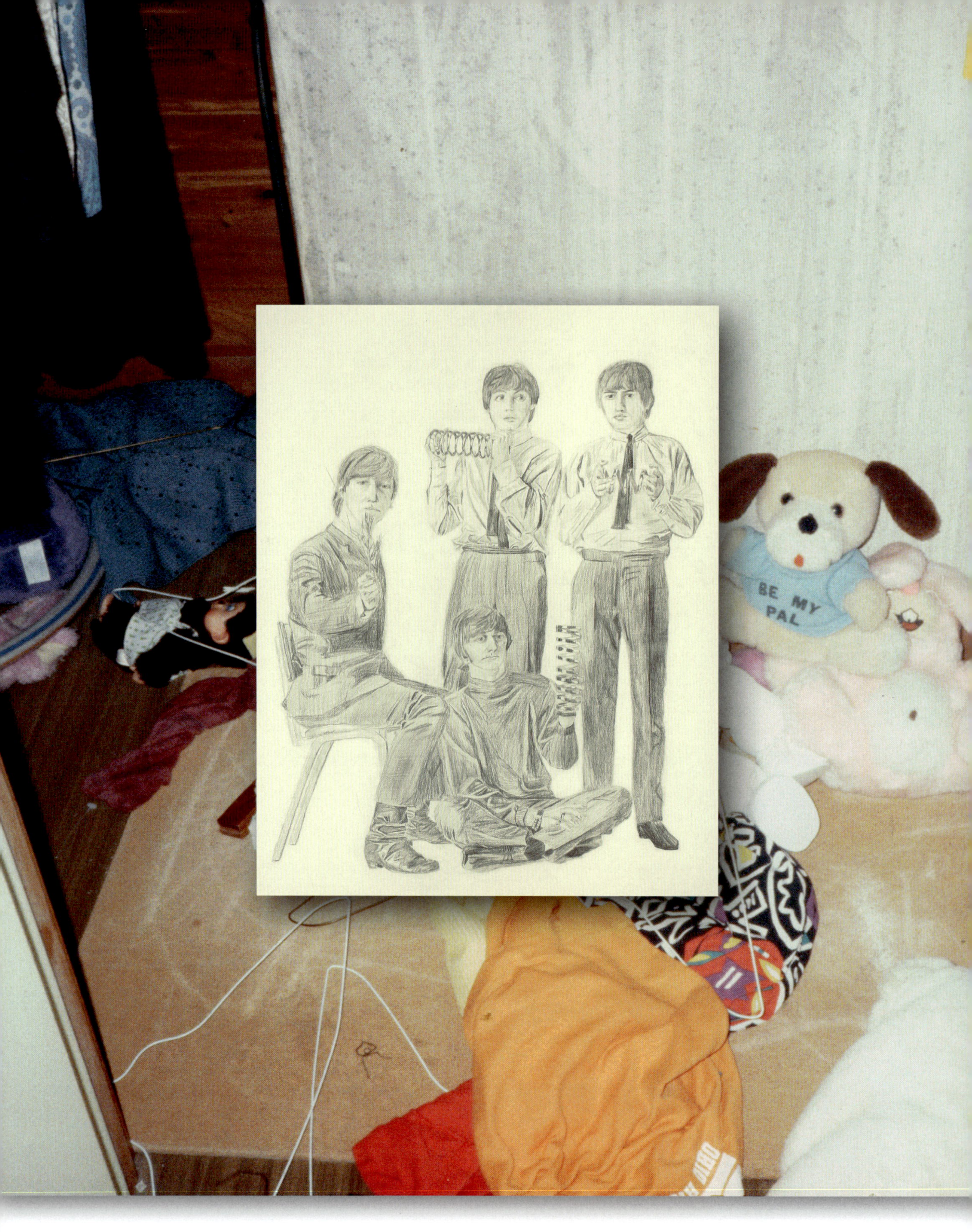

Foreground: *Beatles*, 1987, graphite on paper, 22 × 17 in. (55.9 × 43.2 cm)
 Background: Closet in childhood home, Norwalk, Ohio, 1986

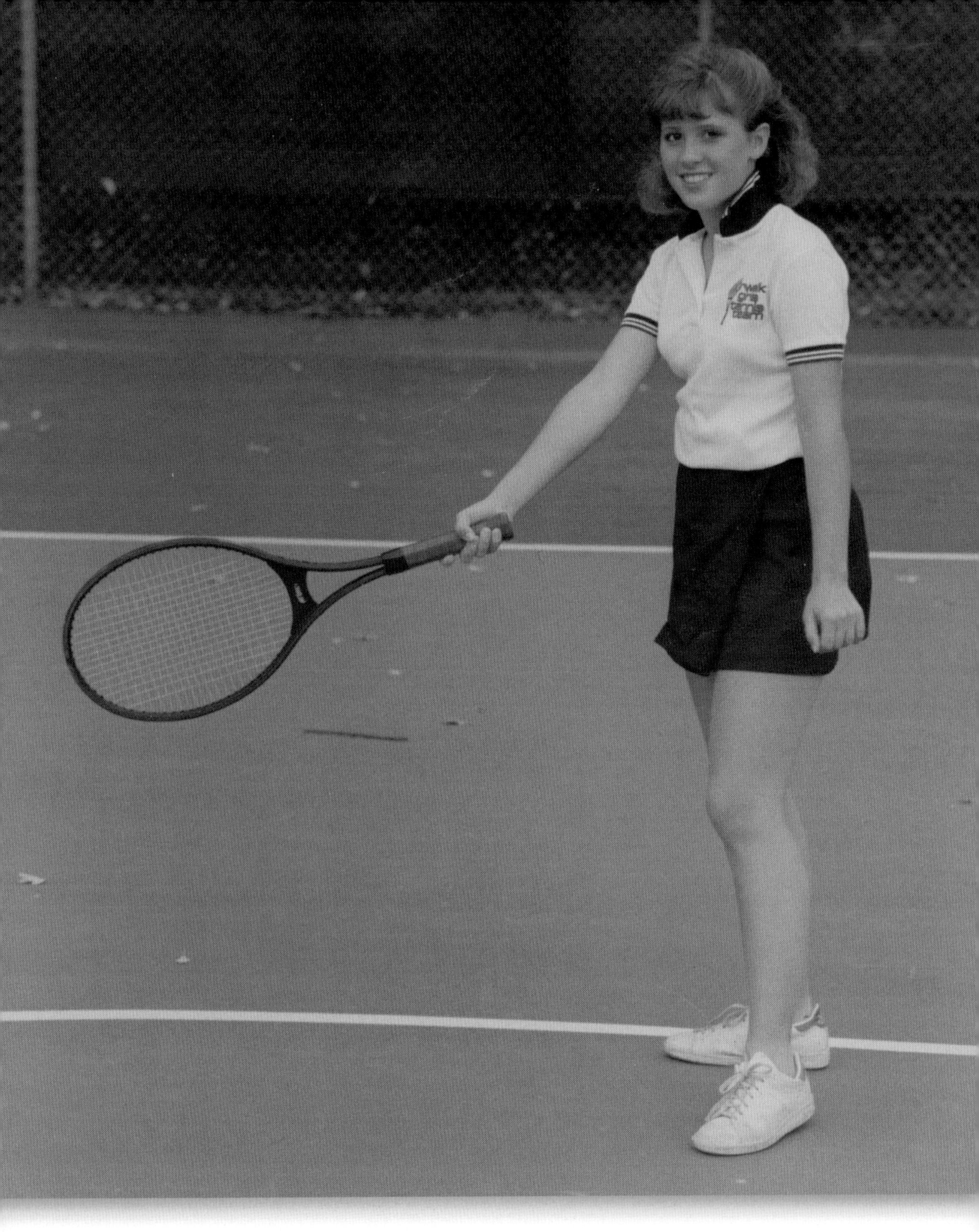

Norwalk High School yearbook photo, 1986

TENNIS, TRIGONOMETRY, TORNADOES:
A MIDWESTERN BOYHOOD
DAVID FOSTER WALLACE

When I left the boxed township of Illinois farmland where I grew up to attend my dad's alma mater in the lurid, jutting Berkshires of western Massachusetts, I right away developed a jones for mathematics. I'm starting to see why this was so. College math evokes a Midwesterner's sickness for home. I'd grown up inside vectors, lines and lines athwart lines, grids—and, on the scale of horizons, broad curving lines of geographic force, the weird topographical drain-swirl of a whole lot of ice-ironed flatland that sits and spins atop plates. I could plot by eye the area behind and below these broad curves at the seam of land and sky way before I came to know anything as formal as integrals or rates of change. Calculus was, quite literally, child's play.

In late childhood I learned how to play tennis on the blacktop courts of a small public park carved from farmland. This was in my home of Philo, Illinois, a tiny collection of com silos and war-era Levittown homes whose native residents did little but sell crop insurance and nitrogen fertilizer and herbicide, and collect property taxes from the young academics at nearby Champaign-Urbana's university, whose ranks swelled enough in the flush late 1960s to make an outlying oxymoron like "farm and bedroom community" lucid.

Between the ages of twelve and fifteen I was a near great junior tennis player. I cut my competitive teeth beating up on lawyers' and dentists' kids at little Champaign and Urbana country club events, and was soon killing whole summers being driven through dawns to tournaments all over Illinois, Indiana, and Iowa. At fourteen I was ranked seventeenth in the United States Tennis Association's Western Section ("Western" being the creakily ancient USTA's designation for the Midwest; farther west were the Southwest, Northwest, and Pacific Northwest sections), fourth in the state of Illinois, and around one hundredth in the nation, having flown in 1976, at the regional association's expense, to the US National Junior Hardcourt Championships in Kalamazoo, Michigan, where in the second round I got my rural ass handed to me by a California kid named Scott Davis, who's now a marginal figure on the pro circuit.

My flirtation with tennis excellence had way more to do with a weird proclivity for intuitive math, and with the township where I learned and trained, than with athletic talent. Even by the standards of junior competition, in which everybody's a tight bud of pure potential, I was a pretty untalented tennis player. My hand-eye was okay, but I was neither large nor quick, had a near concave chest and wrists so thin I could bracelet them with a thumb and pinkie, and could hit a tennis ball no harder or truer than most girls my age. What I could do—in the words of my township's juniors' coach, a thin guy who chewed Red Man and spat into a Folgers can—was "Play the Whole Court." This was a tennis cliché that could mean any number of things. In my case, it meant I knew my limitations and the limitations of the courts I played on, and adjusted thusly. I was at my best in bad conditions.

Now, conditions in Central Illinois are from a mathematical perspective interesting and from a tennis point of view bad: summer heat and wet-mitten humidity; moths and crap gnats forming an asteroid belt around each tall lamp at night, the whole lit court surface aflutter with spastic little shadows; mosquitoes that spawn in the fields' furrows and in the conferva-chocked ditches that box each field; and, most of all, wind.

The people I know from outside it distill the Midwest into blank flatness, black land and fields of green fronds or five o'clock stubble, gentle swells and declivities that make the topology a sadistic exercise in plotting quadrics, highway vistas so same and dead they drive motorists mad. Those from Indiana, Wisconsin, and northern Illinois think of their Midwest as agronomics and commodities futures and corn-detasseling and bean-walking and seed-company caps, apple-cheeked Nordic types, cider and slaughter and football games with white fog banks of breath exiting helmets. But in the odd central pocket that

 Originally published in *Harper's Magazine* 284 (December 1991): 68–75, 78. Wallace was an American novelist and essayist.

is Champaign-Urbana, Rantoul, Philo, Mahomet-Seymour, Mattoon, and Tolono, Midwestern life is informed and deformed by wind. To the west, between us and the Rockies, there is basically nothing tall, and weird zephyrs and stirs join breezes and gusts and thermals and downdrafts and whatever out over Nebraska and Kansas, and move east like streams into rivers and jets and military fronts that gather like avalanches and roar in reverse down pioneer ox trails toward our own unsheltered asses. Nobody I knew in Philo combed his hair because why bother.

The worst was spring, boys' high school tennis season, when the nets would stand out stiff as proud flags and an errant ball would blow clear to the easternmost fence, interrupting play on the next several courts. Summers were manic and gusty, then often, around August, deadly calm. The wind would just die, some days, in August, and it was no relief at all; the cessation drove us nuts. We realized afresh how much the wind had become part of the soundtrack to life in Philo. The sound of wind had become, for me, silence. When it went away, I was left with the squeak of the blood in my head and the aural glitter of all those little eardrum hairs quivering like a drunk in withdrawal.

To your average outsider, Central Illinois looks ideal for sports. The ground, seen from the air, strongly suggests a board game: anally precise squares of dun or khaki cropland all cut and divided by plumb-straight tar roads. From ground level, the arrayed fields of feed corn and soybeans look laned like sprint tracks or Olympic pools, replete with the angles and alleys of serious tennis.

The terrain's strengths are its weaknesses. Because the land seems so even, designers of clubs and parks rarely bother to roll it flat before laying the asphalt for tennis courts. The result is usually a slight list that only a player who spends a lot of time on the courts will notice. Since tennis courts are for sun-and-eye reasons always laid lengthwise north-south, and since the land in Central Illinois rises very gently as one moves east toward Indiana, the court's forehand half, for a rightie facing north, always seems physically uphill from the backhand. The same soil that's so full of humus farmers have to be bought off to keep markets unflooded splits asphalt courts open with the upward pressure of broadleaves whose pioneer-stock seeds are unthwarted by a half-inch cover of sealant and stone. So all but the very best maintained courts in the most affluent Illinois districts are their own little rural landscapes, with tufts and cracks and underground-seepage puddles being part of the lay that one plays.

Tennis-wise, I had three preternatural gifts to compensate for not much physical talent. The first was that I always sweated so much that I stayed fairly well ventilated in all weathers. Oversweating seems an ambivalent blessing, and it didn't exactly do wonders for my social life in high school, but it meant I could play for hours on a Turkish-bath July day and not flag a bit so long as I drank water and ate salty stuff between matches. I always looked like a drowned man by about game four, but I didn't cramp, vomit, or pass out, unlike the gleaming Peoria kids whose hair never even lost its part right up until their eyes rolled up in their heads and they pitched forward onto the shimmering concrete.

A bigger asset still was that I felt extremely comfortable inside straight lines. This was environmental. Philo is a cockeyed grid: nine north-south streets against six northeast-southwest, dozens and dozens of gorgeous slanted-cruciform corners (the east and west intersection-angles' tangents could be evaluated integrally in terms of their secants!) around a three-intersection central town common. Most of my memories of childhood, whether of furrowed acreage or a harvester's sentry duty along R.R. 104W or the play of sharp shadows against the Legion Hall softball field's dusk, I could now reconstruct on demand with an edge and protractor.

I liked the sharp intercourse of straight lines more than the other kids I grew up with. I think this is because they were natives, whereas I was an infantile transplant from Ithaca, New York, where my dad had Ph.D.'d. So I'd known, even as a baby, horizontally and semiconsciously, something different, the tall hills and serpentine one-ways of upstate New York. I'm pretty sure I kept the amorphous mush of curves and swells as a contrasting backlight somewhere down in the lizardy part of my brain, because the Philo children I fought and played with, kids who knew and had known nothing else, saw nothing stark or new-worldish in the township's planar layout, prized nothing crisp.

My first really detailed memory is all sharp edges. I was helping a neighbor kid help his mother till a new vegetable garden out in their backyard one April. The garden's outline was a perfect square, with five quincunx subareas—the center for hallowed zucchini—laid out in an H of popsicle sticks and twine. We little boys removed rocks and hard clods from the lady's path as she worked the Rototiller, a rented, wheelbarrow-shaped, gas-driven thing that roared and snorted and bucked and seemed to propel its mistress rather than vice versa, her feet leaving drunken prints in the earth. In the middle of the tilling my friend's baby brother, maybe like four at the time and wearing some kind of fuzzy red Pooh-wear, came tear-assing out into the backyard crying, holding something really unpleasant-looking in his upturned palm. It turned out to have been a rhomboid patch of mold from some exotic corner of their damp basement. It was a sort of nasal green, black-speckled, vaguely hirsute. Worse, the patch of mold looked incomplete, gnawed on; some nauseous stuff was smeared around the little kid's mouth. "I ate this," he started crying as his mother shut down the tiller and came to him. My friend and I were grossed out as only kids can get grossed out by smaller kids' repulsive snafus. But the little kid's mother, who now that I think about it disappeared under vague medical circumstances a couple years later, went utterly nuts:

"Help! My son ate this!" she yelled, over and over, holding the speckled patch aloft, running around and around the garden's quadrants while my neighbor and I gaped at our first real adult hysteria, the sobbing little kid forgotten by all of us.

"Help! My son ate this! Help!" she kept yelling, running in tight complex little patterns just inside the H of string that marked the garden's quincunx; and I remember noting, and being alone in noting, how even in trauma her flight lines were plumb, her footprints Native American—straight, her turns, inside the ideogram of string, crisp and martial. She ran and yelled and turned and yelled and ran. My friend's dad, who had a pipe sticking out of his face, had to go get the hose.

Unless you're just a mutant, a virtuoso of raw force, you'll find that competitive tennis, like money-pool, requires geometric thinking, the ability to calculate not merely your own angles but the angles of response to your angles. Tennis is to artillery and air strikes what football is to infantry and attrition. Because the expansion of response possibilities is quadratic, you are required to think n shots ahead, where n is a hyperbolic function limited by (roughly) your opponent's talent and the number of shots in the rally so far. I was good at this. What made me for a while near great was that I could also admit the differential complication of wind into my calculations. Wind did massive damage to many Central Illinois junior players, particularly in the period between April and July when it needed

lithium badly, tending to gust without pattern, swirl and backtrack and die and rise, sometimes blowing in one direction at court level and in another altogether ten feet overhead. The best planned, best hit ball often just blew out of bounds, was the basic unlyrical problem. It drove some kids near mad with the caprice and unfairness of it all, and on real windy days these kids, usually with talent out the wazoo, would have their first apoplectic racket-throwing tantrum in about the match's third game and by the end of the first set would have lapsed into a kind of sullen coma, bitterly expecting to get screwed over by wind, net, tape, sun. I, who was affectionately known as Slug because I was so lazy in practice, located my biggest tennis asset in a weird robotic detachment from whatever unfairnesses of wind and weather I couldn't plan for. I couldn't begin to tell you how many tournament matches I won between the ages of twelve and fifteen against bigger, faster, more coordinated, and better coached opponents simply by hitting balls unimaginatively back down the middle of the court in schizophrenic gales, letting the other kid play with more verve and panache, waiting for enough of his ambitious balls aimed near the lines to curve or slide via wind outside the green court and white stripe into the raw red territory that won me yet another ugly point. It wasn't pretty or fun to watch, and even with the Illinois wind I never could have won whole matches this way had the opponent not eventually had his small nervous breakdown, buckling under the obvious injustice of losing to a shallow-chested "pusher" because of the shitty rural courts and rotten wind that rewarded cautious automatism instead of verve and panache. I was an unpopular player, with good reason. But to say that I did not use verve or imagination was untrue. Acceptance is its own verve, and it takes imagination for a player to like wind, and I liked wind.

I started to win a lot. At twelve, I began getting entry to tournaments beyond Philo and Champaign and Danville. I was driven by my parents or by the folks of Gil Antitoi, son of a Québecois-history professor from Urbana, to events like the Central Illinois Open in Decatur, a town built and owned by the A. E. Staley processing concern and so awash in the stink of roasting corn that kids would play with bandannas tied over their mouths and noses; like the McDonald's Junior Open in the serious–corn town of Galesburg, way out west by the river, where in 1974 Antitoi so pummeled Hans Block, son of a prosperous hog farmer who was later to become the most hated man in the Midwest as Reagan's secretary of agriculture, that Hans Block, ranked eighth in Illinois in Twelve and Unders, was never seen on a court again; like the Prairie State Open in Pekin, insurance hub and home of Caterpillar tractor; like the Midwest Junior Clay Courts at a chichi private club in Peoria's pale version of Scarsdale.

Over the next four summers I got to see way more of the state than is normal or healthy, albeit most of this seeing was at a blur of travel and crops, looking between nod-outs at sunrises abrupt and terribly candent over the crease between fields and sky, riding in station wagons' backseats through Saturday dawns and Sunday sunsets. I got steadily better; Antitoi, unfairly assisted by an early puberty, got radically better.

By the time we were fourteen, Antitoi and I were the Central Illinois cream of our age bracket, usually seeded one and two at area tournaments, able to beat all but a couple of even the kids from the Chicago suburbs who, together with a contingent from Grosse Pointe, Michigan, usually dominated the Western Sectional rankings. Antitoi and I ranged over the exact same competitive territory; he was my friend and foe and bane. Though I'd started playing two years before he, he was bigger, quicker, and basically better than I by about thirteen, and I was soon losing to him in the finals of just about every tournament I played. So different were our appearances and approaches and general gestalts that we had something of a modest epic rivalry from 1974 through 1977. I had gotten so prescient at using surface, sun, and gusts that I was regarded as a kind of physical savant, a medicine boy of wind and heat, and could play just forever, sending back moon balls baroque with ornate spins. Antitoi, uncomplicated from the git-go, hit the holy shit out of every round object that came within his ambit, aiming always for a backcourt corner. When he was "on," having a good day, he varnished the court with me. When he wasn't at his best (and the hours we spent—David Hurst from Bloomington, Kirk McKenzie and Steve Moe of Danville, and I—in meditation and seminar on what variables of diet, sleep, romance, car ride, and even sock color factored into the equation of Antitoi's mood and level day to day), he and I had great matches, real marathon wind-suckers. Of the eleven finals we played in 1974, I won two.

Midwest junior tennis was my early initiation into true adult sadness. I had, by thirteen, developed a sort of Taoist hubris about my ability to control via non-control. I'd found a way not just to accommodate but to employ the heavy summer winds in matches. No longer just mooning the ball down the center to allow plenty of margin for error and swerve, I was now able to use the currents the way a pitcher uses spit. I could hit curves way out into cross breezes that'd drop the ball just fair; I had a special wind serve that had so much spin the ball turned oval in the air, curved left to right like a smart slider, and then reversed its arc on the bounce. As a junior tennis player, I was for a time a citizen of the concrete physical world in a way the other boys weren't.

My betrayal came at around fifteen, when so many of these single-minded flailing boys became abruptly mannish and tall, with sudden sprays of hair on their thighs and wisps on their lips and ropy arteries on their forearms. My fifteenth summer, kids I'd been beating easily the year before all of a sudden seemed overpowering. In 1977 I lost in the semifinals of two tournaments that I'd beaten Antitoi in the finals of in 1976. The other boy sensed something was up with me, smelled some breakdown in the odd détente I'd had with the elements.

I felt, as I became a later and later bloomer, alienated not just from my own recalcitrant glabrous little body but in a way from the whole elemental exterior I'd come to see as my co-conspirator. I knew, somehow, that the call to height and hair came from outside, from whatever apart from Monsanto and Dow made the corn grow and the hogs rut. My vocation ebbed. I felt uncalled. I experienced the same resentment toward whatever children abstract as Nature that I knew Steve Moe felt when a soundly considered approach shot down the forehand line was blown out by a gust. I began, very quietly, to resent my physical place in the great schema.

It's also true that my whole Midwest tennis career matured and then degenerated under the aegis of the Peter Principle. In and around my township, where the courts were rural and budgets low and conditions extreme, I was truly near great: I could Play the Whole Court; I was In My Element. But the more important tournaments, the events into which my rural excellence was an easement, were played in a real different world: The courts' surfaces were redone every spring at the Arlington Tennis Club, where the National Junior Qualifier for our Section was held; the green of these courts' fair territory was so vivid as to distract, its surface so bare of flaw, tilt, crack, or seam as to be scary and disorienting. Playing on a perfect court was for me like treading water out of sight of land: I never knew where I was out there. The 1976 Chicago Junior Invitational was held at the Lincolnshire Bath & Tennis Club, whose huge warren of courts was enclosed by these troubling green plastic tarps attached to all the fences, with little archer-slits in them at eye level to afford some parody of spectation. These tarps, developed by some windophobe in the early 1970s, cut down the worst of the unfair gusts, but they also seemed to rob the court space of new air: Competing at Lincolnshire was like playing at the bottom of a well. I just wasn't the same, somehow, without deformities to play around. I'm thinking now that the wind and bugs and chuckholes formed for me a kind of inner boundary, my own personal set of lines. Once I hit a certain level of tournament facilities, I was disabled because I was unable to accommodate the absence of disabilities to accommodate. Puberty-angst aside, my Midwest tennis career plateaued the moment I saw my first windscreen.

Still strangely eager to speak of the weather, let me say that my township, in fact all of east-central Illinois, is a proud part of what meteorologists call Tornado Alley. I personally have seen two or three on the ground and five aloft, trying to assemble. The grotesque frequency of tornadoes around my township is, I'm told, a function of the same variables that cause our civilian winds: We are a coordinate where fronts and air masses converge. Most days between late March and June there are Tornado Watches somewhere in our TV stations' viewing area. Watches mean conditions are right and so on and so forth—big deal. It's only the rarer Tornado Warnings, which require a confirmed sighting by somebody with reliable sobriety, that make the civil defense sirens go. The siren on top of the Philo Elementary School was a different pitch and cycle from the one off in the south part of Urbana, and the two used to weave in and out of each other in a god-awful threnody. When the sirens blew, the native families went to their canning cellars or fallout shelters (no kidding); the academic families in their bright prefab houses with new lawns and foundations of flat slab went with whatever good-luck tokens they could lay hands on to the very most central point on the ground floor after opening every single window to thwart implosion from precipitous pressure drops. For my family, the very most central point was a

hallway between my dad's study and a linen closet, with a reproduction of a Flemish Annunciation scene on one wall and a bronze Aztec sunburst hanging with guillotinic mass on the other; I always tried to maneuver my sister under the sunburst.

If there was an actual Warning when you were outside away from home, say at a tennis tournament in some godforsaken public park at some city fringe zoned for sprawl, you were supposed to lie prone in the deepest depression you could locate. Since the only real depressions around most tournament sites were the irrigation and runoff ditches that bordered cultivated fields— ditches icky with conferva and mosquito spray and always heaving with what looked like conventions of copperheads and just basically places you don't want to lie prone in under any circumstances—in practice at Warned tournaments you zipped your rackets into their covers and ran to find your loved ones or even your liked ones and just milled around trying to look like you weren't terrified.

Tornadoes were a real part of my Midwest childhood, because as a little kid I was obsessed with dread over them. My earliest nightmares were about shrieking sirens and dead white skies, a slender monster on the Iowa horizon jutting less phallic than saurian from the lowering sky, whipping back and forth with such frenzy that it almost doubled on itself, trying to eat its own tail, throwing off chaff and dust and chairs. It never came any closer than the horizon; it didn't have to.

I stayed obsessed as I aged, and I know why: Tornadoes, for me, were a transfiguration. Like all serious winds, they were the z-coordinate for our little stretch of plain, a move up from the Euclidian monotone of furrow, road, axis, and grid. We studied tornadoes in junior high: A Canadian high straightlines it southeast from the Dakotas; a moist warm mass drawls on up north from Arkansas. The result was not a Greek *x* or even a Cartesian axis but an alchemical circling of the square. Tornadoes were, in our part of Central Illinois, the dimensionless point at which parallel lines met and whirled and blew up. They made no sense: Houses blew not out but in. Brothels were spared while orphanages next door bought it. Dead cattle were found three miles from their silage without a scratch on them.

The only time I ever got caught in what might have been one was in June 1978 on a tennis court at Hessel Park in Champaign, where I was drilling one afternoon with Gil Antitoi. Though a contemptible and despised tournament opponent,

I was a coveted practice partner because I could transfer balls to wherever you wanted them with the tireless consistency of a machine. This particular day it was supposed to rain around suppertime, and a couple of times we thought we'd heard the tattered edges of sirens out west toward Monticello, but Antitoi and I drilled religiously every afternoon that week on the slow clayish Har-Tru of Hessel, trying to prepare for a beastly clay invitational in Chicago. We were doing butterflies, a real unpleasant drill where his cross-courts alternated with my down-the-lines. Butterflies are primarily a conditioning drill: Both players have to get from one side of the court to the other between each stroke, and once the initial pain and wind-sucking is over, assuming you're a kid who's in absurd shape because you spend countless mindless hours jumping rope or running laps backward or doing straight sprints back and forth along the perfect furrows of bean fields each morning, once the first pain and fatigue of butterflies are got through, if both guys are good enough so that there are few unforced errors to break up the rally, a kind of fugue-state opens up inside you and your concentration telescopes toward a still point and you lose awareness of your limbs and the soft shush of your shoe's slide and whatever's outside the lines of the court, and pretty much all you know then is the bright ball and the octangled butterfly outline of its path across the court, and at Hessel Park the court was such a deep piney color that the flights of the fluorescent balls stayed on one's visual screen for a few extra seconds, leaving trails.

We had one just endless rally and I'd left the planet in a silent swoop when the court and ball and butterfly trail all seemed to surge brightly and glow as the daylight just plain went out in the sky overhead. Neither of us had noticed that there'd been no wind blowing the familiar grit into our eyes for several minutes—a bad sign. There was no siren. Later they said the civil defense alert network had been out of order. The temperature dropped so fast you could feel your hairs rise. There was no thunder; no air stirred. I could not tell you why we kept hitting. Neither of us said anything. There was no siren. It was high noon; there was nobody else on the courts. The riding mower at the softball field was still going back and forth. There were no depressions except a saprogenic ditch along the field of new corn just west. What could we have done? I think we thought it would rain at worst and that we'd play till it rained and then go sit in Antitoi's parents' station wagon. We were both in the fugue-state that exhaustion through repetition brings on, a fugue-state I've decided that my whole time on tennis was spent chasing, a fugue-state I associate too with plowing and seeding and detasseling and spreading herbicides back and forth in sentry duty along perfect lines, up and back, or military marching on flat blacktop, hypnotic, a mental state at once flat and lush, numbing and yet exquisitely felt. We were young, we didn't know when to stop. I was mad at my body and wanted to hurt it, wear it down. Then the whole knee-high field to the west along Kirby Avenue all of a sudden flattened out in a wave coming toward us as if the field were getting steamrolled. Antitoi went wide west for a forehand cross and I saw the corn get laid down in waves and the sycamores lining the ditch point our way. There was no funnel. Either it had just materialized and come down or it wasn't a real one. The big heavy swings on the industrial swing sets took off, wrapping themselves in their chains around and around the top crossbar; the park's grass laid down the same way the field had. It all happened very fast: field, trees, swings, grass, then the feel like the lift of the world's biggest mitt, the nets suddenly and sexually up and out straight as flags, and I seem to remember whacking a ball out of my hand at Antitoi to watch its radical west-east curve, and for some reason trying to run after this ball I'd just hit, but I couldn't have tried to run after a ball I had hit, but I remember the heavy gentle lift at my thighs and the ball curving back closer and my passing the ball and beating the ball in flight over the horizontal net, my feet not once touching the ground over fifty-odd feet, and then there was chaff and crud in the air all over and both Antitoi and I were blown pinwheeling for I swear it must have been fifty feet to the fence one court over, the easternmost fence, we hit the fence so hard we knocked it halfway down, and it stuck at 45°, Antitoi detached a retina and had to wear those funky Jabbar retina-goggles for the rest of the summer, and the fence had two body-shaped indentations like in cartoons where the guy's face leaves an imprint in the skillet that hit him, two catcher's masks of fence, we both got deep quadrangular lines impressed on our faces, torsos, legs' fronts, from the fence, my sister said we looked like waffles, but neither of us got badly hurt, and no homes got whacked—either the thing just ascended again for no reason right after, they do that, they obey no rule, follow no line, hop up and down at something that might as well be will, or else it wasn't a real one. Antitoi's tennis continued to improve after that, but mine didn't.

Deborah Kass: I've taught a couple of truly brilliant classes in my life, and Laura's group was one of them. I was at RISD from 1990 to 1991; it was my first teaching experience and it was such a passionate time. The reading list was incredible: John Berger, *Ways of Seeing*; Griselda Pollock, "Modernity and the Spaces of Femininity"; Susan Gubar and Sandra Gilbert, "Tradition and the Female Talent." And that was just week one. The next week was Mira Schor and Anna Chave. Then "Modes of Disclosure," Ken Silver; bell hooks, "Altars of Sacrifice: Re-membering Basquiat." And my suggested reading included *Feminist Literary Theory* by Mary Eagleton; *Writing a Woman's Life*, Carolyn Heilbrun; *Sexuality in the Field of Vision,* Jacqueline Rose. These books were brand-new then.

Laura was this quiet, very Midwestern young woman. Art students spend a lot of time focusing inward because they need to get in touch with themselves, but her core was clear, so she was looking outside of herself, aware of the art world in a way most undergrads and even grad students aren't. I remember her work, these French-looking silhouettes and pregnant women, with decorative elements like pink stripes. I felt it was totally involved with our reading; when you take baby stuff and pink stuff and slap it on a wall, you are definitely interrogating those tropes. And she was smashing them together with ideas about modernism. Part of her was also very Mary Heilmann, sort of off-the-cuff casual, but deconstructing formalism. I felt very connected to what she was doing, because I was doing another version of it in a certain way.

Laura was part of this crowd that was so good that I sent them to LA for grad school, because that was where it was happening. My friends Millie Wilson, Lari Pittman, Roy Dowell, Catherine Lord, and others were teaching out there and shaking things up. I remember going out to visit; Laura was just starting out and her mother had come out from Ohio to help move these really big paintings around her studio. She was just such a nice girl, who knew *a lot.*

   Deborah Kass, a Brooklyn-based artist, was a visiting artist at Rhode Island School of Design, Providence, in 1990.

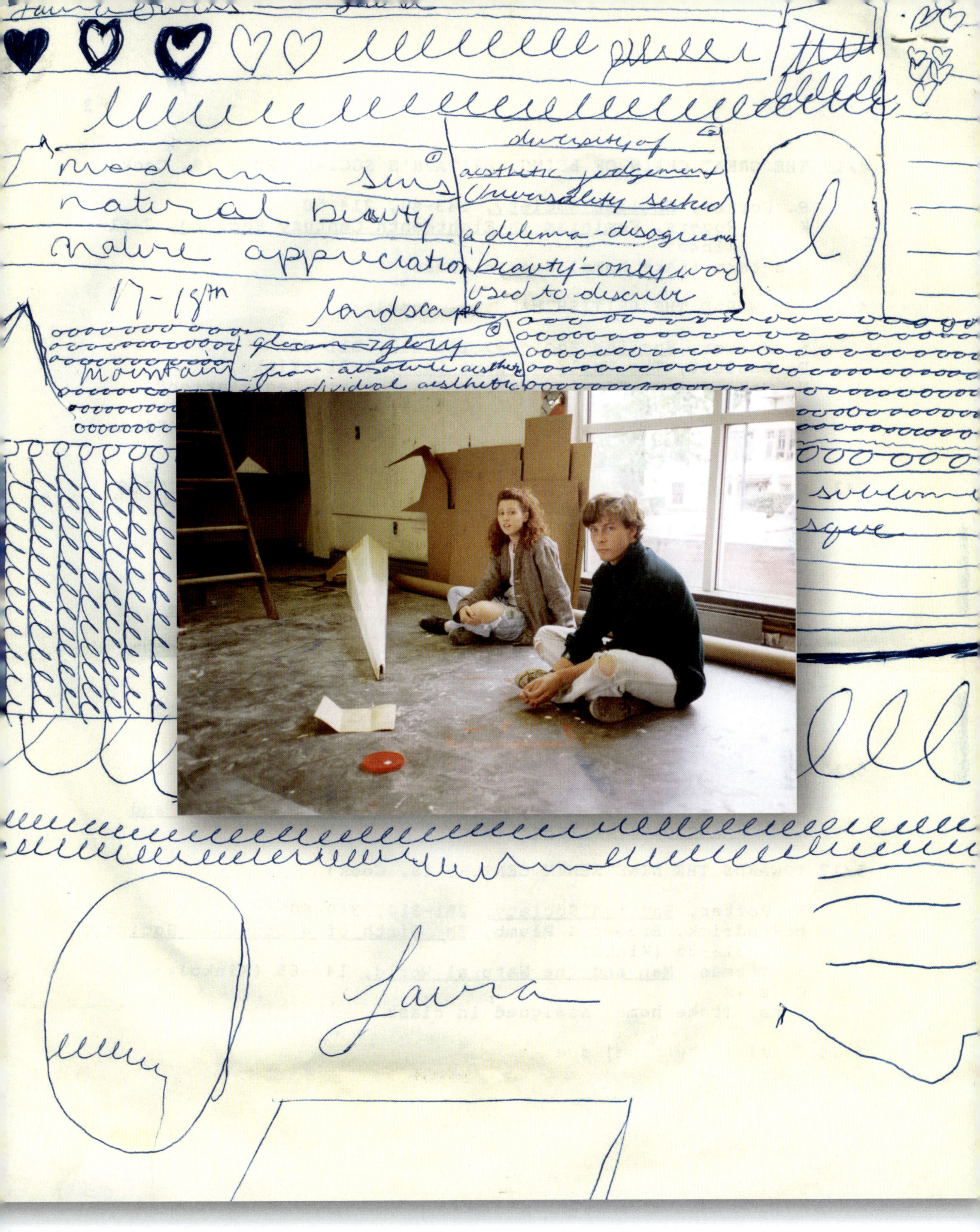

Foreground: Owens and Matt Adelman, Rhode Island School of Design, Providence, 1988
Background: Sketchbook page, ca. 1991

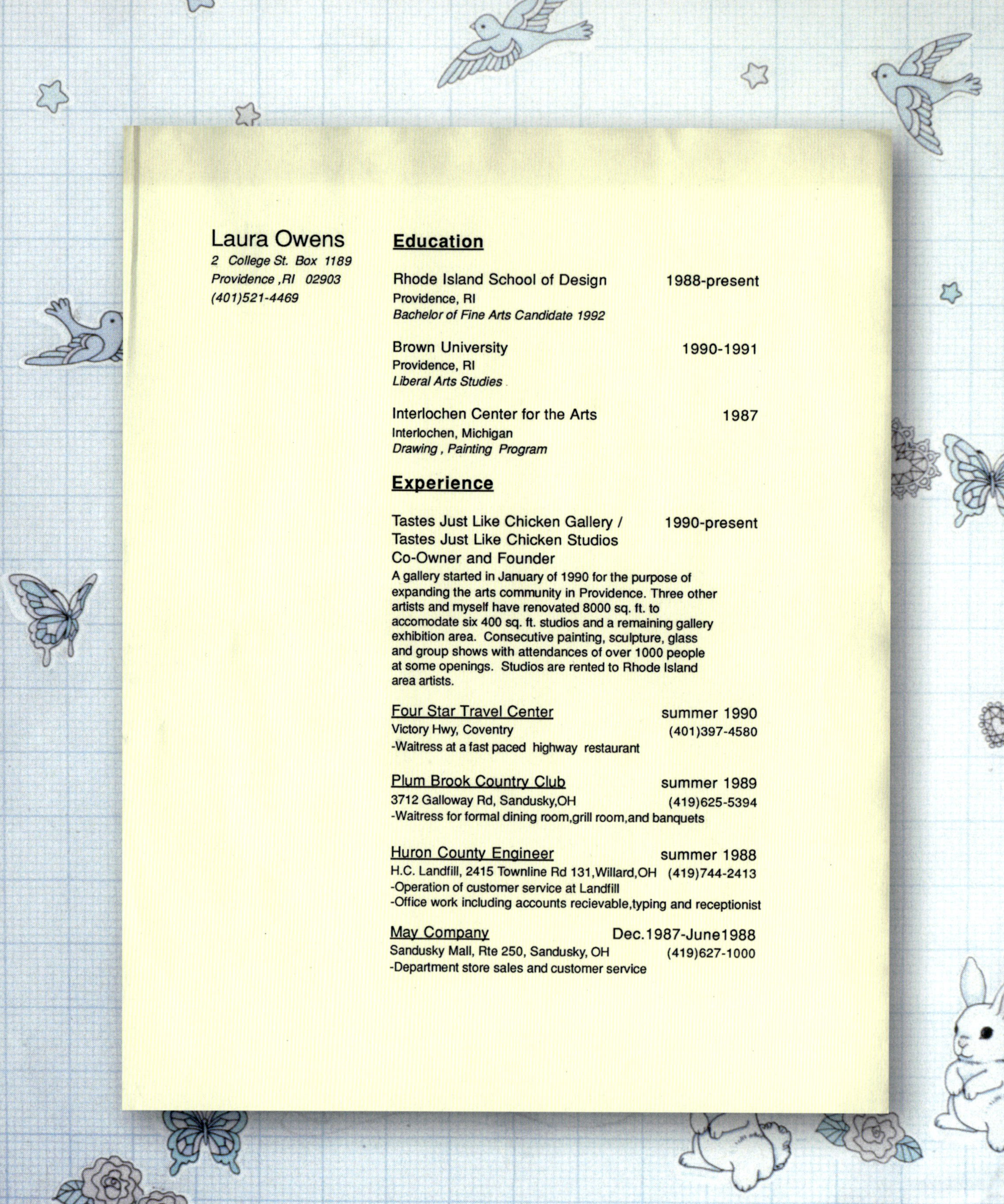

Laura Owens
2 College St. Box 1189
Providence ,RI   02903
(401)521-4469

Education

Rhode Island School of Design   1988-present
Providence, RI
Bachelor of Fine Arts Candidate 1992

Brown University   1990-1991
Providence, RI
Liberal Arts Studies .

Interlochen Center for the Arts   1987
Interlochen, Michigan
Drawing , Painting Program

Experience

Tastes Just Like Chicken Gallery /   1990-present
Tastes Just Like Chicken Studios
Co-Owner and Founder
A gallery started in January of 1990 for the purpose of
expanding the arts community in Providence. Three other
artists and myself have renovated 8000 sq. ft. to
accomodate six 400 sq. ft. studios and a remaining gallery
exhibition area. Consecutive painting, sculpture, glass
and group shows with attendances of over 1000 people
at some openings. Studios are rented to Rhode Island
area artists.

Four Star Travel Center   summer 1990
Victory Hwy, Coventry   (401)397-4580
-Waitress at a fast paced highway restaurant

Plum Brook Country Club   summer 1989
3712 Galloway Rd, Sandusky,OH   (419)625-5394
-Waitress for formal dining room,grill room,and banquets

Huron County Engineer   summer 1988
H.C. Landfill, 2415 Townline Rd 131,Willard,OH (419)744-2413
-Operation of customer service at Landfill
-Office work including accounts recievable,typing and receptionist

May Company   Dec.1987-June1988
Sandusky Mall, Rte 250, Sandusky, OH   (419)627-1000
-Department store sales and customer service

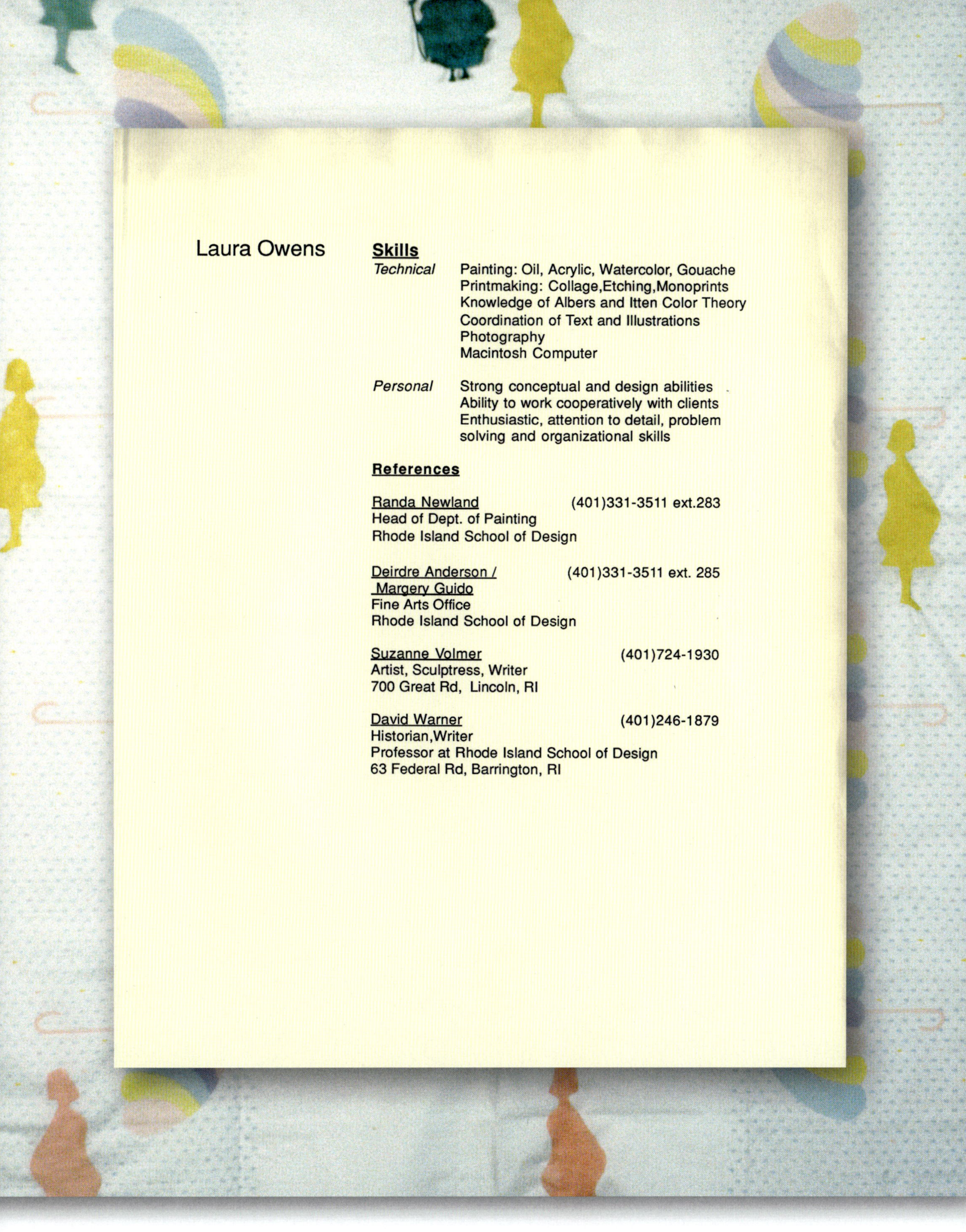

Background: Detail of *Magritte, Me and Two Mirrors*, 1991, collaged paper on party tablecloth, 144 × 36 in. (365.8 × 91.4 cm)

FASCINATIONS — Predominant Images
Home — Domus image — Must have doorway
Little Girl image
☆ Pregnant Women
Clouds
☆ Columns Steeples Architectural details of lightweight elegance
Miniture
(Childrens Illustrated Books)

☆ Stripes ~~~~~~
Polka-dot
☆ Legs top of skirt
Hearts
PAPER
TAPE
Typewritten Word
☆ Definately Phallus References

Why was/is the space inside childrens illustrations much more interesting to me than any paintings space?

? — It is where imaginary movement takes place

I am sure it is not nostalgia for these images for when I was younger I was fascinated by staring at an illustration for hours imagining

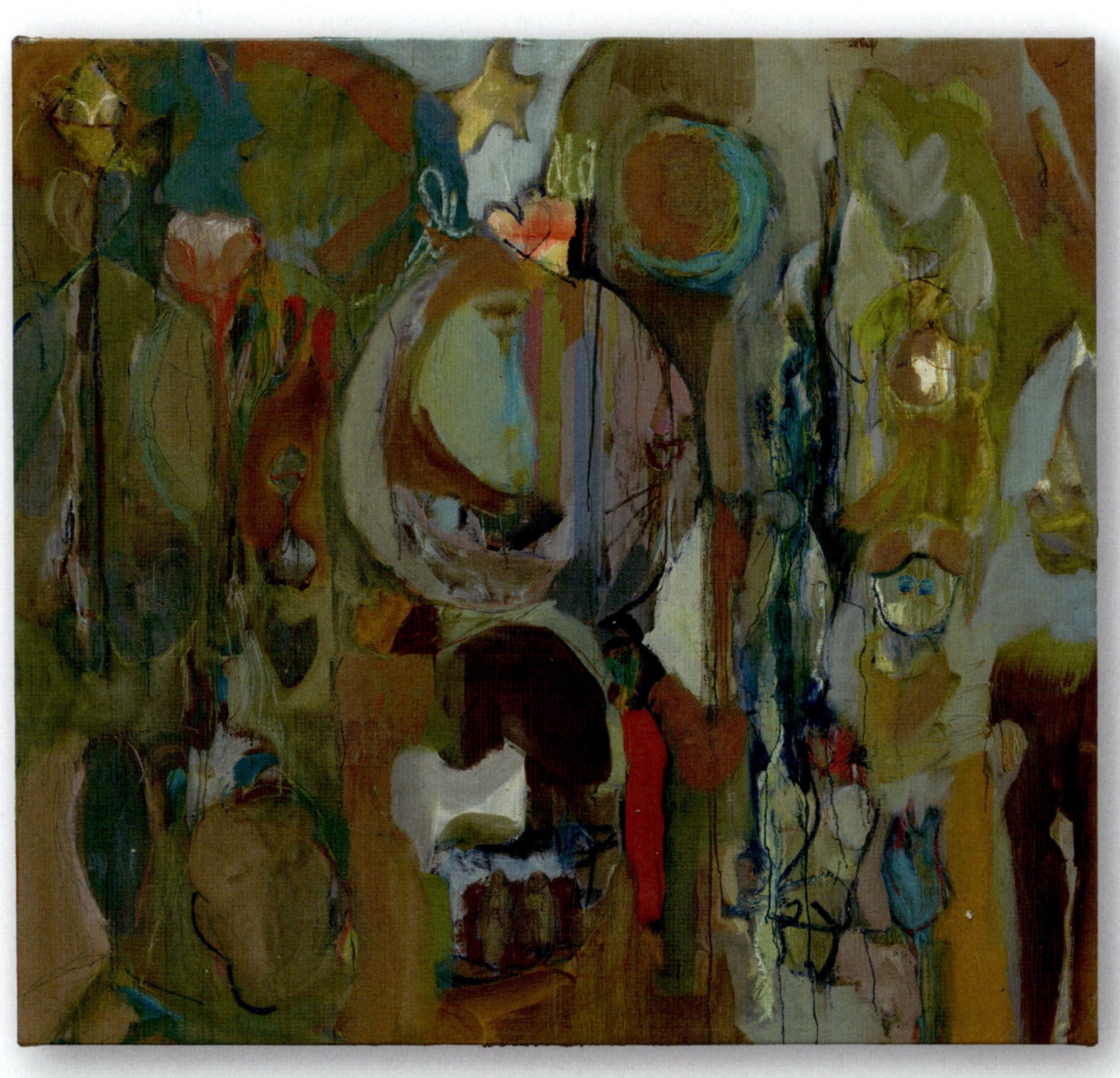

Untitled, 1988–91, oil and pastel on canvas, 66¾ × 71¾ in. (169.5 × 182.2 cm)

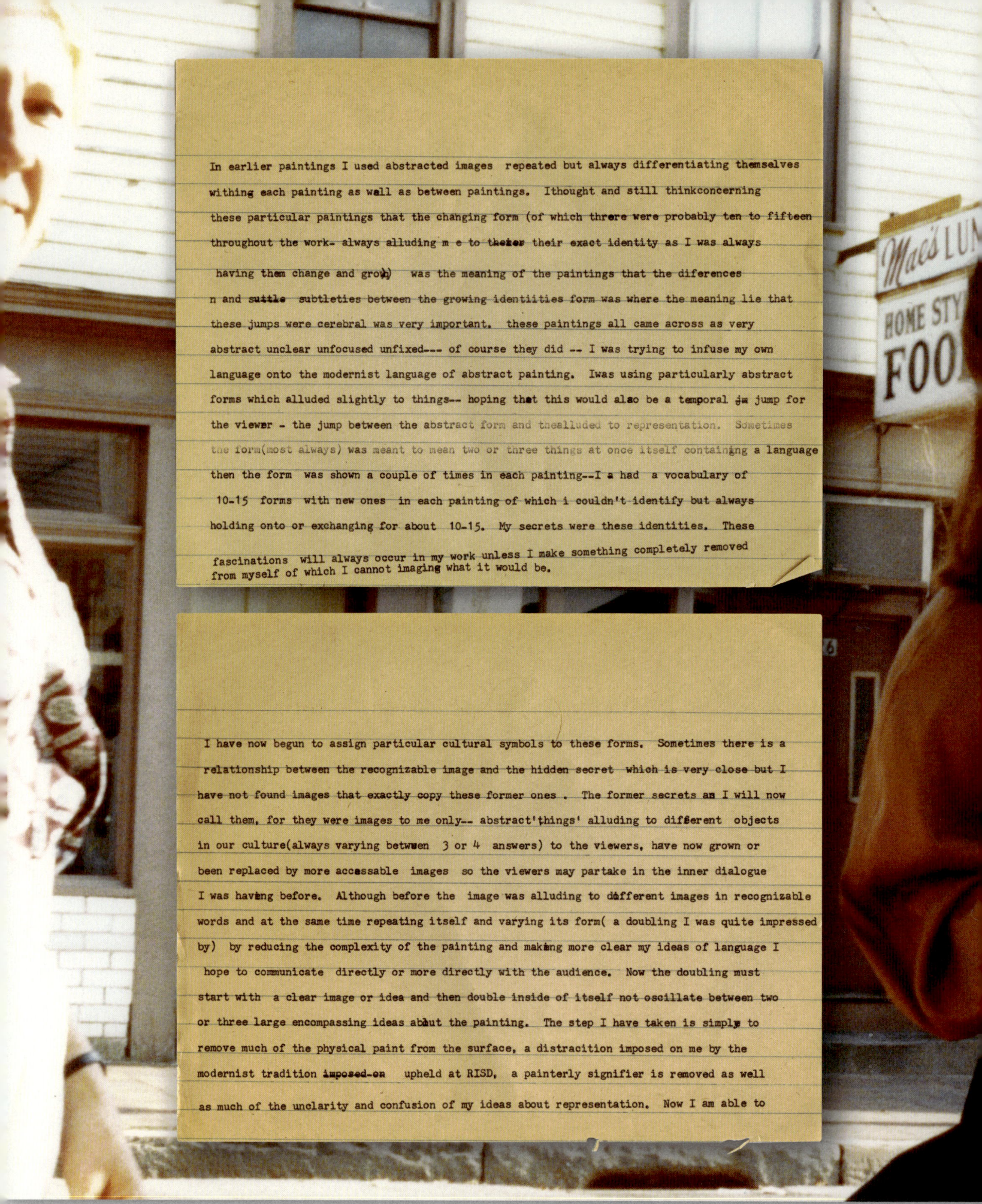

In earlier paintings I used abstracted images repeated but always differentiating themselves
withing each painting as wall as between paintings. Ithought and still thinkconcerning
these particular paintings that the changing form (of which throre were probably ten to fifteen
throughout the work- always alluding m e to theier their exact identity as I was always
 having them change and grow)   was the meaning of the paintings that the diferences
n and suttle subtleties between the growing identiities form was where the meaning lie that
these jumps were cerebral was very important. these paintings all came across as very
abstract unclear unfocused unfixed--- of course they did -- I was trying to infuse my own
language onto the modernist language of abstract painting. Iwas using particularly abstract
forms which alluded slightly to things-- hoping that this would also be a temporal ju jump for
the viewer - the jump between the abstract form and thealluded to representation. Sometimes
the form(most always) was meant to mean two or three things at once itself containing a language
then the form was shown a couple of times in each painting--I a had a vocabulary of
 10-15 forms with new ones in each painting of which i couldn't identify but always
holding onto or exchanging for about 10-15. My secrets were these identities. These
fascinations will always occur in my work unless I make something completely removed
from myself of which I cannot imaging what it would be.

I have now begun to assign particular cultural symbols to these forms. Sometimes there is a
relationship between the recognizable image and the hidden secret which is very close but I
have not found images that exactly copy these former ones . The former secrets an I will now
call them, for they were images to me only-- abstract'things' alluding to different objects
in our culture(always varying betwuen 3 or 4 answers) to the viewers, have now grown or
been replaced by more accassable images so the viewers may partake in the inner dialogue
I was having before. Although before the image was alluding to different images in recognizable
words and at the same time repeating itself and varying its form(a doubling I was quite impressed
by) by reducing the complexity of the painting and making more clear my ideas of language I
hope to communicate directly or more directly with the audience. Now the doubling must
start with a clear image or idea and then double inside of itself not oscillate between two
or three large encompassing ideas about the painting. The step I have taken is simply to
remove much of the physical paint from the surface, a distracition imposed on me by the
modernist tradition imposed on upheld at RISD, a painterly signifier is removed as well
as much of the unclarity and confusion of my ideas about representation. Now I am able to

Foreground: Notes, ca. 1991
Background: Owens, Atwells Avenue, Providence, 1990

use any signifier I wish as I feel empowered by discarding farmalist beliefs completely

Before(and still I believed that I could critique the modernist tradition withing it.

I cannot do that until I have stepped out of it and realized its hegemony over scholarly

painting or true painting by merely being the painting signifier for the past 30 years

Thei Now this type of signifier can be used in a positive way because I can experience

other signifiers as well. Each connotes a varying degree of worth depending on the situation

it is in. For examplre , at RISD the particular signifier which connotesthe most knowing

valuable painting is one that mimicks one of the major tenets of modernism starting with

abstract expression continuing through minimilism. What is needed is , thick oil paint,

a gestalt or focus of climax, basically a mastery of the medium of paint and the gestalt

image. Formalist criticism is predominant, light color wieght focus all validate a good

true painting, Everything else is illustration or not labored enough or unfocused , not

committed--- The entire realm of conceptualization is wiped out of the criterion No concept

is needed not is it welcomed unless it is of the personal spiritual type. Few teachers go

against this type of critique Holly Hughes, Deborah kass and Stuart Diamond are three I know

two go in a different more pluralistic diredtion They are all Part time teachers and pull no

wi

wieght in curriculum or departmental decisions   (i.e. decisions to include

a more diverse teaching staff to include non-formalist modernist painters, more women,

people of color or other marginalized artists, to include in the curriculum manditory

courses on theory and historical precedents set by painters nand issues that are

pertinent to someone painting in the present) Learning to paint (physically) is what

the curriculum containg right now witha year of free reign reign senior year to excel

with a cohesive body of work that its has a content pert pertinent to the particular

student. This would be accomplished easier if throughout the entire course of the 4 years

at RISD the student was given serious liberal arts classes pertaining to critical thinking

and historical events   No theory is better than CAL Arts seems to be the thinking here

At Cal Arts where students are notoriously stifled with theory unable to paint (mentally)

and physically never taught actual painting.   What is Actual Painting RISd doesn't teach

physical painting but a particular physical painting a sort of Frankenthaler- Motherwell

painting (and that is as far as the brigh bridge goes)--maybe some German Expressionsm

it seems to be hot right now. Otherwise the David Parks style is perfectly acceptable and

welcomed -- just learn how to create space through light color and form.

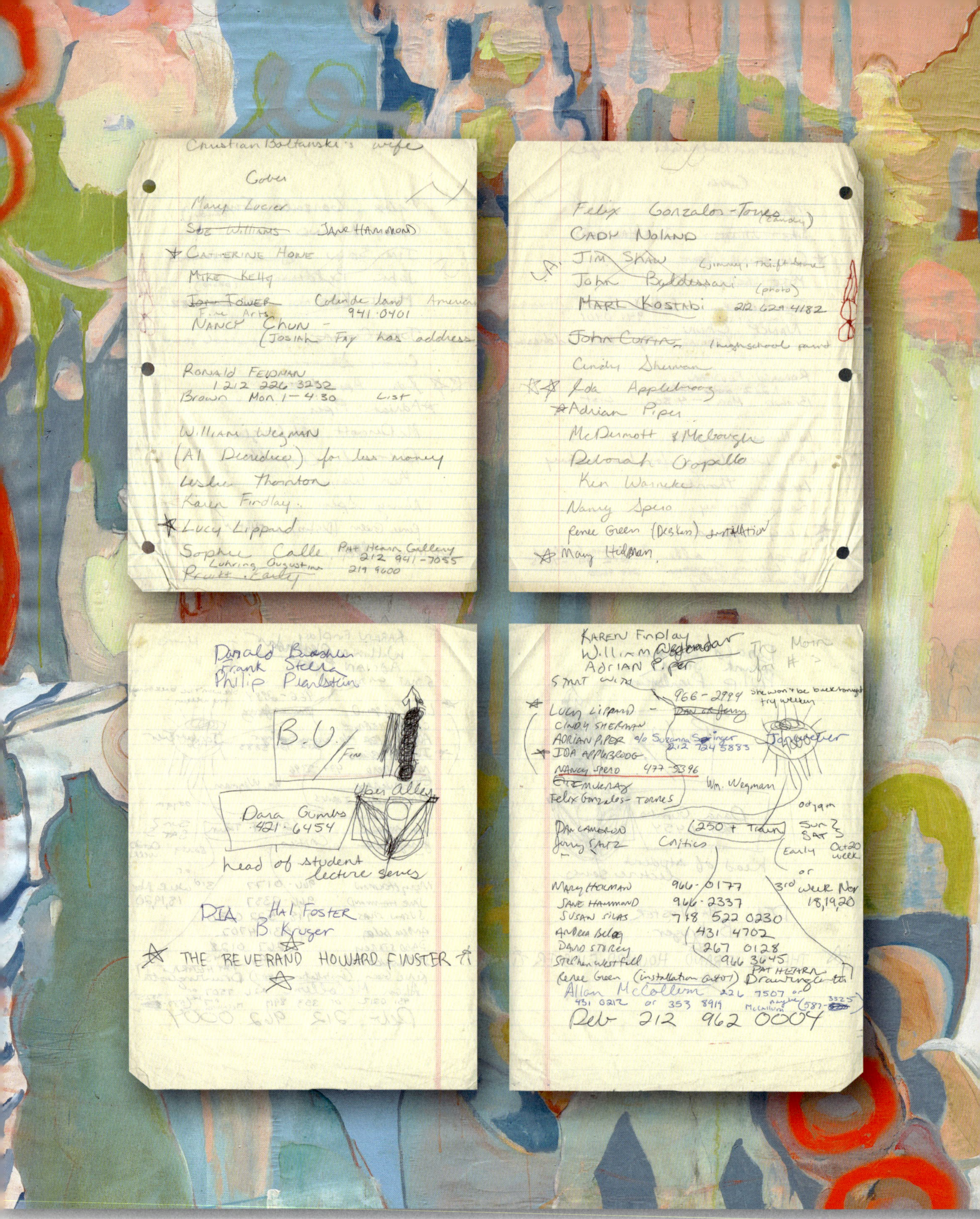

Foreground: Painting Club notes, ca. 1991
Background: Detail of *Untitled*, 1988–91, oil, spray paint, pastel, and graphite on canvas, 68 × 95 in. (172.7 × 241.3 cm)

List of Active Members

PAINTING. CLUB.

#	Printed Name	Signature	Year	Department	Box #
1	Josiah Fay	Josiah Fay	Junior	Paint	446
2	Richard Barlow		SENIOR	PAINT	90
3	Joseph Hartley	Joseph Hartley	SENIOR	PAINT	669
4	Laura Owens		Soph	Paint	1188
5	Jodi Levine				659
6	Nathan Lentz			Architect.	903
7	Philip Anderson			Studio	37
8	Juliana Sohn			Photo	800
9	Bob Bianchini			Illustration	195
10	Richard Herbert.			p.	2099.
11	Sarah Dockter			p.	403
12	Joy Benton				565
13	Bent Dudley			Ip	1986
14				Ip.	1002
15				Ip	684
16	Helen Semidey			ULP	305
17	David Peary				1196
18	Diane Bromberg				248
19	Chrysa Helias			Sculpture	740
20	Adam Frank (Frankk)			LPT.	523
21	Stephanie Snider	S. Snid	SR.	Sculpt.	255
22	Dennis Kuromazy		SR	Sculpt	1507
23	Amelia Biewald		Soph	Paint	233
24	J.A. Williams	Ja Williams	Grad 1	paint	1838
25	Ari Goodknight	AR Goodknight	Soph.	PAINT	757
26	Beth Malamed		Soph	PAINT	1788
27	John Horebschair		soph	PAINT	1175
28	Alice Kennedy	Alice Kennedy	soph	Paint	1150

Laura Owens: My junior year at RISD I realized there was a stranglehold on the painting department—no thinking beyond AbEx was allowed. It's hard to synopsize the stereotypical "boys club" ideas that held sway then, but it was like you had to use oil paint, it had to be Alizarin Crimson and Rich Green. Using certain other colors was not okay. Acrylic paint wasn't considered okay either. It was bullshit. One teacher had insisted all the women in his class paint representationally from still lifes or models. Only men could paint abstractly or use appropriation. I was the only woman painting abstractly. We got in many arguments, and he ended up asking me to work with the only female painting professor instead. Meanwhile, visiting artists and historians like Deb Kass and Mary Anne Staniszewski introduced us to a wide range of writers who contested the department's ideology—like bell hooks and John Berger.

I noticed that we were paying this activities fee as part of our tuition—it was meant to be used for campus socializing. I found out that if we formed a club we could use some of that money. So Josh Hartley and I started a painting club and got a couple thousand dollars and used it to bring in other kinds of artists to counter the very narrow idea of painting espoused by the mostly white, male RISD graduates on the faculty. That's how I met Nancy Chunn—who told me about CalArts—and Sophie Calle, Luis Cruz Azaceta, and a bunch of other people.

Foreground: Phone message from Renée Green, 1991
Background: Painting Club roster, ca. 1991

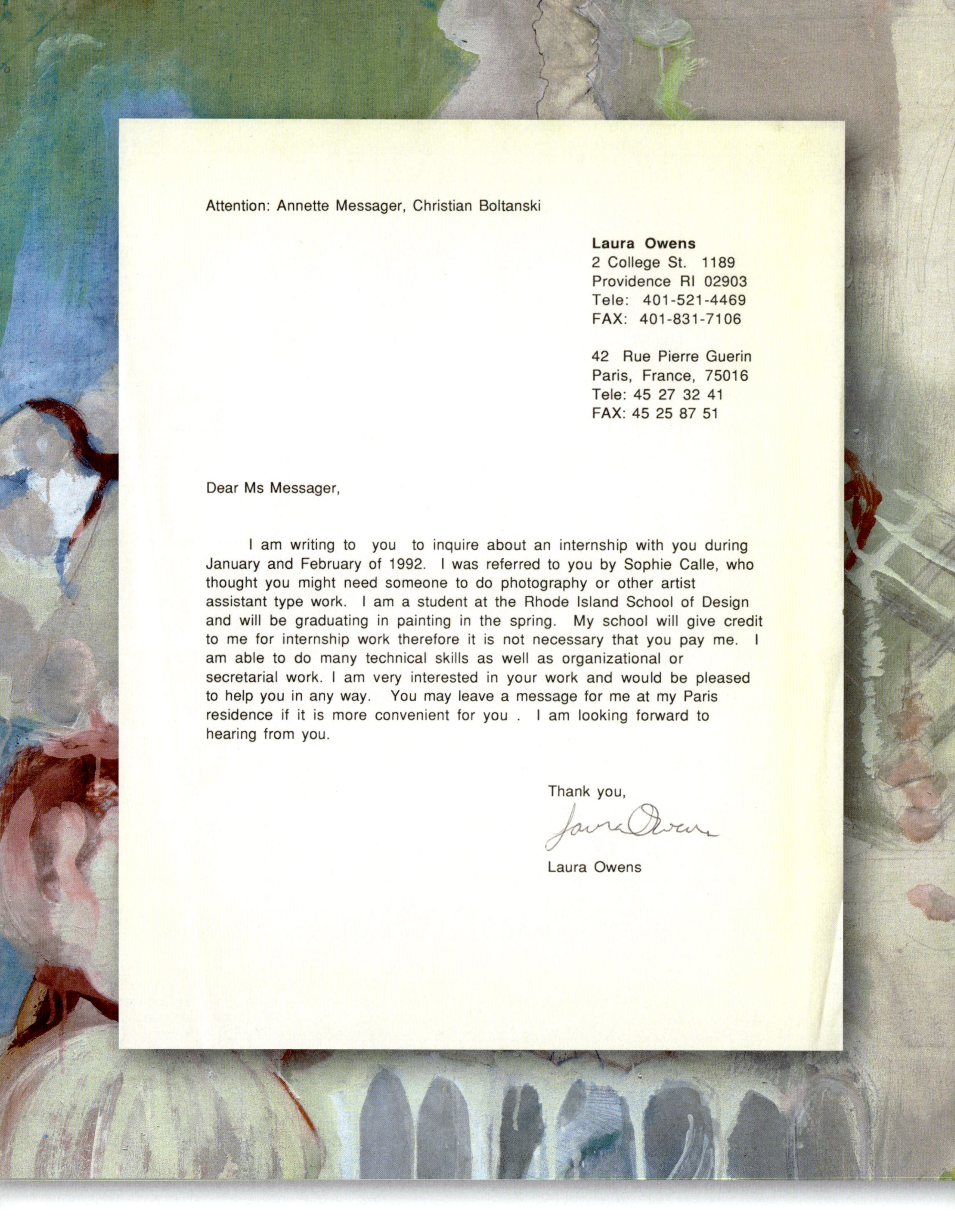

Attention: Annette Messager, Christian Boltanski

Laura Owens
2 College St. 1189
Providence RI 02903
Tele: 401-521-4469
FAX: 401-831-7106

42 Rue Pierre Guerin
Paris, France, 75016
Tele: 45 27 32 41
FAX: 45 25 87 51

Dear Ms Messager,

    I am writing to you to inquire about an internship with you during January and February of 1992. I was referred to you by Sophie Calle, who thought you might need someone to do photography or other artist assistant type work. I am a student at the Rhode Island School of Design and will be graduating in painting in the spring. My school will give credit to me for internship work therefore it is not necessary that you pay me. I am able to do many technical skills as well as organizational or secretarial work. I am very interested in your work and would be pleased to help you in any way.   You may leave a message for me at my Paris residence if it is more convenient for you . I am looking forward to hearing from you.

Thank you,

Laura Owens

Foreground: Letter to Annette Messager, 1991
Background: Detail of *Untitled*, 1988–91, oil, graphite, pastel, and marker on canvas, 68 × 96 in. (172.7 × 243.8 cm)

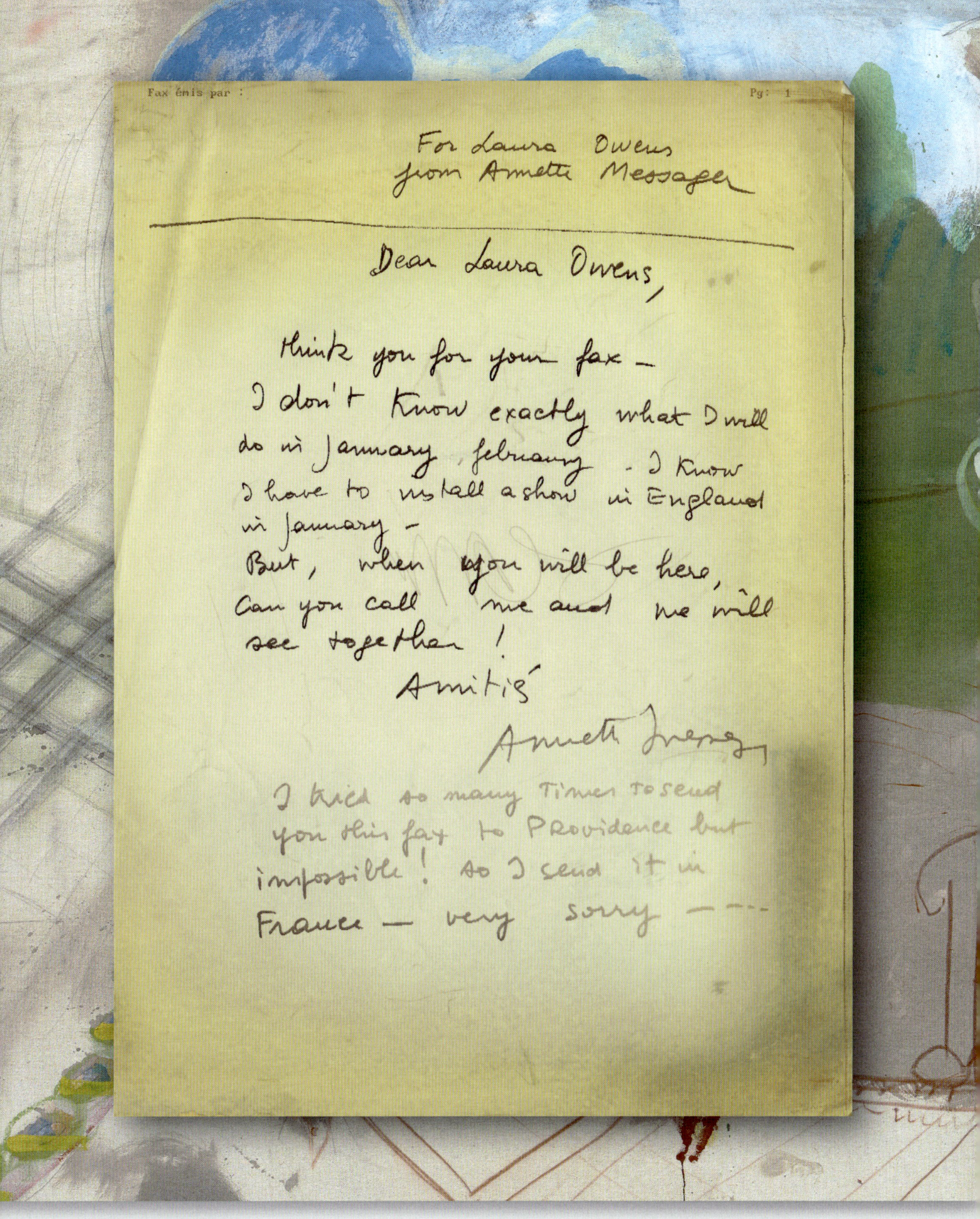
Fax émis par :   Pg: 1

For Laura Owens
from Annette Messager

Dear Laura Owens,

think you for your fax —
I don't know exactly what I will
do in January, february — I know
I have to install a show in England
in January —
But, when you will be here,
Can you call me and we will
see together !
Amitiés
Annette Messager

I tried so many Times to send
you this fax to Providence but
impossible ! So I send it in
France — very sorry ————

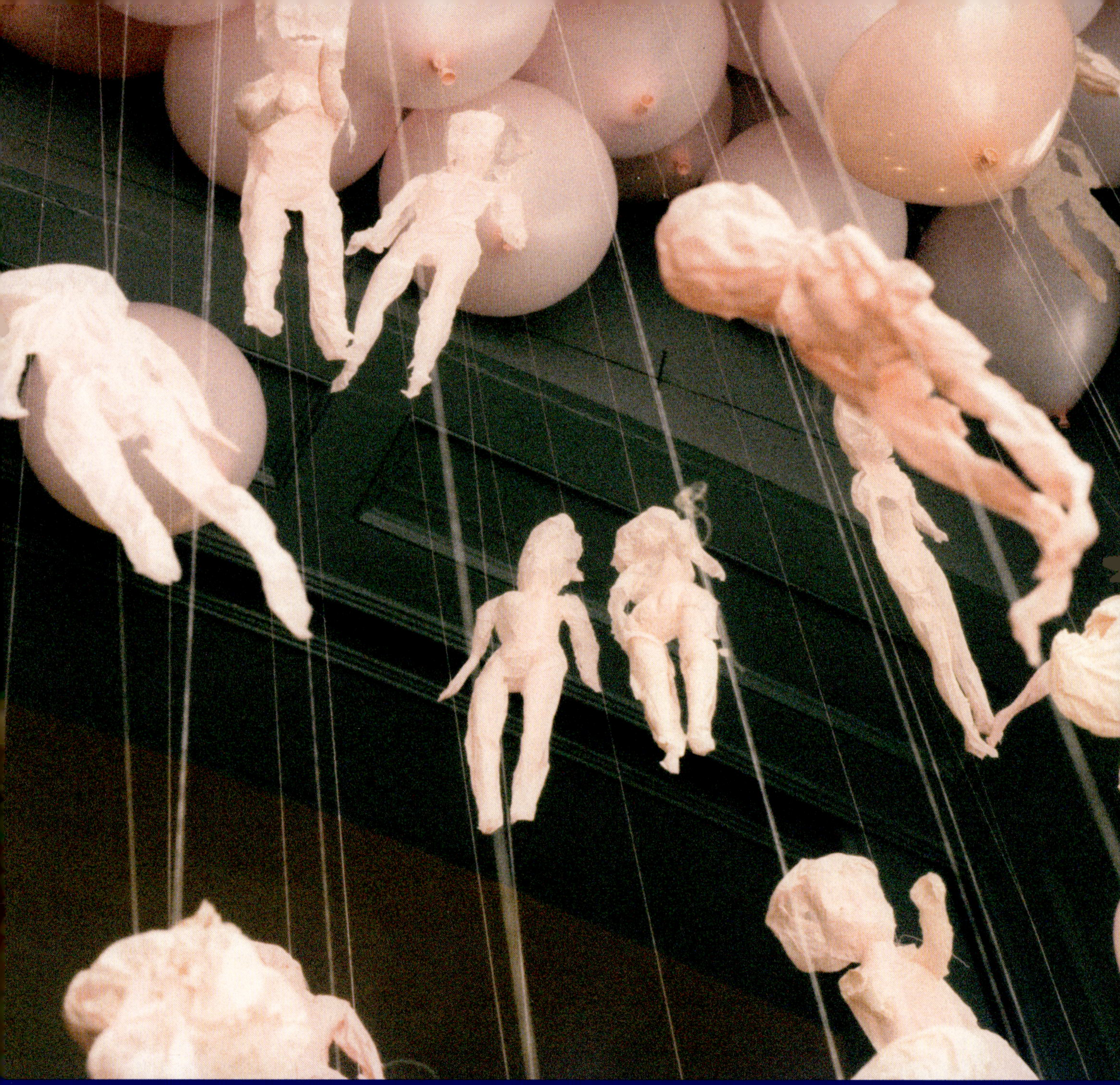

Installation views, senior thesis exhibition, Rhode Island School of Design, Providence, 1992, with *Untitled*, 1992, latex balloons and papier-mâché, dimensions variable

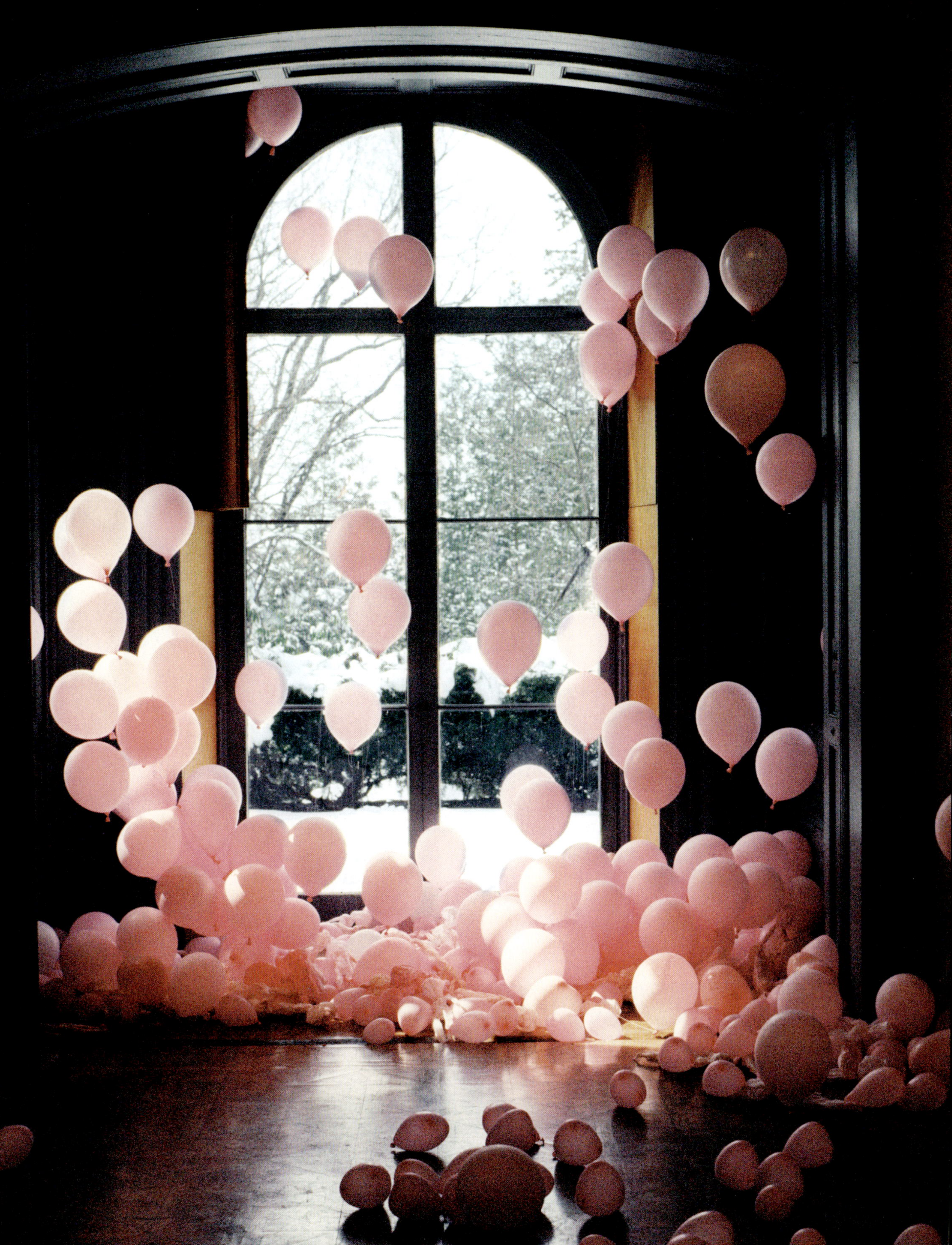

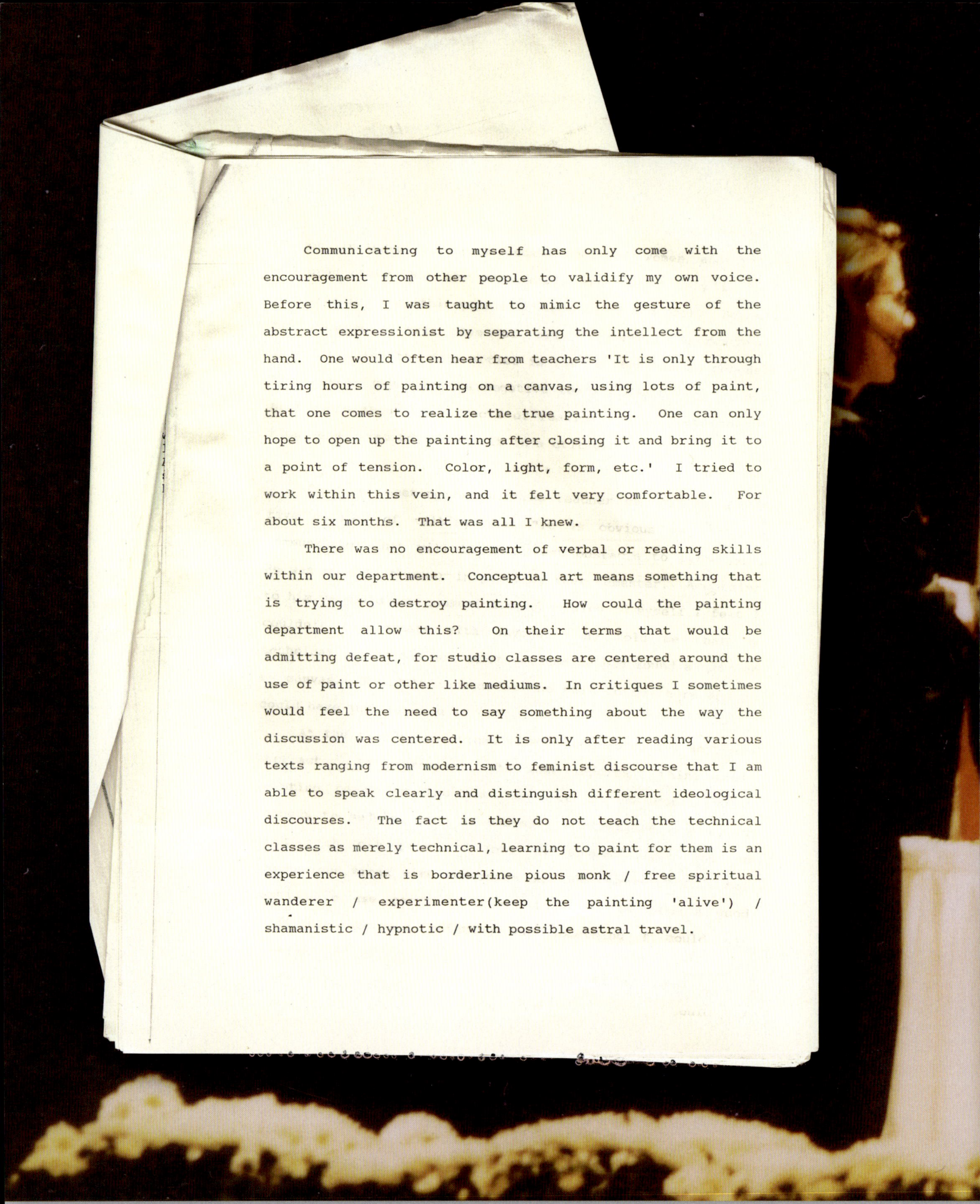

Communicating to myself has only come with the encouragement from other people to validify my own voice. Before this, I was taught to mimic the gesture of the abstract expressionist by separating the intellect from the hand. One would often hear from teachers 'It is only through tiring hours of painting on a canvas, using lots of paint, that one comes to realize the true painting. One can only hope to open up the painting after closing it and bring it to a point of tension. Color, light, form, etc.' I tried to work within this vein, and it felt very comfortable. For about six months. That was all I knew.

There was no encouragement of verbal or reading skills within our department. Conceptual art means something that is trying to destroy painting. How could the painting department allow this? On their terms that would be admitting defeat, for studio classes are centered around the use of paint or other like mediums. In critiques I sometimes would feel the need to say something about the way the discussion was centered. It is only after reading various texts ranging from modernism to feminist discourse that I am able to speak clearly and distinguish different ideological discourses. The fact is they do not teach the technical classes as merely technical, learning to paint for them is an experience that is borderline pious monk / free spiritual wanderer / experimenter(keep the painting 'alive') / shamanistic / hypnotic / with possible astral travel.

We were taught a linear art historical canon freshman year, with only some doubt as to it's validity. We were reminded at the beginning and the end of each semester that Janson included minuscule percentages of women and that cultures other than the Eurocentric are viewed only in the paleolithic, neolithic-primitive section of the book. Beyond this cursory criticism of art historical approaches, literature for the fine artist is left to her/him to choose. Needless to say with the negative reinforcement from studio professors about the effects of reading, no one read theory much less dared to mention it in a critique.

*   *   *

On first meeting my painting teacher he told me after five minutes of talking that "it is obvious we can not communicate, that will be the first obstacle to overcome." He was my only teacher in painting that semester. According to him we could not communicate, according to myself I felt I couldn't communicate with anyone. He told me that my technical skills did not exist because he had found a hair on my canvas. I didn't intend for the hair to be there and he could have just brushed it off.

At the time my paintings were homogeneous, low key, and abstract. In retrospect, the most important thing about painting to me at the time was not to use conventional methods to seduce, such as gestalt, a stretched canvas, or dark rich oil paint. That my unspecificity was an unconscious break with modernism has now become clear. Not wanting to use painting tricks in order to make a good believable abstract painting was something I could not

"WHEN I WAS A YOUNG SOLDIER FOR THE REVOLUTION": COMING TO VOICE

bell hooks

Angela Davis spoke these words. They moved me. I say them here and hope to say them in many places. This is how deeply they touched me—evoking memories of innocence, of initial passionate commitment to political struggle. They were spoken in a talk she gave at a conference focusing on "Poetry and Politics: Afro-American Poetry Today." I began writing poetry when I was young, ten years old. Poetry came into my life, the sense of poetry, with reading scripture with those awkward and funny little rhymes we would memorize and recite on Easter Sunday. Then it came into my life at Booker T. Washington grade school, where I learned that poetry was no silent subject. That moment of learning was pure enchantment, for we learned by listening and reciting that words put together just so, said just so, could have the same impact on our psyches as song, could lift and exalt our spirits, enabling us to feel tremendous joy, or carrying us down into that most immediate and violent sense of loss and grief.

Like many African Americans, I became a writer through making poems. Poetry was one literary expression that was absolutely respected in our working-class household. Nights when the lights would go out, when storms were raging, we would sit in the dim candlelight of our living room and have a talent show. I would recite poems: Wordsworth, James Weldon Johnson, Langston Hughes, Elizabeth Barrett Browning, Emily Dickinson, Gwendolyn Brooks, poetry by white writers was always there in schools and on family bookshelves in anthologies of "great" works sold to us by door-to-door salesmen, book peddlers, who came spreading their wares as though we were a dark desert people and they weary travelers bringing us light from a faraway place. Poetry by black writers had to be searched for, a poem copied from books no one would let you borrow for fear of loss, or taken from books found by puzzled white Southern librarians eager to see that you "read right." I was in high school before I discovered James Weldon Johnson's collection of American Negro Poetry. It had never been checked out of the library even though it had been on the shelves for some time. I would keep this book as long as I could, working to memorize every poem so I would know them all by heart.

For me, poetry was the place for the secret voice, for all that could not be directly stated or named, for all that would not be denied expression. Poetry was privileged speech—simple at times, but never ordinary. The magic of poetry was transformation; it was words changing shape, meaning, and form. Poetry was not mere recording of the way we Southern black folks talked to one another, even though our language was poetic. It was transcendent speech. It was meant to transform consciousness, to carry the mind and heart to a new dimension. These were my primitive thoughts on poetry as I experienced and knew it growing up.

When I became a student in college creative writing classes, I learned a notion of "voice" as embodying the distinctive expression of an individual writer. Our efforts to become poets were to be realized in this coming into awareness and expression of one's voice. In all my writing classes, I was the only black student. Whenever I read a poem written in the particular dialect of Southern black speech, the teacher and fellow students would praise me for using my "true," authentic voice, and encouraged me to develop this "voice," to write more of these poems. From the onset this troubled me. Such comments seemed to mask racial biases about what my authentic voice would or should be.

In part, attending all-black segregated schools with black teachers meant that I had come to understand black poets as being capable of speaking in many voices, that the Dunbar of a poem written in dialect was no more or less authentic than the Dunbar writing a sonnet. Yet

Originally published in *talking back: thinking feminist, thinking black* (New York: Routledge, 2015), 30–43. hooks is a cultural critic and feminist writer based in Kentucky.

it was listening to black musicians like Duke Ellington, Louis Armstrong, and later John Coltrane that impressed upon our consciousness a sense of versatility—they played all kinds of music, had multiple voices. So it was with poetry. The black poet, as exemplified by Gwendolyn Brooks and later Amiri Baraka, had many voices—with no single voice being identified as more or less authentic. The insistence on finding one voice, one definitive style of writing and reading one's poetry, fit all too neatly with a static notion of self and identity that was pervasive in university settings. It seemed that many black students found our situations problematic precisely because our sense of self, and by definition our voice, was not unilateral, monologist, or static but rather multi-dimensional. We were as at home in dialect as we were in standard English. Individuals who speak languages other than English, who speak patois as well as standard English, find it a necessary aspect of self-affirmation not to feel compelled to choose one voice over another, not to claim one as more authentic, but rather to construct social realities that celebrate, acknowledge, and affirm differences, variety. In *Borderlands/La Frontera,* Gloria Anzaldúa writes of the need to claim all the tongues in which we speak, to make speech of the many languages that give expression to the unique cultural reality of a people:

> For a people who are neither Spanish nor live in a country in which Spanish is the first language; for a people who live in a country in which English is the reigning tongue but who are not Anglo, for a people who cannot entirely identify with either standard (formal, Castilian) Spanish nor standard English, what recourse is left to them but to create their own language? A language which they can connect their identity to, one capable of communicating the realities and values true to themselves . . .

In recent years, any writing about feminism has overshadowed writing as a poet. Yet there are spaces where thoughts and concerns converge. One such space has been the feminist focus on coming to voice—on moving from silence into speech as revolutionary gesture. Once again, the idea of finding one's voice or having a voice assumes a primacy in talk, discourse, writing, and action. As metaphor for self-transformation, it has been especially relevant for groups of women who have previously never had a public voice, women who are speaking and writing for the first time, including many women of color. Feminist focus on finding a voice may seem

clichéd at times, especially when the insistence is that women share a common speech or that all women have something meaningful to say at all times. However, for women within oppressed groups who have contained so many feelings—despair, rage, anguish—who do not speak, as poet Audre Lorde writes, "for fear our words will not be heard nor welcomed," coming to voice is an act of resistance. Speaking becomes both a way to engage in active self-transformation and a rite of passage where one moves from being object to being subject. Only as subjects can we speak. As objects, we remain voiceless—our beings defined and interpreted by others. It is this liberating speech that Mariana Romo-Carmona writes about in her introduction to *Compañeras: Latina Lesbians*:

> Each time a woman begins to speak, a liberating process begins, one that is unavoidable and has powerful political implications. In these pages we see repeated the process of self-discovery, of affirmation in coming out of the closet, the search for a definition of our identity within the family and out community, the search for answers, for meaning in our personal struggles, and the commitment to a political struggle to end all forms of oppression. The stages of increasing awareness become clear when we begin to recount the story of our lives to someone else, someone who has experienced the same changes. When we write or speak about these changes we establish our experiences as valid and real, we begin to analyze, and that analysis gives us the necessary perspective to place our lives in a context where we know what to do next.

Awareness of the need to speak, to give voice to the varied dimensions of our lives, is one way women of color begin the process of education for critical consciousness.

Need for such speech is often validated in writings by people engaged in liberation struggles in the Third World, in the literatures of people struggling globally from oppression and domination. El Salvadoran writer Manlio Argueta structures his powerful novel *One Day Of Life* around the insistence on the development of political awareness, the sharing of knowledge that makes the revolutionary thinker and activist. It is the character José who is most committed to sharing his awareness with family and community, and most importantly with Lupé, his friend and wife, to whom he says: "that's why the problems can't be solved by a single person, but only by all of us working together, the humble, the clearheaded ones. And this is very important; you can be humble and live in darkness. Well, the thing is not a matter of being or not being humble. The problem lies in our awareness. The awareness we will have. Then life will become as clear as spring water."

I first read this novel in a course I taught on Third World literature and it was clear then that speaking freely, openly has different meaning for people from exploited and oppressed groups. Non-literary works by writers opposing domination also speak to the primacy of coming to voice, of speaking for the oppressed. In keeping with this emphasis on speech, Alicia Partnoy proclaims in her brave work *The Little School: Tales of Disappearance and Survival,* "They cut off my voice so I grew two voices, into different tongues my songs I pour." Here speech has a dual implication. There is the silence of the oppressed who have never learned to speak and there is the voice of those who have been forcefully silenced because they have dared to speak and by doing so resist. Egyptian writer Nawal el Saadawi protests against such silences in her *Memoirs from the Women's Prison.* She dedicated her book "to all who have hated oppression to the point of death, who have loved freedom to the point of imprisonment, and have rejected falsehood to the point of revolution." Or the resistance to being silenced Theresa Hak KyungCha describes in *Dictee*:

> Mother, you are a child still. At eighteen. More of a child since you are always ill. They have sheltered you from the others. It is not your own. Even if it not you know you must. You are bi-lingual. You are tri-lingual. The tongue that is forbidden is your own mother tongue. You speak in the dark, in the secret. The one that is yours. Your own . . . Mother tongue is your refuge. It is being home. Being who you are. Truly. To speak makes you sad. To utter each word is a privilege you risk by death.

In fiction as well as in confessional writing, those who understand the power of voice as gesture of rebellion and resistance urge the exploited, the oppressed to speak.

To speak as an act of resistance is quite different than ordinary talk, or the personal confession that has no relation to coming into political awareness, to developing critical consciousness. This is a difference we must talk about in the United States, for here the idea of finding a voice risks being trivialized or romanticized in the rhetoric of those who advocate a shallow feminist politic which privileges acts of speaking over the content of speech. Such rhetoric often turns the voices and beings of nonwhite women into commodity, spectacle. In a white-supremacist, capitalist, patriarchal state where the mechanisms of co-optation are so advanced, much that is potentially radical is undermined, turned into commodity, fashionable speech as in "black women writers are in right now." Often the question of who is listening and what is being heard are not answered. When reggae music became popular in the Untied States, I often pondered whether the privileged white people who listened were learning from this music to resist, to rebel against white supremacy and white imperialism. What did they hear when Bob Marley said, "We refuse to be what you wanted us to be"—did they think about colonization, about internalized racism? One night at a Jimmy Cliff concert attended predominantly by young white people, Cliff began a call and response refrain where we the listeners were to say "Africa for Africans." There was suddenly a hush in the room, as though the listeners finally heard the rebellion against white supremacy, against imperialism in the lyrics. They were silent, unable apparently to share in this gesture affirming black solidarity. Who is listening and what do they hear?

Appropriation of the marginal voice threatens the very core of self-determination and free self-expression for exploited and oppressed peoples. If the identified audience, those spoken to, is determined solely by ruling groups who control production and distribution, then it is easy for the marginal voice striving for a hearing to allow what is said to be overdetermined by the needs of that majority group who appears to be listening, to be tuned in. It becomes easy to speak about what that group wants to hear, to describe and define experience in a language compatible with existing images and ways of knowing, constructed within social frameworks that reinforce domination. Within any situation of colonization, of domination, the oppressed, the exploited develop various styles of relating, talking one way to one another, talking another way to those who have power to oppress and dominate, talking in a way that allows one to be understood by someone who does not know your way of speaking, your language. The struggle to end domination, the individual struggle to resist colonization, to move from object to subject, is expressed in the effort to establish the liberatory voice—that way of speaking that is no longer determined by one's status as object—as oppressed being. That way of speaking is characterized by opposition, by resistance. It demands that paradigms shift—that we learn to talk—to listen—to hear in a new way.

To make the liberated voice, one must confront the issue of audience—we must know to whom we speak. When I began writing my first book, *Ain't I a Woman: black women and feminism,* the initial completed manuscript was excessively long and very repetitious. Reading it critically, I saw that I was trying not only to address each different potential audience—black men, white women, white men, etc.—but that my words were written to explain, to placate, to appease. They contained the fear of speaking that often characterizes the way those in a lower position within a hierarchy address those in a higher position of authority. Those passages where I was speaking most directly to black women contained the voice I felt to be most truly mine—it was then that my voice was daring, courageous. When I thought about audience—the way in which the language we choose to use declares who it is we place at the center of our discourse—I confronted my fear of placing myself and other black women at the speaking center. Writing this book was for me a radical gesture. It not only brought me face-to-face with this question of power; it forced me to resolve this question, to act, to find my voice, to become that subject who could place herself and those like her at the center of feminist discourse. I was transformed in consciousness and being.

When the book was first published, white women readers would often say to me, "I don't feel this book is really talking to me." Often these readers would interpret the direct, blunt speech as signifying anger and I would have to speak against this interpretation and insist upon the difference between direct speech and hostility. At a discussion once where a question about audience was raised, I responded by saying that while I would like readers to be diverse, the audience I most wanted to address was black women, that I wanted to place us at the center. I was asked by a white woman, "How can you do that in a cultural context where black women are not primary book buyers and white women are the principal buyers of feminist books?" It seemed that she was suggesting that audience should be determined by who buys certain books. It had never occurred to me that white women would not buy a book if they did not see themselves at the center because, more than any group of people I could identify, white people have travelled the

globe consuming cultural artifacts that did not place them at the center. My placement of black women at the center was not an action to exclude others but rather an invitation, a challenge to those who would hear us speak, to shift paradigms rather than appropriate, to have all readers listen to the voice of a black woman speaking a subject and not as underprivileged other. I wrote *Ain't I a Woman* not to inform white women about black women but rather as an expression of my longing to know more and think deeply about our experience.

In celebrating our coming to voice, Third World women, African American women must work against speaking as "other," speaking to difference as it is constructed in the white-supremacist imagination. It is therefore crucial that we search our hearts and our words to see if our true aim is liberation, to make sure they do not suppress, trap, or confine. Significantly, knowing who is listening provides an indication of how our voices are heard. My words are heard differently by the oppressive powerful. They are heard in a different way by black women who, like me, are struggling to recover ourselves from the ravages of colonization. To know our audience, to know who listens, we must be in dialogue. We must be speaking with and not just speaking to. In hearing responses, we come to understand whether our words act to resist, to transform, to move. In a consumer culture where we are all led to believe that the value of our voice is not determined by the extent to which it challenges, or makes critical reflection possible, but rather by whether or not it (and sometimes even we) is liked, it is difficult to keep a liberatory message. It is difficult to maintain a sense of direction, a strategy for liberated speaking, if we do not constantly challenge these standards of valuation. When I first began to talk publicly about my work, I would be disappointed when audiences were provoked and challenged but seemed to disapprove. Not only was my desire for approval naïve (I have since come to understand that it is silly to think that one can challenge and also have approval), it was dangerous precisely because such a longing can undermine radical commitment, compelling a change in voice so as to gain regard.

Speaking out is not a simple gesture of freedom in a culture of domination. We are often deceived (yes, even those of us who have experienced domination) by the illusion of free speech, falsely believing that we can say whatever we wish in an atmosphere of openness. There would be no need to even speak of the oppressed and exploited coming to voice, articulating and redefining reality, if there were not oppressive mechanisms of silencing, suppressing, and censoring. Thinking we speak in a climate where freedom is valued, we are often shocked to find ourselves assaulted, our words devalued. It should be understood that the liberatory voice will necessarily confront, disturb, demand that listeners even alter ways of hearing and being. I remember talking with Angela Davis a few years ago about the death threats that she often received before speaking. Our conversation had a profound effect on my consciousness, on me as a listener; it changed my understanding of what it means to speak from a radical position in this society. When one threatens—one is at risk.

Often I am amazed as a teacher in the classroom at the extent to which students are afraid to speak. A young black woman student wrote these words to me:

> My voice is not fit to be heard by 120 people. To produce such a voice, my temperature increases and my hands shake. My voice is calm and quiet and soothing; it is not a means of announcing the many secrets my friends have told me—it quiets the rush of the running stream that is their life, slowing to make a mirror to reflect their worries, so that they can be examined and problems rectified. I am not relieved by voicing my opinions. Placing my opinion up to be judged by the public is a form of opening myself to criticism and pain. Those who do not share my eyes cannot see where to tread lightly on me.
>
> I am afraid. I am, and will always be afraid. My fear is that I will not be understood. I try to learn the vocabulary of my friends to ensure my communication on their terms. There is no singular vocabulary of 120 people. I will be misunderstood; I will not be respected as a speaker; they will name me Stupid in their minds; they will disregard me. I am afraid.

Encouraging students to speak, I tell them to imagine what it must mean to live in a culture where to speak one risks brutal punishment—imprisonment, torture, death. I ask them to think about what it means that they lack the courage to speak in a culture where there are few if any consequences. Can their fear be understood solely as shyness or is it an expression of deeply embedded, socially constructed restrictions against speech in a culture of domination, a fear of owning one's words, of taking a stand? Audre Lorde's poem "Litany for Survival" addresses our fear of speech and urges us to overcome it:

> and when we speak we are afraid
> our words will not be heard
> nor welcomed
> but when we are silent
> we are still afraid
>
> So it is better to speak
> remembering
> we were never meant to survive.

To understand that finding a voice is an essential part of liberation struggle—for the oppressed, the exploited a necessary starting place—a move in the direction of freedom, is important for those who stand in solidarity with us. That talk which identifies us as uncommitted, as lacking in critical consciousness, which signifies a condition of oppression and exploitation, is utterly transformed as we engage in critical reflection and as we act to resist domination. We are prepared to struggle for freedom only when this groundwork has been laid.

When we dare to speak in a liberatory voice, we threaten even those who may initially claim to want our words. In the act of overcoming our fear of speech, of being seen as threatening, in the process of learning to speak as subjects, we participate in the global struggle to end domination. When we end our silence, when we speak in a liberated voice, our words connect us with anyone, anywhere who lives in silence. Feminist focus on women finding a voice, on the silence of black women, of women of color, has led to increased interest in our words. This is an important historical moment. We are both speaking of our own volition, out of our commitment to justice, to revolutionary struggle to end domination, and simultaneously called to speak, "invited" to share our words. It is important that we speak. What we speak about is more important. It is our responsibility collectively and individually to distinguish between mere speaking that is about self-aggrandizement, exploitation of the exotic "other," and that coming to voice which is a gesture of resistance, an affirmation of struggle.

Alex Slade: Laura and I met at CalArts when I was a second-year and she was a first-year. She did this show at the Mint Gallery where everything was pink—I feel like we had a critique in Michael Asher's class about that. That show was my introduction to Laura's work, so I didn't really think of her as a painter, I thought of her as an installation artist. At that time it seemed like everybody at CalArts was an installation artist—there were very few real painters, and I think there was pressure to think a lot about installation. And so everyone did, myself included. I stopped taking photographs and started doing installation and sculpture. I had heard that Laura was a painter at RISD, but her first year at CalArts she was doing these installations. I had never really seen anything like Laura's show— it was unusual, especially for that time, when CalArts was very political and everything had a big theoretical component. Laura's show did not have any of that stuff—it was different, and people didn't know what to do with it; it didn't fit into any of the categories we were used to using to talk about artwork.

In those days Sande Cohen was teaching Deleuze and Baudrillard, and we were all into that kind of theory. Blake Rayne and Pieter Schoolwerth always spoke in Michael Asher's class, and they spent a lot of time talking about that stuff. Sharon Lockhart was down at ArtCenter in Pasadena then and I was up at CalArts. I went to all their events and she came up to CalArts to the events that we had. Sharon met Laura through that, and sometimes she would come up for the parties, the openings on Thursdays. It was a weird period at CalArts because Catherine Lord had just come in and eviscerated the program. Richard Hertz ran the program at ArtCenter, and I think he had been at CalArts before that. When Lord arrived, he and Jeremy Gilbert-Rolfe were shown the door. Someone once described her as a humorless Marxist: if you had a sense of humor you had to go somewhere else. When I got there students in the class ahead of me said that the previous year had been the most contentious, awful experience for everybody. There was this intense political correctness that everyone was fighting against, and everybody was frustrated—the people who were fans of Catherine and the people who weren't: there was equal frustration and bitterness on both sides.

You would hear about how CalArts was this theory place, but it wasn't like theory didn't exist down at ArtCenter. Tim Martin was there, and Mike Kelley and Stephen Prina and Jeremy. They were all just as interested in theory as the people at CalArts, but it was a little different. CalArts had Allan Sekula, so it was more along the lines of that traditional *October* crowd, whereas ArtCenter was more art driven than theory driven. So, there was a difference, but it was not as dramatic as it has been made out to be. Essentially the institutions were very different, but I felt like the students in both programs were similar. At CalArts we were really aware of whether or not we were political, whereas I think at ArtCenter that wasn't an issue. The practical difference was that at ArtCenter everything was organized, but at CalArts everything was disorganized. You had to arrange your own studio visits with teachers and be aggressive about doing that. You had to make connections with instructors, whereas at ArtCenter everything was programmed, it was more structured. CalArts was total chaos and it's still that way.

December 20 1992

Mr. William H. Ahmanson
The Ahmanson Foundation Scholarship

Dear Mr. Ahmanson,

I would like to take this time to thank you for your generous support. As a recipient of an Ahmanson Scholarship I would be unnable to attend CalArts without your financial support.

This semester was my first semester as a graduate student at CalArts. I am concentrating in Fine Art, and am using these two years of graduate school to build a portfolio of work. As an artist, it is extremely difficult to make a lot of work while holding down a full time job. At CalArts I have the time to solidify my ideas and concentrate on developing my artwork. Currently I am making sculpture and paintings which pertain to the female body by using images that are found in popular culture. Most of these found images come from a selection of materials used to socially construct what is considered female in our culture. Many of the faculty are also interested in gender analysis and many of the classes at CalArts are focused on this area of study. This is particularly unusual for most art schools, therefore I feel like I have made a wise decision to come to the CalArts graduate program. I found the teachers to be very encouraging and helpful. At my undergraduate school this was not always the case so I am particularly grateful in my present situation.

I am currently involved in many out of school activities which along with my MFA degree should prepare me for the job market. I am working as the Video Associate at L.A.C.E. , a nonprofit arts organization. This is an internship in which part of my pay comes from government work-study. I am responsible for managing and developing the video program.

I am also working with three other women to coordinate a party for youth in South Central Los Angeles scheduled for February 13, 1993, in which we will focus the music, visuals and other party paraphernalia around HIV/AIDS education. Our first group of teenagers happen to be from South Central but we have future plans to move the party to Pasadena and other areas of L.A.

I am also involved in an artist collective (consisting of ten visual artists) called L.A. Matter. We make site specific installations and performances focusing on social issues, particularly those in L.A. Our last show was held at the F.A.R. Bazaar during the month of December.

After graduation I hope to get a job teaching. Most colleges require a graduate degree in order to teach. I cannot express how grateful I am for your scholarship, without it I would not be able to attend CalArts. I feel I would be hard pressed to find another program similar to or even of the same quality as CalArts. I am currently taking out loans for the remainder of my tuition. Without your scholarship I cannot see myself continuing my education at CalArts, the financial burden would really be too much for me to bear. Please accept my sincere gratitude.

Thank you,

Laura Owens

Foreground: Requisite letter of gratitude to William Ahmanson, 1992
Background: Detail of *Untitled*, 1994 (see p. 64)

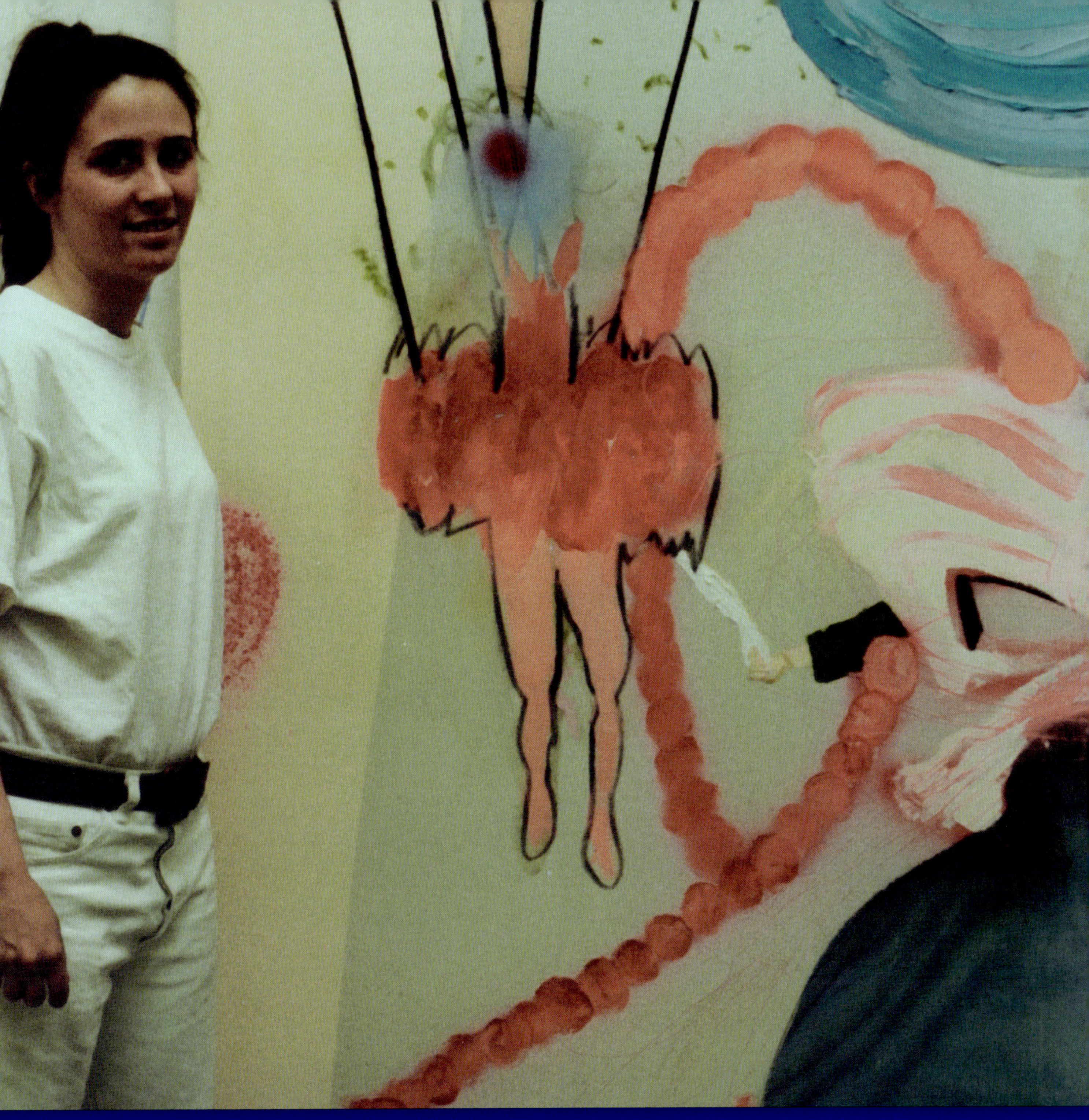

Owens with *Untitled*, 1993, acrylic and oil on canvas, 70 × 56 in. (177.8 × 142.2 cm), California Institute of the Arts, Valencia, 1993

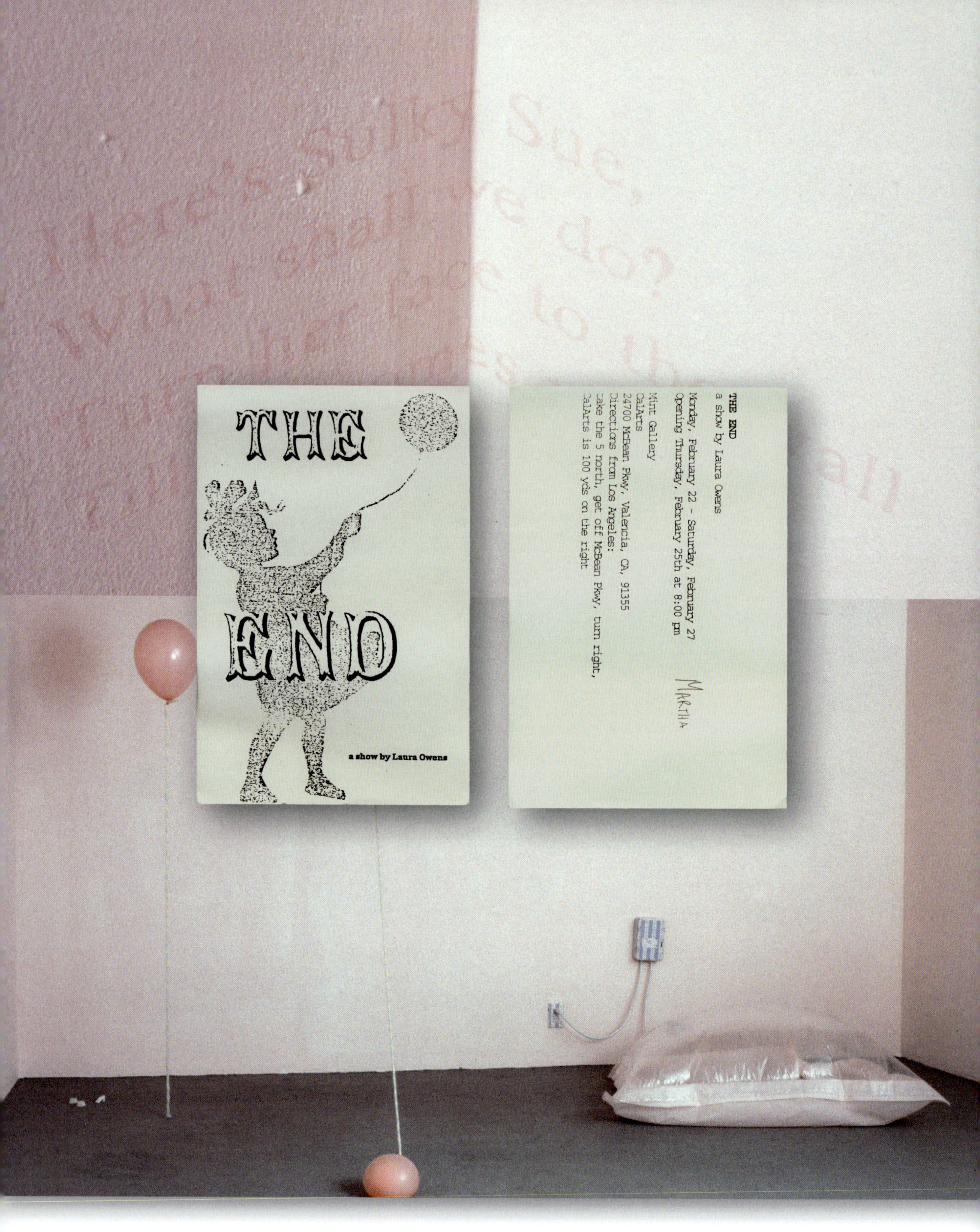

Foreground: Invitation, *The End*, Mint Gallery, California Institute of the Arts, Valencia, 1992
Background: Installation views, Mint Gallery, California Institute of the Arts, Valencia, 1992, with *Untitled*, 1992, house paint, contact paper, plastic, fabric, timer, hairdryer, and balloons, dimensions variable

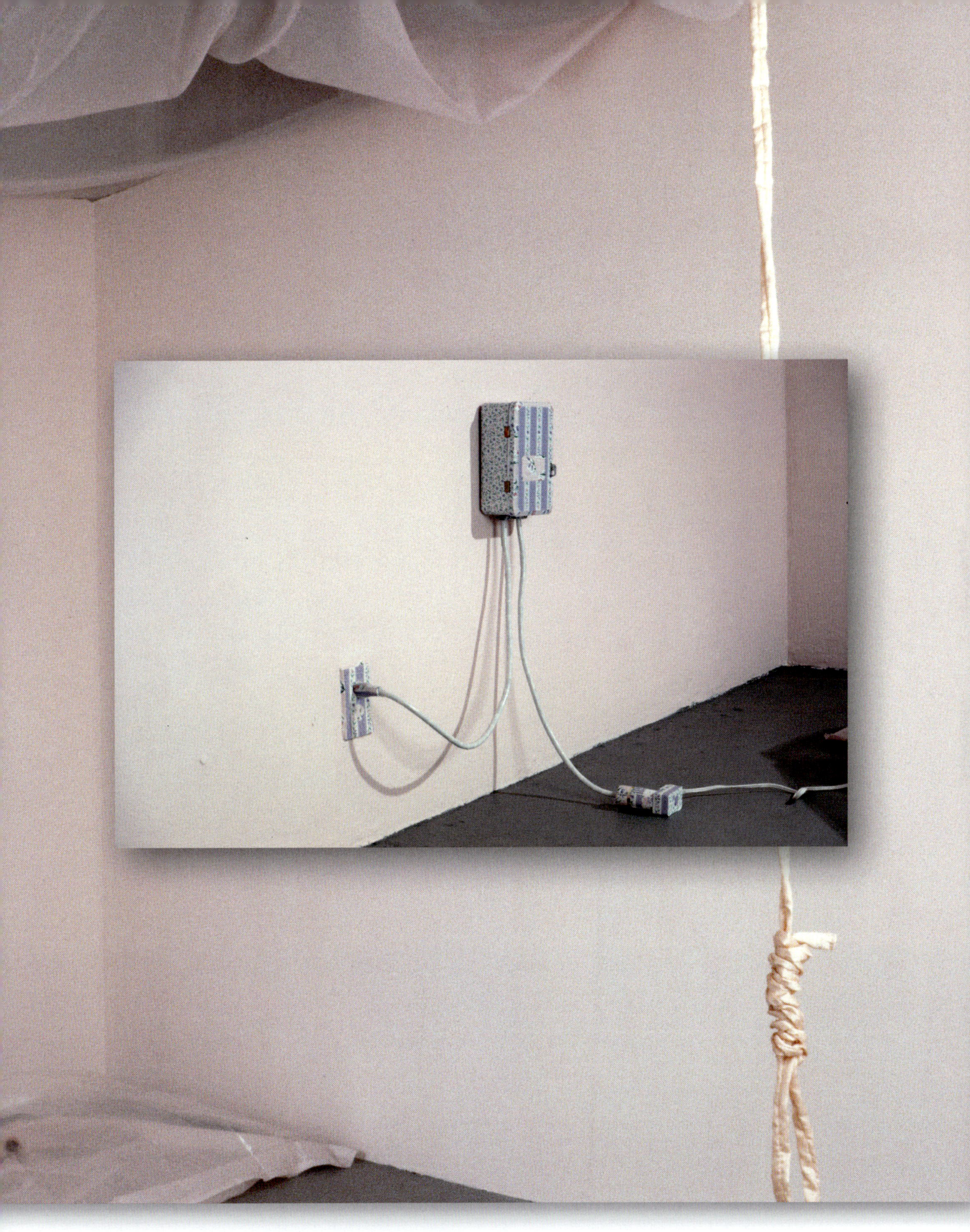

Foreground: Installation view, *The End*, Mint Gallery, California Institute of the Arts, Valencia, 1992, with *Untitled*, 1992, house paint, contact paper, plastic, fabric, timer, hairdryer, and balloons, dimensions variable
Background: Installation view, Mint Gallery, California Institute of the Arts, Valencia, 1992, with *Untitled*, 1992, house paint, contact paper, plastic, fabric, timer, hairdryer, and balloons, dimensions variable

PROPHYLACTIVE

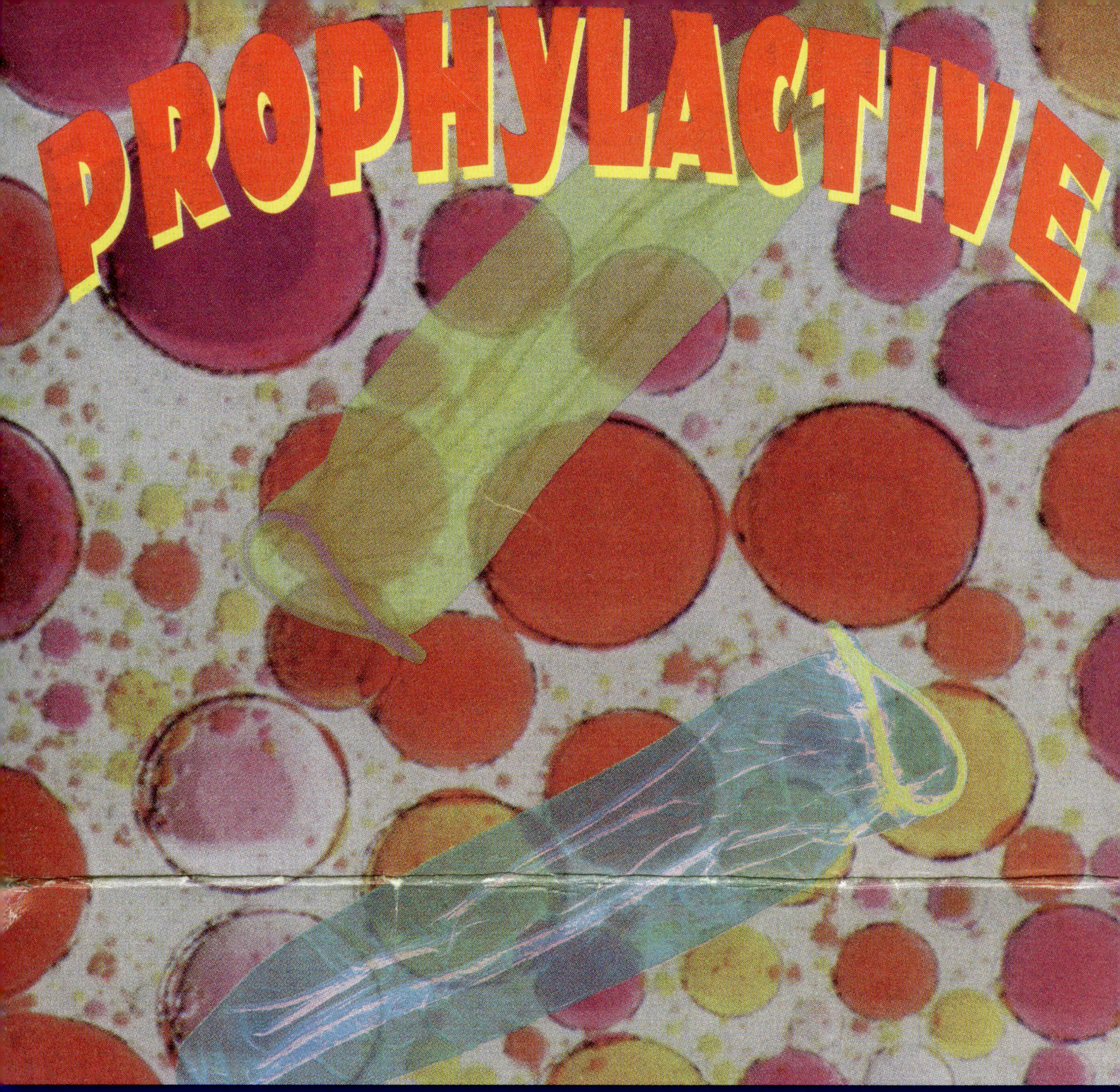

Laura Owens: In the early nineties I went with Diane Bromberg, a friend from RISD, to a Women's Action Coalition meeting in LA. We met Eve Luckring there. The three of us bonded over wanting to empower teenage women from different communities. We decided to throw a rave for teens called Club P, for "prophylactive," but we wrote "Pro-feel-active" to promote getting in touch with feelings and being proactive with one's own sexuality. It grew into a group that became known as REACH LA. We went to after-school programs and met teenagers who would be spokespeople, and we used the analog editing bays at CalArts to compile videos of facts, sex-positive imagery, and demonstrations of safe sex and projected them at our events. We also handed out condoms and educational material. We tried to get teenagers to show up—there was no alcohol or anything like that. Lance May joined us and so did Tessa De Roy, who worked for the ACLU at the time and helped us apply for a Magic Johnson Foundation grant. Eventually it turned into a nonprofit. In 2014 Ethan [Swan] from 356 said, "I've got this proposal from REACH LA to do their Ovahness Ball," a voguing ball that raises money for the organization. I was like, "REACH LA? That's so crazy." They didn't realize I had been involved; on their website it just says the group was started in the nineties by "three women artists."

   REACH LA flyer for Club Prophylactive, ca. 1992

WHAT IS NEEDED FOR CLUB PROPHYLACTIVE

Space $1,000
Security $ 500   ($50 each x 10 guards)
Met. detect $ 250
DJ $ 500
Invite $ 150
Postage $ 100

Visuals: Carol Kest's friend rental of audio/visual warehouse

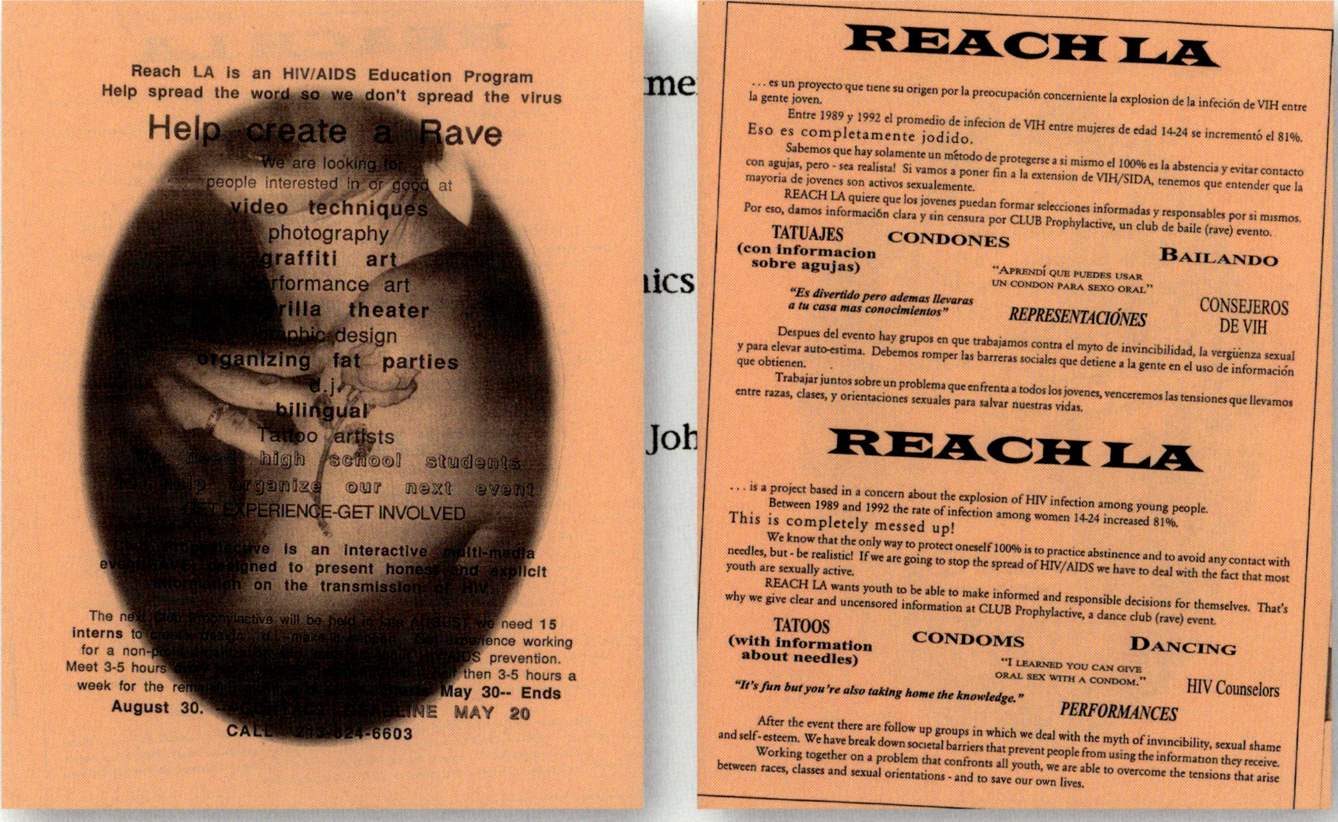

Rework the condom information packet both interms of text and
design...

Gina Lamb for video documentation(or Miguel Arteta)
Press coverage:
Ruben
Lynell
LA Times etc.

Introductions

LOCATION UPDATE:

Warehouse spa... ...dams/28th) owned by Hermandad
Sound, vide... ...etc.

CONFIRM

Day and Time P...
(Project Able p...
Age range (permi...

Performers Wishlist _TLC_

Yo Yo
Salt n Pepa
KRS-1
Queen Latifah
Disposable Heroes
Project ABLE, Int... ...n Revolt, Marcus
"Carmen" Kuilland ... ...ousin?

Additions:

SIGN UPS:

1. SECURITY: Ern...
   How many guar...
   How to contro...

2. ANNOUNCEMENT:
   CHRIS/ CRE-8/
   Distribution?

   Tickets? Flye...
   Cost, buy in...
   distribution

3. SLIDES/VIDEO:
   Laura/Lance p... the week of
   Jan 9 - 16
   Reccommendati...

4. MUSIC/DJs Lis...

5. EDUCATION: Fo... ...ling, condoms
   Translation o...

Foreground: Care package
Background: REACH LA meeting agenda, 1992

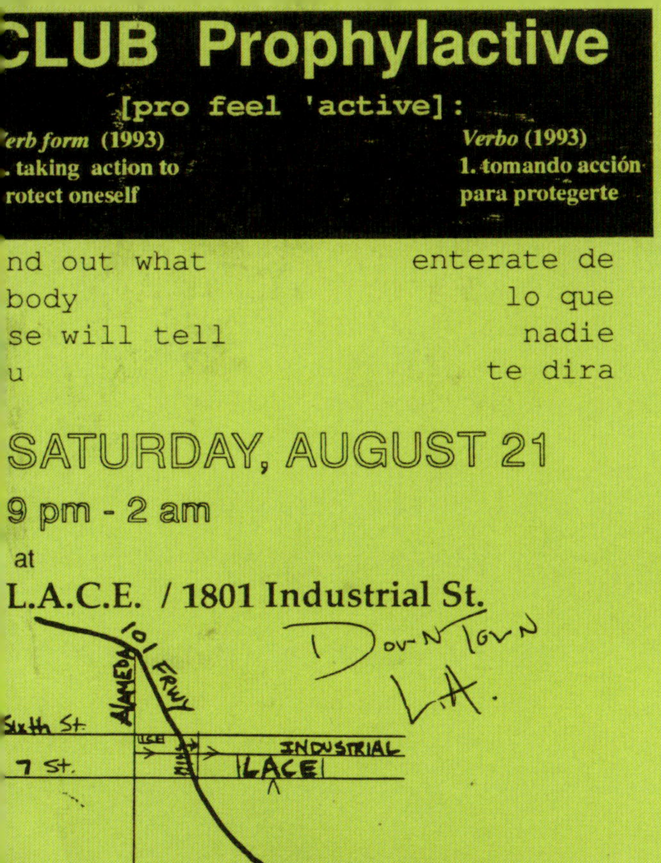
CLUB Prophylactive
[pro feel 'active]:
Verb form (1993)
1. taking action to
protect oneself
Verbo (1993)
1. tomando acción
para protegerte
nd out what
body
se will tell
u
enterate de
lo que
nadie
te dira
SATURDAY, AUGUST 21
9 pm - 2 am
at
L.A.C.E. / 1801 Industrial St.
Downtown L.A.
ALAMEDA
101 FRWY
Sixth St.
7 St.
INDUSTRIAL
LACE
10 FREEWAY
admits two
invitación para dos personas

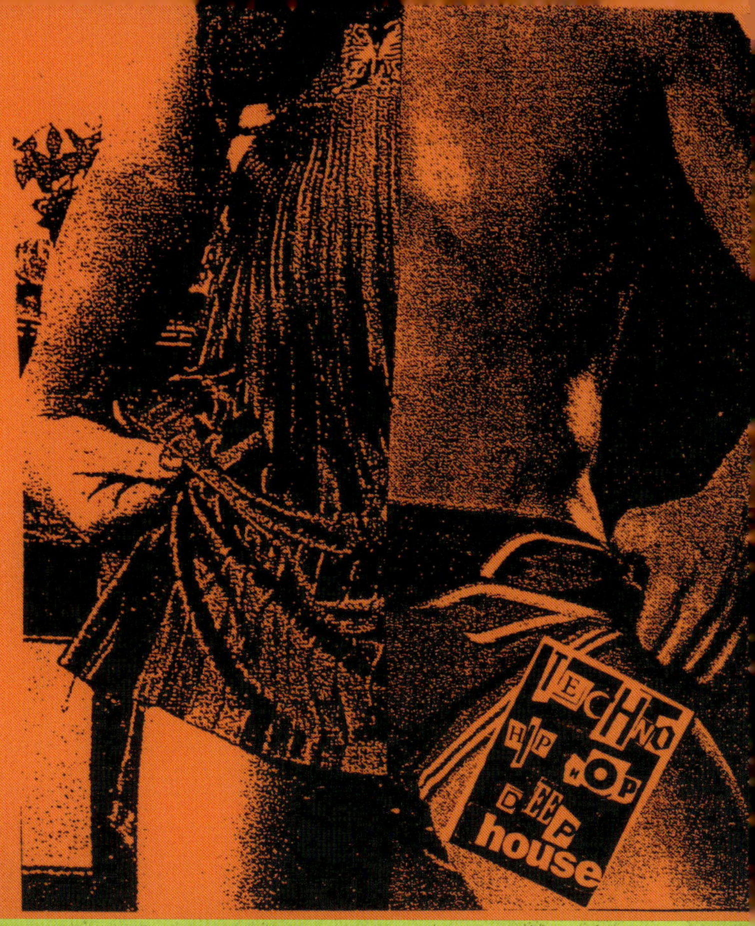
TECHNO
HIP HOP
DEEP
house

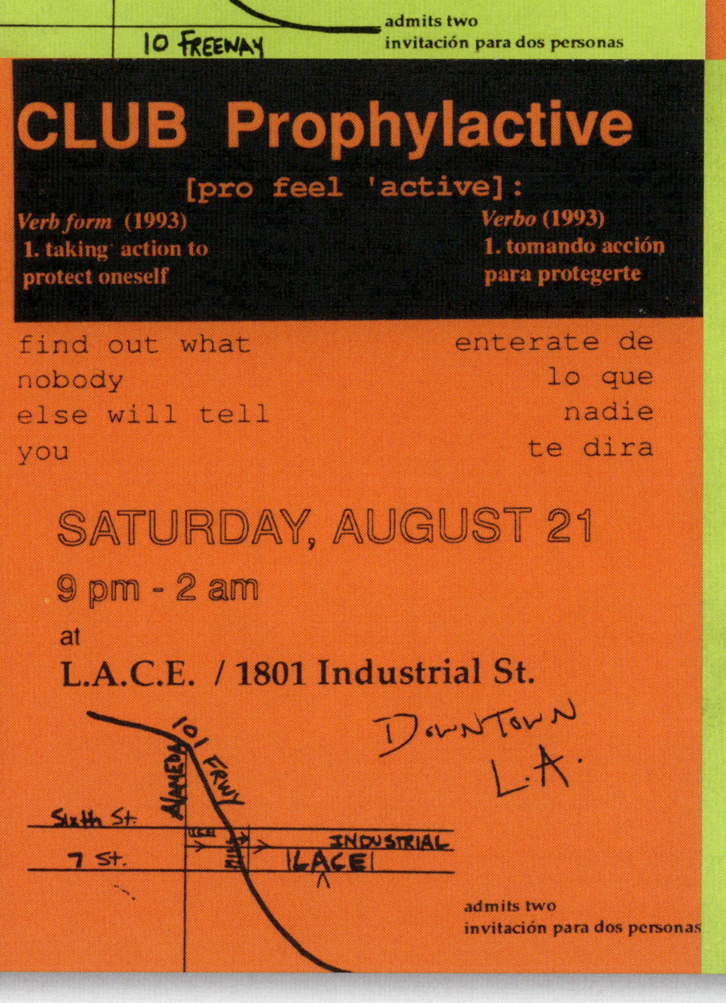
CLUB Prophylactive
[pro feel 'active]:
Verb form (1993)
1. taking action to
protect oneself
Verbo (1993)
1. tomando acción
para protegerte
find out what
nobody
else will tell
you
enterate de
lo que
nadie
te dira
SATURDAY, AUGUST 21
9 pm - 2 am
at
L.A.C.E. / 1801 Industrial St.
Downtown L.A.
ALAMEDA
101 FRWY
Sixth St.
7 St.
INDUSTRIAL
LACE
admits two
invitación para dos personas

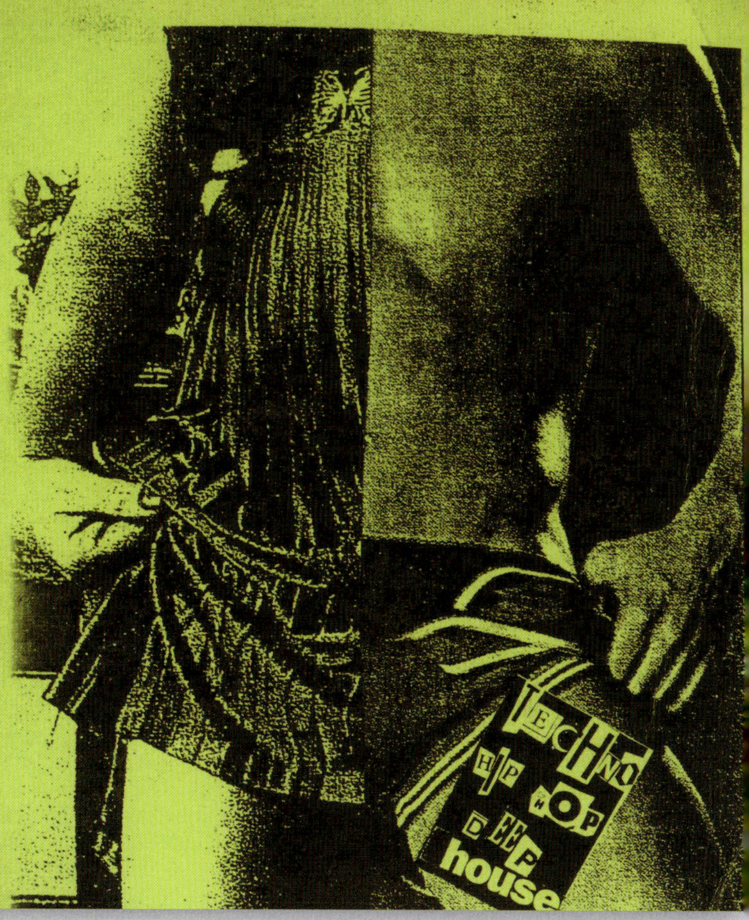
TECHNO
HIP HOP
DEEP
house

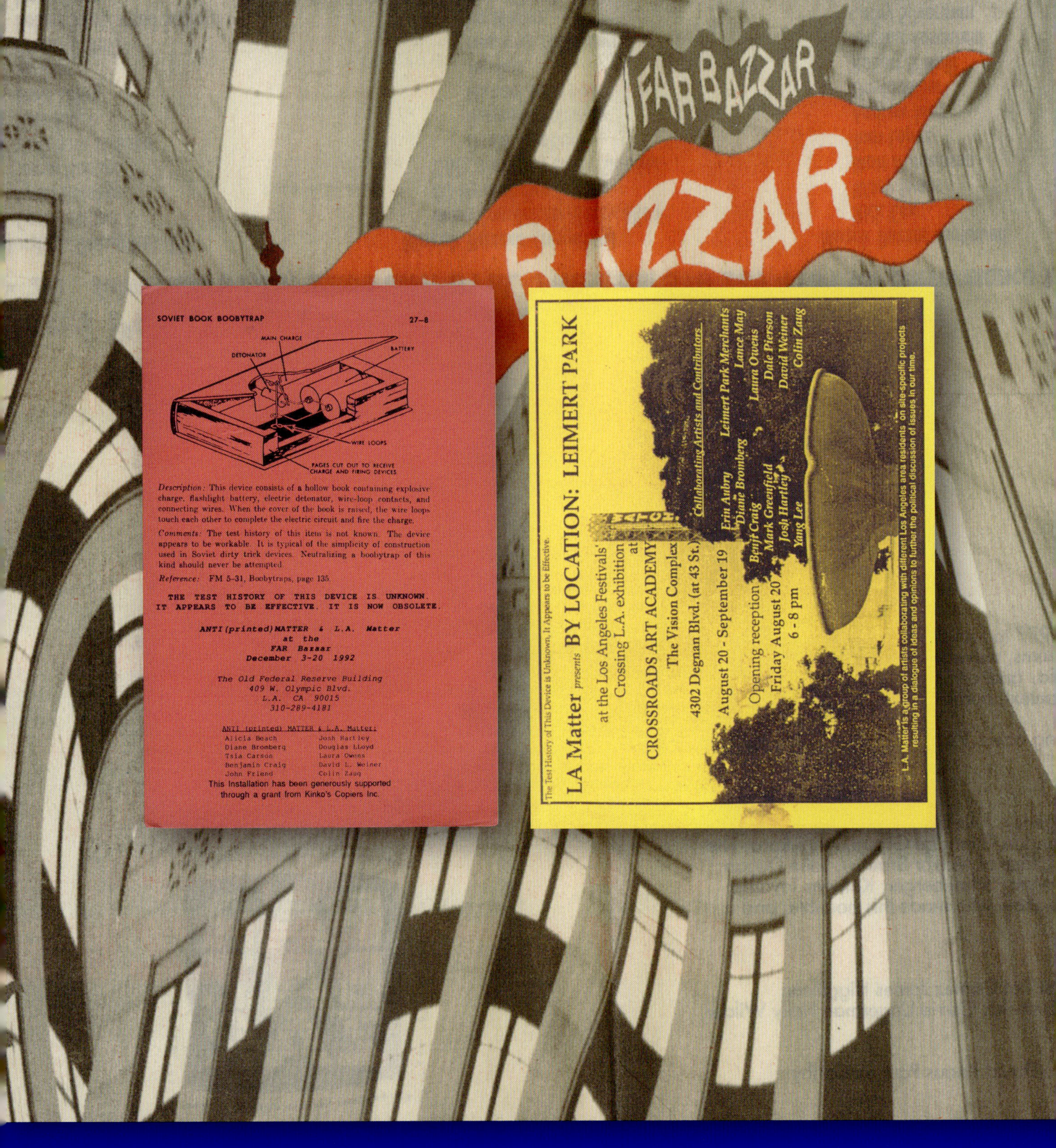

Foreground: *ANTI (printed) MATTER and LA Matter* flyer, FAR Bazzar, 1992; LA Matter invitation, *By Location: Leimert Park*, 1992
Background: FAR Bazzar publication, 1992

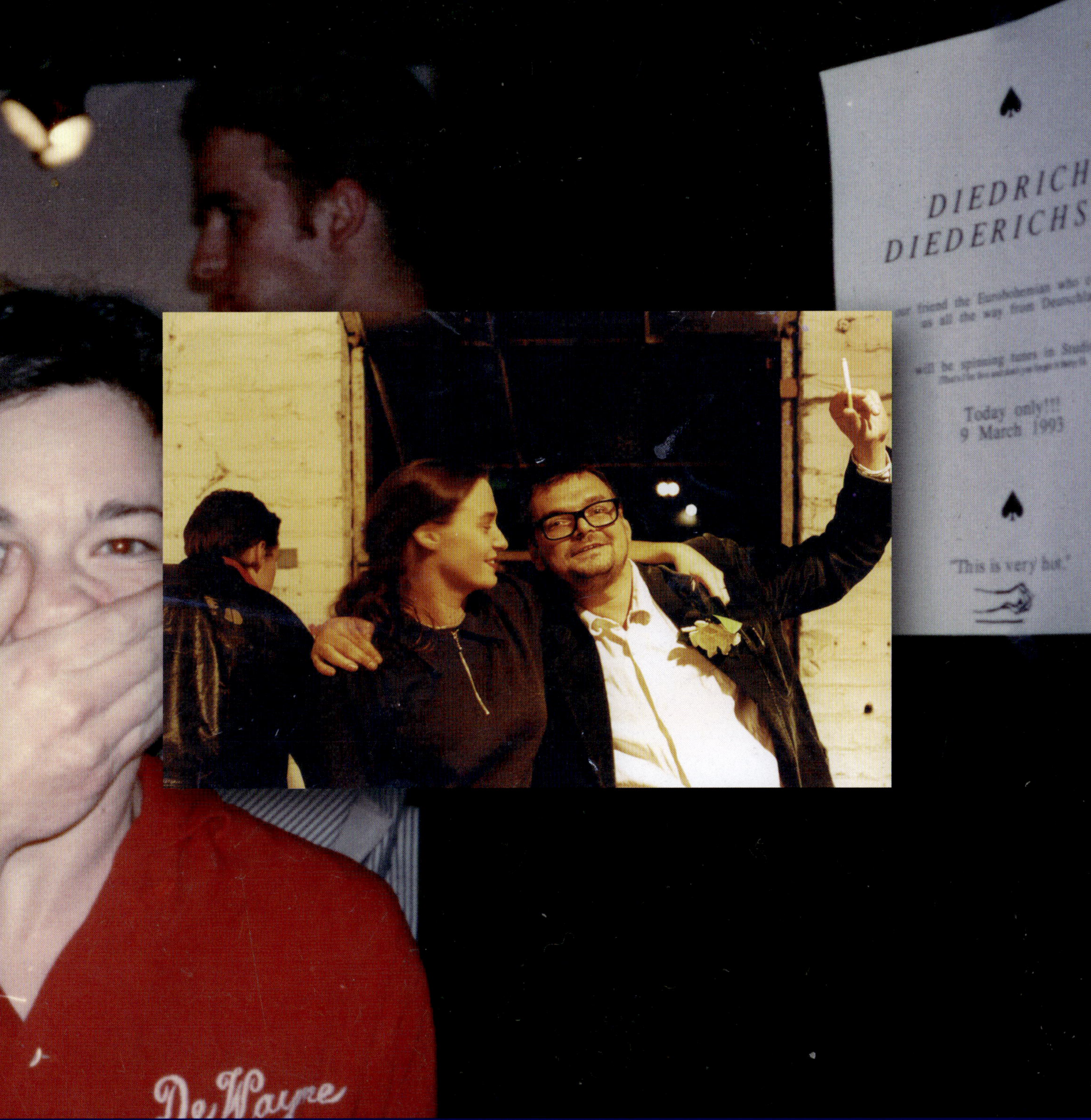

Foreground: Sharon Lockhart and Diedrich Diederichsen, Los Angeles, 1993
Background: Frances Stark, Los Angeles, 1993

REVIEW REPORT

CRITICAL STUDIES UNITS STATUS: GRADUATION__________
COMPLETED TO DATE___n/a_____   MID-RESIDENCE__X____
REMAINING _______________   SPECIAL__________
IN PROGRESS ______________   DATE_March 9, 1993___

Laura Owens   ID #:   35115   BOX #: GZ-24

YEAR LEVEL: MFA-1, 2nd semester   MENTOR: Gaines, Charles

SCHOOL: School of Art   AREA: Program in Art

PERSONS PRESENT FOR REVIEW: C. Gaines, C. Hatch, N. Mitchnick, K. Atkinson

WORK PRESENTED FOR REVIEW: Show: "The End" (an installation--pink room,
nursery rhymes subtly stencilled on the walls, odd objects)

COMMENTS:

You could position yourself more aggressively in your shows without
sacrificing them. It would have been nice if your voice was clearer so
we could have understood what the objects meant to you. I think you
are close, but there is an edge that needs to be exposed yet.

THE FOLLOWING RECOMMENDATION/ACTION IS BASED ON COMPLETION OF ALL WORK

IN PROGRESS:____Approved to advance to MFA2-1 Fall, 1993.__________

DATE OF GRADUATION: 05/01/94

APPROVED BY MENTOR:

APPROVED BY DEAN:

COPIES OF THIS REPORT WILL BE SENT TO THE STUDENT, MENTOR AND DEAN. THE
ORIGINAL WILL BE PLACED IN THE STUDENT'S FILE IN THE REGISTRAR'S OFFICE.

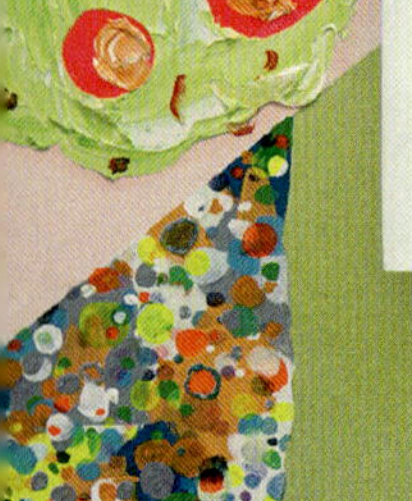

 Foreground: Mentor's report by Charles Gaines, 1993
Background: Detail of *Untitled*, 1994, acrylic, oil, spray paint, and graphite on canvas, 96 × 120 in. (243.8 × 304.8 cm)

April 1, 1993

Dear Charles,

     As I have told you previously I am involved with many
different outside of the studio projects which are additives to a
formulating idea of my art practice. Two of these, PAGES and
R.E.A.C.H. L.A., are currently filing for 501c3 status. I have
worked collaboratively to form each of these organizations and am
on each one's Board of Directors. As of April 14 R.E.A.C.H. L.A.
with the help of Community Partners as an umbrella organization
will attain a temporary 501c3 status. Both of these organizations
mean very much to me and I have put much of my personal time and
money into starting them.
     When I graduate from CalArts I hope to continue to use my
time and money to support these organizations as well as my own
artwork. Right now, I owe approximately $20,000+ in student loans
which will put a particular strain on me financially when I leave
CalArts. This year has been extremely difficult for me
financially. I have worked 14+ hours a week at LACE directing the
video program, 4-8 hours a week in the supershop, and second
semester attained a TA job, yet my friends have continuously had
to loan me money to survive. I am currently indebted to friends
for over $500 in rent and food. I do not own any credit cards but
I feel this is probably the only way I can survive right now.
     I am writing all this to you because it very difficult for me
to communicate this verbally without sounding completely
distressed. I just wanted to let you know my situation, so
hopefully next year my financial aid status will change. Perhaps
through non-workstudy jobs combined with workstudy jobs or through
an increase in scholarship money.

     Thank you,

     Laura Owens

cc:John Bache

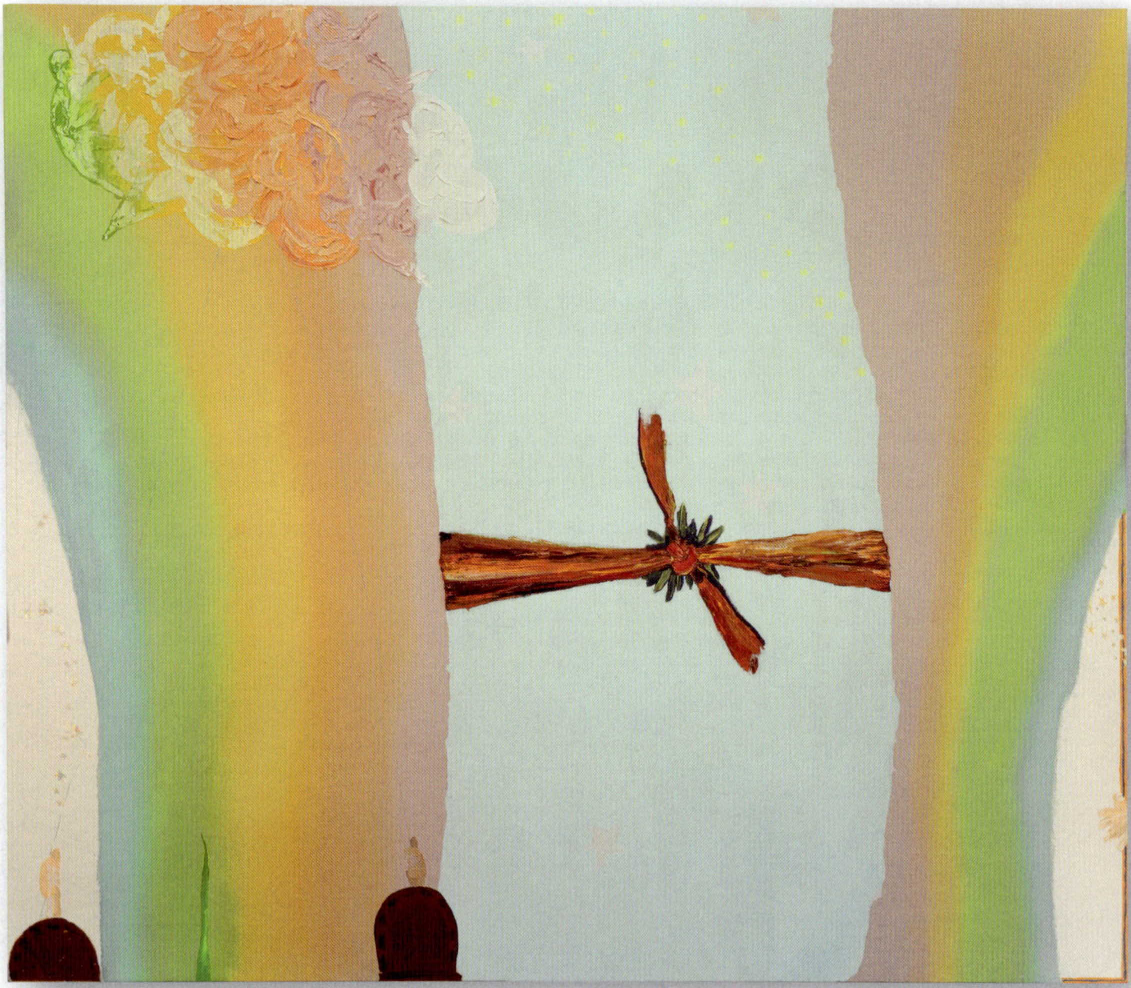

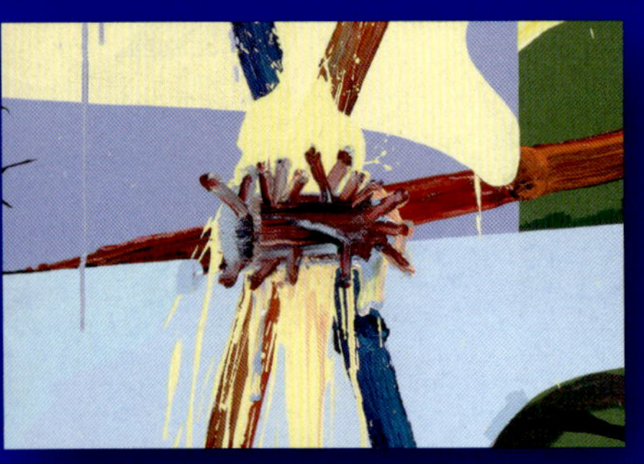

Untitled, 1994, acrylic and oil on canvas, 84 × 96 in. (213.3 × 243.8 cm)

64 Inset: Detail of Fiona Rae, *Untitled (purple and green)*, 1993, oil on canvas, 48⅜ × 92⅛ in. (123 × 234 cm)

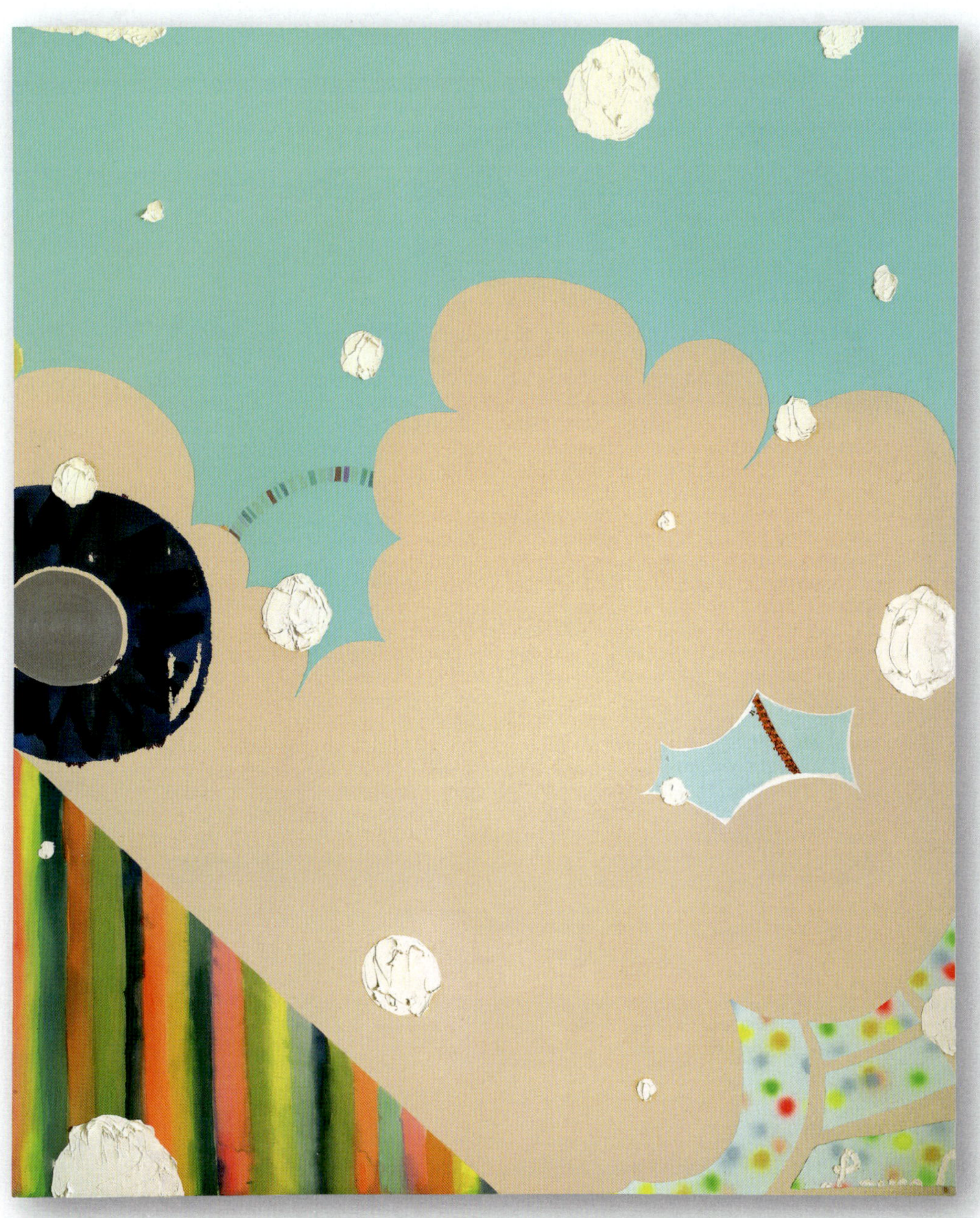

Untitled, 1994, acrylic and oil on canvas, 120 × 96 in. (304.8 cm × 243.8 cm)

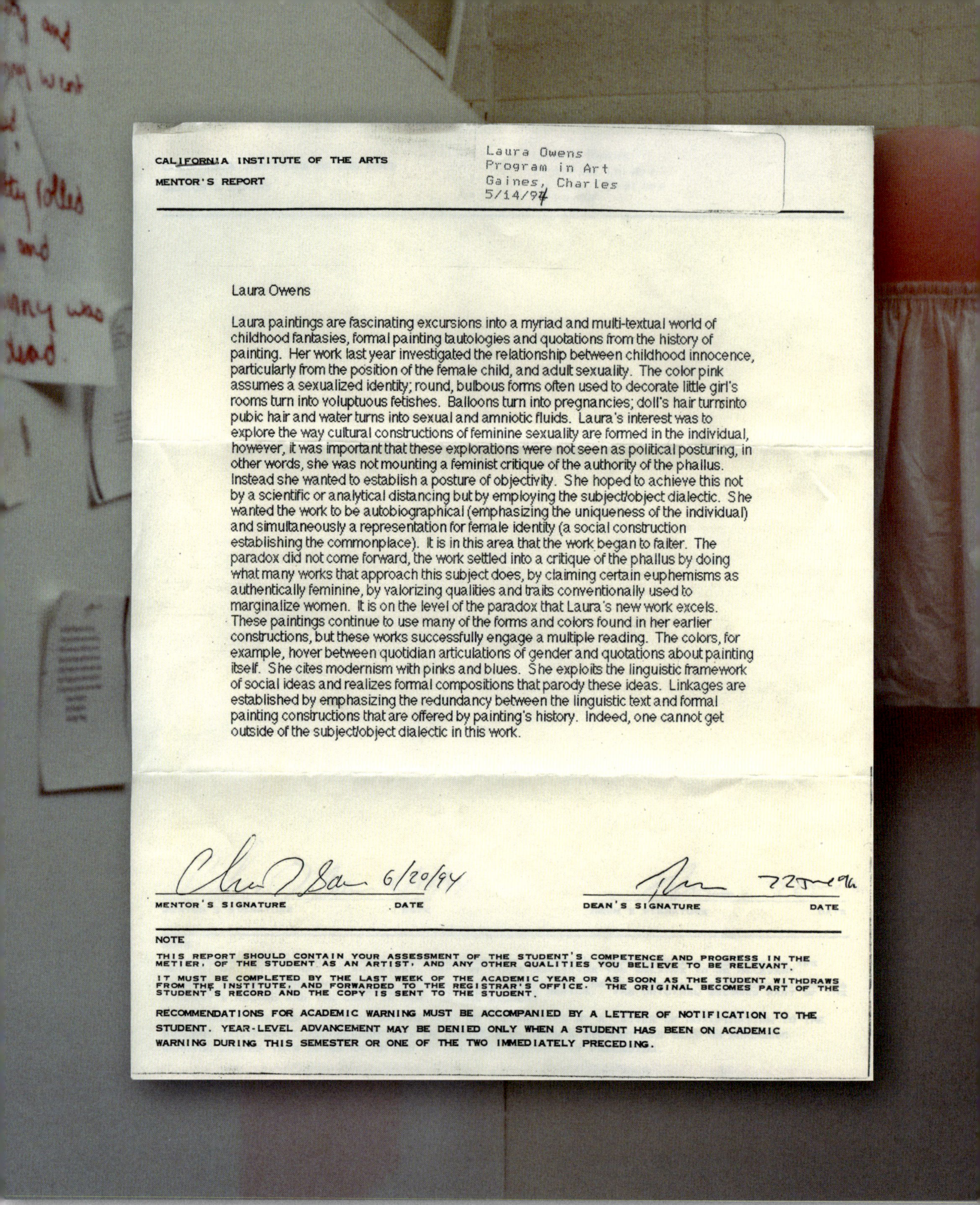

Foreground: Mentor's report by Charles Gaines, 1994
Background: California Institute of the Arts studio, Valencia, 1994

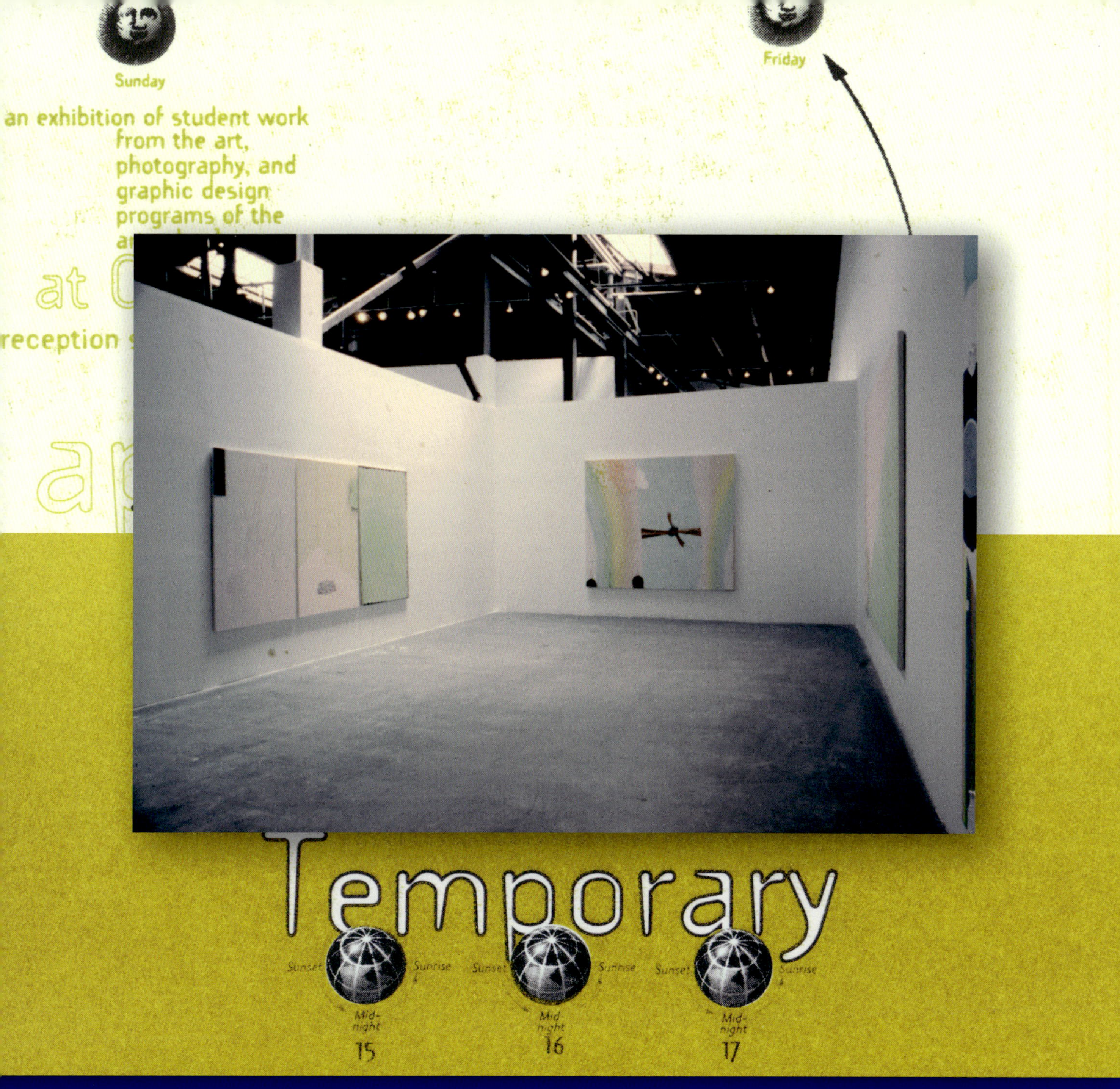

Laura Owens: At CalArts I continued making sculpture and installation, and that made it much easier for the faculty and other students to talk with me. At first I would love my installations, but I'd come in the next day and think they had kind of died. They never had the longevity that even my worst unfinished paintings did. But I kept making sculpture until my last semester. It was just easier to have a conversation around; otherwise it was impossible. The question would be: "Why did you make a painting?" Not, "What is the painting?" Michael Asher once looked at a Monique Prieto painting and said, "I see you've taken this cloth and wrapped it over this wooden structure." He could not help himself: that is the way he saw art. It's a very specific and strict position.

The Northridge earthquake in 1994 pretty much destroyed CalArts; all the classes moved to an unused Lockheed Martin facility. After the earthquake there was—at least for forty-eight hours—a sense of emergency. It was like "What the fuck? Why do I care about this shit I've been so worried about?" I ended up resigning myself to the fact that I really liked looking at paintings and that I wanted to make paintings. I decided everything I was trying to do with installation a painting could do. And that if I wanted the idea of collage, I would use paint to do that. For example, I would stain the canvas to look like gingham instead of just sticking it on.

Foreground: Installation view, *Temporary*, Temporary Contemporary, Museum of Contemporary Art, Los Angeles, 1994, with *Untitled*, 1994, acrylic and oil on canvas, three panels: 70 × 40 in. (177.8 × 101.6 cm) each, and *Untitled*, 1994 (see p. 64)
Background: Invitation, Temporary Contemporary, Museum of Contemporary Art, Los Angeles, 1994

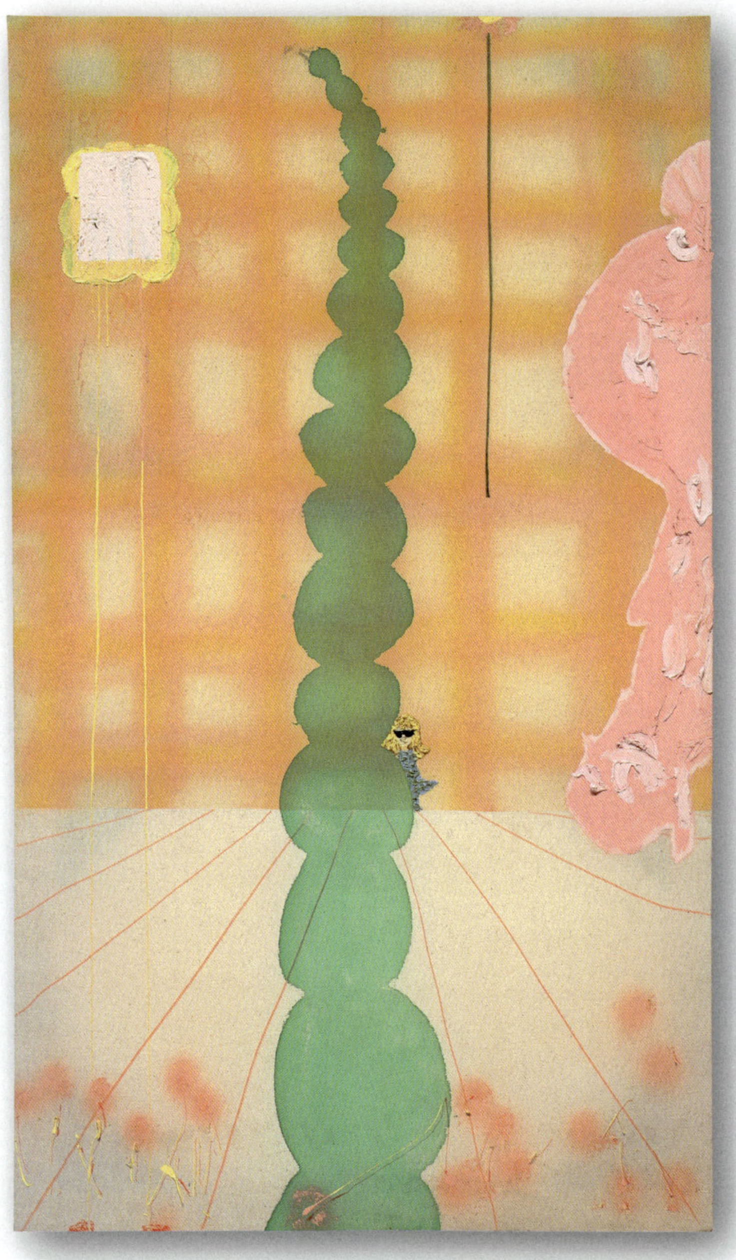

 Untitled, 1994, acrylic and oil on canvas, 70 × 40 in. (177.8 × 101.6 cm)

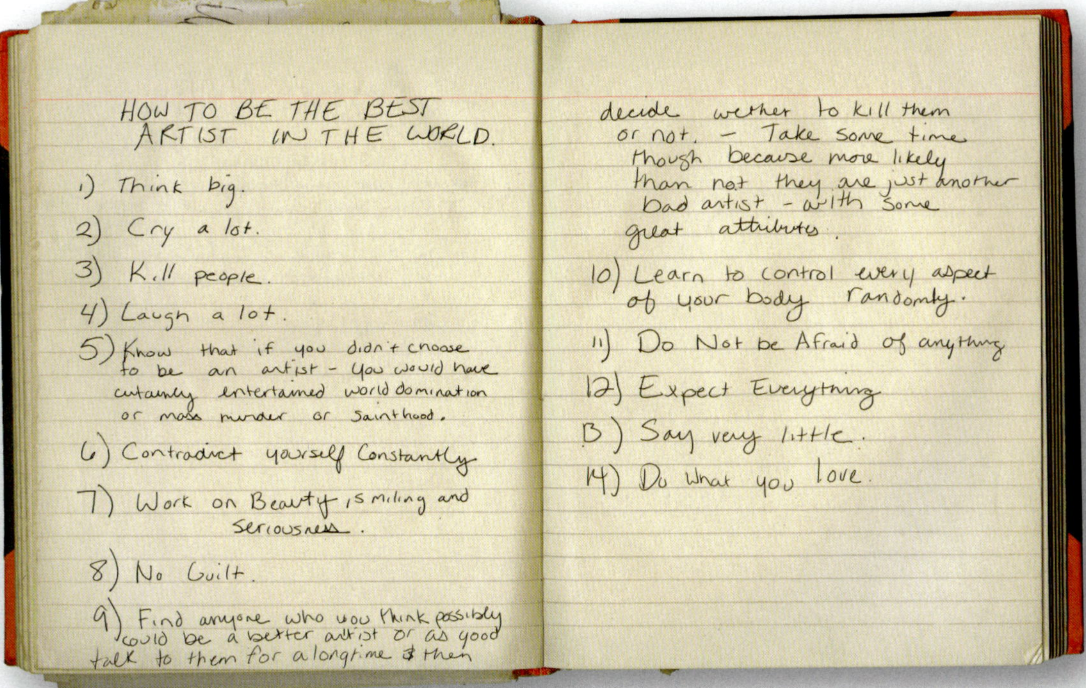

HOW TO BE THE BEST ARTIST IN THE WORLD.

1) Think big.
2) Cry a lot.
3) Kill people.
4) Laugh a lot.
5) Know that if you didn't choose to be an artist - You would have certainly entertained world domination or mass murder or sainthood.
6) Contradict yourself Constantly
7) Work on Beauty, smiling and seriousness.
8) No Guilt.
9) Find anyone who you think possibly could be a better artist or as good talk to them for a long time & then
decide wether to kill them or not. - Take some time though because more likely than not they are just another bad artist - with some great attributes.
10) Learn to control every aspect of your body randomly.
11) Do Not be Afraid of anything
12) Expect Everything
13) Say very little.
14) Do What you love

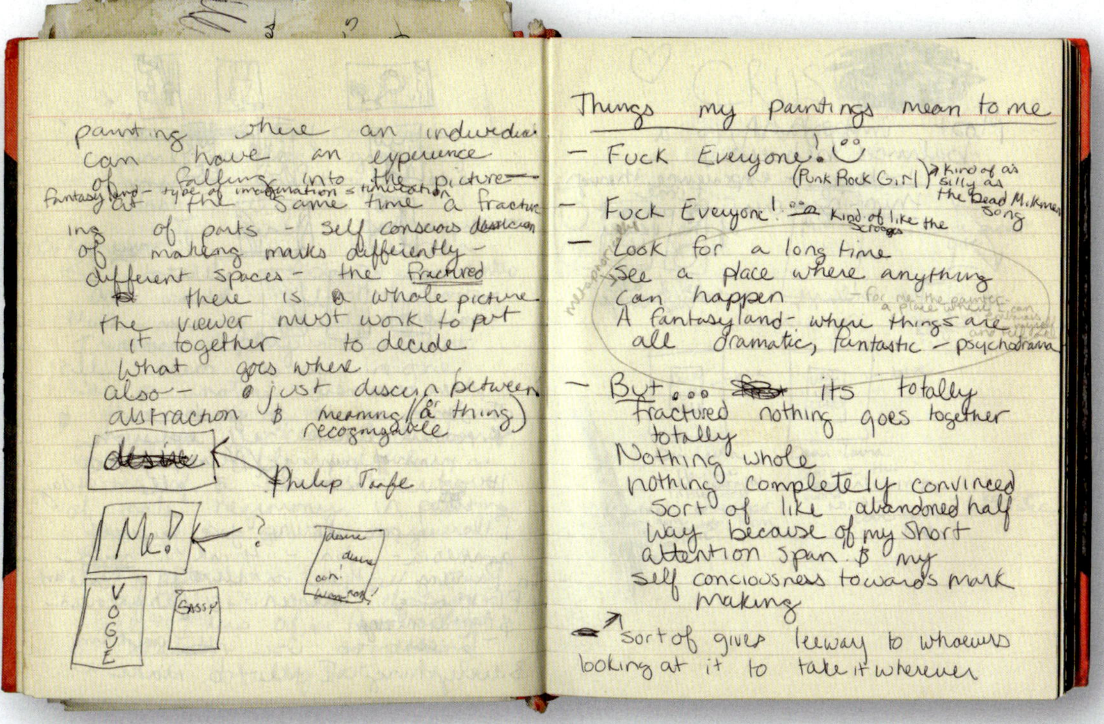

painting where an individual can have an experience of falling into the picture— type of imagination = fantasyland art at the same time a fracturing of parts - Self conscious depiction of making marks differently - different spaces - the fractured there is a whole picture the viewer must work to put it together to decide what goes where
also— a just discern between abstraction & meaning (a thing) recognizable
Philip Taafe
Me!? ?
VOGUE SASSY

Things my paintings mean to me
- Fuck Everyone! (Punk Rock Girl) kind of as silly as the Dead Milkmen Song
- Fuck Everyone! kind of like the Scrooge
- Look for a long time See a place where anything can happen A fantasyland - where things are all dramatic, fantastic - psychodrama
- But... its totally fractured nothing goes together totally Nothing whole nothing completely convinced Sort of like abandoned half way because of my short attention span & my self conciousness towards mark making
sort of gives leeway to whoever looking at it to take it wherever

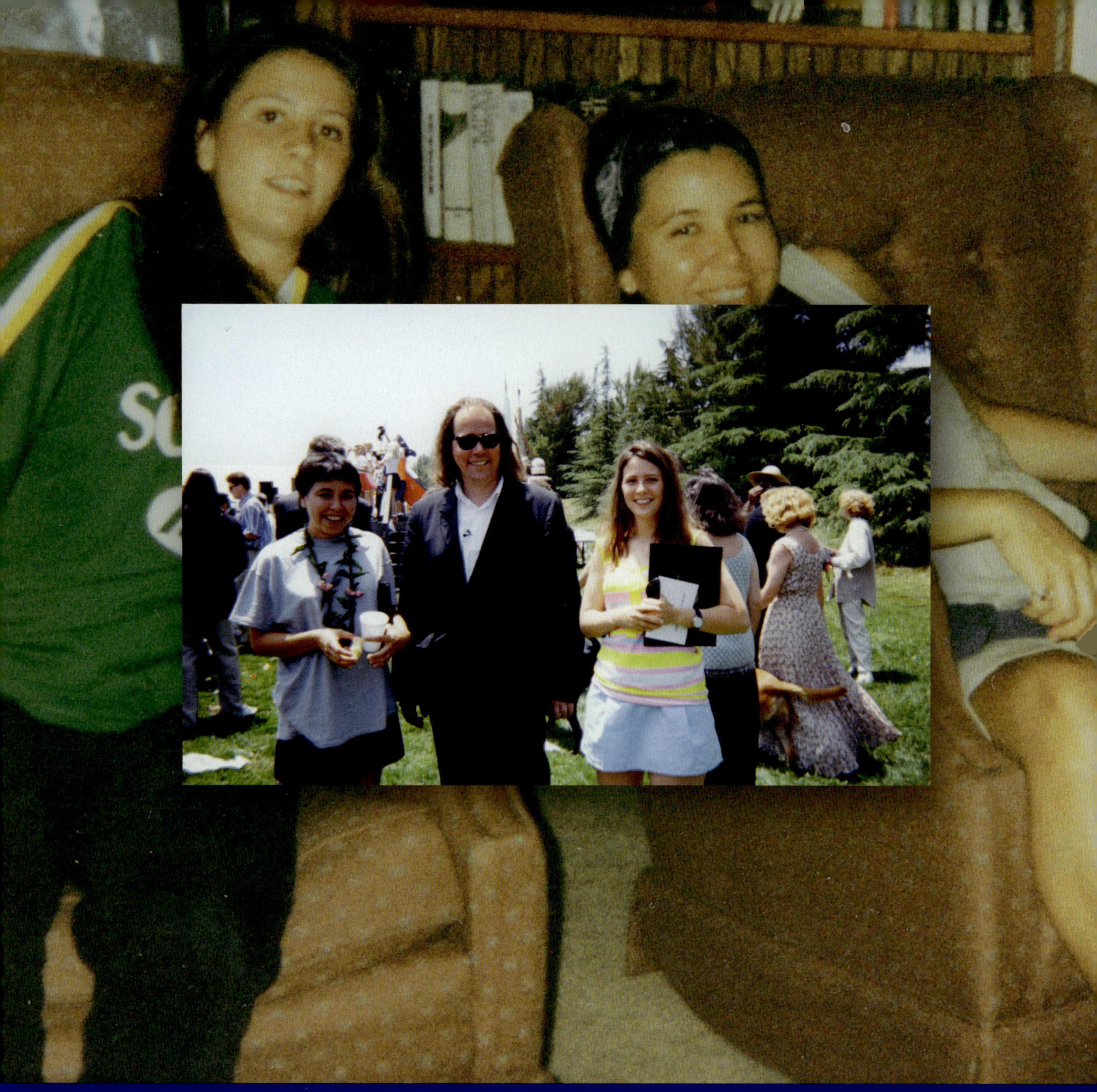

Monique Prieto: Tom Lawson was offered a couple of fellowship slots at Skowhegan if he had students he wanted to send, and he gave them to Laura and me. We made it into a road trip. I was visibly pregnant by that time. I had a pickup truck and I put a shell on it and we packed up and drove cross-country; it was scary and fun. It took us about a week. Skowhegan gave me a thoroughly new perspective. It was my first contact with people coming out of East Coast schools. That they were so comfortable being painters was really interesting. They weren't having big doubts—but the stuff they were making wasn't particularly rigorous either. At CalArts we'd had to sword fight through any critique we brought a painting to; you had to be on top of your game and make a case for it. When we got to Skowhegan some people were still working on the problems of AbEx and how expressive you could be with paint. It was like, "This is all New York wants from you? They don't want some depth or critical distance from your painting?" On one hand it was kind of funny, and on the other it was a relief to know there was a community out there who wouldn't push back so hard if you wanted to show them something. Being pregnant I was not inclined to hang out with the late-night partying/sleeping-around set. We left early; we were feeling done.

Foreground: Monique Prieto, Thomas Lawson, and Owens, graduation reception, California Institute of the Arts, Valencia, 1994
Background: Owens and Monique Prieto in Oregon, en route to Skowhegan School of Painting and Sculpture, Maine, 1994

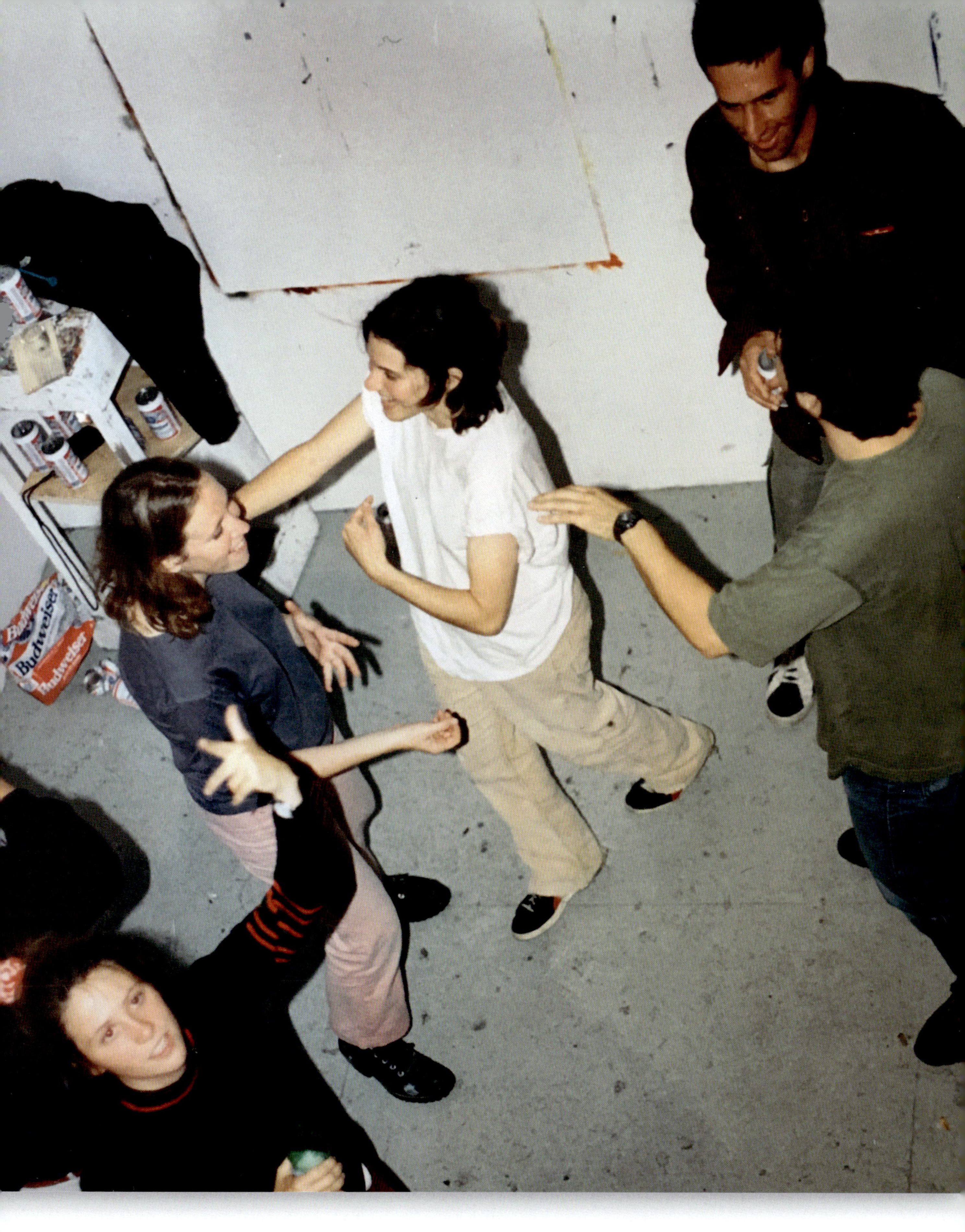

Owens, Rebecca Morris, Ruth Root, and others, Skowhegan School of Painting and Sculpture, Skowhegan, Maine, 1994

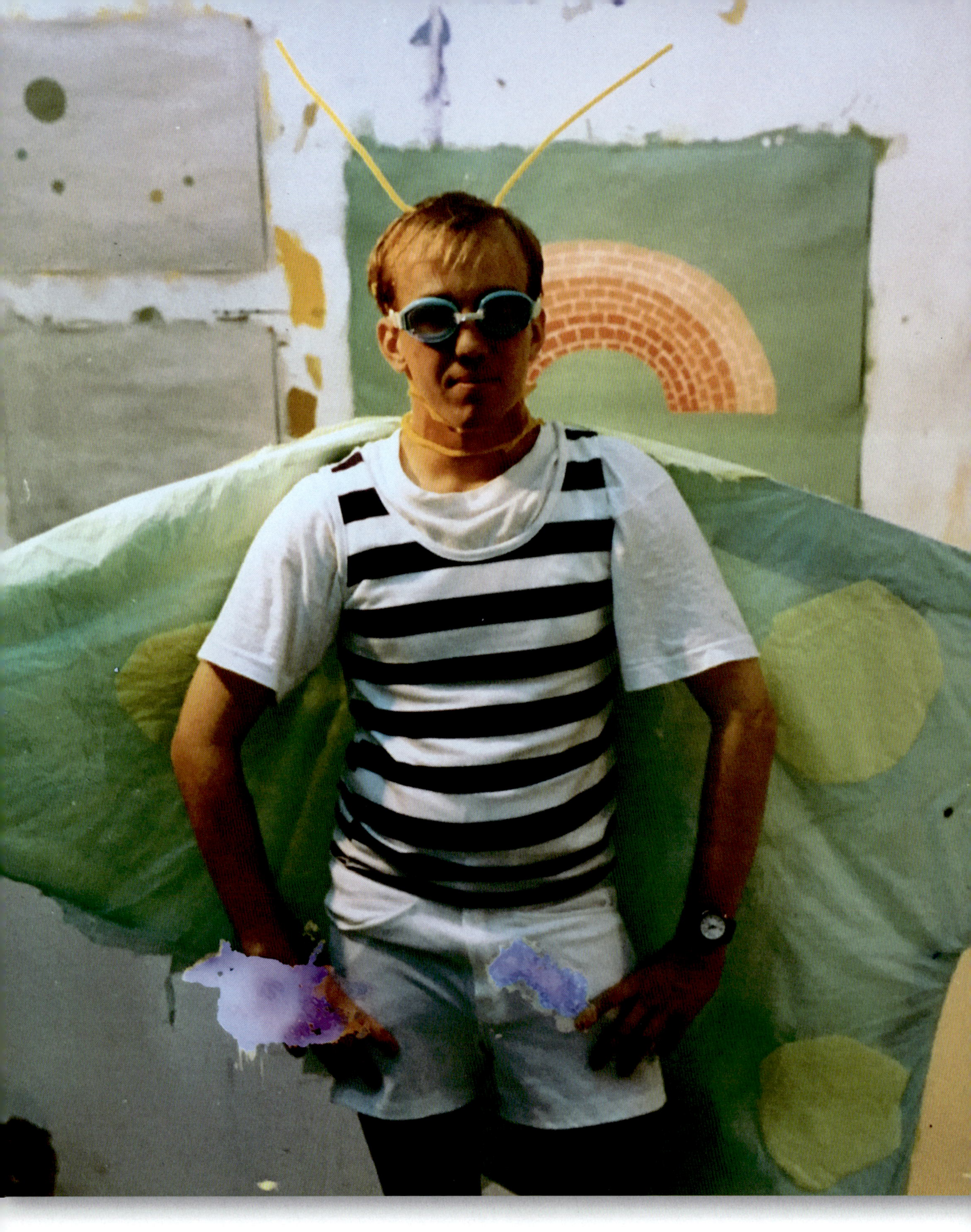

    Scott Reeder, Skowhegan School of Painting and Sculpture studio, Skowhegan, Maine, 1994

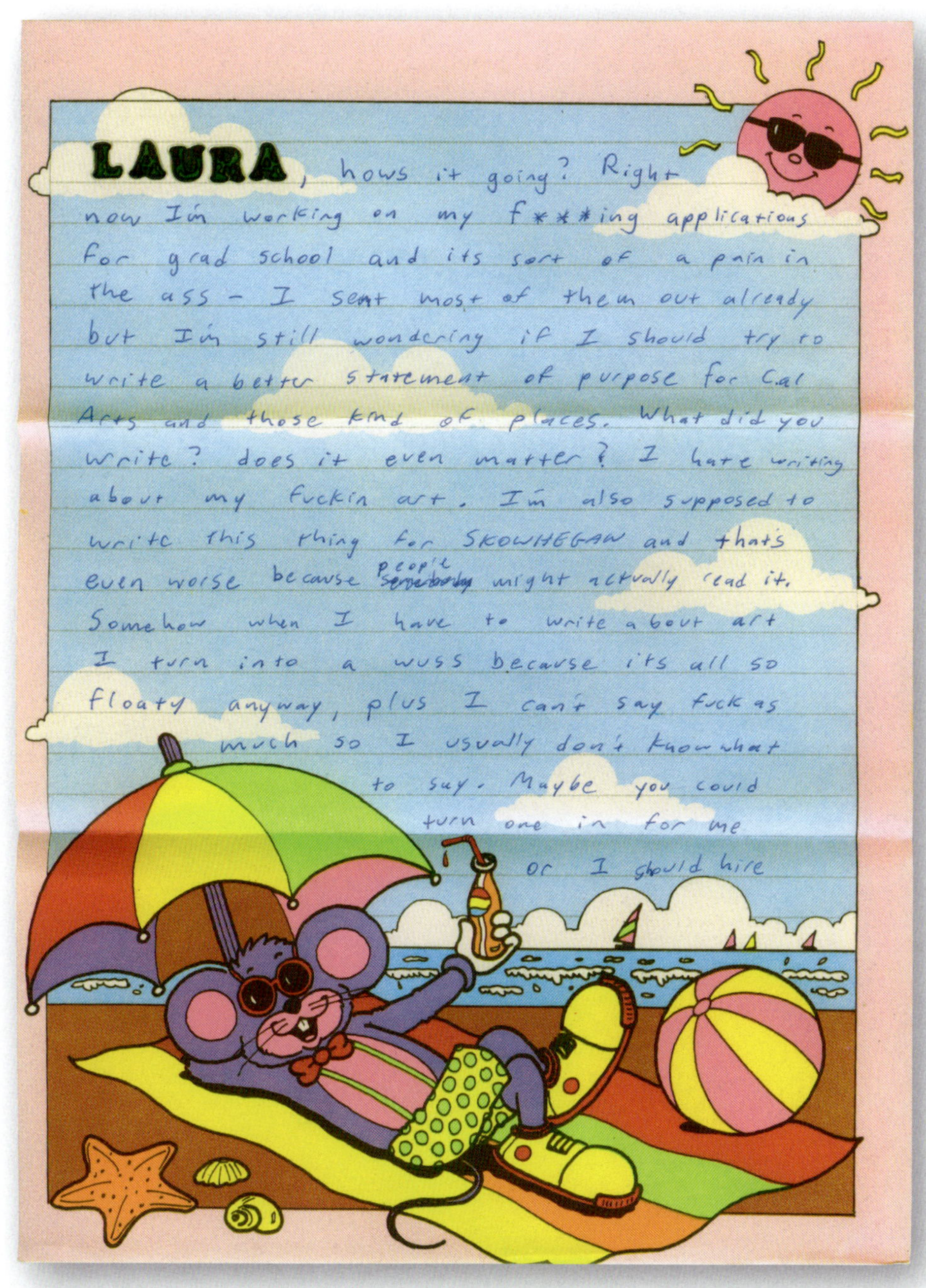

Scott Reeder: Every summer Skowhegan does this thing where the students are sort of forced to donate work to a benefit. One year I was one of the auctioneers and somebody just laid into it and auctioned off a date with me. Laura won, but immediately afterward she told me that she wasn't going to pay, and I made it clear I wasn't going to go out with her for free. And then it became this standoff that lasted the whole summer—she didn't want to pay, and I just thought that on principle she should, because there had been other men and women bidding on me who would've paid, you know? So I just thought it wasn't fair. Eventually somebody set up this donation jar in the cafeteria with a sign that said, "Send our kids to Pizza Hut." And people put money in the jar so we could go on a date there. But neither of us would budge—we both held our ground about it. I can't remember what the winning bid was; I should know. Like, in my prime, how much was I worth?

74   *Untitled*, 1994, acrylic on canvas, 22½ × 19 in. (57.2 × 48.3 cm)

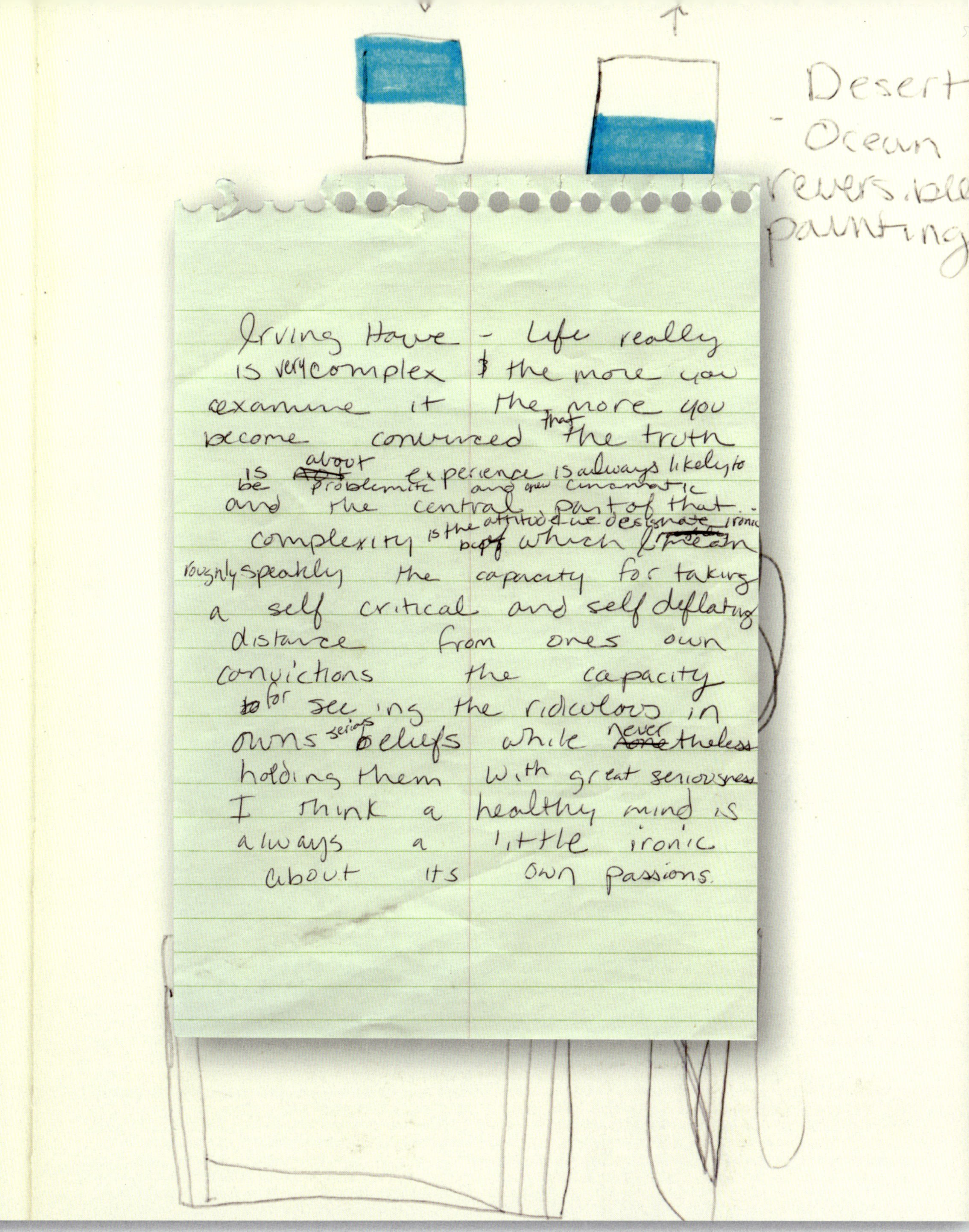

Irving Howe – Life really
is very complex & the more you
examine it the more you
become convinced that the truth
is about experience is always likely to
be problematic and new cinematic
and the central part of that
complexity is the attitude we designate ironic
by which I mean
roughly speaking the capacity for taking
a self critical and self deflating
distance from ones own
convictions the capacity
for seeing the ridiculous in
owns serious beliefs while nevertheless
holding them with great seriousness
I think a healthy mind is
always a little ironic
about its own passions.

Foreground: Notebook page, 1994
Background: Sketchbook page, 1994

Laura Owens: After Skowhegan I found a studio in Eagle Rock where I lived and worked. I had it until 2003 or 2004, and it was $300 a month, which enabled me to make art for ten years without worrying about income. It was a storefront in a 1920s brick building that was about 600 square feet. There was no "For Rent" sign; I just knocked on the door and convinced the landlord, Chuck Thompson, to move his stuff out of the front so I could rent it. After a while I got him to move out of the back space and I subleased it to other artists. Rebecca Morris moved in first, then Sharon Lockhart and Alex Slade, and then Mungo Thomson. Later I needed more space and rented a second storefront in the building; I subleased some of the space behind it to Matt Connors, Edgar Bryan, and Mary Weatherford. Scott Reeder had a studio one block south for a while in the nineties. We would play basketball with Tyson Reeder, Mark Grotjahn, Mari Eastman, and Rebecca. I sold my first painting to Clyde Beswick (who I later learned was compulsively buying art from many young LA artists) after he saw the Dave Hickey–curated show at LACE I was in. I worked at Arcana Books for a while, and also was sort of a studio assistant to Alison Saar and Tom Lawson, and was Alison's babysitter. I was also a babysitter for Leslie Dick. But the bookstore job was a real job; I worked there about four days a week. I also worked for Norm Laich, an artist who owned a vinyl-cutting business.

Foreground: Day planner, 1995

 Background: Eagle Rock studio, Los Angeles, 1994, with *Untitled*, 1994 (see p. 65)

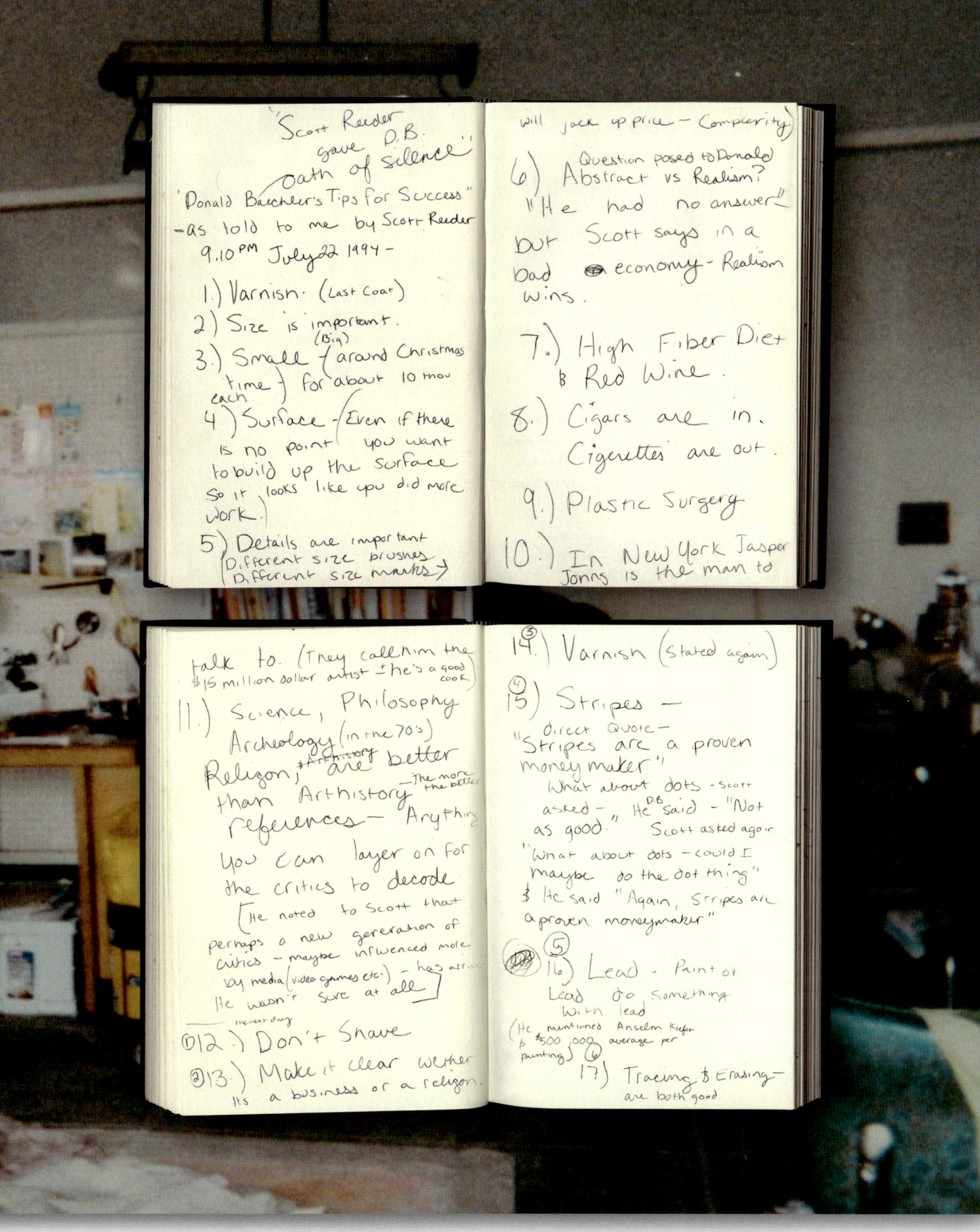

"Scott Reeder
gave D.B.
"Oath of silence"
"Donald Baechler's Tips for Success"
- as told to me by Scott Reeder
9.10 PM July 22 1994 -

1.) Varnish. (Last Coat)
2.) Size is important.
3.) Small (Big) (around Christmas time) for about 10 thou each
4.) Surface - (Even if there is no point you want to build up the surface so it looks like you did more work.)
5.) Details are important (Different size brushes Different size marks →

will jack up price - (Complexity)
6.) Abstract vs Realism? Question posed to Donald
"He had no answer" but Scott says in a bad economy - Realism wins.
7.) High Fiber Diet & Red Wine.
8.) Cigars are in. Cigarettes are out.
9.) Plastic Surgery
10.) In New York Jasper Johns is the man to

talk to. (They call him the $15 million dollar artist & he's a good cook)
11.) Science, Philosophy Archeology (in the 70's) Religion, Art history are better than Art history - The more the better references - Anything you can layer on for the critics to decode
[He noted to Scott that perhaps a new generation of critics - maybe influenced more by media (video games etc.) - has arrived. He wasn't sure at all]
- the next day
①12.) Don't Shave
②13.) Make it clear wether its a business or a religion.

③14.) Varnish (stated again)
④15.) Stripes -
"Direct quote - "Stripes are a proven money maker"
What about dots - Scott asked - He D.B. said - "Not as good." Scott asked again.
"What about dots - could I maybe do the dot thing" & He said "Again, Stripes are a proven moneymaker"
⑤16.) Lead - Paint or Lead - do something with lead (He mentioned Anselm Kiefer & $500,000 average per painting)
⑥17.) Tracing & Erasing - are both good.

Laura Owens: I was very nervous and excited when Rosamund Felsen came to my studio and asked me to do a solo show at her gallery. I probably had more anxiety than I admitted to and I kept getting pretty bad acne. I was working at Arcana Books at the time and making all my stretchers in Monique Prieto's garage. She had bought a table saw so that we could cut the wood ourselves instead of paying someone else.

I overcompensated by making way too many paintings for the space. Nothing was too planned out in terms of scale, and I just kept adding more very small and very large sizes. The shippers had to make two trips from Eagle Rock to the gallery in Santa Monica, and my friends who worked for LA Packing came back after unloading the first batch and told me Rosamund had not been shy in expressing her disappointment in the paintings.

Installing the show was stressful and made me rethink my ideas about making exhibitions. Unlike for the exhibitions that followed, I hadn't thought about the rooms or layout but instead had focused on the combination of and connections between the paintings. Images of several of them appeared in others hanging nearby. I wanted to have a range of marks and used staining, tie-dye, and impasto. References to animation, still life, tennis, basketball, and a variety of other paintings showed up. One work was a zoomed-in crop of a Frank Stella Black Painting with an oversize, elderly finger pointing to its wall label. From far away this painting looked more like an extra-large black-and-white John McLaughlin.

After a day of installing I wanted to remove paintings from the front two rooms, but I felt pressure to hang even more. Lisa Anne Auerbach was asked to leave when she stopped by and told me it looked overhung. Luckily Tom Lawson came by, and Rosamund respected his advice and took a few works out, and he liked the idea of putting a large painting in the hallway. The evening of the opening I don't remember Rosamund leaving her office, and there wasn't any alcohol, water, or even cups. So I gave my credit card to Lisa, who ran out and bought some drinks.

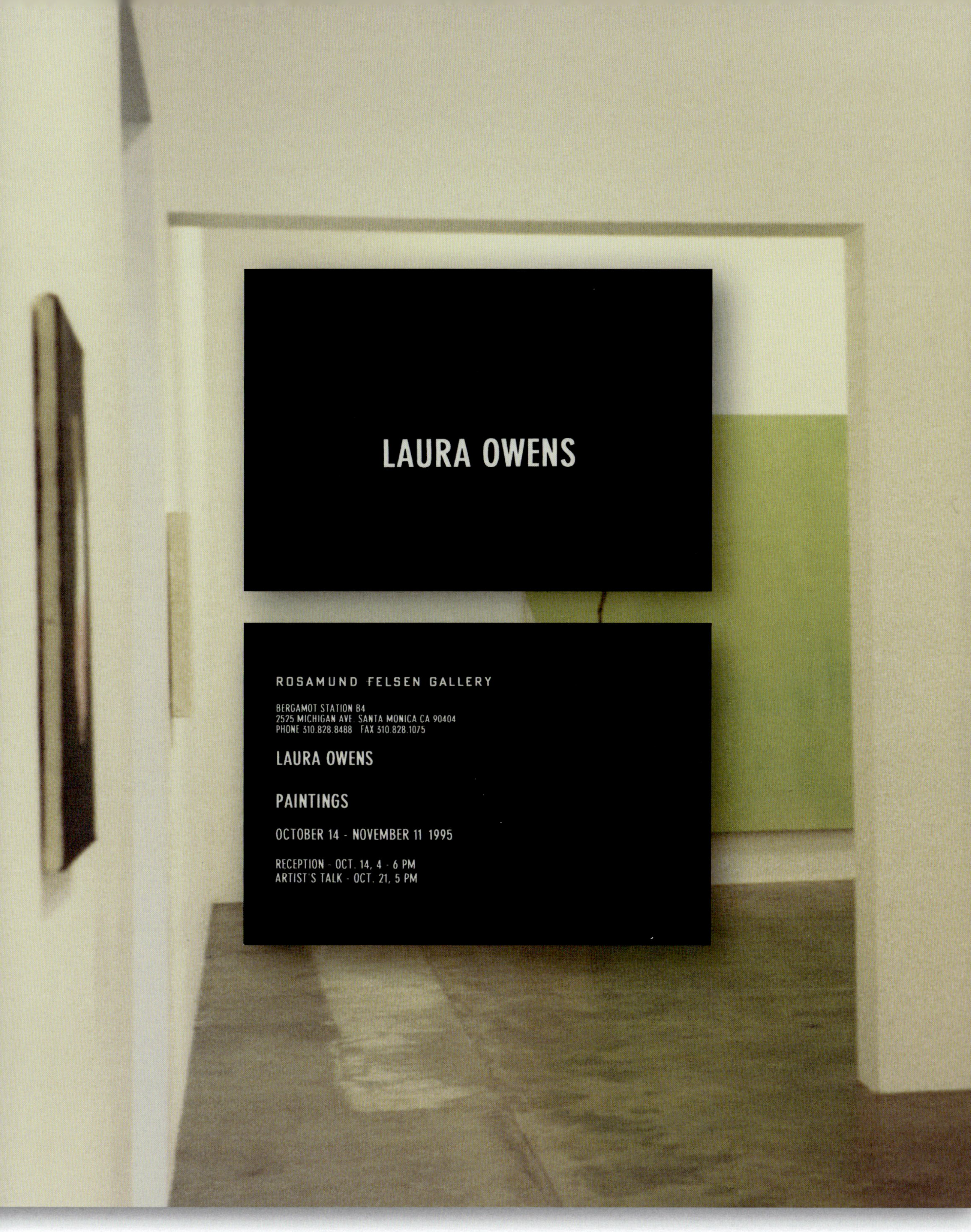

Foreground: Invitation, *Paintings*, Rosamund Felsen Gallery, Santa Monica, 1995
Background: Installation view, Rosamund Felsen Gallery, Santa Monica, 1995, with *Untitled*, 1995 (see p. 85), and *Untitled*, 1995, acrylic
and graphite on canvas, 96¼ × 119 in. (244.5 × 302.3 cm)

ROSAMUND FELSEN GALLERY

Bergamot Station B4
2525 Michigan Avenue
Santa Monica California 90404
TEL 310·828·8488
FAX 310·828·1075

LAURA OWENS

paintings

oct 14 - nov 11, 1995

entry

#1797 ● 1.   Untitled. 1995 *(LO95 16)*
Acrylic, ink, charcoal, pencil on canvas
120 x 96"
$6000.

LAURA OWENS   951013-001
"UNTITLED" 1995
ACRYLIC, INK, CHARCOAL, PENCIL ON CANVAS
120 X 96 INCHES

gallery 1

#1800 ● 2.   Untitled. 1995 *(LO95 14)*
Oil and acrylic on canvas
72 x 60"
$3000.

LAURA OWENS   951013-005
"UNTITLED" 1995
OIL AND ACRYLIC ON CANVAS
72 X 60 INCHES

3.   Untitled. 1995 *(LO95 17)*
Oil, acrylic, enamel, marker, ink, colored pencil, crayon
on canvas
72-1/4 x 84-1/4"
$5000.

LAURA OWENS   951013-005
"UNTITLED" 1995   OIL, ACRYLIC, ENAMEL,
MARKER, INK, COLORED PENCIL, CRAYON ON
CANVAS   72-1/4 X 84-1/4 INCHES

Foreground: Checklist, Rosamund Felsen Gallery, Santa Monica, 1995
Background: Installation view, Rosamund Felsen Gallery, Santa Monica, 1995, with *Untitled*, 1995, acrylic and ink on canvas,
22⅛ × 16¾ in. (56.2 × 42.5 cm)

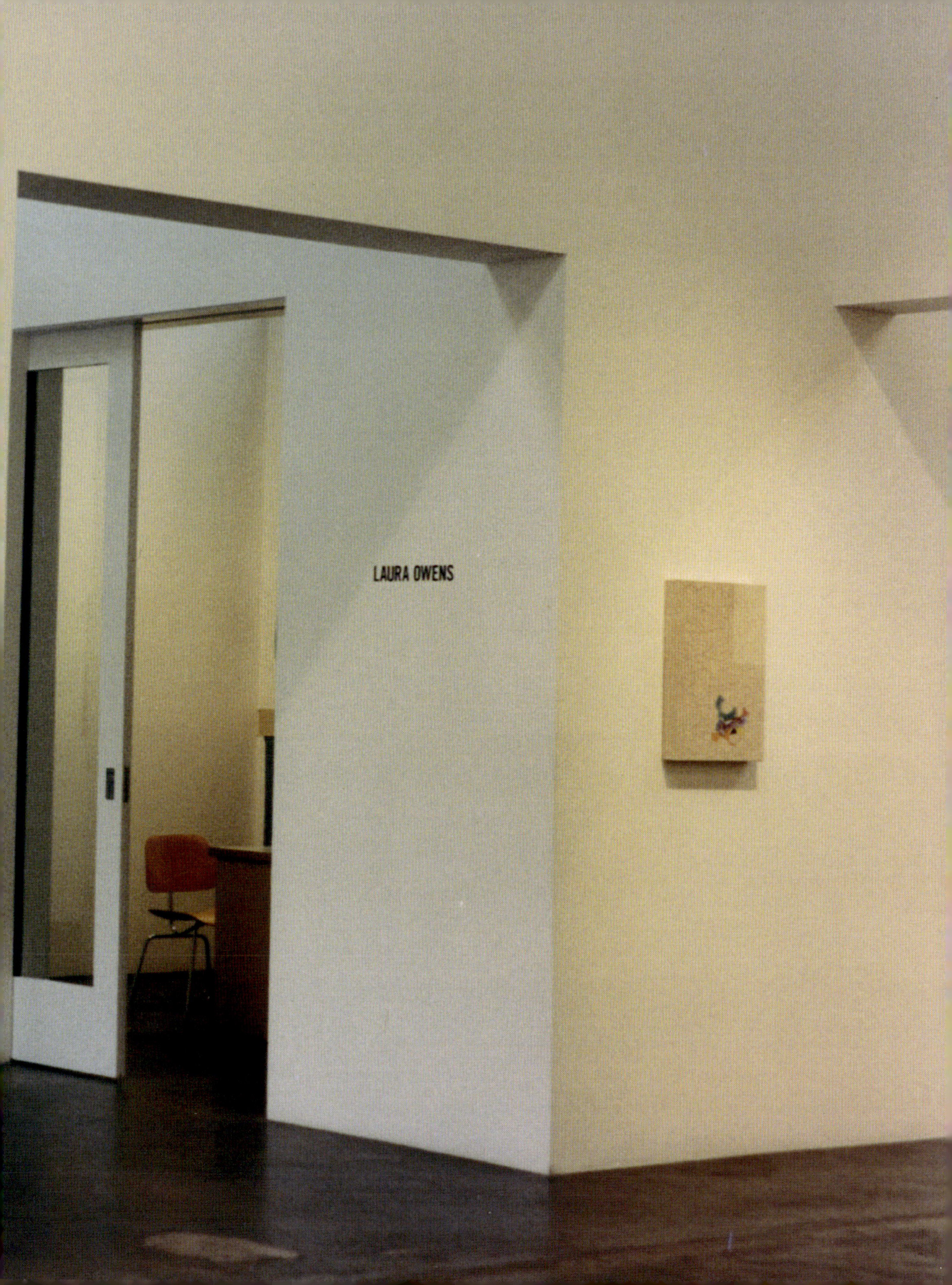
LAURA OWENS

Paul Schimmel: I first saw Laura's work very early on in an exhibition at Rosamund Felsen Gallery in Santa Monica. The show included one of her stained, Color Field–like paintings, and I immediately thought, "Oh, yes, finally, the most disparaged movement in American art returns!" I had my first job at the Museum of Fine Arts, Houston, during the 1970s, and that was the last bastion of Color Field painting, because Clement Greenberg, stains, targets, stripes, and all that shit had by then been banished to the ends of the earth. But sometimes it takes two or three generations to get enough distance from something, and then you can go back. In some corners of LA you could see that it was kind of bubbling up, like in the work of Monique Prieto, who Laura was super close with. I knew from the times when we had shown a Kenneth Noland Target or a Morris Louis at MOCA that artists would say, "Hmm, that looks more interesting than not."

 Foreground: Notebook pages, 1996
Background: Detail of *Untitled*, 1995, acrylic on canvas, 72½ × 60¼ in. (182.9 × 153 cm)

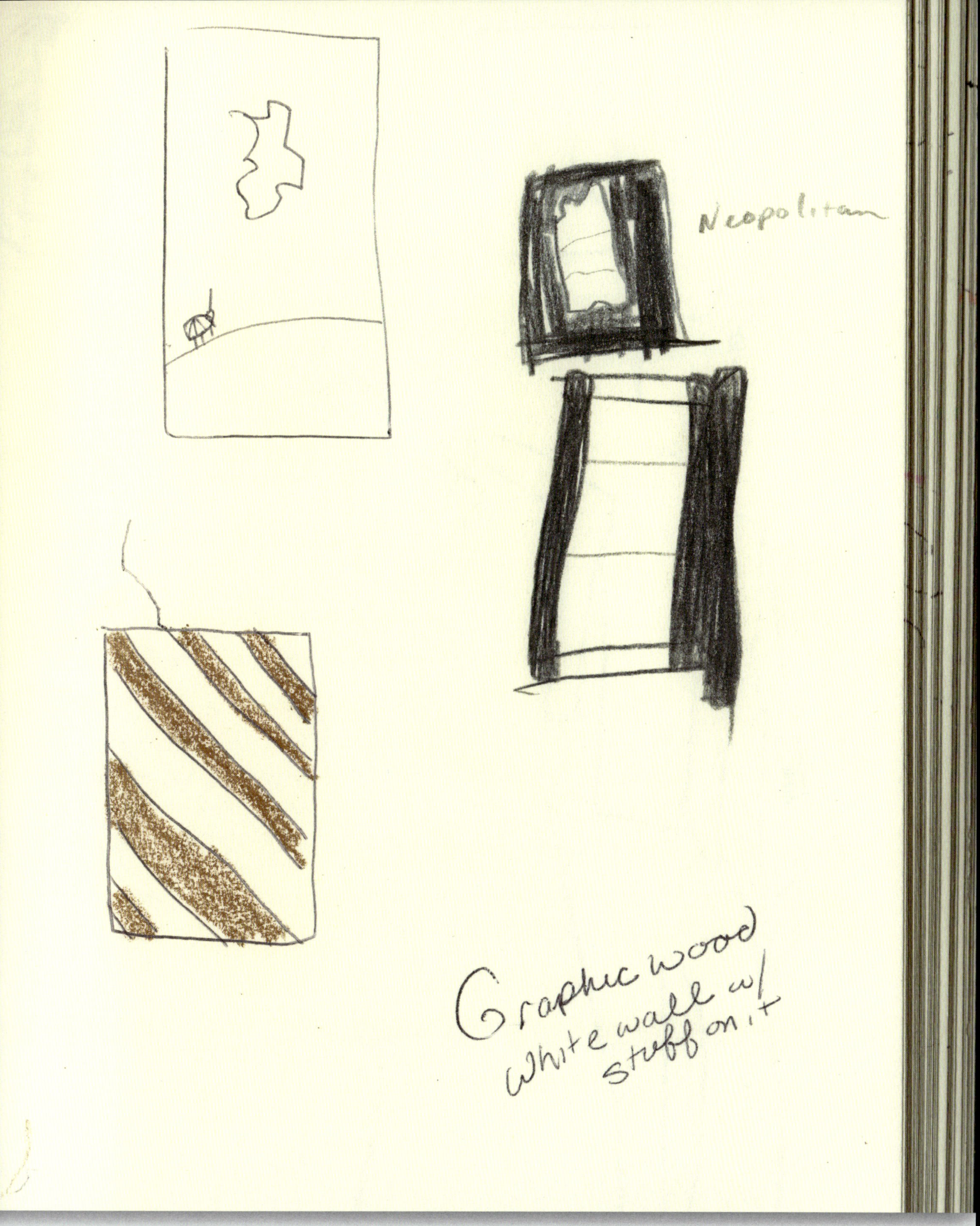

Neopolitan
Graphic wood
White wall w/
stuff on it

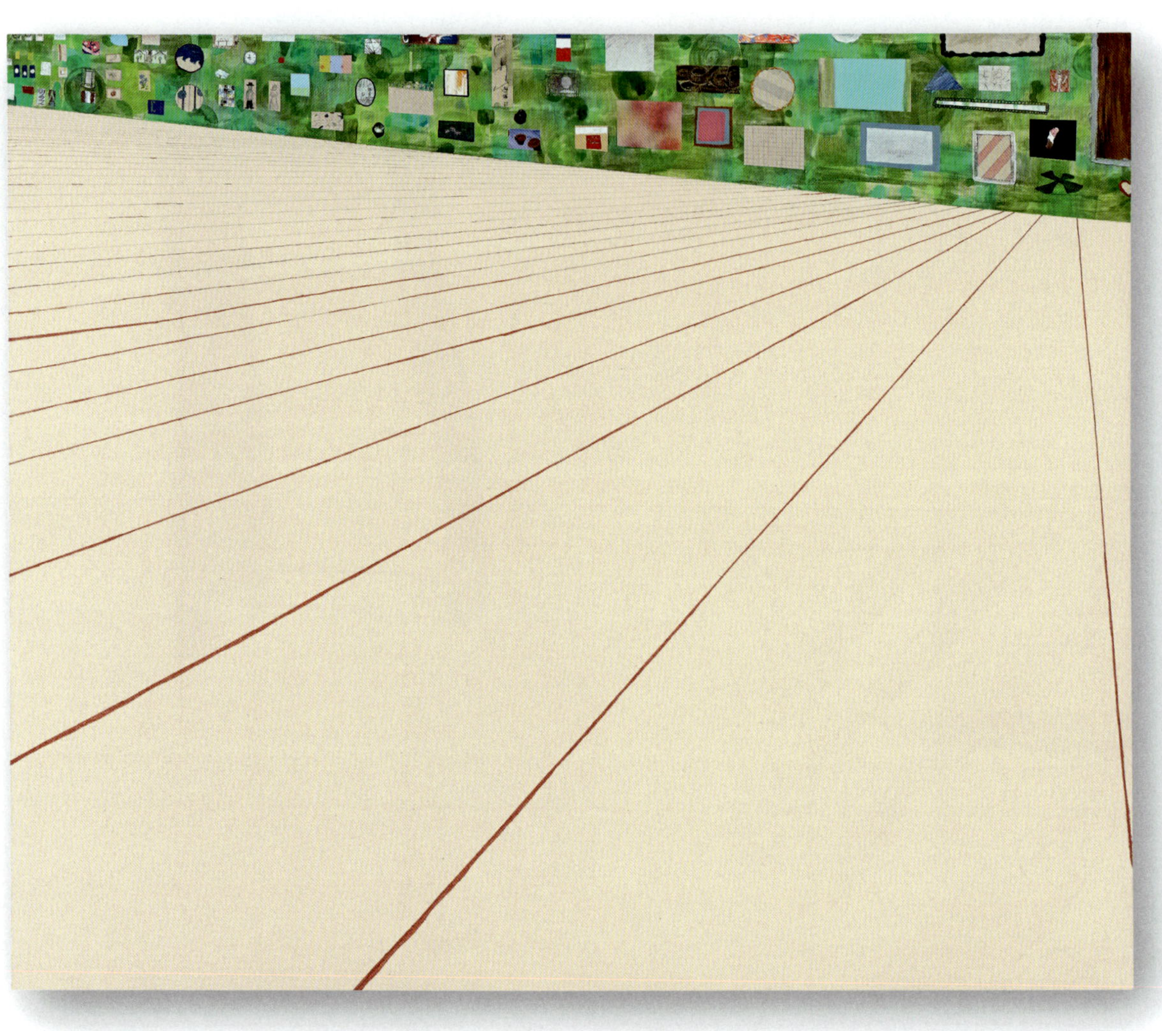

84 *Untitled*, 1995, acrylic, oil, enamel, ink, and marker on canvas, 72¼ × 84¼ in. (183.5 × 214 cm)

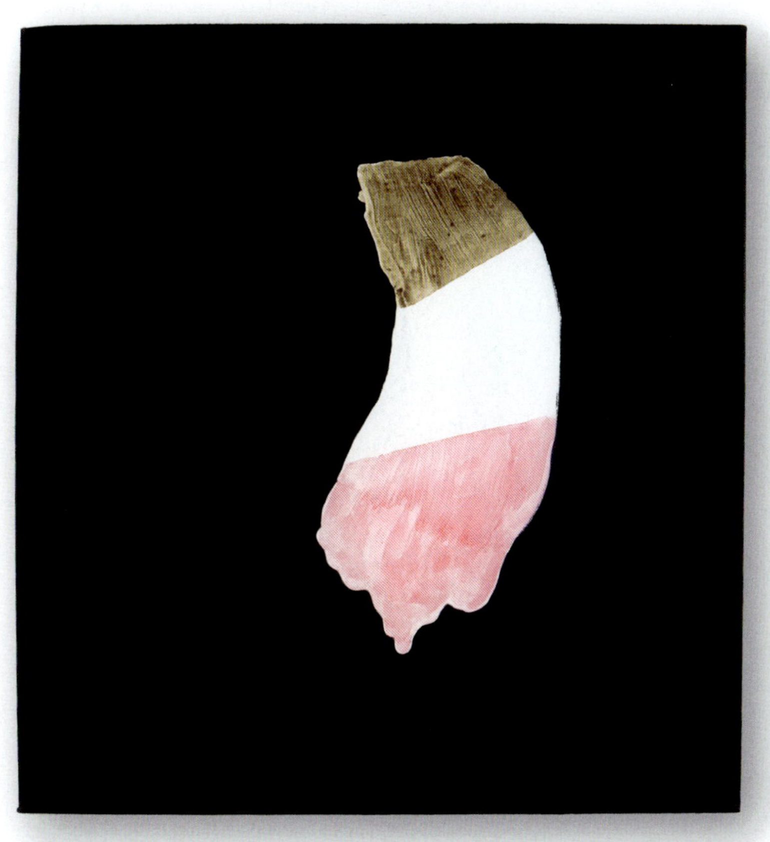

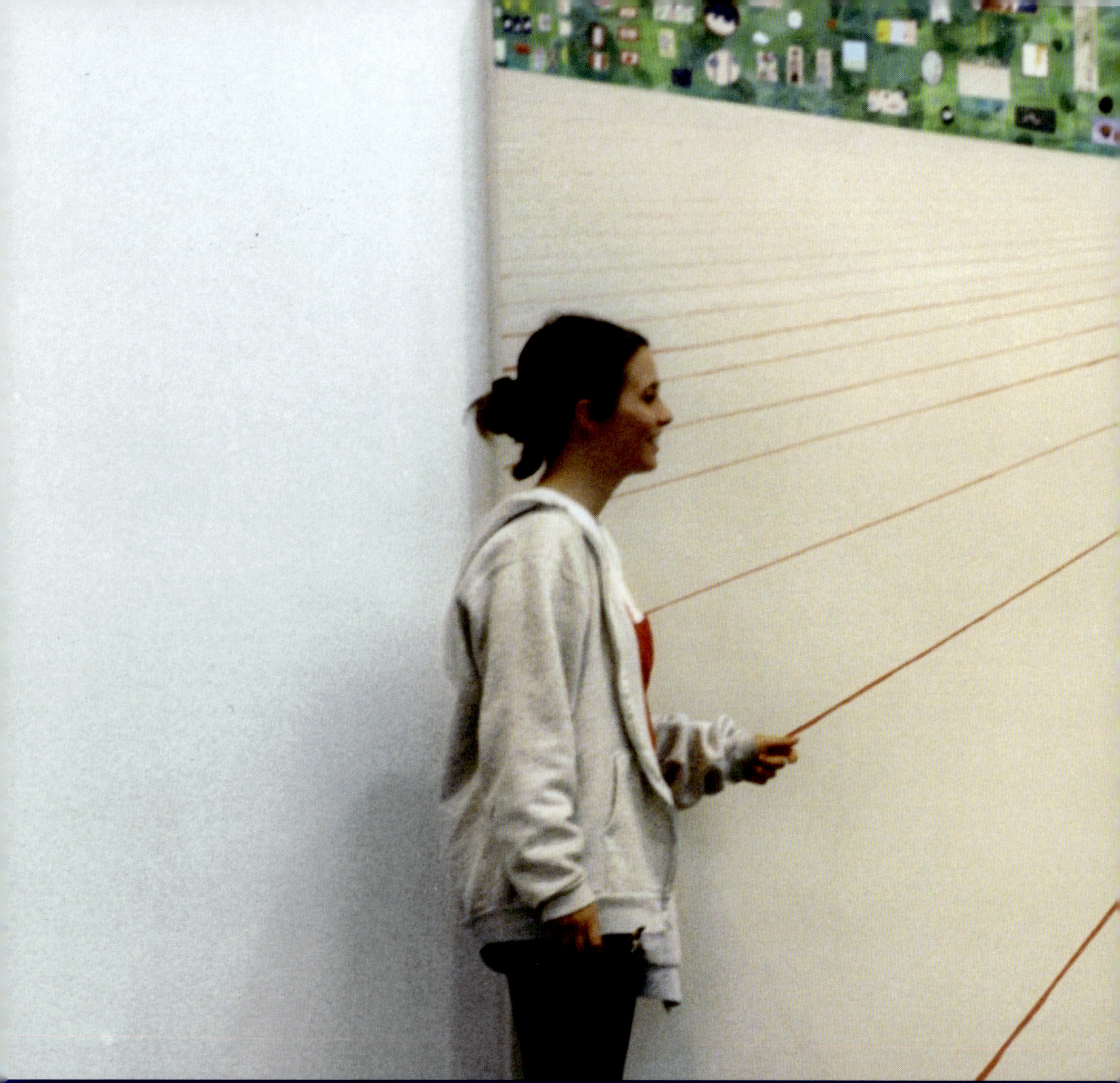

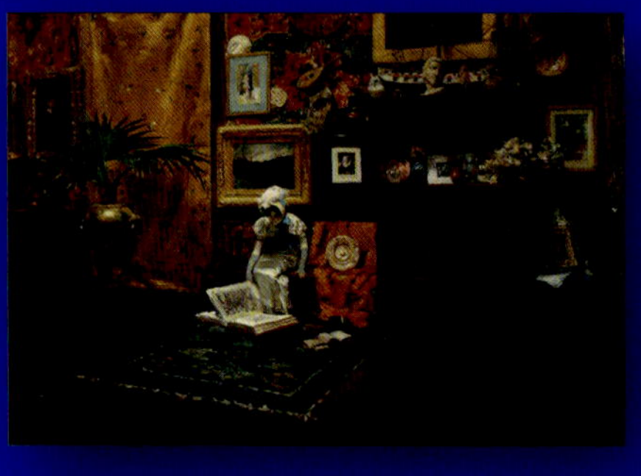

Laura Owens: I started this work after seeing a William Merritt Chase painting at LACMA. I would often go to museums with a sketchbook and make notes about ideas I had for paintings. I drew the perspectival lines directly on the raw canvas to indicate floorboards and gessoed and painted the wall at the top, leaving small white rectangles to fill with paintings. Then it sat in my studio while I worked on all the other pieces for the Rosamund Felsen show. I had started out with the intention of it being a collaborative painting. So whenever anyone would stop by I would ask them if they could paint one of the small works within the work. My mom, my brother, and Lisa Anne Auerbach each made some. Probably other people I can't remember did too. I also painted in some other works from that show along with various paintings I liked at the time, by artists like David Reed, and also a representation of the painting itself—a mise en abyme.

Owens with *Untitled*, 1995 (see p. 84), Rosamund Felsen Gallery, Santa Monica, 1995
Inset: William Merritt Chase, *Studio Interior*, ca. 1882, oil on canvas, 28⅛ × 40⅛ in. (71.4 × 101.9 cm)

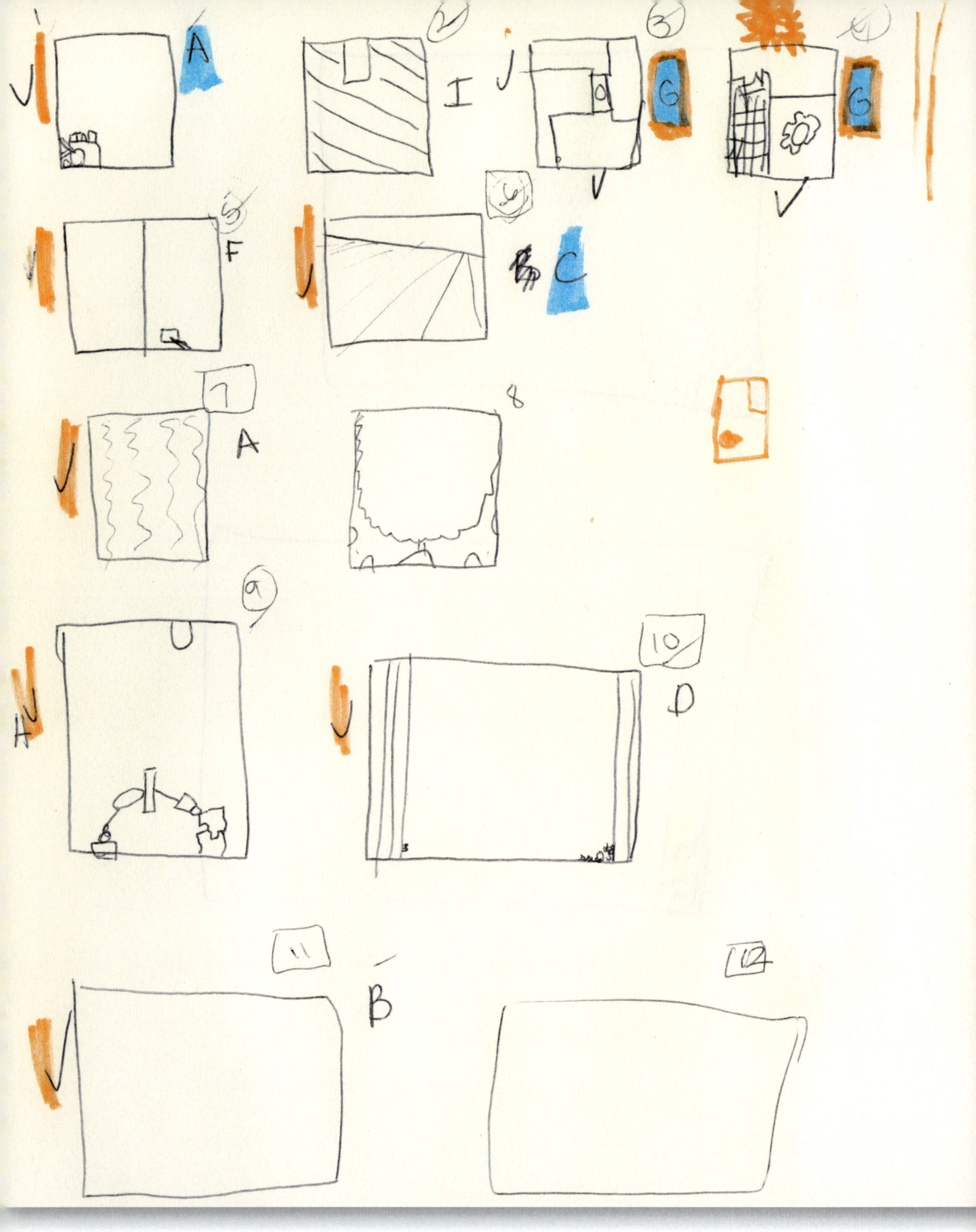

Foreground: *Untitled*, 1995, acrylic and oil on canvas, 72 × 60 in. (182.9 × 152.4 cm)
Background: Sketchbook pages, 1995

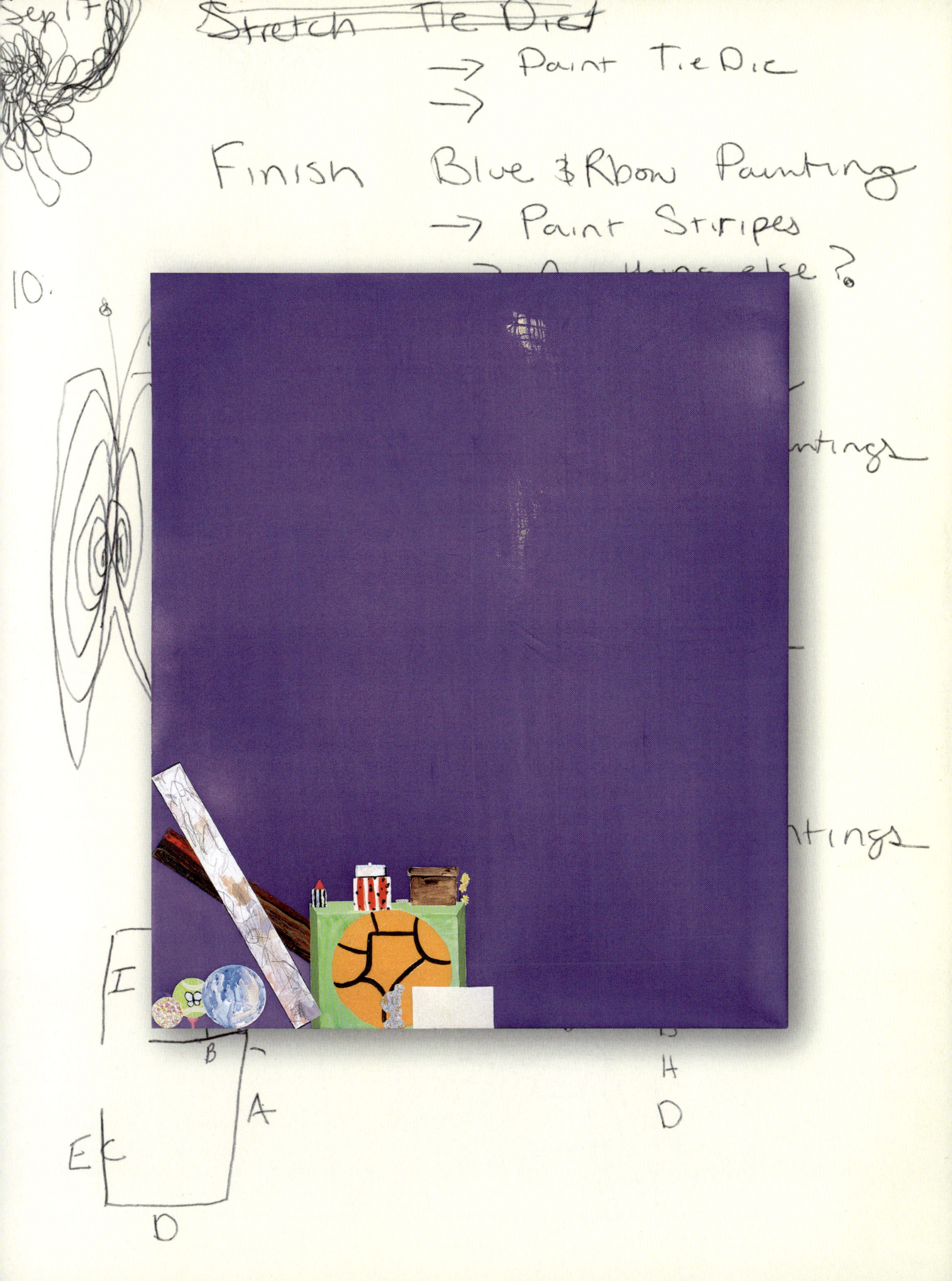

Sept 14
~~Stretch Tie Died~~
→ Paint Tie Die
→
Finish Blue & Rbow Painting
→ Paint Stripes
→ Anything else?
10.
...ntings
...ntings
I
B
A
E
D
H
D

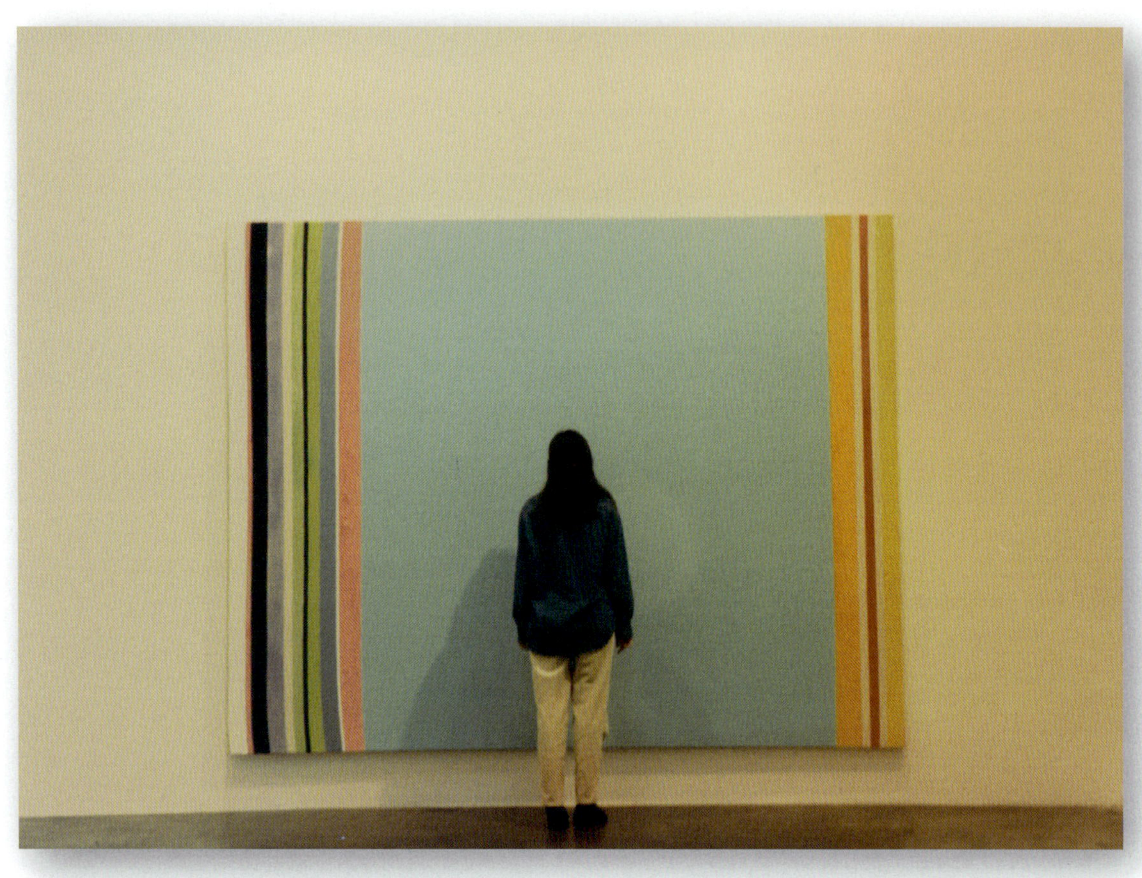

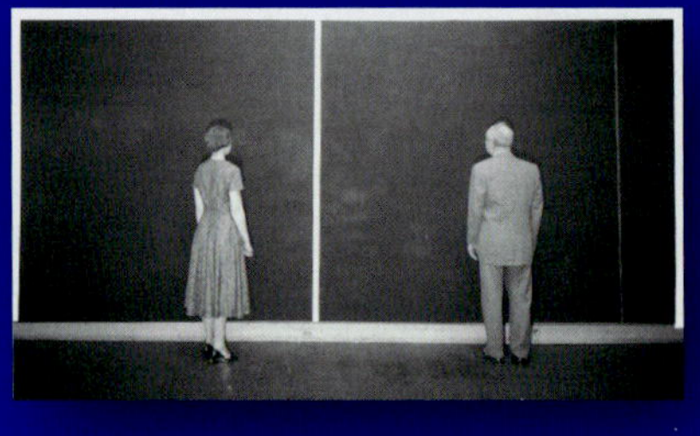

Colleen Grennan with *Untitled*, 1995, acrylic and enamel on canvas, 96½ × 120¼ in. (245.1 × 305.4 cm), Rosamund Felsen Gallery, Santa Monica, 1995

Inset: Barnett Newman, *Cathedra*, 1951, oil and acrylic on canvas, two panels: 95¾ × 213½ in. (243 × 543 cm) overall, Front Street studio, New York, 1958

Foreground: Letter from Rosamund Felsen Gallery, Santa Monica, 1995
Background: Detail of *Untitled*, 1995, acrylic, charcoal, graphite, and ink on canvas, 120 × 96 in. (304.8 × 243.8 cm)

Rosamund Felsen Gallery

Title	Year	Reg#	Medium	Dimensions	Price	Notes
Untitled	1995	LO95 13	Oil & acrylic on canvas	72 x 60"	3000	black & white bricks
Untitled	1995	LO95 14	Oil & acrylic on canvas	72 x 60"	3000	purple
Untitled	1995	LO95 19	Acrylic on canvas	24 x 22"	1200	neopolitan
Untitled	1994	LO95 3	Oil & acrylic on canvas, 3-part	70 x 40" each panel.	5500	triptych
Untitled	1995	LO95 24	Acrylic on canvas	72 x 60 1/4"	3000	tie-dye
Untitled	1995	LO95 25	Acrylic on canvas	72 1/2 x 60 1/4"	3000	snake

Foreground: Comment book, *Paintings,* Rosamund Felsen Gallery, Santa Monica, 1995
Background: Consignment list, Rosamund Felsen Gallery, Santa Monica, 1995

Back in L.A. - things to do.

- Take car for oil → mechanic
- Create Database for storage boxes throw out stuff → remove visual clutter.
- Decide wether to get apartment
    → Get Money from Rosamund!
    or → Build Loft
- Buy Fax - Ans. Machine
- Buy Plants - Flowers
- Buy Bicycle
- Change BANK - open savings account.
- New email
- Muesli → Oatmeal - Brown Rice

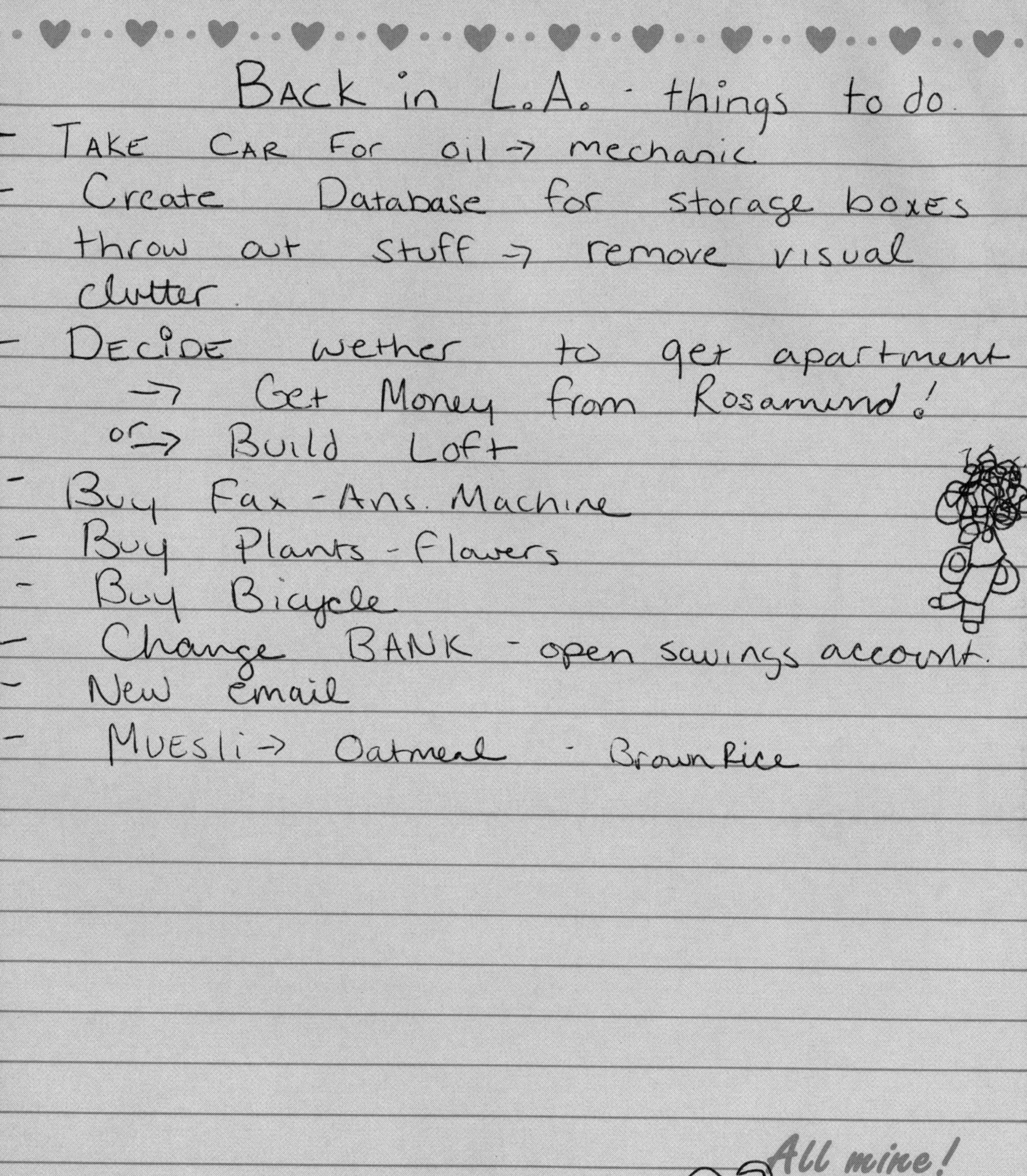

TRIUMPHS, SETBACKS, REAR EXITS, AND CEASE FIRES: SOME AESTHETIC ISSUES CONCERNING ALBERT OEHLEN, AND SOME ARCHITECTURAL AND MUSICAL COMPARISONS
DIEDRICH DIEDERICHSEN

I've rarely had as much fun with any artwork as I've had with the Great Mosque in Córdoba, Spain; John Ford's film *Cheyenne Autumn*; downtown Los Angeles; Archie Shepp's recording of "A Portrait of Robert Thompson (as a young man)" on the LP *Mama Too Tight*; or the CD *Lysol* by the Melvins.[1] Albert Oehlen's new paintings and Don Covay's song "I Was Checking Out, She Was Checking In" take matters a step farther (though I don't mean to imply that farther is necessarily better). I'd like to describe here some aspects of the construction of the works on the first list that appear to have something in common with each other, in order to develop a conception of the aesthetic at work in Albert Oehlen's paintings of at least the last five years, and of the scale relationships, oppositions, and interconnections that are the basic, or even the determining, issues undergirding his work.

I think that what Oehlen likes so much about some of Frank Zappa's recordings also can be found in the examples cited above, even if an exact correspondence between Zappa's nervous, multipartite compositions and the bipartite structures that I am going to describe cannot be so easily drawn. The key is probably that in all of these examples the parts don't act like separate pieces; neither do they form an additive, unified whole, nor establish relations based either on total opposition or subordination of one to the other. In fact, besides those named above, and perhaps Zappa, there are very few works of art that perfectly deploy the many parts of a single experience to create such surprising and disproportionate effects. Although far be it from me to adopt the position of an economist, for whom the most perfect system would be the one employing the fewest elements, it seems true that in Oehlen's work, for example, it's not a question of the number of elements, but of the distinctions among them—

these being as great as possible while still allowing interferences and relationships to develop. It is exactly the distinctiveness[2] of the elements that make them rather indistinct, or hard to distinguish, the virtues of which are precisely what I wish to clarify through the examples cited above and described in what follows.

After many years of trying to clear away misconceptions about the nature of painting through his work, Oehlen reached the point of being able simply to demonstrate his position without having to mount a full frontal assault. The decisions he made in his painting no longer required external justifications for their handwriting, palette, style, degree of flatness, content, or whether they were representational or nonrepresentational, whether they improved our perception or not. It was this decision-making process that allowed new relationships between the still clearly recognizable, distinct elements to be automatically obtained, without their standing for some external legitimation. A section of built-up surface, a bizarre, primary-colored form, a pattern, a partial figure, all appear as so many equal parts. This always surprises people trying to decipher the pictures, and leads to interpretations that say the works are overloaded, when in fact they are simply unhierarchical. This also makes for a pleasant feeling for a viewer who has known distinctiveness only in connection with triumphs and domination of one part over another, and of parts over the whole. It is this experience, rare as it is, that unites my encounter with many of Oehlen's paintings, especially the later ones, and the following examples from architecture, cinema, and music. While the clarity achieved in the examples may be attributed to their structural simplicity, this is hardly the case for Oehlen's works, in which the distinctions may be clear to

Originally published in *Oehlen Williams 95*, ed. Catherine Gudis, exh. cat. (Columbus, OH: Wexner Center for the Arts, The Ohio State University, 1995), 102–17. Translated from the German by Peter Chametzky. Diederichsen is an author, music journalist, and cultural critic as well as a professor at the Academy of Fine Arts, Vienna.

a seasoned observer, but far harder to describe, even for a seasoned commentator.

❙ Catholics conquering the Islamic cultural center of Córdoba in the fifteenth century encountered over three hundred mosques there.[3] They immediately destroyed and razed most of these, and the rest disappeared over time. The persecution of the Jews and Moslems who refused to convert, and of "crypto-Moslems" (those Moslems allowed to convert to Christianity in the first decades of the reconquest, but whose conversion was not considered legitimate in the years thereafter) was sporadically carried out at first, but soon became brutal. This, as well as the other major events of 1492—Columbus's voyage, the expulsion of Arabs and Jews, the conquest of Granada— not only expanded the territory of the Catholic crowns, but also changed territorial thinking itself, making available new spatial and ethnographic conceptions of interior and exterior and of alien and native, all organized around the determining forces of Catholicism and early capitalism.[4]

In the middle of the Córdoba, on the Guadalquivir river, stood what was then the second (and today, the third) largest mosque in the world, La Mezquita (the Great Mosque). Since the year 756, Córdoba had been an Arab residence city and capital of the dynasty of Syrian caliphs founded by the Umayyads. The first Umayyad caliph, Abd al-Rahman I, began the building of the Great Mosque.[5] After the Catholic victory, the mosque was used as a Christian church for a time, before the canons of Córdoba decided to build a Renaissance cathedral right in the middle of it. Charles V (or Carlos Primera, as he's known in Spain)—the ruler on whose empire the sun never set—visited the new Mezquita three years after its completion in 1526. He is reputed to have said that the canons had taken a building that could have been put anywhere in the world, and placed it precisely so that it disfigured another unique and irreplaceable structure.[6] It remains unclear why they let the Great Mosque survive at all, rather than tearing it down as they had done with all the others. Was it respect for its grandeur? Or perhaps to settle an old debt: before the Moorish conquest there had actually been a Christian church on the site, which the Umayyads tore down, but only after they, the conquerors, had bought it from the Christians.

One could argue that the Great Mosque bears witness to the magnitude of the enemy that had been overcome. Its horizontal monumentality—

so foreign to the vertically oriented spires of the Christian vision—might in any case have flattered the Christian conquerors' sense of new connections to global trade and empire. (Indeed, this form is similar in many ways to the architecture of later European market halls—extending even to the French arcades of the nineteenth century—whose massing and colonnades might be said to resemble the porticoes and vast interior spaces of the Great Mosque.) Although there is speculation as to other reasons why the building was spared, suffice it to say that neither the apparently "worldly" Charles, nor his depressed successors ever fundamentally transformed the building. (Charles did proceed, however, as had the canons of Córdoba before him—whom he had upbraided as barbarians—to build "disfiguring" extensions to the Alcázar in Seville and the Alhambra in Granada.) Perhaps the insertion of the cathedral within the mosque at Córdoba ultimately contributed to the fact that the Great Mosque was tolerated in the ultra-Catholic city for almost five hundred years, through the Inquisition, Counter-Reformation, Catholic Fundamentalism, and Fascism.

When you stroll through the seemingly endless forest of columns in the mosque, you get the feeling of being led nowhere. The repetition and lack of a discernable hierarchy invites the type of unrestricted roaming that appeals to tourists, but which they usually automatically abandon in the

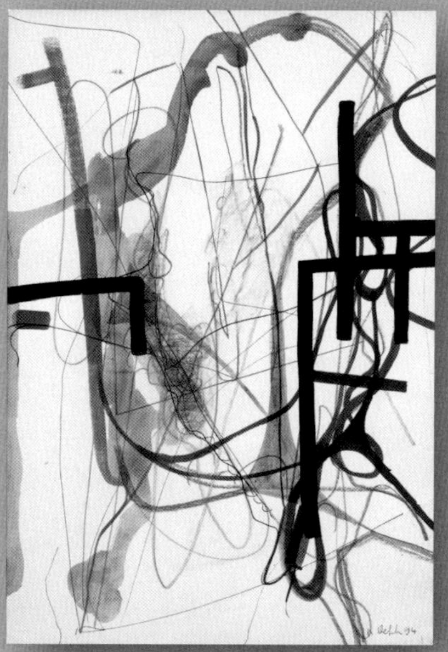

Albert Oehlen, *Ohne Titel* (Untitled), 1994, mixed media on paper, 26¾ × 18 in. (68.5 × 46.3 cm)

structured spaces of churches and cathedrals. This is not to say that people behave totally without inhibition in the mosque: they still speak in hushed tones as if they're in a church. Although the portal of the cathedral could certainly be circumvented, as it's right in the center of and surrounded by the mosque, generally one enters the pompous, showy, plateresque cathedral through the front entrance, and finds oneself in a space that displays its current function in its every detail. One surfaces from an indistinct historical meditation (of a mosque no longer true to its original religious intents) into an unequivocal, historically continuous, ongoing religious space that leaves nothing unresolved and allows the (religiously) disinterested tourist no other reaction than the usual astonished upwards gape. But following the church's main axis down the nave to the altar offers the only opportunity in the world to *pass through* a cathedral: visitors leave through the rear exit and once again are in the mosque, where most linger for just as long as in the first stages of their visit. Although the mosque does not have a single nameable "attraction"—the space itself is the attraction—most of one's time is spent in it. Many visitors, who by this point have gotten the taste for ambling and don't want to go back into the church at all, try to avoid it, circumventing it to get back again to where they started at the main entrance. In winter or summer the temperate, limitless space is endlessly inviting.

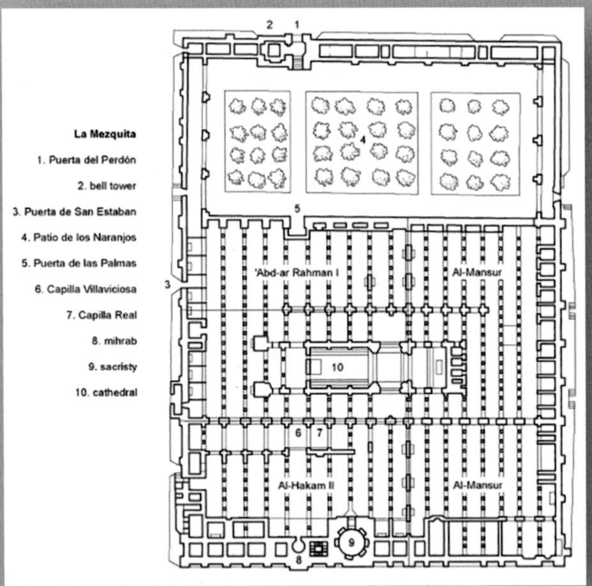

Floor plan, La Mezquita, Córdoba, Spain, showing additions and alterations

It remains unclear whose victory or triumph this monstrous construction documents. Charles's original idea is quickly revealed to be nonsense: the mosque is not disfigured or debased by the church. Wrapped loosely around the tense Christian core, the mosque seems to have the last, relaxing word.

But the church's "come hither" quality is also to dramatic effect. One can imagine how, historically, a strong symbolic pressure to convert was brought to bear upon Jews, Arabs, and others who were forced to continually pass through the "pagan" building. Even believers must have experienced the sense of passage that the architecture reinforced—from the sinful and disbelieving world of temptation to the refuge of the church and out again into a miserable world. Probably, though, today's impression was also valid in the past: the church's symbolic world, enveloped by a second zone of symbolism invoked by the mosque surrounding it, holds an attraction or fascination because it remains ambiguous and unresolved.

II In the 1960s a phase began in the work of John Ford that as a whole has always fascinated me, that I've called his "decadent period." In it, the director takes the liberty of dismantling the mythological foundations of his own "great works."[7] For example, *The Man Who Shot Liberty Valence* (1961) questions the authenticity of the film's genre, while *Donovan's Reef* (1963) takes apart its stars—John Wayne and Lee Marvin—letting them stumble as mindless brawling rowdies through a plot that has almost nothing to do with the roles they play. And *Cheyenne Autumn* (1964) offers an apology to the indigenous inhabitants of North America for the way they had been demonized in Westerns.[8] But what interests me here is not so much what today looks like a particularly radical form of self-reflexiveness or deconstruction, but rather that which corresponds formally with the Córdoba Mezquita. In the movie, the Cheyenne trek on and on, hour after hour, soaking wet, hungry, and defeated, through the overly long film's winter version of Ford's favorite Southwestern landscape, and, except for a few cuts to Washington, DC, where we get to see Edward G. Robinson as Carl Schurz, nothing happens. Since Ford doesn't allow any "action," the film illustrates its protagonists' suffering especially well. By its nature "misery" cannot be portrayed as a sudden catastrophe, especially not in the cinema, but only as something endured over time. Ford's proverbial camera searches out the proverbial Monument Valley horizon as if he had already read his European admirers.[9] In the middle of this hyper-Ford landscape (which lacks every element that goes into a normal Ford narrative) and after half the film is already over, the master built in an interlude that seems to try to cram an entire

Western into thirty minutes. The Cheyenne reach Dodge City and suddenly all the conventional Western tropes rush by as if in fast-forward: the saloon with piano, horses, cowboys, honky-tonk singer, brawls, Hollywood stars, and even Wyatt Earp and Doc Holiday. But, as in the cathedral-inside-the-mosque, one exits this episode out the back, and is returned to the Cheyenne for a while, banished again to their fate.

Interestingly, it was this structural aspect of the film that bothered the studio and distributor most, and not the impoverished plot, excessive length, or possibly controversial theme. They tried to get around this in various ways. The film was shown first with an intermission just before the Dodge City episode, which gave people the comforting feeling of having wandered into a different film. Later the episode was totally cut out. Ford's idea that you couldn't undo thousands of other Westerns by showing the other side just once, and that once and for all he had to push the Western itself to the point of a burlesque farce, is effective in large part because of his artistic integrity and renown as a director of Westerns. Even when he turns his virtuosity against himself, he doesn't betray it.

But moral content is not the only basis for this island of action amid an unmoving sea of affliction. Certain European theorists (of the *Cahiers du Cinéma* circle) were at the same time developing the idea of wandering from one film into another. However, their genre critique can hardly be separated from their infatuation with it, and from this dilemma a new genre ultimately developed: the *nouvelle vague* cinema, which is characterized, among other things, by providing a European critique of Hollywood and a Hollywood critique of Europe. Both are given equal emphasis, and the charm resides precisely in the fact that neither simplification is allowed to carry the day.

Ford, though, was much tougher: it has often been remarked upon that a movie theater is like a church, in that one is not allowed to leave too early or through an unmarked exit (Roland Barthes, for instance, stressed the pleasurable feeling of being trapped in cinema's front rows). The film can be about or show anything, any type of imaginary escape—except from one film into another.[10] Ford, it would seem, could risk making this quite radical gesture, unsettling the basic structural principle of his own films, more easily than, say, Godard—for whom film was problematic in a similar way as the Great Mosque was for Charles V and his successors. In all the centuries following the canons of Córdoba, no other worldly ruler or artist could make such disruptive moves. It's possible that the revisions of the canons as well as Ford actually did much to secure the place of their respective religions (and for Ford I'd say this was cinema, and not the Western) by leaving the thorniest question of final victory or defeat of the arch rival unresolved. Instead of celebrating, they refute the validity of the entire preexisting scenario.

III Contemporary urban theory is oriented more and more towards Los Angeles, in a critical as well as a celebratory sense. For art theorists, the most influential urbanists today are the LA specialists Edward Soja and Mike Davis. They have become as known for their urban studies of LA as Richard Sennett has, for instance, for his work on New York and as Henri Lefebvre on Paris. Urban planners and local politicians from Frankfurt am Main to Marseille argue increasingly about possibilities gleaned from Los Angeles.[11] On the one hand, Los Angeles appears to be the antipode to the old European utopias, invented purely by capitalism and placing its faith in progress. On the other hand, it is also the testing ground for new and more or less subtle forms of segregation in the increasingly "overburdened" multicultural metropolises of the twenty-first century. Other city administrators are looking to it first to avoid problems, second to discover solutions, and third to find nice names for pernicious measures. Los Angeles in the present seems to be exemplary and avant-garde in advancing into the future predicted by Gilles Deleuze in his essay, "Postscript on the Society of Control."[12] What Michel Foucault called the society of discipline is transformed into what Mike Davis describes, and Deleuze calls, the society of control, which is what happens when "Gang-free Parks," "Gated Neighborhoods," "Citizen Patrols," etc., treat people simply as objects to be controlled and regulated, and no longer even as economic subjects to be exploited or militarized.

Davis has described the creation of a pseudo-urban "downtown," whose location could be anywhere in the city, not only in terms of the licentious mobility of California capitalism, but also for its use of digital, smart, and sensitive monitoring technologies, which play a particular role in the struggle with segregation being fought with the most varied of weaponry, from the National Guard to helicopters to anti-gang laws and the like.[13] But downtown LA also contains aspects of the cathedral-in-the-Mezquita, or of the Dodge City episode in the middle of the Cheyenne's hunger march: once you've passed through it, you're right back where you started from. A difference is also apparent. While the ultimate victor remained undecided in Córdoba, and *Cheyenne Autumn* operated on another level, involving the metahistory of film itself, the message of LA comes through pretty clearly. One drives through endless monotonous stretches of LA, and then encounters the concentrated, gleaming citadels of power downtown, only to leave it again, and usually into particularly depressed areas (especially if one leaves from the south or east). The message seems clear: the vertical in the midst of the horizontal scores a symbolic triumph.

On the other hand, the concentrated verticality appears also to ask in exactly those "problem" groups that were segregated out and that form a tract of criminality and poverty surrounding downtown. They seem to be the literal underworld necessary to stage this triumph. Or are they the hypostatization of what is otherwise absent in LA, a staged version of the traditional urban fabric, which, beside the upwardly striving economic power symbolized by skyscrapers, crowds into the smallest possible space in an exaggerated version of a colorful, multicultural street life complete with retailing, drug traffic, and homelessness? In contrast to Córdoba or Dodge City, long before you get to downtown LA it's obvious that you can pass right through it. The surprise of this bypassable center resides, actually, in its real content: an enactment of New York–style street life, a staged modernism that makes no claim to be totalizing, a bold realization of the architectural fantasies of pure capitalism. This exists next to real social distress on one side, and really picturesque historical re-creations on the other.[14] Capitalism presents a carnivalized version of itself, even as, beyond downtown, its real and chronic effects can still be observed. Under extremely unequal conditions of poverty and possibility one finds omnipresent palm trees and an architectural illusion of equality. Impressions can therefore be deceiving.

Carnivalized capitalism is more coherent and monolithic than it appears, and the apparent architectural homogeneity of the tracts surrounding downtown are deceptive about the tremendous social and economic inequality. This capitalism, as it proudly proclaims, can't be dismissed anymore as a carnival. The spectacle directs a dose of homeopathic subversion and comedy against itself, even at the level of urban and architectural planning. This is poverty behind tall palms, a reality that can't be captured, that photography cannot expose. In such a situation appearances are always deceptive (not about some hidden reality, but rather about that which is seen), meanings are ambiguous, new, and unclear. It demands to be spoken about in terms of Córdoba, and the degree of balance achieved between the preexisting structure and the one inserted into it. The horizontal destruction of the rest of LA's public space demanded the insertion of a simulated city, which could be both in the tradition of other "fortresses" there, such as the Times Building and the walled villas, but which also had to look totally new in order to survive.

Building-into appears to be the opposite procedure of an active war, in which the conqueror comes upon a fortification that he besieges, razes, or conquers. A new ring is created from the outside around that which already exists. The citadel, the vertical, the center, the cathedral is always already there, and new settlements grow up around it. In today's American urban agglomerations, though, tracts of "livable," less traveled, gang- and drug-free zones, in which the political decision makers and ruling classes live, ring and imprison inner cities, places that the African American poet Wanda Coleman has compared with concentration camps.[15] The old center is no longer what once dominated, but rather the always-already-marginalized, which, unlike, the disempowered and conquered center, possesses no negotiable cultural capital, no "tradition" or "seniority." In this context, the gesture of planting something in the center is really strange, regardless of whether it's done in triumph, as a show of power, as a critique of power, or in the name of art. The American example shows that all the possible combinations in the center-periphery relationship can be plotted along a matrix:

	POWER	TRADITION/IDENTITY	CULTURAL CAPITAL
1. Conventional Conquest			
Periphery	+	-	-
Center	-	+	+
2. American Cities Today			
Periphery	+	-	+
Center	-	+	-
3. Córdoba Mosque			
Periphery	-	+	+
Center	+	-	+
4. Dodge City			
Periphery	-	+	-
Center	+	-	-
5. Downtown Los Angeles			
Periphery	-	+	-
Center	+	-	+

Note: Around all of matrix 5 there is a tract from matrix 2. The direct periphery of downtown is a ring of powerlessness. Around this is a suburban, predominantly powerful zone made up of wealthy, or at least better-off, areas.

The different power relations and very different historical situations determining our examples appear to explain the aesthetic peculiarity of the impassible being passable. Planting-in-the-middle only occurs when normal means of postponing or carrying on power struggles fail or are halted or have been stretched to the limit (California represents what the German economist Robert Kurz has called "capitalism that is no longer able to exploit").[16] In the examples described here a point of virtual stasis is achieved, scored either as an ambivalent draw, or locked in a cease-fire imposed by a concerned artist.

IV Power struggles are nowhere so strongly symbolized and so unresolved in their outcomes as in music. The old opposition of music and architecture (which was particularly dear to surrealists) attributes freedom to music and control to architecture. It is more rarely held, though just as plausibly, that music is actually similar to exterior architecture, in that it forces itself upon us internally and psychologically. The basic architectural problem that I've been discussing here is also familiar to music. To pass through a space in order to return to where one was to begin with is a general principle of musical composition, familiar in *Lieder* and sonatas and jazz. The difference resides in the fact that the two elements are a function of each other, and not of the introduction of radically disjunctive oppositions. The latter was introduced to music, as to most other arts, through collage techniques, which in fact were often also conceived in relationship to harmony, balance, or composition. In the compositions of Pere Ubu, for instance, a rock guitar plays on one track, while one hears synthesized high-pitched whistling from another. The Jesus and Mary Chain juxtaposes feedback and acoustic, folksy guitar melodies.[17] I am trying to find even more extreme oppositions, or better, not exactly oppositions, but elements that seem so erratic and "distinct" that they would normally only be possible in an environment dedicated to contrariness.

Archie Shepp recorded the LP *Mama Too Tight* on the Impulse label in 1967. It came out a little before Coltrane's death the same year. The first side stays within the general orbit of collective free improvisation, an area Coltrane had been expanding on in terms of the radicalness of the musical "freedom" and the number of players involved. Shepp went a step farther by eliminating the piano—and, to a certain extent, its limiting and defining function—from his arrangements. Instead, he worked with six wind instruments and a rhythm section: a tenor saxophone, clarinet, trumpet, two trombones, and a tuba. This wind ensemble was neither divided up into the traditional separation of brasses and reeds, nor did it coalesce in a single unit. The traditional wind ensemble—harmonizing, cooperating, following orders—is broken up into a bunch of lone musicians. They're not soloists, though. Rather, the juxtaposition of their improvisations defines the collective as a group in which each can take any part and all have an equal voice. Collective free improvisation had never been taken so far. Previously, the traditional foreground-background hierarchy had been maintained, or else a clear separation of the functions of the heterogeneous instruments had produced something more like the Communist "from each according to his abilities, to each according to his needs." In Shepp all the instruments are equally loud, and all play about the same theme with about the same authority. Constant, breathtaking motion produces an extreme cacophony, for which a pause would mean immediate dissolution. This continues with varying intensities, motives, and volumes— blues themes and Duke Ellington's "Prelude to a Kiss" crop up—over the first two parts of the three-part "A Portrait of Robert Thompson (as a young man)." After a quarter of an hour the anarchic web of voices issues into a march, "Dem Basses." It's certainly a halting march, but even so it creates an extreme contrast to the utopian musical explorations that precede it. The enormous, striking contrast offers no alternative sequential passage back to the start. But another level is preserved in intonation and playing style, and one can clearly discern the identity of the familiar voices. This checks the antithesis from becoming too extreme. The listener emerges from the short stretch of the march with its rigid rhythms and extremely organized ensemble and individual parts, and recognizes the anarchic voices again, now somewhat reined in. This creates the impression that they had either just been parodically "playing around," or that their first incantation was simply an extended prelude to the basic problem expressed here: where anything is allowed, too extreme display will ultimately bring forth a tyrant.

Or, could it be that freedom is not complete without the possibility of its negation? First of all parodic and carnivalesque, the form of expression here owes much, rhetorically, to the whole African American tradition of "signifying." In any case, the negation is serious and total, particularly because the march is so cheerful. The concept of freedom developed by the extreme distinctions here goes beyond conventional philosophical terms. This piece was recorded after the murder of Malcolm X, and at the time of the emergence of the Black Panther Party. For an explicitly political artist like Shepp, questions of power play on a number of different levels. Who codifies jazz? (In the liner notes he talks about how, if jazz is "valorized," it will be torn out of the ghetto to become part of bourgeois culture.) What is a collective? To whom do particular symbols belong, and above all, how do the various different musical concepts such as "harmony," "atonality," "composition," and "improvisation" relate to each other? A few very general historical facts, or a few biographical ones about Shepp, though, cannot account for any correspondence between the power struggle within the music with one outside of it (not as reflection or criticism, but as something playing through it). Rather, the correspondence resides in the aesthetic phenomenon of "distinctions" between elements, which probably owes as much to coercion as to any inner compulsion for struggle.

V Even before their most recent records gained notoriety on the art scene, the Melvins qualified as a new breed of rock musicians. Since 1986 they have been one of the bands oriented towards metal and hard rock that has been able to take out of context and to celebrate the genre's flourishes, explosive force, and dramatic turning points. On their 1992 record *Lysol*, just before they signed with a major label, they took this to the limit: for all the CD player knew, *Lysol* consisted of a single song. There were even two undocumented cover versions on the record, of songs by Alice Cooper and Flipper. From the appropriate roar of the bass at the beginning, to the minute-long drum intros in the middle, to the relatively conventional song at the end, a good half-hour later, the record attempted nothing other than to preserve and extend for as long as possible all of metal's tried and true but all too quickly fading flourishes, freed from their dependence on fixed locations in predetermined scenarios. "Distinctions" become here practically pure qualities, independent of context. The only necessary context would be the knowledge of metal history and, with it, a memory of the flourishes that have been extracted from it, as well as knowledge of how they became codified. Maybe with this the program of drawing

distinctions comes to its conclusion. We now know its meaning: to use encoded communication with people who can still remember the emotional necessity that produced the code in the first place, and who also know that necessity no longer exists. The initial contribution in each case would be to test which codes can be so employed in each particular era. And to take pleasure in them, even if and when the code has been broken.

VI The perfect balance that I've been trying to find in the depiction of symbolic and real power struggles has, to my knowledge, only once found totally adequate expression in terms of both form and content. Don Covay's song "I Was Checking Out, She Was Checking In" (1974) sets itself up as a "deeply emotional" song with all kinds of dramatic excesses and clichés. Over the course of the five-minute ballad nothing happens but that the narrator keeps repeating what happened to him in the parking lot of the motel in which he's just cheated on his wife: she comes into the same lot he's about to leave, with her own lover. The narrator celebrates, declaims, intones as if possessed, but leaves totally up in the air whether he's happy that he doesn't have to bear alone the moral burden of betraying the marriage, or whether he's enraged that his wife has cheated on him. Perhaps he's just fascinated by the absurdity of the situation? Despite chorus and bridge and all the organizational ingredients that make the emotionalism of a normal soul ballad clear, the atmosphere here remains unvaryingly charged to the end, multiplying the possible meanings to the max. Not a picture-puzzle, not a Mona Lisa smile, rather it's a totally clear and distinct articulation of two or three normally competing feelings. By God, it's all unresolved.

It's a conceit of hermeneutics to read aesthetic phenomena or procedures as metaphors for social or political processes. One can get close to an artwork and draw certain conclusions from the examination. But this ruins one's eyes. One can also do the opposite, and circle around it very broadly. Whether the examples discussed here used metaphor, allegory, or directly historical methods to describe unclear, unclarified, or still unresolved power situations, they can all be described as cases in which distinctions were called forth by a pressure corresponding to a particular power relationship.

It would be appropriate now to take the further step of applying the microphysical methods of describing power relations developed by Michel Foucault. They are in fact not so different from purely aesthetic depictions of proportional relationships. This is exactly the method of analysis of Albert Oehlen (but with something more particular added), which hopefully will be quite clear if one approaches his paintings over the circuitous routes I've set up. To simplify the formulation, one could say that the left, before Foucault, only analyzed power morally, historically, and narratively, and not strategically. The description of power relations with and since Foucault has tended to a quasi-scientific, even microphysical form that avoids any possible intervention or historicity. The painting of distinctions (not understood as having a metaphorical or allegorical relation to anything in the world) represents the representability and attainability of power relations beyond those which exist and can be identified. This allows one to imagine other relations, to deal with existing ones differently, as well as offering protection from them. The creation can also be enjoyed in a different way, by opening up possibilities, neither as commentary nor as reflection, but fictionally, using a vocabulary specifically derived from conflict. One emerges unharmed, and lands better equipped back in the social world. To get there, though, one has to go through something that contains as much of the world as possible, but is itself clearly a treatment, which one can never encounter again. The more distinctions appear as art, the stronger the user becomes in dealing with everything else.

Notes

1 Shortly after *Lysol* came out, the manufacturer of Lysol disinfectant protested the title. The name has been blacked out or decaled over on recent issues, leaving the record untitled. (Issued in 1992 by Boner Records, PO Box 2081, Berkeley, California, 94702-0081.)

2 The word in German, *Ausgepragheit*, cannot be precisely translated as either "distinctiveness" or "distinction." For the most part, the word "distinctions" will be used here, although in many ways "distinctiveness" or "pronouncedness" might be more apt translations.

3 The historical term *Reconquista* (Reconquest) used to describe this period is a perfect example of how attempts to establish political legitimation for territorial rights to southern Spain for over seven hundred years have been mystified.

4 See, for instance, Bernard Vincent, *L'année admirable* (Paris: Aubier, 1991).

5 Burchard Brentjes, *Die Kunst der Mauren* (Cologne: DuMont, 1992).

6 Rudolf Lothar, *Die Seele Spaniens* (Munich: Georg Müller, 1916). In more recent texts this story is either disputed or omitted.

7 In fact, Albert Oehlen and I once organized a film screening that we called "The Best Films in the World." We showed Fassbinder's *Satansbraten* (Satan's Brew, 1976), Brian De Palma's *The Fury* (1978), and John Huston's *Fat City* (1972) and *Donovan's Reef* (1963).

8 John Ford said: "I had wanted to make it for a long time. I've killed more Indians than Custer, Beecher and Chivington put together, and people in Europe always want to know about the Indians. There are two sides to every story, but I wanted to show their point of view for a change. Let's face it, we treated them very badly—it's a blot on our shield; we've cheated and robbed, killed, murdered, massacred and everything else, but they kill one white man and, God, out come the troops." Quoted in Peter Bogdanovich, *John Ford* (Berkeley: University of California Press, 1978), 104.

9 For example, Frieda Grafe and Enno Patalas, "Es war einmal ein Ford," in *Im Off—Filmartikel* (Munich: Hanser, 1974).

10 And if that should occur, then it could only go in one direction. Even in a perfectly innocuous postmodern entertainment such as Woody Allen's *Purple Rose of Cairo* (1985), the old game of the real and the imaginary only plays in a single direction; Steve Martin's *Dead Men Don't Wear Plaid* (1982) requires a distanced audience that after decades of cultural reflexivity recognizes its quotations for what they are. *Cheyenne Autumn* contained two complete films and a movement between them at a time when people still regarded going to the movies like going to church.

11 For instance, in Frankfurt there are many theorists, architects, urbanists, and city planners working for the Social Democrats and Greens in city administration who are considering the future of the Rhein/Main region in terms of greater Los Angeles.

12 Gilles Deleuze, "Postscript on the Society of Control," *October* 59 (Winter 1992): 3–7.

13 Mike Davis, "The Ecology of Fear," in *Open Magazine Pamphlet Series* (Westlake, NJ: New Press, 1992) and *City of Quartz* (New York: Verso Press, 1990), 221 ff.

14 For example, Olvera Street—part of La Placita, the first public plaza of Los Angeles—was the center for daily life and trade for the early settlers, and remained so from the 1780s through the mid-nineteenth century; since moved and now surrounded by freeways and freeway ramps on two sides, and Chinatown and the Civic Center on its other opposing sides, the marketplace-turned-tourist-attraction illuminates starkly contrasting moments and lifestyles.

15 Wanda Coleman, *Berserk on Hollywood Boulevard* CD (New Alliance Records, 1992).

16 Robert Kurz, *Der Kolleps der Modernisierung—Vom Zusammenbruch des Kasernensozialismus zur Krise der Wello Konomie* (Frankfurt am Main: Eichborn 1991).

17 For example, Pere Ubu's "Non Alignment Pact," on *The Modern Dance* LP (Phonogram, 1977) and The Jesus and Mary Chain's *Psychocandy* LP (WEA, 1985).

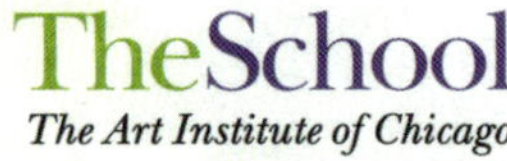

TheSchool
The Art Institute of Chicago

January 12, 1995

Laura Owens
5117 Eagle Rock Blvd.
Los Angeles, CA 90041

Dear Laura:

This is just a confirmation letter concerning your upcoming visit to The School of The Art Institute this Spring. The week of your visit will be March 4 to March 8. As you know, you will need to make and pay for your own travel arrangements. Please be sure that you arrive sometime during the later afternoon or evening of Sunday, March 3. Your last appointment with us on Friday, March 8 will end at 4 p.m. You may plan your return for anytime after that up until Sunday, March 10 in the morning. It is up to you. As soon as you make your arrangements please let me know. I will, of course meet you at the airport. (Sometimes flights are cheaper into Midway as opposed to O'Hare.)

Your honorarium will be $1,500. Your slide lecture has been scheduled in our School Auditorium on Tuesday, March 5 at 10 a.m. The rest of the week will include individual critiques with graduate and advanced undergraduate students.

Please let me know if you have any questions, 312-345-3593. On behalf of the Painting and Drawing Department, we look forward to your visit.

Sincerely,

Rebecca

Rebecca Morris, Graduate Program Coordinator
Painting and Drawing Department

112 South Michigan Avenue   312.899.5100
Chicago, Illinois
60603-3103

[Background article — Benjamin Weissman, "Openings: Laura Owens," partially obscured:]

rom Frank Stella's
de hood to the hi
stractions of artist
nd Fabian Marcacc
es to make the glo

nptiness, every co
utterance—whethe
stly present or totally absent (well, how *did*
rush strokes get there, Doctor?)—has been
hearsed, walked through, and played out.

Articulating reality was once a decent enough pursuit. It still is, depending on how far you take your
idea of what reality is and what it is to represent it.

etting up out o
t. That's where L
nger to late-cen
he manages to r

nusual and inte
Los Angeles (an
d while. Her p
es: their blank
es, and muted M
vulnerability. T
. And gigantic,
ith you, my dea
some hybrid of
"Little Red Rid
nowing and dia
ely innocent, an
r to find out wl
e tries to eat her
ot the only one v
n, or for him to
kes her. Like a le
g in her head; sh
from the sweet
While the surfac
ttle resemblance
s share his rever
he trail of a nor
here areas of co
unks of a painti
, pleading with
l be there, if ar
hey were solids,
into cartoony s
mushy smear th
benign lump, all within an airy, heady sp
ventions remain resolutely nonrepresen
her, painting is painting, not a story.

Foreground: Letter from Rebecca Morris, 1995
Background: Benjamin Weissman, "Openings: Laura Owens." *Artforum* 34, no. 3, November 1995

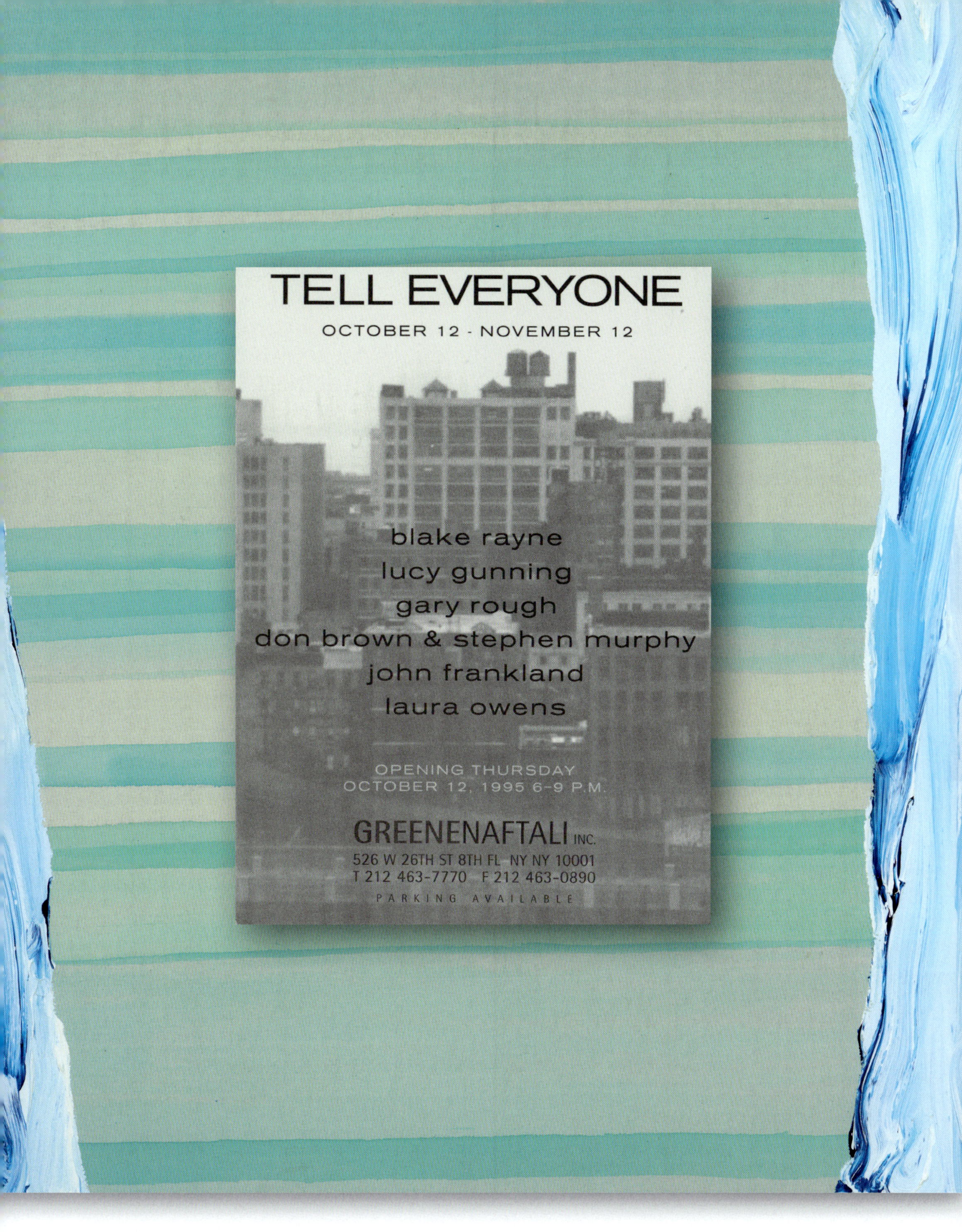

Foreground: Invitation, *Tell Everyone,* Greene Naftali Gallery, New York, 1995
Background: Detail of *Untitled*, 1995, acrylic on canvas, 66 × 60 in. (167.6 × 152.4 cm)

For immediate release

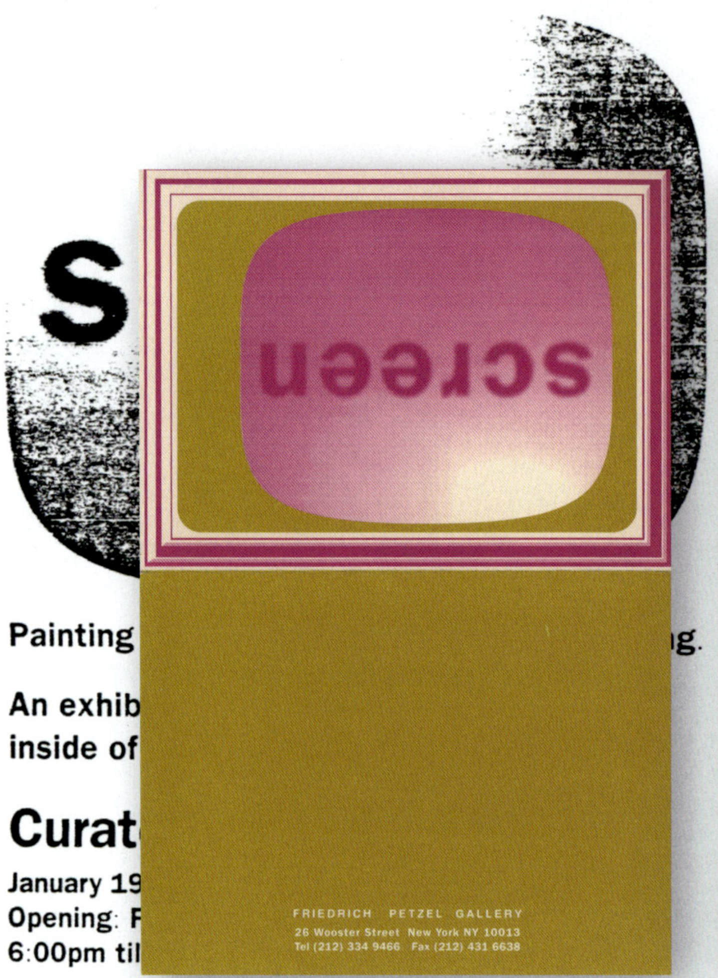

> **Lisa Anne Auerbach:** *Laura and I talked a lot about how influential television was to her as a kid and even as an adult. I remember very vividly a conversation when she told me about going down to her basement in Ohio when she was growing up and watching TV. I don't think she told me what it looked like, but I have this vision in my head of her as a child staring at a television. I wasn't a TV watcher, so it was always really exotic to me that she was so inspired by stuff she saw on TV and I would try and see how that led to what she was making. I don't know if I could ever really make the connection. Sometimes she gets this sort of vacant expression and you can just imagine that with a TV in front of it. Or you wonder suddenly if while you were talking to her you became the image on the TV. Like how do you relate to a world with this filter of television? I don't know if she still watches TV. This is a conversation we had probably in the 1990s about growing up, and I just kept thinking, "Wow, this is such a different thing—how did she become an artist out of this obsession with popular culture, and how does that manifest itself? Should I have watched more TV? Would I be a painter too?"*

Foreground: Invitation, *Screen: Painting on Television, Television on Painting*, Friedrich Petzel Gallery, New York, 1996

 Background: Press release, Friedrich Petzel Gallery, New York, 1996

March 14 1996

To: David Reed   Fax # 212.571.2188

From : Laura Owens tel and fax 213.255.8829

Hi David!! Long time no speak. Hope you are well. I went to the opening of a new show at the Temporary Contemporary last night. It's called Hall of Mirrors:art and film since 1945. My friend Sharon Lockhart is in it. Anyway It is in many ways an awesome show and I think you would love it. It is mostly film, video and photo with lots of Hollywood crossover. I think the only paintings were Warhols-- I wasn't able to spend lots of time looking at the show so I'm not sure. Also Sharon has a show up at Blum and Poe which is equally awesome. I think the same pictures will be at Petzel's in September so you'll get to see. Monique is having a one person show at Bravin Post Lee in April. I saw the paintings -- they are so great.
I am leaving on a world tour in two weeks so I will miss her opening.   I will be in New York March 28-30 so maybe if you are around we could have coffee or something-- if you have time. From New York I go to Berlin for a month to work in a studio at Bethanien. It's like a fellowship program -- Sharon got a studio for a year but is unable to use it because she is teaching at UCLA. So instead of giving it up she 'curated' a show where one or two people go for a month and have a little show in the studio at the end of the stay. After Germany I have really sketchy plans to go to Italy for two weeks. I have never been so I figured I better have a look-see. Then I will fly back tío L.A. I am pretty bummed that I will completely miss Monique's show - hopefully you will tell me how it all unfolds.   I am still pretty unsure where and when I will show in New York. I am kind of thinking/hoping Pat Hearn might work out.   I am so confused about the whole idea.
Thanks so much for wanting to see my work at Rosamunds. I feel really ambivalent about that show. It was nice to have some sort of general support. I felt really frazzled while you were here.   I realized a couple days after you left that I had that crazy flu everyone got.
So, say hello to everyone. I'll give you a call when I get to New York.

Talk soon,

Laura

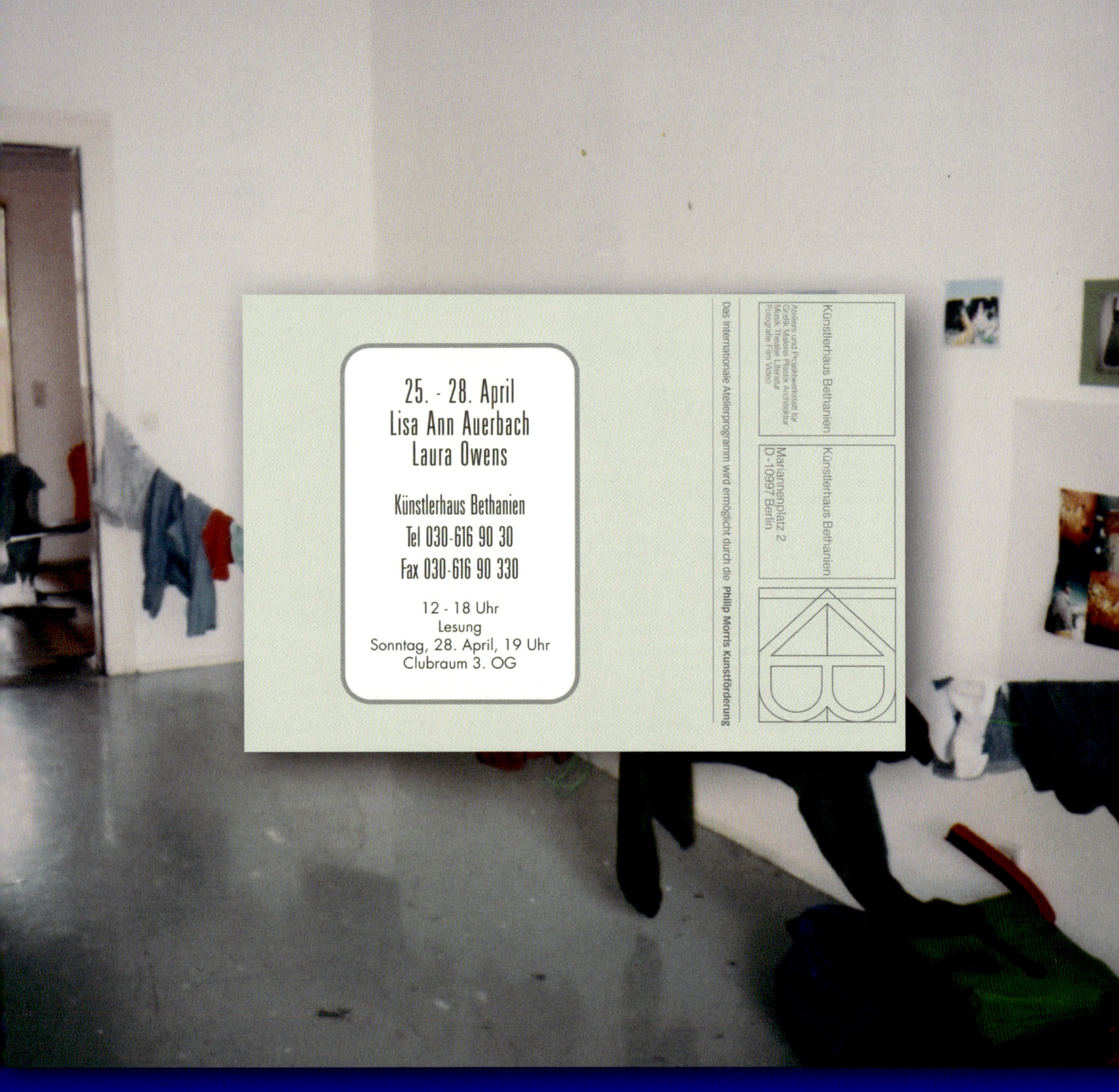

Lisa Anne Auerbach: Sharon Lockhart got a grant to go to Berlin and do a year at the Künstlerhaus Bethanien, but she couldn't get funding to go for the whole time. She decided to invite some of her friends to spend a month each there. Laura and I went together. I would wake up really early every morning and go and see Berlin, and she would stay in the studio most of the time. She was sick for a while, but one day she decided to make a giant painting of a hallway with a bunch of little paintings by different people at the bottom. I think I made one of them. I remember helping her deal with the logistics of being in Berlin and getting stretcher bars and canvas and everything back to our place. She was getting on the subway with these giant canvases. I was out sightseeing all the time. I was like, I'm in Berlin, I've got to see every single museum and the Nazis and all this shit. She wasn't really interested in hanging out or sightseeing, but she was very interested in getting serious with this painting stuff. And she was very serious about going to the bar at night. I remember instances of dancing on tables—it was joyous and celebratory, and probably the reason that she wasn't getting out of bed as early as I was. Also, I was making photographs, so that's something that I would do out in the world, but she's a painter and was making things in the studio, so that was very different.

Foreground: Invitation, *Studio 246,* Künstlerhaus Bethanien, Berlin, 1996
Background: Künstlerhaus Bethanien studio, Berlin, 1996

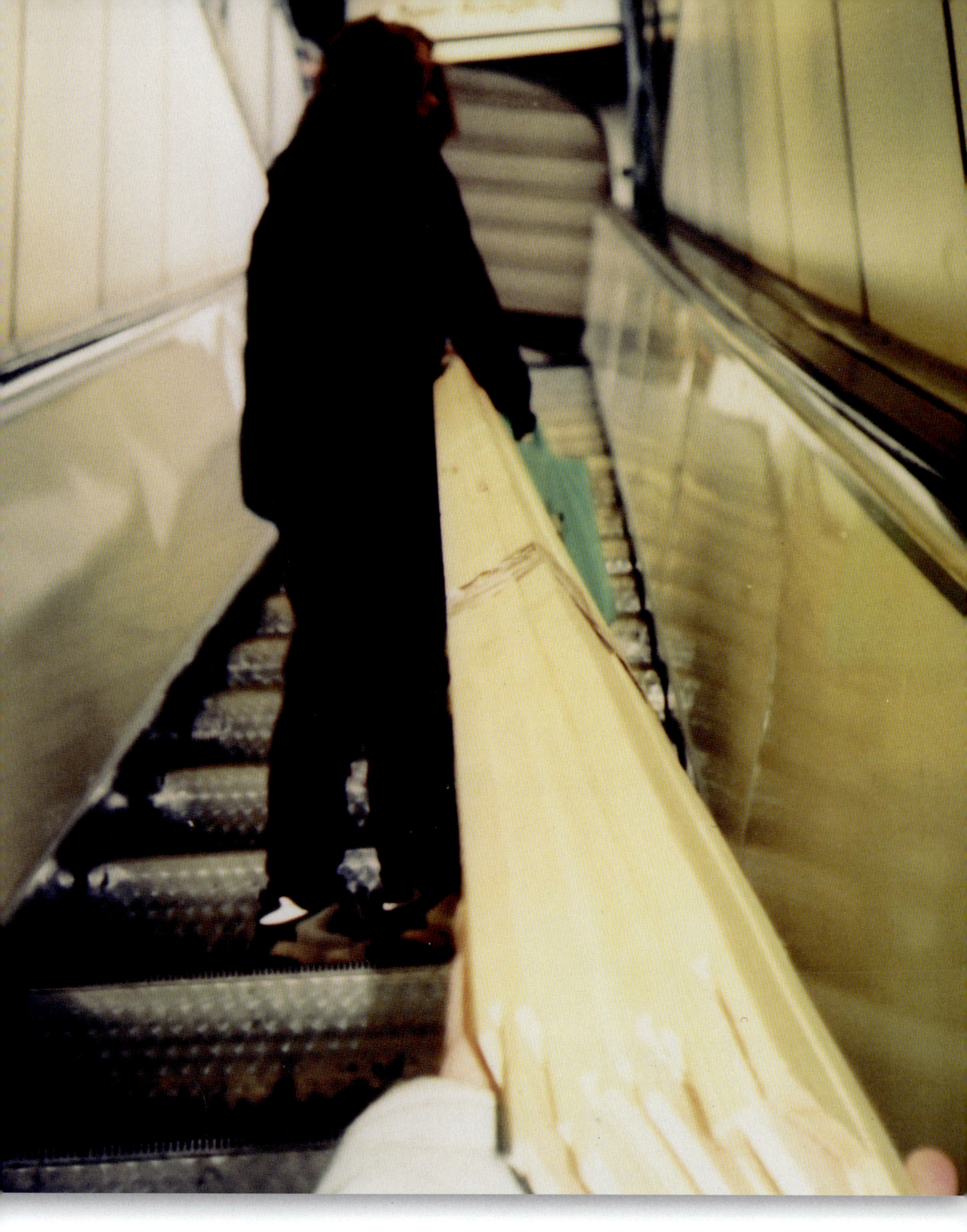

Owens and Lisa Anne Auerbach with stretcher bars, U-Bahn, Berlin, 1996

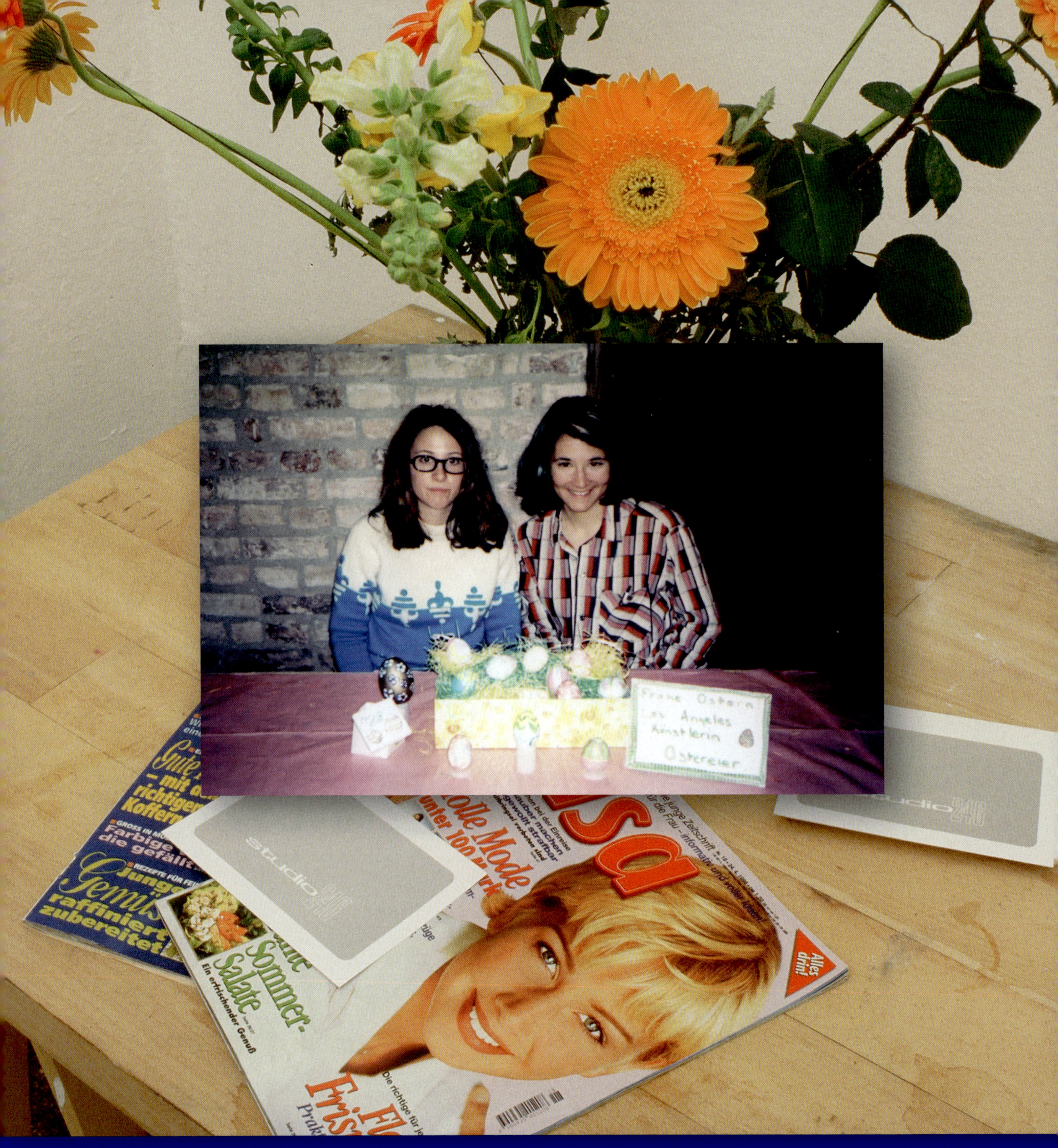

Laura Owens: Lisa and I arrived in Berlin and had no money. We asked the director at Künstlerhaus Bethanien, where we were doing the residency, if he knew of any jobs—babysitting, anything. He suggested that we make some kind of craft object and take it to Spandau Citadel for a craft fair and sell it. It was a disaster. We hollowed out a couple dozen eggs we had spent our last deutsche marks on. We painted them, but pretty abstractly. We had to take multiple buses to get to Spandau in freezing cold weather. They gave us a table and we quickly realized that the level of craft at this fair was very high and we looked like fools. Pretty much everyone laughed at our eggs and we sold none.

Foreground: Owens and Lisa Anne Auerbach at an Ostermarkt (Easter market), Spandau Citadel, Berlin, 1996
Background: Installation view, *Studio 246*, Künstlerhaus Bethanien, Berlin, 1996

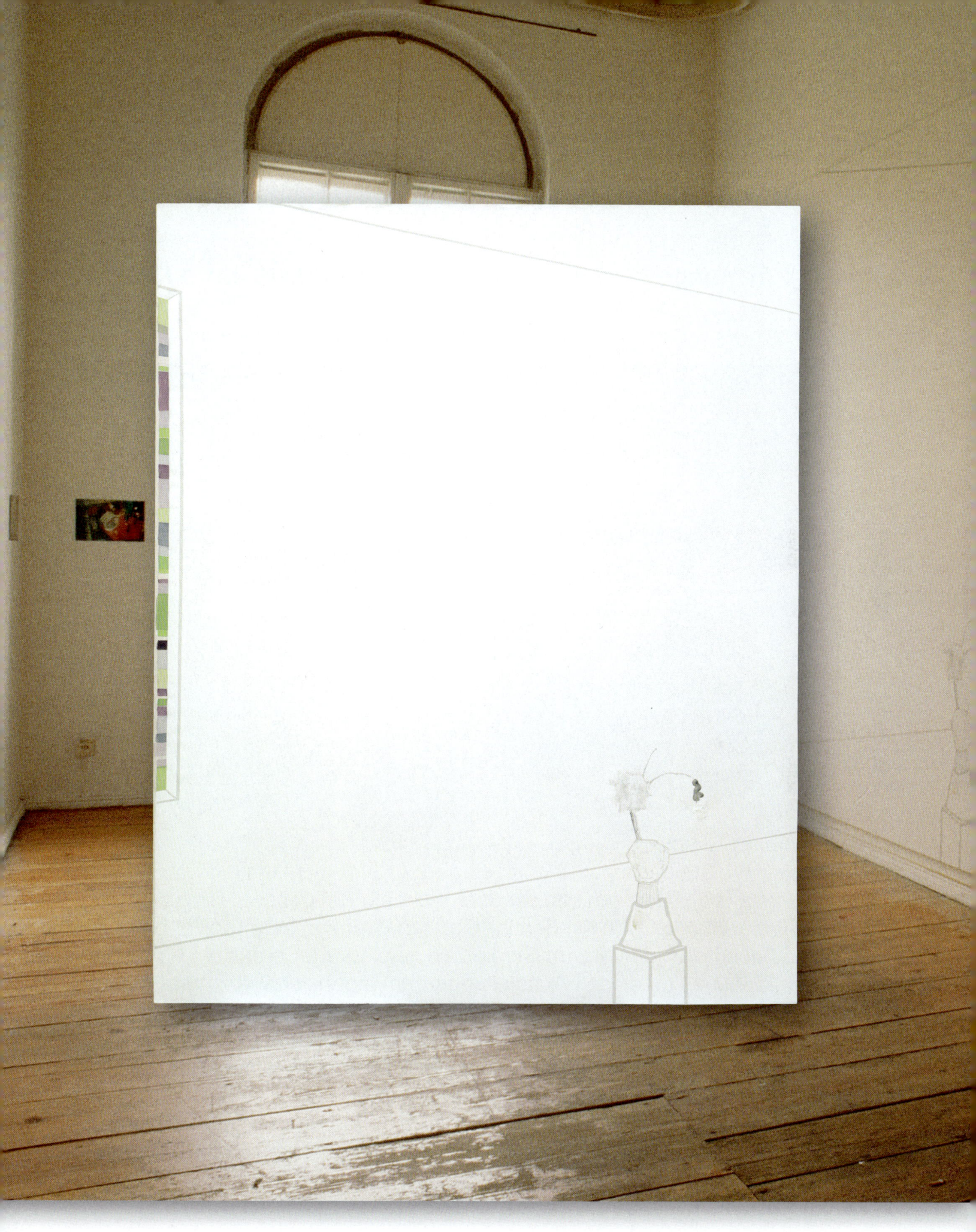

Foreground: *Untitled*, 1996, acrylic on canvas, 120 × 96 in. (304.8 × 243.8 cm)
Background: Installation view, *Studio 246*, Künstlerhaus Bethanien, Berlin, 1996, Owens and Lisa Anne Auerbach, *Untitled*, 1996, and
  Untitled, 1996

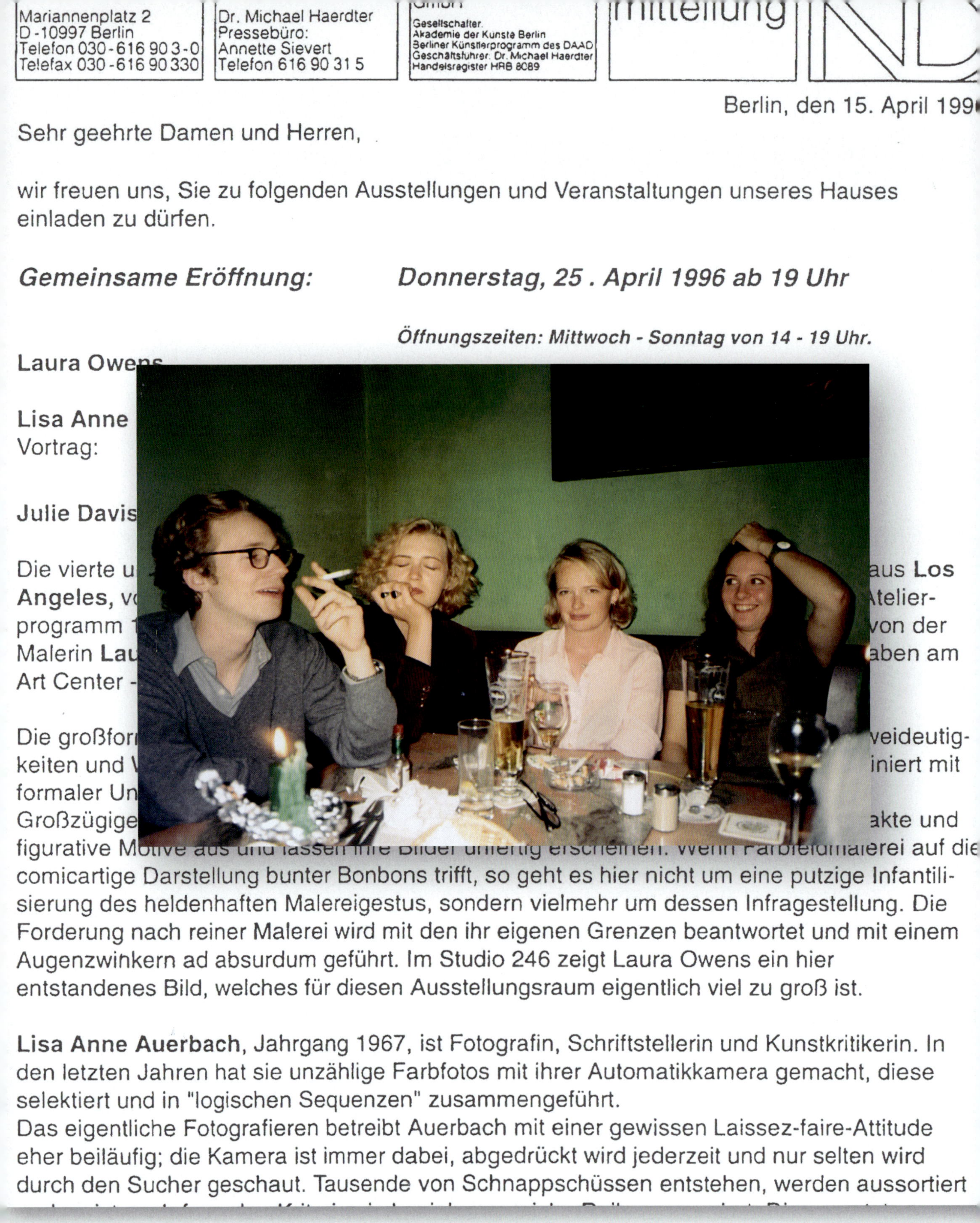

Mariannenplatz 2
D -10997 Berlin
Telefon 030 - 616 90 3 - 0
Telefax 030 - 616 90 330

Dr. Michael Haerdter
Pressebüro:
Annette Sievert
Telefon 616 90 31 5

GmbH
Gesellschafter.
Akademie der Künste Berlin
Berliner Künstlerprogramm des DAAD
Geschäftsführer: Dr. Michael Haerdter
Handelsregister HRB 8089

mitteilung ND

Berlin, den 15. April 199[6]

Sehr geehrte Damen und Herren,

wir freuen uns, Sie zu folgenden Ausstellungen und Veranstaltungen unseres Hauses einladen zu dürfen.

Gemeinsame Eröffnung: *Donnerstag, 25 . April 1996 ab 19 Uhr*

Öffnungszeiten: Mittwoch - Sonntag von 14 - 19 Uhr.

Laura Owens

Lisa Anne [...]
Vortrag:

Julie Davis [...]

Die vierte u[nd ...] aus **Los Angeles**, vo[...] Atelier-programm 1[...] von der Malerin **Lau**[...] aben am Art Center - [...]

Die großform[...] veideutig-keiten und V[...] iniert mit formaler Un[...] Großzügige[...] akte und figurative Motive aus und lassen ihre Bilder unfertig erscheinen. Wenn Farbfeldmalerei auf die comicartige Darstellung bunter Bonbons trifft, so geht es hier nicht um eine putzige Infantili-sierung des heldenhaften Malereigestus, sondern vielmehr um dessen Infragestellung. Die Forderung nach reiner Malerei wird mit den ihr eigenen Grenzen beantwortet und mit einem Augenzwinkern ad absurdum geführt. Im Studio 246 zeigt Laura Owens ein hier entstandenes Bild, welches für diesen Ausstellungsraum eigentlich viel zu groß ist.

Lisa Anne Auerbach, Jahrgang 1967, ist Fotografin, Schriftstellerin und Kunstkritikerin. In den letzten Jahren hat sie unzählige Farbfotos mit ihrer Automatikkamera gemacht, diese selektiert und in "logischen Sequenzen" zusammengeführt.
Das eigentliche Fotografieren betreibt Auerbach mit einer gewissen Laissez-faire-Attitude eher beiläufig; die Kamera ist immer dabei, abgedrückt wird jederzeit und nur selten wird durch den Sucher geschaut. Tausende von Schnappschüssen entstehen, werden aussortiert [...]

Foreground: Martin Klosterfelde, Annette Sievert, Charline von Heyl, and Owens, Berlin, 1996
Background: Press release, *Studio 246*, Künstlerhaus Bethanien, Berlin, 1996

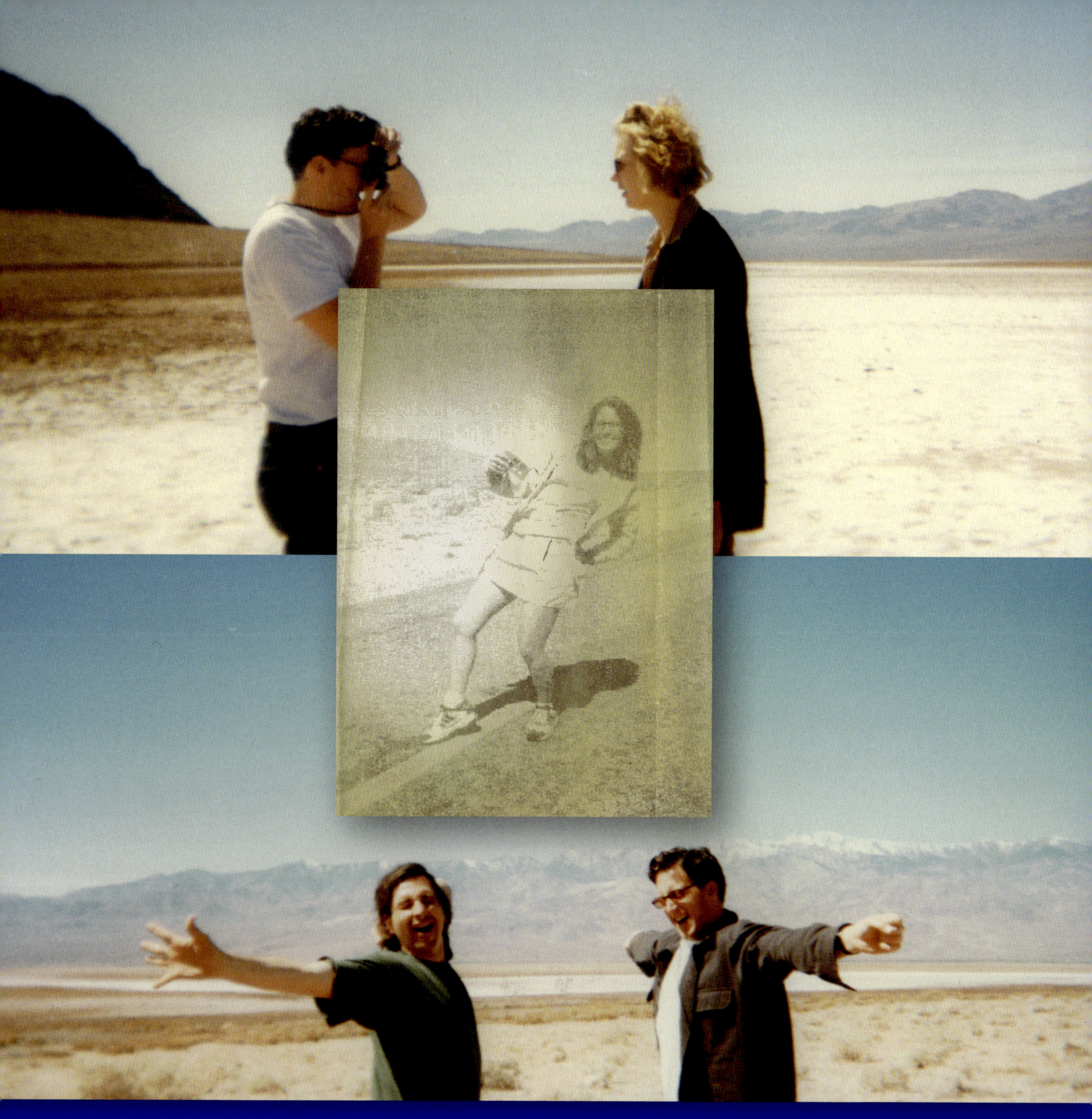

T. J. Wilcox: A group of us went to Death Valley and stayed at an old-fashioned motor court motel. On our first morning we headed for the dry lakebed, which was ringed with mountains and brilliant blue sky. Laura and I drove ahead together and our pals followed five minutes behind us. The road twisted through extreme rock formations, and Laura said, "I've got a great idea." She wanted to make it look like we'd had a fight and I had knocked her out and left her for dead. She sprawled in the middle of the road across the yellow meridian while I hid behind the rocks with the car so I could watch them arrive, which we thought was going to be so funny. We waited and waited, with Laura lying in the middle of the road. Eventually our friends arrived, stopped, and ran over to Laura as she played dead. Ultimately they realized she was okay, but instead of laughing they were scared and mad. We got in so much trouble but continued to think it was hilarious. This scenario Laura created of her body lying in the road, spilled across the yellow line in this otherworldly landscape, was a fantastic and risky image to make. It was provocative and far outside the boundaries of permissible humor.

Foreground: Owens, Death Valley, California, 1996
Background: Top, T. J. Wilcox and Annette Sievert; bottom, Alex Slade and T. J. Wilcox, Death Valley, California, 1996

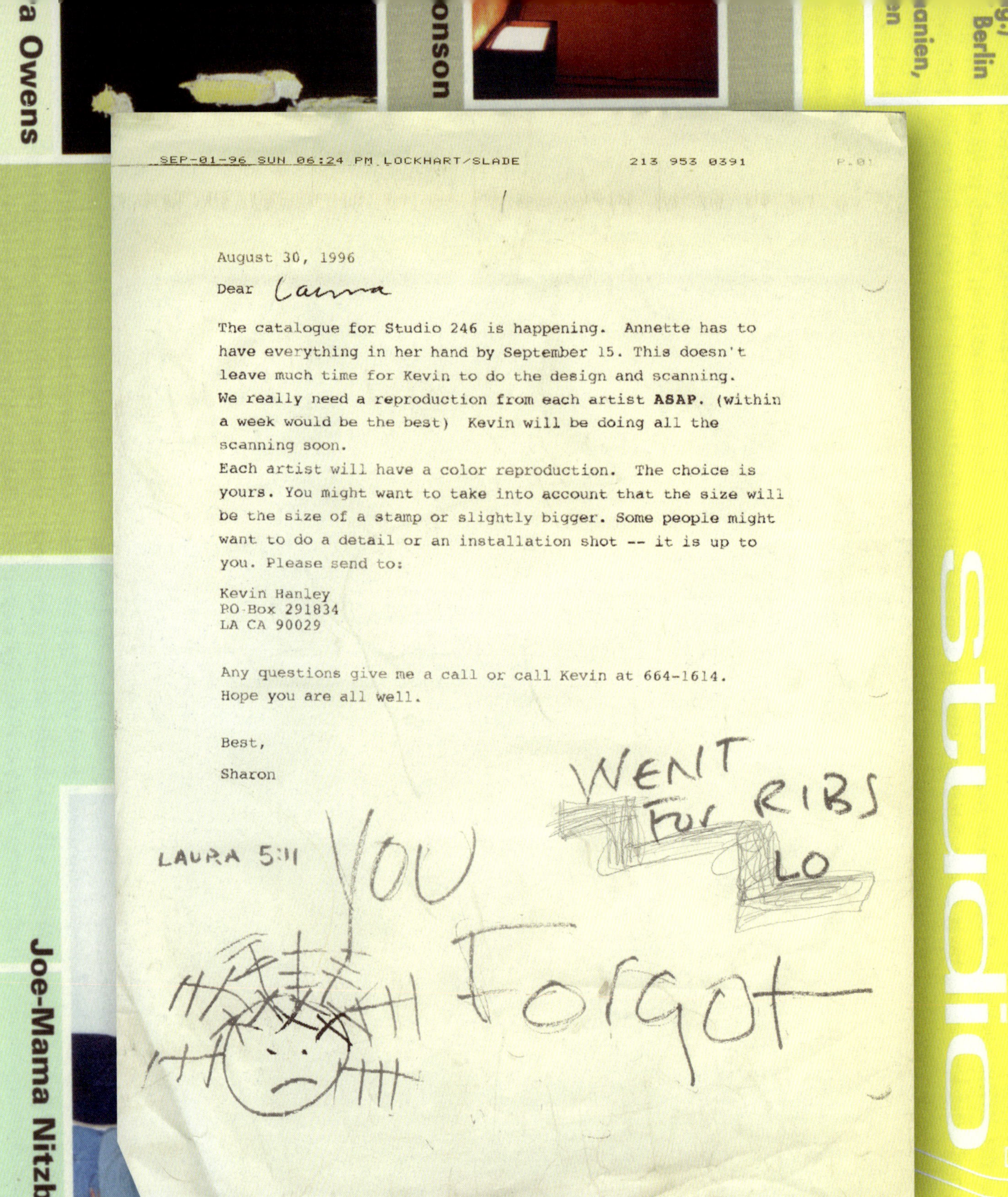

SEP-01-96 SUN 06:24 PM LOCKHART/SLADE   213 953 0391   P.01

August 30, 1996

Dear Laura

The catalogue for Studio 246 is happening. Annette has to
have everything in her hand by September 15. This doesn't
leave much time for Kevin to do the design and scanning.
We really need a reproduction from each artist **ASAP**. (within
a week would be the best) Kevin will be doing all the
scanning soon.
Each artist will have a color reproduction. The choice is
yours. You might want to take into account that the size will
be the size of a stamp or slightly bigger. Some people might
want to do a detail or an installation shot -- it is up to
you. Please send to:

Kevin Hanley
PO Box 291834
LA CA 90029

Any questions give me a call or call Kevin at 664-1614.
Hope you are all well.

Best,

Sharon

Foreground: Fax from Sharon Lockhart, 1996
Background: Invitation, *Studio 246*, Marc Foxx, Santa Monica, 1996

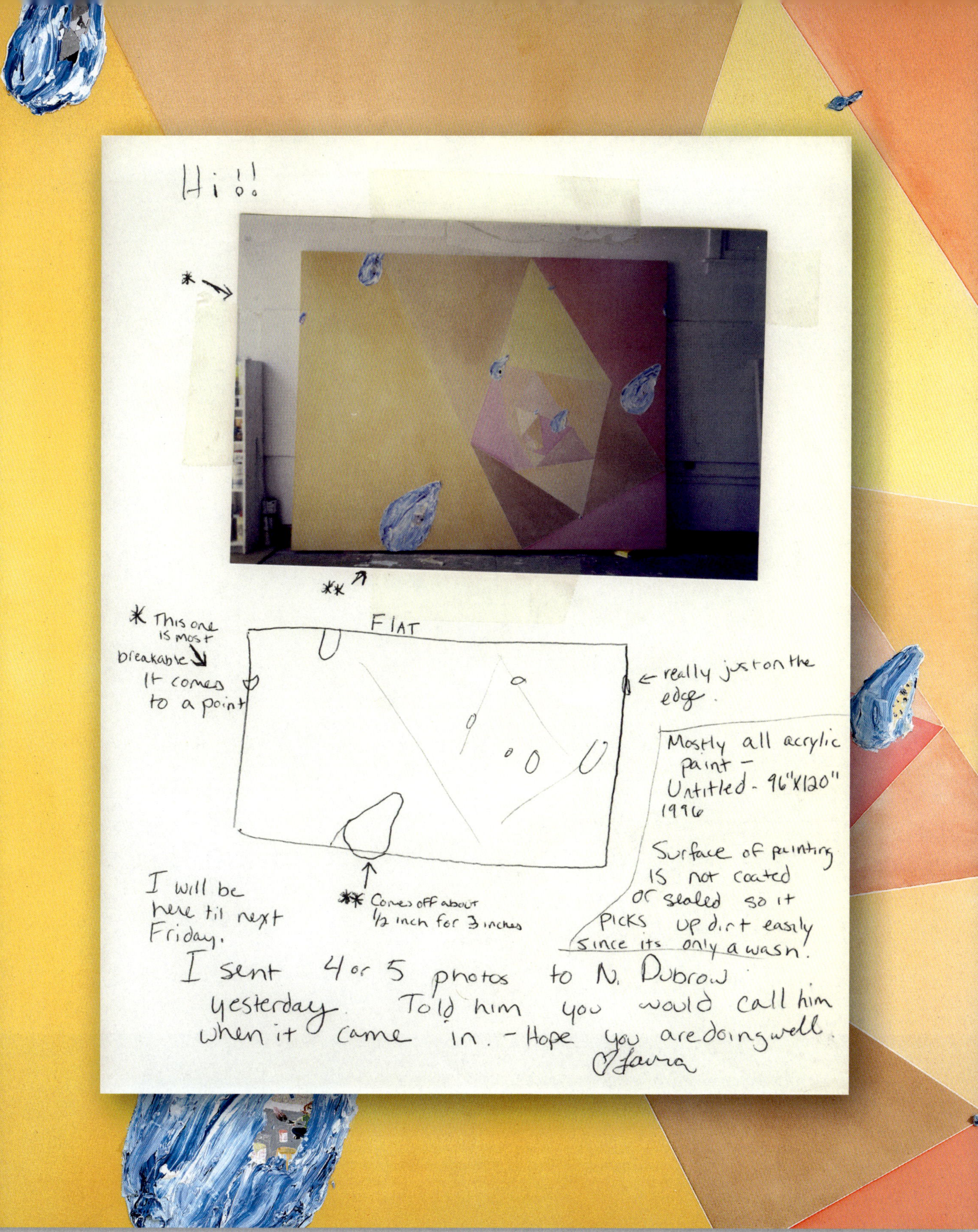

Foreground: Packing instructions to Gavin Brown for *Untitled*, 1996, acrylic on canvas, 96 × 120 in. (243.8 × 304.8 cm)
Background: Detail of *Untitled*, 1996

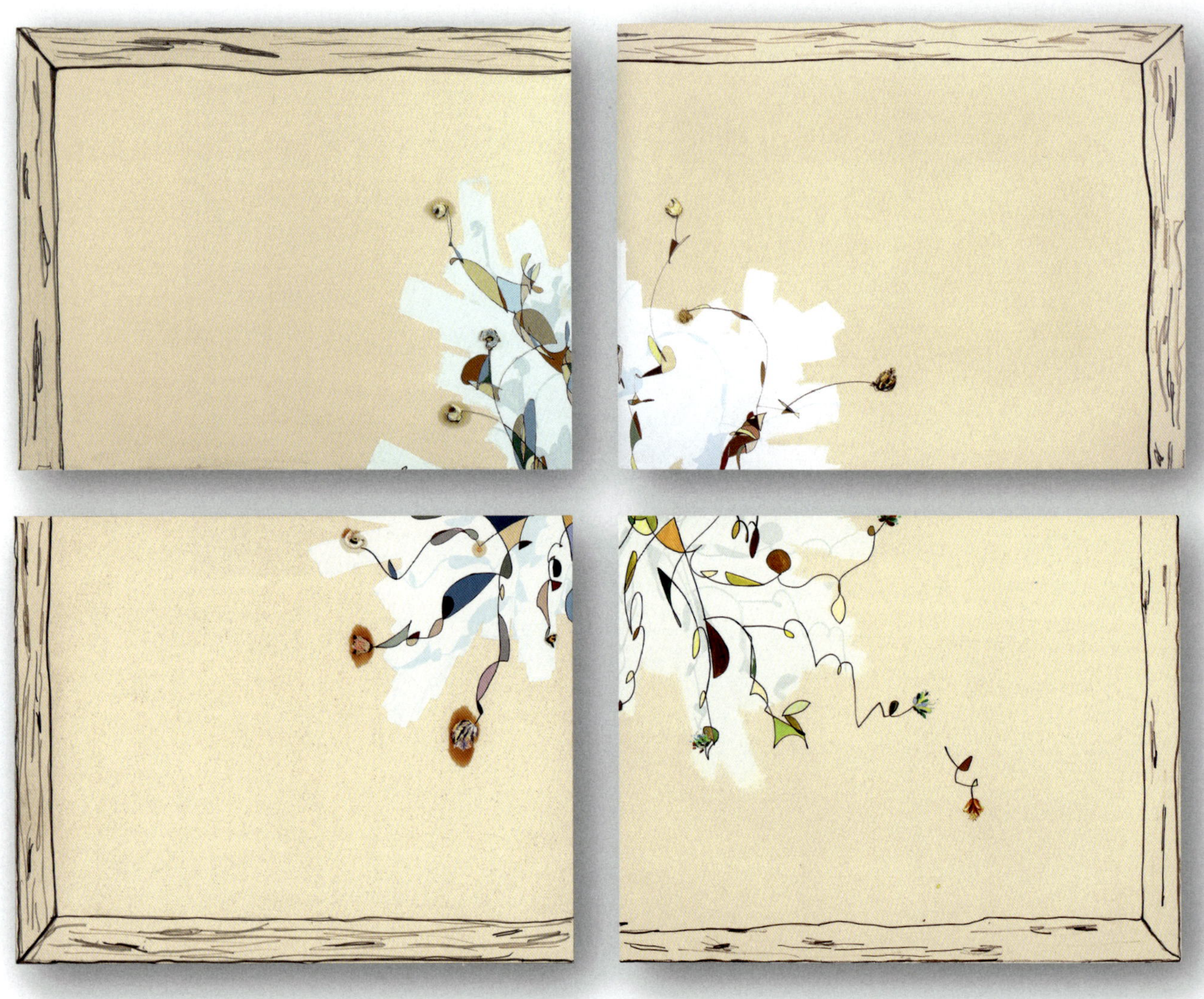

Clockwise from top left: *Untitled*, 1996, acrylic and oil on canvas, 48 × 60 in. (121.9 × 152.4 cm); *Untitled*, 1997, acrylic and oil on canvas, 50 × 41 in. (127 × 104.1 cm); *Untitled*, 2002, acrylic, oil, and marker on canvas, 48 × 59½ in. (121.9 × 151.1 cm); and *Untitled*, 1997, acrylic and oil on canvas, 48 × 60 in. (121.9 × 152.4 cm)

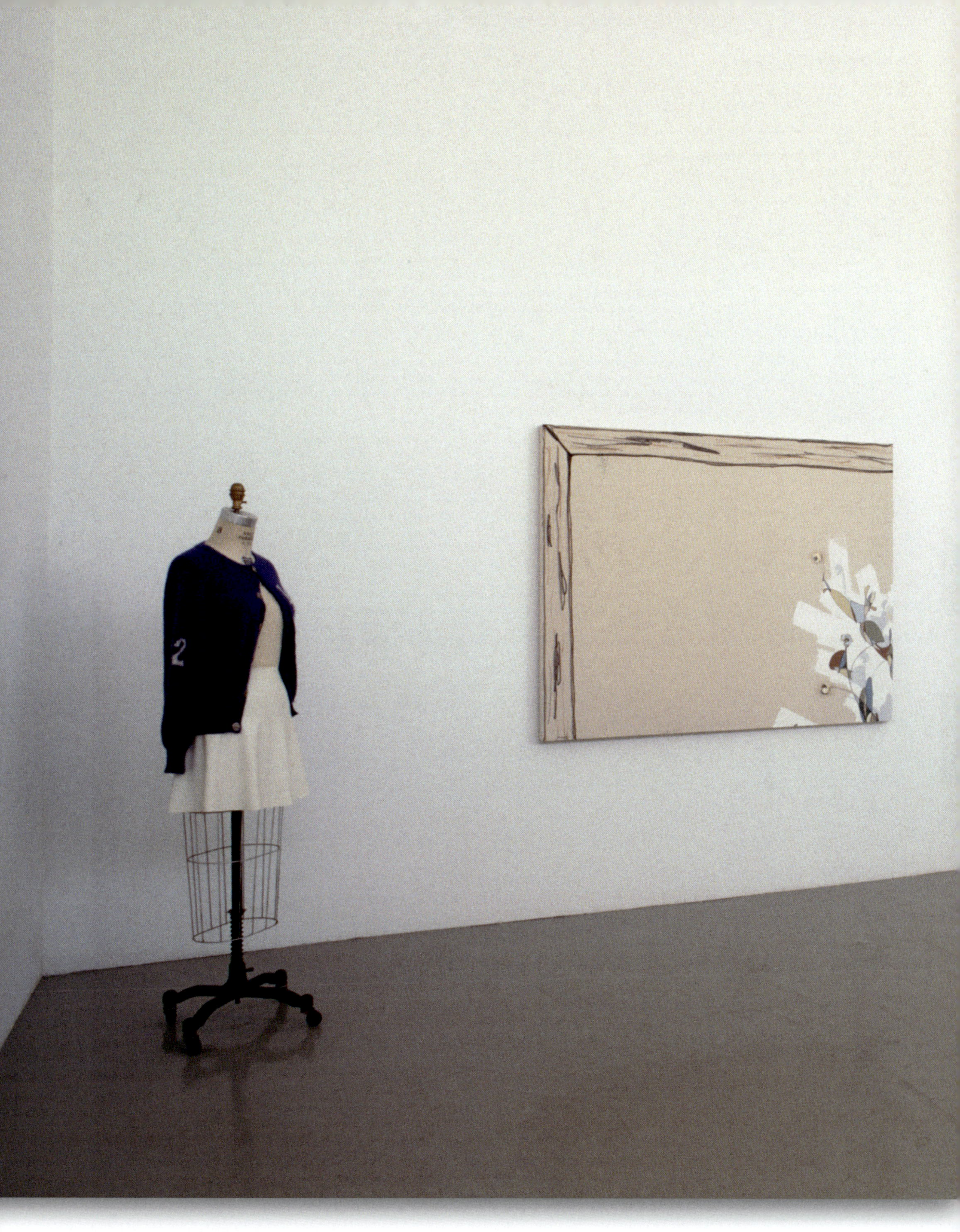

Installation view, *Studio 246,* Marc Foxx, Santa Monica, 1996, with Lisa Anne Auerbach, *Sandy Koufax Sweater*, 1996, wool, dimensions variable, and *Untitled*, 1996 (see p. 114)

P a t   H e a r n   G a l l e r y

The Speed of Painting:
Laura Owens, Monique Prieto, Steven Parrino, Scott Reeder
and Donald Morgan/Scott Reeder collaboration

As a viewer engaged in the process of reading contemporary art, I am continually reminded that the speed at which I receive an artwork is determined by my willingness to meet the work halfway. It is not enough that the work alone arrive with content.

The development of art theory over the past thirty years has evoked an increased awareness of potential languages within an extended field of art making, while simultaneously confusing the legibility of contemporary art. If what is understood to be credible in contemporary art today relates to some notion of postmodern culture, it is important to remember that that which is called postmodern derives itself, to some degree, from modernism. A categorical rejection or deification of particular languages within this field (such as painting) is generally consistent with those on a quest for some notion of the "avant garde", or equally as treacherous, the ignorant "painting only" lover: "I know what I like".

This impulse is often channeled through and perverted by other aspects of contemporary culture. By refusing to consider beyond these reflexive judgments this misdirected nostalgia ensues passivity, leaving the myth of the artist (the voice with the last word) intact. This passivity requires no commitment and keeps the viewer "safe".

In this position there is no meeting ground, no receiver, no exchange, no reflection, no transportation of ideas, the viewer looks but never arrives. What you see is what you get---

> *the vulnerability of looking*
> *the density of simplicity*
> *the speed of painting*
> *the emperor does have new clothes*
> *the marginal center*
> *the trendy receiver*
> *the ignorant lover*
> *the limitations of vision*
> *the vision*
> *the place of arrival*
> *the point of departure*
> *the speed of . . .*
> *no end in sight*

Pat Hearn, September 1996

530 West 22nd Street N.Y.C. 10011 212 727 7366 fax 212 727 7467

  Foreground: Press release, *The Speed of Painting*, Pat Hearn Gallery, New York, 1996
Background: Shipping manifest, Pat Hearn Gallery, New York, 1996

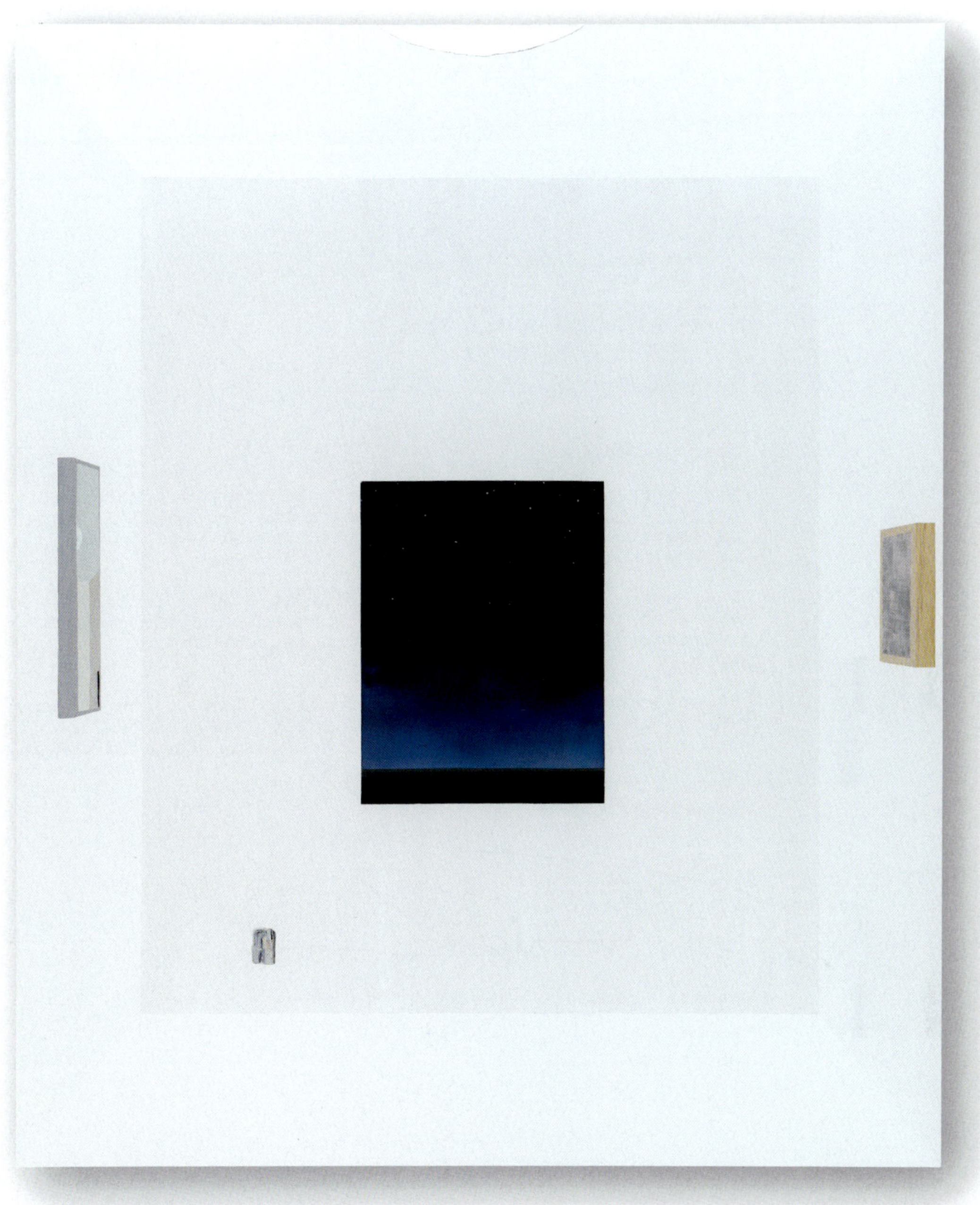

Untitled, 1996, acrylic on canvas, 120 × 96 in. (304.8 × 243.8 cm)   **117**

Laura Owens
5121½ Eagle Rck Blvd., Apt. D
Los Angeles, CA 90041

20 December 1996

Dear Ms. Owens:

I am very pleased to inform you that your work entitled
<u>Untitled</u> of 1996 has been added to the Guggenheim museum's
permanent collection through the generosity of Norman
Dubrow.

This work is an important addition to our collection and we
are glad to have the opportunity to enhance our current
holdings with such an outstanding representation of your
work.

As an acknowledgement of your contribution to the museum,
we enclose a lifetime Artist Courtesy Pass which allows you
and a guest free admittance to the museum whenever we are
open.

With best wishes,

Thomas Krens

TK/elr
enclosure

GUGGENHEIM MUSEUM

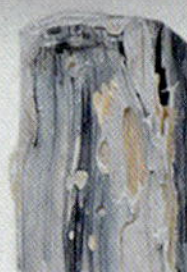

 Foreground: Letter from Thomas Krens, 1996
Background: Detail of *Untitled*, 1996 (see p. 117)

Dec. 2, 1997

Laura Owens
5121½ Eagle Rock #D
LA CA 90041

Dear Laura,

Thank you for sending me the polaroids of your London show. I like all the paintings, but I am really floored by the "illusionistic painting of a pseudo-museum space with an easel." I hope that it went to a good collection. I think that it is one of your best paintings to date.

I told you that the three paintings of yours that I bought have been given to, and accepted by, three New York museums — they are, for your records:

Guggenheim Museum — "Untitled (Night Sky)"
Metropolitan Museum — "Untitled (Teardrops or Raindrops)"
Whitney Museum — "Untitled (Sky, Clouds, Snowflakes)"

I am happy that you are keeping me informed about what you are doing, and I hope that you will continue to do so.

continued best wishes,   Sincerely yours,
                                Norman Dubrow

Foreground: Letter from Norman Dubrow, 1997

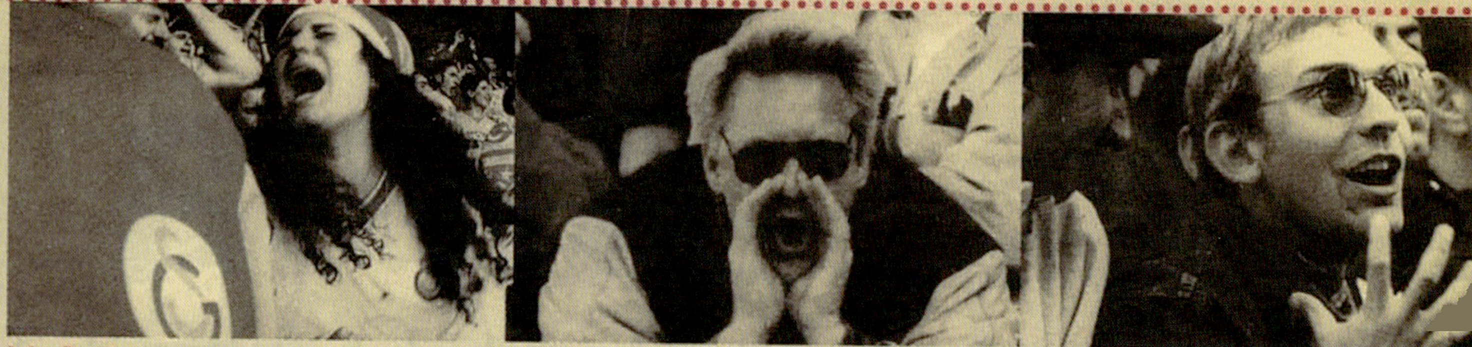

Andrea Bowers

It seems that almost everyone who moves to Los Angeles develops increasingly complex and out of control allergies; an aggravated sensibility, a feeling of being constantly undetermined by unknown forces, becomes the ruling condition of everyday life. Sunny optimism is darkened by the squally clouds of paranoia.

Hot

Selected by Thomas Lawson

Edward Weston's photograph of a crudely-made sign for a coffee shop stuck out in the California desert resonates with this disquiet and pathos— I almost sneeze just looking it. A giant cup and saucer loom large in the foreground, yet are oddly lost in the vast landscape that rolls out to a distant mountain range. The sign is not very well made. Its edges are bashed and bruised by the wind, the lettering is not quite convincing. Its placement out in the inhospitable desert offers hope to the coffee-drinking traveler, despair to the coffee maker imprisoned under the open sky. Looking at this now, I still feel overwhelmed by the struggling, hopeless optimism it captures. The picture so eloquently expresses a weirdly hypnotic combination of confidence and delusion: setting down roots as convincingly as the tumbleweed.

The transient nature of Los Angeles has become something remarked too often; yet it is hard to deny the flux of the place. People come and go.

They come with fantasies and hopes, and find traffic management and gridlock. They rarely find a destination, only a rest stop, a coffee break. From the U.S. they come looking for the glamour of the entertainment industries, but from around the Pacific, and from Mexico and Central America, they come looking for jobs and security. As a result, cultures shift, merge, and split apart again, as does the ground beneath our feet. The persistent ambiance is one of distrustful spectatorship, the anomie of post-suburban life.

The one allergy I brought with me from New York is that activated by curatorial attempts to make thematic statements out of modest group shows. My organizing principle for any exhibition has always been driven by the simple desire to see artworks I like — that I find interesting, challenging, amusing — gathered together. The pleasure of a show like this is found in the discoveries made possible by the actual grouping of works.

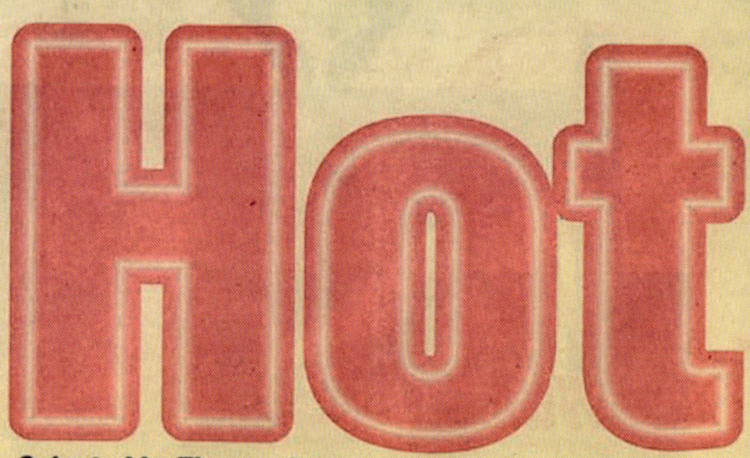

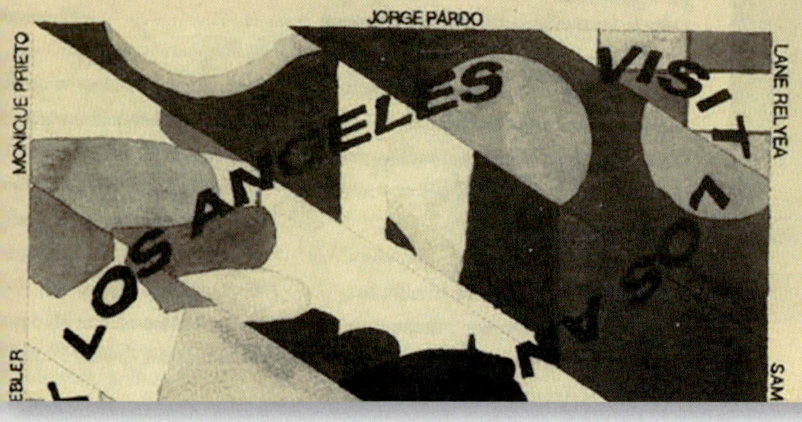

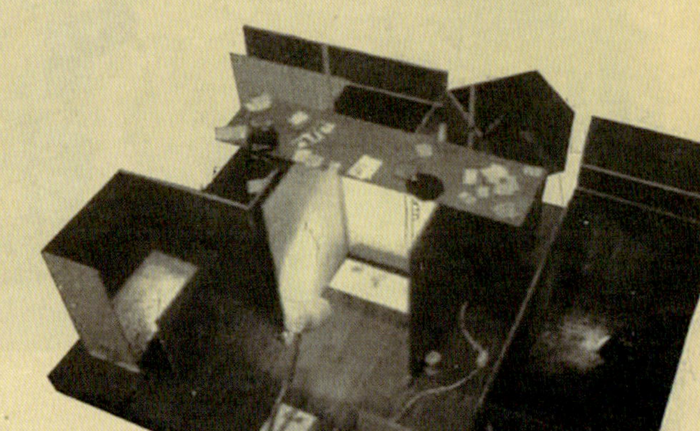

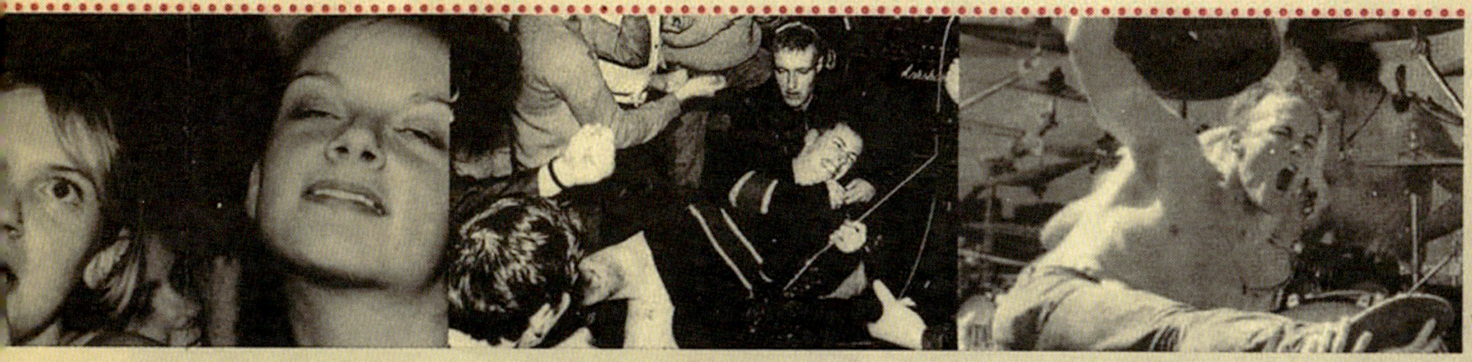

Coffee

Having said that, I will go on to claim that the art selected here does share something more than the fact that it was recently made in Los Angeles. Mostly this is manifest in the hybrid sense of unease that animates the work, a kind of provisional, improvisational refusal to find closure, to make the big, destiny-defying statement. There is no particular allegiance to medium or category, but an openness to association, an interest in mixing material and information from familiar sources in mass culture, esoteric themes from academe, and insider references to contemporary art. There is an attempt to find a beauty, or at least the pathos of an ordering, in the clutter of rescued banality. In that attempt a whole range of interesting questions about aesthetics, spectatorship, class alienation and humor are thrown together to form a puzzle which can only be partially solved by recourse to the idea of "art from Los Angeles."

—Thomas Lawson

Thomas Lawson is an artist and the Dean of the School of Art at the California Institute of the Arts. He exhibited at Artists Space in 1977, and curated the show "Scottish Artists" at the gallery in 1979. From 1979 to 1991, Artists Space acted as the conduit for Real Life, a publication he co-founded with Susan Morgan.

....

"Hot Coffee" is made possible in part by contributions from The Peter Norton Family Foundation, the Jerome Foundation, and the New York State Council on the Arts. Additional support was provided by Dean Valentine, Ruth and Jacob Bloom, Shoshana Wayne Gallery, Tina Petra and Ken Wong, and Barry Smooke.

Laura Owens

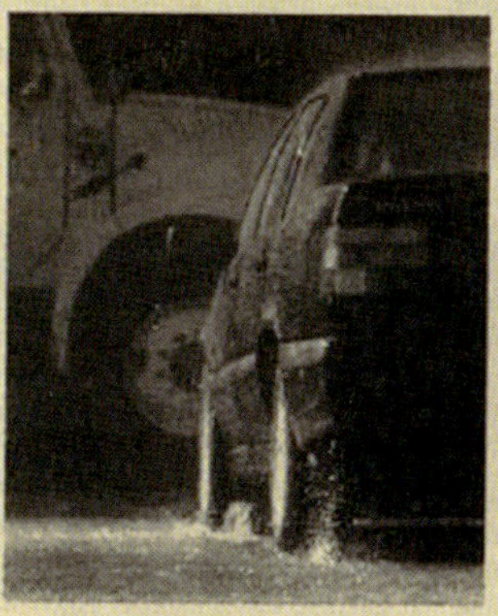

Kent Young, *Untitled*, 1996

Programming Attitude: An Interview with Laura Owens

by Rebecca Morris

RM: There is a lot of talk about L.A. being a great place for young artists. Is this true?

LO: L.A. is a great place to live, for young people in general and especially for young artists. It doesn't take too much to have a nice life here. It is affordable and beautiful. I think most people who do not live here are intimidated by the expansive decentralized urban sprawl. I love to drive so that is not a problem for me. There are a lot of young artists living in different pockets around the city. I think because there are so many young art school graduates from Pasadena Art Center, Cal Arts, U.C.L.A., Otis, etc., many are deciding to stay in L.A. and make it work for them. There isn't a gold mine of opportunity out here; it is more a quality of life.

RM: Who are your friends in L.A.? Are they primarily artists, and do you talk about your work with them? Do these relationships involve studio visits, insights and exchange of ideas—do they affect your studio work?

LO: I have some close friends who are artists, writers, and musicians. We don't talk about my work. We just hang out more or less. None of my friends, except one, are primarily making paintings. We have similar tastes in many ways, which have nothing to do with the mediums in which we work. At the same time, we are all making very different-looking objects, so it is interesting to look for the connections. I am planning on doing a show sometime in the future with Frances Stark and Sharon

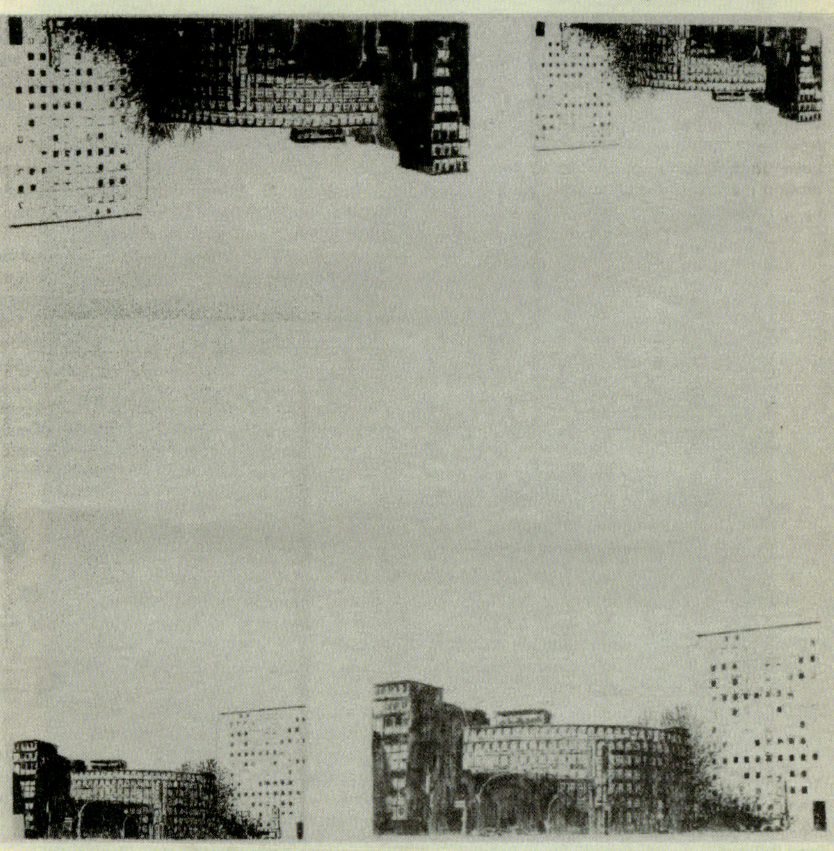

Frances Stark
Hamburg, 1995
carbon on paper

RM: What is it about working in L.A. that seems right to you, that makes you committed to staying there?

LO: The friends I have made out here make me feel committed to staying. Also the ability to be isolated within a huge urban environment is somehow stabilizing and allows me the freedom to work. I can walk out my door, go to the store, go to the mall and not run into anyone I know, unlike New York where it is inevitable you will see people you know at every bar, coffee shop, or street corner. Also there are many public parks, tennis courts, hiking trails, beaches, and other places where I try to maintain a year-round outdoor healthy experience. These things make me feel like a normal person, not like an artist in a claustrophobic, forced community. The art world is here, you just have to drive to it, instead of being constantly immersed in it.

Lockhart. I know there are certain connections, but because they are not readily obvious, it is difficult to identify them.

RM: How do you feel about people thinking that you have an L.A. aesthetic?

LO: No one in L.A. has ever said that. I think it's just people trying to get a handle on something they know nothing about. Stereotyping makes you feel good about yourself, like you know what's up. It's a way to stop thinking. Human beings are inherently lazy. People will use any and every opportunity to avoid thinking. They categorize, box things up and put them on a shelf.

RM: How do you generate ideas for your work?

. I think about two dimensional flat surfaces—
w I receive them in the world, what their curren-
is, and the many ways of interpreting an illusion.
 to the library, the movies and museums. I watch
ot of television every day and use a computer
ost every day. All of this enriches and tests my
racy in two dimensional visual culture. I don't
e ideas directly from any particular place. I want
make paintings that are simply about looking at a
nting, so fundamentally, that is where I start,
ugh other stuff floats in and out.

: Currently, what are your major influences and
y?

. That's hard to answer. I feel open and con-
ted to most 20th century art; I like to look at
erything and read everything. I listen to the Beach
ys, Snoop Doggy Dog and Gary Numan—they
uence me in some way. I'm a sucker for anyone
h a 'vision' and a sense of humor, of lightness:
ston Sturges films, Ad Reinhardt writing, Barnett
wman painting. The Mondrian retrospective
w me away. I love the film maker, Chris Smith,
o made "American Job". I just saw the Magritte
w in L.A. and thought I would hate it because
images are so trite, but I loved it. I am addicted
Seinfeld. I am becomming interested in the
ightenment, primarily the writing and the gar-
s. I could keep going. I don't know how all of
 influences me, but it does inspire me.

: You've mentioned that you want to present an
itude" in your work. What does that mean?

Perhaps that isn't the best word. I believe it is
re important to decide how to approach making
than to decide what to make. Developing an
que attitude is a program from which you make
rk. It is rewritten everyday and is not fully defin-
. It is the infrastructure. When I lecture to art
dents, I tell them this rather than why I made this
nting or that painting. A long time ago "attitude"
ght have been known as "ethics," or "morals."
t wouldn't make any sense now.

: You use formulas and techniques for making
listic work, i.e. the rules of classical art training,
you play with these rules. Why?

I'm interested in visual perception, though I'm
sure why—perhaps it is because it is taken for
nted, or maybe it is because I dislike literal

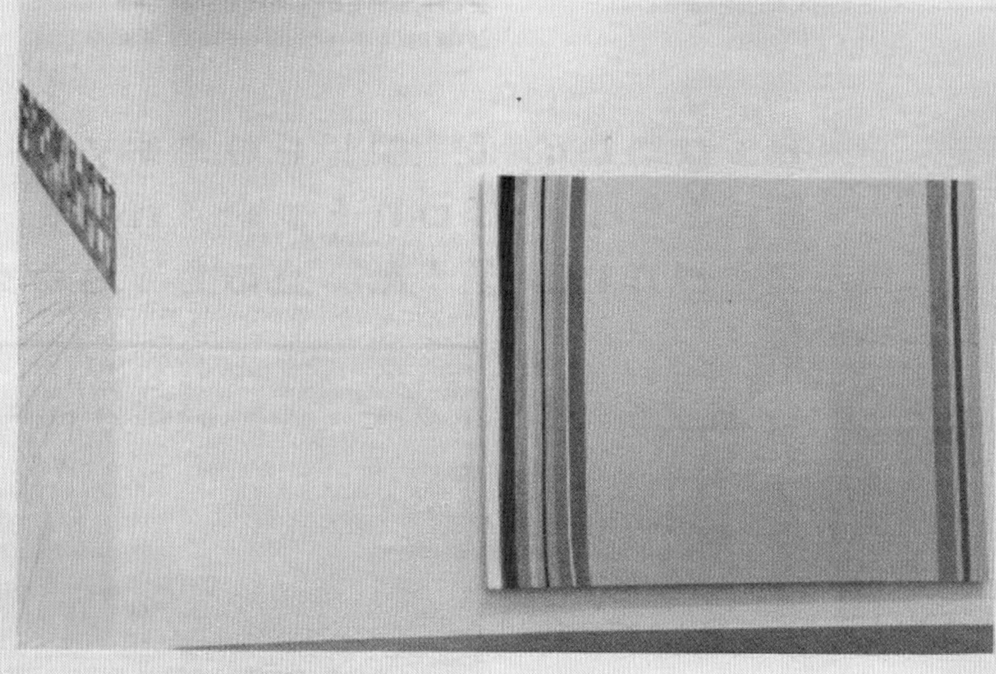

Laura Owens
Untitled, 1995
installation view

metaphor and the symbolic in art. I have a distaste
for work that tries to describe "something else"; the
passive. I don't want to be shuttled to the past or
transported to the future. When I think about perception, I am thinking about the person looking at
the artwork. I never think about "breaking the
rules," for that involves posturing and an antagonistic approach.

RM: Why do you dislike the literal metaphor, the
symbolic in art?

LO: It is boring and uninteresting, which usually
means the expectations surrounding the piece were
very low. When visual art depends heavily on a literal metaphor, or on symbolism, the work is often
not as interesting as the intended reference. This
creates a pathetic and dependent relationship. It's
like a cover song, not only is it rarely as good as the
original, it's completely parasitic. Art that goes outside of itself and bounces back, generates meaning
and is much more interesting. Passive objects are
the complete absence of anything problematic,
which is just lame. A painting like Manet's
"Dejeuner Sur L'Herbe," was completely unsettling,
if not shocking. It was very problematic and it was,
and is, very interesting. However, to be shocking for
that sake alone is infantile and boring. I also think
that art has to question itself, you can't just fill in the
blanks according to the guidelines and get an "A"
because you tried hard and did what you were told.

Rebecca Morris is a painter living in Chicago.

T. J. Wilcox: Laura was in New York and a bunch of us, including Gavin Brown, went to dinner after a group show she was in at Pat Hearn's. We were all sitting at this outdoor restaurant on Eighth Avenue between Twenty-Second and Twenty-Third. I remember that night so vividly, because it's weighed on my conscience ever since. Laura and Gavin were courting at that point, and it was becoming clear that she was probably going to work with him but she hadn't actually pulled the trigger. She kind of pulled me aside and was like, "T. J., I've been talking to Gavin and he's really weird. And you work with him, can I trust this guy? Do you think that I should show my work with Gavin?" And I said, "Oh, yes, absolutely. He's great. You should." I said that with no reservations. Very shortly after that she agreed to work with Gavin. He's a complicated guy, in the best possible way. But I've always thought, "God, when this thing hits the fan, I'm going to hear from Laura, 'You told me he was a reasonable person and that I could trust him.'" I think that it has more or less worked out, but I've always felt a little guilty for getting that involved.

When Laura decided to work with Gavin he was so thrilled. He still had the gallery on Broome Street, where I'd had my first show. And there was just no question of showing her paintings there—they would have had to be folded in half to be shown in that space. So Gavin rented a space to show Laura's work. That was stepping up as an art dealer to a degree that was unimaginable for those of us who were working with the gallery then, because everything was on a shoestring, as it had to be, I'm sure. We were so impressed that she was coming to town and was going to get this huge gallery space, we thought that was so grand and impressive. It was right by the entrance to the Holland Tunnel, a former bank or something that had just closed. They were trying to lease it, and Gavin talked the guy into renting it to him for a month or two for Laura's show. What I really remember about the installation was that the volume of the space

   T. J. Wilcox is a New York–based artist.

really suited those canvases. It was really tall—it could easily have been too tall or not tall enough or whatever. But there was a happy relationship between the canvases and the volume of the room. And I specifically remember that the first canvas you saw coming in was one of the seagull canvases, which just was so huge and broke so many rules about what you were supposed to do as an artist, as a painter. There were many things that were wrong about that painting, that absolutely were not permissible; she was breaking the rules with that canvas. It worked fantastically, and it was exciting to see her paintings like that. I remember standing in the doorway with Gavin and just saying, "This is so great you got this space. It's so essential you got this space and it's so fantastic that you're showing Laura. This is going to drive people crazy." And I think it did.

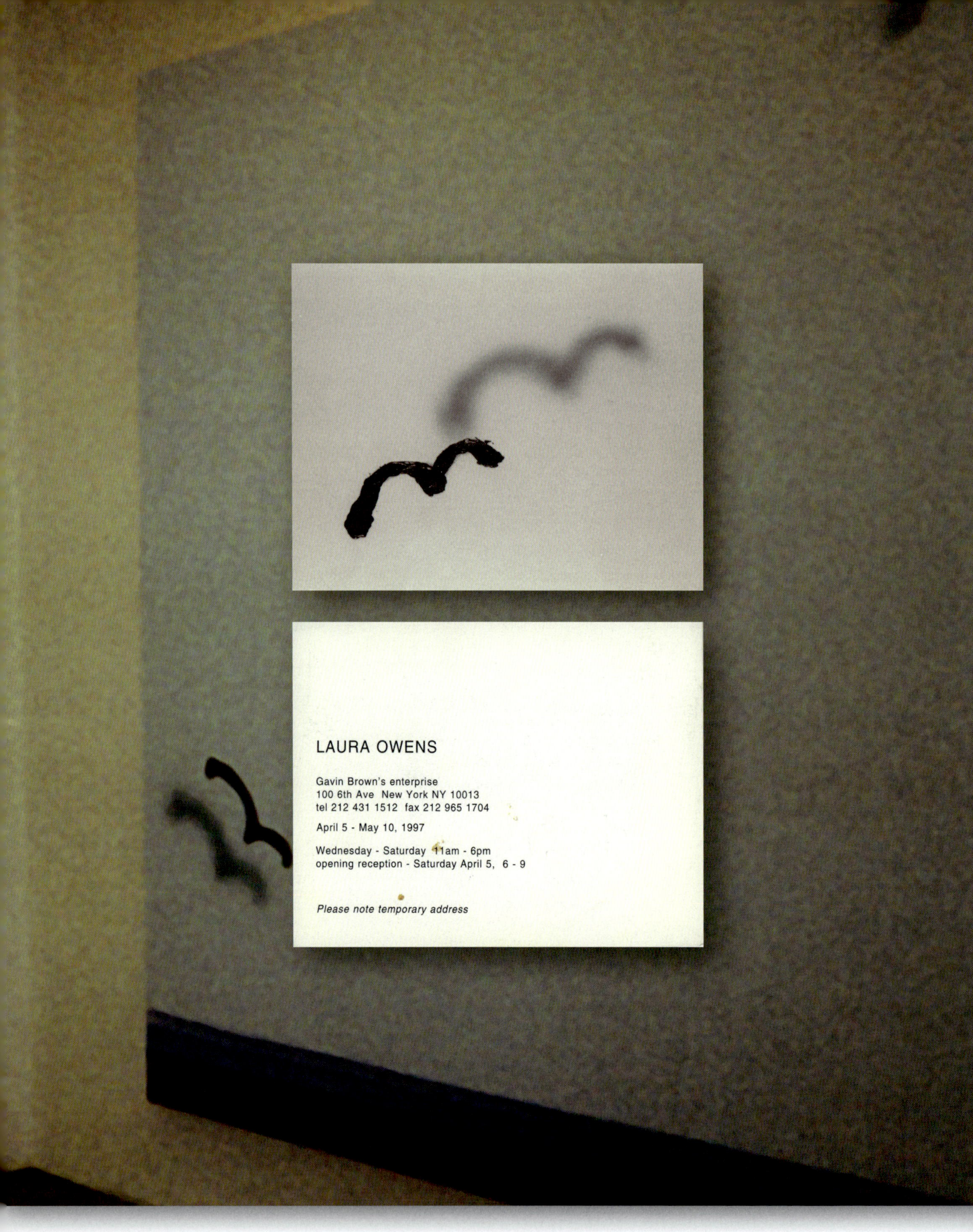

Foreground: Invitation, Gavin Brown's enterprise, New York, 1997
Background: Installation view, Gavin Brown's enterprise, New York, 1997, with *Untitled*, 1997 (see p. 134)

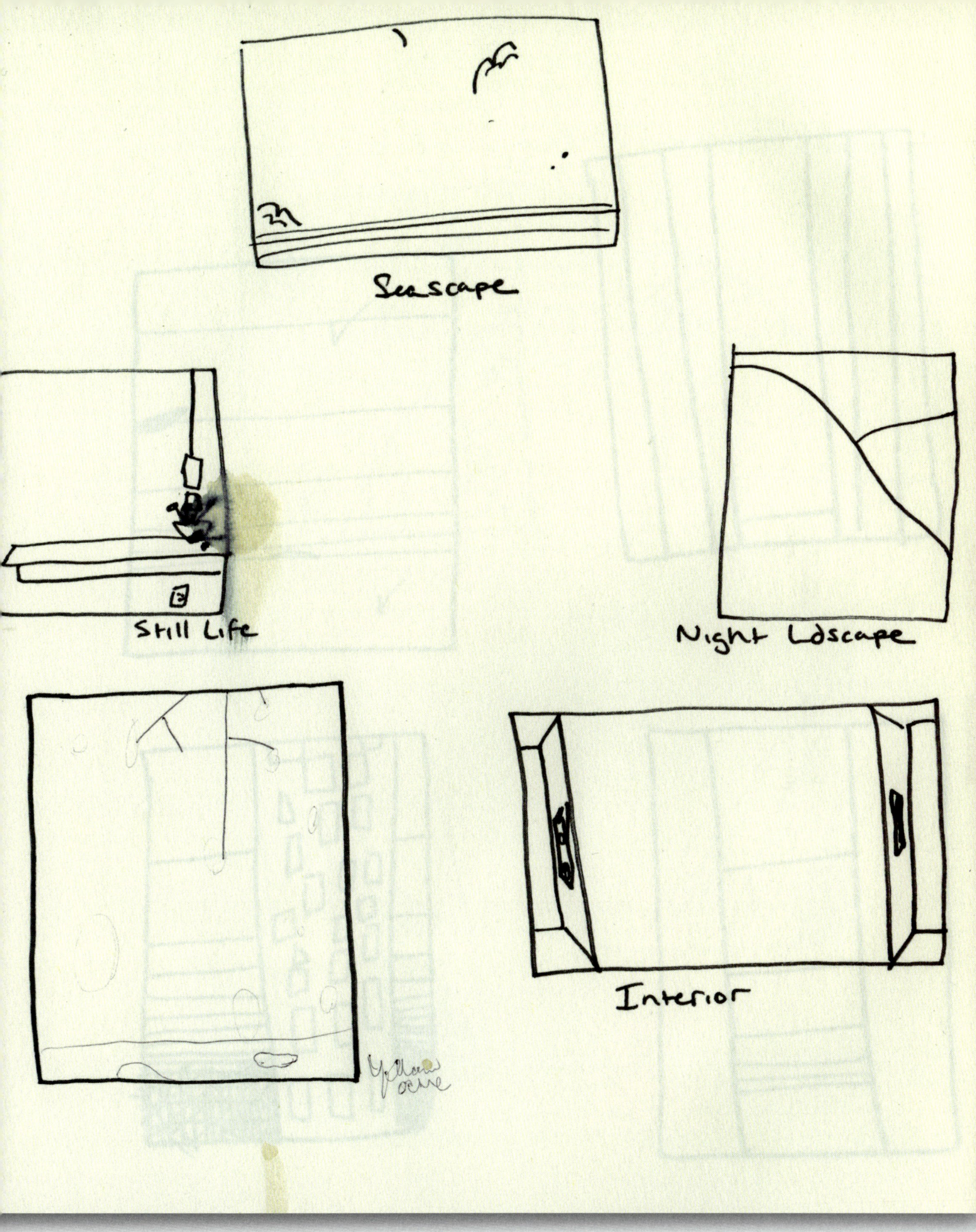

Seascape
Still Life
Night Ldscape
Interior
Yellow ochre

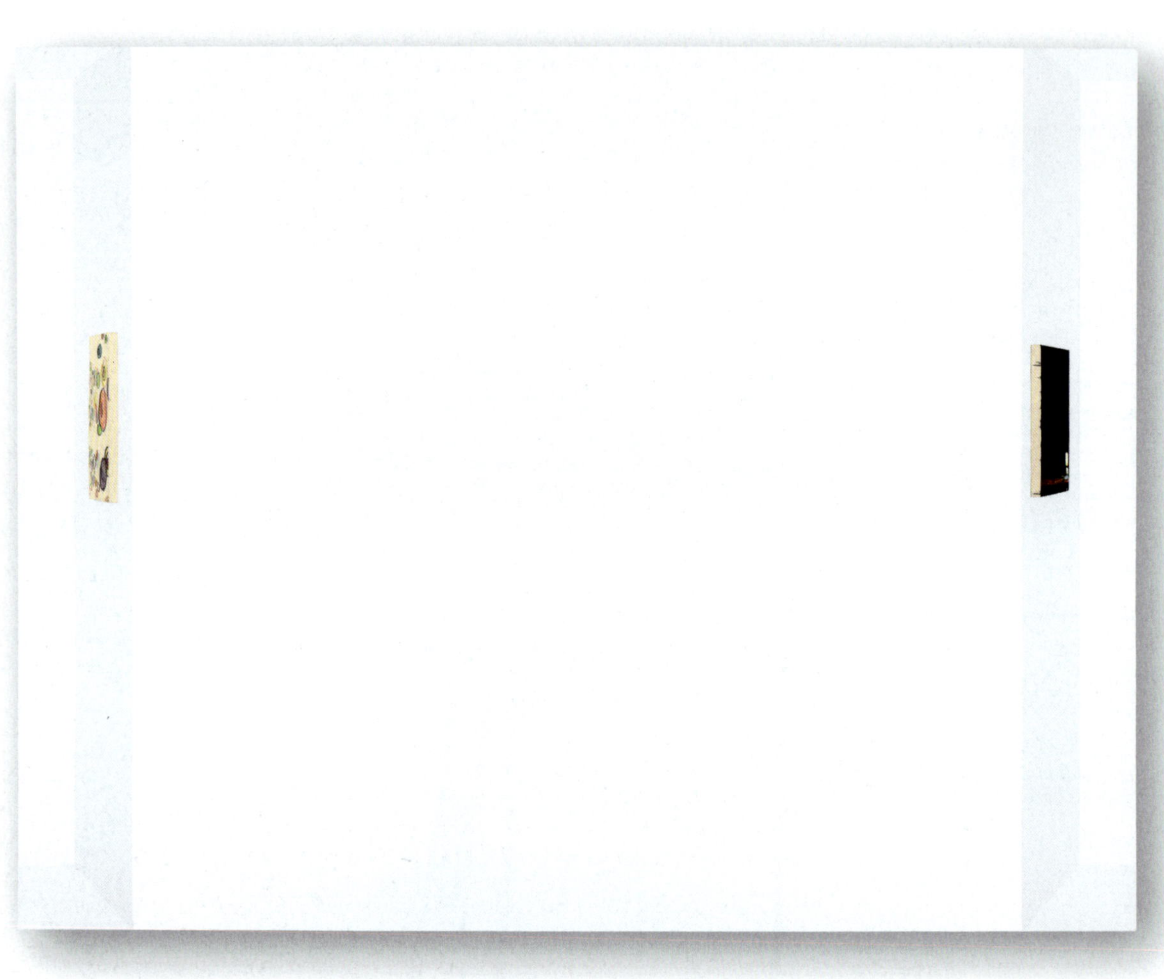

   Untitled, 1997, acrylic and modeling paste on canvas, 96 × 120 in. (243.8 × 304.8 cm)

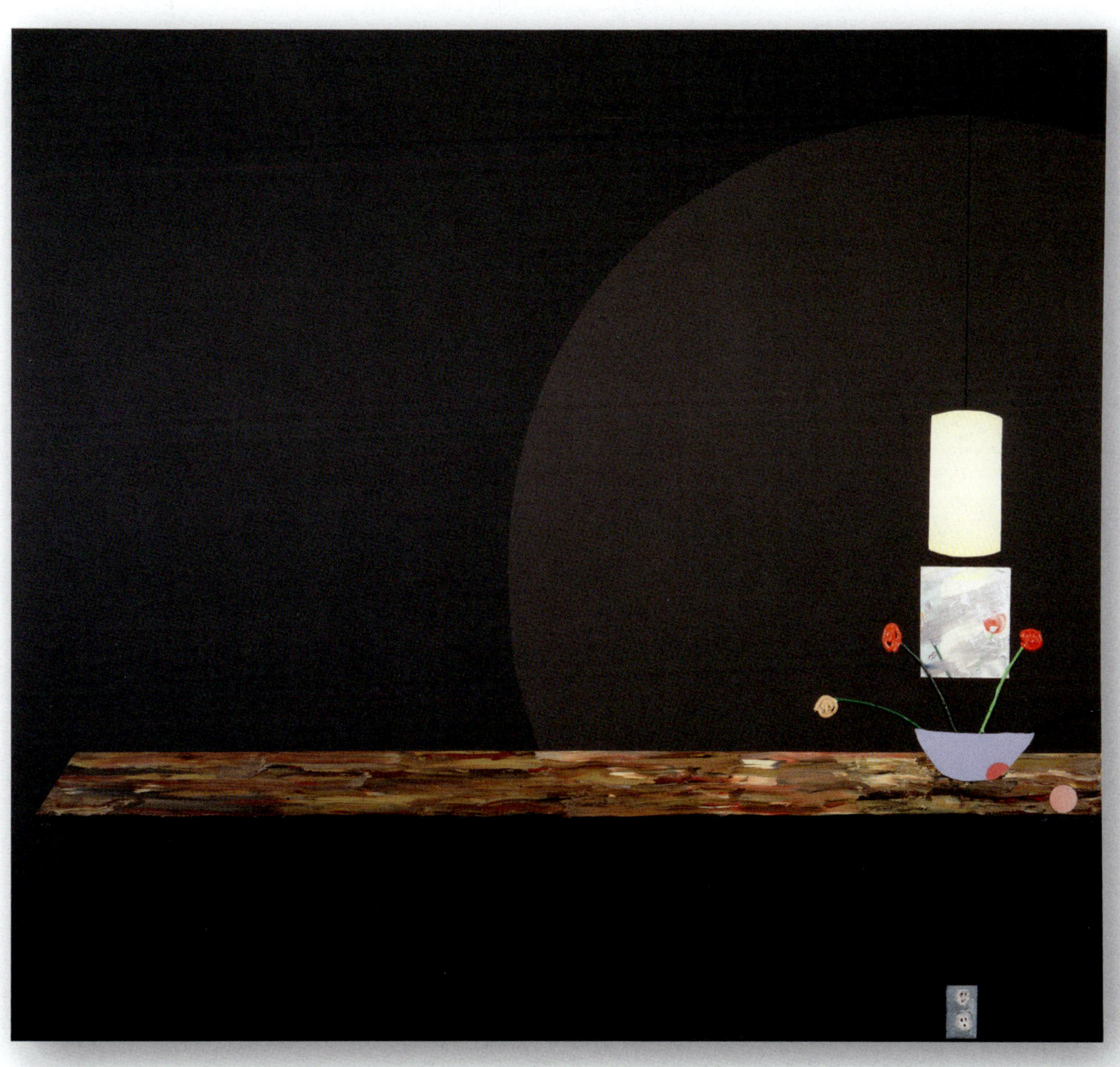

Untitled, 1997, acrylic and oil on canvas, 78 × 84 in. (198.1 × 213.4 cm)

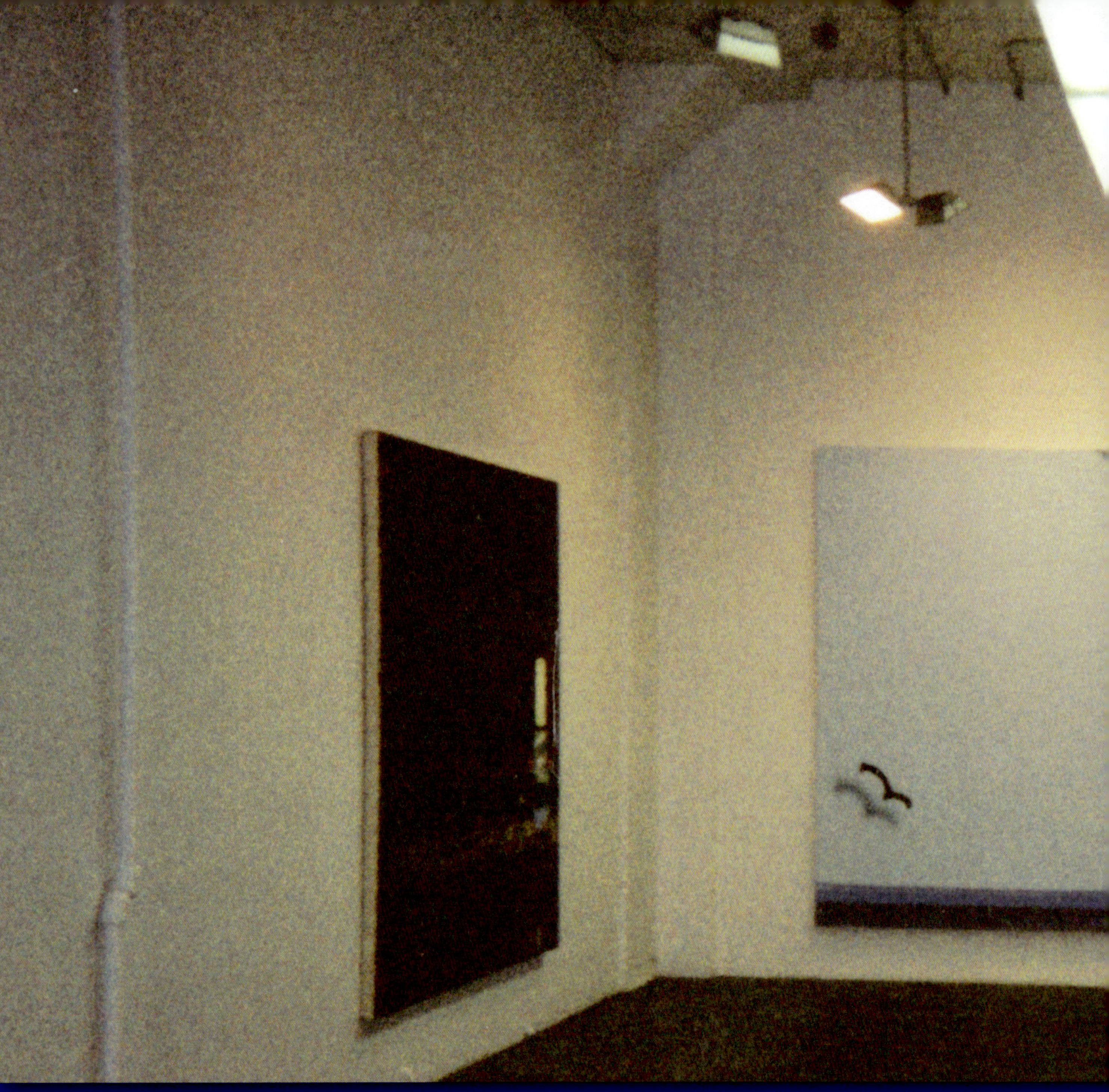

Installation view, Gavin Brown's enterprise, New York, 1997, with *Untitled*, 1997 (see p. 129); *Untitled,* 1997 (see p. 134); and *Untitled,* 1997, acrylic and oil on canvas, 84 × 78 in. (213.4 × 198.1 cm)

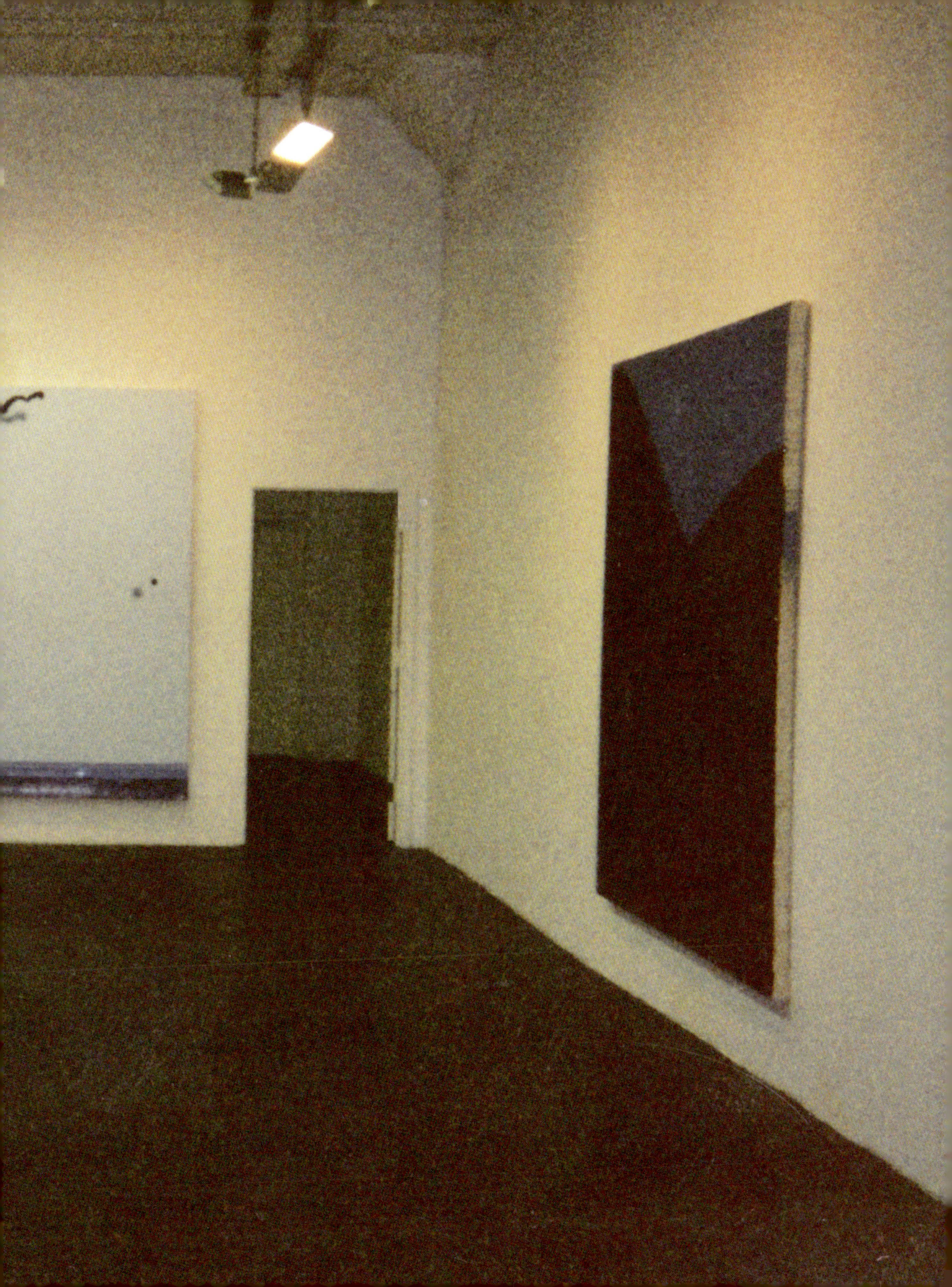

7·30·97

Gavin,
      Hope you get this — I'm
thinking you are at the
beach.   Sorry to bother you
with all   this crap but...
I   will need slides of   last 2 ptngs
I sent you $ the panting the
Met has $ the Artists Space / Saatchi
panting by beginning of September
to Apply for Tiffany Grant. I t
would be best to just send me 4x5's
$ then I can dupe slides from that.
Also I have   no $ to
make panting for   Sadies show
maybe you could send me $ for
the rest of   Cesar's panting   or Dean's
painting. Hoping to find money
soon so I can make the work.
Also P.S. One might fly me to
N.Y. to do Mural project - Do you know

when T.J.s film will screen
so I could maybe come for
that?
    I am meeting with Guenzai
tomorrow about a show either
with Sharon Lockhart or Jorge.
I had a meeting w/ Tim Blum
& Jeff Poe. I don't know
what I can stomach.
I am definately doing Independent
show in Spring — I think the
best way is just try to presell
some paintings from studio. I
guess just depends how much it all
costs I'm thinking — total $3000 to
rent space, hire student, invitations &
possibly ad — [Artforum is probably too expensive]
Anyway — hope you are having a fun
summer. Talk to you soon.
                        ♡ Laura

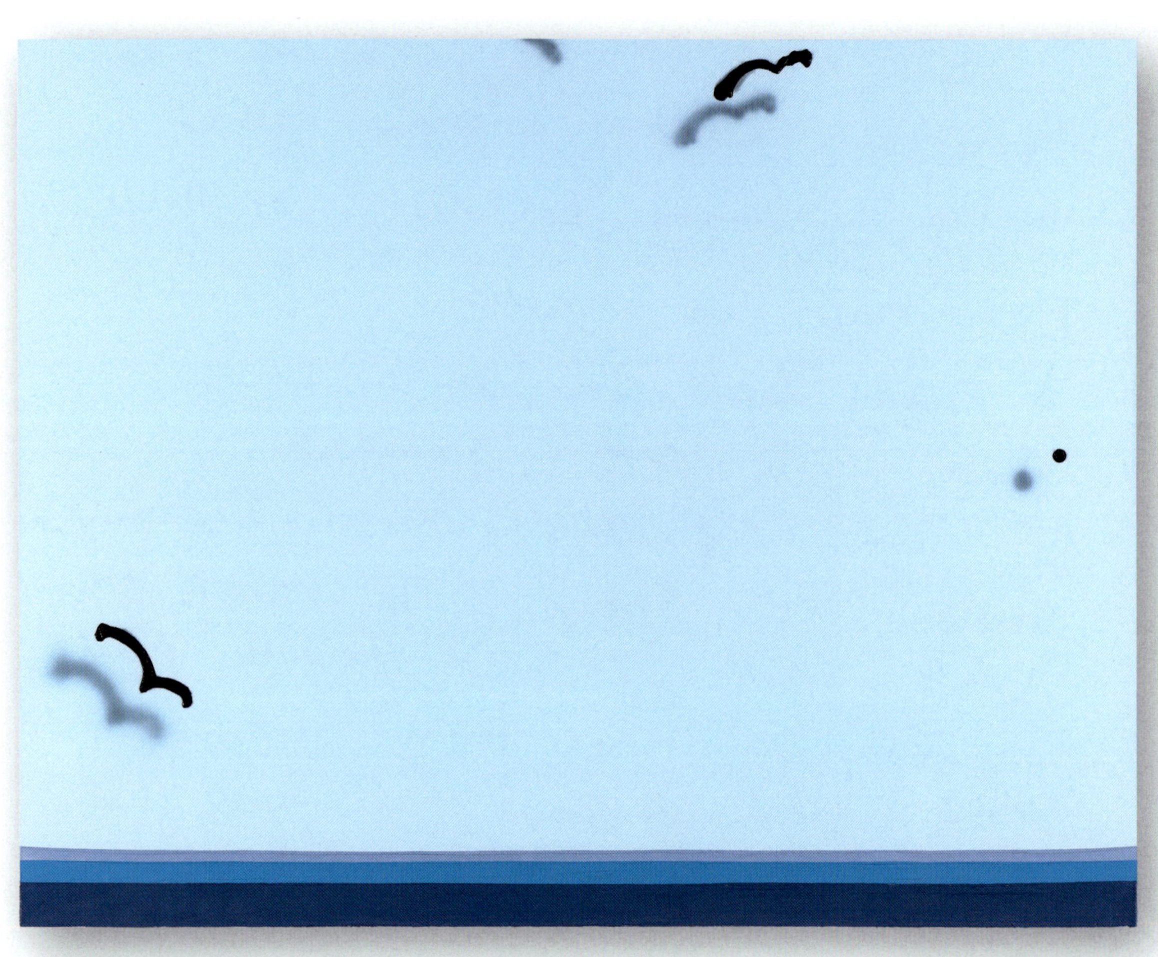

134   *Untitled*, 1997, oil, acrylic, and airbrushed oil on canvas, 96 × 120 in. (243.8 × 304.8 cm)

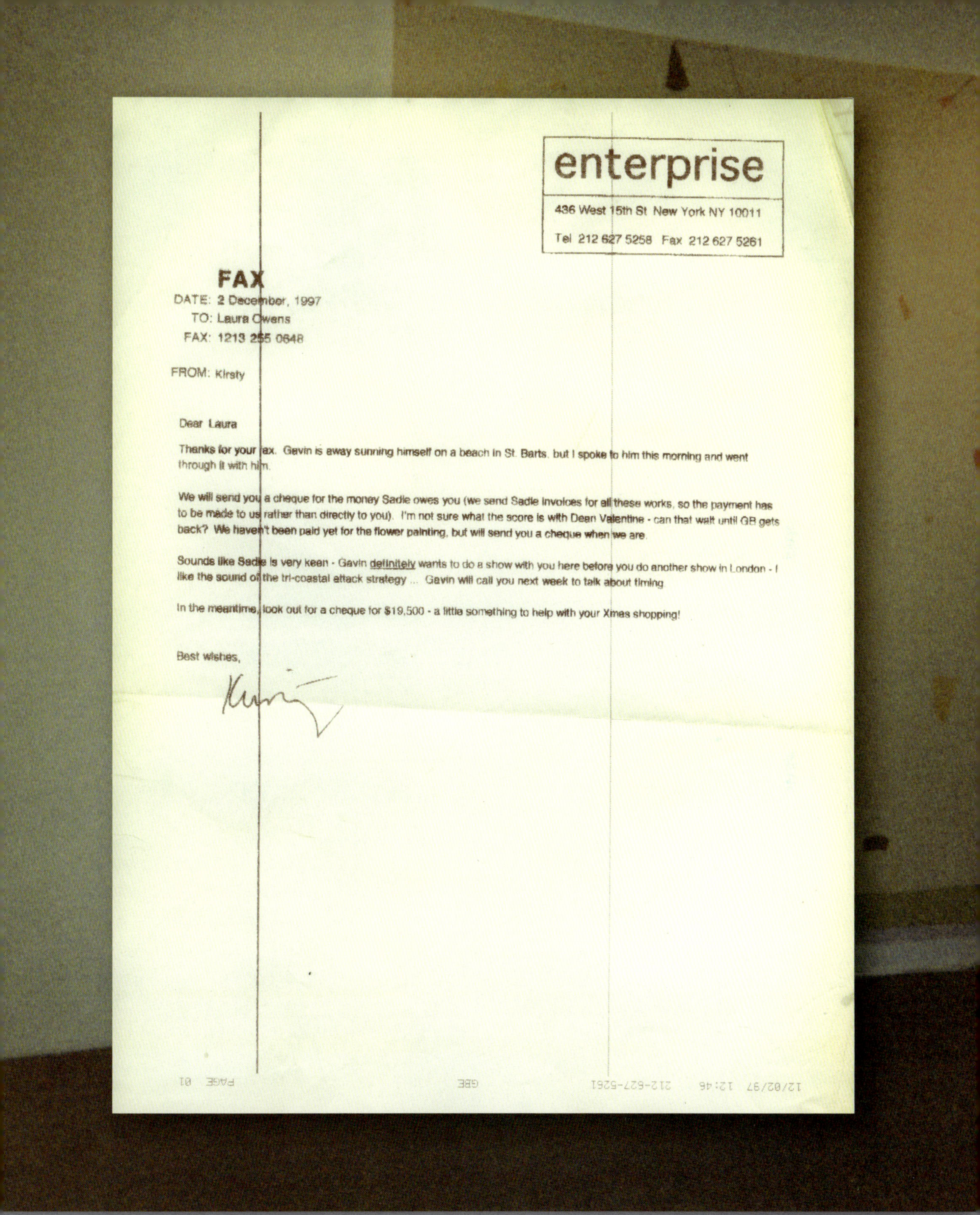

FAX

DATE: 2 December, 1997
TO: Laura Owens
FAX: 1213 255 0648

FROM: Kirsty

Dear Laura

Thanks for your fax. Gavin is away sunning himself on a beach in St. Barts. but I spoke to him this morning and went through it with him.

We will send you a cheque for the money Sadie owes you (we send Sadie invoices for all these works, so the payment has to be made to us rather than directly to you). I'm not sure what the score is with Dean Valentine - can that wait until GB gets back? We haven't been paid yet for the flower painting, but will send you a cheque when we are.

Sounds like Sadie is very keen - Gavin _definitely_ wants to do a show with you here before you do another show in London - I like the sound of the tri-coastal attack strategy ... Gavin will call you next week to talk about timing

In the meantime, look out for a cheque for $19,500 - a little something to help with your Xmas shopping!

Best wishes,

Foreground: Fax from Kirsty Bell, 1997
Background: Installation view, Gavin Brown's enterprise, New York, 1997, with *Untitled*, 1997, acrylic on canvas, 120 × 96 in. (304.8 × 243.8 cm)

dec. 17 97

Dear Gavin,

Here is a list of payments that are still outstanding. I really need you to pay this before
I start sending you more paintings. Thanks.   Laura

Dean Valentine painting(plein?)
Untitled 1997 96" x 120" (white room). 1900.00

Cesar Reyes
Untitled 1997(nightscape) 2600.00

Untitled 1997 (2 flowers) 4500.00

                                 TOTAL $9000.00

P.S. I am also wondering what
if anything happened to a small
painting I gave you in April
that was brown & baby blue.
about 22" x18".
Thanks! ♡ Laura

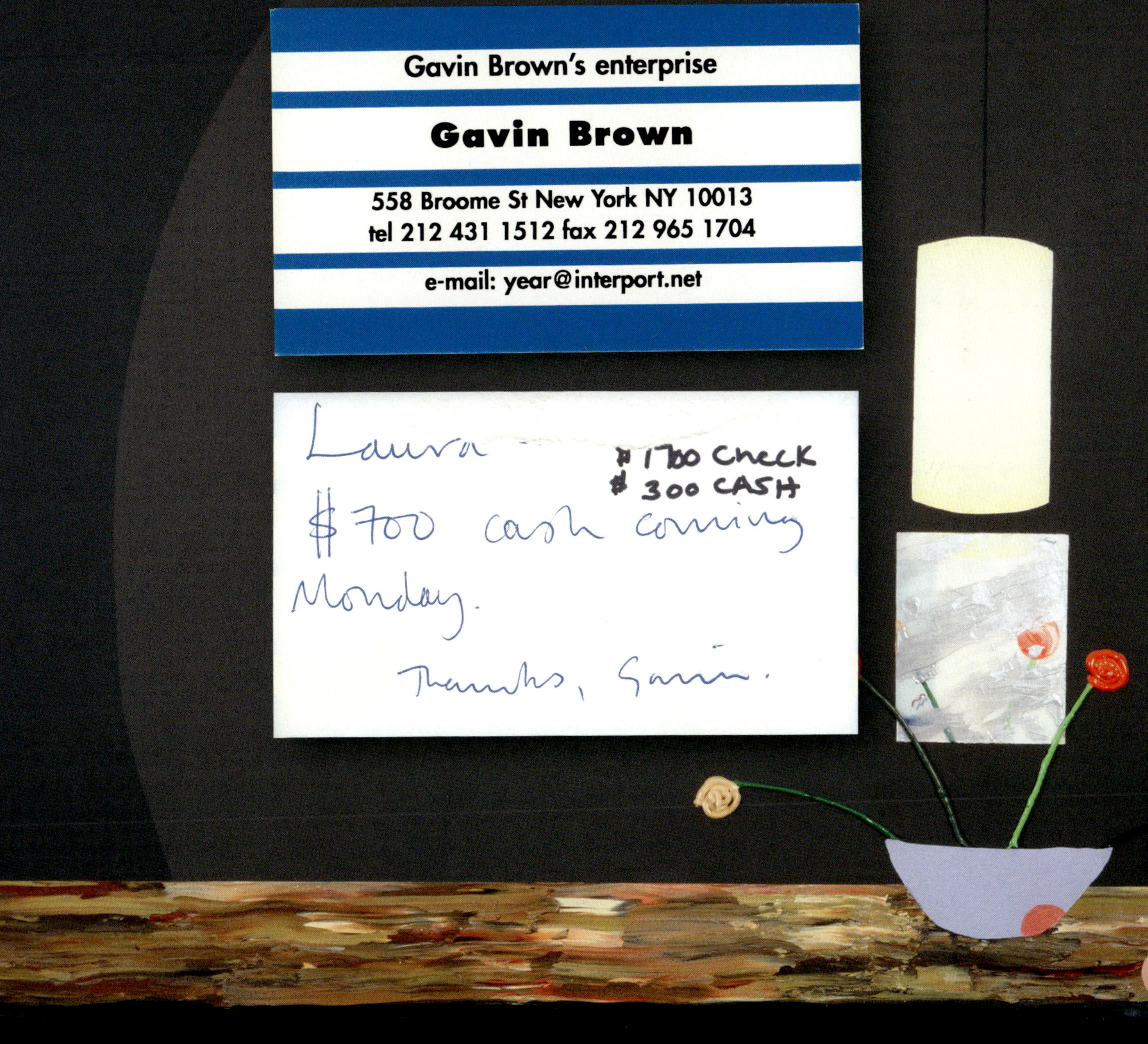

Foreground: Business card with note from Gavin Brown, 1997
Background: Detail of *Untitled*, 1997 (see p. 129)

HOW SHOULD A PAINTING DO?
BRUCE HAINLEY

Before we start looking, let's reflect where we are. This location was designed for you to train your eyes and senses on objects and talk to your neighbor or yourself about what it is you are looking at. It happens all the time here, and it should be easy to guide yourself. At least it should be easy to find the art. It could be obvious that it is in here. Outside of here there are large problems that are not art problems. Inside-the-art problems are only in the art objects. You know what I mean. When you look at these objects, do you think they are looking at you? Don't you think they are human, too? You see the birds but they don't see you. For many years we have been scouting locations to hang paintings. We are looking for rooms to make photographs of hanging paintings. Images of exhibitions are wonderful narrations. Projections. There's a static image inside the moving image. How can this be? You might want to walk around and film the space, and there's a space in the painting ready for projection. Take a picture. What do you think about when you read the words in the painting? How are they different from the didactics on the wall telling you my name, the date, and the lender? Where is the painting? It's easy to find, right? They work in spaces to make them art spaces. We changed a bar into an art gallery. How rude! The bar is sad. Alfred Barr started this art museum. Do you think he's happy? If you're not ready to go home, can I get a "Hell no!"? He made an art gallery into a bar. More humans used this space before this painting walked in and made it an art space, okay? Whoa, better? Worse? Is this our house? Is this our party? We can do what we want, right? Once upon a time there was a ginormous monster who loved a princess and her name was Lala and she hated him because he had really fierce jaws. But one day, her mother, the Queen, said she had to marry but she didn't want to so she ran away. That's it. I'm going to marry her anyway. Quitting is beginning. Let's quit together. Let's leave this space alone. This is our house. This is our roof. Let's hang, hang out, and hang ourselves together and alone. In order to begin, please quit what you are doing. Here are our surrogates, they are young and dumb. Get an up-close view of what's your favorite without scaring them. We could go all night.

—Laura Owens, 2014

That goon was inaugurated today. He bellowed words that have never been used in any previous inauguration speech: *bleed, carnage, stealing, stolen, rusted, tombstones, trapped, depletion, flush, sad* **were just a few of them, all delivered to exploit as much fearmongering as possible. Some said passages of the speech parroted lines lifted from the monologue of a blockbuster villain. Are those words now outside or inside here (not quite the** *here* **Laura refers to above, but not exactly unrelated to it either)? Some will have noticed I've slipped into the familiar, referring to the artist by her first name. Confronting the problems she raises of outside and inside, of large problems that may not be the problems of art, which has its own variously sized problems, it strikes me right now that not calling her Laura would seem odd, akin to providing "alternative facts" or giving purchase to those who might think that this text is in any way unbiased or "objective" (it isn't). Shut up, kiss me, hold me tight.**

I'd wanted to write something about her painting of sky and sea (*Untitled***, 1997; see p. 134), with birds (I always imagine them to be gulls) held variously aloft as if on the paused poles of an invisible merry-go-round, calliope music waning. I would rather stare out at the sea than do anything else. This desire would seem to be a retreat from the large problems outside, many of which just got larger.**

Man looking into the sea,
taking the view from those who have as much right to it as you
                                        have to it yourself,
it is human nature to stand in the middle of a thing,
but you cannot stand in the middle of this;
the sea has nothing to give but a well excavated grave.

These are the opening lines of Marianne Moore's poem "A Grave" as it appeared in her *Selected Poems* **(1935), a volume with an introduction by T. S. Eliot published long before mankind turned the ocean toxic, creating the largest trash dump on the planet—a so-called "patch" or "vortex" of plastic and particulates in just one northern Pacific section of the Seven Seas is "about the size of Texas." I won't get into the waters' rising temperatures or spikes in the ocean's acidification. Above the grave, Moore discerns that "the birds swim through the air at top speed, emitting cat-calls / as heretofore." She continued to seek, having already sought, ways to**

     Bruce Hainley is a writer in Los Angeles who is also associate chair of graduate art at ArtCenter College of Design in Pasadena.

question man's supposed priority, and she freaks her poem with his variegated rapaciousnesses, desecrations. On some level the poet trains her extraordinary skills of observation on things that unman anyone in the vicinity. If you are still following my train of thought, do you think we're more outside or inside the matter at hand?

I don't know where you'd have to be positioned to have this view (the painting's vantage). On a pleasure craft at sea? Or situated in a theater, since the painting plays with the vernacular of a theatrical backdrop, one that might be rolled in and offstage quickly? Any land seems far away behind us. Mostly sky, with a shimmer of horizon, a placid bit of waves with possible wrinkles, and then the immediate woolly blue. Swimmingly, the seagulls float with their shadows above it all—one appearing at the top only as a fading afterthought of a wing's silhouette. It's a largish painting made up of four different blues or blue-grays, along with black and a murky pewter or porpoise. Painted sky, painted horizon, painted waves, painted immediacy, painted seagulls and shadows floating above it all, in oil, acrylic, and airbrushed oil on canvas. Some of the paint spread thick as royal icing, elsewhere pooled like molasses, but the main field of "sky," its beachy light full of glare, pristine as a new screen. *Before the ubiquity of "smart" phones and social media* is a more accurate date for when the painting was made than 1997, however much the artist seems to have prepared for someone to pose for a selfie in front of it and seem briefly unmoored.

However long ago it was, it wasn't a time before drop shadows, which arrive, waggishly, as if from a 1980s infomercial for the marvels of desktop publishing and classy, home-office graphic design. What are the shadows supposed to be falling on? And what to do with—I haven't even mentioned it!—the lone black dot (cursor? period at the end of whatever visual "sentence" the artist with paint articulates?) and its even more impish trace? Everything about the picture, its scenography, seems poised, pointedly (?), at its negation, or, rather, not its *negation* but its becoming merely something *signified*. Is having only a single one a witty rejoinder to Georges Seurat's points? "What the dot seemed to promise, at least for a while, was a truly naïve visualization of the singular and uniform as the same thing," T. J. Clark, fiery éminence grise, proposes in *Farewell to an*

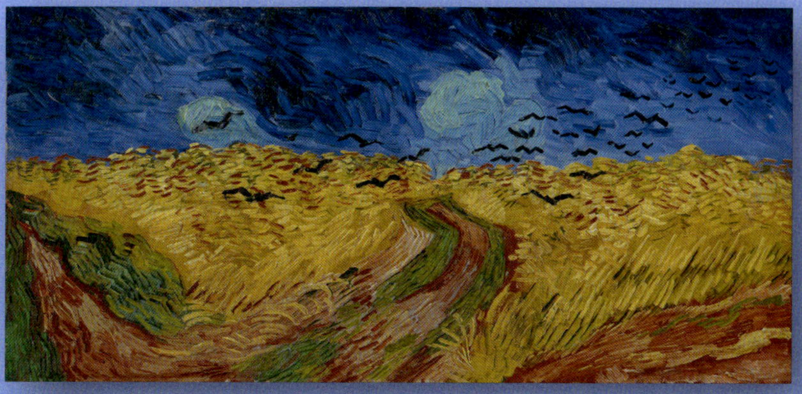

Vincent van Gogh, *Wheatfield with Crows*, 1890, oil on canvas, 19⅞ × 40½ in. (50.5 × 103 cm)

Idea (1999), licking his chops at the possible consequences. "The dot exploded the opposition. And this was wonderful. It planted a bomb in the middle of the bourgeois idea of freedom—and order, and individuality, and Art-ness, and taste, and 'touch,' intuition, variety, expressiveness. All the aesthetic categories of the nineteenth century, including most of the modernist ones, disappeared down the black hole of Seurat's technique." Laura paints the escape velocity from that sticky black hole, but it leaves an airbrushed residue.

Some might not quite see direct ways to tally the nineteenth century in this painting, and yet there is that point or dot. A working theory: all the colors that make up the scene arrive courtesy of Vincent van Gogh's *Wheatfield with Crows*, particularly via the sky above that turbulent sea of grain. Many consider it the last work he painted—July 1890, Auvers-sur-Oise—before killing himself, and Joan Mitchell would eventually reply to its entreaties (see *No Birds*, 1987–88). Van Gogh's birds would seem to be "drop-shadowed" by the thick strokes of oil paint rumbling in the stormy sky and clouds they depict. Of course, I could get to the art historical in a more synchronic manner: around the time Laura was sorting out how a painting should do, Vincent Fecteau, in the midst of some of his earliest pieces, placed seagulls, inverted, little, marker *W*'s, flying around Zenith televisions and down numbing corridors; Jonathan Livingston Seagull and his siblings aflight, worn down to forlorn doodles. What does it mean to take some schlock or kitsch aspect of culture (Jonathan Livingston Seagull, a sea view) and find in it a trapdoor to profundity?

I attended Laura's wedding to my friend Sohrab and now consider her a friend, one I never expected to have or get to know given that I was once very shitty in print about some of her paintings. That was a while ago, and there's much more thinking

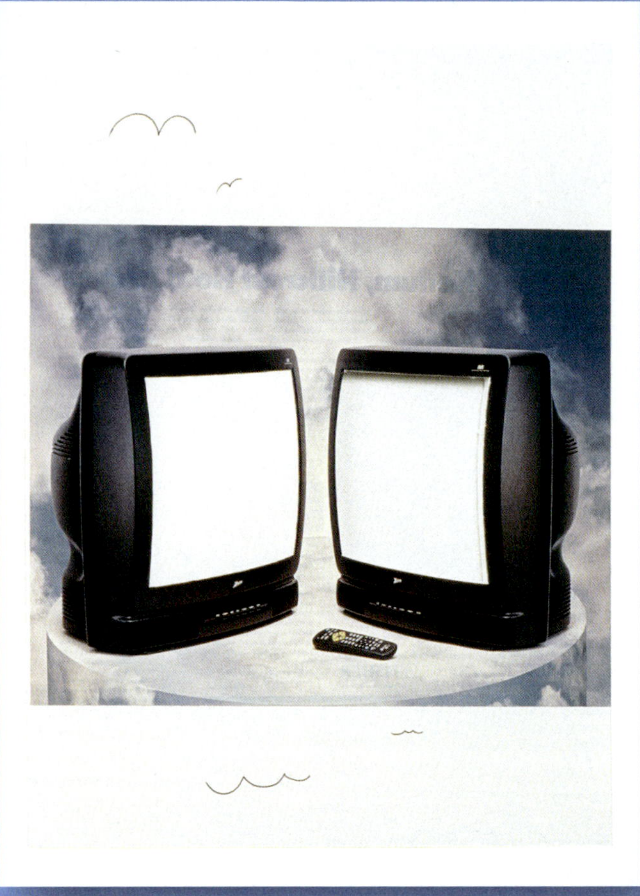

Vincent Fecteau, *Untitled*, 1996, foamcore, collaged printed paper, and ink, 13¾ × 10¾ in. (34.9 × 27.3 cm)

to be done about friendships, cohorts, and crews in relation to art, but all of it inflects how one might determine "outside" and "inside" and why of all the matters in Laura's statement on which one might dwell I've been thinking mostly about these three sentences: *Outside of here there are large problems that are not art problems. Inside-the-art problems are only in the art objects. You know what I mean.* John Ashbery, giving a needed slap on the wrist to those who questioned the "use" of his poetry in a wounding world, once cautioned not to "confuse it with the Salvation Army." Which is only to say that his retort isn't alien to what Laura is asking anyone to consider. While I don't believe those lines to be a cry of *ars gratia artis*, I do believe they're worth unfurling in relation to the *Jetztzeit* and what it puts to the test in terms of outside and in.

Last summer I went to hear Laura and Suzanne Hudson discuss monochromes. There are many worse ways to consider her painting of sky and sea and seagulls and shadows than as a confrontation with the fraught history, manifold pleasure,

and theoretical minefield of the monochrome. One of the first monochromes they talked about was by Felix Gonzalez-Torres. He made a four-panel painting, one for each of four colors. The museum in Los Angeles that owns this painting and that hosted the talk between the two women hasn't shown it for more than fifteen years, despite other works by Gonzalez-Torres being perennial curatorial favorites. There is a frequent waxy buildup of piety around this artist, but when Laura read the statement he wrote in 1988 to accompany the work's first installation (along with several of his timeline Photostats), at the New Museum, New York, something burned all of it away. She read the text with gusto and, I'd like to claim, with something that felt like *identification* with his sense of how a painting should do—especially when she came to the penultimate paragraph of Gonzalez-Torres's call to arms and somewhat crestfallen (?) acknowledgment of what will and more than likely won't precipitate from any painting:

It is a fact people are discriminated against for being HIV positive. It is a fact the majority of the Nazi industrialists retained their wealth after war. It is a fact the night belongs to Michelob and Coke is real. It is a fact the color of your skin matters. It is a fact Crazy Eddie's prices are insane. It is a fact that four colors—red, black, green and white—placed next to each other in any form are strictly forbidden by the Israeli army in the occupied Palestinian territories. This color combination can cause an arrest, a beating, a curfew, a shooting, or a news photograph. Yet it is a fact that these forbidden colors, presented as a solitary act of consciousness here in SoHo, will not precipitate a similar reaction.

Although the Palestinian flag, its colors, and their use in artwork of "political significance" have not been banned in Israel since 1993, when the Oslo peace accords were signed, many of these facts still have a hold on reality, some pulverizingly so.

The 2016 audio files about Laura's paintings now available at why11.com are randomized by some algorithm it is beyond my ken to try to explain: you rarely find the same response—encountering,

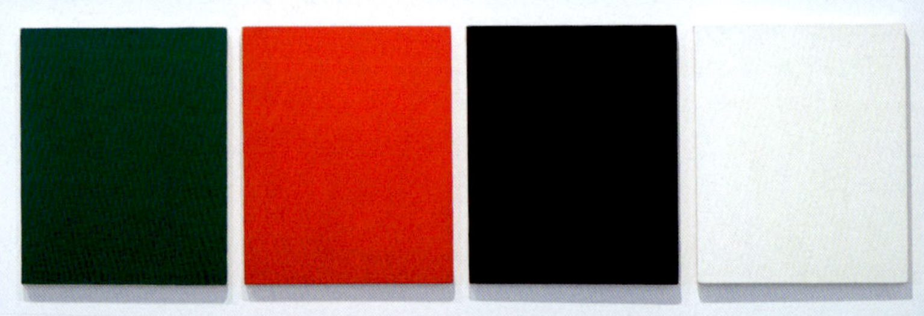

Felix Gonzalez-Torres, *"Forbidden Colors"*, 1988, acrylic on panel, four parts: 20 × 16 in. (50.8 × 40.6 cm) each, 20 × 68 in. (50.8 × 172.7 cm) overall

variously, bits of music; the artist speaking, sometimes quickly name-checked ("Hi, this is Laura Owens"), sometimes not; the voices of unidentified assistants; alternately a computer's "voice" from a text-to-speech program in both "male" and "female" modes. Since each time you choose a given work from the drop-down menu a different didactic clip plays, the effect is both specific and shifting. The statement that opens this text, which I heard when I selected "Painting 089" and have almost never hit upon again, glides through a range of discourses and concerns, beginning with the here and now of how any viewer sees or "engages" with a painting or its reproduction as well as trafficking in the strange, specific sitedness of how and where paintings arrive, only to be reproduced even more than they are to be seen. Call it a blunt coming to terms with the fact that most paintings are seen, if at all, by an audience who sees them online, on some device, a device Laura's voice in this clip asks the listener to quit.

With its "blank" space glaring and so much of its technique seemingly shrugging off "artness," *Untitled* (1997), long before there really were any smart devices to quit, nevertheless unexpectedly, proleptically, highlights this technological condition or situation, all the while beckoning human interference/participation and simultaneously turning the human into nothing but a prop. Laura's most recent interventions—from a painting, somewhat like a matryoshka doll, with other paintings and a book "hidden" beneath or within it (*Untitled*, 2014, see pp. 558–59) to an entire suite of paintings embedded within gallery walls behind wallpaper (as in her exhibition *Ten Paintings*, 2016, see p. 598)—deal with this situation and thwart it with even more intensity: she takes for granted that her paintings will be "seen" with or through "smart" phones or on social media and utterly fucks with this mediation, as if painting can only be seen in some place beyond the site of both the actual and the mediated. Glancing back at the tradition that precedes her seascape while also staring out at some horizon (call it the future), Laura waves so long to the aesthetic categories of the twentieth century in a manner not that different from Seurat's adieu to those of the nineteenth. The painting cues what lies ahead, just out of view, rumbling like a storm approaching—the twenty-first century (its "smart" glare, its glare smarting), inescapable as a black hole, fuzzy as an airbrushed drop-shadow dot and its attendant physics, somehow retro and avant simultaneously.

This is why whatever we encounter are surrogates, young and dumb as we are standing in front of the new, things we never really see (or *that cannot be seen*), which is weird to articulate, but I think not untrue. As much as the statement and its gentle visual training glide into and out of a childlike storytelling, perhaps to be taken as one kind of account (certainly no worse, often so much better, than others) of dealing with the world, it does more than merely allude to the fact that domesticity entails more work for women—often a ginormous amount, especially when they're mothers—than for men, no matter what else the mothers may do, no matter at what pitch.

By the time you're reading this description of a description, the goon, that rough beast, will have, possibly, slouched his way to (almost, but let's hope not) a year in office. What will the world be like? I don't know. Better? Worse? I don't know. Masha Gessen has stated that her worst fear is him bringing about nuclear holocaust. That's a large problem, maybe the largest, and it's outside, suppurating. Remaining vigilant to the inside-the-art problems—there are some that are only in art objects, whether we know which ones she means or not, whether we agree with her or not—enables Laura to make more than a few paintings that are the most powerful retort, including joy even, to the situation at hand, in some way because she allows herself to fail in not always making a painting that is "powerful" or a "retort" to anything at all. Instead, in that refusal, there remains a way of being steadfast to the local concerns of art— which is to say, in allowing it to be what can be, will be, and could be, which is hard to know and sometimes difficult to see.

It is a fact people are discriminated against for being HIV positive. It is a fact the majority of the Nazi industrialists retained their wealth after war. It is a fact the night belongs to Michelob and Coke is real. The Palestinian cause remains dire. It is a fact the color of your skin matters. Crazy Eddie now sits at the left hand of power, which has so many left hands, no right at all. Who is your crew? How do they assemble? Do they eschew mourning for possibility? How should a painting do? How does anyone look to sea? Pick your battles. Shut up, kiss me, hold me tight.

The epigraph is a transcription of a stop from Owens's audio tour for her exhibition at Sadie Coles HQ, London, 2016. The audio, accessed January 13, 2017, at why11.com, was initially created for *The Forever Now: Contemporary Painting in an Atemporal World* at the Museum of Modern Art, New York, 2014.

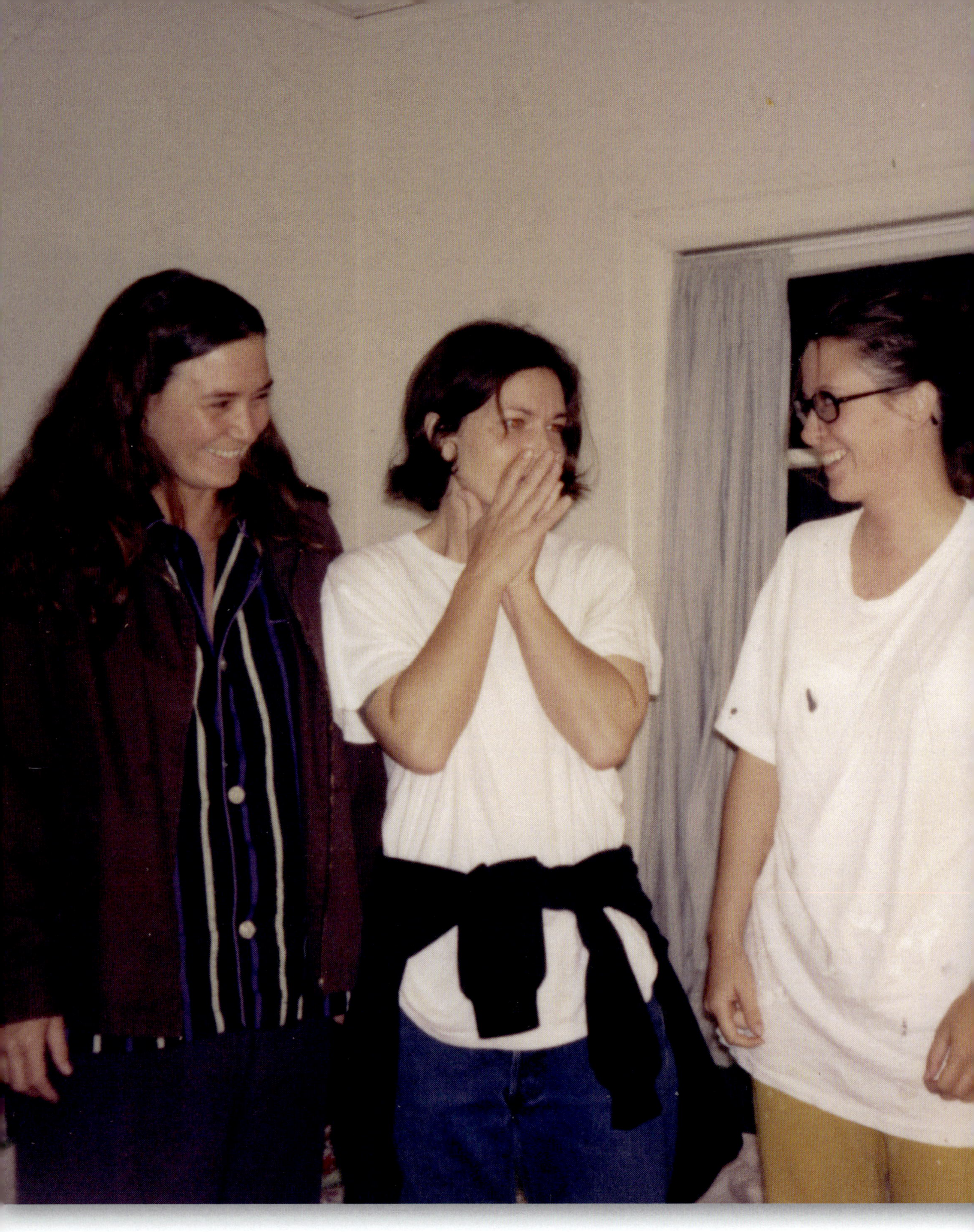

142 Sharon Lockhart, Frances Stark, and Owens, Los Angeles, 1997

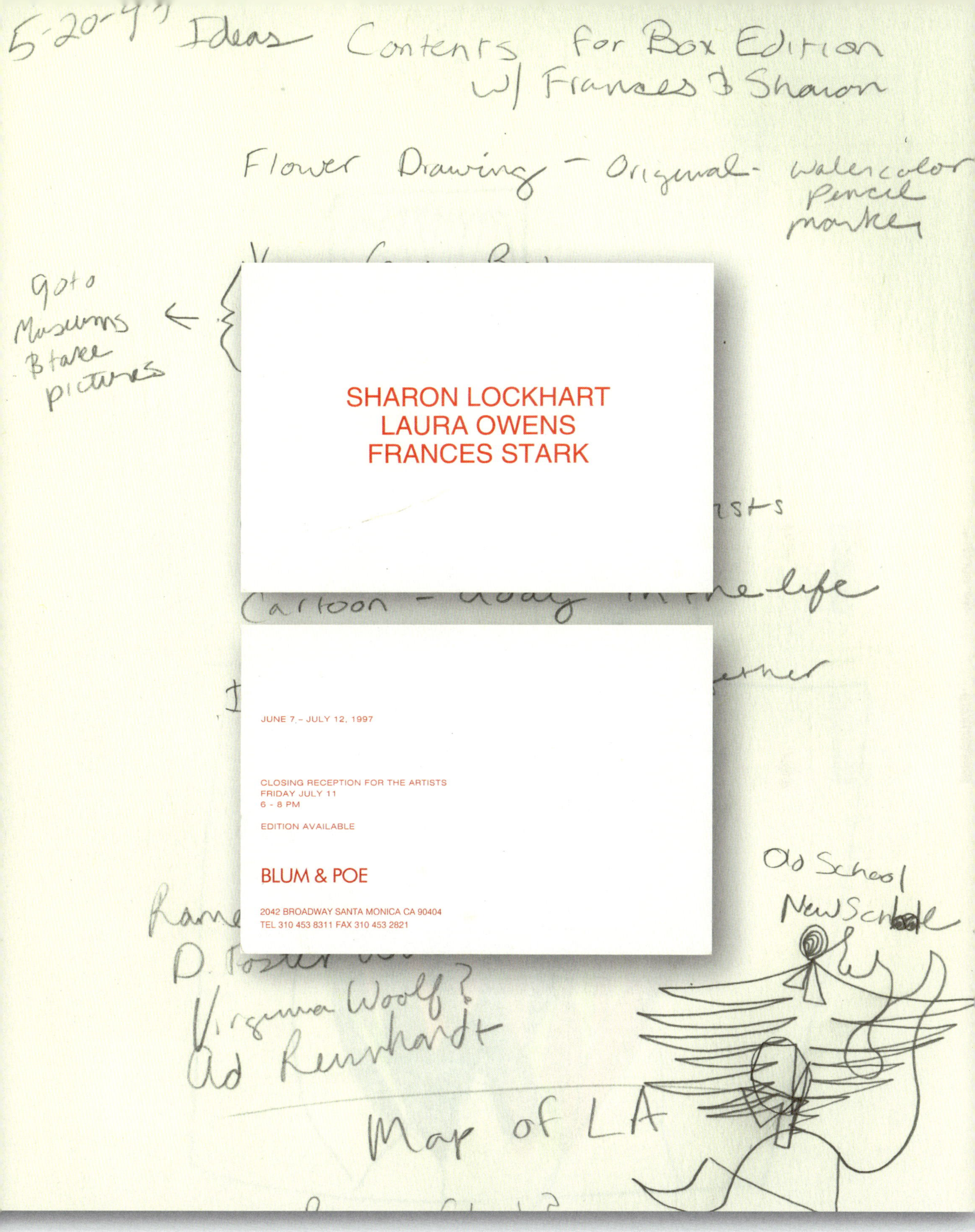

Foreground: Invitation, *Sharon Lockhart, Laura Owens and Frances Stark,* Blum & Poe, Santa Monica, 1997
Background: Sketchbook page, 1997

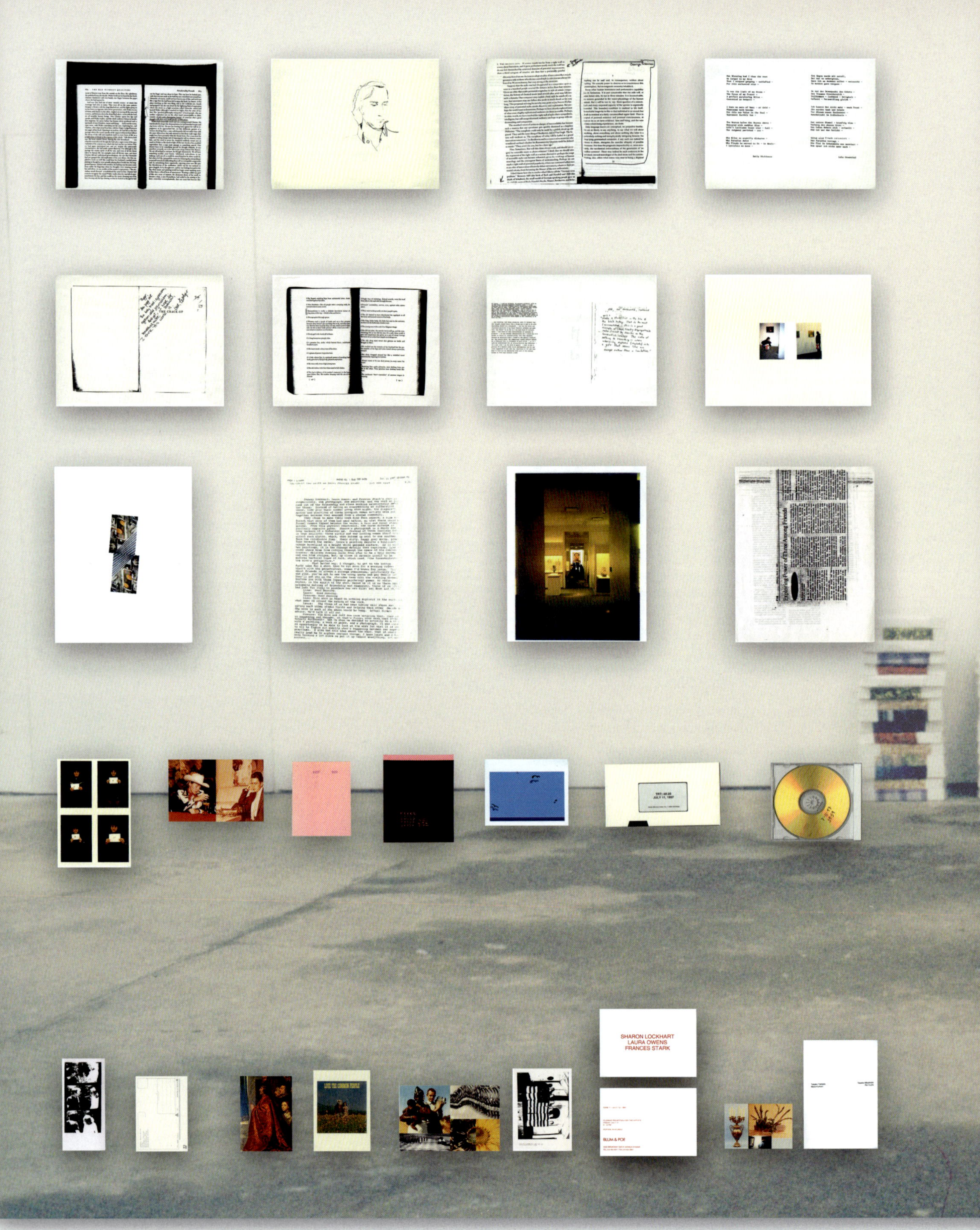

Foreground: Sharon Lockhart, Owens, and Frances Stark, contents, *Box Edition*, 1997
144 Background: Installation view, *Sharon Lockhart, Laura Owens and Frances Stark*, Blum & Poe, Santa Monica, 1997

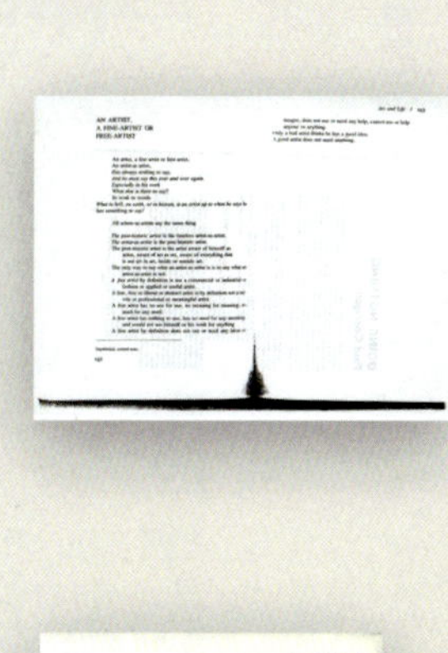
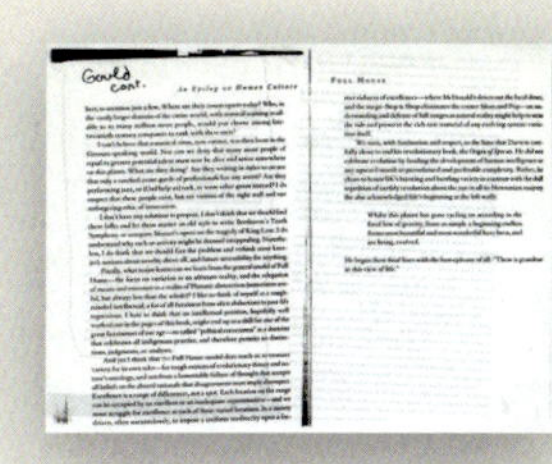
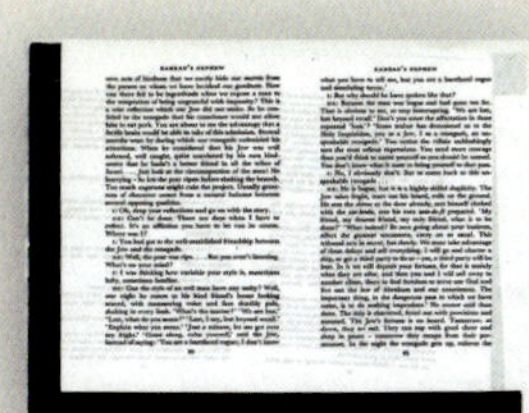
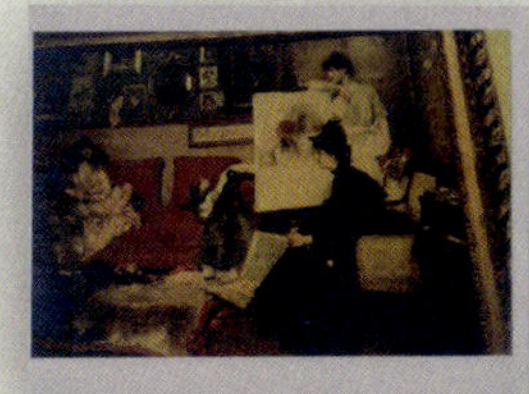
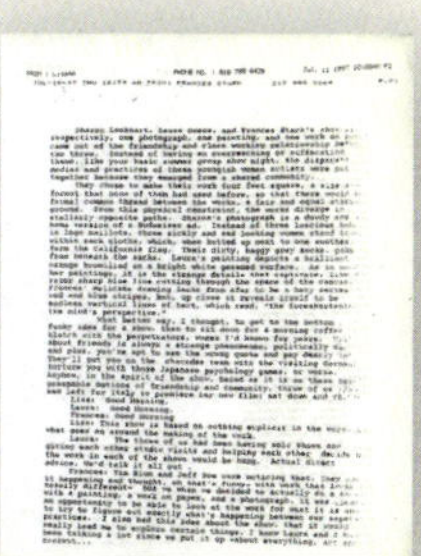
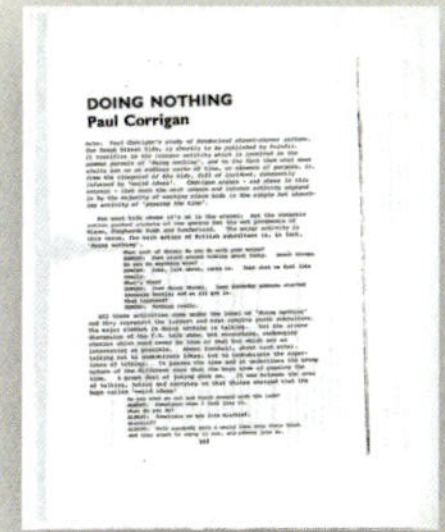
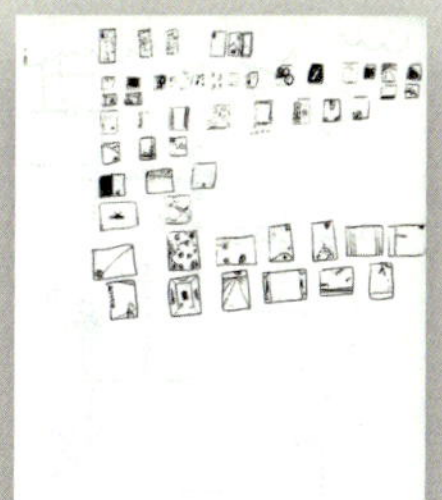
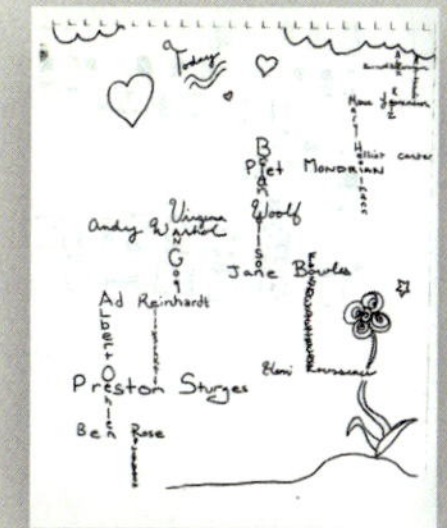
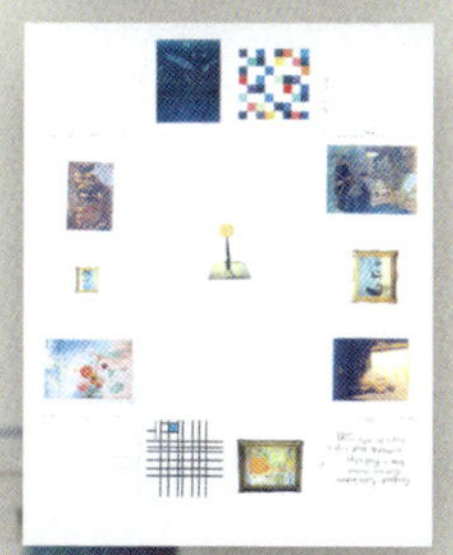
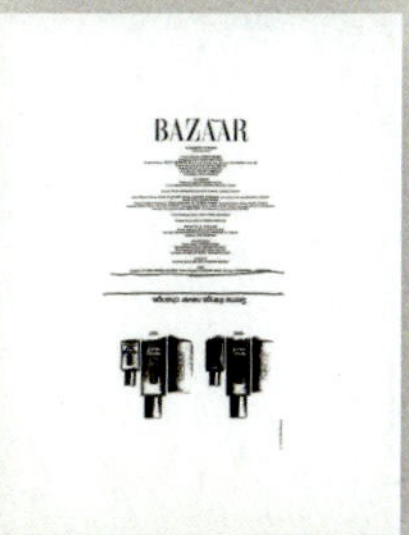
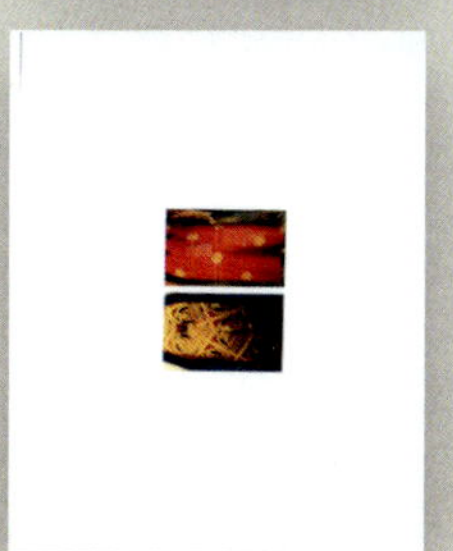
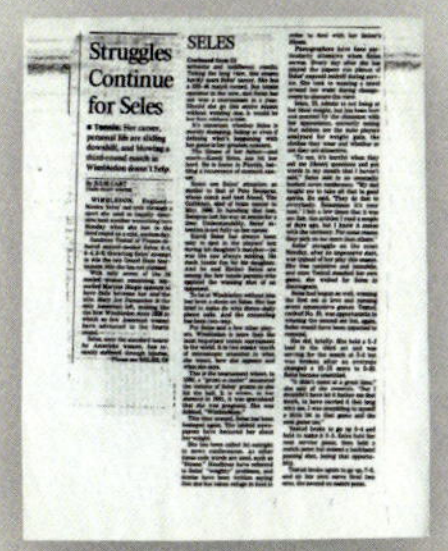
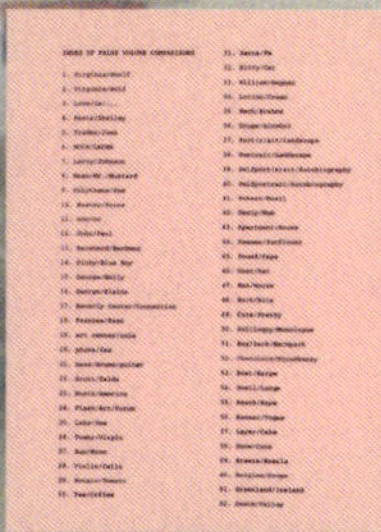
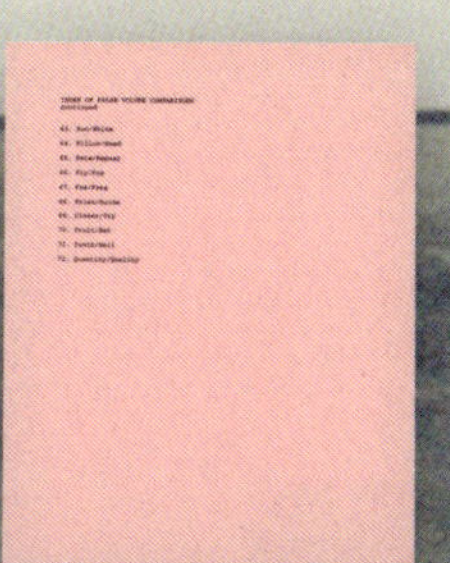
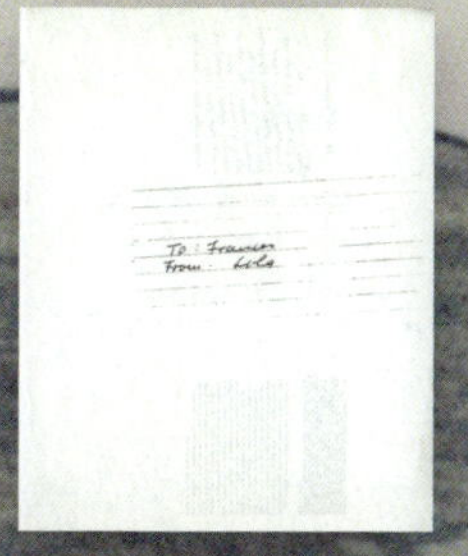
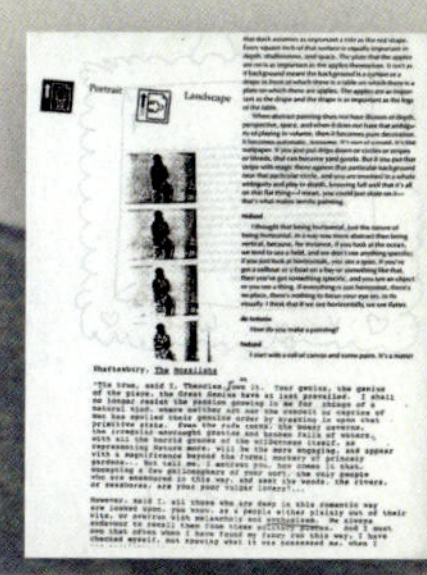
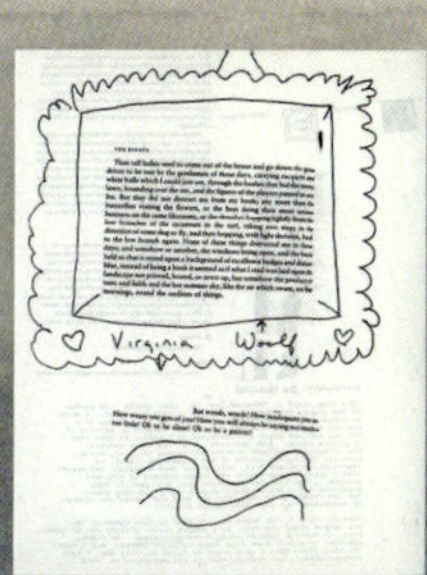
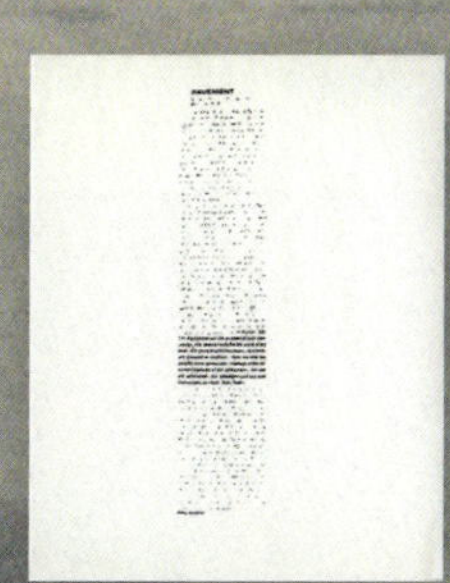

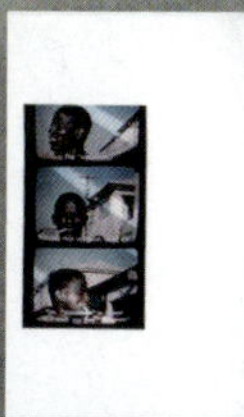

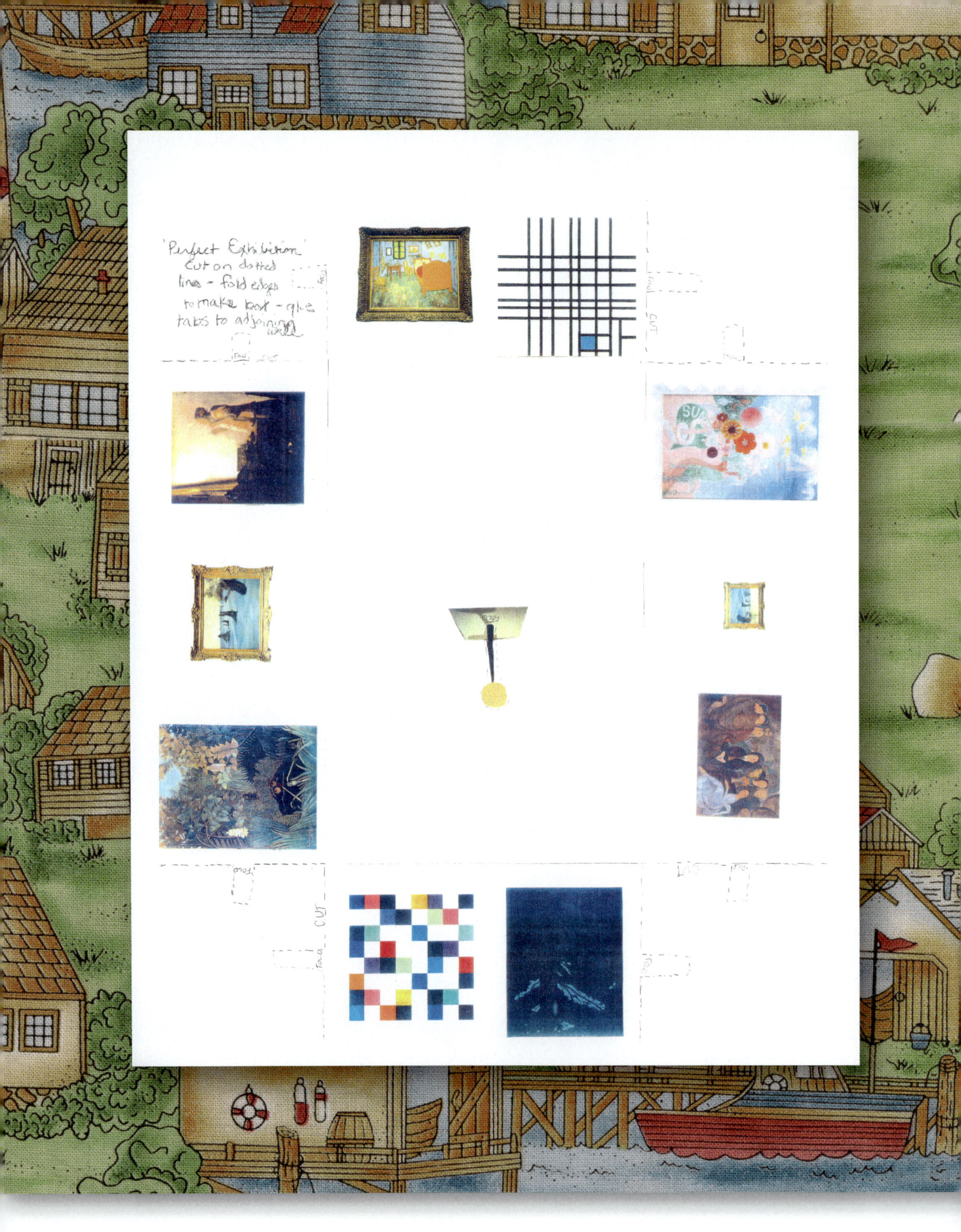

Foreground: Sharon Lockhart, Owens, and Frances Stark, photocopy, *Box Edition*, 1997
Background: Sharon Lockhart, Owens, and Frances Stark, sleeve fabric, *Box Edition*, 1997

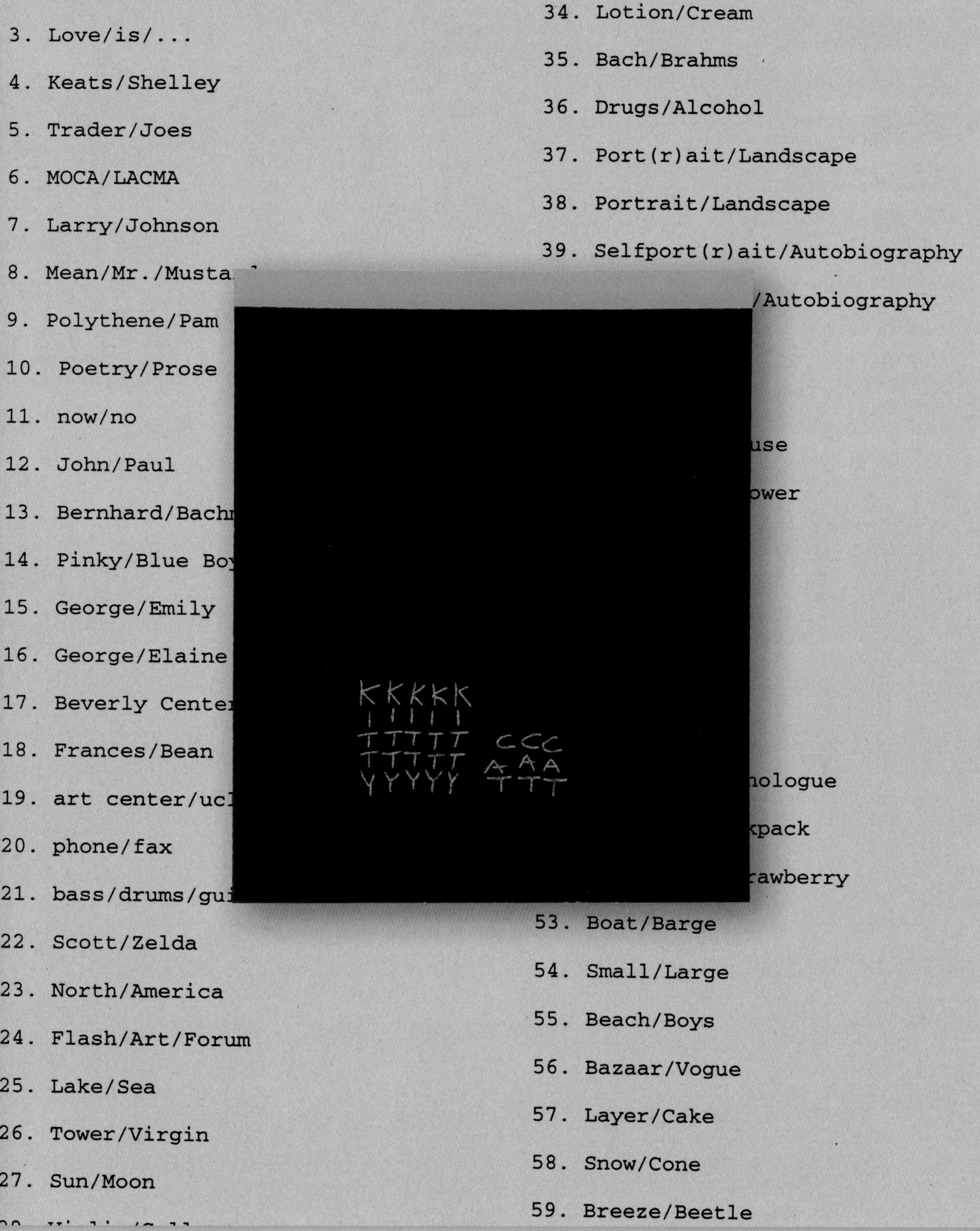

2. Virginia/Wolf

3. Love/is/...

4. Keats/Shelley

5. Trader/Joes

6. MOCA/LACMA

7. Larry/Johnson

8. Mean/Mr./Musta...

9. Polythene/Pam

10. Poetry/Prose

11. now/no

12. John/Paul

13. Bernhard/Bach...

14. Pinky/Blue Bo...

15. George/Emily

16. George/Elaine

17. Beverly Center

18. Frances/Bean

19. art center/ucl...

20. phone/fax

21. bass/drums/gui...

22. Scott/Zelda

23. North/America

24. Flash/Art/Forum

25. Lake/Sea

26. Tower/Virgin

27. Sun/Moon

34. Lotion/Cream

35. Bach/Brahms

36. Drugs/Alcohol

37. Port(r)ait/Landscape

38. Portrait/Landscape

39. Selfport(r)ait/Autobiography

.../Autobiography

...use

...ower

...nologue

...kpack

...rawberry

53. Boat/Barge

54. Small/Large

55. Beach/Boys

56. Bazaar/Vogue

57. Layer/Cake

58. Snow/Cone

59. Breeze/Beetle

Foreground: Sharon Lockhart, Owens, and Frances Stark, carbon transfer paper, *Box Edition*, 1997
Background: Sharon Lockhart, Owens, and Frances Stark, printout, *Box Edition*, 1997

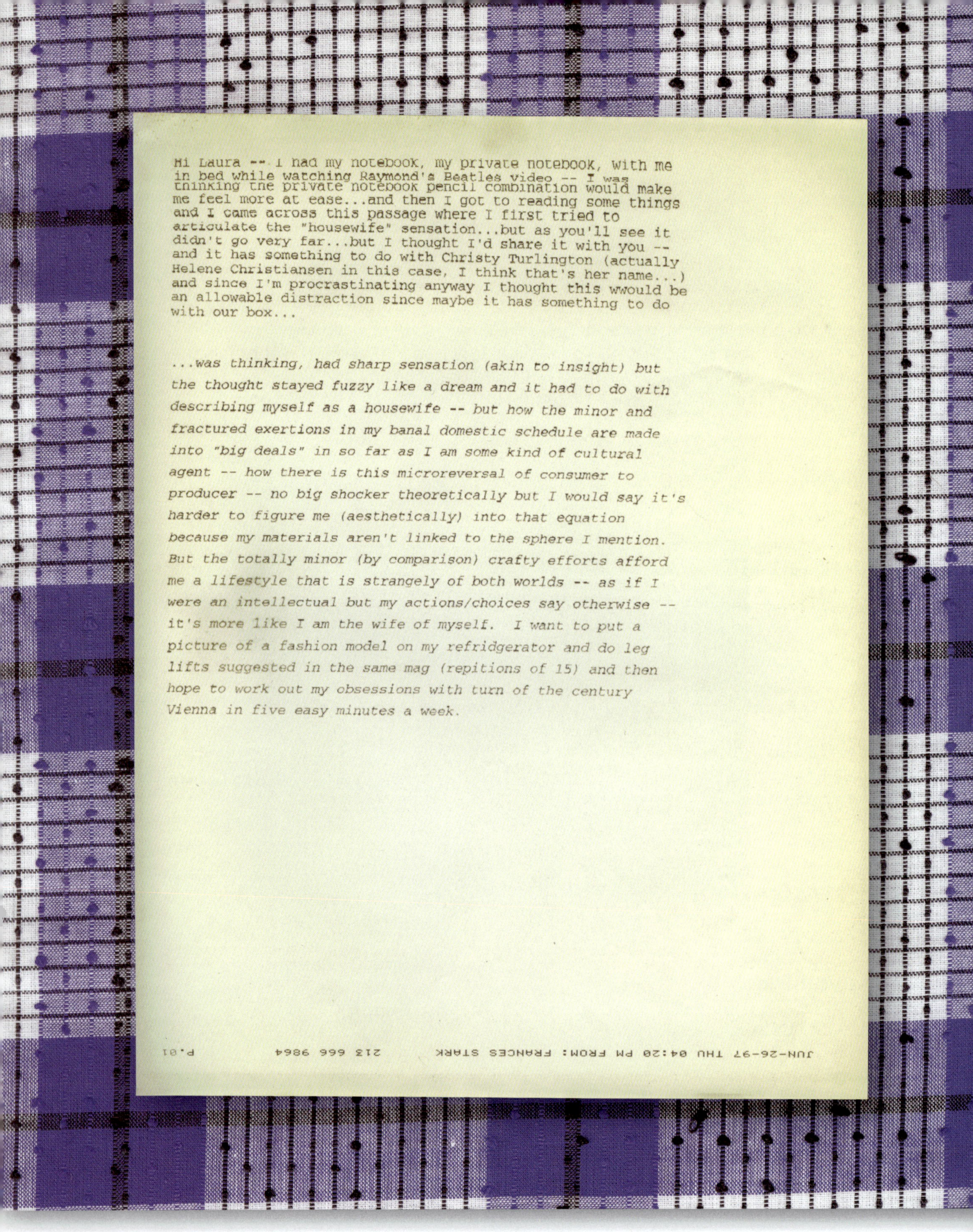

Hi Laura -- I had my notebook, my private notebook, with me
in bed while watching Raymond's Beatles video -- I was
thinking the private notebook pencil combination would make
me feel more at ease...and then I got to reading some things
and I came across this passage where I first tried to
articulate the "housewife" sensation...but as you'll see it
didn't go very far...but I thought I'd share it with you --
and it has something to do with Christy Turlington (actually
Helene Christiansen in this case, I think that's her name...)
and since I'm procrastinating anyway I thought this wwould be
an allowable distraction since maybe it has something to do
with our box...

...was thinking, had sharp sensation (akin to insight) but
the thought stayed fuzzy like a dream and it had to do with
describing myself as a housewife -- but how the minor and
fractured exertions in my banal domestic schedule are made
into "big deals" in so far as I am some kind of cultural
agent -- how there is this microreversal of consumer to
producer -- no big shocker theoretically but I would say it's
harder to figure me (aesthetically) into that equation
because my materials aren't linked to the sphere I mention.
But the totally minor (by comparison) crafty efforts afford
me a lifestyle that is strangely of both worlds -- as if I
were an intellectual but my actions/choices say otherwise --
it's more like I am the wife of myself. I want to put a
picture of a fashion model on my refridgerator and do leg
lifts suggested in the same mag (repitions of 15) and then
hope to work out my obsessions with turn of the century
Vienna in five easy minutes a week.

Foreground: Fax from Frances Stark, 1997
 Background: Sharon Lockhart, Owens, and Frances Stark, sleeve fabric, *Box Edition*, 1997

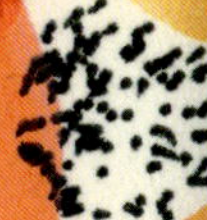

OH, ON HOUSEWIFE, continued

april 7
"Made a short list in the line @
the bank today. That is the most
I accomplished... this is a good
example of that Freaky disproportionate
ratio I want to describe in the
housewifish analogy. The ratio of
Nothing to something — when
interiority explodes (implodes) into
a gift that seems like an
escape rather than a limitation."

Foreground: Fax from Frances Stark, 1997
Background: Sharon Lockhart, Owens, and Frances Stark, watercolor, *Box Edition*, 1997

Nov 7

Dear Tim and Jeff,

        I am very sorry that we had to have a confusing and upsetting
conversation in my studio today.   I realize we have had very
different impressions about our relationship.   I am very grateful to
you guys for bringing Dean Valentine to my studio.   I also really
enjoyed doing the group show and working on the multiple together.
When I talked to you during the show to tell you my plans about
working on a show on my own in L.A. I did not mean to say I want
Blum and Poe to represent my work. I am sorry that that is what you
heard. I realize I have been way too ambiguous and that is because I
was unsure of how or who I want to work with in L.A.   At the time of
our conversation I did have an idea for a site specific show and I
wanted to throw that at you to see what your thoughts were.   At that
time I realized you did want to work with me and that you did want to
support the show and/ or sell the work.   I left that conversation
thinking I would do some footwork and work out my ideas and see what
happens. I do not recall saying I want to work with Blum and Poe in
L.A. or that I would do a show in your gallery at some time in the
future. For me I was still thinking about my position in L.A.,
unfortunately my ambiguousness has lead to much misunderstanding.
Recently I have decided to have Gavin represent my work, anyone I
work with will have to respect this decision.
Our conversation this morning was very inappropriate and has made me
very uncomfortable.   At this time I do not wish to work with your
gallery.   I do not wish to burn bridges or blow things out of
proportion either. I hope you can respect my decisions.

Best,
Laura

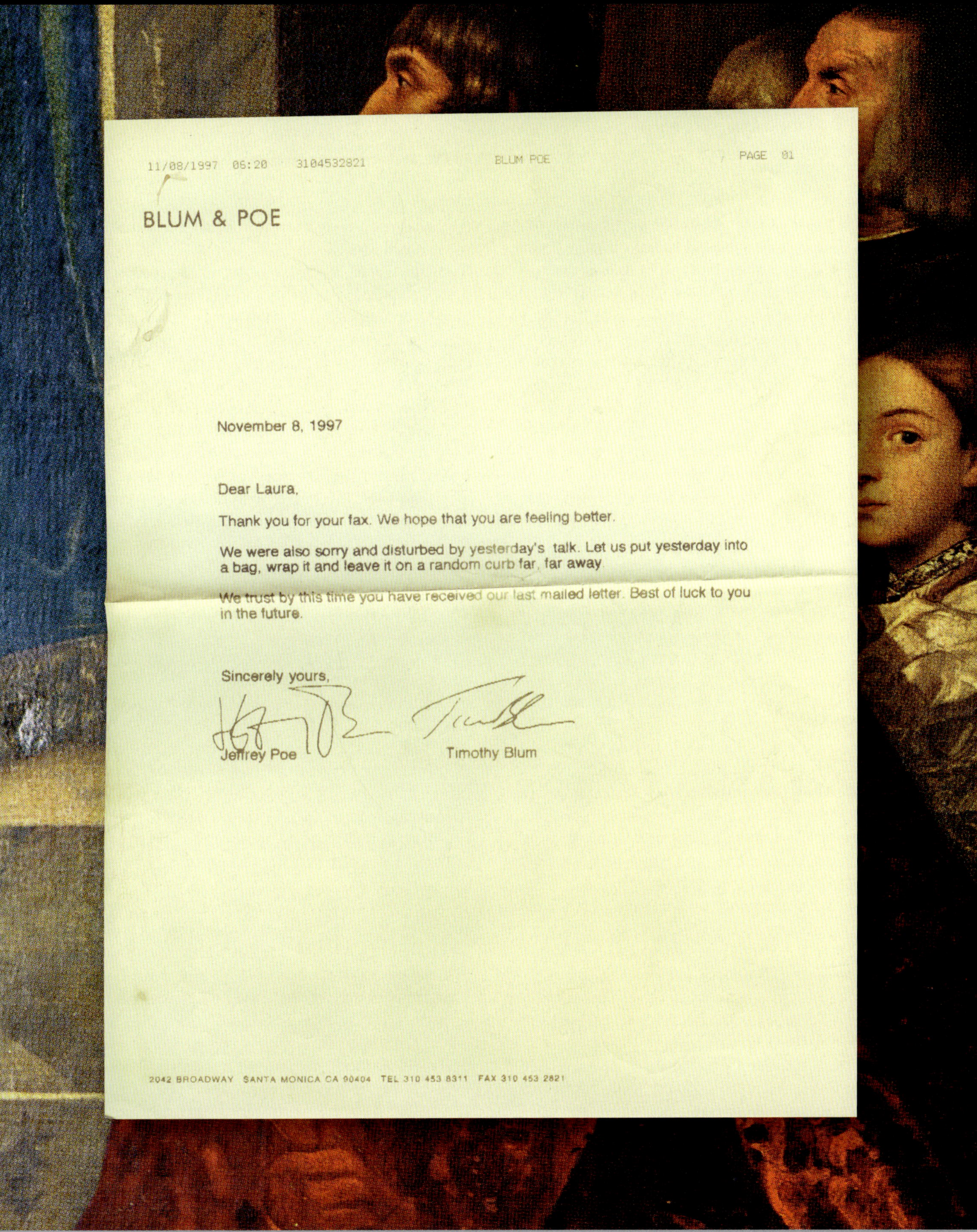

Foreground: Fax from Jeffrey Poe and Timothy Blum, 1997
Background: Sharon Lockhart, Owens, and Frances Stark, postcard, *Box Edition*, 1997

FLAG GIRL
JENNY JASKEY

It's no small feat to will oneself an artist. Part of claiming that title as a young woman these days is putting everything on the line. You scrape together enough cash to get a studio, pay off your student loans (tuition at the top ten MFA programs now averages $38,000 per year), and haul your belongings to a city where there are enough artists around to have both antagonism and admiration built into the scene. Especially in these tender years, maybe the biggest challenge— and the greatest fun—of becoming an artist lies in finding one's peers. Every generation has to make the terms of debate their own, and defining what questions are urgent enough to be worth asking is never separate from the music you're listening to, the drugs you're on, the childhood movies you remember, the politician you did or didn't vote for, or what national trauma's got everyone exercised. When the artistic will is tested and the questions come into focus, it's not only book learning but also a life (and a practice) with peers that makes the work. That may be why we make so much of an artist's early career. The urgency of things— of establishing artistic identity and ensuring survival—is most palpable in those years.

Laura Owens completed her MFA at California Institute of the Arts (CalArts) in Valencia, California, in 1994, a year after her fellow artists Sharon Lockhart and Frances Stark graduated from ArtCenter College of Design in nearby Pasadena. After meeting as students, the three women began getting together regularly at their studios. They belonged to a set of young LA artists—including Jorge Pardo and Jason Rhoades—for whom the social context of making and exhibiting art was particularly important. Sometimes those dynamics were explicitly incorporated in the material or logic of a given piece, sometimes not. Either way, they mattered to these artists. That art need not be located strictly within the confines of an obdurate object was, for them, becoming a given.[1]

This was the first bloom of a relationally oriented 1990s generation of artists. The dealers Tim Blum and Jeff Poe were starting their eponymous gallery in a small Santa Monica storefront. By spring 1996 they were representing Sharon Lockhart. It wasn't long before Blum & Poe proposed a group show with Lockhart and her two friends; the dealers hoped to make sense of the local scene at a time when a "movement"— defined by formal aesthetic congruity across art objects—otherwise seemed difficult to identify, not to mention undesirable.[2] As Frances Stark said in a joint interview with Owens around the opening of the show, Blum and Poe had observed the artists visiting each other's studios and offering one another advice: "They noticed and thought, 'Oh, that's funny,' since our work looks so totally different. . . . [The exhibition] became an opportunity to look at the work for what it is and to try to figure out exactly what's happening between our separate practices. I know Laura and I have been talking [about the show] since we put it up— about context."[3]

Titled simply *Sharon Lockhart, Laura Owens and Frances Stark*, the Blum & Poe exhibition billed itself as "an investigation into the nature of discourse and dialog among friends." It eschewed the typical group show format that thematized "obvious similarities between artists of a particular moment in time."[4] The result was an exhibition with only three works—one painting (Owens), one drawing (Stark), and one photograph (Lockhart)— whose only obvious commonality was their dimensions, an arbitrary 48 × 48 inches. Each piece took up one wall of the small gallery. Lockhart appropriated Arthur J. Telfer's photograph *Flag Girls, Cooperstown, NY* (1918), in which six teens pose on a stage, swaddled, pageant-queen-like, in sections of fabric that together make one large American flag. Lockhart's photograph was just as amateurish but oriented to the local context: in her photo, Lockhart, Stark, and Owens are each

    Jenny Jaskey is executive director and curator of the Artist's Institute, New York.

wrapped in a section of a DIY-style replica of the California state flag that has been fashioned from a sheet tenatively pinned with felt cutouts of its iconic red star and grizzly bear. The result was a feminist and California icon. Like the Cooperstown women, the artists stand at attention, heads in quarter-profile. They share the self-serious expressions of Telfer's subjects, yet their white socks peek out from beneath the drapery, a subtle touch that gives the image an airy, casual quality, as of the art studio. From Owens there was a painting of an engorged flower bud whose electric-pink and orange petals protrude from a too-slim bough: globby leaves of green and yellow paint top the branch, giving dimensionality to the canvas while casting small shadows on its bright-white background. And finally, there was a subtle contribution from Stark: an unframed drawing on paper that from far away looks like an exercise in exaggeratedly deliberate line drawing à la Agnes Martin. Look closer and you can see the phrase "a foreshortening of the mind's perspective" handwritten over and over again vertically, so that it can be read both down and across the piece as a double acrostic.

It would be difficult to find many obvious correspondences between these three works without jumping through some serious mental hoops. This must be what led more than one critic to call the exhibition "cryptic."[5] But the fact that the works *didn't* obviously relate to one another was the artists' point. Their goal was for the show to celebrate friendship and dialogue, not sameness. Their conversation materialized in an edition of forty-eight glossy white cardboard boxes produced over the show's run and exhibited at its closing

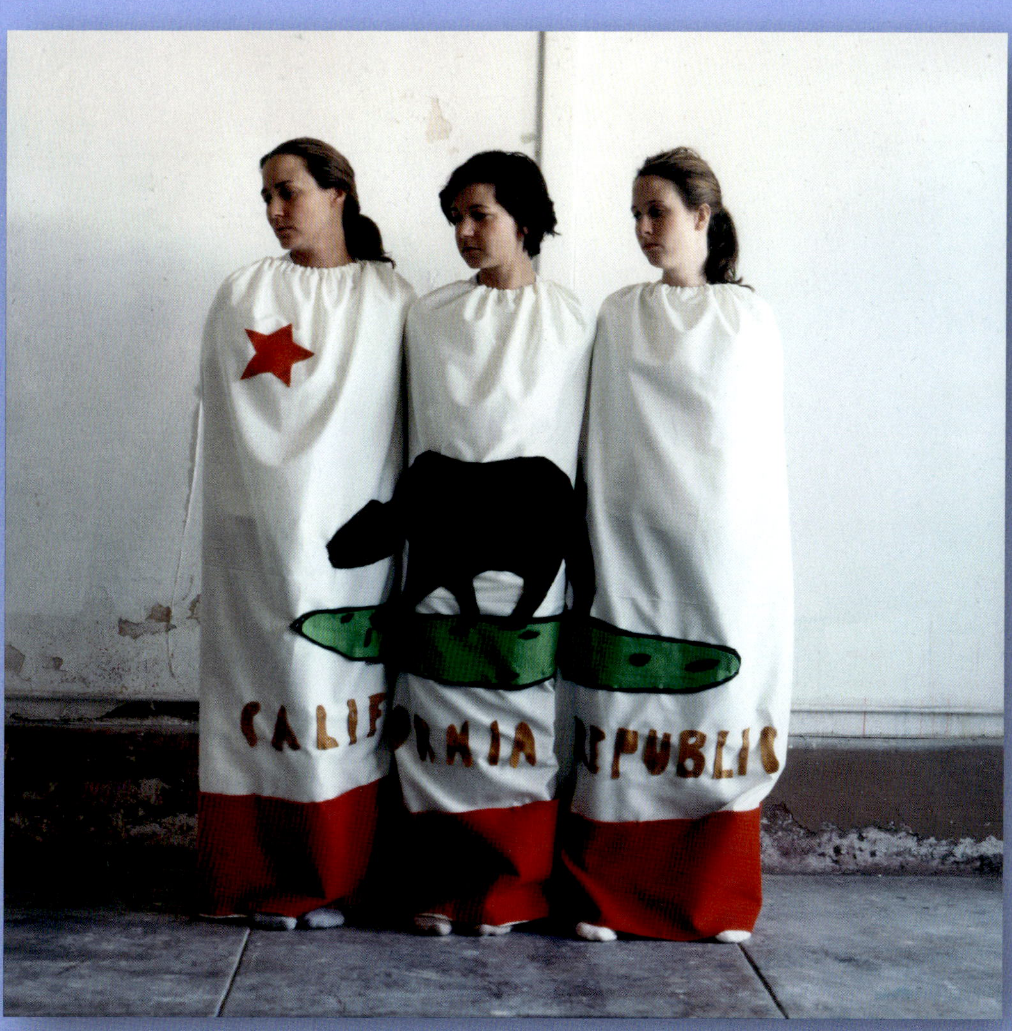

Sharon Lockhart, *Untitled*, 1997, chromogenic print, 48 × 48 in. (121.9 × 121.9 cm)

reception. Bound in a variety of colorful patterned fabrics, the boxes made you feel a bit like you'd opened up a desk drawer from grad school days: here were a heap of photocopies of articles and studio notes, art postcards and personal photographs, and even a CD–ROM and VHS cassette featuring sequences of favorite music and video clips.[6] In one photocopy, someone had drawn Scrabble-like, interlocking arrangements of painters' names—Albert Oehlen, Preston Sturges, Ad Reinhardt, Ellsworth Kelly, Ben Rose, and Roy Lichtenstein—surrounded by doodles of hearts, clouds, and a flower. (True to the collaborative spirit of the women's dialogue, no authorship was attributed to these pages, but one suspects Laura's hand. Her Scrabble obsession is well documented.) Then there were photocopies of underlined passages from books (F. Scott Fitzgerald's *The Crack-Up*; Denis Diderot's *Rameau's Nephew*; Robert Musil's *The Man Without Qualities*; Stephen

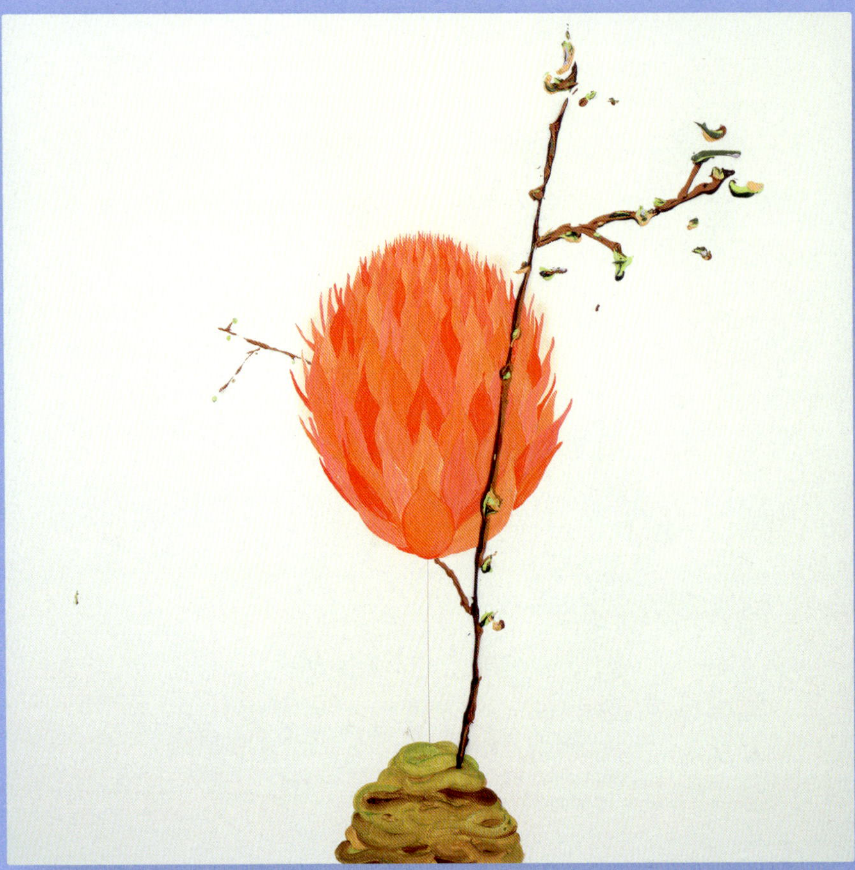

Untitled, 1997, acrylic on canvas, 48 × 48 in. (121.9 × 121.9 cm)

Lockhart's photographs and films only become possible through years-long relationships with her subjects; Stark has infused her day-to-day process with a hands-on pedagogical mission; and when Owens wanted to show new paintings in Los Angeles after a decade-long hiatus from exhibiting locally, she founded the art space 356 Mission. This enabled her *Twelve Paintings* to sit within a framework of other exhibitions and events that invigorated them, whether or not the works thematically related.

A few weeks after the exhibition at Blum & Poe opened, Owens remarked: "I would hope that curators might look at it and think, 'Okay, I'm going to have a show that totally falls apart. . . .'" Sometimes falling apart is the surest way for women to get it together.

Jay Gould's *Full House: The Spread of Excellence from Plato to Darwin*, to name a few). And in a rather arty-recursive move, the women also included materials related to the exhibition: the Blum & Poe invitation card; copies of the show's reviews in the *Los Angeles Times* and *LA Weekly*; and even photos of the boxes themselves, stacked up in the gallery.

Perhaps surprisingly for a group of artists interested in dialogue, there was nary a gallery panel discussion, document-lined vitrine, or theory-heavy press release in sight. Nor were there artworks explicitly making "the social" their primary form or content. Instead, the women's relationships and discussions appear as traces, hidden away in boxes as cheap copies, a CD mix, and film clips that operated as means to the art rather than its ends.[7] This non-instrumental attitude toward personal relations—with its emphasis on relationships but not *relational aesthetics*, sociality but not *social practice*—is an ethos that, for all three artists, has held steady throughout the past two decades. In fact, it's rare to read a text on any of the three now without finding at least a passing mention of these "extracurricular" pursuits.

Notes

1 The exhibition *Public Offerings*, curated by Paul Schimmel at the Museum of Contemporary Art, Los Angeles, in 2001, addressed the relational dimension of this generation of LA artists directly. As artist and critic Lane Relyea writes in his essay for the catalogue that accompanied the show: "For [Jorge] Pardo and most of the other LA artists in this exhibition, the real isn't manifested in any single, inscrutable material object. . . . Rather it inheres in strings of relationships, in the tenuous and intimate connections that make up an artist's scene or the ecology of his or her practice, in the interlocking and occasional slippage of components within those systems, and in their dense circulation of information (of objects, people, money, press camaraderie, gossip)." See Lane Relyea, "LA–Based and Superstructure," in *Public Offerings*, ed. Paul Schimmel, exh. cat. (Los Angeles: Museum of Contemporary Art, 2001), 255.

2 In her review of the Blum & Poe exhibition Susan Kandel writes, "It's (usually) a suicide mission to group of-the-moment-artists under the pretext of a theme." See "Exploring the Power of Three Among Friends," *Los Angeles Times,* July 4, 1997. Similarly, in *LA Weekly* Lisa Anne Auerbach notes: "Whether or not the show comes together as a cohesive statement is immaterial to the artists, who feel that implicit connections between artworks that come from a shared sense of community are ultimately more important than thematic associations." See "Sharon Lockhart, Laura Owens and Frances Stark at Blum & Poe," *LA Weekly,* June 27–July 3, 1997, 57.

3 Auerbach, "Sharon Lockhart, Laura Owens and Frances Stark at Blum & Poe," 57.

4 "Sharon Lockhart, Laura Owens, and Frances Stark," press release, Blum & Poe Gallery, Santa Monica, June 7–July 12, 1997.

5 See, for example, Kandel, "Exploring the Power of Three Among Friends," 18.

6 Among the media included were clips from John Cassevetes's *Woman Under the Influence;* an odd cartoon whose theme song is "If I Can't be a Painter, I'll be a Millionaire"; and a shot of the ecstatic champion of the 1993 United States National Spelling Bee, who happens to resemble Owens in her lithe frame, blonde hair, and glasses.

7 Writing about Laura Owens's Los Angeles project space 356 Mission, Linda Norden observes: "Evidence of how Owens's ongoing, live exchanges factor into her paintings and their conceptualization is obviously a lot harder to track. But it's as interesting to follow what she's made of 356 S. Mission as it is to analyze a given painting, if only because it gives real insight into such things as her keen sense of location and place as inhabited space, and of the range of 'traces' people, not just painters, leave." Linda Norden, "Monkey Grammarian," in *Laura Owens* (New York: Rizzoli, 2015), 218.

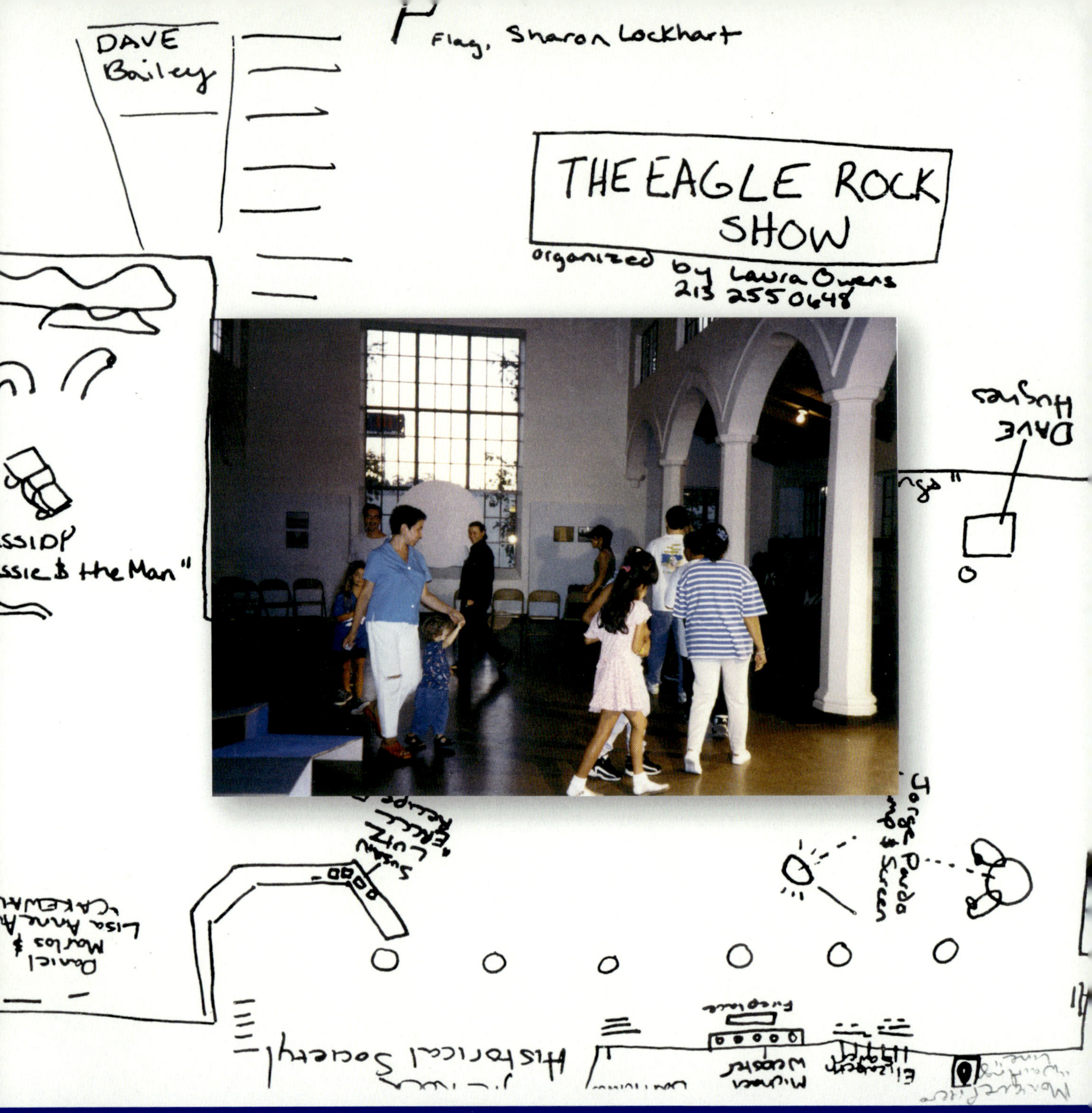

Foreground: Cakewalk, *The Eagle Rock Show*, Eagle Rock Community Cultural Center, Los Angeles, 1997
Background: Floor plan, *The Eagle Rock Show*, Eagle Rock Community Cultural Center, Los Angeles, 1997

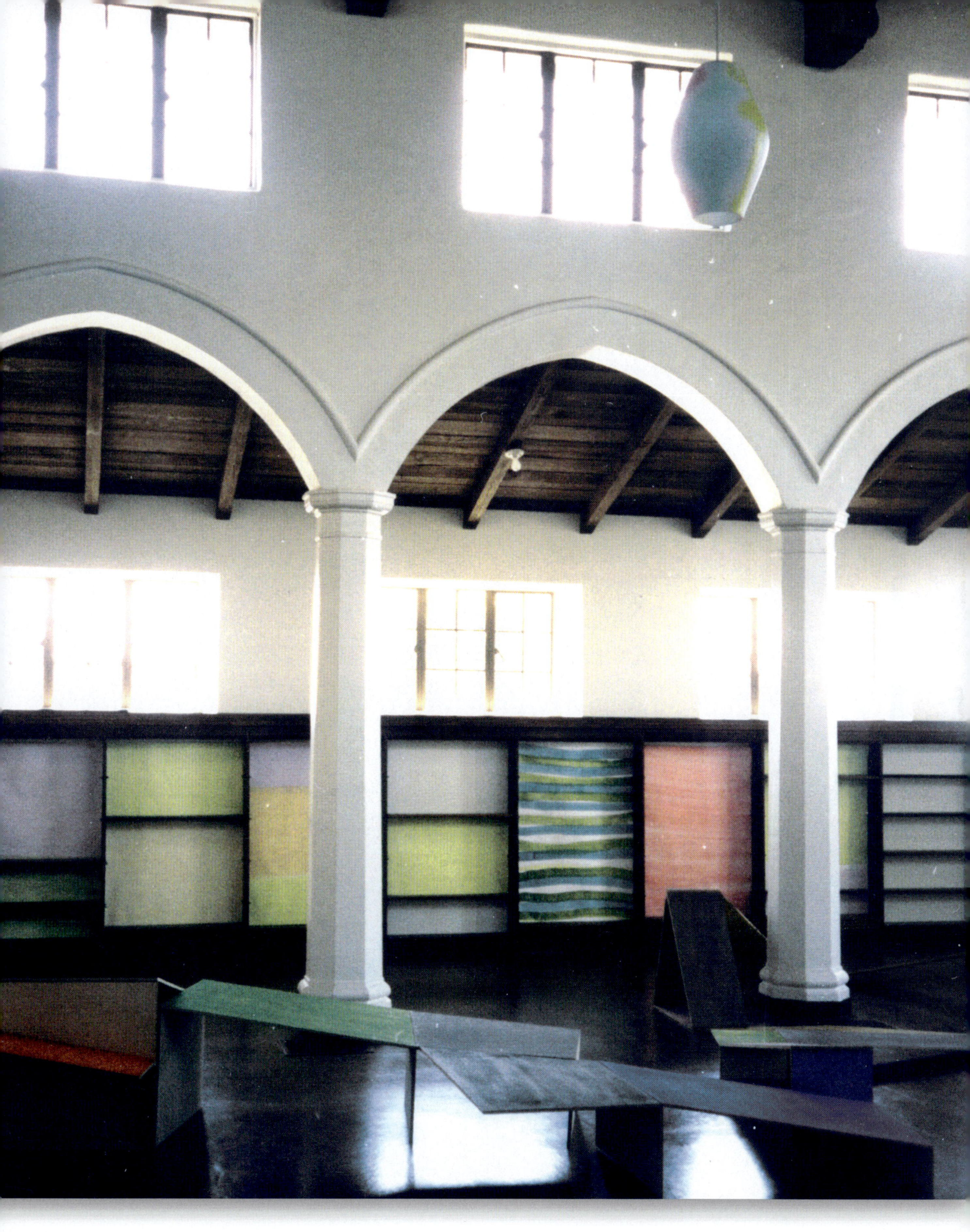

Foreground: Installation view, *The Eagle Rock Show*, Eagle Rock Community Cultural Center, Los Angeles, 1997, with *Untitled*, 1997, watercolor on paper, dimensions unknown; Alex Slade, *Ahistorical Walk through Eagle Rock*, 1997, acrylic on wood, dimensions unknown; and Jorge Pardo, *Untitled*, 1997, glass, electrical fixture, paint, 12 x 8 x 8 in. (30.5 x 20.3 x 20.3 cm)

Eric Palgon: It was my junior year at UCLA, which would have been 2003, and I took Laura's advanced painting class. I think there was a little bit of a buzz because she was so young; she was about thirty and pretty successful. On the first day of class she took us into a small room and played a Pavement song on a boom box. She played that song "Stereo" . . . "Hey, listen to me, I'm on the stereo." She played it really loud, and she said, "Okay, some of you guys might know this song, but I want you to listen to it." She played it and people who knew the song laughed or whatever. And then she asked us, "How is this song a painting?" So we broke it down hierarchically, because that song, and a lot of Pavement songs, did this thing where the instruments seemed to do their own thing but also came together. In retrospect, that was an easy way to read her work too.

Maybe that same day, the first day of class, maybe even in that little room, she said this thing that I really remember. She said, "Everyone is going to try to tell you not to do it. Curators, art historians, galleries, collectors, they're all going to make you feel like you're doing something wrong. But you know what, if we all quit making art, they'd all be out of jobs." It was really Team Art. It was cool. It was a funny thing to say, but it was very empowering to hear someone who was having a lot of success saying that to students—I don't think she'd seen a single painting by any of us when she said that.

There was a core group of students at UCLA that were pretty ambitious and earnest. It was a great time, and Laura's energy seized on that moment. We had one exchange I remember. I was making these drawings on mat board, and one of them that I thought was really good was in this massive stack of paintings that were kinda falling on top of each other. My drawing was in there somewhere, getting smooshed and dinged up. So as I'm working to get this

    Eric Palgon is a California-born, New York–based artist and a former student of Owens's.

drawing out from the pile, she's kind of shaking her head. When I finally get it out—I don't even think she looks at the drawing. She's just shaking her head and gives me that incredulous Laura look and says, "How can you expect me to look at this drawing when you don't even care about it?" The drawing was pretty beat up, but I still thought it was presentable. I told her, "I don't think better materials will make me a better artist." She stared at me and said, "Is that what you think?" That is what I thought. But I think she was right and I was probably only a little bit right.

I don't think Laura has a dogma or an approach. She has certain things she likes to say, like, "Everyone is a folk artist." She was pushing that for a long time. She's a motivator, she's a big supporter, she's very Team Art. And I'm not saying that she's soft. When she comes into the studio she has really good insight. I just wouldn't say it's dogmatic. When I was in my twenties I got into "bad painting" and started saying to a lot of people that I thought making "good" art was a stupid mandate. Like why can't people make C art? Why does everything have to be an A? Or why can't people do minor projects instead of major projects? I don't think Laura would have said the same things in the same way, but she presented a good example of following your interests, whatever they are, with her early paintings. Embracing kitsch images or children's illustration . . . her follow-through was incredible. It's not that she chose children's illustration and then it's hokey, it's that she did it big and with total conviction. She paints through art history and samples from textiles and crafts . . . she sets an example of "do your interest." I remember when we first got our studios in my junior year she said, "Put up images of stuff you like. Just put up tons of stuff you like in your studio." That was her way of saying, "This is what's important." She's always trying to empower you.

September 29 1997

Laura Owens

Senior Seminar

Language surrounding works of art , whether it is anecdotal,
historical, or critical, occupies a space. This class will attempt to
look at and locate that space and relate it to the space that physical
objects occupy. How does the academic setting frame the way language
is formed around works of art? How does one institution or teacher
differ from another? How does the title of an art work relate to the
object? Looking at the space of 'critique' and the many methods will
hopefully allow us a somewha't open space within the classroom to look
at works of art and to listen to one another.

Requirements for the class.

1. One oral presentation on contemporary art around midsemester.
(Another handout will describe in detail)

2. Present your own work in an informal manner within class. (i.e.
ideas, works in progress and/or finished work)

3.End of semester slide presentation of finished work accompanied by a
more formal lecture and discussion.

4. Class participation in all discussions.

5. You can miss one or two classes, however a third absence will
result in an incomplete.

I will be planning at least one field trip and one visiting lecturer.
To be announced at a later date.

Choose one of these artists to do an oral presentation on—
write your name after the artists name:

Polly Apfelbaum________________________________
Bernard Frize__________________________________
Kaus Merkel____________________________________
Fiona Rae______________________________________
Lydia Dona
Carl
Fabi
Moir
Lari
Juan
Adri
Mari
Manu
Jona
Moni
Udom
Eliz
John
Sean
Albe
Mary
Beat
Luc

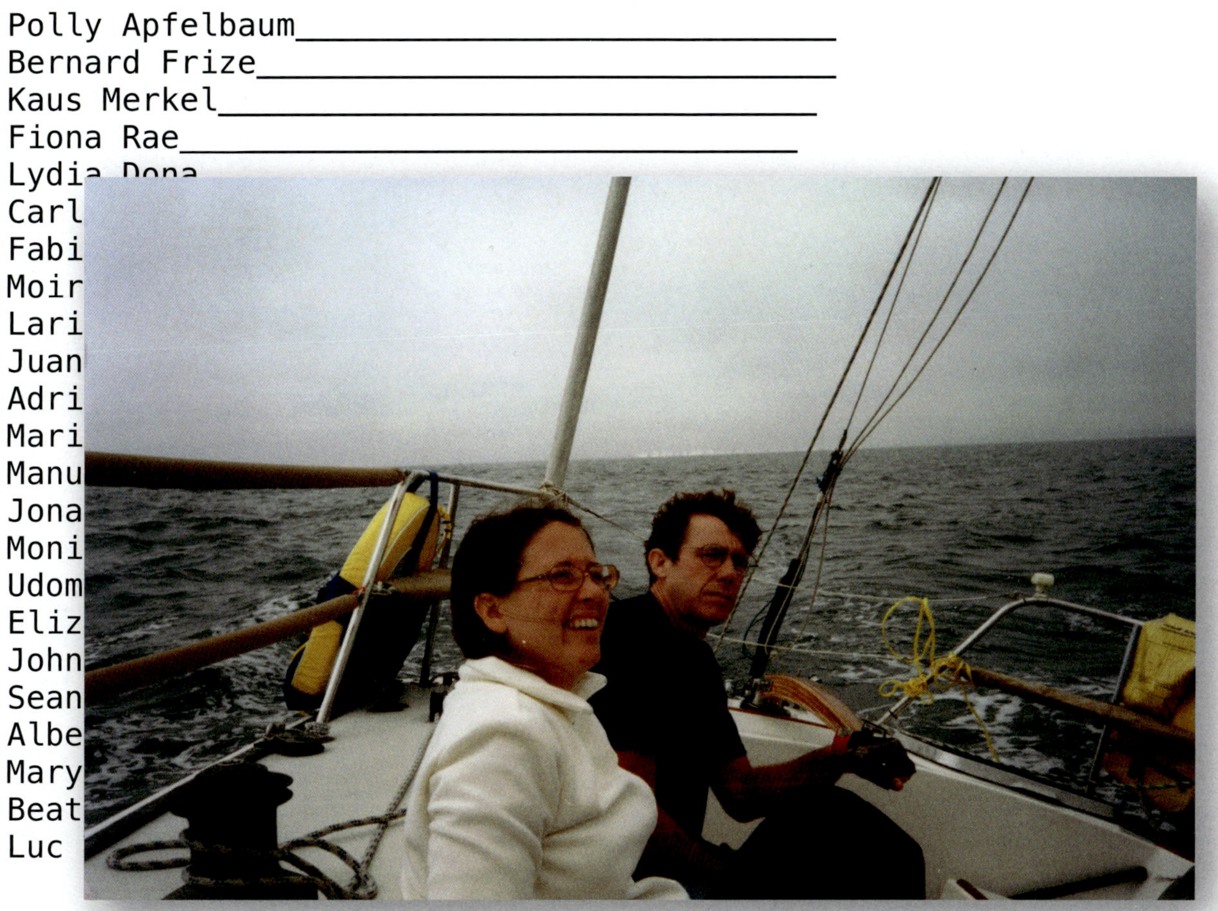

Foreground: Owens and Charles Ray, Southern California coast, ca. 2001
Background: Prompt for class assignment, University of California, Los Angeles, 1997

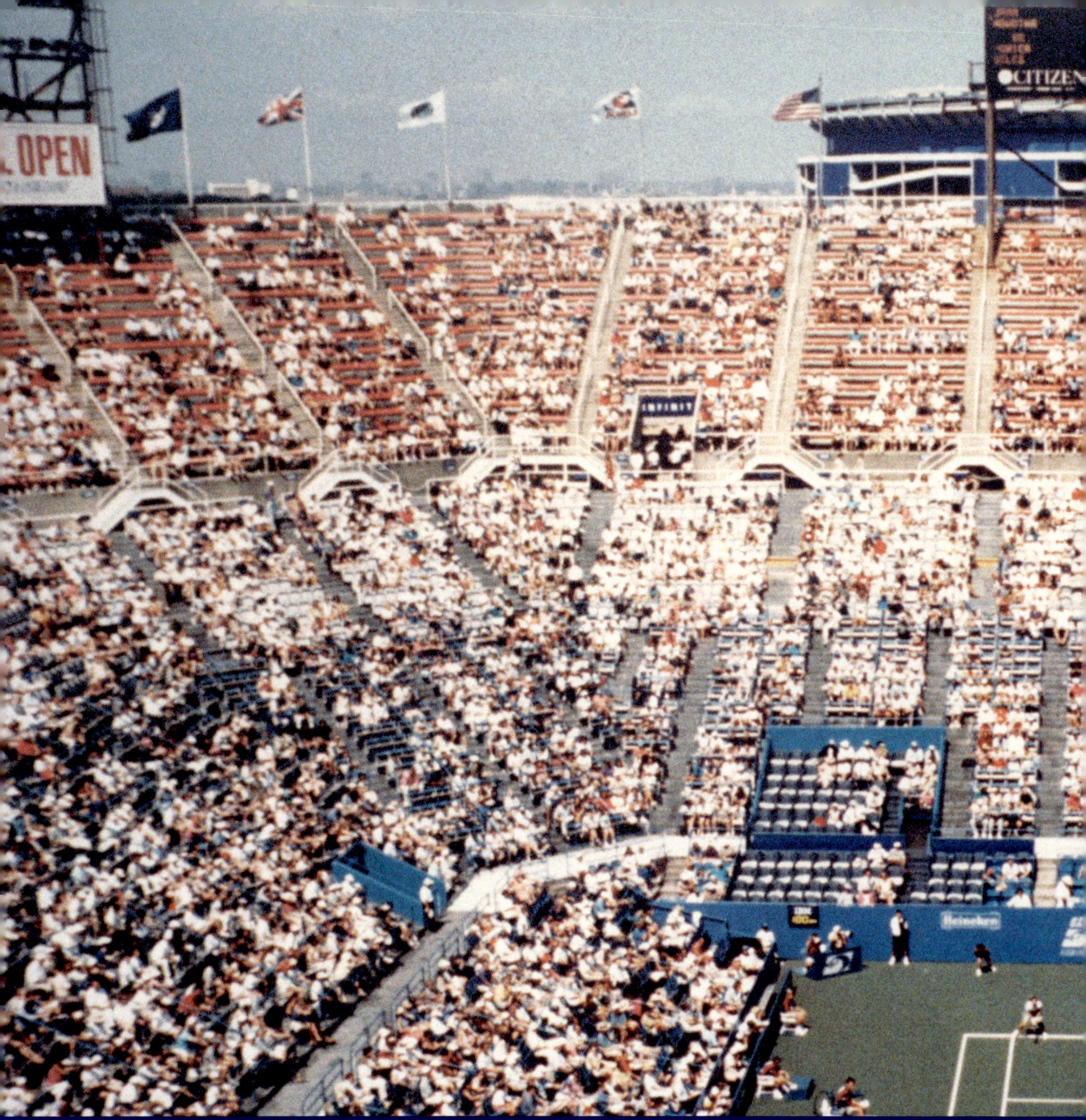

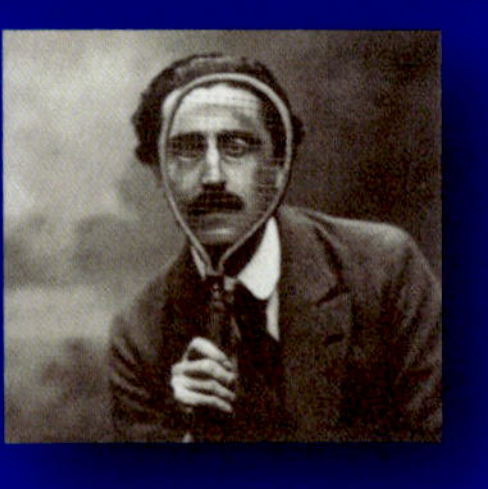

Laura Owens: When I was first asked to give lectures I often referred to images by Charles Schulz, ideas from Dada, and some quotes by Monica Seles—particularly ones where she referred to tennis as being her life but acknowledged that it was only a game. For me this attitude was similar to a kind of lightness I had learned from Mary Heilmann and her approach to being an artist, which emphasizes being serious about not being serious. Alex Slade knew I was a fan and gave me this photo of Seles playing at the US Open.

Foreground: Monica Seles quote in Julie Cart, "It's All Relative," *Los Angeles Times,* July 31, 1997
Background: Monica Seles on court at bottom, US Open, New York, 1995
Inset: Paul Dermée, originally published in *Dada 7: Dadaphone*, March 1920

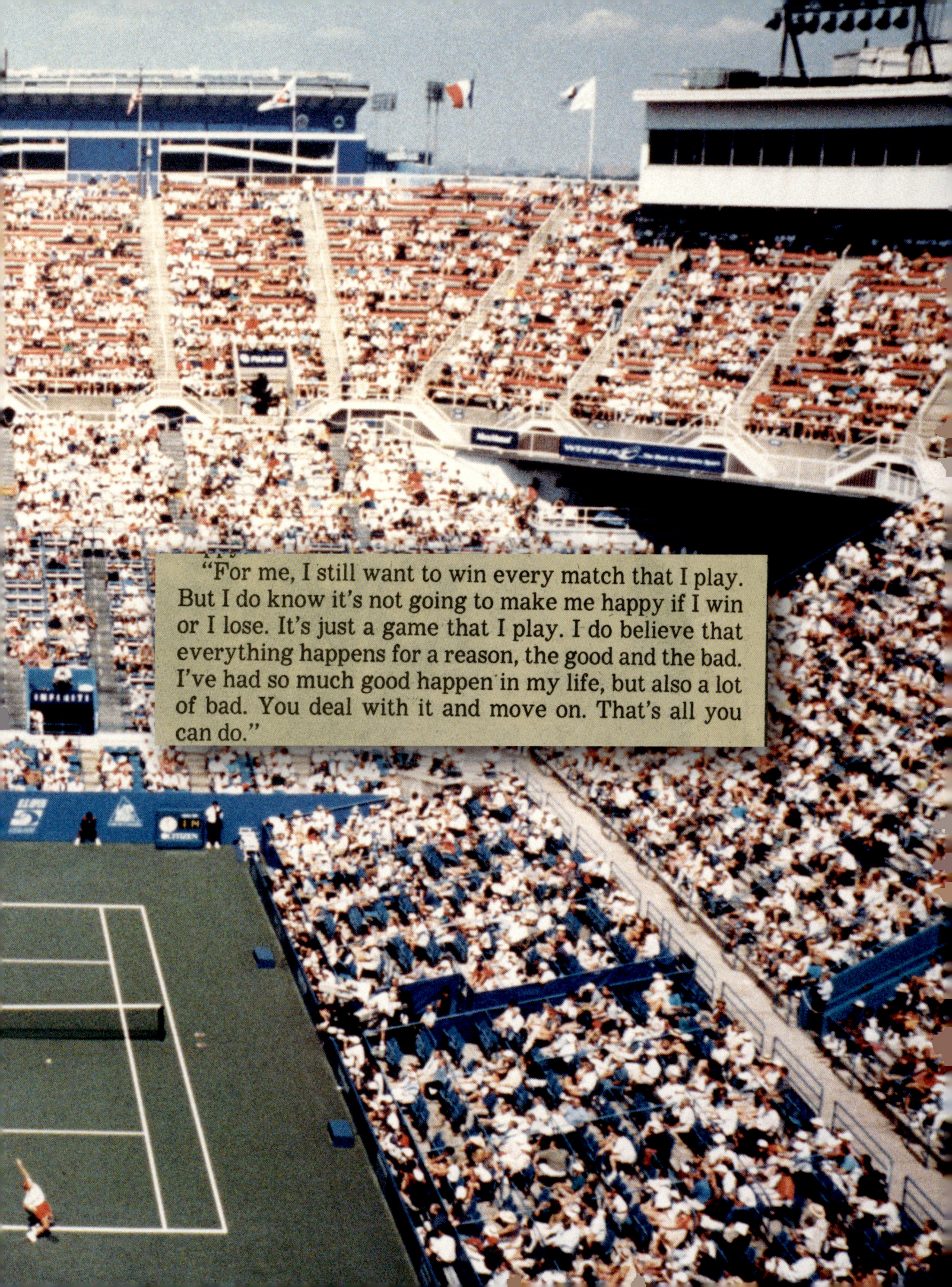

"For me, I still want to win every match that I play. But I do know it's not going to make me happy if I win or I lose. It's just a game that I play. I do believe that everything happens for a reason, the good and the bad. I've had so much good happen in my life, but also a lot of bad. You deal with it and move on. That's all you can do."

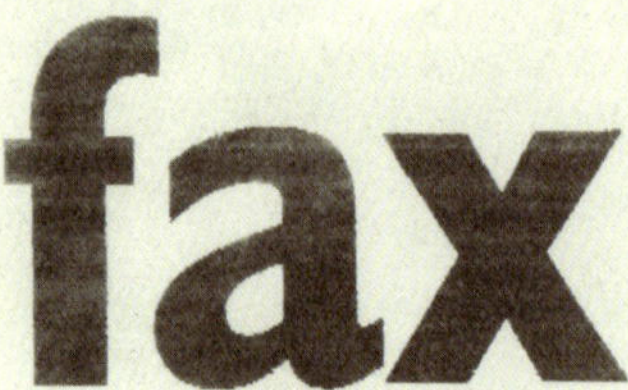

27/05/1997 14:55   +44-171-434-2228   SADIE COLES HQ   PAGE 01

To: Laura Owens

Fax: 001 213-255 0648

From: Sadie Coles

Date: 27 May 1997

Pages: 1 page(s) including this page.

Dear Laura,

I got to New York for one day to see the show. Gavin was kind enough to keep it up for an extra day so that I could see it and I was really amazed by the paintings. Having only seen one previously (at Artist's Space) it was wonderful to have my horizon (quite literally) broadened and questioned by the paintings in the exhibition. It was a real breath of fresh air, particularly for a European, something akin to seeing a different sense of space, colour and light when you experience a radically different landscape.

Gavin and I spoke about the possibility of inviting you to show here in London some time in the Fall. I realise you need to meet me in person and suggest that I will come to Los Angeles over the summer. Is that soon enough? It is a long summer here (what with Venice, Munster and Documenta) but from July it gets a bit more possible to make a long haul trip. It would, however, be good to know if you can commit in principle to the idea of an exhibition.

In the meantime I can give you more of an idea about the other people I am working with. The first exhibition in my space was new paintings by John Currin, the second new sculpture and photographs by the British artist Sarah Lucas. I organised a second, larger exhibition for Sarah in an empty building in London which complements the gallery show and is open at the same time. The third show is with Simon Periton, and I am hoping to do exhibitions with Keith Edmier, Elizabeth Peyton, Danny Oates, Don Brown, Nicola

Sadie Coles HQ

35 Heddon Street London W1R 3LL
Tel: 44 (0)171 434 2227
Fax: 44 (0)171 434 2228

Foreground: Fax from Sadie Coles, 1997
164 Background: Detail of *Untitled*, 1997 (see p. 172)

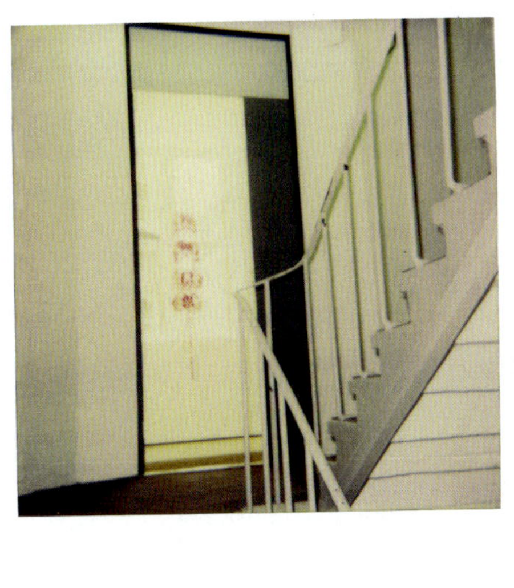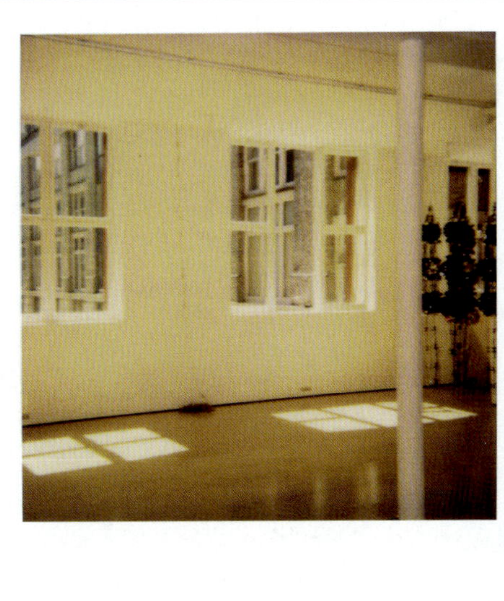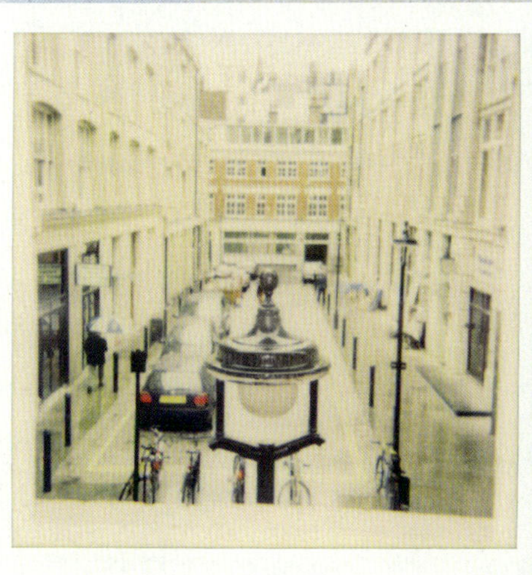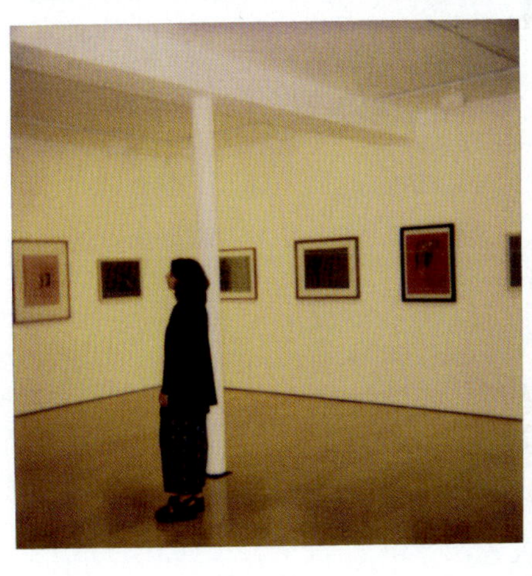

Foreground: Polaroids of Sadie Coles HQ, London, 1997

7-25-97

Sadie,

Got the package — I have
a lot of questions. I couldn't quite
tell. how a painting can clear turns
up the stairwell & into the gallery —
also into the office. I want to make
2 8'x10' horizontal ptngs & probably three
other medium (7x8 or 5x6' or 6'x7' or 3'x4') or
small ptngs — 1 - 8'X10' would go
on the back gallery wall — I am
thinking of casting a shadow of the pole
on that one — The other — [more tricky]
would go in the office? On the small 123"
wall — just fitting → If it doesn't clear
the turn — I might be able to cut that
one in 1/2 & bend it & reassemble — Is
there 9'x11' of floor space to reassemble?
Could you also take a picture looking
straight out the window → down the street I
assume. Also it would be helpful for scale
to see a person in the space. That's it for
now. On → could you tell me where North East West
South — is in the gallery. Thanks Laura Owens

Floor plan, Sadie Coles HQ, London, 1997

8/31/97

Dear Sadie,

I just spoke to the people at the " Highland Gardens" They have a room and are located in Hollywood. (pretty close to where I live)   The room is $60 a day for pleasure (business is more) I guess maybe don't fax your letterhead. I have not seen it but Petzel and the germans stay there and I am told there is a pool and its slightly kitschy hollywood but nice.   There are many options in making your plans. I am planning to pick you up at the airport and drive you around Wed., Thurs, Fri. however Friday at midnight I leave to go to maine. From that point on if you would like you are more than welcome to stay in my apartment in Eagle Rock and borrow my car or if you don't know how to drive you can hire an art student as driver for 75-100 per day. Or if you want to relax a little more we can move you to a hotel near the beach and spend the day walking around santa monica/beach area which is nice. I don't recommend staying in Hollywood and walking around.   I am trying hard to remember this really nice inexpensive hotel that Claudio Guenzani stays in at the beach.   I can probably find out in the next couple of days.

    Anyway I recommend at least Wed and thursday night staying at the Highland Gardens . You can fax Marie in Reservations with a Visa or Mastercard at 213 850 1712 or call 213 850 0536.   I am looking forward to meeting you. I will pick you up at the airport-- Perhaps its safest if I meet you outside the gate. I assume I will recognize you , but really have no idea what you look like.   I am nondescript, long brown hair, short .

    Again I am looking forward to meeting you and I really appreciate you coming out to L.A. to talk about the work and the show.
Best,

Laura Owens

Sadie Coles   HQ

35 Heddon Street London W1R 7LL England   T +44 [0] 171 434 2227   F +44 [0] 171 434 2228

attention

Laura Owens

at

001 213-255 0648

from

Sadie Coles

date/pages inclusive

1 September 1997

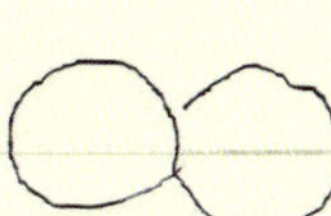

Dear Laura

You can't believe the commotion here over the *Princess Diana* tragedy.
I'm glad to be leaving. It is so hypocritical.

I have faxed Highland Gardens for 3-5 - it sounds absolutely fine.
Thank you for that suggestion. I too am looking forward to spending
time with you and am very grateful to you for offering to help me see
the sights (and particularly galleries etc). I cannot drive - at least not
until I get my license back.

One way to recognise me is to get this month's *Art and Auction*. There
is a picture of me that is pretty accurate - PLEASE DO NOT IMAGINE I
ACTUALLY SAID ANY OF THE QUOTED THINGS. It is a crummy bit
of journalism. Otherwise I am 5'7" with short dark hair and no
interesting bits. Do you want anything from England? Tea, marmite,
art stuff?

Best wishes

Sadie

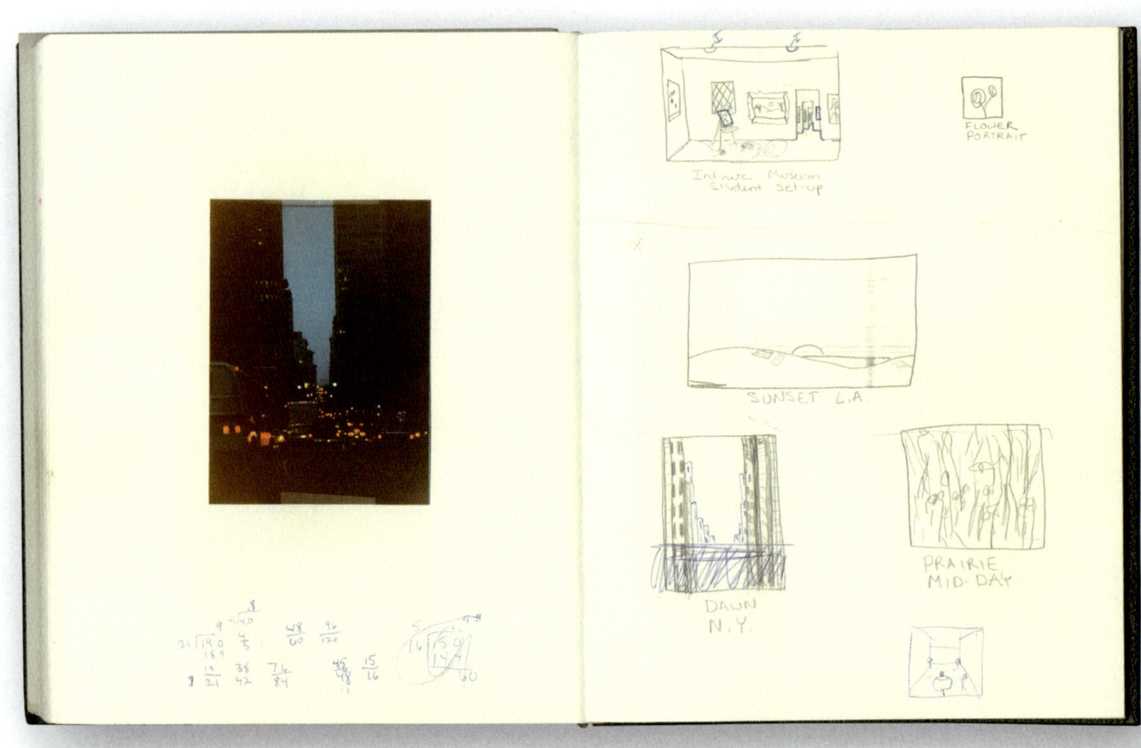

Laura Owens: I would usually start out on my studio couch with a sketchbook, making little rectangles and writing lists of words, ideas, or what I was thinking about. Inside the rectangles I would very quickly draw random ideas I had for paintings. In essence it's note-taking. So in this sketchbook I wrote something like, "What would be the hardest painting to make? A sunset painting, because it's a cliché." I was thinking about my trip to Sadie Coles in London and showing my art for the first time in a different country. Also about time and space and how to represent the space between the paintings. I wrote, "Dawn in New York, noon in the Midwest, and sunset in LA." Times of the day and stretches of land. It was a portrait of America, but also an organizing principle and a metaphor for types of light and space in between the work. Having these loose terms helped me make decisions and start painting. I was looking at a lot of Shaker quilts and folk art—that's in the bright, saturated colors. The shadow on the potted plant is definitely a high-noon shadow. Since I had never visited the gallery I asked Sadie to send pictures and a floor plan. I noticed there was a pole right in the center and opposite the largest wall was a bank of windows. I imagined that at sunset the pole would potentially cast a shadow, so I painted a trompe l'oeil one on the right two-thirds of the largest work, so the shadow determined the painting's off-center placement within the gallery.

Sadie Coles   **HQ**

LAURA OWENS

**Paintings
22 October-22 November 1997
private view Wed 22 Oct 6-8pm**

Viewing the paintings of Laura Owens is a happily engulfing experience. You are gently asked to consider, and re-consider, all possible angles in our wider periphery vision: inside/outside, upside down, open/closed, near/far. Her cool and detached constructions, where noisy questions about perspective, spatial definition, and representation ricochet across quiet canvases, have fun with our logical desire for a more scientific scrutiny.

One of the paintings in this exhibition is a view through the receding doorways of the central gallery of a museum. The physical space is economically mapped out in large, flat areas of colour with minimal detail. In each room, edges of paintings can be glimpsed (the jewels in this composition being where the eye would naturally concentrate), and only here is the paint intensively worked.

Zooming in and out of view is our relationship within and comprehension of the 2-D visual plane. Owens is unafraid to keep one eye on Barnett Newman and the other on David Hockney as she steers us on a well thought-out route through the contradictions of our visual readings.

Laura Owens lives and works in Los Angeles. She has had solo exhibitions at Gavin Brown's Enterprise in New York and Rosamund Felsen Gallery, Santa Monica. This is the UK first exhibition by Laura Owens.

For photographs and information please call Sadie Coles and Pauline Daly at Sadie Coles HQ on 0171 434 2227 or fax on 0171 434 2228.

35 Heddon Street London W1R 7LL England
T +44 [0] 171 434 2227 F +44 [0] 171 434 2228

Reg in England no 3211376
Vat no 690 6671 06

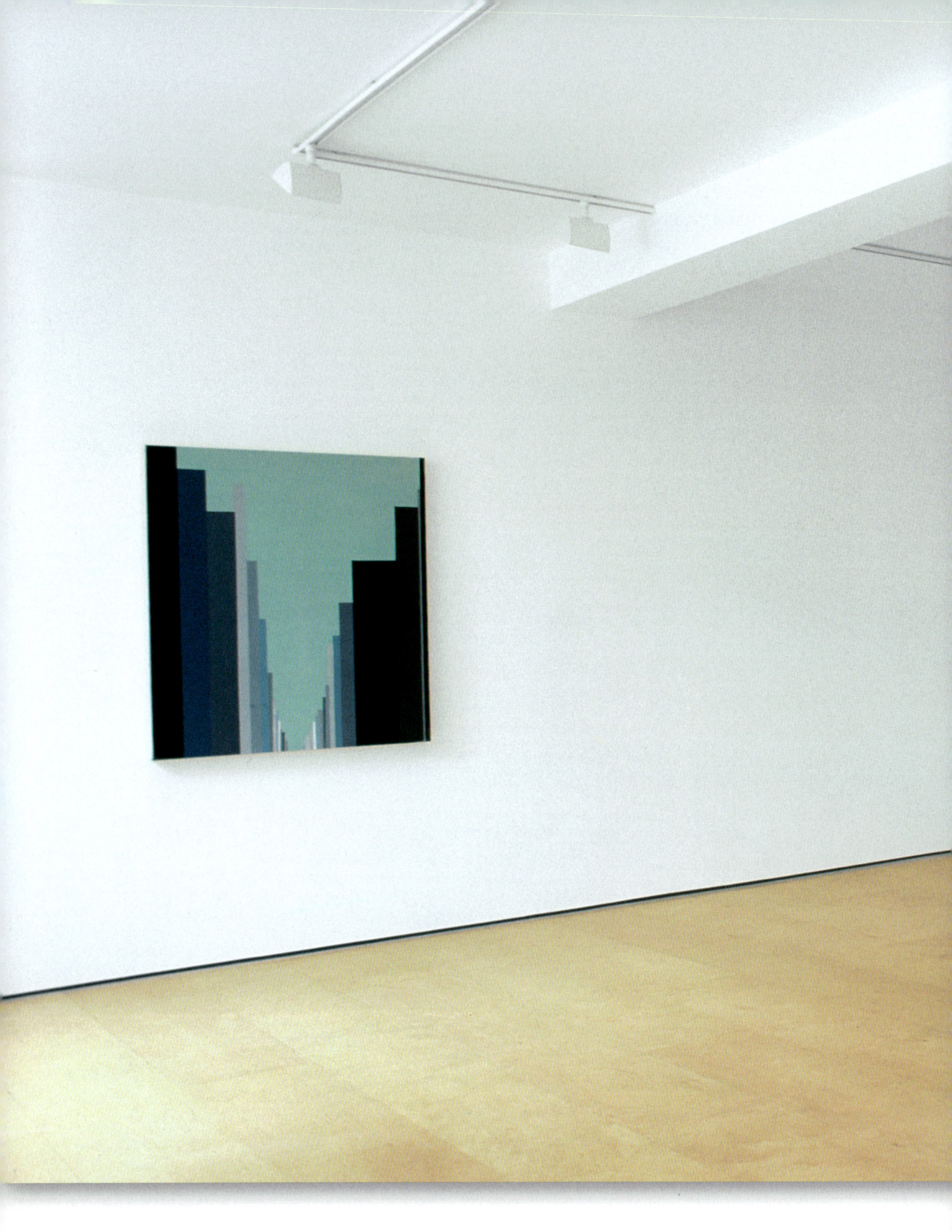

Installation view, Sadie Coles HQ, London, 1997, with *Untitled*, 1997, acrylic and oil on canvas, 49¾ × 45½ in. (126.4 × 115.6 cm), and *Untitled*, 1997, acrylic and oil on canvas, 96 × 120 in. (243.8 × 304.8 cm)

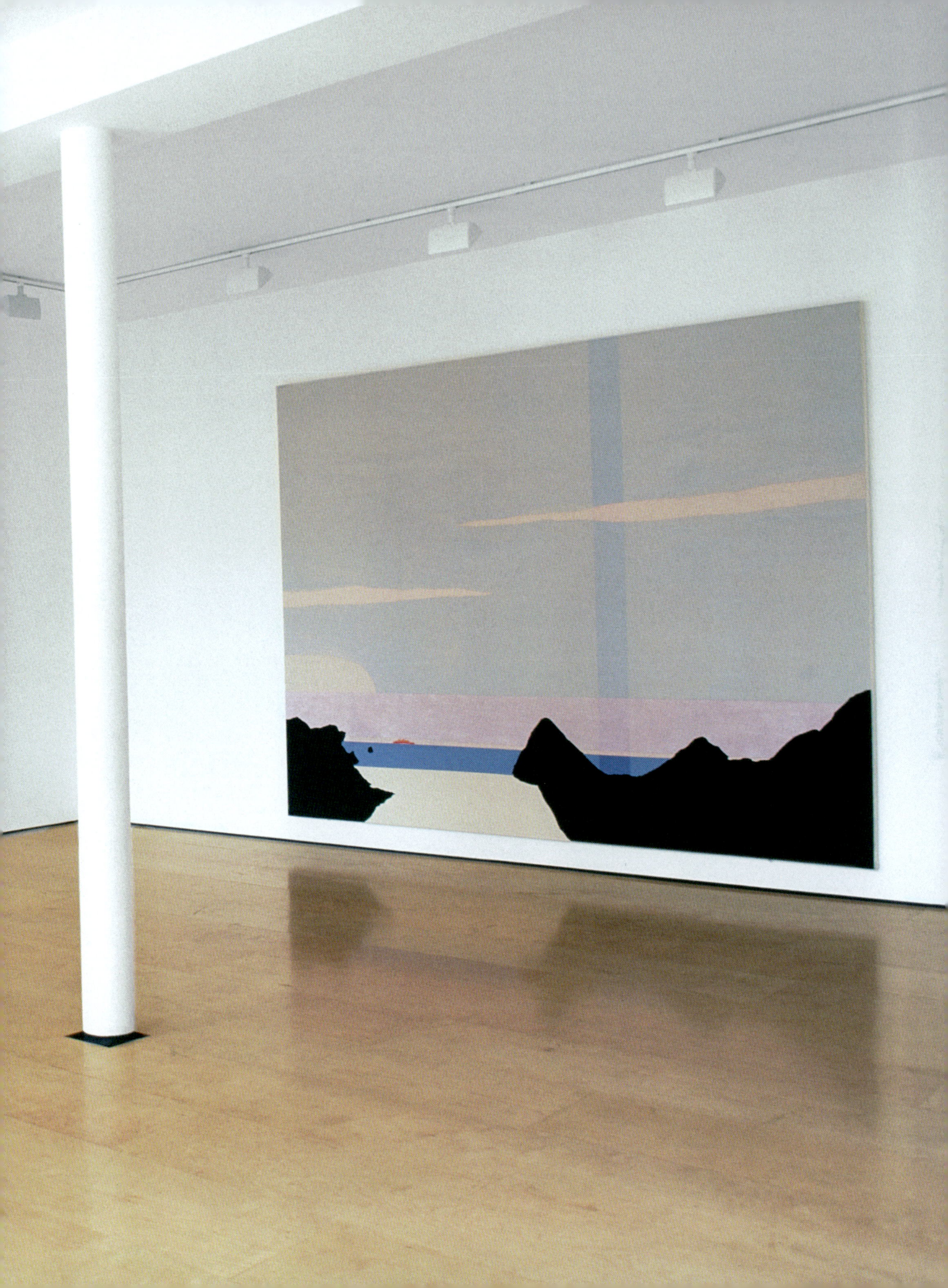

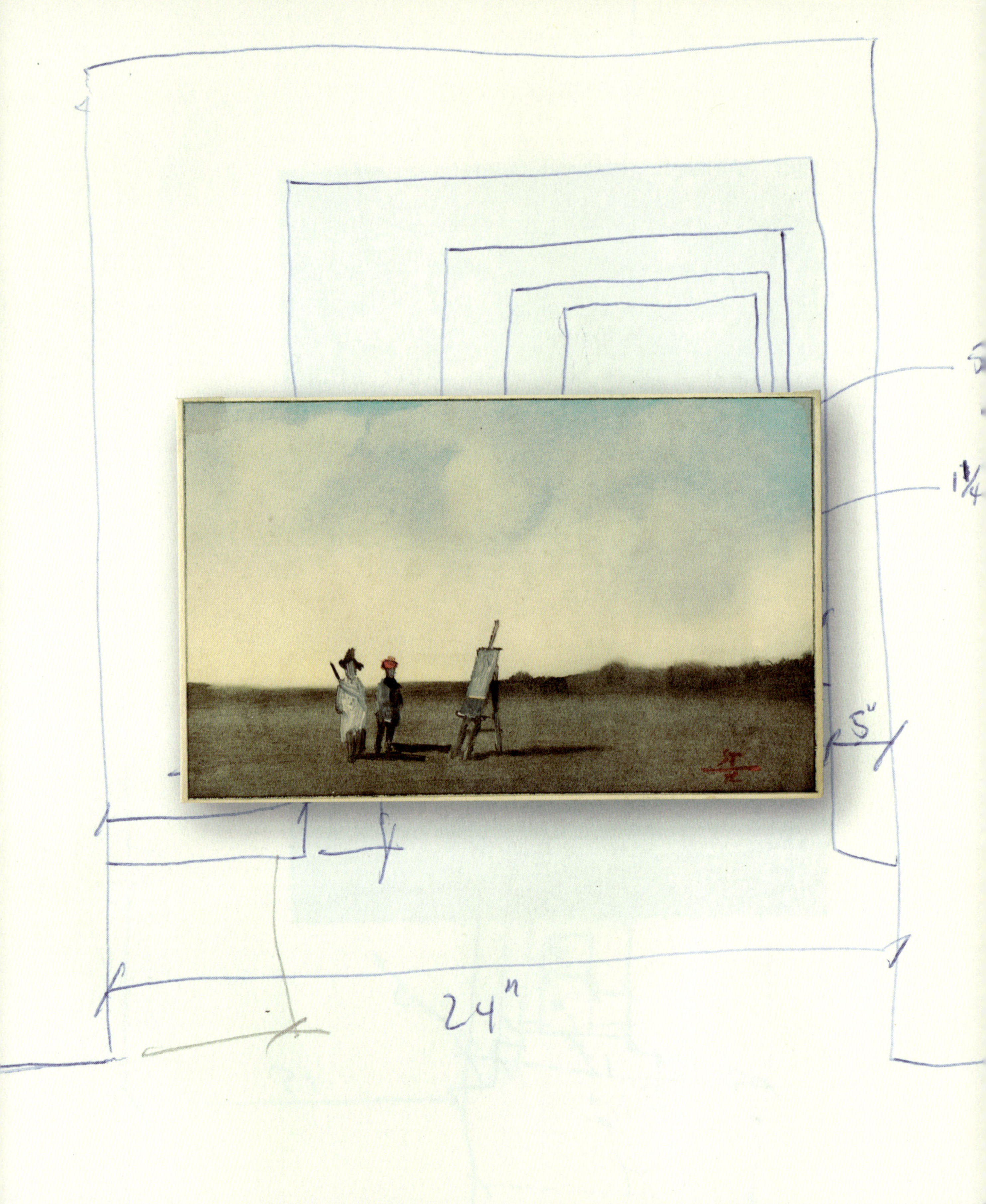

Foreground: Invitation, *Steinberg,* Galerie Maeght, Paris, 1973
 Background: Sketchbook page, 1997

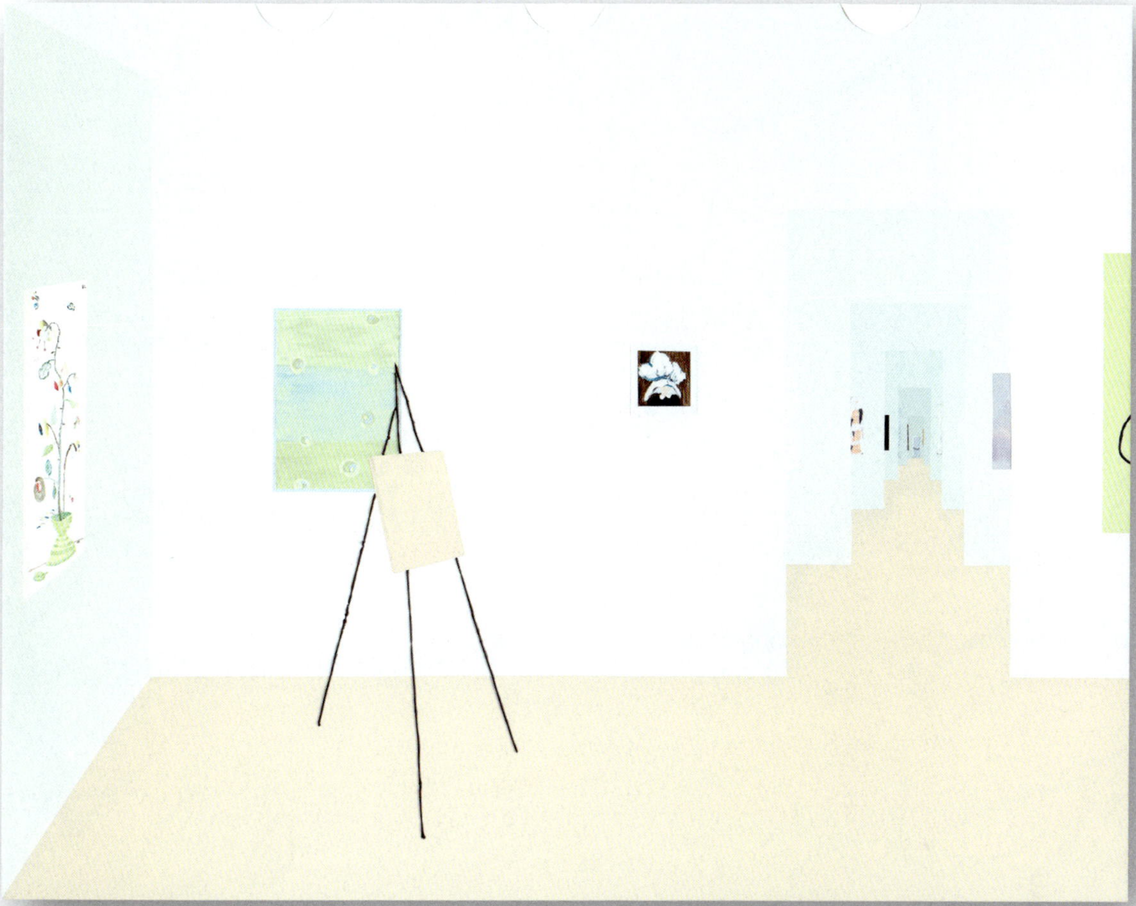

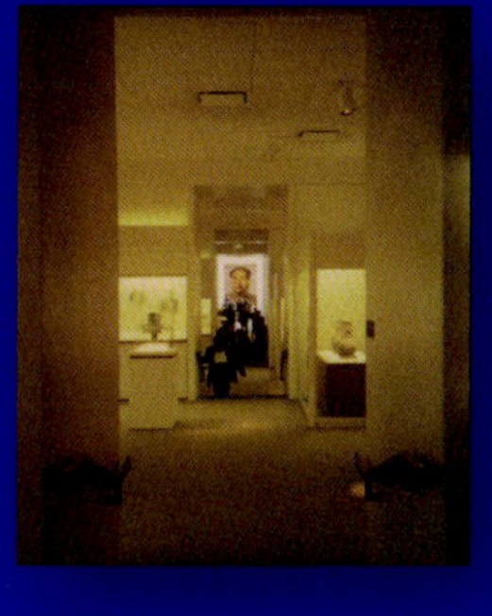

Laura Owens: When I was working at the School of the Art Institute of Chicago in 1997 I had a point-and-shoot camera and took a lot of pictures while walking around the museum. One of them was of a floor-to-ceiling Andy Warhol Mao painting, seen through the Asian art wing. It was very large, but it seemed like a postage stamp receding at the end of all those rooms, a football field away. I had that photo hanging in my studio for years, and when Sadie showed me pictures of her gallery I wanted to do something like that in the office. I thought it would be funny to do a painting that covered the entire wall and was composed of many smaller paintings, adding more space to the office and also camouflaging the work's size. The painting alludes to things I was looking at, like a van Gogh that was in the Norton Simon Museum. I added an easel and an industrial push door at the end of the hallway instead of the Mao. I thought this was a funny nod to the formalist rule about never having a hole in a composition. It reminds me of this postcard of a Saul Steinberg painting that I found later, in Italy, and kept hanging in my studio for several years.

Untitled, 1997, acrylic and oil on canvas, 96 × 120 in. (243.8 × 304.8 cm)
Inset: Research photograph by Owens, Art Institute of Chicago, 1997

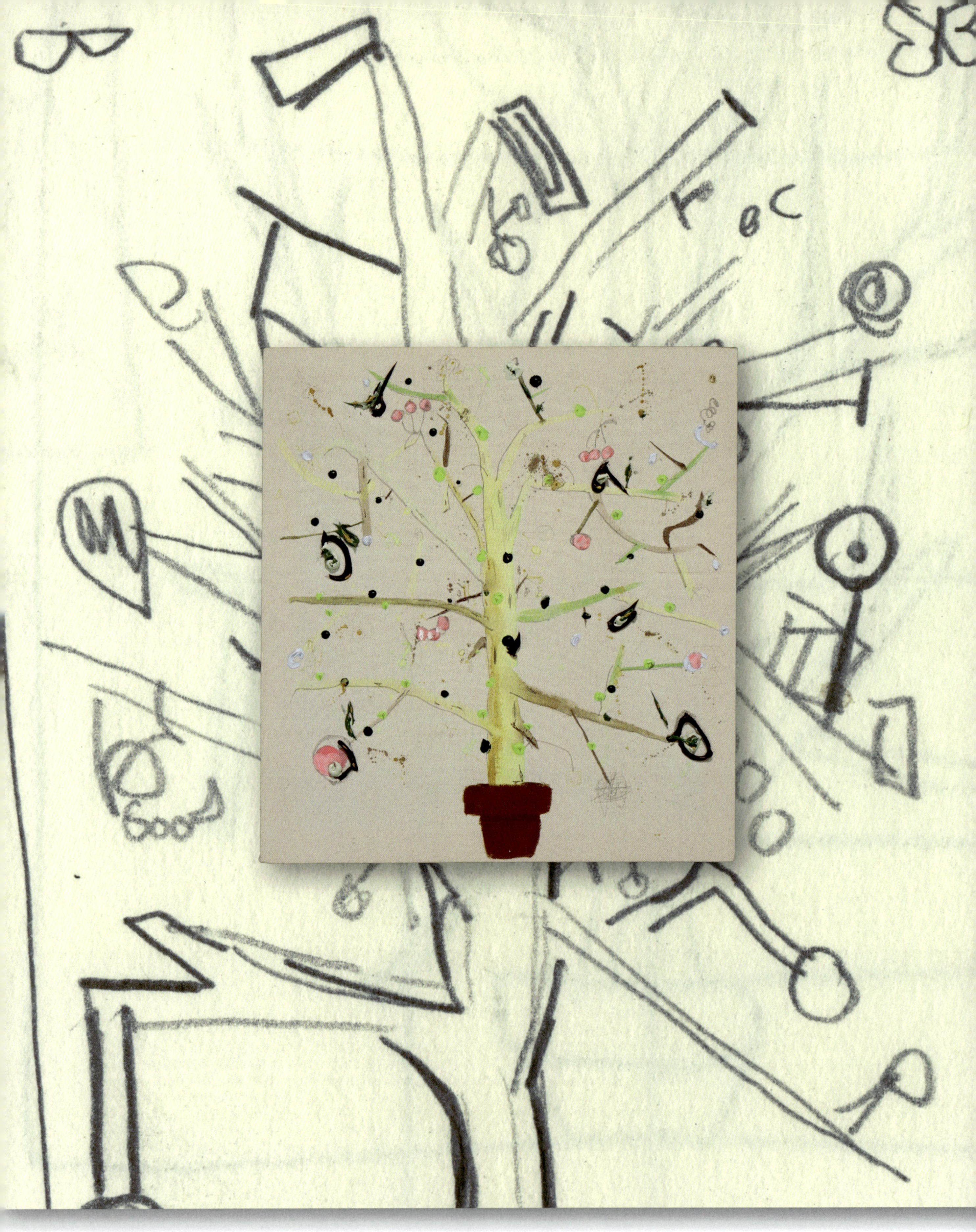

Foreground: *Study for Untitled*, 1997, acrylic and oil on canvas, 22 × 20 in. (55.9 × 50.8 cm)
Background: Sketchbook page, 1997

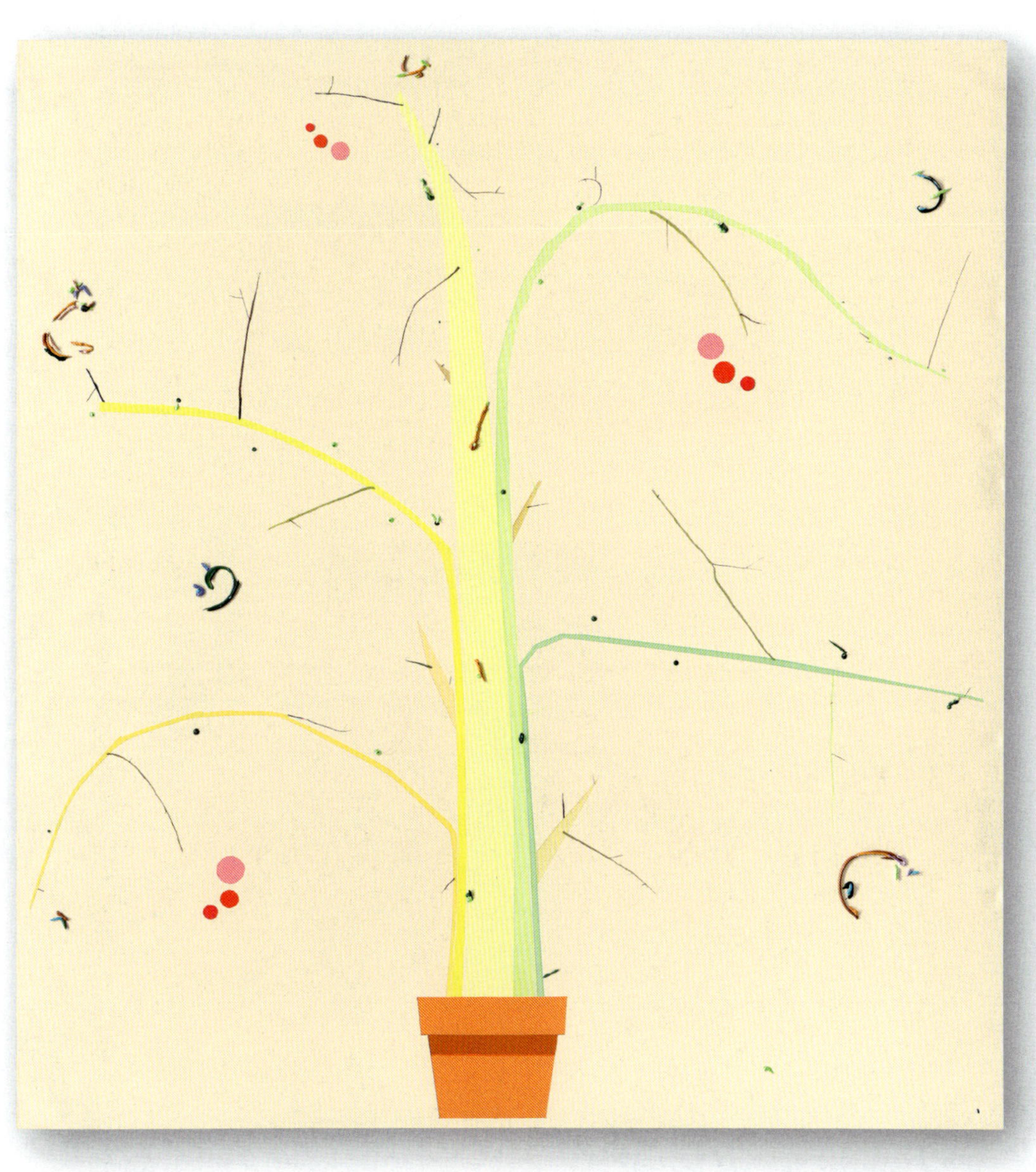

Untitled, 1997, acrylic and oil on canvas, 84¼ × 75½ in. (214 × 191.8 cm)

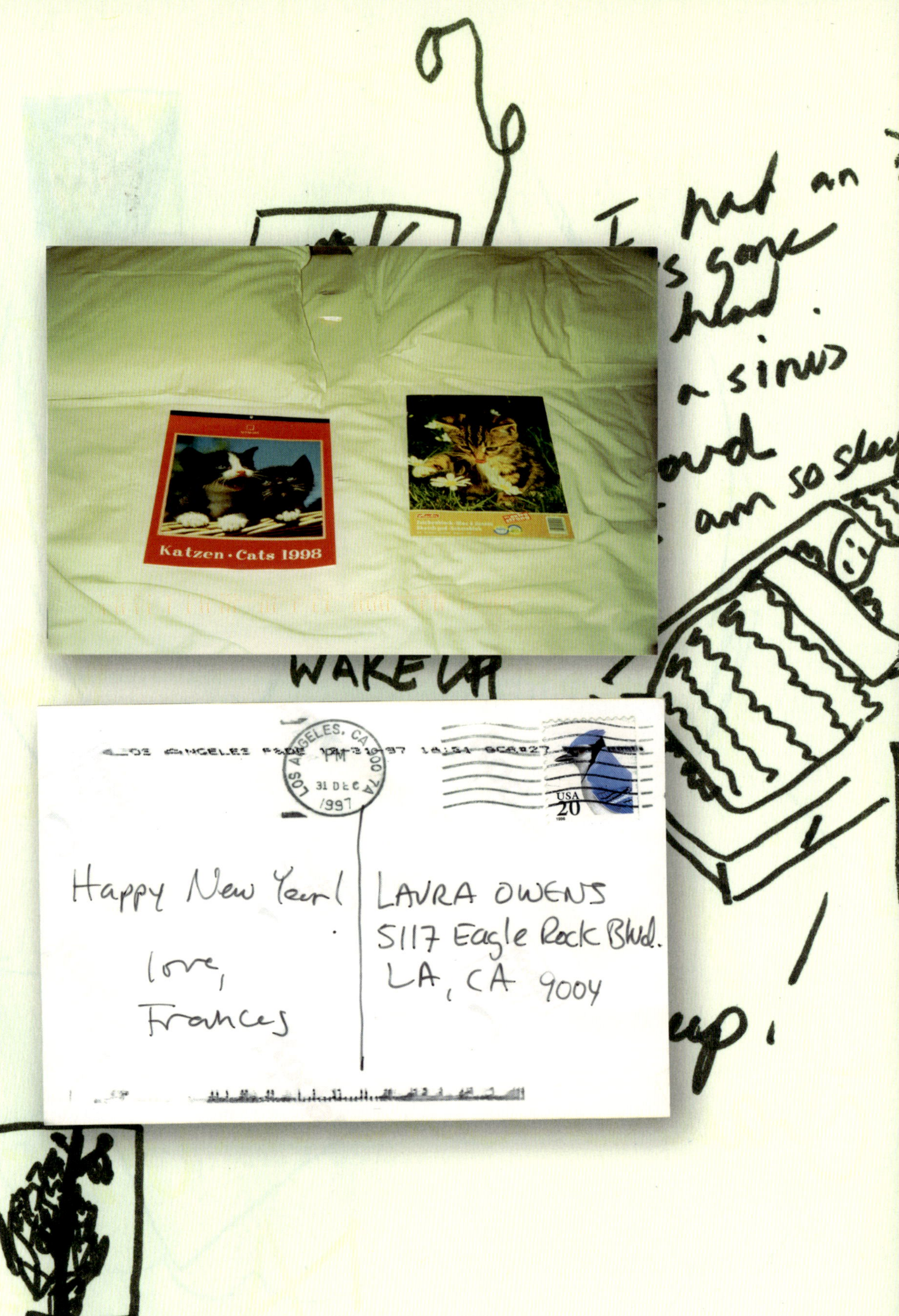

Foreground: Postcard from Frances Stark, 1997
178   Background: Sketchbook pages, 1997

Virginia Woolfe

???

IDEAS

E KELLY

Henri Rousseau

Roy
Lichtenstein

BARNETT
NEWMAN

3/5

This day

FLORINE STETTHEIMER

NEWMAN

Marie

Keith
HARING

Laurencin Van Gogh

Matisse

John
McKracken

Mary
Heilmann

EXCERPT FROM *THE ARCHITECT AND THE HOUSEWIFE*
FRANCES STARK

I In Los Angeles, in the spring, at a table, on the beach, Michael Lin told me about his last project *Interior* and showed me his plans for *Complementary*. We spoke of his interests in pursuing a dialogue between the public space of the exhibition and the private space of the domestic interior. He told me the project, *Complementary*, was to culminate in book form. If I wanted, I could contribute some text. Then and there I had a heading in my head, a heading in my head not altogether un-complementary in and of itself, under which a textual exploration of *Complementary* might fall. In Taipei, in summer, at a table, under some air conditioning, the heading that was in my head is going from my head now to the paper, towards that aforementioned book, which I have to assume you are now holding, in which case you are also about to encounter below the heading mentioned above, beneath which you will not find an analysis or interpretation of Michael Lin's *Complementary*. Instead you'll find my monologue, my contribution to the dialogue. But briefly, before I begin, I'm just going to pull a quote from a book I found lying on Michael Lin's desk. The book is by Oscar Wilde and it's called *The Critic as Artist*. I opened it up because on the cover, in addition to the title, it said: with some remarks on the importance of doing nothing and discussing everything, and my eyes landed on the following sentence: "If you wish to understand others you must intensify your own individualism."

The Architect & The Housewife
I have had complaints about my couch, which bisects my living room diagonally, orienting the viewer towards a rather delightful view overlooking the city and its backdrop of hills, behind which the sun can be seen disappearing nightly. Although not lacking a handful of admirers, the couch seems to provide inadequate comfort to most visitors, either they say so directly, or more often express their discomfort silently by choosing to make themselves comfortable at the kitchen table in the adjoining room, from which you only have a view of purple and pink flowers. The couch is a Danish Modern design, smaller than your average couch, with quite thin square cushions, extremely attractive actually. However, I don't think the design is the problem. The problem, rather, lies in the fact that directly behind the couch, meaning directly behind the head of anyone sitting on the couch, is my desk. It's technically just a table, a long one, slightly longer than the couch and only an inch or so taller than the top of the couch. The large rectangular surface of the desk is covered in that dark chocolatey-brown, fake wood veneer. Its edges are curved, lined with dark brown plastic trim about an inch thick. Its base, collapsible if necessary, is made of thin, cheap metal, painted, of course, dark brown. Usually the entire surface of the desk is covered—my computer, loose papers, books and stacks of this and that. So, not only is it just a desk behind the seated person's head, but an unruly mess made up of stacks of loose papers that can and do easily stray from the boundary of the table-desk toward the head and shoulders of a seated guest. It's a mess because it lacks any of the simple and ingenious design conveniences which might usually be incorporated into a well-made desk in order to keep papers and various other desk-dwelling items under control. I failed to mention that the table/desk lies flush with the back of the couch diagonally bisecting my living room in order to leave all possible wall space open. I use the desk for writing and the walls for making drawings, which I may as well tell you, are made up of writing. So you see this curious arrangement (of my couch and my desk, not my writing and my writing-drawing) is predicated on the fact that not only is my living room my living room but my living room also serves as my studio.

The dilemma of having a couch in my studio is perhaps an interesting one. If I can't get sufficiently engaged in a book, or making a drawing I might

 Excerpted from *The Architect & the Housewife* (London: Book Works, 1999). Stark is an interdisciplinary artist and writer based in Los Angeles.

end up staring into space. You can't stare into space forever, so I might start to look around and begin thinking to myself, this house is too messy or not nice looking enough or those drawers should be cleaned out or perhaps if I got a different piece of furniture for over there I could rearrange this here and my life would run more smoothly. I am sparing you the details of my toil which aspires to productivity, suffice it to say it is not hard not to experience, on a regular basis, the loneliness, the anxiety, the constant urge to redecorate I imagined a housewife might feel.

The possibility of becoming an active consumer can drive me out of the house—once entering Ikea, or even Office Depot—wherever—the world opens up in terms of what me and my home, office, studio can become. On two separate occasions I bought a pillow from a chain store called The Pottery Barn. Both times I resented the homogeny of the store, but both times I thought to myself "My head deserves the luxury this pillow has to offer." The first pillow purchase actually can be broken down into two parts. Part one is I simply bought a pillow without a case at Ikea, the first throw-pillow I ever bought in my life, by the way. In the do-it-yourself spirit of Ikea,[1] I planned to sew my own case out of something special. I don't really sew, but it seemed simple enough. Several weeks passed without me sewing a case. One day my father and baby brother drove into town. We planned to drive to the museum where one of my drawings happened to be hanging in an exhibition. We got in the car to go there but first we needed to eat. In our search for a meal we could all agree on we got completely off track and far from the museum. By the time we finished eating it was quite late and we were running out of time, and because adult things are harder to do with a six year old in tow, we ended up at the mall across the street instead of the museum. That is where the first shop that sucked me in spat me back out again with a baby blue angora pillow case. That was part two of pillow purchase number one. Pillow purchase number two is like this. I was feeling heartbroken and unable to work. My friend Laura, a painter, learned of my useless condition and decided I needed escape. She drove me to a heavily populated shopping area. We walked into a series of stores that sold housewares and took turns interpreting the merchandise. We ended up at The Pottery Barn and she bought a variety of blue floral pillows in different sizes whereas I selected a large summery two-tone green silk. But this second trip to The

Pottery Barn, with another woman artist instead of my father, coincided with the moment at which I recognized there was a novice homemaker-cum-consumer in me that was eager to get out and find a rug, an inoffensively scented candle or a pillow at precisely the time I should be sitting at the chocolatey fake wood table pushing through a difficult piece of work.

The kind of anxiety associated with working alone in a domestic environment is precisely what brought the housewife to mind. I have sometimes found myself envying a male friend, here or there, who happened to be engaged in large-scale art projects, out in the open air, or inside institutions with many people running around to ensure an imminent production. Was I not unlike a housewife, toiling within the confines of my home and serving as both hostess and docent of my tiny quarters? Were these men not unlike architects in that they were constantly carrying out plans—giving instructions, making constructions?

The impetus behind these categorizations had a little bit to do with the idea of couples. I knew of some couples in the art world where the female part of the couple happened to be engaged in works that were more studio oriented, in that they were either paintings or some other type of practice which typically has to be carried out alone in the studio whereas their partners were involved in projects that were sculpture-oriented and employed many more people in their realization. I thought about the studio works and how their viewing demanded a certain kind of intimacy and physical proximity to the viewer and how the men were making work that—although in some cases dealing explicitly with issues of domesticity— surrounded a viewer, was public, or involved some kind of environment or activity that accommodated more people at one time than could stand in front of a painting or read a tiny text in a drawing on the wall. It wasn't that the females weren't getting as much attention as the men, it was just a difference which made me consider whether or not I was somehow involved in an extremely conservative, not to mention lonely, practice. The painter Laura and I decided to pursue this extreme binary of the architect and the housewife as a way of reflecting on and examining current art practices around us. This construction, as simplistic and reductive as it might sound, started to prove effective. In fact more than just elucidating differences in interior versus exterior sites of production, we began to consider whether "interiority" and "exteriority" were types of meaning-production as well, interiority evoking more of a Romantic tradition and exteriority being perhaps more in line with the avant-garde. Maybe, maybe not. I can imagine *The Architect & The Housewife* as a heading over almost any discussion regarding post-studio art practices which focus on decorative and design issues, whether in a public or private space. I can imagine its applicability to those works which seek to examine or at least evoke modernism's failures or successes, its utopian designs-for-living, or to those works which rely heavily on a public setting or large quantities of institutional commerce to bring the final product, object, and/or site into being, and last but not least those practices which seemingly overlook their complex reliance on the architecture and structure of the "art world," still insisting that the hand-made portable object is capable of producing meaning within its limited frame.

But first, back to basics. I presume a housewife is someone who will stay and maintain the home, decorate, arrange, rearrange, prepare, wash, put things away, bring them out again—the house not being a site of accumulating production but a site of a series of simultaneous productions which bear no evidence of productivity—save for the fact that the home isn't falling apart. A supposedly good housewife maintains a busy environment which should appear as if nothing has ever happened. Nothing is being built per se. The architect, on the other hand, solves problems the public doesn't think about but which affect their consciousness of the environment, from things as essential as material, lighting and scale to more socially articulated needs like safety, cost, codes etcetera.

The exteriority I have so far mentally ascribed to "the architect" has to do with elaborate extensions, disruptions and transformations into and of material reality. And, by extension, the act of writing, with a special emphasis on fiction, seems to demand very little in terms of outside space—no commerce, a budget of mostly just living expenses, minimal materials—not much of a production. The production doesn't extend into or employ much of the exterior environment. Publication and distribution are different matters entirely since the formal completion of the work of fiction does not depend on the realization of either. However in the case of this writing here I wanted to break out the confines of a personal interior and experience Taiwan. Flying halfway around the world to look at an exhibition and make a short

piece of writing, for which I would receive a small payment, is a way for me, personally, to upset my imaginary position in my binary configuration. Recall the famous piece of writing by Virginia Woolf, *A Room of One's Own*. This text, written in 1928, was meant to address the slippery topic of women and fiction. In it she writes: "A woman must have money and a room of her own if she is to write fiction." Isn't she suggesting that a main prerequisite to productivity is privacy? A woman, if she is occupying and/or upkeeping everyone else's rooms is going to have a difficult time getting any work done. Sure, she can enjoy many other "rooms," consuming culture with the best of men, but when it comes to producing culture it might not only be a question of where she will do it but also a question of where you will consume it. Think of literature as an interior event, the mind or imagination being the place where the text unfolds. And consider the interior of the head— the particular bodily limits of your own perception and yet the seeming limitlessness of though.

Now think of the interior of a home, to which a housewife has historically been expected to attend. Traditionally it is meant to provide her partner with a restorative and pleasant atmosphere so that he can continue his hard work in the public sector. Here I am talking about European bourgeois society around the turn of the century at which time something called "Neurasthenia" was a common form of nervous exhaustion thought to be brought about by excessive use of the brain.[2] Businessmen were advised to temper their neurasthenia by going home to a completely soothing environment. Patterns found in decorative art objects which adorned the home were meant to offer repose in the domestic setting.

Consider now the boundaries of the studio—not a home and not just a room. I came across a particularly striking phrase of Daniel Buren's in an essay published in *October* magazine called "The Function of the Studio." Here is Buren's phrase, his heading: "the unspeakable compromise of the portable work of art." The compromise Buren finds unacceptable is that if a work is produced in a studio it is automatically wedded to that space, it somehow lives perfectly in that space, yet its portability is some kind of breach in integrity, meaning that it compromises itself by having to leave its home and go to a supposedly neutral gallery or museum space. This is at once declaring that a work should completely take into account that the museum or gallery space is nowhere near neutral and that somehow if one denies the works' relation to its space, one is on some level choosing to ignore the values the museum/gallery architecture ascribes to the work, and the work itself is simply a piece of merchandise that shuttles easily from the studio into the marketplace. By the time I came across this I had already been ruminating on Michael's pillows. It is interesting how the paintings of the pillows conjure up both the portability of painting as a practice, as well as the portability of the pillows themselves, a major contribution to their use value. Also *Complementary* exhibits a self-consciousness of its status as an exhibition. Not only does its intervention into the architecture offer a better view of outside to its viewers, it allows for more natural light to be shed onto the work, and that view is made available to you now seeing as how the show documented itself. Okay, so I have just put the ideology of institutional critique into a convenient nutshell but let's put scholarship aside for the sake of letting Buren's "unspeakable compromise" resonate poetically under my compromise heading—granted it's an extremely subtle poetic.

There are a few ways to read the word "compromise," one being more drastic than the other. The drastic way, which is surely what he meant, is "to make liable to suspicion, danger or disrepute." But I also think of a compromise as simply a settling of differences—for instance, something a couple must do to stay a couple. I have learned that the fabric used and reproduced in *Complementary* is a fabric associated with the wedding night. So, as it turns out, there are couples all over the place here and with a title of a show that means "offsetting mutual lacks" you can bet there's no way to have a hermetically sealed art discussion, there have to be men, women, unhappiness, happiness, weddings, divorces, and sex. I mean I won't explicitly discuss these things I just don't want you to forget about the fact that a

home is usually designed for a family which starts with a couple, which is usually made up of two people who at some time in their compromising and complementary relationship have rolled around naked together on some pillows or some equivalent thereof. That reminds me of something. Adolf Loos, the Austrian architect, famous for his manifesto against décor, once wrote "All art is erotic." He didn't mean it as a compliment. Sure this is seriously taken out of context, but wait.

The architect, R. M. Schindler, also Austrian, designed his own residence in Los Angeles to be occupied by two couples. He seemed to be aspiring to a different kind of domesticity. Each couple would have their own bedroom and places in the house in which they did their work and studies, with several common indoor/outdoor living areas. The house is too complicated to describe here in detail but the pertinent part for our story is that the two couples did not end up occupying the place harmoniously and it ended up just being the home of Schindler and his wife, Pauline. Finally that couple, too, disintegrated. They divided the house and lived there, separately, together. His wife began to hang wallpaper and install carpeting, decorating her part of the house exactly the way she wanted, and here I might add that pink was her favorite color. Her husband would draft her letters which went something along the lines of "I am sure you are familiar with the reasoning for my choice of materials and that what you have done is completely incongruent with my design and destroys the integrity of the structure," something along those lines, "signed R. M. Schindler, Architect." So much for compromise.

Famous architects throughout history have also been known to design chairs. Adolf Loos, Le Corbusier, Mies van der Rohe, Eero Saarinen, Frank Gehry and so on, even Schindler. The specificity of the challenge lies in the intimacy with which a body is to interact with a chair, an intimacy far greater and literally more pressing than between a body and a building. Here there is a direct correlation with contemporary artists' desire to address private individual comfort from the standpoint of an extremely public and social oriented tradition. Domesticity, interior design, and private vs. public space surface as issues in the works of many young contemporary, internationally renowned artists (which might be squeezed into the "architect" category), artists whose practices are in line with Daniel Buren's oppositional ideology. In a lot of instances the work directly involves seating: the upholstering of chairs, a pier on which to venture out, buy a pack of cigarettes, smoke and enjoy the view, a private island, the transformation of a public Donald Judd sculpture into a bench at which to sit with friends, drink alcohol and listen to music, a building turned into a lamp with a rug laid out in front of it. Some of these projects were taken from *The Sculpture Projects in Munster,* 1997, which culminated in a five hundred and forty page catalogue of the exhibition. Interestingly enough, Daniel Buren not only participated in the project but contributed a manifesto-like text to the catalogue. I was reclining on a rug under a lamp next to a stack of art catalogues at Michael's house leafing through this gigantic catalogue thinking about how despite the fact that Buren's critique of the portable object is now pretty much the dominant ideology, there surely is no shortage of the most portable object of all time, the book, and here I refer specifically to the art catalogue, which ensures that a work—no matter how problematic or ephemeral, no matter how casual or whimsical—remains a work of art, and a portable one at that.

Another book I happened to find at Michael's house, aside from the Oscar Wilde one, was *The Sense of Order: A Study in the Psychology of Decorative Art* by E. H. Gombrich. This book is so great I'm sad to have to go back to LA without it. Several days after picking up Wilde's *Artist as Critic* (which sort of gave me the go-ahead to be myself in this piece, so to speak) I started reading the Gombrich book. I couldn't believe its pertinence. Just that day I had come so close to buying a different book by Gombrich, my first one by the way, as with the Ikea throw pillow, but I decided, it'll be cheaper in the States. And now here was Gombrich again, this time tempting me to just copy half of his book by hand and put it in the catalogue instead of my own writing. And not only that. Right at a critical point where designers were considering themselves equals with painters he quotes *The Critic as Artist* (auspicious or what?):

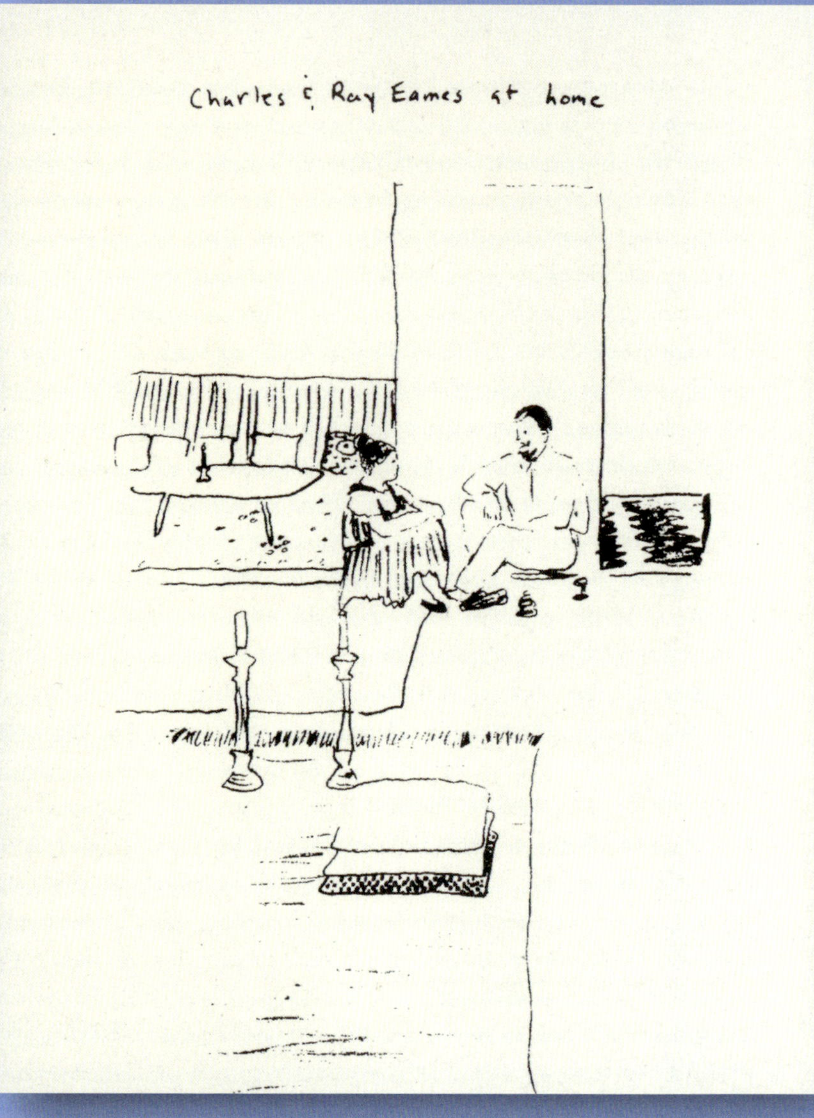

Frances Stark, *Charles and Ray Eames at Home*, 1999

The art that is frankly decorative is the art to live with. It is, for all visible arts, the one art that creates in us both mood and temperament. Mere colour, unspoiled by meaning, and unallied with definite form, can speak to the soul in a thousand different ways. The harmony that resides in the delicate proportions of lines and masses becomes mirrored in the mind. The repetitions of patterns give us rest.

Now bear with me, I am about to put that Loos business about all art being erotic into context for you. According to Gombrich "the emancipation of pattern design into a dependent art with growing pretensions foreshadowed the divorce between decoration and functional fitness." He quotes Loos, who vehemently requests the divorce, from his 1908 essay *Ornament und Verbrechen.* But before that he briefly points out that as early as 1892 the American architect, Louis Sullivan, had written: "it would be greatly for our aesthetic good if we should refrain entirely from the use of ornament for a period of years in order that our thoughts might concentrate acutely upon the production of buildings well formed and comely in the nude." Here it sounds like Sullivan is only calling for a friendly separation instead of a divorce. And I know with Sullivan they get back together, and I know this because I know Sullivan was obsessed with decoration until his very old age because in fact I happen to have a tattoo of one of the drawings he made after he had stopped making buildings. So, you can imagine my excitement when I first read those few sentences heretofore left out from in front of "All art is erotic": "The man of this century who tattoos himself is a criminal or a degenerate. . . . The urge to ornament one's face and everything within each is the very origin of the visual arts. It is the babbling of painting." According to Gombrich abstraction in painting didn't occur until after this complicated and competitive intermingling of decorative art with high art. And speaking of babbling, I have babbled on long enough but I'd like to bring this full circle if I can, and bring your attention now to an image of a perfect couple, a perfect marriage, where the gesture of placing a pillow in just the right spot has made history.

Charles & Ray Eames at Home [drawing reproduced here] shows three pillows of the same size placed on top of each other, on a rug, on the floor, offering contrasts in color and tone. At other times, more pillows were used and the grouping was placed slightly differently on the rug and in relation to the other objects. On the Sofa Compact in the late 1960s and for much of the 1970s, two patchwork pillows complemented each other and contrasted with a larger striped one.[3]

Notes

1 Possibly traceable back to Carl Larsson, a big influence in Swedish design movements. See "The Ideal Swedish Home: Carl Larsson's Lilla Hyttnas" by Michelle Facos in *Not at Home: The Suppression of Domesticity in Modern Art and Architecture*, ed. Christopher Reed (Thames & Hudson, London, 1996).

2 This and the following quote come from the essay "Hi Honey, I'm Home: Weary (Neurasthenic) Businessmen and the Formulation of a Serenely Modern Aesthetic" by Joyce Henri Robinson. This essay can also be found in *Not at Home*.

3 Pat Kirkham, *Charles and Ray Eames: Designers of the Twentieth Century* (Cambridge, MA: Massachusetts Institute of Technology, 1995), 188–89.

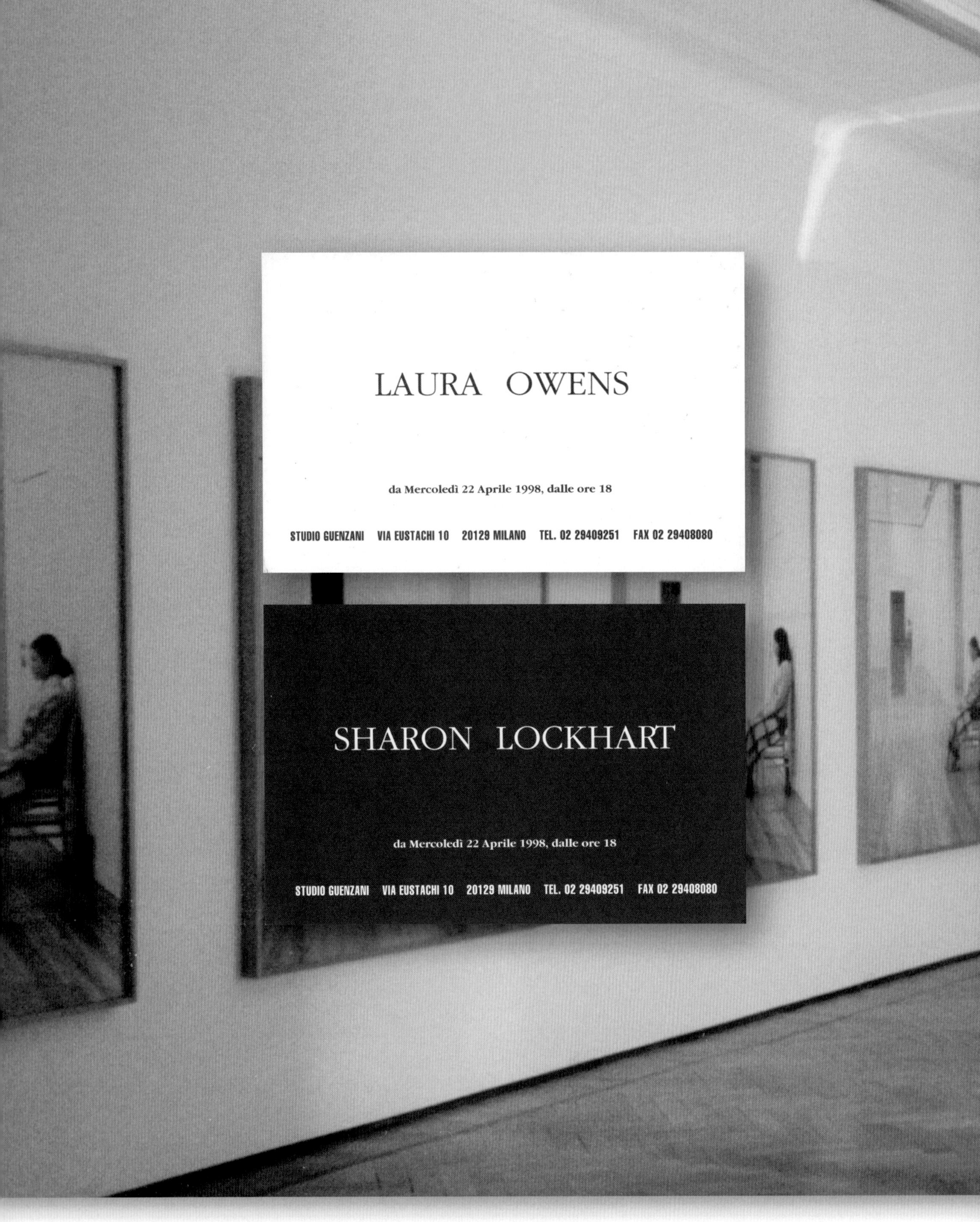

Foreground: Invitation, *Laura Owens and Sharon Lockhart*, Studio Guenzani, Milan, 1998
Background: Installation view, Studio Guenzani, Milan, 1998, with Sharon Lockhart, *On Kawara: Whole and Parts, 1964–95, Museum of Contemporary Art, Tokyo, January 24–April 5, 1998*, 1998, chromogenic prints, four parts: 64½ × 49 in. (163.8 × 124.5 cm) each, and *Untitled,* 1998, acrylic on canvas, 96 × 84 in. (243.8 × 213.4 cm)

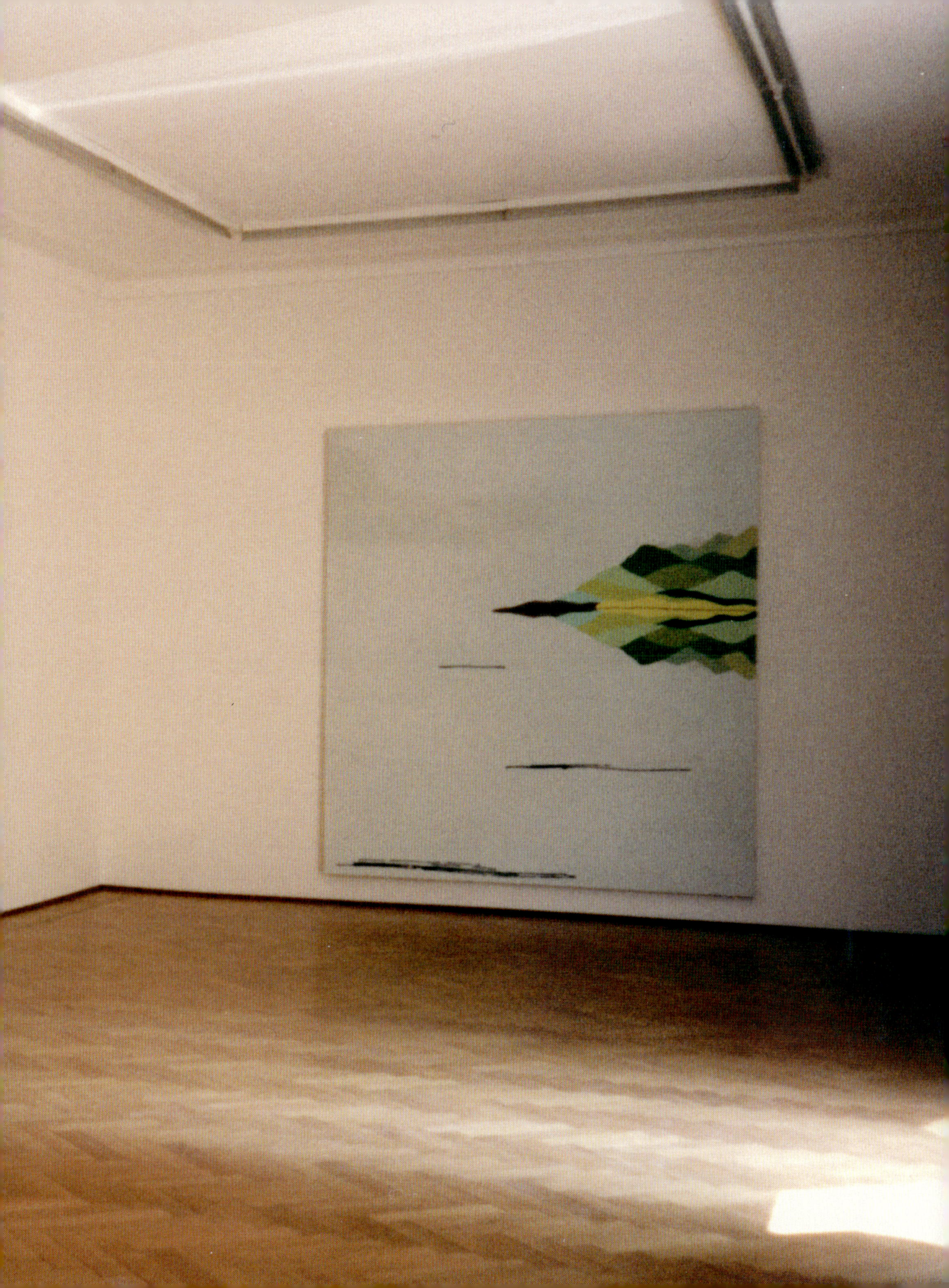

Foreground: Fax from Sadie Coles with notes by Owens, 1998
188   Background: Desktop calendar, 1998

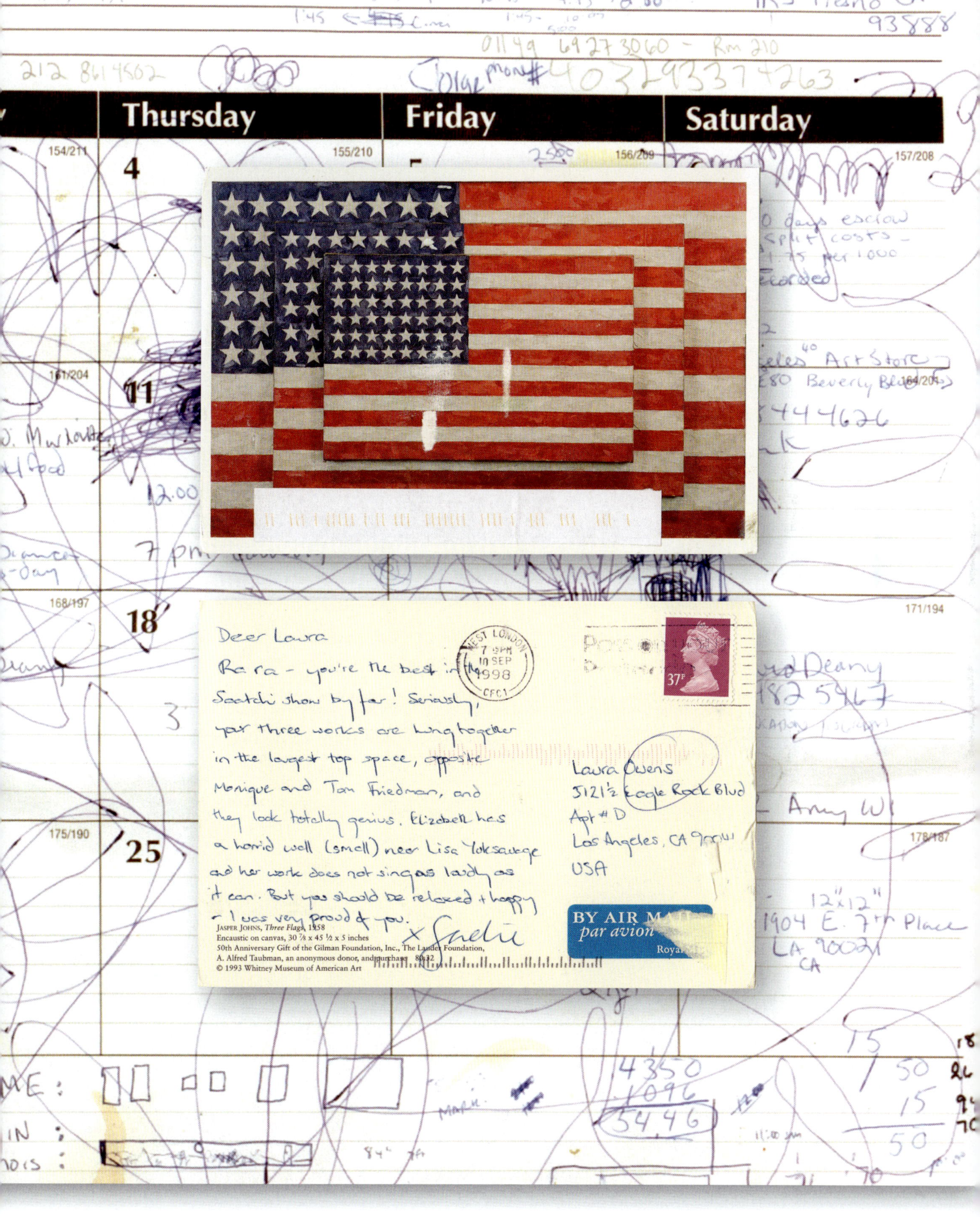

Foreground: Postcard from Sadie Coles, 1998

Mungo Thomson: Laura did a show with Jorge Pardo at Patrick Painter, and they were "just" making bedroom sets. The claims that they were making were not that grand and at the same time super ambitious. It's a funny sort of inversion. Coming from New York to LA and spending time with them and in that milieu was really interesting. Laura has that famous line, "Make the painting you want to be with," or whatever. And Jorge had this thing where he was saying, "If you don't like it as art, at least it's a lamp and you can read by it." There was a kind of stunt to his approach that was a little bit to do with what he could get away with. There's this way that that show had more to do with LA and lifestyle than with aiming for the canon, but in a funny way it was aiming for the canon anyway. There's a slyness to those operations that I really appreciated coming from New York, and it's part of what sold me on LA. The show was dealing with taste in a way that understood it as a driving factor in contemporary art. It played with the rules on the ground, and that's something that Jorge did a lot and it's something that Laura did as well. When they were together they amplified it in each other. The question was, "Would you like to live with this?" I think the acknowledgment of the ultimate destination of art as largely domestic is Michael Asher-esque; thinking the game all the way through to the end in that sort of structural, metadiscursive way is interesting and was different from what other painters working at that time were doing.

  Mungo Thomson is a Los Angeles–based artist and wrote about Owens in *Parkett* 65, September 2002.

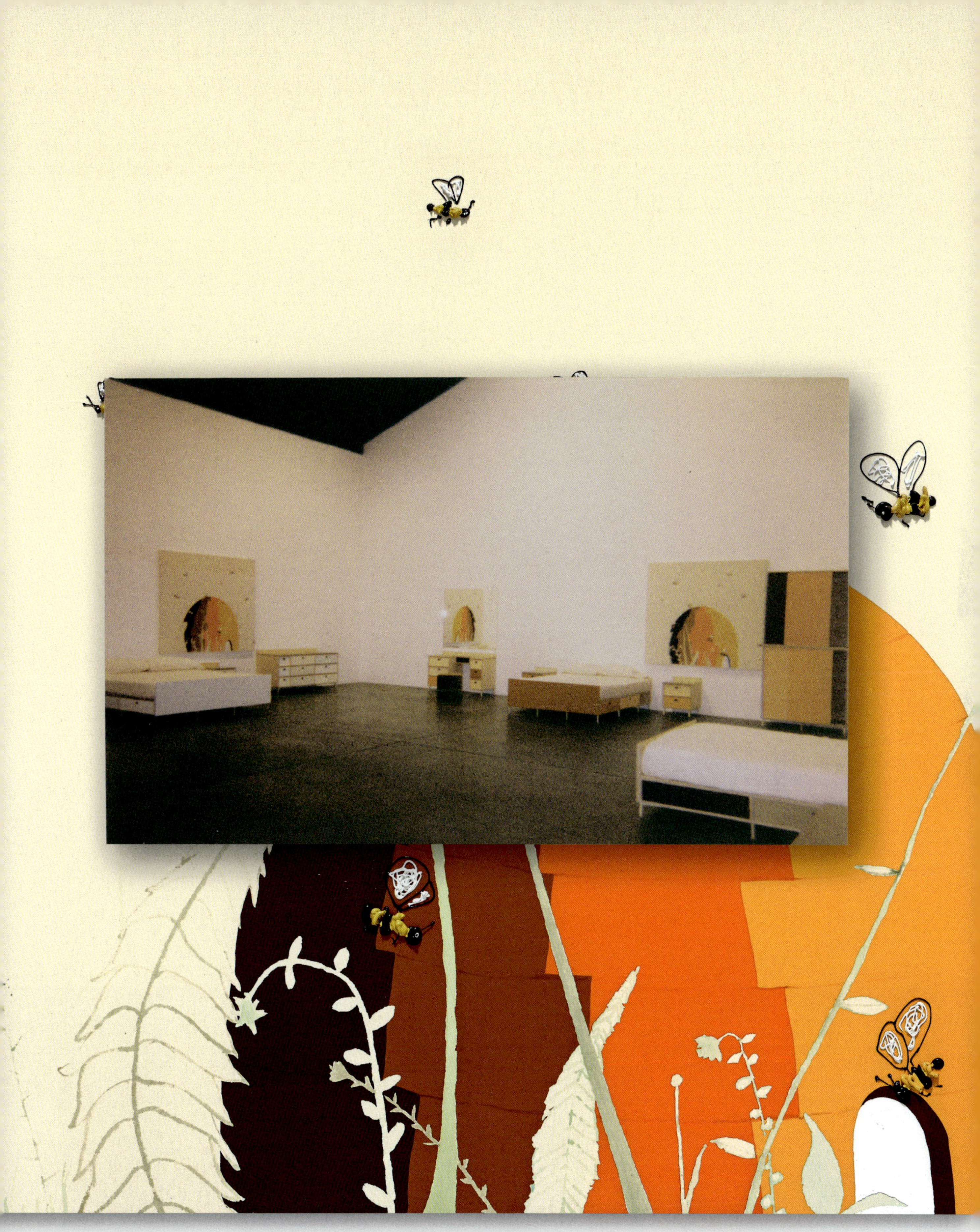

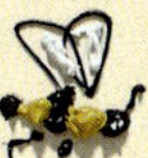

Foreground: Installation view, *Jorge Pardo*, Patrick Painter, Inc., Santa Monica, 1998, with Jorge Pardo, *Untitled*, 1998, mixed media, dimensions variable; *Untitled*, 1998, acrylic on canvas, 66 × 72 in. (167.6 × 182.9 cm); Jorge Pardo, *Untitled*, 1998, mixed media, dimensions variable; *Untitled*, 1998, acrylic on canvas, 66 × 72 in. (167.6 × 182.9 cm); Jorge Pardo, *Untitled*, 1998, mixed media, dimensions variable
Background: Detail of *Untitled*, 1998, acrylic on canvas, 66 x 72 in. (167.6 x 182.9 cm)

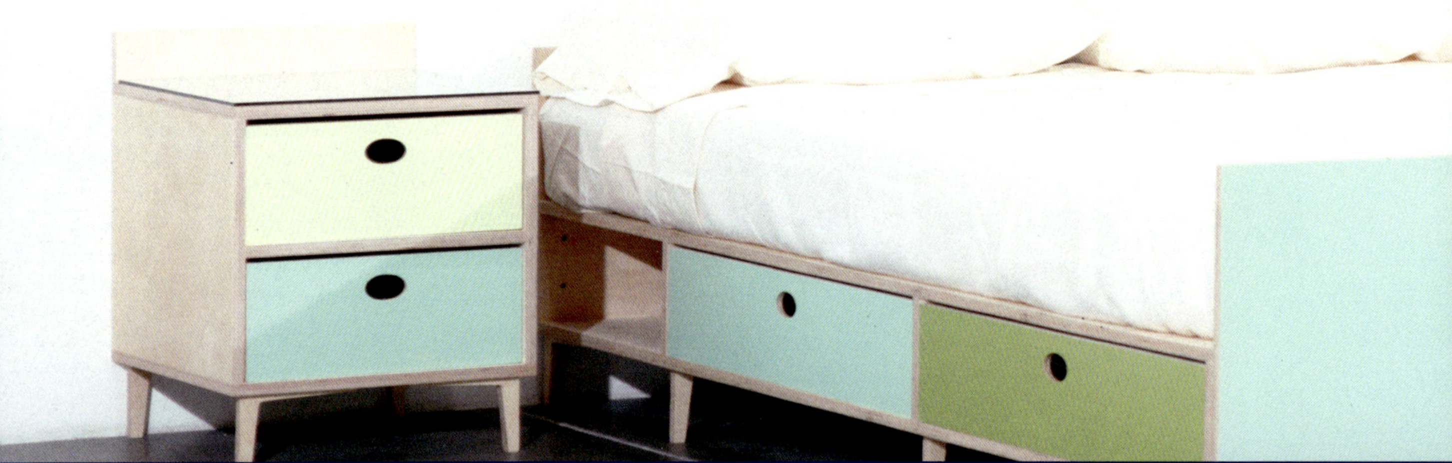

Installation view, *Jorge Pardo*, Patrick Painter, Inc., Santa Monica, 1998, with Jorge Pardo, *Untitled*, 1998 (see p. 191), and *Untitled*, 1998, acrylic on canvas, 66 × 72 in. (167.6 × 182.9 cm)

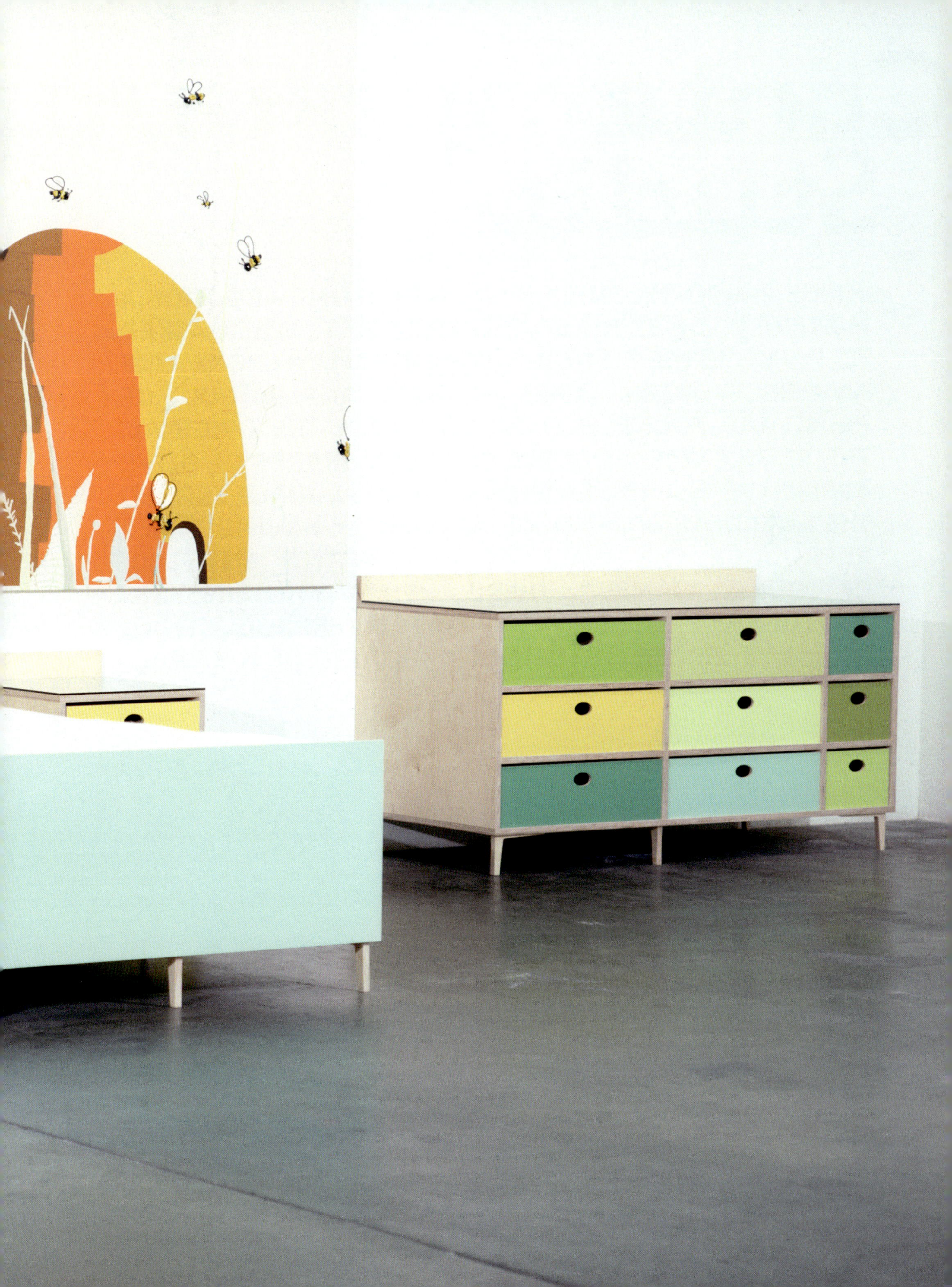

Contemporary Studio

JORGE PARDO RECENTLY MADE A PAINTING ABOUT/OF A MISTAKE MADE BY HIS STUDIO ASSISTANT. WHEN ASKED TO PAINT JORGE'S STUDIO (WHICH REALLY LOOKS LIKE AN OFFICE) GREEN, JAMES, HIS ASSISTANT, RAN OUT OF PAINT AND FOUND IT HARD TO MATCH THE ORIGINAL. THE RESULT WAS A COUPLE OF CLOSE SHADES OF OLIVE APPLIED WITH A ROLLER BRUSH. IN TURN, JORGE TURNED THE ANECDOTE OF MISTAKE INTO ART BY HAVING JAMES REPRODUCE THE WALL AS A PAINTING ENTITLED, OF COURSE, "JAMES." THERE ARE MANY INTERESTING MEANINGS PRODUCED BY THIS OVERPRODUCTION; FOR MY PURPOSES, IT PAINTS A PICTURE OF A STUDIO.

Laura Owens

My friend Frances and I have been talking for months about "the Architect and the Housewife" a fictional course of study we planning to (not) teach. Brewing in our brains has been some unattainable m idea that looks at the multiple and varied sites of production that artists presently using—how these definitions don't fit as binary categories to drop an name under, but do work towards undefinable modes of production convenie overlapping under one roof. To put it more bluntly, do you fax your drawin Cologne? Or do you draw alone at home? Well, no one does either exclusi but faxing fabrication plans and the-studio-is-my-living-room are two comm practices among artists. I talked with some friends about the way they conceive and use their studios. This is not a survey of practices in Los Angeles. These just my friends. So, I played dumb and went and asked them a lot of questio thought I knew the answers to, and was pleasantly surpri

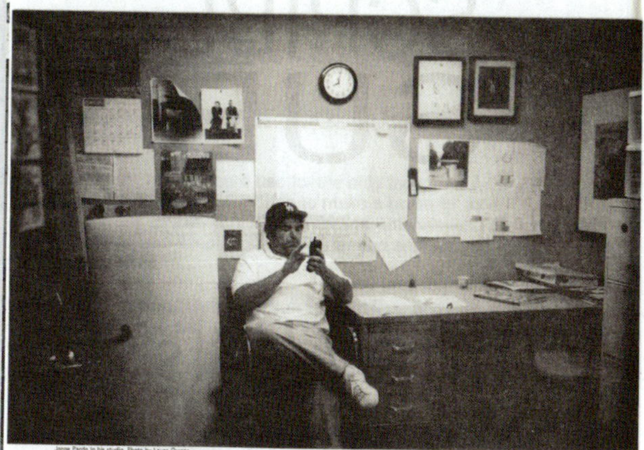

Jorge Pardo in his studio. Photo by Laura Owens.

Jorge Pardo

Me Again: Do you have a studio?
Jorge Pardo: Yes, it's separate from where I live, an old 6000 square foot factory I share with three other artists. I have an office there, I fabricate pieces, make models, or generally just hang around. Sometimes we make big projects but I don't want to do that anymore.

Do you use your studio for fabrication or to think of ideas? The studio is not the only place to get ideas. I go there mostly to make phone calls and do stupid clerical stuff.

Do you work with other people around? Yes, there are always other people around. It is a very communal space. I like that. I get a lot of ideas from other people.

Is your studio practice more like a business or religion? It is closer to a business.

Do you ever make work outside of your studio? I make work that goes through the studio and I make work in other places that never goes through the studio. Maybe I will be traveling for a month or two and then I will make a piece, and the piece maybe gets fabricated in France or some place like that.

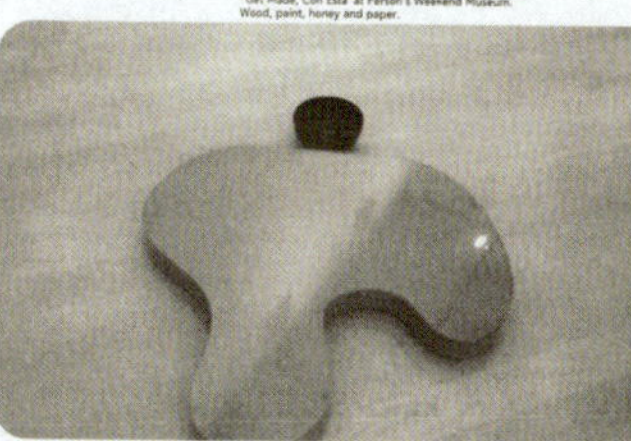

Jorge Pardo
"Get Made, Con Esta" at Parson's Weekend Museum. Wood, paint, honey and paper.

Do you just fax specifications? How do you make work outside the studio? The same as I make it in the studio. I come up with something I want to make and then I either make it myself or I try to find people to help me make it.

What is the most important tool you use in your studio? My phone. I seem to use it more than anything else. I like to be on the phone. Talking to people about certain processes, how much it costs, how long something takes…I have a drawing board I use a lot. Actually the most important tool I use in my studio right now is my assistant Eric Blumberg. He helps me with everything. He gets materials, makes things, coordinates shipping, he'll give me a last minute opinion, he sketches things and makes detailed fabrication drawings, lots of things.

So how much time do you spend working in your studio as opposed to else where? About half and half. The studio is not a place to get away and think. I do that in my car or at home. When I go to the studio it is to execute something that is already in motion. Generally I go to the studio to make something - not for some process of ideation. I don't use the studio for that anymore. Six or seven years ago when I had a full time job at the library it was more of a necessity to have a place to get away from work. Now that I primarily make art I think of the studio as a different place.

Monique Prieto

Me: What is your studio like?
Monique Prieto: I have a converted studio on the first-floor of our two story house. I split the floor with my husband, Michael, who has a recording/music studio there as well.

Do you go to your studio to think about ideas, or do you do that somewhere else? I think of ideas mostly in the studio.

Can you work with other people hanging around in your studio? I find it difficult but it depends what stage of the work I am at. I can if I am putting coats of paint on something that is already established. If I am thinking then it is better to be alone. But it's not always an option.

What are the most important tools you use in your studio? I couldn't do without my computer, and I couldn't do without a dictionary. In fact if I don't have a dictionary and thesaurus around I can't get things done.

Do you have a phone in your studio? No.

Do you listen to music? Yes.

Music with words? Yes, it gives me something to think about while I am working.

While you are thinking of ideas? Sometimes music will work its way into my ideas. A song might clarify a previous idea for a painting.

Do you ever ask people what they think in the middle of your process or ask for advice? I don't mind people seeing things unfinished but I don't consult, and I don't really appreciate input. If I get to a point where somethings is pretty much finished and I am deciding if it works or not then I will ask for advice.

Who do you ask? My husband—but I don't always take his advice.

Do you ever think of going to the studio as going away from motherhood responsibilities to have your own thoughts? Maybe a break from domestic life, but motherhood, that's just what I am now. I do manage to shut off the dishes and the laundry but I never shut off being a mother. So, the studio is a place to efficiently satisfy part of my life that isn't satisfied elsewhere. But I have to do it in small increments.

Do your kids come in your studio more than other people? Yeah, I more readily have Guillermo (age 3) and Emmett (almost 1) in the studio than anyone else. Yet it is the one room in the house I have complete control over.

Is L.A. a bigger version of the studio, inspiration and otherwise? Because I have lived here all my life, I have images of LA, I recall and use.

Like architecture? No, just the relationship between things. Peoples' expectations and what is actually presented to them.

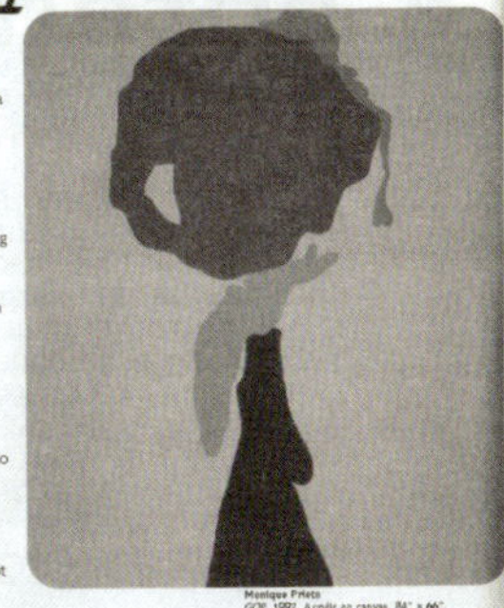

Monique Prieto
GOP, 1997. Acrylic on canvas, 84" x 66".

Is it the funny juxtapositions or is it more of a pathos-ridden sad idea? No, not sad. Just an observation or thought about why these things might be.

You mean like when someone has a really expensive shiny new car and yet they are still stuck in a traffic jam along with every other person? Yeah, I guess it is really about people's hopes and if they are maintaining their optimism. How they balance and juggle what they have with what they want and what is in front of them that they can't quite see.

There seems to be a range of approaches to making art, from treating it like a business to treating it like a religion or belief system. Where do you see your approach? Is it like going to a job or just another part of your home? It's not like going to another part of my home, it is like going to a really great job, unlike any other I have ever had.

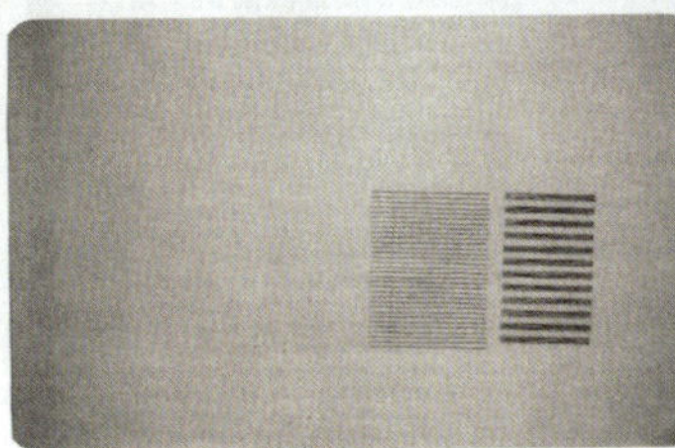

Frances Stark
Untitled (music is different), 1997. Carbon on paper, 25 1/2" x 40".

Frances Stark

Me again: Do you have a studio?
Frances Stark: No (laughing). We are sitting in it. It's my living room, I guess I refer to it as a studio/workspace but I walk two feet to my kitchen or my bedroom.

So you don't mind that your life spills into your studio space? I kind of can't see it any other way. It would be nice if it was bigger, but there isn't much to separate from, I don't have a family or a lot of guests.

Do you think of ideas in the studio or somewhere else? I guess I do a lot of the work here just sitting staring at the wall. It's not just a place for executing the work. I also get a lot of ideas in bed.

What is the most important tool you use in your studio, your computer? The computer is less of a tool than the printer. It is really old and obsolete so I use it like a typewriter. Of course books, literature, that's where a lot of ideas come from. I read in bed or at my desk. And the dictionary.

Laura Owens: When I did the show at Sadie Coles in London in 1997, I thought about the space between the paintings as a portrait of America. After that I thought it would be interesting to try to have an exhibition that expanded that space to thousands of miles. I would have three shows—located in LA, Chicago, and New York—that would be one show in my mind. I took the train cross-country to install the works. I made a preliminary trip to look for the American prairie in Illinois and see the gallery at Loyola University, north of Chicago. It was a shallow, eighty-foot-long space enclosed in glass with only one large wall. Perpendicular to the gallery were windows that looked out over Lake Michigan. I decided I would make a forty-foot painting for that space using one piece of canvas on one stretcher in situ.

In LA several of the paintings I made responded to the site of the gallery or were relational to my experience of living there. There was a diptych of a landscape that hung in a corner, a small painting made from a photo of Descanso Gardens, and a painting that looked like a graphite and watercolor drawing of a tree that was perpendicular to a window looking out on Wilshire—it was exactly the size of the window. And then there was a painting I made in the gallery that fit floor to ceiling; the majority of it was done with the same house paint they used on the gallery walls. I made it in a couple days, after they had deinstalled the previous show. It was very camouflaged in the space.

Then I got on the train and went to Chicago. I had sketches, I'd planned where I was going to get the paint, and I had asked the curator to help make the stretcher in the gallery beforehand. When I arrived I saw that he was still trying to put it together and that it was made out of scenic flats. Prior to getting there I had imagined working on the painting alone on the floor and periodically having one or two people help me lift it up to look at it. I realized once it all got put together and stretched that it weighed so much and was so unwieldy that it would take twelve people to lift it. So I had to completely change the plan for how I would be working.

    I had made most of the work for the New York show on Fifteenth Street in Maine at "Kamp Kippy." Gavin had just moved into the Passerby space, and I asked him for the dimensions and height of the walls. He gave me the wrong height, and one large white painting I'd made to fit (like at ACME.) extended over the floating wall by a couple of inches. I thought of this mismatch as a perfect portrait of my relationship with Gavin at the time. The beehive painting was inspired by a pillow I'd bought at an estate sale that got me thinking, "Why can't a very kitsch crewel embroidery object be a motivation to talk about abstraction in painting?" One of the last paintings I made was based on a glossy computer printout that I had made from this Kid Pix program. I'd had the printout in my studio for about a year, and my mom suggested I make a painting like that when I was having anxiety about getting the rest of the work for the show finished.

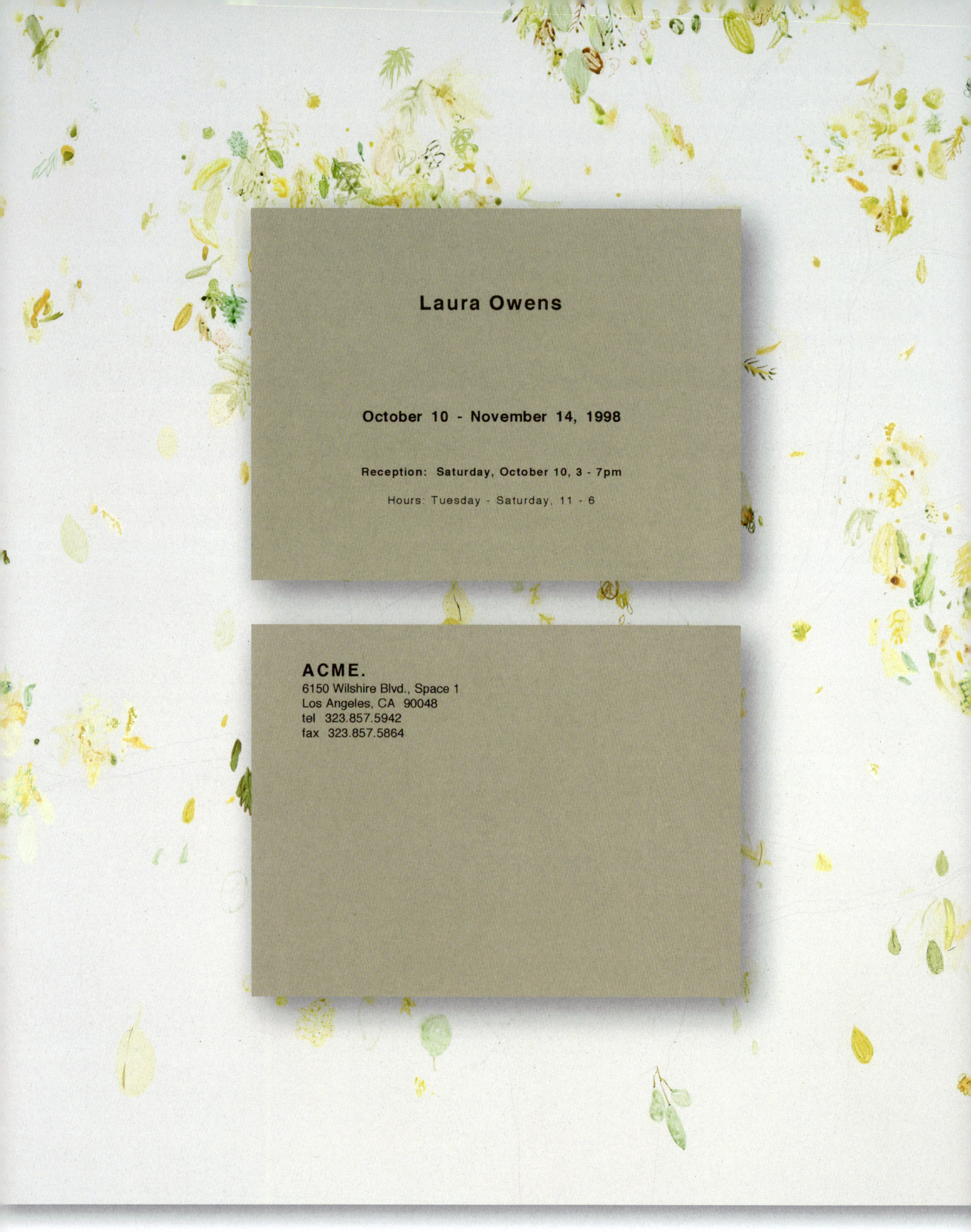

Foreground: Invitation, ACME., Los Angeles, 1998
Background: Detail of *Untitled*, 1998, acrylic and graphite on canvas, 96 × 75 in. (243.8 × 190.5 cm)

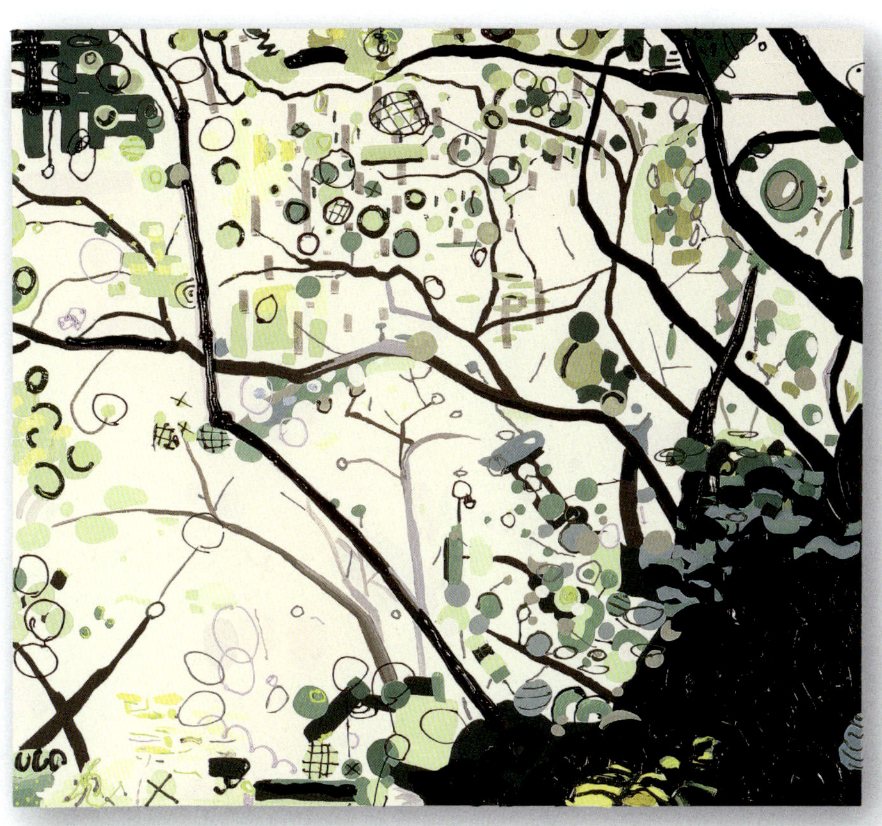

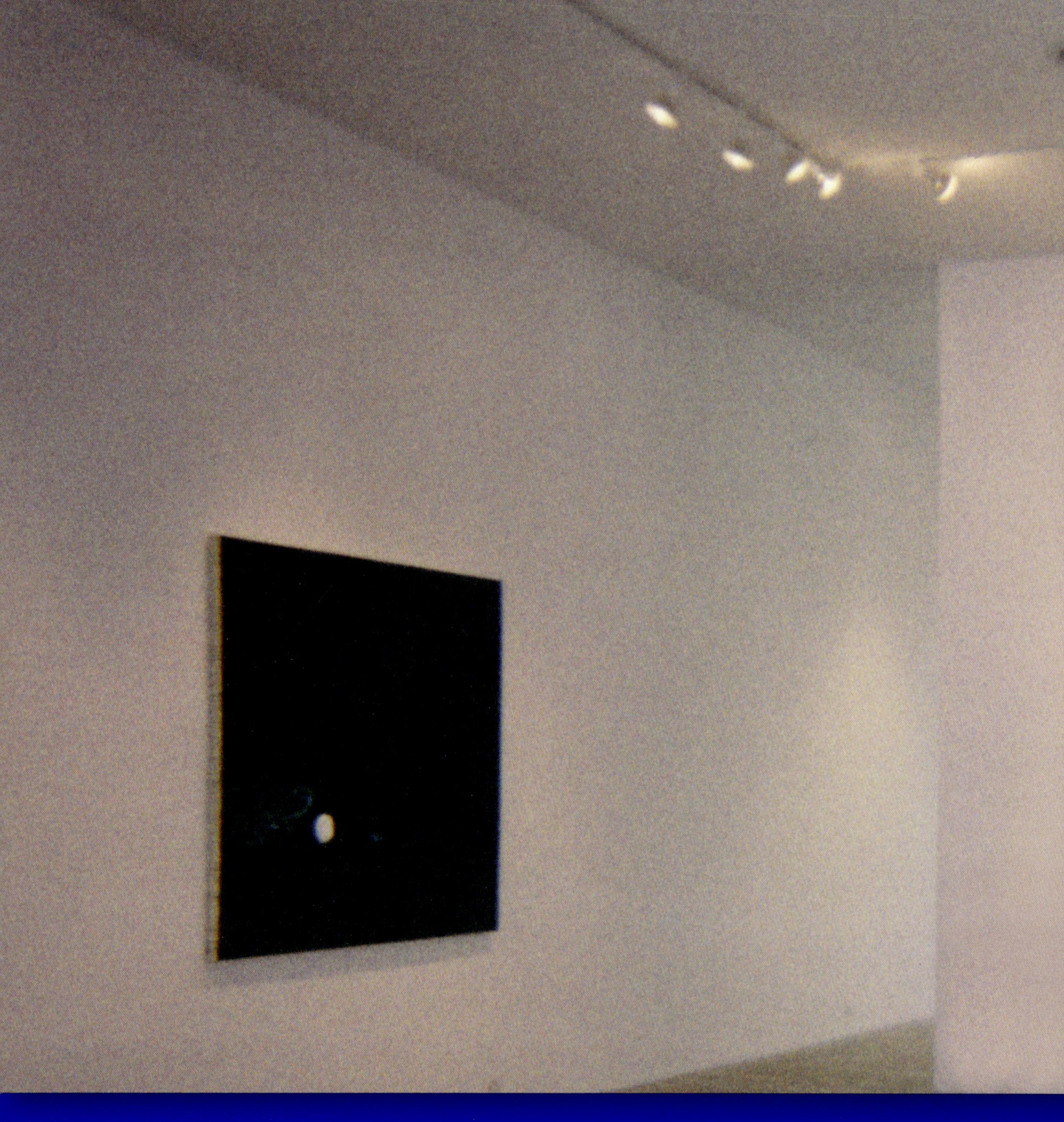

 Installation view, ACME., Los Angeles, 1998, with *Untitled,* 1998, acrylic and oil on canvas, 64 × 72 in. (162.6 × 182.9 cm), and *Untitled* (see p. 263)

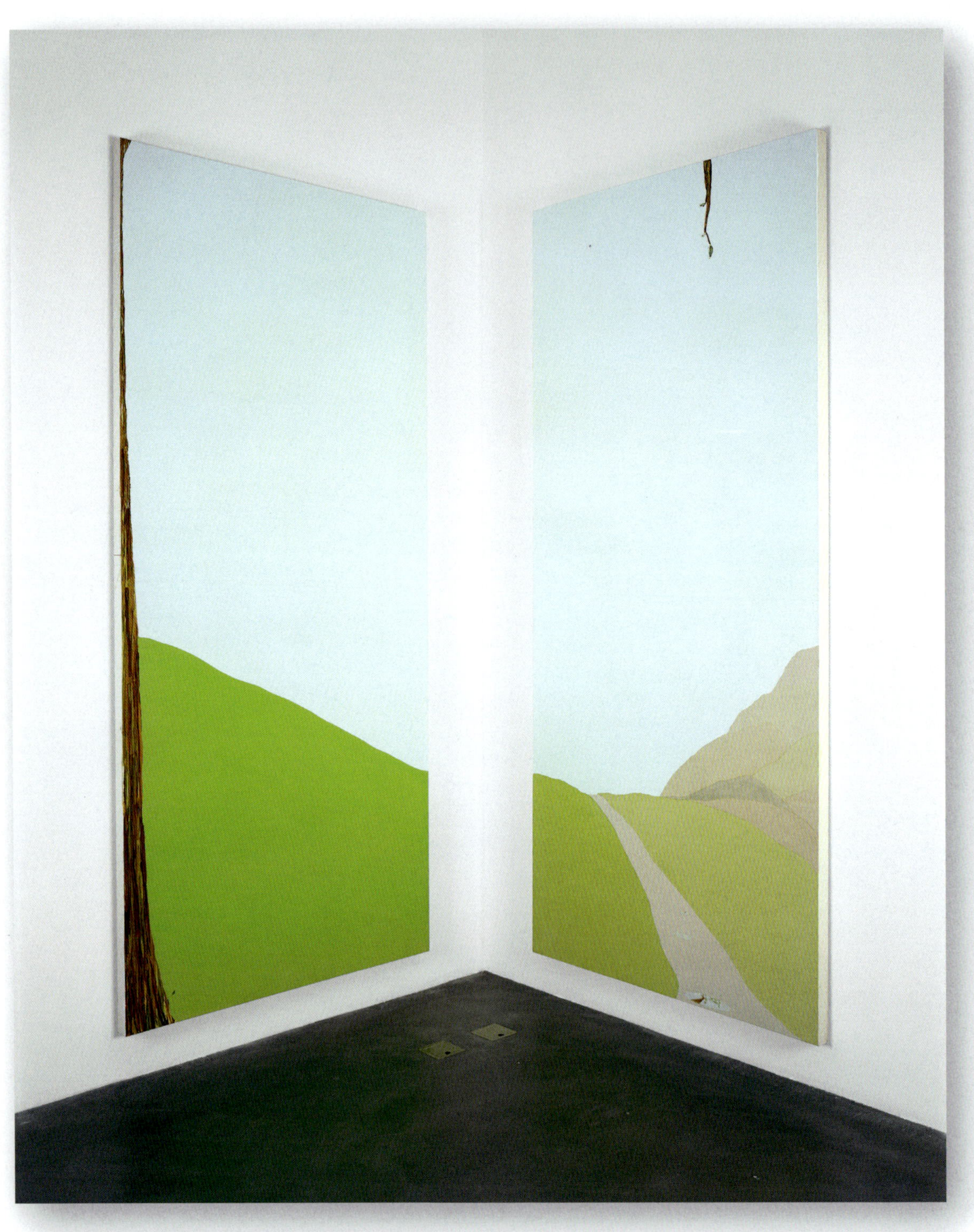

   Untitled, 1998, acrylic, oil, and graphite on canvas, two panels: 114 × 50 in. (289.6 × 127 cm) each

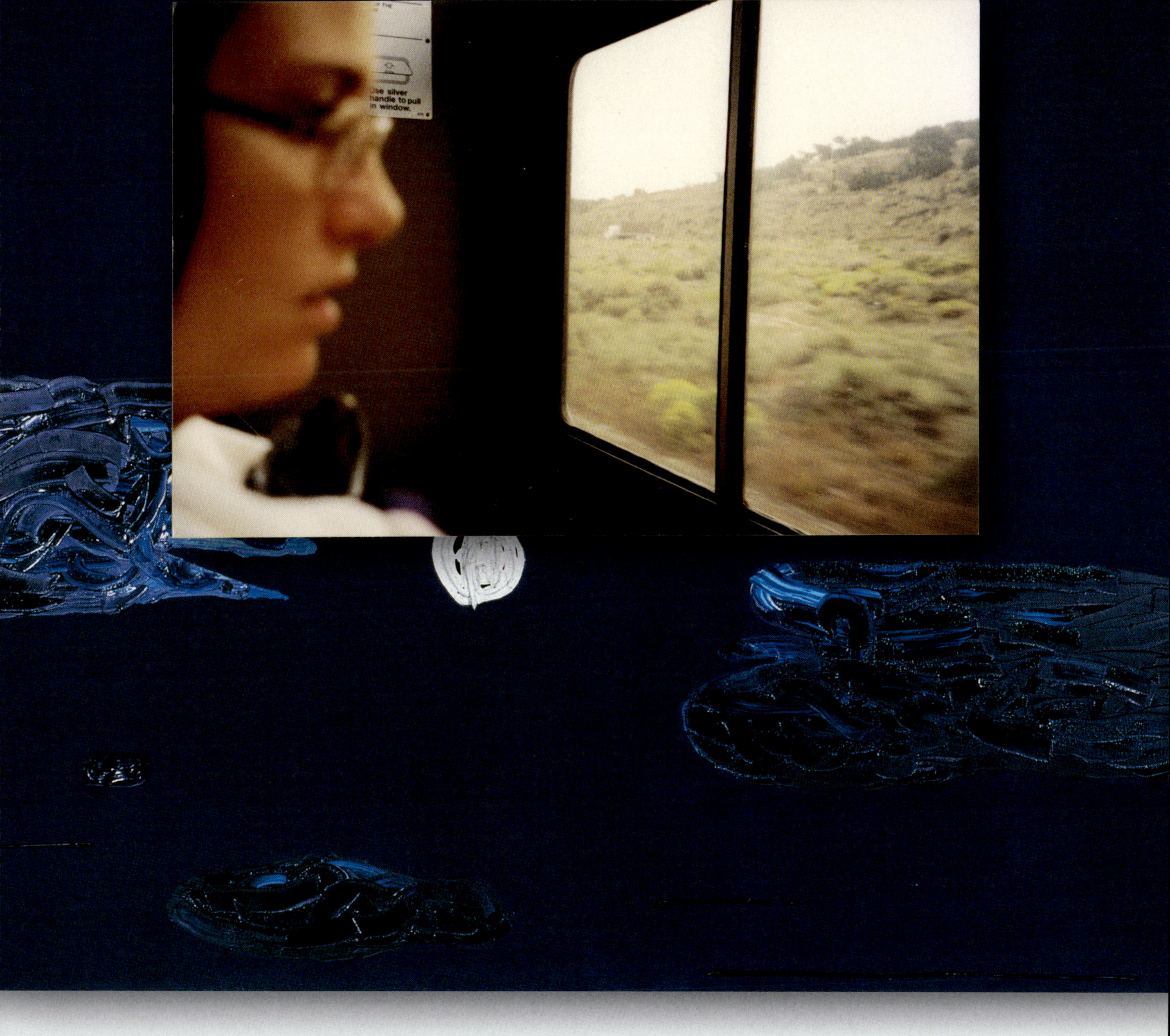

Foreground: Owens, train trip to Chicago, 1998
Background: Detail of *Untitled*, 1998 (see p. 200)

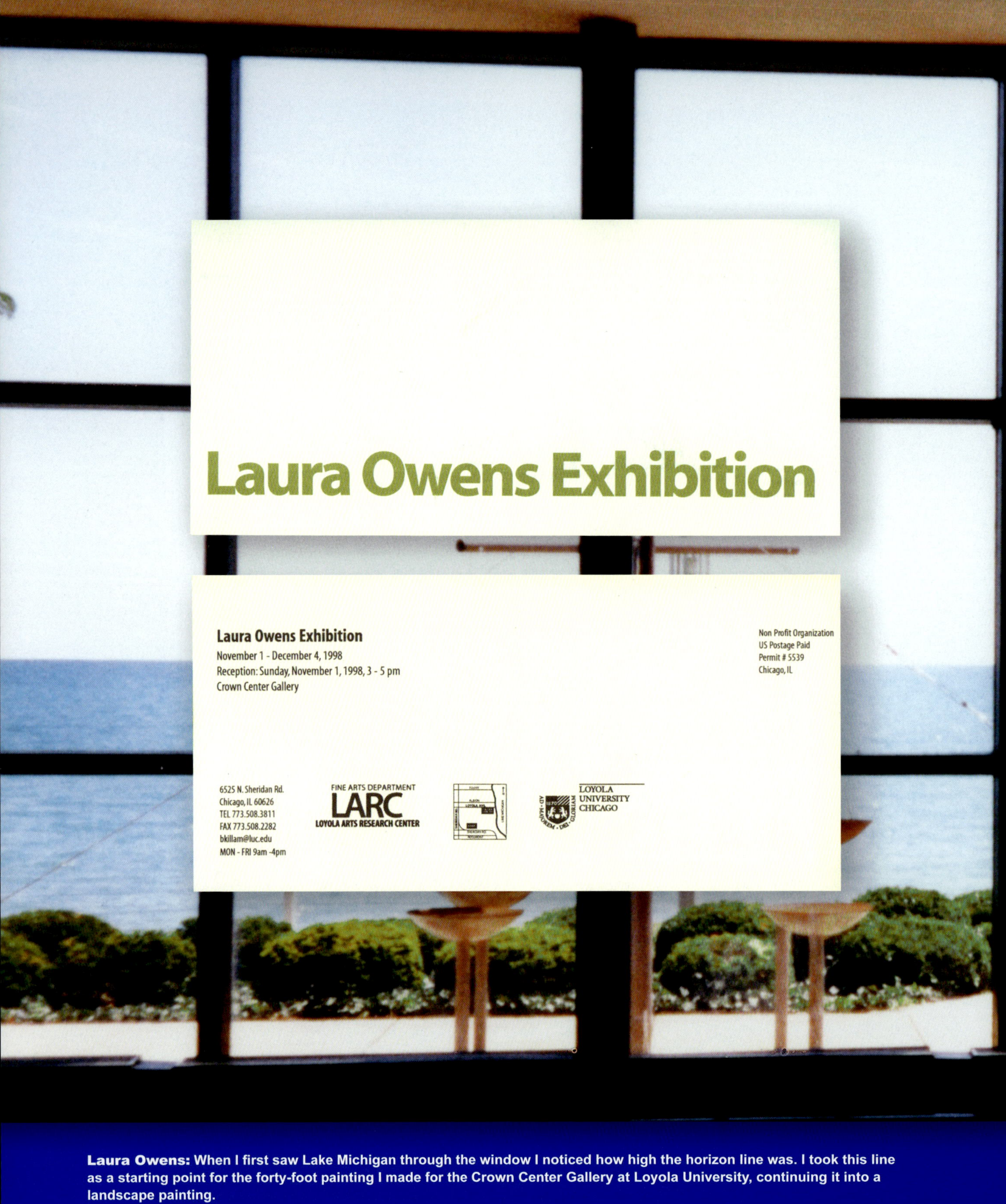

Laura Owens: When I first saw Lake Michigan through the window I noticed how high the horizon line was. I took this line as a starting point for the forty-foot painting I made for the Crown Center Gallery at Loyola University, continuing it into a landscape painting.

Foreground: Invitation, Crown Center Gallery, Loyola University, Chicago, 1998
Background: View of Lake Michigan, Crown Center Gallery, Loyola University, Chicago, 1998

& guess for some reason & really want to make a big painting like this & & like the "no pressure" situation of Chicago as sort of a practice run for this way of making paintings. At the same time I feel slightly demoralized doing a show for nothing & practically paying out of pocket — Anyway I guess I already made a decision to do it a long time ago. David Pagel Interviewed me & 5 other people for Sunday times. I + was real stupid but super positive.

I hope everything is going really well with the bar. Very excited to see where its at when & come. & might stop by or come back for Sep. 11 opening. Probably just see the show on my way back through — 30th September.
Thanks again. ♡ Laura

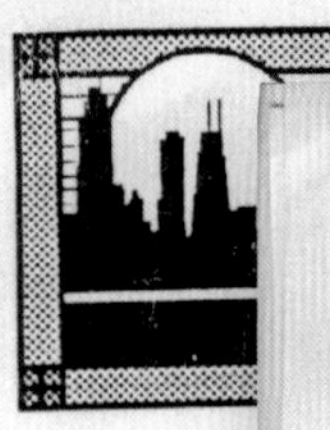

dable Prices

Dear (

Welco

Enclo   da
Centr   the
buildi

There
callin

Suite
Suite
Suite
Suite
Suite

In cas
apart   g
Throu   n
callin   y the
sigr

Chec   t
Passi
made

Thank   gain
soon.

Since

Marc Aguila
Linda Davis

05/14/?? 01:21   212-627-5261   GBE   PAGE 01

Brad Killam
Fine Arts Department
Loyola University Chicago
6525 N. Sheridan Road
Chicago
IL 60626

Our ref: GB/2046

28 July, 1998

Dear Brad

I spoke to Laura this morning - it's good she was able to visit you in Chicago and go through the plans for the show in October. Attached is a breakdown detailing what she will need to make the painting in Chicago. It would be good to know what your budget is at this stage in relation to this breakdown. Also, please let us know if you have heard anything from the Stones.

I will be away now until the end of August, but Gavin will be here so you can contact him directly or our assistant Anton.

With best wishes,

Kirsty Bell

Laura —

This is what Kirsty faxed Brad. It seems pretty harmless to me. He must be going through some kind of POT PARANOIA

Foreground: Fax from Gavin Brown's enterprise, 1998

Illinois

GET A MILLION MILES FROM MONDAY.

8/91   04:13   212-627-5261   GBE   PAGE 01

Is there anything missing? xK

LAURA OWENS: CHICAGO SHOW

TO: Laura
     512
     Los

Thank you
We have
you with t

<u>Schedule</u>

19 October: LO arrive Chicago

20 October: deinstall previous show; begin to put together stretcher and strech canvas

21 -31 October: make painting (must have access to space as late and early in day as poss.)

1 November: Show opens

<u>Assistants</u>

- 4 people (at least) to stretch canvas - including LO and BK

- 1 person full-time to paint long even coats once canvas is stretched and sand but also do detail
  work

- 3 people on-hand to move painting

** Laura said you had mentioned working with students which would be fine, although there must
also be someone there full time who is competent and reliable. Ideally that would be Laura's
assistant from LA - would this will be possible within your budget?

<u>Materials</u>

- Strecther ready to assemble: 111" x 480", drills, hammers, measuring tape, screws

- Canvas: 12' x 42' piece

- Dropcloths: 2mm weight, enough to cover gallery floor (so canvas doesn't get dirty)

- 3 stapleguns

- 3 canvas pliers

- 2 hot pots to boil water (to even out glitches)

- Sandpaper

- 3 fans for during painting

** Once canvas is stretched it may need to be restretched so Laura will need access to all materials
& equipment for the full time

<u>Sundry expenses</u>

- $300 for house paint (must have access to a paint store that sells quality latex house paint)

- $100 for incidental supplies eg. brushes, tubes of paint etc.

- $75 to UPS art supplies from LA in early October

- $150 for dropclothes, masking tape, other hardware

FULT HI
LAKE M
BLUFF R
FULTS

Description
WITHIN TH
ALSO CON
BOTTOMS
PRESERV

Directions
5 MILES N

GOOSE
5010 NO
MORRIS

Description
GOOSE LA
WATCHING
10:00 TO 4:

Directions
GOOSE LA
TOWN ROA

1 - 8 0 0 - 2 C O N N E C T

T T Y   1 - 8 0 0 - 4 0 6 - 6 4 1 8   •   h t t p : / / w w w . e n j o y i l l i n o i s . c o m

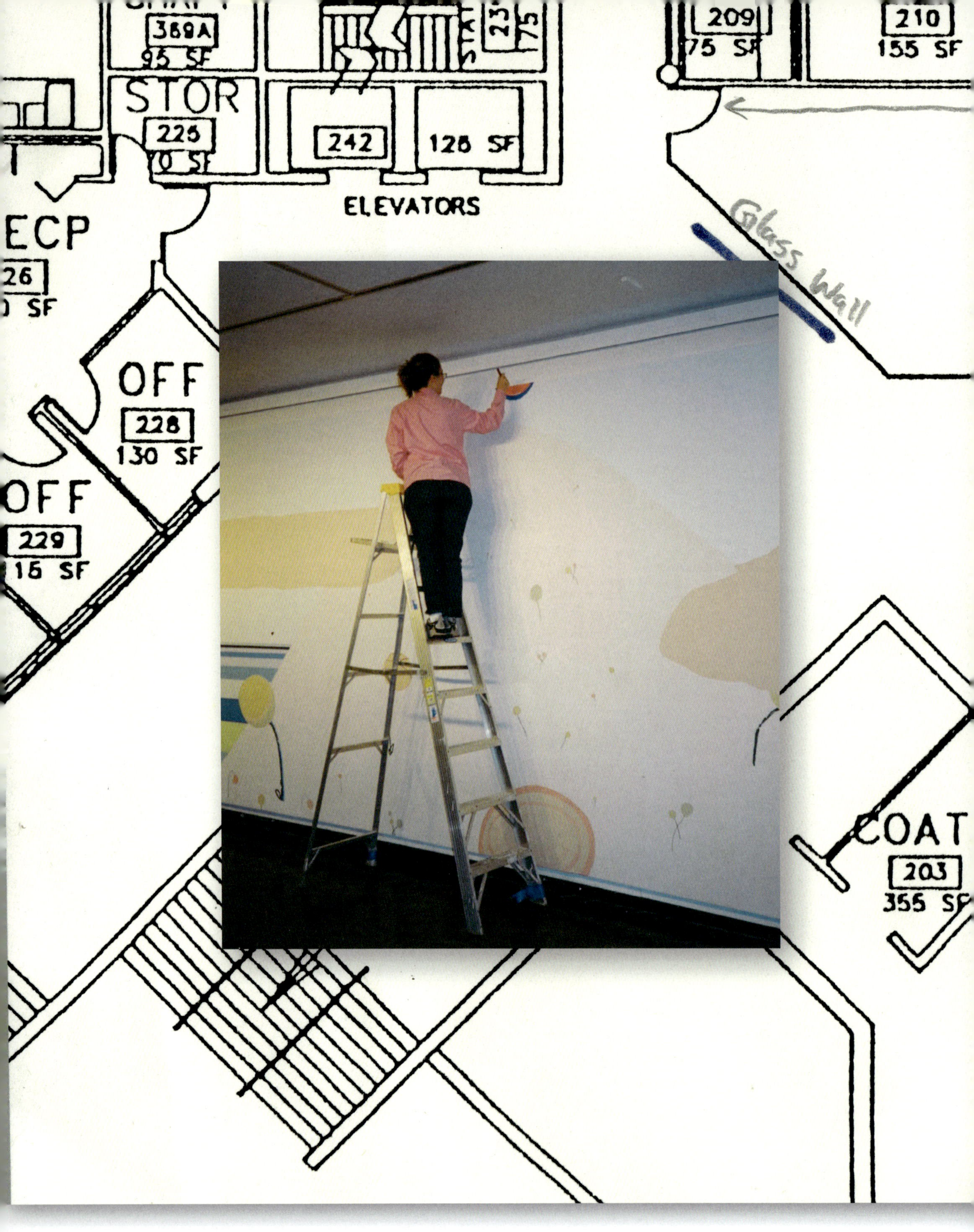

Foreground: Owens with *Untitled*, 1998 (see p. 210), Crown Center Gallery, Loyola University, Chicago, 1998
 Background: Floor plan, Crown Center Gallery, Loyola University, Chicago, 1998

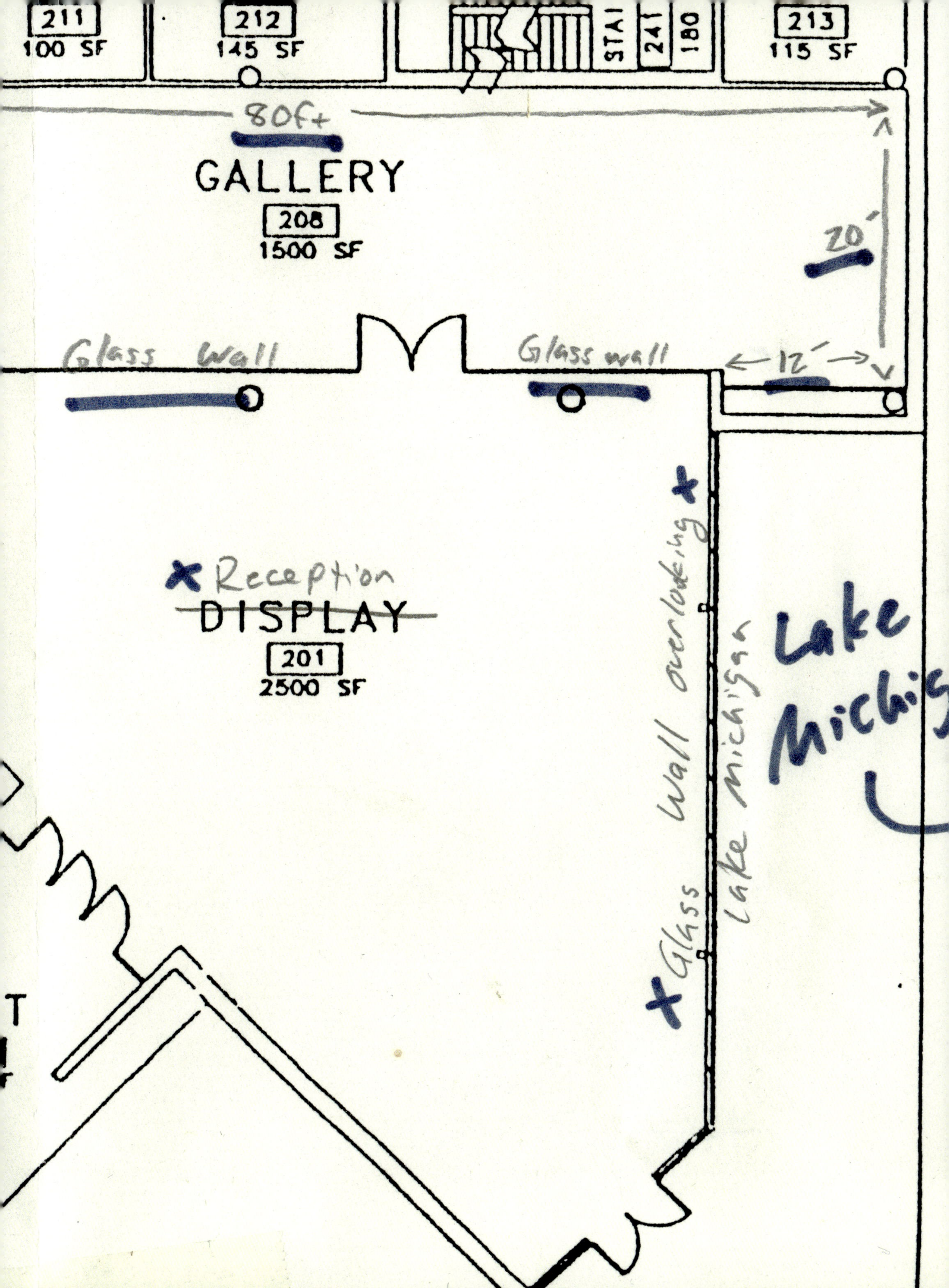
211
100 SF
212
145 SF
STAI
241
180
213
115 SF
80f+
GALLERY
208
1500 SF
20´
12´
Glass wall
Glass wall
Reception
DISPLAY
201
2500 SF
Glass wall overlooking lake michigan
Glass
Lake Michig

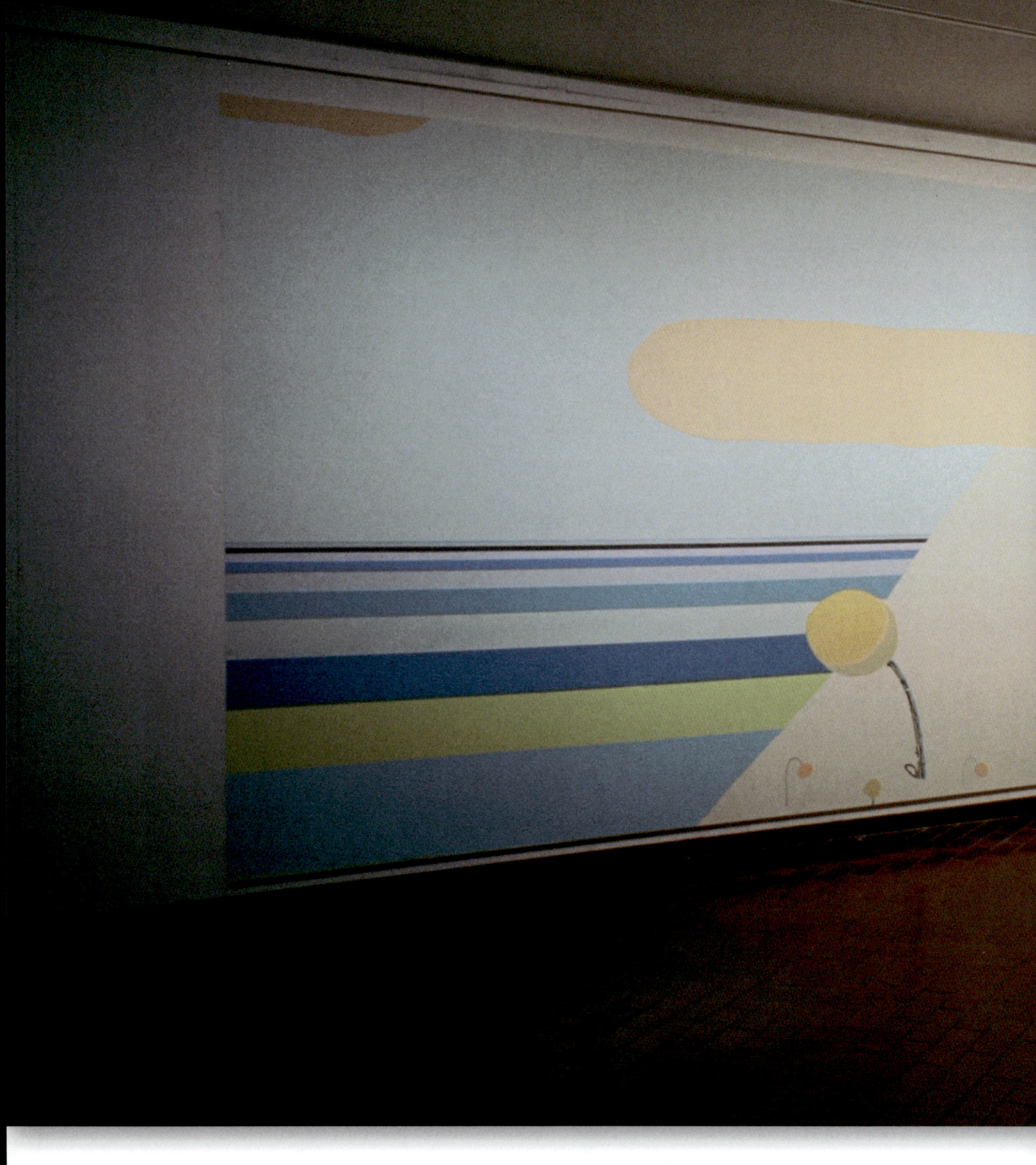

Installation view, Crown Center Gallery, Loyola University, Chicago, 1998, with *Untitled*, 1998, acrylic and enamel on canvas, 111 × 480 in. (281.9 × 1219.2 cm)

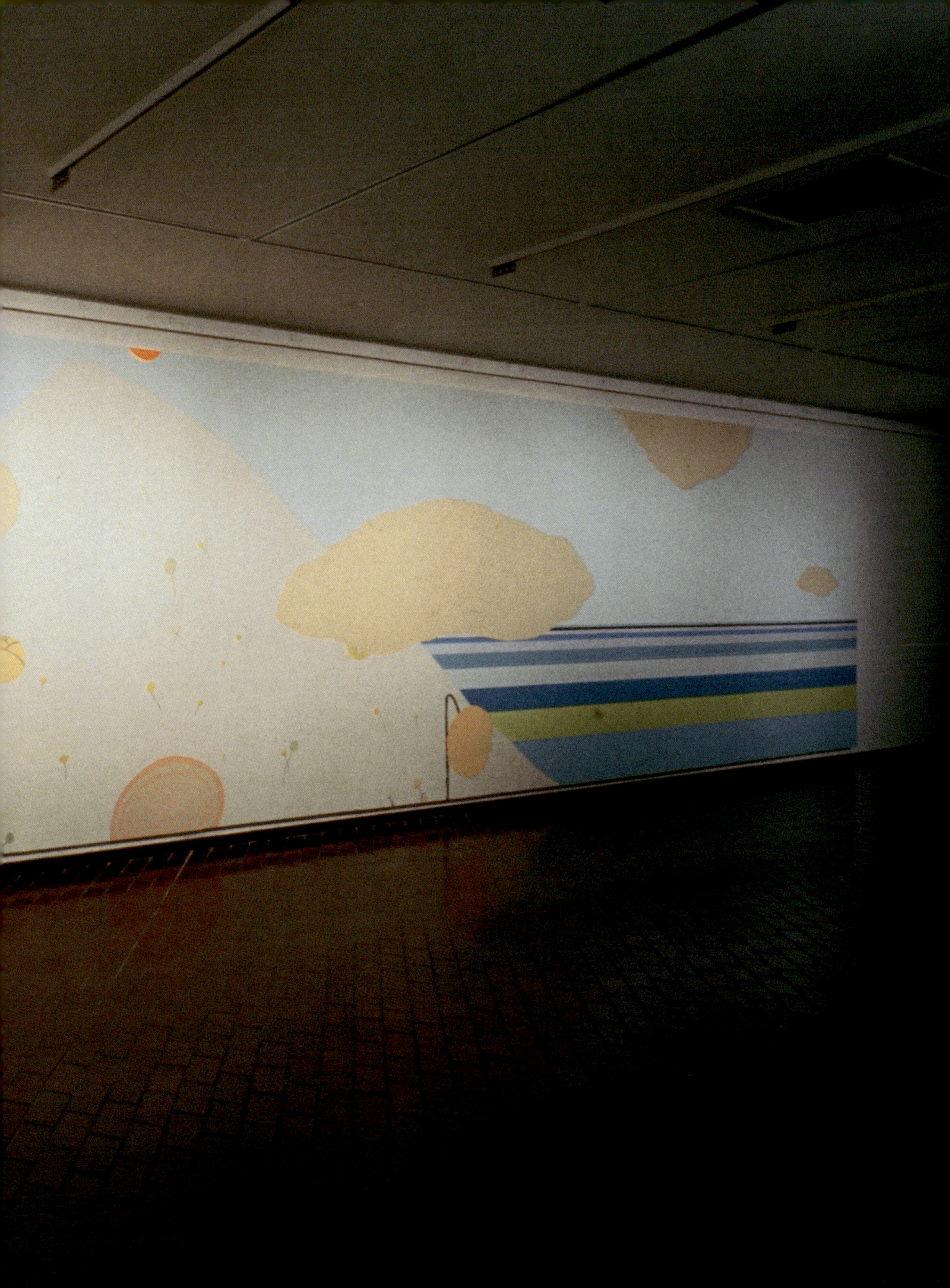

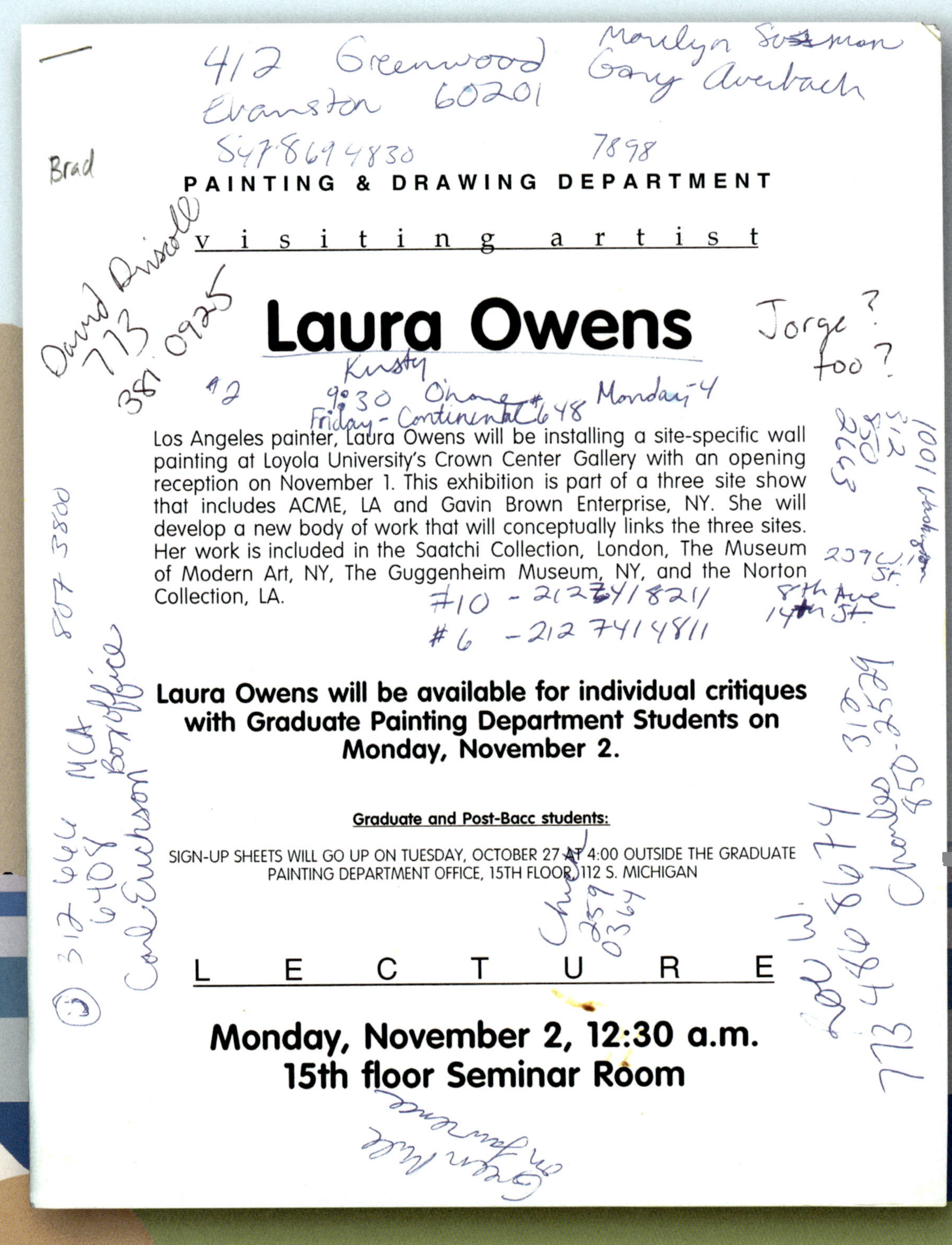

Foreground: Flyer with notes by Owens, 1998
Background: Detail of *Untitled*, 1998 (see p. 210)

January 11, 1999

Laura Owens
5121 1/2 Eagle rock Blvd.
Apt. D
Los Angeles, CA 90041

Dear Laura,

Greetings for the new year, hope your holiday was a warm and festival time. As you may have heard on the news, ours was a bit different.

Following up with the finishing touches of your exhibition, I'm glad to report that all of your assistants have been paid in full. However, your disbursement has been altered. Allow this attempt to explain.

Three factors play a role in the Chairman's(my boss) decision to require me to re-submit a check requisition for you.

1. The University is going thru major restructuring in a process called "Loyola 2000". Basically this means that the entire university is being asked to cut their current budgets by 11% by the end of the current fiscal year. Preposterous, I agree.

2. I submitted my resignation in early December (January 15 departure) and since have had all my affairs micro-managed, especially budget.

3. We overspent budget for your show by $741.67. Thus, the chair of the department withheld approval of the requested $747.33 for your honorarium and supplies reimbursement. He argued that we have already spent too much.

My rebuttal has a positive ending. I argued persuasively that you worked extremely hard for two solid weeks and that you should receive some compensation. The compromise is to still honor the $400.00 honorarium. I've enclosed a copy of that paperwork for your peace of mind, a check will come.

I must apologize for such an administrative nightmare, sparked by the tending of my resignation. I'm sure the run-around has put a sour spin on this place for you. On a better note, New Art Examiner is rounding up writers to produce a nice piece about your work. I'm not sure of the publication date, but would guess the March or April issue.

Thank you again for such a wonderful exhibition and breathtaking painting. Though Loyolan's may be rather short sighted , your show here had a significant impact in all the right places. Truly the best painting to be displayed in Chicago in a long, long time.

Best Regards for the new year.

Brad Killam

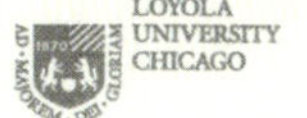

FINE ARTS DEPARTMENT
LARC
LOYOLA ARTS RESEARCH CENTER

Edward Crown Center
for the Humanities–219
6525 North Sheridan Road
Chicago, IL 60626-5385
TEL: (773) 508-3811
FAX: (773) 508-2282
EMAIL: bkillam@luc.edu

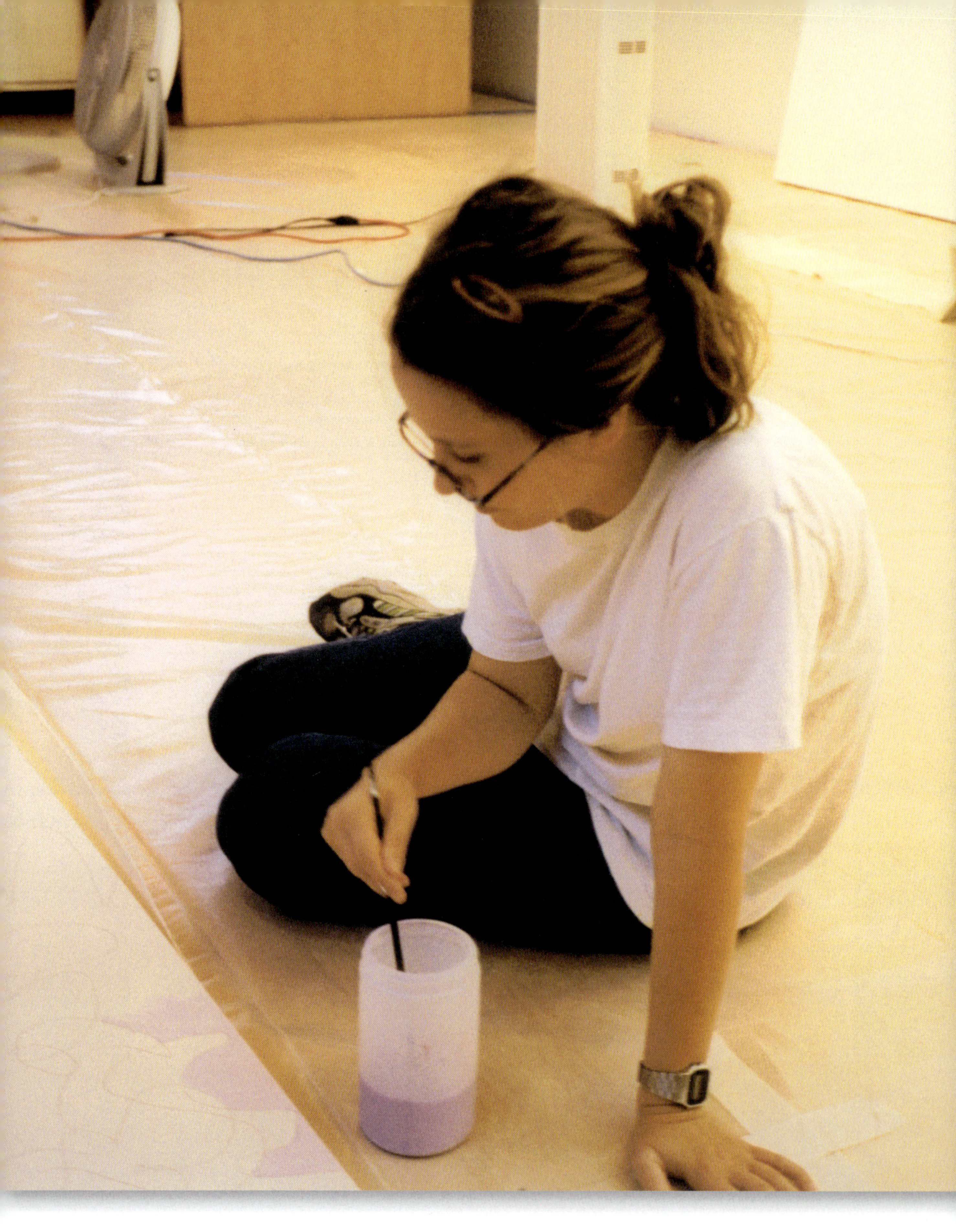

  Owens with *Untitled*, 1998 (see p. 220), "Kamp Kippy" (Acadia Summer Arts Program) studio, Mount Desert Island, Maine, 1998

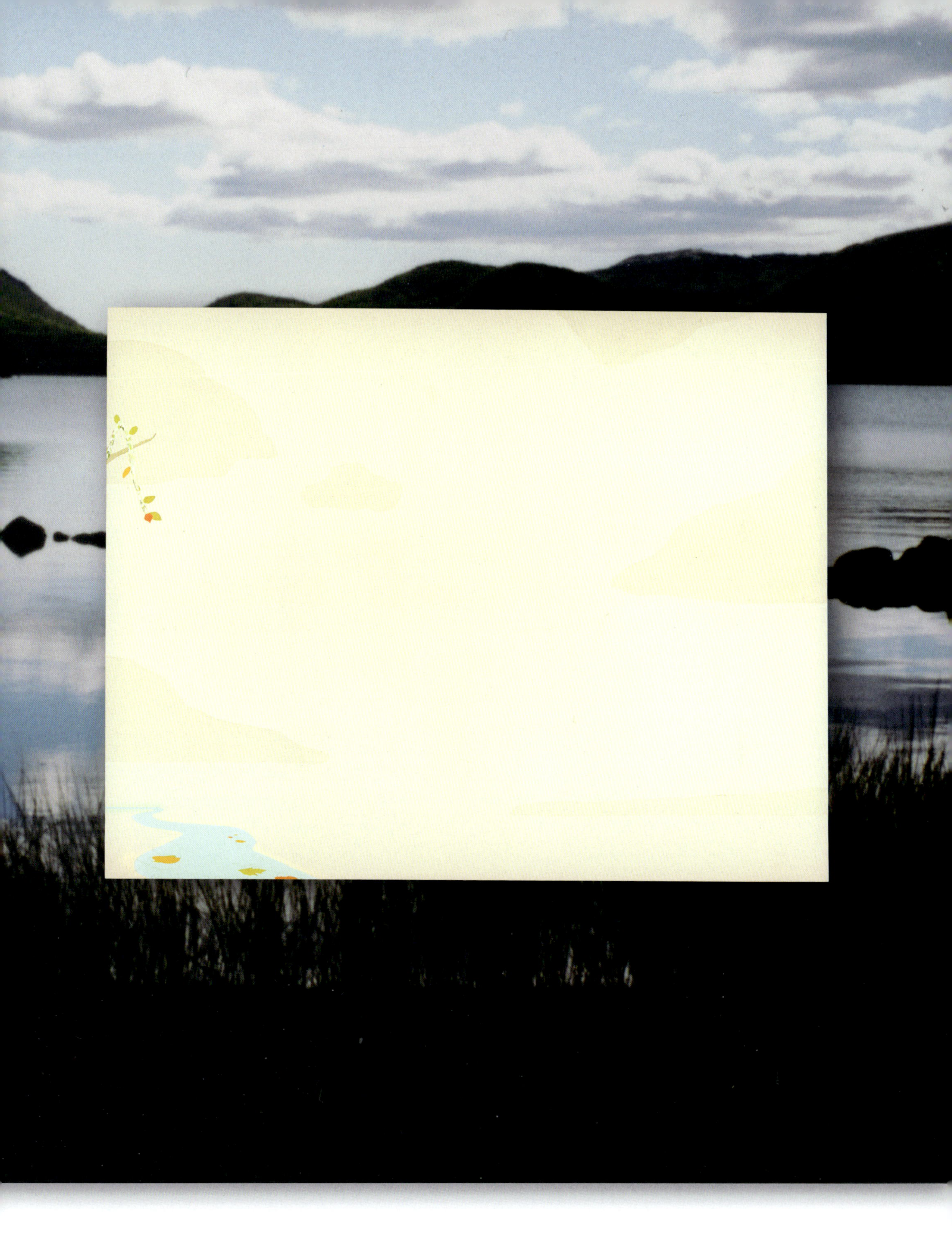

Foreground: *Untitled,* 1998, acrylic and enamel on canvas, 96 × 120 in. (243.8 × 304.8 cm)
Background: Research photograph by Owens, Deer Isle, Maine, 1998

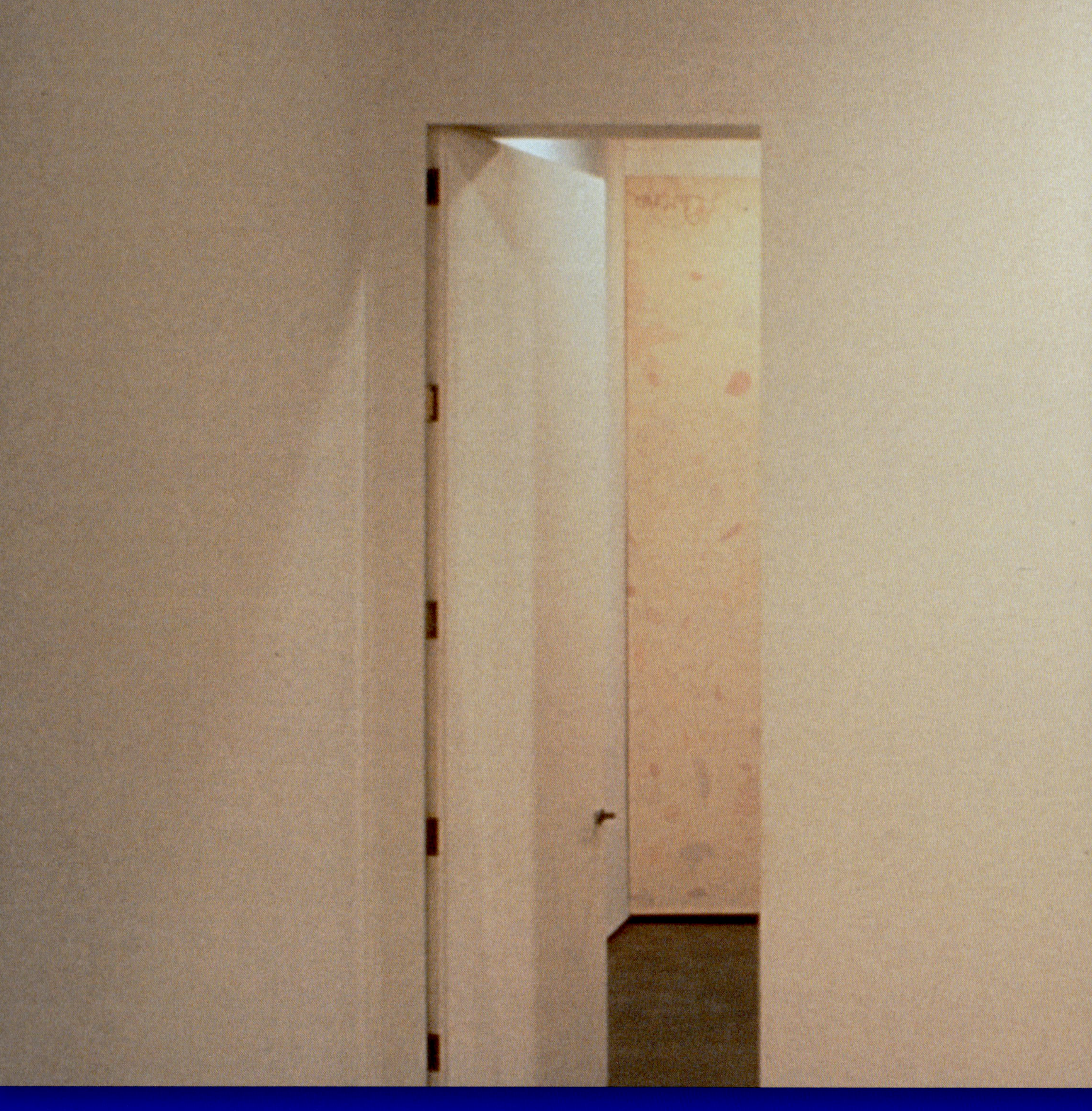

Laura Owens: I was invited to Kamp Kippy as Jorge Pardo's guest and decided to make most of the work for the New York show there. I ordered a stretcher that was the width of the door to Gavin's office and really tall. I thought it would be funny if, looking through the door from far away, it seemed like there was a really huge painting in the office, but it actually was just tall and thin. I started making an all-over pattern on the raw canvas with a Space Pen. I filled in some of the shapes with thin washes of acrylic. I was very inspired by a show of fifty years of textiles after the Bauhaus that I'd seen at the Art Institute while teaching there. All of the yardage in that show was shown stretched in three-foot-by-ten-foot samples hung on the wall. When I walked into the show I had the realization that they were paintings, and that the history of textiles was an important part of the canon of painting and should not be omitted or segregated to a different department but embraced. After I had done the washes I didn't know how to finish the painting so I just thought, "I know, I'll sign it." When I lifted it up to look at it, it was upside down—that was an unplanned accident but it immediately felt right, and the work was finished.

Foreground: Invitation, Gavin Brown's enterprise, New York, 1998
Background: Installation view, Gavin Brown's enterprise, New York, 1998, with *Untitled*, 1998 (see p. 220), and *Untitled*, 1998 (see p. 215)

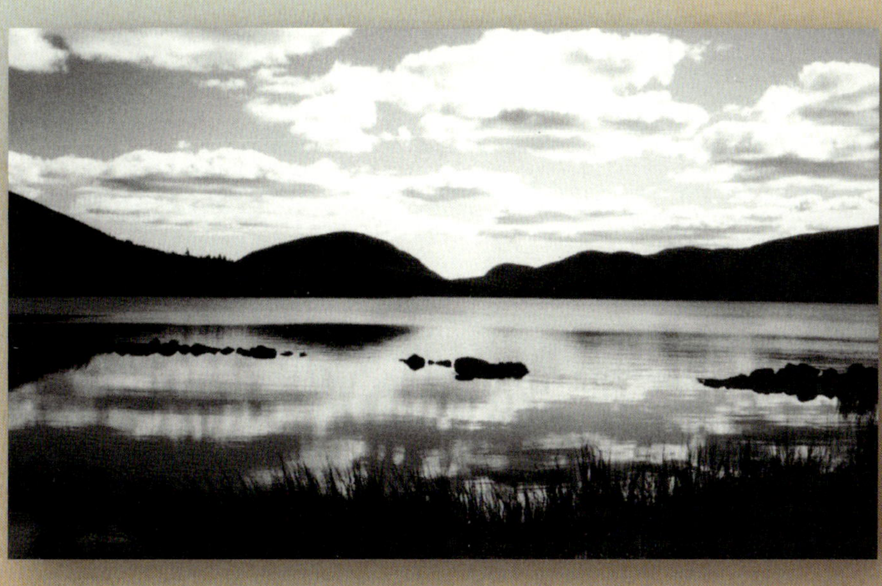

LAURA OWENS

October 17 - November 14, 1998

Gavin Brown's enterprise, corp.
436 W15th St New York NY 10011
tel 212 627 5258 fax 212 627 5261
e-mail: passerby@bway.net

Tuesday - Saturday 10 am - 6 pm
Opening reception: Friday October 16, 6 pm - 9 pm

Dear Gavin & Kirsty,

Hi from L.A. I am sorry I have not sent the painting yet. I guess I
am having a few doubts about it. Anyway I am working on the bigger
one. I am supposed to have a studio visit with Moca committee on the
28th. I think it would be good to have something to show them. I
think we said to ship the painting the 22nd is it a problem for you
to get a week later? I am trying to ask Connie Butler how much it
really matters if they see actual work or not, so I will let you know
what she says.   Also I am trying to order about 15 stretchers for all
these shows in the fall.   Can you please fax me a floor plan and
ceiling height , what fits in the door etc.   I wanted to come see the
space but   I can't come until June.   Also I am thinking of going to
Maine, kippy invited me, in September. Can you guys ship paintings
from Maine? It would be nice to make some of the work in Maine, like
2 paintings.   Tomorrow I am having a lunch with David Maupin.   I
know.
Did you send a check for the 3750 (Hussenot ptng) ? Did the Venice
gallerist pay for her painting? All the stretchers are going to cost
around $5000 and I am broken.

Call me later tommorrow afternoon if you can.

xxxoxoxoxoxooooooooooooooo
Bye-Bye, Laura

Foreground: Letter to Gavin Brown and Kirsty Bell, 1998
Background: Floor plan, Gavin Brown's enterprise, New York, 1998

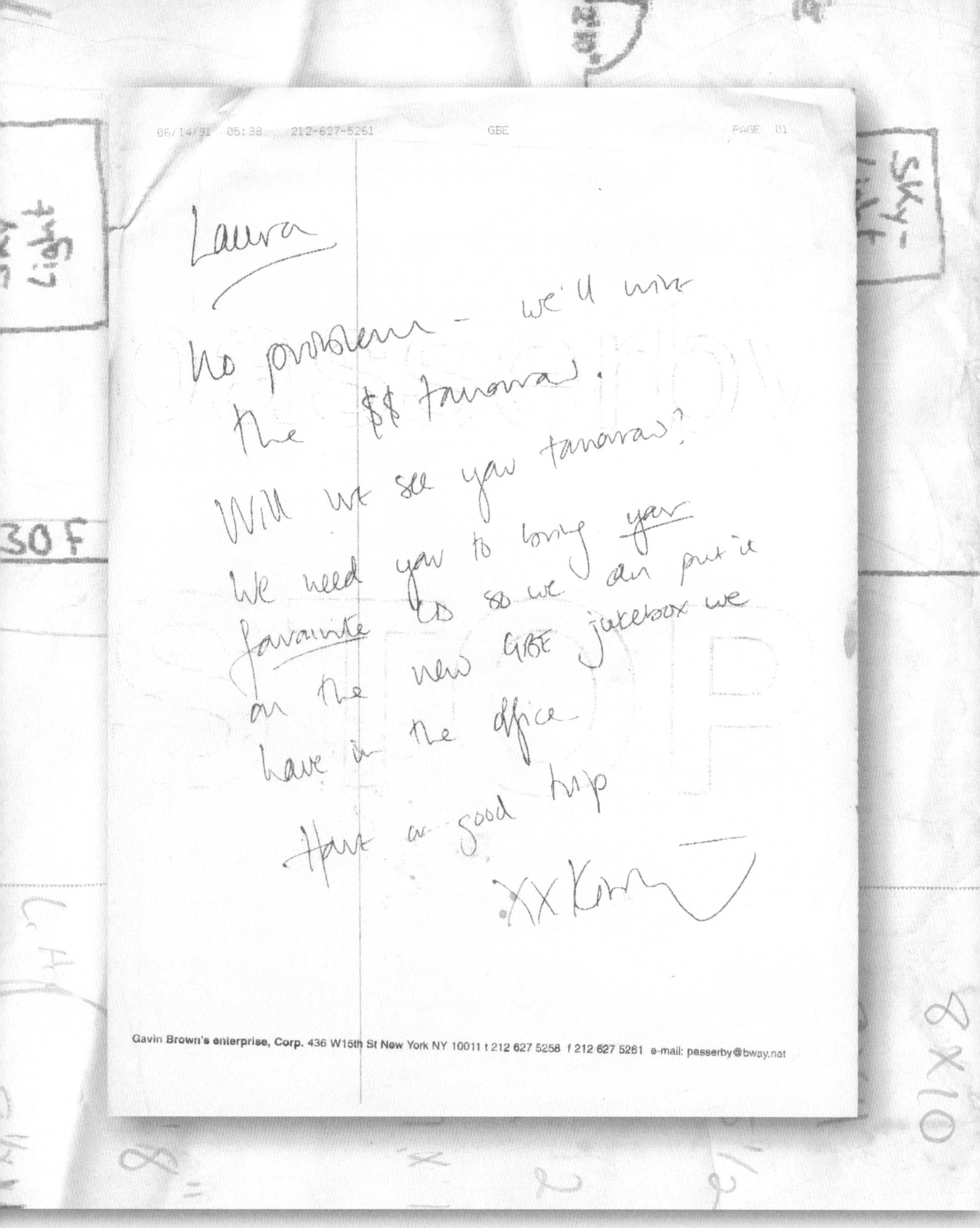

Foreground: Fax from Kirsty Bell, 1998

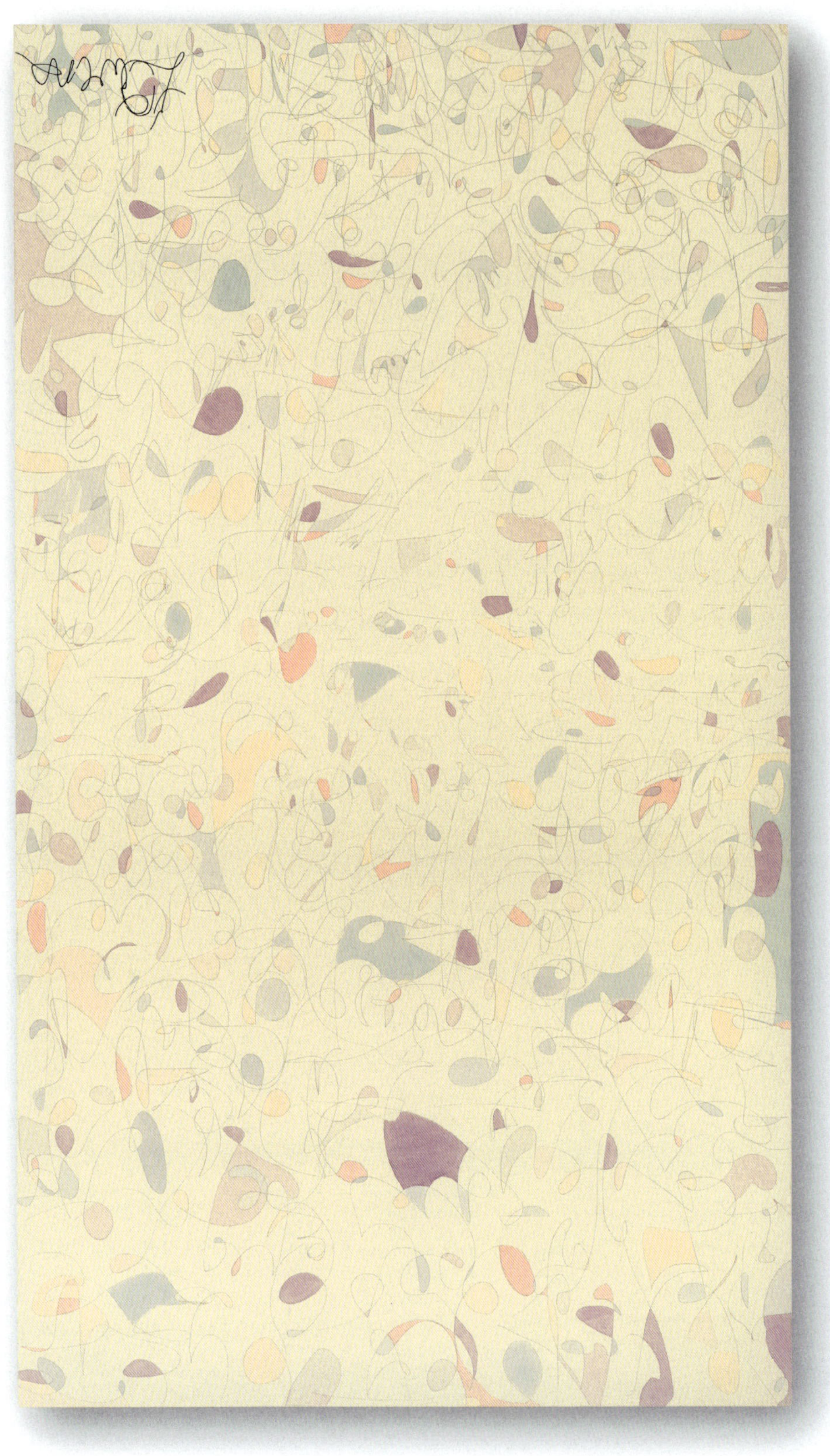

 Untitled, 1998, acrylic and pen on canvas, 144 × 84 in. (365.8 × 213.4 cm)

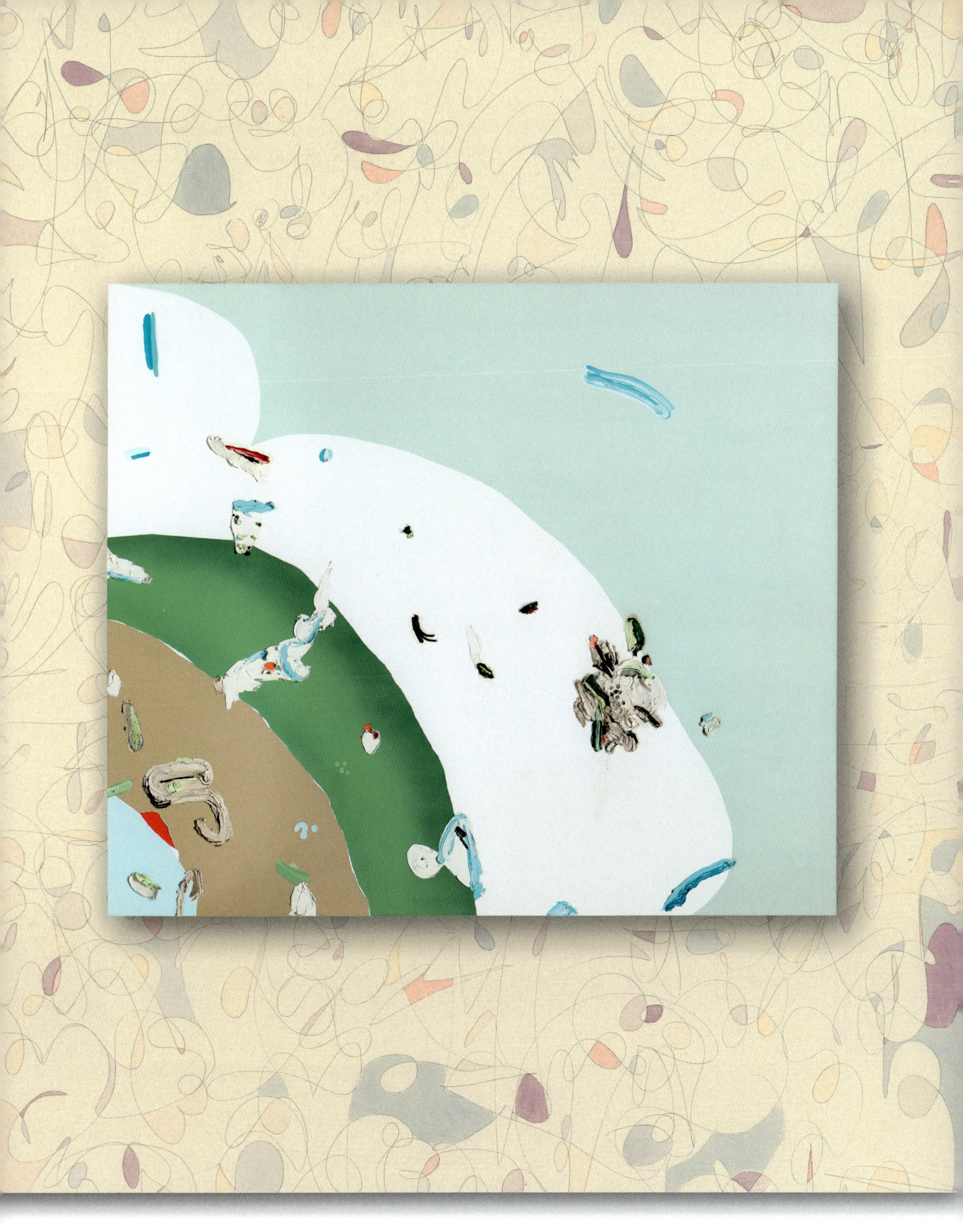

Foreground: *Untitled,* 1998, acrylic and oil on canvas, 84 × 96 in. (213.4 × 243.8 cm)
Background: Detail of *Untitled*, 1998 (see p. 220)

Dear Gavin & Kirsty

Can you Please wire me reimbursement of train ticket $836? I am leaving & won't be able to deposit a check.

Thanks a lot!!!

♡ Laura

Routing # 3210 7000 7

Acct # 270 409 4453

LAURA Ann Owens
5121½ EagleRockBlvd, Apt D
Los Angeles CA 90041-1155

CALFED
5015 EagleRockBlvd
LA CA
90041

Foreground: Letter to Gavin Brown and Kirsty Bell, 1998
Background: Gavin Brown, New York, 1998

LAURA OWENS PRICE LIST
May 1998

I	18 x 20 inches	$3,000
	22 x 22 inches	
	24 x 24 inches	
	26 x 26 inches	
I	36 x 36 inches	$4,000
III	48 x 48 inches	$5,000
	48 x 50 inches	
IV	48 x 60 inches	$6,500
V	66 x 72 inches	$8,000
	72 x 60 inches	
VI	78 x 84 inches	$10,000
	84 x 96 inches	
VII	96 x 120 inches	$11,000

Drawings

10 x 7 inches	$800
9 x 12 inches	$600
14 x 16 inches	$1200
9 x 40 inches	$1400
22 x 30 inches	$1800
34 x 50 inches	$2500

25" x 40" $2,300

ACME Drawings
drawings   7" X 11" $600

GALERIE GISELA CAPITAIN

Laura Owens
USA Los Angeles

Fax

October 21, 1998

Dear Laura,

Hopefully you are doing well. How was New York? Charline told me very good things about your exhibition at Gavin Brown's. I hope I can see it when I will be in New York on November 18th.

In the meantime you may have gotten my message on your answering machine. I hope, it was understandable for you. Again, I would like to express my congratulations and my respect for the show I have seen in Los Angeles. Stephen Prina and I had talked about your way of pushing the genre of landscape painting to such a remarquable extreme point.

I am very much interested in your work and I would like to invite you to do an exhibition in my gallery in the coming year. It would be phantastic if possible!!!

I am looking forward to hear from you.

My best regards,

Gisela Capitain

Nov. 27. 1998

Dear Gisela,

Thank you for your message
I am planning to come to
Cologne Dec. 12-19. I would
love to get together, talk
see your gallery, etc.

I am also leaving to go to
London for a few days during
that time., but for sure,
let's get together.
Hope you are well.
Sincerely, Laura

Nov. 27 1998

Dear Peter Doig,

Hi! Hope you are well! Cesar Reyes gave me your #. I have been thinking about organizing a show in Los Angeles. I would really love to talk to you about it. I am also planning to come to London Dec 13-18. If there is any chance you would want to get together for a little bit I would really appreciate it. I understand I am giving very short notice B its the Holidays but fax me or call if you have any time. My Fax B phone are → ~~███~~ 323. 255 0648 Thanks so much!!
Sincerely,   Laura Owens

226

1·29·99 ·From: Laura Owens · FAX & Phone
323.255.0648

FAXED

Dear Chris,

Hi! Thanks for having me by your studio when I was in London. I really enjoyed it & I especially liked seeing your paintings at the Tate gallery. Very inspiring. Also thanks for thinking about doing this L.A. show. ACME will definitly do it, I'm keeping it open though in case we need a bigger space or whatever.

How is 1999? Are you relaxing? I hope so. I'll probably see you around in New York or London — at your show or my show, hopefully. — Regardless I'll just drop a line — whenever I get more information or ideas about L.A. If you have any ideas etc. ⊕ you can fax or call the # above. Take care,

♡ Laura

P.S. How's the iMac?

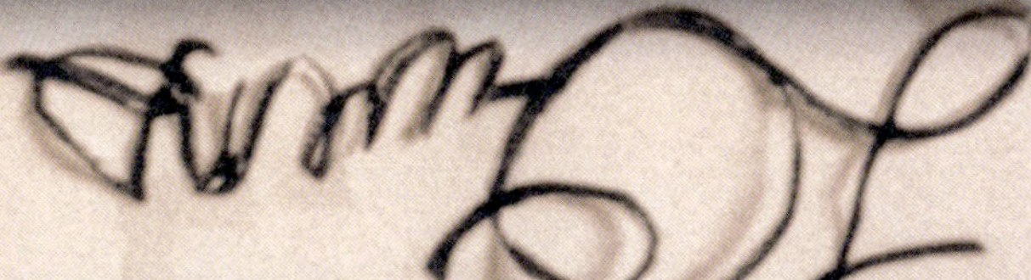

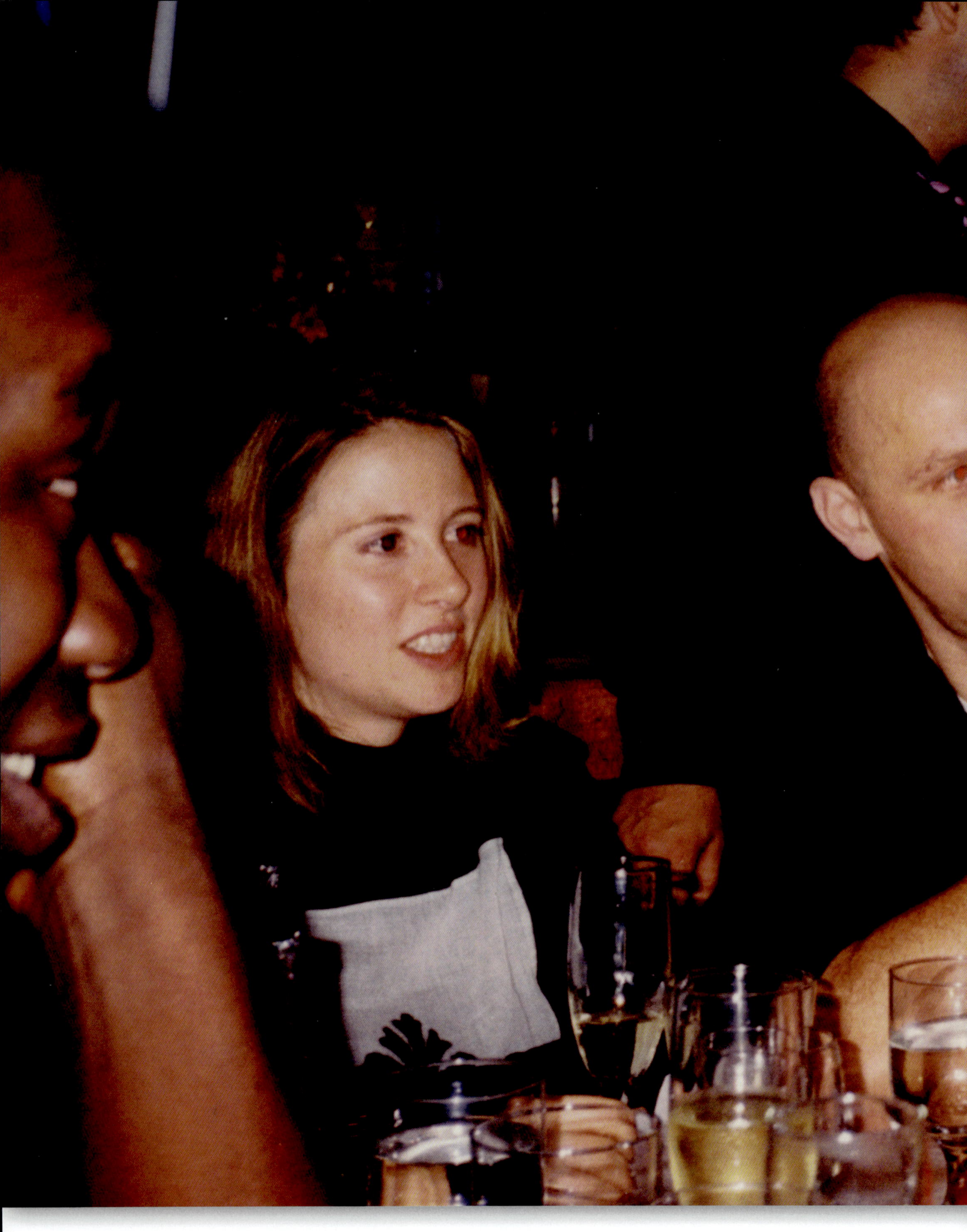

 Chris Ofili, Owens, Peter Doig, and John Currin, with Gavin Brown and Elizabeth Peyton (standing), La Lunchonette, New York, 1999

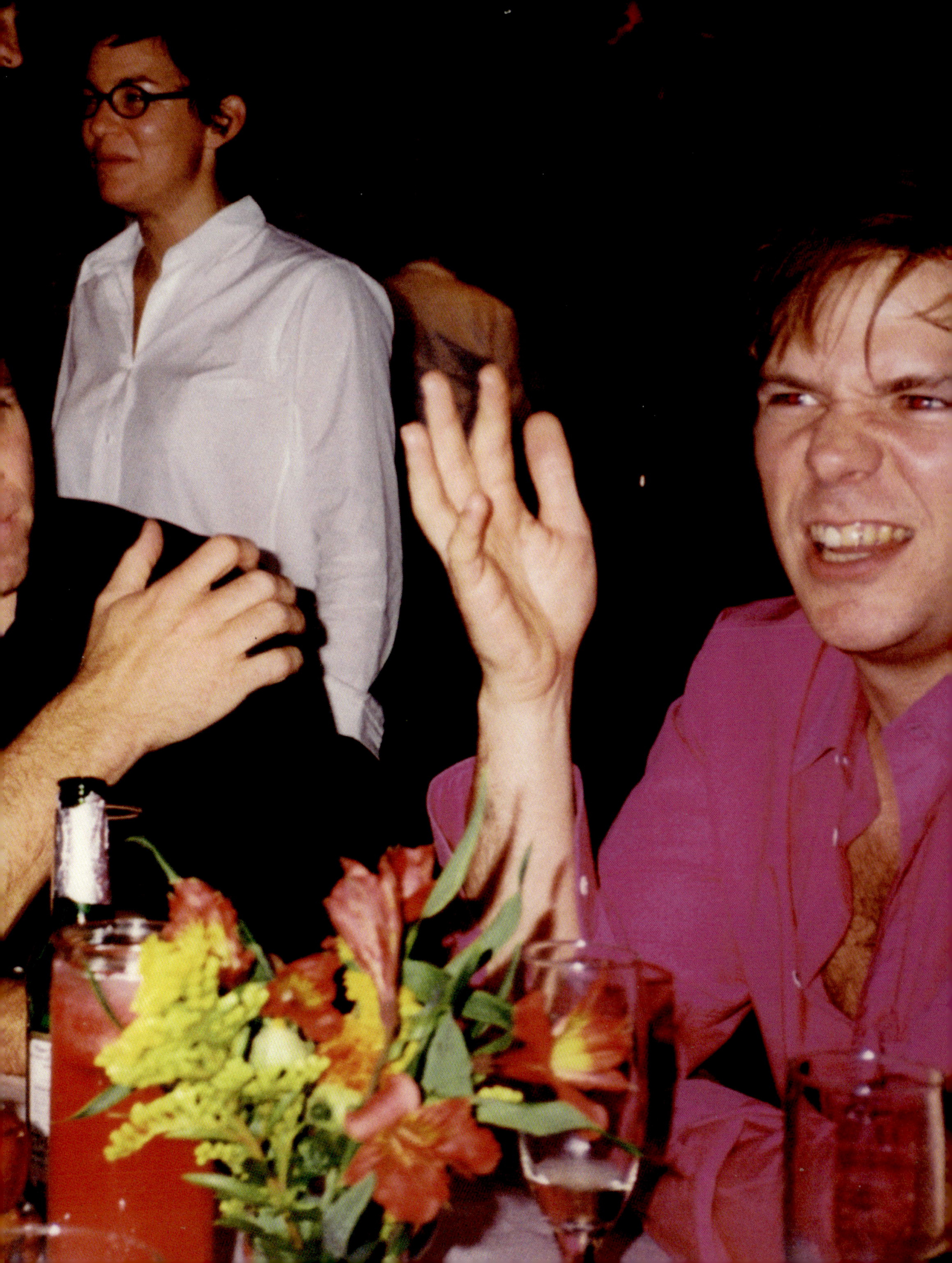

EXCERPT FROM "OUR AESTHETIC CATEGORIES"
SIANNE NGAI

The recent turn to aesthetics [in the academy] has been embraced by some of its advocates as a polemical riposte to critique: a practice increasingly attacked from multiple directions but here specifically for doing artworks the disservice of reducing them to encryptions of history or ideology. But while the new or revived focus on pleasure (and, to a much lesser extent, displeasure)[1] has been vaunted for the way in which it seems to circumvent the reduction of artworks to historical or ideological concepts, our aesthetic experience is always mediated by a finite if constantly rotating repertoire of aesthetic categories. Any . . . cultural criticism purportedly engaged with aesthetics needs to pay attention to these categories, which are by definition conceptual as well as affective and tied to historically specific forms of communication and collective life. But how does one read an aesthetic category? What kind of object is it, and what methodological difficulties and satisfactions does its analysis pose?

[*Our Aesthetic Categories*] makes a simple if no doubt contentious argument about the zany, interesting, and cute: that this quotidian triad of aesthetic categories, for all their marginality to historical accounts of postmodernism as well as to canonical aesthetic theory, is the one in our cultural repertoire best suited for grasping how the concept of "aesthetic" has been transformed by the performance-driven, information-saturated and networked, hypercommodified world of late capitalism. This is because the interesting, cute, and zany index—and are thus each in a historically concrete way about—capitalism's most socially binding processes: production, in the case of the zany (an aesthetic about performance as not just artful play but also affective labor); circulation, in the case of the interesting (a serial, recursive aesthetic of informational relays and communicative exchange); and consumption, in the case of the cute (an aesthetic disclosing the surprisingly wide spectrum of feelings, ranging from tenderness to aggression, that we harbor toward ostensively subordinate and unthreatening commodities). As sensuous, affective reflections of the ways in which subjects work, communicate, and consume (and as the cute and zany in particular show, in ways directly mediated by gender and class), the domestic and commodity-oriented aesthetic of cuteness, the informational and discursive aesthetic of the merely interesting, and the occupational and cultural performance aesthetic of zaniness help get at some of the most basic dynamics underlying life in Western industrial societies. No other aesthetic categories in our current repertoire speak to these everyday practices of production, circulation, and consumption in the same direct way.

It is thus no surprise that the zany, cute, and interesting are omnipresent not just on television and across the Web but also in the postwar literature anthology, where one is likely to encounter an example of each style in rapid succession, from the vertiginous zaniness of Thomas Pynchon to the poet Matthea Harvey's aggressively cute tributes to objects like the bathtub and sugarbowl to the merely interesting serial texts of the conceptual writer Robert Fitterman. But while the uniquely intimate relation of these aesthetic categories to production, circulation, and consumption provides the best explanation for their pervasiveness, the zany, cute, and interesting are important for the study of contemporary culture not simply because they index economic processes but also because they provide traction to a series of long-standing problems in aesthetic theory that continue to inform the production, dissemination, and reception of literature and art in the present. These problems include the close relation between the form of the artwork and the form of the commodity; the ambiguous state of the avant-garde, which in zombie fashion persists

Excerpted and adapted by the author from an essay in *PMLA* 125.4 (Spring 2010): 948–58. Ngai is a cultural theorist and literary critic as well as a professor of English at Stanford University.

even as its "disappearance or impossibility" is regarded as one of postmodernism's constitutive features; the relevance of aesthetic to critical or other nonaesthetic judgments aimed at producing knowledge (or how one is permitted to link judgments based on subjective feelings of pleasure or displeasure to ones with claims to objective truth); the relation between artistic production and labor in a world where immaterial labor is increasingly aestheticized; and the "parergonal" relation between art and theoretical discourse, all the more pressured with the rise of an institutional culture of museums and curricula that has led art and criticism to internalize each other in historically unprecedented ways.[2] While central to some of the most important texts of modern aesthetic theory, these problems have also remained fundamental to contemporary literary practice in ways directly reflected by the three aesthetic categories in my study.

Prompting us to think across our entire system of fine arts, the zany, cute, and interesting are also linked to major representational modes—comedy, in the case of zaniness; romance, in the case of cuteness; realism, in the case of the interesting— as well as to specific forms, genres, and media. As I have argued elsewhere, it is easy to see how the cute becomes a particular problem for twentieth-century poetry, a genre associated commonly (if not always correctly) with small texts focused on domestic objects.[3] Reflecting what Hannah Arendt describes as the "modern enchantment with 'small things' . . . preached by early twentieth-century poetry in almost all European tongues," the "*petite bonheur*" of cuteness, or the "art of being happy . . . between dog and cat and flowerpot," is thus part of the expansion of the charmingly "irrelevant," which she links to the decay of a genuinely public culture: "What the public realm considers irrelevant can have such an extraordinary and infectious charm that a whole people may adopt it as their way of life, without for that reason changing its essentially private character."[4] Since cute things evoke in us a desire to protect them, poetry might be considered cute in another problematic sense. Twentieth-century poetry's smallness in comparison with novels and films, where the proportion of quotable unit— sentence or paragraph, frame or shot sequence— to the work as a whole is substantially lower, has made it excessively protected by copyright and thus, in a certain economic sense, protected from criticism: one literally has to pay in order

to comment. Susan Stewart's wry caveat in the preface and acknowledgments to *Poetry and the Fate of the Senses* ("Like anyone who writes on poetic forms, I have been restricted . . . by the availability of permissions for reproduction"[5]) will be familiar to any critic who has tried to write on the genre, which copyright laws have indirectly defined as unusually tender or vulnerable speech. Poetry's complicated and ambivalent relation to an aesthetic that celebrates the diminutive and nonconsequential becomes all the more problematic in the case of the avant-garde, which has historically defined itself in opposition to everything for which cuteness stands. Yet in examples ranging from Gertrude Stein's homage to lesbian domesticity in *Tender Buttons* to William Carlos Williams's spare objectivist poems about ordinary household objects to Harryette Mullen's exploration of fashion and groceries in *Trimmings* and *S*perm**rk*t,* cuteness remarkably gives us leverage not just on the genre of poetry but also on two problems central to modern aesthetic theory: the ambiguous status of the contemporary avant-garde and the closeness between the artwork and the commodity. As Walter Benjamin writes, "If the soul of the commodity which Marx occasionally mentions in jest existed, it would be the most empathetic ever encountered in the realm of souls, for it would have to see in everyone the buyer in whose hand and house it wants to *nestle*."[6]

If the cute is thus warm and fuzzy, the poetics of the merely interesting is cool, both in the sense of the ironic detachment attributed to *das Interessante,* a style of eclectic novelty first explicitly theorized by Friedrich Schlegel and the German Romantic ironists as part of a larger agenda calling for art to become more reflective or philosophical,[7] and in the technocratic, informatic sense Alan Liu conveys in his book on postmodern knowledge work.[8] And the zany, for its part, is hot: hot under the collar, hot and bothered, hot to trot. Pointing to the intensely embodied affects and desires of an agent compelled to move, hustle, and perform in the presence of others, these idioms underscore that the zany is the only aesthetic category in our repertoire with a special relation to affective or physical effort and is thus an aesthetic whose dynamics are most sharply brought out in performance: dance, theater, happenings, television, film. It is because the zany, interesting, and cute are respectively about performance, information or media, and domestic life—and more specifically about the ambiguous status of performance between labor and play, the ceaseless relaying of artworks through the medium of discourse, and the paradoxical complexity of our desire for a simpler relation to our household commodities—that the deepest content of these aesthetic categories concerns the socially binding processes of production, circulation, and consumption. And it is because the zany, interesting, and cute are about production, circulation, and consumption that they are so important, as a triad, to the genealogy of the postmodern and to our aesthetic theory.

Yet the interesting, cute, and zany are also undeniably trivial. Indeed, in contrast to the powerful moral and political resonances of the beautiful and sublime, each of the aesthetic categories in this triad revolves around a specific type of inconsequentiality: the low affect that accompanies the perception of minor differences against a backdrop of the generic, in the case of the interesting; physical smallness and vulnerability, in the case of the cute; and the flailing helplessness of impotent rage, in the case of the zany. Because of a contradictory mixture of affects underscoring their politically ambivalent nature—for the zany, fun and unfun; for the interesting, interest and boredom; and for the cute, tenderness and aggression—we might say that the cute, interesting, and zany have a certain "mereness" at their cores.[9] Yet this triviality is not itself trivial; it explains why these aesthetic categories are suited for helping us think more deeply about the shifting meanings of the aesthetic, art, and even culture in our time, a period in which, with the integration of "aesthetic production . . . into commodity production generally," as Fredric Jameson notes, the "frantic economic urgency of producing fresh waves of ever more novel-seeming goods (from clothing to airplanes), at ever greater rates of turnover, now assigns an increasingly structural function and position to aesthetic innovation and experimentation."[10] In addition to posing unprecedented challenges for our understanding of the new and avant-garde, this increasing interpenetration of economy and culture has wrought two significant changes for the concept of art as such, Jameson notes: the weakening of art's capacity to serve as an image of nonalienated labor (which it has arguably done since the eighteenth century) and the loss of art's more specifically modernist, twentieth-century mission of producing perceptual shock.[11] With

the waning of these older vocations for art and aesthetic experience, minor aesthetic categories crop up everywhere, testifying in their ubiquity to how aesthetic experience, radically generalized in an age of design and advertising, becomes less rarefied but also less intense. The romance of cuteness, the comedy of zaniness, and the realist and information-oriented aesthetic of the interesting are thus important to autonomous art's attempts to reflect on the smoothness of its integration in mass culture. What better way to get traction on art's diminishing role as the privileged locus for modern aesthetic experience than an aesthetic category of and about inconsequentiality? As styles about our complex and often conflicted affective relations to commodities, labor, and media or communicative systems, the cute, zany, and interesting are also suited for helping us figure out what the discourse of aesthetics might mean or become in the wake of aesthetic idealization—when reverence for the aesthetic as such, though still advocated by many, no longer seems self-evidently desirable or even defining of what an aesthetic attitude is.

Notes

1 It is worth noting how quickly displeasure seems to drop out of the picture not just in contemporary aesthetic theory but also in *The Critique of Judgment*, where Kant first mentions "dissatisfaction without any interest" side by side with "satisfaction without any interest" but never gives us an account of what the former is (leading to much debate about whether or not Kantian aesthetics can genuinely account for the ugly). See Immanuel Kant, *The Critique of Judgment*, trans. Paul Guyer and Eric Matthews (Cambridge, UK: Cambridge University Press, 2001), 96. Would the widely held idea that aesthetic judgments have no place in critique be less prevalent if it were recognized that the aesthetic includes displeasure as well as complicated mixtures of displeasure and pleasure? This is in fact the case for all the aesthetic categories featured in my study.

2 On the "disappearance or impossibility" of the avant-garde, see Fredric Jameson, *Postmodernism, or, The Cultural Logic of Late Capitalism* (Durham, NC: Duke University Press, 1991), 167. On the "parergon" as index of the relation between art and theory, see Jacques Derrida, *The Truth in Painting*, trans. Geoffrey Bennington and Ian McLeod (Chicago: University of Chicago Press, 1987).

3 See Sianne Ngai, "The Cuteness of the Avant-Garde," *Critical Inquiry* 31, no. 4 (2005): 811–47.

4 Hannah Arendt, *The Human Condition* (Chicago: University of Chicago Press, 1958), 52.

5 Susan Stewart, *Poetry and the Fate of the Senses* (Chicago: University of Chicago Press, 2002), ix.

6 Walter Benjamin, *Charles Baudelaire: A Lyric Poet in the Era of High Capitalism,* trans. Harry Zohn (London: New Left, 1973), 55; emphasis added.

7 See Kathleen M. Wheeler, ed. *German Aesthetic and Literary Criticism: The Romantic Ironists and Goethe* (Cambridge, UK: Cambridge University Press, 1984). See also Friedrich Schlegel, *On the Study of Greek Poetry,* ed. and trans. Stuart Barnett (Albany: State University of New York Press, 2001).

8 See Alan Liu, *The Laws of Cool: Knowledge Work and the Culture of Information* (Chicago: University of Chicago Press, 2004).

9 I discuss this idea in depth in Sianne Ngai, "Merely Interesting," *Critical Inquiry* 34, no. 4 (2008): 777–817.

10 Jameson, *Postmodernism,* 4.

11 Ibid., 146–47, 121–22.

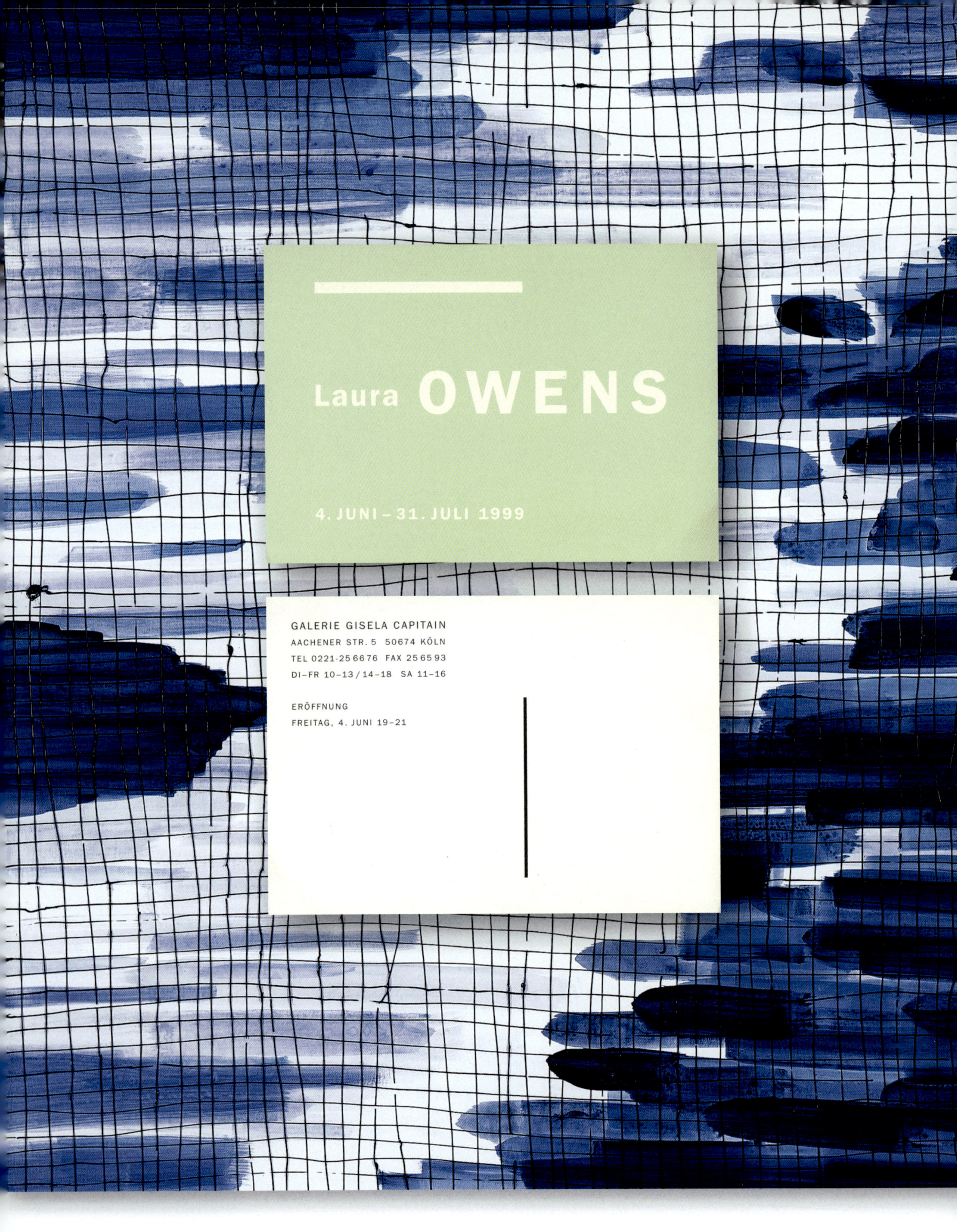

Foreground: Invitation, Galerie Gisela Capitain, Cologne, 1999
Background: Detail of *Untitled*, 1999 (see p. 236)

Untitled, 1999, acrylic and oil on canvas, 96 × 84 in. (243.8 × 213.4 cm)

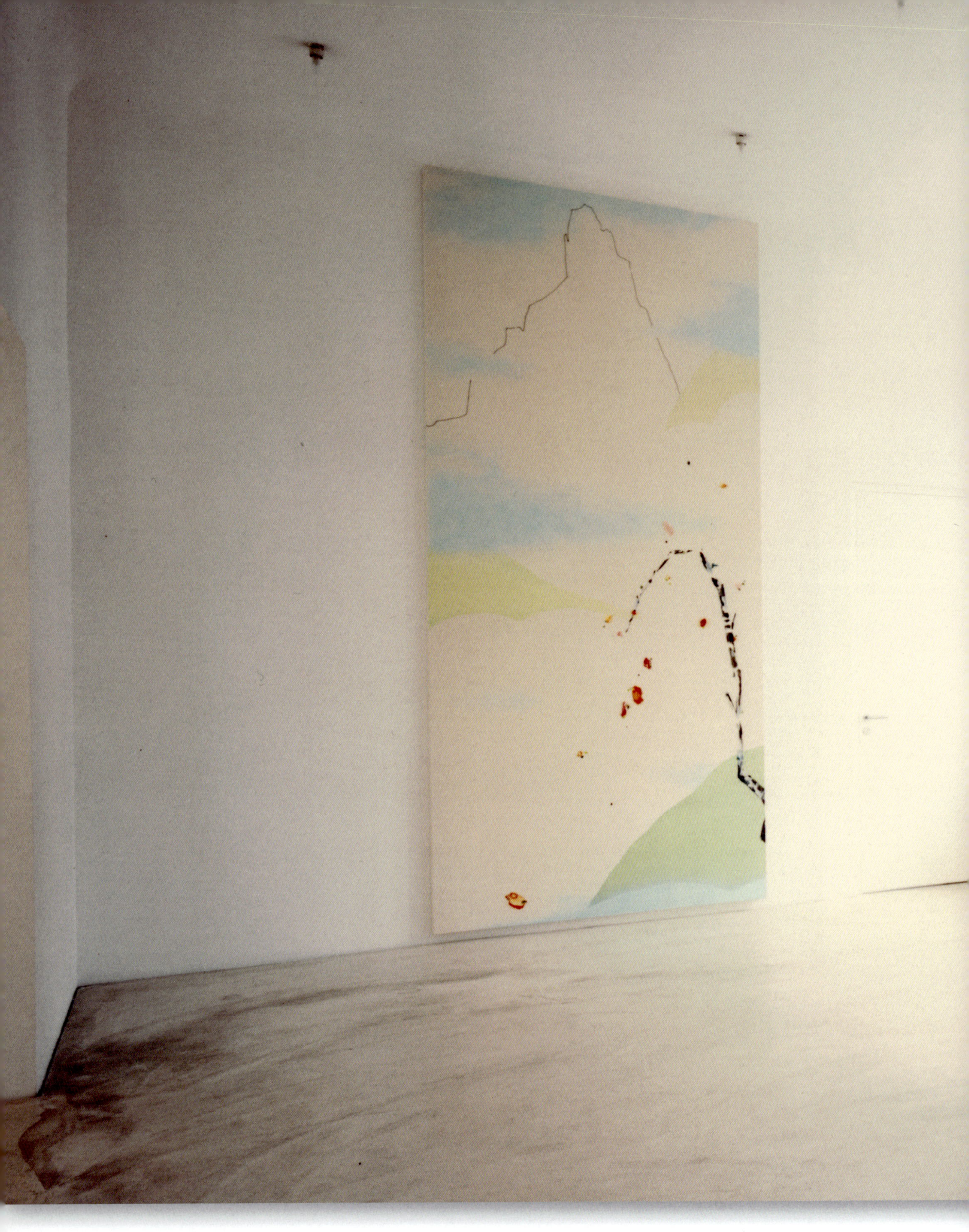

Installation view, Galerie Gisela Capitain, Cologne, 1999, with *Untitled*, 1999, acrylic and oil on canvas, 150 × 60 in. (381 × 152.4 cm), and *Untitled*, 1999, acrylic on canvas, 64 ½ × 49 ½ in. (163.8 × 125.7 cm)

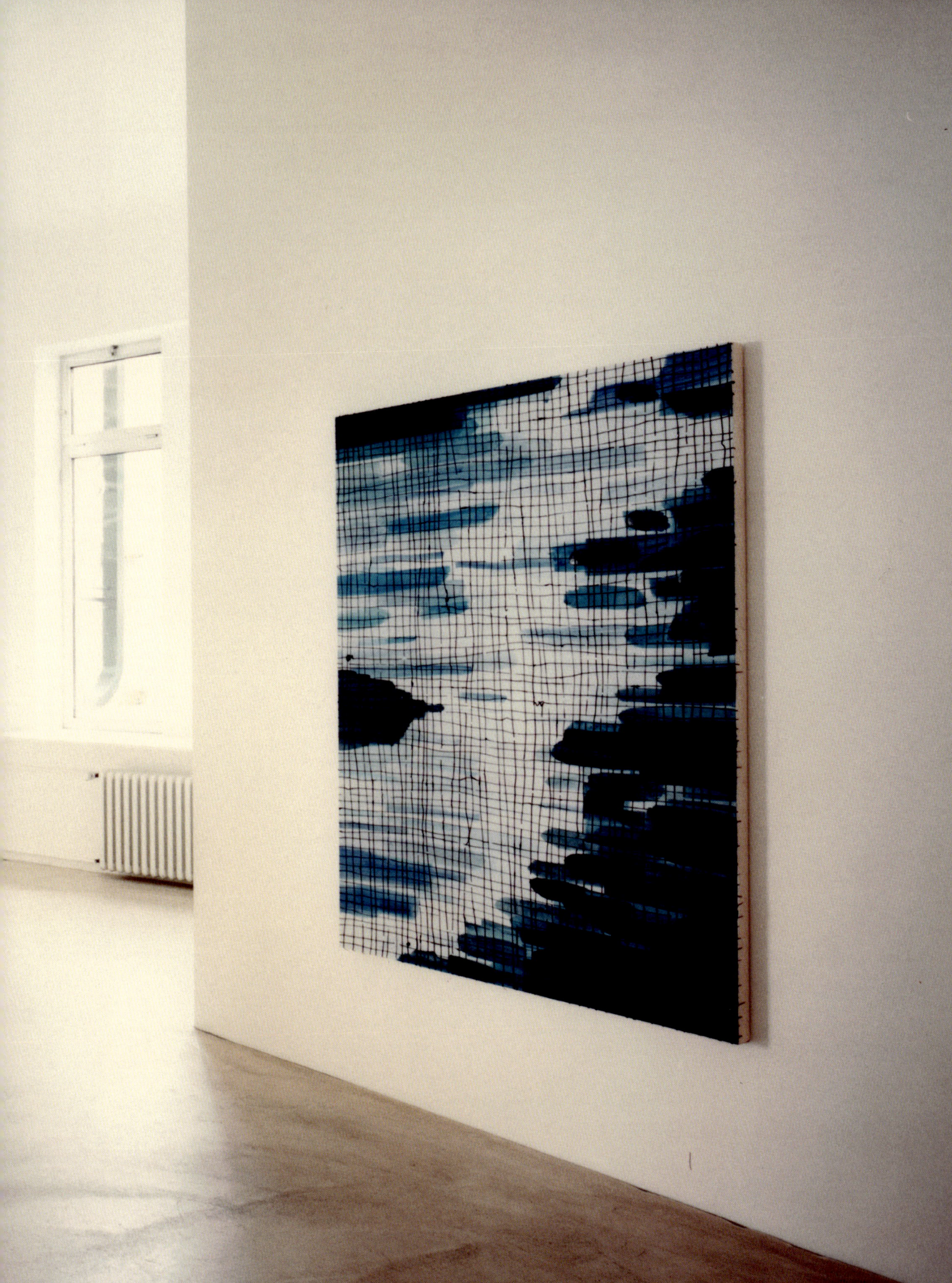

CONGRAJULATIONS
June 4 1999
Dear Laura
Congratulations!!
I hope you have
a great night
in Koln
xxx T.J
ORRY
THGR
LOVE

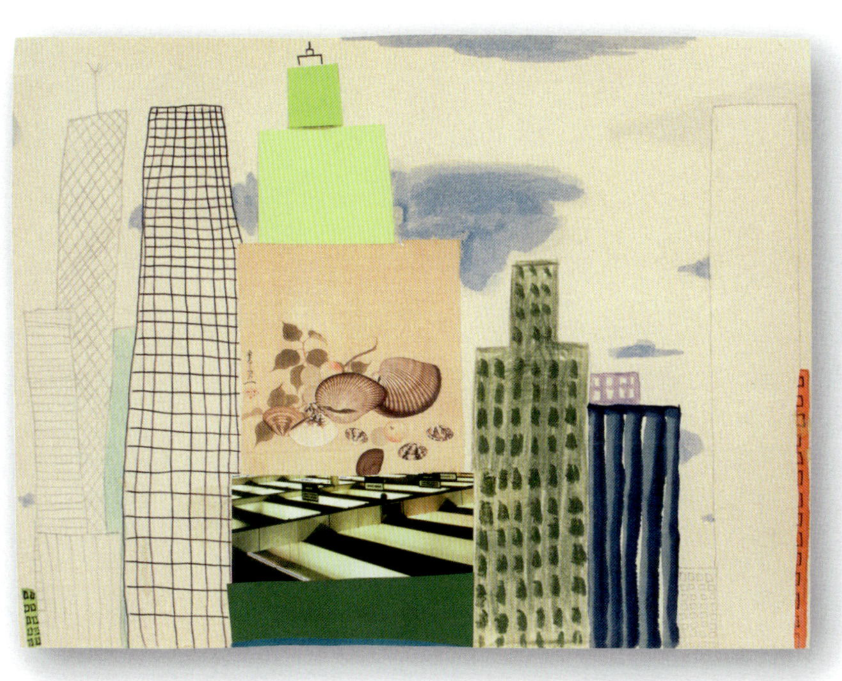

Untitled, 1999, watercolor, graphite, and photo collage on paper, 9 × 11 ½ in. (22.9 × 29.2 cm)

Laura Owens
5121 1/2 Eaglerock Blvd #D

USA Los Angeles, CA 90041

VIA FAX

November 17, 1999

Dear Laura,

Hoping this finds you well and having heard that you had a
brilliant opening in London I a approaching concerning a
very different kind of story.

In December I will meet my best girl-friends from study-
time again for doing Christmas-baking. I really would love
good chance to be the winner of the baking contest, which
my girl-friends has always under fail!

may I kindly ask to send the recipe over to me whenever you
have a minute - or is this a Owens-family secret?

Best wishes,

Stefanie Jansen

11-23-99

Dear Steffi,

Sorry It has taken me so long to respond. I have been in New york having a little vacation. Hope you are doing well.   The recipes are by no means a family secret, in fact they are just from the cereal box and the chocolate chips bag. I don't know if they sell the rice krispies in Germany, but all you need is a box of Rice Krispies, a bag of Marshmallows, margarine and vegetable spray. You melt 3 tablespoons margarine in a pan on the stove then stir in 10 ounces of marshmallows (probably just the whole bag)then after they melt you slowly stir in 6 cups of Rice krispies. Then you just spray a baking pan with vegetable oil and spray a spatula with vegetable oil and sort of spread the gooey mess in the pan and flatten it out. Then you just let it cool.

The chocolate chip cookies are slightly more complex. First combine 2 1/4 cups all purpose flour,1 teaspoon baking soda and 1 teaspoon salt in a small bowl. Beat 1 cup of soft butter, 3/4 cup granulated sugar, 3/4 cup packed brown sugar and 1 teaspoon vanilla extract in a large mixing bowl. Add two eggs, one at a time and beat after each egg. Then gradually add in flour mixture. Stir in 12 ounces of chocolate chips (also nuts if you want) and then drop portions of about one tablespoon of cookie dough onto an ungreased baking sheet a couple inches apart. Bake in preheated oven at 375 degrees Fahrenheit for 9 to 11 minutes. Let stand for 2 minutes then remove to wire racks to cool completely. This will make about 60 small cookies.

Hope this helps.

Also the inventory number for the painting is LO133. Hope you are well and having a nice time around the holidays.

Best wishes,

♡ Laura

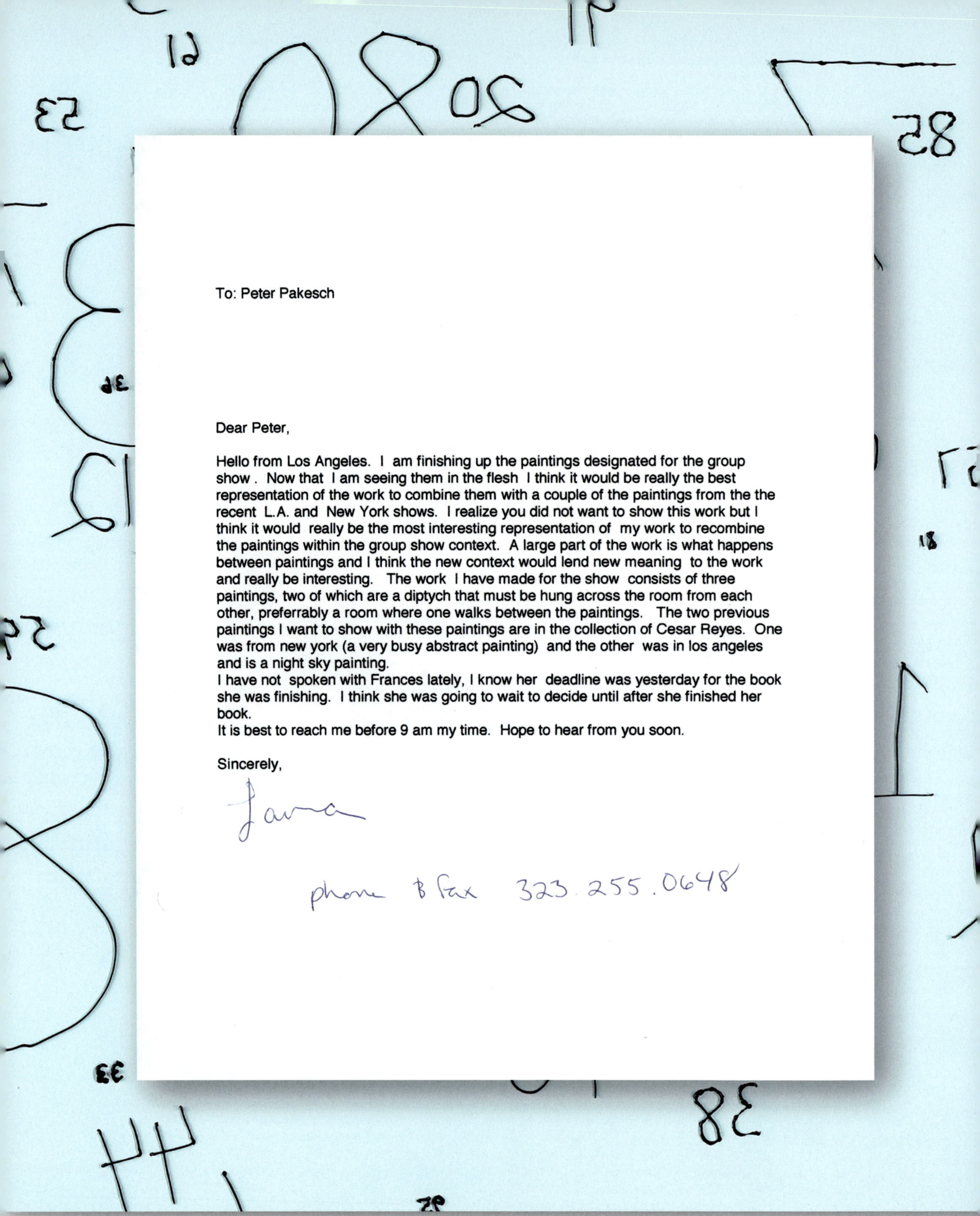

To: Peter Pakesch

Dear Peter,

Hello from Los Angeles. I am finishing up the paintings designated for the group
show . Now that I am seeing them in the flesh I think it would be really the best
representation of the work to combine them with a couple of the paintings from the the
recent L.A. and New York shows. I realize you did not want to show this work but I
think it would really be the most interesting representation of my work to recombine
the paintings within the group show context. A large part of the work is what happens
between paintings and I think the new context would lend new meaning to the work
and really be interesting.   The work I have made for the show consists of three
paintings, two of which are a diptych that must be hung across the room from each
other, preferrably a room where one walks between the paintings.   The two previous
paintings I want to show with these paintings are in the collection of Cesar Reyes. One
was from new york (a very busy abstract painting) and the other was in los angeles
and is a night sky painting.
I have not spoken with Frances lately, I know her deadline was yesterday for the book
she was finishing. I think she was going to wait to decide until after she finished her
book.
It is best to reach me before 9 am my time. Hope to hear from you soon.

Sincerely,

Laura

phone & fax 323.255.0648

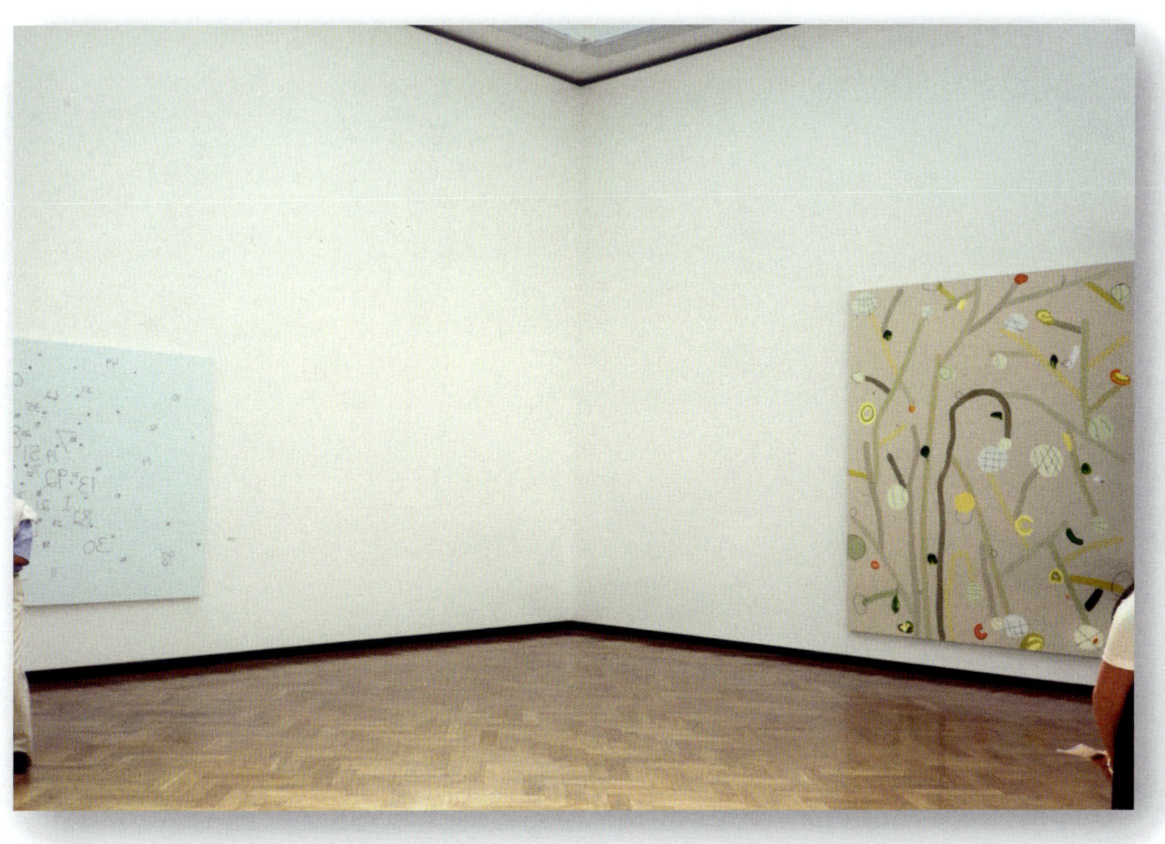

Background: Installation view, *Nach-Bild,* Kunsthalle Basel, 1999, with *Untitled*, 1999 (see p. 244), and *Untitled*, 1999, acrylic and oil on
canvas, 120 × 96 in. (304.8 × 243.8 cm)

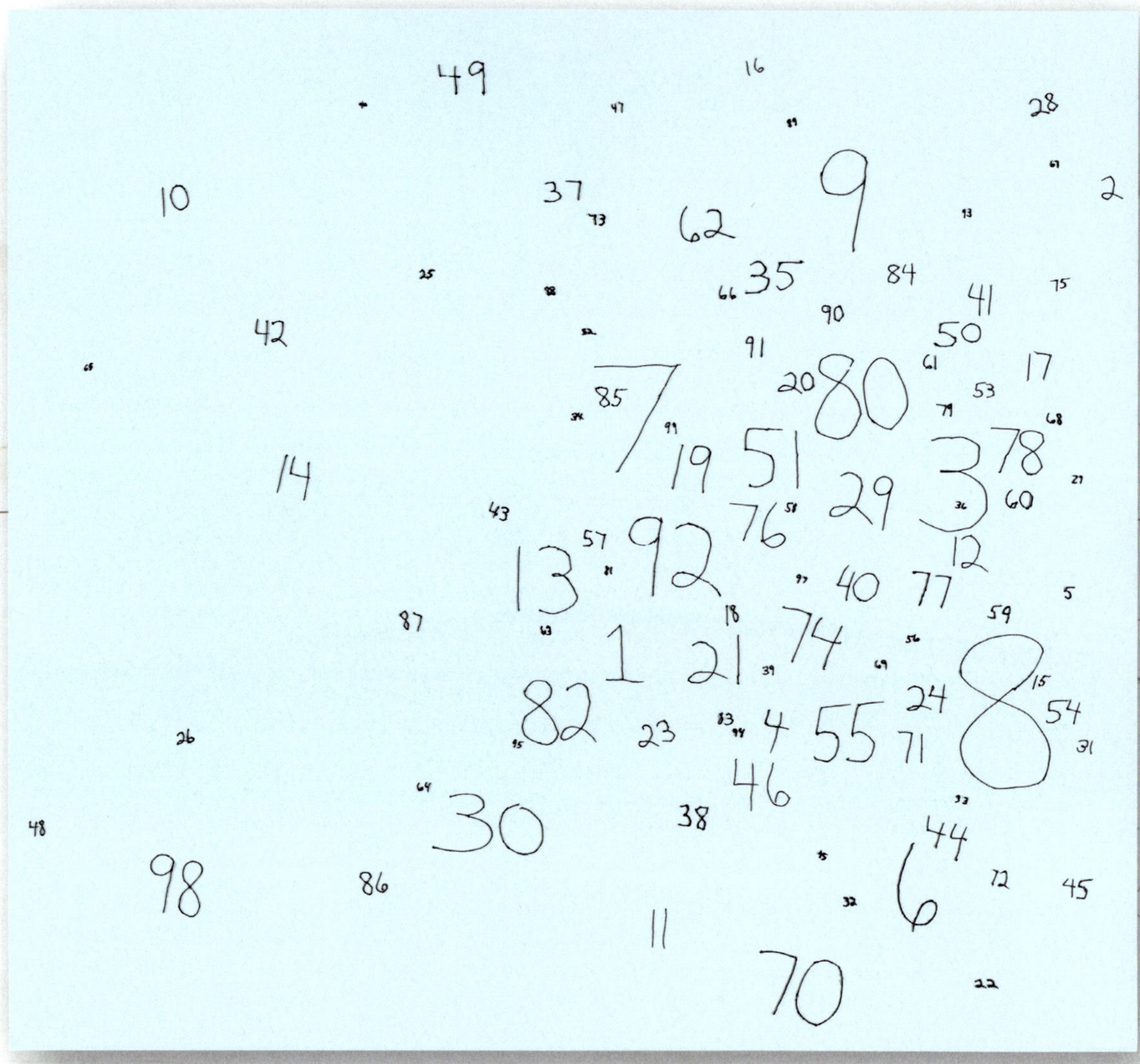

Foreground: *Untitled*, 1999, acrylic on canvas, two panels: 78 × 84 in. (198.1 × 213.4 cm) each
Background: Preparatory drawing, 1999

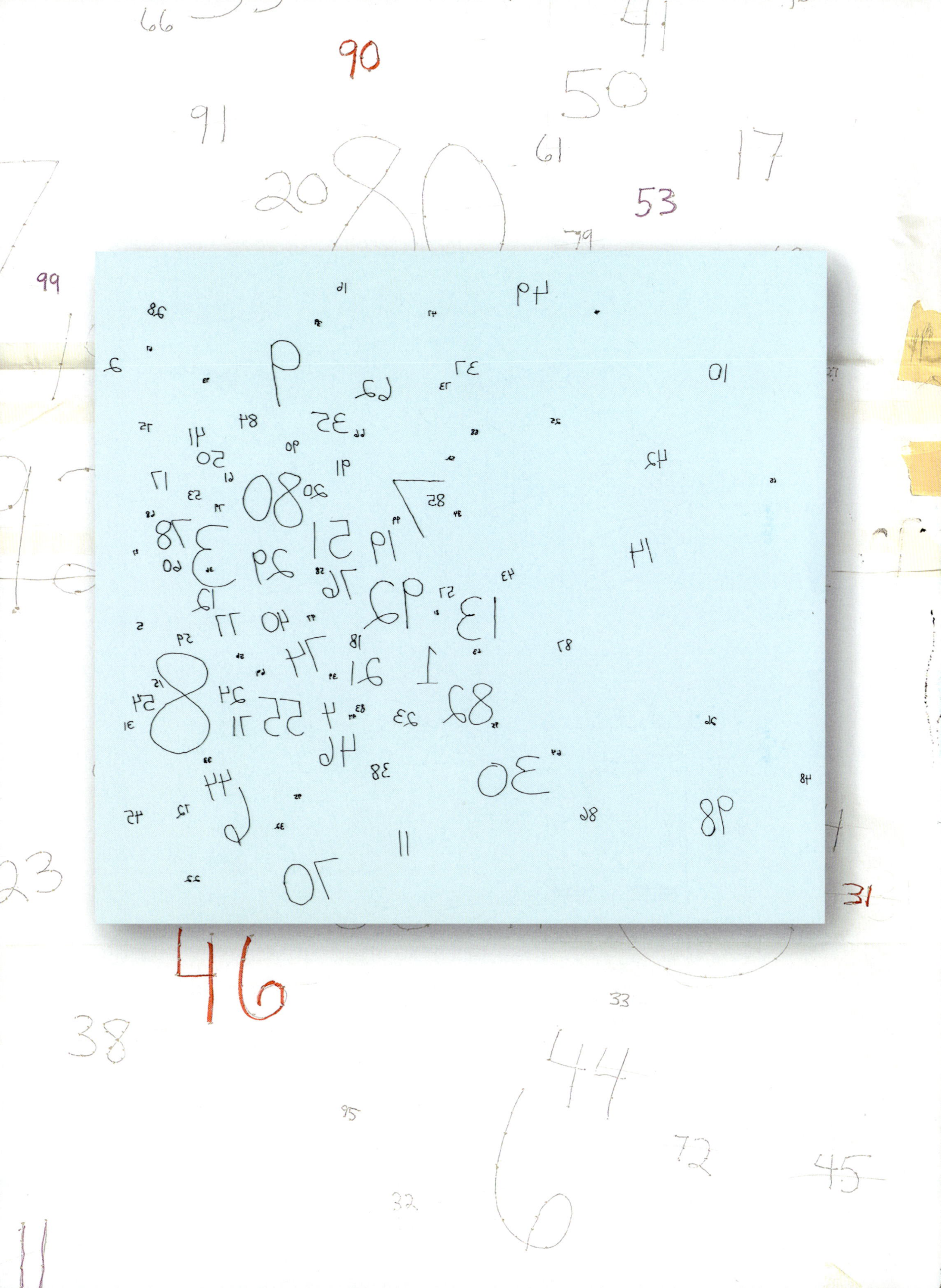

to Laura Owens

Dear Laura,

Unfortunatly I can't get the proportion right. The

space is big + high it is an cube of aprox 8 × 7 × 7 m.

All the best

GESAMT SEITEN 01

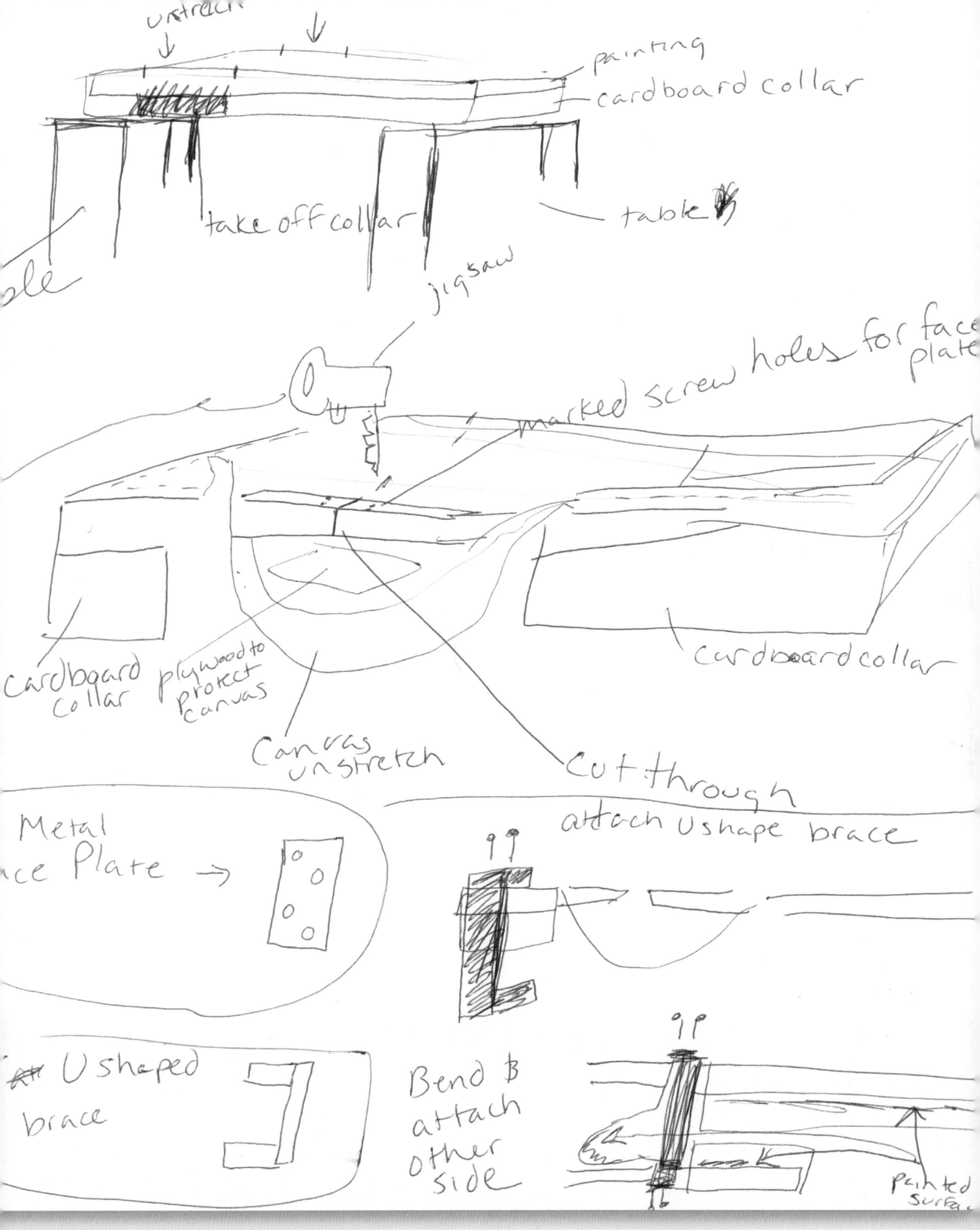

Packing instructions for *Nach-Bild*, Kunsthalle Basel, 1999

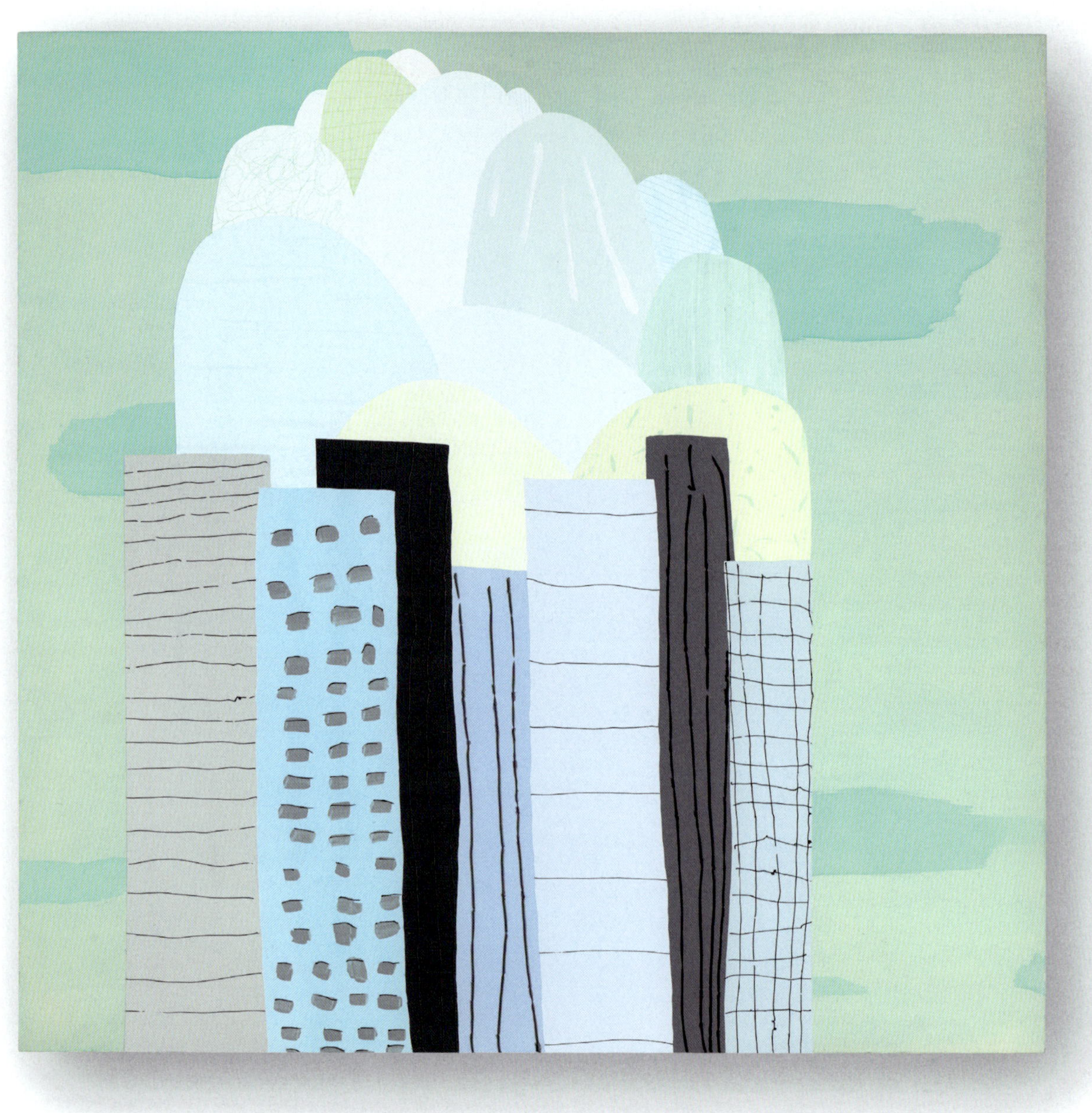

248 *Untitled*, 1999, acrylic and oil on canvas, 120 × 120 in. (304.8 × 304.8 cm)

FAX

DATE: 29 June, 1999
  TO: Laura Owens
  FAX: 1323 255 0648
FROM:

Dear Laura

I hope you got the check by now. Congratulations again.

The response to the work was incredible, if a little overwhelming. It made the installation seem somewhat frustrating although of course that is what made it so brilliant and irresitable to people. Everything seems to be moving up a notch in terms of activity and I want to make sure we understand each others expectations and that we have a good, clear plan for the future. There was a lot of serious interest from public and private collections which was generated at the fair, and as a result there are many things I want to talk with you about.   My main concern is that after the effort and expense of the fair, the results of what I initiated there will fall elsewhere. For example, the insurance company want a number of paintings to purchase and donate to Swiss museums and there are also a number of really great collections that are looking for your work. Call me self-centered and greedy but success for you is the reason I am doing this. I have to be realistic about this - it is just bad business for me to go and give it away.

As I'm sure you know, I would like to get some more work but need to figure out with you what the best arrangement would be. I don't want to push you into a situation of overproduction and I know you will be starting to think about Sadie's show soon, but I also want to keep you present and in people's minds here. What I am hoping for is to have a number of new paintings over the next six months that I can show in the back room here and save for Baloise or the other important collections. What do you think of making three new paintings between now and Christmas so that we could hang one great new piece in the back room at the opening of each fall show? On top of this, there are also several good collectors who have been looking for a smaller work of yours for some time . Anyway, that is how the horizon looks from my point of view, but you should tell me what it looks like for you and maybe we can come to some mutually beneficial point that will keep us all happy.

Give me a call when you get a chance and lets talk about this some more.

Gavin xt

Gavin Brown's enterprise, Corp. 436 W15th St New York NY 10011 t 212 627 5258 f 212 627 5261 e-mail: passerby@bway.net

like t   y down
an e: s, set the
ques   nt, and
ques   ly had
another   at, sinc
number   getting
ing at a   me time
will ofte   letely
them. C   ainting.
the worl   some
Which o   anted to
quality,   time, an
painting   way the
When th
different
but whil   s since
somethi   growing
always (do art
vates m   Museum
over eve   ntings—
painting   , Morris
bit scary   er seein

I had be   gs there
you, you

between paintings. When I made   I feel that my paintings are very speci-
this work for the show at Loyola, it   cally American and have a lot to do wi

FROM : MORGAN LAWSON   PHONE NO. : 323 4668007   P01

Dear Laura,

Artforum has just faxed me a copy of the piece w/ some questions that only _you_ Laura Owens can answer:

1. you were born in ___Euclid___, Ohio.
   name of city here

2. you received your MFA in 1994 ______
   year here.

3. Mary Heilman was a visiting artist at ___Cal Arts___
   name of school here

4. "The canvas in forty feet long & nine and a half feet high" ACME says the painting is ten feet high.
   True [X] nine and a half (111 inches actually 9'3")
   True [ ] ten   :) Hi!

   Check one answer.
             thank you for your help. Yours,
                                        Susan

Foreground: Fax from Susan Morgan with notes by Owens, 1999
Background: Susan Morgan, "A Thousand Words: Laura Owens Talks About Her New Work." *Artforum* 37, no. 10, Summer 1999

re fun to be with someone who is
lling to go out on a limb, embarrass
emselves a bit. I thir... ... eeing it from the
tists use a painting t... ... oking at such fore-
erence—a quote, an... ... ive deceives your
ea—and that referenc... ... when you are up
eresting than the work... walk the walk, go
ve a reference gener... ou realize it *is* a

e of the things that'... ... nink that to make
inting is that it has a... ctually big, to liter-
en I first stretched ... gives you a lot of
nvas, it looked huge... ... I'm always inter-
inting was complete... ...se things. □

the image was composed—everything
appeared to snap down to postcard

9-9-99

Please come to my birthday party. free bowling. chinese snickysnacks. cash bar. djs music and more. At the Eagle Rock All Star Lanes, 4459 Eagle Rock Blvd. btwn York & Ave. 45. Thursday Sep. 9, 8-@ midnight. come at 8 don't be late. info 323 255 0648

**Laura Ow... ...intings: Lines
sweep into our peripheral vision, speed along as dar-
ingly as fearless schoolgirls sliding on ice, then burst
unexpectedly into shapes—tiny spiraling volcanoes of
color, wavering horizons, or bulky clouds. If Owens's
style—a surprising blend of mid-century formalism and
Pop mischieviousness—evinces a cagey knowingness,
it also reveals an unabashed delight in the voluptuous-
ness of paint and form. With their light touch and winking**

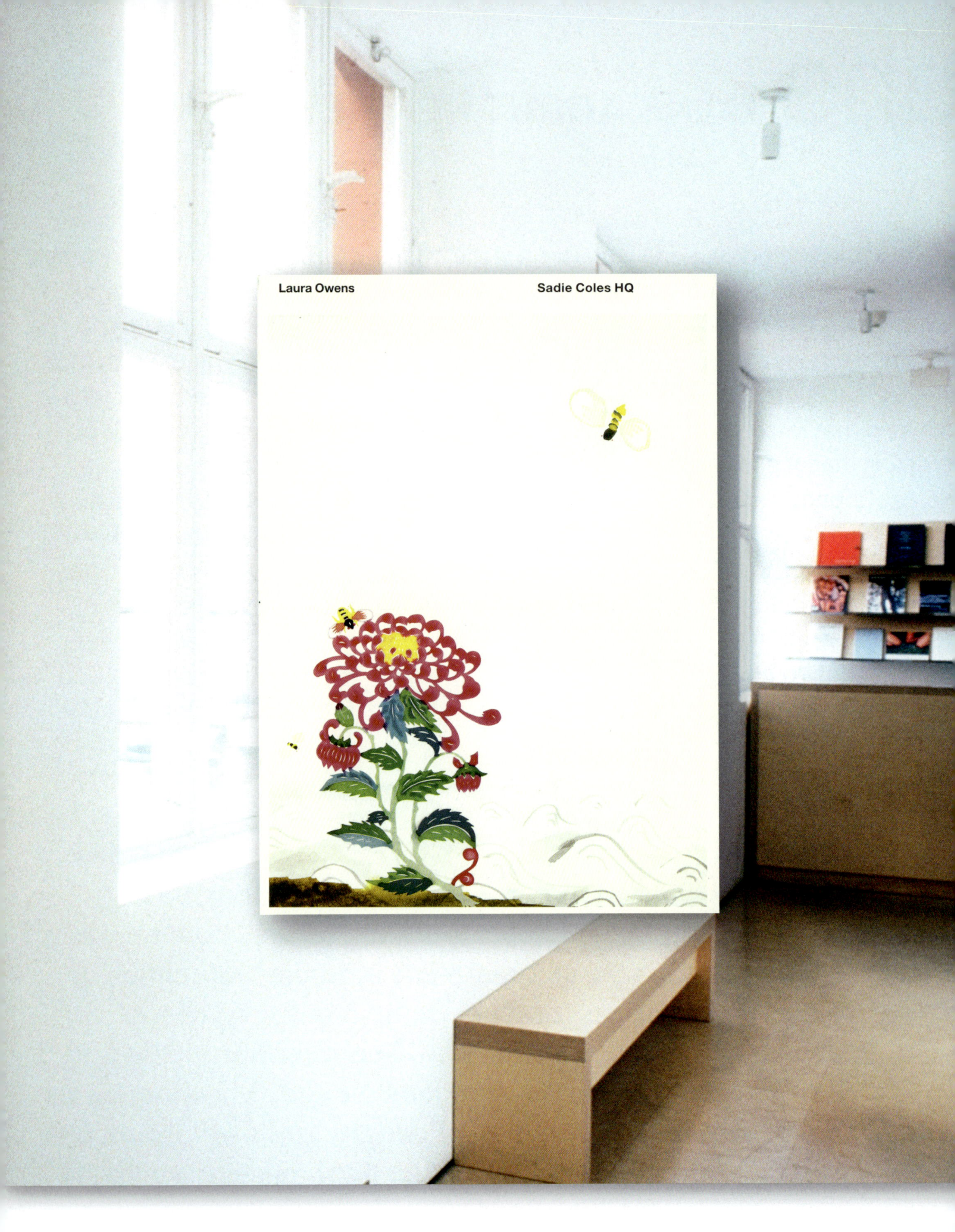

Foreground: Invitation, Sadie Coles HQ, London, 1999
Background: Sadie Coles HQ, London, 1999

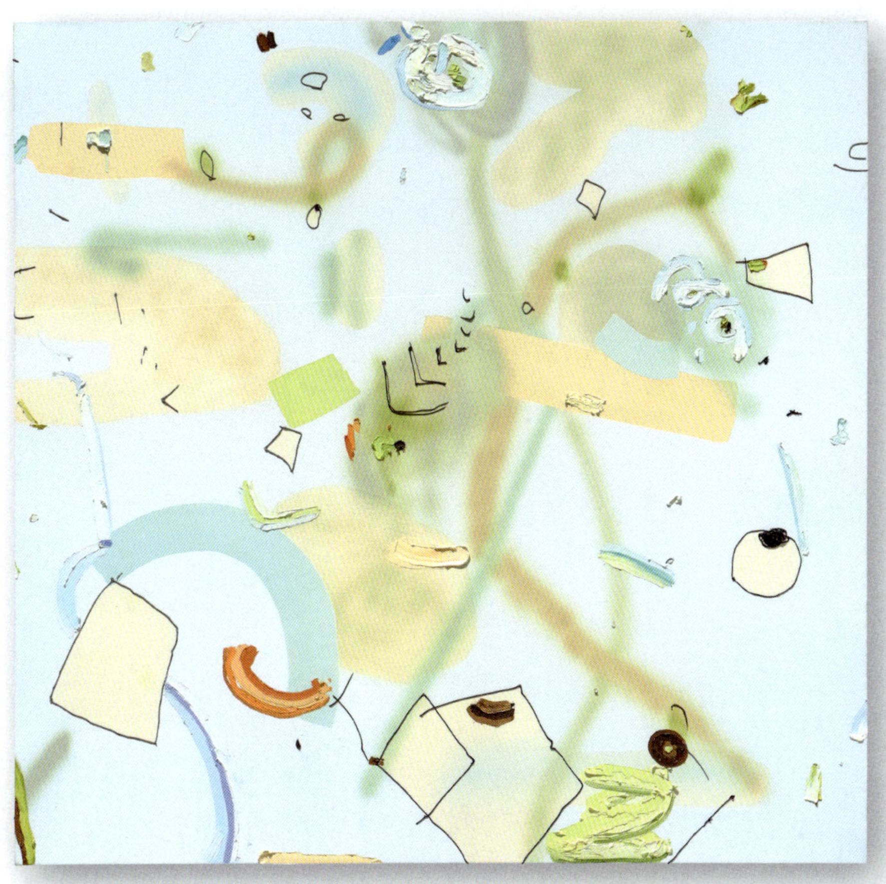

Untitled, 1999, acrylic and oil on canvas, 60 × 60 in. (152.4 × 152.4 cm)

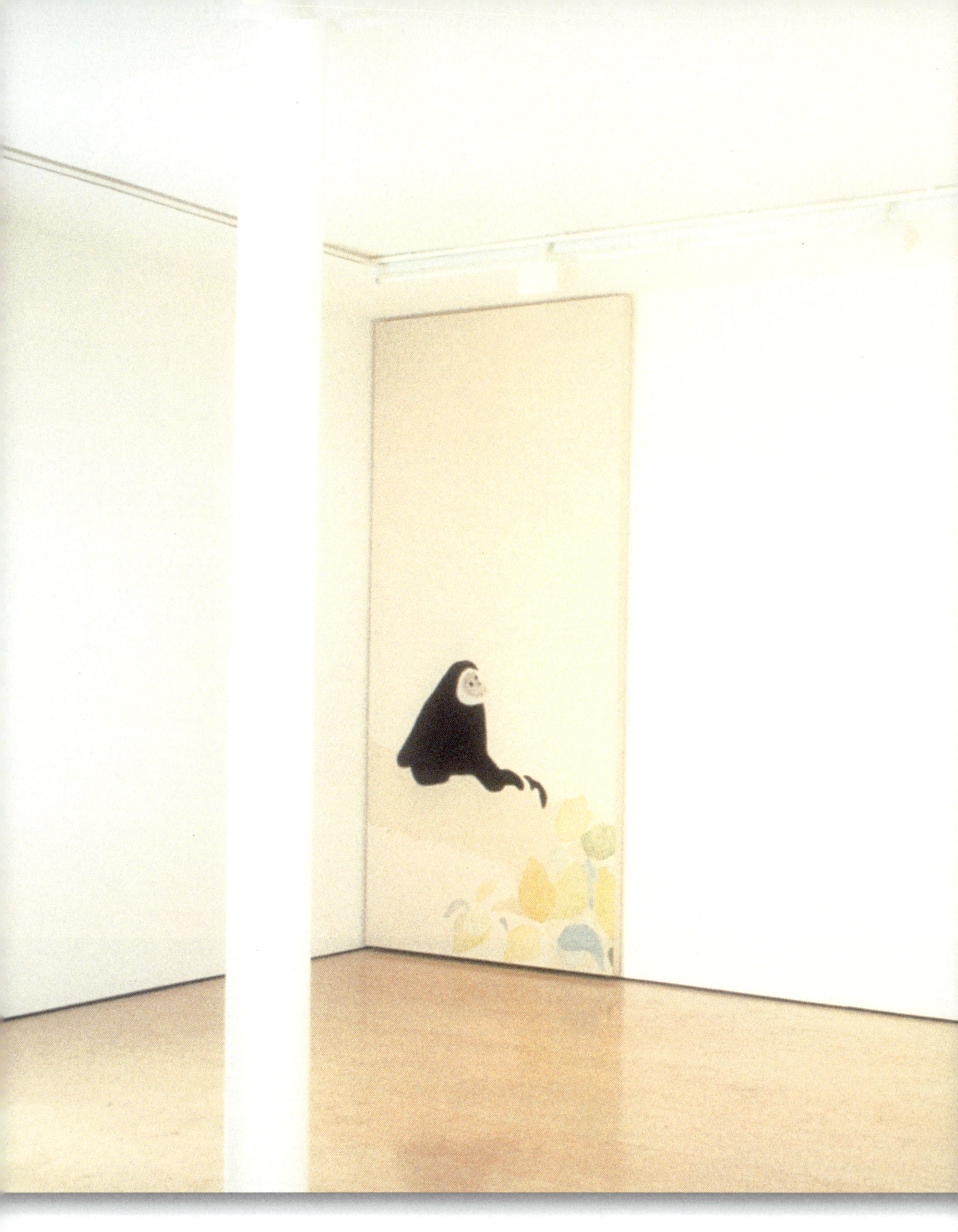

Installation view, Sadie Coles HQ, London, 1999, with *Untitled*, 1999, acrylic and waterproof ink on canvas, two panels: 122 × 60 in.
(309.9 × 152.4 cm) each

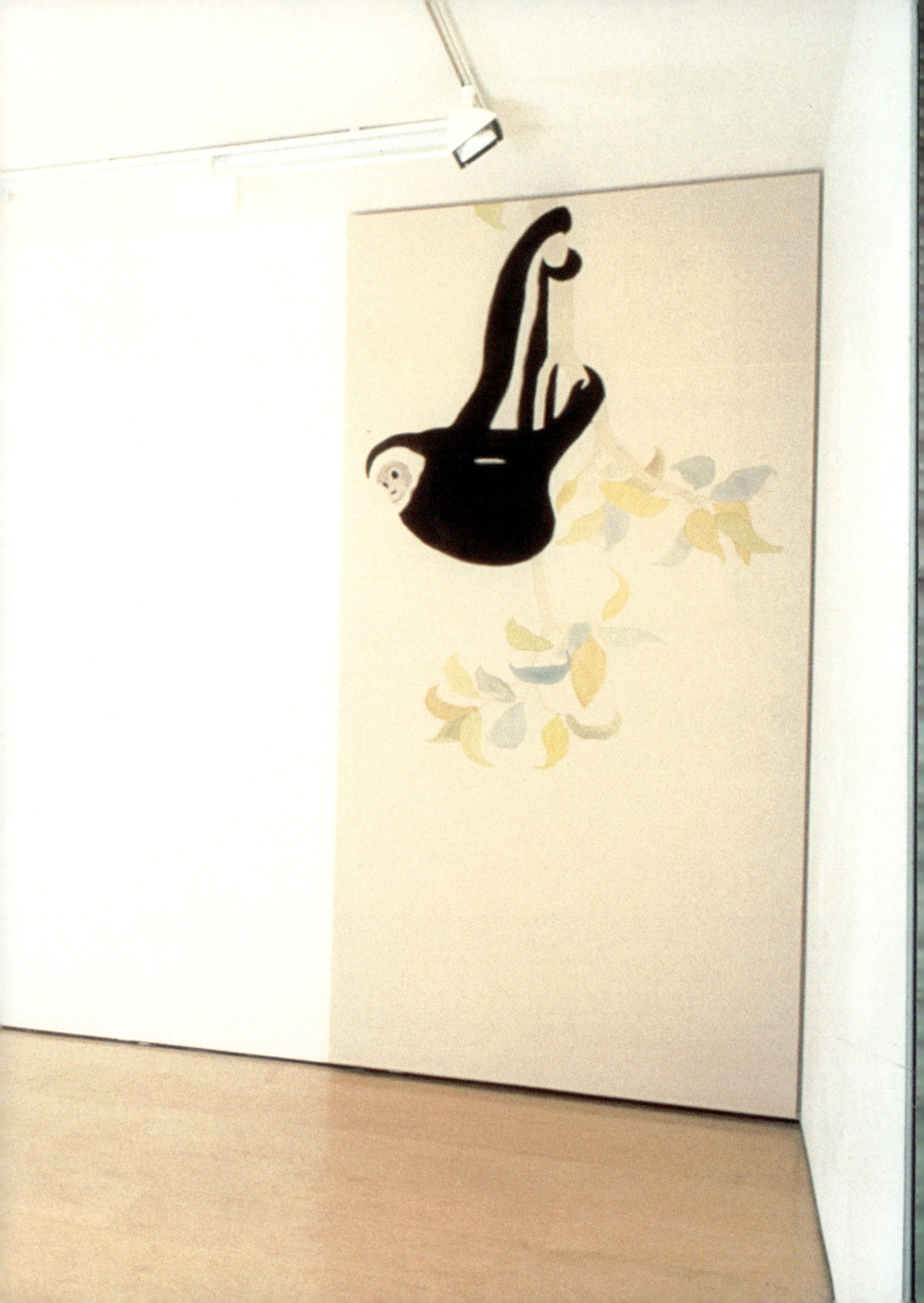

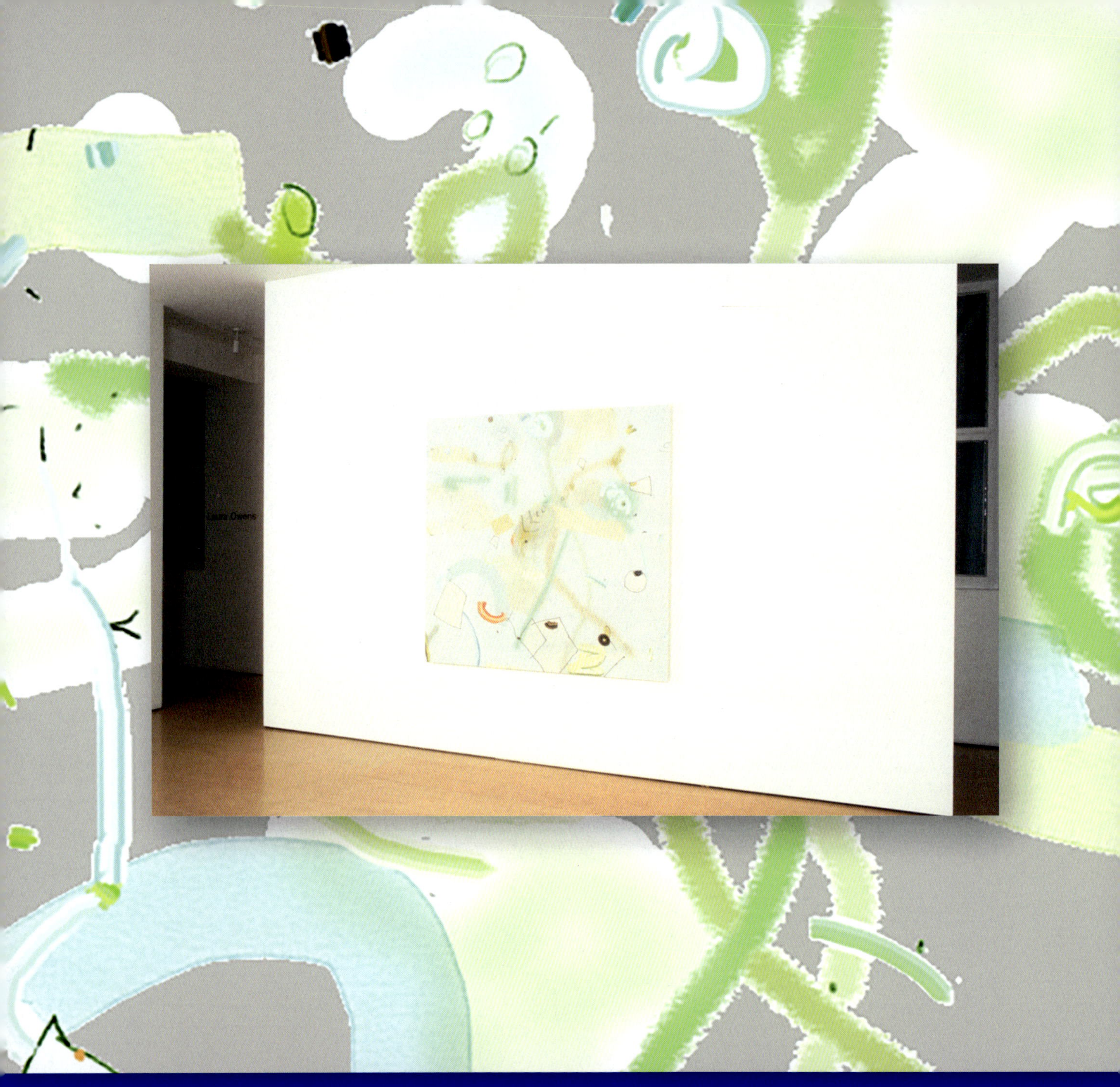

Laura Owens: I made a computer drawing in Corel Painter for a five-by-five-foot painting. Monique Prieto and I both used the program in the early nineties; before that I had used Kid Pix. In these computer sketches I was trying out all the options on the drop-down menu of brushstrokes; many of them were named after historic painters like van Gogh or Seurat, but you could also just choose "palette knife" or "airbrush." After printing the sketches out I would try to interpret the digital brushstrokes back into different ways of applying the paint, impasto, staining, etc.

I wanted a small abstract painting to hang on the floating wall Sadie Coles had recently built at her gallery. It was opposite the diptych of monkeys who empathetically gazed at each other across a large expanse of white wall, and I imagined this sort of mathematical abstract painting opposite that expanse, filling or representing that space between them. After I made the smaller painting I decided I would make another large painting for the very small office Sadie had. I enlarged the "canvas" in Corel Painter to 102 × 122 inches with the original five-by-five-foot painting sitting on the bottom right, and then proceeded to fill up the rest of the expanded surface with more marks, composing the work based on the smaller one that had preceded it. This inverted the idea of the "detail." Together these canvases formed a new kind of diptych, although one whose components hung in different rooms. I liked the idea that this show was composed of two diptychs.

Foreground: Installation view, Sadie Coles HQ, London, 1999, with *Untitled*, 1999 (see p. 253)

256 Background: MetaCreations Painter 6.0 file, 1999

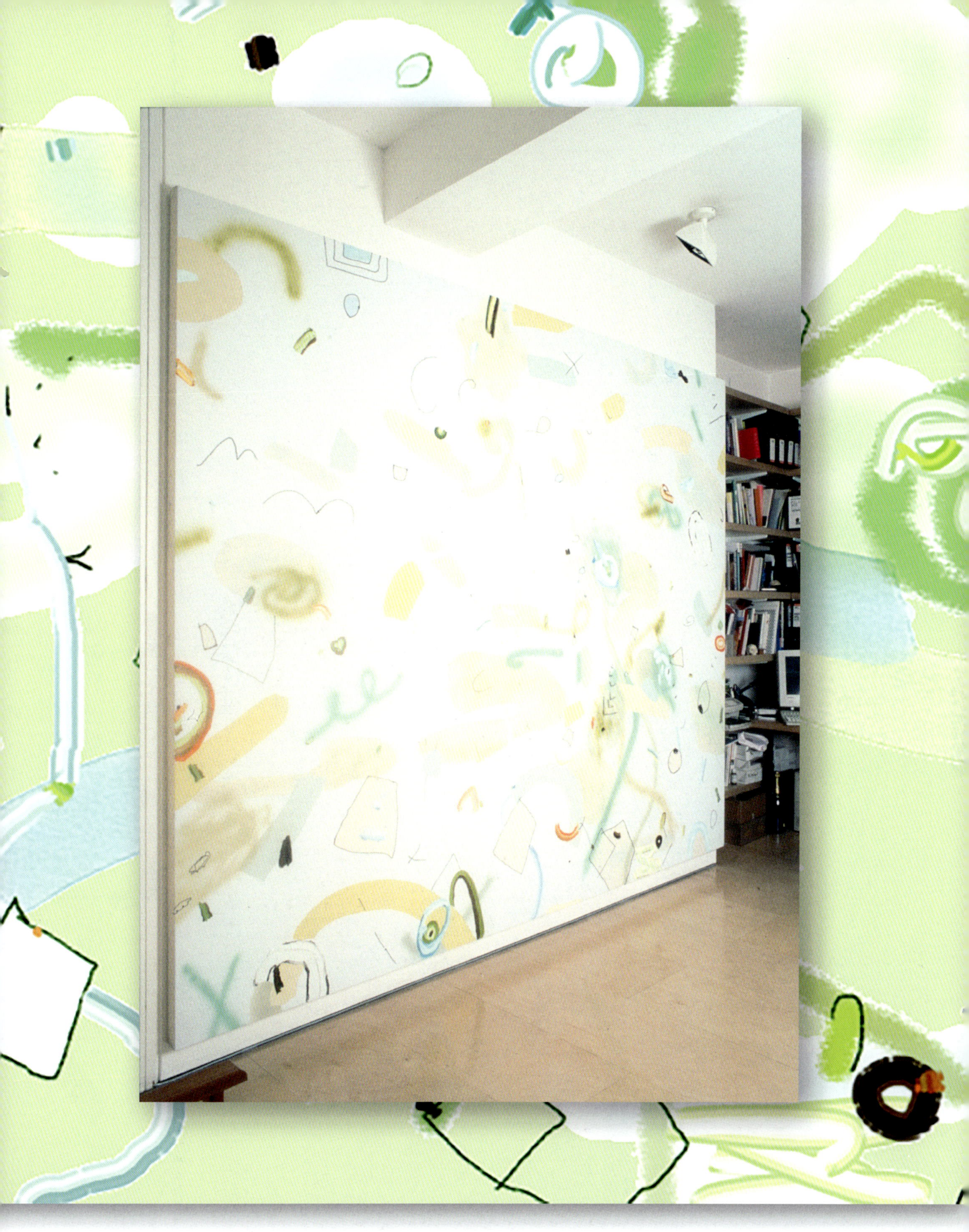

Foreground: Installation view, Sadie Coles HQ, London, 1999, with *Untitled*, 1999, acrylic and oil on canvas, 102 × 122 in. (259.1 × 309.9 cm)
Background: MetaCreations Painter 6.0 file, 1999

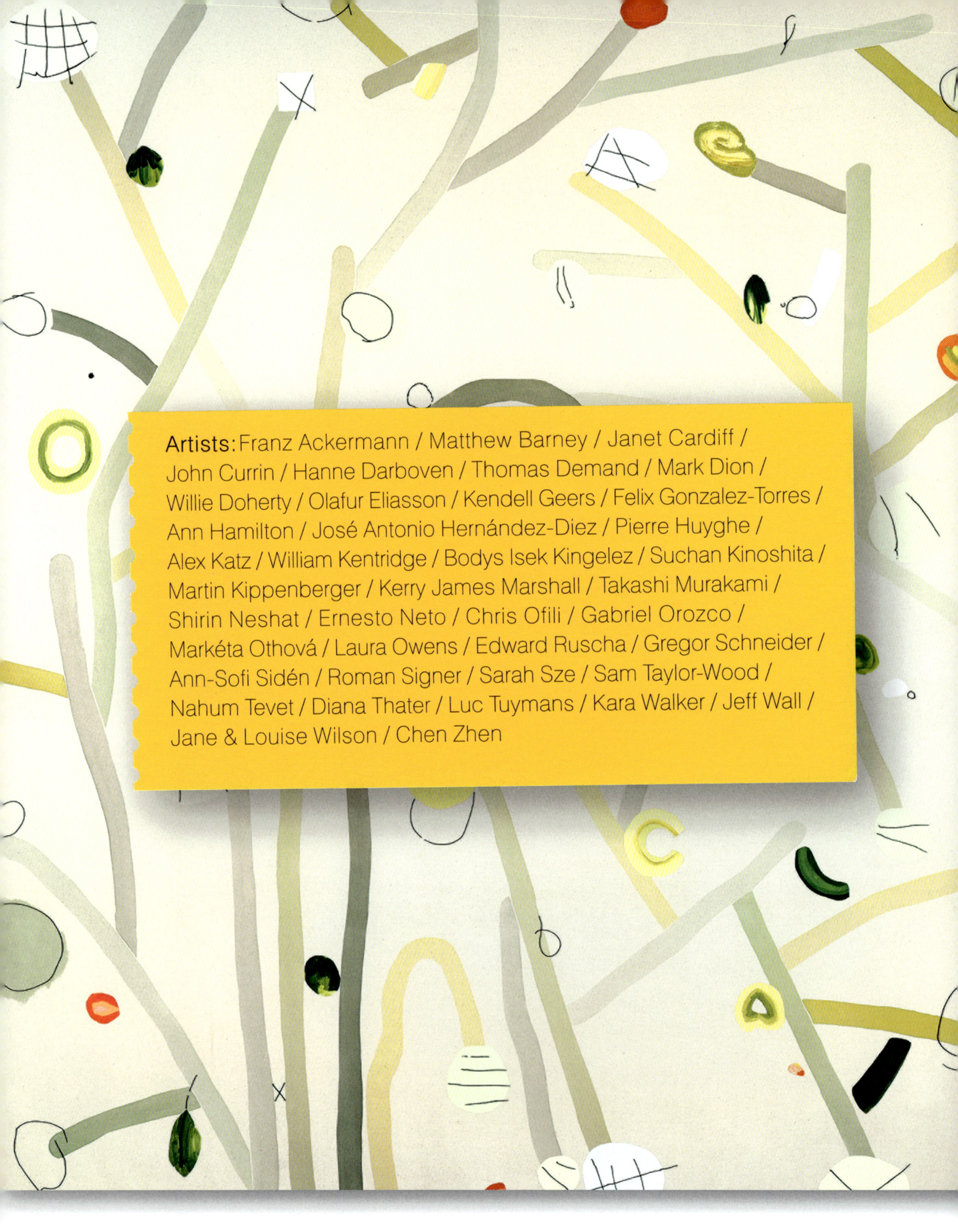

Foreground: List of participating artists, *Carnegie International 1999/2000,* Carnegie Museum of Art, Pittsburgh, 1999
Background: Detail of *Untitled*, 1999 (see p. 243)

CI:99/00
Carnegie International
1999/2000

Carnegie Museum of Art
4400 Forbes Avenue
Pittsburgh PA 15213-4080
Tel 412.622.1907 / 622.5547
Fax 412.578.2546 / 622.3112
www.carnegieinternational.org

July 6, 1999

Ms. Laura Owens
5121 ½ Eagle Rock Boulevard
Los Angeles, CA 90041

Nov 6, 1999 – Mar 26, 2000

Dear Laura,

It was a pleasure speaking with you last week. I am delighted that you have accepted the invitation to participate in the 1999/2000 *Carnegie International* and look forward to working with you on this exciting and important show, one in which your work plays a pivotal role.

As you know, the *Carnegie International* is a century-old survey series of contemporary art from around the world, and has been among the most innovative, influential, and challenging exhibitions presented in North America. Founded in 1896, the 1999 *Carnegie International* will be the 53rd installment in this series, and after the Venice Biennale, is the senior such exhibition worldwide. In 1999 the *Carnegie International* will honor its strong historical commitment to exhibiting the current peaks of visual expression, while also introducing a thematic emphasis focusing on post-conceptual realism and on "multi-internationalism."

The *Carnegie International* opens Thursday November 4, 1999 and will be on view through March 26, 2000. Works by forty artists will be installed at the Carnegie Museum of Art, the Carnegie Museum of Natural History, and the Carnegie Library. I hope you will be present at the opening gala on the evening of November 4. Additional activities are planned for November 5 and 6, details of which will follow later.

My assistant Alyson Baker will soon be sending you a plan and pictures of the gallery I have reserved for your work. As we discussed, it's my hope that you can make a new painting for the *International*: I'm particularly keen for you to take into account the tremendous sight-lines and distances that the gallery affords. A work that can be read from afar as well as close-up seems crucial to your presentation here, in my opinion. Once you've studied the plan and pictures, we can together finalize the selection of works.

With thanks again for your involvement and best regards,

Madeleine Grynsztejn
Curator

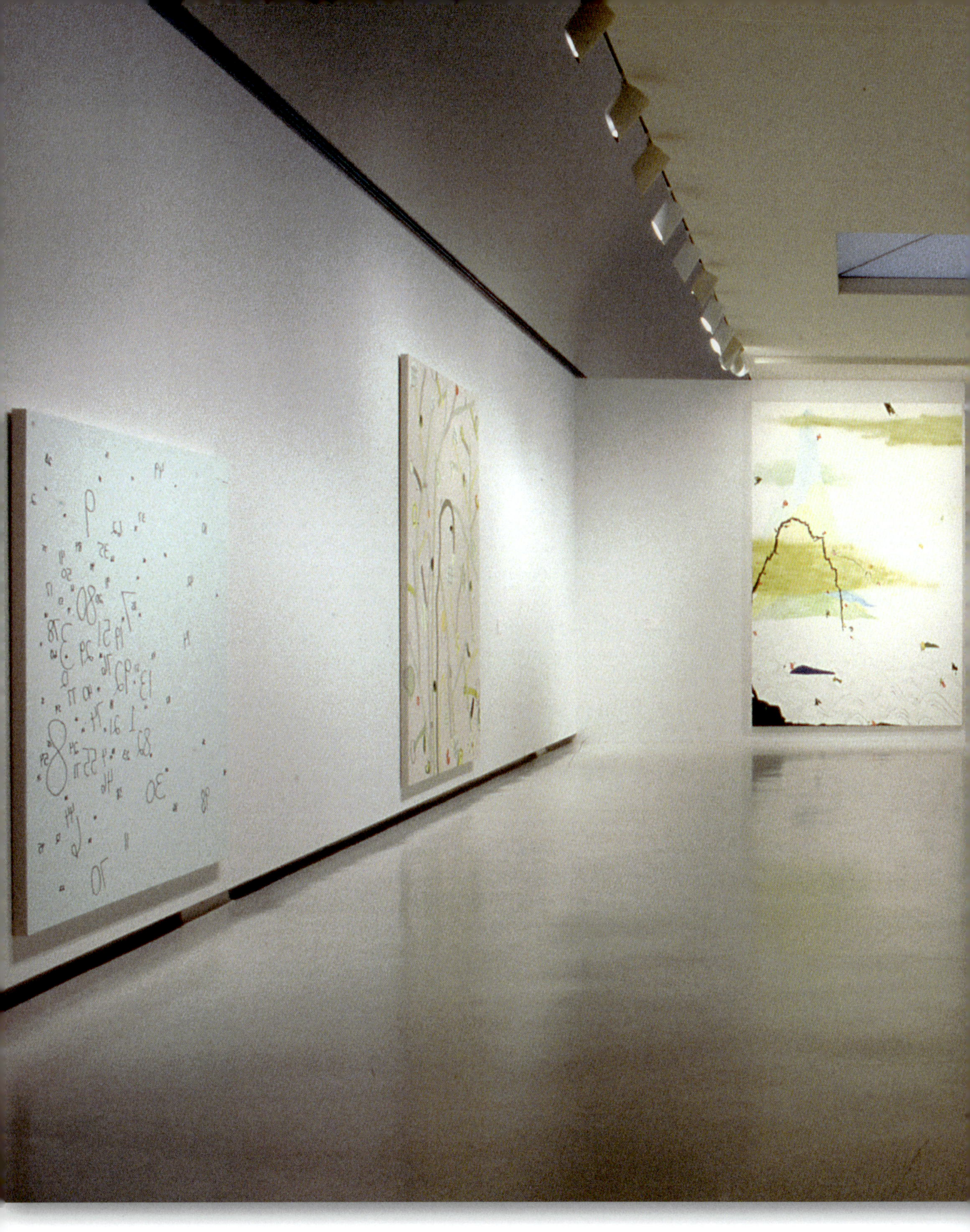

Installation view, *Carnegie International 1999/2000,* Carnegie Museum of Art, Pittsburgh, 1999–2000, with *Untitled*, 1999 (see pp. 244–45); *Untitled*, 1999 (see p. 243); and *Untitled*, 1999, acrylic, oil, and graphite on canvas, 150 × 96 in. (381 × 243.8 cm)

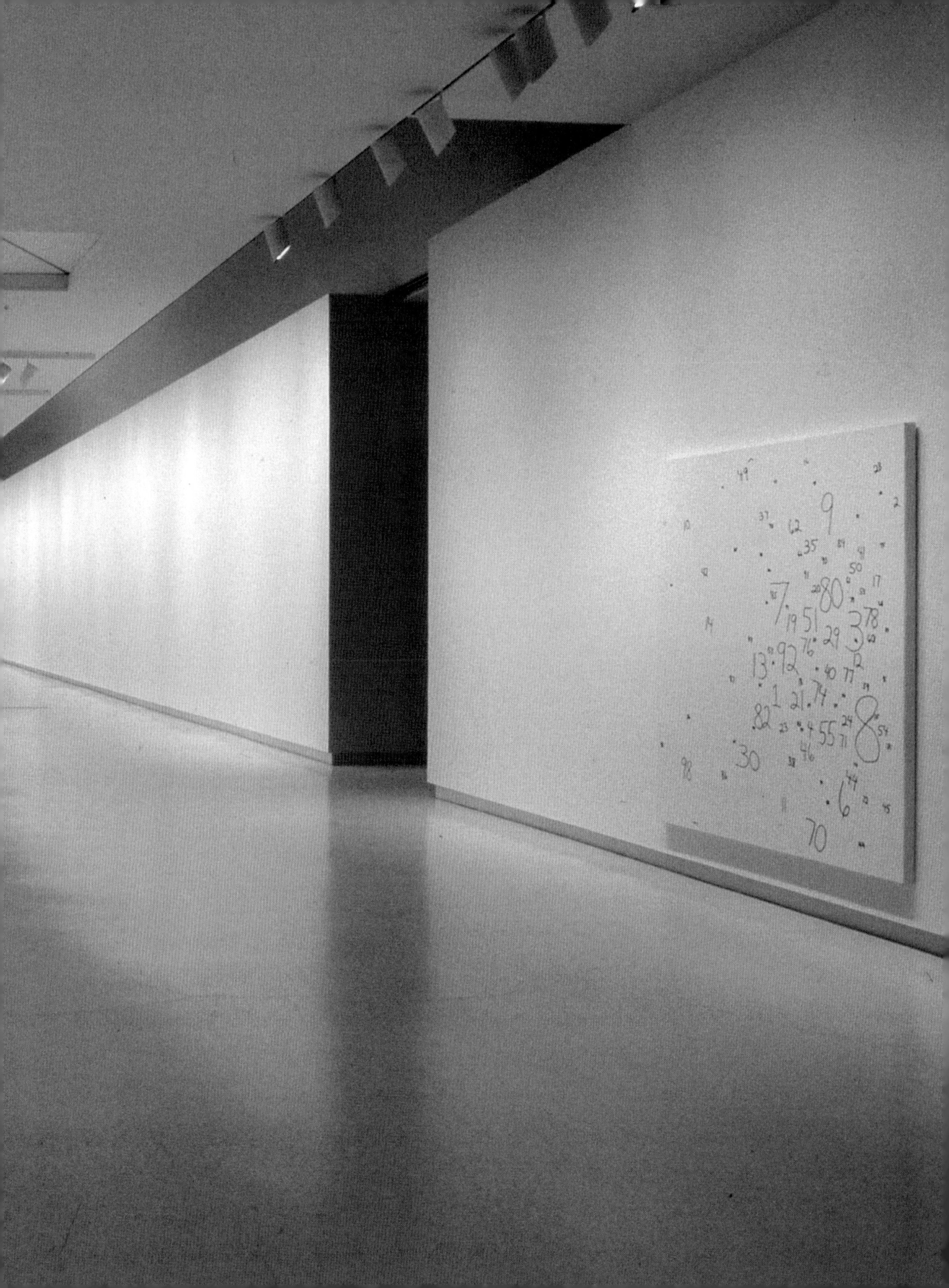

To: Randy Sommer ACME.   Thanks! I'll keep you posted. Terry

TOP SECRET!!!

"Standing Still & Walking in Los Angeles"

Jennifer Bornstein
Evan Holloway
Larry Johnson
Dave Muller/Three Day Weekend
Laura Owens

Terry R. Myers, curator

Gagosian Gallery, L.A.

opening August 6th, 1999

will be accompanied by a publication with an essay by the curator

Dear Laura —

Terry asked if you would be interested in Participating in the above group show with any <u>large</u> work. I said the only available work is the beautiful 14' x 11' white painting in storage. He thought it would be perfect. Bob and I think it is fine. What do you think? I need to get back to Terry asap. Please let me know. Hope you are well.

Hugs & kisses,
Uncle Randy

Untitled, 1998, acrylic and oil on canvas, 168 × 132 in. (426.7 × 335.3 cm)

<u>Ground/Paint</u>: The composition of the ground was undetermined, but is
most likely an acrylic gesso, which was applied by the artist. The tacking
margins were not primed.

The artis[...]   [...]ain field
was late[...]   [...]sh
horizont[...]   [...]appears
continuo[...]

The bott[...]   gray an[...]
brown), [...]   ion of th[...]
paint ma[...]   paint in [...]
two sma[...]   right--
associate[...]   is uncle[...]
as well, [...]   lge, and
small ob[...]   reas hav[...]
ridges o[...]

Please re[...]   [...]ainting
composi[...]

-Crease, [...]
-Dent, to[...]
-2 dents [...]   [...]in lengt[...]
-Multipl[...]   [...]ft of cent[...]
probably[...]
-Bucklin[...]   [...]ely 19".
Puckerin[...]   [...]as is
associate[...]
-Left ed[...]   [...]d area.
-Right e[...]
-To the [...]   [...]ront
(concav[...]   [...]12" in
diamete[...]   [...](since a[...]
other damages are from the reverse [...]
-Crossbar creases, horizontal, from 6 crossbraces.
-Feather cracks with associated tenting of paint in the following areas, low[...]
1/3 of painting:

RIA GERMAN-CARTER, CONSERVATOR OF PAINTINGS
2514 32nd. Avenue • San Francisco, CA 94116 • (415) 753-8540

CONSERVATION EXAMINATION REPORT/TREATMENT PROPOSAL

Artist: Laura Owens

Accession Number: N/A

Title/Date: Untitled, 1998

Dimensions: 168" x 132" x 2"

Medium/Support: Latex and oil or acrylic
on cotton duck

Signature: Not signed on front

Frame: Unframed

Date Examined: 26 October 1999

Client: Gagosian Gallery
456 North Camden Drive
Beverly Hills, CA 90210

(310) 271-9400-Candy Coleman

<u>Description</u>: Minimalist painting (mostly white) with an abstract landscape
form at the bottom, and tan/beige form in the upper right. Heavy
applications of paint are found in two areas: in the bottom right corner, and
in conjunction with the tan/beige form in the upper right.

<u>Condition Summary</u>: The painting is in fair condition. Several areas of
mechanical feather cracks are found in the lower half of the painting.
Buckling is located near the center on both right and left sides. Some creases
near the center on the right and left edges are probably associated with the
buckling--from stresses caused by folding the painting for shipment. (See
diagram for location of damages). Creases from the six crossbraces are
visually disturbing under some lighting conditions.

<u>Auxilliary Support/Support</u>: The painting is attached to a four member
strainer with four corner braces, and six horizontal crossbraces. There are no
vertical crossbraces. The present strainer is inadequate for the size and weight
of this painting. The strainer should have a minimum of five added vertical
crossbraces. It would be preferable to mount the canvas onto a new
expansion-bolt stretcher with adequate support in both horizontal and
vertical dimensions.

The support is a medium weight cotton duck.

  Foreground: Fax from Ria German-Carter, 1999
Background: Conservation examination report from Ria German-Carter, 1999

-Near the left edge, top is 3-1/4" from the left, 19" long, some cupping
paint.
  -Arched crack, 32" from the left, 11" long, some cupping of paint.
  -Branched feather cracks, below arched crack, 27" from the left, 38"
om the b[...]
  -Lo[...]   30" from
ttom, ap[...]
  -Ho[...]   om, 5"
ng. This[...]
  -Bra[...]   in
ameter, [...]

e cracke[...]   upping of
nsolidat[...]   er than
e cracke[...]
acked ar[...]   o remain
plane, a[...]   e not
commer[...]

rface: T[...]   l.

ame: Tl[...]   board.

onserva[...]   cernable
der cert[...]   be
inimize[...]

strongly[...]   dditional
ertical su[...]   ansion
olt stretc[...]   le to
xpand th[...]   n.

acking b[...]   erse are
rongly r[...]   g by the
ossbrace[...]   this

[...]anner, and may appear years after the event. Most of the present dents and
[...]acks were from the reverse, and might have been avoided had backing
[...]oards and carrying handles been installed.

LAURA OWENS UNTITLED, 1998

CREASE
DENT
DENTS/CREASES
6 CROSSBRACES LEAVE CREASES
DENTS WITH ASSOCIATED CRACKS
PUCKERING
BUCKLING FROM FOLDING
DENTS
PUCKERING
BUCKLING FROM FOLDING
PUCKERING
DENTS / DEFORMATIONS (CONCAVE)
AREAS OF MECHANICAL FEATHER CRACKS

Laura —
These are the areas we noted here
at Gagosian

Candy

DAMAGES NOTED 10/26/99
AT ATTHOWE FINE ART STORAGE
SAN FRANCISCO, CA
BY RIA GERMAN-CARTER,

Scott Reeder: Right when I moved to LA, in 1999, Laura and I did a collaborative show at China Art Objects. The main idea was to make this giant painting, this diptych that went between floors. One half was upstairs and the other half was downstairs in the basement. The image was a giant tree, and then underneath it the second half of the painting was roots and little tunnels and burrows with animals in them. We worked on it in the studio together and designed what the composition would look like, then painted all the little elements separately. I would paint ten birds, she would paint ten birds, etc. So it was sort of calculated together, but then we each had different individual elements that we put into it.

At the time, galleries were just starting to move to Chinatown. At China Art Objects you could hear these pachinko machines—that game with the little metal balls—happening next door. It might have been the first gallery there, I'm not sure. You got this idea that around that area there were illegal poker games or gambling going on. The show was loosely like heaven and hell. So the upstairs was heaven, and then the downstairs for whatever reason was already painted red and that was hell. We lit the bottom of the painting with candles and made this little gambling den with a poker table and we had a little bar. We also had this security camera that would have a live feed that showed you what was happening upstairs. We'd noticed that at the openings they would always have DJs and they would try to get people to hang out in the basement, but people wouldn't really do that because they'd feel like they were missing out on what was happening upstairs. So we set up this little monitor in the basement that let you see what was going on up there—that made it even more like a casino. The added element was that most of the footage was a live feed, but then some of it was prerecorded—like someone in a gorilla costume, or a part that made it look like stuff was falling off the painting. We recorded all this stuff ahead of time,

   Scott Reeder is a Detroit-based artist and has collaborated with Owens intermittently over the past twenty years.

and it would just be interspersed with the live feed. People would get really confused. Like when the opening was packed, but then on the monitor the space looked empty, they went upstairs and were like, "What? There's still people here." We were sort of playing around with reality, or time. That show was really fun to do. We also did a weekly poker game through the run of the exhibition. If I remember right I lost a ton of money and Laura made a ton of money. She was a pretty good gambler. I think that China Art Objects show was a little kernel of what 356 would become. At the core is a normal white-cube exhibition space, but with all this ancillary stuff that's really rich. The paintings provided a social space and a context for a lot of other activities.

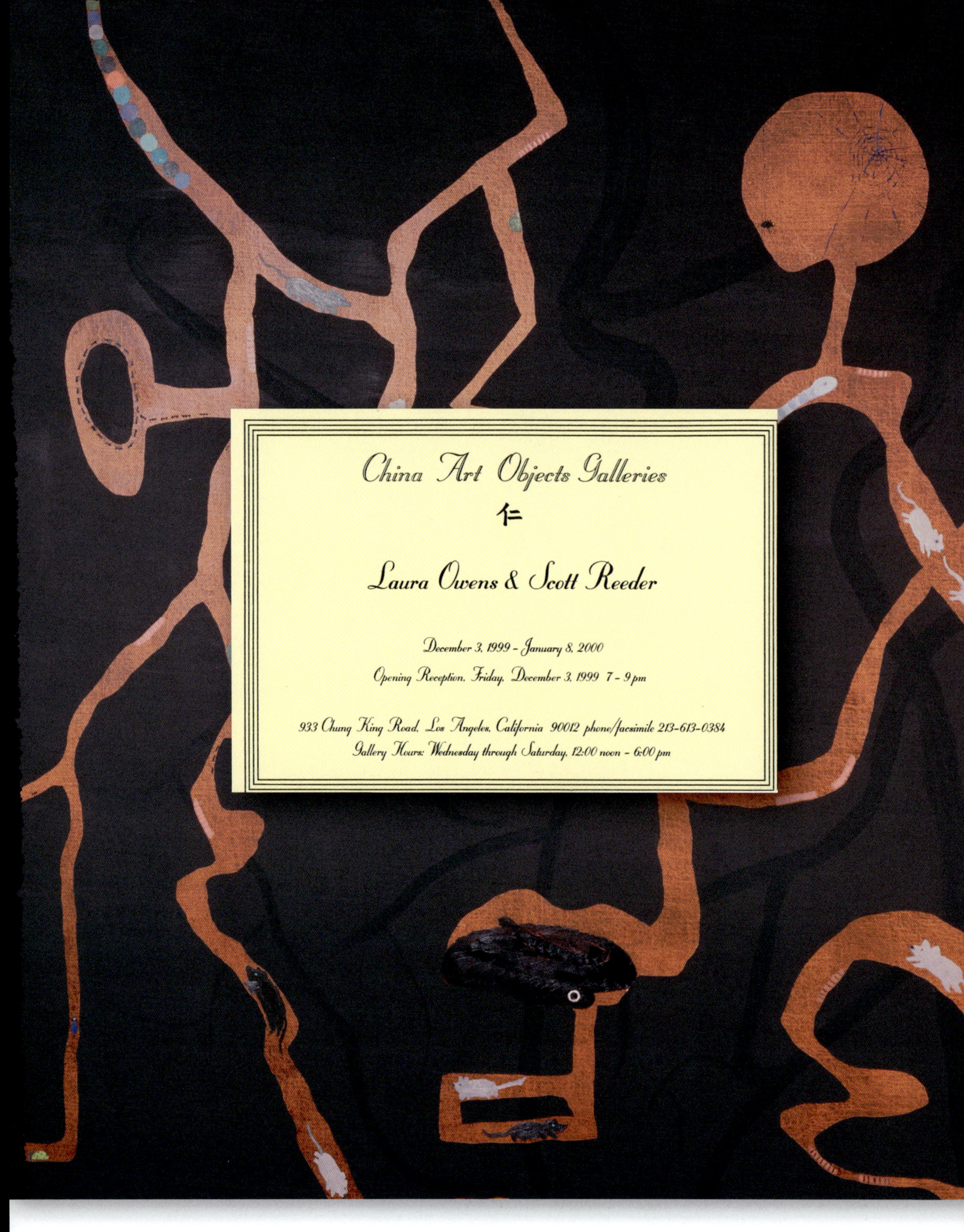

Foreground: Invitation, *Heaven and Hell*, China Art Objects Galleries, Los Angeles, 1999
Background: Detail of Owens and Scott Reeder, *Untitled*, 1999 (see p. 275)

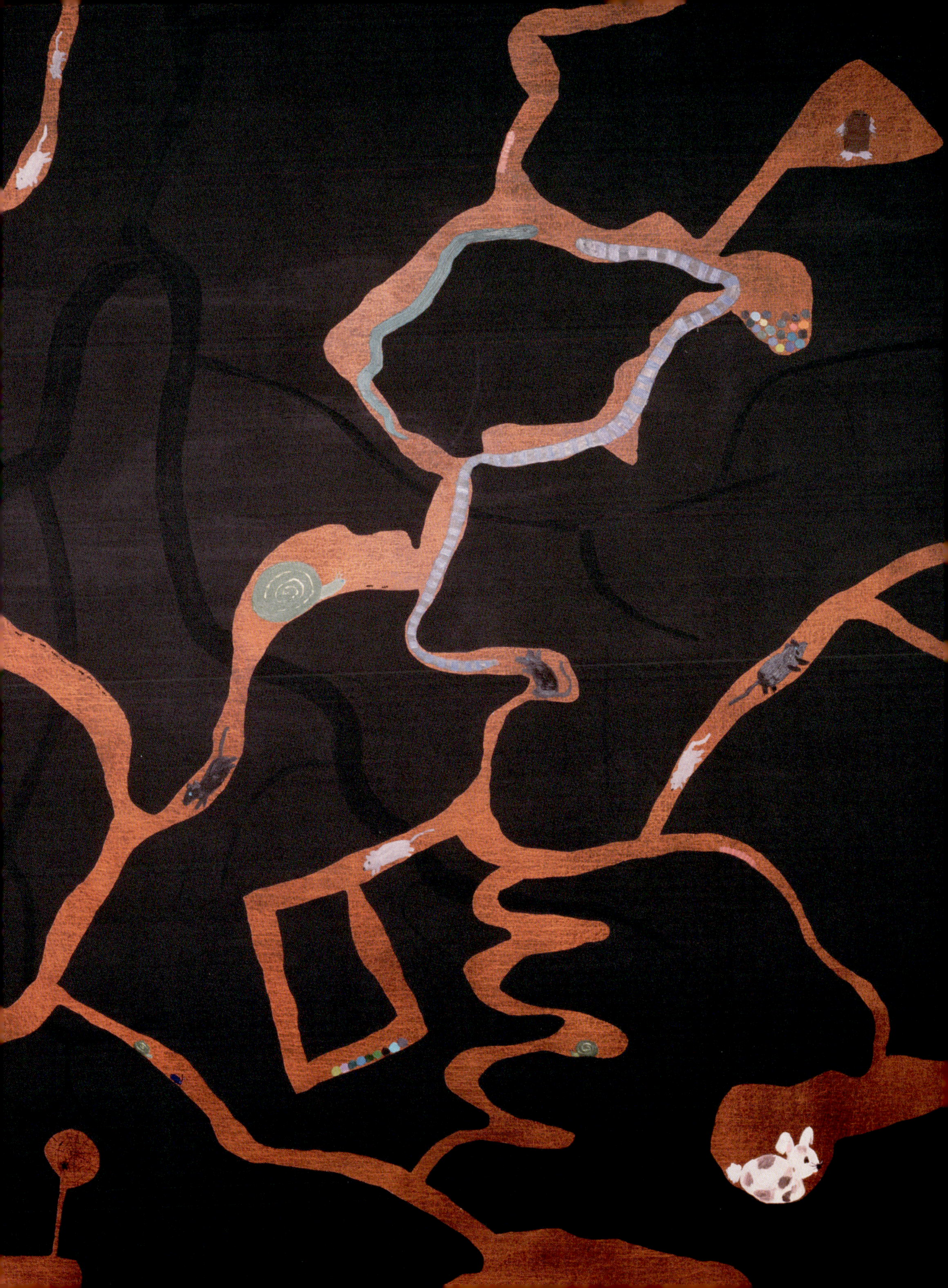

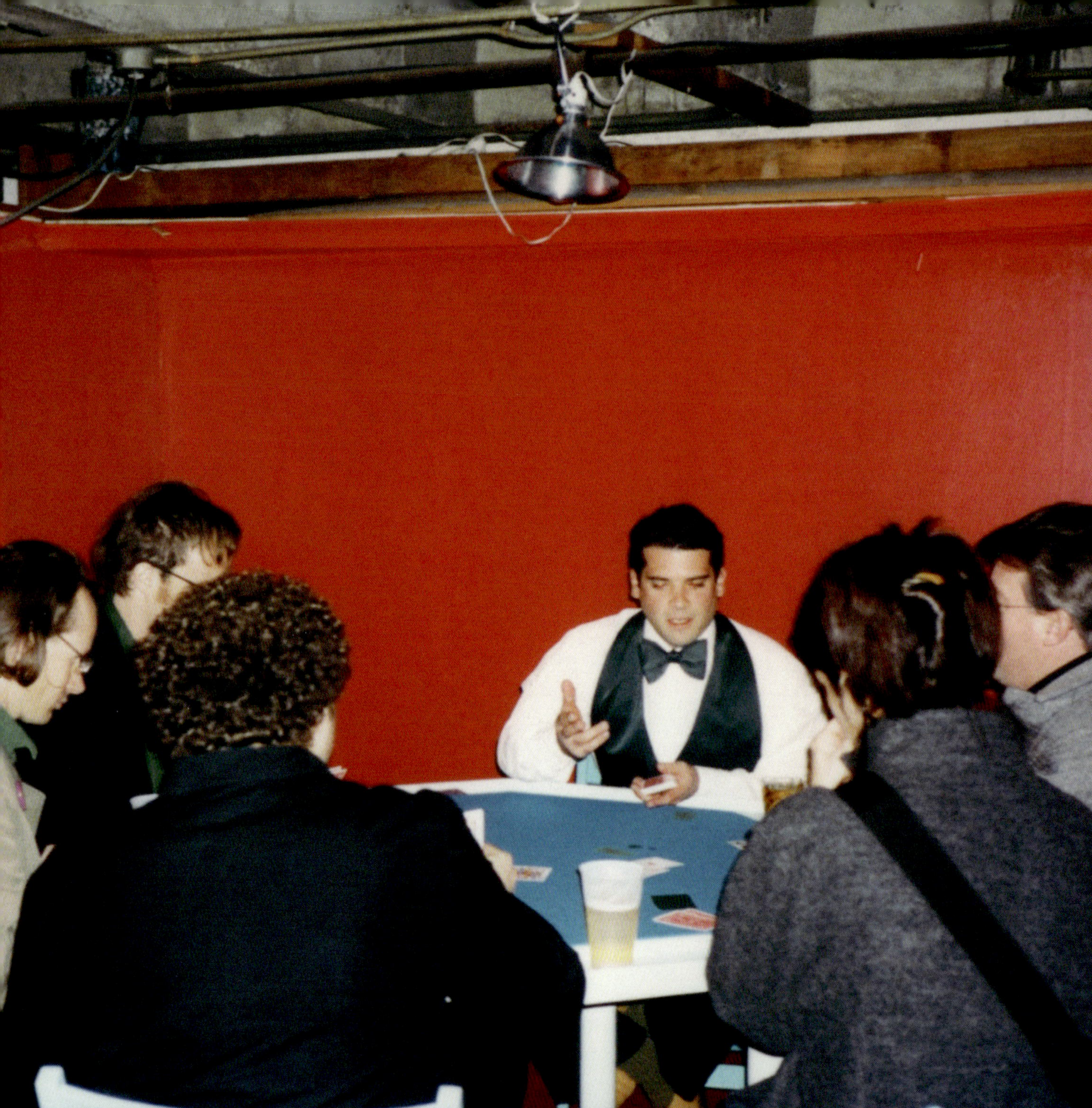

   Poker game in *Heaven and Hell*, China Art Objects Galleries, Los Angeles, 1999

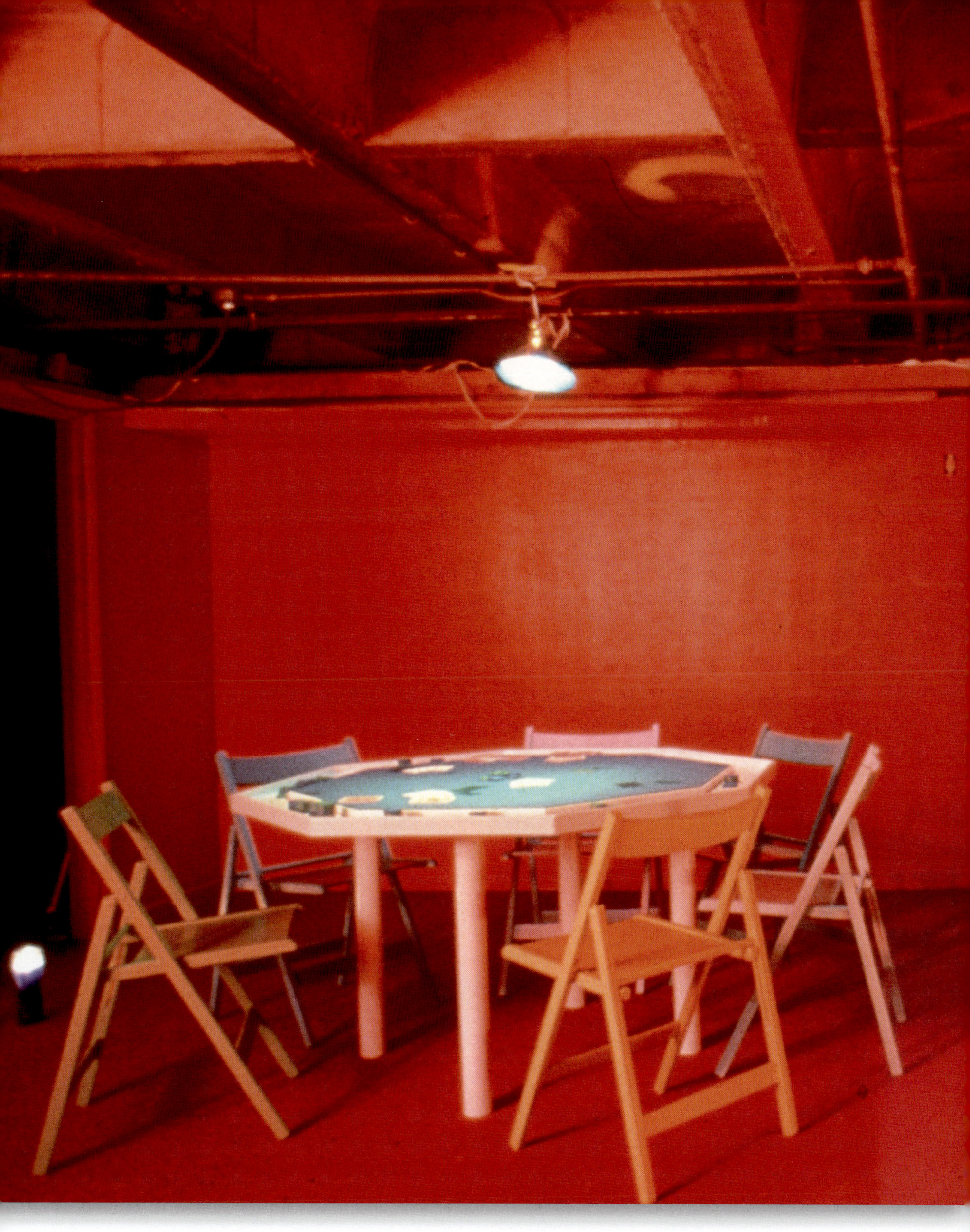

Installation view, *Heaven and Hell*, China Art Objects Galleries, Los Angeles, 1999, with Owens and Scott Reeder, *Untitled*, 1999, wood, felt, and acrylic paint, dimensions variable

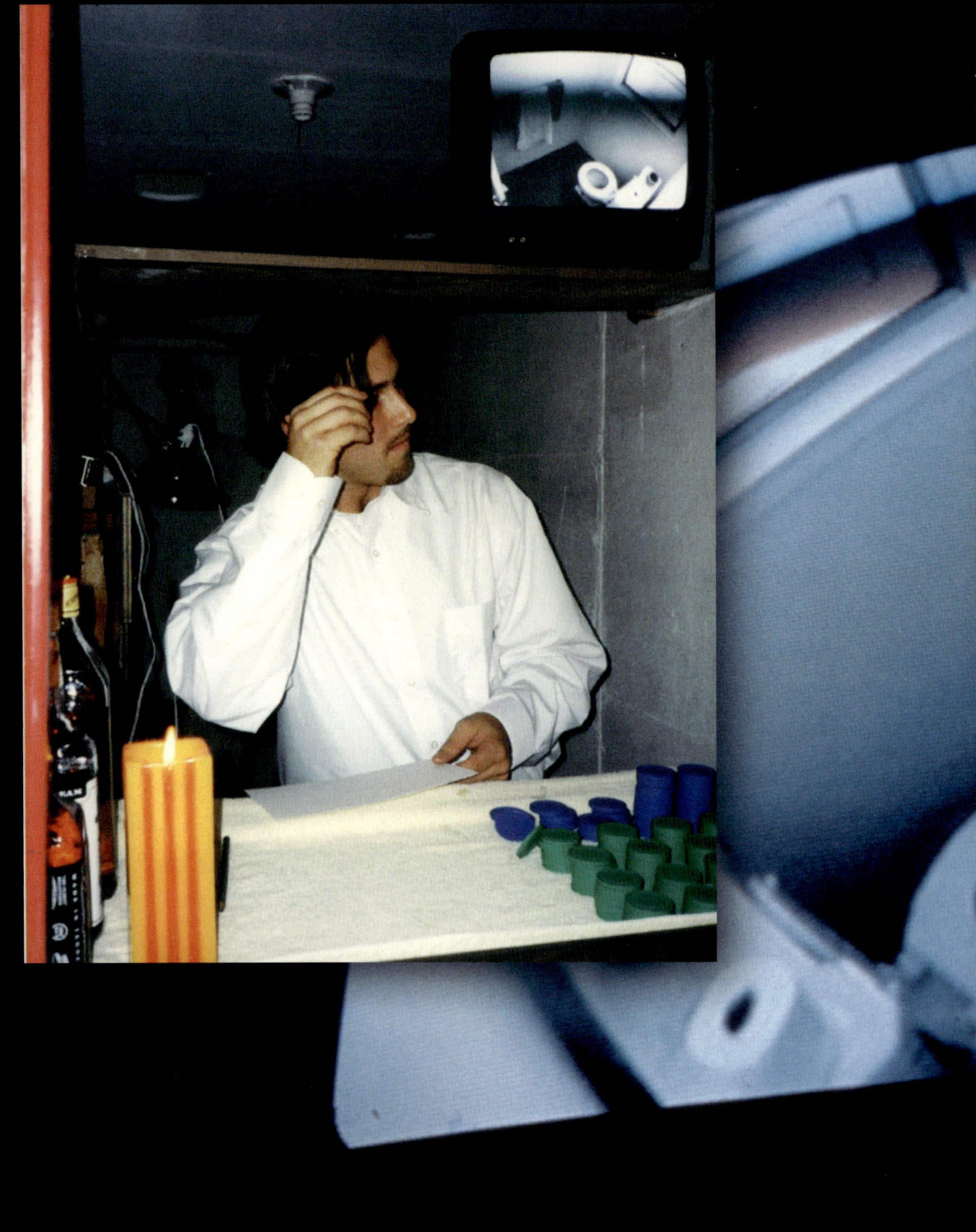

Foreground: Lincoln Owens, *Heaven and Hell*, China Art Objects Galleries, Los Angeles, 1999
Background: Video still, China Art Objects Galleries, 1999

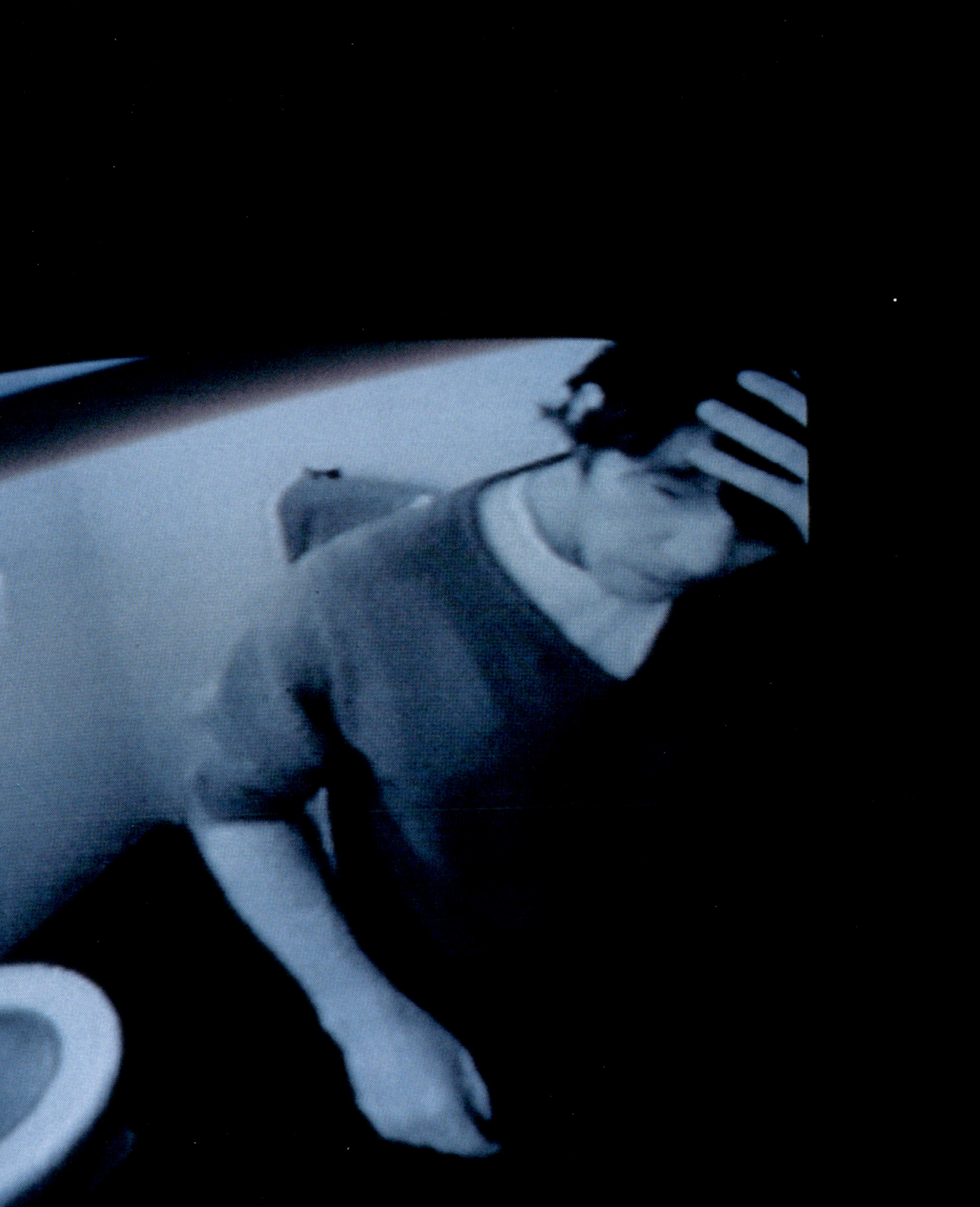

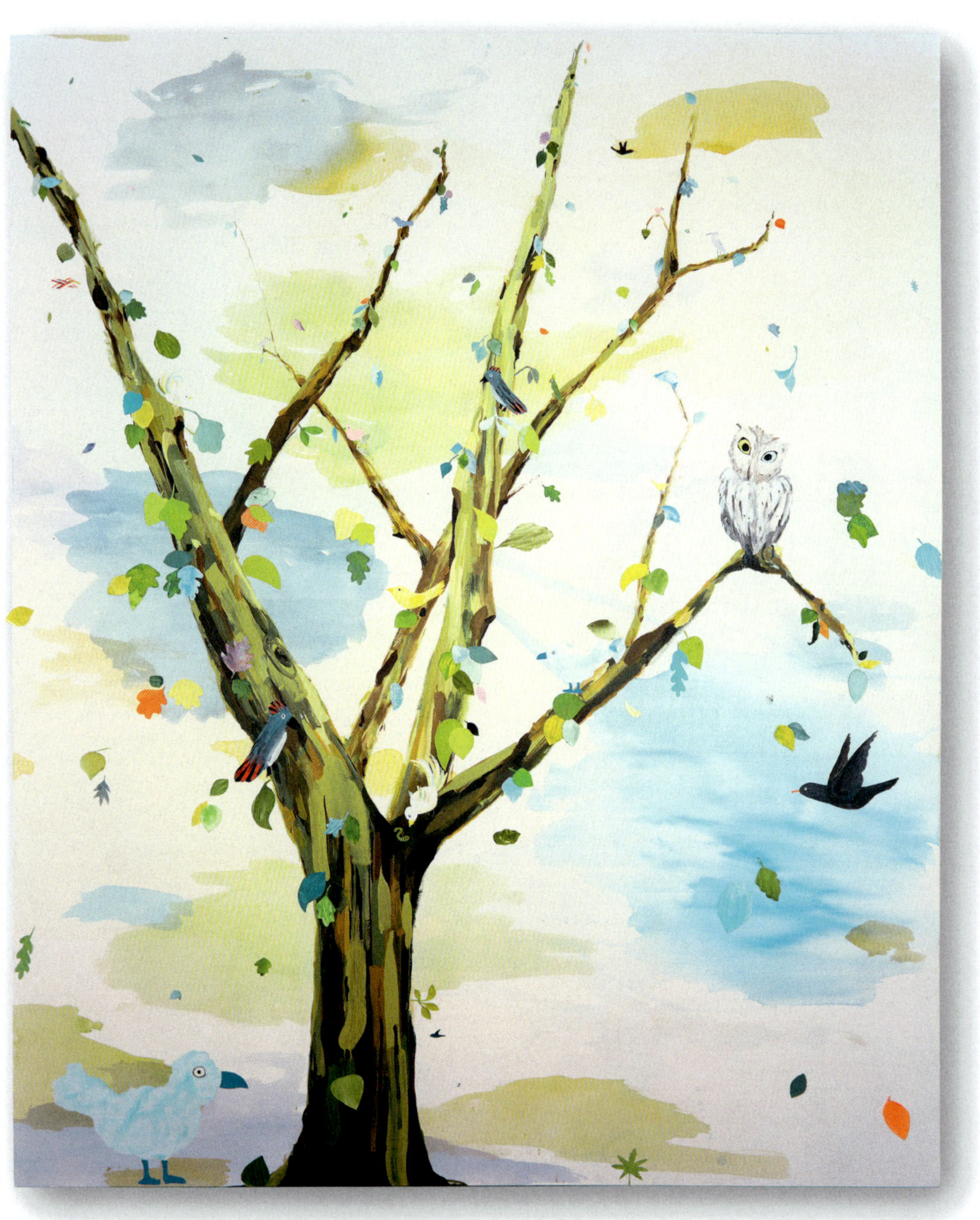

274   Owens and Scott Reeder, *Untitled*, 1999, acrylic, oil, pen, and collaged paper on canvas, 144 × 114 in. (365.8 × 289.6 cm)

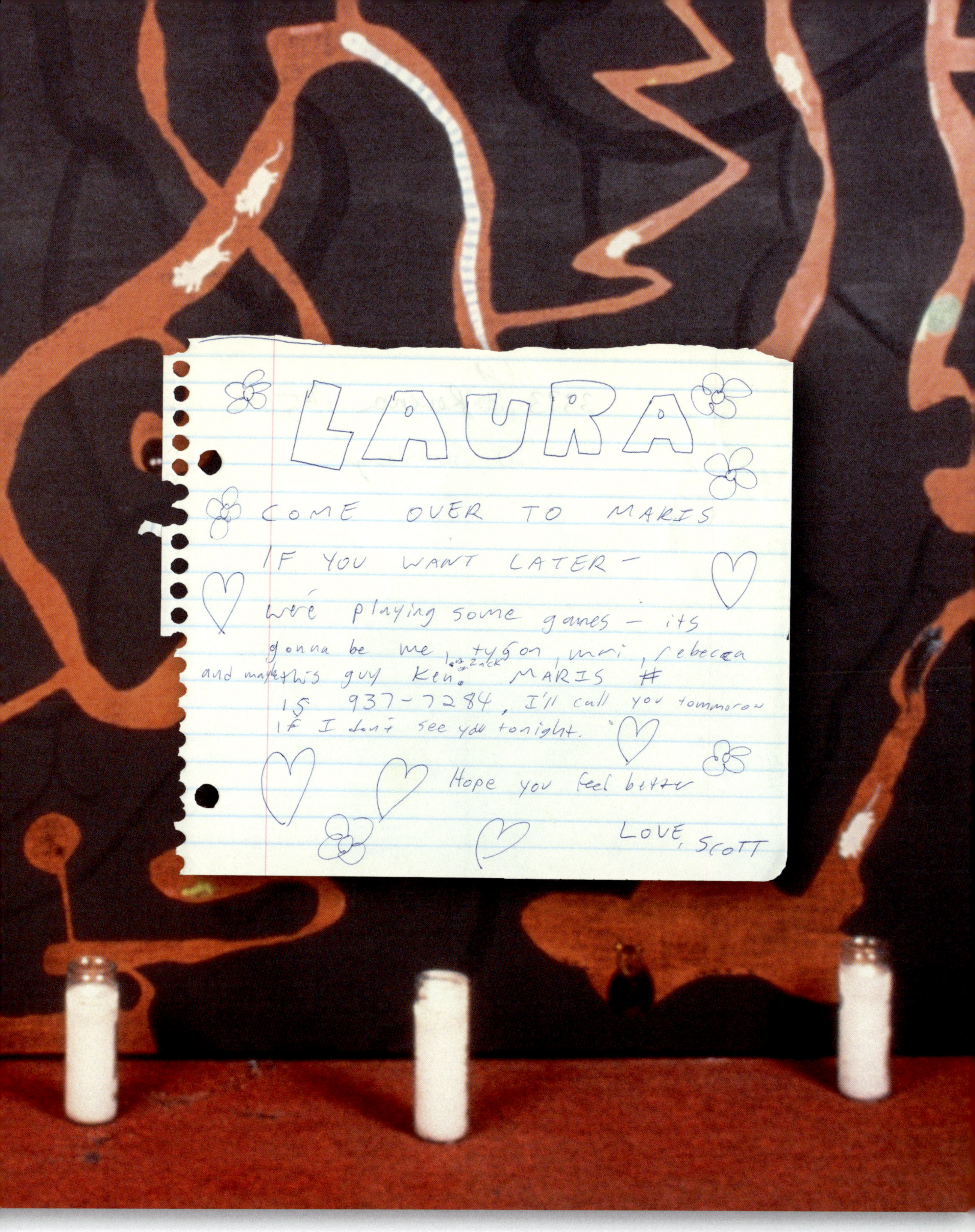

Foreground: Note from Scott Reeder, 1999
Background: Installation view, *Heaven and Hell*, China Art Objects Galleries, Los Angeles, 1999, with Owens and Scott Reeder, *Untitled*, 1999, acrylic and oil on canvas, 80 × 114 in. (203.2 × 289.6 cm)

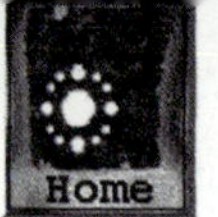

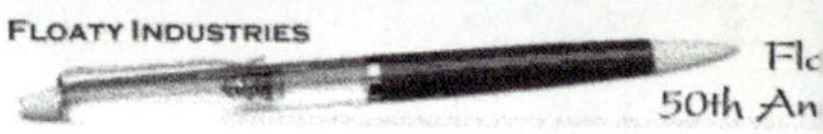

how will i proceed with my paintings

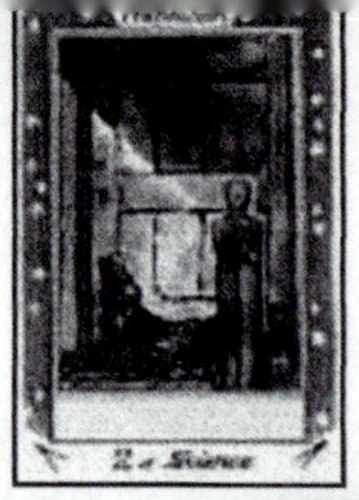
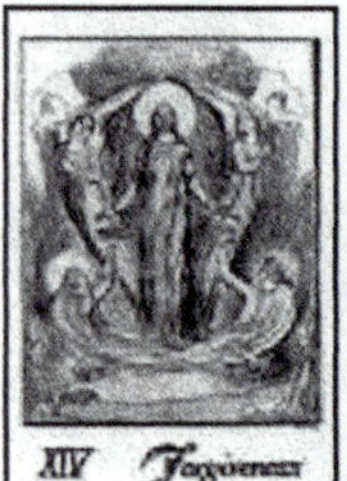
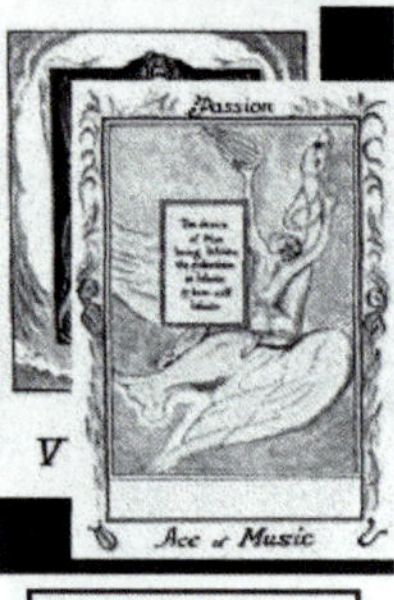
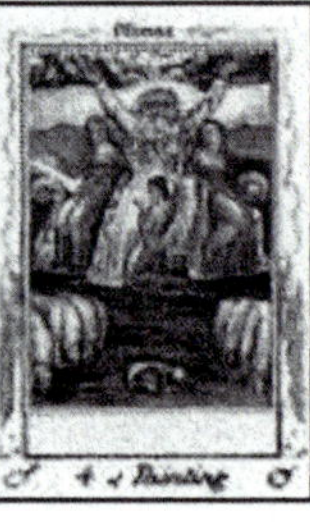
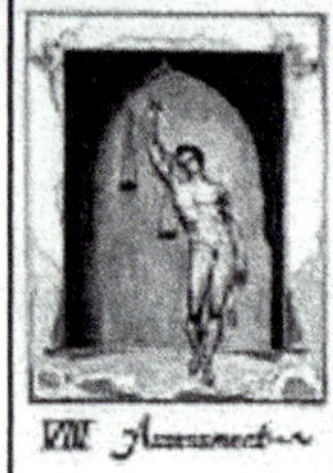

The center card, partially obscured, represents the Creative Project. This card represents the essence of the reading.

Tarot   4/10/99 3:36 PM

VIII ASSESSMENT
A need to be fair and just. A situation involving judgments or balancing the issues. Consideration of commitments, agreements, or negotiations . Weighing the pros and cons of a situation. Evaluating the needs of self versus others. Transcending the limits of a situation by using kindness and imagination.

The rightmost card represents the Manifesting or Culmination of the project. This card tells you how to actually do the work and/or the form it will take when completed. Associated with the Shadow, this card may also indicate something unreal in the outcome, a projection of desire rather than an expression of the spiritual motive.

4 OF PAINTING - MEANS
Material prosperity and contentment. Attachment to money and material goods. Creative achievements using material resources. Consolidation of personnel and materials. Bringing about order and structure. Emphasis on controlling, dominating, or monopolizing. Protecting and maintaining.

In the creative process: Before reaching out for creative inspiration, prepare the groundwork: by appropriately allocating your resources and assigning creative tasks.

[Click here for Full Graphics]

Copyright 1993 Facade Market Concepts, Inc. All rights reserved. All materials contained in this site are protected by

---

Tarot   4/10/99 3:36

V RELIGION
Need or desire for personal guidance. Hypocritical influences may be present (spiritual materialism). Question authority and be suspicious of leaders and gurus. Conventional morality may be a dominant factor. Corruption in high places. Fighting (or giving in to) City Hall. Feeling oppressed by the rules.

The card covering the center card, represents the Creator. This card represents the spiritual impetus or force behind the project. This can be yourself, another person, or, some other creative entity. This card and the above card are a snapshot of the creative synthesis.

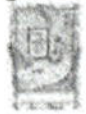

ACE OF MUSIC - PASSION
[The desire of Man being Infinite the possession is Infinite & him-self Infinite]

Release of emotions. Upsurge of creative power. Unlimited potential. Being carried away by your emotions (swept up on wings of song). Feeling a passion for life. Wanting to achieve the highest potentials in yourself and the situation. Following your bliss. Feeling a deep sense of grace and fulfillment. Vulnerability and openness.

In the creative process: A passionate desire to rise above the norm, to soar to personal new heights of creative vision.

The top card represents the Imagination. This card tells you something about the ideation of the project. The spiritual truth overseeing the project.

Laura Owens: At some point I had a theory that there were two types of artists—those that had a hard time starting and those that had a hard time finishing. Really it's the same problem, just in different forms. I constantly felt I had too many ideas or options and couldn't settle on one to start on in any given moment. I often had to force myself or trick myself into starting. Frequently I would give myself an assignment, like remaking a historic painting or painting a sunset. I am very good at procrastinating, and even with only dial-up Internet in my Eagle Rock studio I managed to waste many hours on tarot card websites and playing Bejeweled, which all felt like a necessary part of the process. I also made a serious dive into astrology. There was an endless amount to learn about the energies each planet held, and I related much of what I read to a CalArts class Leslie Dick taught on Freud and Lacan as well as to what I knew about Greek and Hindu mythology. I was particularly interested in Jeff Green's writings about Pluto, but I also worked with several other astrologers, including Christy Walker, who would give me mini tutorials whenever I had a reading. For a while the esoteric bookstores in any city were the first places I would seek out, and I found this macro gazing at connections and planets to be a helpful escape from the negativity and disappointment you can sometimes get caught up in as a young artist.

1999 *Transit Search*
Transiting Planets
Mars Jupiter thru Pluto
Applying Orb 2 Degrees
Separating Orb 2 Degrees

Dec31

Transit list (left margin):

Aspect	Date
☍ MC	Jan1
☌ 4	Jan1
☍ ☿	Jan1
✶ ♄	Jan1
□ ☽	Jan1
☌ 9	Jan1
□ ♀	Jan1
✶ ♅	Jan1
✶ ☽	Jan4
☍ AS	Jan1 / *Mar…*
☌ 7	Jan1
☍ ♇	Jan1
□ 4	Jan2 / *Mar…*
☌ ♀	Jan2
△ ♆	Jan2
□ AS	Jan3
✶ ♂	Jan3
☌ 4	Jan3
△ AS	Feb1
☍ ♀	Mar1
☍ ♅	Mar1
□ AS	Mar1
△ ♂	Mar1
☍ 4	Mar1
✶ ♂	Apr1
☌ 4	Apr1
□ AS	Apr2
☌ ♀	Apr2
☌ MC	Apr2
☌ 10	Apr2
☌ 6	May8
✶ ♅	May8
△ ☽	May1…
□ ♀	Jun1 / *Sep2…*
☍ ♀	Jun2…

Transit list (lower section):

Aspect		
△ ☉	Jun30 Aug30 Oct31 / *Jul27* *Oct2*	
☌ ♀	Jul5 *Jul10* Jul16	
□ AS	Jul8 Aug25 Oct11 / *Jul25* *Sep24*	
☌ △ ♅	Dec3 *Dec6* Dec8	
☌ ✶ MC	Dec18 *Dec21* Dec23	
☌ ✶ ☽	Dec22 *Dec25* Dec27	
☌ □ ♄	Dec23 *Dec25* Dec28	

Laura Owens
Natal Chart
Sep 9 1970
3:25 am EDT +4:00
Euclid, OH
41°N35'35" 081°W31'37"
Geocentric
Tropical
Koch
True Node

Compliments of:–
Rick Levine
Redmond, WA
email: rlevine@stariq.com
http://www.stariq.com
425.882.3481

Aspect Grid

	☽	☉	☿	♀	♂	♃	♄	♅	♆	♇	⚷	☊	As	Mc
☽														
☉	□ 6S08											‖ 0S35		
☿	□ 0A40	☌ 6A48												
♀	S 1A07	∠ 0A50					# 0A56			# 0A12				
♂				✶ 1A51		# 0S43						# 0A40		
♃		∠ 2A42		☌ 1A53	✶ 0A02									
♄		△ 6A24	△ 0A25	S² 1A35						‖ 0S44				
♅	Q 2S37						□ 0S08							
♆		Q 0A10		□ 5S31			☍ 5S46	S 0S47						
♇	□ 4A28		☌ 3S48				△ 4S12		✶ 1A34					
⚷				Q² 0S49	S³ 0A52	∠ 1A28	☍ 1A20							
☊	Q 1S37			△ 0A42	☍ 1S09	△ 1S11			Q² 1A00	□ 4A22	S³ 1A38			
As		∠ 2A19		□ 1A30	⚹ 0S21	□ 0S23	Q 1A05			△ 5A10		△ 5A32		
Mc	△ 3S13	Q² 3S04	S³ 0S24	□ 0A15						Q² 3S14		∠ 1A24	S² 1A32	

Foreground: Natal chart from psychological horoscope by Rick Levine, 1999
Background: Detail of transit chart from psychological horoscope, 1999

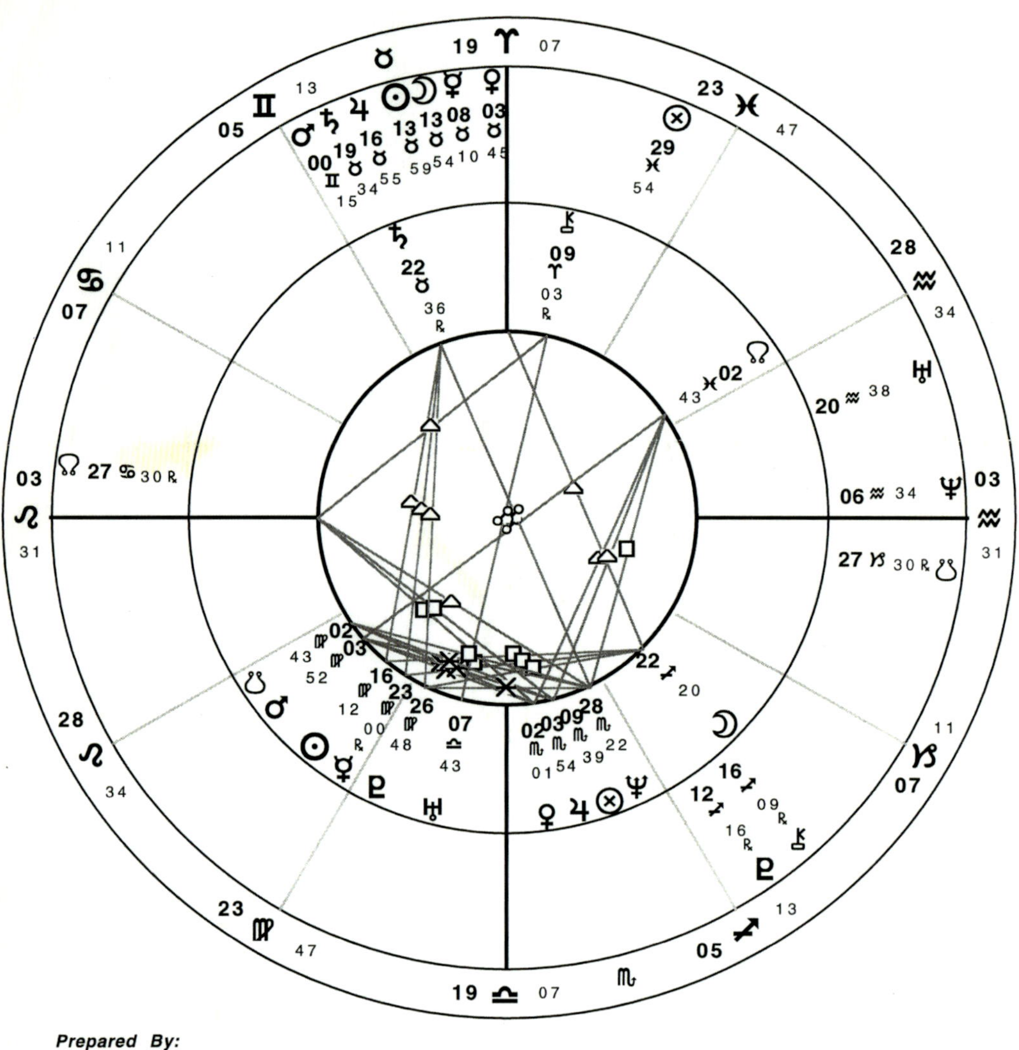

Psychological Horoscope Analysis
for
Laura Owens, born 9 Sep 1970

Nr 25122.23-1

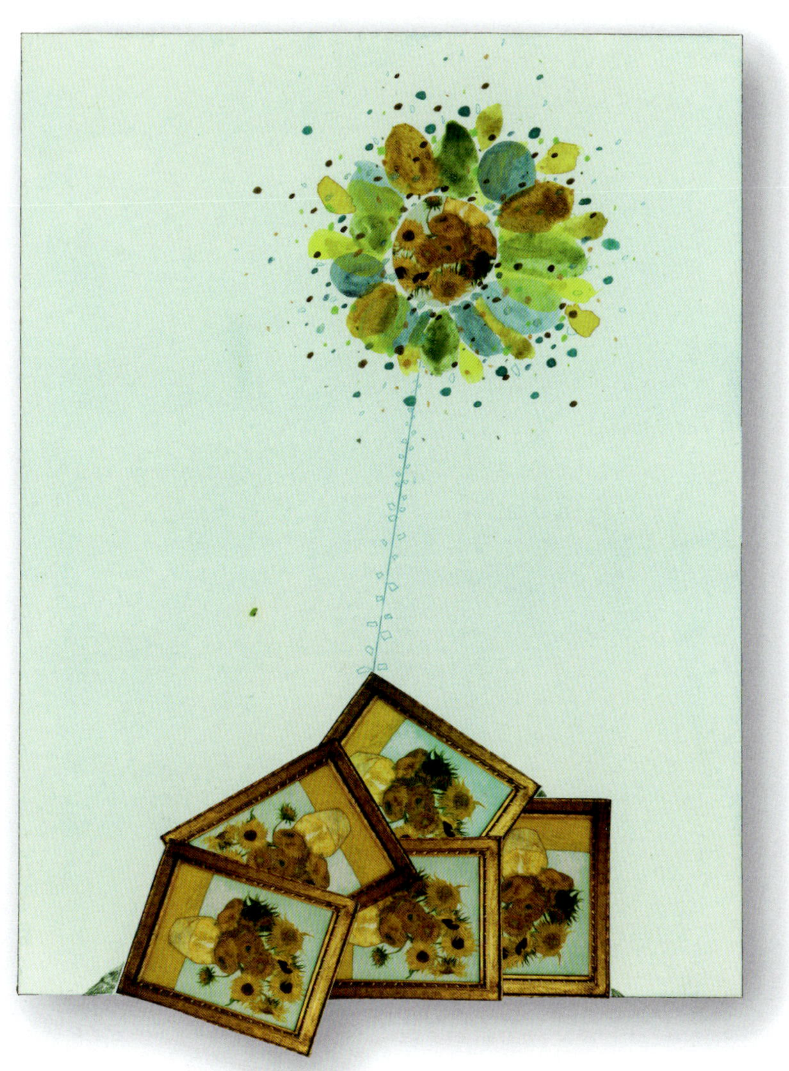

Untitled, 2000, watercolor and collaged paper on paper, 12 × 9 in. (30.5 × 22.9 cm)

Dream

Sat. May 13

Hang show at CAO.
w/ Scott.. Only I'm the only
one - No Work Day of the
opening Get big white pieces
of paper on all the walls
(Gallery D.f.t)   at first

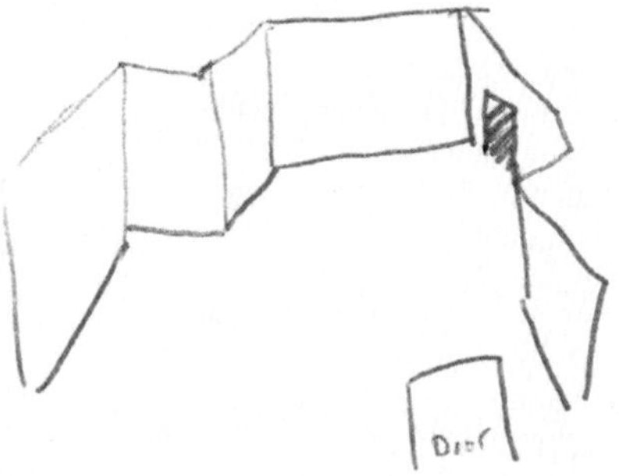

I am going to do big
ptngs on all the walls
then time running out
I take down paper and
instead stick old drawings
up - (decide not to use some walls)
inbetween drawings I draw
pencil lines (like a constellation)
My mom has been there getting
in the way but now she's helping a little
but I wish I could have time to do it

no one will see the
show. Scott comes
in B tells me its bad
it looks pretentious.
I'm kind of mad he
wasn't around but also
sad because I am in
such a whirlwind I can't
even tell that it would
look pretentious
- later I am teaching
a class (Art Center? CalArts)
but it is like the medical
classrooms of the 19th century
(eakins) I start a movement
of Anarchy - I am loud
and everyone warns me that
reviews are going on next
door - but I can't help
Jason Yates puts me on
his shoulders as we m
around the classroom +
shout Anarchy - laughin
- Full Time Faculty
in - I see my nam
in school catalogue in
support of some real
stupid article
(I am really just starting
people come in)

May 8 2000

Pluto by Jeff Green

① - Moving from an individuated state → spiritual state of consciousness (oscillating?)

② - An artist from middle class middle America

③ Prior evolutionary intent (my place of gravitation for "unconscious" emotional "security")
Pluto in Virgo: lessons of personal humility, self doubt, purification & self improvement through intense self analysis
Transitioning from subjective/egocentric to objective progressively egoconcentric
Pierce the balloon of self importance/delusions of grandeur — to learn what you are not with Mercury in Virgo ... 2nd →

Periodic "surveys" of myself to purge & grow mentally emotionally .... to identify w/ larger & larger wholes
Most Virgos hold unconscious 'guilt' for mistakes of not perfect in order to atone → work/service for other — Your own worst enemy - Flaws, shortcomings - - never ready, never good enough ... PROCRASTINATION, not fulfill potential & yet another source of guilt!!! (many lifetimes over. A vicious circle →

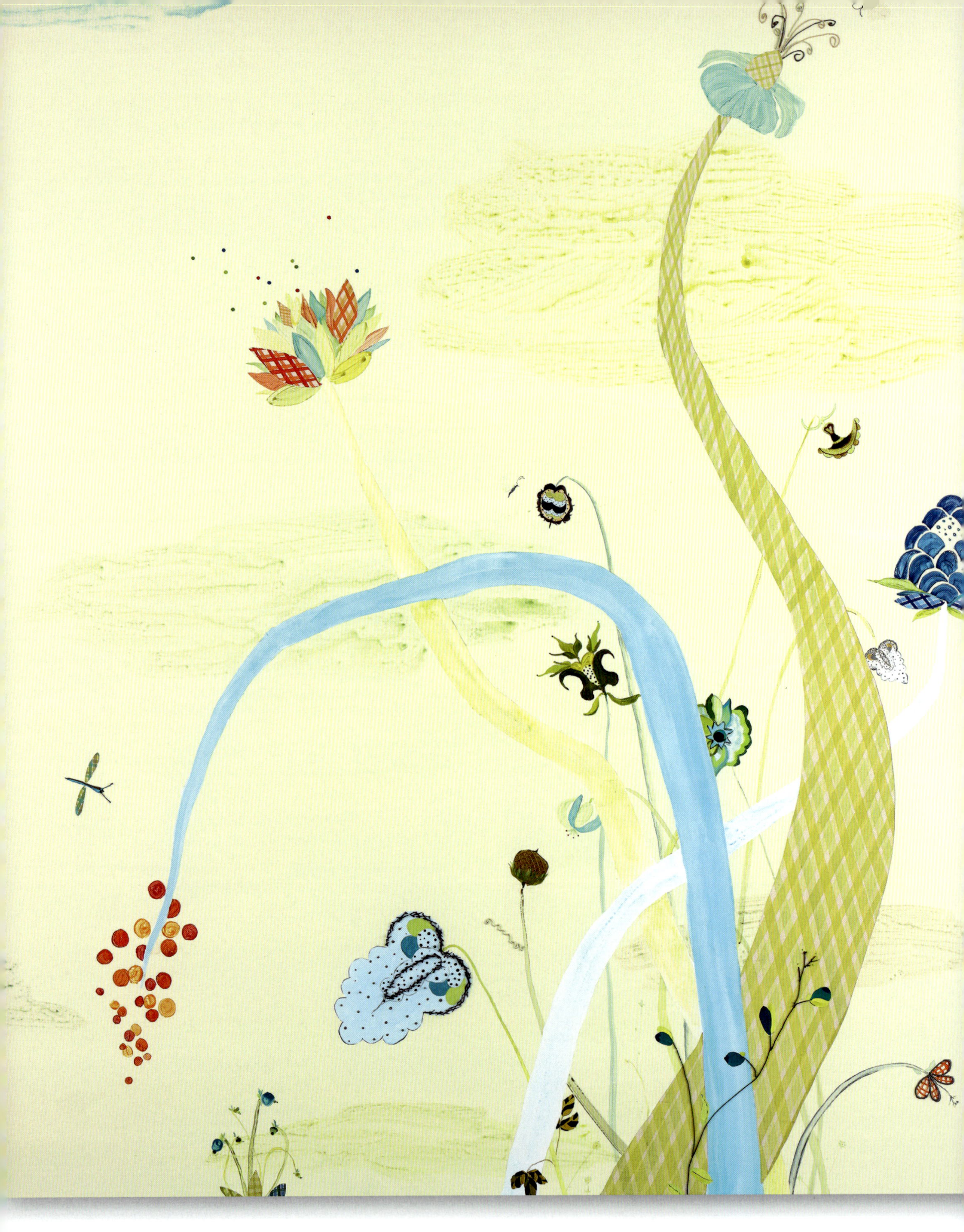

282 Detail of *Untitled*, 2000, acrylic and oil on canvas, 96 × 84 in. (243.8 × 213.4 cm)

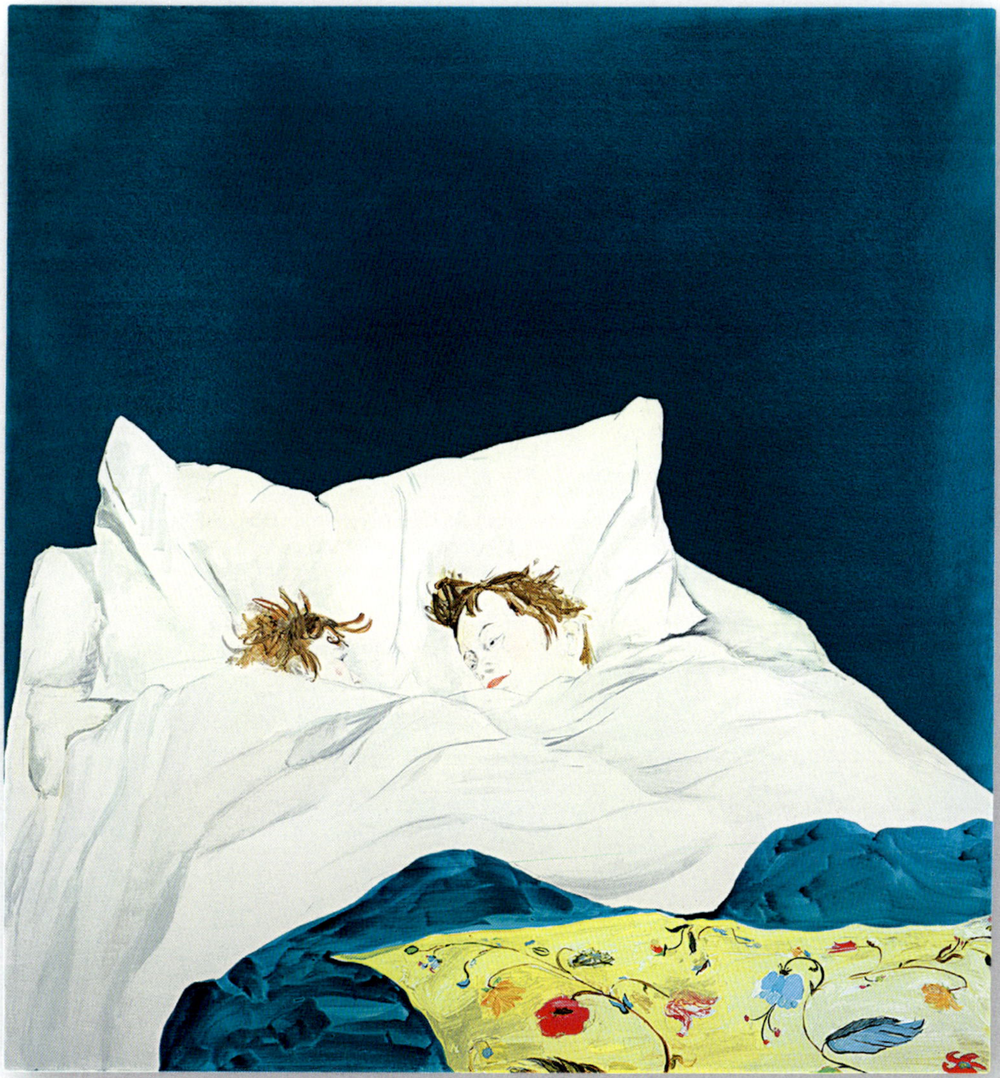

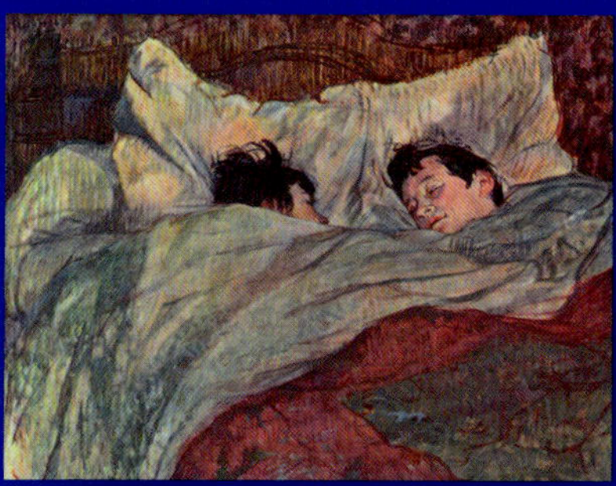

Laura Owens: After making many paintings and drawings using images of animals, I realized I was avoiding the human figure. For the diptych with monkeys that was in my second Sadie Coles show I had started with a painting by an unknown Sung Dynasty artist, *Gibbons Playing in a Loquat Tree,* studied it, and remade it. So I found this Toulouse-Lautrec painting of two people in a bed and decided to remake it. The diptych had been made complete by a twenty-foot expanse of white wall; I decided that here it would make sense for the center of the painting to be an area of flat, white gesso that I would leave blank to represent the space between the two figures and the pillow they were lying on. I painted a quilt on the bed that referred to another painting in the show.

Untitled, 2000, acrylic, oil, and graphite on canvas, 72 × 66½ in. (182.9 × 168.9 cm)
Inset: Henri de Toulouse-Lautrec, *Le lit* (The Bed), ca. 1892, oil on cardboard, 21.1 × 27.6 in. (53.6 × 70.1 cm)

Marion Boulton Stroud-Swingle

4049 Conestoga Road (Rt. 401), Elverson, Pennsylvania 19520-8731
2602 Indian Point Road, Bar Harbor, Maine 04609-9751
1221 North Lake Way, Palm Beach, Florida 33480-3147

8th May, 2000

Laura Owens,
5121 ½ Eaglerock Boulevard, #D,
Los Angeles, Ca 90041-1167.

Dear Laura,

I was happy to get your email recently and I do hope that Peter Doig will be able to join us in Maine this summer.   He is clearly very well thought of as an artist, as Paul Schimmel of LA MOCA also recommended him.

We have just published this new book by "Jorge Pardo" and I wanted you to have a copy of it.   Any comments? Every step of the way on the book, we felt like giving up, but held our tongues!

Looking forward to seeing you in Maine this summer and many thanks for your wonderful recommendations. Do try to get Chris Offili as well.

Best wishes, *love + hugs,*

Kippy

Pennsylvania : Phone 610.363.2330/610.286.6503 *Fax 610.286.5669*
Maine: Phone 207.288.2345 * Fax 207.288.2046 ASAP 207.288.0101
Florida: Phone 561.848.5656 *Fax 561.848.5622* E-mail Kippyss@AOL.com

June 5, 2000

Yes, and hello Laura Owens,

This is Dianna Molzan, former student from Chicago, writing
after three years. Slow, yes, I am, with the verbal. But I
have kept up with your work nonetheless, via periodicals,
exhibits. What I have seen, I admire very much. Me, I have
one year of undergraduate study left. This fall semester, I
will live in Berlin and study video at the Hochschule der
Kunste. I still paint, and now do lots of other things too:
video, text/writing, fashion-less garments. And still I
consider the possibility of moving to Los Angeles for graduate school and beyond. But, so yes, I am writing because,
I would like to get in contact with you before I venture
a trip west in a year or so. I understand that you must be
busy, but if you would please drop me a line sometime through
my e-mail (I do not have your e-mail address), to let me
know that this letter reached you, and to arrange a time
in the future that we can make contact. I would like to ask
you about the schools, exhibit spaces, recommendation stuff.
Also, I have sent you some random bits of projects that I
compiled together. Goodbye then, take care.

Dianna

Dianna Molzan
1302 N Leavitt, #1
Chicago, IL 60622
ph#: 773-395-1931
e-mail: dorkface5@hotmail.com

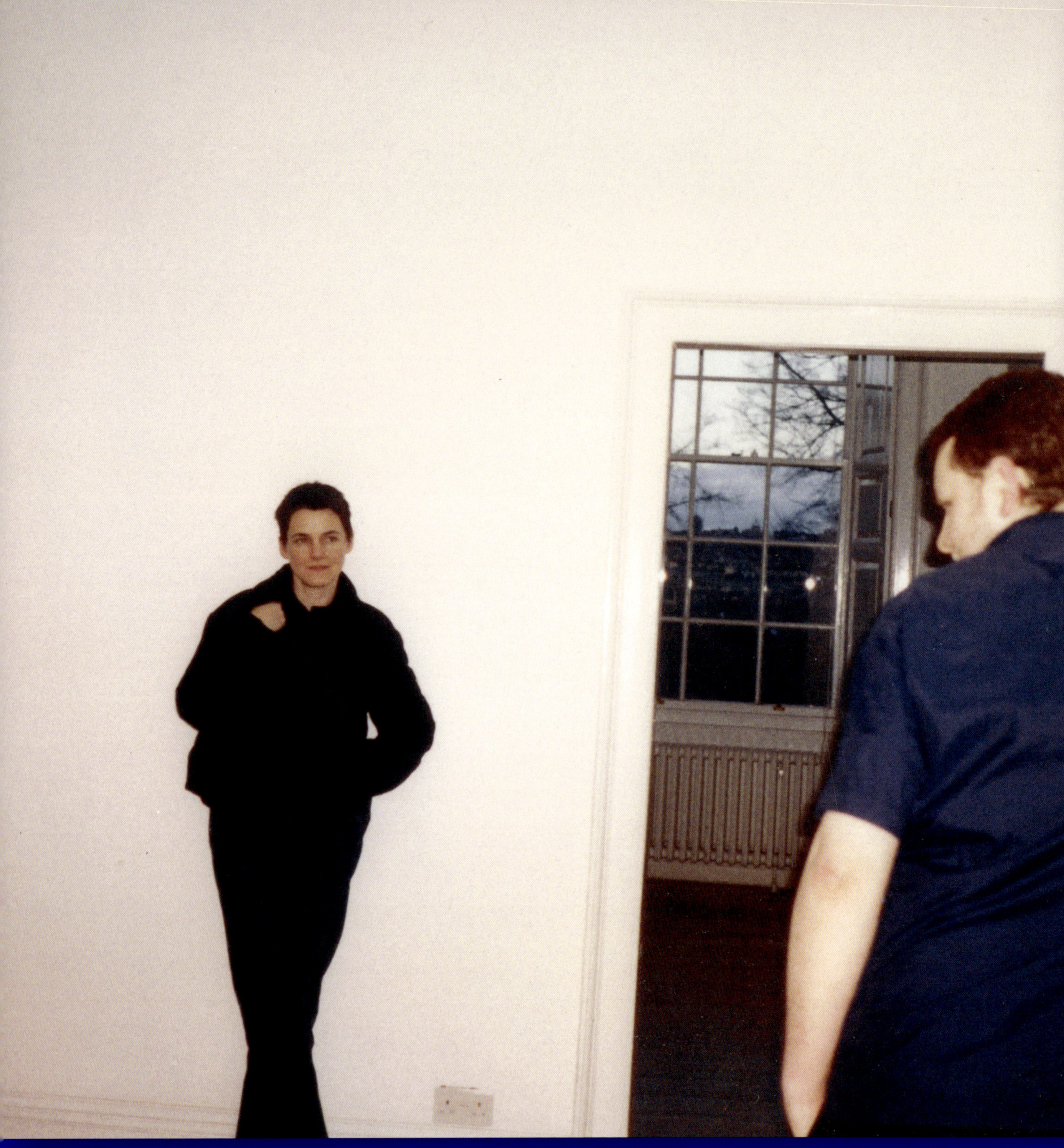

   Sadie Coles and Graham Donk, Inverleith House, The Royal Botanic Garden, Edinburgh, UK, 2000

10 livereviews

A natural talent in all its glory

VISUAL ART
Laura Owens: New Work
Royal Botanic Garden, Inverleith House, Edinburgh
Until July 30

SINCE her graduation from the California Institute of the Arts in the early 1990s, Laura Owens has been gleefully hailed as a new hope for contemporary painting. These new works fall into two loose groupings.

First are the two big canvases, each with rooms of their own. Both are exuberant riots of colour, from the palest avocado to looming midnight blues, with great carefree splodges of paint and taught, pacy lines that spiral into little whirlwinds of detail. Then there are the groups of smaller works that draw on a combination of collage and swiftly executed drawing. These combine whimsical little touches – a ladybird plods through cutesy flora – with the same living, breathing wholesomeness of the grand paintings.

This exhibition's greatest success, though, is the setting. The works by Owens were made in part as a response to the botanical teaching diagrams of John Hutton Balfour, and the dialogue between the scientific illustration on show and the art proper extends outward into the Botanical Gardens. This has a curious looping effect, where the real nature on the doorstep of Inverleith House is laid bare by Balfour's firm eye for precise detail, exuberantly celebrated by Owens and finally framed by the gallery windows. It is almost as if the trees shifting in the wind outside bleed into the paintings.

This, is then, is a case of believe the hype. The unique presentation of the paintings and drawings makes for essential viewing and highlights the fact that, while Owens is a lauded artist marrying stunning technique with a seemingly symbiotic relationship with her subject, her work is as accessible as a walk through the Gardens.
Jack Mottram

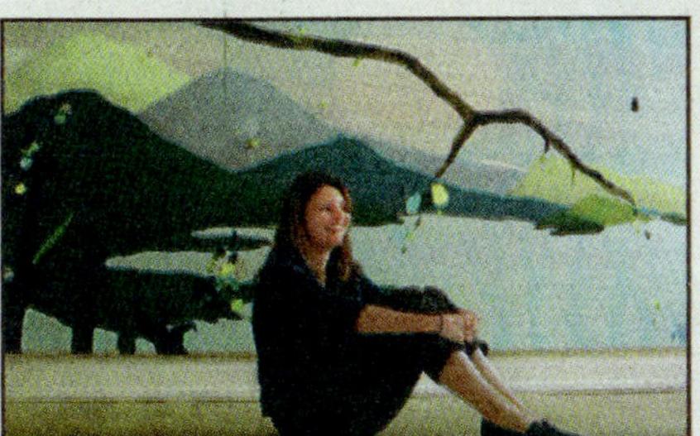

Laura Owens' work combines whimsical detail with grand gestures

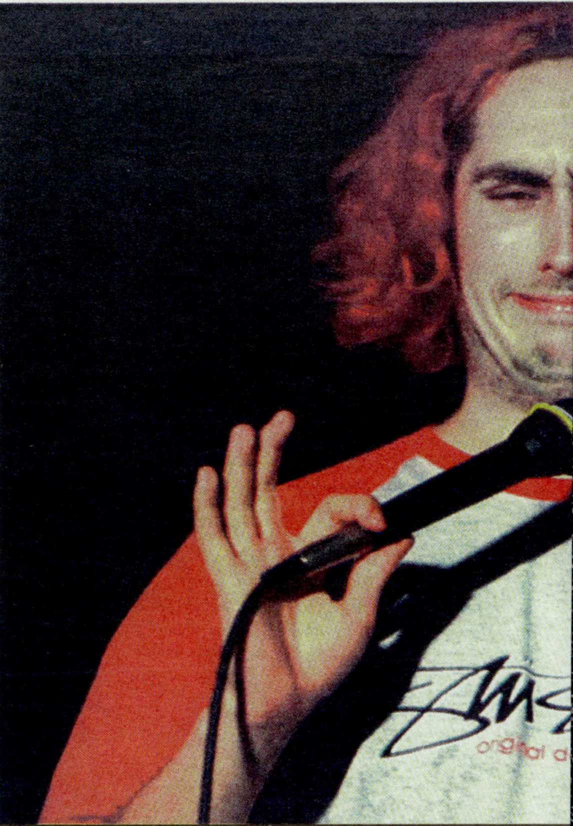

Red-hot funnyman Ross Noble jets off on another wild flig

SCARLET F

COMEDY
Ross Noble
Jesters, Mansions Cafe Bar, Glasgow
Also at The Stand, Glasgow, July 8-9; The Stand, Edinburgh, July 9; Gilded Balloon, Edinburgh, August 4-28

AS grand entrances go it's fairly feeble. No rising up from beneath the stage on a giant shell, no descending on a crescent moon, no roaring in from stage left astride a smoke-belching Harley. Ross Noble – the man heavily tipped to win the Perrier Award at this year's Edinburgh Fringe – arrives 90 minutes late, running in from the back of the hall, a bulging bag of clothes slung over one shoulder, his bright

most at home, radiatin of relaxation and comfe the room is immediate and drawn into his world. He's like a com around him, inhaling high on his seemingly non-sequiturs and fligh wizard, a true star.

This isn't observatic are no isn't-it-funny-w thats. "Sorry," he war haven't noticed anythi linear trajectory either. on anything," he says turned a disability into off his audience and im

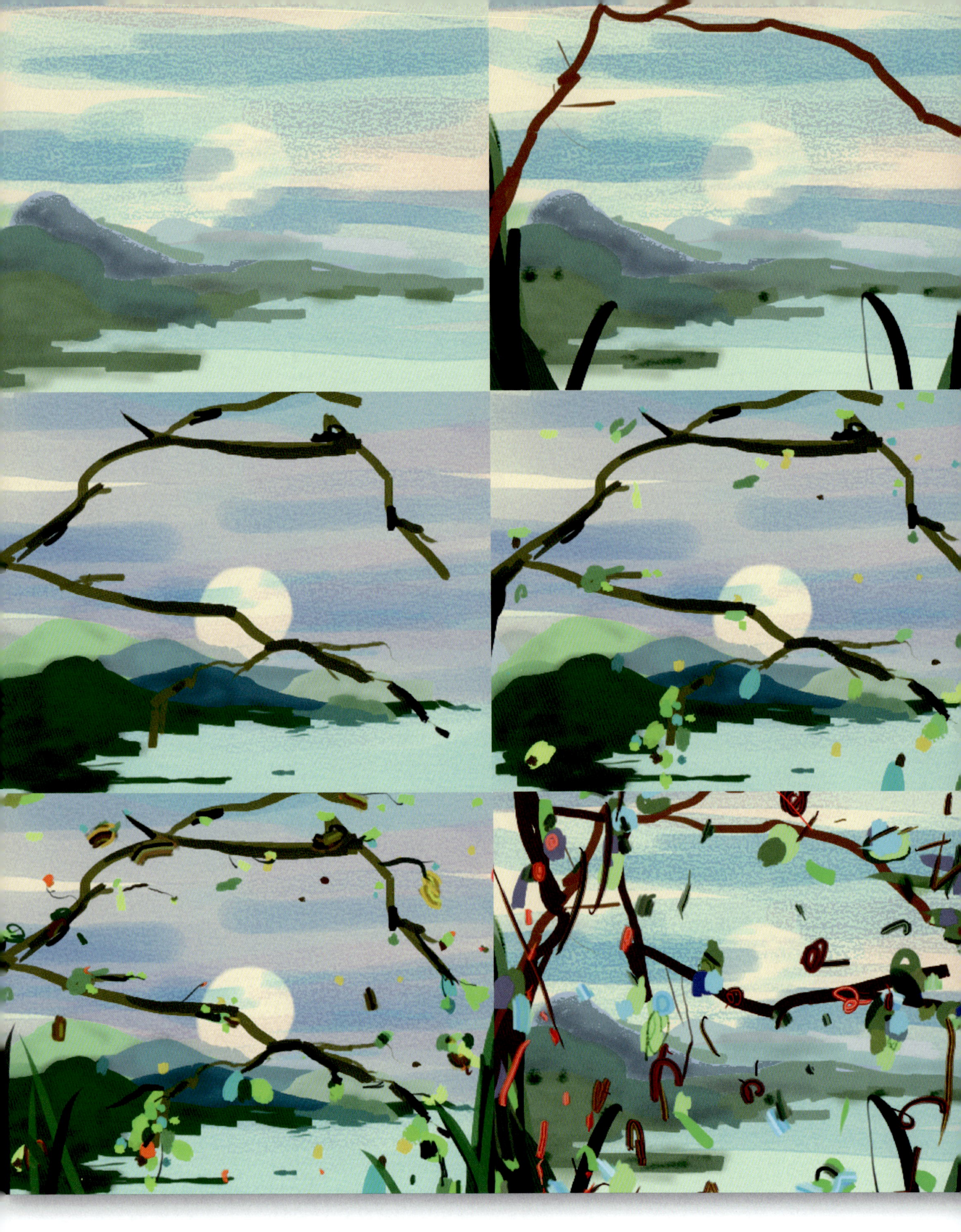

    Corel Painter 6.1 files, 2000

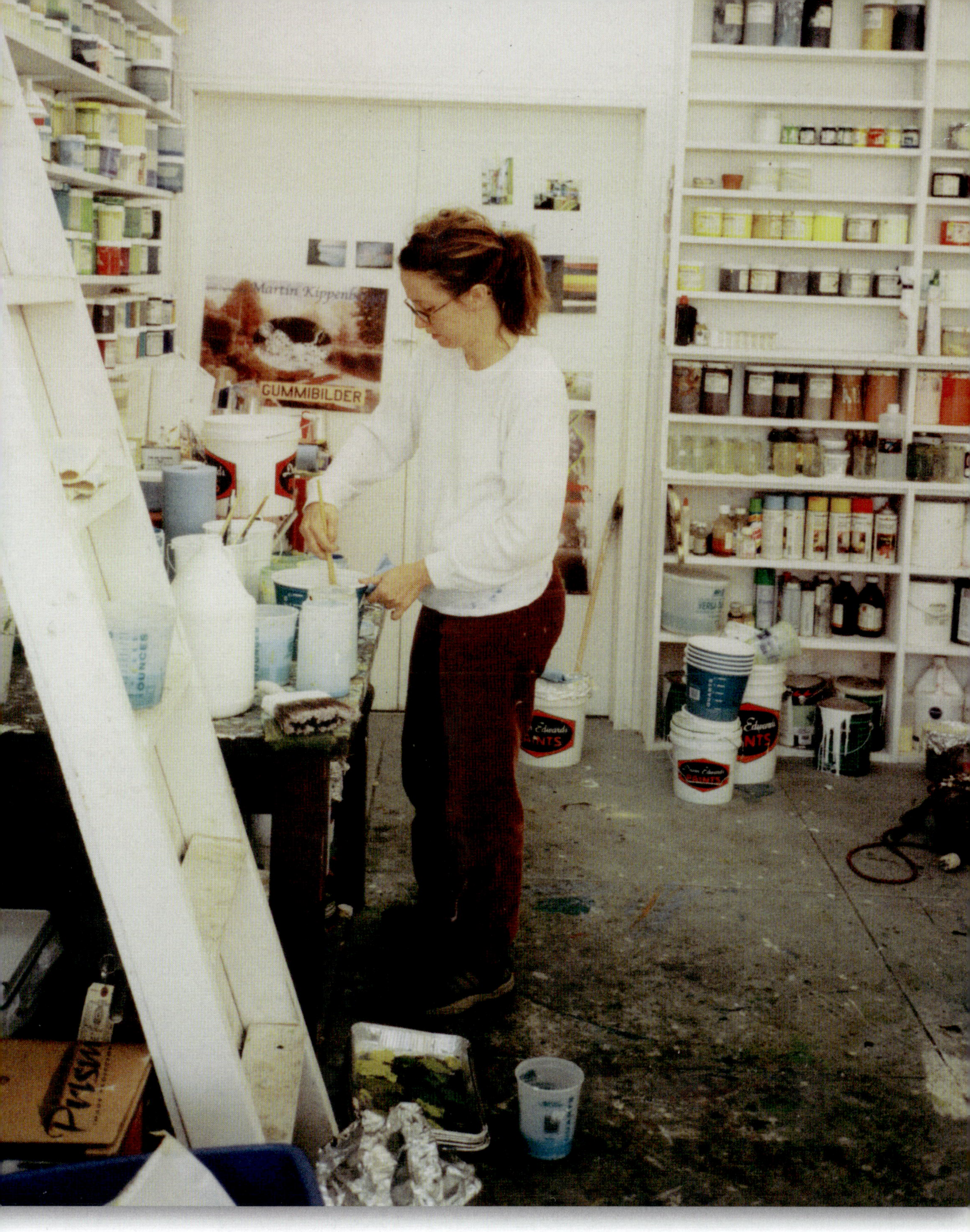

Owens, Eagle Rock studio, Los Angeles, 2000

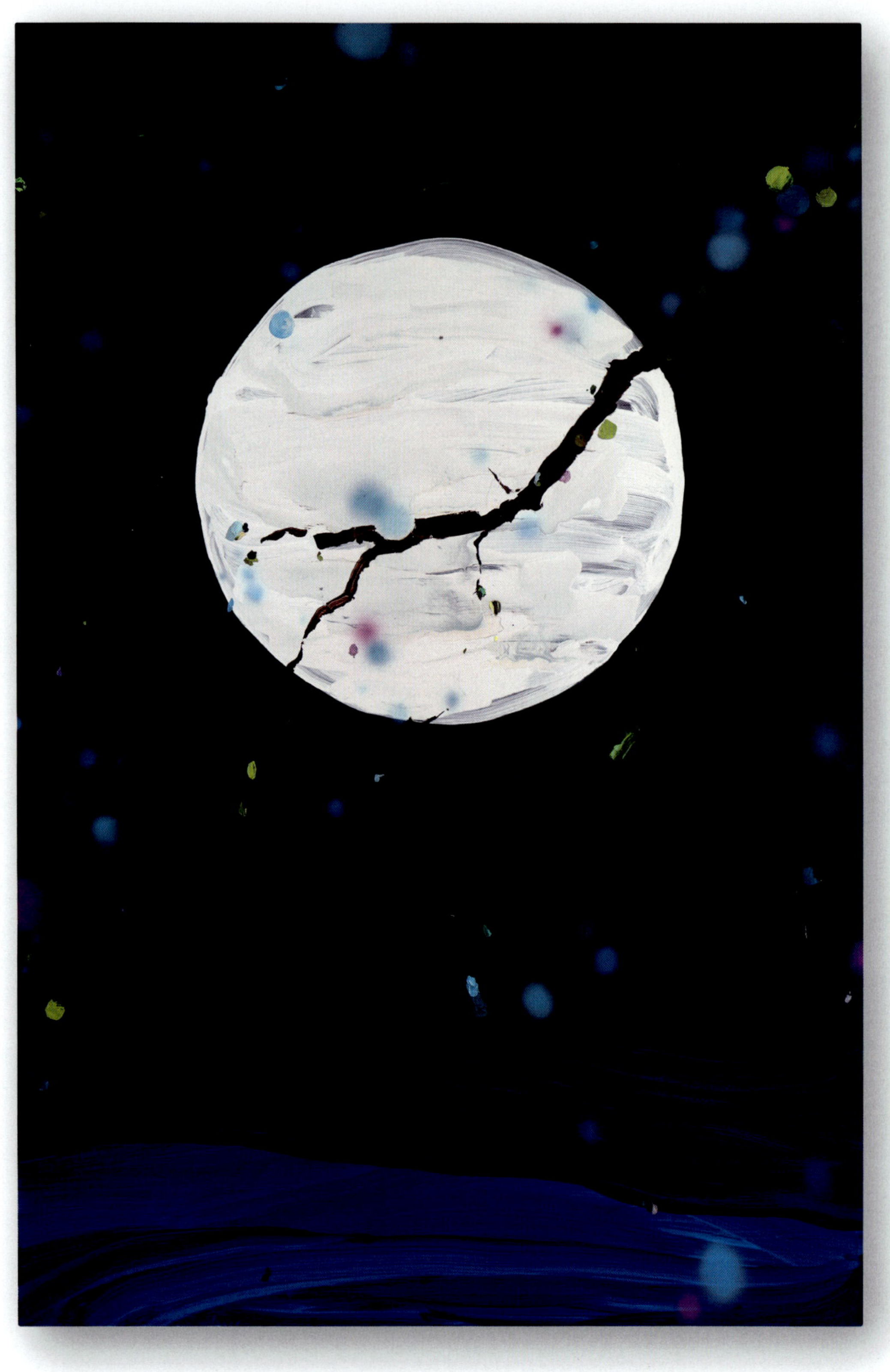

  Untitled, 2000, acrylic and oil on canvas, 111 × 72 in. (281.9 × 182.9 cm)

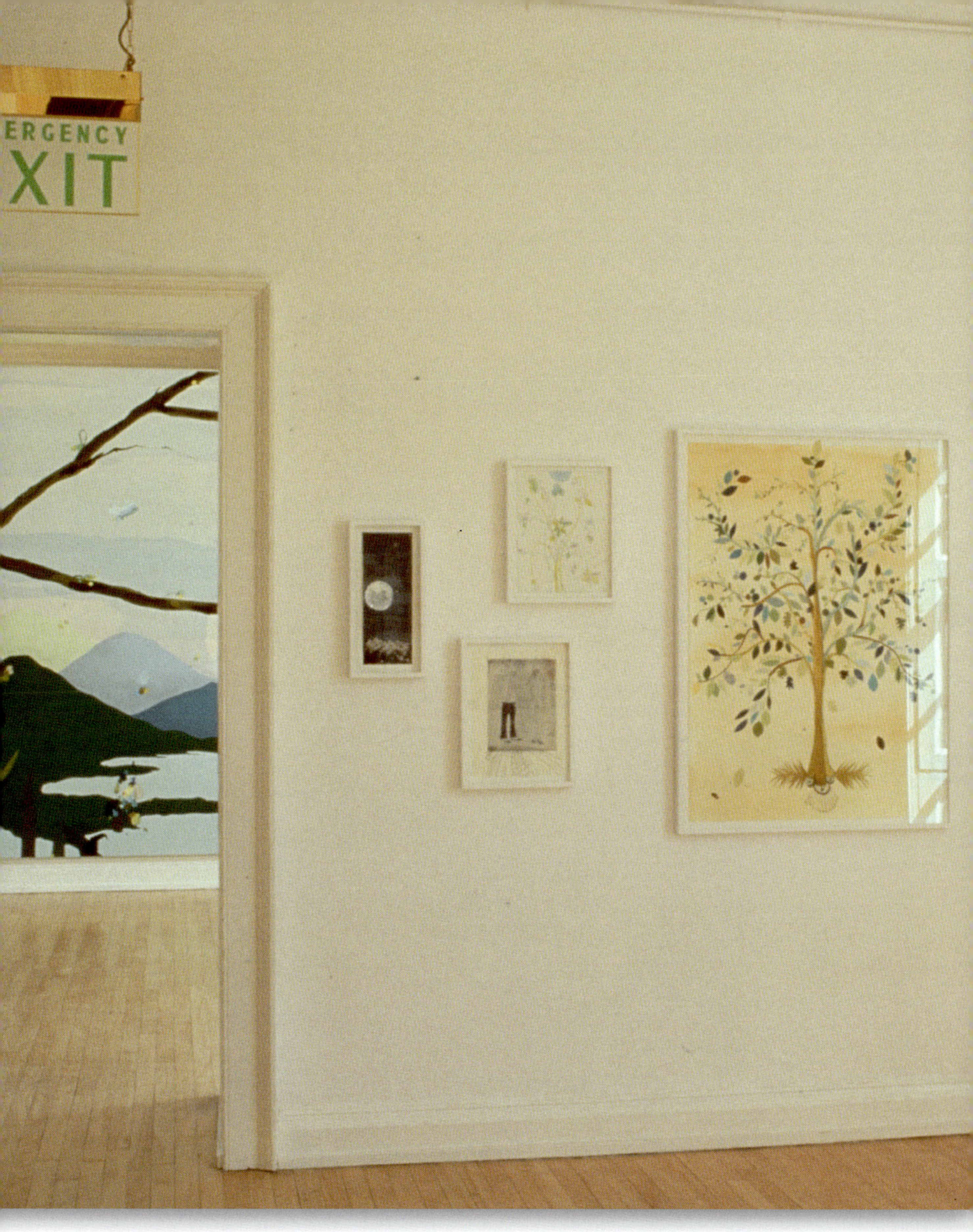

Installation view, Inverleith House, The Royal Botanic Garden, Edinburgh, UK, 2000, with *Untitled*, 2000 (see p. 293); *Untitled*, 2000, watercolor, ink, and collage on paper, 13¼ × 4⅞ in. (33.7 × 12.4 cm); *Untitled*, 2000, graphite, colored pencil, and collage on paper, 13 × 9¼ in. (33 × 23.5 cm); *Untitled*, 2000, watercolor, graphite, and paint marker on paper, 12¼ × 9 in. (31.1 × 22.9 cm); and *Untitled*, 2000, acrylic, watercolor, graphite, and collage on paper, 39 × 27½ in. (99.1 × 69.9 cm)

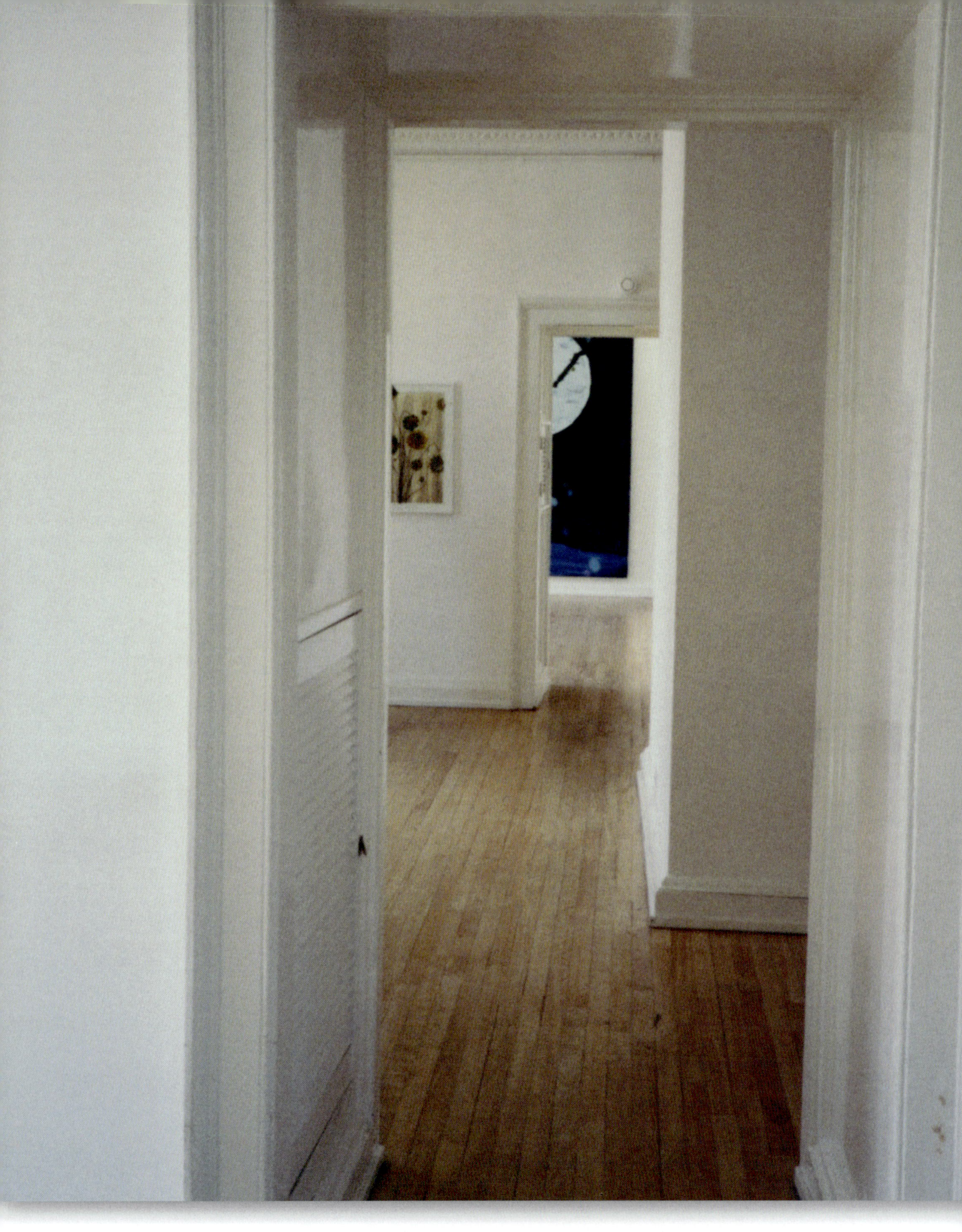

Installation view, Inverleith House, The Royal Botanic Garden, Edinburgh, UK, 2000, with *Untitled*, 2000, acrylic, watercolor, and collage on paper, 24 × 18 in. (61 × 45.7 cm), and *Untitled*, 2000 (see p. 290)

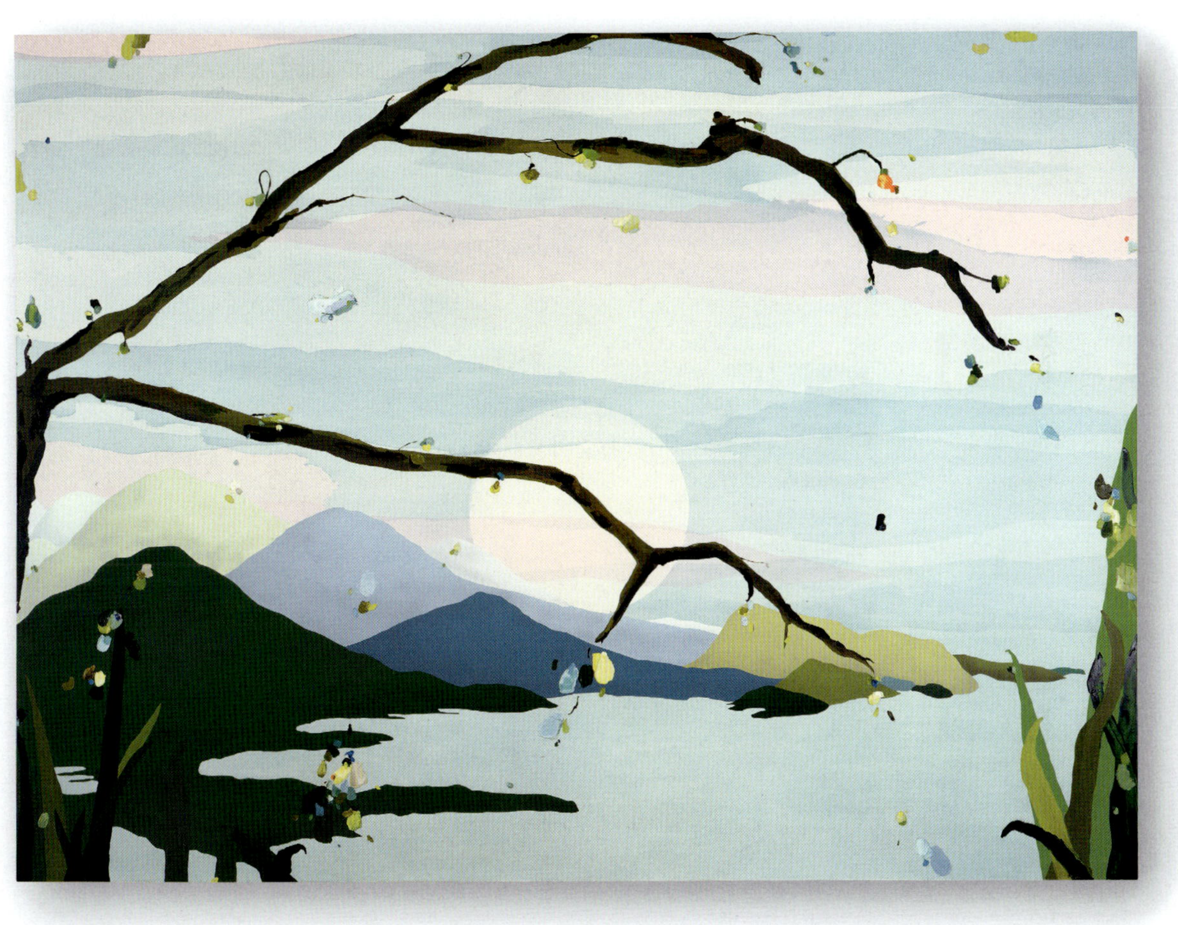

Untitled, 2000, acrylic and oil on canvas, 108 × 132 in. (274.3 × 335.3 cm)

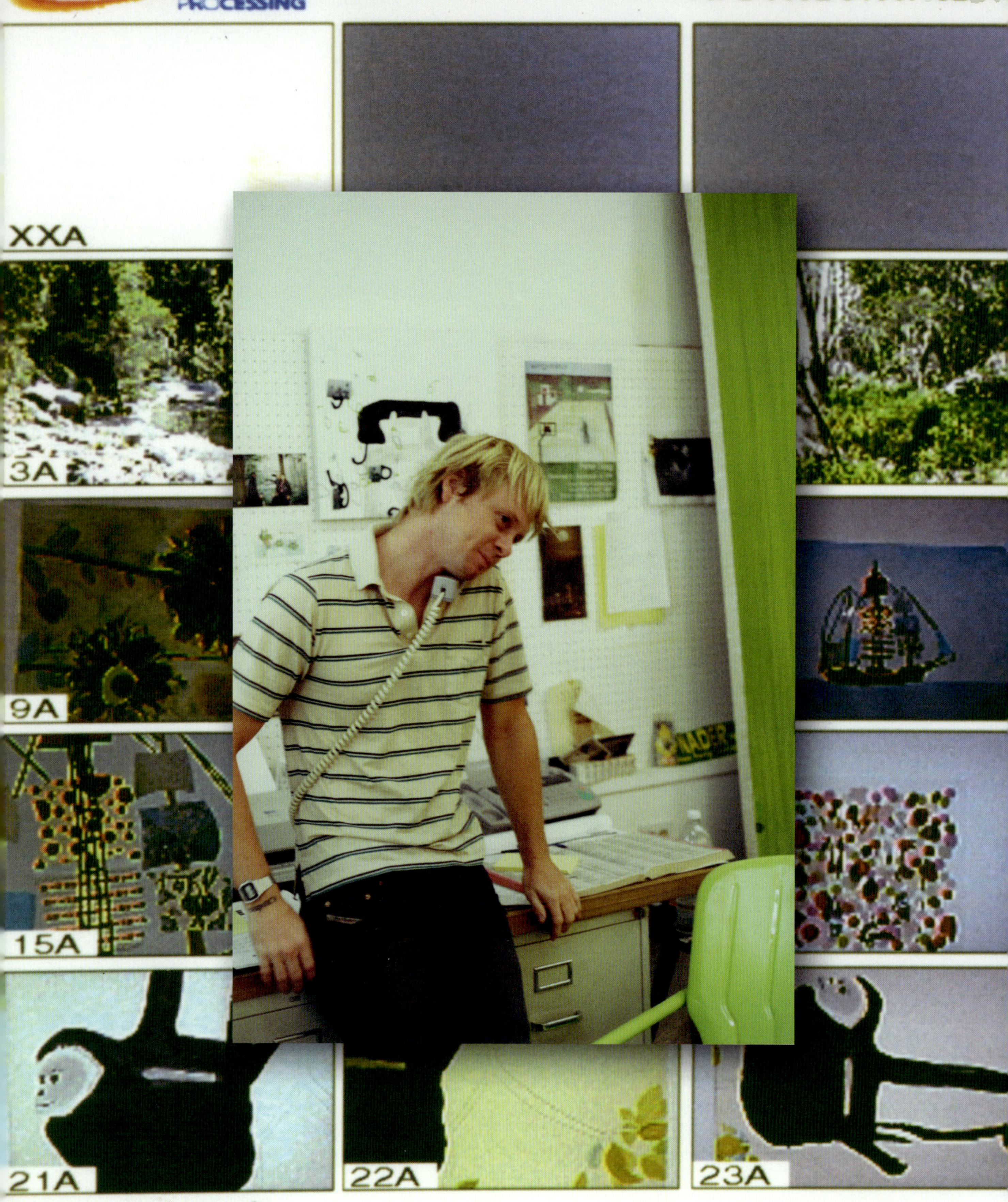

Foreground: Edgar Bryan, Eagle Rock studio, Los Angeles, 2000
Background: Digital contact sheet of 35mm photographs, 2000

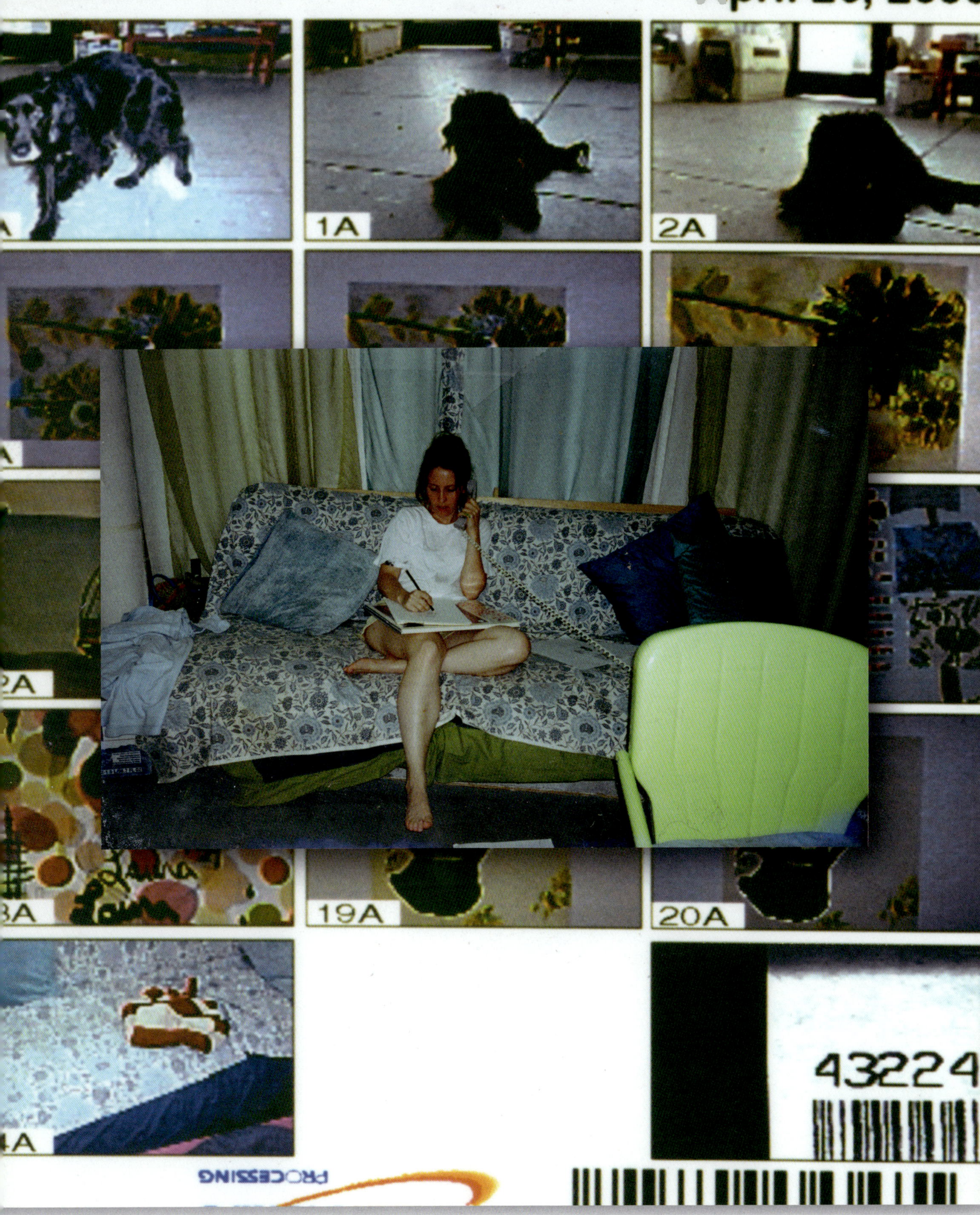

Foreground: Owens, Eagle Rock studio, Los Angeles 2000

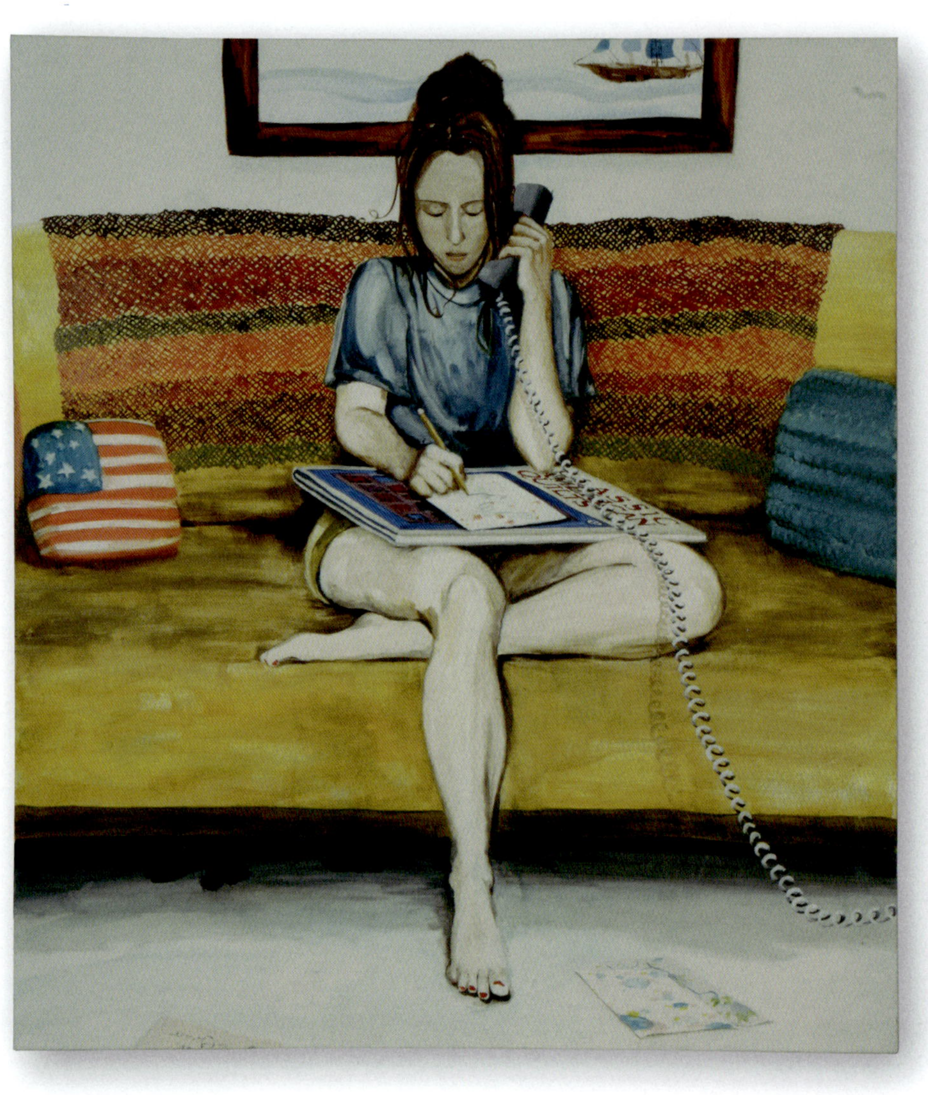

Edgar Bryan and Owens, *Untitled*, 2000, acrylic and oil on canvas, two panels: 62 × 54 in. (157.5 × 137.2 cm), 58 × 46 in. (147.3 × 116.8 cm) each

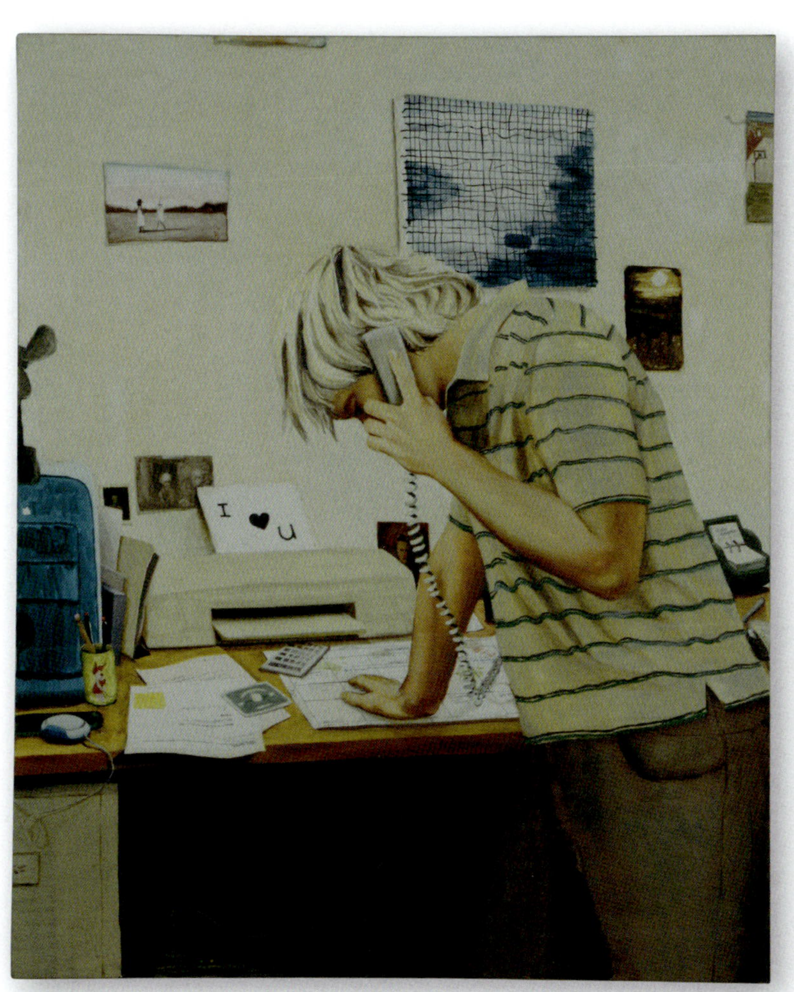

I ♥ u

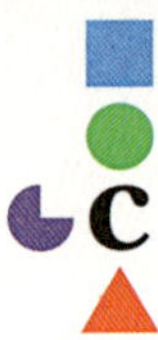

8 January 2001

Laura Owens
5121 1/2 Eagle Rock Blvd., #D
Los Angeles, CA 90041

Dear Ms. Owens,

I am sending along for your review and comment a Xerox copy of the spread from the forthcoming *Public Offerings* catalogue featuring your work. Please review the pages for appropriate orientation and cropping of images, accurate caption information, and, in general, to ensure that none of your work has been misrepresented. The deadline for your response is noon P.S.T. on Thursday, January 11.

The enclosed pages are consistent with the general design of the plate section in the catalogue. However, please note that these pages were printed at a low resolution that has caused some distortion of the images; of course, they will not appear this way in the final publication. Also, be aware that the spread has been reduced to 80% of its original size in order to produce the enclosed copies.

If you have any questions about the images or captions we have used to represent your work, or any general concerns about the catalogue, please do not hesitate to contact exhibition director Ciara Ennis by phone (213.621.1720), fax (213.620.8674), or e-mail (cennis@moca.org).

With best wishes,

Elizabeth Hamilton
Editorial Assistant

The Museum of Contemporary Art
and The Geffen Contemporary
250 South Grand Avenue
Los Angeles, California 90012
213/621-2766 Fax 213/620-8674
www.MOCA-LA.org

Foreground: Letter from Elizabeth Hamilton, 2001
Background: Layout for Paul Schimmel, ed., *Public Offerings*, exh. cat., Museum of Contemporary Art, Los Angeles, 2001

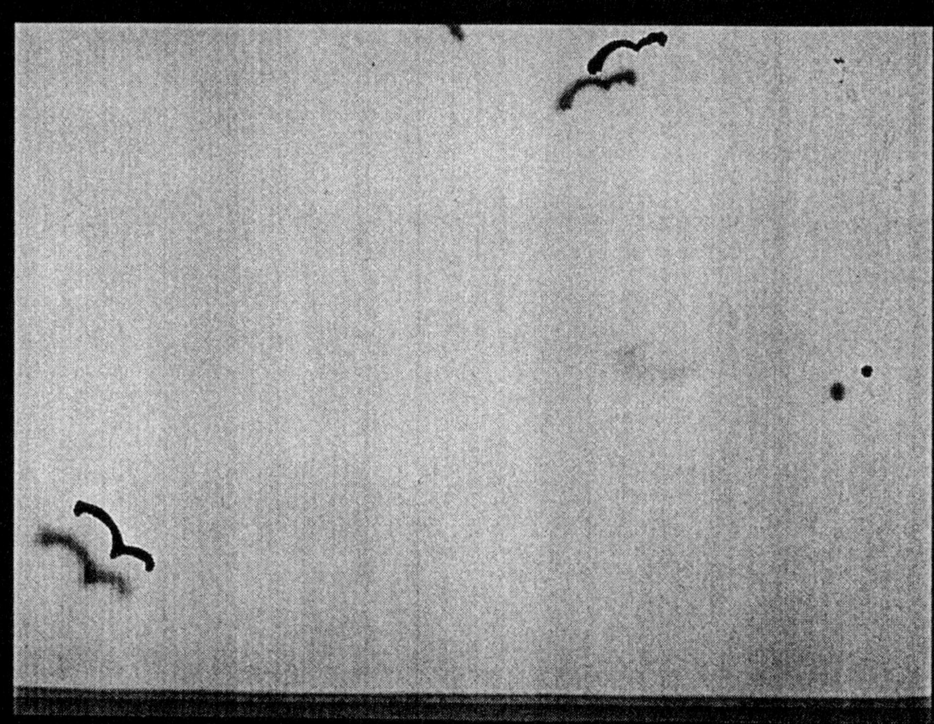

Untitled, 1997

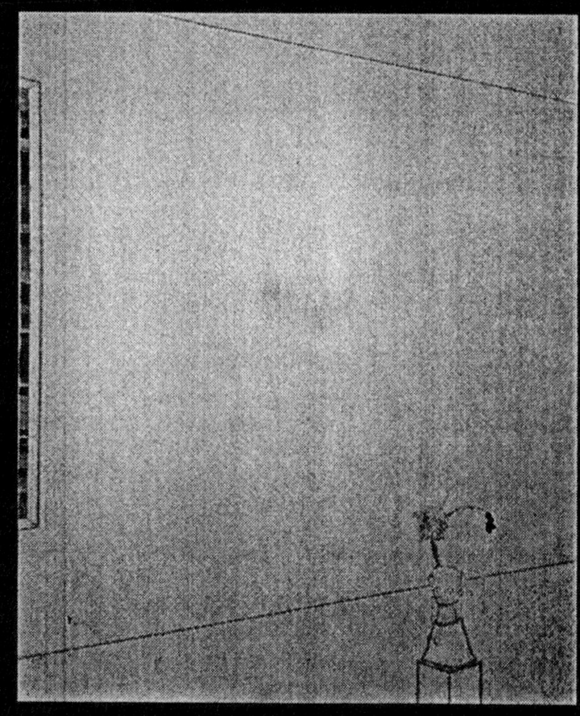

Untitled, 1996 153

Exponent of a new generation of women ar

Owens admits to influences, especially from Mary Heilman or Helen Frankenthaler. But she also says, "I feel c
st 20th-century   he often we
um and the Cle   lso by Richa
pression on he   Providence
to the Skowhe   e California
encia. Her first   Gavin Brow
She rapidly est   new genera
n as "L. A. Wom   California f
iflage on the s

The status c   oes not view
tation marks w   vels of refle
esign and Hard   ssailability,
hat Benjamin   ity for some

Date: Sat, 3 Feb 2001 16:15:38 -0800
To: laura_owens@prodigy.net
From: Gavin Brown <passerby@bway.net>
Subject: WOMEN ARTISTS BOOK (images)

oops...just sent this to your old address too.

Laura,
I know Kirsty already forwarded this to you, but I am not sure if there was
any communication about it after that since she is away. If you do want to
be included in the book, will you please let me know which images you would
like us to send them?
Thanks,
Corinna

Cologne, 15.01.01

Dear Gavin Brown,

TASCHEN Publishers is planning to publish a book entitled WOMEN ARTISTS.

The book will list in alphabetical order the 100 most important female
artists of the last 50 years. Each artists will be represented with a
portrait, her dates, a longer text about her life and work, a number of
reproductions of her work and ? if possible ? some biographical
photographs.
The book will consist of about 600 pages and have a format of ca. 26 x
20 cm and will be translated into several languages and sold throughout
the world.
Laura Owens should absolutely be included in this publication.
Accordingly we would be very pleased, if you could send us labelled
transparencies of her most important works, as well as three
installation shots of her biggest shows, a portrait (of which the
reproduction rights are settled), a biography and ? if available ? some
biographical photographs.

Once we have selected the pictures, we will send you a statement of
release granting us permission in writing to reproduce your photos.

We hope very much that you will be able to support us in this project
and look forward to a fruitful collaboration with you.
If you require any further information, please do not hesitate to
contact us.

Sincerely yours,

Uta Grosenick
TASCHEN GmbH

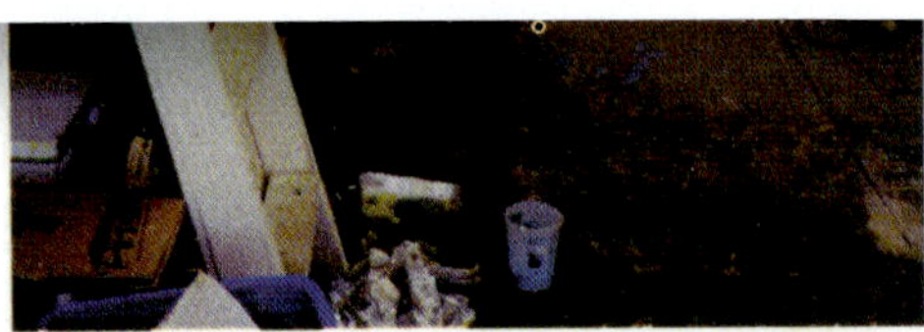

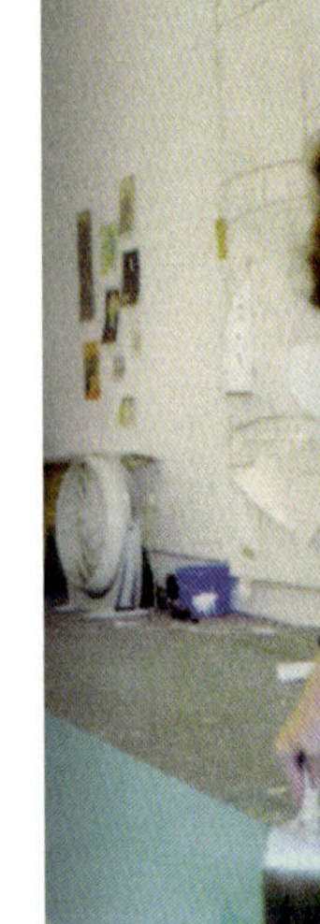

Foreground: Email from Corinna Durland, 2001
Background: Holger Liebs, "Laura Owens." Uta Grosenick, ed., *Women Artists in the 20th and 21st Century*. Taschen, 2001

Date: Sat, 3 Mar 2001 20:44:30 +0100
To: laura_owens@prodigy.net
From: Meyer + Kainer <contact@meyerkainer.at>
Subject: exhbition

Dear laura,

I would like to talk with you about the idea of showing female painters,
not exclusivly, but as a new point of our programm.

In history the tradition of painting is a story of men and in Europe one
can have the impression, that it remains the same since sixteen hundred -
most of the painters showing in Galleries and Museums in Italy, in Germany,
in England, in Spain are men - which is okay - I think Gerhard Richter is a
great painter..... but.....

We would love to show other positions - not only female, but new positions
and I think new positions in painting are mostly coming from woman.

We would like to make the strong position of woman more visible.

So - we start with Mary Heilmann - the opening will be at 2 nd May .

We will show Sarah Morris and we hope to work with Monique Prieto, Marlene
Dumas a. o.

AND WE REALLY HOPE TO WORK WITH YOU.

It would be very important for us to have you in our small family.
I could come any time to Los Angeles, to speak with you.

I would be great to hear your thinkings.

with kind regards

Renate

Galerie Meyer Kainer
Eschenbachgasse 9
A-1010 Vienna
Austria

Tel +43 (0) 585 72 77

SOMEWHERE ELSE COMPLETELY
FRANCINE PROSE

The four walls of the rectangle cannot possibly contain an art that exists on, explores, and explodes so many different borders. Looking at Elizabeth Murray's work, you feel that all those extrusions and protrusions, splashes and bubbles, stalks and diamonds and handles projecting into space, all those empty gaps carved out to create more edges *inside* the painting are not so much the reasoned product of an aesthetic or choice but rather of a necessity, of an obsessive desire to create new boundaries to approach, to straddle and bravely cross.

These exuberant paintings compel us—with the lightest touch, as if we are being gently but firmly prodded with one of their fingerlike forms—to confront and reexamine the most profound demarcations: between the comical and the horrific, the earthy and the transcendent, the ego and the id, the idyll and the nightmare, the child and the adult, the recognizable and the unnameable, the instinctive and the cerebral, the natural and the artificial, the visionary and the reportorial, the idea and the execution. To say nothing of that border that's almost too terrifying to mention—the big one, between life and death, being and nonexistence.

Elizabeth Murray's art reminds us of, insists upon, and celebrates the joys of living in the world, the satisfactions of color and form, of work and dreams, the sheer pleasure a painter takes in playing with paint. And yet it never lets us forget how easy it would be to shut our eyes for a heartbeat, to drop our guard for an instant—and to go spinning into free fall off the edge of the planet.

Looking at Elizabeth Murray's work, I find myself drawn to that interface between the animate and the inanimate, the mysterious and the mundane— a border that (as in an animated cartoon) rapidly transforms itself into a road that I can travel back to my earliest and most inchoate experience of art. For one of the tricks at which art excels—the sleight-of-hand that Elizabeth Murray so deftly performs—is to operate on our consciousness like a sort of protracted déja vu, allowing us to grasp at and then lose, to nearly recover and then surrender, some long-lost, buried memory or chimerical sensation that eludes us, skirting the edges of our peripheral vision, vanishing like a vivid dream at the moment of awakening.

Over the years, I've come to understand that what Elizabeth Murray's paintings evoke for me are the childhood hours I spent delighting in the golden age of children's entertainment, those final decades before the grown-ups decided that kids had to be saved from their own desire to be scared out of their wits. I've never forgotten the anxious giddiness with which I followed the adventures of Koko the Clown, the perils of Betty Boop, watched Farmer Gray chase his deeply alarming mice across our ten-inch TV screen. But only now, as I look at Elizabeth Murray's work, can I summon a sense of what it must have been like to see all that shape-shifting and metamorphosis, to observe the stunning ease with which household objects learned to walk and talk—to see it before I was old enough to know precisely how much of what I was seeing was possible, or *real*.

I was an infant when we got a television set. At that point, my observational experience of the world was too narrow and limited for me to know, or much care, if a clown could materialize out of a bottle of ink, or if the engine of a train could turn into a giant, predatory mouth, ready and eager to swallow whatever was loitering on the tracks. For all I knew about palm trees, they bent and swayed and sang hula songs along with an invisible ukulele; for all I knew about adult emotion, huge drops of water flung themselves off the grown-ups' foreheads when they were anxious or perplexed. I could have been that North African neighbor Paul Bowles describes—the man who goes to see his first film, which happens to be *The Ten Commandments*, and leaves the theater horrified, convinced that Cairo has been destroyed. For

Originally published in *Elizabeth Murray: Paintings 1999–2003*, exh. cat. (New York: Pace Wildenstein, 2003), 6–11. Prose is a critic and novelist based in Brooklyn.

both that Moroccan and myself, there was, I am sure, something powerful and ineffably strange about that innocent confusion. The limits of the visible world have never been and will never again be stretched so widely, never permitted to accommodate so much mystery and wonder.

Never, that is, until I became acquainted with Elizabeth Murray's paintings, which—perhaps because they embody suggestions of cartoonishness but are more elemental, less narrative and complex, more elusive and allusive than cartoons—re-create for me that state of pure receptivity, of unblinkered consciousness, the visceral chill-down-the-spine of recognizing everything I saw with absolute conviction and at the same time not knowing in the slightest what in the world I was seeing. Which is, of course, part of what art does, what art *is*: it resonates with the familiar and at the same time resists every attempt to explain or describe or reduce it. Perhaps that's why, in interviews, Elizabeth Murray demurs when asked what exactly she had in mind at the start—or the end—of a painting. For always, what's most interesting about a painting or novel or poem has occurred in that interval after the initial impulse is overruled or forgotten, and a new imperative takes over, conveyed by the sort of celestial dictation that the artist takes and that makes a work of art appear to have a life of its own.

In fact, so much life has been compressed into Elizabeth Murray's art that it's stating the obvious to remark that the effect is eruptive. Her images seem not merely rebellious but caged, confined against their will: forces struggling to escape from the bounds of the painting. Possibly that's why it's so hard to imagine the work at an earlier state—to believe that the vibrant form before us was ever a blank, featureless construct of stretchers and bare canvas. Elizabeth Murray's work is indelibly marked with her hand, her signature, her personality, and yet she manages to make the mind and hand of the artist disappear into something that appears to have given birth to itself, and to have always existed.

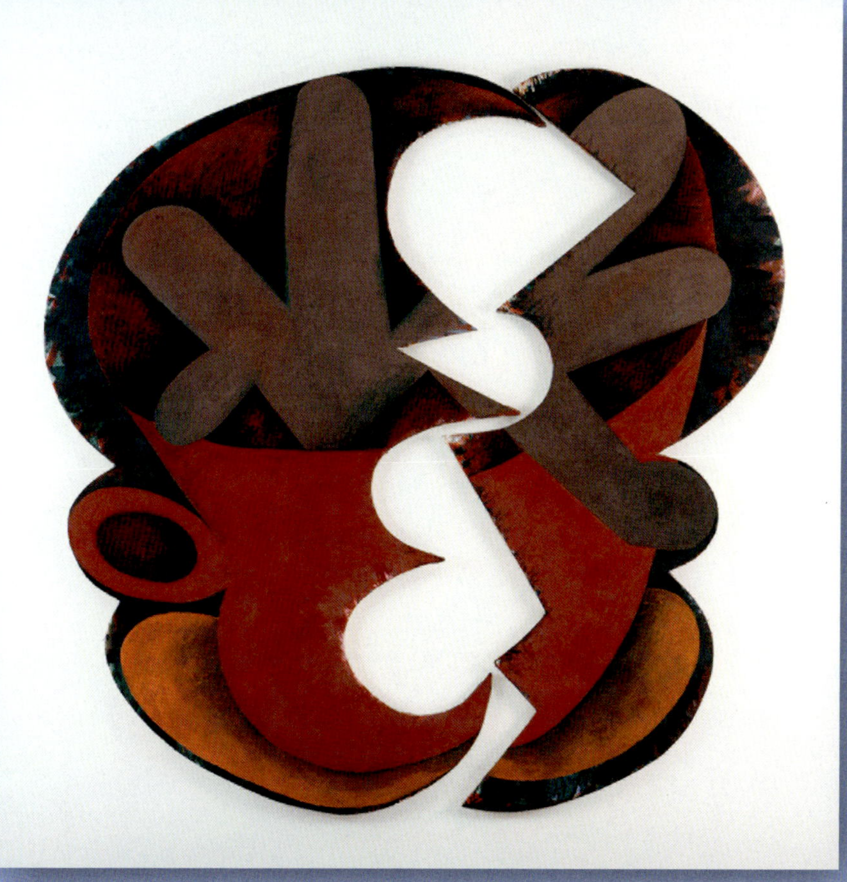

Elizabeth Murray, *Yikes*, 1982, oil on canvas, two panels: 115 in. × 113½ in. (292.1 × 288.3 cm) overall

In a smarter and wiser, more hip and sophisticated world than our own, we would never need to address a subject that inevitably seems to arise in relation to Elizabeth Murray's work—that is, the whole issue, of the domestic. A more intelligent world would know that *domestic* is a perfectly neutral word, universal in its significance, since all of us live—or have at one time lived—in households, or at least houses. *Domestic* can be, and often is, used in a harmless, nonpejorative way—for example, when we remark that domestic objects have regularly and consistently appeared in the work of such geniuses as Velázquez, Vermeer, Cézanne.

The problem (the intermittently squeaky wheel that demands our attention) is when *domestic* is used as codespeak to mean *feminine* or *female*, which is further codespeak for *weak* and *second-rate*. That the word might be used this way is an especial danger when the maker of domestic images happens to be an actual female. All this seems especially puzzling and illogical in regard to Elizabeth Murray. Because if *domestic* is being

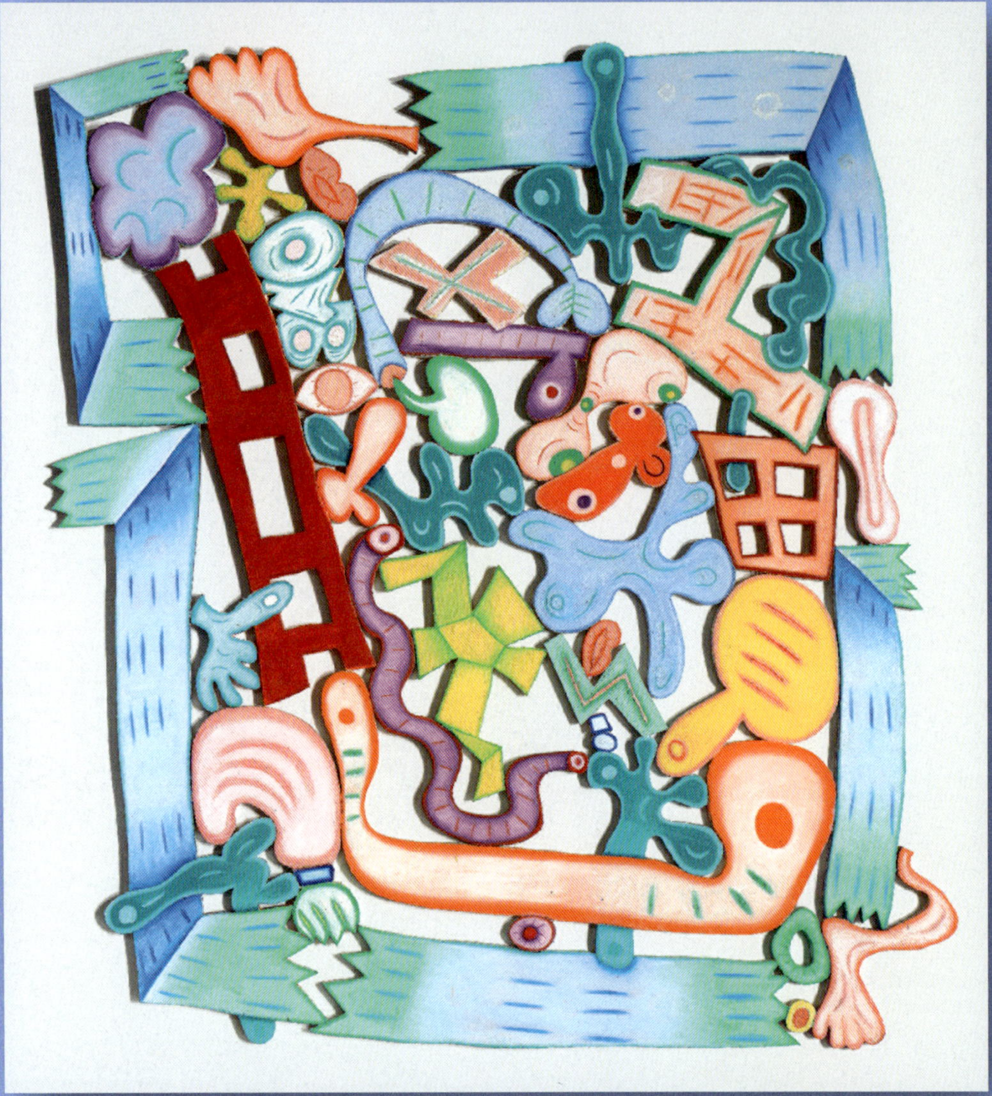

Elizabeth Murray, *Cloud 9*, 2002, oil on canvas, 93 × 84 in. (236.2 × 213.4 cm)

used to mean *trivial*, *mild*, *humble*, *predictable*, *timid*—that is, more codespeak for *female*—Elizabeth Murray's paintings certainly aren't *that*. On the shallowest level, the domestic objects in her painting are a great deal more proactive and even ferocious than their ceramic counterparts in many Old Master paintings. No sensible person would pour hot coffee into one of Elizabeth Murray's cups, or stuff a T-shirt into the bureau drawers already spitting their contents back. Meanwhile, it takes great courage (a word that this use of *domestic* does not associate with the domestic, that is, the female) for a female artist to avoid self-censorship if what burbles up from the id happens to be coffee cups and bureau drawers—in other words, *domestic* images, in the sense of *art lite*.

In fact, Elizabeth's Murray's paintings are anything but lightweight. Far from being humble and timid, they're—given her very particular balance of image and abstraction—confrontational and even pushy in the way they force you against yet another border, a tough demarcation often misidentified as one of gender, or sociology, when in fact that division has more to do with temperament, consciousness, and metaphysics.

That is the separation between those who can lose themselves in idea, in pure form and abstraction, and those who—like Orpheus, like Lot's wife—are sooner or later moved to look back over their shoulders at the raucous and precious world. It is again too simple to say that this division breaks down along the lines of male and female, domestic and hunter-gatherer, since there are men and women in both groups, great abstractors from Thomas Aquinas to Agnes Martin, and those to whom household objects sing their siren song: Manet, Philip Guston.

Of course, fewer women have the option, the luxury of choosing which group they want to belong to, particularly when they have children, whose very real and pressing needs often make it harder to focus exclusively on the far horizon. But is it better to fixate on the abstract and airy than on the here and now; or is it, in fact, more admirable and difficult to cultivate the sort of double vision that allows us to keep watch over both frontiers at once? In any case, Elizabeth Murray's work insists on its right *not* to shrink itself into categories and limits, not to fit itself into a realm that filters out the wondrous detritus of human life, our coffee cups and shoes. Because the (one would think) self-evident fact that the domestic *is* the world is something that, until recently, art has effortlessly understood, but which (briefly, we can only hope) it lately seems to have forgotten.

The bold, innovative new paintings take these tensions and reconciliations even further. They invite us to look at the most recent work, and then back at the earlier images, and to track the ways in which these resolutely nonrepresentational paintings plainly show us how the world has changed over the last several decades. Like the culture in which we live, the new works have grown more urgent, more fragmented, unstable, fragile and vertiginous. Paintings such as *Cloud 9* and *Rocker* suggest that we might as well be Dorothy in *The Wizard of Oz*, at the very moment—or the very moment before—Aunt Em's house is picked up and carried away by the swirling cyclone.

Yet here is the ultimate paradox: Looking at Elizabeth Murray's work provides so much interest and pleasure that it helps us forget the increasingly dangerous circles in which we seem to be spinning. Jittering, exploding, jumping on or off the walls, her paintings still find the time and space to extend a hand and help us over the most important boundary that art can lead us across— that is, the border between being here, confined in our bodies and minds, and being set free from all of that: being somewhere else completely.

Laura Owens: Jennifer Gross, curator of contemporary art, invited me to do a residency at the Isabella Stewart Gardner Museum. They have an incredible collection, but the circumstances were very odd because the museum had suffered one of the worst art thefts in history, but the residents were invited to live there in an adjacent carriage house. I had to go through a mantrap every time I entered the property and present a list of any guests in advance. The guards there are amazing people with a lot of institutional knowledge, and one of the highlights is a flashlight tour they take you on in the dead of night when no one is around. Because Mrs. Gardner had started her collection after her only son died at a very young age, the museum reflects the person who made it with incredible specificity. Her will states that nothing about the installation can be changed, and many of the sculptures, paintings, and textiles symbolically represent her and her family. I think Mrs. Gardner was an installation artist; she created a story using found works of art from multiple eras and cultures. It's all done through these gazes, or angles—she would even angle a painting off the wall so that a figure can look into another room, its sightline moving you through the space. This over-the-top installation made me think, "What if I can get all this stuff I'm trying to do with my exhibitions and between the paintings into one painting?" So that your eye is moving forward, sideways, and back into deep space. I tried to use all these animals to shoot you around, and to let a painting be an autonomous object that can contain the whole idea of space in and of itself—and make you think about deep space and how space gets made. I also just felt like I had been relying too much on artwork being born out of the exhibition site. So I decided to try to do something different. While in Boston I was very lonely. I ended up frequenting an esoteric bookstore on the edge of Cambridge and buying a new astrology book almost every day. I taught myself astrology and was looking at Mrs. Gardner's chart.

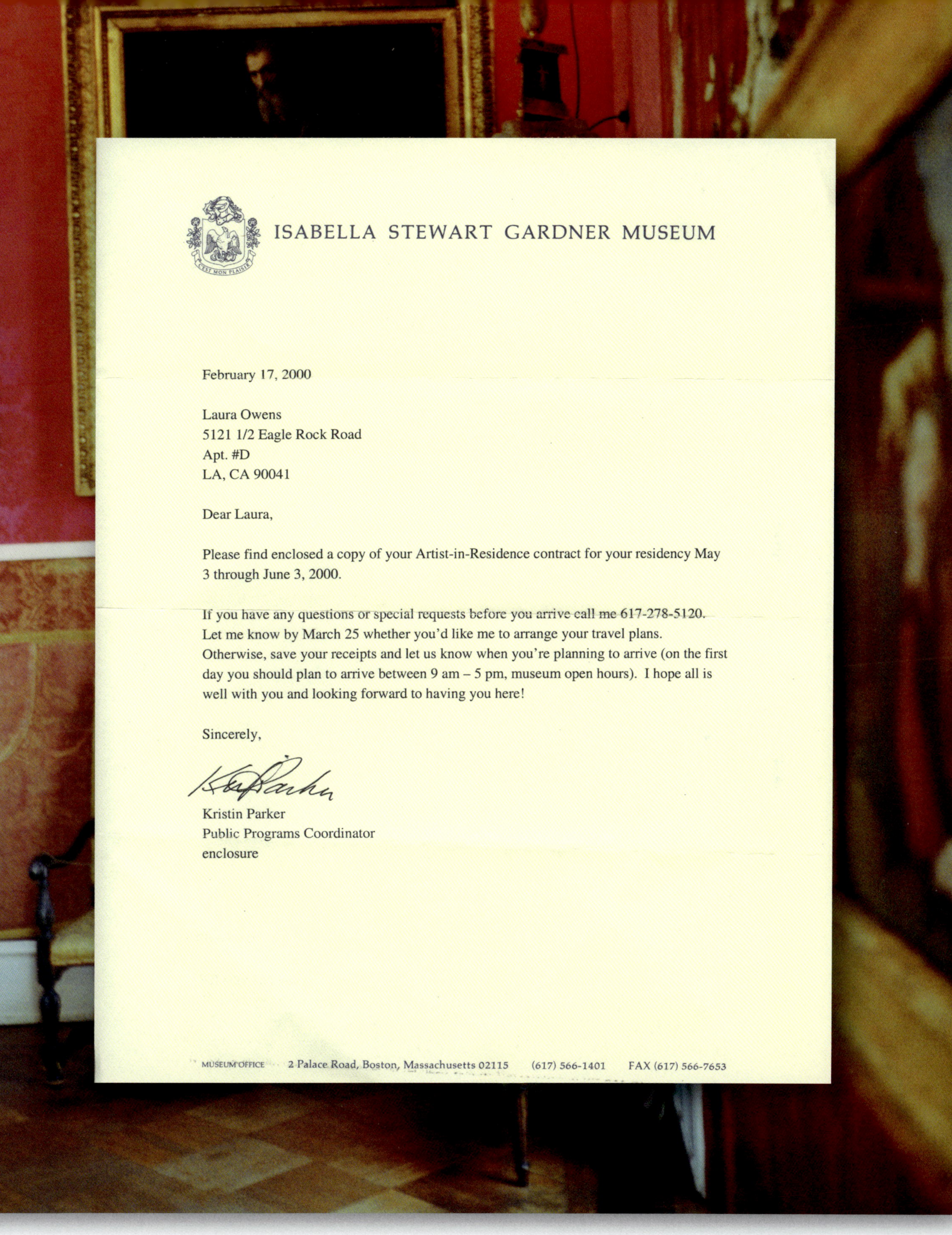

ISABELLA STEWART GARDNER MUSEUM

February 17, 2000

Laura Owens
5121 1/2 Eagle Rock Road
Apt. #D
LA, CA 90041

Dear Laura,

Please find enclosed a copy of your Artist-in-Residence contract for your residency May 3 through June 3, 2000.

If you have any questions or special requests before you arrive call me 617-278-5120. Let me know by March 25 whether you'd like me to arrange your travel plans. Otherwise, save your receipts and let us know when you're planning to arrive (on the first day you should plan to arrive between 9 am – 5 pm, museum open hours). I hope all is well with you and looking forward to having you here!

Sincerely,

Kristin Parker
Public Programs Coordinator
enclosure

MUSEUM OFFICE   2 Palace Road, Boston, Massachusetts 02115   (617) 566-1401   FAX (617) 566-7653

Foreground: Letter from Kristin Parker, 2000
Background: Research photograph by Owens, Isabella Stewart Gardner Museum, Boston, 2000

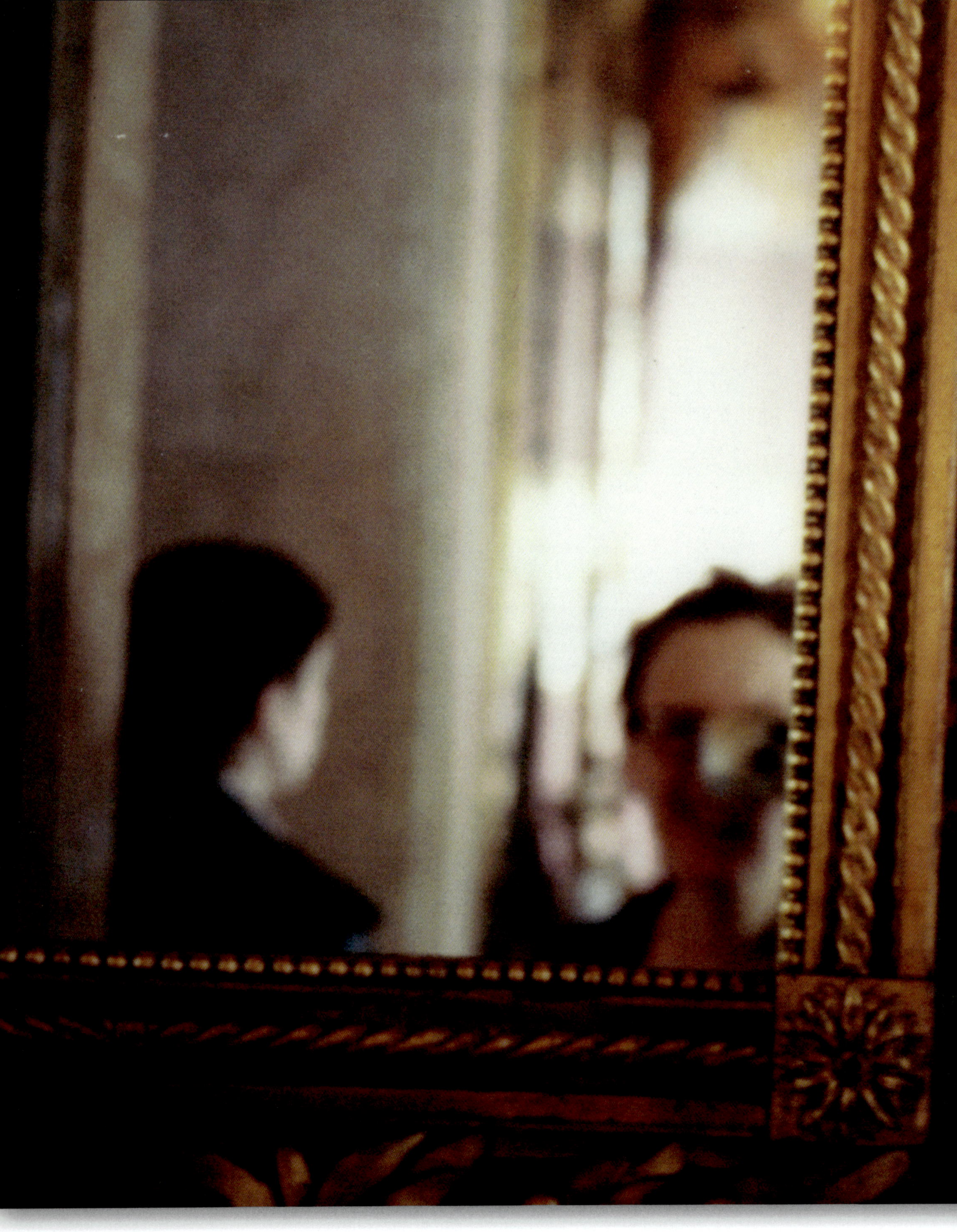

308   Research photograph by Owens, Isabella Stewart Gardner Museum, Boston, 2000

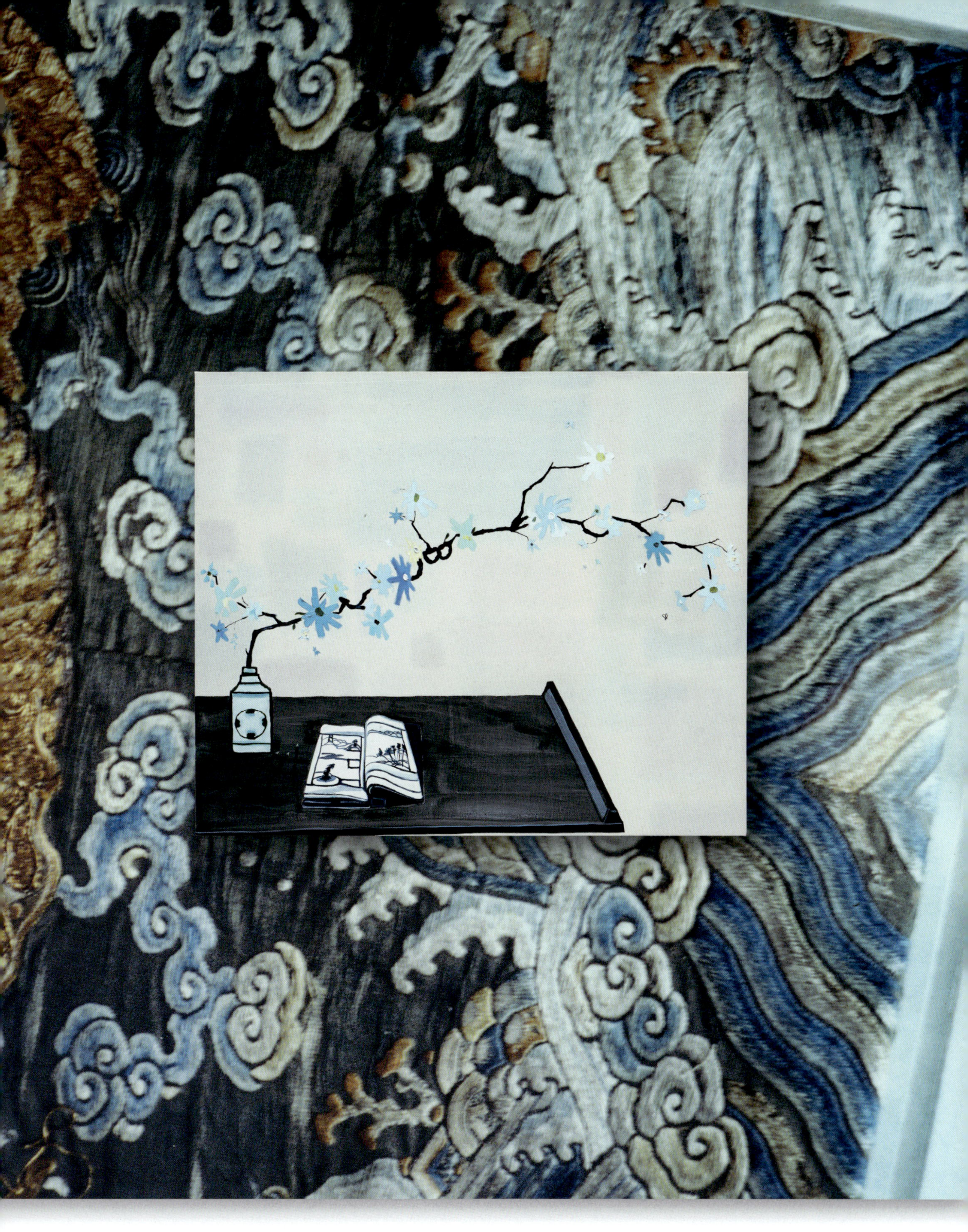

Foreground: *Untitled*, 2001, acrylic and oil on canvas, 46 × 54¼ in. (116.8 × 137.8 cm)
Background: Research photograph by Owens, Isabella Stewart Gardner Museum, Boston, 2000

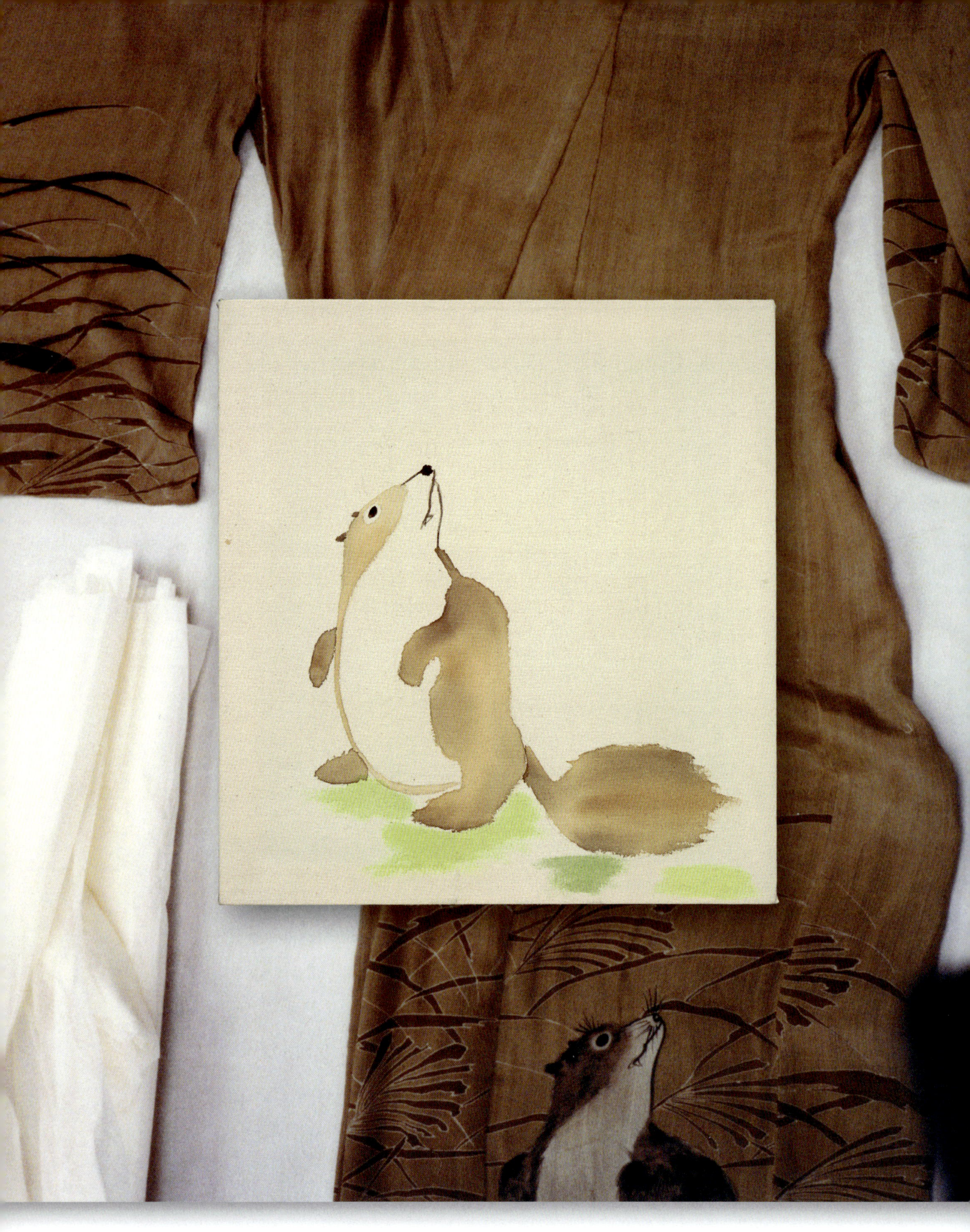

Foreground: *Untitled*, 2001, acrylic on canvas, 24 × 22 in. (61 × 55.9 cm)
 Background: Research photograph by Owens, Isabella Stewart Gardner Museum, Boston, 2000

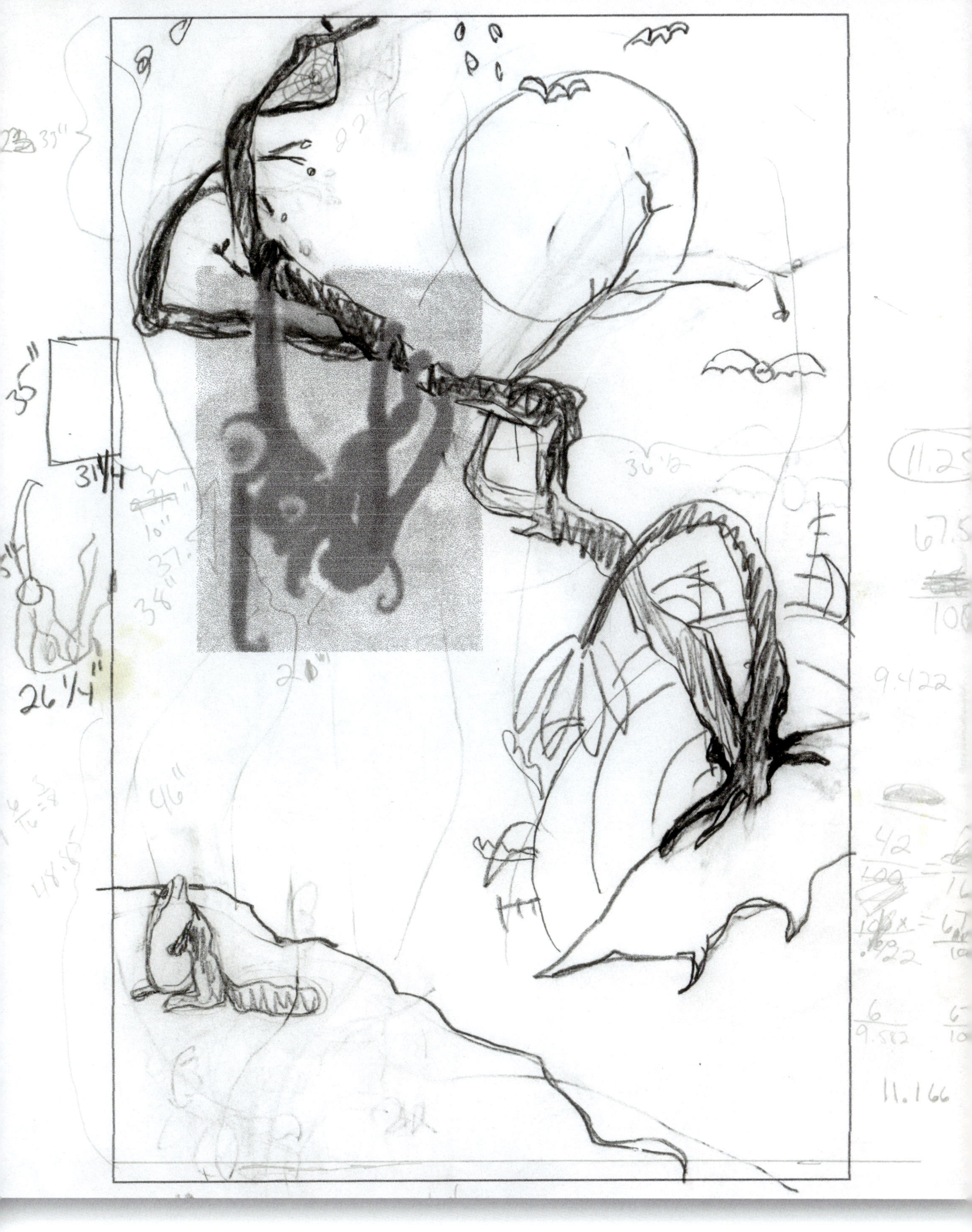

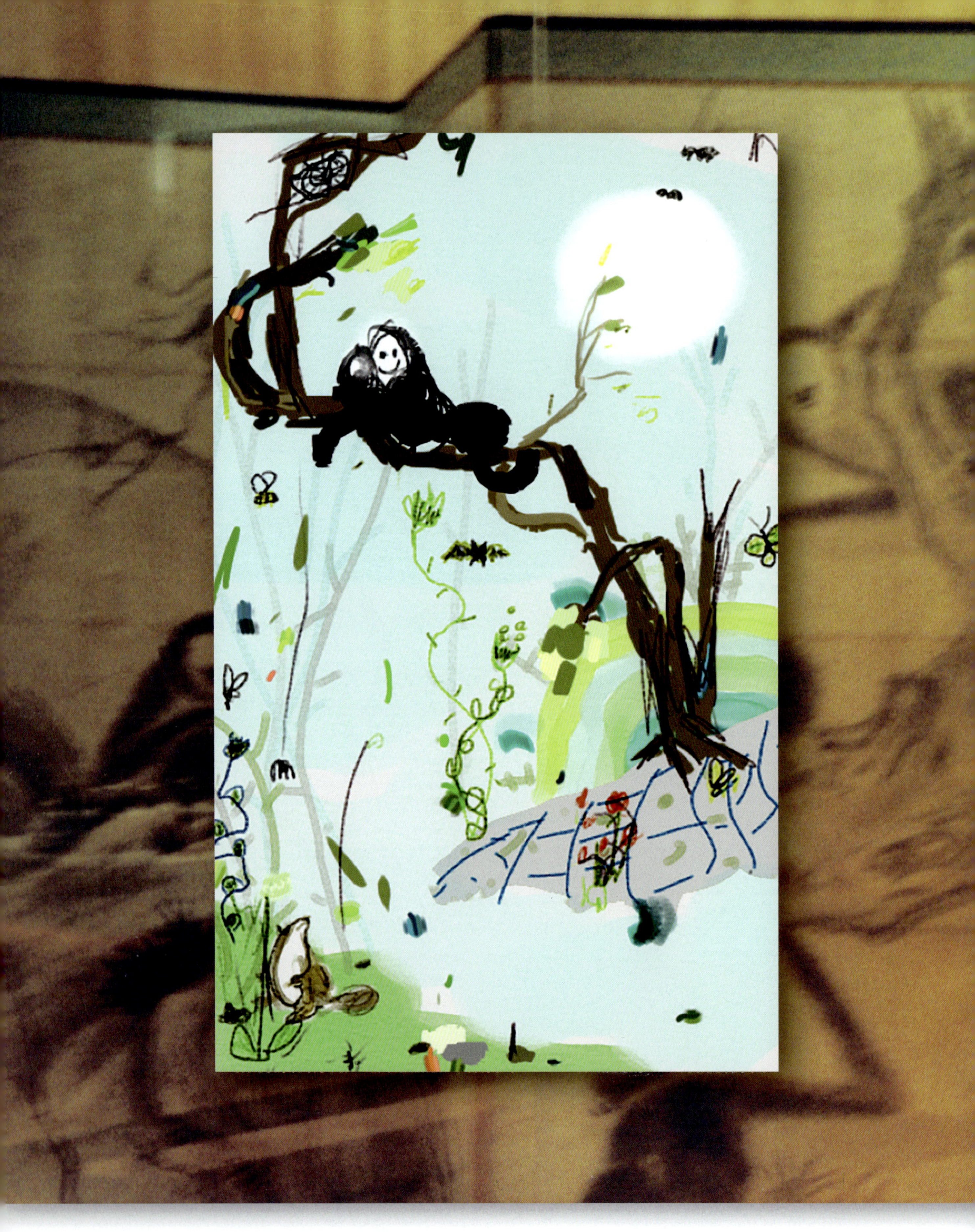

Foreground: Corel Painter 7 file, 2001
Background: Research photograph by Owens, Isabella Stewart Gardner Museum, Boston, 2000

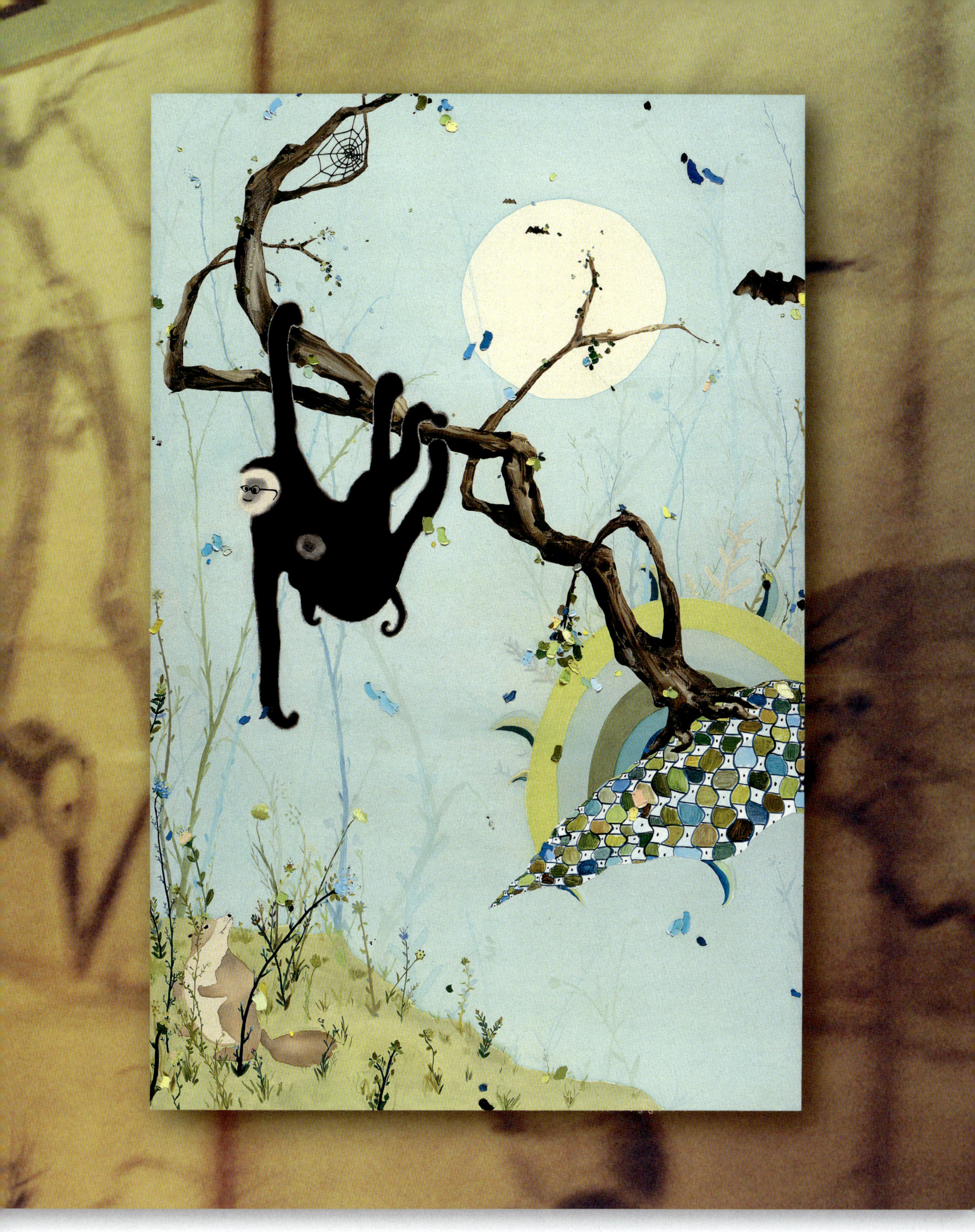

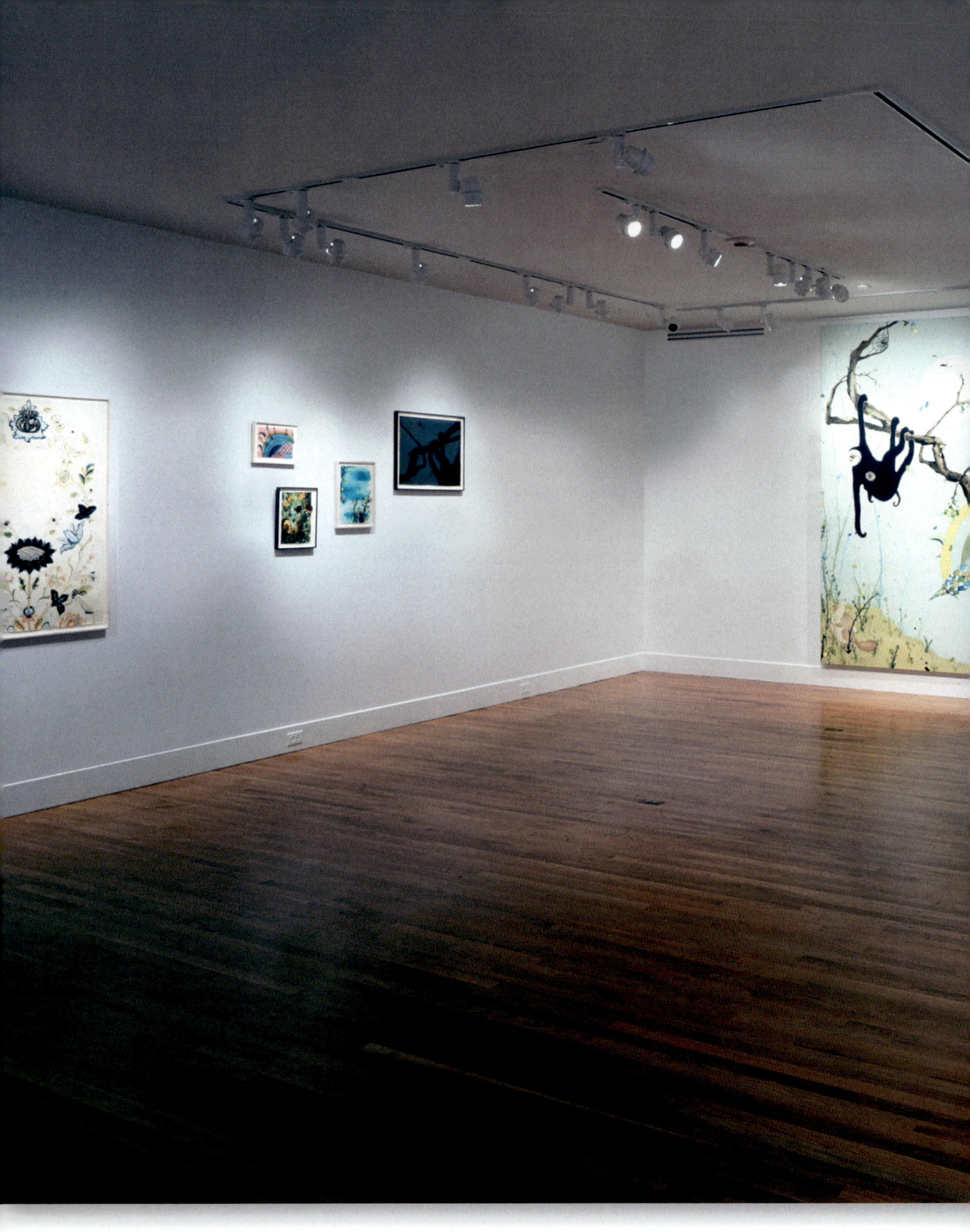

Installation view, Isabella Stewart Gardner Museum, Boston, 2001, with *Untitled*, 2001, watercolor and graphite on paper, 44 × 30¼ in. (111.8 × 76.8 cm); *Untitled*, 2001, watercolor, felt, and collage on paper, 7 × 10 in. (17.8 × 25.4 cm); *Untitled*, 2001, watercolor, felt, and collage on paper, 12 × 9½ in. (30.5 × 24.1 cm); *Untitled*, 2001, watercolor, graphite, and collage on paper, 14 × 10 in. (35.6 × 25.4 cm); *Untitled*, 2001, watercolor and oil on paper, 18 × 24 in. (45.7 × 61 cm); and *Untitled*, 2001 (see p. 313)

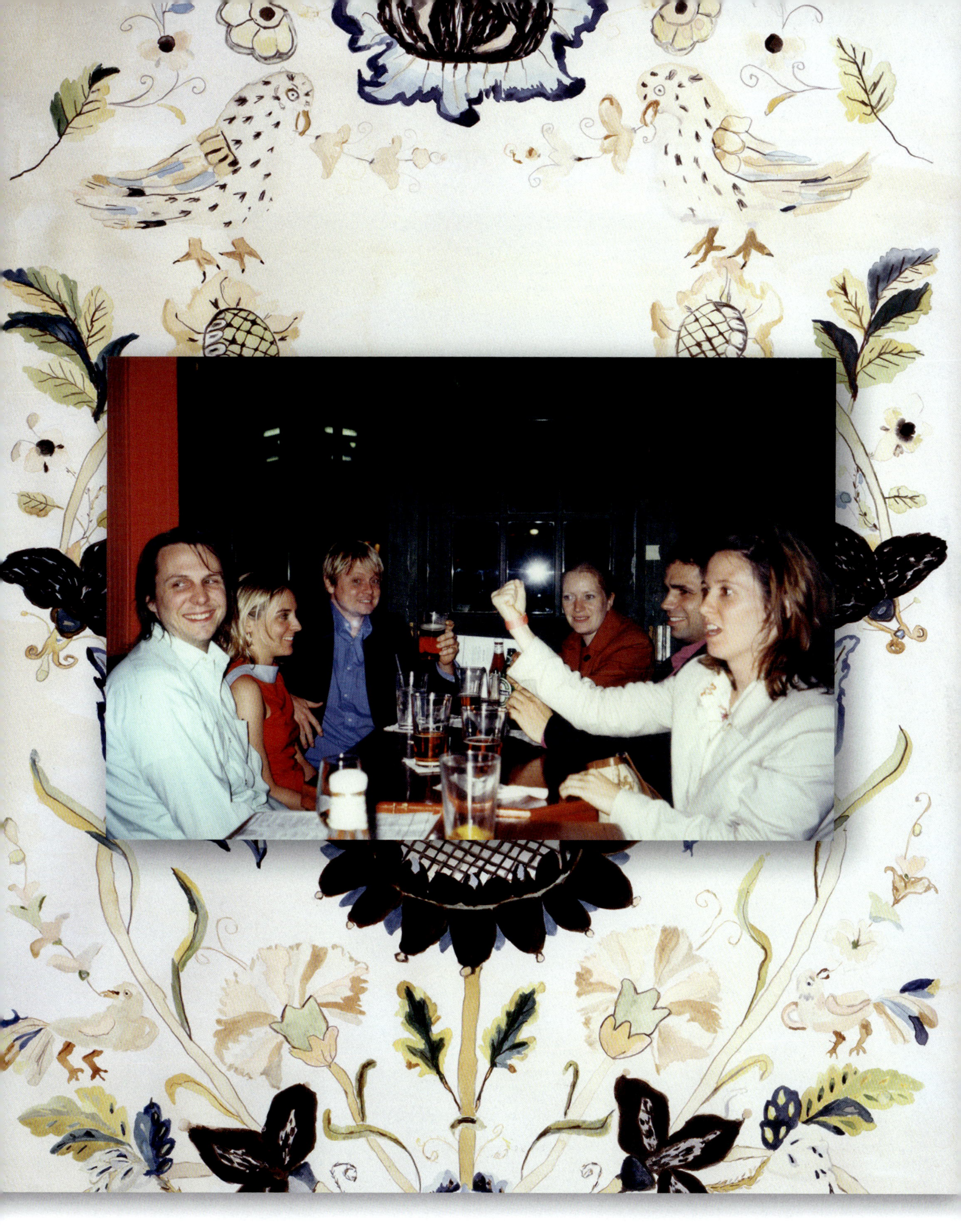

Foreground: Donald Morgan, Jessica Jackson Hutchins, Edgar Bryan, Kirsty Bell, Gavin Brown, and Owens, Boston, 2001
Background: Detail of *Untitled*, 2001 (see p. 314)

artin, Michael Webster, Monique Prieto, Adrian Williams, Jonathan
ford, Ruth Root, Florian Maier-Aichen

together in an open studio exhibition:
5117 Eagle Rock

les wants to throw a   Have you called
do you think? Her p

E   CALL   AND
S   GOING   KS.

Foreground: Invitations, *more! more! more!*, Chicago Project Room and Eagle Rock studio, Los Angeles, 2001

 Background: Invitation draft, Eagle Rock studio, Los Angeles, 2001

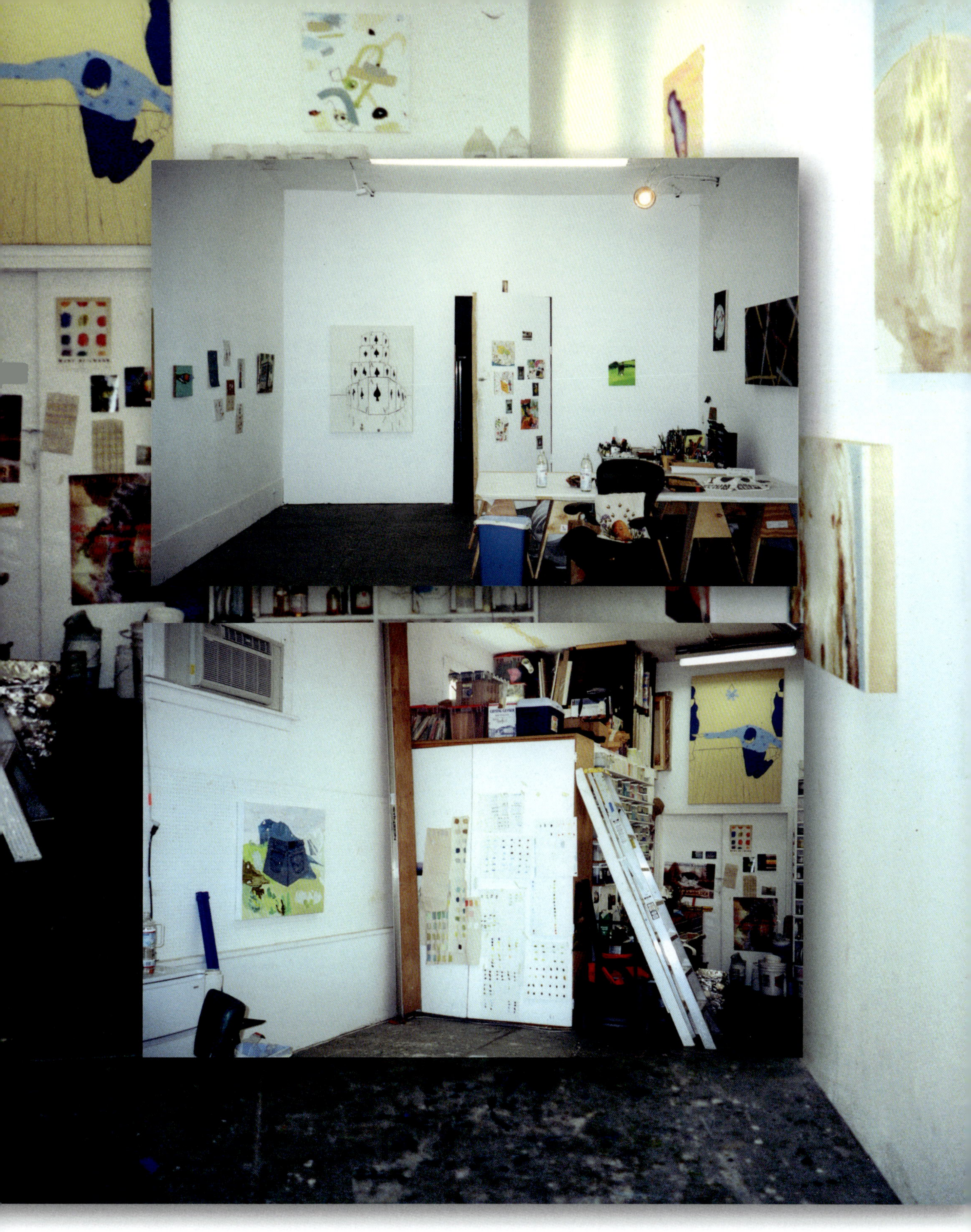

Installation views, *more! more! more!*, Eagle Rock studio, Los Angeles, 2001

thing like that here in the past."

Not on this scale, at least. Back in the early 1990s, the Michigan Avenue galleries in Santa Monica, led by Food House, were the place for all things raw and exciting in the L.A. art world, but when the galleries relocated to 6150 Wilshire Boulevard in 1998, the scene lost much of its youthful energy. "As soon as those guys moved to Wilshire, and Food House changed its name to Acme, they became a lot more polished and established," says video artist Jessica Bronson, who lives and works in a white modern house hanging off the side of a grassy hill in Highland Park and shows at Goldman Tevis Gallery in Chinatown. "I think that created a need for another group of galleries which would encourage a similar kind of raw energy and enthusiasm."

Enter Chinatown, a charming, if largely neglected, clutch of streets ideally situated a couple of blocks from L.A.'s Museum of Contemporary Art (the museum now runs bus tours to the Chinatown galleries) and a 10-minute drive from Eagle Rock, Highland Park and Mount Washington. Hanson and Intra recognized the area's potential immediately. "We loved the architecture," says Hanson, referring to the neighborhood's whimsical rooftops and wishing wells, "and I liked the fact that Chinatown was on the opposite side of town from everything else that was going on in the commercial art world in L.A. It seemed kind of adventurous and exciting." Hanson pauses and chuckles. "It was also the only place we could afford."

The gallery was an immediate hit,

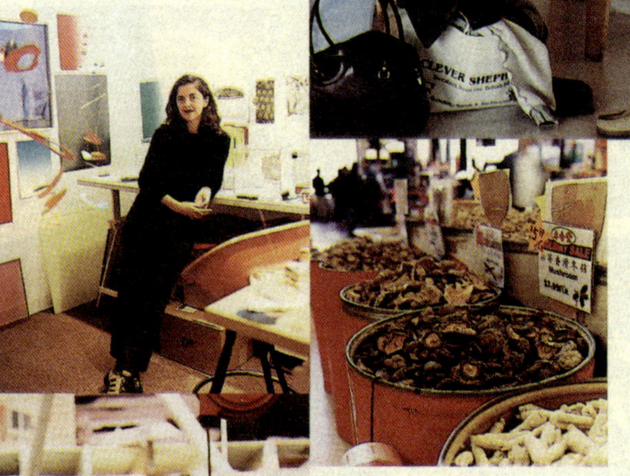

Clockwise from top: Painter Mari Eastman in her Lincoln Heights studio; a Chinatown herbal apothecary; artist Mike Kelley in his Eagle Rock studio; artist Pae White in her Highland Park studio.

"No one can afford to live on the West Side anymore," says Mike Kelley, who was a pioneer when he moved to Eagle Rock in 1989.

making a name for itself with unconventional openings like Laura Owens and Scott Reeder's collaborative 1999 show "Heaven and Hell," which featured a hellish gambling den in the basement of the gallery. "For the first six months that China Art Objects was open, it had this really amazing feeling," says Owens, who had previously only shown at the West Side's Acme Gallery. "The openings weren't like normal art openings; they had a very present-tense feel to them." Owens recalls one show that featured a Frances Stark video of her cat listening to a Black Flag album in her apartment. "It was incredibly compelling, but you didn't know whether it was art or not, and that was so exciting; it hadn't been defined yet."

In the minds of many young artists, it was Owens and Reeder's show that served as proof that L.A. was a good place to make and show work. "I think it made a lot of people realize that you didn't have to move to New York to have a career as an up-and-coming artist," says painter Mari Eastman, who moved to L.A. in 1998, after graduating from the School of the Art Institute of Chicago.

Pardo and Muller pioneered the East Side back in the early Nineties. Muller has held several of his wildly popular "Three Day Weekend" collaborative shows in his Highland Park studio, and as part of a 1993 show at MOCA, Pardo rebuilt a house on Mount Washington—in which he now lives—and the museum ran buses of visitors up to see it. But it wasn't until Owens, almost a cult figure, moved to the neighborhood that the hordes of young art-school grads started following.

Not surprisingly, a collection of new galleries has popped up, including Goldman Tevis, Acuna-Hansen and UCLA painting professor Roger

But not everybody is gung ho about the East Side's transformation. "The problem with gentrification is that it f--s everything up," says Kelley, whose folk-inspired multimedia art also has an in-your-face quality to it. "You have to think to yourself, Well, do I want a bar and a bookstore, or do I want to be able to afford to stay in my apartment?"

Kelley's probably not far off the mark. As the scene explodes—and the prices of L.A. artists' work continue to rise—others will be pushed out of the neighborhood. "It's crazy how much money these kids are making right now," says junk-shop Pop artist Jim Shaw, who lives in a charming Craftsman house in the hills of Highland Park. "Nobody ever made money like that when I was young," he continues, not without a note of bitterness in his voice. "Until the Laura Owens School of Colorful Painting happened to Los Angeles, the idea of getting $10,000 a pop straight out of school was unheard of. It took me 20 years to get anything like that."

China Art Objects' Hanson and Intra, while clearly in favor of the area's development, are nevertheless aware that they are playing with fire. "I hope it doesn't get out of control," Hanson says. "Right now there's still a good balance. You can still walk down the street late in the evenings and hear the families playing mahjongg upstairs, and I'd hate to lose that. We don't want to get this reputation as these colonists coming in, you know?" —KIMBERLY CUTTER

Clockwise from top: Painter Laura Owens in her Eagle Rock studio; Chinatown hot spot Hop Louie; artist Jorge Pardo in his Chinatown studio; China Art Objects' Steve Hanson and Giovanni Intra.

Celebs like Christina Ricci, Gwen Stefani, Beck, Mario Testino and Iggy Pop mingle on Chung King Road.

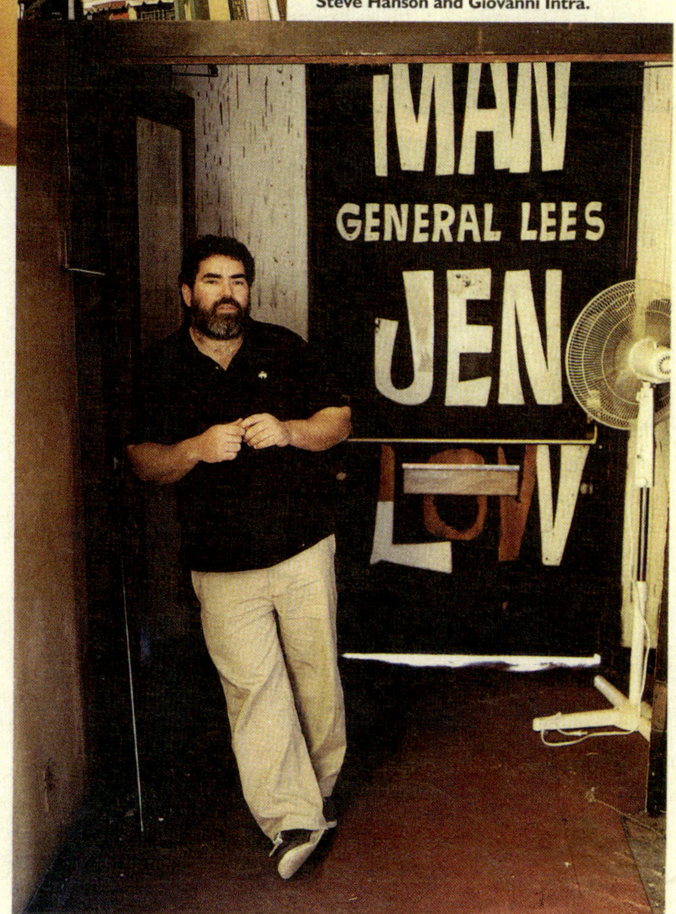

Ford. "The neighborhood definitely has a more commercial feeling now, but hopefully, in exchange, it's also gained longevity," says Owens, who has a two-year waiting list for her innocent, cartoonlike paintings.

"It's wild around here these days," adds Hanson, who has been coming to Chinatown since it was a haven for punk clubs like the Hong Kong Cafe in the early 1980s. "It used to be that you'd tell people you were looking for a space in Chinatown and they'd be like, 'Oh, God, don't go down there—it's dangerous.'" Hanson's monthly rent—for the moment—is only $540. "Now there's a line around the block of people trying to get spaces here," he says.

One of the neighborhood's more recent tenants is artist Miltos Manetas, who hosted the after-party for artist Vanessa Beecroft's performance of *VB46* at his project space, Electronic Orphanage. (The performance itself, however, was across town at the blue-chip Gagosian Gallery.) On weekends, celebs like Christina Ricci, Gwen Stefani, Beck, Mario Testino and Iggy Pop mingle on Chung King Road amid the throng of pierced and shaved art students who hop from gallery opening to gallery opening, clutching spring rolls and plastic cups of wine. And once the galleries close up shop for the night, the crowd migrates to the high-kitsch, pagoda-style bar Hop Louie or the Friday-night dance club Firecracker at Grand Star.

And the scene is not limited to Chinatown. Downtown L.A. is undergoing its own makeover, with hotelier Andre Balazs putting up another Standard while the El Dorado Hotel is being resurrected just down the street. When New York art dealer Gavin Brown brought the performance art-cum-rock diva band Fischer Spooner to L.A. last winter, he set them up in the Standard's construction site and re-created his Passerby bar for the after-party at Project, a nearby gallery.

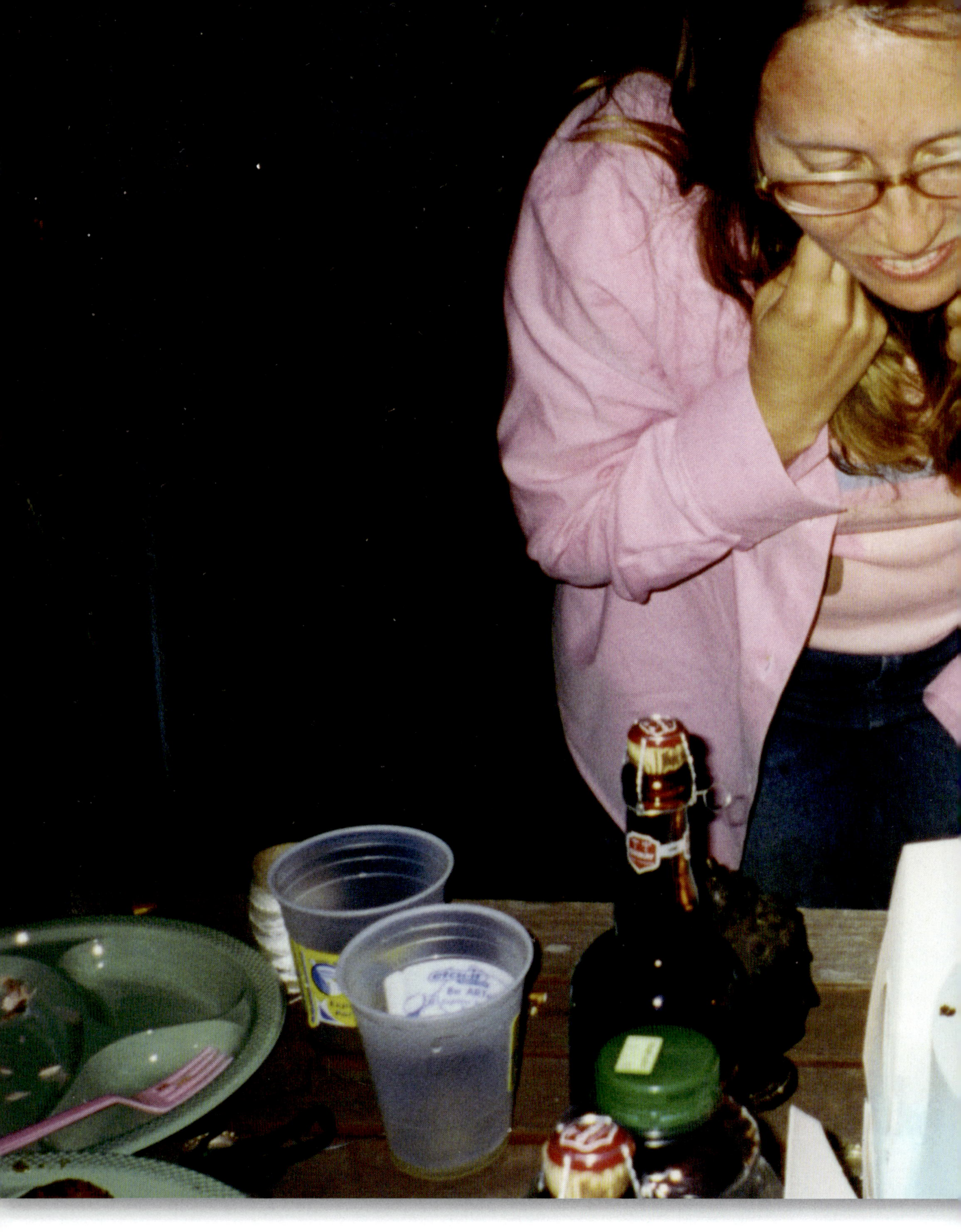

     Owens at her birthday party, Los Angeles, 2002

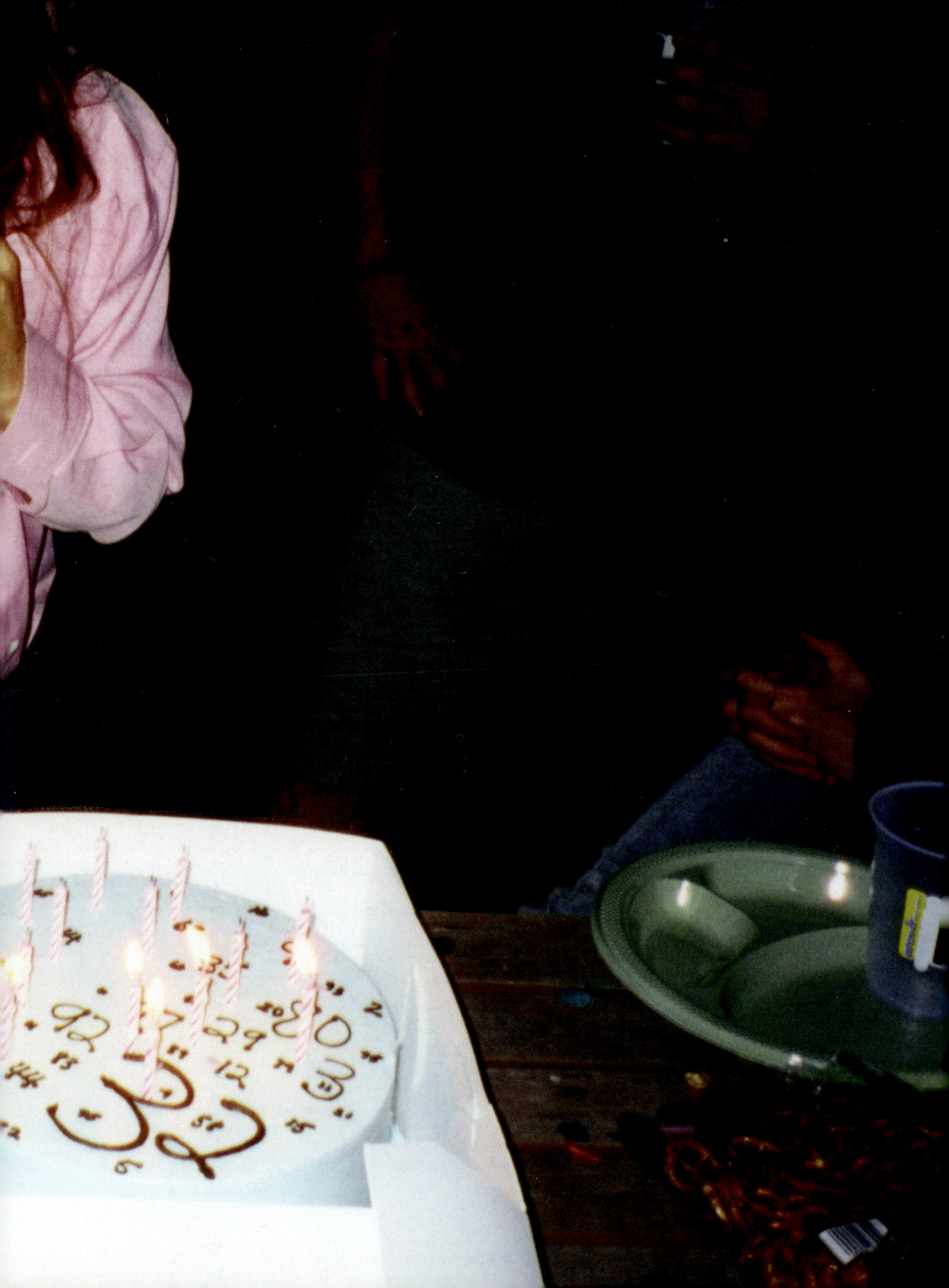

Chris Ofili: *Cavepainting* was very much Laura's initiative. I don't know why she wanted to make an exhibition with Peter Doig and me, but the idea was really great because it was so much about working in the studio—the studio as this kind of cave and a place of creativity and home.

At that time we all showed with Gavin Brown and were making different types of paintings with different voices. I was quite interested, and still am actually, in that Jim Jarmusch film *Ghost Dog: The Way of the Samurai*. There's the samurai, played by Forest Whitaker, and the guy in the ice cream truck, played by Isaach De Bankolé: their relationship is interesting in that one speaks English and the other speaks French, and neither of them can speak the other's language but they're very, very good friends. So you have this interaction in the film through a series of conversations, and they're missing each other's statements but there's a strange kind of comprehension. I think in some way the show seemed to be about that too. We spoke in different languages but somehow there was a comprehension of what one another was trying to say.

We all went to Los Angeles and installed it together. I didn't really get too involved in the hang, but Laura and Peter nailed it pretty easily. I think I made everything new for the show, and around that time was the beginning of my interest in the natural world, or being closer to the natural world through Trinidad. Peter and I had been there at that point and it was really starting to kick in, so it was new territory and quite exciting. I don't think I had ever been to LA before, or if I had it's not somewhere that I was familiar with then. Even now it's a place that always seems almost like another planet—very established but very far away. Maybe that's what Laura is like as well.

At the time of *Cavepainting* Laura seemed very clear-sighted and focused, very inquisitive and in some ways like a maverick. She's tough but also embraces a kind of vulnerability. She always seems

 Chris Ofili is a British painter who lives and works in Trinidad and was in the group exhibition *Cavepainting* with Owens in 2005.

to be interested in challenging hierarchies: social hierarchies, political hierarchies, pictorial hierarchies. She's got a very singular vision, and I think she allows whatever she does to be polluted by her personality, infused with "Lauraness." It's not a word that I use often—it's more of an American word—but I've always thought of Laura as kooky. Her paintings are kooky as well. They're a bit tripped out, just in between fairy tale and actual reality. They flirt with being completely flirtatious, being leaves in the wind, but then they seem to insist on having gravity. I like to think of living that way and at times trying to see the world in that way—to catch special glimpses into how the world might actually be if you could just find that slipstream.

If I'm really honest, what struck me then was that Laura was trying to deal with being a female painter and pushing her ambitions beyond the limits of what may be construed as the glass ceiling of her gender. She just seemed very empowered as a woman painter. Her paintings have a very light touch but also a punch and weight that can hold your attention. I don't know how she does it. It's something to do with that slightly crazed look in her eyes that seems to stare right through things. The subjects can seem a bit off, like you don't quite know what you're looking at, or rather the thing that you're looking at seems to be in the wrong context. That destabilizing allows you to stay there a bit longer. I think that's probably what still has me interested in what she's doing.

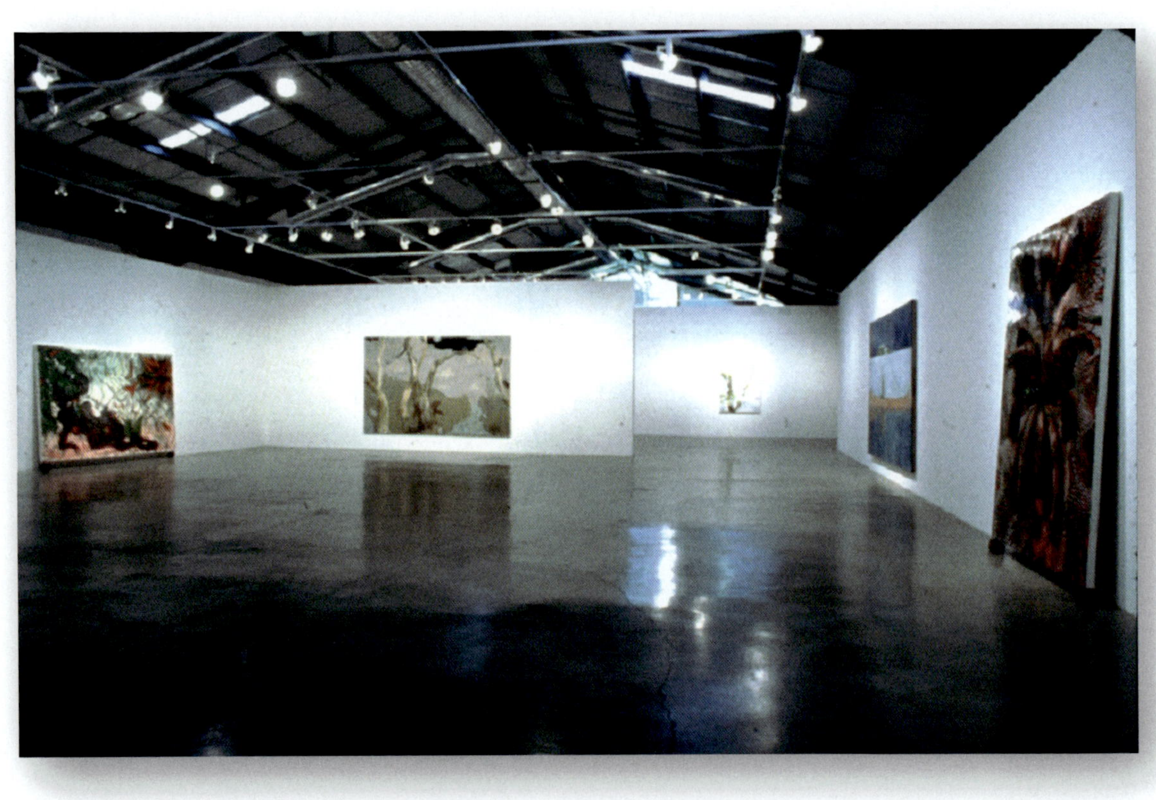

    Installation view, *Cavepainting: Peter Doig, Chris Ofili, and Laura Owens*, Santa Monica Museum of Art, 2002

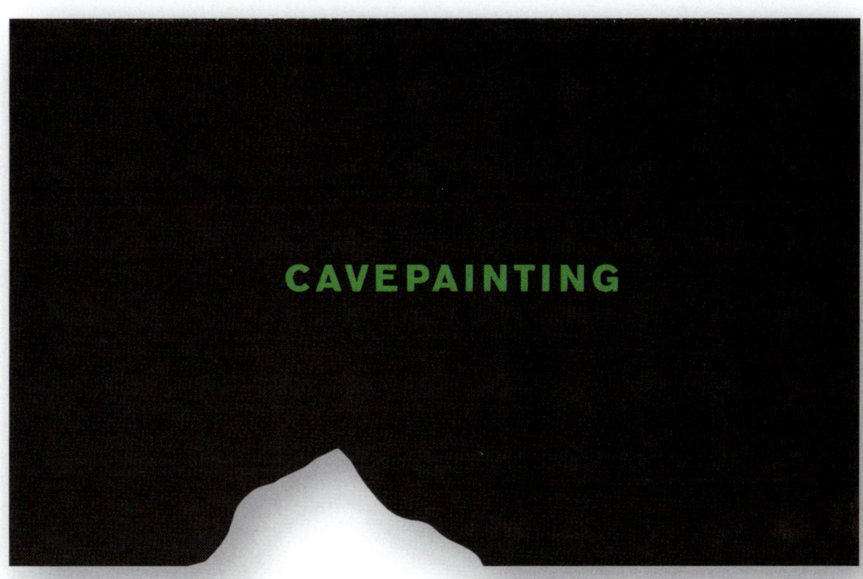

SANTA MONICA : MUSEUM : OF ART

Santa Monica Museum of Art
Bergamot Station G1
2525 Michigan Avenue
Santa Monica CA 90404

Tel 310.586.6488
Fax 310.586.6487
info@smmoa.org
www.smmoa.org

Non Profit
U.S. Postage
P A I D
Service
Mailers

CAVEPAINTING Peter Doig, Chris Ofili, & Laura Owens
February 8, 2002—March 31, 2002

**Opening Reception:
Friday, February 8**

6–7pm
Special Members' Preview:
a unique opportunity to hear Peter Doig,
Chris Ofili, & Laura Owens discuss the
evolution and realization of
CAVEPAINTING

7–9 pm
Public Opening

7–8 pm
Kids' Art Station Workshop
$8 members, $12 non-members
Reservations required,
phone 310.586.6488, ext. 32

March 8, 7pm

Mary Heilmann, distinguished
New York-based painter talks about
the work of Doig, Ofili, & Owens

March 19, 7pm

Exhibition walk through: Commentary,
and conversation with Los Angeles-
based abstract painter, John Millei

Project Room

Mark Leckey "Fiorucci Made Me Hardcore"

The Project Room series is organized
by associate curator Ciara Ennis

Support has been provided by the National Endowment for the Arts; the City of Santa Monica Community Arts Grant Program,
a project of the Santa Monica Arts Commission; the City of Santa Monica Cultural/Arts Organizational Support Grant Program;
the California Arts Council; the Los Angeles County Arts Commission; the California Community Foundation; The Getty
Grant Program; and the Friends and Board of Trustees of the Santa Monica Museum of Art. Special thanks to
The Annenberg Foundation, the Entertainment Industry Foundation, and the Nathan Cummings Foundation
for their generous support of the museum's educational program.

Museum hours:
Tuesday through Saturday
11 am–6 pm
Sunday 12 noon–5 pm

Invitation, *Cavepainting*, Santa Monica Museum of Art, 2002

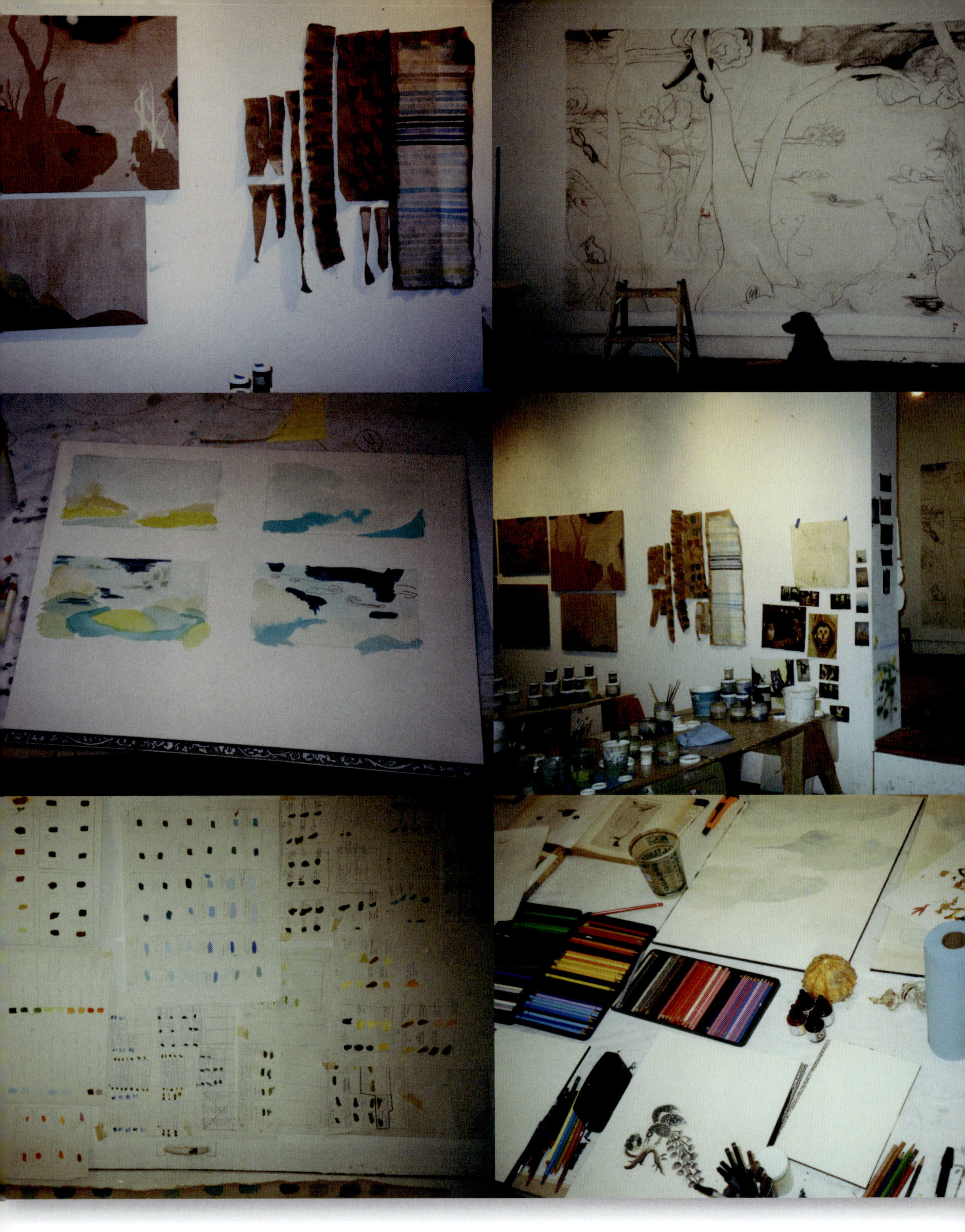

 Eagle Rock studio, Los Angeles, 2002

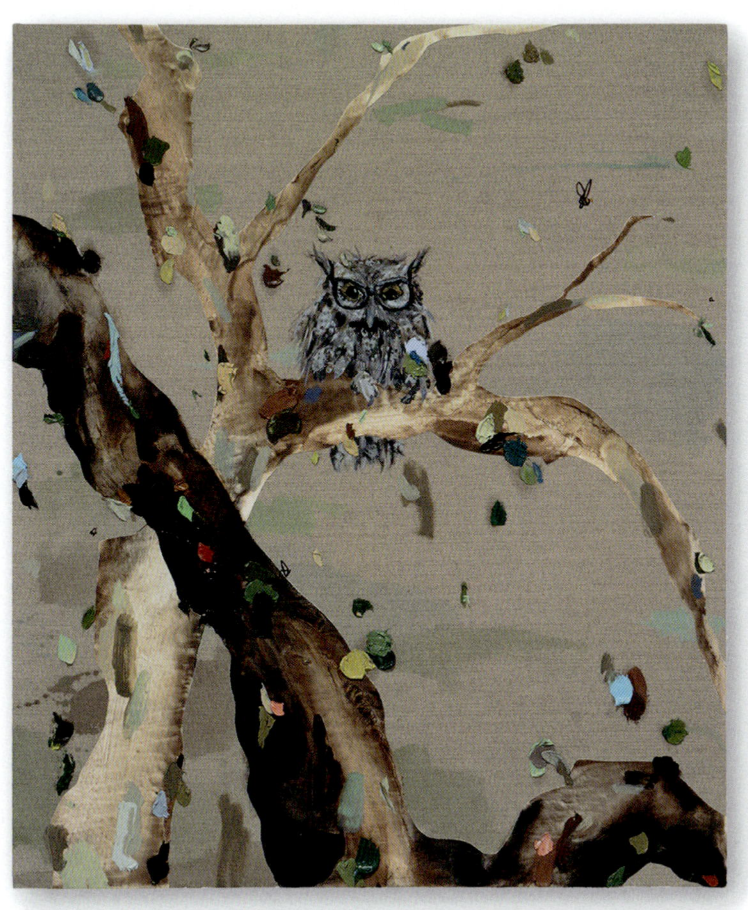

Untitled, 2002, oil and acrylic on linen, 34 × 28 in. (86.4 × 71.1 cm)

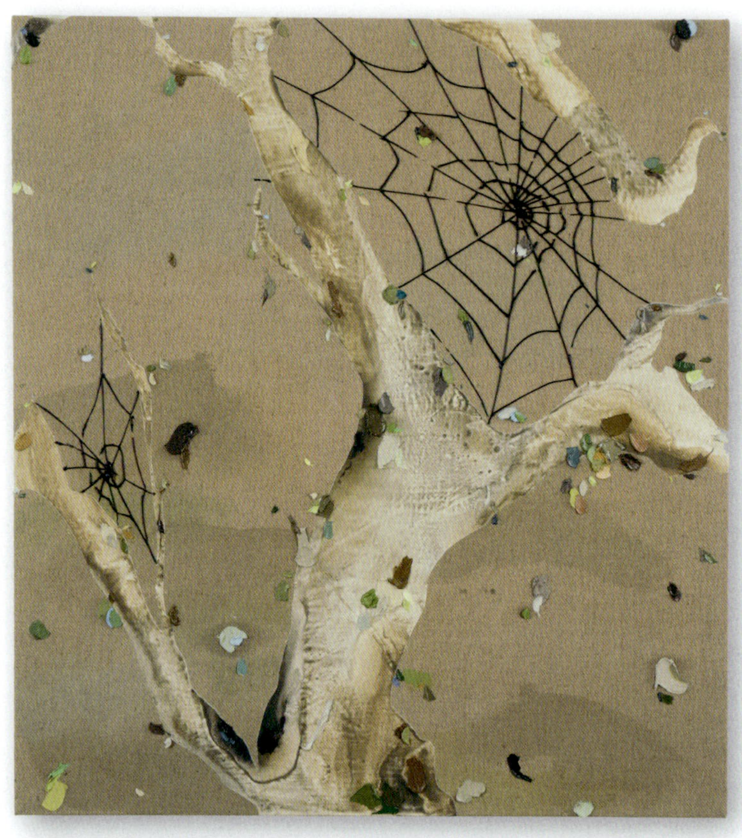

Monique Prieto: When my husband, Michael, and I learned that Laura had never tried backpacking, we planned a four-day beginner trip. I was eight months pregnant with Emmet and I had Guillermo in a backpack. A couple hours into the hike our two dogs, who had gone ahead, suddenly came tearing around the bend back toward us and on their tail was a bear. It was stunning—at first I disconnected and thought, "It's like a cartoon . . ." I had this stick and was saying, "No," to the bear as if it's a dog. I remembered having read about how this kid got rid of a bear by screaming, and I just screamed as loud as I could. My older dog started charging. Laura was screaming too. Michael started lobbing rocks at the bear. It had cataracts and was blind, so it was all smell. His claws were as long as my fingers and he was roaring. I think he thought, "This is too much trouble," and he walked away. Michael and I were like, "Let's keep going," and Laura was like, "I am *not* staying here. Are you kidding?" So we walked down and decided to celebrate. We stopped at Baskin-Robbins and got a cake and called everyone we knew to say, "We're alive!" A few weeks later we dragged Laura to the San Diego Zoo, and when we went to see the polar bears she was not amused and walked off saying, "This is not cute! Who wants to look at bears?"

   Untitled, 2002, oil and acrylic on linen, 36 × 32 in. (91.4 × 81.3 cm)

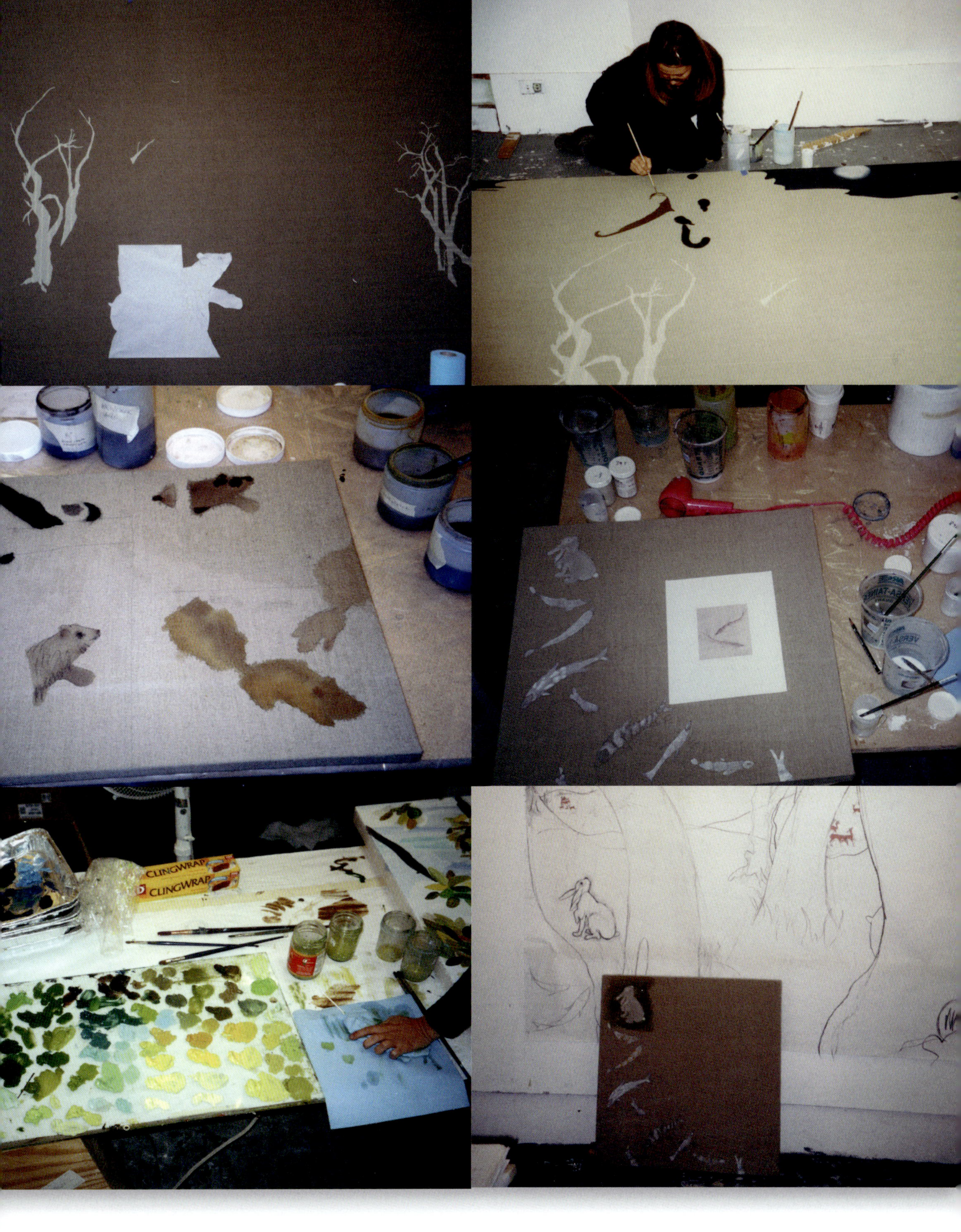

Foreground: Preparatory drawing, 2002
Background: Sketchbook pages, 2002

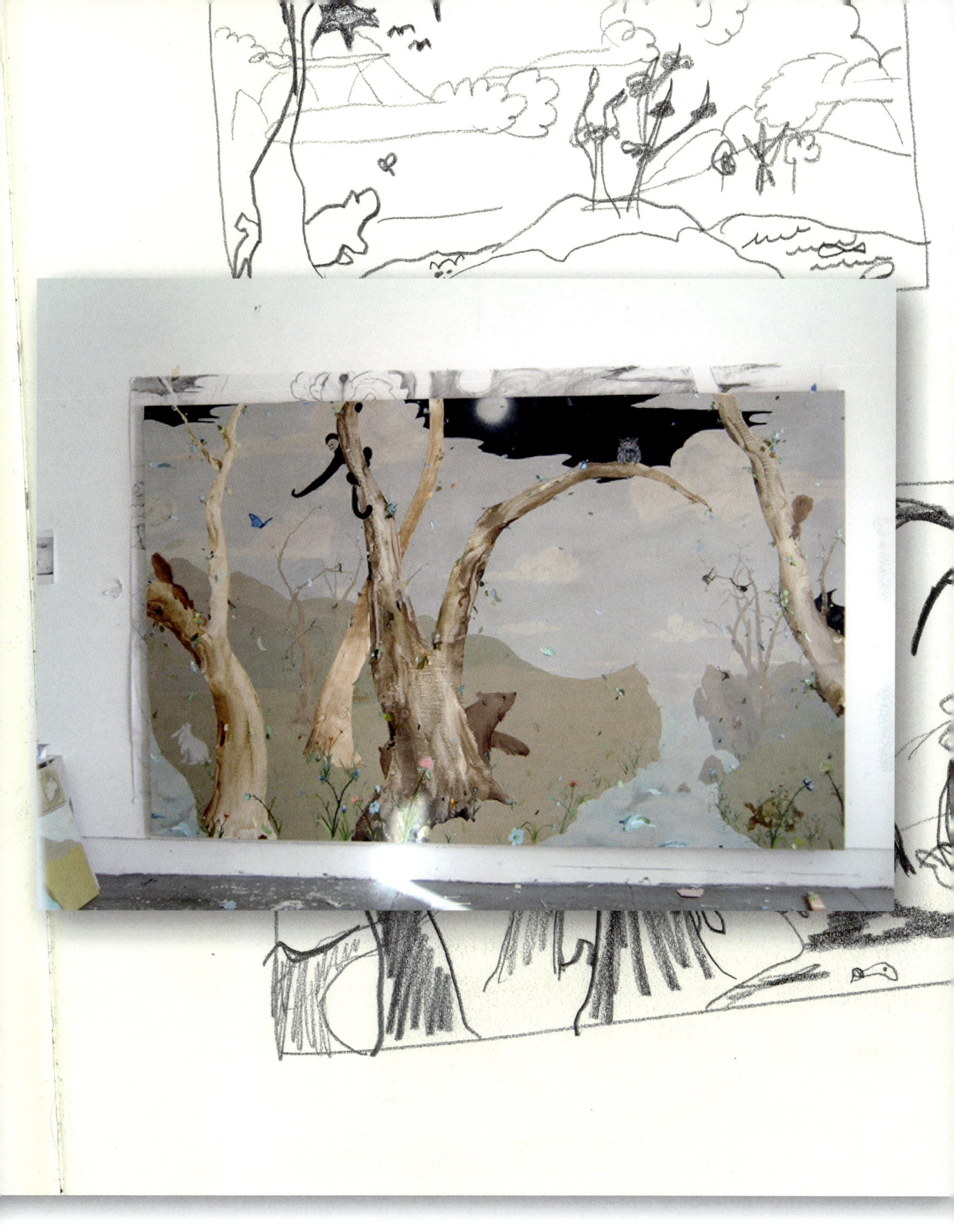

Foreground: *Untitled*, 2002 (see p. 335), on top of preparatory drawing, 2002

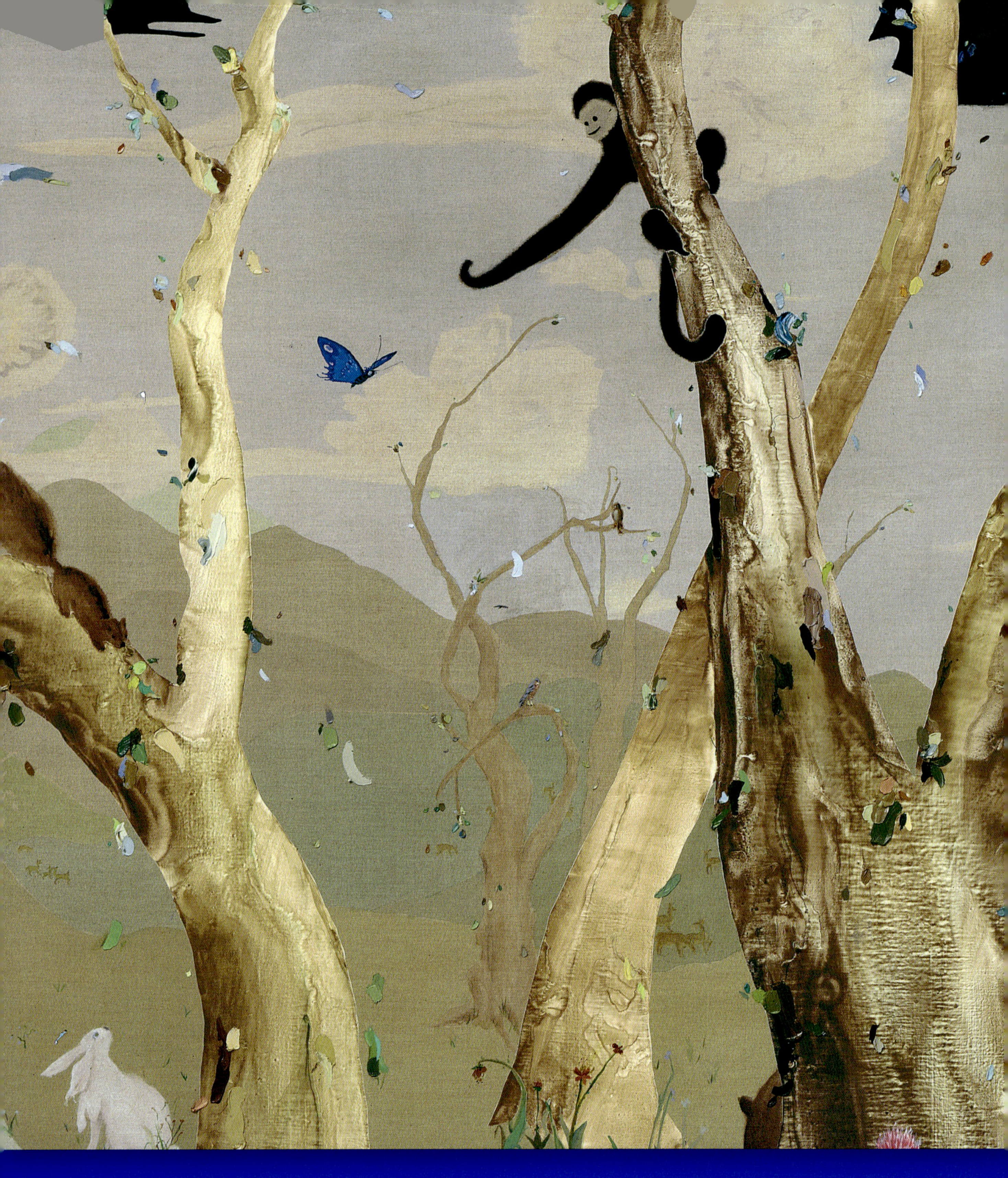

Foreground: Research photograph by Owens, San Diego Zoo, 2002
Background: Detail of *Untitled*, 2002 (see p. 335)

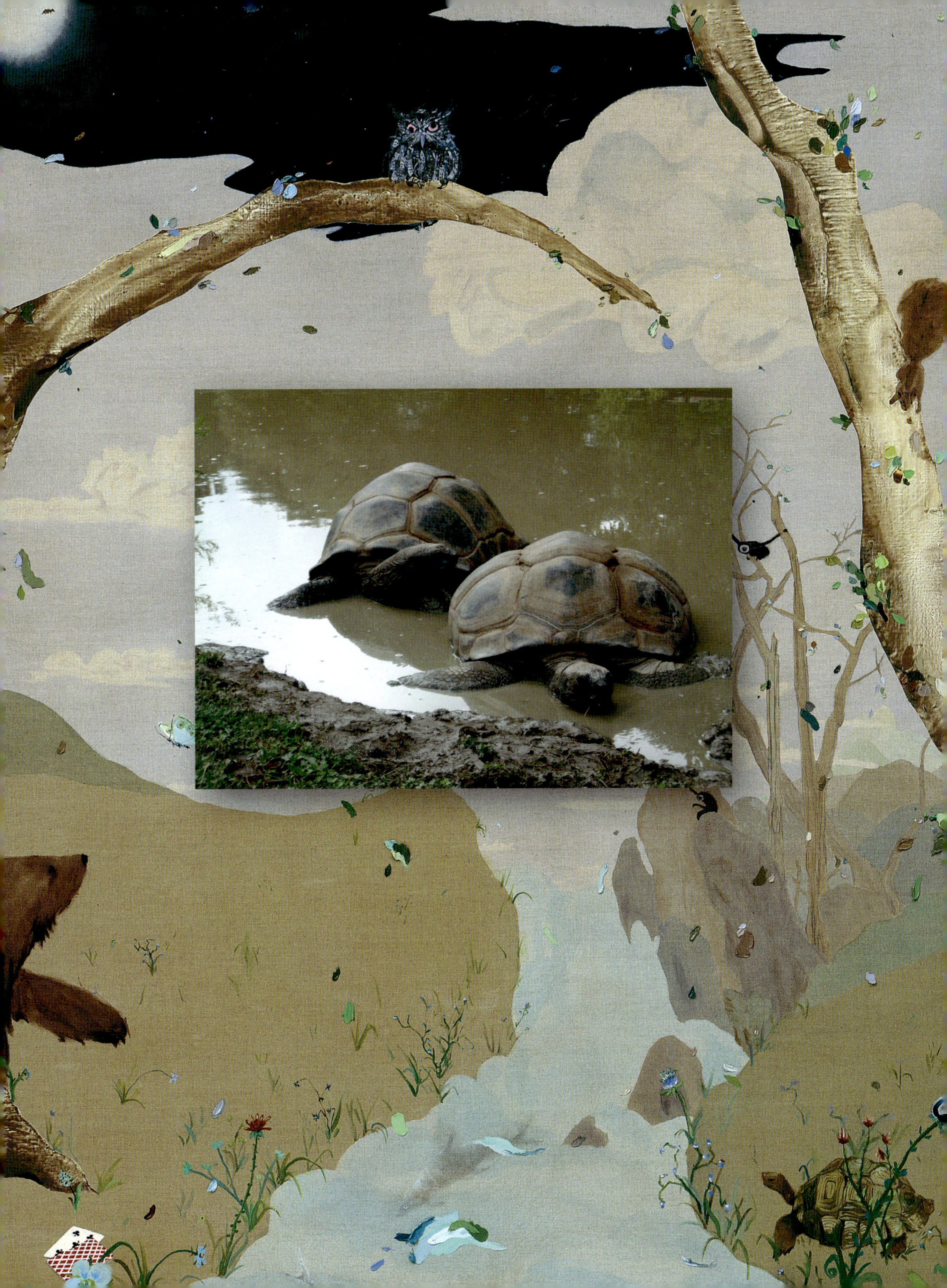

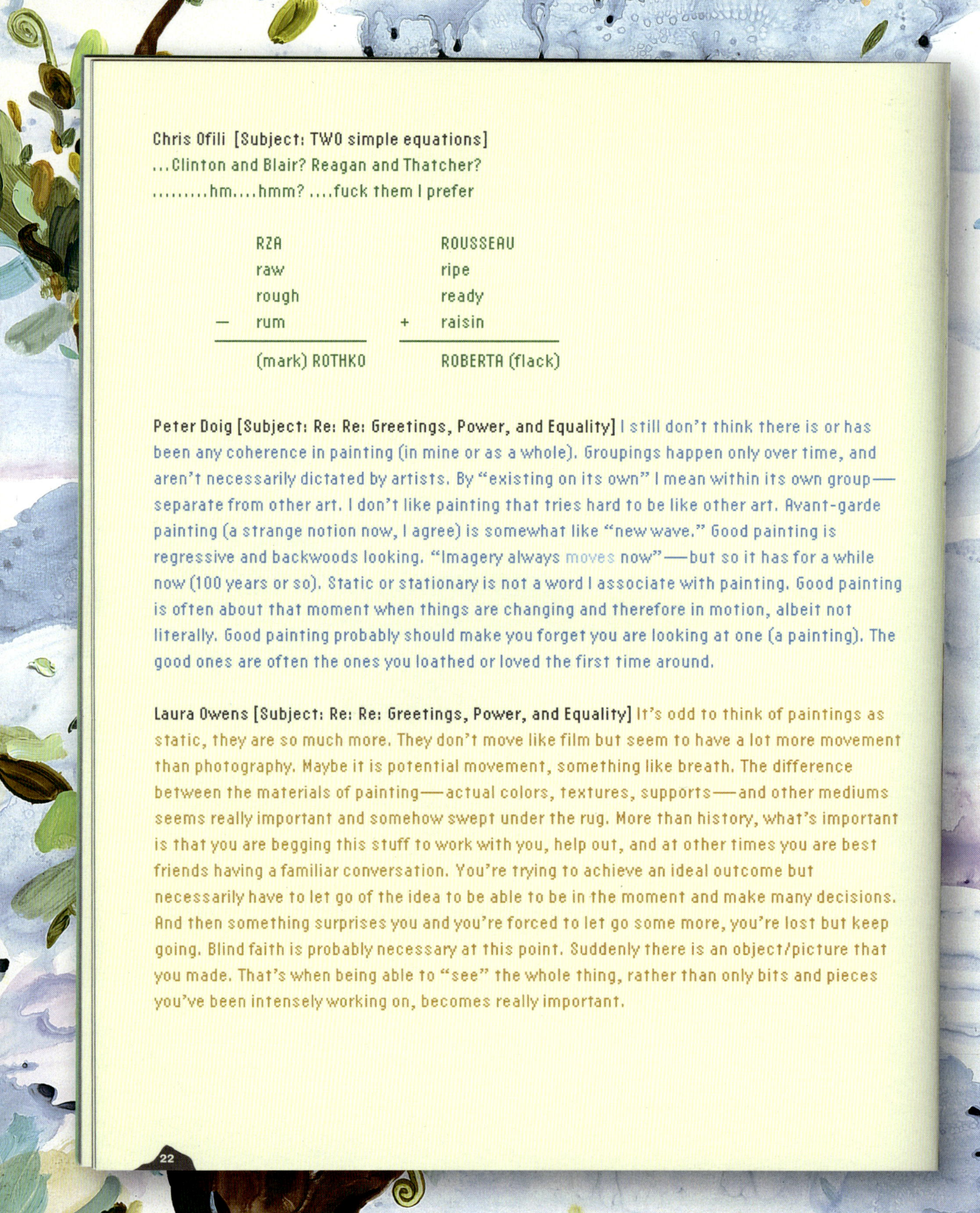

Chris Ofili [Subject: TWO simple equations]
...Clinton and Blair? Reagan and Thatcher?
.........hm....hmm? ....fuck them I prefer

$$-\ \frac{\begin{array}{l}\text{RZA}\\ \text{raw}\\ \text{rough}\\ \text{rum}\end{array}}{\text{(mark) ROTHKO}}\qquad +\ \frac{\begin{array}{l}\text{ROUSSEAU}\\ \text{ripe}\\ \text{ready}\\ \text{raisin}\end{array}}{\text{ROBERTA (flack)}}$$

Peter Doig [Subject: Re: Re: Greetings, Power, and Equality] I still don't think there is or has been any coherence in painting (in mine or as a whole). Groupings happen only over time, and aren't necessarily dictated by artists. By "existing on its own" I mean within its own group—separate from other art. I don't like painting that tries hard to be like other art. Avant-garde painting (a strange notion now, I agree) is somewhat like "new wave." Good painting is regressive and backwoods looking. "Imagery always moves now"—but so it has for a while now (100 years or so). Static or stationary is not a word I associate with painting. Good painting is often about that moment when things are changing and therefore in motion, albeit not literally. Good painting probably should make you forget you are looking at one (a painting). The good ones are often the ones you loathed or loved the first time around.

Laura Owens [Subject: Re: Re: Greetings, Power, and Equality] It's odd to think of paintings as static, they are so much more. They don't move like film but seem to have a lot more movement than photography. Maybe it is potential movement, something like breath. The difference between the materials of painting—actual colors, textures, supports—and other mediums seems really important and somehow swept under the rug. More than history, what's important is that you are begging this stuff to work with you, help out, and at other times you are best friends having a familiar conversation. You're trying to achieve an ideal outcome but necessarily have to let go of the idea to be able to be in the moment and make many decisions. And then something surprises you and you're forced to let go some more, you're lost but keep going. Blind faith is probably necessary at this point. Suddenly there is an object/picture that you made. That's when being able to "see" the whole thing, rather than only bits and pieces you've been intensely working on, becomes really important.

Foreground: Lane Relyea, "Correspondence with Peter Doig, Chris Ofili, and Laura Owens," *Cavepainting: Peter Doig, Chris Ofili, and Laura Owens*, exh. cat. Santa Monica Museum of Art, 2002

 Background: Detail of *Untitled*, 2002, acrylic and oil on canvas, 54 × 48 in. (127.2 × 121.9 cm)

CAVEPAINTING:
Peter Doig, Chris Ofili & Laura Owens

1. Peter Doig
Gasthof zur Muldentalsperre
2001–2002
oil on canvas
Courtesy Gavin Brown's enterprise, New York;
Victoria Miro Gallery, London; and the artist

2. Laura Owens
Untitled
2002
acrylic, collage, a
Courtesy Gavin B
ACME., Los Ange

3. Chris Ofili
Triple Beam Drea
2001–2002
acrylic, oil, leaves
map pins, and ele
elephant dung sup
Courtesy Gavin B
Victoria Miro Ga

4. Laura Owens
Untitled
2002
acrylic and oil on
Courtesy Gavin B
ACME., Los Angeles; and the artist

5. Peter Doig
100 Years Ago(Figure in Canoe)
2001
oil on canvas
Courtesy of Gavin Brown's Enterprise, New York;
Victoria Miro Gallery London; and the artist

6. Chris Ofili
Triple Eye Vision
2000–2002
acrylic, oil, glitter, paper collage, polyester
resin, map pins, and elephant dung on linen,
with two elephant dung supports

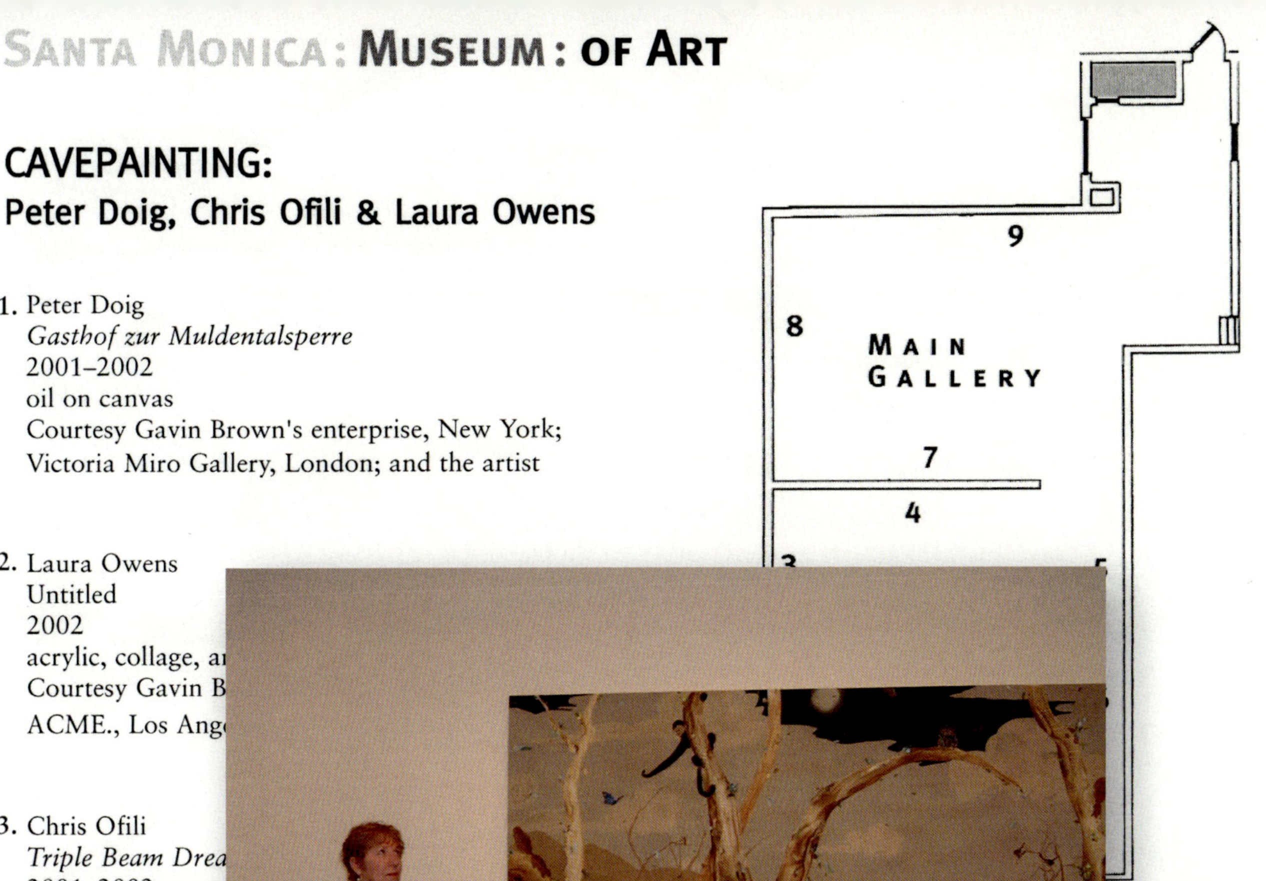

up pins, and ele-
ant dung sup-
ports
Courtesy Gavin Brown's enterprise, New York;
Victoria Miro Gallery, London; and the artist

8. Peter Doig
House of Pictures
2000–2002
oil on canvas
Courtesy Gavin Brown's enterprise, New York;
Victoria Miro Gallery, London; and the artist

9. Laura Owens
Untitled
2002
acrylic and oil on canvas

Foreground: Mary Heilmann with *Untitled*, 2002, acrylic and oil on linen, 84 × 132 in. (213.4 × 335.3 cm), Santa Monica Museum
of Art, 2002
Background: Gallery guide, Santa Monica Museum of Art, 2002

Paul Schimmel: I had always understood that Laura thought a lot about installation, considering the architecture in which her paintings would be hung or referencing the space in which the work would be exhibited rather than the space in which it was made, the studio. That was super apparent in her collaboration with Jorge Pardo at Patrick Painter. He was better known and had kind of a macho thing going. More importantly, he made three-dimensional objects that occupy space, so I assumed it would be a Jorge sculpture show, with Laura providing the decorative elements. But when I walked in I thought, "Oh, Laura just pulled the rug out from Jorge, stole the show!" She wasn't just doing the most beautiful, amazingly original pictures, but dealing with the whole notion of collaboration—of who's "on top," so to speak. And she turned that upside down so that Jorge's sculptures ended up becoming the architecture in which her paintings thrived. She really made architecture the fixed element. She owned it. It became her thing.

It wasn't until a few years later that I really started thinking about giving her a show at MOCA. We were both staying up in Maine at Kamp Kippy. I had already done a series of one-person shows with artists of my own generation, and I really wanted to delve fairly early into the next generation. It was kind of clear to me that Laura was the smartest and most rigorous one—about everything from embroidery to theory—in a way I couldn't fully understand. And she seemed quite prepared for it. As a matter of fact, for somebody who had a very strong regional identity and had grown up with and identified with her own LA generation and the schools, she was also very international in her outlook and was in the process of organizing the *Cavepainting* show in Santa Monica with Peter Doig and Chris Ofili. So she wasn't like, "I don't want to do this. It's going to screw everything up. It's too soon."

There's a tendency for a young artist to say, "Yes, but really the only thing that's good is the thing that's in the studio right now," but

Paul Schimmel is a Los Angeles–based curator and former chief curator of the Museum of Contemporary Art, Los Angeles, where he curated Owens's 2003 exhibition.

Laura was completely open to going through her entire database and telling a much broader story. I would say I gravitated, as probably any curator does, toward the greatest hits, which are usually the more complicated, sort of flashy, and iconographically rich works. But she was quite instructive about balance, in a way that was very unusual for someone of both her youth and immaturity in terms of making exhibitions. She was right to say that you can't just line up all the ducks and not have works that seem less ambitious.

It was relatively easy to come to a kind of a consensus with her on the checklist, but not on the hang. You want to have sort of a chronology that tells the story, even though certain ideas are happening simultaneously. But I think she was, to a large degree, right that at such a young age we shouldn't try to be too rigorously chronological, and that to show this body of work and then that body of work would be to fold it back into a box. The installation process was fairly exhausting. I remember hanging with her, hanging without her, having her come in and move things after I had moved them around. And I would say, "Let me do my curatorial job," and she goes, "No, no, this has to be like this. It's still my painting." So it was really hard when we were laying things out, especially in LA. A show in your hometown is always different than a show anywhere else. And there was this very large-scale painting that she was working on until the very end that was by far the most unknown and unresolved. It was a history painting, full of humor, and there was a feeling of her trying to capture the political moment of that time after 9/11. Yet the specifics of the war were dealt with almost in a parallel fairy tale. It was by no means didactic about what was going on, but one still sensed the Wild West and George W. Bush in it.

The opening dinner was in the lobby at MOCA. Gavin Brown, Sadie Coles, and the two boys that she had been working with for years at ACME. were there. I put one of them at the head table with her, and of course he was a no-show. So at the last minute I put Patrick Painter there, because he would always complain I never invited him to any of the good dinners at MOCA. True to form, he shows up wearing a fricking T-shirt, with cigarettes rolled up in his sleeve, saying, "Oh, fuck, I'm not sure I want to be seated with Laura Lee Woods," who was a big supporter of the exhibition and had acquired a piece. So it was this weird sort of vibe, a premonition of what was to come: The paintings looked good on the wall, but you couldn't get the people to sit in the right places. I suspect the show was easier for her to do, but then harder to live with. She couldn't really know what it felt like to have a museum survey in her thirties until she did it. But it was quite interesting, especially for such a young person, that she had this ability to sort of step outside of herself.

Since then, Laura has shown very little here, and I think LA has really missed her. I remember years after her show one of my favorite trustees giving me a hard time, saying, "You're always so good, but what happened to Laura? She sort of dropped off the face of the earth." And I said, "No. You watch. She's the smartest, the best. She just needed to get distance from her work to move forward." And a little while after that she did a fucking killer show at Kunsthalle Zurich, and I understood she just couldn't do it here. But now, you know, we really need her in LA. Have somebody from a museum here give her a call.

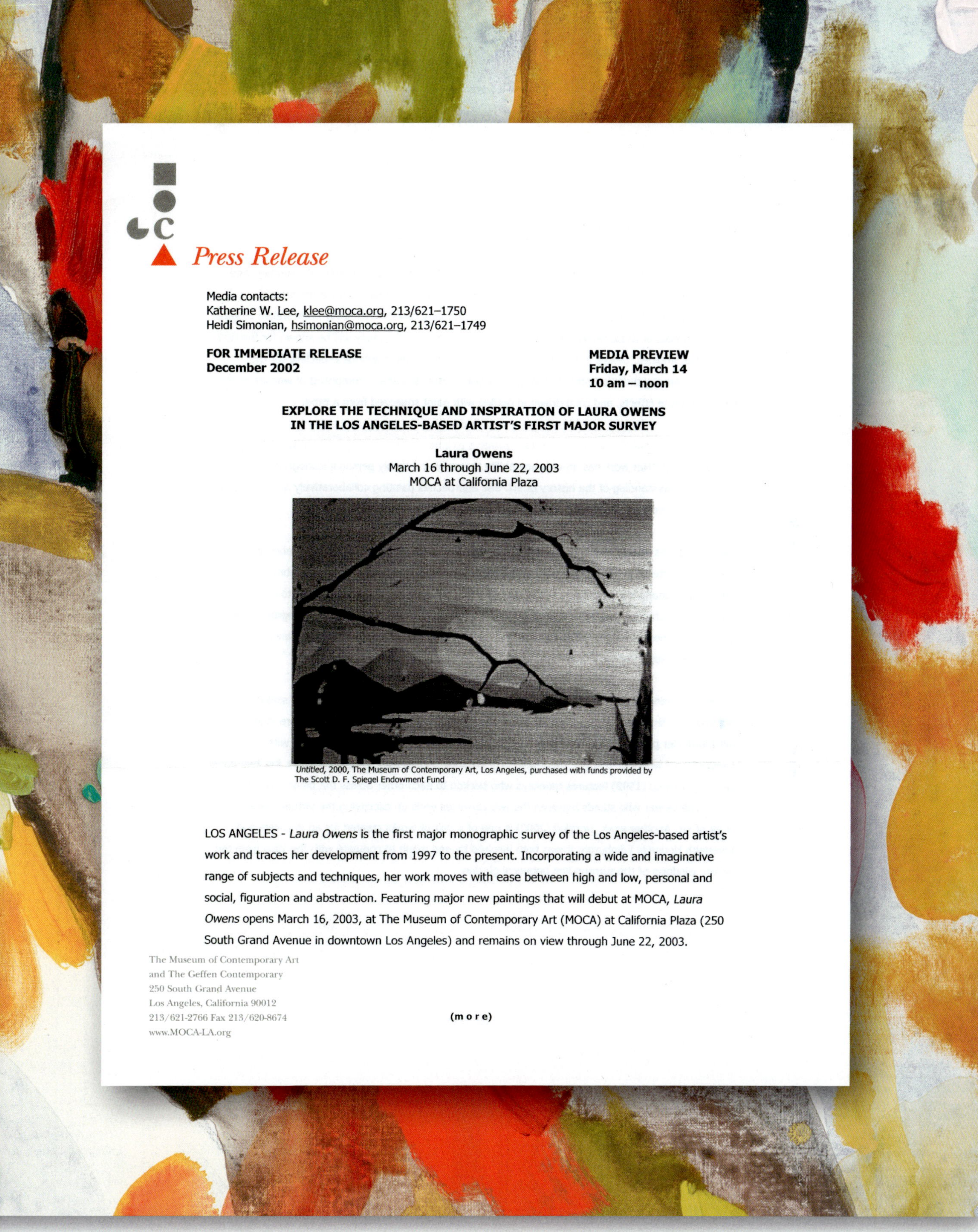

▲ *Press Release*

Media contacts:
Katherine W. Lee, klee@moca.org, 213/621–1750
Heidi Simonian, hsimonian@moca.org, 213/621–1749

FOR IMMEDIATE RELEASE
December 2002

MEDIA PREVIEW
Friday, March 14
10 am – noon

EXPLORE THE TECHNIQUE AND INSPIRATION OF LAURA OWENS IN THE LOS ANGELES-BASED ARTIST'S FIRST MAJOR SURVEY

Laura Owens
March 16 through June 22, 2003
MOCA at California Plaza

Untitled, 2000, The Museum of Contemporary Art, Los Angeles, purchased with funds provided by The Scott D. F. Spiegel Endowment Fund

LOS ANGELES - *Laura Owens* is the first major monographic survey of the Los Angeles-based artist's work and traces her development from 1997 to the present. Incorporating a wide and imaginative range of subjects and techniques, her work moves with ease between high and low, personal and social, figuration and abstraction. Featuring major new paintings that will debut at MOCA, *Laura Owens* opens March 16, 2003, at The Museum of Contemporary Art (MOCA) at California Plaza (250 South Grand Avenue in downtown Los Angeles) and remains on view through June 22, 2003.

The Museum of Contemporary Art
and The Geffen Contemporary
250 South Grand Avenue
Los Angeles, California 90012
213/621-2766 Fax 213/620-8674
www.MOCA-LA.org

(m o r e)

Foreground: Press release, Museum of Contemporary Art, Los Angeles, 2003
Background: Detail of *Untitled*, 2003 (see p. 350)

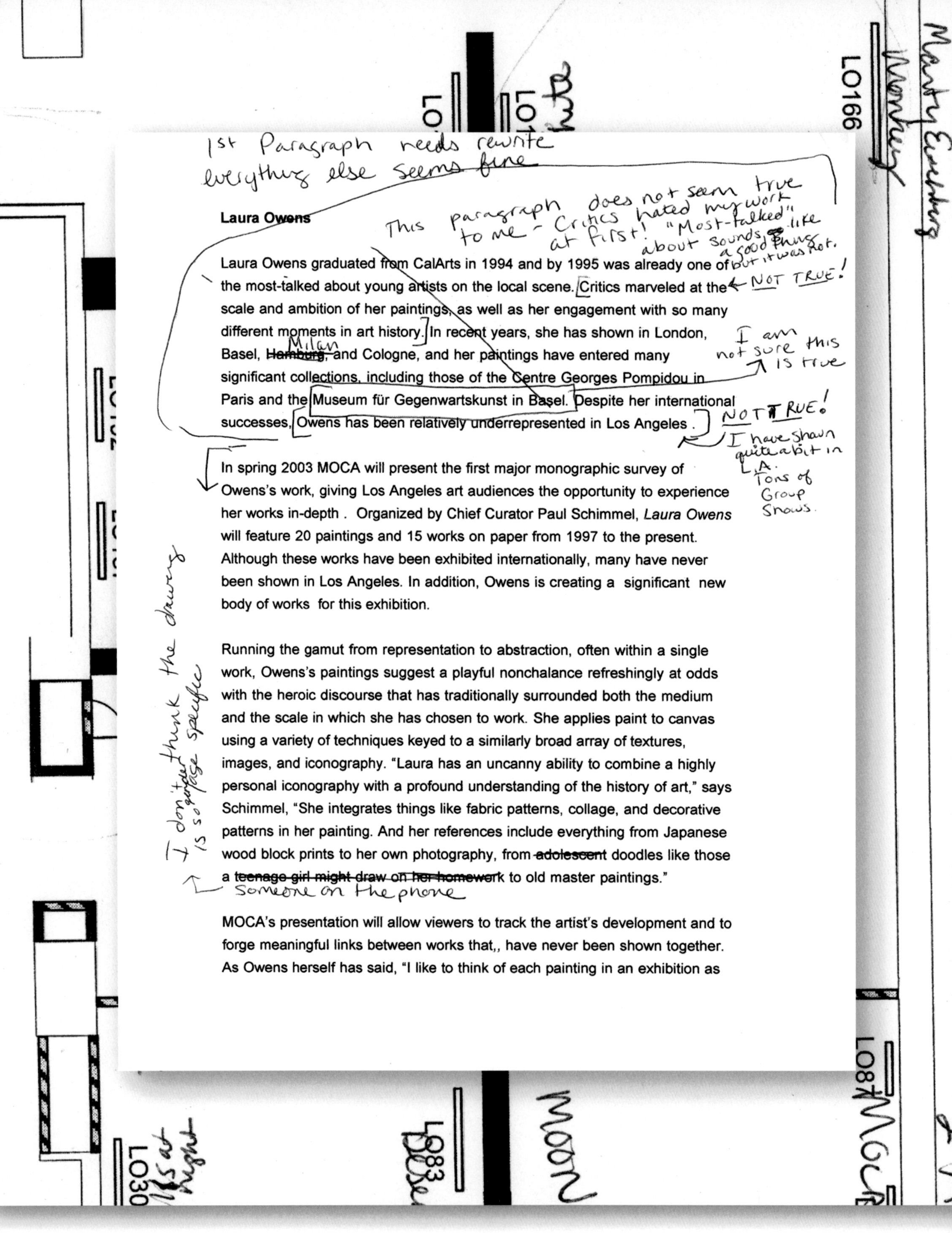

Laura Owens

Laura Owens graduated from CalArts in 1994 and by 1995 was already one of the most-talked about young artists on the local scene. Critics marveled at the scale and ambition of her paintings, as well as her engagement with so many different moments in art history. In recent years, she has shown in London, Basel, Milan, and Cologne, and her paintings have entered many significant collections, including those of the Centre Georges Pompidou in Paris and the Museum für Gegenwartskunst in Basel. Despite her international successes, Owens has been relatively underrepresented in Los Angeles.

In spring 2003 MOCA will present the first major monographic survey of Owens's work, giving Los Angeles art audiences the opportunity to experience her works in-depth . Organized by Chief Curator Paul Schimmel, *Laura Owens* will feature 20 paintings and 15 works on paper from 1997 to the present. Although these works have been exhibited internationally, many have never been shown in Los Angeles. In addition, Owens is creating a significant new body of works for this exhibition.

Running the gamut from representation to abstraction, often within a single work, Owens's paintings suggest a playful nonchalance refreshingly at odds with the heroic discourse that has traditionally surrounded both the medium and the scale in which she has chosen to work. She applies paint to canvas using a variety of techniques keyed to a similarly broad array of textures, images, and iconography. "Laura has an uncanny ability to combine a highly personal iconography with a profound understanding of the history of art," says Schimmel, "She integrates things like fabric patterns, collage, and decorative patterns in her painting. And her references include everything from Japanese wood block prints to her own photography, from adolescent doodles like those a teenage girl might draw on her homework to old master paintings."

MOCA's presentation will allow viewers to track the artist's development and to forge meaningful links between works that,, have never been shown together. As Owens herself has said, "I like to think of each painting in an exhibition as

Foreground: Press release draft with notes by Owens, Museum of Contemporary Art, Los Angeles, 2003
340 Background: Floor plan with notes by Owens, Museum of Contemporary Art, Los Angeles, 2003

COLLECTION OF WORKS IN SAN JUAN ON THE SAME DAY	$	800.00
CASE CONSTRUCTION FOR PUERTO RICO LOANS	$	2500.00
DELIVERY OF CRATE TO AIRPORT FOR SHIPMENT TO MIAMI	$	275.00
AIRPORT SUPERVISION OF DEPARTURE	$	350.00
AIRFREIGHT TO MIAMI @ 2000 LBS	$	5500.00
COLLECTION OF CRATE AT MIA, DELIVERY TO WAREHOUSE	$	
SHUTTLE SERVICE FROM MIAMI TO LOS ANGELES	$	
INTERVENTION, COORDINATION, COMMUNICATIONS	$	350.00

MUNICH AND COLOGNE LOANS

German costs:

PRE-MEASURE ON SITE AT MUNICH ADDRESS	$	65.00
CASE CONSTRUCTION, PACKING	$	2100.00
EXPORT CUSTOMS CLEARANCE	$	115.00
TRANSPORT FROM MUNICH TO FRANKFURT AIRPORT	$	800.00
CONSTRUCTION OF COLOGNE CRATE, PACKING	$	800.00
EXPORT CUSTOMS CLEARANCE	$	115.00
TRANSPORT FROM COLOGNE TO FRANKFURT AIRPORT	$	250.00
AWB/ HANDLING AT THE AIRPORT	$	65.00
SUPERVISION AT FRANKFURT AIRPORT	$	320.00
AIRFREIGHT TO LAX @ 650 KG	$	2200.00
DISBURSEMENT FEE @ 5%	$	80.00
INTERVENTION, COORDINATION, COMMUNICATIONS	$	100.00

U.S. costs:

U.S. CUSTOMS CLEARANCE & SERVICES	$	250.00
P.E.B. PLACEMENT	$	75.00
SUPERVISION OF ARRIVAL	$	475.00
COLLECTION DELIVERY TO MOCA	$	275.00
INTEVENTION, COORDINATION, COMMUNICATIONS	$	175.00

ZURICH AND MILAN LOANS

Milan costs:

Note: As there is no longer service from Italy to LAX, we have anticipated that the Milan loans would arrive via Zurich.

CASE CONSTRUCTION, PACKING, ITALIAN LOAN	$	715.00
COLLECTION AT ONE MILAN ADDRESS	$	540.00
ITALIANCUSTOMS EXPORT FORMALITIES	$	517.00
ROAD TRANSPORT FROM MILAN TO ZURICH	$	1037.00
INTERVENTION, COORDINATION, & COMMUNICATIONS	$	150.00

Continued.....

Foreground: Shipping estimate, Museum of Contemporary Art, Los Angeles, 2003

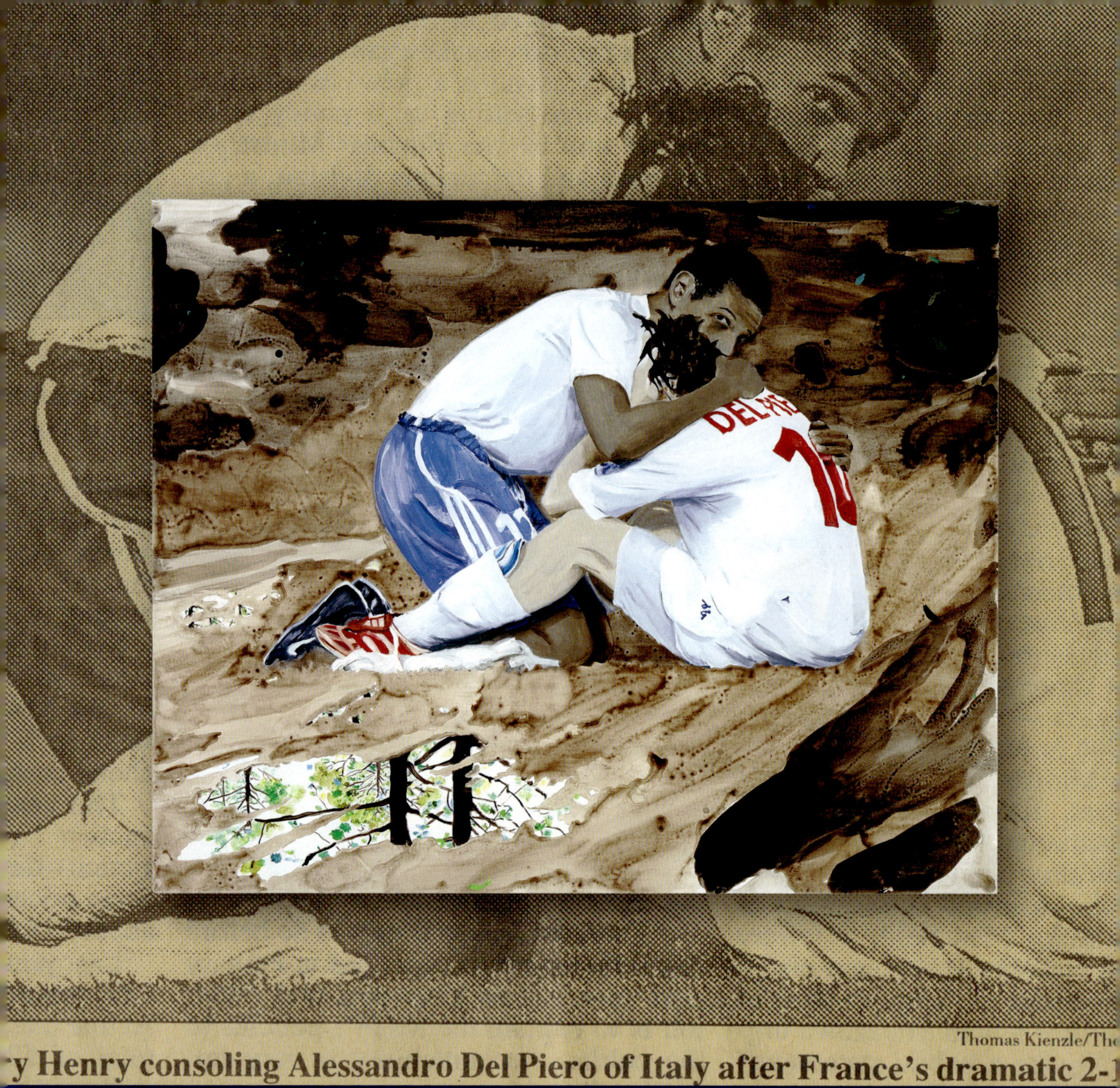

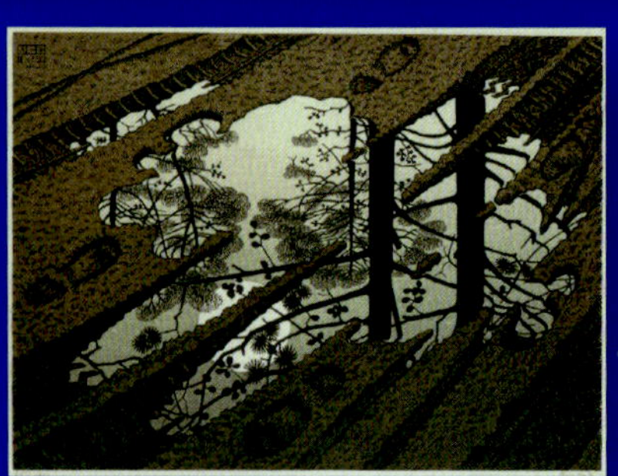

Laura Owens: I had this newspaper clipping from the UEFA Euro 2000 Final hanging in my studio for a long time. For me the image related to a series of paintings that included the monkey diptych with the twenty-foot wall between the canvases, the Toulouse-Lautrec couple in bed that has a white space between the two people, and the kissing couple that share the same blank space as a nose. Here the two figures become one and, almost like with sculpture, the shape of the negative space between them seemed very important. I was thinking a lot about Charles Ray's *Unpainted Sculpture* and how the unseeable space inside can be just as important as what is seen. Then I added the Escher in the reflection on the water; I had been looking at his work a lot at the time.

Foreground: *Untitled*, 2003, acrylic and oil on linen, 43 × 52 in. (109.2 × 132.1 cm)
Background: Research material, 2000

 Inset: M. C. Escher, *Puddle,* 1952, woodcut, 9½ × 12½ in. (24 × 31.9 cm)

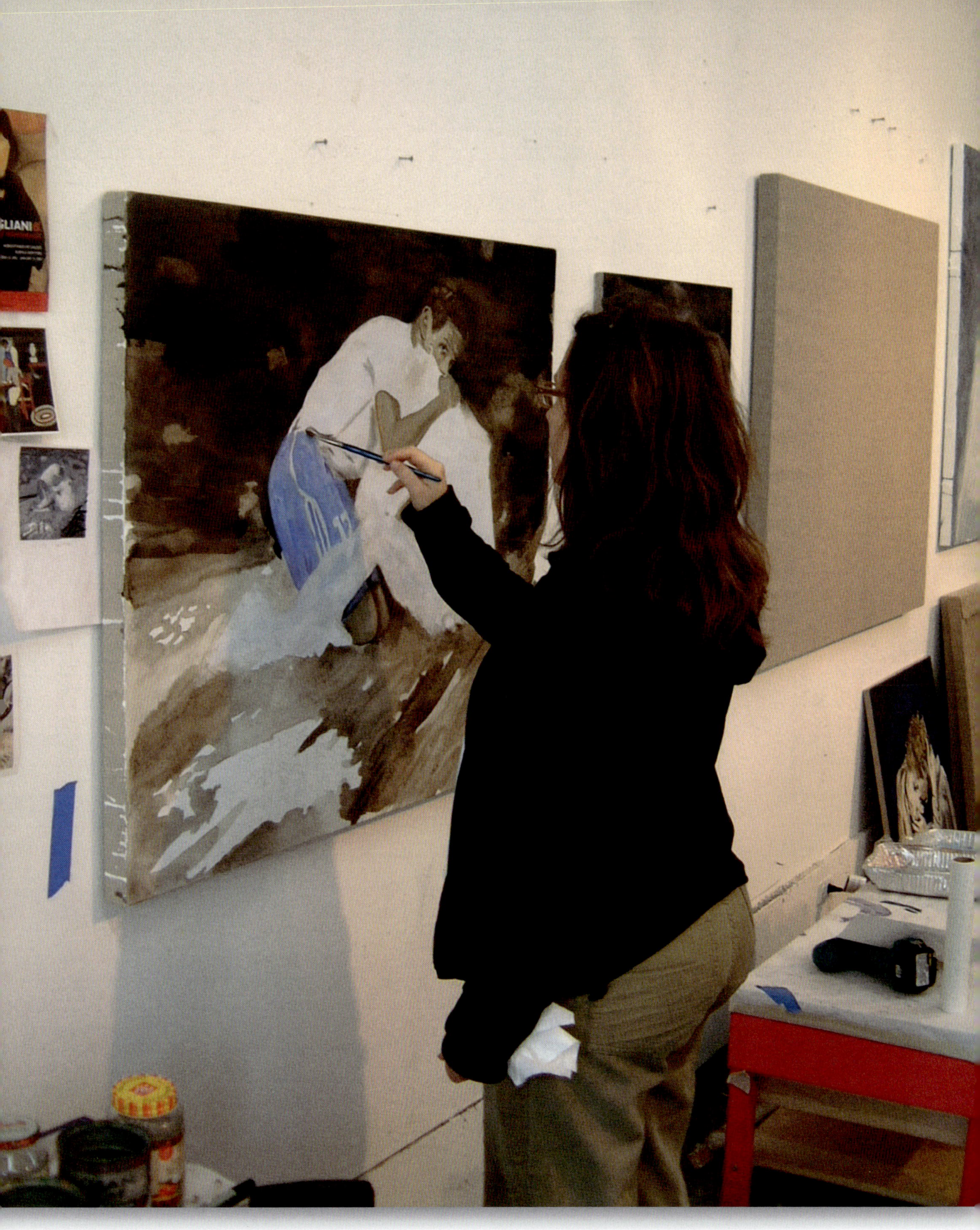

Owens with *Untitled*, 2003 (see p. 342), Eagle Rock studio, Los Angeles, 2003

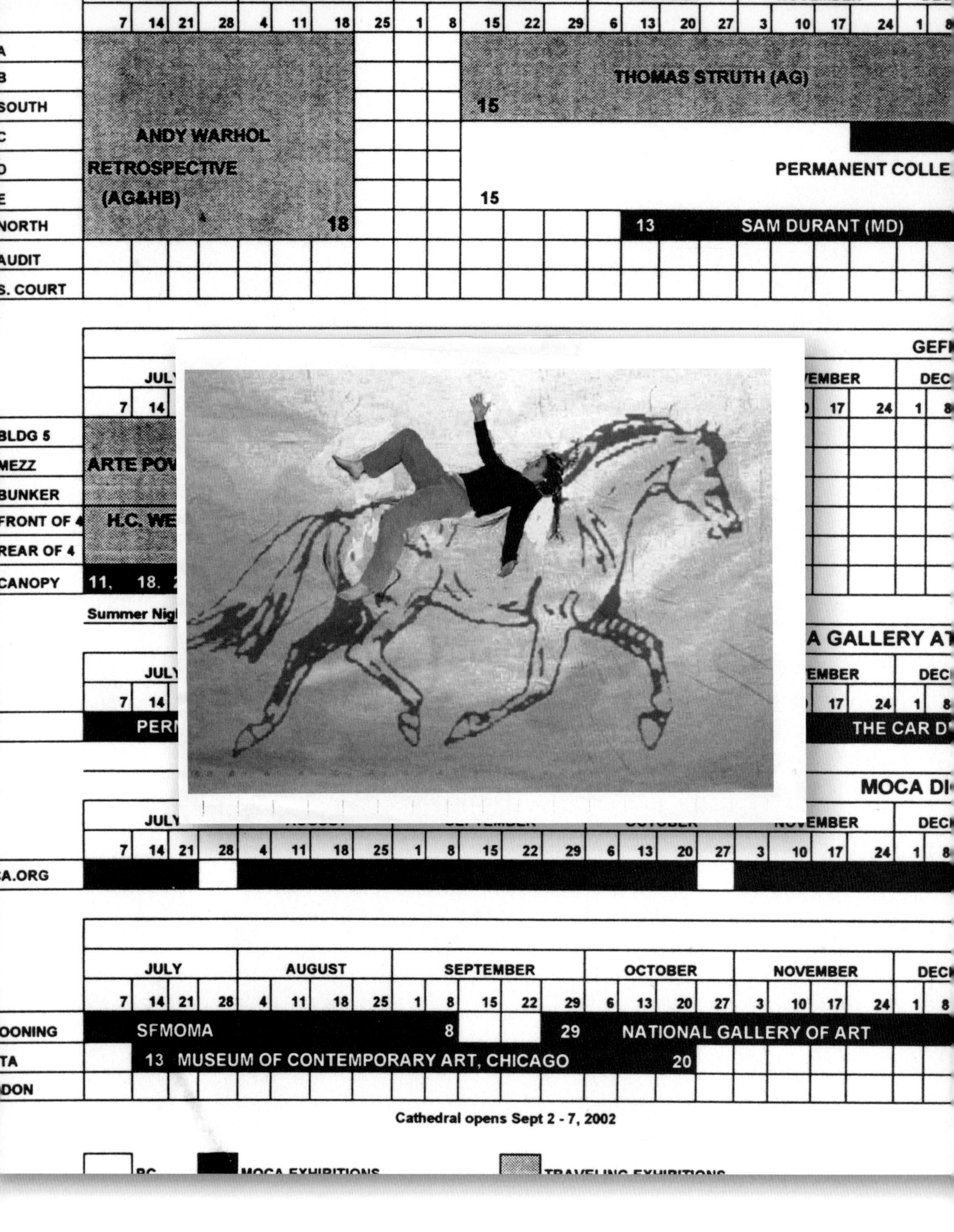

Foreground: Research material, 2003
344 Background: Exhibition schedule draft, Museum of Contemporary Art, Los Angeles, 2002

LUCIAN FREUD (PS & RM)

5   9   25

O CATTELAN (AR)   **GALLERIES AND DATES TO BE DETERMINED**

9   16   **LAURA OWENS (PS)**   22

EMPORARY

JANUAR

29   5   12

CIFIC DES

JANUAR

29   5   12

J MAYS (BH

ALLERY

JANUAR

29   5   12

CTION

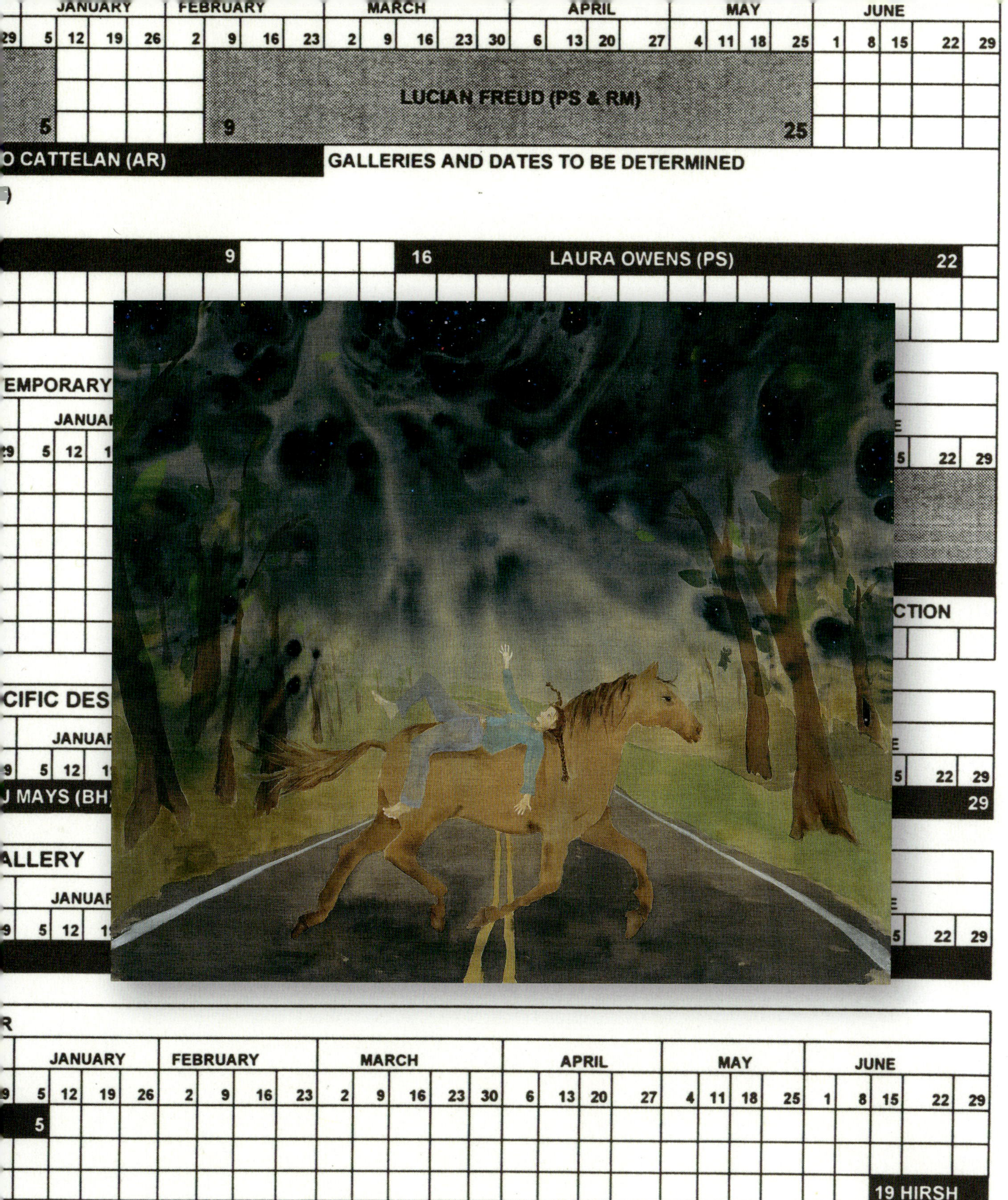

5

19 HIRSH

L.A. Auto Show 1st week Jan 2003

Foreground: *Untitled*, 2003, acrylic and oil on linen, 84 × 90 in. (213.4 × 228.6 cm)

LAURA OWENS

Pick up List· JAN 9 2003 –
morning?

① · 84" × 80"

② Blum

③ 24"

④ 42"

⑤ 77"

⑥ 77"

⑦ 77"

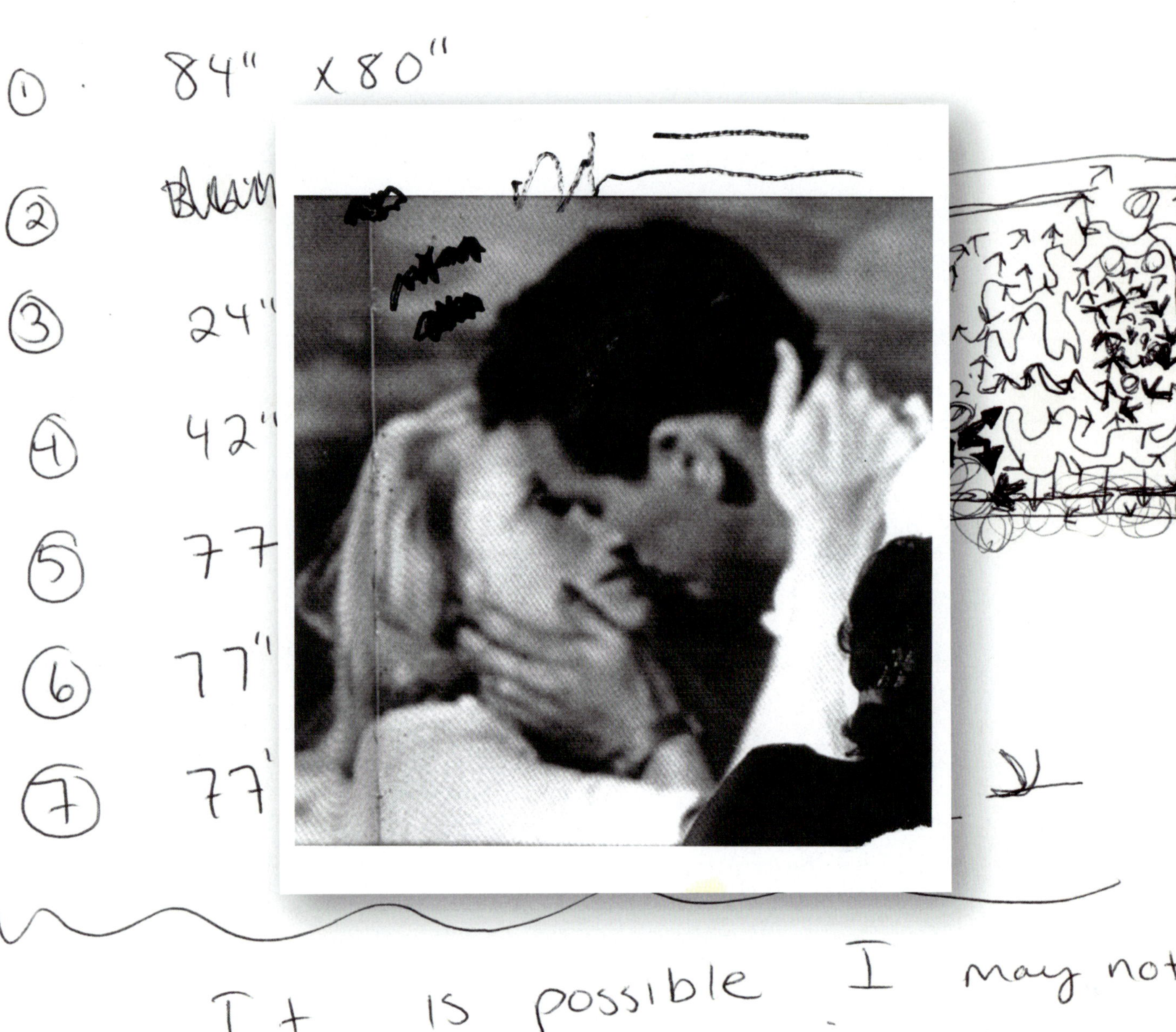

It is possible I may not
finish #6 or #7 in time.

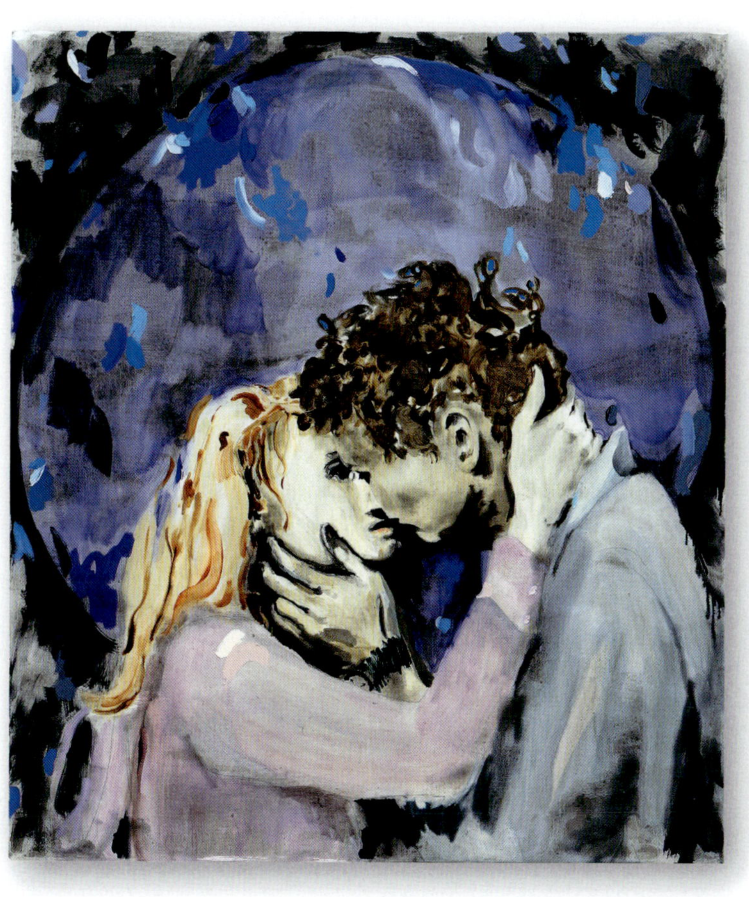

Untitled, 2003, acrylic and oil on linen, 42 × 36 in. (106.7 × 91.4 cm)

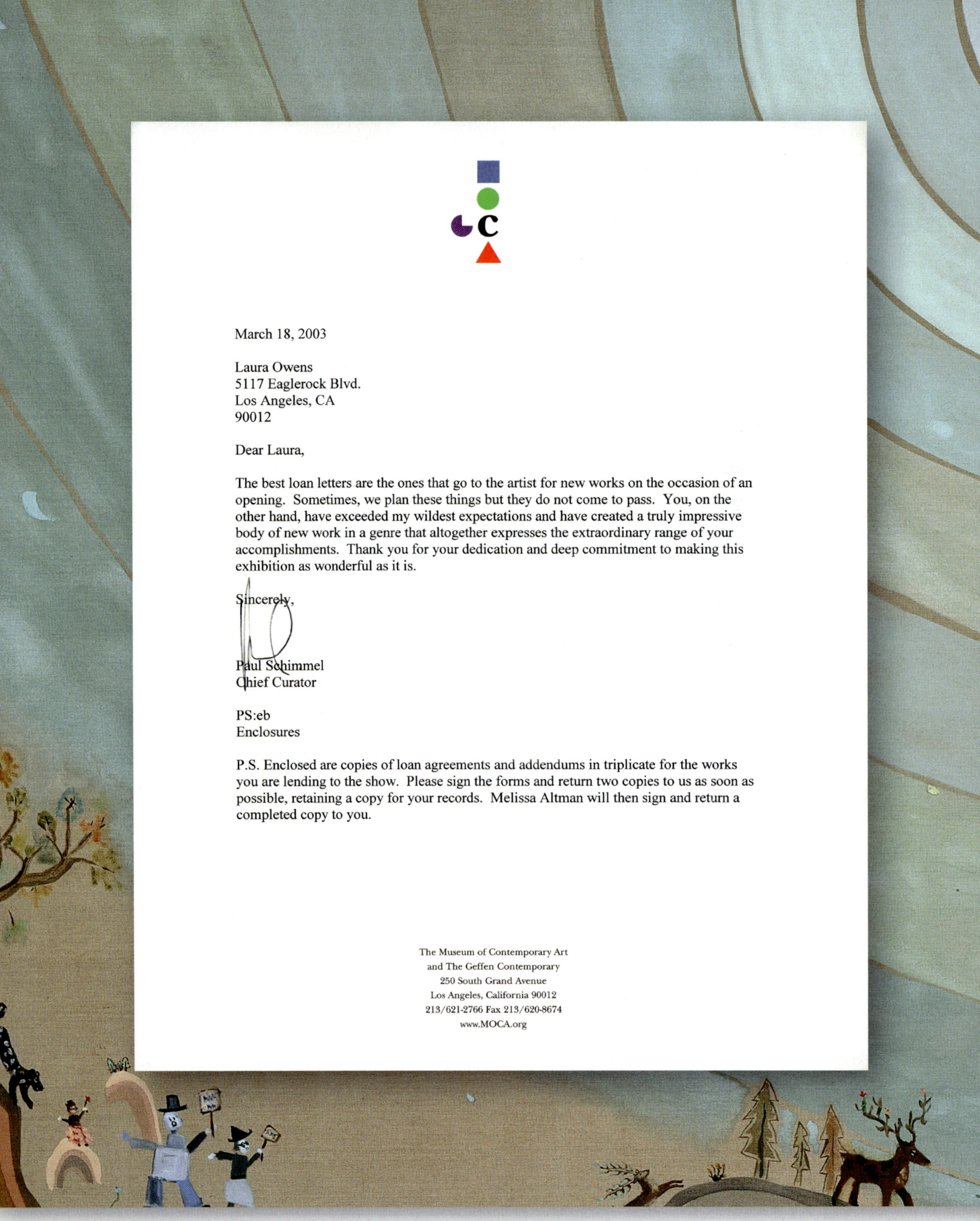

March 18, 2003

Laura Owens
5117 Eaglerock Blvd.
Los Angeles, CA
90012

Dear Laura,

The best loan letters are the ones that go to the artist for new works on the occasion of an opening. Sometimes, we plan these things but they do not come to pass. You, on the other hand, have exceeded my wildest expectations and have created a truly impressive body of new work in a genre that altogether expresses the extraordinary range of your accomplishments. Thank you for your dedication and deep commitment to making this exhibition as wonderful as it is.

Sincerely,

Paul Schimmel
Chief Curator

PS:eb
Enclosures

P.S. Enclosed are copies of loan agreements and addendums in triplicate for the works you are lending to the show. Please sign the forms and return two copies to us as soon as possible, retaining a copy for your records. Melissa Altman will then sign and return a completed copy to you.

The Museum of Contemporary Art
and The Geffen Contemporary
250 South Grand Avenue
Los Angeles, California 90012
213/621-2766 Fax 213/620-8674
www.MOCA.org

Foreground: Letter from Paul Schimmel, 2003
Background: Detail of *Untitled*, 2003 (see p. 349)

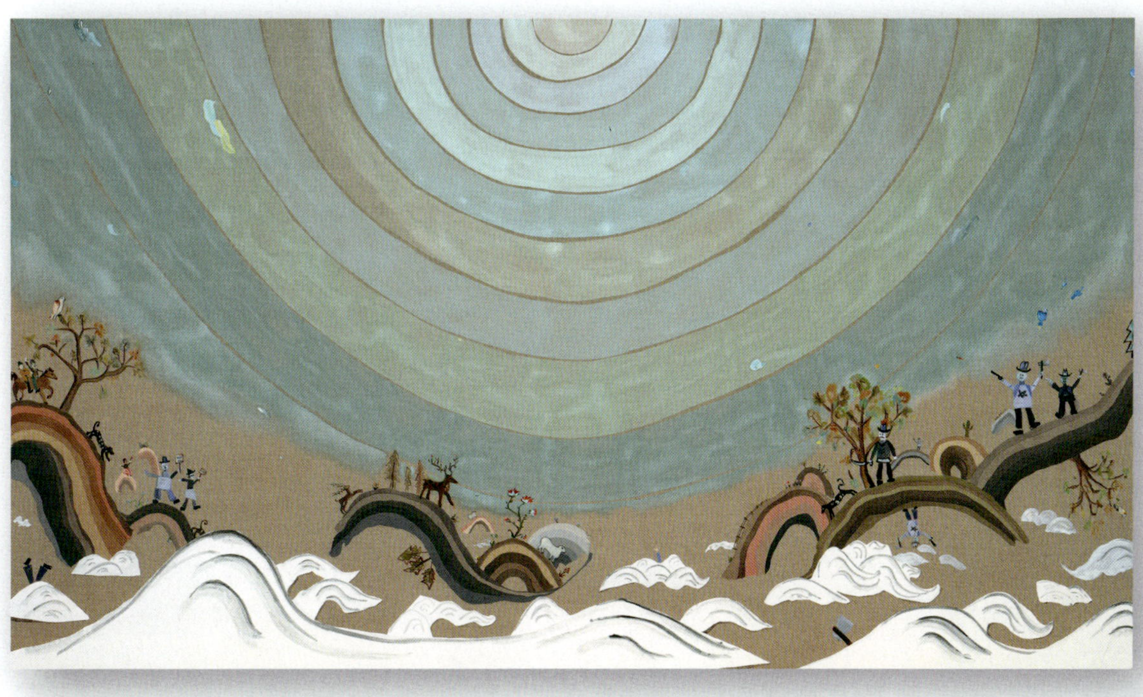

Untitled, 2003, acrylic and oil on linen, 111 × 189 in. (281.9 × 480.1 cm)

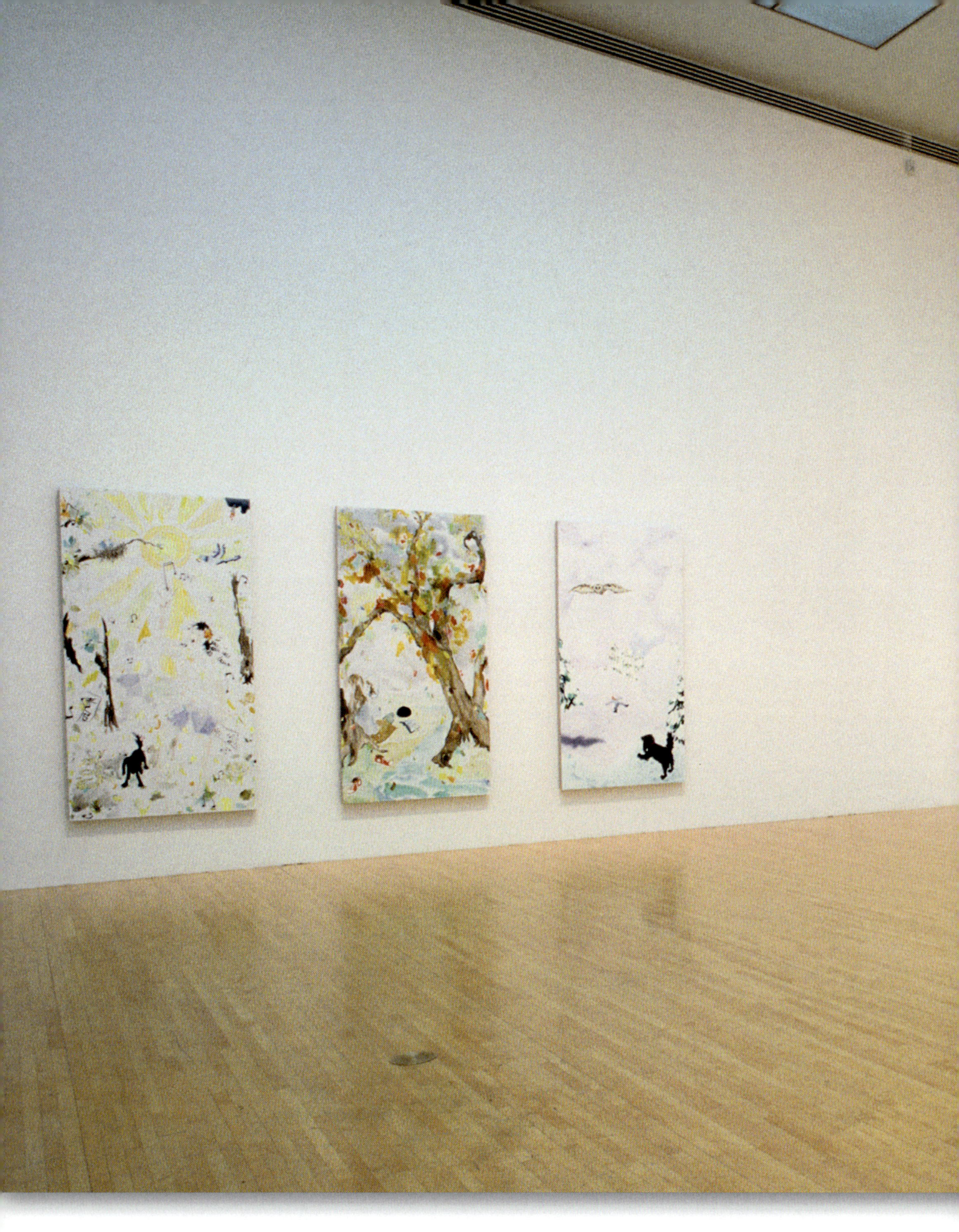

Installation view, Museum of Contemporary Art, Los Angeles, 2003, with *Untitled*, 2003, acrylic and oil on linen, three panels: 77 × 38 in. (195.6 × 96.5 cm) each; *Untitled*, 2003 (see p. 349); *Untitled*, 2003, acrylic and oil on linen, 34 × 36 in. (86.4 × 91.4 cm); and *Untitled*, 2003 (see p. 342)

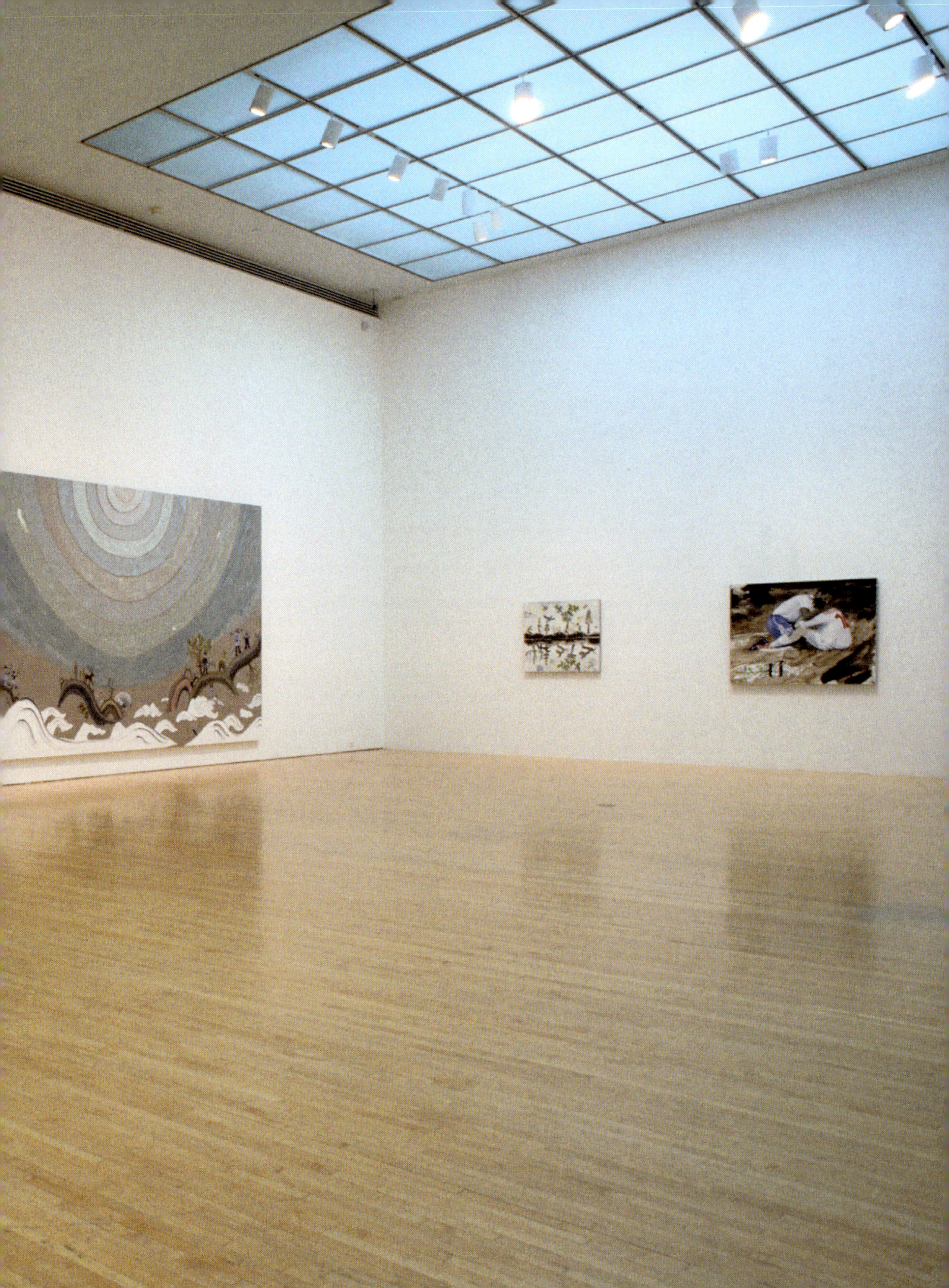

S A M M L U N G   G O E T Z

Oberföhringer Str. 103 81925 München Tel.: 089/95939690 Fax: 089/959396969

F A X

An:	Museum of Contemporary Art
z. Hd.:	Melissa Altman
Fax-Nr.:	001-213-6208674
Datum:	17.10.2002
Seiten:	1 incl. Deckblatt
Betreff:	Laura Owens

Dear Melissa,

Miss Goetz has received the loan request signed by Paul Schimmel for the works by Laura Owens from her collection.

As a matter of fact we have had some earlier inquiries about possible loans from gallerists of Laura Owens, but something was never really clear, so we have promised already two of her works for an important painting exhibition at Kunstmuseum Wolfsburg from February to End of May 2003.

These two works are both from 1999, LO 113 (the black grid over variations of blue), and a work I do not have a LO number but is the large grey grid -fence - structure with a few green weeds and some insects - a very minimal structure on white ground.

Two other works LO 174d and LO 149d are recently on loan to the Moma Queens till End of January. All other works are free for your exhibition but we would require a climate controlled loan crate for LO 167 and a consolidated colimate controlled loan crate for all the other smaller ones.

Are you still interested in lending these? Please confirm and I would process our loan-agreement, we are working exclusively with, including insurance over our insurance partner - AXA.

Best Rainald Schumacher

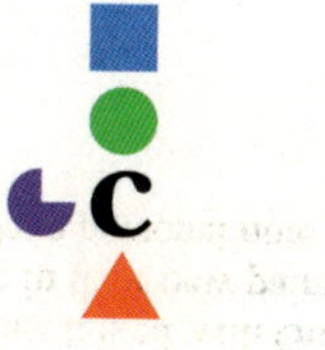

October 23, 2002

Laura Owens
5117 Eaglerock Blvd.
Los Angeles, CA
90012

Gavin Brown
Gavin Brown's Enterprise, Corp.
436 W15th St
New York, NY 10011

Dear Laura,
Dear Gavin,

This is quite a problem. I am surprised that Wolfsburg acted preemptively since they knew of our exhibition. When I had last talked with Guys about her work they had not even decided if Laura was going to be in their new painting exhibition. I think if Mrs. Goetz is to change her mind it will take a personal note from both of you, especially Laura.

Sincerely,

Paul Schimmel
Chief Curator

PS:eb

Enclosure

The Museum of Contemporary Art
The Geffen Contemporary
The MOCA Gallery at the Pacific Design Center
250 South Grand Avenue
Los Angeles, California 90012
213/621-2766 Fax 213/620-8674
www.MOCA.org

354   Installation view, Museum of Contemporary Art, Los Angeles, 2003, with *Untitled*, 1999 (see p. 254), and *Untitled*, 2000 (see p. 290)

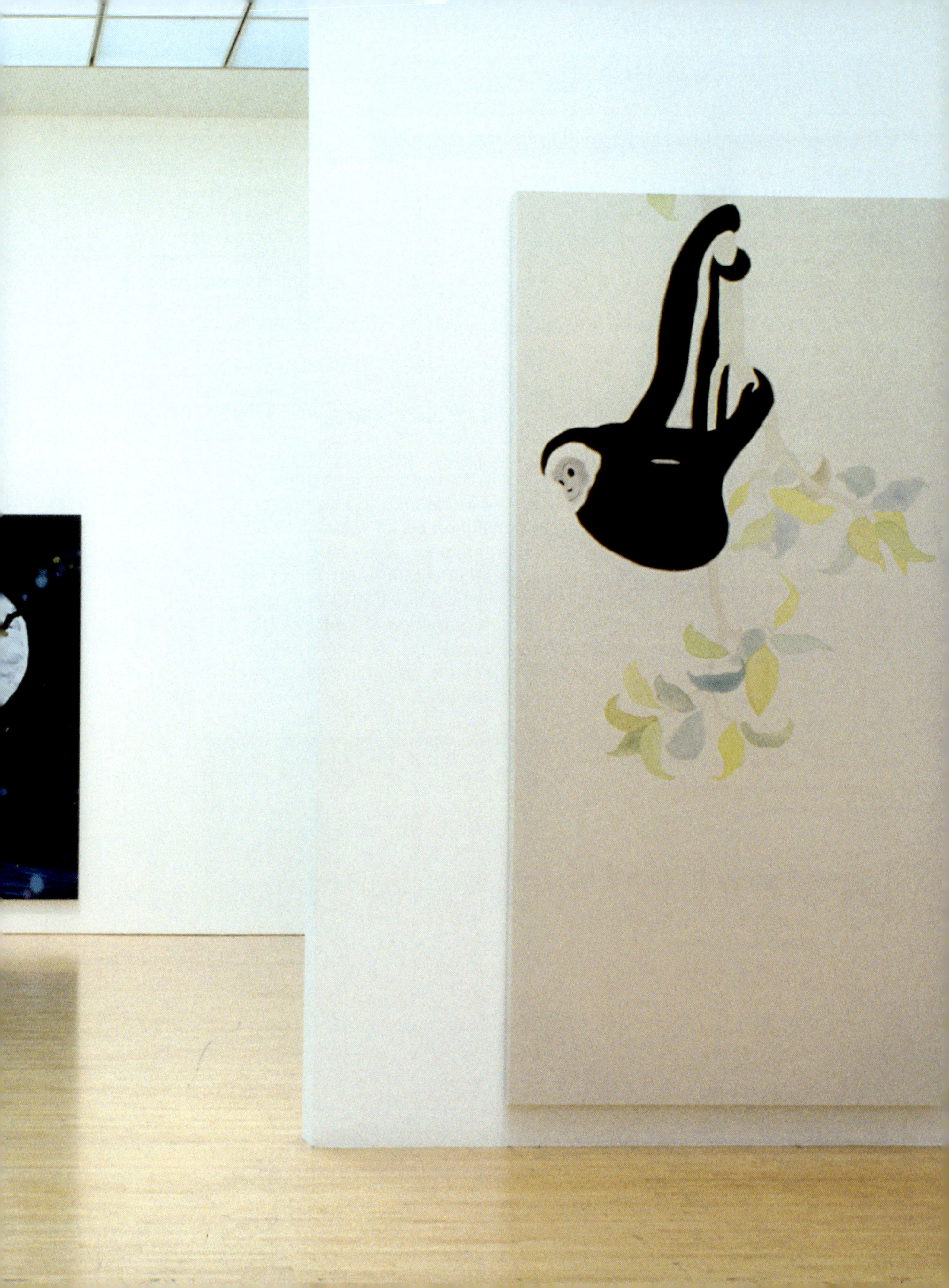

Name	Party	Decline
Aberle, Matt & Scott Cutler	2	Armstrong, Richard
Alexander, Mary & Alfrida King	2	Bilger, Arthur
Burton, Betye & Elizabeth Algermissen	2	Bryant, Don
Byrne, Blake & guest	2	Dictrow, Joel
Capitan, Gisela	1	Einstein, Mandy
Cohen, Arthur Jeanne	2	Eisenberg, Rebecca
Cypres, Kathi & Gary	2	Gersh, David
Eastman, Mari & Charles Irvin	2	Heilman, Mary
Gross, Jennifer	1	Lovelace, Lillian
Guenzani, Claudio	2	Potter, Brenda
Handle, Carl & Mika Yoshitake	2	Shaye, Bob
Hendrickson, Carol & Dick	2	Hockney, David
Johnson, Paul	1	Murkoff, Eric
Kabler, Jamie		
Katzenstein, Rannee		Toby
Lawson, Tomas & Susan		il
Maier-Aichen, Florian		
Mark, Lisa & Channing		eil
Morgan, Donald		
Nimoy, Susan & Leonard		Beth
Norris, William & Jane		udd
Owens, Laura & Edgar		
Owens, Lincoln & Aime		
Owens, Lisa		
Reeder, Scott & Alisha		
Regen, Shaun		
Roach, Dennis & Stephanie	2	
Schimmel, Paul & Yvonne	2	
Schorr, Lenore & Herbert	2	
Schwartz, Sam & Shanit	2	
Siegel, Mark & Christina Slawson	2	
Siegel, Rebecca & Emily	2	
Simchowitz, Jennifer	1	
Sobel, Dean	1	
Sommers, Randy & Robert Gunderman	2	
Soros, Jeffrey & Catharine	2	
Strick, Jeremy & Wendy	2	
Thomson, Mungo & Kerri Tribe	2	
Tuttle, Bob	1	
Weintraub, Richard and Liane	2	
Whipple, Sarah & Rhan Small	2	
Winter, Jeffrey	1	
Woods, Laura Lee & Bob	2	
Total	76	

9 LAURA OWENS Owens's current show at the Los Angeles Museum of Contemporary Art is full of invention and affection. At yet another panel on painting a few years ago, Owens responded to a question about what direction the medium might take by quoting KRS-One, who responded to a similar question, "Where is hip-hop going?" with "You all *are* hip-hop. Where are *you* going?" In Owens's case I'm happy to follow, just to see what's going to happen.

Tom
Donald

Foreground: Dave Muller, "Top Ten." *Artforum* 41, no. 10, Summer 2003
Background: RSVP list, Museum of Contemporary Art, Los Angeles, 2003

Ms. Owens,

Sorry this note has been delayed. We sent it to your old address and it was returned to us.

CALARTS
STUDIES · DANCE · FILM/VIDEO · MUSIC · THEATER

California Institute of the Arts
24700 McBean Parkway
Valencia, California 91355-2397

661 253 7820 tel
661 254 8352 fax
www.calarts.edu

Laura Owens
5121 Eagle Rock Boulevard
Los Angeles, California 90041

Dear Laura,

Congratulations on your beautiful show at MOCA. I looked for you at the opening--Leslie Dick described your beige coat and your red high-heeled shoes, which shouldn't have been difficult to miss--but I still missed you. Rarely do I leave a show thinking that I want to live with one of the works, but I felt that way about a great number of paintings. I hope I'll have the opportunity to express my admiration to you in person in the not-too-distant future.

Again, congratulations.

Sincerely yours,

Steven D. Lavine
President

SDL/jsm

Foreground: Letter from Steven D. Lavine, 2003
Background: Banner, Museum of Contemporary Art, Los Angeles, 2003

The work I want to make....

feeling unsupported in the actual making of it.

 The technical capibilities.
I am unable technically to do some of the things I wish to...

Studio size and setup is a constraint
Some equipment is not sufficient
i.e. projector,

I am unable to work some things because I am not technically that proficient
photoshop
computer stuff
projecting can not be done alone or with out someone who is pretty good at it.

The material and logistical problems. A lot of which I have a hard time figuring out by mys
or is actually impossible for just one person to do.

An assistant. someone who works in the studio, mixing paint doing logistical studio work,

Cleaning up
Mixing paint
gesso
preparing stretchers

==========

Running errands
Foreseeing problems... running out of a paint, getting a linen to match existing to do
studies.
Seeing that the stretchers are too weak etc.

=======

Physically I am incapable of making approximately 50% of my paintings without help.
Mostly because they are too big and unwieldy. Or because of sanding..or other issues.

Most importantly though is time constraints.

I find most of my time managing someone to do the previous stuff and make sure it is
working out.

Also a lot of times keeping up with requests from galleries, schools, former students,
curators, studio visits, lectures, but also ....
Bills, housecleaning, managing finances, working with architect---This falls under a larger
category of How In The Long Term Do I Make Things Bettter.
Looking for a building to buy. Thinking about moving to the Desert... these are all things I
spend time on because I think it will somehow make things easier in the category of "Makii

Paintings, thinking of Artworks, thinking about large Projects,,,, will be more relaxed and better if my studio/setup is better and more comfortable.

2 things that are thought to make things better....
move studio closer or in home

isolate studio away from big city/ phone.

This relates also to Less REsponsibilities create more time for working on art work.

....

Feeling unsupported

Feeling like I have to ask Edgar to help me in order to make my paintings.

This is partly because of the previous reasons.. and also because he knows a lot about my process and can easily figure out problems. Also though he is a good painter and can see how to fix or create things easily.

Feeling like anyone I hire has a long learning curve and is ultimately very hard to trust with important things... like

painting on the painting

paying bills, managing finances

communicating with colleagues and requests

These are all things ultimately I have never had luck with hiring people.

Edgar can help me with these but we are married, live together and there is a familiarity.

One idea:

Perhaps the gallery should employ and manage assistants and the studio.

an accountability

Is there a model of a business plan for an artist.

A successful example, an artist? do they have a business manager? a studio manager? where did they find these people?

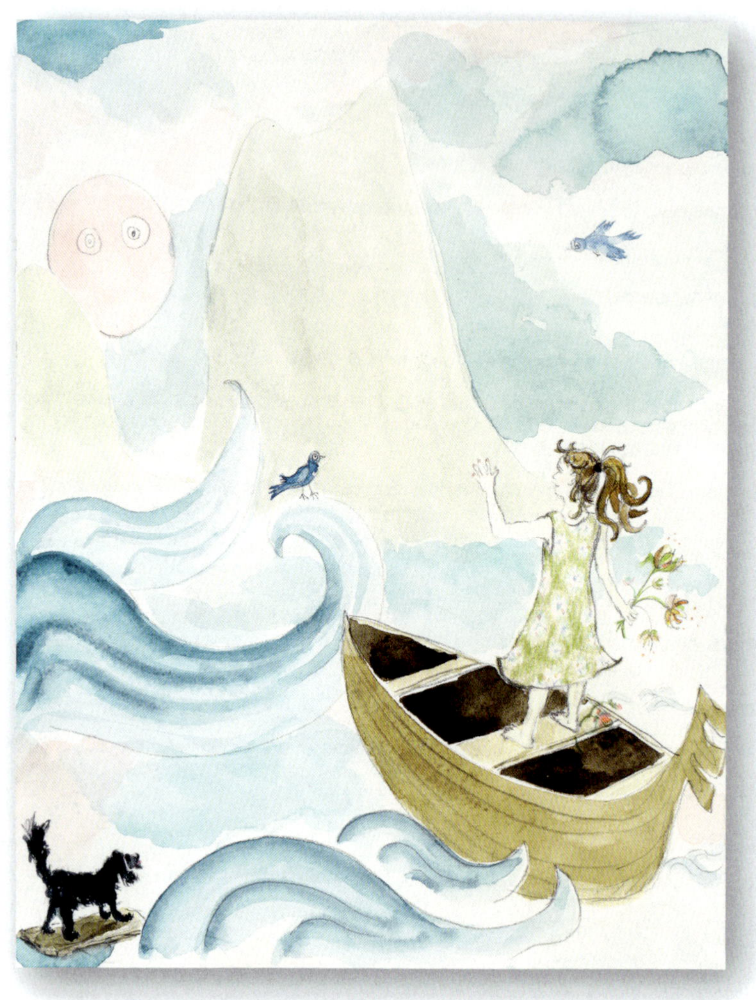

Laura Owens: Corinna Durland emailed me repeatedly to ask if I would participate in a feature in *Vogue* magazine that was to be illustrated by self-portraits by women artists. I said no several times because my work didn't really deal with self-representation, and I thought it was a leap away from what I was thinking about. But after many "please, we need you in the article" emails, I said I would try and make something. I made a watercolor of a girl on a boat talking to the sun and a bird sitting on a wave—it's ambiguous. My dog Lucy was floating on a piece of driftwood next to me. I sent the image off to *Vogue* and Anna Wintour rejected it.

360 *Untitled*, 2003, watercolor on paper, 12 × 9 in. (30.5 × 22.9 cm)

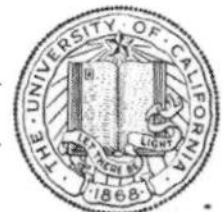

BERKELEY • DAVIS • IRVINE • LOS ANGELES • MERCED • RIVERSIDE • SAN DIEGO • SAN FRANCISCO   SANTA BARBARA • SANTA CRUZ

VISUAL ARTS DEPARTMENT 0327
(858) 534-2860
FAX: (858) 534-8651

9500 GILMAN DRIVE
LA JOLLA, CALIFORNIA 92093-0327

May 20, 2003

Laura Owens
PO Box 411902
Los Angeles, CA 90041

Dear Laura:

One of the least agreeable aspects of my job as department chair is sometimes having to deliver disappointing news. I'm writing to let you know that the department has decided to offer our studio artist position to another candidate. This search was unusually difficult for us, because all the candidates were exceptional in their different ways. Finally, though, we could only make one hire.

We thank you for your interest and for taking the time to come to meet with us here in San Diego. We were all gratified to have had the opportunity to meet you and to get to know your work better. We wish you well.

With best regards,

Susan Smith
Chair

Interview with *Laura Owens*

by Benjamin Weissman

Laura Owens is one of my favorite people alive. A truly adorable character—odd, sweet, humble, funny, super smart. The second she exited CalArts, her meteoric rise in American painting was launched, a career that's been fun to watch and cheer about. Laura's been touring the planet doing exhibitions, teaching, giving lectures, being held captive at small eccentric museums, making art under the guise of fellowship, and shaking the hands of various Counts and Countesses who find themselves unable to live without a "Laura Owens." Knees scraped, eye glasses in need of a pushback, Laura always looks like she's just fallen off a bicycle. She has big, amazing, wonder-eyes that take in double the normal dose. A face that's perpetually bewildered, stunned, and a mouth slightly ajar—these charms and countless others contribute to making her the memorable creature she is. Laura doesn't pussyfoot around—she's tough and blunt and always says what's really on her mind. A rare gift in these *if-you-don't-have-anything-nice-to-say-don't-say-it* days. I count on Laura for her candid takes on things. She has one of the best belly laughs in the world: big, messy, and out of control. When you tell her something true, yet unbelievable, she'll invariably say, "Shut up!" but it's said in a green light, tell-me-more kind of way. We conversed below via electronic mail.

Ben: To hell with the first snow question.

Laura: I liked the snow question…I am just slow. I don't know how common it is but I remember once getting about three to four feet of snow in Ohio then having a warm day where it melted about six inches then a new storm blew through that night and froze the water. Anyway, being only about 40 pounds at the time it was like walking on a frozen pond but it was all super fluffy snow underneath. I punched a few holes in the ice and dug out different sections of snow making an underground house which I was able to sit up in. I brought all my toys and moved out

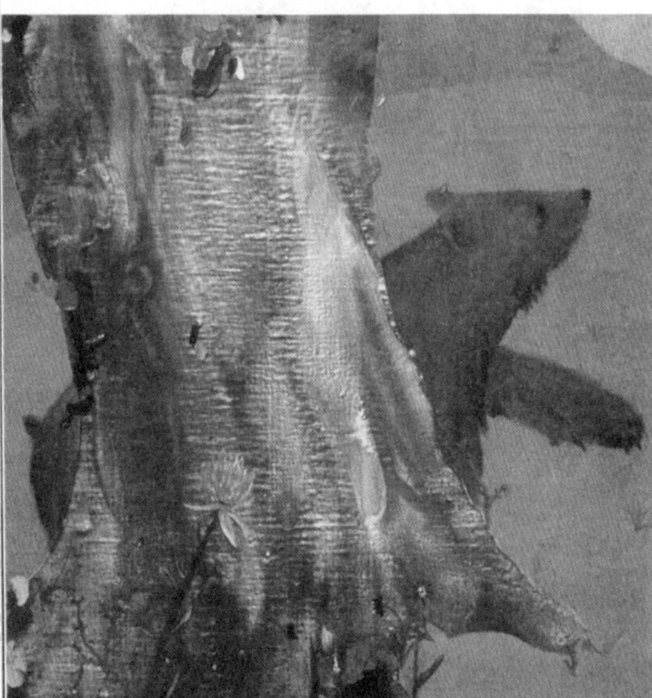

Foreground: Benjamin Weissman, "Interview with Laura Owens." *Cakewalk* 5, Winter 2003
Background: Detail of *Untitled*, 2003, acrylic and oil on canvas, 84 × 80 in. (213.4 × 203.2 cm)

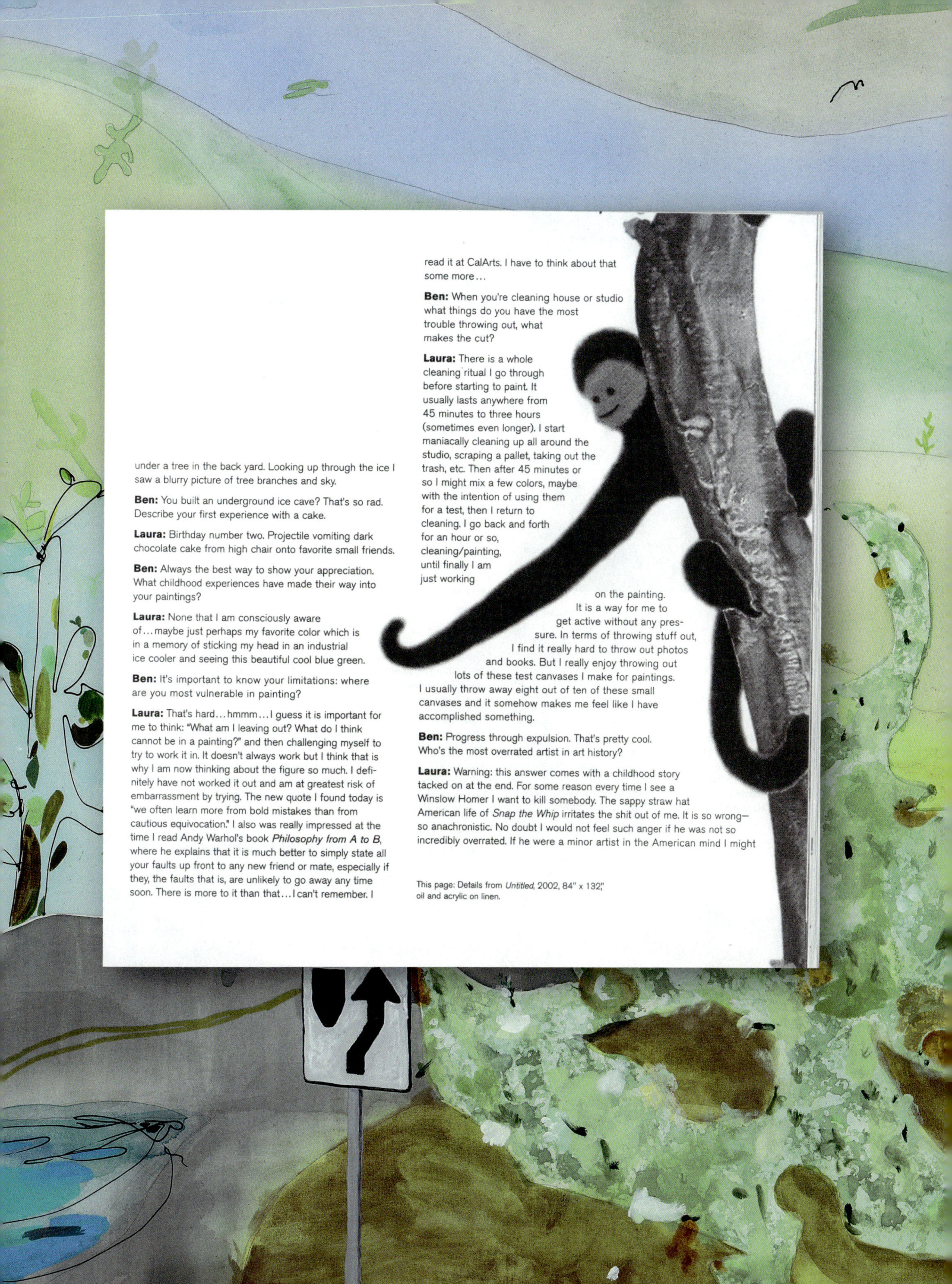

read it at CalArts. I have to think about that some more…

Ben: When you're cleaning house or studio what things do you have the most trouble throwing out, what makes the cut?

Laura: There is a whole cleaning ritual I go through before starting to paint. It usually lasts anywhere from 45 minutes to three hours (sometimes even longer). I start maniacally cleaning up all around the studio, scraping a pallet, taking out the trash, etc. Then after 45 minutes or so I might mix a few colors, maybe with the intention of using them for a test, then I return to cleaning. I go back and forth for an hour or so, cleaning/painting, until finally I am just working on the painting. It is a way for me to get active without any pressure. In terms of throwing stuff out, I find it really hard to throw out photos and books. But I really enjoy throwing out lots of these test canvases I make for paintings. I usually throw away eight out of ten of these small canvases and it somehow makes me feel like I have accomplished something.

Ben: Progress through expulsion. That's pretty cool. Who's the most overrated artist in art history?

Laura: Warning: this answer comes with a childhood story tacked on at the end. For some reason every time I see a Winslow Homer I want to kill somebody. The sappy straw hat American life of *Snap the Whip* irritates the shit out of me. It is so wrong— so anachronistic. No doubt I would not feel such anger if he was not so incredibly overrated. If he were a minor artist in the American mind I might

under a tree in the back yard. Looking up through the ice I saw a blurry picture of tree branches and sky.

Ben: You built an underground ice cave? That's so rad. Describe your first experience with a cake.

Laura: Birthday number two. Projectile vomiting dark chocolate cake from high chair onto favorite small friends.

Ben: Always the best way to show your appreciation. What childhood experiences have made their way into your paintings?

Laura: None that I am consciously aware of…maybe just perhaps my favorite color which is in a memory of sticking my head in an industrial ice cooler and seeing this beautiful cool blue green.

Ben: It's important to know your limitations: where are you most vulnerable in painting?

Laura: That's hard…hmmm…I guess it is important for me to think: "What am I leaving out? What do I think cannot be in a painting?" and then challenging myself to try to work it in. It doesn't always work but I think that is why I am now thinking about the figure so much. I definitely have not worked it out and am at greatest risk of embarrassment by trying. The new quote I found today is "we often learn more from bold mistakes than from cautious equivocation." I also was really impressed at the time I read Andy Warhol's book *Philosophy from A to B*, where he explains that it is much better to simply state all your faults up front to any new friend or mate, especially if they, the faults that is, are unlikely to go away any time soon. There is more to it than that…I can't remember. I

This page: Details from *Untitled*, 2002, 84" x 132," oil and acrylic on linen.

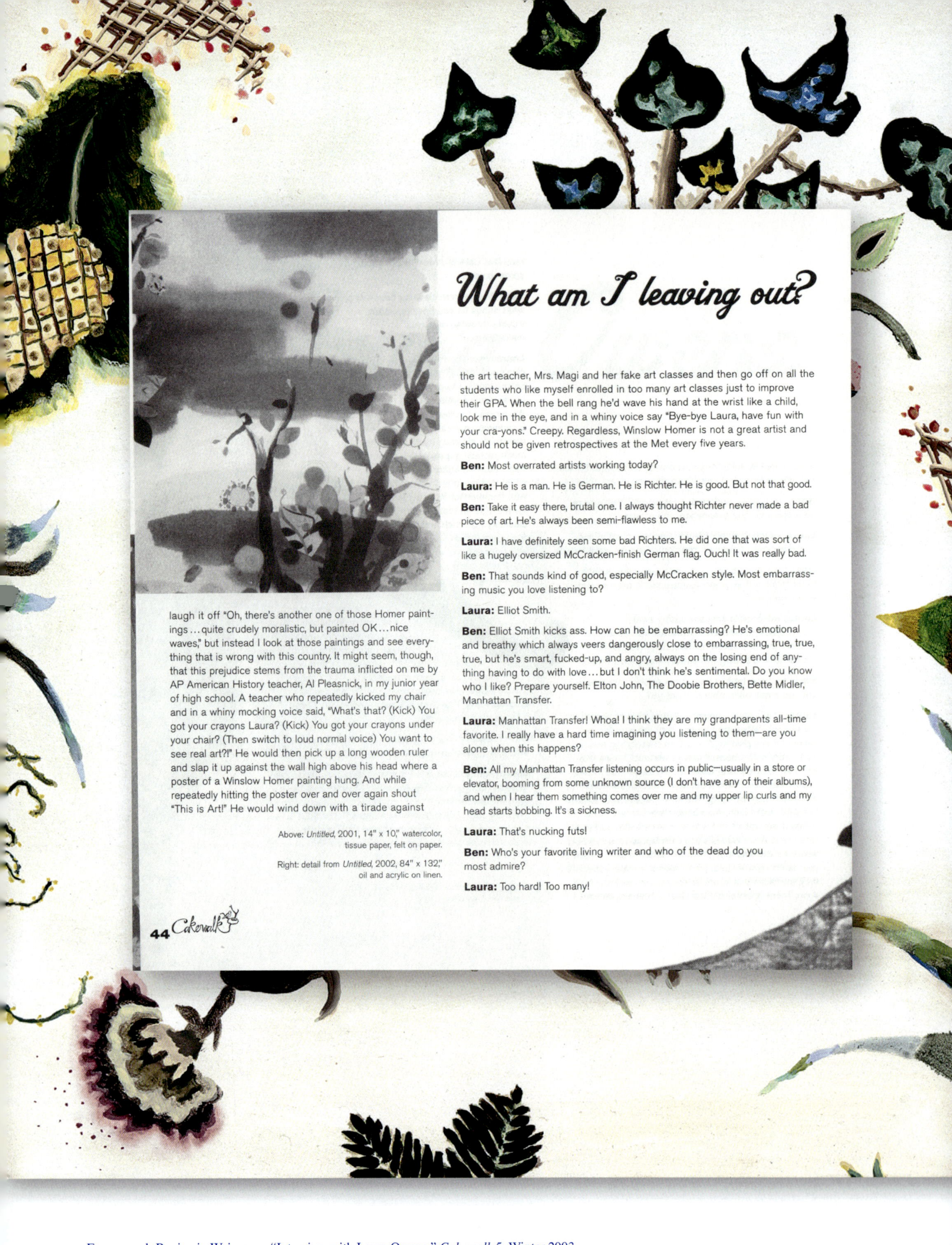

What am I leaving out?

the art teacher, Mrs. Magi and her fake art classes and then go off on all the students who like myself enrolled in too many art classes just to improve their GPA. When the bell rang he'd wave his hand at the wrist like a child, look me in the eye, and in a whiny voice say "Bye-bye Laura, have fun with your cra-yons." Creepy. Regardless, Winslow Homer is not a great artist and should not be given retrospectives at the Met every five years.

Ben: Most overrated artists working today?

Laura: He is a man. He is German. He is Richter. He is good. But not that good.

Ben: Take it easy there, brutal one. I always thought Richter never made a bad piece of art. He's always been semi-flawless to me.

Laura: I have definitely seen some bad Richters. He did one that was sort of like a hugely oversized McCracken-finish German flag. Ouch! It was really bad.

Ben: That sounds kind of good, especially McCracken style. Most embarrassing music you love listening to?

Laura: Elliot Smith.

Ben: Elliot Smith kicks ass. How can he be embarrassing? He's emotional and breathy which always veers dangerously close to embarrassing, true, true, true, but he's smart, fucked-up, and angry, always on the losing end of anything having to do with love…but I don't think he's sentimental. Do you know who I like? Prepare yourself. Elton John, The Doobie Brothers, Bette Midler, Manhattan Transfer.

Laura: Manhattan Transfer! Whoa! I think they are my grandparents all-time favorite. I really have a hard time imagining you listening to them—are you alone when this happens?

Ben: All my Manhattan Transfer listening occurs in public—usually in a store or elevator, booming from some unknown source (I don't have any of their albums), and when I hear them something comes over me and my upper lip curls and my head starts bobbing. It's a sickness.

Laura: That's nucking futs!

Ben: Who's your favorite living writer and who of the dead do you most admire?

Laura: Too hard! Too many!

laugh it off "Oh, there's another one of those Homer paintings…quite crudely moralistic, but painted OK…nice waves," but instead I look at those paintings and see everything that is wrong with this country. It might seem, though, that this prejudice stems from the trauma inflicted on me by AP American History teacher, Al Pleasnick, in my junior year of high school. A teacher who repeatedly kicked my chair and in a whiny mocking voice said, "What's that? (Kick) You got your crayons Laura? (Kick) You got your crayons under your chair? (Then switch to loud normal voice) You want to see real art?!" He would then pick up a long wooden ruler and slap it up against the wall high above his head where a poster of a Winslow Homer painting hung. And while repeatedly hitting the poster over and over again shout "This is Art!" He would wind down with a tirade against

Above: *Untitled*, 2001, 14" x 10," watercolor, tissue paper, felt on paper.

Right: detail from *Untitled*, 2002, 84" x 132," oil and acrylic on linen.

44 Cakewalk

Foreground: Benjamin Weissman, "Interview with Laura Owens." *Cakewalk* 5, Winter 2003
Background: Detail of *Untitled*, 2003, acrylic and oil on linen, 26 × 24 in. (66 × 61 cm)

What do I think cannot be in a painting?

Ben: Bad answer. You're going to think I'm a real psycho for asking you this. But what is a woman? What's it like for you to be a woman or a girl? Please explain.

Laura: This question is impossible. I have nothing to compare it to. I tried to recall all those various incarnations as men, boys, animals and insects. Kind of murky. I do think I felt a lot more solid and sure of myself pre-puberty. I am hoping that comes back after menopause. Why do women wear make-up and perfume? Because they are ugly and they smell bad. I guess that's a funny joke. Maybe not. It's hard to generalize about an entire sex. They do make babies. I think that is way cool. I love that boobs are functional. I like hour glass shaped ladies. The more curvy the better, I guess it just looks right to me. I don't know what else to say….

Ben: That's a cool answer. Remember that art collective Pleasure Function? Jenny Holzer and Dick Prince were in it, Fend, Peter Nadin? Maybe you were like 13 when this was going on. All the rage. Very socialistic. Kind of cool. Your "functional bosom" comment reminds me of them.

I want to talk about your writing. It kicks ass. What you do with written language, this fantastic blasted out imagination has similarities to your paintings. Maybe not. I'm forcing a comparison. But one can be made. Talk about your impulse to write stories.

Laura: I feel like I have a lot of stories playing in my head all the time. I also have a vague distant view of this really important story that I want

or need to write. I guess I wish I could articulate them and so writing is starting to do that. I think I have quite a ways to go though and I get sort of stuck a lot.

Ben: Let's talk about cake again. Name all the cakes you've made in your life?

Laura: Chocolate. That's the only kind I have ever made. I used to make microwave chocolate cakes when I came home after high school.

Ben: Answer this: Why do wedding cakes always suck? Shouldn't an important event require a perfect cake?

Laura: I have tasted these wedding cakes from Hansen's that were awesome. I just stopped eating sugar a couple weeks ago so I am not the best person to ask. Food rituals seem like they are pretty ancient. I am into barbecues.

Drain my blood and

Ben: I concur. Marinated animals sizzling on a grill is a beautiful thing. As far as cakewalks go, talk about walking the cake, describe a personal cakewalk, when has it been too easy for you?

Laura: Sadly, I am too neurotic to let anything be too easy. I try though.

Ben: What's the most useful thing you've learned about painting in the last two years?

Laura: It takes exactly six times the amount of time you think it takes to do anything. Realizing this made me have less anxiety and be more patient.

Ben: What's the worst thing about sex?

Laura: I guess the worst is when you feel like no one will ever want to have sex with you for the rest of your life.

Ben: Is there one part of your body that amuses you more than another?

Laura: I am trying to get into my body. I think I have been floating about three feet above for quite sometime. Bumping into things a lot, not good.

Ben: Please explain why video installation art is so deep and cool and exciting and speaks to core of who we are as knuckle-walking beasts?

Laura: Huh?

Ben: Exactly. You and I were once talking about a certain some-one's vacant video work and you said the funniest, most graphic thing I've ever heard. You said, "Drain my blood and burn it."

Laura: Yeah, I guess I didn't like it very much.

Ben: Yeah, just a little. Let's continue on. What historical event rocked your world the most?

Laura: The Northridge earthquake happened my last semester of grad school. I was pretty sure the building I was in was going to fall over. It didn't. But I stopped worrying about making art so much and just made stuff I liked and wanted to see.

Ben: That is gnarly. Do you have any recurrent nightmares?

Laura: Nope.

Ben: Lucky you. What's cool about Ohio?

Laura: I have no idea. I haven't been there in so long. I am sure there is something cool about it now. When I was younger there were a lot of clubs and thrift stores in Cleveland that were cool.

Ben: What's the most ghoulish thing a collector ever said to you?

Laura: Someone once very early on brought over two collectors to my studio who came over and walked around the perimeter looking at stuff, whispering to each other and then walked outside and never said a word.

Ben: That's not polite. Did you smack them?

Laura: I kicked them.

Detail from *Untitled*, 2002, 84" x 132," oil and acrylic on linen.

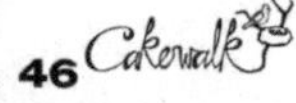

46 *Cakewalk*

Foreground: Benjamin Weissman, "Interview with Laura Owens." *Cakewalk* 5, Winter 2003
Background: Detail of *Untitled*, 2003 (see p. 350)

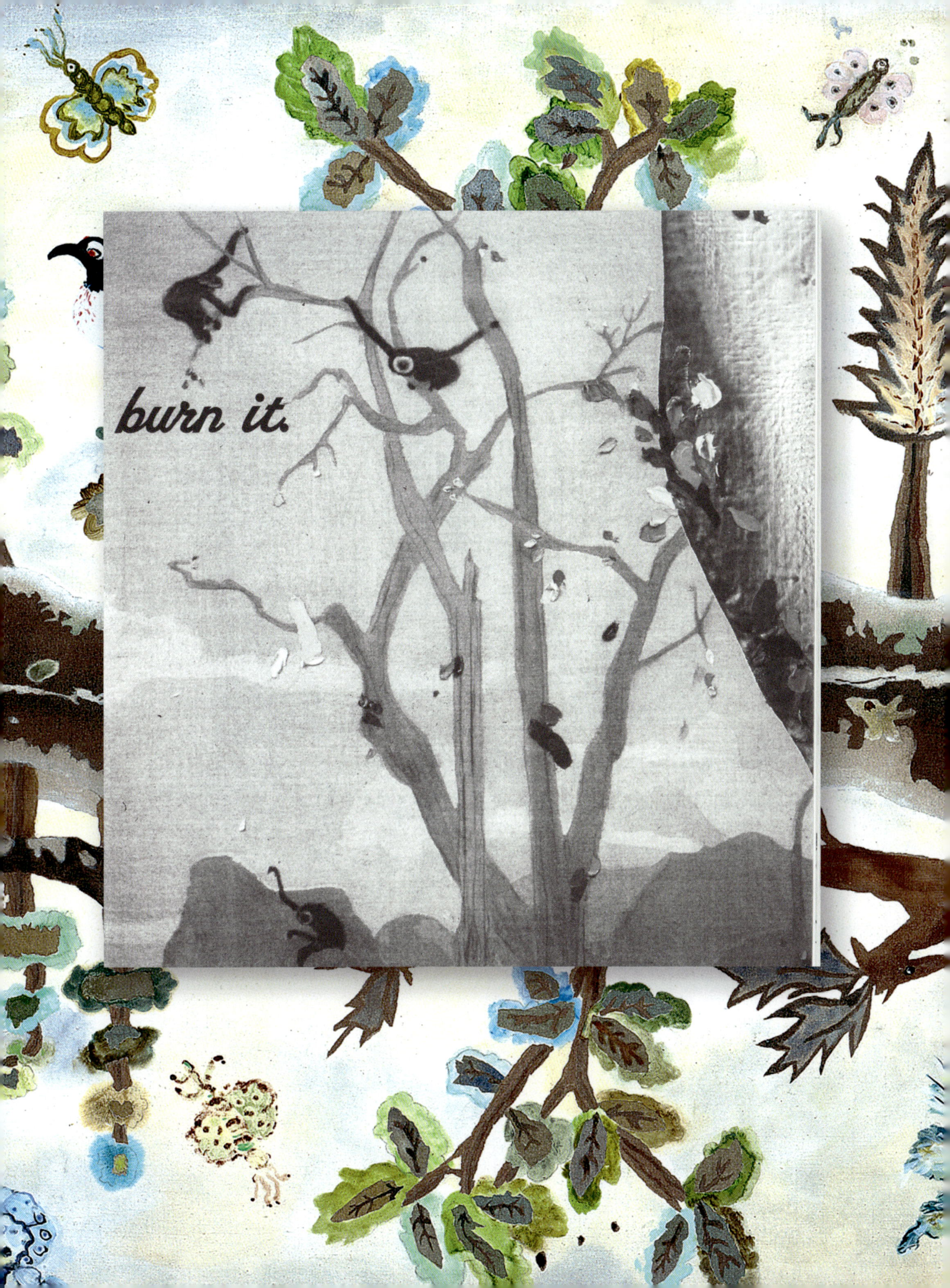

burn it.

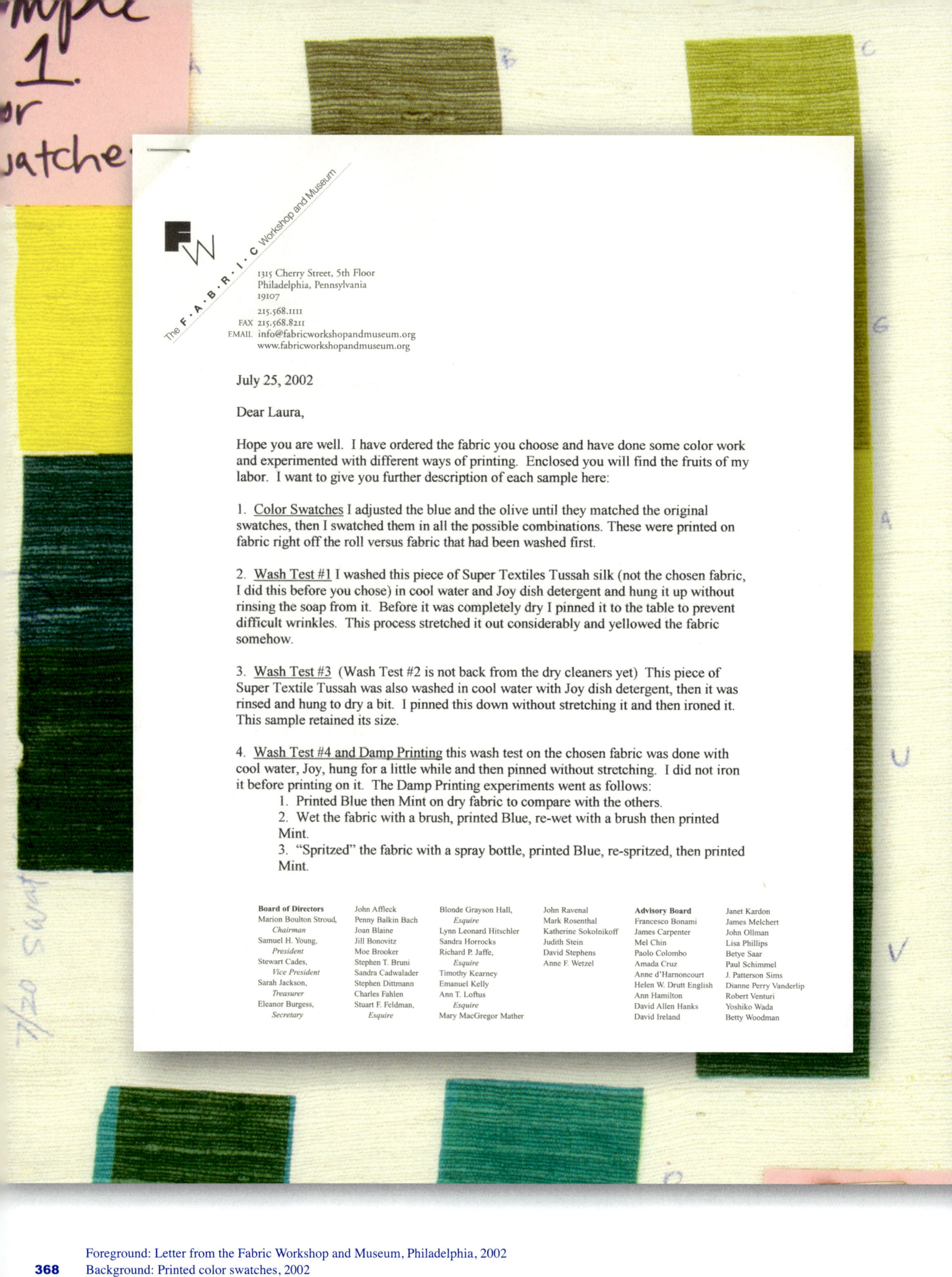

The **F·A·B·R·I·C** Workshop and Museum

1315 Cherry Street, 5th Floor
Philadelphia, Pennsylvania
19107

215.568.1111
FAX 215.568.8211
EMAIL info@fabricworkshopandmuseum.org
www.fabricworkshopandmuseum.org

July 25, 2002

Dear Laura,

Hope you are well. I have ordered the fabric you choose and have done some color work and experimented with different ways of printing. Enclosed you will find the fruits of my labor. I want to give you further description of each sample here:

1. <u>Color Swatches</u> I adjusted the blue and the olive until they matched the original swatches, then I swatched them in all the possible combinations. These were printed on fabric right off the roll versus fabric that had been washed first.

2. <u>Wash Test #1</u> I washed this piece of Super Textiles Tussah silk (not the chosen fabric, I did this before you chose) in cool water and Joy dish detergent and hung it up without rinsing the soap from it. Before it was completely dry I pinned it to the table to prevent difficult wrinkles. This process stretched it out considerably and yellowed the fabric somehow.

3. <u>Wash Test #3</u> (Wash Test #2 is not back from the dry cleaners yet) This piece of Super Textile Tussah was also washed in cool water with Joy dish detergent, then it was rinsed and hung to dry a bit. I pinned this down without stretching it and then ironed it. This sample retained its size.

4. <u>Wash Test #4 and Damp Printing</u> this wash test on the chosen fabric was done with cool water, Joy, hung for a little while and then pinned without stretching. I did not iron it before printing on it. The Damp Printing experiments went as follows:
    1. Printed Blue then Mint on dry fabric to compare with the others.
    2. Wet the fabric with a brush, printed Blue, re-wet with a brush then printed Mint.
    3. "Spritzed" the fabric with a spray bottle, printed Blue, re-spritzed, then printed Mint.

Foreground: Letter from the Fabric Workshop and Museum, Philadelphia, 2002
Background: Printed color swatches, 2002

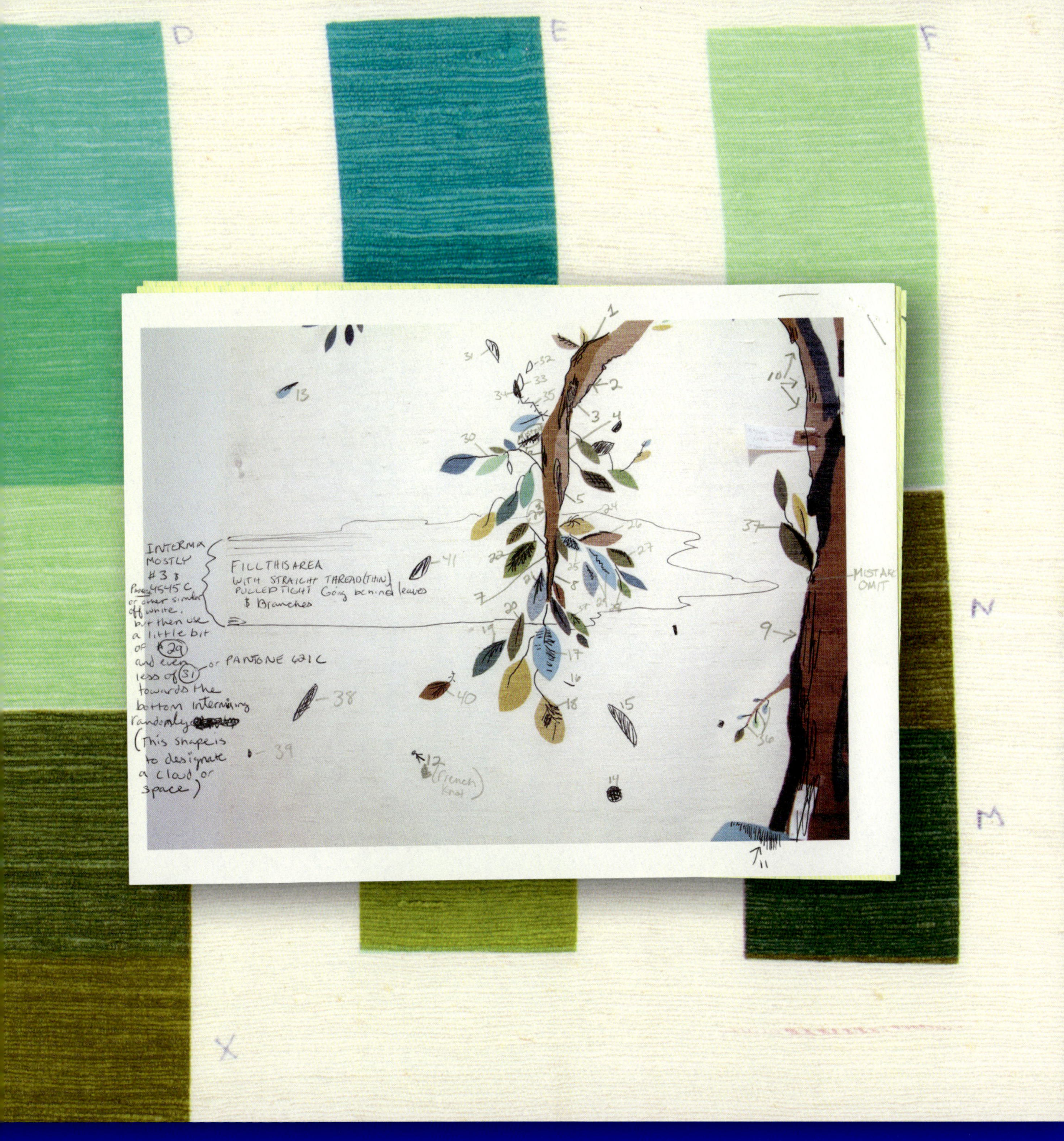

Foreground: Preparatory drawing, 2002

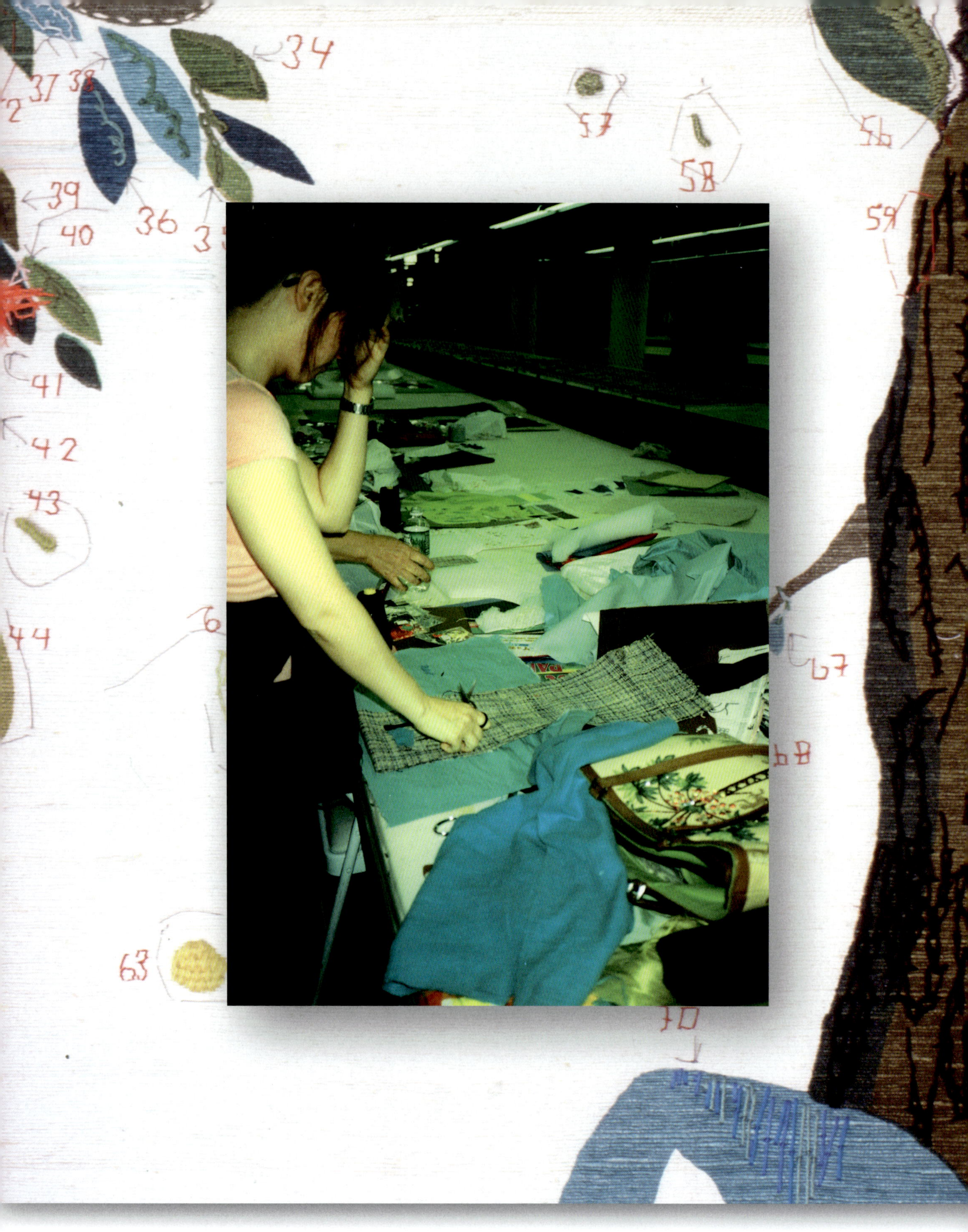

Foreground: Owens, Fabric Workshop and Museum, Philadelphia, 2002
Background: Preparatory fabric swatch, 2002

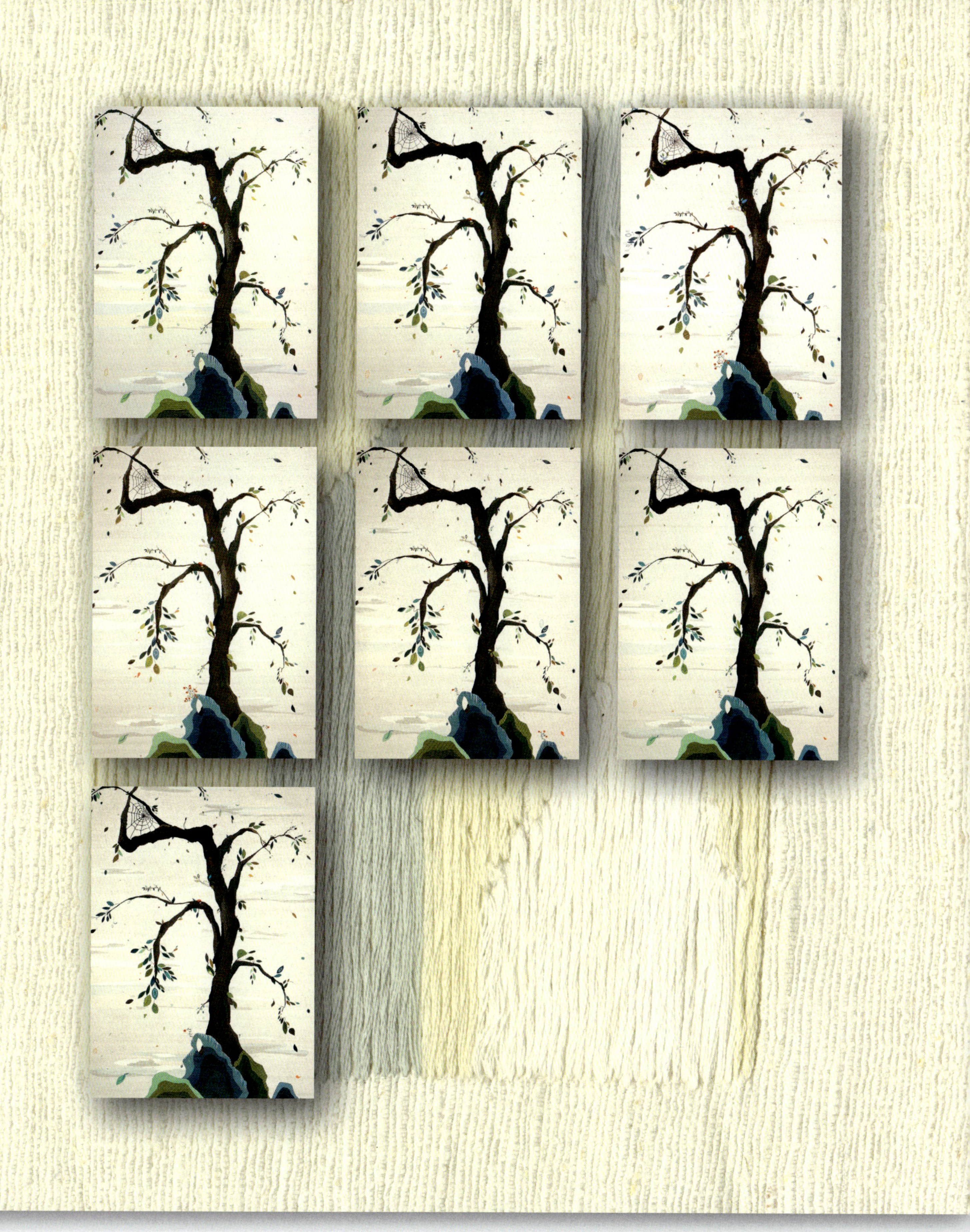

THE CREATION OF FEMININITY
ROZSIKA PARKER

Needlework is the favourite hobby of two percent of British males, about equal to the number who go to church regularly. Nearly one man in three fills in football coupons, in an average month, or has a bet.[1]

The Guardian was no doubt confident that its coverage of a Government survey of changing trends in leisure activities was eye-catching, and that this opening sentence was guaranteed to amuse by its incongruity. The unspoken assumption implied by the juxtaposition of male needleworkers and churchgoers is that these men are pious, prim and conformist. Real men gamble and fill in football coupons; only sissies and women sew and swell congregations.

The sexual division that assigns women to sewing is inscribed in our social institutions, fostered by school curricula which still direct boys to carpentry and girls to needlework. Even in today's progressive schools the assumptions and divisions remain intact. An enthusiastic report on a large suburban primary school praised the diligent, pioneering teaching practised by the staff. Two photographs illustrated science teaching methods: in one, a small group of boys were shown unselfconsciously engrossed in a "wave power machine"; in the other, two smiling girls displayed copper atoms embroidered in silk.[2]

The role of embroidery in advertising and commercial design also endorses the notion that a man who practises embroidery is imperilling his sexual identity. Embroidery is invariably employed to evoke the home. The cover of a brochure produced by a British home removal firm illustrates an embroidery of a house, the stock motif of so many samplers, and bears the embroidered words "Home Moving Guide." Embroidery connotes not only home but a socially advantaged home, securely placed in the upper reaches of the class structure. An advertisement for embroidery patterns promises that "the tapestries are a pleasure to make and once completed will elegantly grace any home and become much valued family heirlooms."

It is not only home and family that embroidery signifies but, specifically, mothers and daughters. Heinz based an advertising campaign for tomato ketchup on a picture of a sampler stitched with the words, "If other ketchups were as rich, then I'd say so stitch by stitch. Ann and Lucy James (but mostly Lucy)." The sampler associates tomato ketchup with the ideal of childhood as sincere, innocent and pure.

Embroidery also evokes the stereotype of the virgin in opposition to the whore, an infantilising representation of women's sexuality. Thus Lil-lets the menstrual tampons were recently packed in a box masquerading as fabric, embroidered with pastel flowers to represent menstruation as natural and entirely nonthreatening. The conflation of embroidery and female sexuality, both innately virginal and available for consumption, is blatantly expressed in the title bestowed on a porn magazine, the *Rustler Sampler,* which offered "nearly two hundred, yes, two hundred juicy, picture-packed pages." The word "Sampler" evokes an image of innumerable passive, powerless women just waiting to be selected and roped in by the "Rustler." Embroidery has become indelibly associated with stereotypes of femininity.

I shall define briefly what I mean by femininity. In *The Second Sex*, 1949, Simone de Beauvoir wrote: "It is evident that woman's 'character'—her convictions, her values, her wisdom, her morality, her tastes, her behaviour—are to be explained by her situation."[3] In other words, femininity, the behaviour expected and encouraged in women, though obviously related to the biological sex of the individual, is shaped by society. The changes in ideas about femininity that can be seen reflected in the history of embroidery are striking confirmation that femininity is a social and psychosocial product.

Originally published in *The Subversive Stitch: Embroidery and the Making of the Feminine* (1984, London; repr., New York: Routledge, 1989), 1–16. Parker was a British psychotherapist and feminist art historian.

Nevertheless, the conviction that femininity is natural to women (and unnatural in men) is tenacious. It is a crucial aspect of patriarchal ideology, sanctioning a rigid and oppressive division of labour. Thus women active in the upsurge of feminism which began in the 1960s set out to challenge accepted definitions of the innate differences between the sexes, and to provide a new understanding of the creation of femininity. In consciousness-raising groups and campaigns we compared our experiences at work, at school, at home, in relationships, as mothers, as daughters and sisters. The workings of sexism were scrutinised in the division of labour in and out of the home, in sexuality, the family, health care, child care, language, the law, education, the arts, the media and government policy. How race, class and sex intersect to shape women's lives became clearer.

Institutional discrimination co-exists and interacts with the mechanisms and effects of psychic subordination, though obviously rigid divisions cannot be drawn between internal and external oppression. The complex of emotional attitudes of passivity, submission and masochism which guarantee the subordination of women cannot simply be shrugged off or discounted. Juliet Mitchell, in *Psychoanalysis and Feminism*, 1974, observed that:

> . . . the status of woman is held in the heart and the head as well as in the home: oppression has not been trivial or historically transitory—to maintain itself so efficiently it courses through the mental and emotional bloodstream. To think that this should not be so does not necessitate pretending it is already not so.[4]

Many feminists have looked to psychoanalysis and Marxist theory to provide an account of how masculinity and femininity are constructed and reproduced historically. The family was identified as the place where the "inferiorised psychology"[5] of women was reproduced and the social and economic exploitation of women as wives and mothers legitimised. Writing of the construction of femininity in the family, anthropologist Gayle Rubin in an essay in *Towards an Anthropology of Women*, 1975, commented: "One can read Freud's essay on femininity as a description of how a group is prepared to live with oppression," and she makes clear how painful the process is. "It is certainly plausible to argue that the creation of 'femininity' in a woman in the course of socialisation is an act of psychic brutality."[6]

It is, however, important to distinguish between the construction of femininity, lived femininity, the feminine ideal and the feminine stereotype. The construction of femininity refers to the psychoanalytic and social account of sexual differentiation. Femininity is a lived identity for women either embraced or resisted. The feminine ideal is an historically changing concept of what women should be, while the feminine stereotype is a collection of attributes which is imputed to women and against which their every concern is measured. Millicent Fawcett, the nineteenth-century British feminist, declared, "We talk about 'women and women's suffrage,' we do not talk about Woman with a capital W. That we leave to our enemies."[7]

In other words, there is a significant difference between acknowledging the construction of femininity in the family and its maintenance in social institutions, and accepting the cultural representation of women imposed upon us. The feminine stereotype categorises everything women are and everything we do as entirely, essentially and eternally feminine, denying differences between women according to our economic and social position, or our geographical and historical place. In fact, what Gayle Rubin termed "the act of psychic brutality" meets with resistance at all levels, in different ways at different historical moments.

What, then, is the purpose of the feminine stereotype? In *Old Mistresses: Women, Art and Ideology*, 1981, Griselda Pollock and I looked at the role of the feminine stereotype in the writing of art history. We asked why painting by women has been set apart from painting by men and why women's art, in all its diversity, has been described as homogeneous. We revealed the feminine stereotype to be one of the major elements in the construction of the current view of the history of art.[8] The particular way women's work is presented—the constant assertion of the feminine weakness of women's art—sustains the dominance of masculinity and male art.

The situation of embroidery is more elusive. When women paint, their work is categorised as homogeneously feminine—but it is acknowledged to be art. When women embroider, it is seen not as art, but entirely as the expression of femininity. And, crucially, it is categorised as craft. The division of art forms into a hierarchical classification of arts and crafts is usually ascribed to factors of class within the economic and social system, separating artist from artisan. The fine arts—painting and sculpture—are considered the proper sphere of the privileged classes while craft or the applied arts—like furniture-making or silver-smithery—are associated with the working class. However there is an important connection between the hierarchy of the arts and the sexual categories male/female. The development of an ideology of femininity coincided historically with the emergence of a clearly defined separation of art and craft. This division emerged in the Renaissance at the time when embroidery was increasingly becoming the province of women amateurs, working for the home without pay. Still later the split between art and craft was reflected in the changes in art education from craft-based workshops to academies at precisely the time— the eighteenth century—when an ideology of femininity as natural to women was evolving.

The art/craft hierarchy suggests that art made with thread and art made with paint are intrinsically unequal: that the former is artistically less significant. But the real differences between the two are in terms of *where* they are made and *who* makes them. Embroidery, by the time of the art/craft divide, was made in the domestic sphere, usually by women, for "love." Painting was produced predominantly, though not only, by men, in the public sphere, for money. The professional branch of embroidery, unlike that of painting, was, from the end of the seventeenth century to the end of the nineteenth century, largely in the hands of working-class women, or disadvantaged middle-class women. Clearly there are huge differences between painting and embroidery; different conditions of production and different conditions of reception. But rather than acknowledging that needlework and painting are different but equal arts, embroidery and crafts associated with "the second sex" or the working class are accorded lesser artistic value.

The classification of embroidery is a difficult task. To term it "art" raises special problems. Moving embroidery several rungs up the ladder of art forms could be interpreted as simply affirming the hierarchical categorisations, rather than deconstructing them. Moreover, to describe embroidery as "art" is to fail to distinguish it from painting, concealing the profound differences that have developed historically between the two media. However, to call it "craft" is no solution. Embroidery fails to comply with the utilitarian imperative that defines craft—because much of it is purely pictorial. Traditionally, women have called embroidery "work." Although to some

extent an appropriate term, it tends to confirm the stereotypical notion that patience and perseverance go into embroidery—but little else. Moreover, the term was engendered by an ideology of femininity as service and selflessness and the insistence that women work for others, not for themselves. I have decided to call embroidery art because it is, undoubtedly, a cultural practice involving iconography, style and a social function.

That embroiderers do transform materials to produce sense—whole ranges of meanings—is invariably entirely overlooked. Instead embroidery and a stereotype of femininity have become collapsed into one another, characterised as mindless, decorative and delicate; like the icing on the cake, good to look at, adding taste and status, but devoid of significant content.

The association between women and embroidery, craft and femininity, has meant that writers concerned with the status of women have often turned their attention towards this tangled, puzzling relationship. Feminists who have scorned embroidery tend to blame it for whatever constraint on women's lives they are committed to combat. Thus, for example, eighteenth-century critical commentators held embroidery responsible for the ill health which was claimed as evidence of women's natural weakness and inferiority. In the nineteenth century, women wanting to be taken seriously in supposedly "male" spheres deliberately declared their rejection of embroidery to distance themselves from the feminine ideal. In Helen Black's late nineteenth-century publication, *Notable Authors of The Day*, 1893, consisting of interviews with novelists, Adeline Sargeant stated, "I have done some elaborate embroidery in my time but now I never use the needle for amusement, only for necessity."[9] She asserts her seriousness and her disdain for feminine frivolity. The majority of interviewees, however, stress their needlework. For although writing novels was, by then, an acceptable activity for women, professionalism was frowned upon. Women therefore covered themselves with their amateur "work." Mrs. L. B. Walford, for example, is described as "wearing a pretty blue tea gown richly embroidered in silk by her own hand,"[10] and Helen Mather is offered as a "great needlewoman, not only are the long satin curtains by her own hand but the pillows, cushions and dainty lampshade."[11]

To reject embroidery, as Adeline Sargeant did, was to run the risk of appearing to disparage other women, or to endorse the stereotypical view of the art propounded by a male-dominated society. For purely tactical reasons therefore, women who might have been critical of embroidery praised it. Thus the more enlightened seventeenth-century women educationalists had included needlework in their curriculum largely to provide an acceptable face for women's education. Nineteenth-century writers defended embroidery, claiming it as an unappreciated art form. Some believed in raising the status of women, not by dismissing women's traditional creative activity, but by demanding that its true worth be recognised. In her novel *The Beth Book*, 1897, Sarah Grand offers embroidery as evidence of women's superiority. Beth embroiders, selling her work secretly through the discreet commercial outlets provided by the Arts and Crafts Movement to market "ladies' work." For Sarah Grand embroidery represents the beauty of the female imagination, its spiritual clarity in contrast to male pedestrian rationalism. But this attempt to validate women's work ultimately reinforces the rigid sexual categorisation and justifies the separate spheres.

Novels like *The Beth Book* are a rich source of information on attitudes towards embroidery, which is, from the eighteenth century onwards, repeatedly used to signify femininity. Through the work of four novelists I shall show briefly how each employs embroidery to comment on the position of women in society. May Sinclair takes the identification between embroidery and feminine purity to suggest that women's sexuality is innately pure and innocent, but corrupted by men. Nevertheless women's purity as embodied in embroidery has the potential power to transform patriarchal corruption. Walter Majendie in *The Helpmate*, 1907, is unfaithful to his wife with an embroiderer called Maggie, and the delicacy of her work signifies that Maggie is the seduced not the seducer. Finally her embroidery draws Majendie's family's attention to her existence; she is "tracked down by the long trail of her beautiful embroidery."[12] The work is ultimately responsible for revealing to the man the errors of his ways: "He hated to see his innocent child dressed in the garment which was the token and memorial of his sin."[13]

May Sinclair and Sarah Grand represent that tendency in nineteenth-century feminism which, by positing women's essential spiritual superiority, inadvertently confirmed the oppressive Victorian stereotype of "The Angel in the House." Twentieth-century novelists largely write about embroidery and femininity not as a superior essence of women, but as the product of sexual difference, of family life, and the mother/daughter relationship in particular.

Edith Wharton in *The Age of Innocence,* 1920, conjures the archetypal scene in which a mother and daughter embroider together for Newland Archer, the son of the family:

> After dinner, according to immemorial custom, Mrs. Archer and Janey trailed their long silk draperies up to the drawing room where, while the gentlemen smoked below stairs, they sat beside a Carcel lamp with an engraved globe, facing each other across a rosewood work-table with a green silk bag under it, and stitched at two ends of a tapestry band of field flowers destined to adorn an "occasional" chair in the drawing room of young Mrs. Newland Archer [the son's future wife].[14]

Economically and ideologically, Janey—the unmarried, upper middle-class daughter—is destined to remain at home, locked into "genteel" pursuits with her mother. Young Mrs. Newland Archer, on the other hand, has escaped through marriage, but her own mother's influence, encapsulated in embroidery, follows her and, with peer-group pressure, ensures that she reproduces the sexual hierarchy of her own family:

> She was not a clever needle-woman: her large capable hands were made for riding, rowing and open-air activities; but since other wives embroidered cushions for their husbands she did not wish to omit this last link in her devotion . . . she was simply ripening into a copy of her mother, and, mysteriously, by the very process, trying to turn him into a Mr. Welland [her father].[15]

Edith Wharton exemplifies two common uses of embroidery in women's novels. First, the image of the woman who is clumsy with the needle is repeatedly employed to counter the feminine stereotype and to combat the way in which embroidering was used to justify the sexual division of labour. Women are so nimble-fingered, it's claimed, but women's embroidery has everything to do with their place in society and nothing to do with the size of their fingers. At the same time Edith Wharton, through embroidery, demonstrates the extraordinary power of social ideology.

Colette similarly employs embroidery to undermine the stereotype and to illuminate femininity. She, however, is less fatalistic than Edith Wharton. Demonstrating a different dynamic, she suggests that the construction of femininity is rarely complete and that it can be ruptured; and that, moreover, femininity contains its own curious power.

When her daughter Bel-Gazou was nine, Colette's friends expressed their surprise and disapproval that the child was unable to sew. Anxious not to fail as a mother, and concerned that her child fulfil the social expectations that confront her, she urges Bel-Gazou to take up needlework. She remembers, however, the way her own mother had reacted when she had embroidered as a child: "When I was a young girl, if I ever happened to occupy myself with needlework, Sido always shook her soothsayer's head and commented 'you will never look like anything but a boy who is sewing.'"[16] It was her mother's attitude that enabled Colette to practise embroidery and to insist that other areas of creative work were as appropriate for women.

She does, however, have mixed feelings when her own daughter embroiders. Her women friends applaud: "Just look at her, isn't she good," but secretly Colette disagrees:

I shall speak the truth: I don't much like my daughter sewing. When she reads, she returns all bewildered and with flaming cheeks from the island where the chestful of precious stones is hidden, from the dismal castle where a fair-haired orphan child is persecuted. She is soaking up a tested and time-honoured poison whose effects have long been familiar. If she draws, or colours pictures, a semi-articulate song issues from her, unceasing as the hum of bees around the privet. It is the same as the buzzing of flies as they work, the slow waltz of the house painter, the refrain of the spinner at her wheel. But Bel-Gazou is silent when she sews, silent for hours on end, with her mouth firmly closed, concealing her large, new-cut incisors that bite into the moist heart of a fruit like little saw-edged blades. She is silent, and she—why not write down the word that frightens me—she is thinking.[17]

The child's silence, her thoughts kept to herself, signify her separateness from her mother. Colette conjures up an ideal past when embroidery maintained the mother-child bond rather than underlining separation and the child's approaching adulthood. She thinks of

young embroiderers of bygone days, sitting on hard little stools in the shelter of their mother's ample skirts! Maternal authority kept them there for years and years, never rising except to change the skein of silk, or to elope with a stranger . . .

What are you thinking about, Bel-Gazou?

Nothing, Mother, I'm counting my stitches.[18]

Colette's sense of anxiety when faced with her silent stitching child conveys the two sides of embroidery. Eyes lowered, head bent, shoulders hunched—the position signifies repression and subjugation, yet the embroiderer's silence, her concentration also suggests a self-containment, a kind of autonomy.

The silent embroiderer has, however, become a part of a stereotype of femininity in which the self-containment of the woman sewing is interpreted as seductiveness. The following scene from a story in *Cosmopolitan* magazine can also be found in innumerable romantic novels:

you never saw a woman sit so still. Her stillness seemed part and cause of that still summer. Day after day she sat in a basket chair on the stones beneath the pretty white iron spiral staircase, sewing among her roses. . . . Rose's hands seemed usually to be still, though the needle was always threaded. She drove men demented.[19]

In fiction the silence and stillness of the sewer can mean many things from serious concentration to a silent cry for attention, but in terms of the stereotype it is a sexual ploy. If a woman sits silently sewing she is silently asking for the silence to be broken. The stereotype denies that there is anything subversive in her silence by asserting that it is maintained for men. Yet the way the intimations of autonomy are so resolutely quashed by the stereotype suggests that there is something disturbing in the image of the embroiderer deep in her work.

The manner in which embroidery signifies both self-containment and submission is the key to understanding women's relation to the art. Embroidery has provided a source of pleasure and power for women, while being indissolubly linked to their powerlessness. Paradoxically, while embroidery was employed to inculcate femininity in women, it also enabled them to negotiate the constraints of femininity. Observing the covert ways embroidery has provided a source of support and satisfaction for women leads us out of the impasse created by outright condemnation or uncritical celebration of the art. Nevertheless, it would be a mistake to underestimate the importance of the role played by embroidery in the maintenance and creation of the feminine ideal. During the seventeenth century the art was used to inculcate femininity from such an early age that the girl's ensuing behaviour appeared innate. By the eighteenth century embroidery was beginning to signify a leisured, aristocratic life style—not working was becoming the hallmark of femininity. Embroidery with its royal and noble associations was perfect proof of gentility, providing concrete evidence that a man was able to support a leisured woman. Moreover, because embroidery was supposed to signify femininity—docility, obedience, love of home, and a life without work—it showed the embroiderer to be a deserving, worthy wife and mother. Thus the art played a crucial part in maintaining the class position of the household, displaying the value of a man's wife and the condition of his economic circumstances. Finally, in the nineteenth century, embroidery and femininity were entirely fused, and the connection was deemed to be natural. Women embroidered because they were naturally feminine and were feminine because they naturally embroidered. Then embroidery was blamed for the conflicts provoked in women by the femininity the art fostered. By the end of the century, Freud was to decide that constant needlework was one of the factors that "rendered women particularly prone to hysteria" because day-dreaming over embroidery induced "dispositional hypnoid states."[20]

The subject matter of a woman's embroidery during the eighteenth and nineteenth centuries was as important as its execution in affirming her femininity (and thus her worth and worthlessness in the world's eyes). It was expected to reflect the current feminine ideal, which was held to be the highest, yet paradoxically most natural, achievement of women. If the content conformed to the ideal it supposedly won the needlewoman love, admiration and support. By examining the content of embroidery throughout [*The Subversive Stitch*], we will see how women responded to the current ideologies of femininity from the Renaissance onwards, how they used these ideologies and were used by them.

The iconography of women's work is rarely given the serious consideration it deserves. Embroidery is all too often treated only in terms of technical developments. One reason why the subject matter of embroidery is summarily dismissed is that embroiderers employ patterns. The interpretation, adaptation and variation of pattern is an integral aspect of the activity and it is therefore assumed that stylistic and technical properties are all that concern the embroiderer. However, needlewomen chose particular patterns, selecting those images which had meaning for them. The enormous popularity of certain images at different moments indicates that they had specific importance and powerful resonance for the women who chose to stitch them. Where embroiderers have actually employed

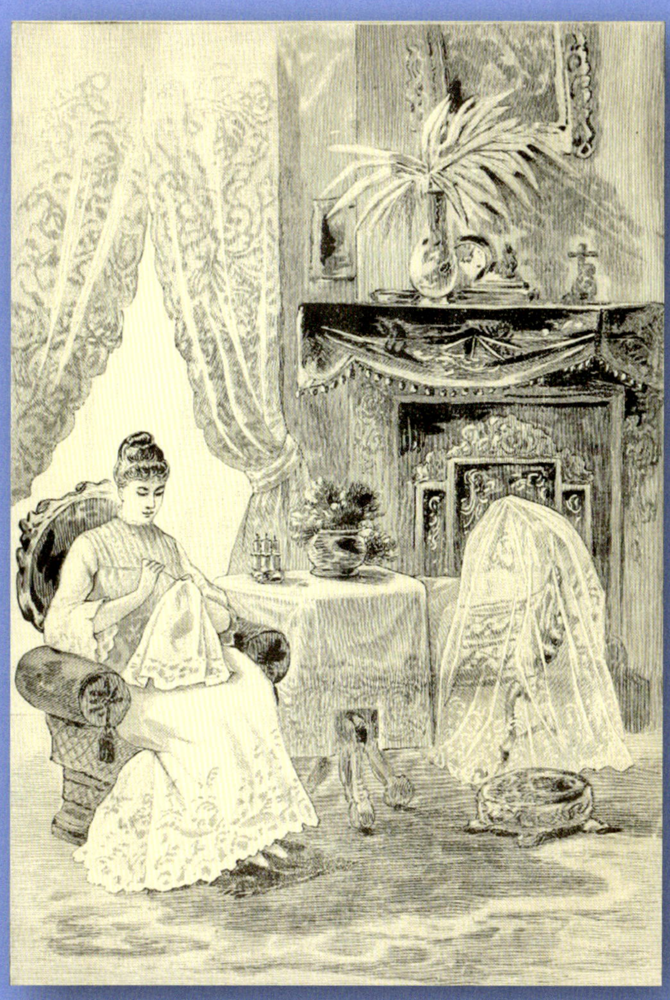

Frontispiece from John D. Reed and Eliza M. Lavin, *Needlecraft: Artistic and Practical*, Butterick, 1889

contemporary paintings as patterns, we can perceive what could or could not be stitched by women, and how they were able to make meanings of their own, by observing which they selected and where they departed from their models. Nevertheless, the meanings of any embroidered picture have to be carefully considered within their historical, artistic and class context. What a picture conveys often relates to the needs of a woman's class as much as to her experience as a woman at that time, as well as to the dominant concerns of contemporary paintings and to the history of embroidery.

Sometimes embroiderers reinforced the feminine ideal in their work, comfortingly concealing the disjunctures between the "ideal" and the "real" by the words and images they stitched—"Home Sweet Home." At other times they resisted or questioned the emerging ideology of feminine obedience and subjugation, as in the following seventeenth-century sampler verse:

When I was young I little thought
That wit must be so dearly bought
But now experience tells me how
If I would thrive then I must bow
And bend unto another's will
That I might learn both care and skill
To Get My Living with My Hands
That So I Might Be Free From Band
And My Own Dame that I may be
And free from all such slavery.
Avoid vaine pastime fle youthful pleasure
Let moderation allways be thy measure
And so prosed unto the heavenly treasure.

The verse is a curious mixture of piety and rebellion, resentment and acquiescence. Because samplers were becoming the place where moral sentiments were impressed upon young girls, they were sometimes also the place where conflicts underlying the ideology were expressed.

Such overt recognition of the clash between individual ambition and the ideology of femininity is rare indeed. More often the embroiderers' desire was to achieve exactly what was expected of them, developing satisfying and praiseworthy levels of skill. From our vantage point, it is all too easy to sneer at the Victorian embroiderer completing yet another pair of slippers stitched with a fox head, or at the eighteenth-century embroiderer reproducing in thread the moralising, sentimental domestic genre paintings of her time. But rather than ridiculing them, or turning embarrassed from our history, we should ask why they selected such subjects, what secondary gains they accrued from absolute conformity to the feminine ideal, and how they were able to make meanings of their own while overtly living up to the oppressive stereotype.

Sometimes the secondary gains, or the ways women made meanings of their own, are covert indeed. The ubiquitous late eighteenth-century mourning pictures, for example, overtly conform to the ideology of wifely obedience and fidelity. Whatever the complexity and ambivalence of a woman's personal response to bereavement, embroidering conventional memorial pictures provided the security of social approval. Women are depicted in silk tending the family tomb. In Chapter Six I describe how these pictures related both to the expansion of domestic mourning ritual and to contemporary attitudes to death represented in neo-classical art. But a comparison between paintings by men of mourning women and embroidered mourning pictures by women reveals significant differences. Embroiderers endow their *mourners* with particular prominence and power,

even as they manifest their allegiance to the ideology of the "virtuous widow."

While recognising the varied ways in which women have conformed to and resisted the dictates of femininity in their work, it is important to remember that embroidery has been and is a source of artistic pleasure to many women. Olive Schreiner, in her novel *From Man to Man,* 1927, evoked the satisfaction of needlework, particularly the narcissistic pleasures it provided:

All her life she had dreamed of having a dress made of thick black silk, with large blue daisies with white centres embroidered in raised silk work all over it at intervals. Her mother had had such a bit of silk in a patchwork quilt she had brought from England with her.[21]

Embroidery summons up both "advanced" civilisation and very early childhood when a primal, unproblematic unity with the mother still existed. However, the work provides narcissistic pleasure not only because it evokes the love and unity of early childhood; but also because women were taught to embroider as an extension of themselves; and quite crudely because embroidery is used on clothing where it provokes admiration. Urged to embroider clothing and furniture, encouraged to see it as the natural expression of their nature, women were still accused of vanity when they embroidered for themselves. The stereotype of embroidery as a vain and frivolous occupation, like the stereotype of the silent, seductive needlewoman, controls and undermines the power and pleasure women have found in embroidery, representing it to us negatively.

Nevertheless, women have found gratification in the activity. Olive Schreiner conveys the immense creative satisfaction it provides:

Slowly the scores of little tucks and fine embroidery shaped themselves. At the end of the week there were two tiny armholes. At the end of a fortnight the long white rope with its delicate invisible stitching was also complete . . .[22]

She also perceived the bond that embroidery forged between women; sewing allowed women to sit together without feeling they were neglecting their families, wasting time or betraying their husbands by maintaining independent social bonds:

They were unalike physically and mentally but they had tastes which harmonised. While Veronica sat upright on a high-backed chair knitting heavy squares for a bed quilt,

Mrs. Drummond, on a low settee, with her head a little on one side, chose carefully the shades of silk for an altar cloth which she was making.[23]

The women's choice of work indicates the different personalities; that they both engaged in domestic art reveals what they share as women in society.

After placing embroidery at the centre of women's lives, Olive Schreiner makes a plea that it be recognised as art, as a creative expressive activity, but nevertheless betrays her kinship to the attitude towards needlework manifested by the contemporary novelists Sarah Grand and May Sinclair:

The poet, when his heart is weighted, writes a sonnet, and the painter paints a picture, and the thinker throws himself into the world of action; but the woman who is only a woman, what has she but her needle? In that torn bit of brown leather brace worked through and through with yellow silk, in that bit of white rag with the invisible stitching, lying among fallen leaves and rubbish that the wind has blown into the gutter or street corner, lies all the passion of some woman's soul finding voiceless expression. Has the pen or pencil dipped so deep in the blood of the human race as the needle?[24]

While placing embroidery as an art like poetry and painting, Olive Schreiner reasserts its association with femininity. It is the bearer of women's soul. The images of the white rag with the invisible stitching, the yellow silk besmirched and trodden underfoot silently suggest a comparison with women's fate in the streets. Olive Schreiner maintains the link between embroidery and feminine purity, thus presenting it as a sexual characteristic, and failing to establish it as an art form equal to painting and poetry. In part this reflects Olive Schreiner's own ambivalence towards the domestic labour she describes: "The worst of this book of mine is that it's so womanly. I think it's the most womanly book that ever was written, and God knows I've willed it otherwise."[25] But the effect of the passage is largely determined by the hierarchical categorisation of art forms in our culture. By claiming that embroidery should be valued because of its intimate associations with women's lives and domestic tradition, Olive Schreiner inevitably though unwittingly discounted it as art.

The extraordinary intractability of embroidery, its resistance to redefinition, is the result of its role in the creation of femininity during the past five hundred years.

Notes

1 John Ezard, "Victorian Touch to Credit Cold Britain," *The Guardian* (London), December 6, 1979.

2 Adrian Hopkins, "Firm but Not Fixed in Their Ways," *The Guardian*, March 30, 1979.

3 Simone de Beauvoir, *The Second Sex* (London: Penguin Books, 1972), 635.

4 Juliet Mitchell, *Psychoanalysis and Feminism* (London: Penguin Books, 1974), 363.

5 Ibid.

6 Gayle Rubin, "The Traffic in Women: Notes on the 'Political Economy of Sex,'" in *Toward an Anthropology of Women*, ed. Rayna R. Reiter (New York: Monthly Review Press), 196.

7 Millicent Fawcett, "England: The Woman's Suffrage Movement," in *The Woman Question in Europe*, ed. Theodore Stanton (New York: G. P. Putnam's Sons, 1884), 6.

8 See Rozsika Parker and Griselda Pollock, *Old Mistresses: Women, Art, and Ideology* (London: Routledge & Kegan Paul), 1981.

9 Helen Black, *Notable Authors of the Day* (Glasglow: David Bryce and Son, 1893), 169.

10 Ibid., 27.

11 Ibid., 78.

12 See May Sinclair, *The Helpmate* (London: Constable, 1907), chapter 29.

13 Ibid., chapter 31.

14 See Edith Wharton, *The Age of Innocence* (London: Penguin Books, 1974), chapter 5.

15 Ibid., see chapter 31.

16 Colette, *Earthly Paradise* (London: Secker and Warburg, 1966), 205.

17 Ibid., 214–16.

18 Ibid.

19 Jane Gardam, "Dead Heat," *Cosmopolitan*, July 1981.

20 Joseph Breuer and Sigmund Freud, *Studies on Hysteria*, in *The Complete Works of Sigmund Freud*, vol. 2, ed. James Strachey (London: The Hogarth Press), 12.

21 Olive Schreiner, *From Man to Man* (London: Virago, 1982), see chapter 11.

22 Ibid., chapter 9.

23 Ibid., chapter 6.

24 Ibid., chapter 9.

25 Ruth First and Ann Scott, *Olive Schreiner* (London: André Deutsch, 1980), 175.

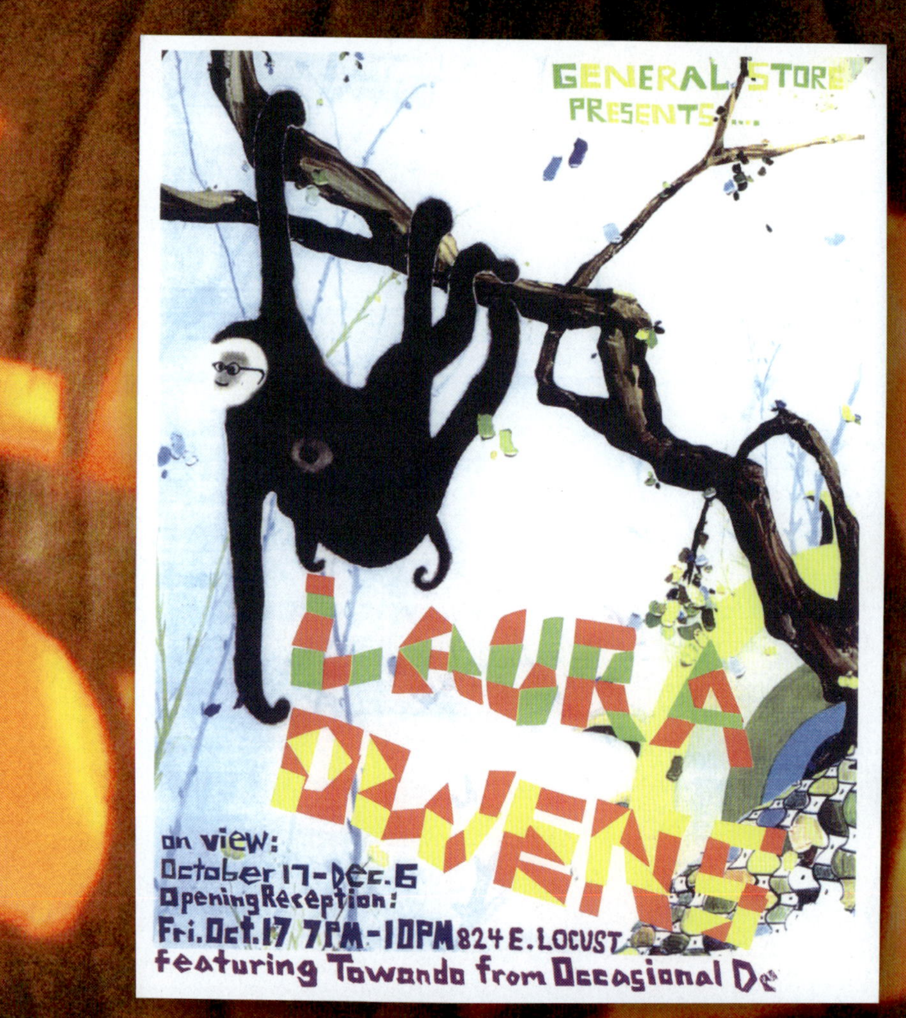

Foreground: Invitation, General Store, Milwaukee, 2003
Background: Jack-o'-lantern, Milwaukee, 2003

MANIFESTO

(For Abstractionists and Friends of the Non-Objective)

BE A FORCE

Don't shoot blanks

Black and Brown: that shit is the future

Triangles are your friend

Don't pretend you don't work hard

When in doubt spray-paint it gold

Perverse formalism is your god

You are greased lightning

Bring your camera everywhere

Never stop looking at macramé, ceramics, supergraphics, and Suprematism

Make work that is so secret, so fantastic, so dramatically old school/
new school that it looks like it was found in a shed, locked up since the 1940s

Wake up early, fear death

Whip out the masterpieces

Be out for blood

You are the master of your own universe

Abstraction never left, motherfuckers

If you can't stop, don't stop

Strive for the deeper structure

Fight monomania

Campaign against the literal

ABSTRACTION FOREVER!

Rebecca Morris, *Manifesto: For Abstractionists and Friends of the Non-Objective* (2004–5), poster version, 2007. Originally published in *Artforum* on the occasion of Morris's eponymous exhibition at Galerie Barbara Weiss, Berlin, 2006

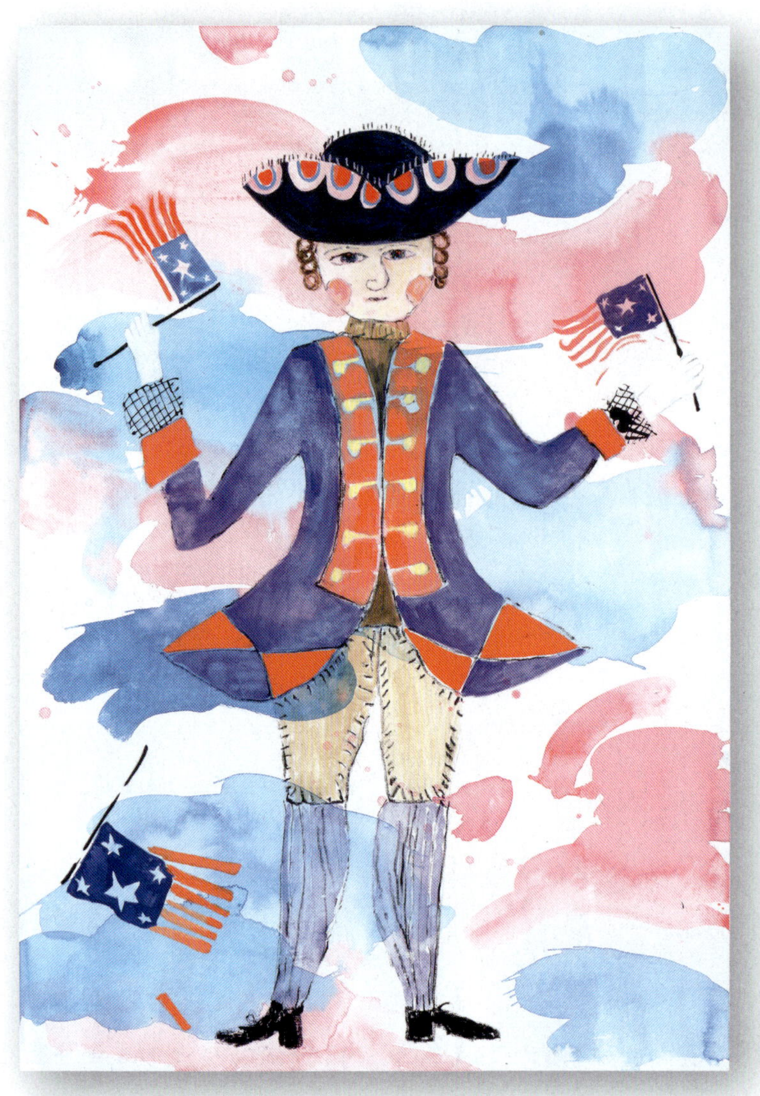

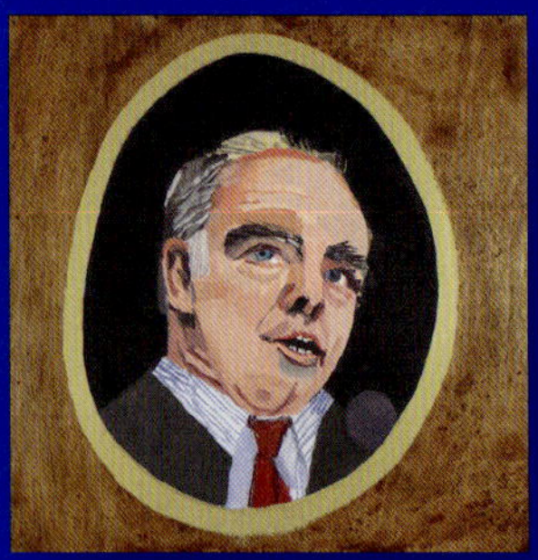

Untitled, 2004, oil and acrylic on canvas, 70 × 46½ in. (177.8 × 118.1 cm)

 Inset: Jonas Wood, *Dean*, 2003, oil on wood, 20 × 19 in. (50.8 × 48.3 cm)

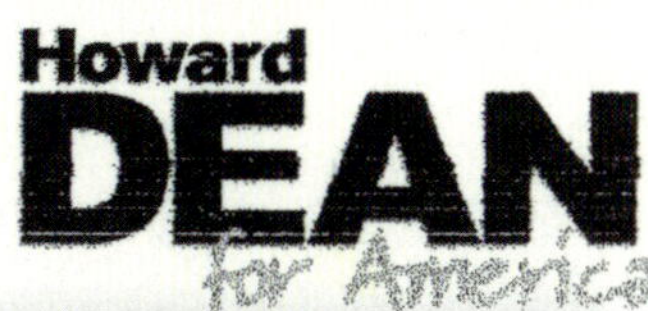

Sign

Join our
active, a

From: **laura_owens** laura_owens@prodigy.net
Subject: FW: We are all in this together
Date: May 29, 2003 at 6:01 PM
To: edgar27@earthlink.net, carol hendrickson carolhendrickson@earthlink.net, Richard D. Hendrickson rhendri@earthlink.net, Rachel Kushner rachelkush@earthlink.net, Marie Rafalko mrafalko@earthlink.net, catherine eastman marieastman@earthlink.net , Angel Chen angeldome@hotmail.com, Anne Collier anneccollier@hotmail.com, Donald Morgan mistermorgan@earthlink.net, Max Lesser youngmax@earthlink.net, Mungo Thomson mungothomson@earthlink.net, kerry tribe kerrytribe@earthlink.net, kirsten everberg keverberg@earthlink.net, kevin Hanley kevin@microint.org, Karl Erickson kheone@earthlink.net, Mary Weatherford maryweatherford@earthlink.net, Gavin Brown gavin@gavinbrown.biz, ben vida benjaminvida@hotmail.com, Trinie Dalton triniedalton@earthlink.net, dwayne moser dwaynemoser@hotmail.com, eric steinman ericsteinman@sbcglobal.net, Owens, Lisa OwensL@leukemia-lymphoma.org, bill owens williamowens@theowenslawfirm.com, Lincoln lincoln.owens@earthlink.net, Nate Lentz natelentz@sbcglobal.net, LAW OFFICE lawoffice4@earthlink.net, ruth root ruthroot@earthlink.net, sarah whipple sarahwhipple@hotmail.com, Alex Slade alexslade@yahoo.com, Scott Reeder scott@0tv.com

Hi ,

I have talked to some of you about how I met Governor Howard Dean last week and talked with him at a question and answer house party. I was pretty impressed, I felt him to be genuine and have a real idea of what it is going to take to beat Bush. He is not as liberal or progressive as one might think, but whenever he does take a more centrist position, it is always backed by a rational or factual basis on what he believes will actually work.
He also has a strike back mentality which most of the democratic party has never heard of. He doesn't believe in letting the opposition get away with anything and at the same time rationally calling them on their hypocritical doublespeak. Anyway I pass this along to you because I think if you have any interest in learning more about a candidate I believe is worthwhile, you could sign up for his email list and just learn more about where he stands on the issues.

Thanks! Laura

ps. his point below about economic policy starving off basic education healthcare and social security, in other words reverse everything back to pre-Roosevelt, can find some substantiation in the new report out today that Bush withheld a study by Paul O'Neill about the impact of baby boomer retirement in his budget proposal . It entails chronic deficits of 44,200bn in current US dollars which is equal to 10 times current deficit or 4 years of Us economic output or 94%of all US householder assets. you choose!

From: Dean for America <info@deanforamerica.com>
Organization: Dean for America
Reply-To: Dean for America <info@deanforamerica.com>
Date: Thu, 29 May 2003 12:56:33 -0500
To: laura_owens@prodigy.net
Subject: We are all in this together

May 29, 2003

Dear Laura,

We are in a battle for our country's heart, soul, and future.

With the President's proposed budget and the $350 billion tax cut package he signed yesterday, it has become clear what this President is attempting to do, and why we must repeal the entire package of cuts: both those signed today and those passed in 2001. I will not go along with it. I believe the majority of Americans do not want to go along with it either, but I need your help.

We can beat Bush in 2004, but we need to build a grassroots movements unlike any other in history. The most effective way to build this movement is through the internet, and through building our email list. **Please forward this email** to all your friends who would be interested, and ask them to join this movement. They can sign up for Dean for America at:

http://www.deanforamerica.com.

Let me be clear. The Bush economic plans are a fundamental assault on the basic American ideals that we all share -- an assault on our schools, our health care, our environment and our social security. The tax cuts are part of a radical agenda to dismantle Social Security, Medicare, and our public schools through financial starvation.

Please submit these names on the web at **www.deanforamerica.com/doubledean**,
or by emailing them in Excel format to **doubledean@deanforamerica.com.**

You can also FAX this sheet to **802/651-3299.**

A Painter's Vote

Laura Owens

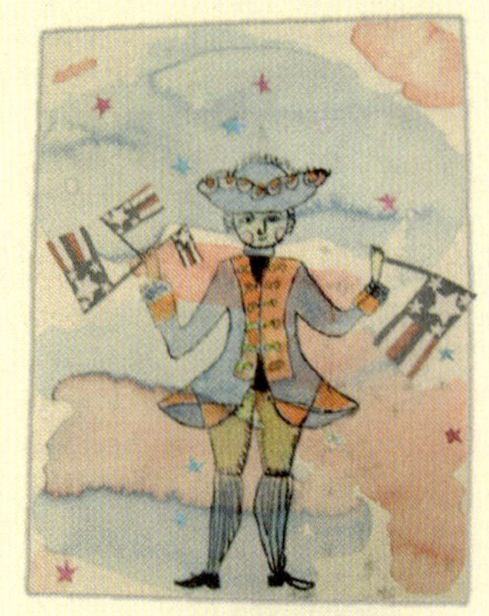

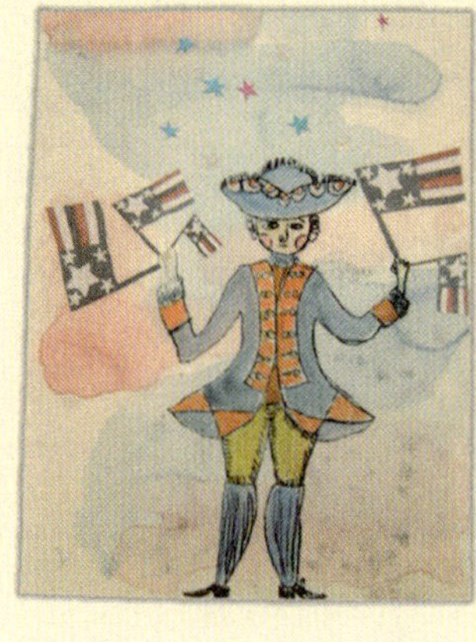

There is a certain self-consciousness that comes with getting involved in any cause or subscribing to any belief system. In the past I like to think I was easy going and fun to be around but now I'm afraid my compulsive obsession with politics is thoroughly annoying to many of my friends. I have poured money into PACs and candidates, begged friends to give money and artworks for fundraisers, written letters, participated in phone banking and signature drives. My current plans include moving back to Ohio to register voters in a key swing state over the summer. Wanna come?

Although it is now a hazy memory, the turning point must have been logging onto the PNAC (Project for the New American Century) website. It was like finding the anti-conspiracy. With radical zeal for intervention and superpower domination, the neo-conservative foreign policy of preemption and regime change had been laid out by Wolfowitz in his Defense Planning Guidance way back in 1992. Rumsfeld, Cheney, and many more with strong ties to the administration have been waiting patiently for the opportunity to enact their hawkish military strategy for years, announcing it to the world, forming think tanks, writing papers—it was all there.

My first impulse was to raise money or start working for the Democrats. But it looked as if they had all taken the little blue pill, standing and applauding Bush's hawkish State of the Union address and promising to sign his resolution. As leader of the house at the time, Dick Gephardt in particular seemed almost to run to the Rose Garden and shake hands with Bush in order to prevent dissent or even discussion amongst house Dems.

In contrast, Howard Dean spoke out against the "unilateral invasion" and even stridently attacked those congressional Dems who, with their eyes on the '04 election, were trying to hedge their bets vis-à-vis the war. Recently his campaign has assumed the position of an insurgent tough guy who will stand up to the radical ideas of the president. With a no-frills bottom-up organizational structure fueled mainly by small donations and encouraging active participation via blogs, meet-ups and a DIY spirit, the campaign has seen a steady rise to the top of the rather large heap. (The Draft Wesley Clark people seemed also to be riding this same spirit but that quickly fell apart when Clark hired top-down management-style campaign staff, many of whom had worked for the Clintons.) However before Dean could catch fire in terms of fundraising and endorsements, a steady stream of "Stop Dean" voices could be heard from the top of the Democratic Party.

Al From and Bruce Reed head the Democratic Leadership Council, one of many centrist groups who refer to themselves as the New Democrats. They were the driving force behind Bill Clinton's '92 victory and have issued regular scathing memos warning of the downfall of the Democratic Party if Dean wins the primary. On May 15 From wrote, "What activists like Dean call the Democratic wing of the Democratic Party is an aberration: the McGovern-Mondale wing, defined principally by weakness abroad and elitist, interest group liberalism at home. That's the wing that lost 49 states in two elections, and transformed Democrats from a strong national party into a much weaker regional one." The DLC represents the pro-NAFTA, middle-class tax cuts and welfare reform move over to the swing voter in the center strategy that worked so well for Bill Clinton.

Or did it? Maybe Clinton's charisma and the Ross Perot campaign were key. One could also argue that the "move to the center" strategy is more specifically a winning fundraising strategy, appealing to professionals who tend to be pro-business, fiscal conservatives, yet social liberals. The downside has been that, over the past decade, in trying to appeal to that elusive swing voter, the Clinton/DLC strategy alienated many so-called traditional democrats. Since '98 the Democrats have been bleeding seats in the house and senate, and the erosion of the base cost Gore the election when the "dissent" vote, a crucial two percent, went to the Greens in 2000.

Why the resistance to Dean from the leadership? Is it that he is "out of the mainstream"? In a recent article in *The New Republic*, Ryan Lizza writes: "The division in the party over Dean is less about ideology than about power." Lizza observes that Dean's insurgency candidacy, if successful, would mean a great upset for those at the top of the Democratic Party. People like Terry McAuliffe and other Clintonites who lead the party would likely be out of power and out of their offices as leaders of the DNC. New speculation about Hillary jumping into the race this June to save the party was tinged with this Washington elite versus the little guy from Vermont dramatic arch.

Which is not to say that there aren't important differences when it comes to strategic vision. The pro-Dean camp

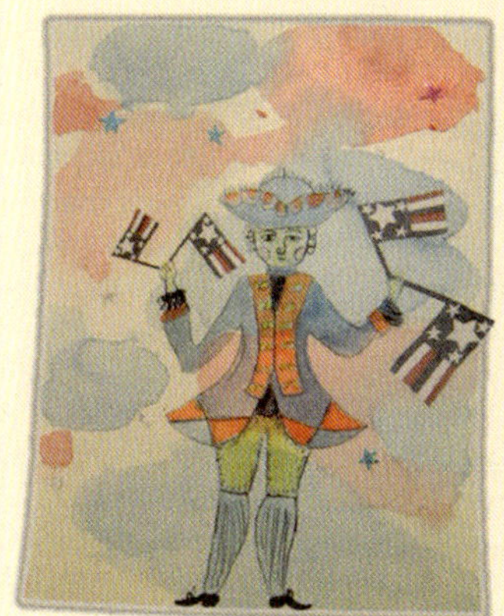 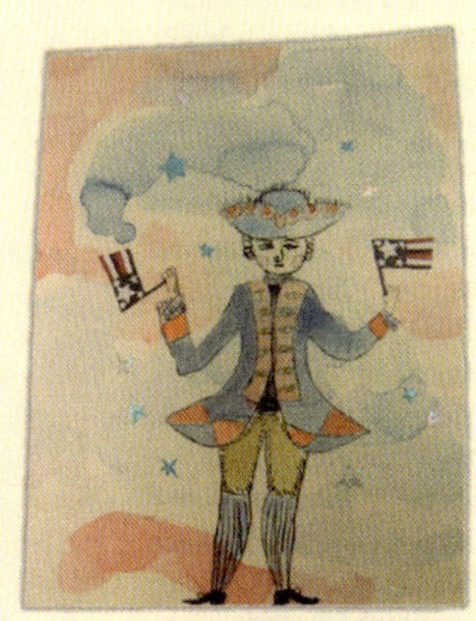 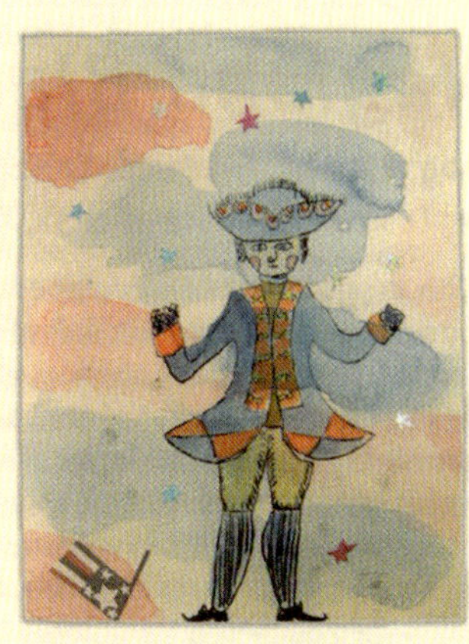

argues that bringing back that crucial two percent dissent vote and mobilizing an activist get-out-the-vote campaign in swing states, thus inflating their base vote, is key to the election. One thing all Democrats agree on is that the Republicans have been out-organizing them for many years now, whether by getting out their base vote, having the whole party stay on the talking-points memo of the week, or simply making the call to Roger Ailes at *Fox News*.

The DLC sees swing voters as a unified block that sits perfectly in the middle of an imaginary line reading left to right. Move over to the center, take your base for granted, and you win. But independent and centrist are not the same thing. The independent voter may be just that, independent, waiting to the last minute, and voting not on issues but emotionally. Living in a state that just got Schwarzeneggered, one is acutely aware of the importance of "gut" feelings. Think of Dole falling off the stage, Papa Bush's vomiting in Tokyo, Carter's lame attempt to Rambo the hostages back, and the aptly named Gray Davis. Unfortunately, "*Quien es mas machos?*" might be the important swing-voter question.

But the result of this counterproductive struggle within the party is paranoia. And a person can't be tough and paranoid at once. What's that? I think I hear Karl Rove chuckling in the background.

Of course, the conservatives have been delighting in sowing discord on many Sunday morning talk shows as well as on the conservative side of the *New*

York Times editorial page. Safire and Brooks are the first to speculate on Clinton conspiracies and Dean debacles. Hello! Shouldn't we be suspicious? When Tucker Carlson comes on CNN wearing a Dean pin, the "Dean is McGovern" meme starts spinning through the papers and the blogs go through yet another paranoid all-night parlor game of "what if we pick the wrong guy?".

Yet an overwhelming sense of fear and doubt on the part of the Democrats is understandable when you look at the cable TV and radio propaganda machine arrayed against them. If you haven't been watching *Fox News*, *Hannity and Colmes*, *The O'Reilly Factor* or *Scarborough Country*, it's almost impossible to understand the fluidity with which the administration can deliver their message. If you thought Rush Limbaugh going to rehab might have lowered the volume of the right-wing message machine, you are sadly out of touch. The level of confidence—or as Bush likes to say, "resolve"—that exists within the Republican party is unmatched. Week after week they are the ones who are "framing" the debate which results in dissenting voices sounding shrill, wimpy, and whiny. Certainly, the "Dems are weak on military and foreign policy" meme could be linked to a lack of coherence/confidence in the message as well as an unwillingness or inability for most to be perceived as the tough guy.

Other efforts by the right involve creating hostility between candidates' blogs by sending in factional trolls (sometimes termed "freepers" in reference

to the Free Republic website) posing as candidate X's supporter in order to disrupt candidate Y's blog. Reporting on family feuds within the party seems to be at an all-time high right now, and hopefully this is more about a story that sells than the real feeling amongst Dems on the street. ABB is a term used on various weblogs to connote "Anyone But Bush" and recently, after much argument, there is a growing consensus that at a certain point all this energy and devotion to particular candidates will be used in a concerted effort to get behind "the one." At the Harkin steak fry, a forum for the candidates in Iowa, keynote speaker Bill Clinton recently echoed this consensus when he asked the audience by all means to fall in love with one of the candidates, but come next summer let's all fall in line.

That said, I have no doubt that the future will see Dean as a pivotal figure in twenty-first-century American electoral politics, even if he falls off the planet today. His bottom-up organizational structure found its partner in the inherently DIY, rhizomatic, *social* structure that is the internet, thus initiating what seems like a new day in American political life. The DNC have been following Dean's success on the internet by starting their own blog, "Kicking Ass," thus capitalizing on the tougher-sounding message that has worked so well for him. No more little blue pills and handshakes, we're kickin' ass now.

THE THIRD DEGREE *is a regular column by different writers on rotating critical issues. Los Angeles-based **LAURA OWENS** is a well-known painter and web enthusiast.*

From: laura_owens laura_owens@prodigy.net
Subject: Bush resume
Date: May 1, 2003 at 6:40 PM
To: Ali Subotnick a.subotnick@parkettart.com, bill owens williamowens@theowenslawfirm.com, Gavin Brown gavin@gavinbrown.biz, catherine eastman marieastman@earthlink.net, Richard D. Hendrickson rhendri@attbi.com, Donald Morgan mistermorgan@earthlink.net, kirsten everberg keverberg@earthlink.net, Karl Erickson kheone@earthlink.net, Ferguson, Russell rferguson@arts.ucla.edu, carol hendrickson carolhendrickson@earthlink.net, Rachel Kushner rachelkush@earthlink.net, bill owens williamowens@theowenslawfirm.com, Mary Weatherford maryweatherford@earthlink.net, Max Lesser youngmax@earthlink.net, Mungo Thomson mungothomson@earthlink.net, michael webster michaelwolfwebster@earthlink.net, Karl Erickson kheone@earthlink.net

George W. Bush's Resume (Please distribute far and wide)

Past work experience:

1. Ran for congress and lost.

2. Produced a

3. Bought an
bankrupt short

4. Bought the
land using tax-
Cubs.

5. With fathers

6. Accomplish
made Texas th
Houston as the
the Texas gove

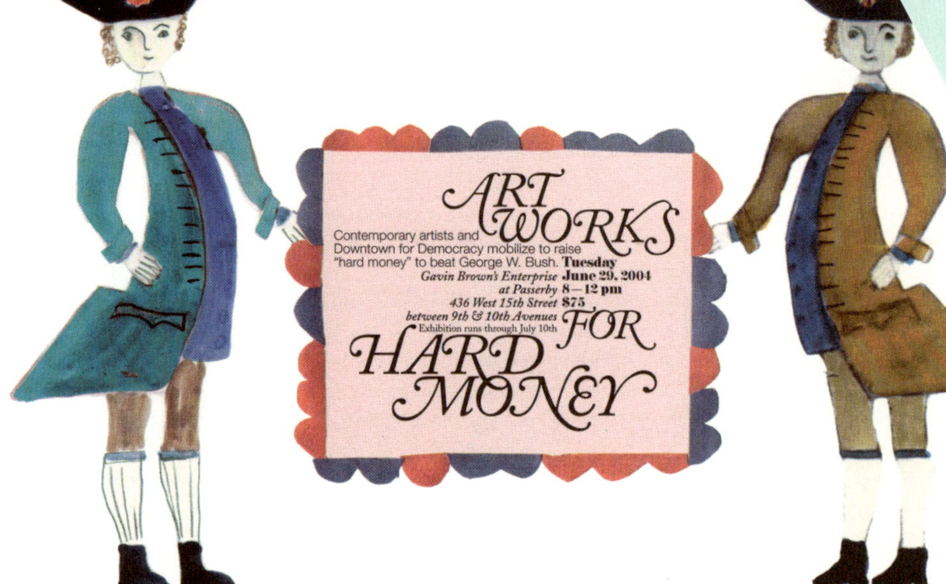

6. First p

7. First president in US history to

8. First year in office set the all-time record for most days
any president in US history.

9. After taking the entire month of August off for vacation, presided over
the worst security failure in US history.

10. Set the record for most campaign fund-raising trips than any other
president in US history.

11. In his first two years in office over 2 million Americans lost their
jobs

jobs.

12. Cut unemployment benefits for more out of work A[m]
president in US history.

13. Set the all-time record for most fore[

14. Appointed more convicte[d
any president in US hist[

15. Set the r[
preside[

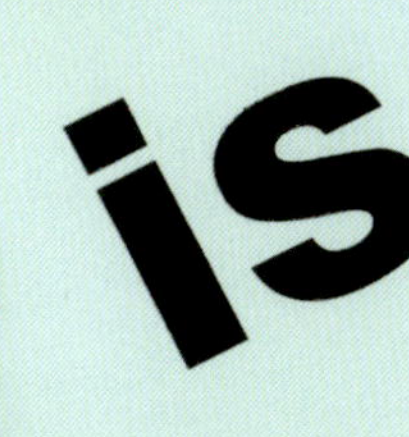

[c]orruption was revealed.

[t]he m[

[m]embers of his cabinet
[h]istory. (the 'poorest' multi-
tanker named after her).

24. First president in US hi[story
simultaneously go bankrup[

25. Presided over the bigge[
in any country in the history[

26. First president in US hi[

27. Created the largest gov[
the United States.

28. Set the all-time record f[
more than any president in[

29. First president in US hi[story
from the human rights com[

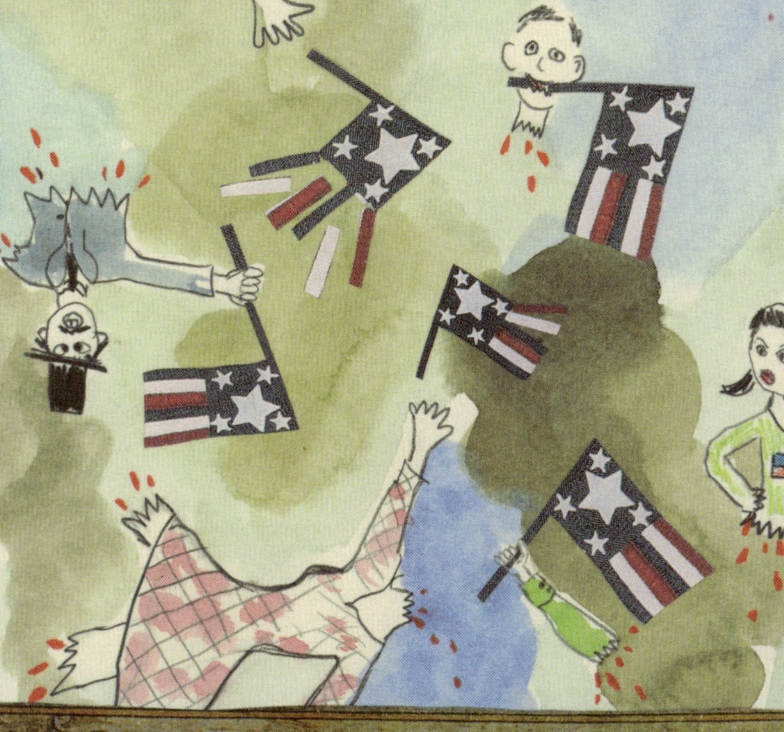

[US] history to have the United Nations remove the US
[ ]oard.

[ ]nd balances, and have the least amount of
[ ] any presidential administration in US history.

[ ]ations irrelevant.

[ ]ernational Criminal Court.

[ ]pectors access to US prisoners of war and by default and
[ ] Geneva Conventions.

[US] history to refuse United Nations election inspectors (during the 2002 US elections).

[ ]world) record holder for most corporate campaign donations.

[ ]me campaign contributor presided over one of the largest corporate bankruptcy frauds in world history (Kenneth Lay,
[ ]n Corporation).

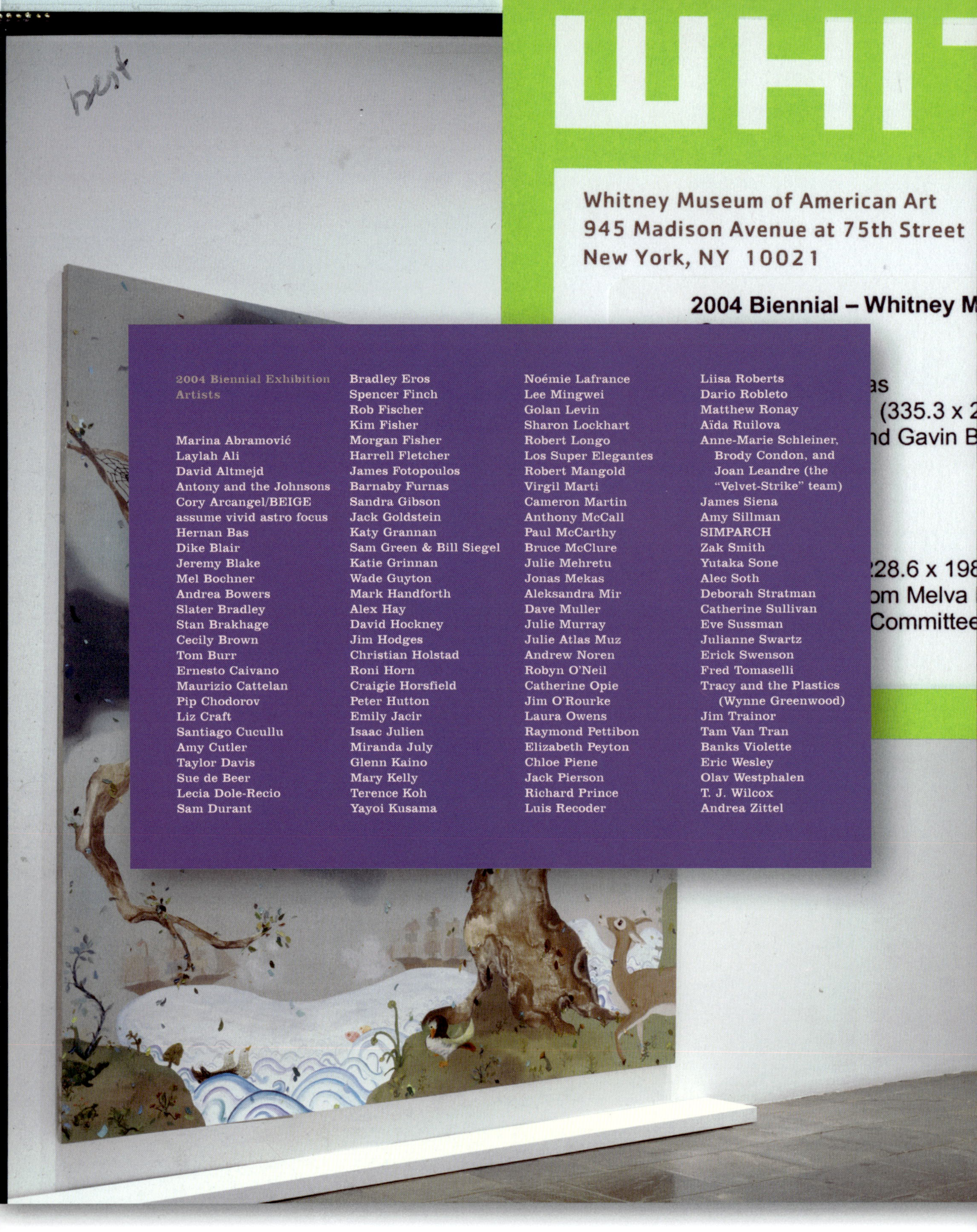

Foreground: List of participating artists, *Whitney Biennial,* Whitney Museum of American Art, New York, 2004
Background: Color transparency featuring *Whitney Biennial*, Whitney Museum of American Art, New York, 2004, with *Untitled*, 2004
(see p. 389), and Cecily Brown, *Black Painting 2*, 2003, oil on linen, 90 × 78 (228.6 × 198.1)

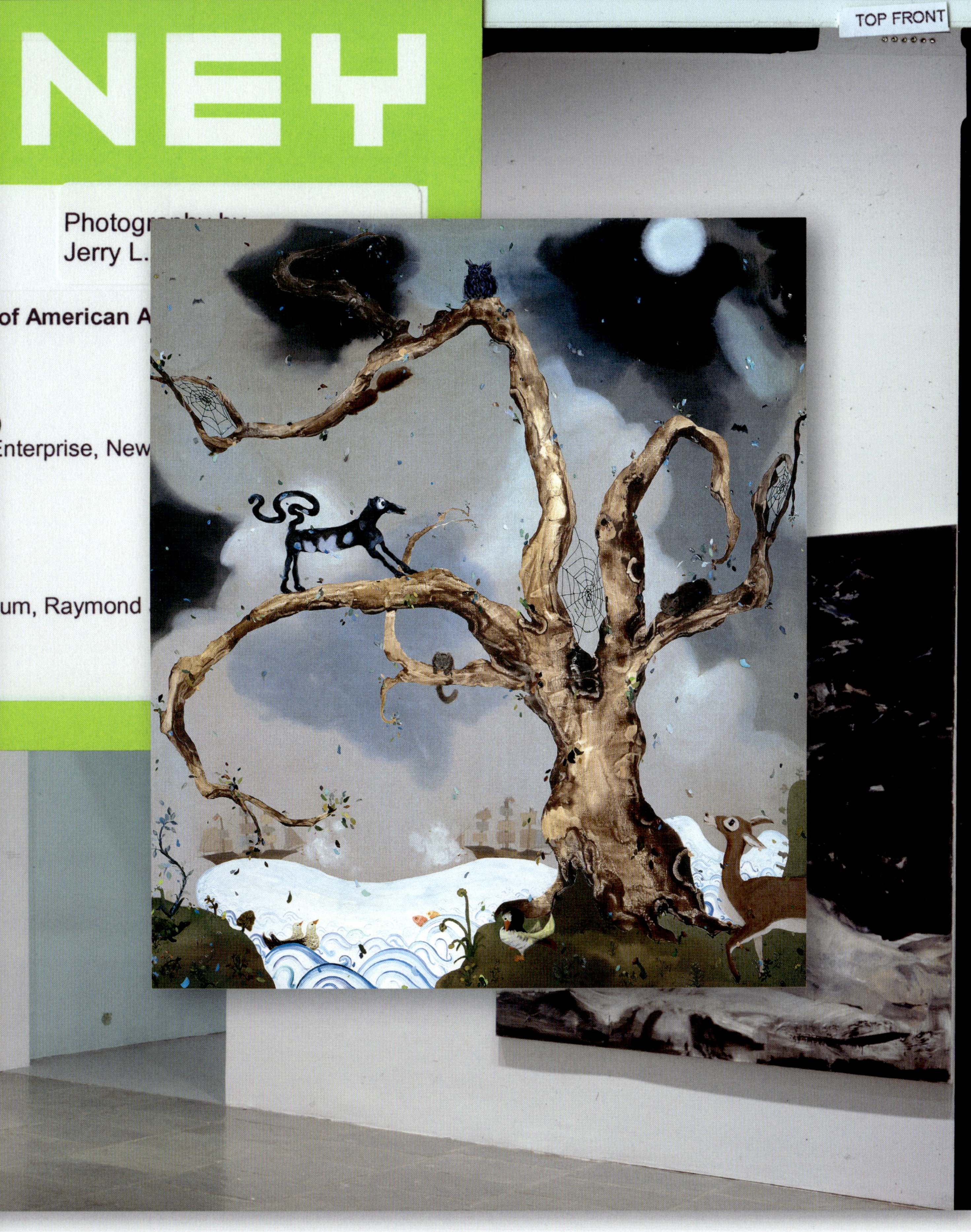
NEY
Photography by
Jerry L.
of American A
Enterprise, New
um, Raymond
TOP FRONT

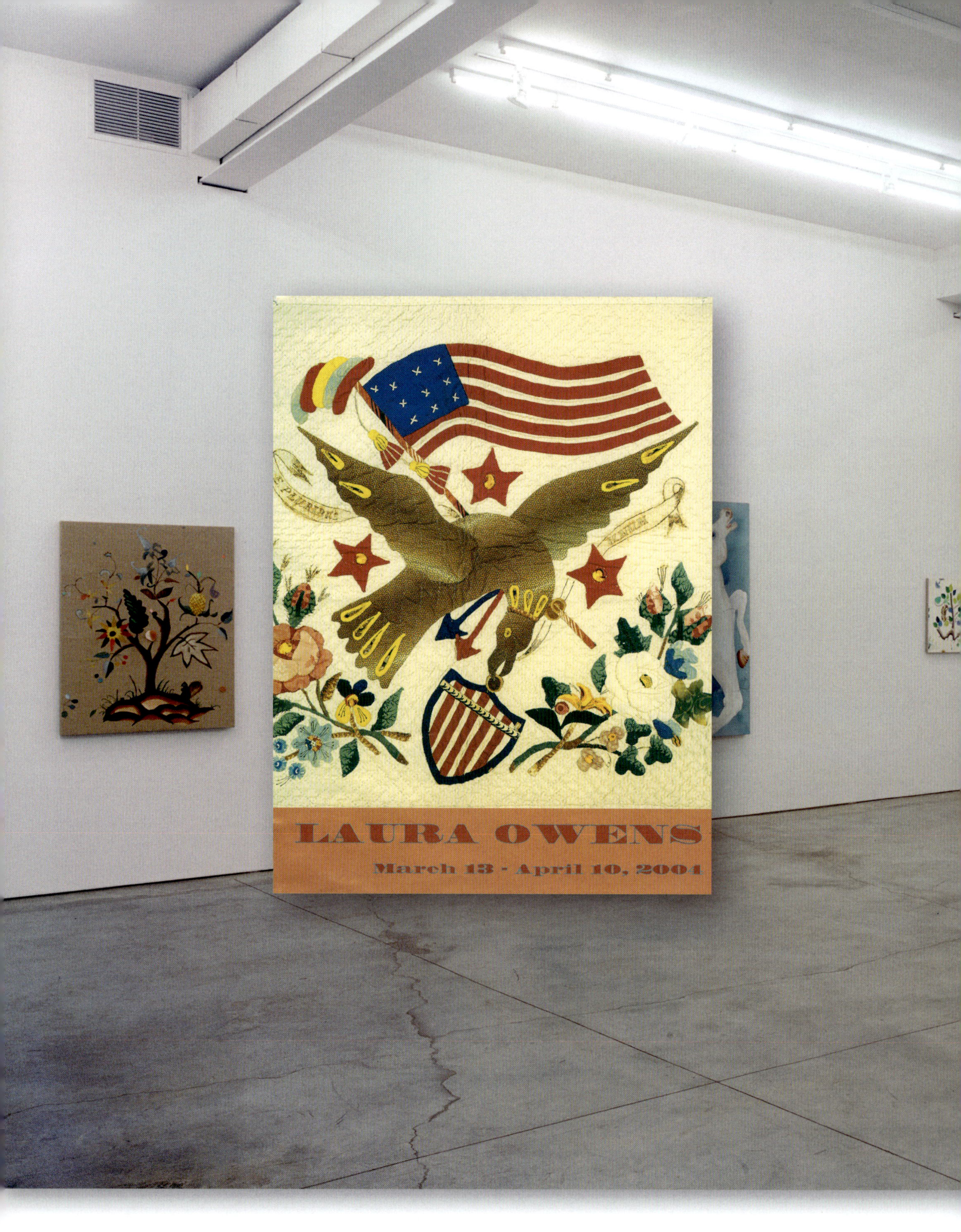

Foreground: Invitation, Gavin Brown's enterprise, New York, 2004
Background: Installation view, Gavin Brown's enterprise, New York, 2004, with *Untitled*, 2004, acrylic and oil on linen, 44¾ × 34¾ in.
(113.7 × 88.3 cm); *Untitled*, 2004 (see p. 391); and *Untitled*, 2004, oil on linen, 24 × 18 in. (61 × 45.7 cm)

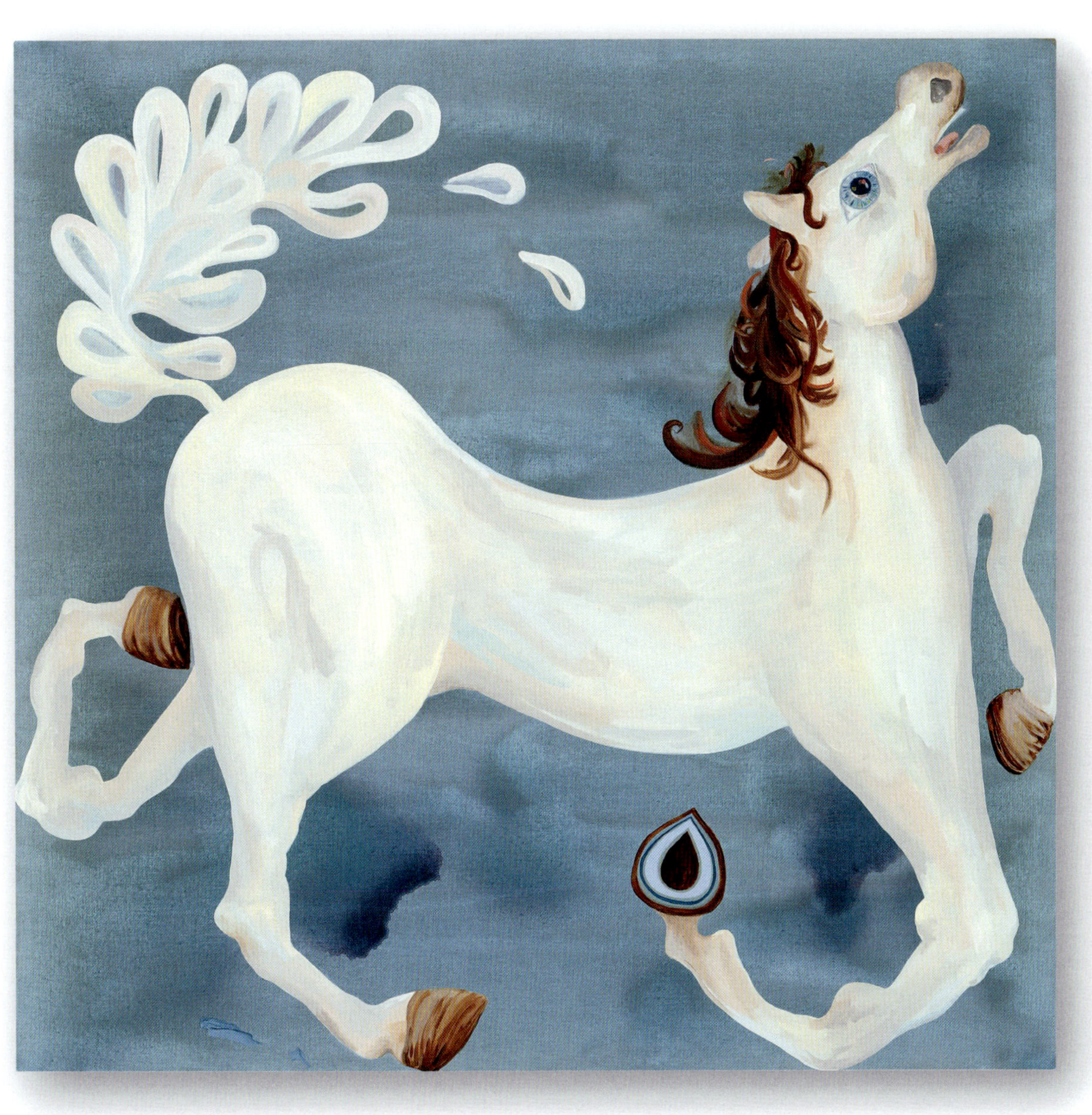

Untitled, 2004, acrylic and oil on linen, 66 × 66 in. (167.6 × 167.6 cm)

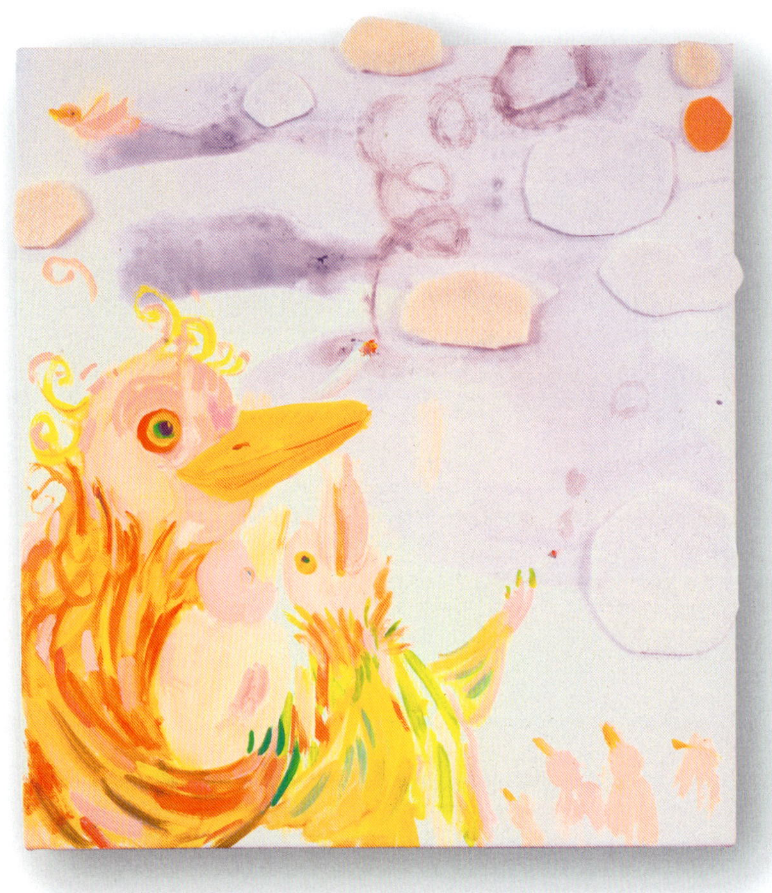

392 *Untitled*, 2004, oil and felt on linen, 18 × 16 in. (45.7 × 40.6 cm)

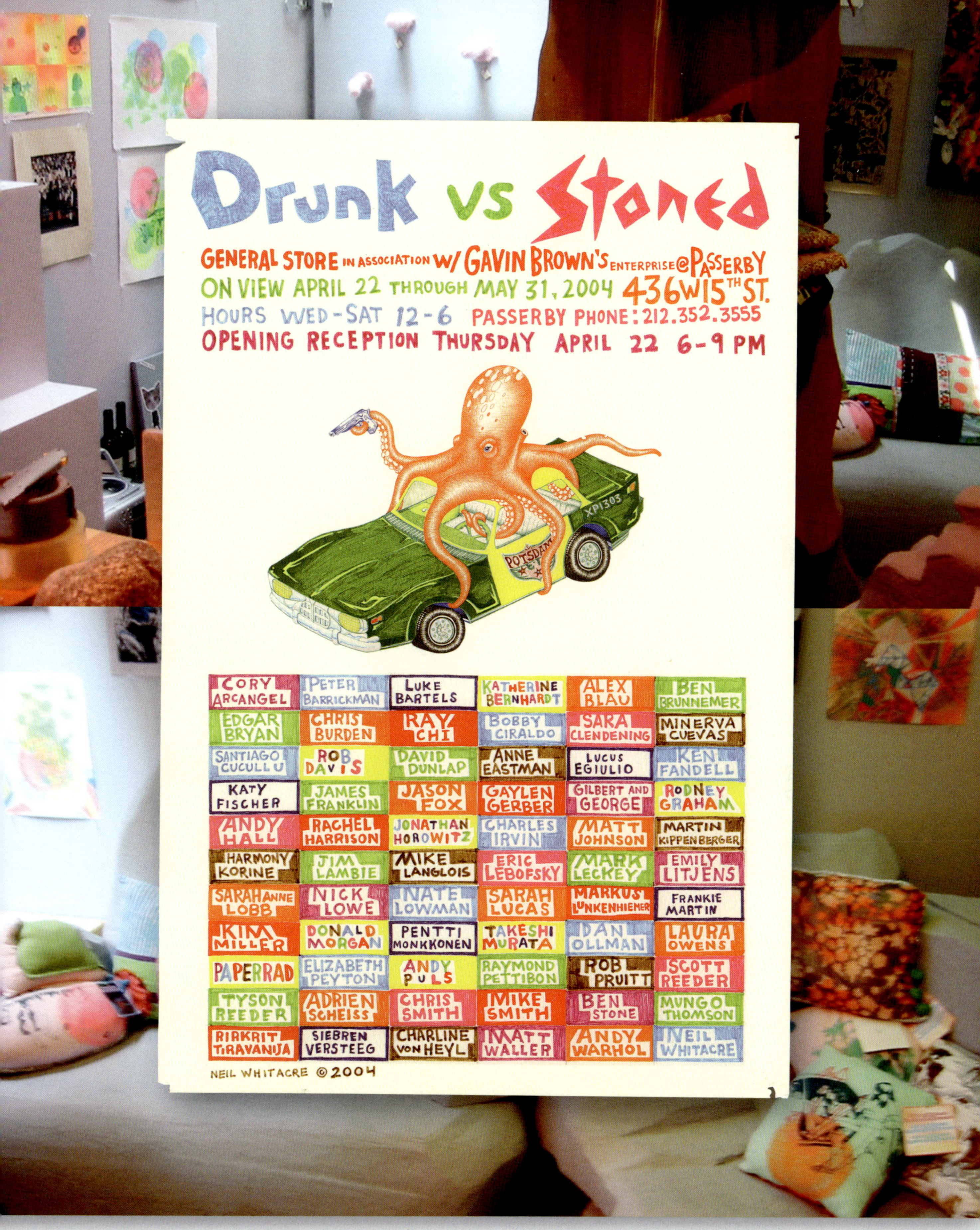

Foreground: Invitation, *Drunk vs. Stoned*, Passerby at Gavin Brown's enterprise, New York, 2004
Background: Installation views, Passerby at Gavin Brown's enterprise, New York, 2004

From: **Laura Owens** laura_owens@mac.com
Subject: cake
Date: March 8, 2005 at 5:42 PM
To: tribe kerry kerrytribe@earthlink.net
Cc: Thomson Mungo mungothomson@earthlink.net

Hi,

I would like to make a real drawing for the cake. I need dimensions and shapes of all the tiers.

Thanks!
xoxoLaura

ps did you VOTE?

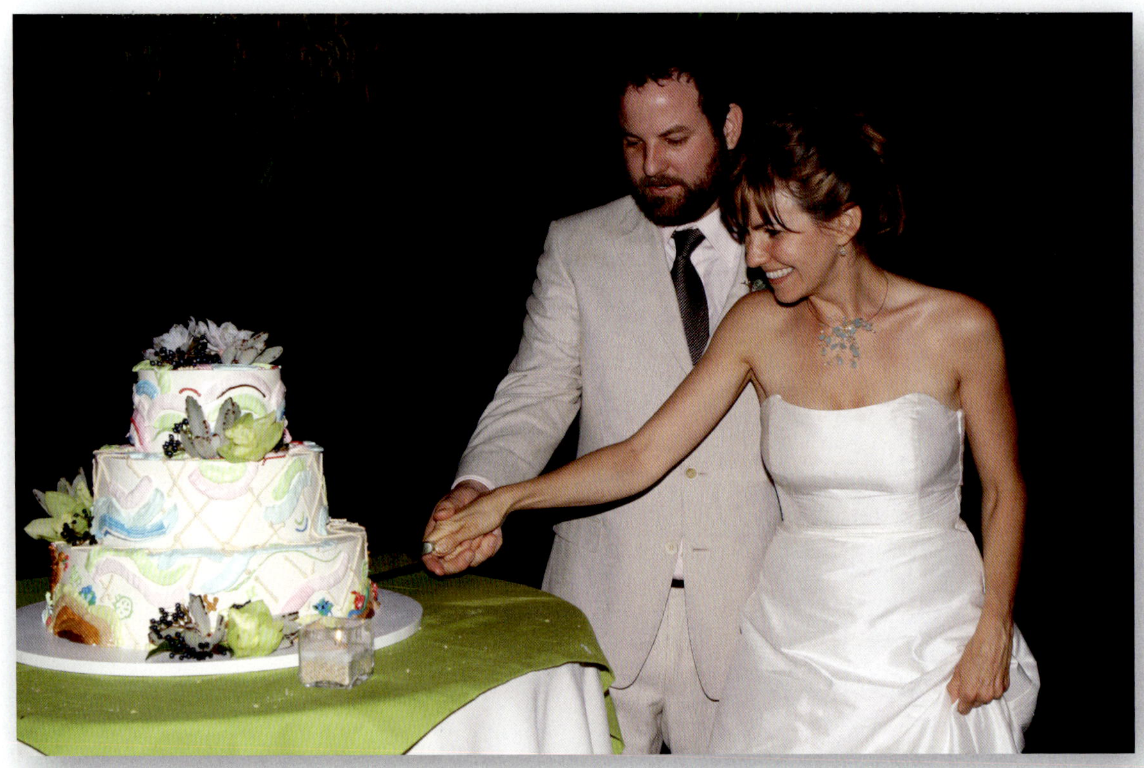

 Foreground: Mungo Thomson and Kerry Tribe, Twentynine Palms, California, 2005
Background: Email to Kerry Tribe, 2005

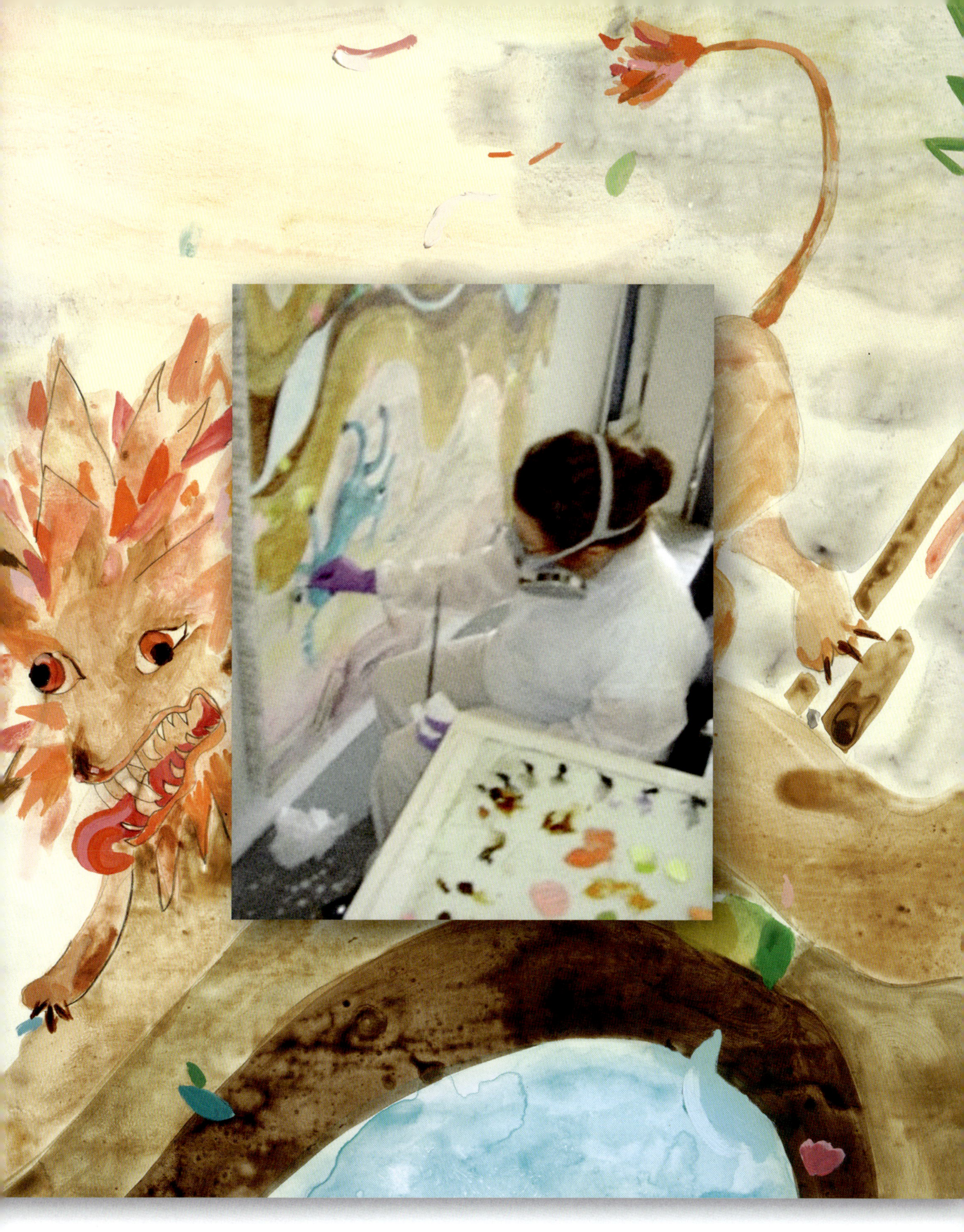

Foreground: Owens with *Untitled*, 2005, Eagle Rock studio, Los Angeles, 2005
Background: Detail of *Untitled*, 2005, acrylic, oil, and felt on linen, 108 × 60 in. (274.3 × 152.4 cm)

Sunday **October 23, 2005**

my brain spins – too many thoughts.. muddled
remembering things   I forgot to do   mid thought
wanting to clear space, time for painting
→ things I want to do→   make lists of things I wa
   todo, have a routine   so I feel there is alwa
   a space & time for painting , exercise etc.
   organize my interests — make sketches of my
   interests   so I remember them   when feeling
   So muddled

Drawings – tight compact motors that churn &
   burn & brighten out of dark smoldering layers
All my work   seems so thin – when I am in
I see it filling up. but later it feels thin—
→More interconnected, interlocking shapes and spaces
Making the drawings — unbreakable — like engineering for
big bridges, trusses, joists etc.

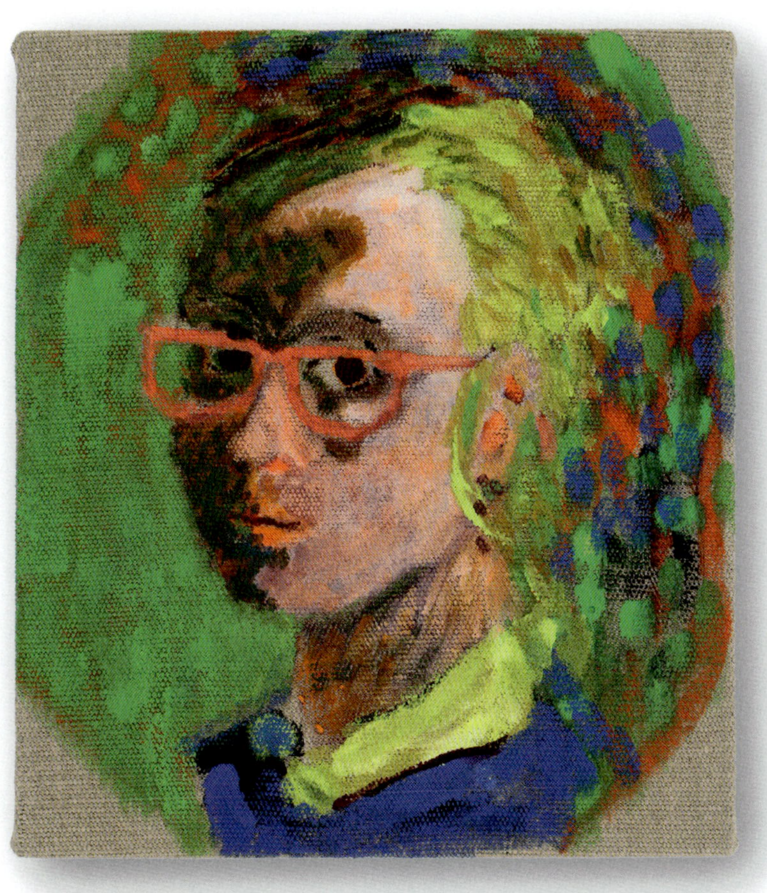

Untitled, 2006, acrylic and oil on linen, 14 × 12 in. (35.6 × 30.5 cm)

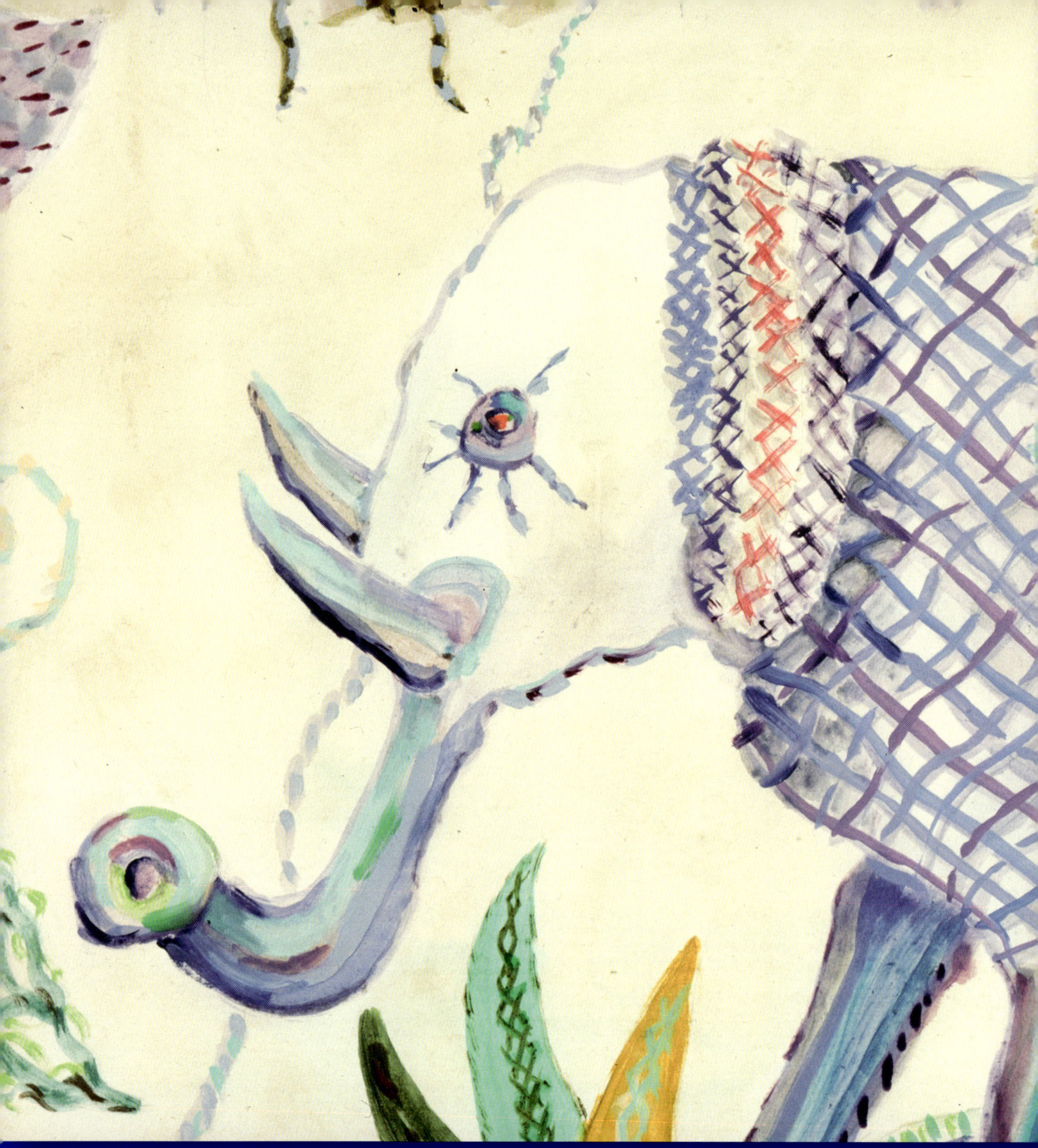

Foreground: Fax from Kirsty Bell, Tony Just, Udomsak Krisanamis, Tim Neuger, Elizabeth Peyton, Burkhard Riemschneider, and Spencer Sweeney, 2006

Background: Detail of *Untitled*, 2005, oil and acrylic on linen, 11 × 14 in. (27.9 × 35.6 cm)

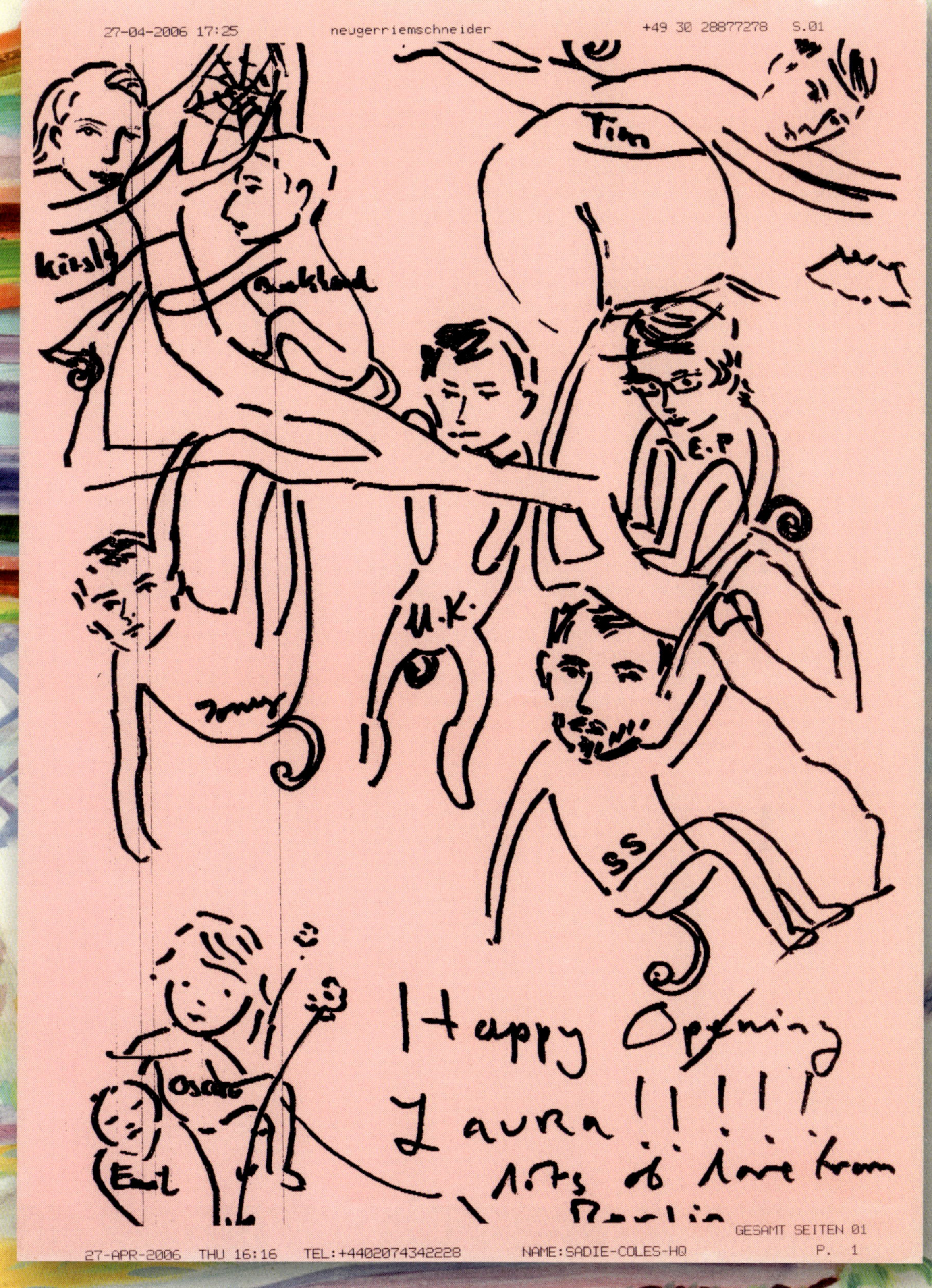
Tim
E.P
kirsty
Aukland
U.K
ss
Oscar
Earl
Happy Opening
Laura !!!!!
lots of love from
Berlin

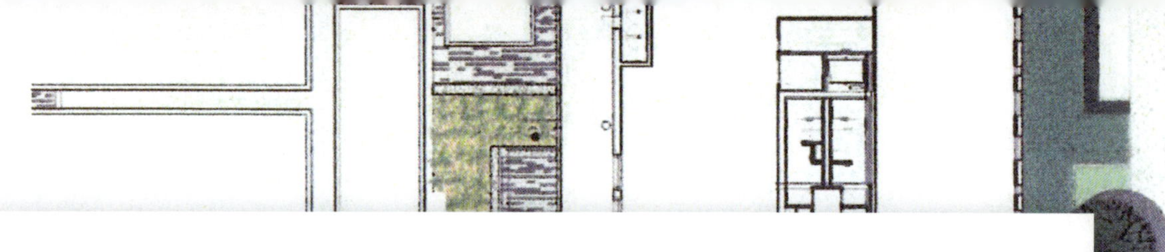

Laura Owens   Thu, Apr 6, 2006 7:11 PM

Subject: amazing invitation
Date: Wednesday, April 5, 2006 8:14 PM
From: ACME. <info@acmelosangeles.com>
To: Laura Owens Studio <lowensstudio@covad.net>

Dear Laura and Elizabeth,
Yesterday I received a call from a woman in the US State Dept.
A new Embassy for the US is being built in Beijing to open in May of 2008.
The woman, Virginia Shore, would like to see if you are interested in making
a painting for permanent installation and acquisition in the new building. It will
be the largest embassy ever built by the US. Several other major American artists are making
work for the building (Rauschenberg, Kelly, Puryear, Anne Chu, Louis Bourgeoise,
Donald Lipski). She talked of a ten by twelve foot or so sized ptg. to go on the main interior entrance wall
next to a Maya Lin piece.
She sent me drawings of the conceived building and some details. Are you interested enough to take a look
so I can get back to her?
If so, please let me know and I will forward the info to you. A budget is revealed as
well. It is limited overall, so she told me people(artists and dealers) are willing to work
with her given the nature of the site. She can spend $85,000.
I think it is worth thinking about and it is quite flattering to you. I told her you had a new baby and a busy schedule
with upcoming shows. She is very hopeful you will say yes, given it is only one painting
and that some of your imagery has been affected by Asian painting.
Let me know if you want to talk about this. She seemed pretty normal on the phone
and is familiar with your work.
Thanks, Laura.
Hope all is well.
Best to Edgar from us,
Randy

____

ACME.

Page 1 of 2

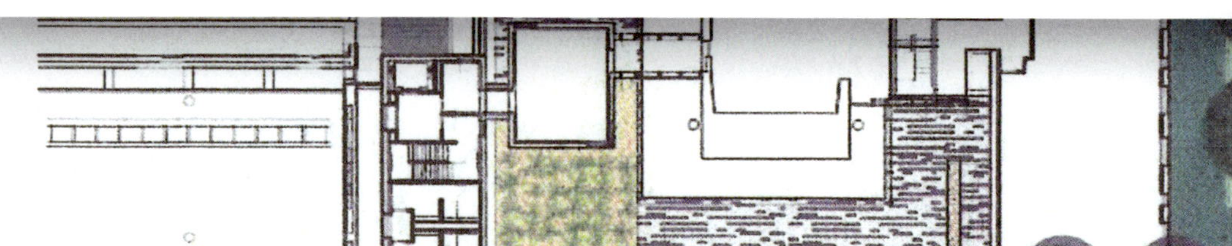

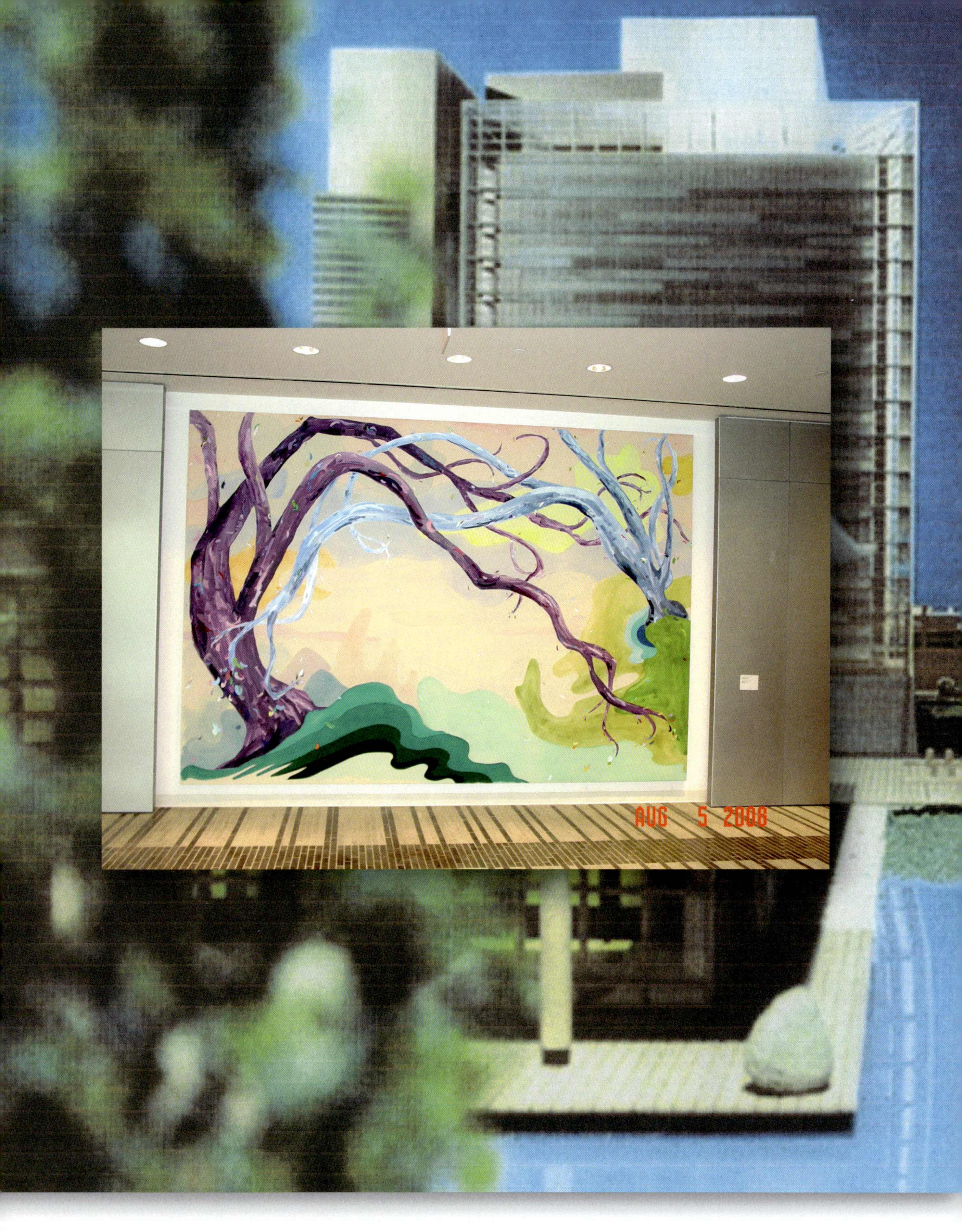

Foreground: Installation view, *Landscapes of the Mind: Art Collection of the United States Embassy*, United States Embassy, Beijing, 2008, with *Untitled*, 2007, acrylic and oil on canvas, 120 × 168 in. (304.8 × 426.7 cm)
Background: United States Embassy, Beijing, digital rendering, 2006

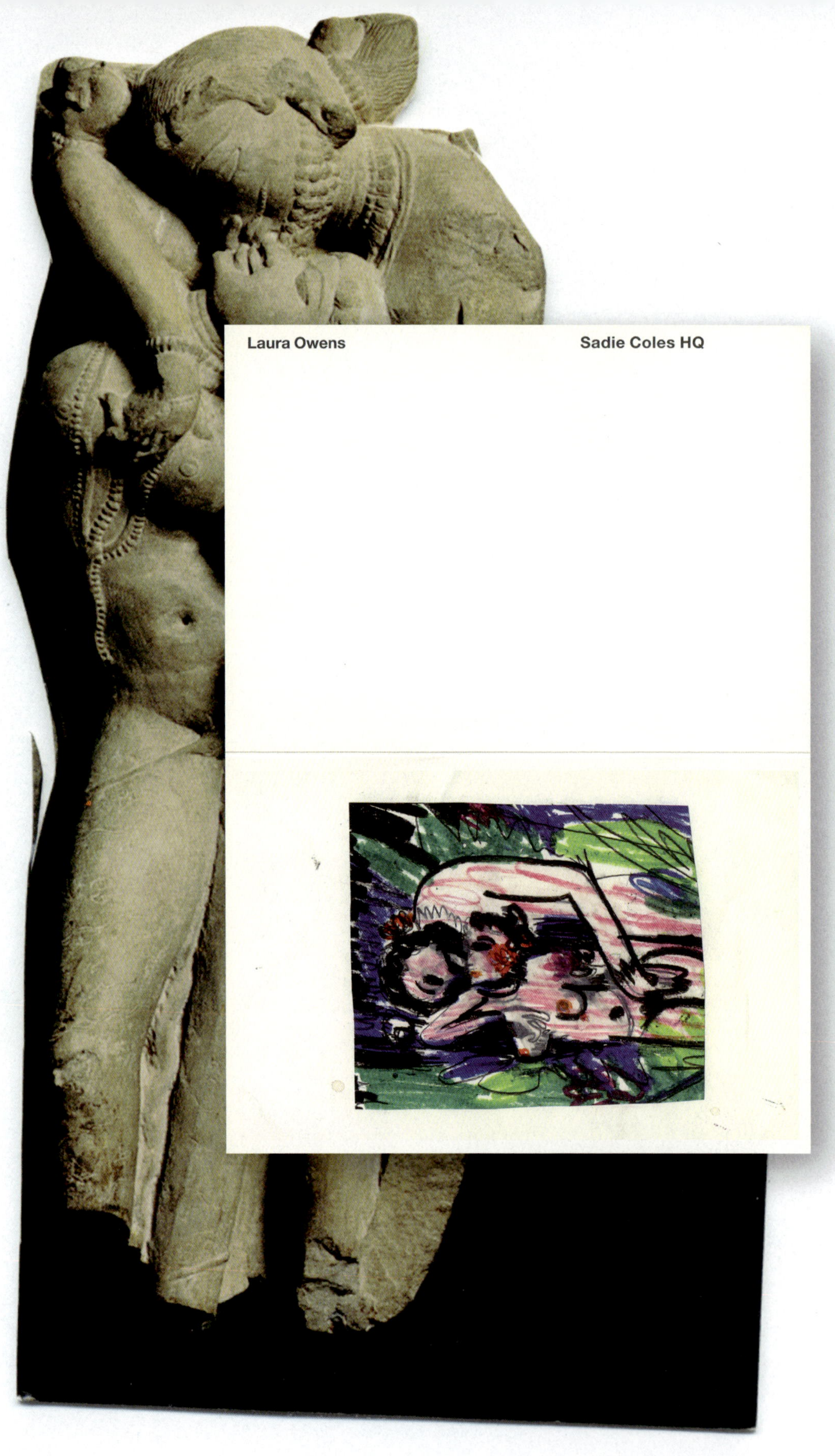

Foreground: Invitation, Sadie Coles HQ, London, 2006
Background: Research photograph by Owens, 2006

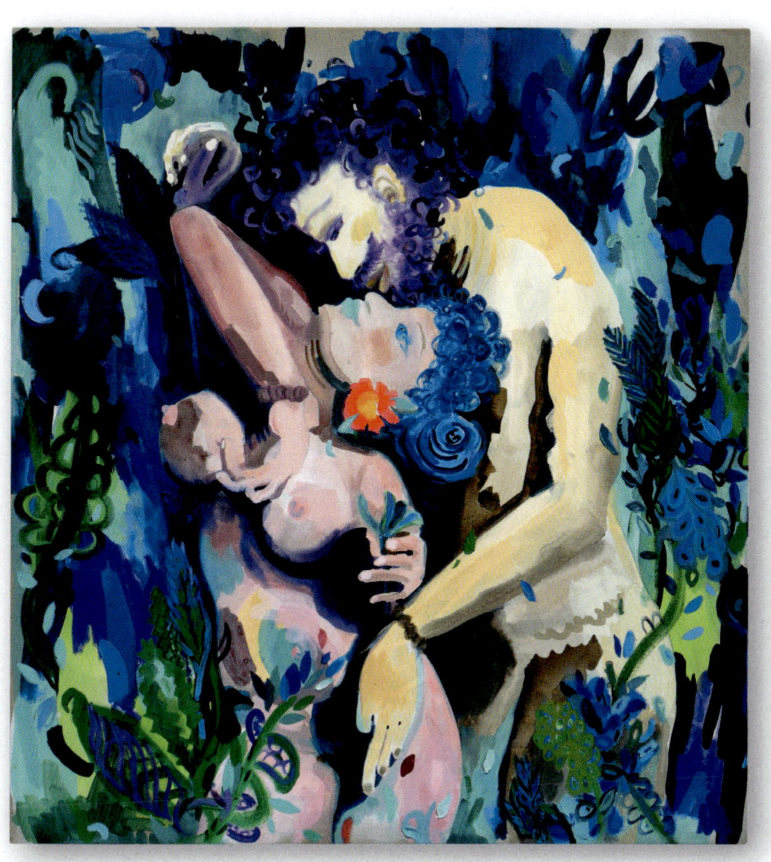

Untitled, 2006, acrylic and oil on linen, 48 × 43 in. (121.9 × 109.2 cm)

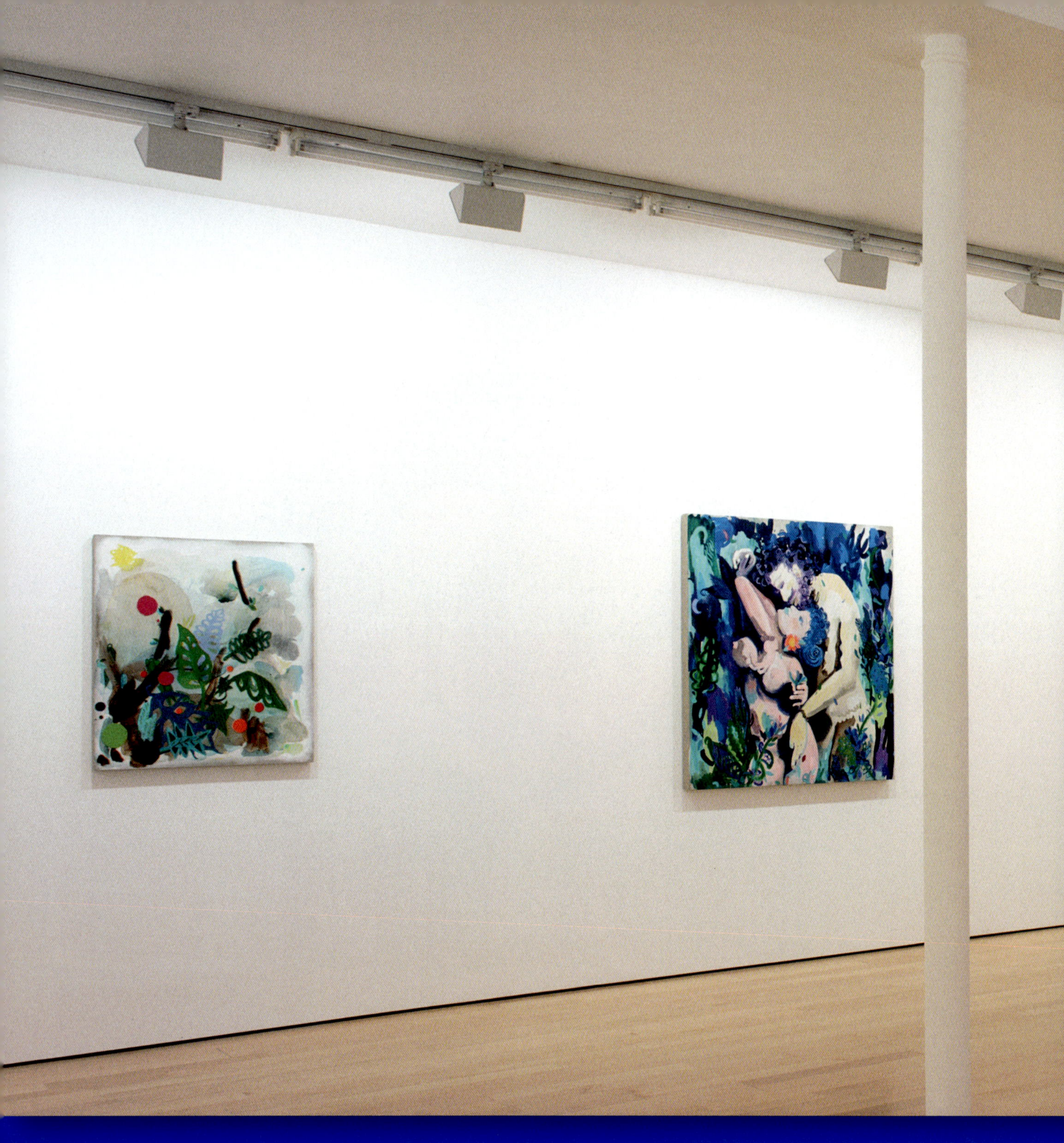

Installation view, Sadie Coles HQ, London, 2006, with *Untitled*, 2005, acrylic, oil, and felt on linen, 33 × 30 in. (83.8 × 76.2 cm); *Untitled*, 2006 (see p. 403); *Untitled*, 2006 (see p. 408); and *Untitled*, 2006, acrylic, oil, and felt on linen, 84 × 108 in. (213.4 × 274.3 cm)

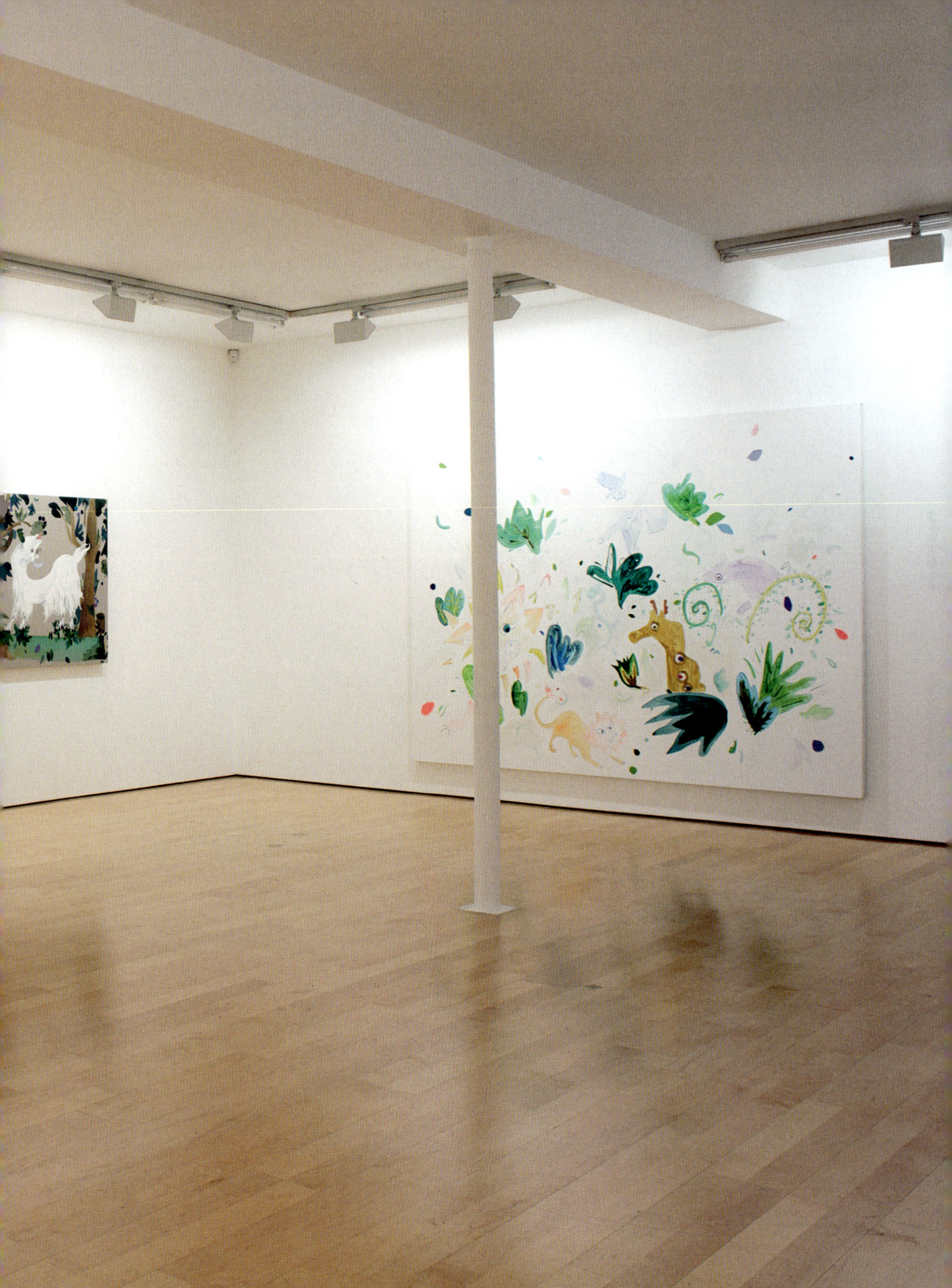

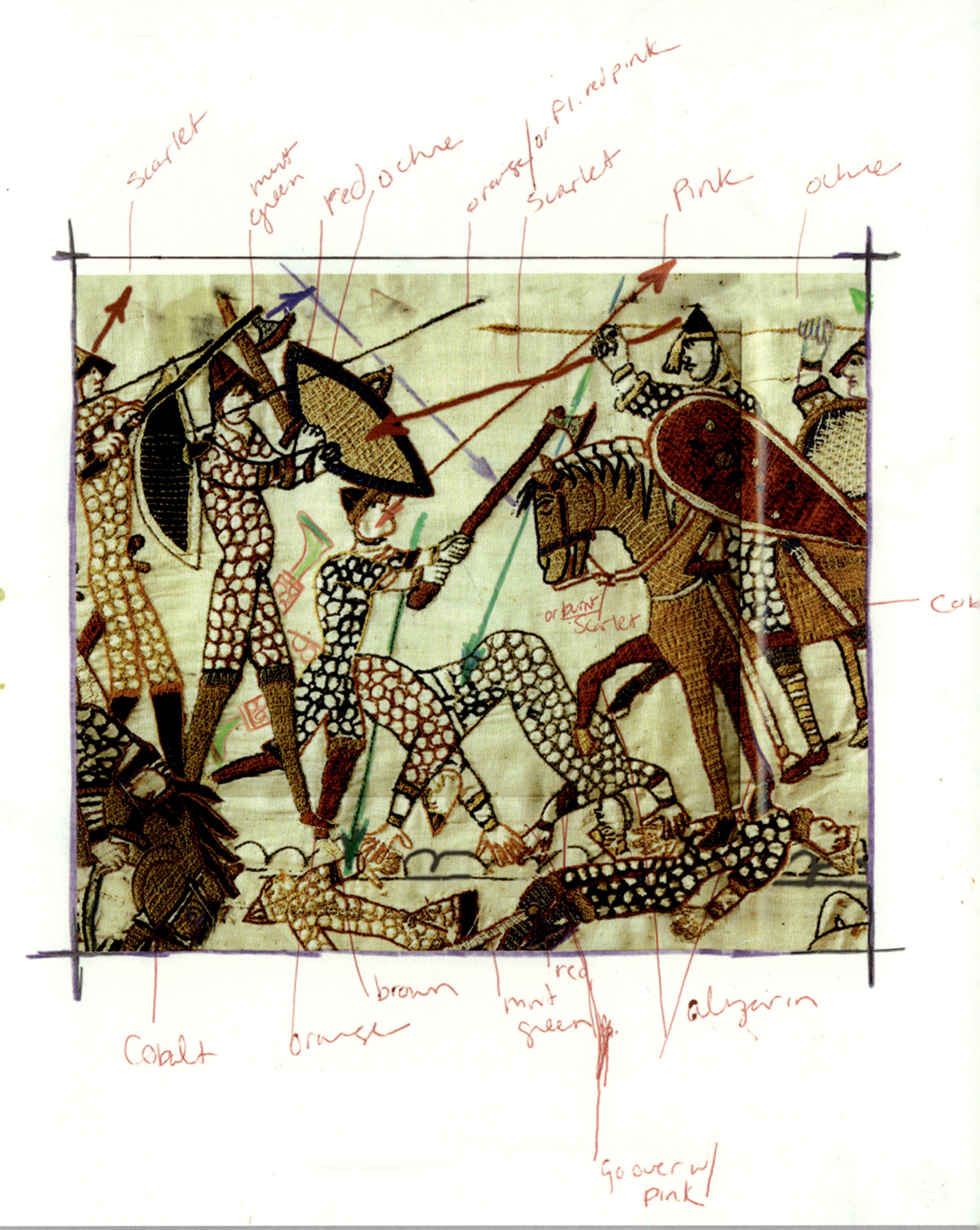

Scarlet
mint green
red ochre
orange/or Fl. red pink
Scarlet
Pink
ochre
Cob
or burnt Scarlet
Cobalt
orange
brown
red mint green
alizarin
red
Go over w/ Pink

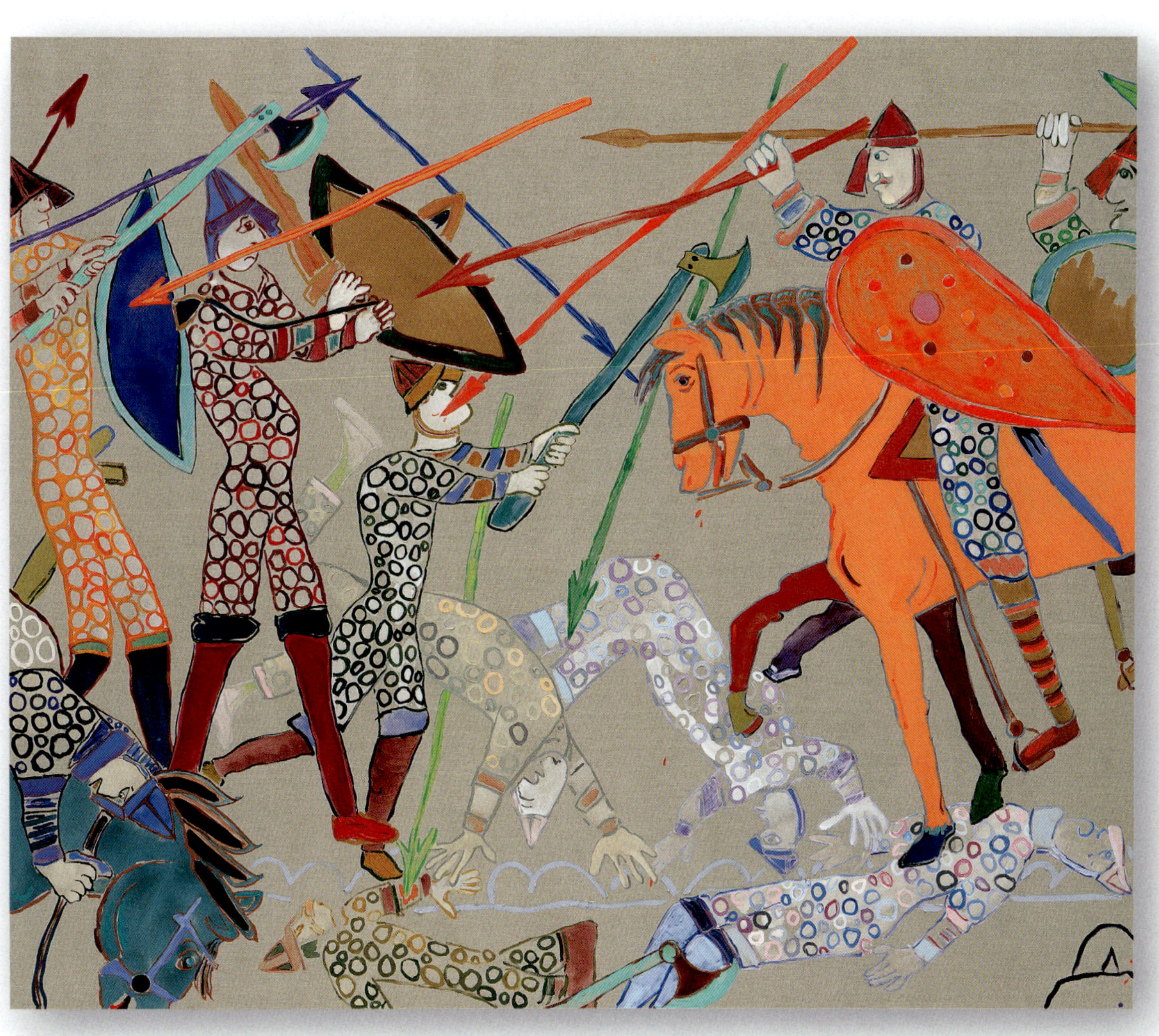

Untitled, 2006, acrylic and oil on linen, 84 × 96 in. (213.4 × 243.8 cm)

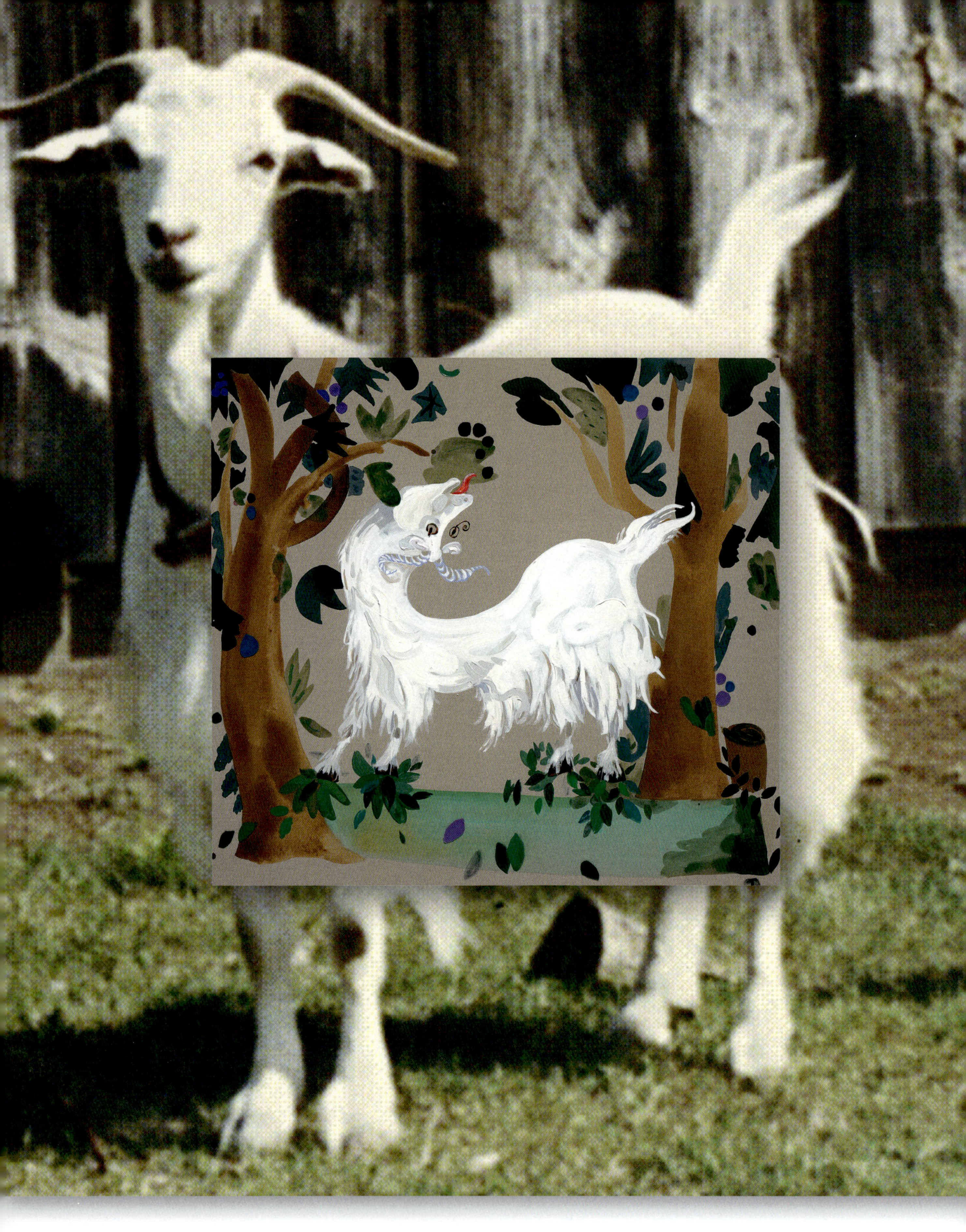

Foreground: *Untitled*, 2006, acrylic, oil, and felt on linen, 43 × 46 in. (109.2 × 116.8 cm)
Background: Research photograph, 2006

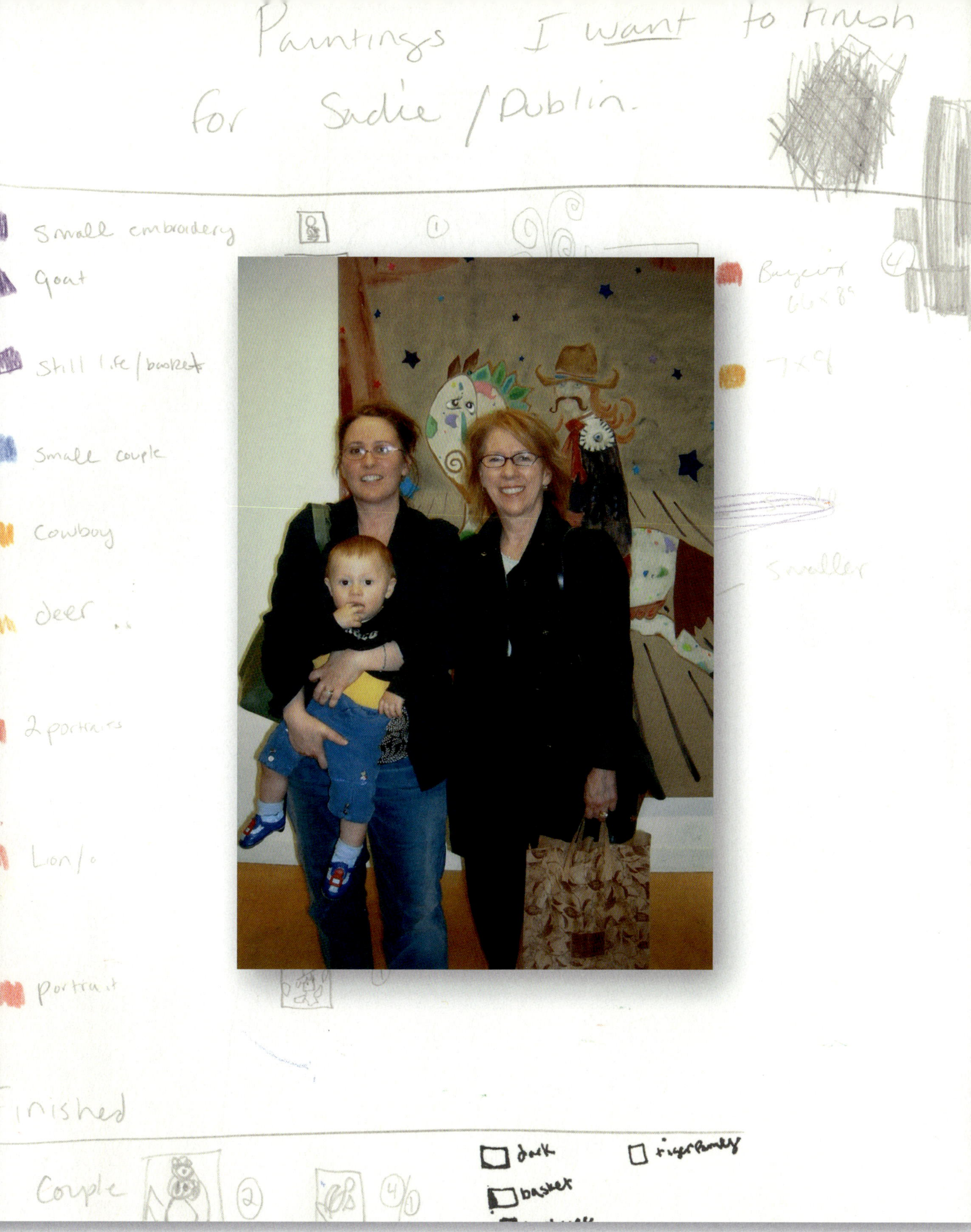

Foreground: Owens; her son, Henry Bryan; and her mother, Carol Hendrickson; with *Untitled*, 2006, acrylic, oil, and felt on linen,
80 × 60 in. (203.2 × 152.4 cm), Sadie Coles HQ, London, 2006
Background: Notes, 2006

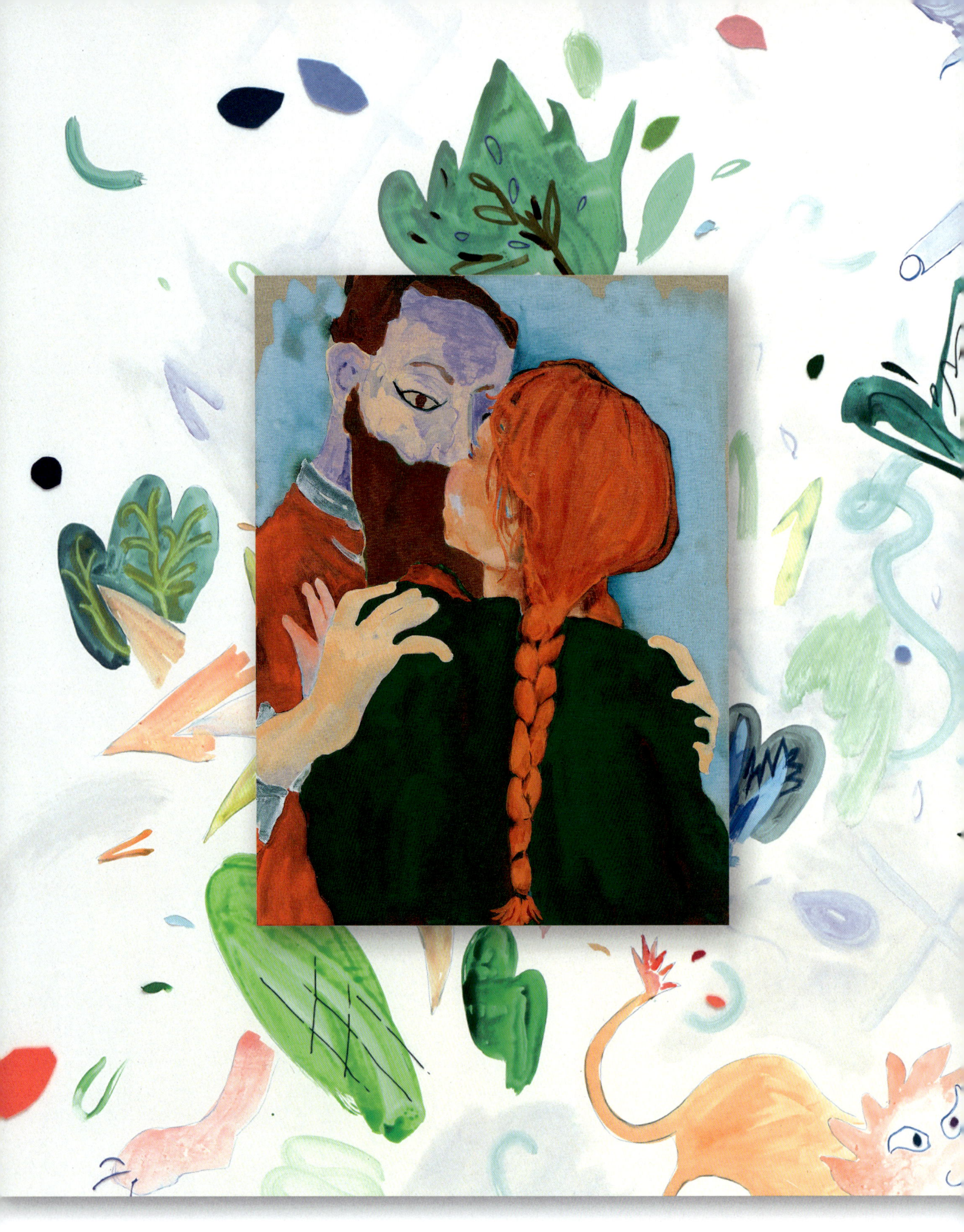

Foreground: *Untitled*, 2006, acrylic and oil on linen, 29¼ × 21¼ in. (74.3 × 54 cm)
Background: Detail of *Untitled*, 2006 (see p. 404)

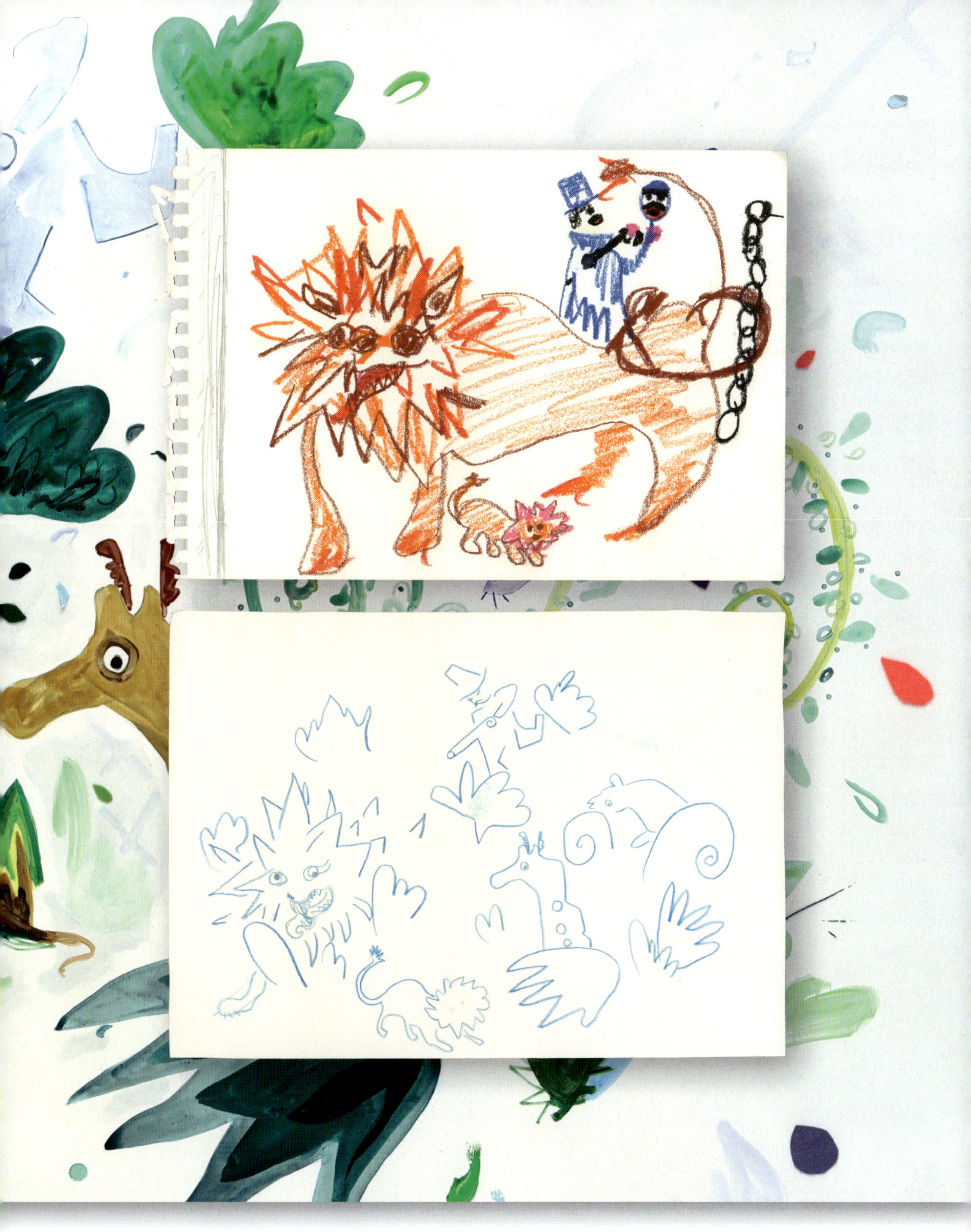

Laura Owens Mon, Apr 10, 2006 11:54 AM

Subject: FW: List of Paintings to Loan/Kunsthalle
Date: Saturday, April 8, 2006 1:52 PM
From: Gavin Brown <Gavin@GavinBrown.biz>
To: Laura Owens <laura_owens@mac.com>, Laura Owens Studio
<lowensstudio@covad.net>, beatrix ruf <ruf@kunsthallezurich.ch>
Cc: Corinna Durland <corinna@GavinBrown.biz>

Dear Laura and Beatrix,

As I mentioned on the phone, I think you need to coordinate your approach
with Beatrix. Some museums (and perhaps some collectors) will need a letter
from you explaining that the loan of their painting is crucial to the show.

The same is true of Dallas. These two should be the first letters written by
both you and Beatrix and I think it should be done as early next week as
possible.

Beatrix what do you think? Can we draw up a strategy for each of these by
Monday - so we are all on the same page. Who should contact them first etc -
perhaps at the same time. Either way soon.

On another note - in my opinion - for what its worth - I think that the
inclusion of 'older' works would make a richer exhibition. Not for its own
sake but lets include them in the pool. If there are associations and
relationships lets not discount them. In the end I think the work is not so
'old'.

LO001
Metropolitan Museum of Art - I am researching who at the Met to talk to. But
I would think, considering it is the Met that this will need LO's input.

LO138
Swiss Re London (Bank) - Beatrix - Corinna tells me you work wit hthese
people - so it should not be a problem?

LO166 & LO232
MOCA - Laura - Paul has been alerted but I think that a call from you on
Tuesday would be good - their ideas about costs could be an issue. Beatrix -
perhaps you could talk directly to him?

LO207
David Teiger/MoMA - I could call him but I think a letter from Beatrix and
Laura would be effective

LO253
Dallas Museum - Jack Lane (Director), Charlie Wylie (curator), Suzanne
Weaver (curator)

LO254
Art Institute of Chicago - I have been in contact with James Rondeau - he
says its fine - Beatrix - you could pick it up from here?

LO030 - Moores - gallery painting - they get nervous about loans and have
made specific requirments in the past with Peytons
LO078 - thea - signature painting - should not be a problem
LO192 - marty eisenberg - he is a workhorse with the loans - always does it
but bitches about it - a presonal appeal from LO would make everything go

Page 1 of 2

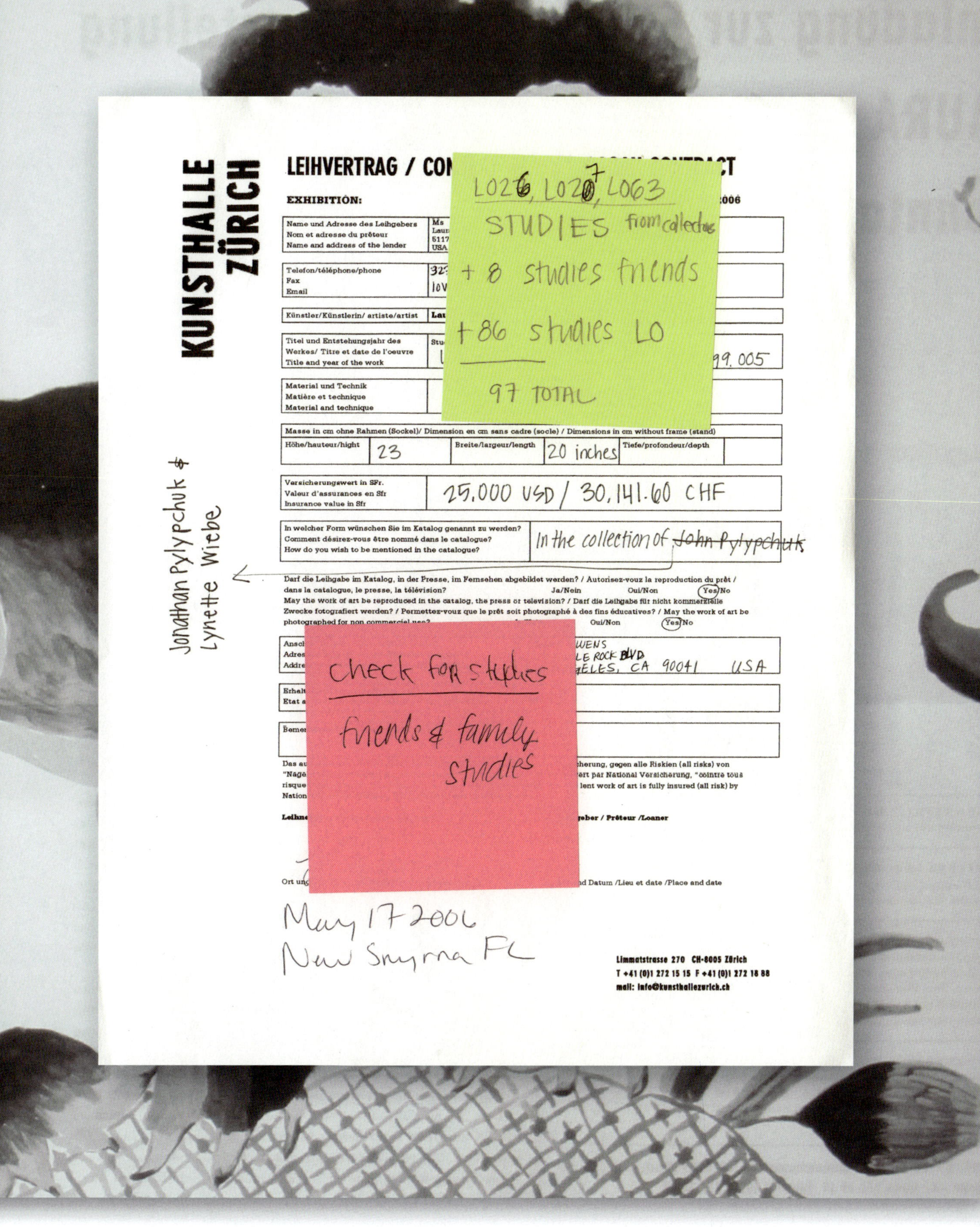

KUNSTHALLE ZÜRICH

LEIHVERTRAG / CON... CONTRACT

EXHIBITION:

2006

Name und Adresse des Leihgebers
Nom et adresse du prêteur
Name and address of the lender
Ms
Laur...
5117
USA

Telefon/téléphone/phone
Fax
Email
323
lov

Künstler/Künstlerin/ artiste/artist
Lau...

Titel und Entstehungsjahr des
Werkes/ Titre et date de l'oeuvre
Title and year of the work
Stu...
U...
99.005

Material und Technik
Matière et technique
Material and technique

Masse in cm ohne Rahmen (Sockel)/ Dimension en cm sans cadre (socle) / Dimensions in cm without frame (stand)
Höhe/hauteur/hight   23   Breite/largeur/length   20 inches   Tiefe/profondeur/depth

Versicherungswert in SFr.
Valeur d'assurances en Sfr
Insurance value in Sfr
25.000 USD / 30,141.60 CHF

In welcher Form wünschen Sie im Katalog genannt zu werden?
Comment désirez-vous être nommé dans le catalogue?
How do you wish to be mentioned in the catalogue?
In the collection of John Pylypchuk

Darf die Leihgabe im Katalog, in der Presse, im Fernsehen abgebildet werden? / Autorisez-vouz la reproduction du prêt /
dans la catalogue, le presse, la télévision?   Ja/Nein   Oui/Non   Yes/No
May the work of art be reproduced in the catalog, the press or television? / Darf die Leihgabe für nicht kommerzielle
Zwecke fotografiert werden? / Permettez-vouz que le prêt soit photographé à des fins éducatives? / May the work of art be
photographed for non commercial use?   Oui/Non   Yes/No

Ansch...   ...WENS
Adres...   ...LE ROCK BLVD
Addre...   ...GELES, CA 90041   USA

Erhalt...
Etat a...

Bemer...

Das au... ...cherung, gegen alle Riskien (all risks) von
"Nagé... ...ert par National Versicherung, "cointre tous
risque... ...lent work of art is fully insured (all risk) by
Nation...

Leihne... ...eber / Prêteur /Loaner

Ort un... ...nd Datum /Lieu et date /Place and date

Limmatstrasse 270 CH-8005 Zürich
T +41 (0)1 272 15 15 F +41 (0)1 272 18 88
mail: info@kunsthallezurich.ch

Jonathan Pylypchuk &
Lynette Wiebe

L026, L020, L063
STUDIES from collection
+ 8 studies friends
+ 86 studies LO
———
97 TOTAL

check for studies
———
friends & family
studies

May 17 2006
New Smyrna FL

Dear Frank and Nina Moore.

I hope this letter finds you well, I am writing because I would like ask that you consider loaning some of your paintings from your collection, on quite short notice. The Zurich Kunsthalle & Beatrix Ruf have invited me to do a survey show of my work. I had the opportunity to either do it quite soon or much later — and I thought it would be really great to do it sooner. However it sometimes makes it difficult to get all the best paintings. I really feel it is important to show two paintings of yours. ▭ - 8 x 10 feet and a smaller one ▭ — both untitled — so hopefully the pictures make it clear which ones I mean. I realize you have loaned them already quite a bit, however this is my first solo museum show in Europe & they are such important paintings I know they

Foreground: Letter to Frank and Nina Moore, 2006
Background: Installation view, studies, Kunsthalle Zurich, 2006

will be missed if we cannot include them.

We are planning to show a range of work from 1994-2006 and do a pretty extensive catalogue. I think it will be really a great opportunity for me and the work will see a whole new audience.

I really hope you will consider this loan. I know it is really very short notice, the show will open June 11, I apologize for any inconvenience this might cause.

Thanks for considering it... I am sure Corinna Durland or Beatrix Ruf will be in touch shortly... If you have any questions my studio number is 323 255 1104 -- Thanks again,
Laura Owens

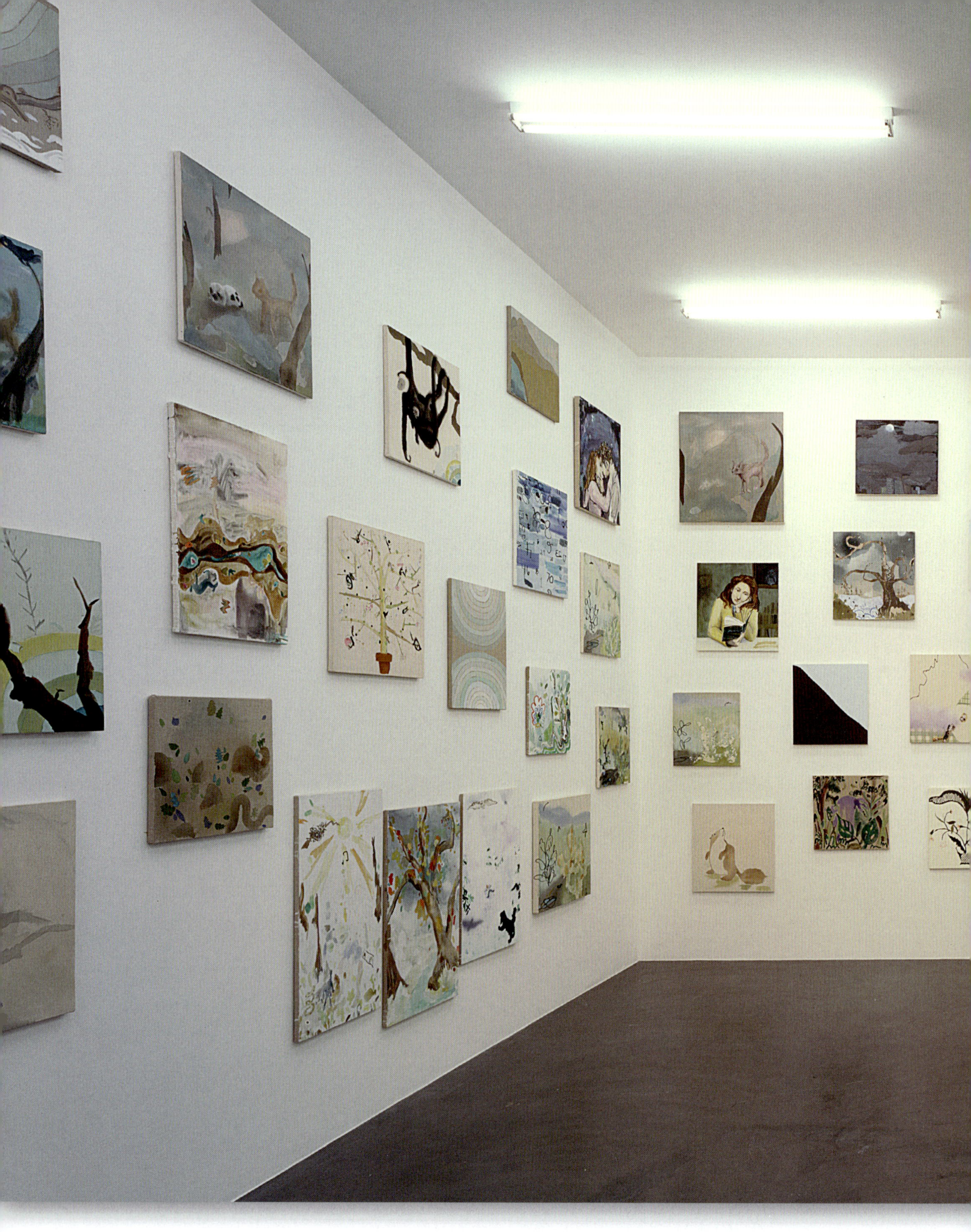

    Installation view, studies, Kunsthalle Zurich, 2006

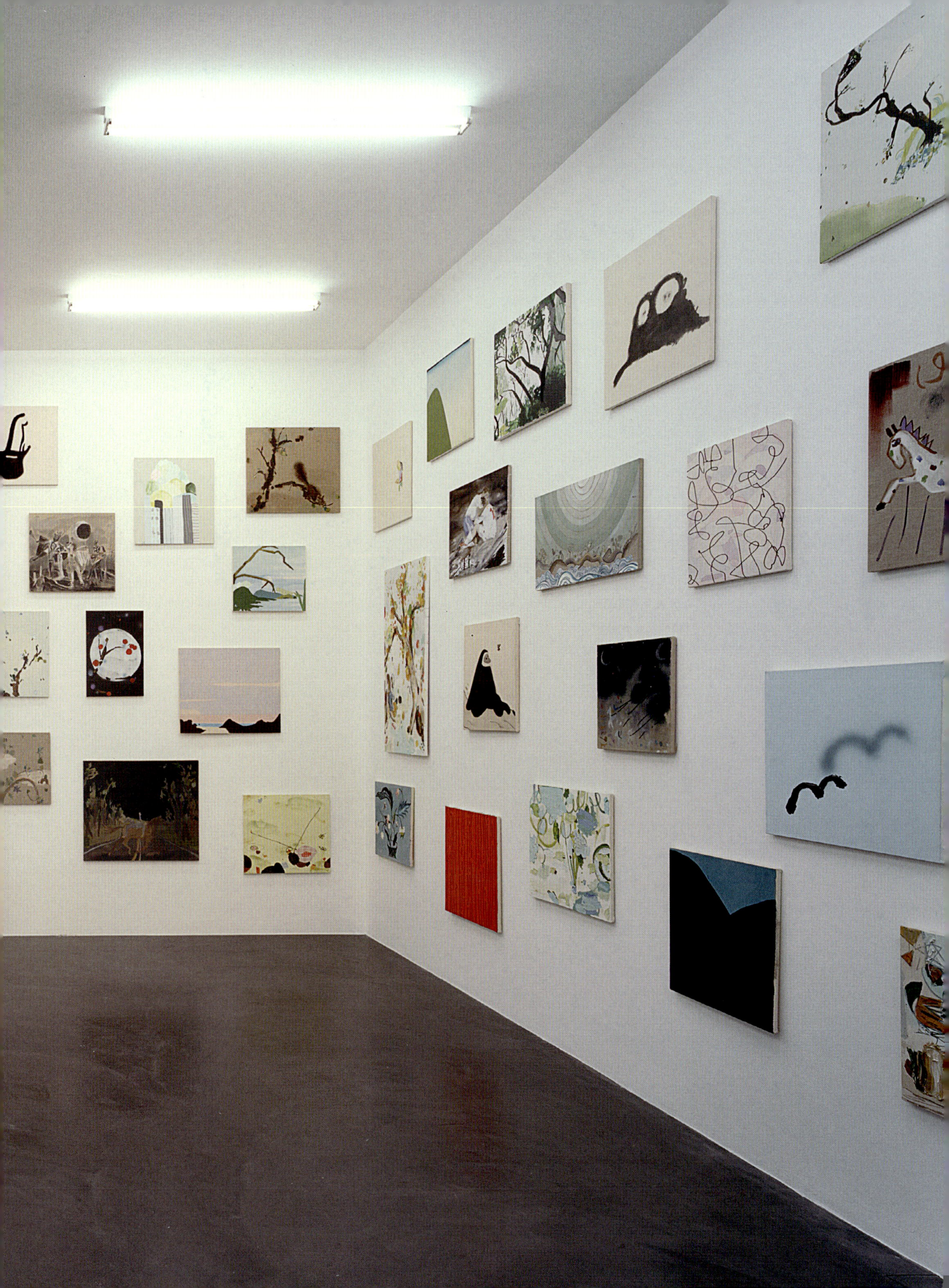

ON LAURA OWENS'S IDEA OF EDGES
KIRSTY BELL

"So anyway with the idea of edges . . . ," Laura Owens writes in an open letter for her 2006 exhibition at Gavin Brown's enterprise in New York. She is discussing the work she made in her parents' newly renovated garage after moving back to Cleveland. Returning to Ohio, where she grew up, was a way of zooming out of the art world's myopic New York/Los Angeles axis and also, paradoxically, a means of focusing more closely on the texture of her everyday life. The resulting paintings pay more attention to the edges of the canvas, creating additional "manufactured edges" that compete with the actual edges, as she writes in the letter-cum-press release. But they also allow free rein to certain other edges of her painterly practice. This period was an experiment in doing away with the notion of untraversable boundaries between the professional life of an artist and the personal stuff that surrounds it, in allowing both to intermingle and play out on the field of the canvas. It is not incidental that when she moved to her parents' house she brought along her baby son, Henry.

———

Owens has always had a particular relationship to edges: she seems congenitally disposed to overstep them. Edges of authorship are challenged by her liberal borrowings from works by other artists. Edges of individual canvases are broken open, forming diptychs that wrap around corners and create imagined connections in the in-between space. Edges of disciplines are in turn transgressed by bringing textiles, photography, text, or embroidery into the frame of painting. She also oversteps edges of taste, indulging in the decorative, the flamboyant, the childlike, the illustrative. There is always more room to be surprised, however. I remember clearly the shock of seeing her first figurative painting—with real people, not just animals—in 2000. Only their heads were visible, resting on a pair of pillows, while the rest of their bodies were covered by an expanse of monochrome sheeting and patterned bedspread much more in keeping with what we'd come to expect from her at that time (see p. 283). Though Owens is a master of composition, and the dynamism of her works has much to do with her sophisticated resolution of the problems that occur within the picture plane, it is at the edges, in the paintings' self-conscious and awkward relations to external aspects such as architecture, interior space, landscape, time, geography, subject matter, style, discipline, and sometimes even politics, that their restlessness is found.

When I think about her painting practice, the difficulties in particular come to mind, despite the fact that the works themselves are characterized by levity and assuredness. Our own relationship, though it began in a professional context, quickly developed into a friendship, and as such always intermingles talk of art, work, and the rest of life, so I witnessed firsthand many of the attendant anxieties that accompany the making of her paintings: the impending deadlines, the juggling of conflicting responsibilities, the inevitable obstacles that seem to keep the figment of a smoothly running studio practice constantly at arm's length. (As I write this, a 2003 painting immediately springs to mind: a gray road winds through a scumbly green landscape; in the foreground is an "obstacle warning" road sign, an arrow weaving to avoid a blockage (see p. 363). To me, that piece has always seemed emblematic of this daily struggle.) I recently read through our email correspondence from the last fifteen years or so and found it to be filled with troubles of many scales, encountered both inside and outside the edges of art:

~ "I actually got really sick on Thursday night finishing up the paintings. I think it was turpentine and exhaustion . . ."

~ "My tomatoes got eaten by a variety of caterpillars and snails, I couldn't bring myself to buy the granules that are supposed to kill them . . ."

    Kirsty Bell is an art critic and writer based in Berlin.

~ "I am freakin' but I am just going to go for it and hopefully everything will work out . . ."

~ "The roof is off my house and I think there was a squirrel in my kitchen . . ."

~ "I have been trying to read a book called *Getting Things Done* for a week now and it's pretty pathetic. The irony there is a little hard to take . . ."

Once we both had children the frequency of our email exchanges decreased, while their references to the basic, recurring problem of the struggle to *get things done* increased:

~ "We have had such a crazy year; next year I am hoping and planning will be quite slow and boring . . ."

~ "I am always strategizing ways to childproof a room completely . . . but it never seems to happen, they always find something to get into . . ."

~ "We are trying to figure out how to be less stressed out . . ."

~ "I did manage to finish things . . . but it was really hard . . ."

~ "We are all pretty good. . . . Just crazy with kids and work . . ."

While preparing a text about her in 2004 I naïvely asked her if she saw painting as a kind of escape from the petty difficulties of the everyday. "No, I wish it were," she replied. "I feel like it's an awkward colliding with yourself and the present moment. All your dissatisfactions with yourself come up one by one and you have to let them pass by, and then you are aware of yourself painting almost too much, and then at some point you let that go. . . . When it's going really well you feel sort of insane . . . you don't relate to everything . . . [to] all your friends [or to] the world in the same way, somehow everything else seems rather unreal and the painting seems real."

———

When Owens moved back to Ohio in 2006 it was not only a geographic zooming-out but also a way of zooming in—of checking in, perhaps, and trying to draw the reality of painting and the reality of everything else closer together. She did this through considering the effects that a change of place and working routine might have on a body of work and through paying attention to the texture

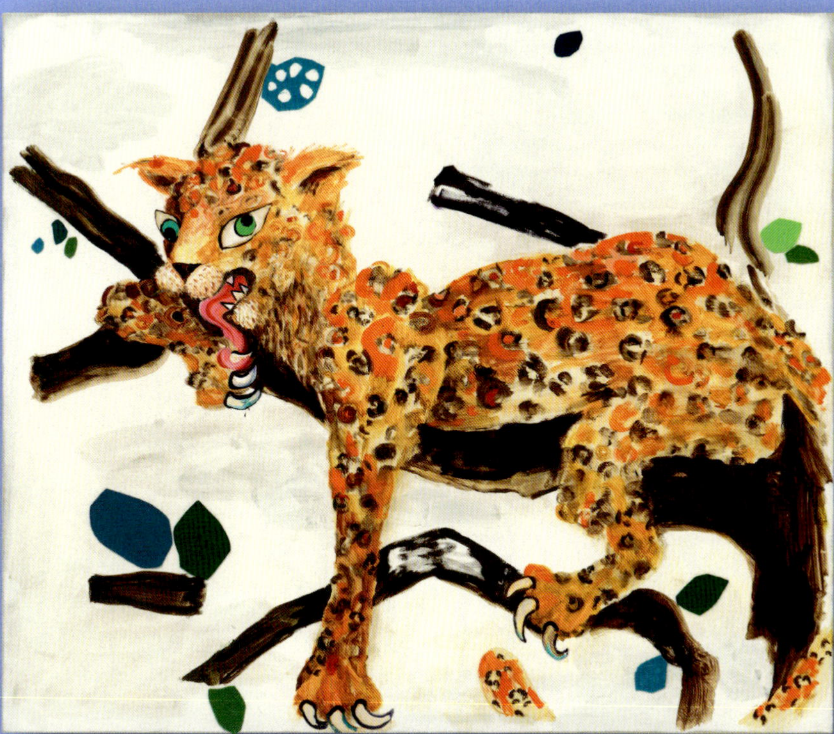

Untitled, 2006, acrylic, oil, and felt on linen, 37¾ × 43 in. (95.9 × 109.2 cm)

of everyday routines, accompanying thought processes, and proclivities and allowing for a kind of "unmediated content" to flow into her paintings. For Owens it had long been a matter of strategy— if not principle—to have an open-door policy when it came to making her work. She wrote in 2004: "I feel like my number one goal in making a new painting is to try to give myself some new small (or large) amount of freedom where I was previously restricting myself. Being aware that I am making a painting and not painting a something is one big way to do this. It is easier said than done though."

The whole body of work from Ohio, like those that followed in the subsequent three or four years, is an effort not to avoid but rather to embody the life changes that occur when confronted with the task of bringing up children. Her paintings from this period are full of bucolic images of love: between mothers and children, or fathers and mothers, naked and often surrounded by animals in Edenic landscapes (see p. 424). They are about being a parent but also about childhood as an Arcadian state: her son's childhood, but also hers, and the memories embodied in her childhood home, or in someone else's picture-book idea of childhood. As usual, the paintings' imagery borrows liberally from other artworks, textiles, Persian miniatures, illustrations. She cites Roy Lichtenstein and Henri Matisse as influences, as well as Marie Laurencin,

in compositions in which formal unity itself was the very point. These new works are conspicuous in their unmediated content and lack of connections. They make porosity their subject matter and engage in a constant prodding at the boundaries and limitations—*the idea of edges*—in an effort to gain, or enforce, elasticity. They not only represent planes, forms, colors, and spaces or people, animals, gardens, and oceans but also tentatively aim for emotional states—love! joy! pleasure!—uncircumscribed by intellectual mediation or conceptual master planning. These works are aimed right at the messy edges where the identity of an artist or painter is in constant collision with other simultaneous identities as lover, mother, teacher, colleague, or friend. Their all-embracing content is an ambitious attempt to reconcile these roles.

———

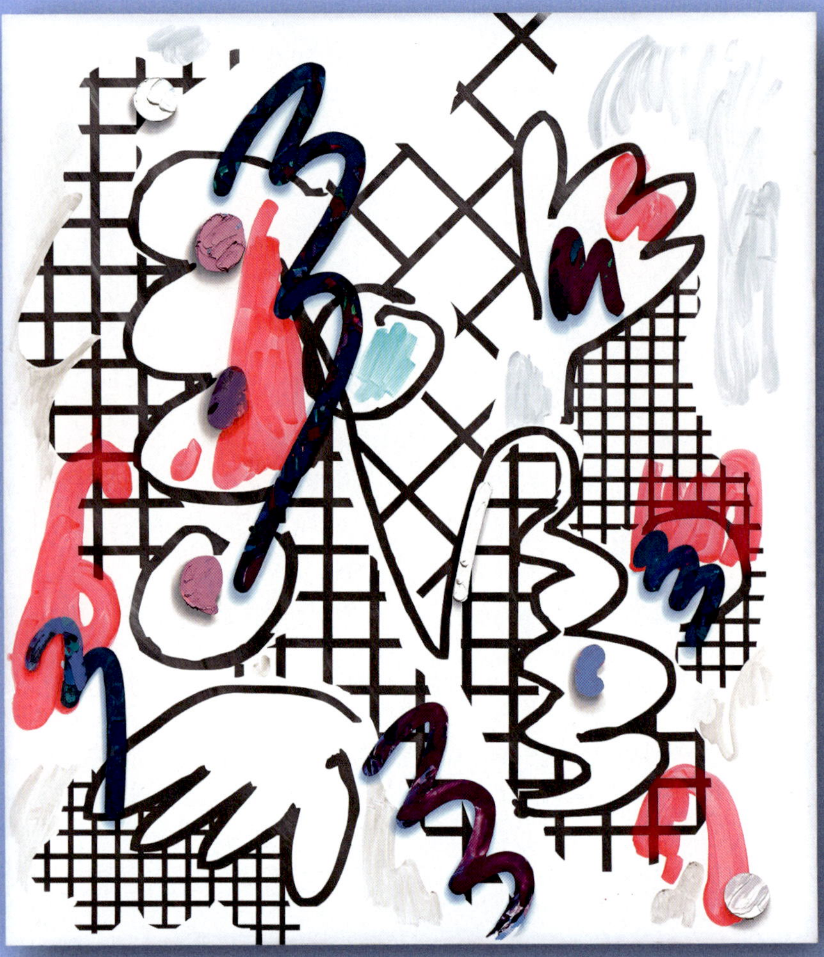

Untitled, 2013, acrylic, oil, resin, and charcoal on linen, 137½ × 120 in. (349.3 × 304.8 cm)

whose works, she says in her press release–letter, "always fuzz out around the edges." In these wildly colored and fantastically animated paintings (the debt to Matisse is clear) the smart compositions of her earlier works have been abandoned for an ornamental looseness as paint and narrative components slide laterally across the surface. She describes the Ohio works, which were installed salon style for the show at her New York gallery, as a diagram of her desk with all its accumulated pictures, books, reference material—snapshots of the things she had on her mind (see pp. 424–25). The works are an exercise in examining whether anything and everything that happened to be in the studio could become a work of art, without the need for an overarching connection.

In previous bodies of work—even those that were already largely figurative, featuring pastoral landscapes full of luscious plants and frolicking animals or decorative still lifes lifted from ornamental textiles—fragments from a variety of stylistic sources were often combined

After her stay in Ohio, Owens continued to work in an absorptive, uncensoring manner, switching between a studio in her backyard in the Eagle Rock neighborhood of Los Angeles and a small garden shed at the house in Orient, Long Island, where she spends the summers. It was the scale of her studio in Orient, along with the experience of borrowing books from the local library there, that led her to begin creating handmade books. As this interest developed and the unique book became an important format and ongoing part of her work, books also became a repository for her unchecked flow of ideas. In 2011 she wrote: "Recycling the studio practice just seems like a good way to let go of something or show something that would otherwise not make it into a painting or drawing. I think the threshold for a book is very low!! Which is good." The result was a siphoning-off of this kind of content, which freed up the canvas again to articulate different kinds of edges.

In summer 2009 Owens began a series of seven still-life paintings: sketchy collections of seaside subject matter and other still-life paraphernalia—starfish, seashells, fruit, ropes, nets, a typewriter—centralized on raw linen. When she brought these works back to Los Angeles a few years later to finish them she became stuck, until she hung them in a row on her studio wall and realized that she wanted to make them a single work by orchestrating their edges into a larger whole (see p. 480). To achieve this she added a cutout grid pattern between the individual paintings—a kind of wooden trellis that gave them the appearance of growing organically on a predetermined structure. This superimposed grid structure has many precursors in Owens's work: as an impastoed screen in 1999 (see p. 237), or in the recurrent patches of cross-hatching that suggest a unified background in a number of her compositions. In a small picture from 1998 the stretcher's wooden cross-frame is depicted on the surface with a thorny rose twisting its way through it. The trellis—a compositional device in which geometric structure meets organic element—became central to her subsequent bodies of work, beginning with the pieces shown in *Pavement Karaoke/Alphabet* (2012, see p. 492) and *Twelve Paintings* (2013, see p. 510), as a kind of shorthand for structuring depth of field. In her paintings made between 2006 and 2011 the compositions are generally spread laterally across the canvas with little perspectival play, emphasizing instead the horizontal connections between elements or between the different works hanging together in a space. Although these lateral connections are still implied through the serial nature of many of Owens's later works, now the spatial experience of her work is countered by the autonomy of the stand-alone paintings, in which the trellis becomes a code that articulates layers of content within the canvases. In these later works, the nature of Owens's subject matter has also modulated. While it may still be personal (in the choice of the classified ads they picture; the plasticized paint daub as signature; the storybook illustrations on school exercises, annotated with children's stories), it is no longer "unmediated content" but is sublimated by the works' overriding structure.

In Owens's book *Claire Van Vliet 1* (2011), a tribute to the eponymous artist, printer, and bookmaker, each page shows a cross-hatching of paint, with the grid's internal squares cut out to reveal a further cross-hatching in a different color on the next page, and so on, until the final page. This dynamic cross-hatching suggests another use of the trellis, here as a way of choosing whether to cover something up or to reveal it. It is a strategic device. It is not that the personal is no longer in there, it may be simply be out of sight.

Except where noted, all quotations are from email correspondence between Laura Owens and the author, 2001–11. The full text of the open letter Owens wrote for her exhibition at Gavin Brown's enterprise, New York, 2006, may be accessed at Artmap, https://artmap.com/gavinbrown/exhibition/laura-owens-2006.

Gavin Brown's Enterprise
620 Greenwich Street, 212-627-5258
Greenwich Village
December 1, 2006 - January 13, 2007
Reception: Thursday, November 30, 6 - 8 PM

To Whom it May Concern,

For this new body of work, I decided to move back to Ohio. I recently renovated my parents' garage and have been working in this new and also very old context. I grew up here and hadn't been back for any length of time since I was a teenager. It's been interesting. Election season, and Ohio suddenly feels like the center of the world…. I thought I had escaped, not so!

I was really disappointed to find out the Cleveland Art Museum would not be open until 2011! They have t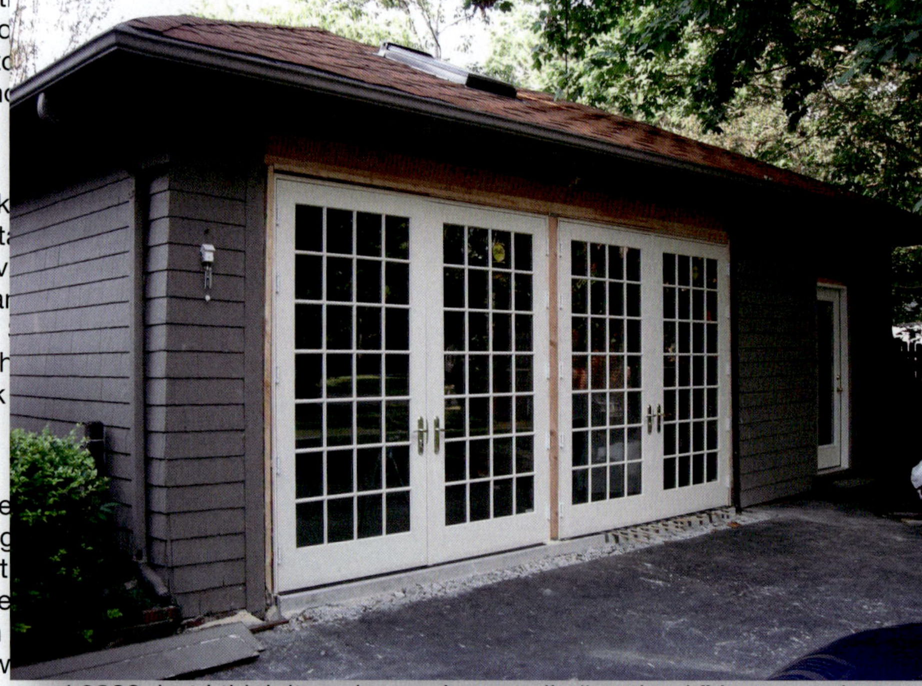

nothing compared

concerted effort to

grandparents, who

didn't find it (yet);

As far as the work

unified…. For insta

edges of the canv

way it is primed an

additional edges.

there are two or th

more ways to talk

space.

Just saw a picture

me, his use of edg

In general I think t

relationship I have

Barnes collection

triptych and the w

to do this since around 2003; but I think its only now I am really "getting it" in any real way.

I also had been a real nut for Marie Laurencin when I was in college. I just bought a catalogue of hers. In many ways her paintings always fuzz out around the edges or create a lot of inner edges that are fuzzy and shifting. Sort of the opposite of Matisse in terms of structure, but similar in some ways to what I am thinking about.

So anyway with the idea of edges….

I also wanted to play around with the edges of the gallery. Where the work is in the gallery, thinking about the different spaces. Waking up some spaces, putting other spaces to sleep. This will be determined by the installation, and so it's sort of a whole lot of b.s. to tell you how it's working in a press release….

Also with the edges of the show… hoping to leave up some of Jenny's work… bring in some of Rob's… sort of to soften the edges of the show (in terms of time)... To not erase and break completely, but to get more close to what I see as reality… not cut nice and

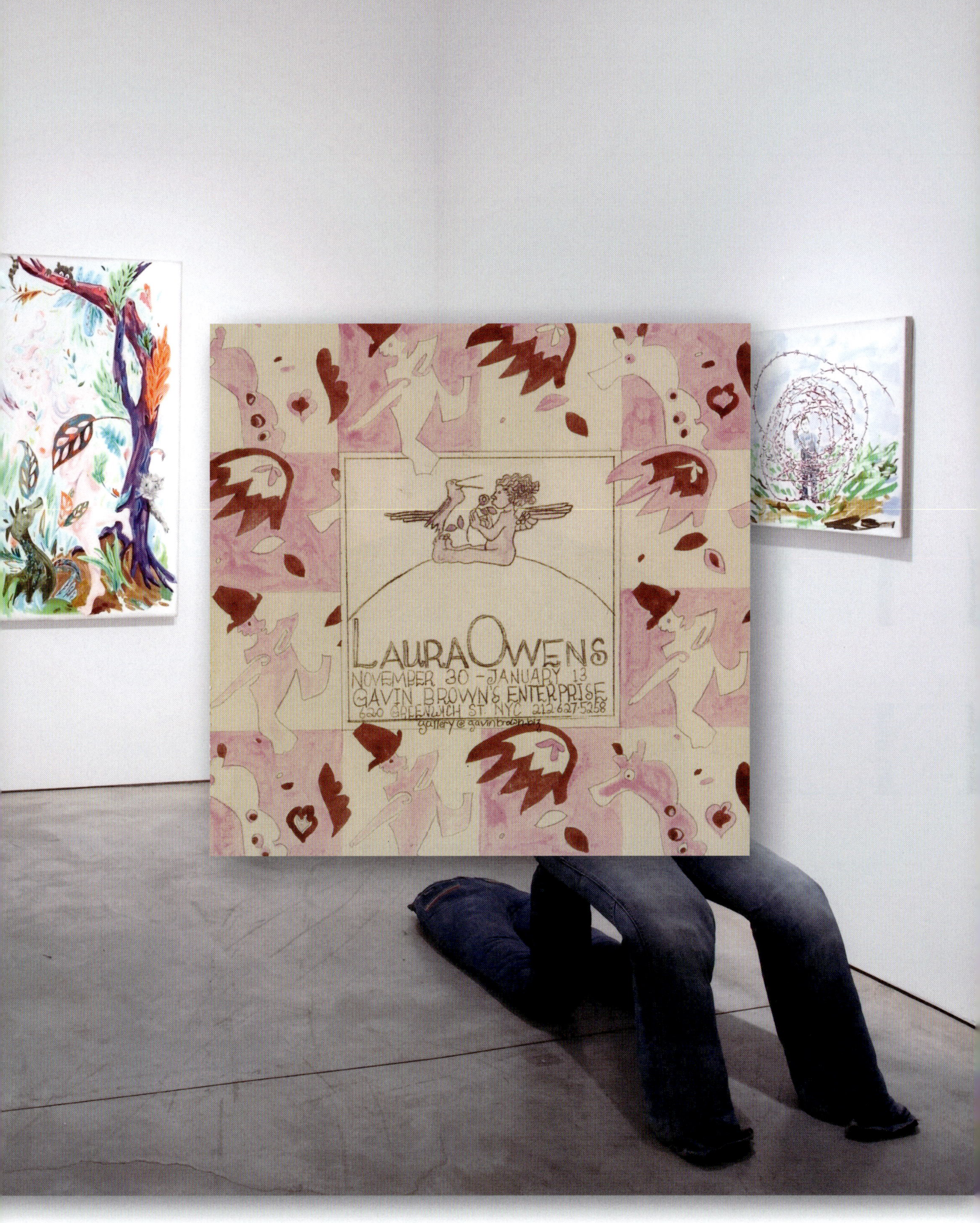

Foreground: Announcement, Gavin Brown's enterprise, New York, 2006
Background: Installation view, Gavin Brown's enterprise, New York, 2006, with *Untitled*, 2006, acrylic and oil on linen, two panels: 56 × 40 in. (142.2 × 101.6 cm) each, and *Untitled*, 2006 (see p. 426), and Rob Pruitt, *Esprit de Corps: Bench, Touché*, 2006, denim and concrete, 22 x 61 x 24 in. (55.9 x 154.9 x 61 cm)

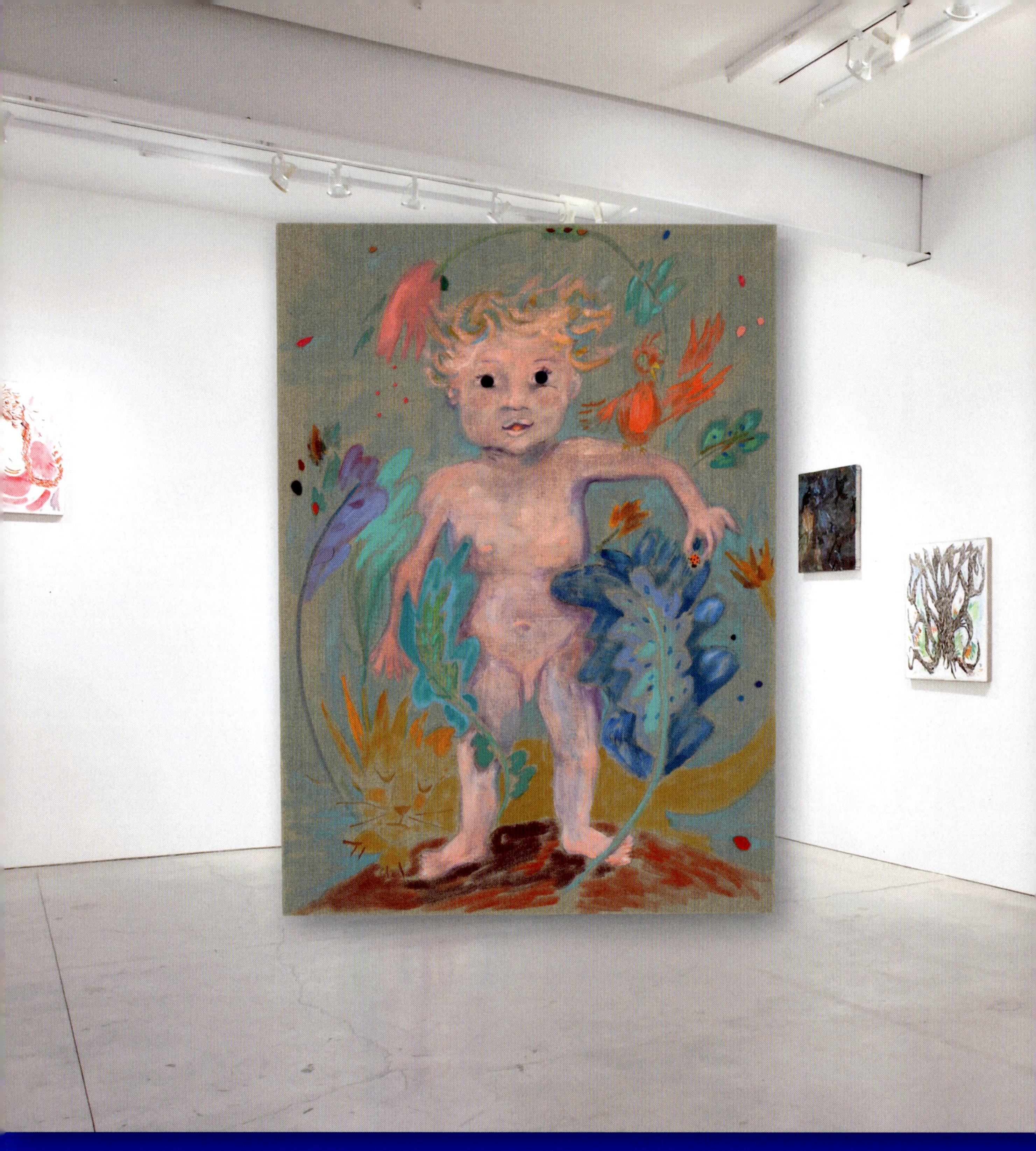

Foreground: *Untitled*, 2006, acrylic, oil, and felt on linen, 49 × 35 in. (124.5 × 88.9 cm)
Background: Installation view, Gavin Brown's enterprise, New York, 2006, with *Untitled*, 2006, acrylic and oil on linen, 33 × 30 in. (83.8 × 76.2 cm); *Untitled*, 2006, acrylic and oil on linen, 28 × 30 in. (71.1 × 76.2 cm); *Untitled*, 2006, acrylic and oil on linen, 34 × 34 in. (86.4 × 86.4 cm); and *Untitled,* 2006, acrylic and oil on linen, 108 × 144 in. (274.3 × 274.3 cm)

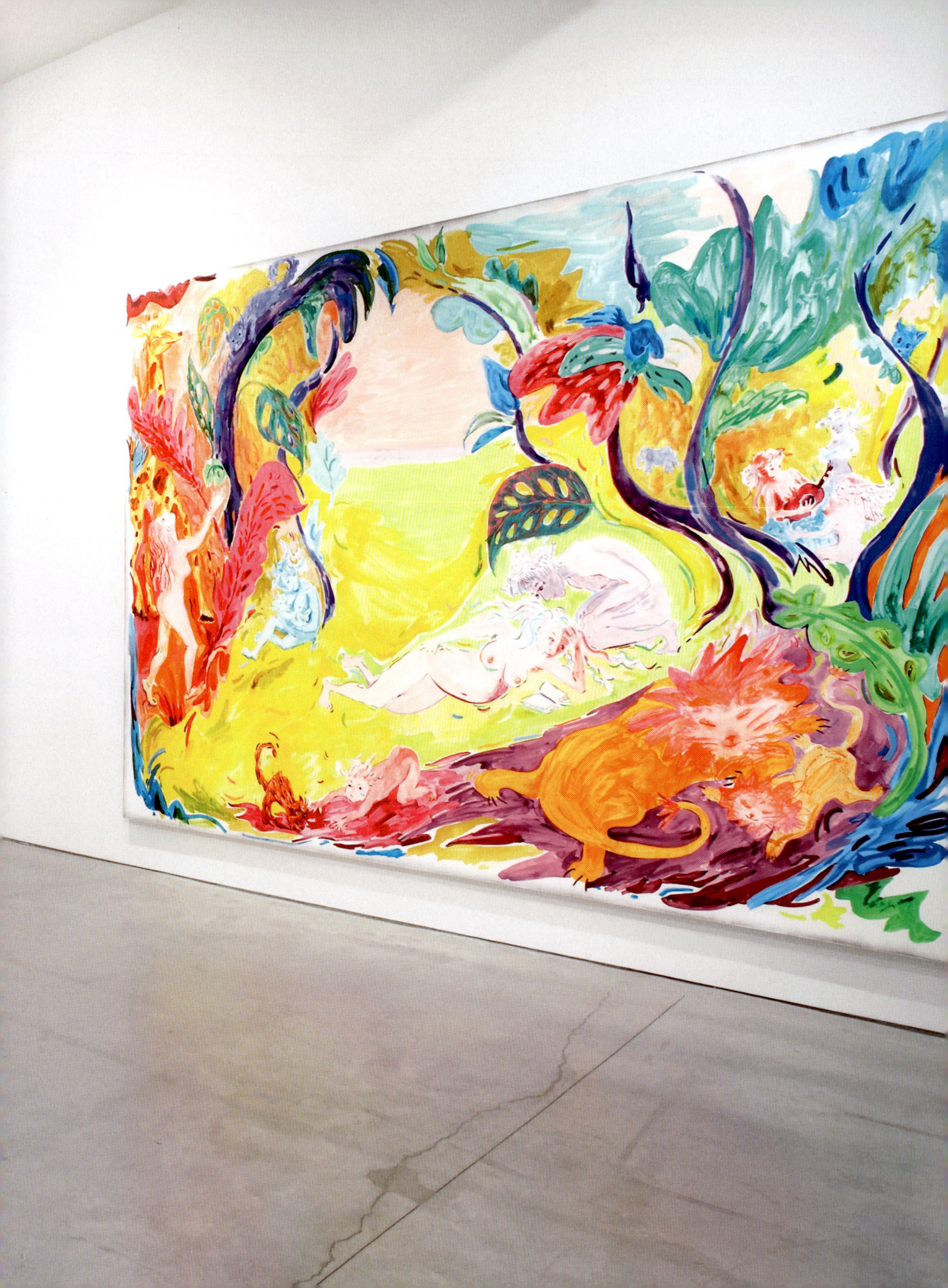

From: **Laura Owens** laura_owens@mac.com
Subject: to do
Date: October 15, 2006 at 8:49 PM
To: Mungo Thomson mungothomson@earthlink.net

1Get the ny times magazine.
2read the Q and A with John Ashcroft
3 as you note answer to visual arts question,
firmly hold onto your head as it is likely to pop off at this point, ...mine just did.

ps can we collaborate on something?... my head has popped off and I am not doing so well.. I think making a collaborative piece about it might help.

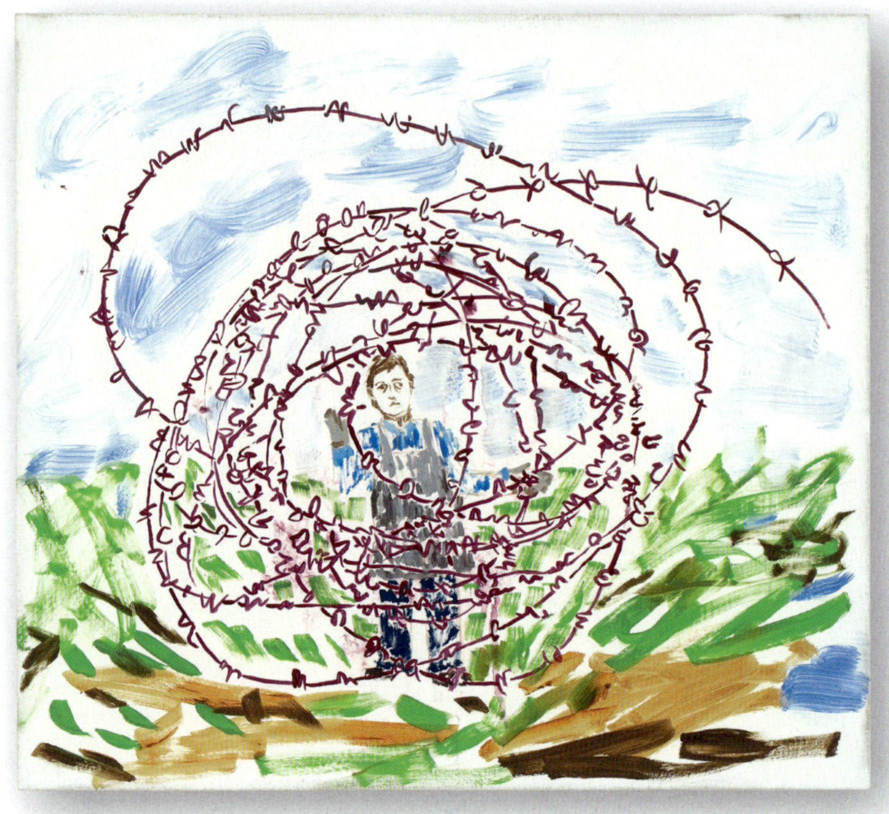

Foreground: Owens and Mungo Thomson, *Untitled*, 2006, acrylic and oil on linen, 20 × 24 in. (50.8 × 61 cm)
 Background: Email to Mungo Thomson, 2006

LAURA OWENS
Untitled
2006
oil and acrylic on linen
9 1/4 x 7 inches
LO 340

$ 45,000

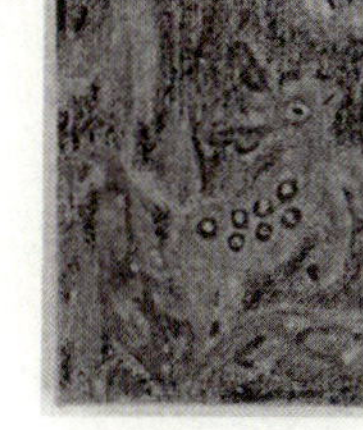

LAURA OWENS
Untitled
2006
oil, acrylic and wood on linen
12 1/4 x 10 inches
LO 341

$ 50,000

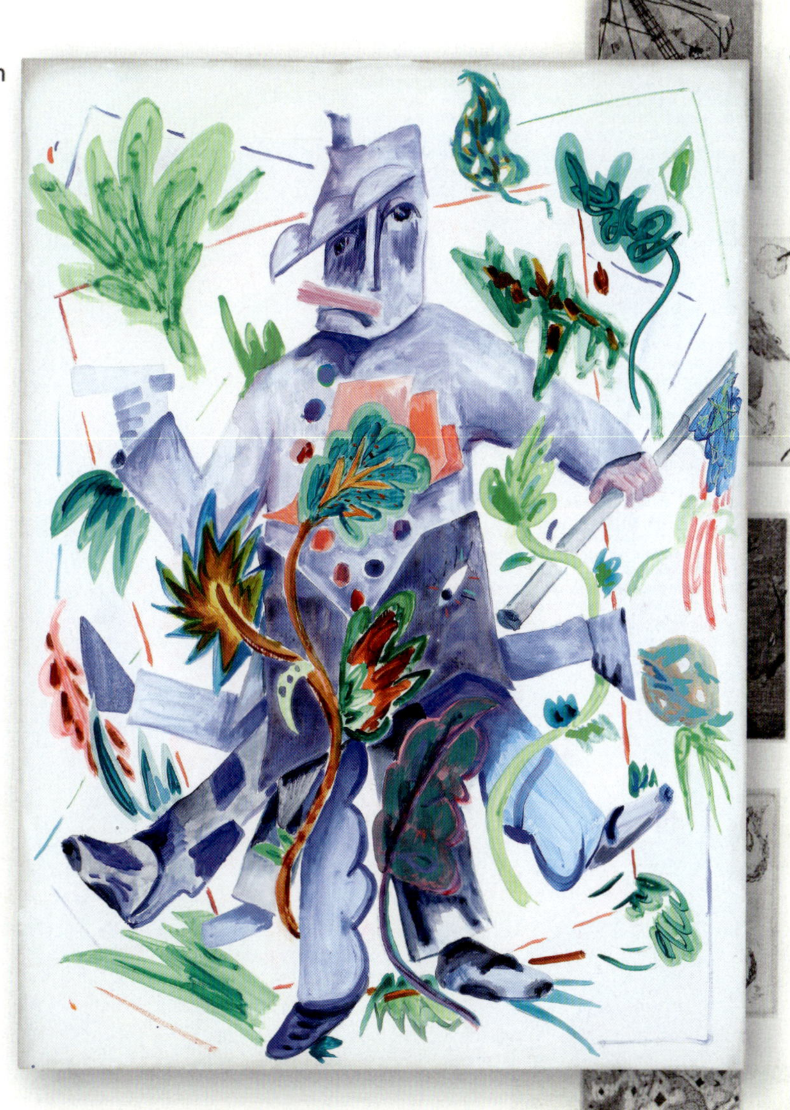

LAURA OWENS
Untitled
2006
oil and acrylic on linen
18 x 20 1/4 inches
LO 342

$ 65,000

LAURA OWENS
Untitled
2006
oil and acrylic on linen
30 x 28 inches
LO 343

$ 65,000

LAURA OWENS
Untitled
2006
oil and acrylic on linen
34 x 34 inches
LO 344

$ 70,000

LAURA OWENS
Untitled
2006
oil, felt, and acrylic on linen
39 1/2 x 35 inches plus 1" felt overhang
LO 345

$ 85,000

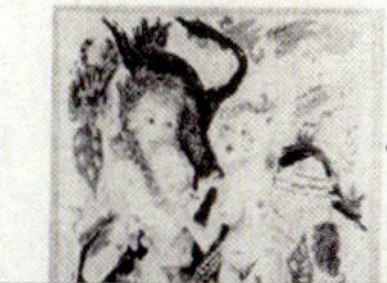

LAURA OWENS
Untitled
2006
oil and acrylic on linen
43 x 45 inches

Foreground: *Untitled*, 2006, acrylic and oil on linen, 56 × 40 in. (142.2 × 101.6 cm)
Background: Price list, Gavin Brown's enterprise, New York, 2006

From: **Gavin Brown's Enterprise** gallery@gavinbrown.biz
Subject: An End for Passerby
Date: August 3, 2007 at 7:01 AM
To: laura_owens@mac.com

Dear Laura,

We at Gavin Brown̦s enterprise are not-so-pleased to announce that as of
February 1st, 2008, the West 15th gallery space at Passerby will be no
longer (Passerby the watering hole will also be deep-sixed). Whether this
forthcoming absence is significant or not we can̦t say. Perhaps you̦ll
want to cheer its passing with a drink at Pastis. But, footnote or not,
Passerby is one more splattered bunny in a growing line of cultural
road-kill on the New York super-highway of averageness.

In anticipation of the inevitable, we̦re launching a creative venture to
revivify the spirit of New York (in the nostalgic imagination), and maximize
the spirit of the Passerby space. What that spirit is need̦nt be named.
Whatever your memory animates for youŠ

For five months September 1st, 2007 until Passerby is exeunt the gallery
will be host to an array of projects. There will be site-specific artisțs
projects, haphazard compound exhibitions, endurance performances, endurance
serendipities, repasts, confabs of the best variety, and whatever else
allows for a supple/unkempt amalgam that will to the death resist
recognition, reject success, reuse tired old ideas and reanimate our lost
city. A standard-bearing website will be host to projects as well.

We̦re writing to you in hopes that you̦d like to join us back in the bunker,
contribute in some form to this amalgam, and help define its ultimate
musculature. Any proposals/ideas you have for the space (whether through
your own work or the work of others) are welcome for due consideration.

Remember the New York of possibilities one more (last) time. And Passerby
as one of its ill-fated kids (maybe ganged-up on by some upstarts). We̦re
hoping you might be able to excavate the magics perched/puckered in its
walls. Whatever it meant to you or still-can-mean. Sloping drywall, charred
beams, and gnarly bricks: funked-up skylights and paint-pocked floors.
Pre-Morimoto, pre-Zwirnerplex, pre-Maritime. Whatever encomium feels good:
love the old boy (bring him some fly new socks).

Any proposals are needed sooner than later. Sometime in August would be
great. We would love the opportunity to work with you on this project, and
hope to hear from you.

Warmest sincerities, regardless

GBE

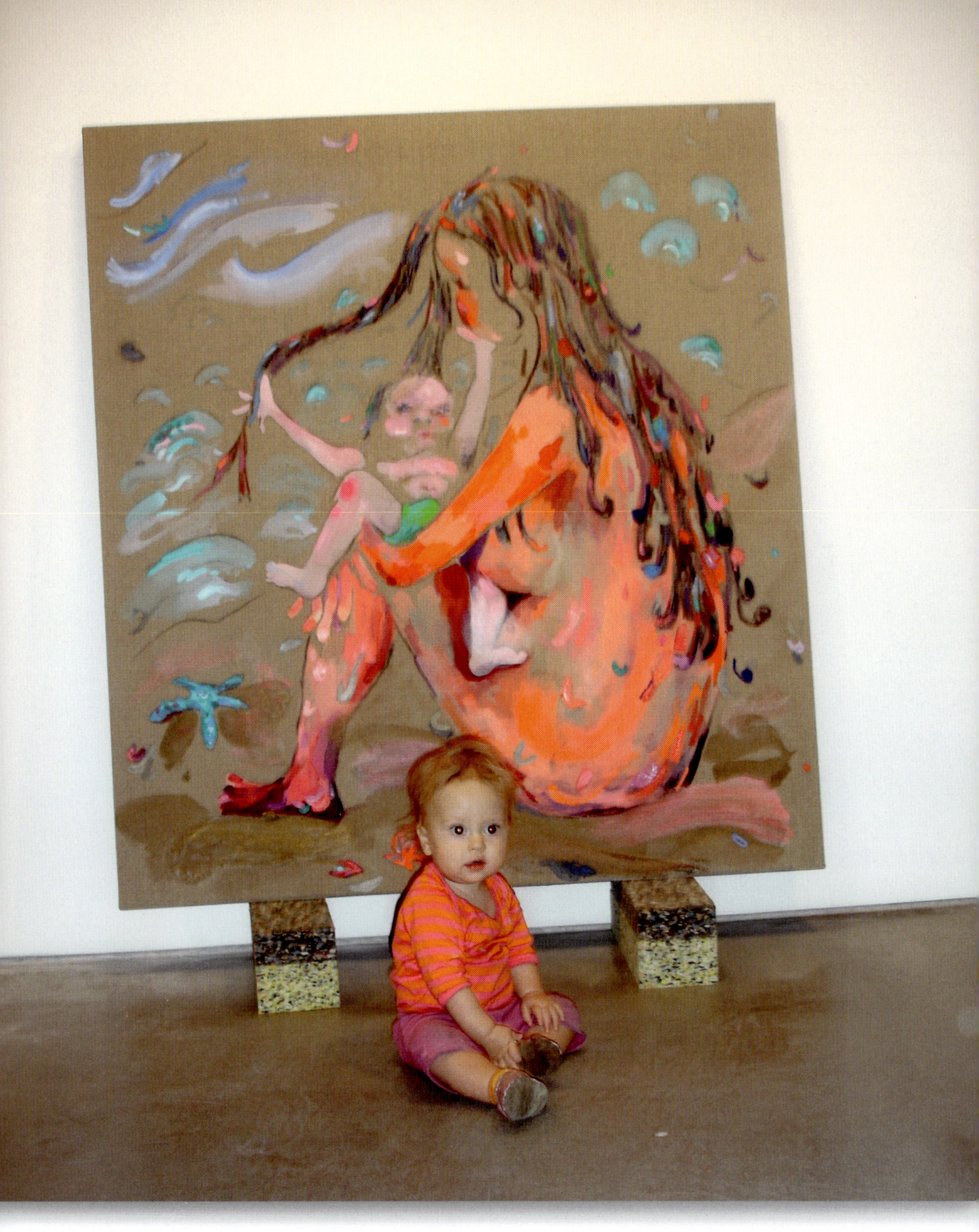

Owen's daughter, Nova Bryan, with *Untitled*, 2008, acrylic and oil on linen, 54 × 48 in. (137.2 × 121.9 cm), Sadie Coles HQ, London, 2008

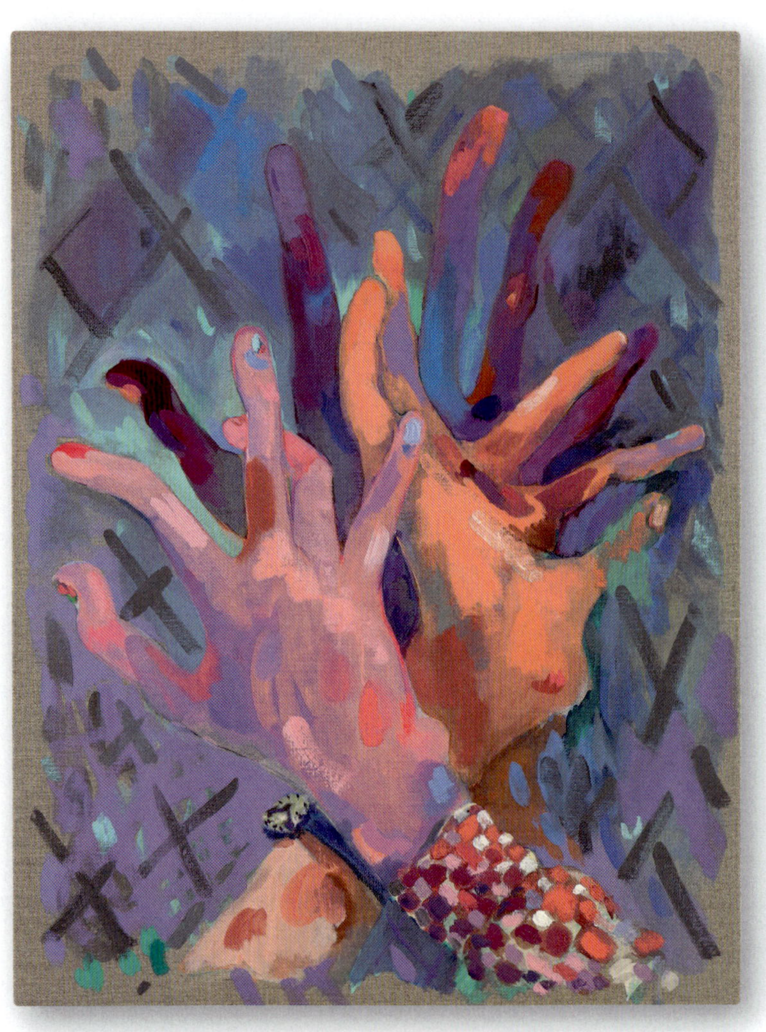

    Untitled, 2008, acrylic and oil on linen, 25 ½ × 19 in. (64.8 × 48.3 cm)

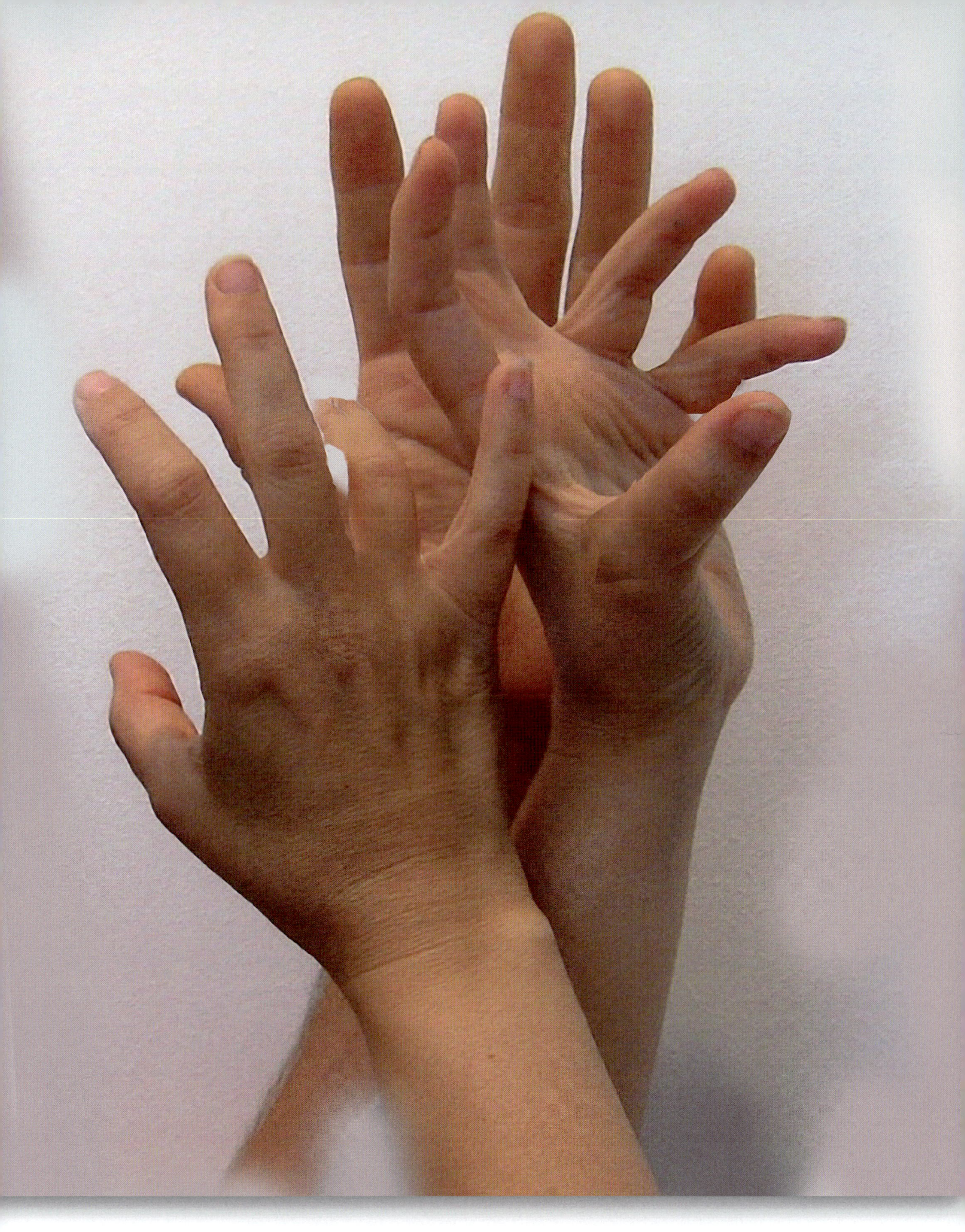

Adobe Photoshop CS4 file, 2008

Laura Owens: One summer I was going to the public library to enjoy the air conditioning and the quiet and I found a small Skira book on Cézanne and a book about Matisse that had been printed in the 1940s. Both were well printed, using older, tipped-in images on smooth, warm paper, and they had a patina created by many hands and years. I felt like I was looking at pictures of art but also holding art objects in and of themselves. I had really grown tired of seeing my drawings in frames; I wanted people to be able to feel the textures of the papers I was drawing on. So I decided to make handmade books that the viewer could touch, hold, and flip through at will. I started off by trying to just copy the small Cézanne book in its entirety, teaching myself to sew and bind. I did a page-by-page replica by hand and remade all the drawings and paintings. After this I read a lot of books about bookmaking and found Jennifer Phiffer and Vi Ha, who taught me techniques and helped me learn how books are assembled. I made many books that were homages to women, including artists Marie Laurencin, Lila Katzen, Vanessa Bell, and Bridget Riley; embroidery designer Erica Wilson; chess grandmaster Judit Polgár; and artist and book designer Claire Van Vliet. These books were unique and shown in groups of six or more on tables I constructed. It was important to me that they be displayed in groups representing different sizes, construction methods, and content, and that they were engaged with by viewers. I never wanted anyone to use gloves when handling them, as I feel this makes them less accessible; also, people are more clumsy with gloves on and tend to bend the pages. I really liked presenting these smaller, interactive, time-based works alongside the paintings, and I hoped people would see the connections between the two forms.

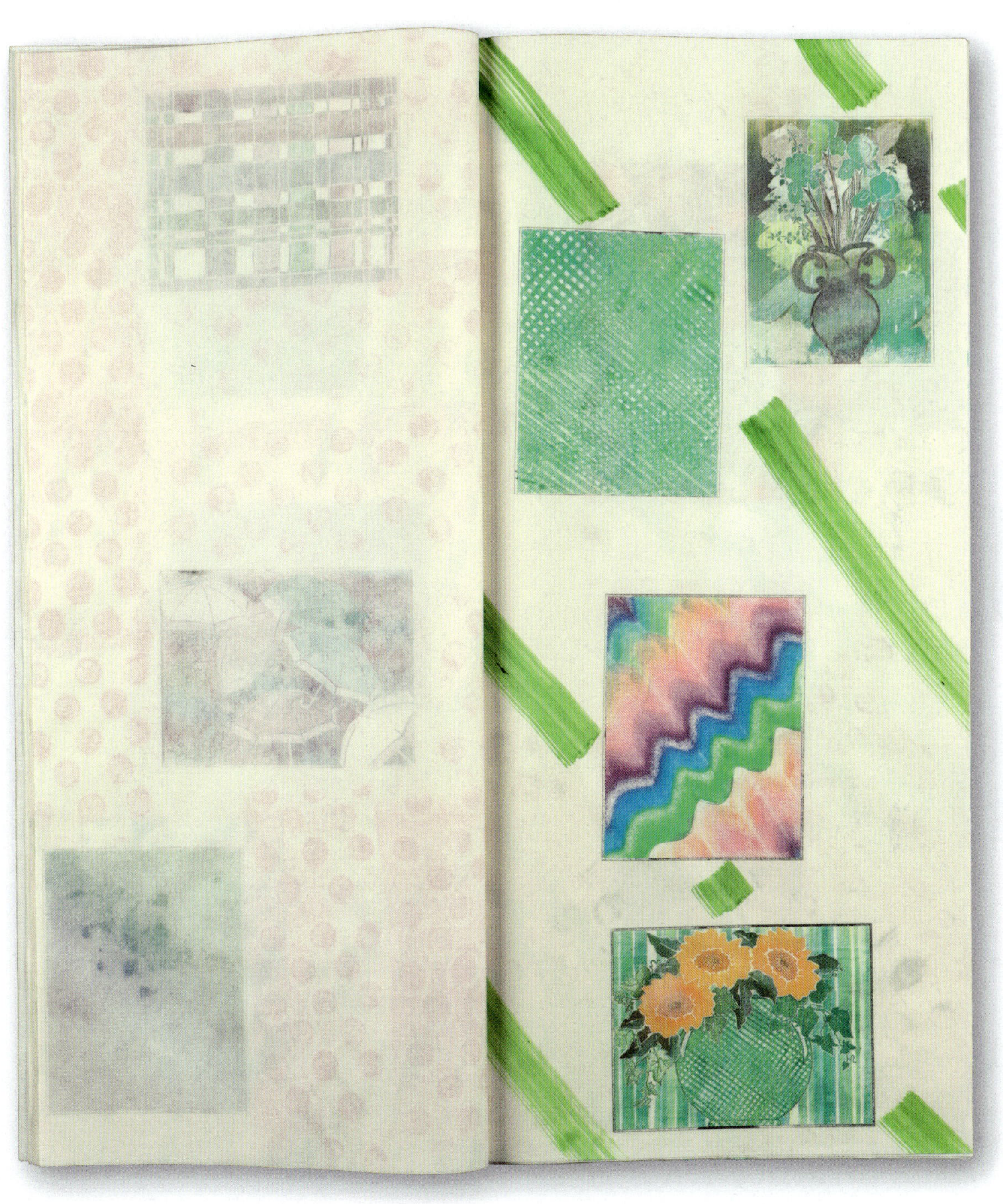

Happy Father's Day, 2011, paper, vinyl paint, acrylic, wintergreen transfer, and thread, 21½ × 10¼ in. (54.6 × 26 cm)

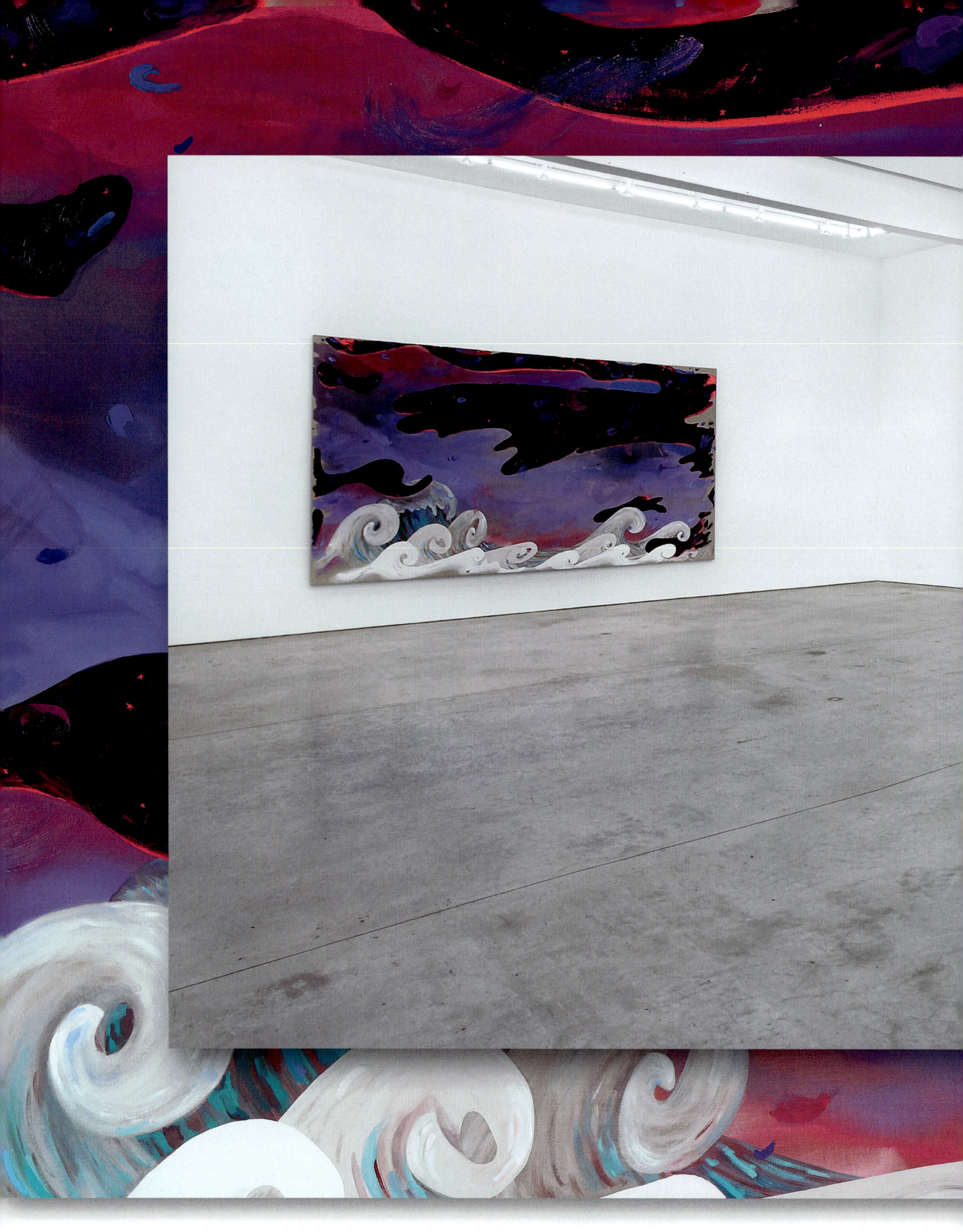

Foreground: Installation view, Gavin Brown's enterprise, New York, 2009, with *Untitled*, 2009, acrylic, oil, vinyl paint, and graphite on linen, 90 × 168 in. (228.6 × 426.7 cm), and *Untitled*, 2009, oil, vinyl paint, and charcoal on linen, 107 × 95 in. (271.8 × 241.3 cm)

 Background: Detail of *Untitled,* 2009

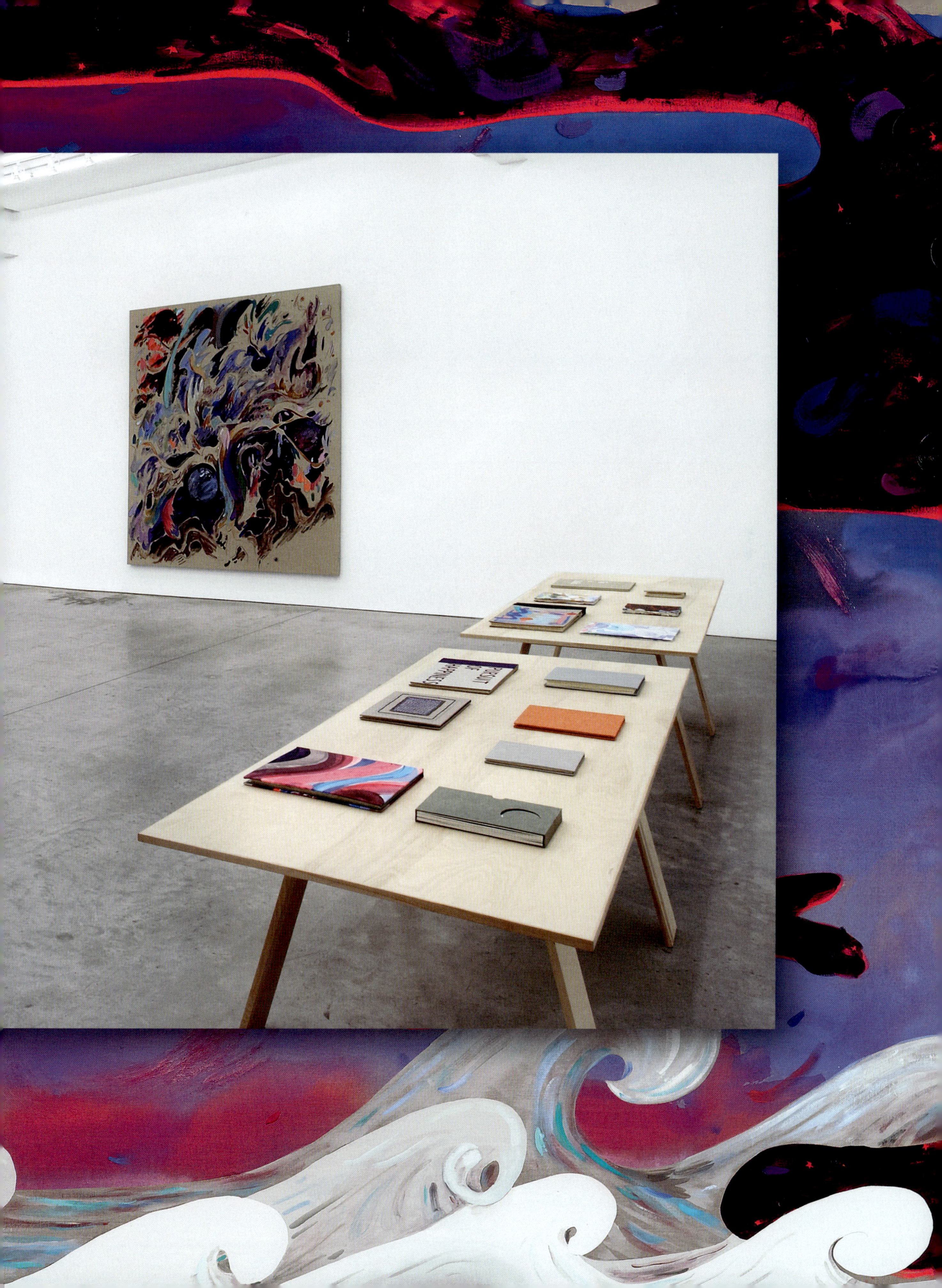

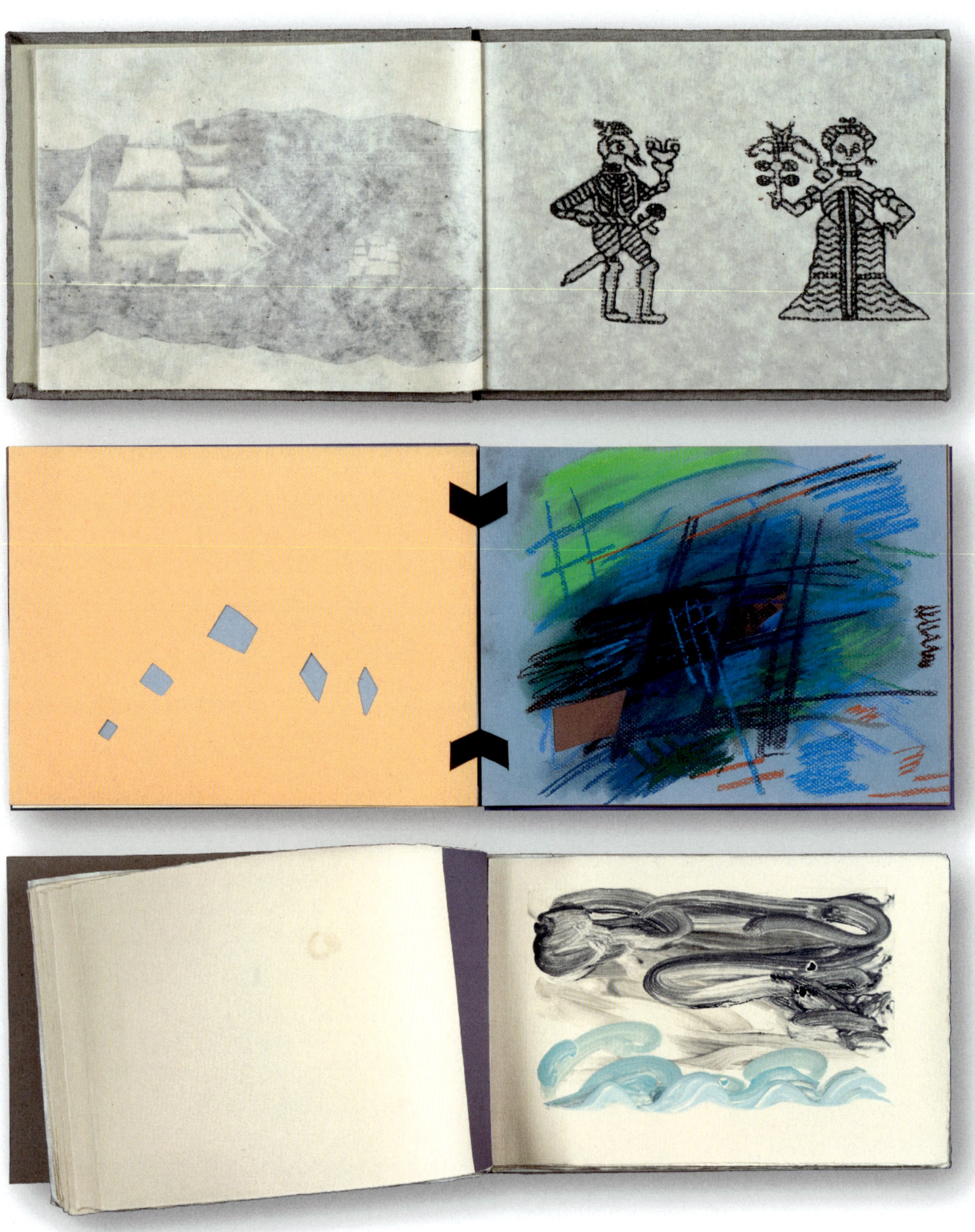

   Pages from *Embroidery Book*, 2009; *Claire Van Vliet 2*, 2011; and *Landscapes and Still Lifes*, 2009

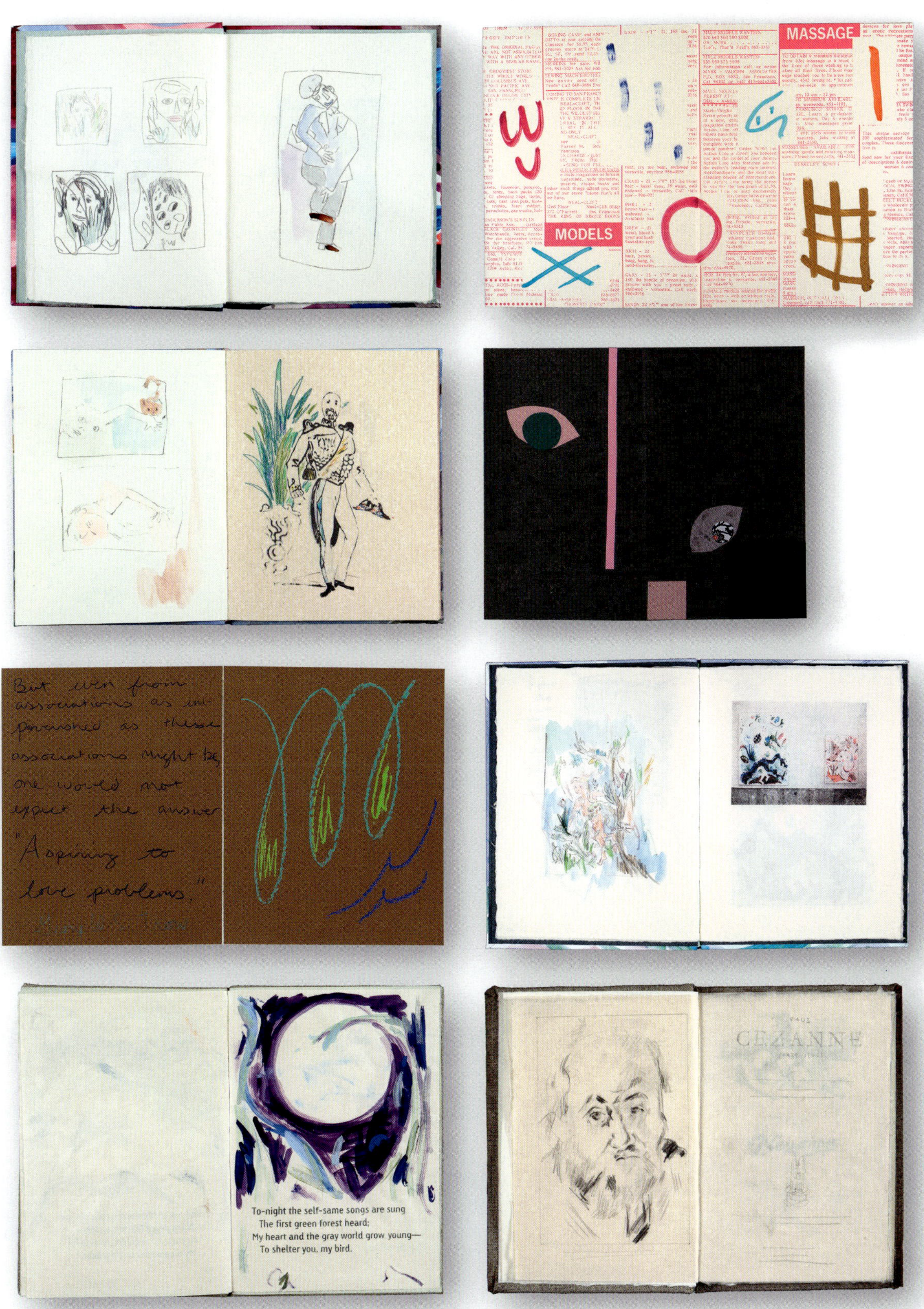

Clockwise from top left: Pages from *Large Sketchbook 2007–2009*, 2009; *Untitled*, 2012; *Moon*, 2009; *Small Sketchbook 2005–2009*, 2009; *Cézanne*, 2009; *To a Child*, 2009; *"Problems" by George W. S. Trow*, 2011; and *De Chirico and Sketches*, 2009

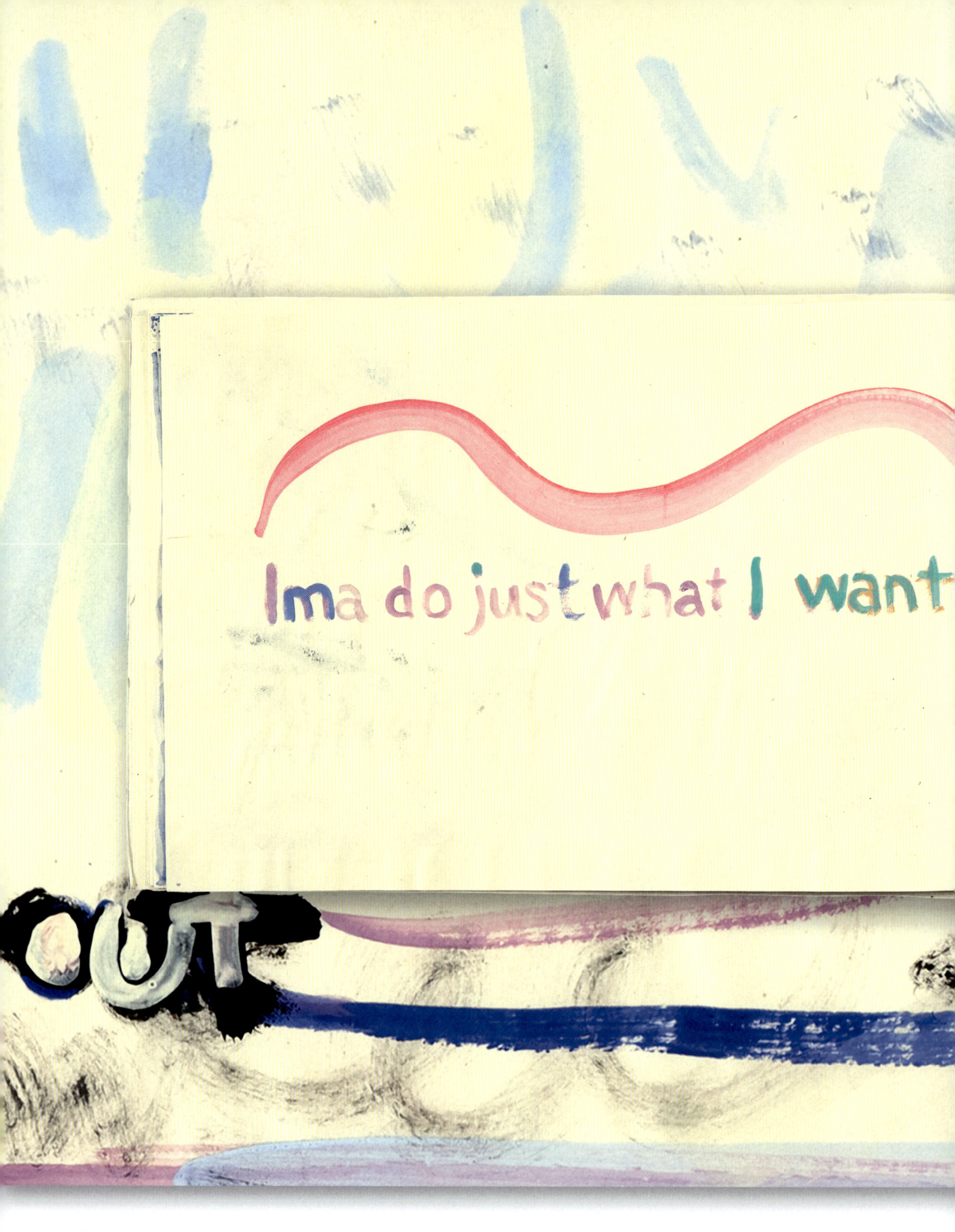

Foreground: Pages from *Pursuit of Happiness [nightmare]*, 2009, vinyl paint, watercolor, and gouache on paper with linen, thread, and binder's board, 11 × 15¾ × ½ in. (27.9 × 40 × 1.27 cm)

438   Background: Detail of *Pursuit of Happiness [nightmare]*, 2009

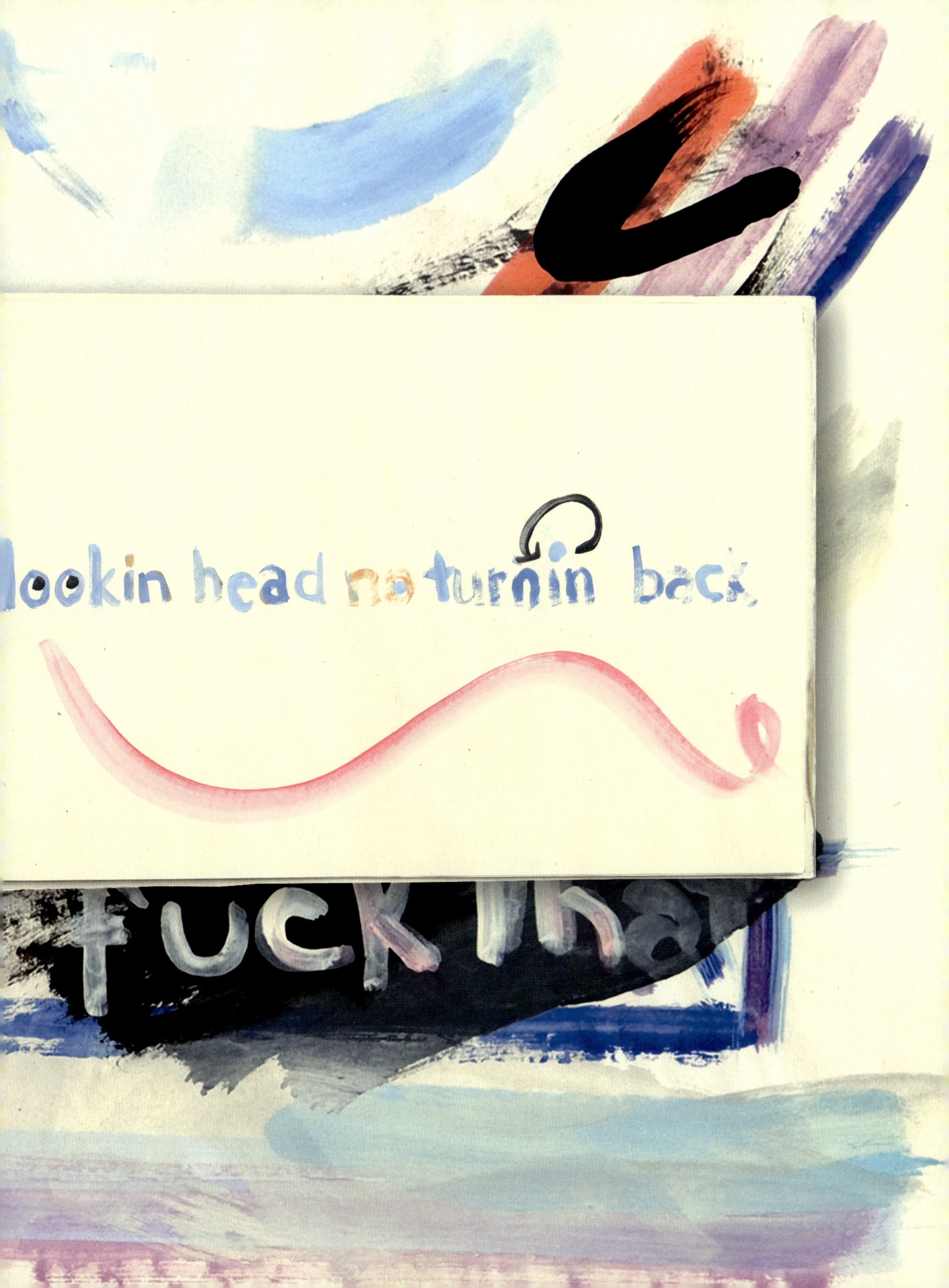

lookin head no turnin back
fuck that

You Stole My Book

You stole my book at the Basel Art Fair in 2010. Could you send it back to P.
411902 Los Angeles CA 90026. Thanks.

← back to Laura Owens

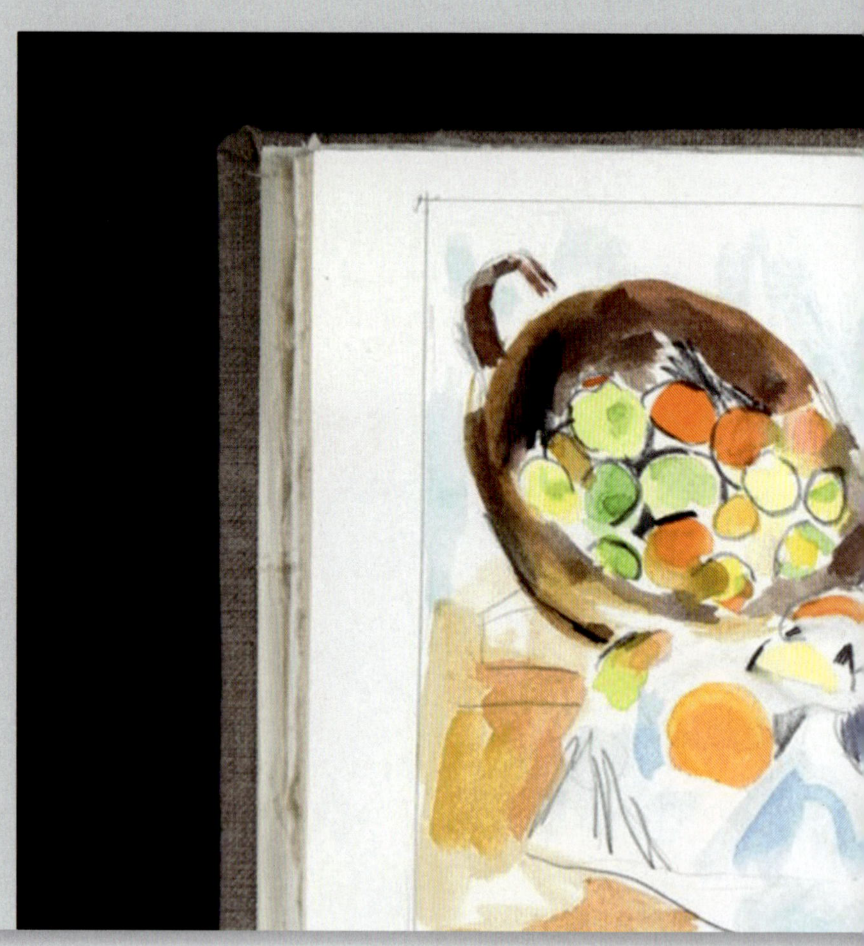

  Screenshot of youstolemybook.com, 2010

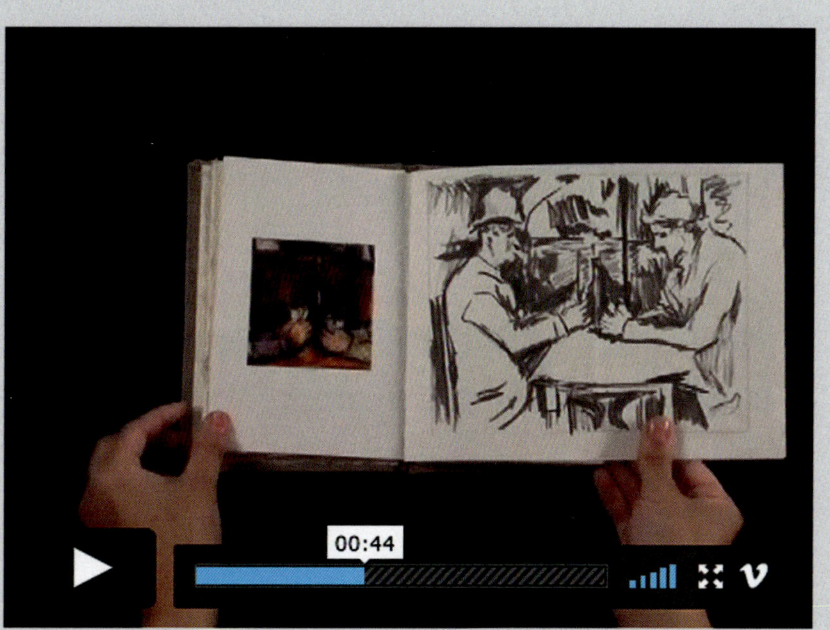

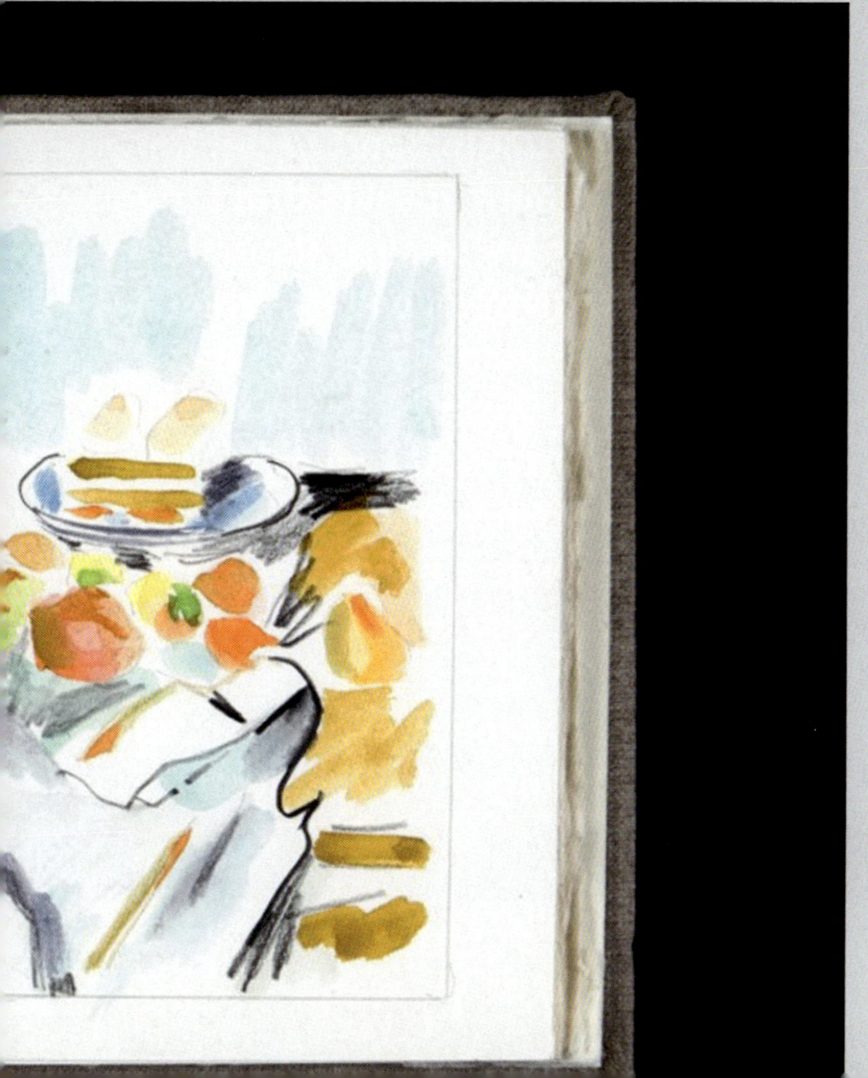

Edgar Bryan: The first clock painting was of a grandfather clock that was about six feet tall; it was in a show at Sadie Coles HQ. Laura would often make paintings or drawings on these huge pieces of watercolor paper that she would paint with a color and then let dry. Later she would cut out shapes and glue them on. In that first painting, the clock hands are made of paper. That was definitely the starting point for wanting to make a painting with a real clock, with hands that really moved. I think it was as simple as that.

We tried all kinds of things to make it happen. First we used regular clock hands and motors we bought at a clock store. There's a heavy-duty motor and a regular one. You could kind of make that work if you glued paper onto the hands. Those clock motors work for years because the clock hands are balanced and extremely light, so there's no extra stress. We were making the hands heavier, but we still had to keep them balanced. We were doing a lot of gluing of these things in the studio. And then Laura thought maybe it would be better if the hands moved at a different speed. So I went to Chinatown and bought these little things that turn—they had lights in them and each one had a picture of Jesus on it. I took them apart to get the motors out. What I didn't know until I took them apart is that they would turn really fast, but they had these gears to slow them down. So I was rebuilding these things on the backs of canvases, which was so much work. I was spending hours and hours assembling them. And then we brought in an expert who made this module and had it 3-D printed. It had a little memory card and you could program it and use a remote control to operate it. It could go any speed, any direction you wanted and it was powerful because it was a servomotor. He developed it really fast, and after that it was easy to make a bunch of Clock paintings.

In the end there turned out to be a size that made sense for Laura and allowed a seriality. She made nine paintings, to be hung in a

     Edgar Bryan is a Los Angeles–based artist who has collaborated with Owens on many projects.

grid. Some of them were moving, some of them weren't. That was the first presentation. She wanted it to look like, "Here's a piece of paint here, here's a piece of paint here, and here's a piece of paint here that's literally moving and turning." I'm pretty sure it came out of her desire to be as radical in a painting as you can be. Like instead of being super minimal—"there's nothing in this painting, it's so radical"—it was like, "I'm going to play with kitsch here. I'm going to have clock hands that turn, and it's literally going to be one of my paintings that's moving, with paint floating around." I feel like a lot of her motivation is to be surprising within her paintings. To see what a painting can be and what it can do. And if it's eccentric, all the better.

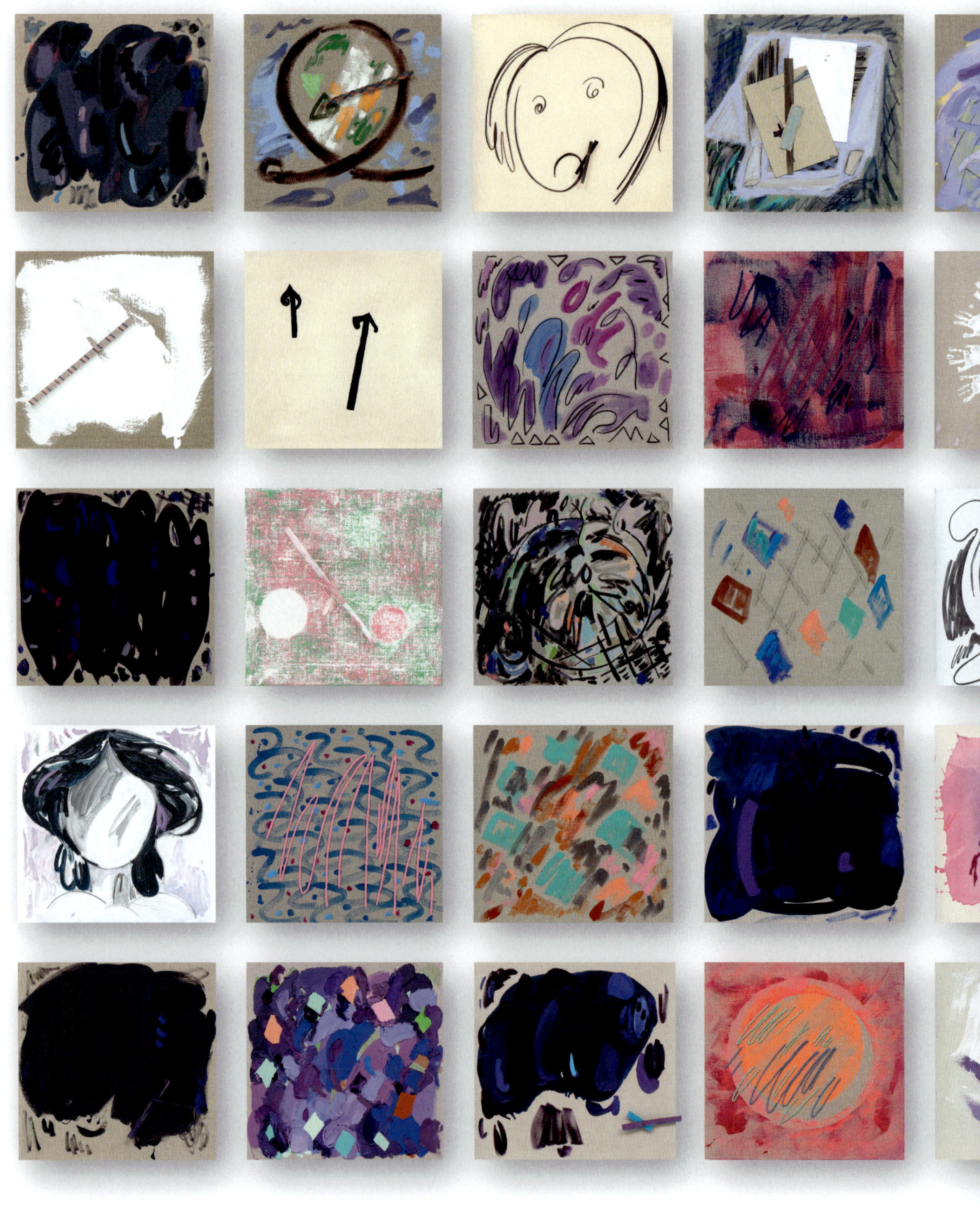

Detail of *Untitled*, 2011–12, acrylic, oil, vinyl paint, charcoal, collage, mica, clock motors, mechanical parts, and yarn on linen and canvas, 92 panels: 24 × 24 in. (61 × 61 cm) each

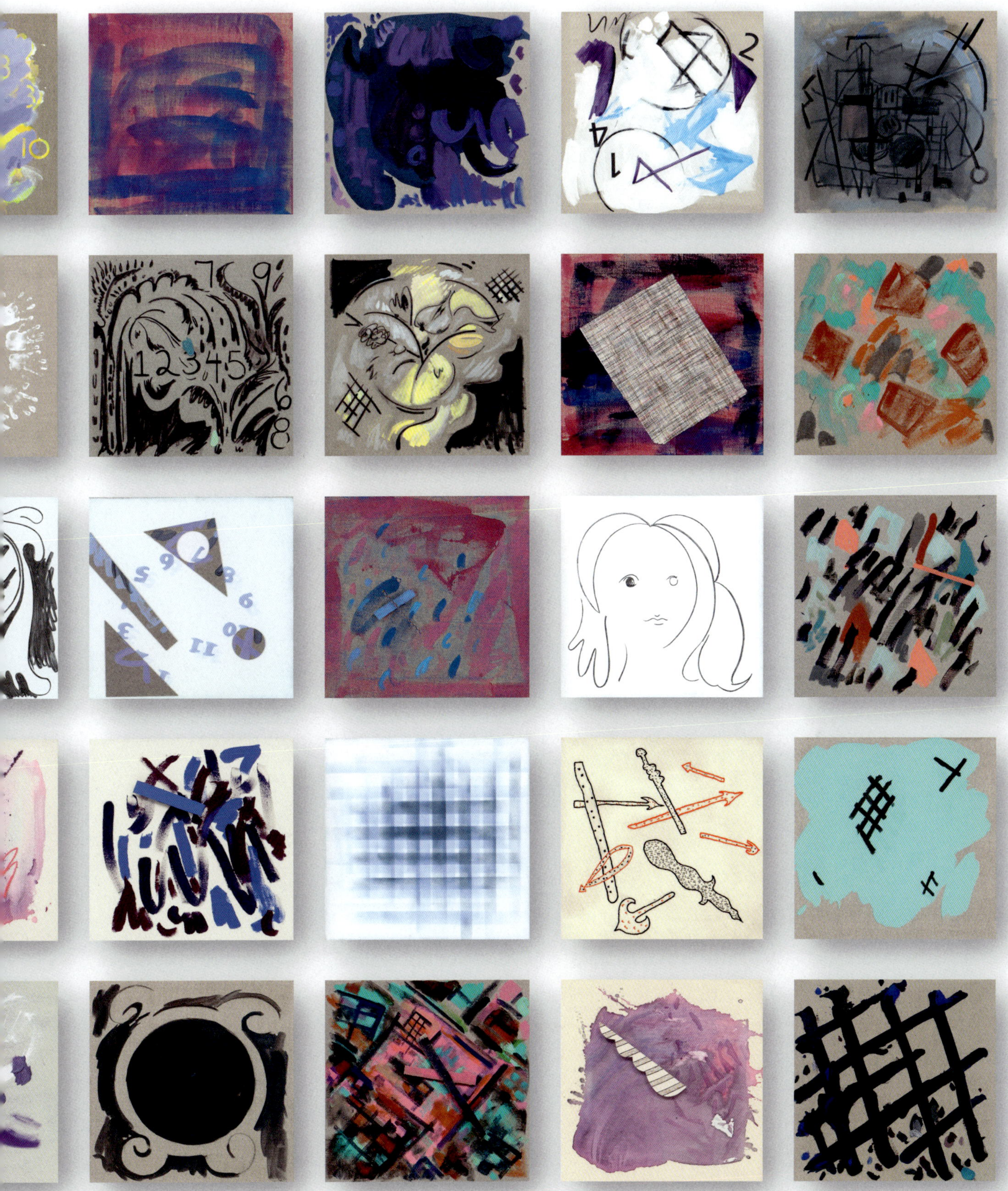

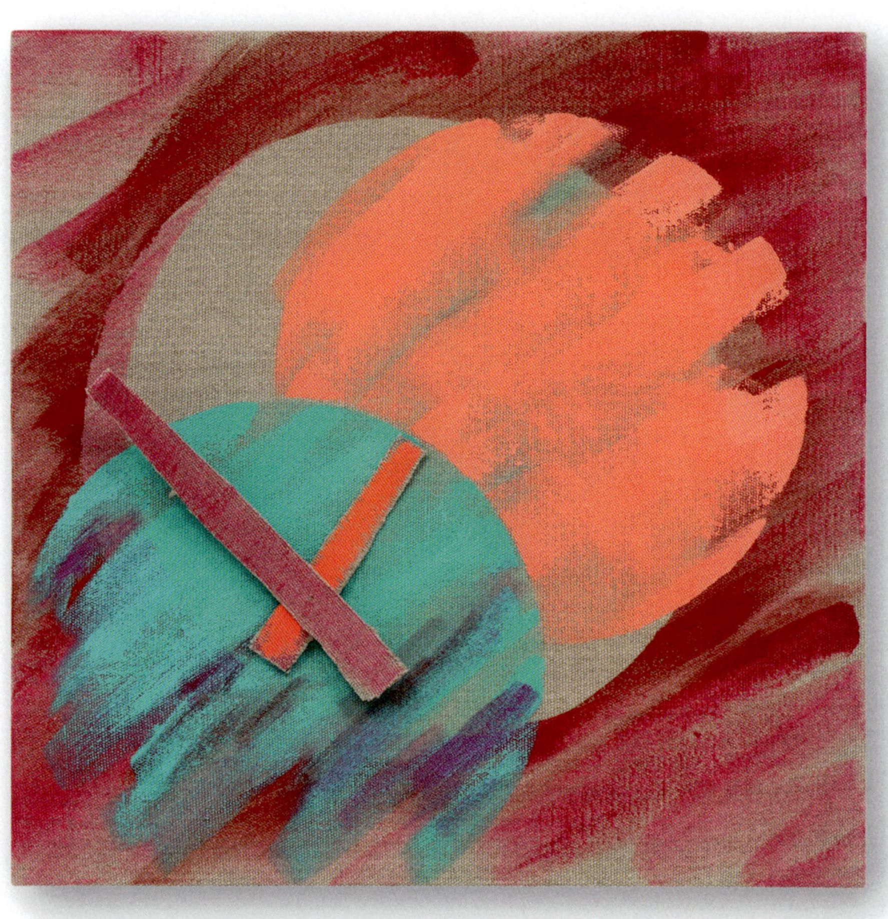

446   Detail of *Untitled*, 2011–12 (see p. 444)

Clocks paintings and books.

I am interested in the way the idea of a clock and the idea of painting could cross over or interpolate. Clockness could be the generative motor for making paintings and their production could reiterate and inform the artists studio practice.

By overlaying the idea of clock onto a painting it opens up many linguistic twins. For example the hands of a clock, hand of the artist, face of a clock/portraiture. The idea of time or telling the time is removed in any real sense.
But the idea of duration or that a painting would create temporal experiences, is literalized with the movement of parts of the composition. This reiterates the already existing temporal experience of looking at a painting, seeing it from the side, far away , up close as well as subjectivity of the viewer.

A book can stand in for a work of art, and be just a book at the same time. It allows a new surface for ideas of both language, drawing, photography, sculpture and painting to take place. The book has its own craft history, its own traditional and nontraditional constructions. Unlike art it is more democratic in nature. One can hold a book, its temporal nature unfolded by the viewer. At the same time this intimate experience mimics our experience with a painting.

A book like a clock is both familiar and mass produced. The unique book or clock exists in the world of artisans and craft. Penetrating both the artisan and familiar nature of these objects allows a painting to expand its own linguistic edges and points to our limited definitions of what a painting can be.

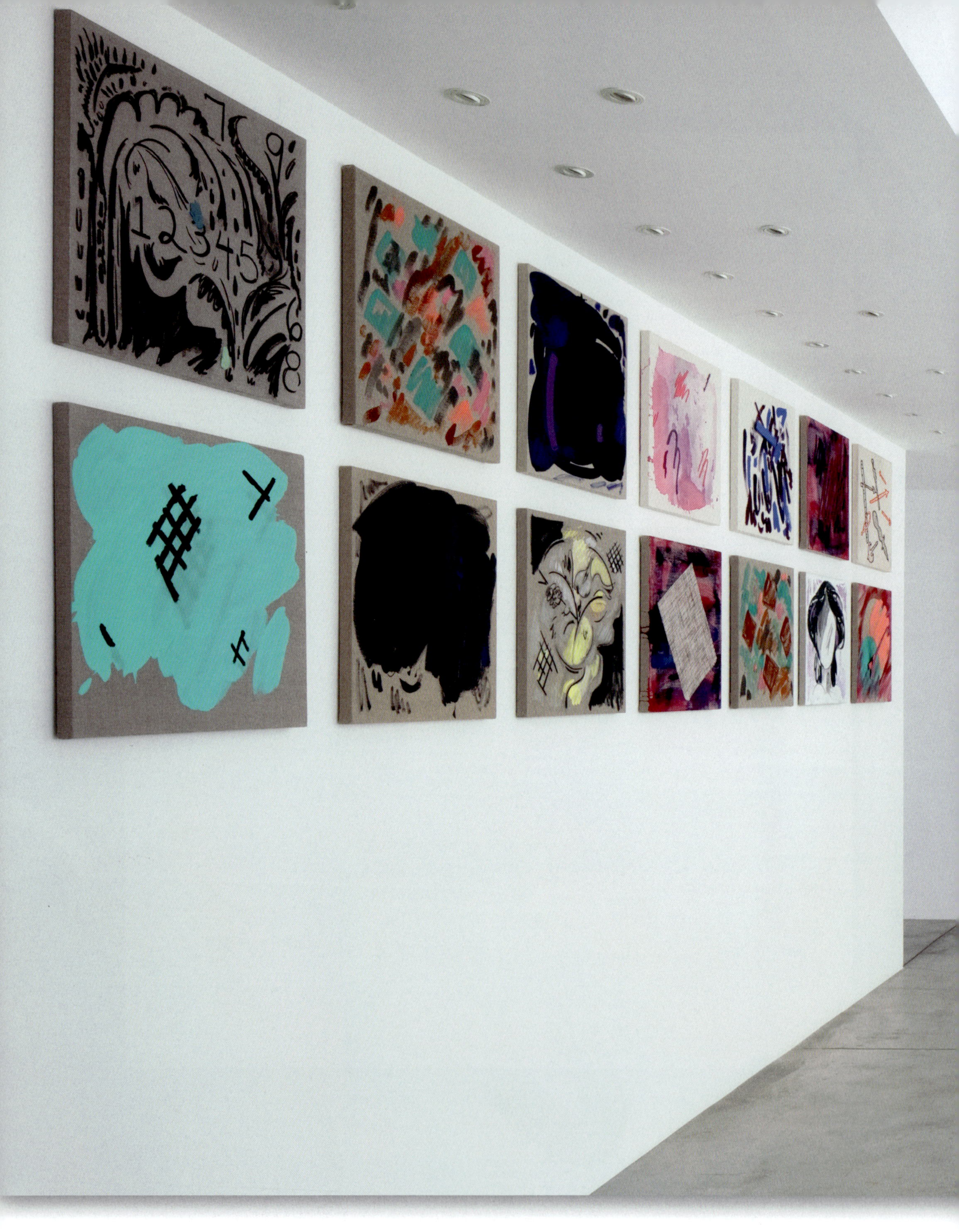

Foreground: Detail of *Untitled*, 2011–12 (see p. 444)
Background: Installation view, Galerie Gisela Capitain, 2011, with *Untitled*, 2011–12 (see p. 444)

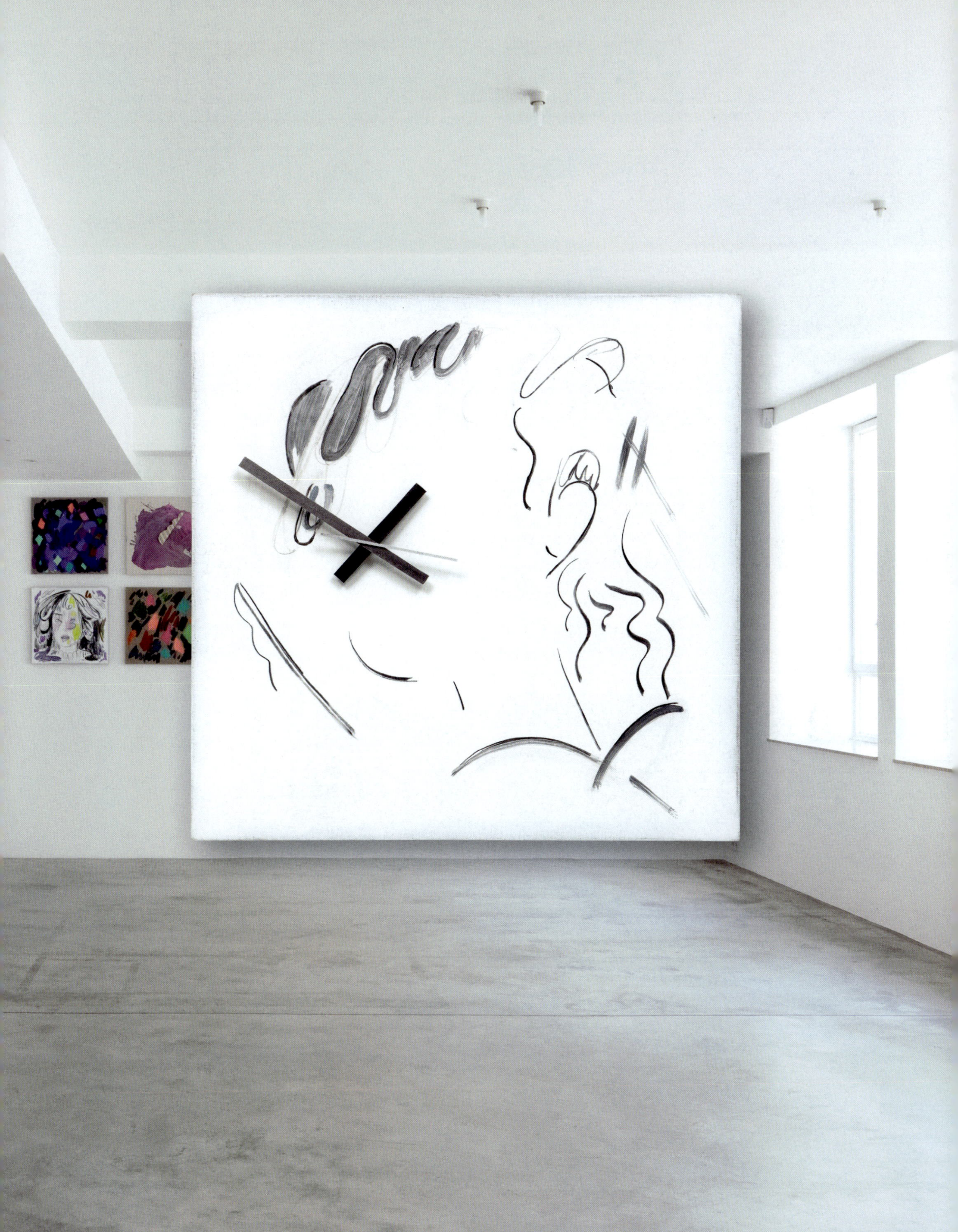

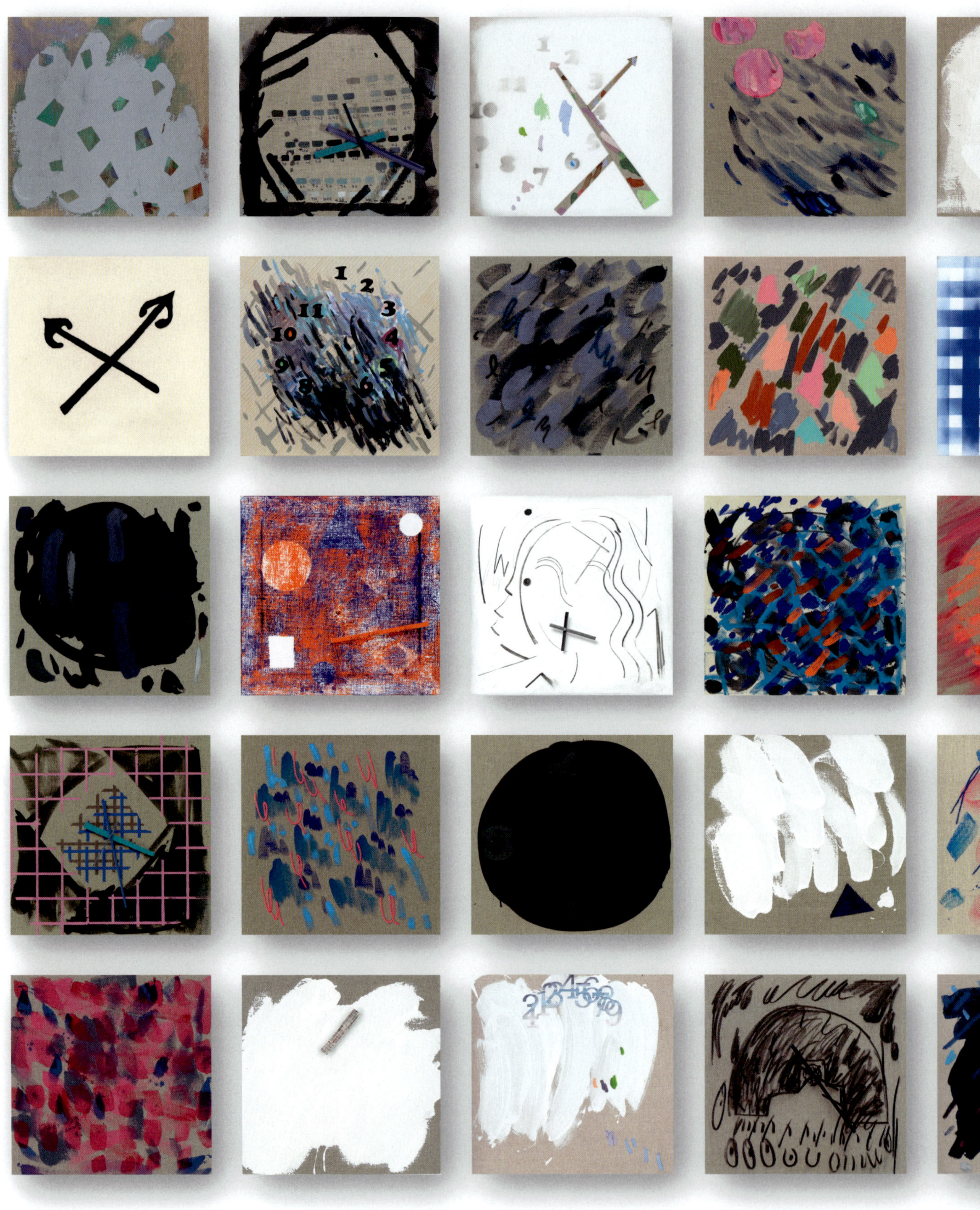

  Detail of *Untitled*, 2011–12 (see p. 444)

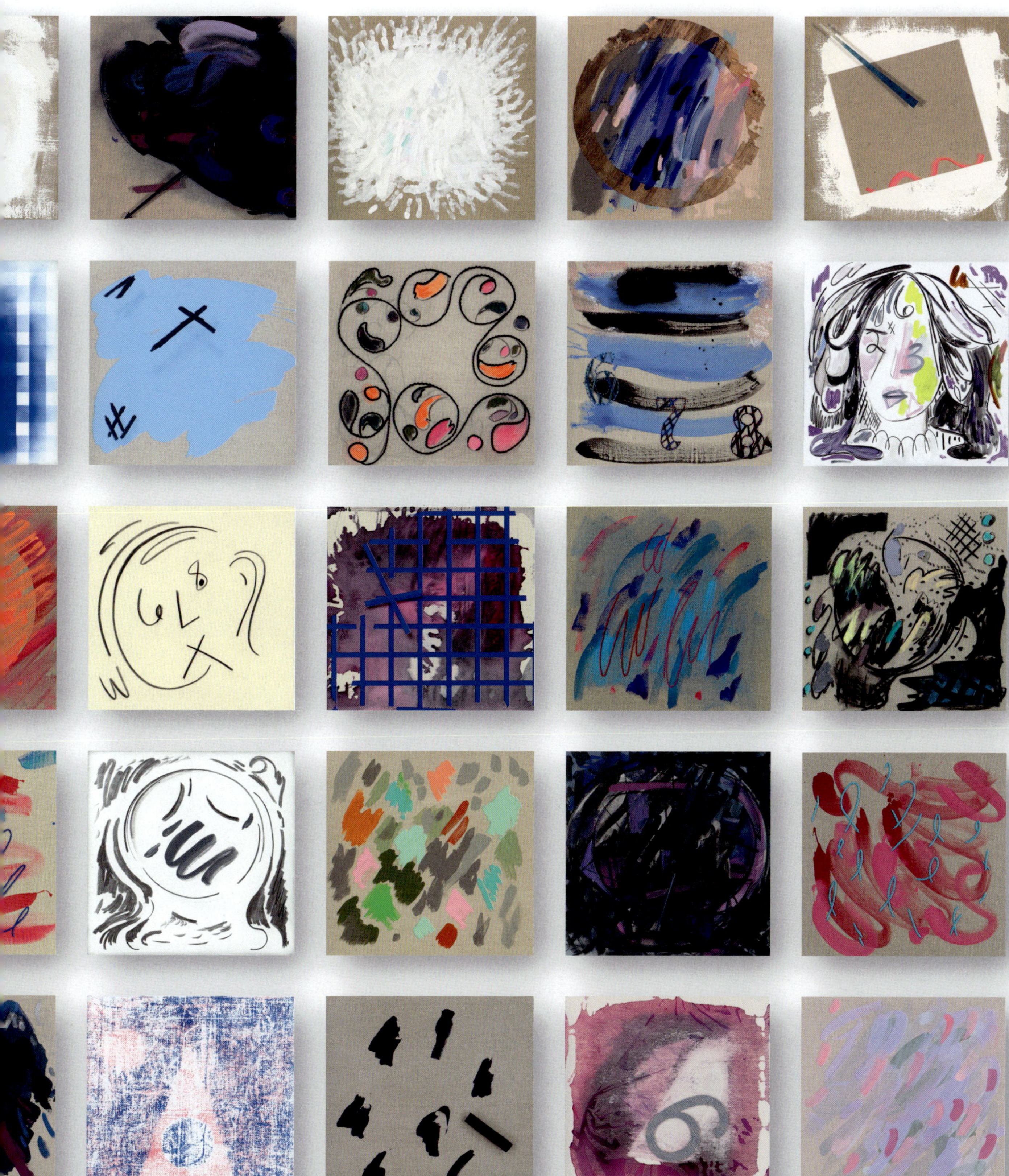

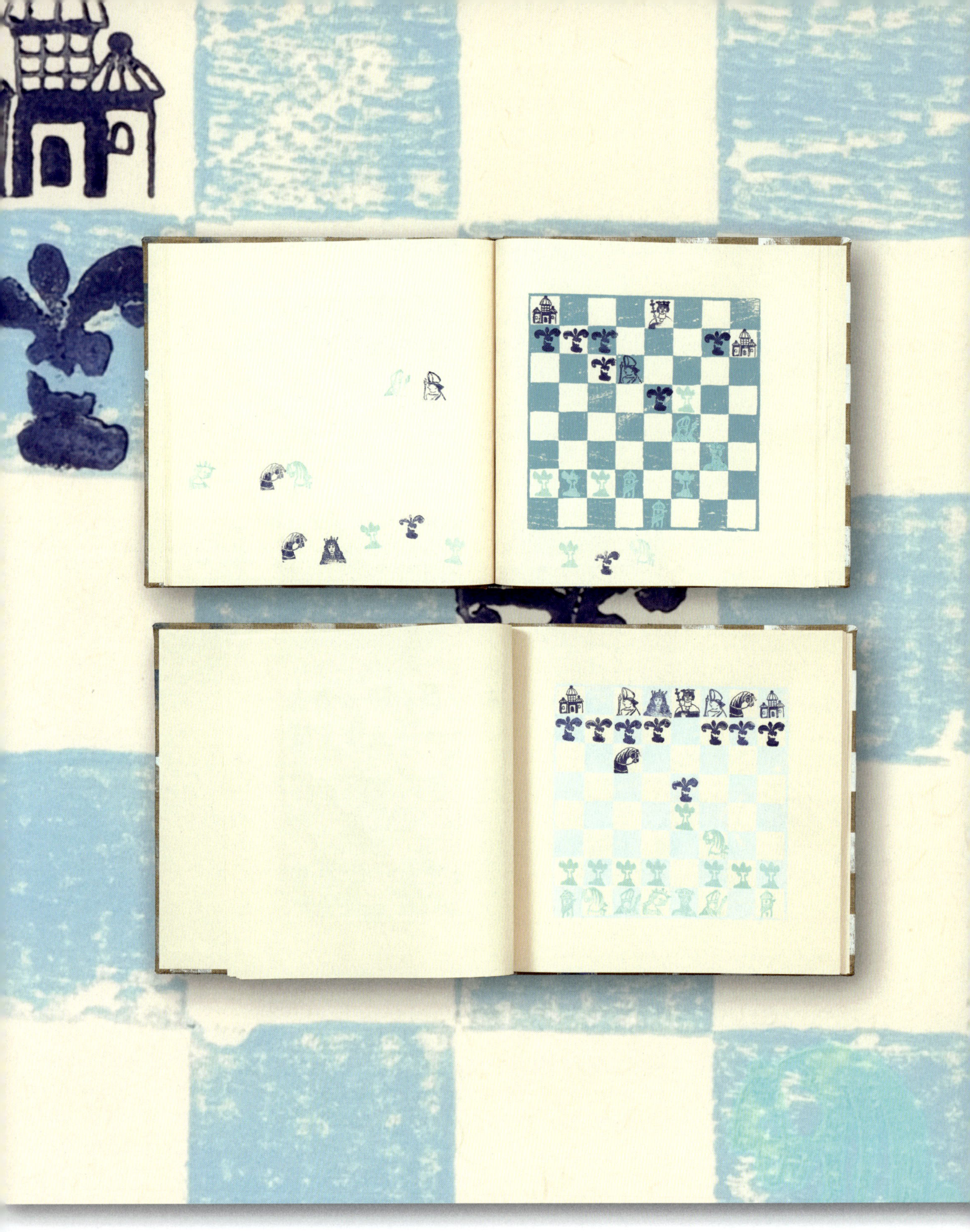

Foreground: Pages from *Kasparov-Polgar*, 2011, acrylic, oil, and vinyl paint on paper with linen, thread, and binder's board, 12¼ × 12¼ × ¾ in. (31.5 × 31.5 × 1.8 cm)

452   Background: Detail of *Kasparov-Polgar*, 2011

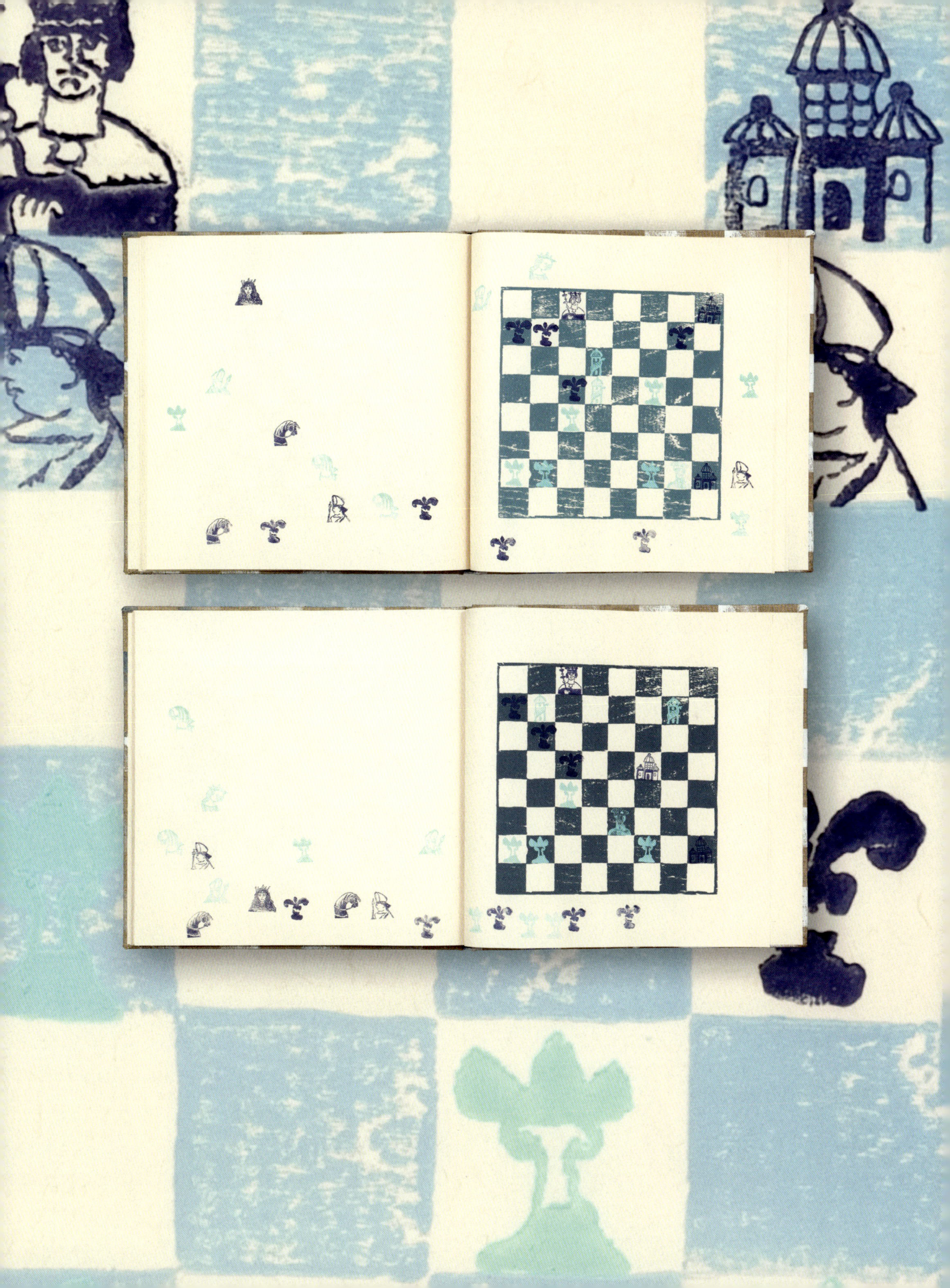

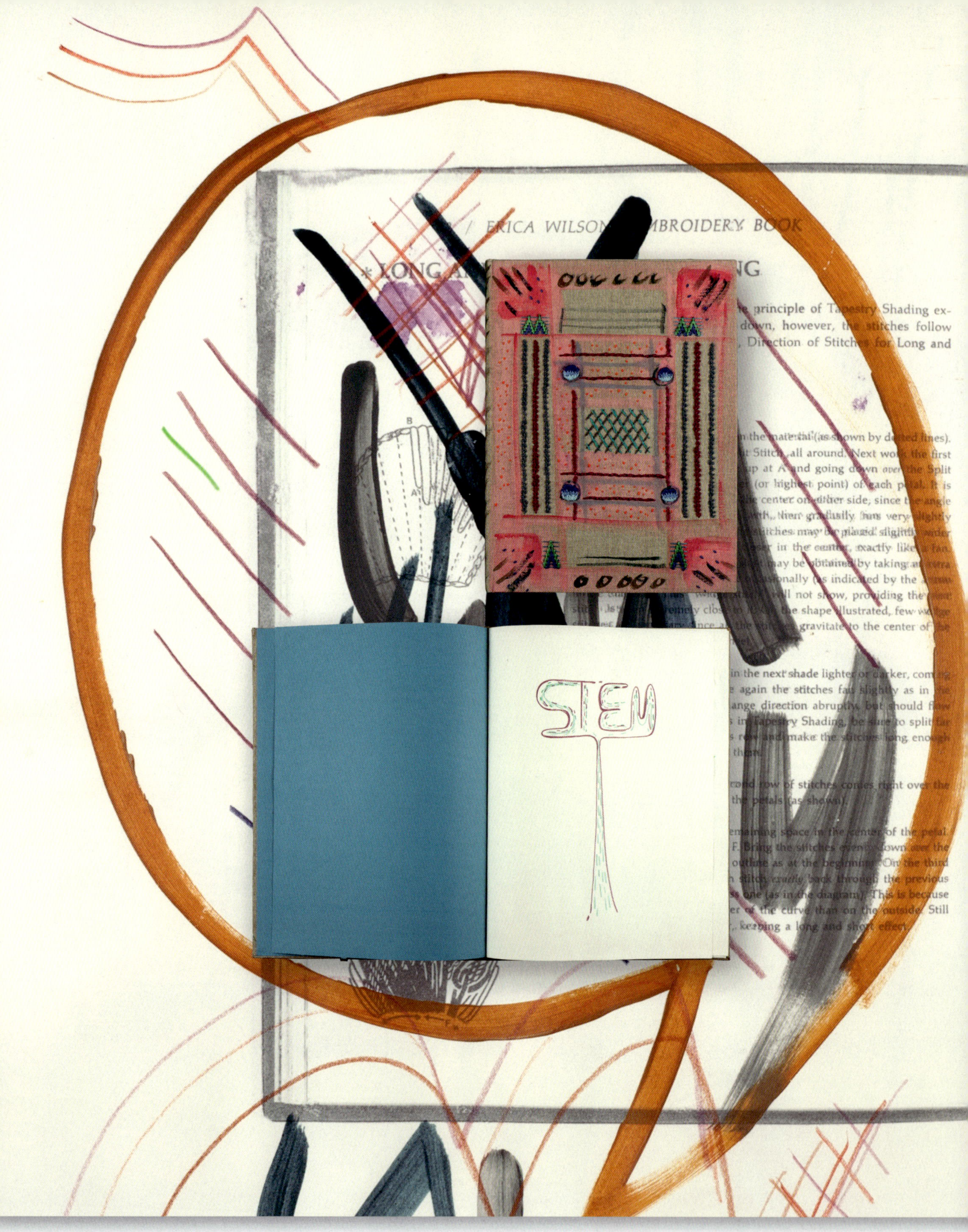

Foreground: Pages from *Stem*, 2011, vinyl paint, colored pencil, watercolor, graphite, wintergreen transfer, acrylic, and embroidery floss on paper with linen, thread, and binder's board, 17 × 12¼ × ½ in. (43.2 × 30.1 × 1.3 cm)

  Background: Detail of *Stem*, 2011

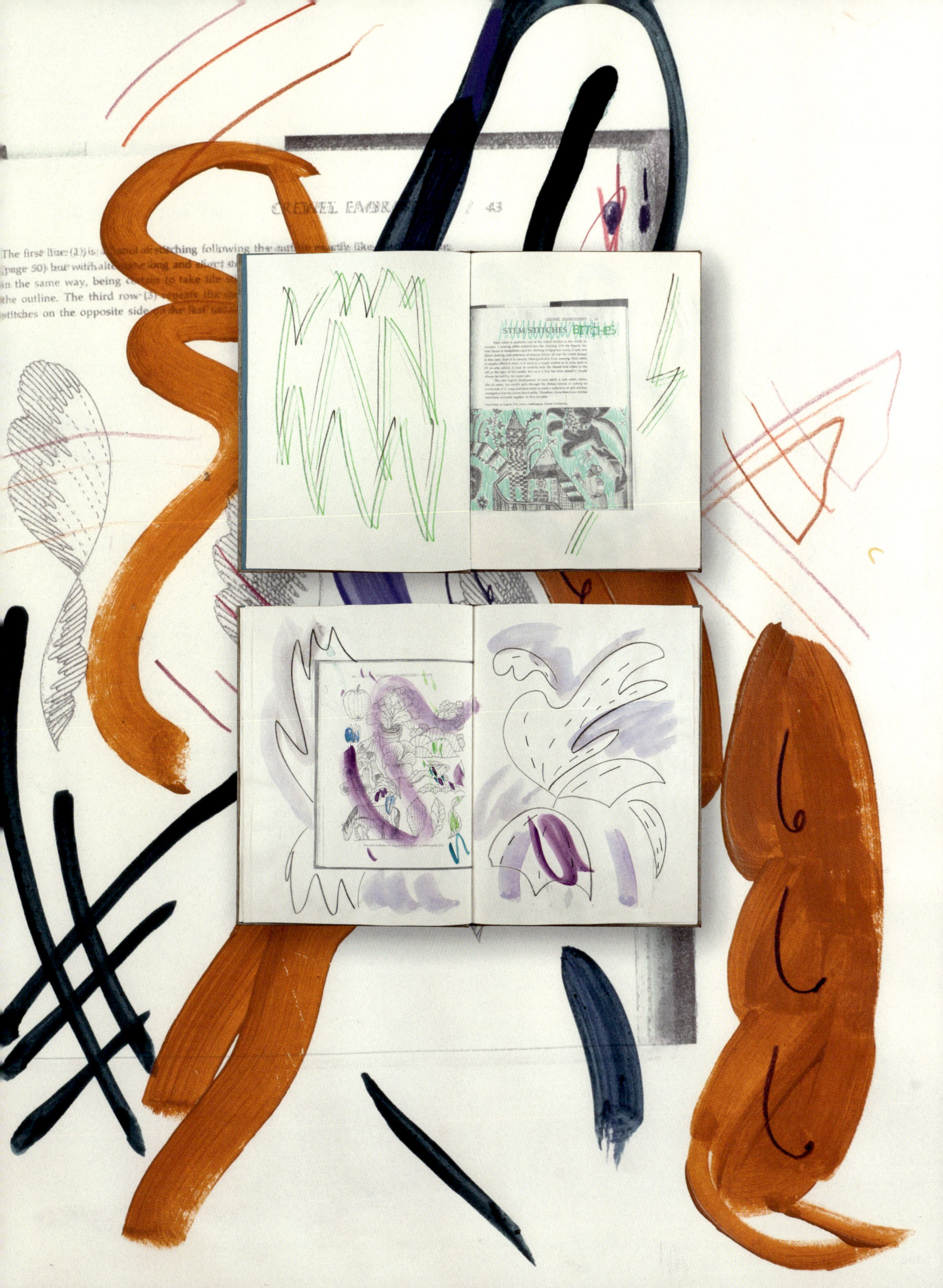

STEM STITCHES BITCHES

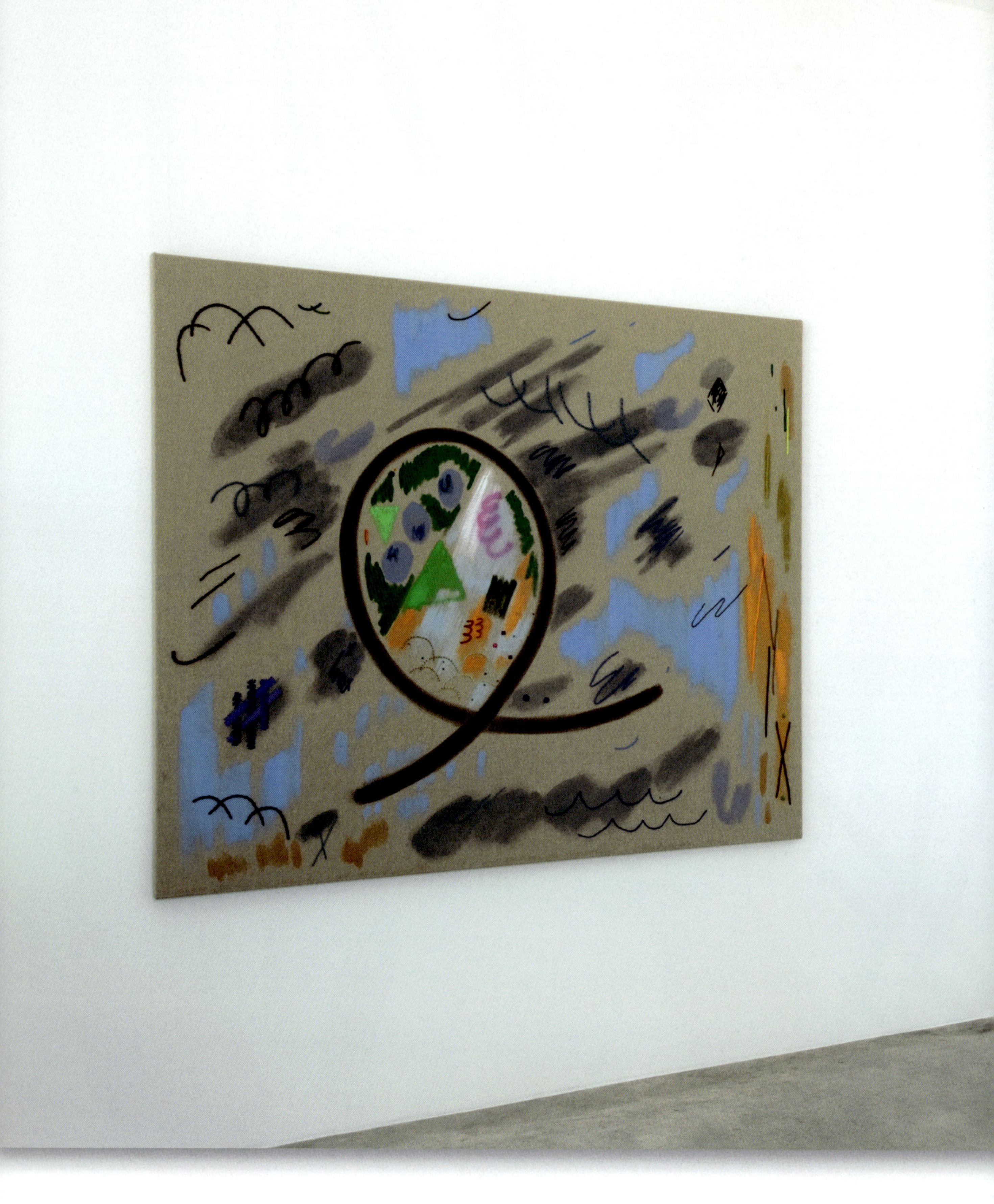

Installation view, Galerie Gisela Capitain, Cologne, 2011, with *Untitled*, 2011, acrylic, vinyl paint, and yarn on linen, two panels:
64 × 72 in. (162.6 × 182.9 cm) each

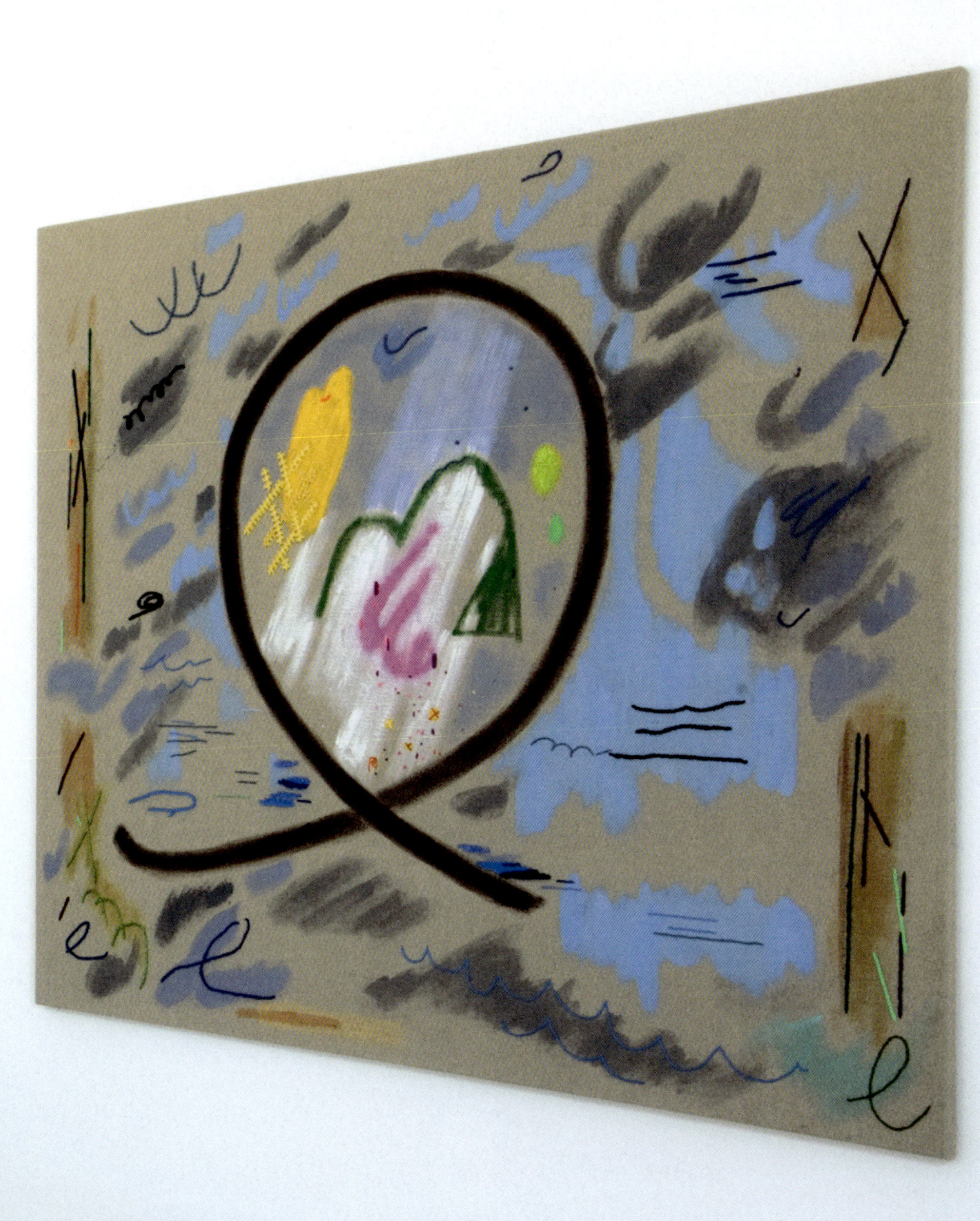

INSTALLING A MECHANICAL MOTOR

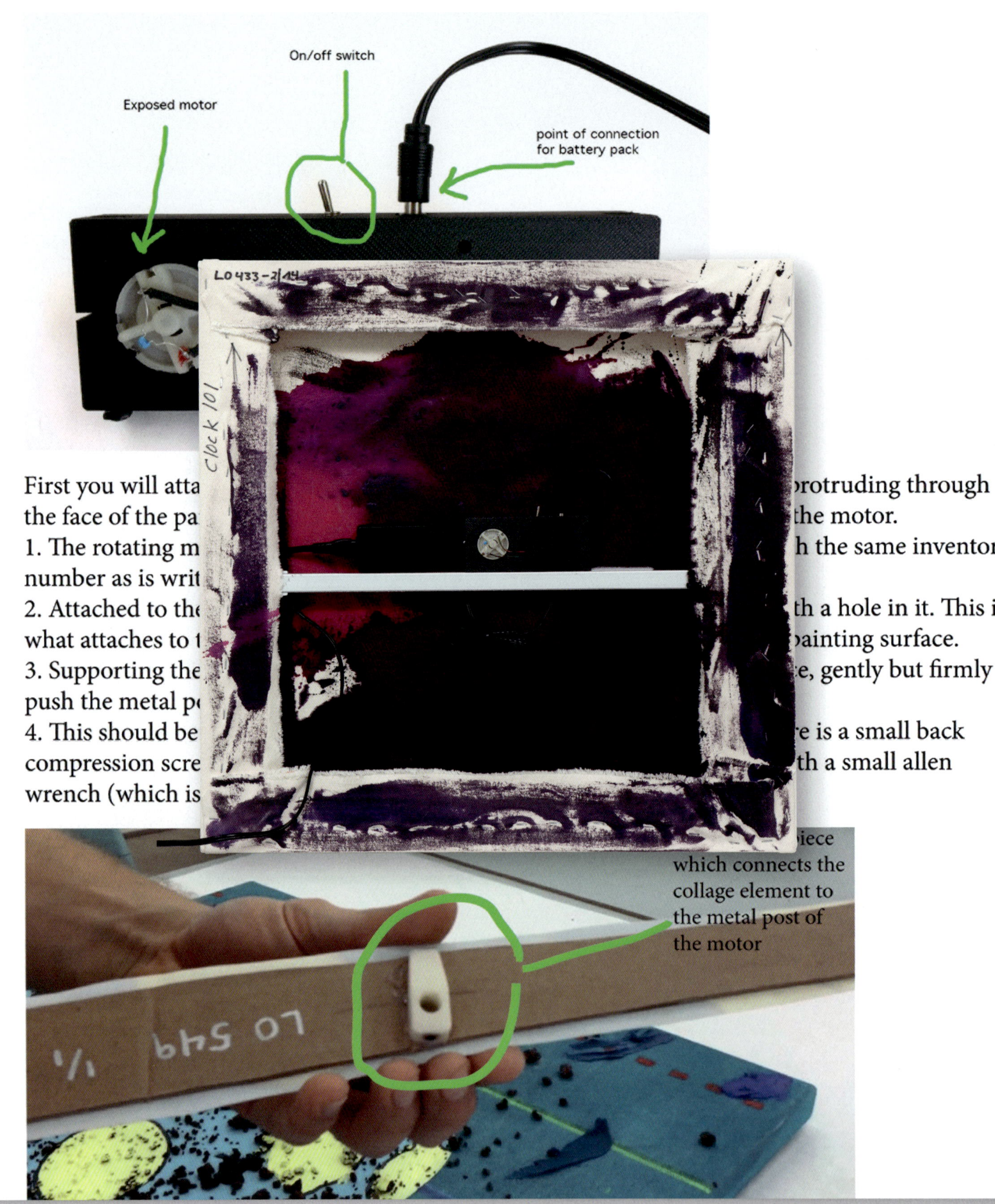

First you will atta... ...rotruding through
the face of the pa... ...the motor.
1. The rotating m... ...h the same inventory
number as is writ...
2. Attached to the... ...th a hole in it. This is
what attaches to t... ...painting surface.
3. Supporting the... ...e, gently but firmly
push the metal po...
4. This should be... ...e is a small back
compression scre... ...th a small allen
wrench (which is...

Foreground: Verso details of *Untitled*, 2011–12 (see p. 444)
Background: Installation instructions for *Untitled*, 2011–12 (see p. 444)

Clock Motor Installation

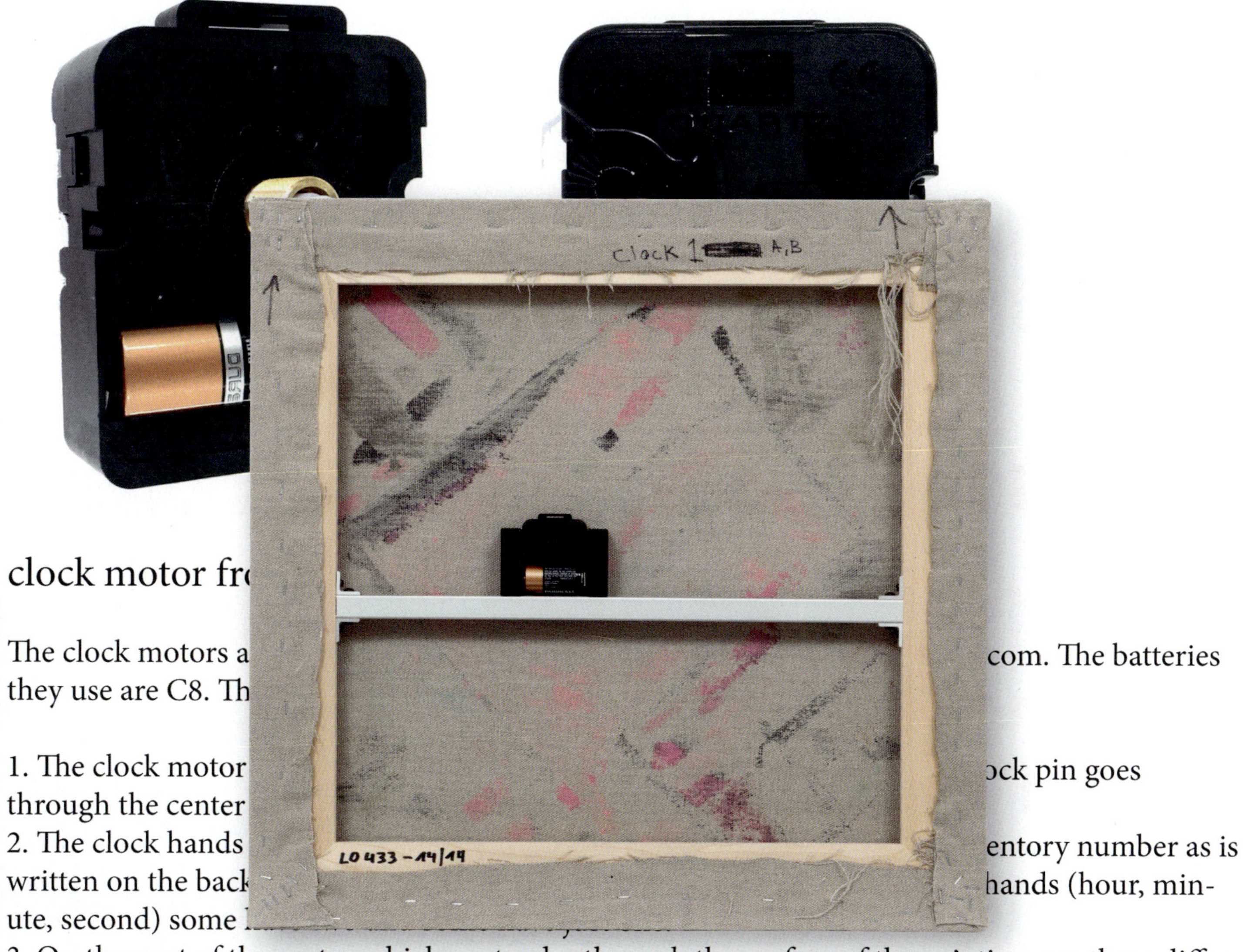

clock motor fr...

The clock motors a... com. The batteries
they use are C8. Th...

1. The clock motor ... ock pin goes
through the center ...
2. The clock hands ... entory number as is
written on the back ... hands (hour, minute, second) some ...
3. On the post of the motor which protrudes through the surface of the painting, are three different fittings for three different sizes of holes in the clock hands.
4. The hour hand has the largest hole, and it is fitted on first. Holding the hand on either side of
the aperture, push it down firmly onto the post. You will feel a slight click.
5. The minute hand is installed next in the same fashion.
6. Between the minute and second hand is a small nut which must be tightened on the post before installing the second hand.
7. The second hand acts as a cap and is firmly but gently pushed on.
8. Upon installation, install the battery in the back. The second hand should immediately begin
to move.
***** After installation, monitor the painting to make sure clock hands can complete full rota-
tions. The hands are very light and flexible and might need to be bent slightly to insure they do
not get caught on each other or against the painting.

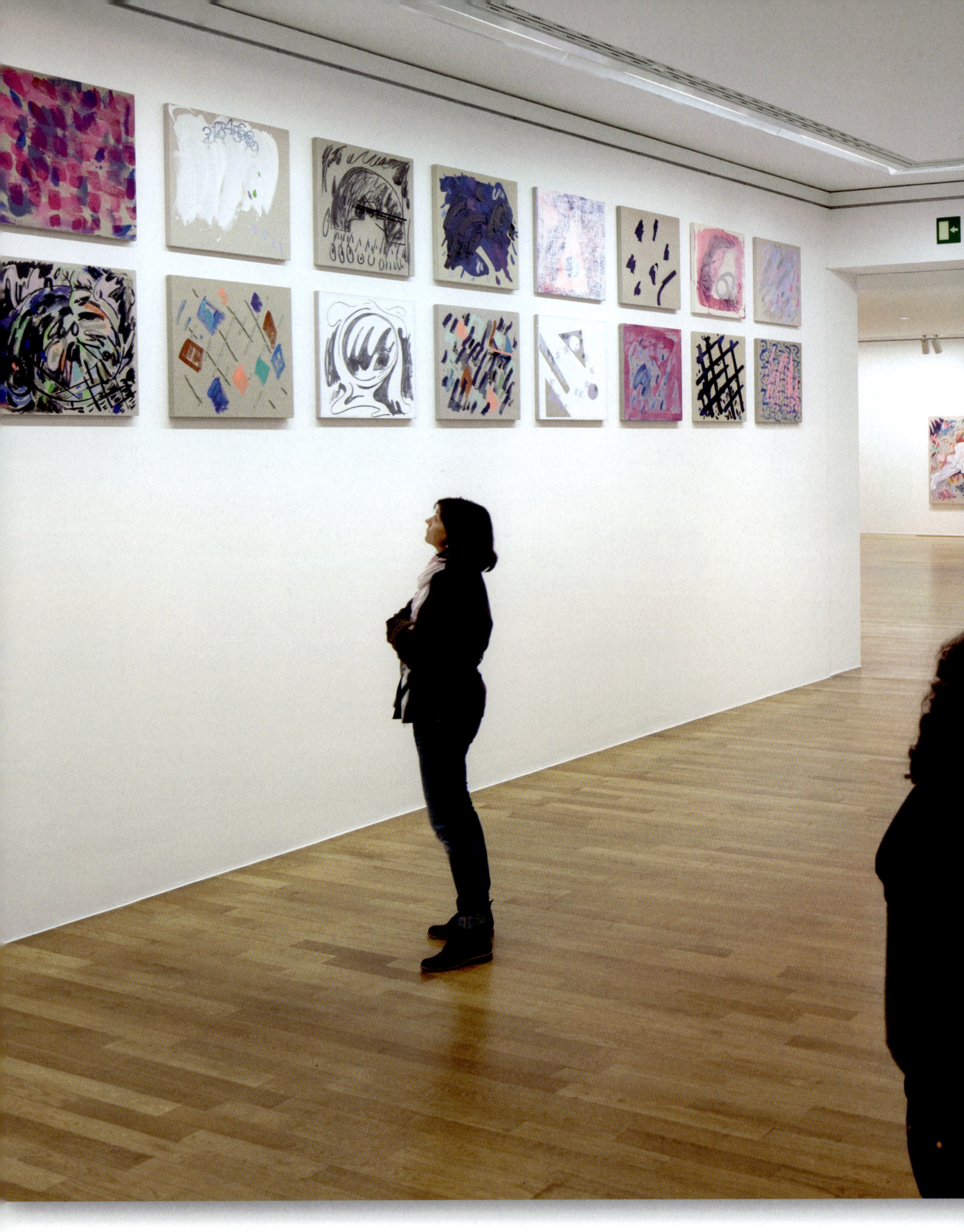

  Installation view, Kunstmuseum Bonn, Germany, 2011, with *Untitled*, 2011–12 (see p. 444)

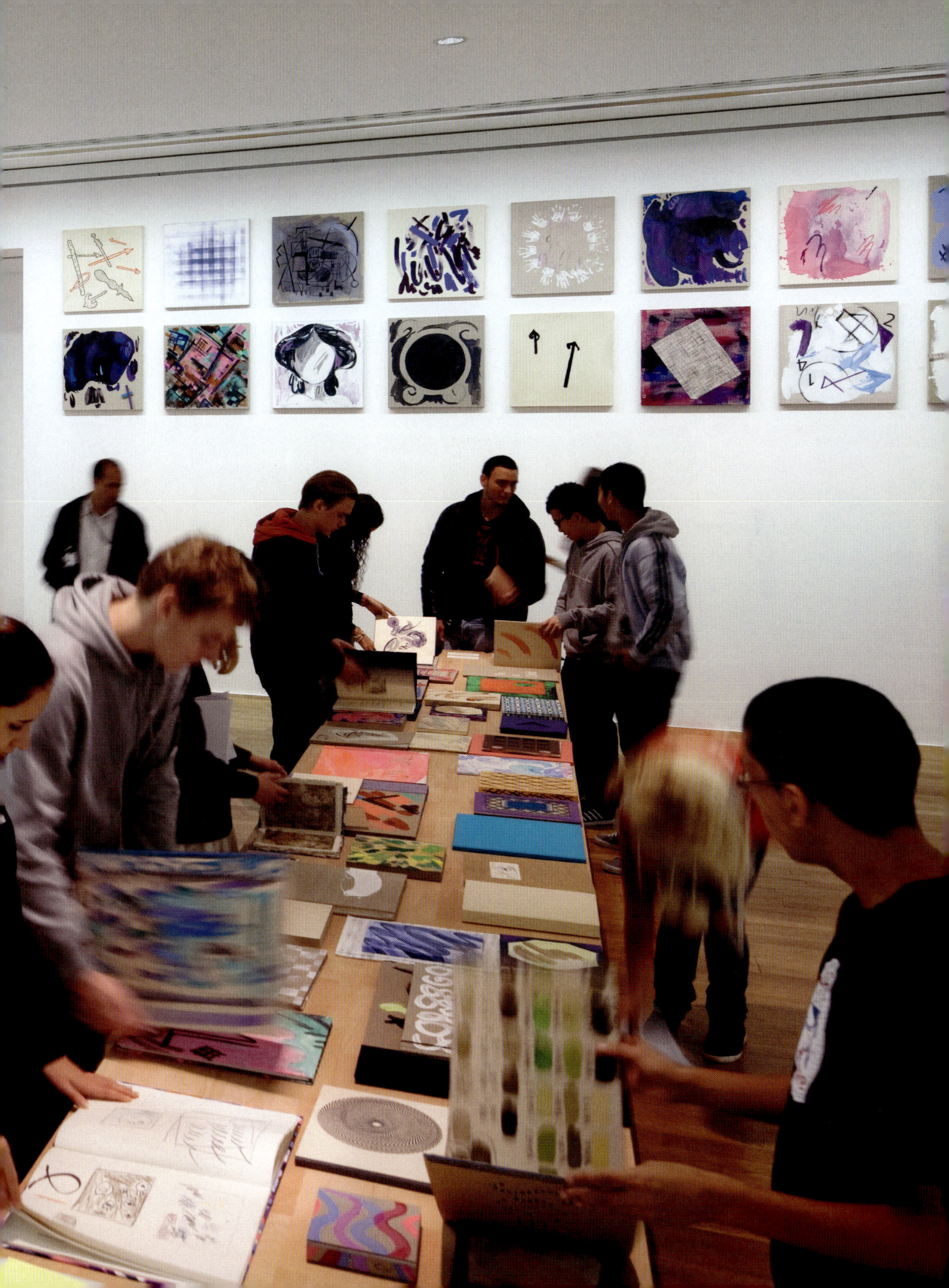

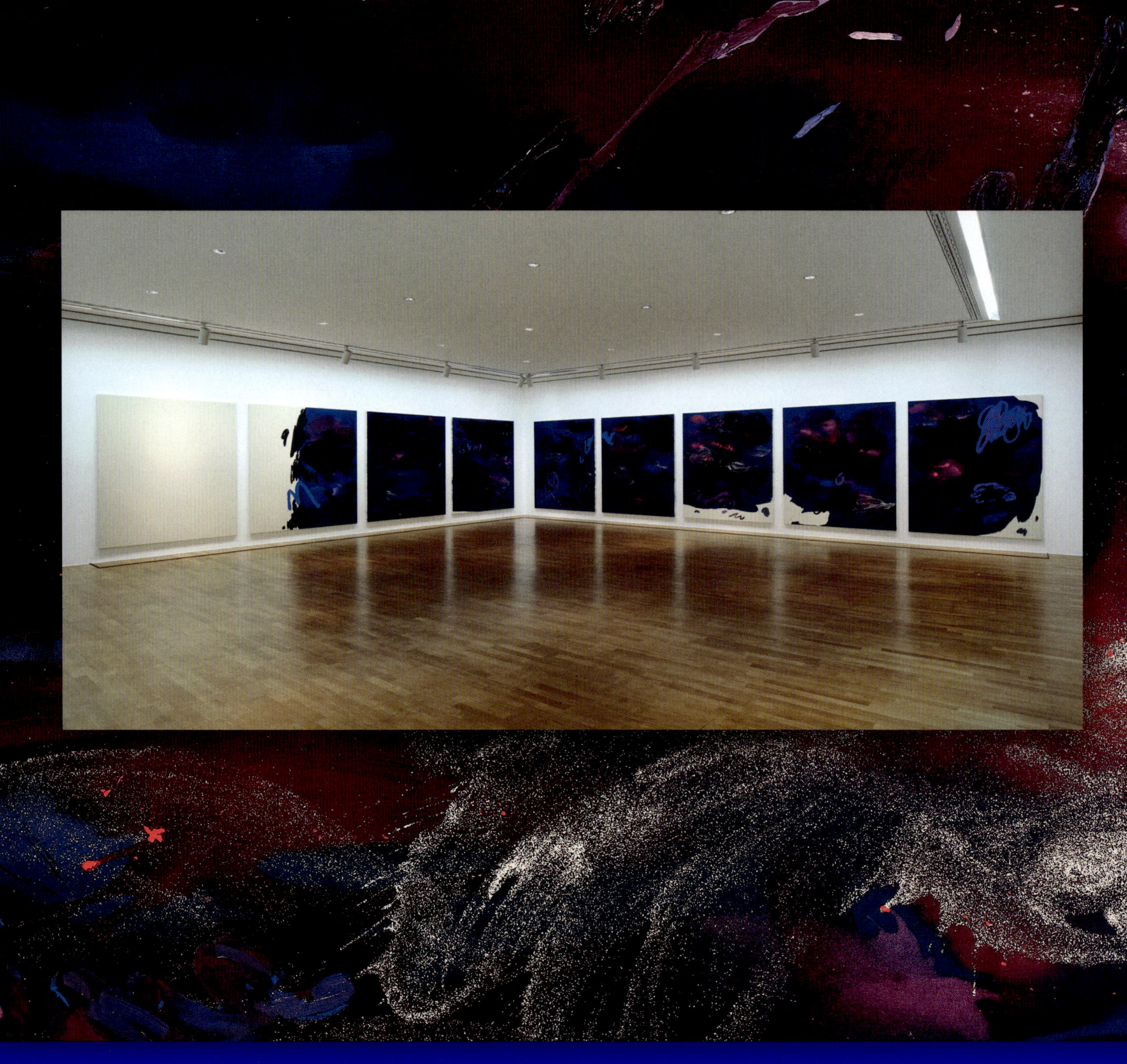

Foreground: Installation view, Kunstmuseum Bonn, Germany, 2011, with *Untitled*, 2011, acrylic, oil, vinyl paint, and mica flakes on canvas, nine panels: 96 × 84 in. (243.8 × 213.4 cm) each

 Background: Detail of *Untitled*, 2011

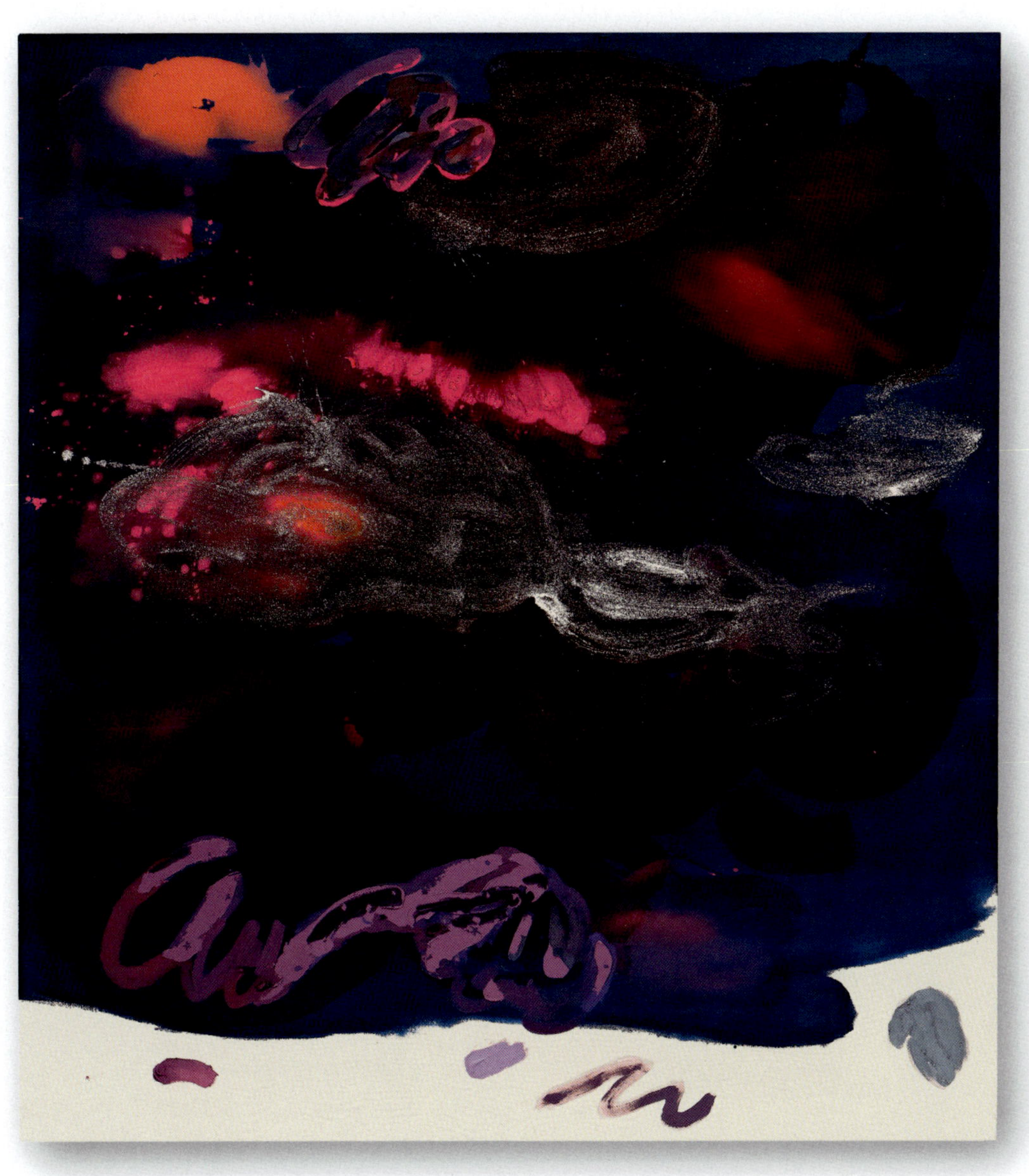

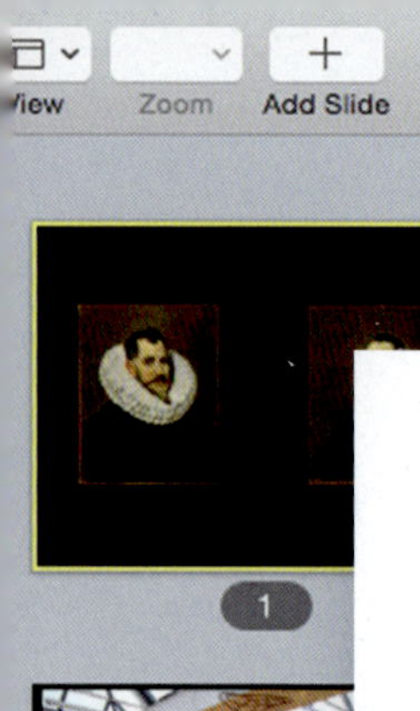
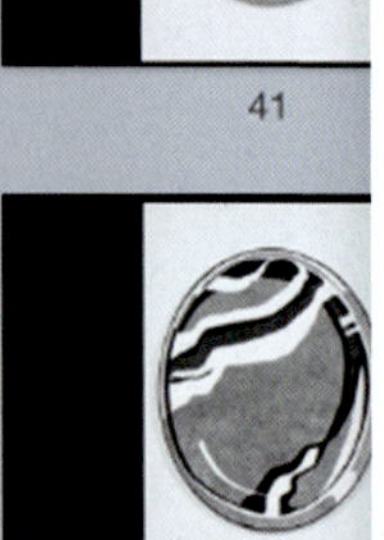
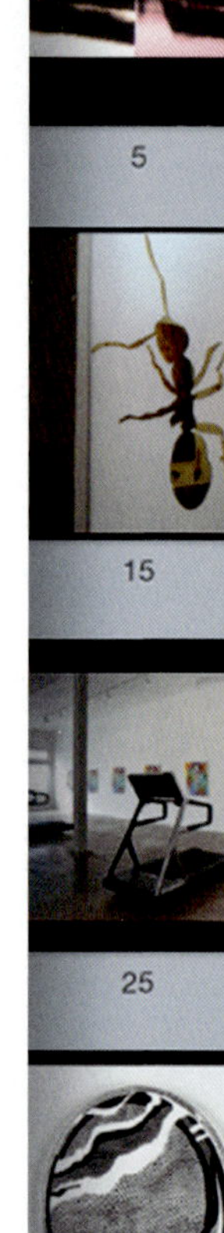
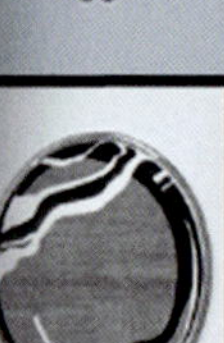
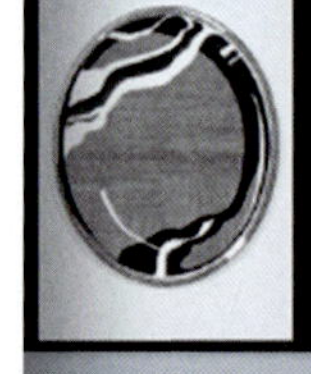

OVERDUIN AND KITE

PROUDLY PRESENTS

MERLIN CARPENTER

"FOR IMMEDIATE RELEASE"

PLEASE READ

Ed Lehan asked me for a painting that was hanging in my flat. I gave him one. It was made in 1990 & meant to be a generic abstract. Now I said OK if I give you a painting then you must make me 20 copies, 20 identical, readymade, abstract paintings. OK this happened and here they are, they are about not being an assistant and not having one, ethical pure exploitation, and like totally also about how in the intervening 20 years, a generic abstract definitely means something different to back then, it incorporates "net" knowledge, curation and post-nonirony like the change from acid house rave music to the garage music of today's London scene.

- Merlin 27.1.2011

Oakwood

Foreground: Press release, *Merlin Carpenter,* Overduin and Kite, Los Angeles, 2011
Background: PowerPoint presentation, 2012

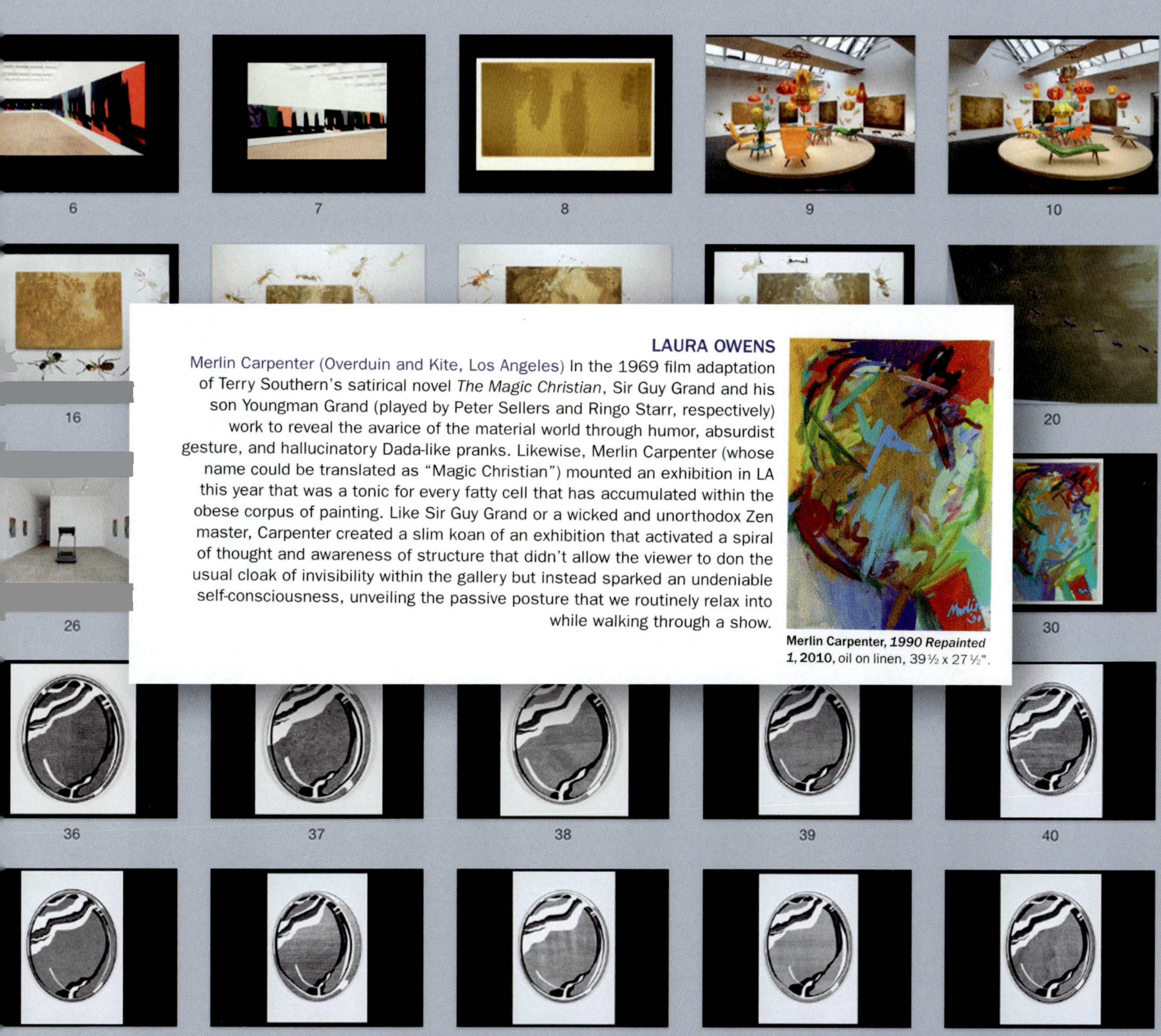

LAURA OWENS

Merlin Carpenter (Overduin and Kite, Los Angeles) In the 1969 film adaptation of Terry Southern's satirical novel *The Magic Christian*, Sir Guy Grand and his son Youngman Grand (played by Peter Sellers and Ringo Starr, respectively) work to reveal the avarice of the material world through humor, absurdist gesture, and hallucinatory Dada-like pranks. Likewise, Merlin Carpenter (whose name could be translated as "Magic Christian") mounted an exhibition in LA this year that was a tonic for every fatty cell that has accumulated within the obese corpus of painting. Like Sir Guy Grand or a wicked and unorthodox Zen master, Carpenter created a slim koan of an exhibition that activated a spiral of thought and awareness of structure that didn't allow the viewer to don the usual cloak of invisibility within the gallery but instead sparked an undeniable self-consciousness, unveiling the passive posture that we routinely relax into while walking through a show.

Merlin Carpenter, *1990 Repainted 1*, 2010, oil on linen, 39½ x 27½".

Laura Owens: Andrew Berardini asked me to give a lecture at the Mountain School in 2012. I had been thinking about three painting shows I had seen recently and how they all similarly referred to and insisted on the labor of the studio assistant, using it as a conceptual underpinning of the work. I was struck by how this idea explicated in a painting might mean something. In 2011 Jorge Pardo had done a show at neugerriemschneider where he asked several assistants to paint the same dark, forested landscape. He covered the paintings with collaged ants that made their way around the gallery walls, sometimes forming microscopic portraits of his head or those of the assistants. Chairs and couches and tables were on a rotating platform at the center of the gallery. This reminded me of one of my favorite pieces by him. He had asked James, his studio assistant, to repaint his office. James ran out of the drab, olive-green paint he used and went to get more but couldn't match the color, so the office was painted two-tone in a somewhat haphazard way. Jorge then asked him to repeat this mistake on a large canvas, almost as a funny punishment. It reminded me of something I had read about Warhol mentioning the productive nature of his assistants' misunderstandings of his instructions. I also discussed a 2011 Merlin Carpenter show that told the story of his exchange with his former assistant Ed Lehan. And I included Jonathan Horowitz, who for a 2012 exhibition asked nineteen different assistants to reproduce a Lichtenstein mirror painting by hand, essentially making individual self-portraits via mirror.

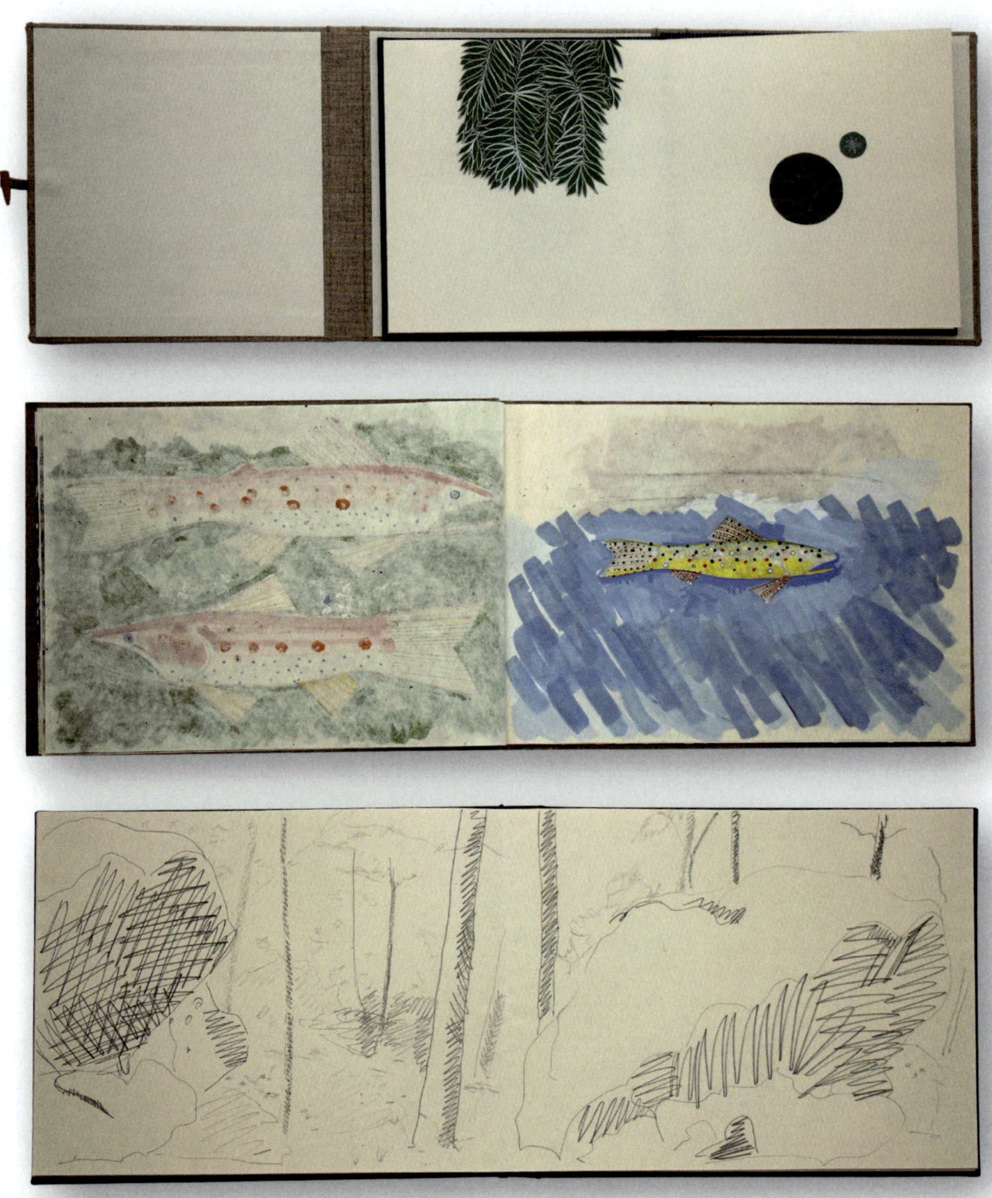

This page, from top: *Untitled* by Katy Fischer, 2010; *Untitled (Fish)* by David Korty, 2011; *Rocks Trees Woods* by Mary Weatherford, 2011. Opposite page, clockwise from top left: *Untitled* by Andreas Reiter Raabe, 2014; *Untitled* by Michael Dopp, 2013; *Lost Angeles* by Nick Herman, 2015; *Untitled* by Eric Palgon, 2011; *Cultural Differences* by Euan Macdonald, 2014; *Untitled* by Monique van Genderen, 2014; *Untitled* by Roger Herman, 2012; and *California Raisins* by Tyson Reeder and Wallace Whitney, 2015

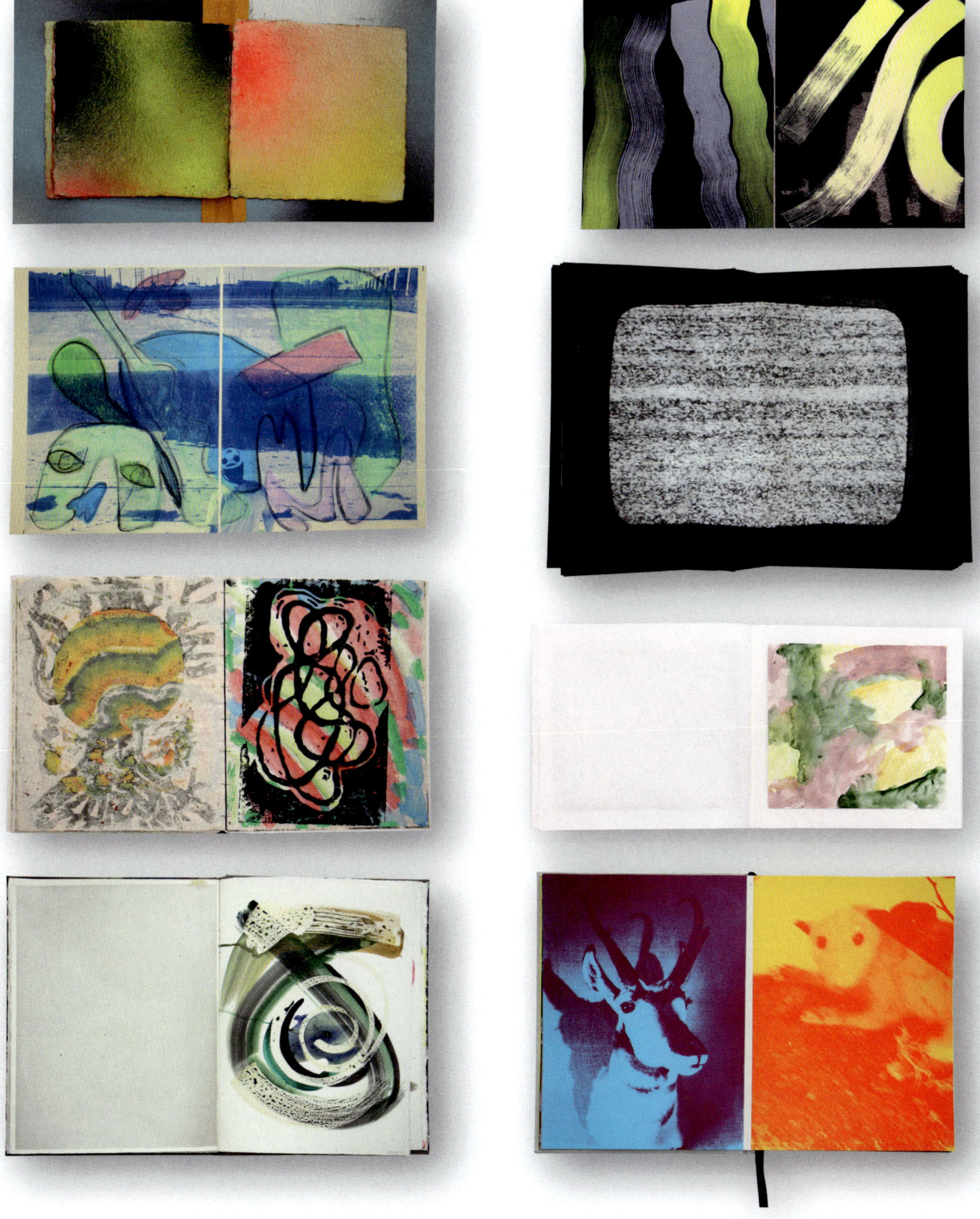

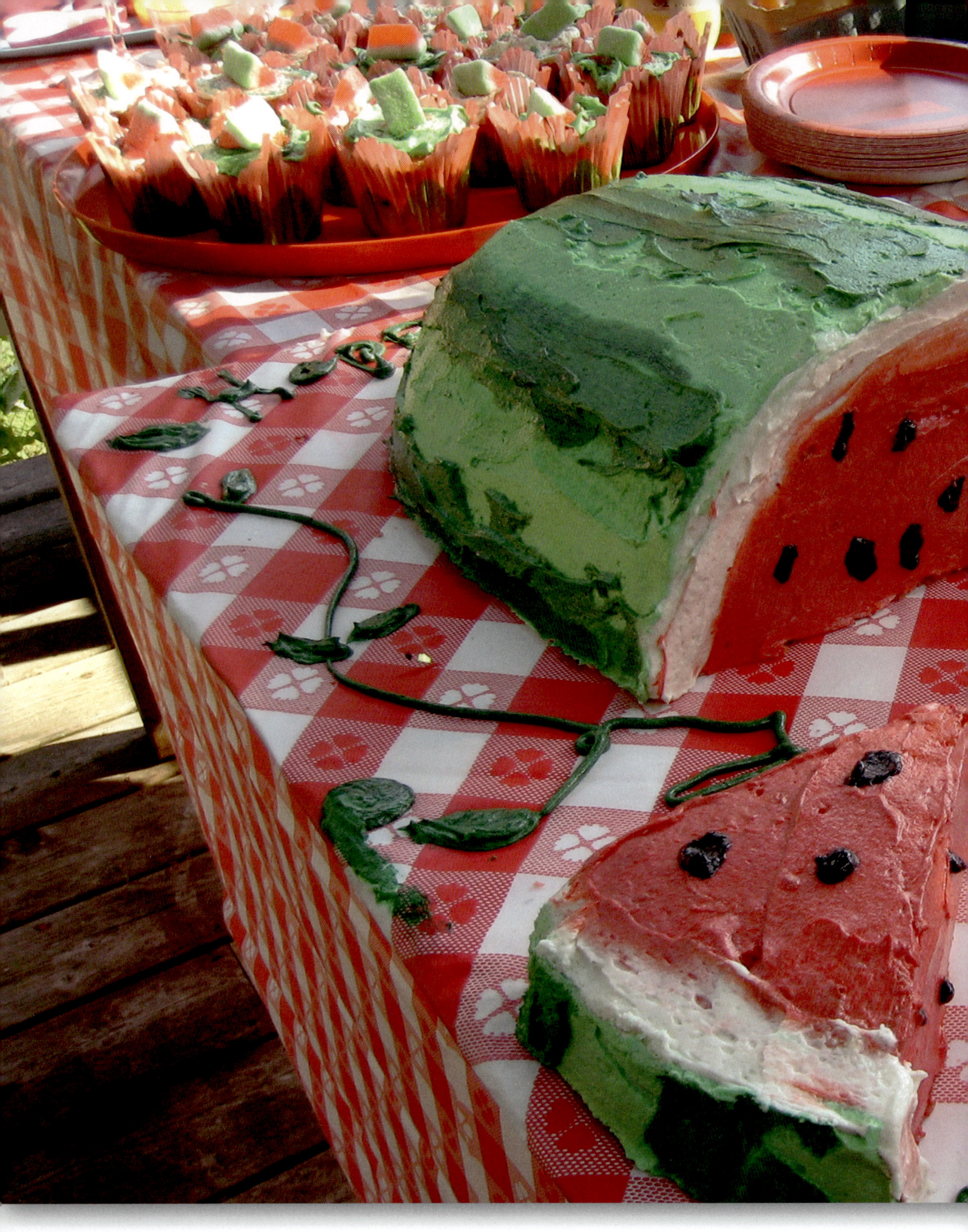

 Birthday cake made by Owens for Henry Bryan, Orient, New York, 2011

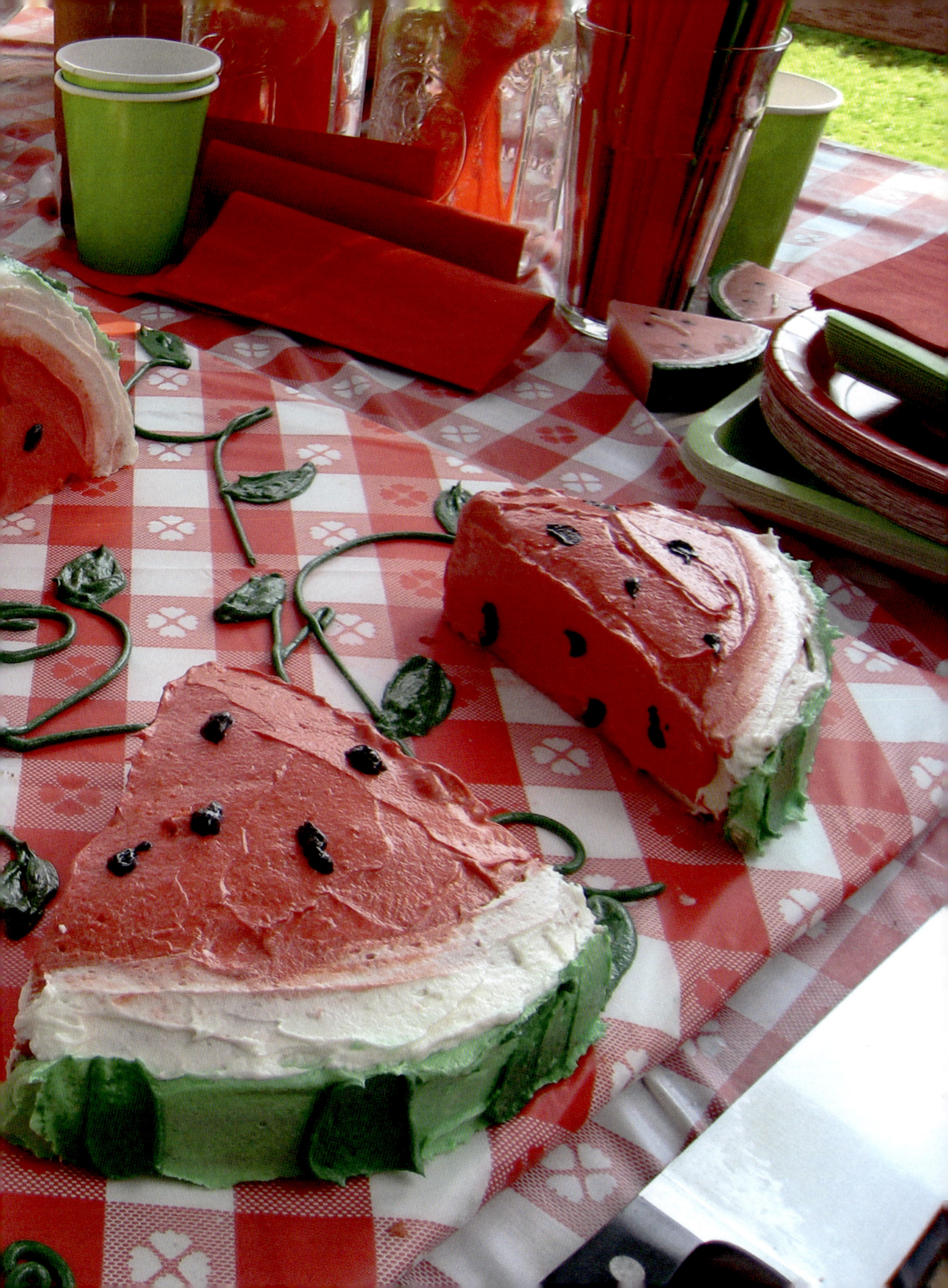

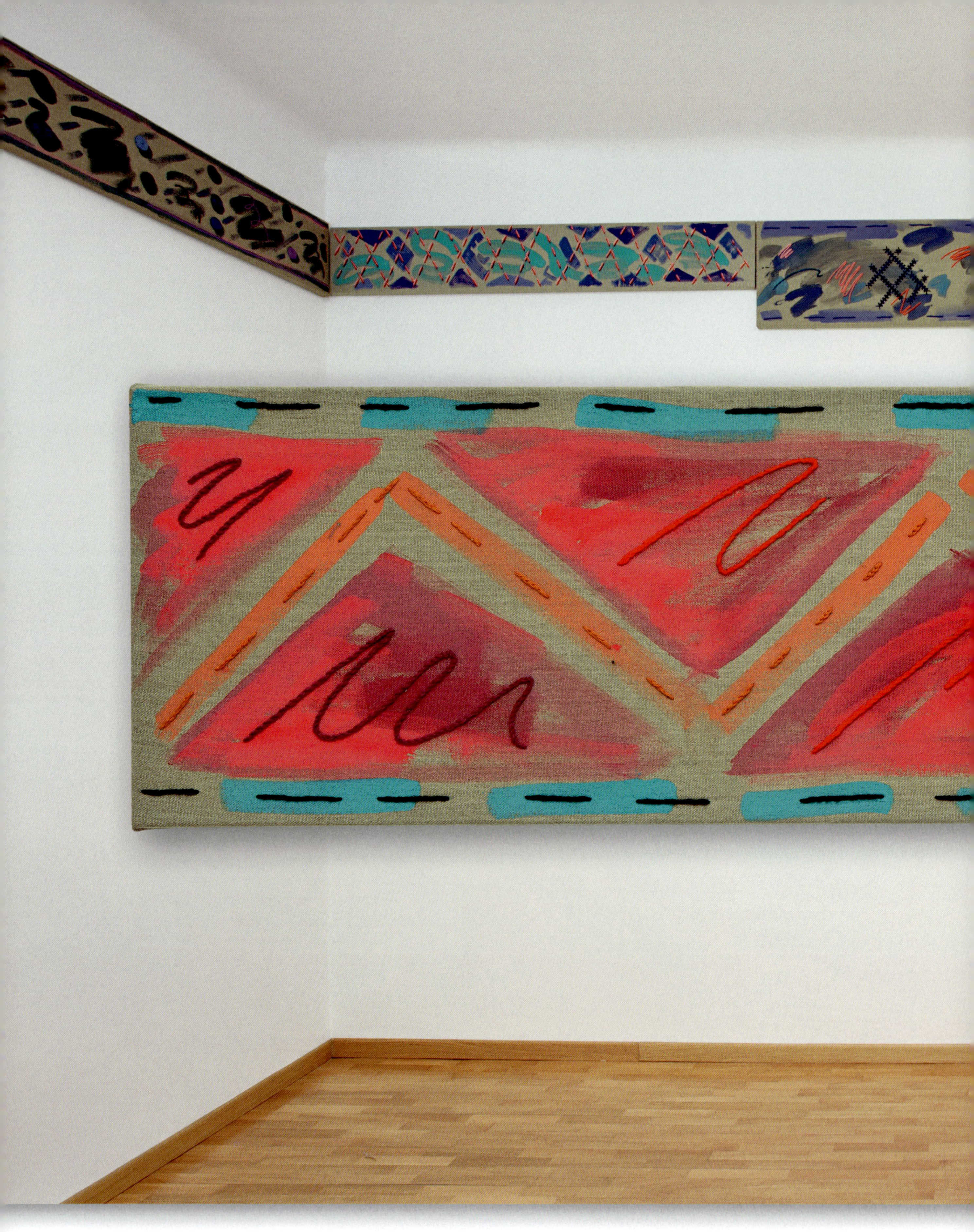

Foreground: Detail of *Untitled*, 2012, vinyl paint and yarn on linen, 15 × 53½ in. (38.1 × 135.9 cm)
Background: Installation view, *Pure Perception: Kristin Baker, Laura Owens, Mai-Thu Perret, Amanda Ross-Ho*, Galleria Monica De Cardenas, Milan, 2012, with *Untitled*, 2012, 11 × 73 in. (27.9 × 185.4 cm), 10 × 64 in. (25.4 × 162.6 cm), 15¾ × 84⅛ in. (40 × 213.7 cm), 10 × 39 in. (25.4 × 99.1 cm), and 11 × 60 in. (27.9 × 152.4 cm), all vinyl paint and yarn on linen

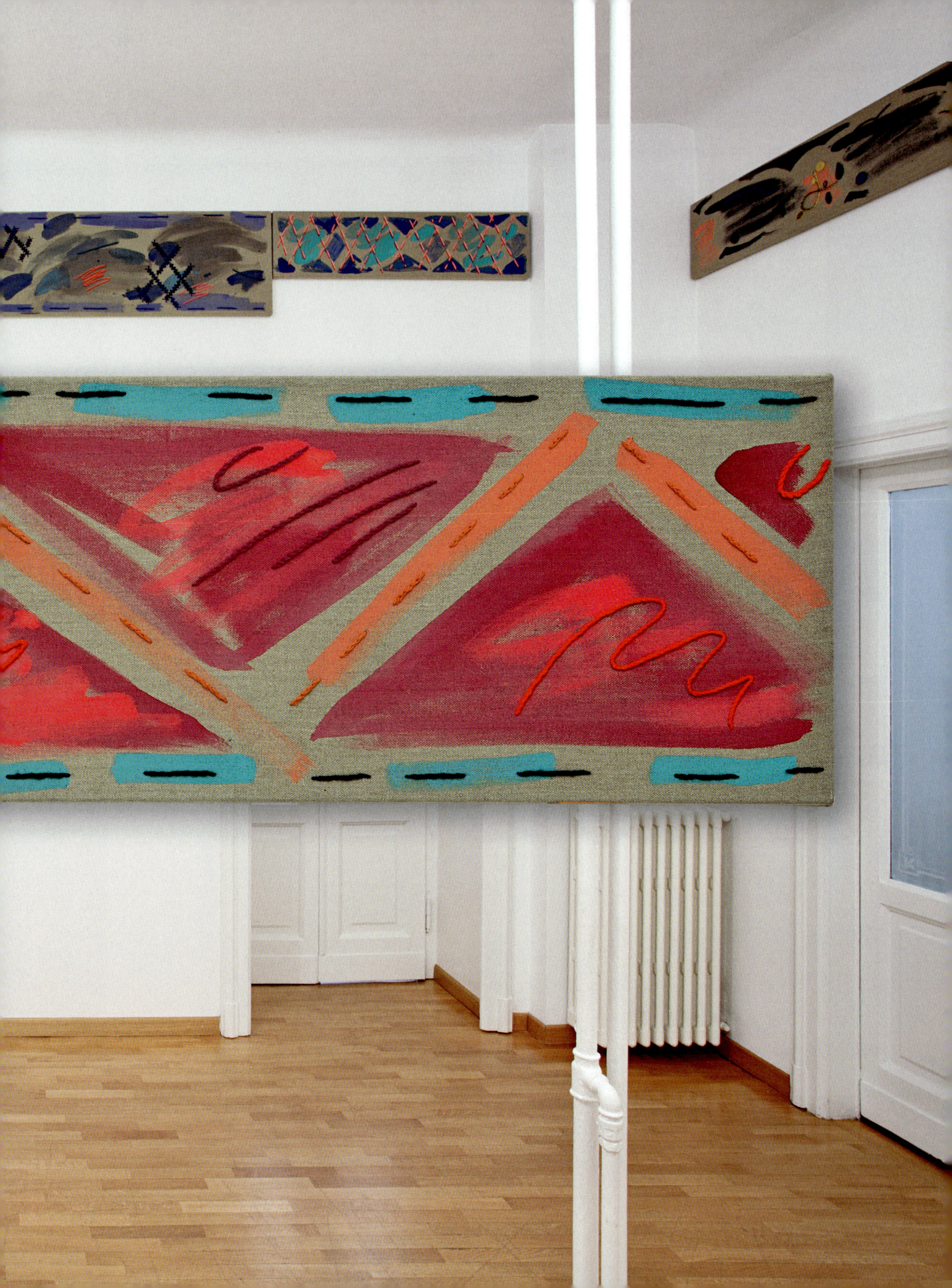

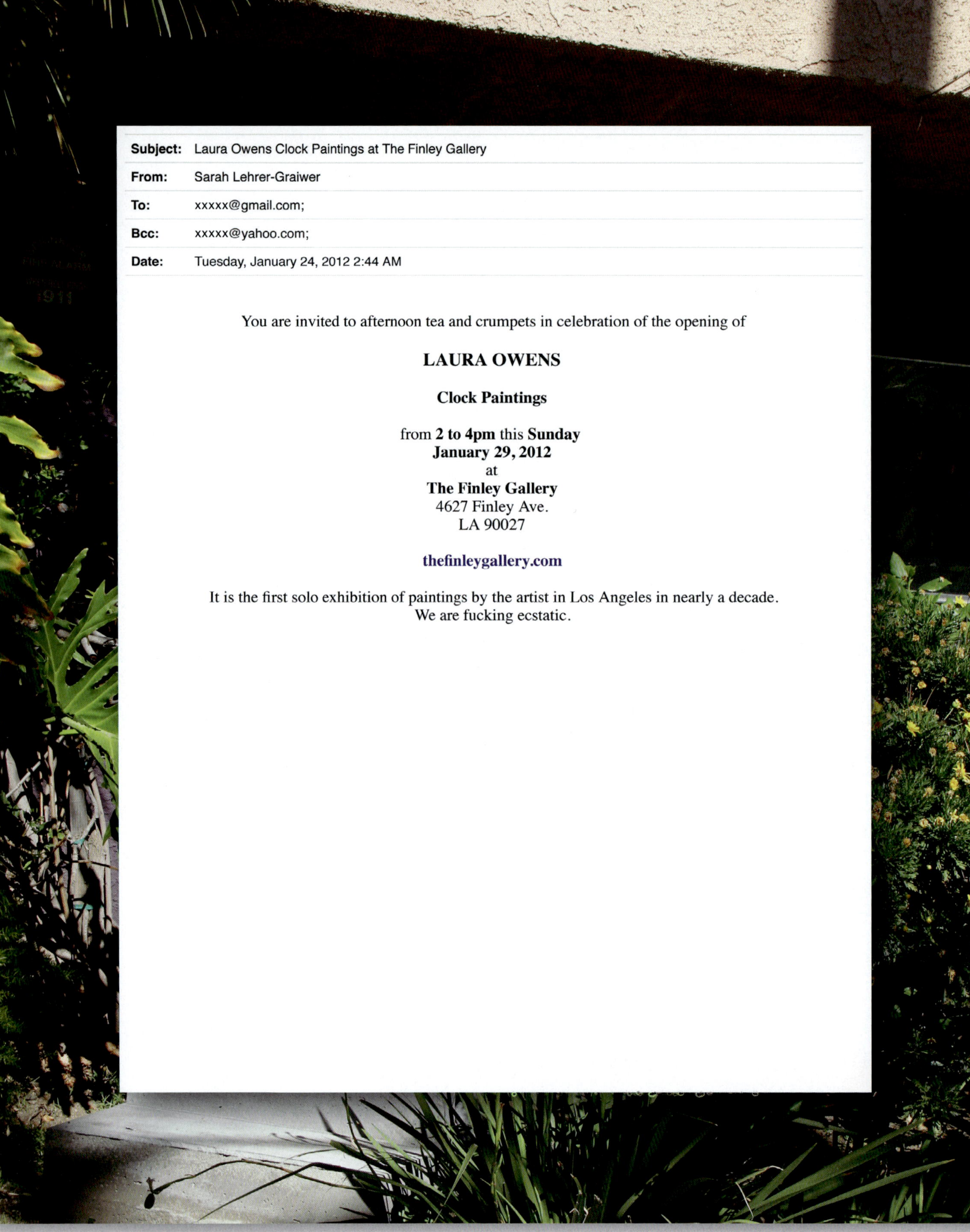

Subject: Laura Owens Clock Paintings at The Finley Gallery
From: Sarah Lehrer-Graiwer
To: xxxxx@gmail.com;
Bcc: xxxxx@yahoo.com;
Date: Tuesday, January 24, 2012 2:44 AM

You are invited to afternoon tea and crumpets in celebration of the opening of

LAURA OWENS

Clock Paintings

from 2 to 4pm this Sunday
January 29, 2012
at
The Finley Gallery
4627 Finley Ave.
LA 90027

thefinleygallery.com

It is the first solo exhibition of paintings by the artist in Los Angeles in nearly a decade.
We are fucking ecstatic.

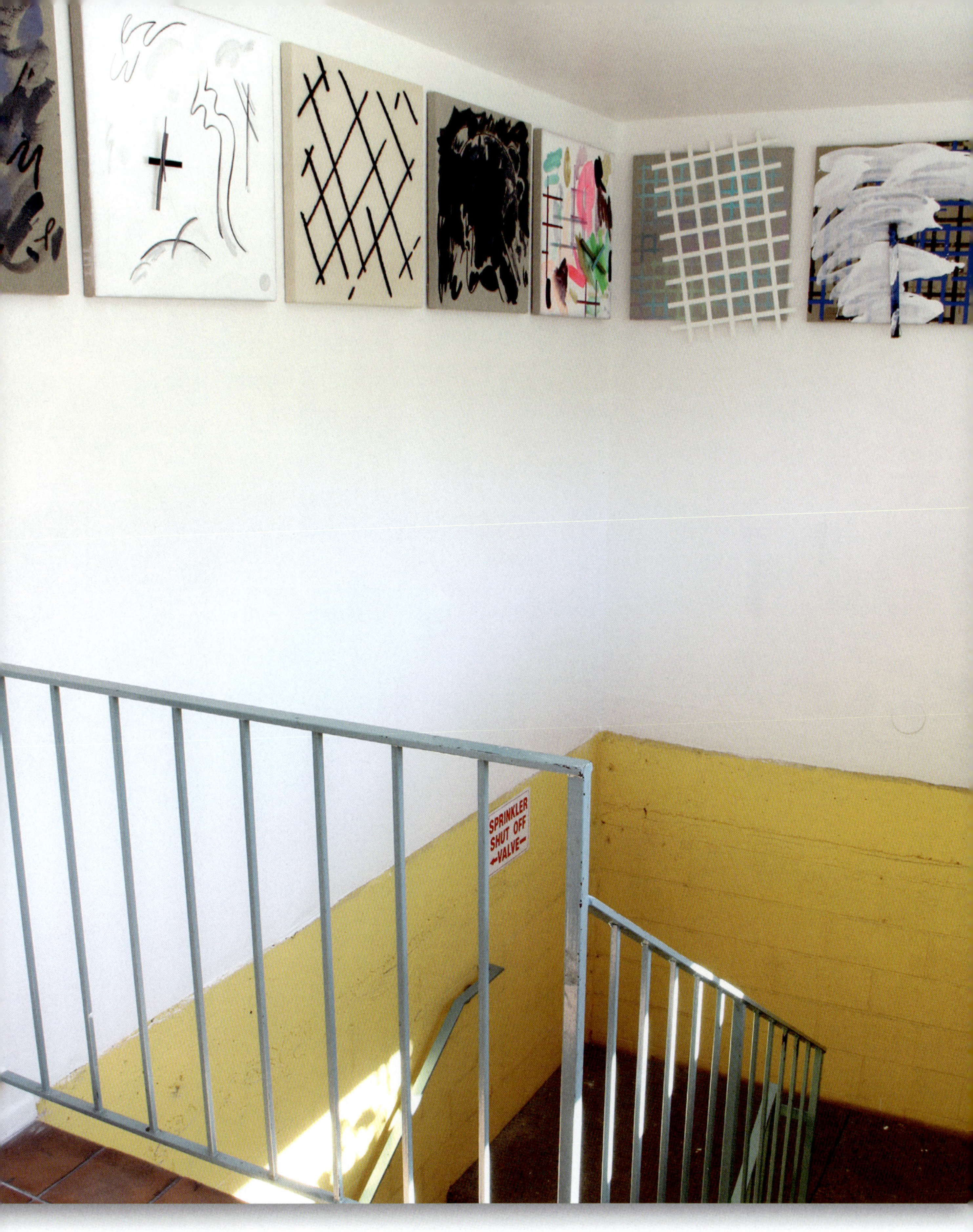

Installation view, *Clock Paintings*, The Finley, Los Angeles, 2012, with *Untitled,* 2011–12 (see p. 444)

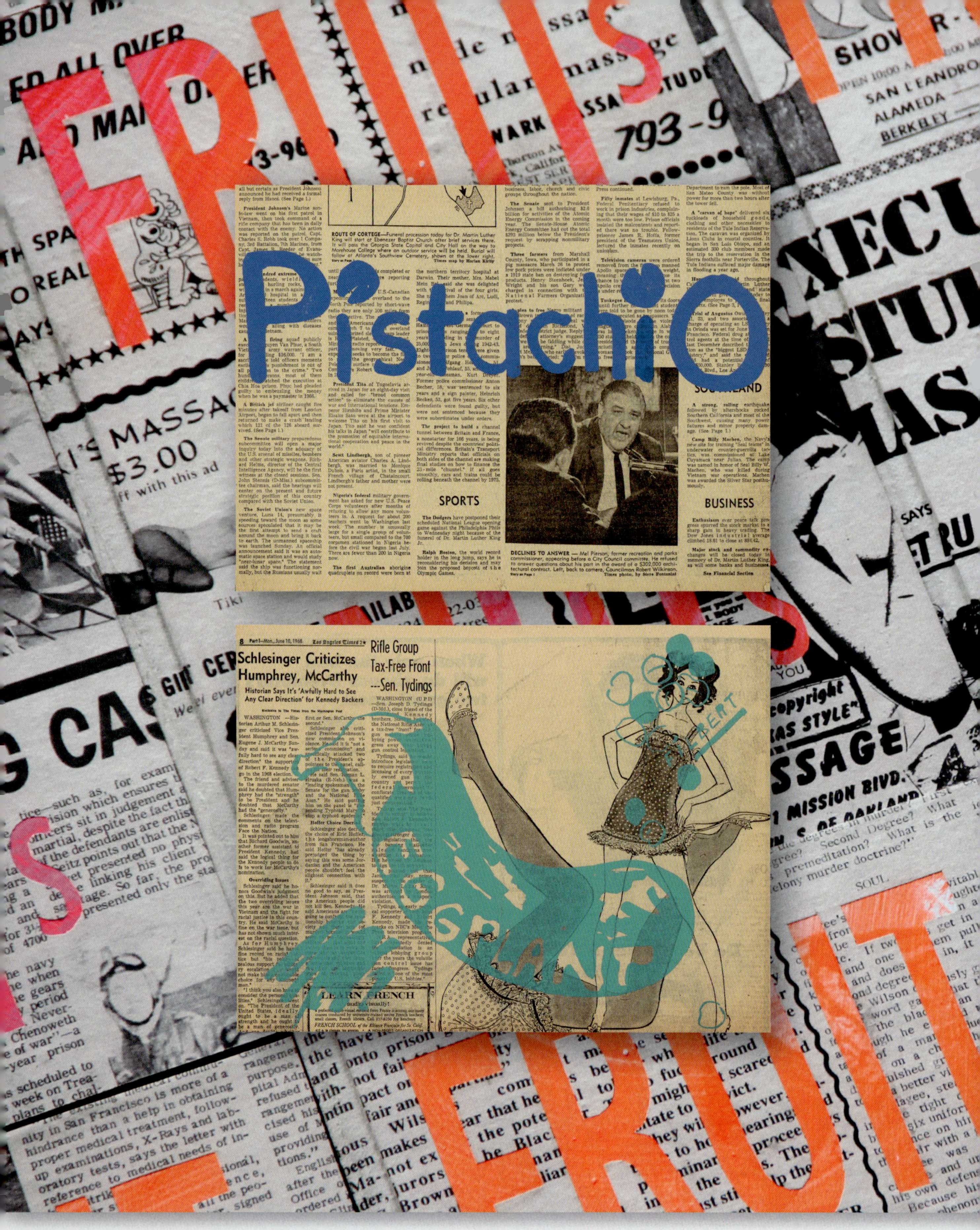

Foreground: Pages from *Fruits and Nuts*, 2011, silkscreen ink on California newspapers from the 1960s, 11 × 7 × ¾ in. (27.9 × 17.8 × 1.9 cm)

 Background: Detail of *Fruits and Nuts,* 2011

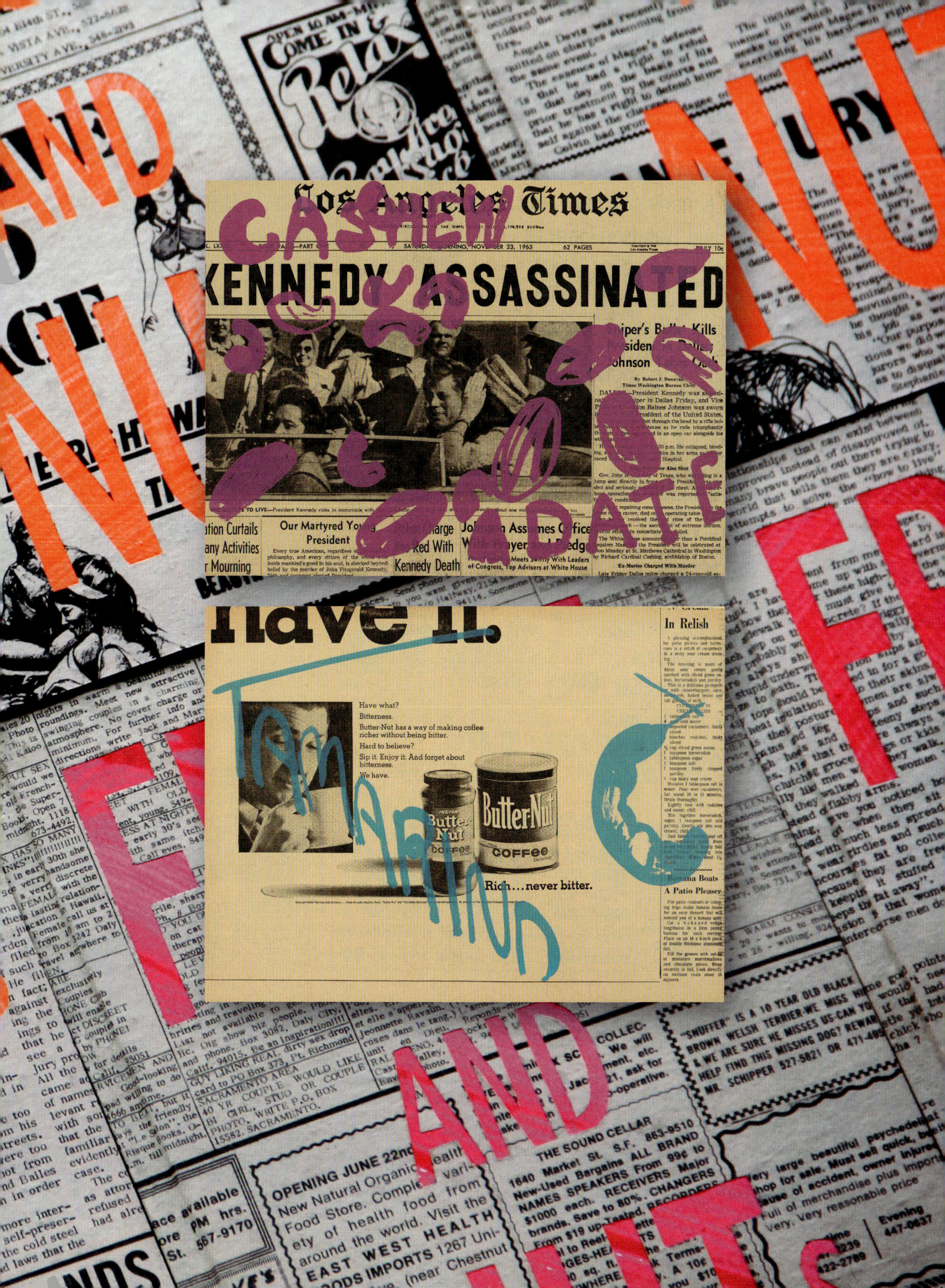
Los Angeles Times
KENNEDY ASSASSINATED
Sniper's Bullet Kills President in Dallas; Johnson Sworn
Our Martyred Young President
Johnson Assumes Office
Have it.
Have what?
Bitterness.
Butter-Nut has a way of making coffee richer without being bitter.
Hard to believe?
Sip it. Enjoy it. And forget about bitterness.
We have.
Butter-Nut coffee
Rich...never bitter.
In Relish
Banana Boats
A Patio Pleaser
THE SOUND CELLAR
OPENING JUNE 22nd
EAST WEST HEALTH

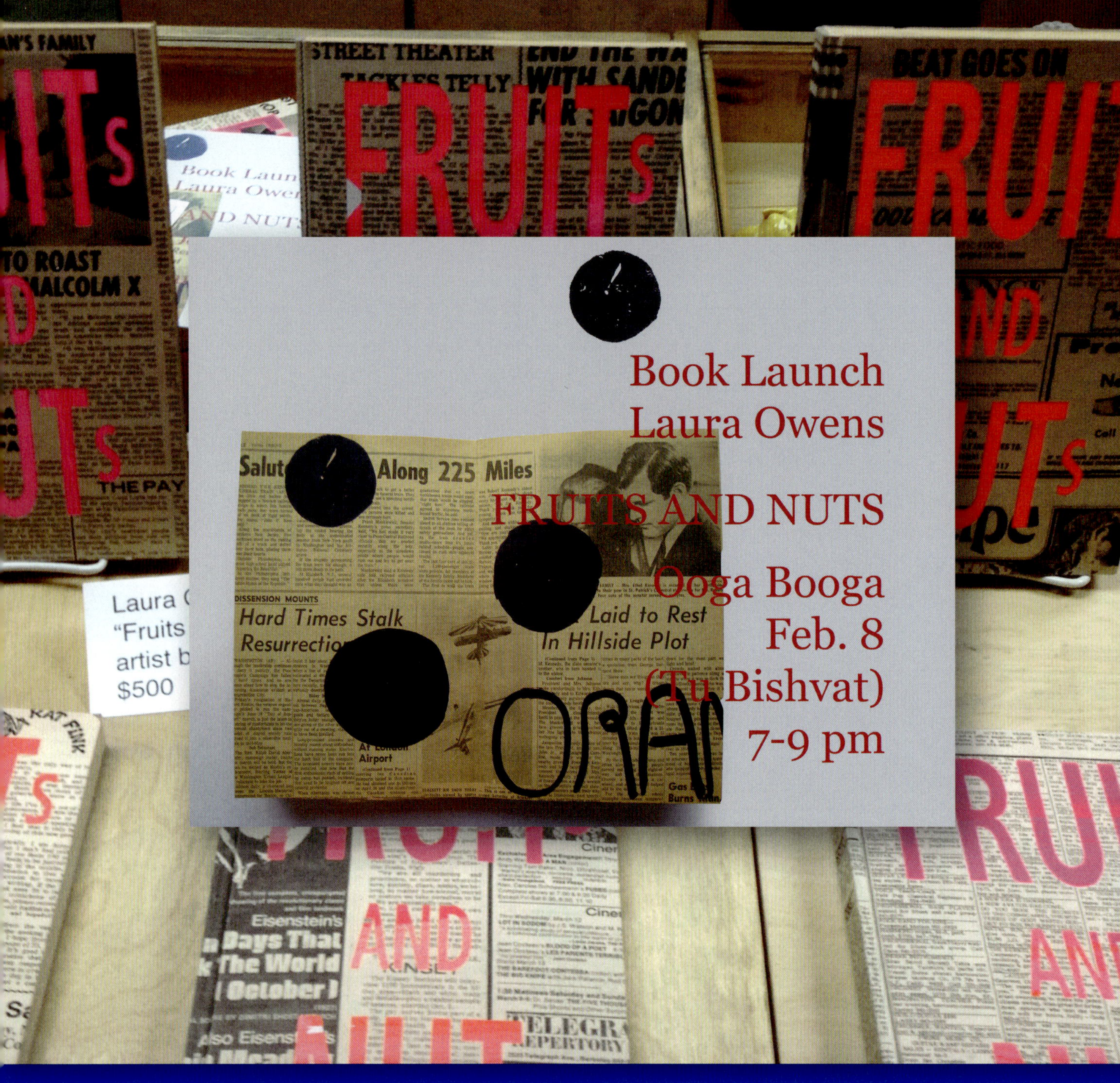

Jennifer Phiffer: Around 2010 a girl I worked with at a bindery who also worked for Laura's studio called to ask some technical questions about some of their projects. Laura wanted me to teach her more about bookmaking in general, which morphed into having me build books for her. She uses a lot of nontraditional materials and methods, which has been very exciting. Some of the first projects we did together were combination books and boxes. There was a Japanese box that was trifold and incorporated a bone enclosure clasp, and there were some very straight-ahead, long-stitch, or what's known as library-stitch, regular sewn books. And then she procured hundreds of historical newspapers to use in various ways. I helped to preserve them by misting them with a liquid that makes the paper's pH neutral. I can't say it makes it acid-free because that's a misnomer, there's no such thing. But it makes it age more slowly. With *Fruits and Nuts* it was especially important for the pages to lie flat so that you could have graphics completely cover each spread. So no sewing, no structure in the gutter. We chose a technique I had gotten good at that mimicks children's board books, which use a structure bookbinders call barrel binding. For that method it's incredibly important to have a carrier page for the newspaper to lie on, because if you can keep it from being mechanically folded and have something else do that folding and carry most of the weight, that will preserve the newspaper better over time. There won't be quite so much stress there.

Foreground: Invitation, *Fruits and Nuts* book launch, Ooga Booga, Los Angeles, 2012
Background: *Fruits and Nuts* book launch, 2012

Mythologies of Painting

"Why do people think artists are special? It's just another job."   Andy Warhol

The dominant cultural cliché of the artist as romantic genius is a slippery non-locatable identity. For those artists painting today, that necessarily brings self-conscious awareness to all studio practice. This class will pay special attention to the techniques, material, colors and gestures that artists use to embrace, perform, consciously ignore or subvert the standard mythologies.

We will look at Pablo Picasso, Jackson Pollock, Francis Picabia, Martin Kippenberger, David Hammons, Julian Schnabel, Mary Heilmann, Silke Otto-Knapp, Merlin Carpenter, Dan Colen. And many others……

Studio Elective

Prerequisite:	Painting II or equivalent
Credit/Hours:	2 credits, 3 hours
Enrollment:	16 max
Required Text:	TBA
First Day Materials:	TBA

Day:	Thursday
Time:	3:30 – 6:30pm
Instructor:	Laura Owens and Edgar Bryan
Location:	G219/G220

Course Goals

Students will be introduced to different materials and techniques in painting. Students should develop a sensitivity to the variety of gestures that make up the lexicon of painting and how their use conveys different meanings.

Students should develop a sense of the complex use of signifiers in works, and how the same gestures can be used to convey different, often opposing narratives.

Students should develop critical thinking skills about their own work, how the gestures convey meaning.

Students are expected to exhibit a serious investigation into their practice, and growth should be apparent throughout the semester. An emphasis will be placed on growth exhibited between mid-term and final critique.

Description for class taught with Edgar Bryan, Otis College of Art and Design, Los Angeles, 2012

FALLEN FRUIT
JONATHAN GOLD

Visitors to the Norton Simon Museum, the collections jimmied into the corpse of the former Pasadena Art Museum, come to admire the handsome Frank Gehry garden, the shimmering tiles by Edith Heath, and what is probably the most impressive group of Rembrandt paintings on the West Coast. There are Degas ballerinas by the bushel, Rubens by the acre, and Venetian cityscapes sufficient to decorate the parlor of any eighteenth-century earl. Simon, or his consultants, had a decent eye—his Cranach looks like a Cranach, and the Ingres portrait is really fine. There may not be much competition, but the Simon is probably the best small art museum in California, and as much as one personally might mourn the superb contemporary-art museum that was vaporized to accommodate the ketchup millionaire's dream, as a fact on the ground the Simon is admirable.

But a casual visitor, someone there because her guidebook tells her that she should come have a look at the Van Gogh, may be understandably puzzled by what seems to be the institution's emphasis on *Still Life with Lemons, Oranges and a Rose* by Francisco de Zurbarán, a seventeenth-century Spanish painter who was unlikely to have come up in the Renaissance-art survey course she took as an elective sophomore year. The museum's gallery map features the Zurbarán on its cover, and the gift shop is stocked with replicas of the painting in every possible size and form. It was the star of the small Norton Simon exhibition in New York's Frick last year. More to the point, the Norton Simon's galleries are laid out in a way that makes it almost impossible to avoid, a flash of yellow in a room just off the most glamorous corridor, a magnetic yellow positioned to distract you as you rush toward the Botticelli.

When Simon bought the painting, in the early '70s, it was the third-most expensive Old Master ever sold, a stand-in for the Velázquez that would never hit the auction block, and the $2,725,000 cost figured into the allure of what is, after all, a picture of some fruit. Zurbarán, its painter, was a friend of Velázquez and an admirer of Caravaggio; his work, chiefly pious religious scenes painted for his court patrons in Seville, is often compared favorably with them both. If you are an aficionado of the way a saint's loose white robe puddles around his holy ankles, Zurbarán is the Baroque-era painter for you.

But *Still Life* is charismatic for a picture of fruit, a three-part composition of nipply lemons, oranges, and an untouched cup of water positioned on a silver tray. An oddly specific light illuminates the composition—early morning sun, perhaps—streaming through a window above and to the viewer's left, focused sharply enough to render the left face of the oranges bright, washed out, although the shadows are almost black. The wooden table on which they sit appears to receive barely enough light to do a crossword puzzle. To the right of the oranges, the sunlight glints from the rim of a porcelain drinking cup filled with water; a white rose stained pink at its edge glows softly as if illuminated from within. On the left are four lemons: some are as defined by their sunken areoles and proud nipples as a vintage *Playboy* centerfold. Another, in the foreground, appears to have the outline of a face with a jutting, crooked nose. If you squint, it is almost a match for the head of the leathery crone who cradles the newborn Virgin in another Zurbarán painting mounted a few feet to one side. The rough-skinned oranges are heaped in a finely woven basket and wreathed with an arrangement of dark leaves and virginal white blossoms that seem less to grow from the fruit than to have descended from heaven.

The museum abounds in other fruit-filled still lifes of the era, and they thrum with life—the yellowing edges of leaves signifying decay, the lumps and hollows hinting at sweet temporality, even the turnips and loamy potatoes that look like tomorrow's dinner. Ants, butterflies, worms, and

 Originally published in *Slake* 1 (Summer 2010): 22–23. Gold is the restaurant critic for the *Los Angeles Times*.

beetles skitter along the edges of the displays, nibbling or sucking out juice.

Fruits are pure sex, the naked reproductive organs of a tree—juicy; plump with fertility; cleft with alluring, syrup-crusted fissures. When we look at Chardin's cherries or a Cézanne peach, what we see is possibility. What we see when we look at Zurbarán's citrus may be the opposite of that—this is among the chastest damned fruit in existence, unviolated ornamental fruit meant to be admired rather than eaten. There are no crumbs. Not a bite is missing. The lemons are actually citrons, whose rind is fragrant but whose flesh is all but inedible; the oranges, like most in Seville at the time, are almost certainly bitter. These will never be eaten.

In fact, Zurbarán mostly hides the naughty bits as completely as Raphael does the genitals on his half-robed saints, except for for a solitary, lovingly rendered crater, the stem end of the closest of the oranges, at the exact center of the painting—thrust out quite directly at the viewer, the pucker at the center of the world. Centered between the virginal chalice on one side and the voluptuous citrons on the other, the dark, bottomless pucker invites what is sometimes known as the male gaze.

The saintly glow of the fruit is indistinguishable from the one of the face of Zurbarán's St. Francis on the painting next to this, or rather to that of the skull to which the saint kneels. There are no glints of light on the oranges themselves—no shine, just brilliantly rough surface. The fruit has no physical presence; it is impossible to imagine plucking it from its basket, to smell it, to feel the heaviness of its juice in your palm. But you want to—you ache for sensation, driven by its sheer, pornographic unavailability. It is no wonder Zurbarán's oranges enraptured a millionaire.

You don't want to eat this fruit. You want to fuck it.

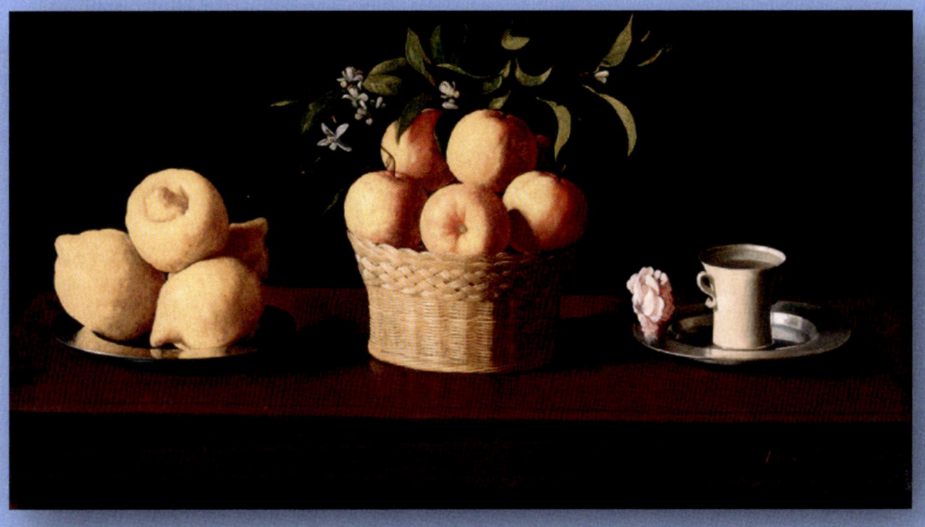

Francisco de Zurbarán, *Still Life with Lemons, Oranges and a Rose*, 1633, oil on canvas, 24½ × 43⅛ in. (62.2 × 109.5 cm)

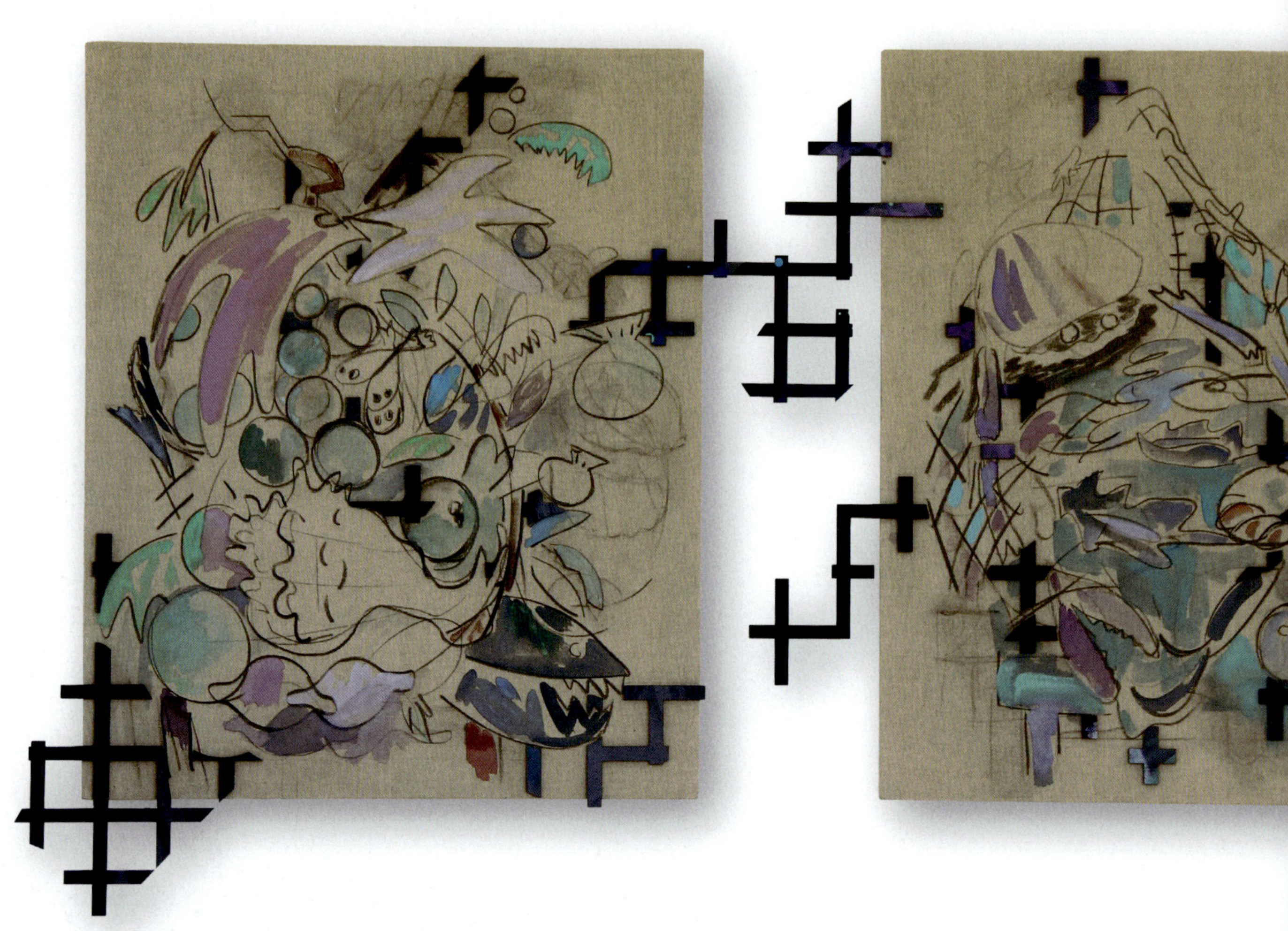

Foreground: Detail of *Untitled*, 2012, oil, vinyl paint, charcoal, and wood on linen, seven panels: 42⅛ × 34⅛ in. (107 × 86.7 cm) each

 Background: Detail of *Untitled,* 2012

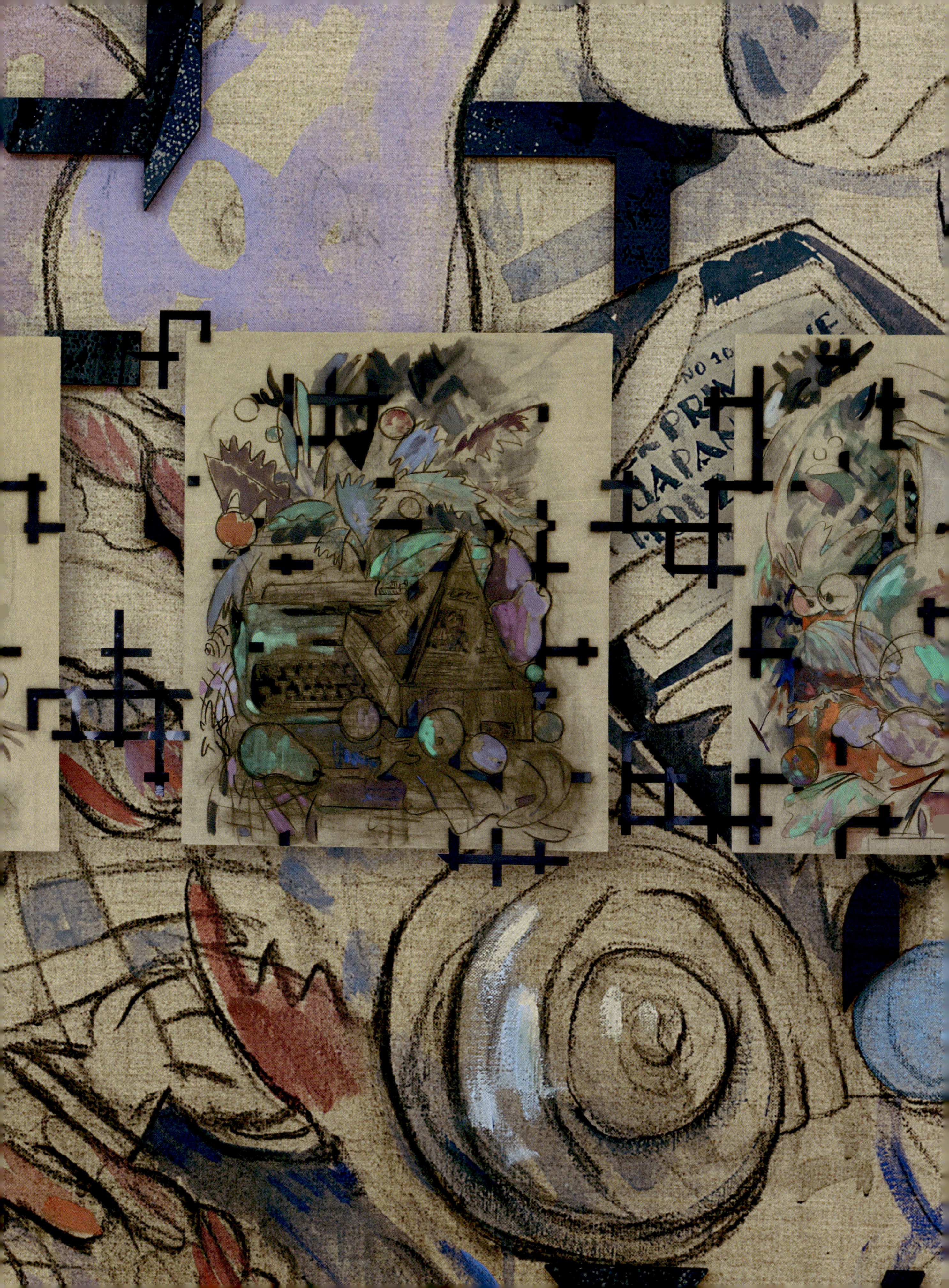

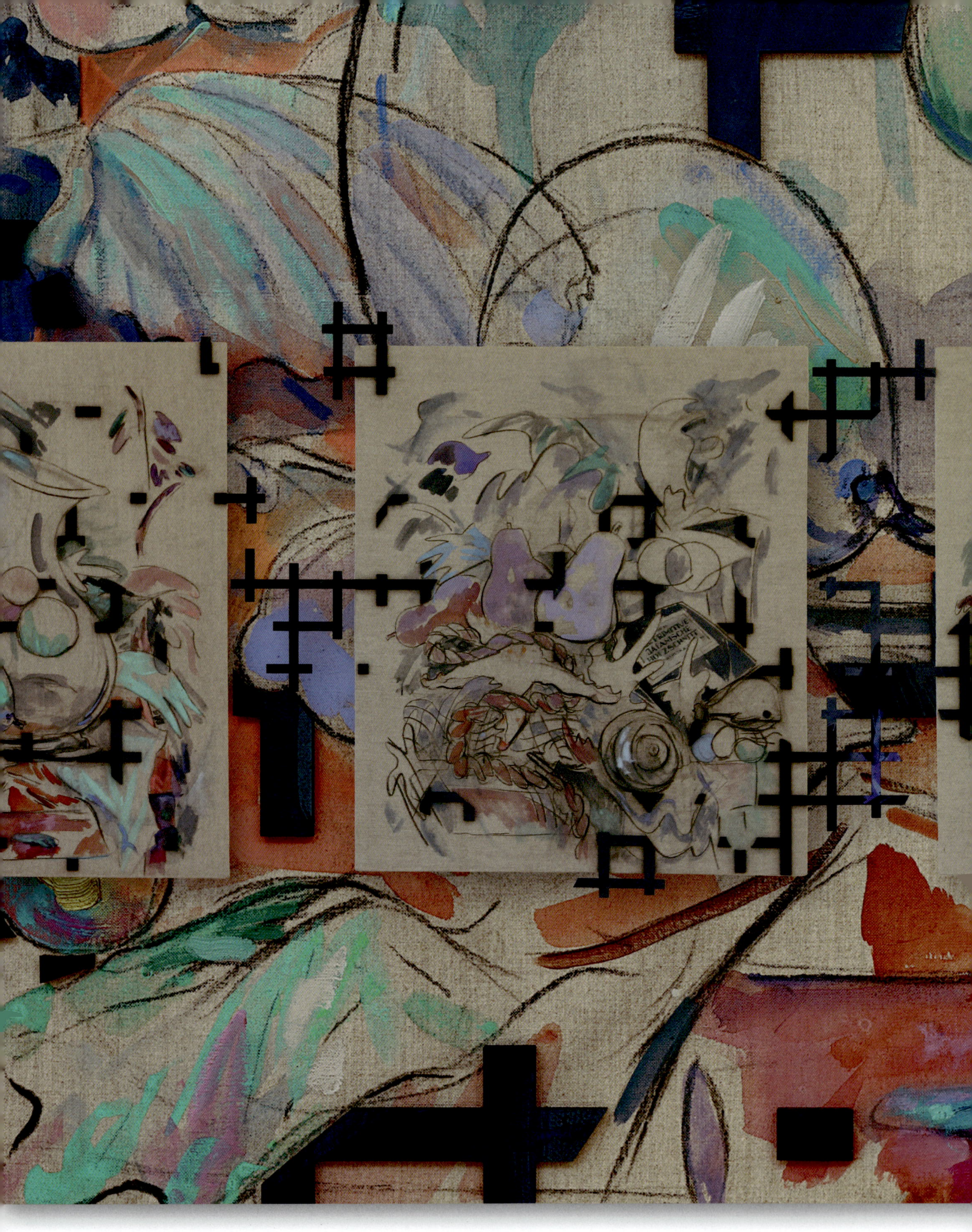

Foreground: Detail of *Untitled*, 2012 (see p. 480)
Background: Detail of *Untitled*, 2012

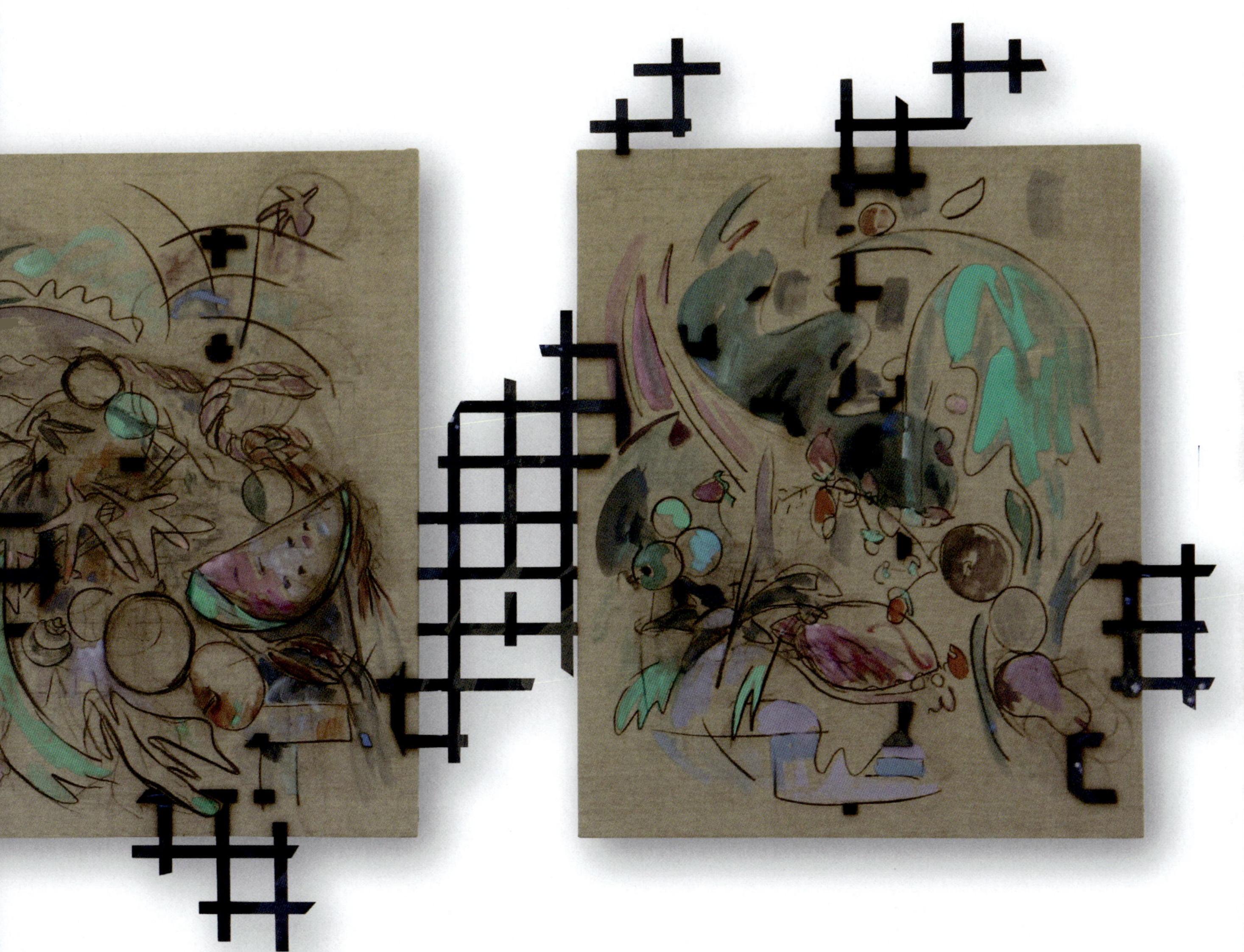

Calvin Marcus: I think there was this strategic thing about the *Pavement Karaoke* show. Laura had talked a lot in the studio about wanting to make a serialized type of painting that followed a rigid structure—whether in terms of size, scale, or content. She had generally been pursuing one-off paintings, and it was pretty typical of her to have a show where there'd be one landscape-oriented painting of waves or something, and then on an adjacent wall there'd be a self-portrait or another kind of painting. It seemed like she made a conscious decision to say, "I want to make this painting show that feels . . ." the opposite of what she had been doing.

Such a thing as "pavement karaoke" was too emo to actually exist; the irony of the idea was funny to Laura. It was supposed to coincide with an actual event where people would get together and do cringey karaoke that didn't sound so good—it wasn't hits, it wasn't Tears for Fears or whatever. Eventually she did do all these funny karaoke nights, but I don't know if they happened in London, where the paintings were shown. They were large-scale works with screenprinting over the entire surface of raw or primed canvas. The painting was very thick, which is something we figured out with the paint chemist guru Robert Doak. Then we ordered these weird dead-stock chemicals that were somewhere in a storage unit in Detroit and mixed them with different oils and mediums and then eventually with paint. I have no idea how those blobby marks are holding up now, hopefully okay. Besides that, we did collage with gingham fabric and also glued rocks onto the canvases. Some works also had drop shadows emulated with screenprinting. That seemed to me to be about creating illusionistic space in a way that was connected to the motifs that were generated by the eraser tool in the digital sketches for the works. We were also using masking tape to make resists that would pop out from under layers of impasto painting. And we were burning full screens of grids of different sizes and thicknesses that

     Calvin Marcus is a Los Angeles–based artist and worked in Owens's studio in 2010–13.

would be hand-masked and printed to outline the shapes of letters—like the *P* or the *A* or the *V*.

All of that seemed fairly analog, whereas the next works, like the ones in *Twelve Paintings*, were created almost entirely on the computer and then physicalized. It seemed like it was in between these two projects that the screenprinting became more intricate. But it was still pretty crude. The screenprints that we made for *Twelve Paintings* and *Pavement Karaoke* didn't correlate to just one painting. I think that now when Laura makes a painting those screens are used just to make one mark or print one section. We used to make a dozen screens with grids and use them on fifteen different paintings, masking them off by hand on one and then on another using the full one. Now it seems like the entire image is created digitally and then everything else is made afterward to generate the painting. I think that's why the paintings today for the most part occur on smooth, sanded, gesso surfaces as opposed to on raw canvases—the gesso surface is more controlled, and it can act more like a sheet of computer paper, whereas the other stuff is just more squirrelly, it shrinks.

We moved the studio from Echo Park to 356 halfway through production for *Pavement Karaoke*. We did all the screenprinting that needed to happen at 356. Then the works were sized, unstretched for the panels, restretched on the frames, and then, one by one, as they were finished, they were brought to Echo Park, where there was a whole other team of people helping mix the big, thick marks and doing the drop shadows. I showed up and Gavin Brown was standing on a ladder painting drop shadows. Laeh Glenn, John Seal, and Andrew Cannon were too—basically all of Laura's friends were there to help get the paintings out the door. I ordered pho for everyone and was there for moral support.

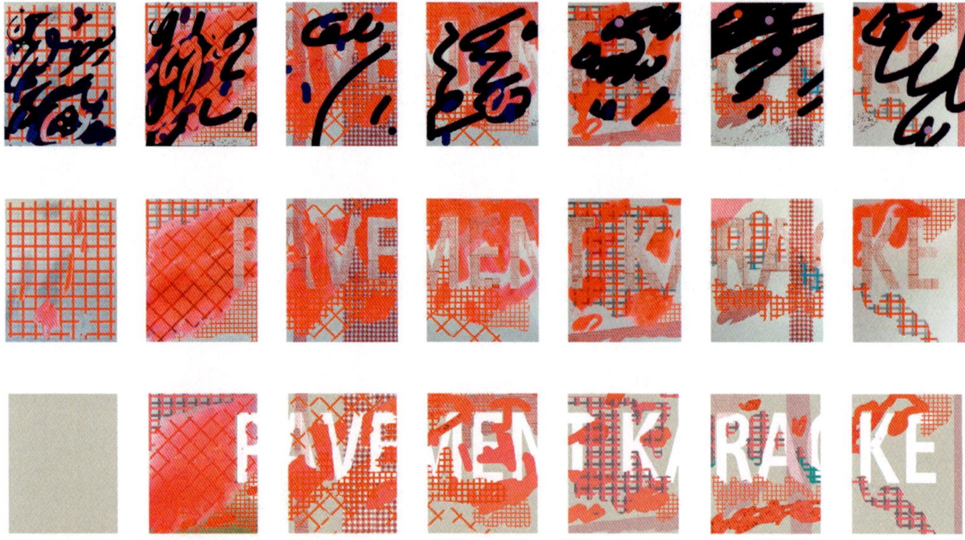

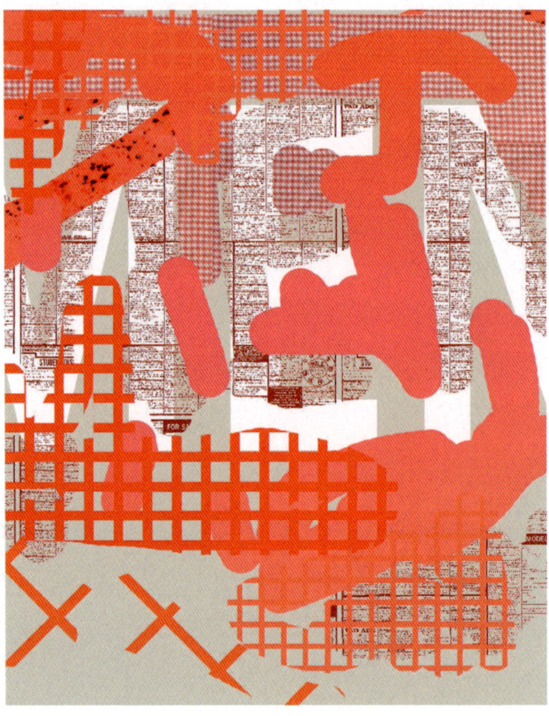

The process started with rough thumbnail sketches done in Photoshop and Corel Painter. The seven paintings were conceptualized first as a sentence, and then took on individual attributes as layers of collage and paint were added.

As each layer is finished, the work is photographed and loaded back into the computer, where the next steps are considered and adjusted according to the actual painting.

The computer was an integral part of the process, not just for sketching and concpetualizing, but also for precisely measuring masked areas. The computer files were frequently projected onto the canvas to mask off a specific shape, or to visualize a certain course.

Foreground: Production notes, 2012
Background: Production notes, 2012

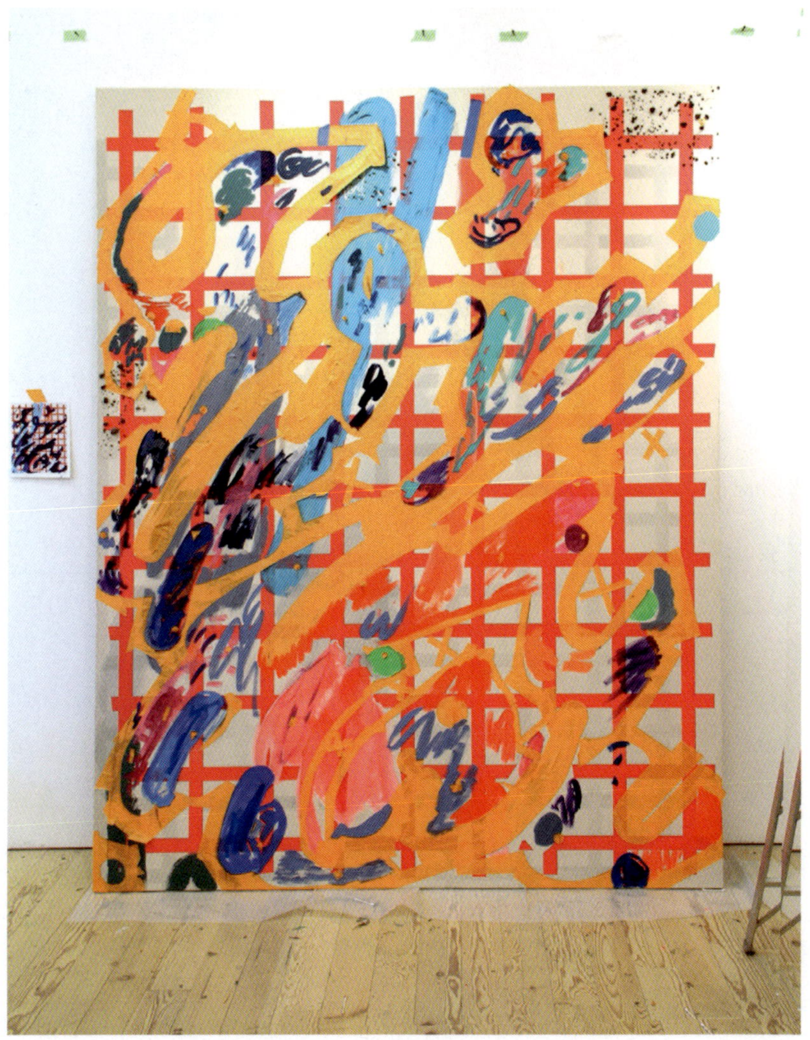

After the underpaintings were completed, The oil marks were masked with tape. Laura added several
layers of oil paint, starting with bright colors and covering with thick dark paint.

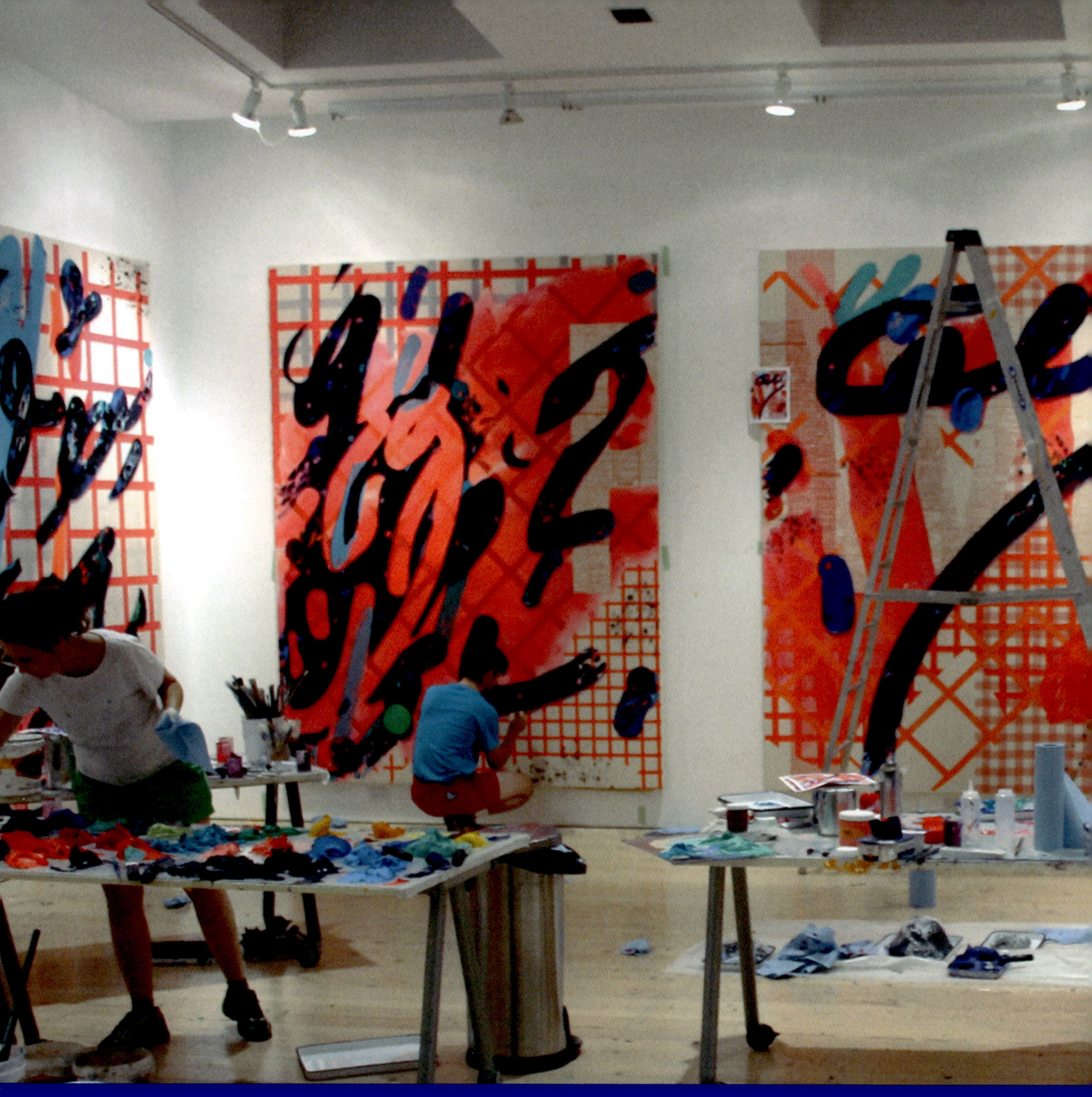

Owens, John Seal, Laeh Glenn, Gavin Brown, and Calvin Marcus with *Untitled*, 2012 (see p. 491); *Untitled*, 2012 (see p. 492); *Untitled*, 2012 (see p. 492); *Untitled*, 2012 (see p. 492); and *Untitled*, 2012 (see p. 492), Echo Park studio, 2012

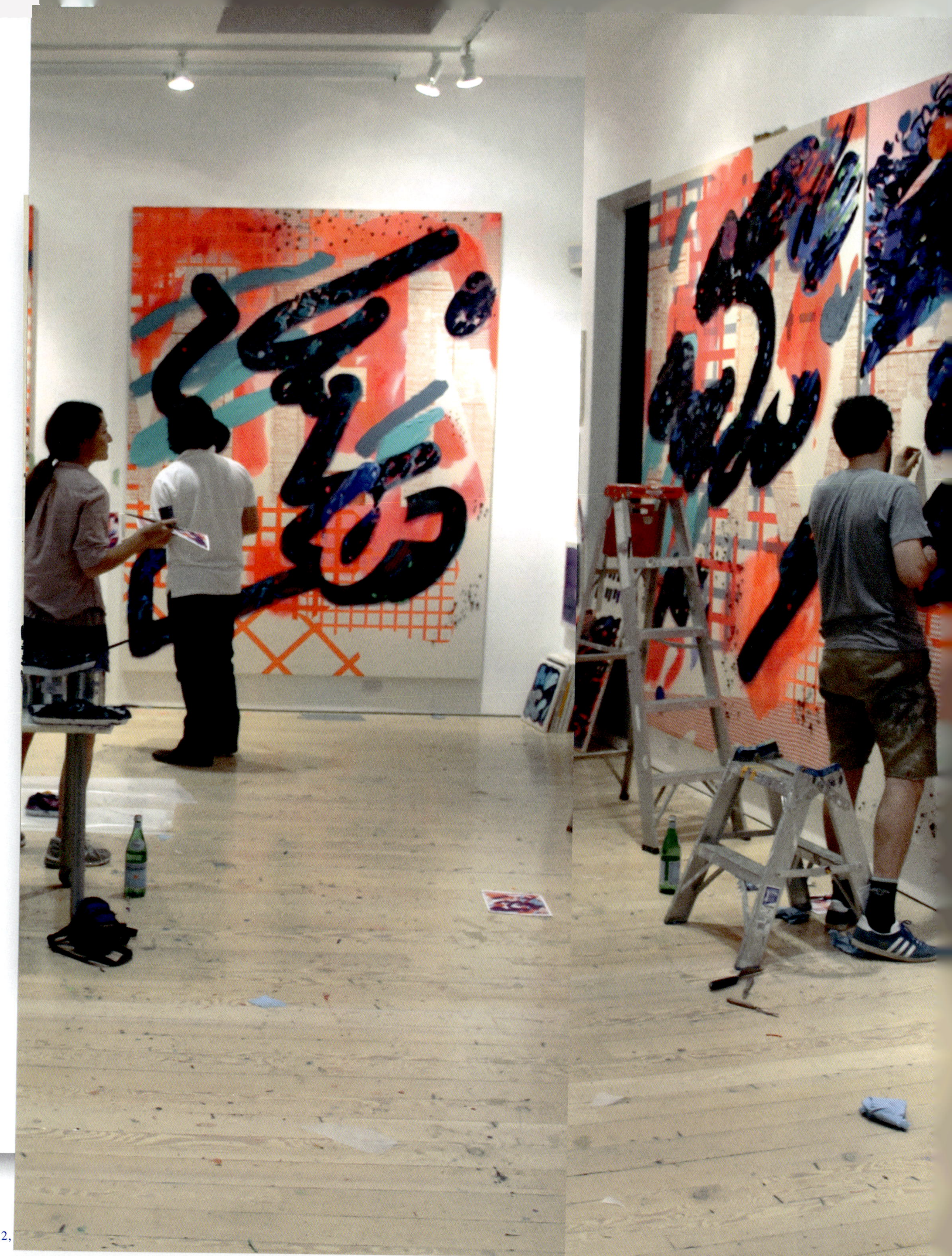

Untitled, 2012,

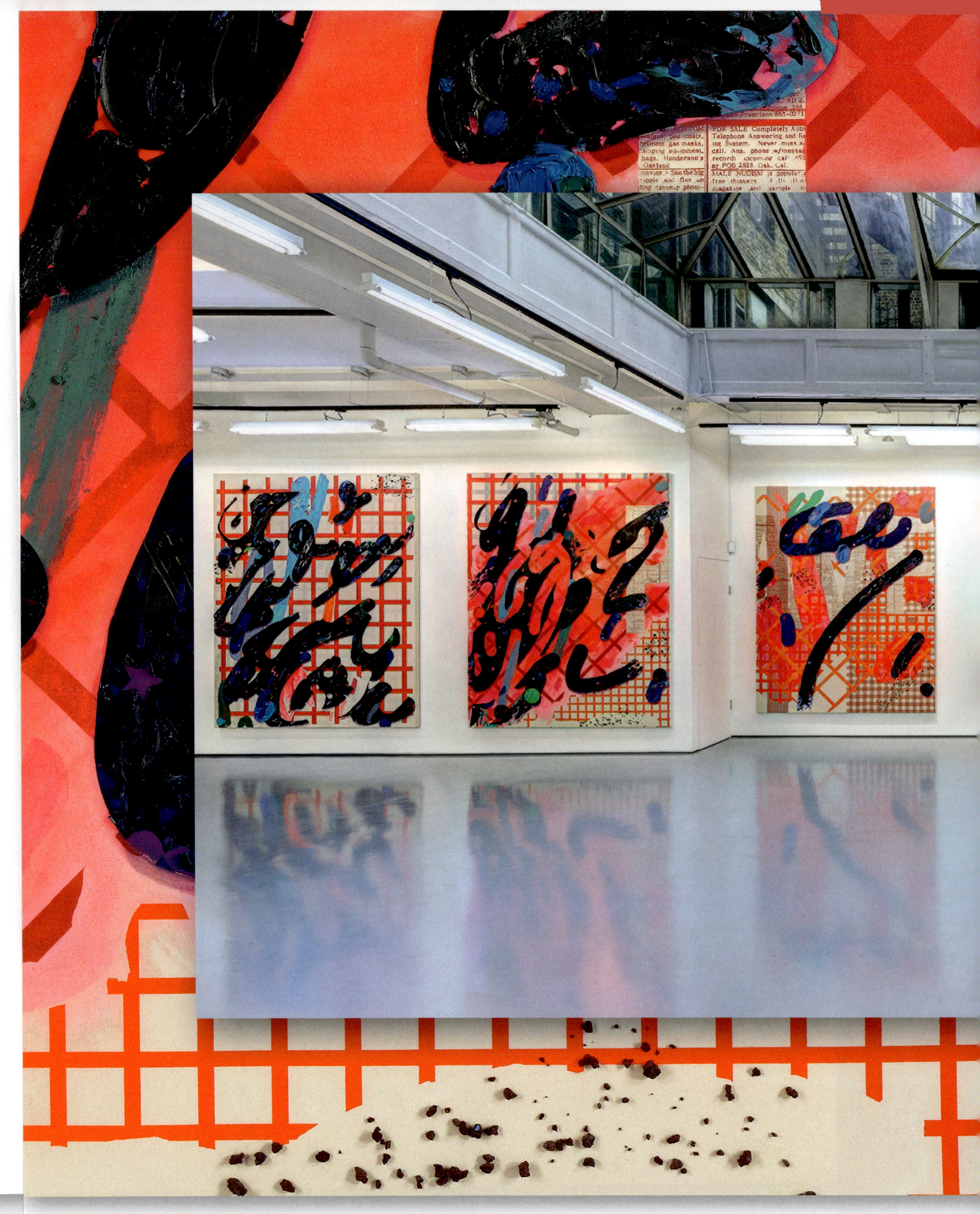

Foreground: Installation view, *Pavement Karaoke/Alphabet*, Sadie Coles HQ, London, 2012, with *Untitled*, 2012 (see p. 491); *Untitled*, 2012, acrylic, oil, vinyl paint, resin, and pumice on canvas; *Untitled*, 2012, *Untitled*, 2012, *Untitled*, 2012, *Untitled*, 2012, and *Untitled*, 2012, acrylic, oil, vinyl paint, resin, pumice, and fabric on canvas, 108 × 84 in. (274.3 × 213.4 cm) each
Background: Detail of *Untitled*, 2012

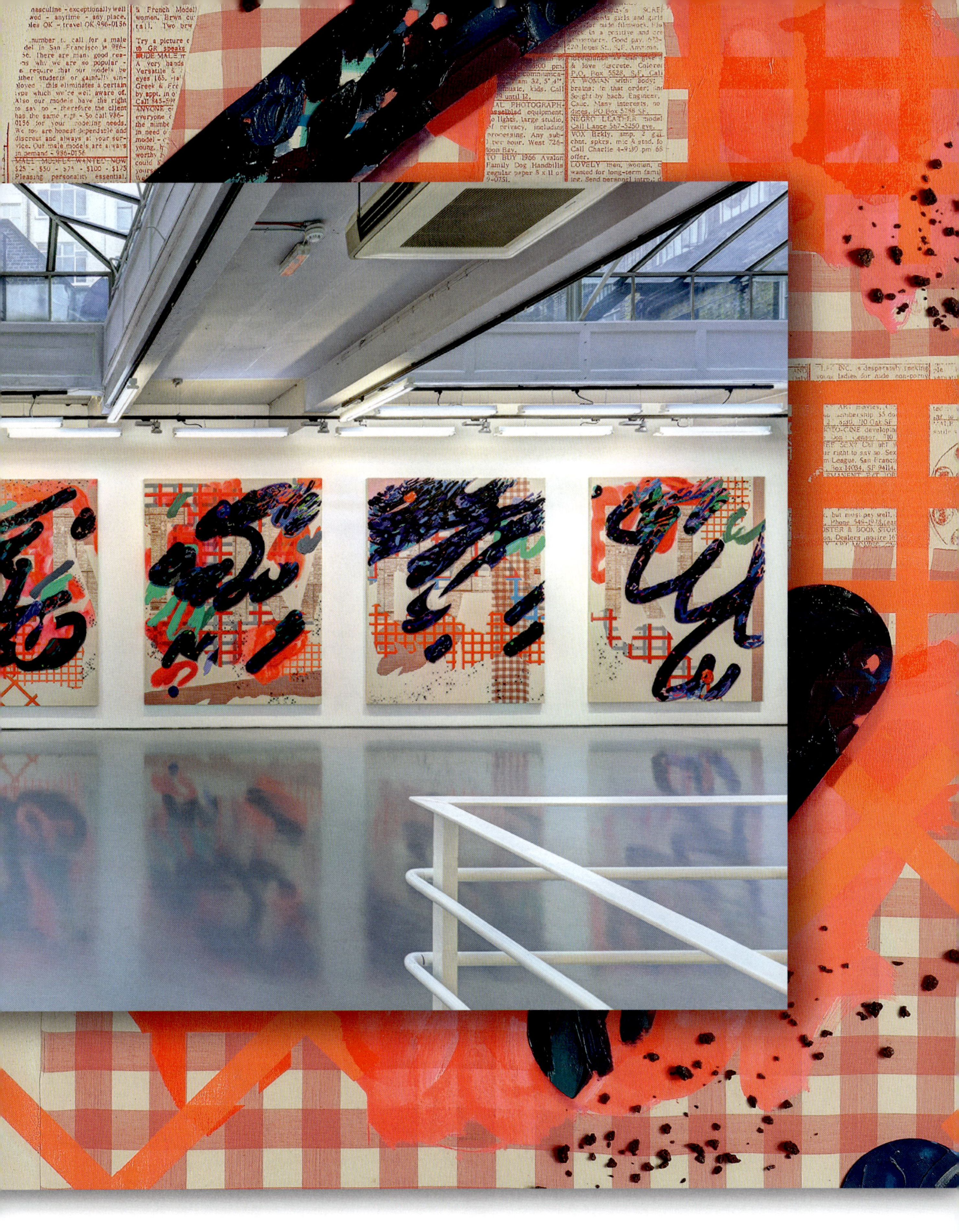

ALPHABETS

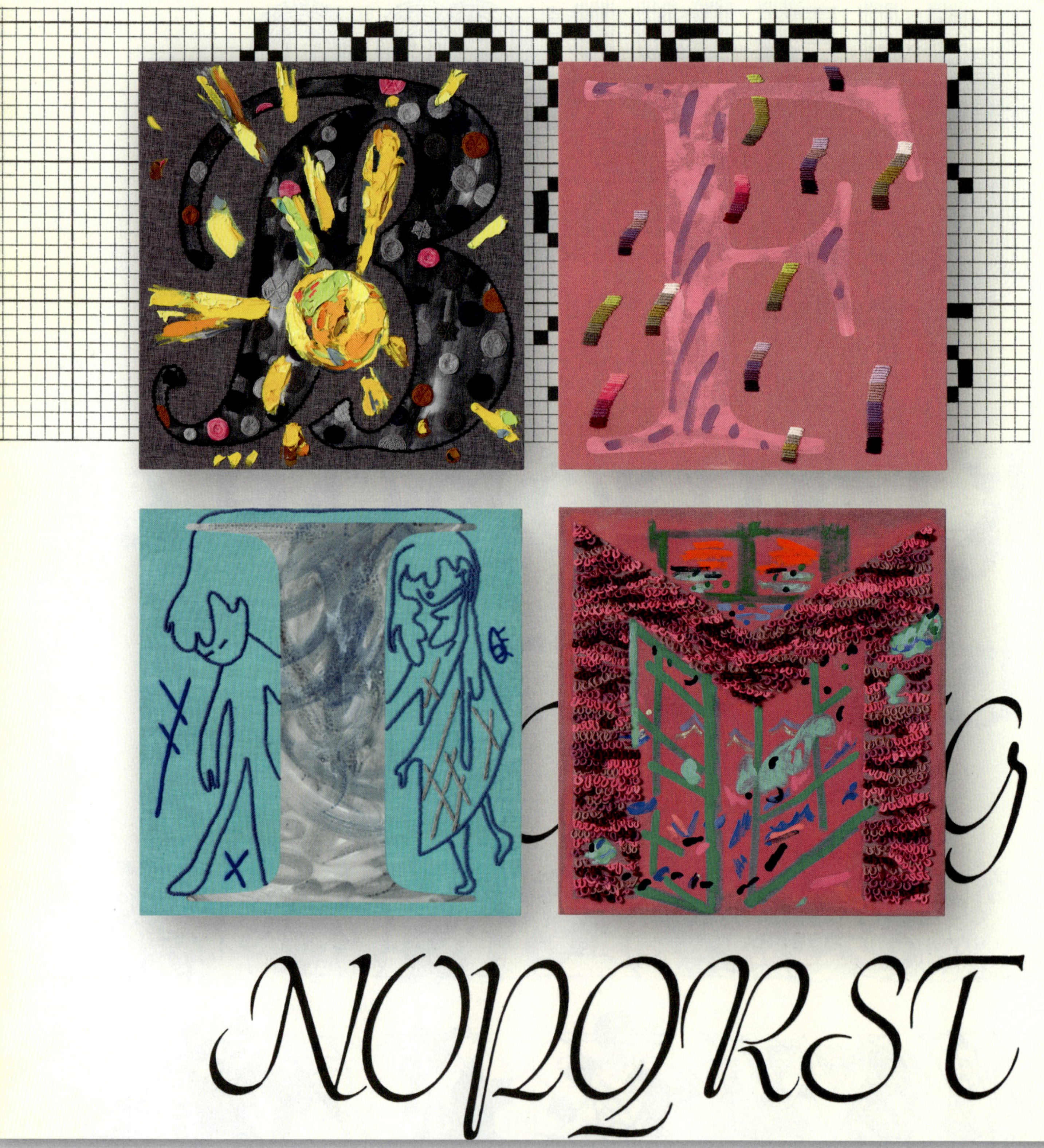

Foreground: Detail of *Untitled*, 2012, acrylic, oil, vinyl paint, charcoal, yarn, and cord on hand-dyed linen, 33 panels: 35½ × 33¼ in. (90.2 × 84.5 cm) each

 Background: *Erica Wilson's Embroidery Book*. Charles Scribner's Sons, 1973

ALPHABETS

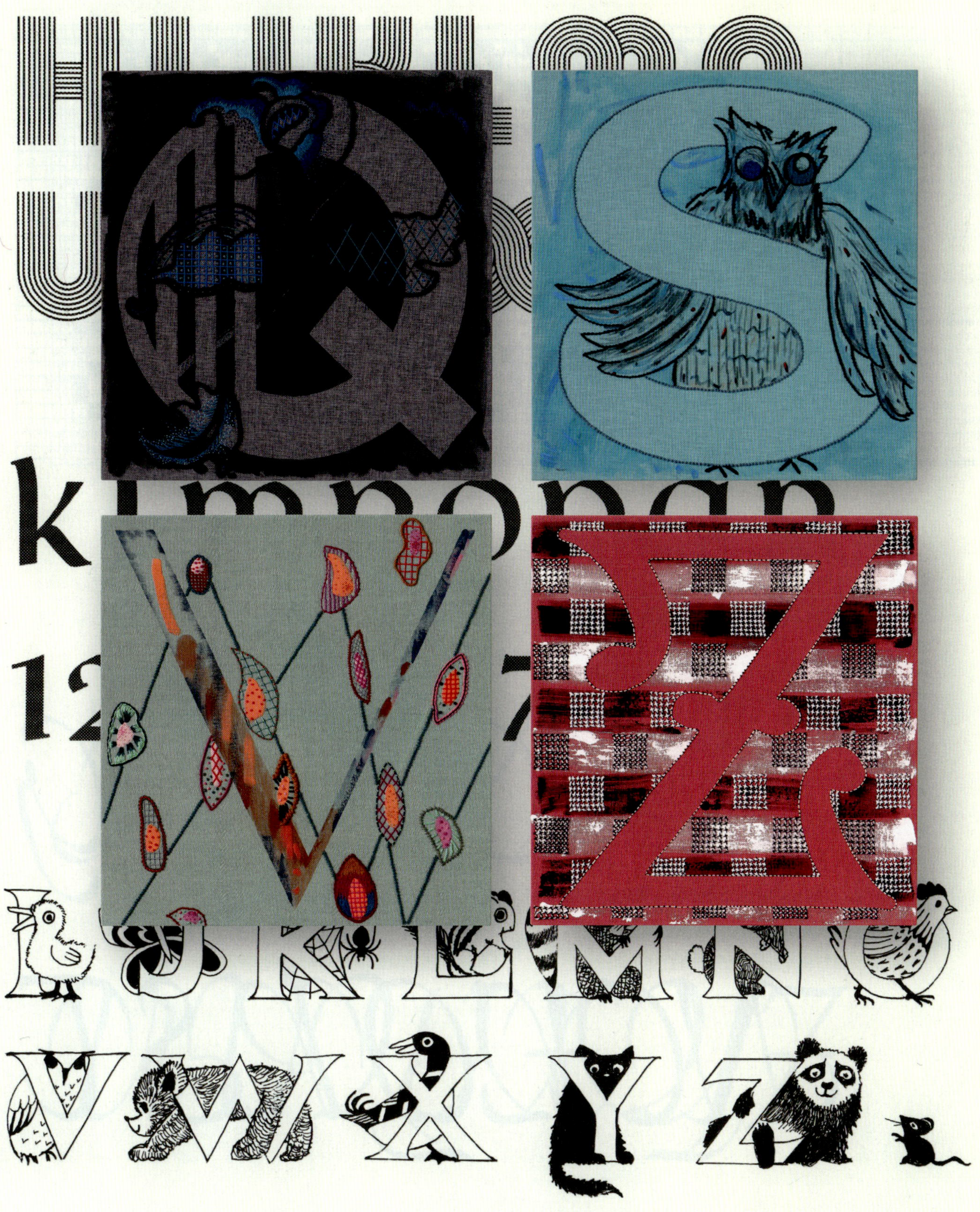

Andrew Cannon: When I started working for Laura in late 2010, her studio was behind her house in Echo Park, and all of the production happened in a single room or out on the patio. At the time she was working on big groups of paintings—the clocks, the gridded still lifes, the panorama of nine blue washes—that took up all of the available space. When the studio moved to 356 S. Mission Rd, the immediate difference was how much room there was to spread out. *Pavement Karaoke*, the panoramic group of seven paintings shown at Sadie Coles in fall 2012, was started in her Echo Park studio but quickly moved to 356 when it became apparent that the printing process would require more space than any of her previous work. Laying the canvases out on the floor and on the walls allowed us to work on them almost all at once.

For *Twelve Paintings,* Laura expanded in every direction, working on mural-size pieces in new ways and with many more assistants. The printing process she used had been established with *Pavement Karaoke.* Screenprinting and adhesive vinyl stencils cut on a plotter replaced steps that had previously required tediously masking off parts of the painting with tape. There were only six fifty-five-by-eighty-inch screens used for *Twelve Paintings,* but they were printed through vinyl stencils or masked directly on the screen.

The size of the paintings, 137½ × 120 inches, was determined early on. It's just a few feet shy of the ceiling height and the largest width able to fit out of the building's biggest exit—a square door at the loading dock that spans ten feet and two inches at its diagonal. Five of the linens were prepared by brushing on milk-thin layers of gesso. Dozens of layers were applied, with wet sanding between coats, to achieve a surface almost like thick, hot-pressed watercolor paper. Laura had done this on a small scale before, but at that size the process became far trickier, and took about four months in all.

The process of building up layers was different for each painting

    Andrew Cannon is a New York–based artist and worked in Owens's studio in 2010–15.

but followed the same general progression. Each work started with a drawing in Photoshop. All of the paintings were side by side in the file, and elements like the six silkscreen patterns or the width of a brush would repeat. After each new step was finished on the actual painting, the work would be photographed and brought back into Photoshop to plan the next layer. Some layers were improvisatory while others were rigidly translated from the file into vectors and masks.

Laura always planned for the paintings to have heavy impasto. For *Pavement Karaoke*, we experimented with various additives to find the consistency of paint she was looking for—something between frosting and taffy. Robert Doak, a paint manufacturer in New York, suggested a clay powder that turned out to be the solution. Mixing the powdered clay with stand oil took a full day and always gave us something slightly different. This mixture was combined with Goop, a mayonnaise-like medium that Doak sold us by the gallon. Between the clay, the Goop, and the paint, we mixed hundreds of pounds of material for *Twelve Paintings,* much of which went on studies.

The classified ads used in several paintings were picked from copies of the *Berkeley Barb* spanning the years 1962 to 1970. Laura originally collected back issues of the *Barb* for *Fruits and Nuts*, an artist's book produced at the studio and published by Ooga Booga in 2011–12. Following this, we made composite pages with Laura's selections from a decade of classified ads, which were enlarged as screenprints for the *Pavement Karaoke* paintings. Those screens appeared in one of the works from *Twelve Paintings* as well; however, the larger texts that act as backgrounds in several of the paintings were made with adhesive vinyl stencils from new composites, which allowed Laura to paint in washes of acrylic rather than a flat application of silkscreen ink.

Laura is infamous for holding up shipping companies to keep painting until the last possible moment. With no shipping schedule to worry about, *Twelve Paintings* was finished the morning of the opening. Laura and several others were up until dawn mixing paint and applying the last impasto marks.

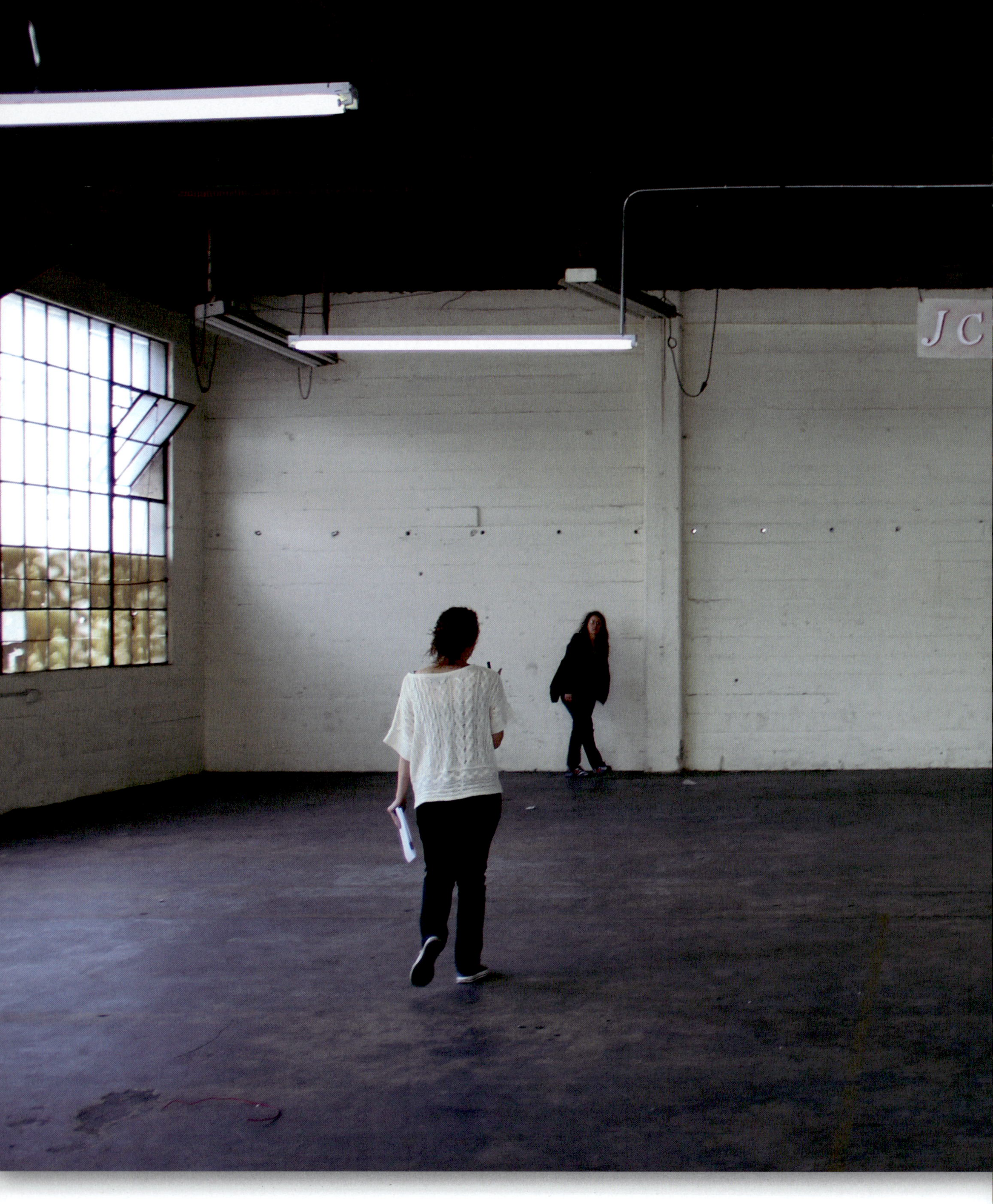

     Corinna Durland and Owens, 356 S. Mission Rd., Los Angeles, 2011

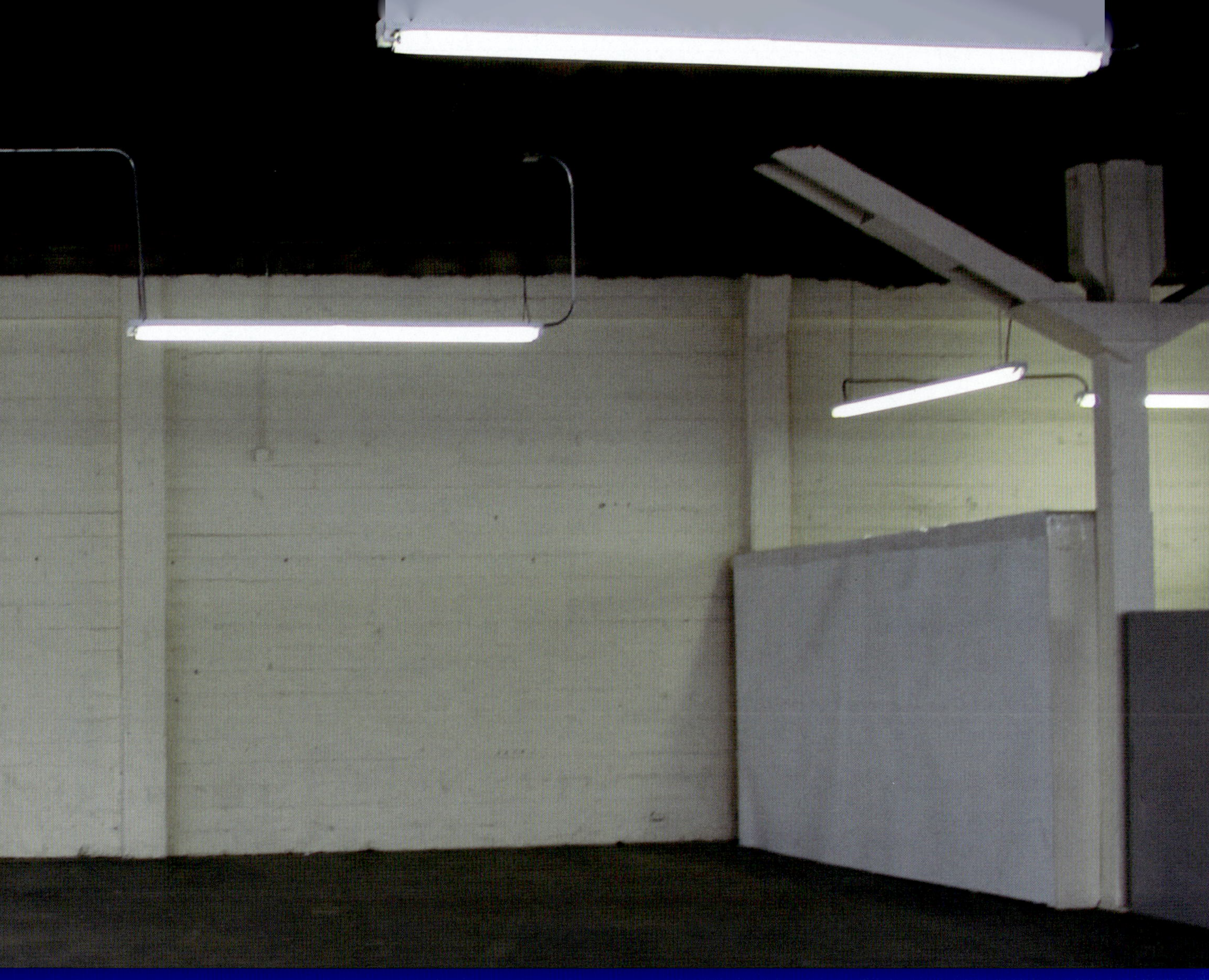

Corinna Durland: As we started looking for locations for *Twelve Paintings*, the parameters were not specific. Laura envisioned a space with strong architectural features or a context that would inform the work. It would start as a studio and become an exhibition space. It was very important to her that the work be made on-site. We saw many possibilities, including a 1970s-era church, an abandoned bank, an old theater, a defunct Michaels craft store downtown, some neglected buildings on Pico Boulevard, storefronts on MacArthur Park, and a Glidden paint store in East Hollywood. All of them were interesting, but none seemed exactly right.

Laura called in November 2011 to say she had seen something amazing. There were three buildings available along an industrial stretch of South Mission Road in Boyle Heights. By February 2012 a lease had been signed for 356 S. Mission, a vast poured-concrete structure built in 1926 for a lithography company. The building's scale didn't seem to make Laura nervous. She knew the paintings would be large and was even concerned that viewers wouldn't be able to get enough distance from them. She does not often think small.

After the installation of the paintings, the spirit of freedom, experimentation, and invention allowed by the space seemed to continue to extend beyond the canvases and back into the building itself—from the entrance, where Ooga Booga takes the place of a reception area; to the film screenings and performances; to the artists' residencies; to the youth workshops; to the continuing exhibitions; and to the building next door that Laura took over for a studio.

PREMISE
"ALL BIG PAINTINGS"   NOT VARIED SCALE
"ALL SAME SCALE"   SELF-PUBLISHED
"NOT A GALLERY"   LOCAL
"MADE ON SITE"   NOT HAD SOLO SHOW
                              IN LA SINCE MUSEUM
"LOCAL GAL MAKES.....o   MID-CAREER SURVE

WHOSE S
WHOSE LIN
WHAT ARE

PREVIOUS RE   ACT?

CLOCKS
GRID

BOOKS

CURRENT C ALPHABET

PAVEMENT
KARAOKE

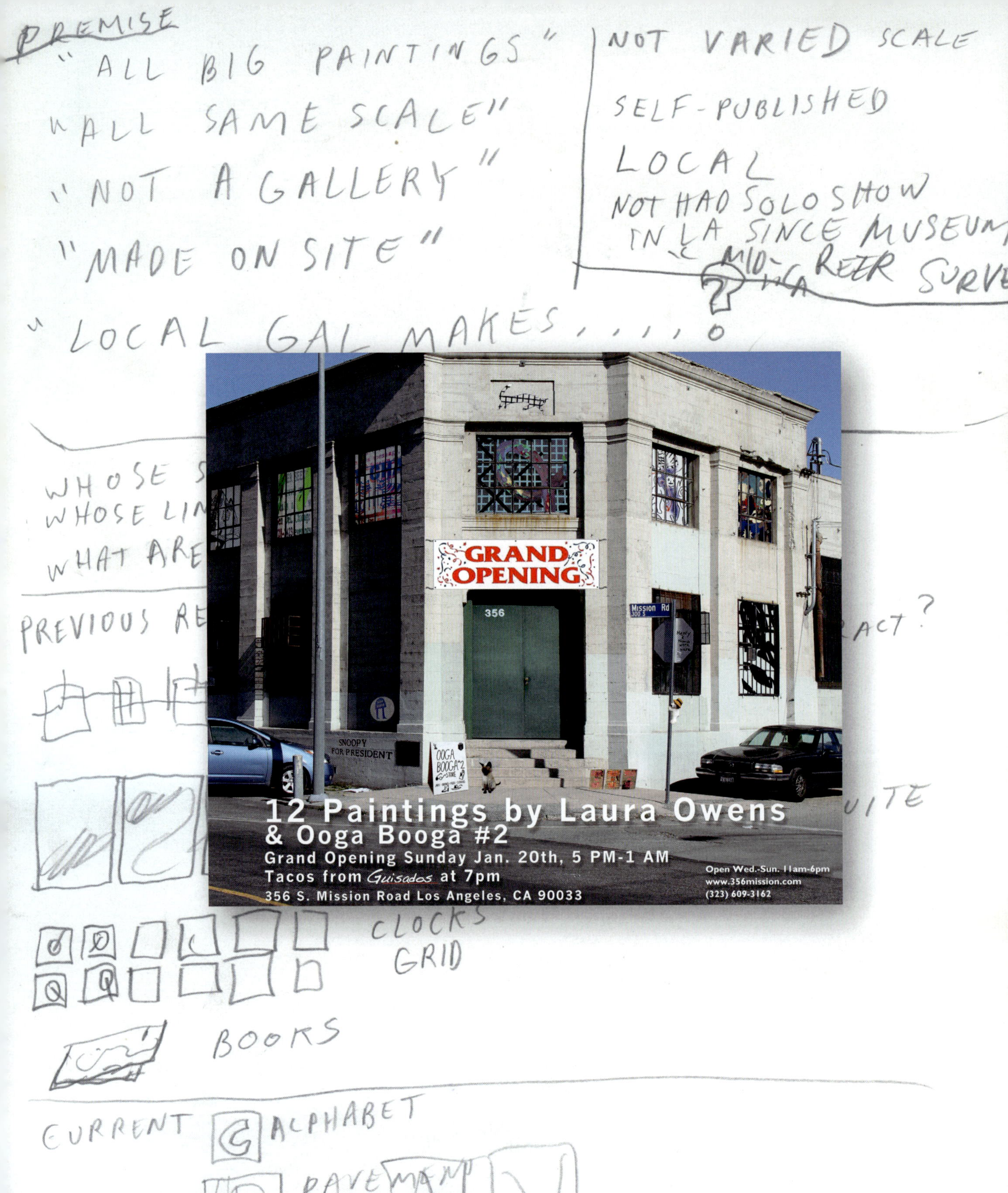

Foreground: Invitation, *Twelve Paintings*, 356 S. Mission Rd., Los Angeles, 2013

 Background: Notes by Eric Palgon, 2013

On November 17, the artist Laura Owens will host an exhibition of her paintings at 356 S. Mission Road in Boyle Heights. It will be the first exhibition of her work in Los Angeles in nearly ten years. The previous solo exhibition being the survey the Museum of Contemporary art devoted to her in 2003.

Los Angeles has a unique history of artists working independently and improvising their own spaces for site specific and event based works. The project that Laura has undertaken taps into that spirit of community and context driven production in Los Angeles. After a year of looking at various types of spaces, from disused churches to abandoned movie theaters, she decided on 356 S. Mission, an industrial building in Downtown LA. It was built in 1926 for a lithography studio, but has also had a life as a warehouse for Liberace's pianos and later for tween girl clothing. Now the space is both a studio and a place of exhibition. Laura has been working in it for the past year, making the many of the studio into the one of the exhibition.

Laura became well known in the 90's for paintings that were strikingly individualistic, self contained worlds of painterly techniques and references. For the past several years she has challenged that mode of working, focusing on groups of works where the individual paintings step back into a gestalt, and meaning is contingent on the proximity and arrangement of discreet gestures within the group. For instance, her 2010-2012 untitled series of ninety-four clock paintings have been shown in various groupings and arrangments, and with each exhibition the constellation changes. The paintings are an interdependent system that generate meanings between themselves, but are not single works. Similarly, series of paintings shown recently at the Kunstmuseum Bonn and NY Frieze, investigate a deflation of the autonomous painting, looking instead for a dispersed meaning outside the painting's edges.

The new group of 11 x 10' paintings are a hybrid of her modes of working from the past two decades. They were made while she designed the walls of the exhibition and planned their placement, a hyper-determined process that includes the space in the paintings. And while the works are the same size, they assume individual poses, while still being held in an array by the exhibition. The exhibition will be open for six months,or until it is not longer interesting. It is an artists studio and exhibition space, a gathering place, a bookstore, a concert hall, an outdoor movie theatre, a cantina, a residency…..

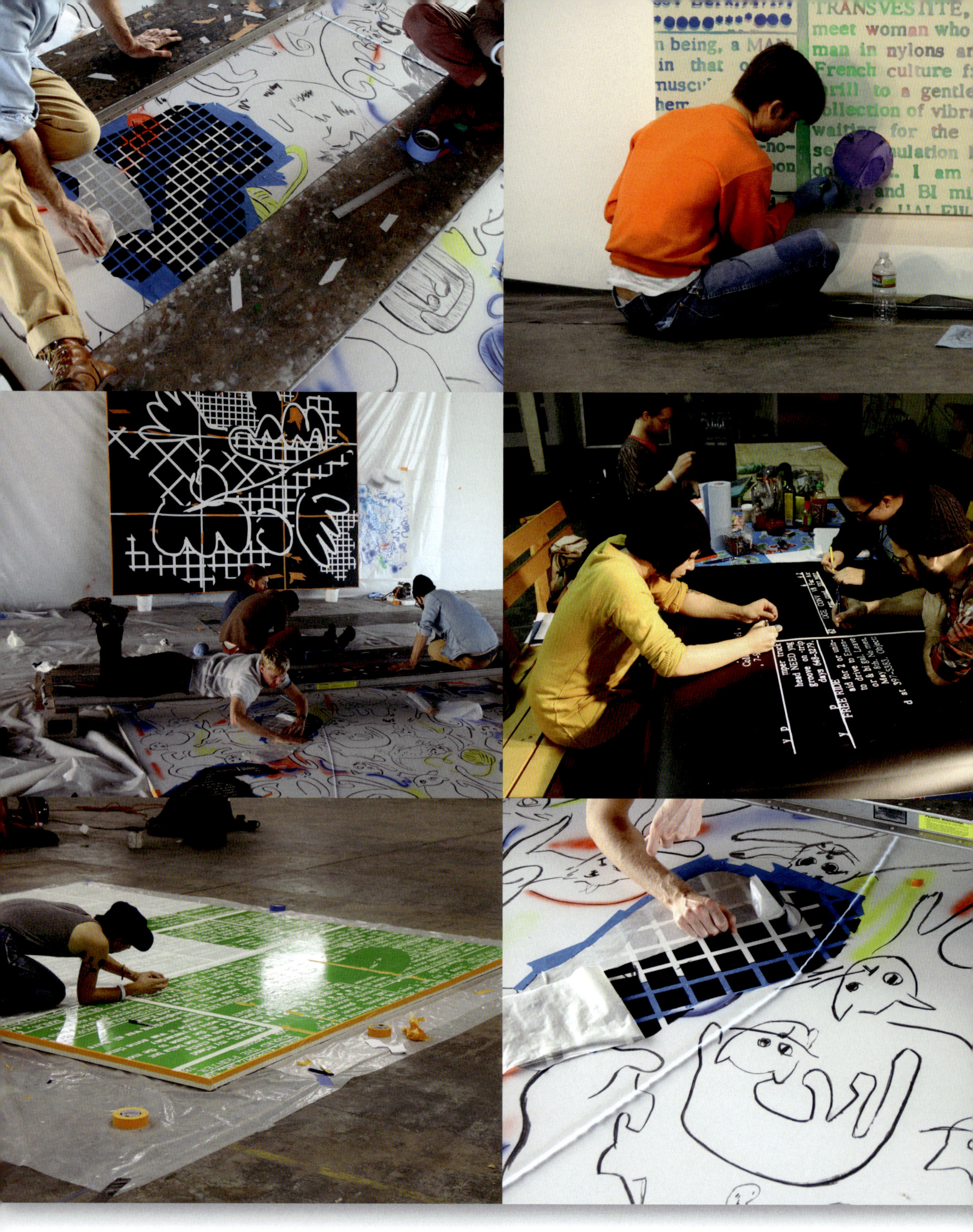

Foreground: Notes, 2013
Background: Alexia Bernal, James Herman, Ann Leese, Alex Meadows, Justin Olerud, James Seal, and Josh Stone, 356 S. Mission Rd., Los Angeles, 2013

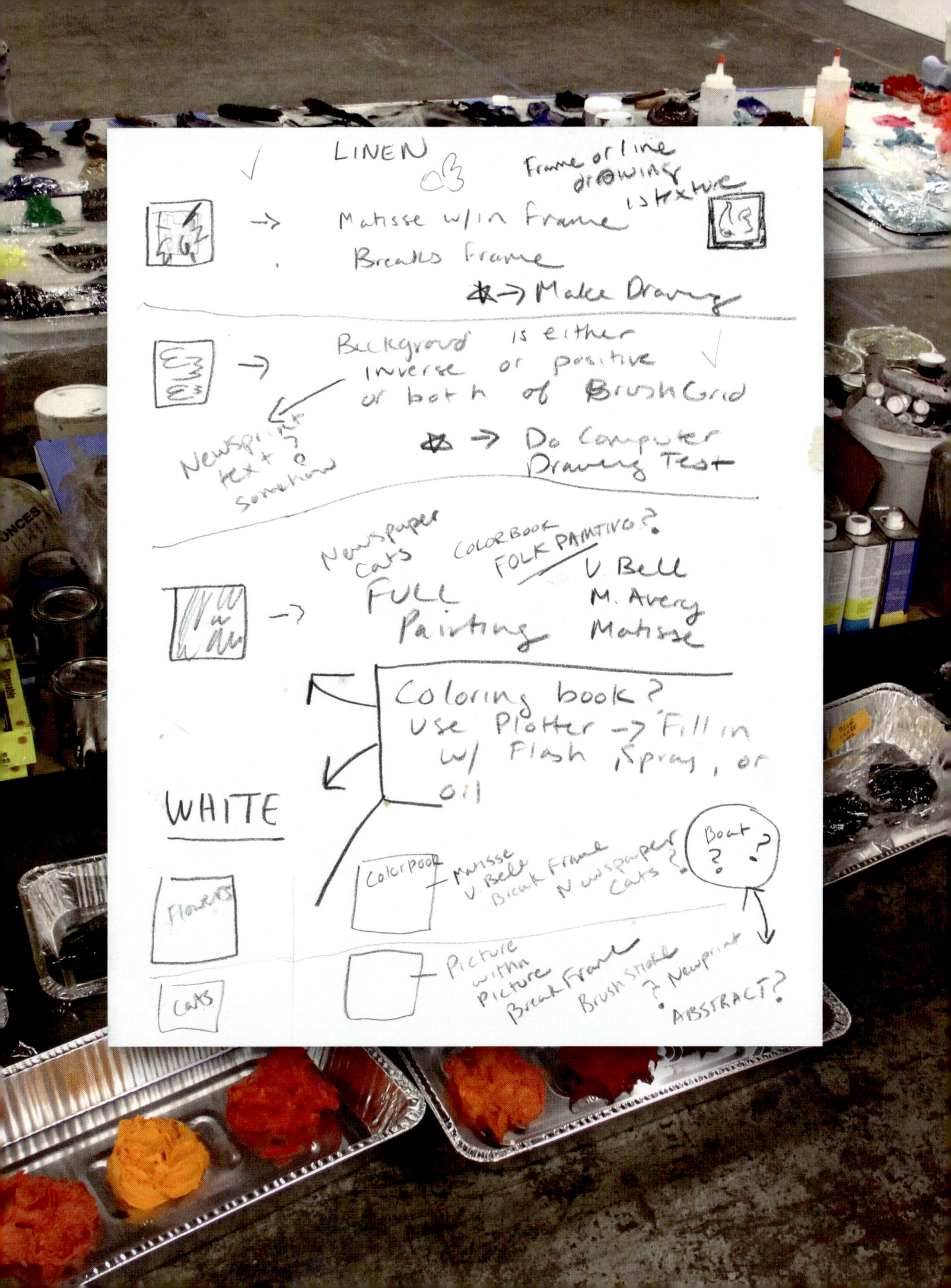
LINEN
Frame or line drawing is texture
Matisse w/in frame
Breaks frame
Make Drawing
Background is either inverse or positive or both of BrushGrid
Newsprint text somehow
Do Computer Drawing Test
Newspaper Cats
COLORBOOK
FOLK PAINTING?
V. Bell
M. Avery
Matisse
FULL Painting
Coloring book?
Use Plotter → Fill in w/ Flash, Spray, or oil
WHITE
Flowers
Cats
Colorbook
Matisse
V. Bell
Break Frame
Newspaper Cats?
Boat ? ?
Picture within Picture
Break Frame
Brush Stroke
? Newprint
ABSTRACT?

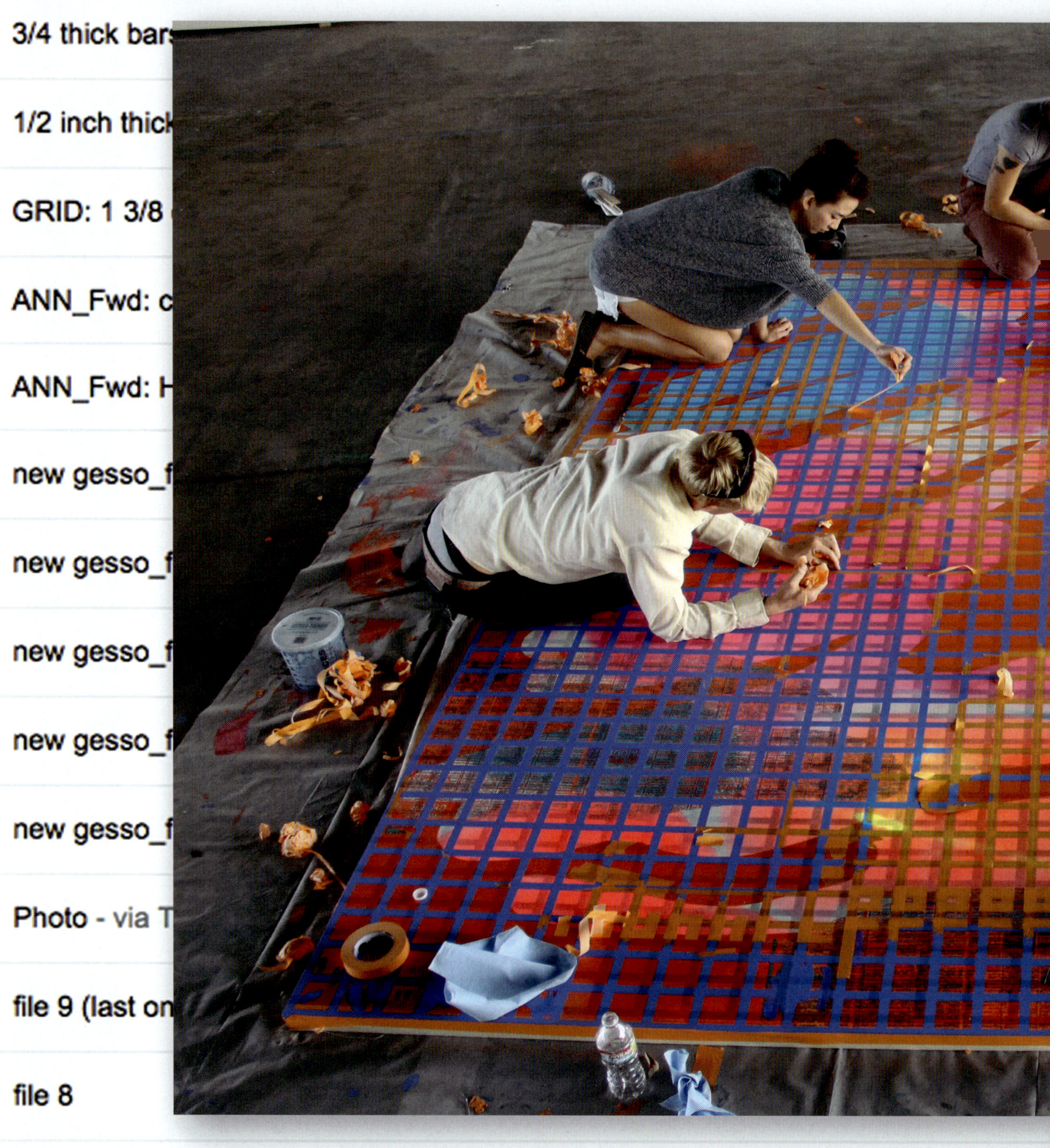

Foreground: James Herman, Ann Leese, Justin Olerud, and John Seal with *Untitled*, 2013 (see p. 506), 356 S. Mission Rd., Los Angeles, 2013

 Background: Screenshot of Andrew Cannon's email inbox, 2013

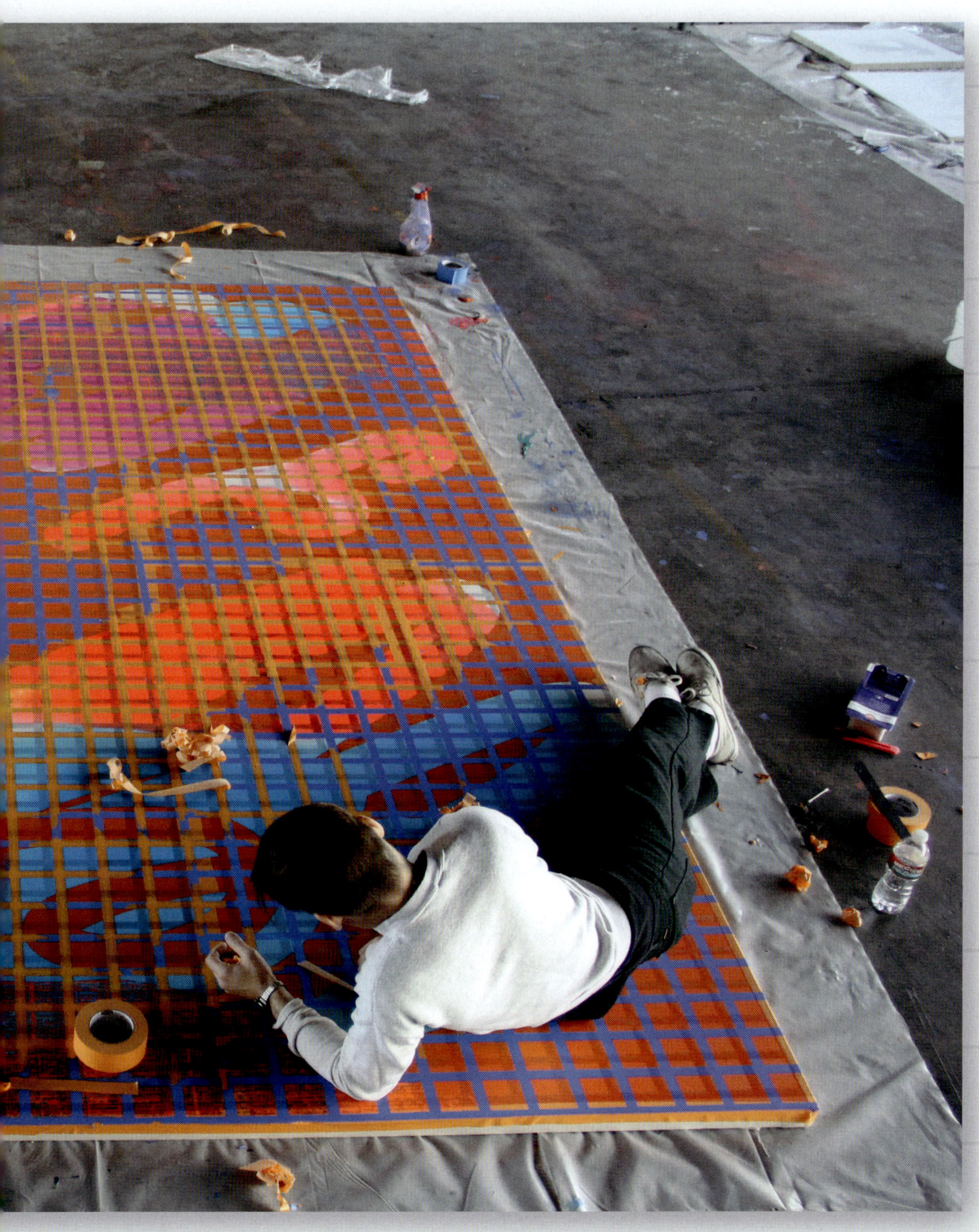

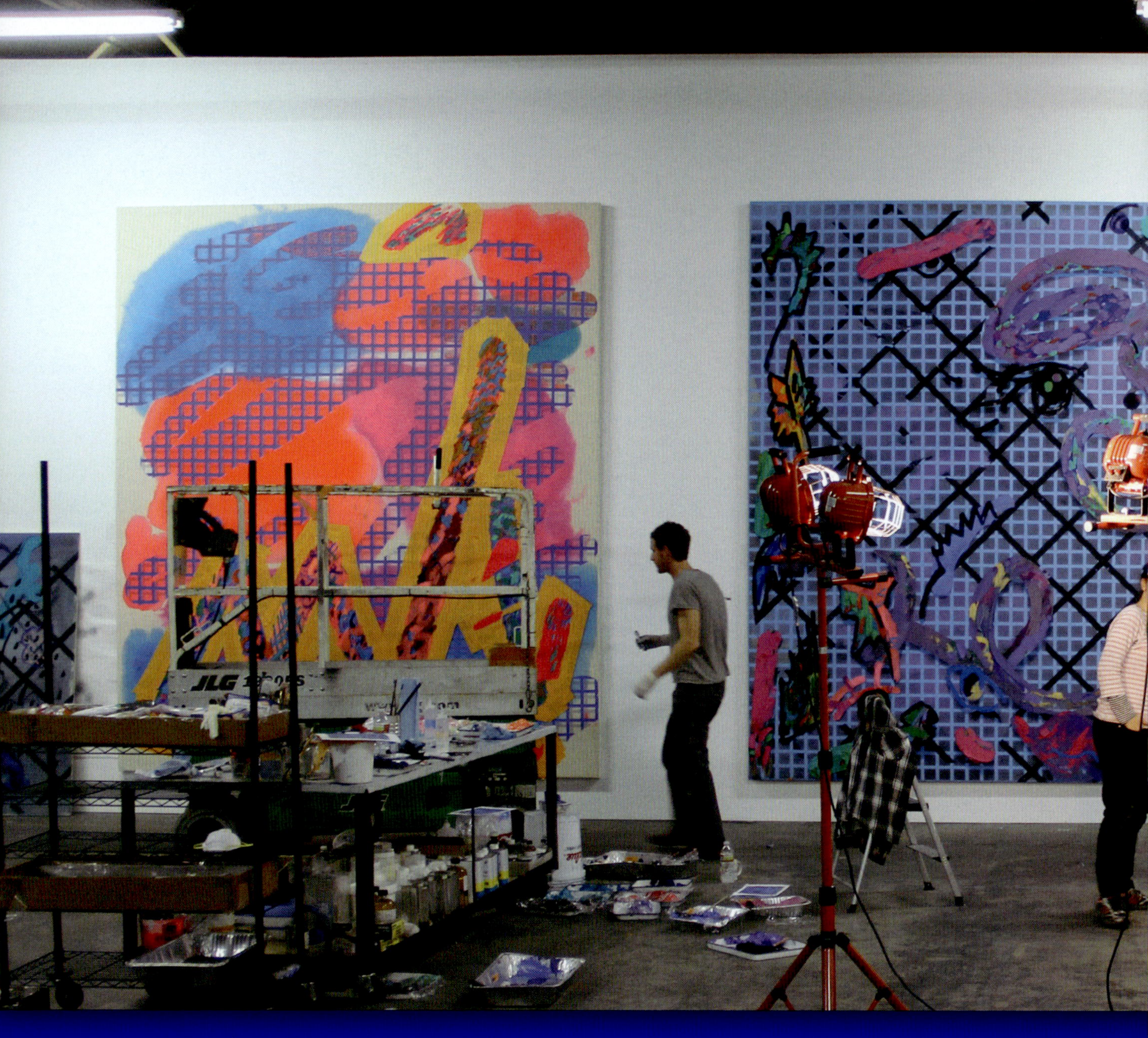

Scott Reeder: In 2012 Laura and I went on a vision quest to Joshua Tree and talked about doing another show together. It had been maybe thirteen years since we did the China Art Objects show. We just drove around Joshua Tree, making drawings and brainstorming about what it could be like to do a show together more than ten years later. We had a bunch of different ideas, but I remember one thing we agreed on was making these giant paintings that would have functioning doors on them. So you could walk through a painting, you know, with a door in it. And it's funny, in the end we didn't do a collaborative show together, but she did that *Twelve Paintings* show and started 356 Mission and then invited me to do *Moon Dust*. So we didn't do something together, but after that vision quest thing in Joshua Tree we both did these big, dramatic, kind of theatrical shows that had a social or narrative aspect. I feel like the Mission Road space is kind of like a painting with a door in it, where the painting is an anchor, but then there's all this other activity beyond it.

Leon Benn, Owens, and John Seal with *Untitled*, 2013, acrylic, oil, vinyl paint, and resin on canvas, 137½ × 120 in. (349.3 × 304.8 cm); *Untitled*, 2013 (see p. 512); *Untitled*, 2013 (see p. 510); *Untitled*, 2013, acrylic and oil on canvas, 108 × 83½ in. (274.3 × 212.1 cm); and *Untitled*, 2013, acrylic, oil, and vinyl paint on canvas, 137½ × 120 in. (349.3 × 304.8 cm), 356 S. Mission Rd., Los Angeles, 2013

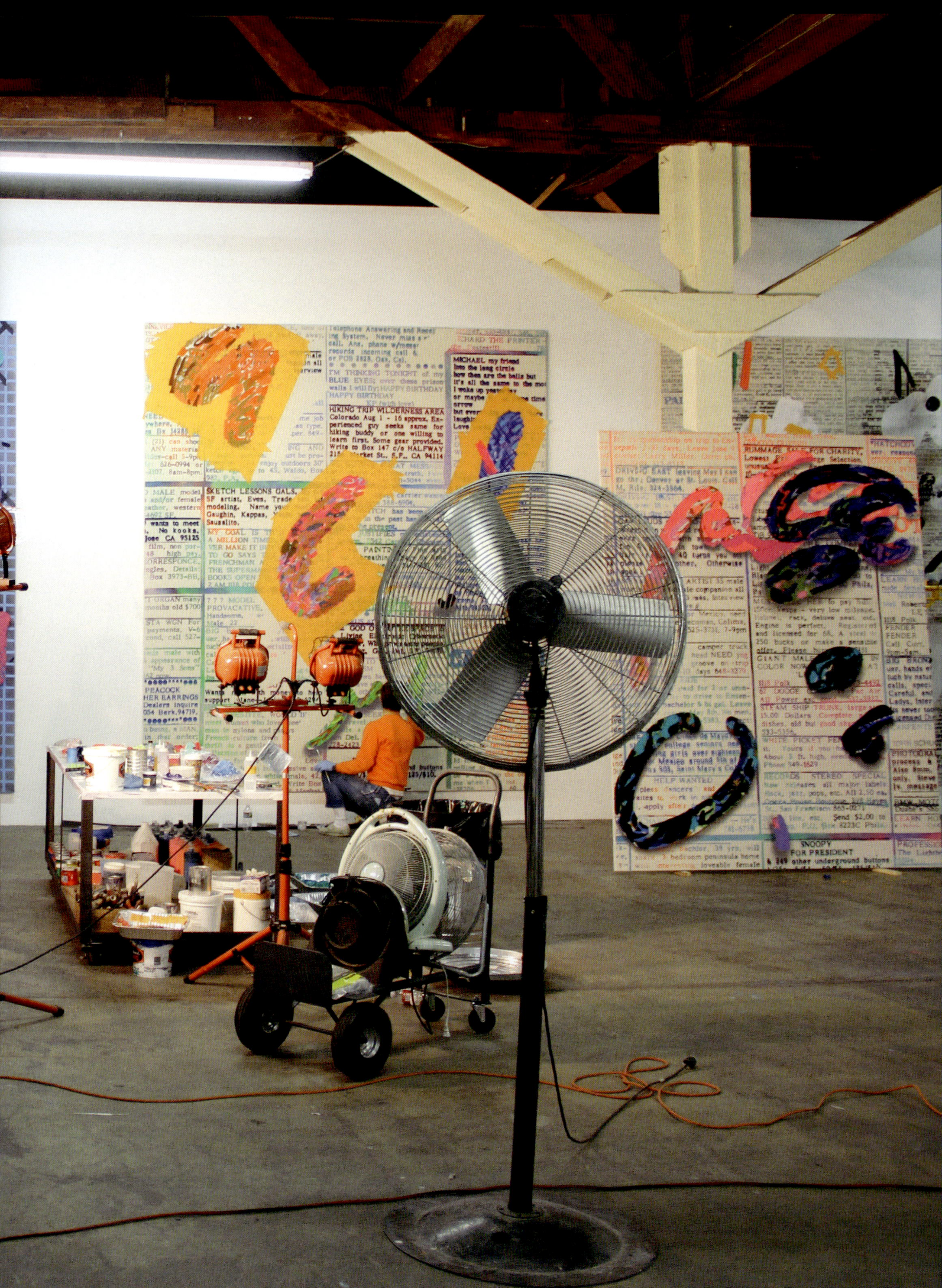

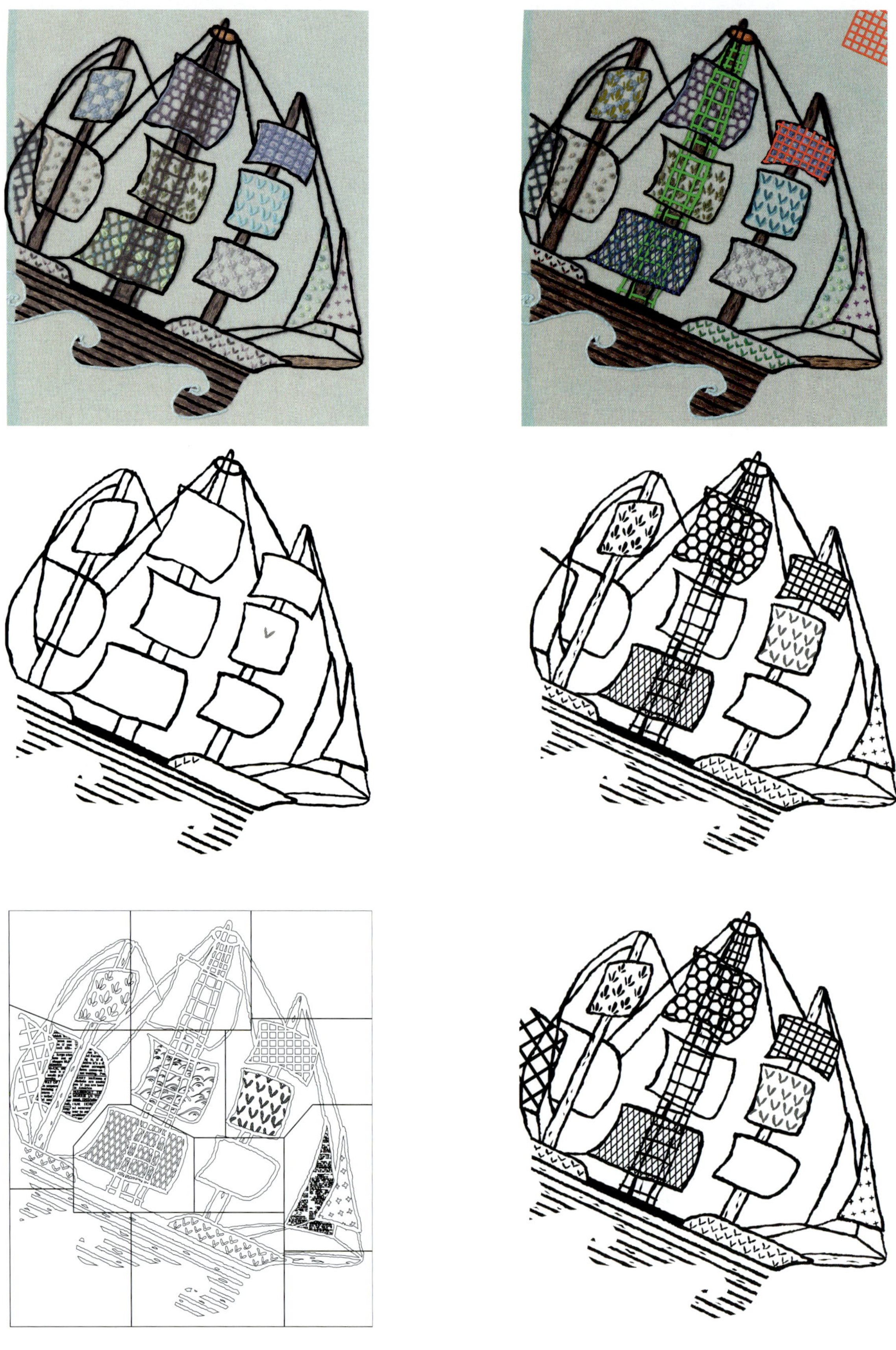

  Adobe Illustrator CS6 files, 2012 (top and middle rows); Adobe Illustrator CS6 files, 2013 (bottom row)

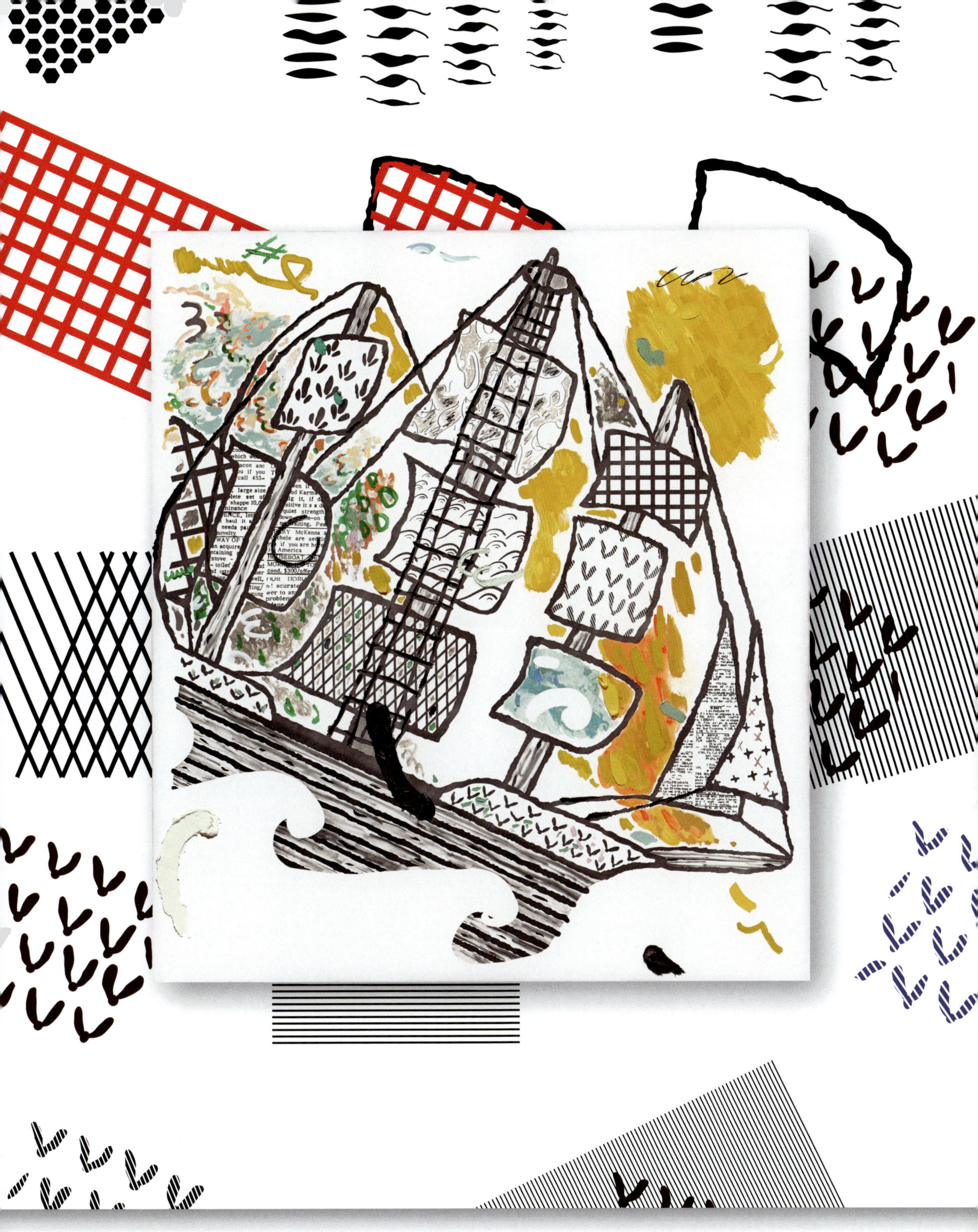

Foreground: *Untitled*, 2013, acrylic, oil, vinyl paint, and charcoal on linen, 137½ × 120 in. (349.3 × 304.8 cm)
Background: Adobe Illustrator CS6 file, 2012

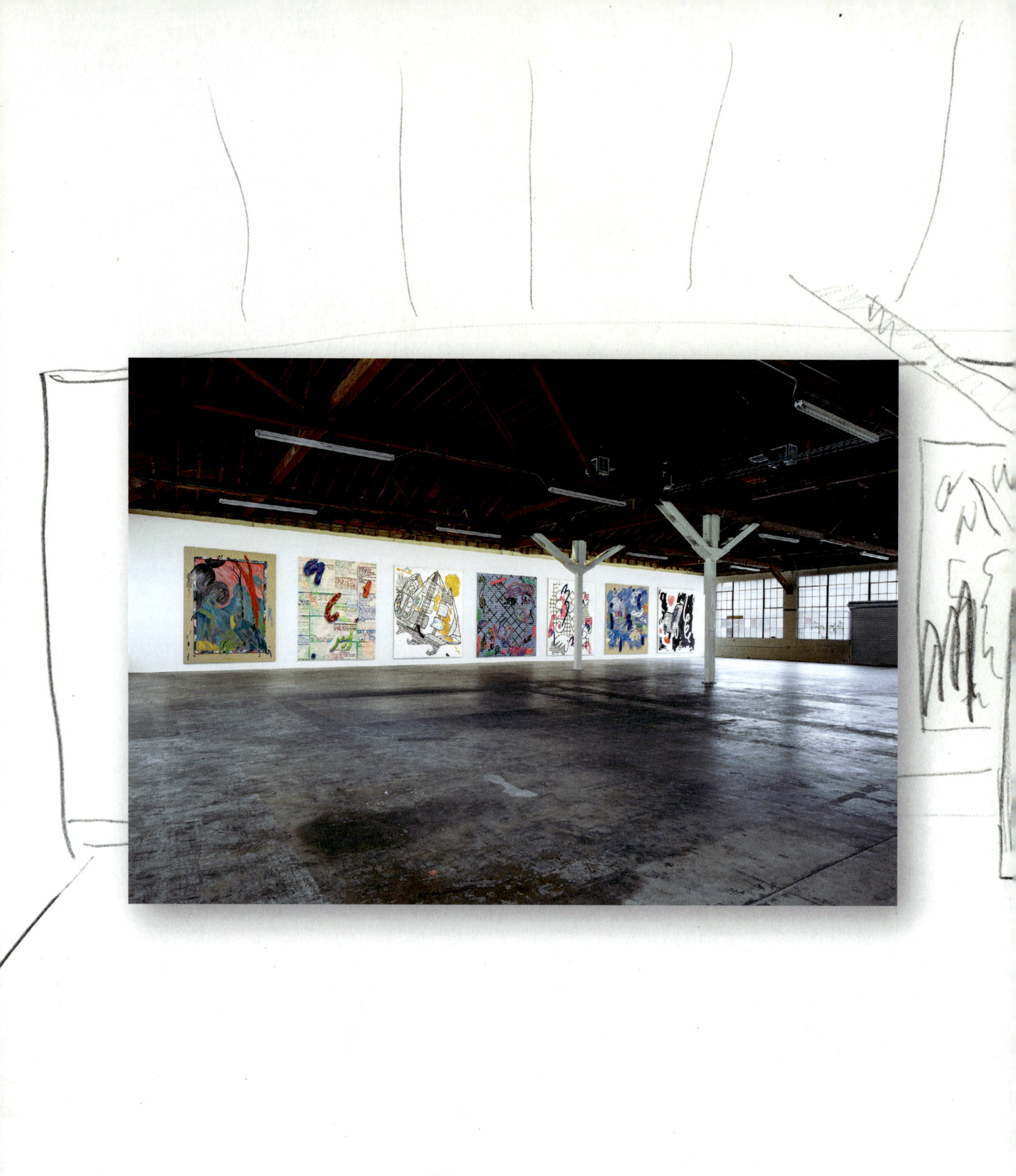

Foreground: Installation views, *Twelve Paintings*, 356 S. Mission Rd., Los Angeles, 2013, with *Untitled*, 2013, acrylic, oil, and vinyl paint on linen; *Untitled*, 2013, acrylic, oil, and vinyl paint on canvas; *Untitled*, 2013 (see p. 509); *Untitled*, 2013 (see p. 512); *Untitled*, 2013 (see p. 420); *Untitled*, 2013, acrylic, oil, and vinyl paint on linen; and *Untitled*, 2013, acrylic, oil, and resin on linen, 137½ × 120 in. (349.3 × 304.8 cm) each

 Background: Sketch, 2013

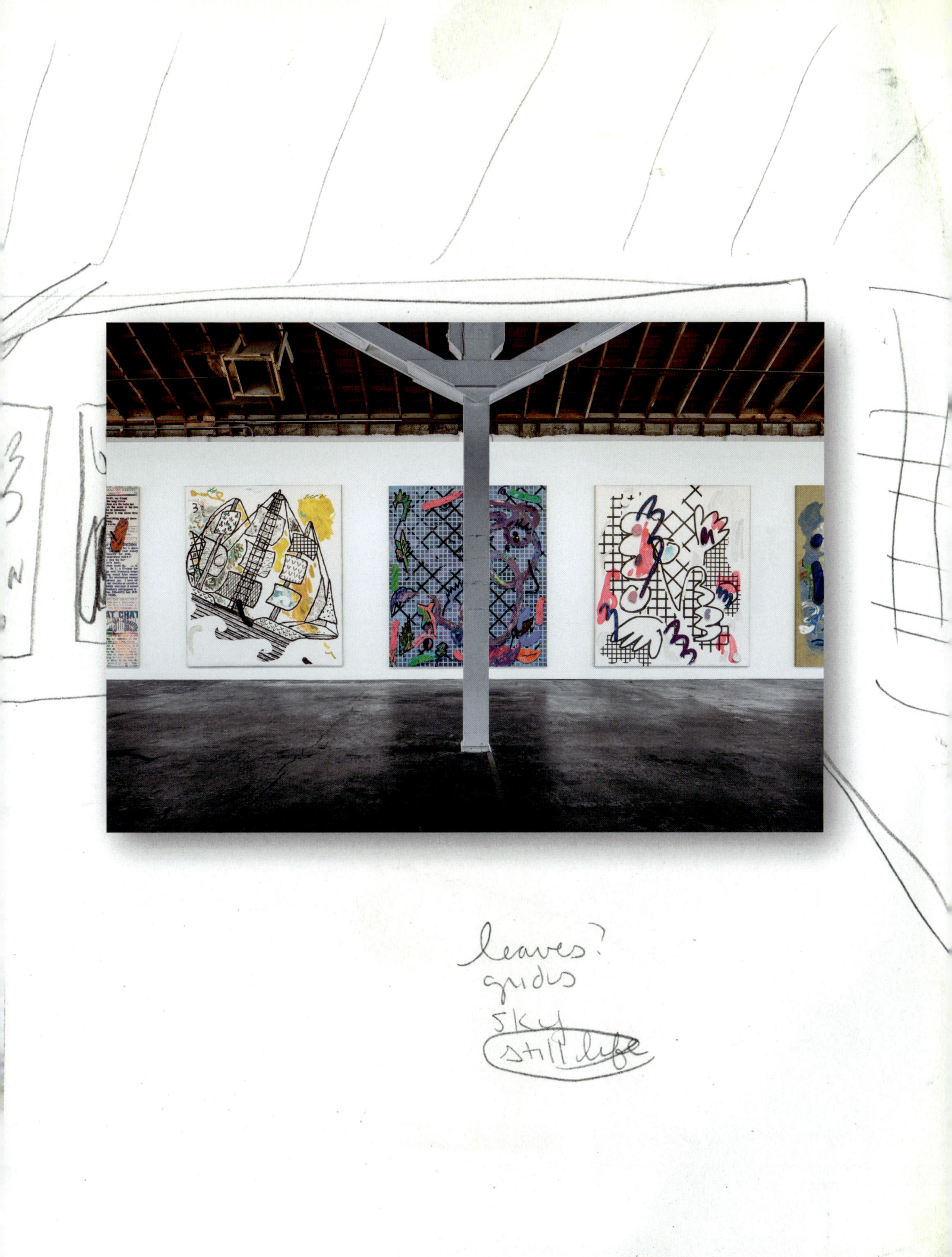

leaves?
grids
sky
still life

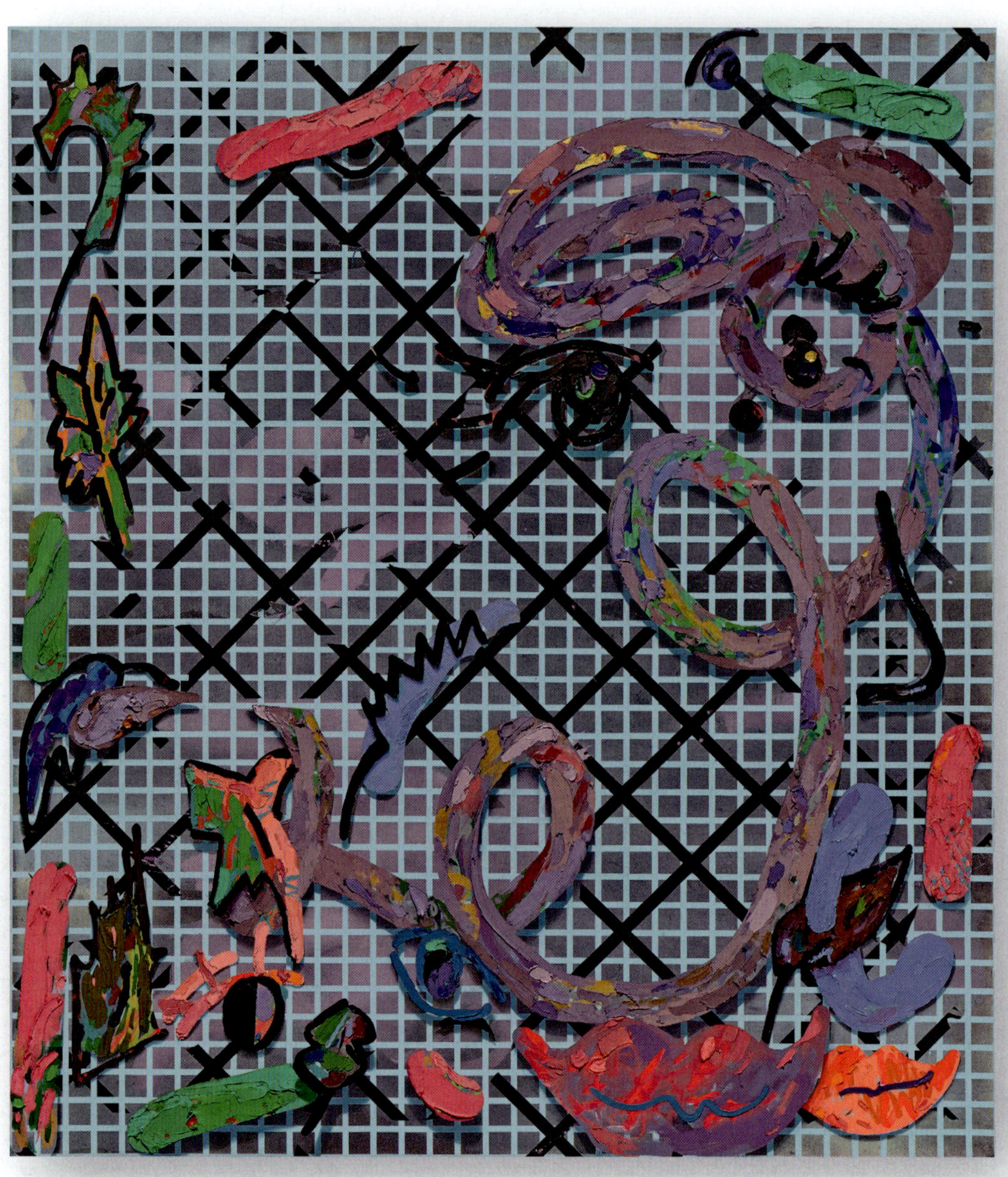

512 *Untitled*, 2013, acrylic, oil, and vinyl paint on canvas, 137½ × 120 in. (349.3 × 304.8 cm)

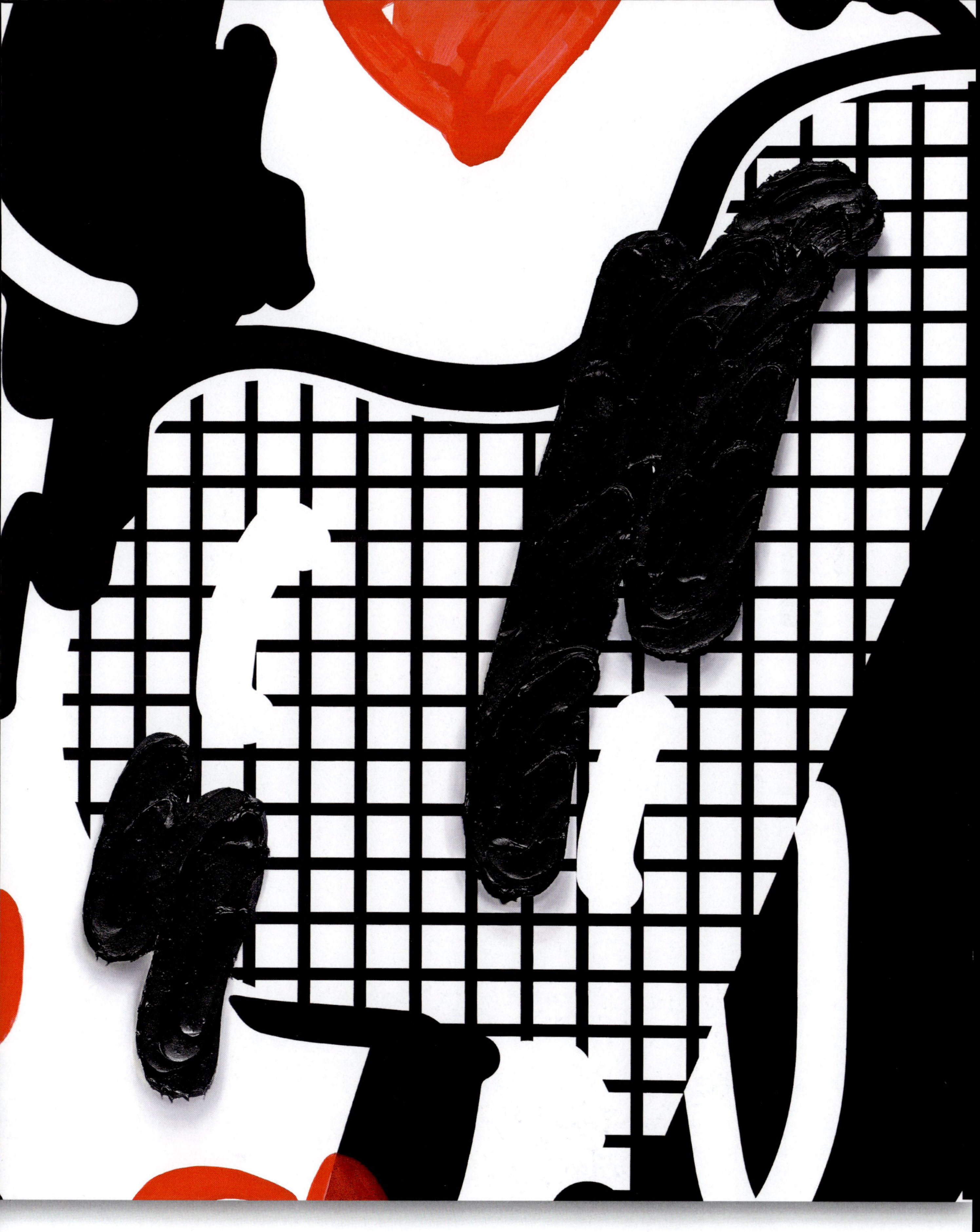

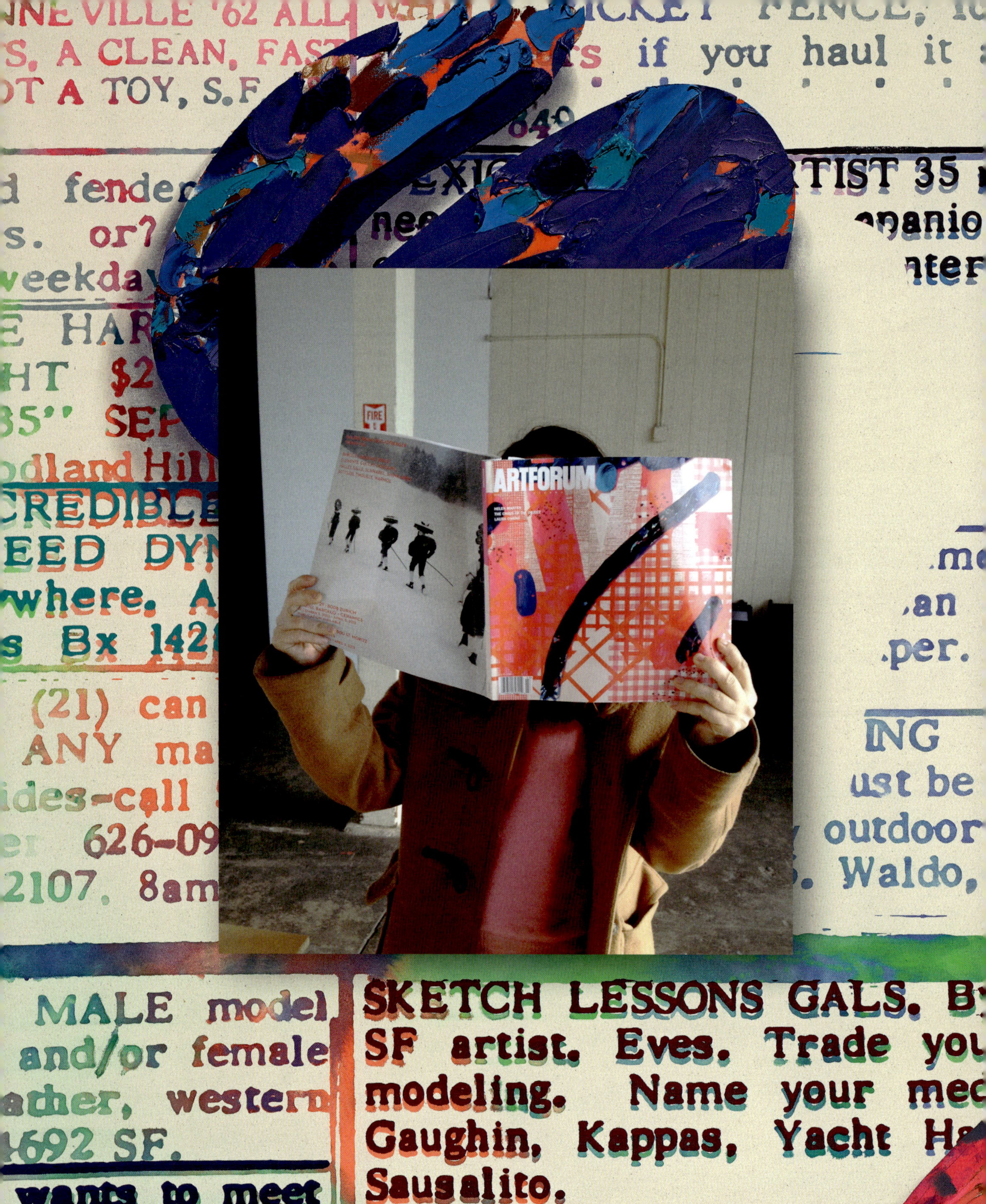

Foreground: Owens with *Artforum*, 356 S. Mission Rd., Los Angeles, 2013
Background: Detail of *Untitled*, 2013 (see p. 510)

514

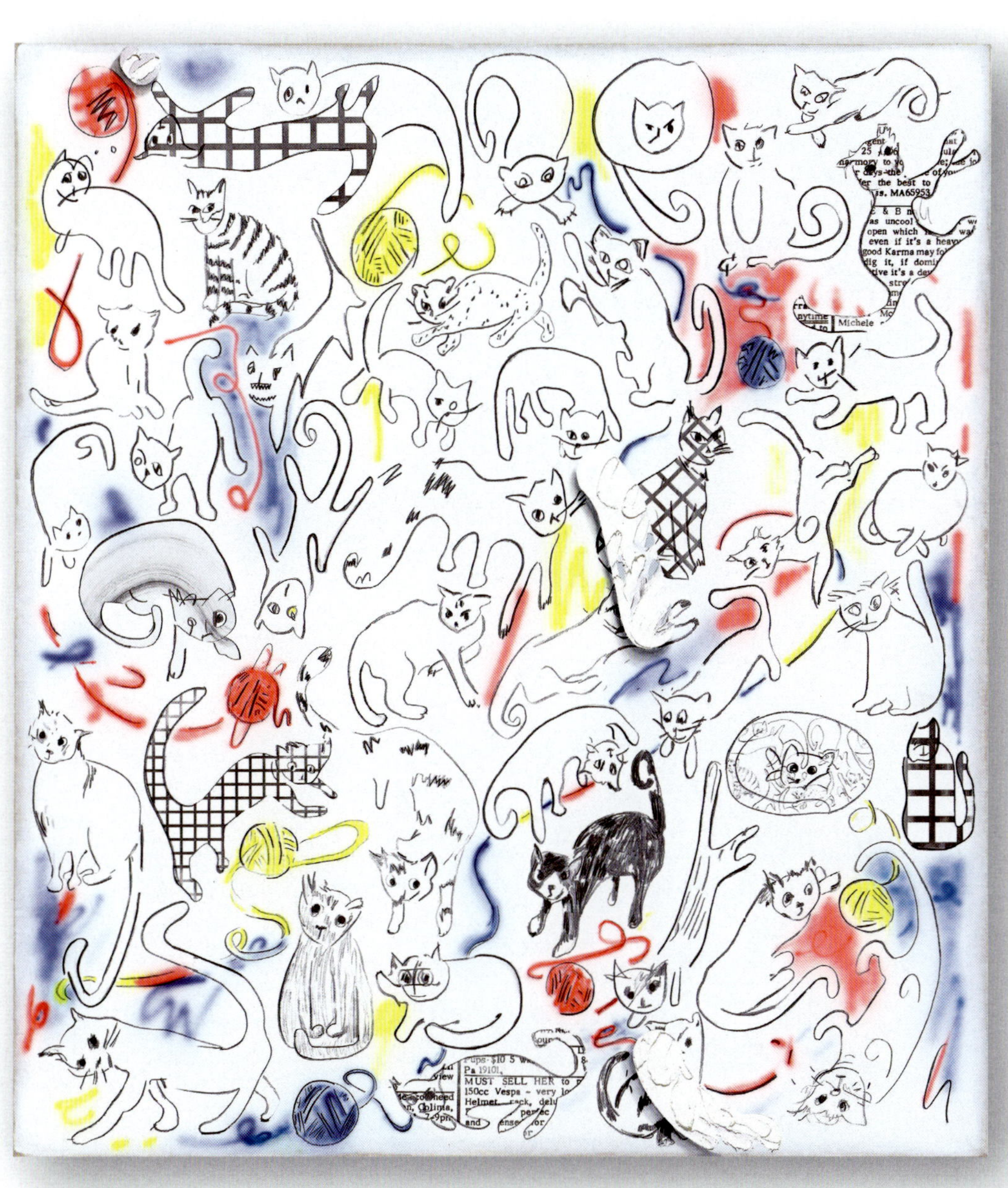

Untitled, 2013, acrylic, oil, and charcoal on linen, 137½ × 120 in. (349.3 × 304.8 cm)

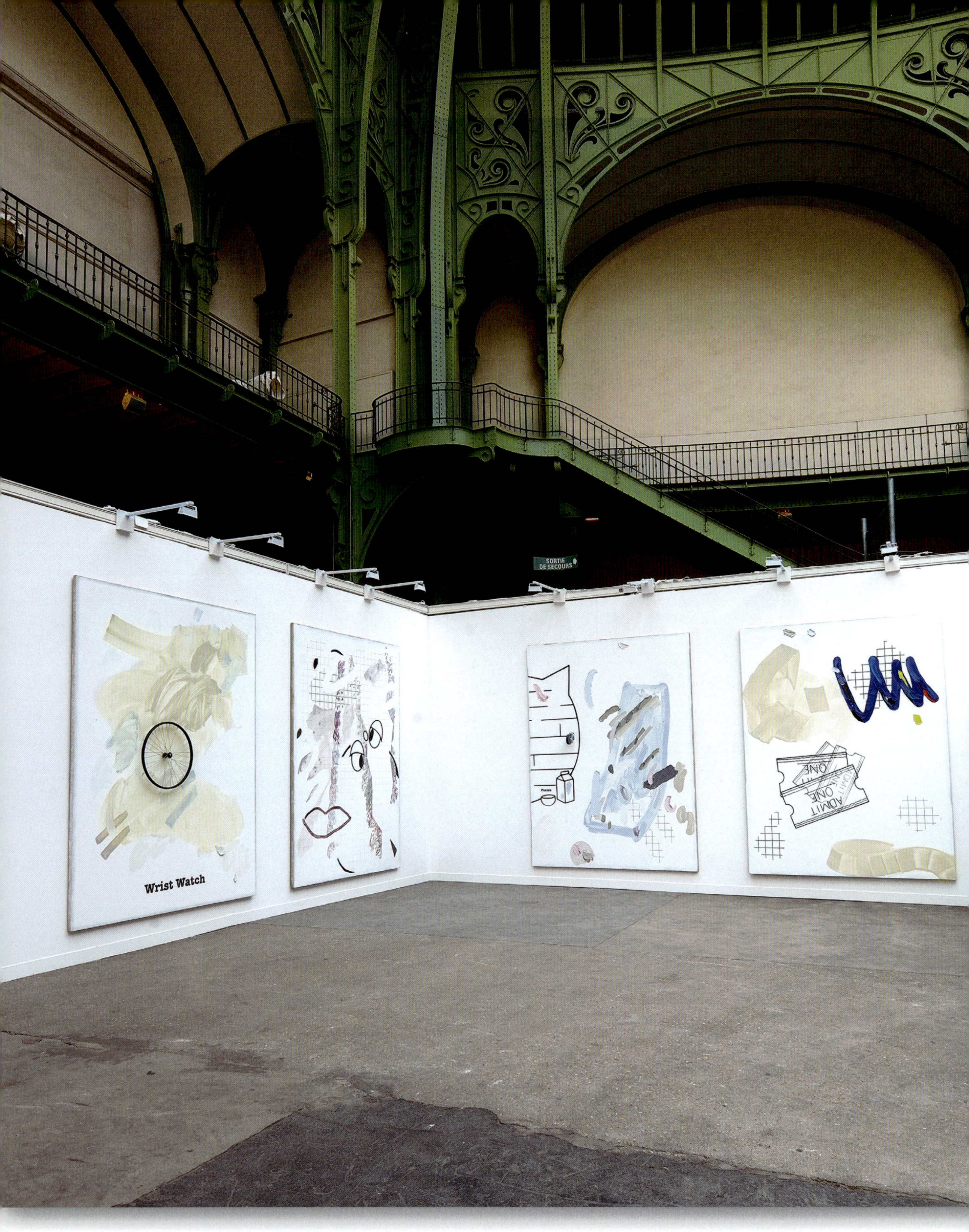

Installation view, Gavin Brown's enterprise at Foire Internationale d'Art Contemporain, Paris, 2013, with *Untitled,* 2013, oil, vinyl paint, charcoal, and wheel on linen, 108 × 84 in. (274.3 × 213.4 cm); *Untitled,* 2013, oil, vinyl paint, and charcoal on linen, 108 × 84 in. (274.3 × 213.4 cm); *Untitled,* 2013, oil, vinyl paint, charcoal, and caster wheel on linen, 108 × 84 in. (274.3 × 213.4 cm); and *Untitled,* 2013, oil, vinyl paint, and charcoal on linen, 108 × 84 in. (274.3 × 213.4 cm)

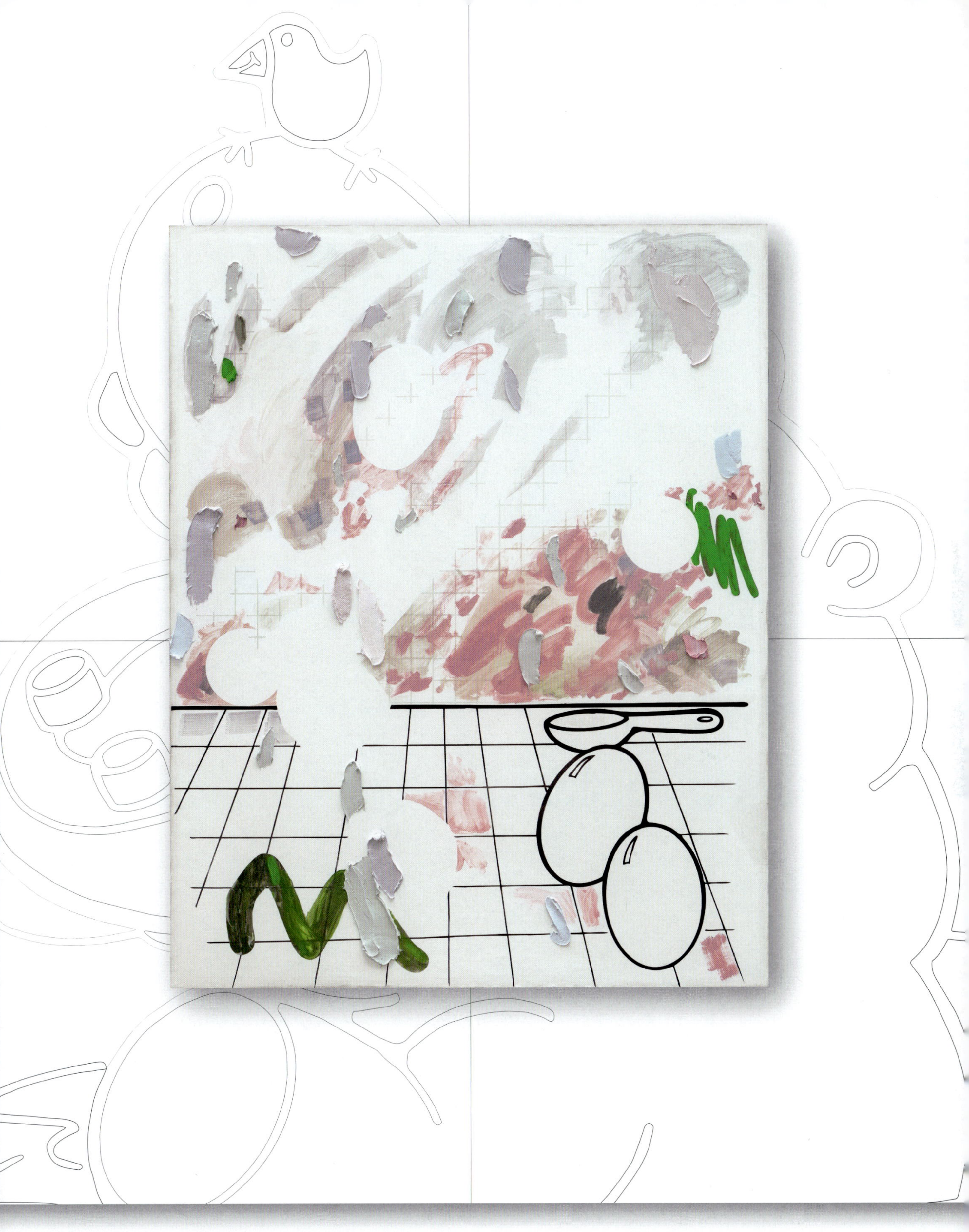

Foreground: *Untitled*, 2013, oil, vinyl paint, and charcoal on linen, 108 × 84 in. (274.3 × 213.4 cm)
Background: Adobe Illustrator CS6 file, 2013

as much as we think this is him being crazy and old-man-like, I have met a lot of people in the art world that think this way

On Jan 29, 2013, at 1:09 PM, Mungo Thomson wrote:

http://galleristny.com/2013/01/georg-baselitz-says-women-dont-paint-very-well/

x Mungo

mungothomson.com

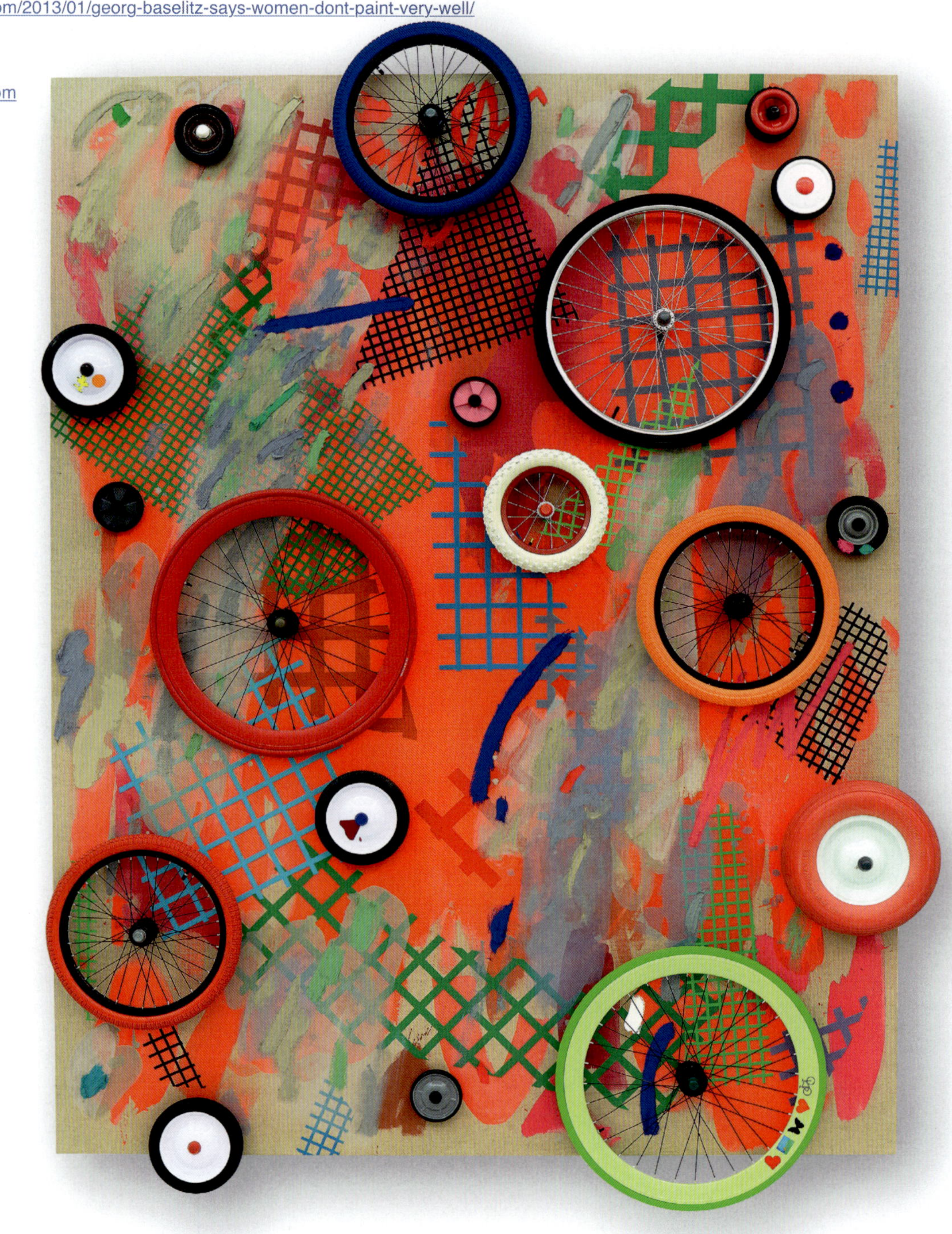

Foreground: *Untitled*, 2013, acrylic, vinyl paint, and wheels on linen, 108 × 84 in. (274.3 × 213.4 cm)

  Background: Emails with Mungo Thomson, 2013

eone draf tea. Someone else felt that a specific kind of taco eaten a particul
phic location was like a drug. The spices generated a certain kind of energy, or, perh
memory. It was 2012.

02, "thoughts mixed and burned with gasoline" turned to Orange County, a web with
The Citadel, Eden-Olympia. The commingling of purposefulness and aimlessness w
ood to be the effect of Junkspace.

81, Peter Schjeldahl took a trip to Los Angeles and wrote a short essay damning ou
ure of cultural irrelevance, lest it somehow invert each and every one of its unique
s. He wrote, "he effect of a li
s independer one and you'll
.] Los Angele spaces--fenced
das of self-ma dreamy, zinging
where in part as theater, Sch
the point.

cipants in the jouissance: th
attered aroun

86, a pedestr e sidewalk nea
of Wilshire an an on televisio
ot fooled by h he intended
ance of variou f his speech wa
d from his ima ord.

opper walks t assemble a me
fe goals by wa he specific alie
at produced t e somewhere,
ating this ama lays stacked t
that person horny? Do they have a gaping flesh wound? A fixed quantity of gasoline
ed to smog today. It is 1999.

Mall of America is constructed in 1992. The FDA urges surgeons to abandon silicone
implants and the first McDonald's franchise is opened in China. In the words of Fren
ologist Marc Augé, "Place and non-place are rather like opposed polarities: the first
ompletely erased, the second never totally completed; they are like palimpsests on
ambled game of identity and relations is ceaselessly rewritten."

Gavin Brown's enterprise and Venus Over Manhattan present...

Made in Space

Curated by Peter Harkawik and Laura Owens

Lucas Blalock
Derek Boshier
Jedediah Caesar
Joshua Callaghan
Vanessa Conte

Michael Decker
Gabrielle Ferrer
Laeh Glenn
Hannah Greely
Marcia Hafif

Peter Harkawik
Cannon Hudson
Jim Isermann
Patrick Jackson
David Korty

Liz Larner
William Leavitt
Tala Madani
Josh Mannis
Max Maslansky
Jesse Mockrin

Rebecca Morris
Davida Nemeroff
Eric Orr
Jorge Pardo
Marina Pinksy
Allen Ruppersberg

Asha Schechter
Peter Shire
John Seal
Mungo Thomson
Aaron Wrinkle

JULY 11 - AUGUST 10

VENUS OVER MANHATTAN
980 MADISON AVE
THIRD FLOOR
NY NY 10075

JULY 11 - AUGUST 10

GAVIN BROWN'S ENTERPRISE
620 GREENWICH ST
NY NY 10014

Foreground: Invitation, *Made in Space*, Gavin Brown's enterprise and Venus Over Manhattan, New York, 2013
Background: Press release, Night Gallery, Los Angeles, 2013

Ethan Swan: One of the the first things I went to after moving to Los Angeles was Asha Schechter's *Transparency Book* launch at Ooga Booga #2. Everybody was hugging or talking or happy to see each other; it felt like a community made visible. And it wasn't exclusive, which was really compelling. I had been in New York for eight years before that and it felt really different, it reminded me more of the underground music scene than an art world event. I started working at 356 four months later. In the beginning there was a vague awareness that there would be some events on the horizon, and that some other things were planned, but there wasn't a sense of what needed to happen for the space to work, or even a sense of what Laura and Wendy and Gavin expected. The way I always think of it is as an artist's space first. Laura loved the experience of using the building as a studio and then showing her work where it was made, and that's still the foundation for most of the shows. It's pretty rare that we don't have the artist spending time in the building; there aren't shows that just get unpacked and put on the wall. Everything takes a really intense series of interactions to figure out how to work within the setting and use the idiosyncrasies of the building and explore some of the possibilities there that don't exist at every gallery.

I often describe 356 as essentially an artist-run space. It's Laura Owens, who has shown a lot of different places; Gavin Brown, who has exhibited artists' work in a lot of different places; and Wendy Yao, who has this really democratic relationship with creative work, and they're making a space where more stuff can happen. These experiences that they've all had produced this idea of putting the artist's voice first as much as possible. We always want the artist to do everything—the flyer for the show, for instance. We would like it best if the artist made it, but we understand that some artists don't want to. Starting with Scott Reeder's show, we have done an

     Ethan Swan is a Los Angeles–based musician and has been the director of 356 S. Mission Rd. since 2013.

interview for every project. The interview stands in for the press release because it includes information about the show but presents it in a way that focuses on the artist and the way they talk about their work instead of projecting some kind of interpretation. This is the thing that I go back to time and time again.

When 356 first started, Laura had a list of all the artists she would love to present. Maybe a year ago we sat down and looked at that list, and we had done a lot more of the things on it than I had thought we could. Michael Clark's performance was something that seemed so difficult to achieve with the scale and scrappiness of 356 in comparison with the level of production that he's used to working with, but his is one of the most memorable projects in the gallery's history. Not just because it breaks with his usual process but because he's an artist who really understood the space. He didn't try to force it to do something it couldn't, but instead used it in the way that made the most sense in terms of his practice. We always say, "Have we found the limits of what this room can do?" And I think there are points at which we're like, "Oh, we kind of know, this is what a painting show looks like here. This is what a video show looks like. This is what sculpture looks like." And then Trisha Baga figured out a new, cool way to use the room that highlighted parts of the building I never think about. When something like that happens you realize there is still a lot more possibility. It is a commercial gallery—the way the whole thing is sustained is through the sale of art—and watching that work or not work over the years has been really complicated and interesting and harrowing. As the expectations for success adjust or are adjusted in terms of just needing the place to work, that's the goal. I don't think anybody was ever like, "This is going to make a huge amount of money. What a great investment." But we've always thought about what kinds of events or exhibitions need to take place in the space and from there tried to figure out how we can make them happen. That way of prioritizing has been very powerful for me.

Three months after I started working at 356 we had this band called C.R.A.S.H. play outside in the area where we keep the dumpsters. It was this funny thing where basically you couldn't see them unless you climbed up on a bench and looked over the fence. And a guy who was watching them got his phone slapped out of his hand and got knocked around a little bit, because it was a punk show and people were bumping into each other. The next day he called the gallery and he was very upset about what had happened. He had this feeling like, "I'll bet you guys don't have insurance and I could shut you down immediately because you don't have the permits to do what you are doing." In talking about that he said, "You can't show millions of dollars' worth of paintings one week and then have some shitty punk band the next." I just remember thinking, "If we can't, then there's no reason to have the space." Right? Because I think that some of this comes from Ooga Booga but it also comes from Laura and Gavin. I will say that on a very fundamental level, very rarely have I gone to something around Los Angeles without seeing Laura there. She's very present and has a keen awareness of what's happening here, and I think that really benefits how the space works because I think she has a sense of what's missing and what works and what would be helpful for people. So we tend toward those kinds of things, and this idea of having a punk band play adjacent to the expensive paintings is just so great for the space. And I would say it's also a great thing for Los Angeles. Because it's not a strategy to get more people in the door, or different audiences in the door. It's more like, "What else do we care about?" And I like that feeling. That's one of the things about this space that I'm proudest of.

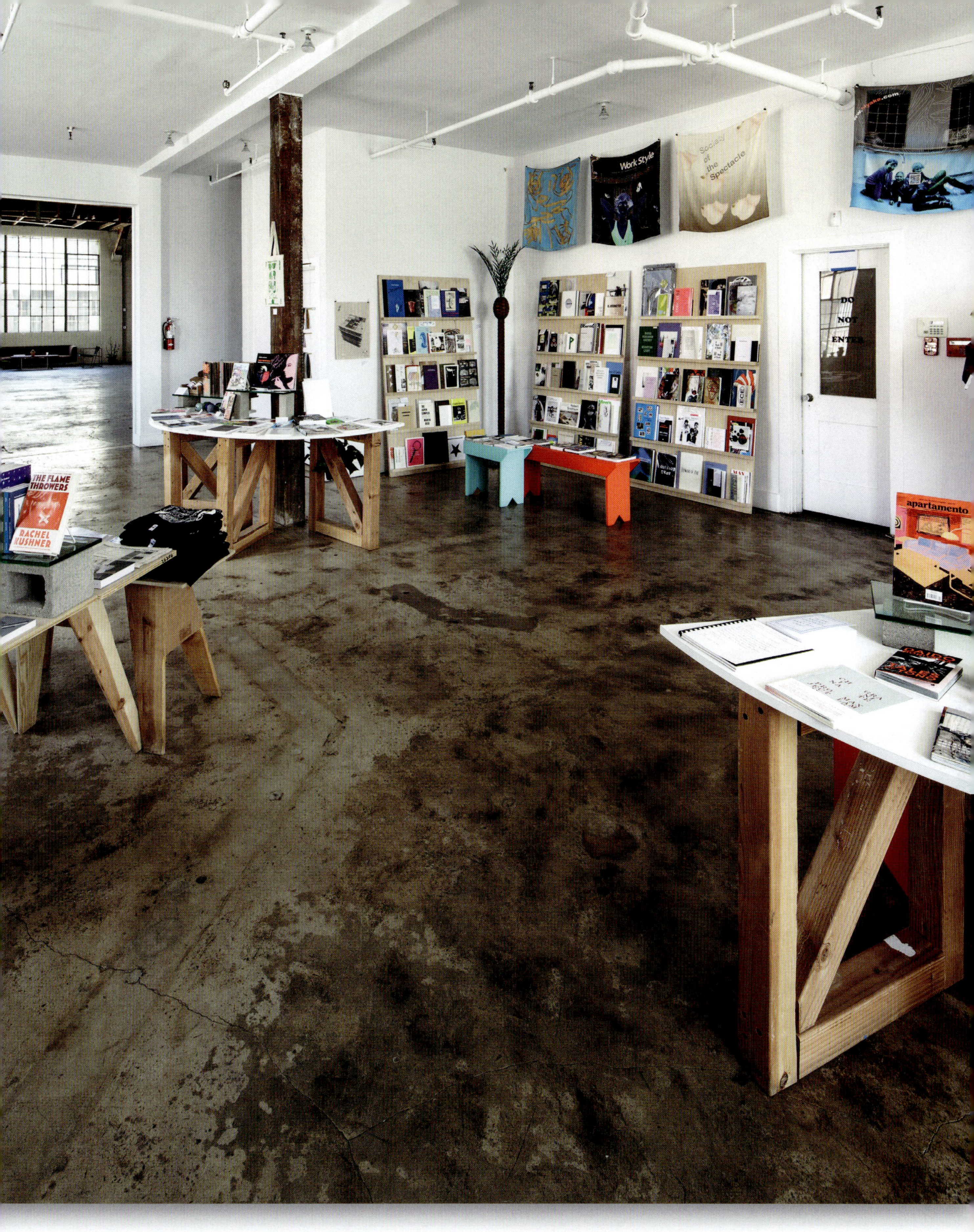

Ooga Booga #2, 356 S. Mission Rd., Los Angeles, 2013

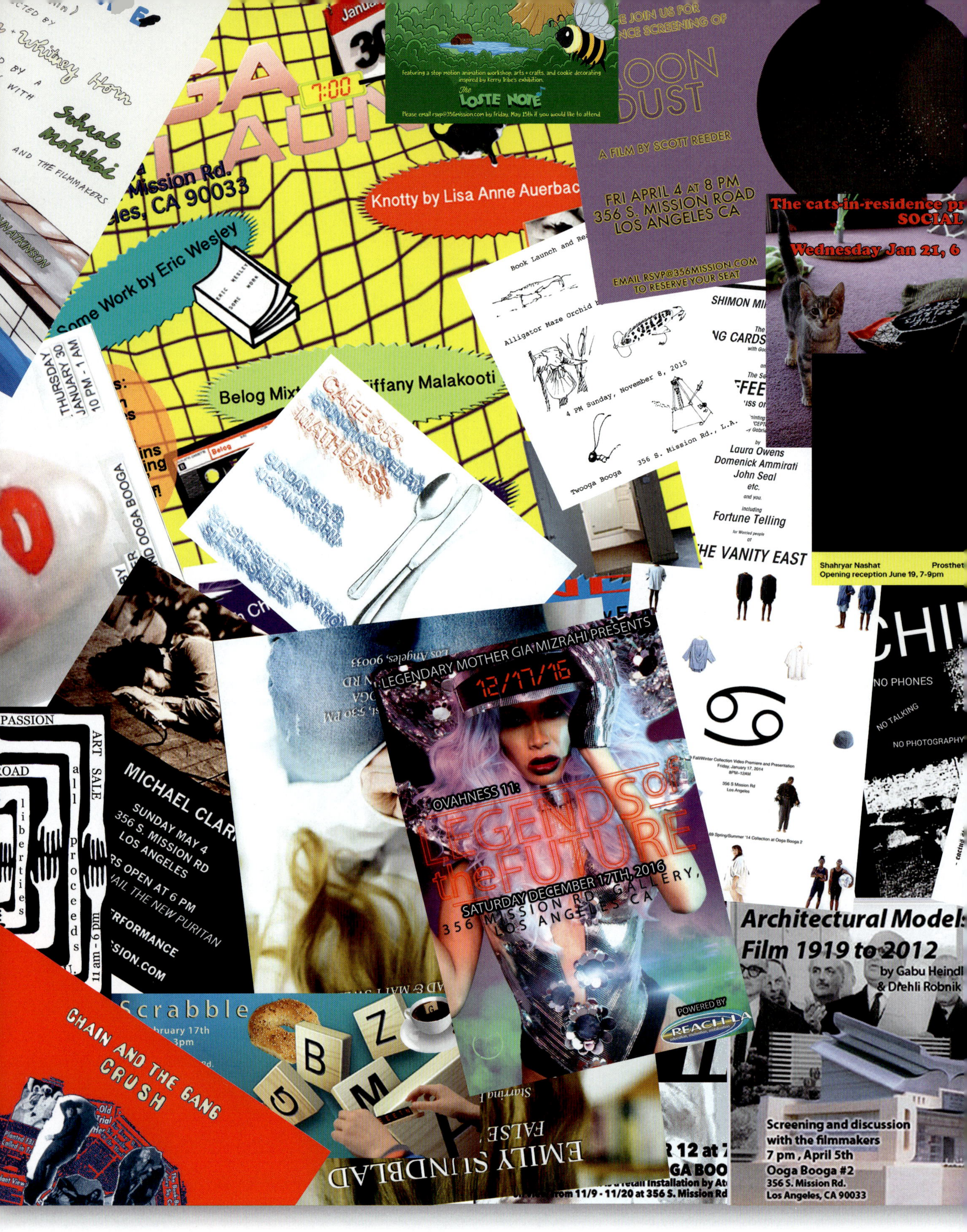
Schuab Mohebbi
AND THE FILMMAKERS
7:00
Knotty by Lisa Anne Auerbach
Some Work by Eric Wesley
Belog Mixt
Tiffany Malakooti
THURSDAY JANUARY 30 10 PM - 1 AM
CAFE 356
MATH BASS
SUNDAY 5/18
The LOSTE NOTE
featuring a stop motion animation workshop, arts + crafts, and cookie decorating inspired by Kerry Tribe's exhibition.
Please email rsvp@356mission.com by friday, May 15th if you would like to attend
MOON DUST
A FILM BY SCOTT REEDER
FRI APRIL 4 AT 8 PM
356 S. MISSION ROAD
LOS ANGELES CA
EMAIL RSVP@356MISSION.COM
TO RESERVE YOUR SEAT
The cats-in-residence pr
SOCIAL
Wednesday Jan 21, 6
Book Launch and Re
Alligator Maze Orchid
4 PM Sunday, November 8, 2015
Twooga Booga
356 S. Mission Rd., L.A.
SHIMON MI
NG CARDS
FEE
Laura Owens
Domenick Ammirati
John Seal
etc.
and you.
including
Fortune Telling
for Worried people
at
THE VANITY EAST
Shahryar Nashat   Prosthet
Opening reception June 19, 7-9pm
PASSION
ART SALE
all liberties
all proceeds
ROAD
MICHAEL CLAR
SUNDAY MAY 4
356 S. MISSION RD
LOS ANGELES
RS OPEN AT 6 PM
AIL THE NEW PURITAN
RFORMANCE
SION.COM
LEGENDARY MOTHER GIA MIZRAHI PRESENTS
12/17/16
OVAHNESS 11:
LEGENDS of the FUTURE
SATURDAY DECEMBER 17TH, 2016
356 MISSION RD GALLERY,
LOS ANGELES CA
POWERED BY
REACH LA
Los Angeles, 90033
NO PHONES
NO TALKING
NO PHOTOGRAPHY
Fall/Winter Collection Video Premiere and Presentation
Friday, January 17, 2014
8PM-12AM
356 S Mission Rd
Los Angeles
Spring/Summer '14 Collection at Ooga Booga 2
CHI
Architectural Models
Film 1919 to 2012
by Gabu Heindl
& Drehli Robnik
Screening and discussion
with the filmmakers
7 pm , April 5th
Ooga Booga #2
356 S. Mission Rd.
Los Angeles, CA 90033
Scrabble
February 17th
3pm
CHAIN AND THE GANG
CRUSH
EMILY SUNDBLAD
FALSE
R 12 at 7
GA BOO
from 11/9 - 11/20 at 356 S. Mission Rd

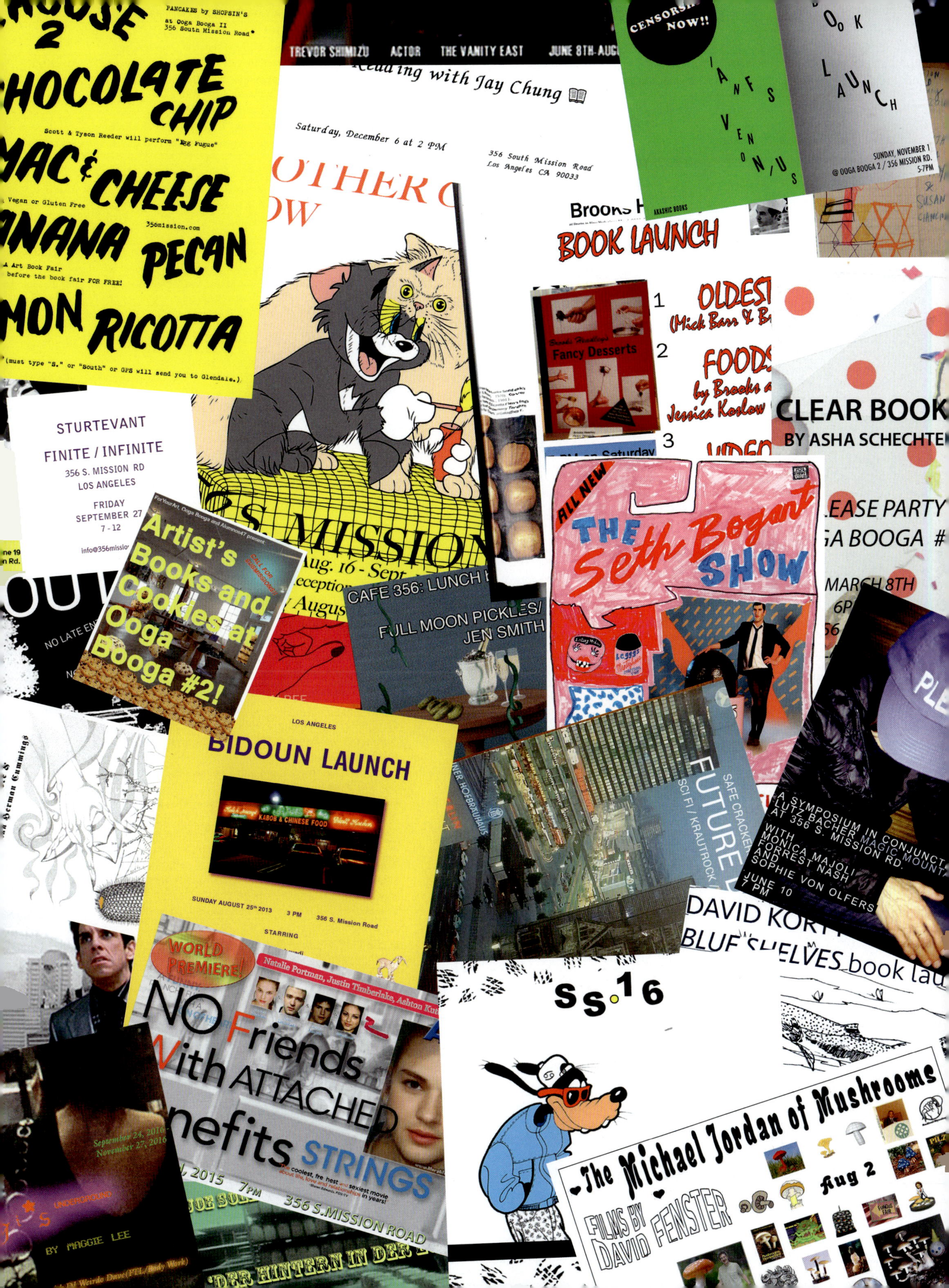
2
HOUSE
CHOCOLATE CHIP
MAC & CHEESE
BANANA PECAN
MON RICOTTA
PANCAKES by SHOPSIN's
at Ooga Booga II
356 South Mission Road
Scott & Tyson Reeder will perform "Egg Fugue"
Vegan or Gluten Free
356mission.com
Art Book Fair
before the book fair FOR FREE!
(must type "S." or "South" or GPS will send you to Glendale.)
STURTEVANT
FINITE / INFINITE
356 S. MISSION RD
LOS ANGELES
FRIDAY
SEPTEMBER 27
7 - 12
info@356missio
Artist's Books and Cookies at Ooga Booga #2!
OUT
NO LATE EN
BY MAGGIE LEE
TREVOR SHIMIZU   ACTOR   THE VANITY EAST   JUNE 8TH-AUG
Reading with Jay Chung
Saturday, December 6 at 2 PM
356 South Mission Road
Los Angeles CA 90033
OTHER
SHOW
S. MISSION
Aug. 16 - Sep
CAFE 356: LUNCH
FULL MOON PICKLES/
JEN SMITH
LOS ANGELES
BIDOUN LAUNCH
KABOB & CHINESE FOOD
SUNDAY AUGUST 25th 2013   3 PM   356 S. Mission Road
STARRING
WORLD PREMIERE
Natalie Portman, Justin Timberlake, Ashton Kut
NO Friends With ATTACHED enfits STRINGS
coolest, fre hest and sexiest movie
about life, love and relationships in years!
2015   7PM   356 S. MISSION ROAD
DER HINTERN IN DER
CENSORSH
NOW!!
I
A
N
F
S
V
E
N
O
N
/
U
S
BOOK LAUNCH
SUNDAY, NOVEMBER 1
@ OOGA BOOGA 2 / 356 MISSION RD.
5-7PM
Broons H
AKASHIC BOOKS
BOOK LAUNCH
Brooks Headley's
Fancy Desserts
1   OLDEST
(Mick Barr & B
2   FOODS
by Brooks a
Jessica Koslow
3
Saturday
CLEAR BOOK
BY ASHA SCHECHTER
ALL NEW
THE Seth Bogart SHOW
LEASE PARTY
GA BOOGA #
MARCH 8TH
6P
56
FUTURE
SCI FI / KRAUTROCK
SAFE CRACKER
A SYMPOSIUM IN CONJUNCT
LUTZ BACHER MAGIC MOUNT
AT 356 S. MISSION RD
WITH
MONICA MAJOLI
FORREST NASH
AND
SOPHIE VON OLFERS
JUNE 10
7 PM
DAVID KORT
BLUE SHELVES book lau
PLE
Ss.16
The Michael Jordan of Mushrooms
FILMS BY DAVID FENSTER
Aug 2
PILZ

5/2/17	Opening Reception for "Sunlight arrives only at its proper hour"
5/5/17	CHILL OUT Relaxing Clothing presents ADSL Camels + DJ's
4/14/17	Sayonara Jupiter Opening Reception
4/12/17	Reza Abdoh: Theatre Visionary (104min., 15)
4/1/17	David Reed Exhibition Opening Reception
3/26/17	Deadlines and Divine Distractions Reading
3/16/17	Sara Knox Hunter West Coast Book Launch and Reading
3/6/17	Chain and The Gang and Crush in Concert
3/4/17	Clara Cakes Cookbook Release Party
2/12/17	Artists' Political Action Network Organizing Meeting
2/1/17	Fridays in February: FAVORITE FOOD: A ceramics workshop for high school students led by Cassie Griffin
1/27/17	Opening Reception for Trisha Baga's exhibition "Biologue"
1/21/17	Amplify Compassion: Art Sale to benefit the ACLU
1/14/17	Brian Sharp opening reception
1/11/17	Premiere of The Smell Virtual Reality Tour
1/8/17	Closing Reception for John Seal's exhibition "While There Is Still Life to Live"
1/7/17	Clemency for Leonard Peltier Letter Writing Action + Presentation by Rigo 23
12/18/16	LAFMS BOX BOX BIG MOUTH BIG SOUNDS Launch
12/17/16	Ovahness 11: Legends of the Future - hosted by REACH LA
12/11/16	Art Center Talks: Book Launch & Panel Discussion
12/4/16	Opening Reception for John Seal's exhibition "While There Is Still Life to Live"
12/1/16	Honored In Vision: A World AIDS Day Event - hosted by REACH LA
11/27/16	What's NOW: An opportunity to meet with activists, nonprofits, and community groups to mobilize our dismay
11/20/16	Everything I Want To Eat: Sqirl and the New California Cooking Book Launch & Apartamento #18 Magazine Launch
11/17/16	Iman Issa + Diana Nawi in conversation - hosted by Artadia as part of Art & Dialogue: Los Angeles
11/13/16	Vanity East Opening Reception for Eric Wysocan's exhibition "REBREATHER"
11/12/16	Opening Reception of ATELIER E.B.'s retail installation "Inventors of Tradition II" and Screening
11/6/16	Copiapoa: Cactus under the influence of Fog - a Presentation by Cactus Store & Christian Herman Cummings
10/30/16	A Talk by Bob Nickas - 100 Paintings / 100 Years: 1915 - 15
10/20/16	Thomas Bayrle and Bernhard Schreiner Record Launch of Warp Weft LP
10/10/16	West Coast Premiere of "Cordelia", a Film by Veronica Gonzalez Peña
9/24/16	Opening Reception of Maggie Lee's exhibition "Gigi*s Underground"
9/21/16	Screening of Maggie Lee's film "Mommy" at Cinefamily
9/17/16	Vanity East Opening Reception for Chris Domenick's & Em Rooney's exhibition "After The Sun"
9/11/16	Opening Reception for Wu Tsang's exhibition "The Luscious Land of God is Sinking"
8/23/16	GIVE ME THE NIGHT: A benefit show for The Smell with performances by The Seth Bogart Show (live), Snake Jé (ex-Mika Miko, ex-Crazy Band), Fictitious Business DBA The Geminis, VIP and DJ M Suarez
8/14/16	YOU SAD LEGEND: A performance by Wu Tsang and boychild, featuring Patrick Belaga
7/28/16	Screening of Moyra Davey's film "Les Goddesses" with an introduction by Suzanna Zak
7/21/16	Screening of Agnes Martin's film "Gabriel" co-presented with LACMA in conjunction with the exhibition Agnes Martin
6/30/16	Screening of "My Name is Lutz"
6/24/16	Record Release Party and Concert for Elizabeth Cline's "The Edge of Forever"
6/18/16	Dog Star Orchestra Concert "The Density of Silence (0'00", part 2)" - Performing works by John Cage, Michael Pisaro, Cassia Streb, Christine Tavolacci, and Colin Wambsgans
6/12/16	Schimpfluch Gruppe Noise Show with Solo Performances by Rudolf Eb.er, dave phillips and Joke Lanz
6/10/16	PLEASE: A symposium in conjunction with Lutz Bacher's exhibition "Magic Mountain" - Participants include Monica Majoli, Forrest Nash and Sophie von Olfers
5/29/16	David Korty Blue Shelves Book Launch, Slideshow Presentation of "on trout and fly tying" and Screening of "The Educated Trout"
5/21/16	Opening Reception of Lutz Bacher's exhibition "Magic Mountain"
5/12/16	Dos Mega in Concert
5/4/16	Lucky Dragons Record Release for "Ooga Booga Bongo Music"
4/29/16	Flat Worms and Susan Record Release and Concert
4/27/16	Wayne Koestenbaum in conversation with Matt Connors
4/22/16	Just Speak Nearby (Day 2): Dialogues, lectures, Performances and Screenings
4/21/16	Just Speak Nearby (Day 1): Trinh T. Minh-ha Lecture and Screening of her film "Reassamblage"
4/16/16	SAFE CRACKERS Presents FUTURE DAYS: Sci Fi/ Krautrock/ Trip Hop
3/20/16	"The Trial of Anne Opie Wehrer and Unknown Accomplices For Crimes Against Humanity" by Robert Ashley (Night 2)
3/19/16	"The Trial of Anne Opie Wehrer and Unknown Accomplices For Crimes Against Humanity" by Robert Ashley (Night 1)
3/19/16	Opening reception for Wayne Koestenbaum's exhibition "A Novel of Thank You and Other Paintings"
2/27/16	STUDIOO MANUEL RAEDER Talk at Ooga Booga 2
2/19/16	Screening of Space Oddities Phase II: 2 New Films by Margo Victor
2/12/16	STUDIOO MANUEEL RAEDER launch at Ooga Twooga
2/10/16	Barbara Kasten in conversation with Martine Syms - Moderated by Alex Klein
2/7/16	Screening of The Wooster Group's "White Homeland Commando" and Discussion w Kate Valk, Elizabeth LeCompte & Lewis Klahr
2/4/16	Sam Ashley and John Krausbauer in Concert
2/3/16	Book Launch for Samara Golden's "The Flat Side of The Knife"
1/30/16	Drawings by Susan Cianciolo - Presented by Ooga Booga / 356 Mission at Paramoun Ranch
12/23/15	Waiting Bodies: An Evening of Mark Morrisroe films
12/20/15	the MOVEMENT Movement: a performance - Led by Mecca Vazie Andrews
12/3/15	Laura Owens & Jordan Wolfson Joint Book Launch and Discussion
11/19/15	Book launch for "Mad Like Artaud" by Sylvère Lotringer with the West Coast Premi his Film "The Man Who Disappeared"
11/13/15	A Coupla White Faggots Sitting Around Talking: Gary Indiana in Film and Video - Presented by Dirty Looks, Semiotext(e) and 356 S. Mission Rd.
11/12/15	Susan Cianciolo: Early Films - Screening and Conversation with Susan Cianciolo an Aaron Rose, Moderated by Sophie von Olfers
11/8/15	Book Launch and Reading of William Leavitt's "Alligator Maze Orchid" (15, publishe Ooga Booga)
11/5/15	Screening of Maggie Lee's film "Mommy" and a Performance by Brendan Fowler
11/1/15	Book Launch for Ian F. Svenonius' "Censorship Now!"
10/24/15	Performance of Robert Morris' "RADIF IV" and Discussion Between Robert Morris Rebecca Morris
10/17/15	Wynne Greenwood: Screening Selections from "TRACY + THE PLASTICS" - New Documentation
10/15/15	A Lecture by Hamza Walker "Rebecca Morris and the Revenge of P&D"
10/11/15	Unveiled: A Symposium on Gary Indiana with Kate Durbin, Bruce Hainley, Chris K Sylvere Lotringer and Michael Silverblatt
10/10/15	Ovahness 10: Tens Across the Board - Hosted by REACHLA
10/8/15	Gary Indiana opening reception and performance
10/2/15	Closing Party for Seth Bogart's exhibition "The Seth Bogart Show"
9/24/15	Lonnie Holley Live Performance organized in conjunction with "All The Instruments Agree" festival at the Hammer Museum
9/12/15	69 Spring/Summer 16 presentation
9/11/15	Opening Reception for Rebecca Morris' exhibition "Rose Cut"
9/3/15	Opening Reception of Seth Bogart's exhibition "The Seth Bogart Show"
8/2/15	Summer Screening Series: "The Michael Jordan of Mushrooms" and performance by Pics
8/1/15	SOME CLEANING: A Choreographic Service by Adam Linder (3)
7/30/15	Summer Screening Series: "No Friends With Attached Benefits Strings" - Presented b
7/26/15	Summer Screening Series: Pestoni's Picks: You Are My Everlovin Enema Bandit Hare
7/25/15	SOME CLEANING A Choreographic Service by Adam Linder (2)
7/23/15	Summer Screening Series: L.A. REBELLION Screening and Discussion
7/19/15	The Vanity East Opening Reception for "Masculini"
7/18/15	Summer Screening Series: FUTURE DAYS: Sci Fi movies, Krautrock, and Trip Hop / presented by SAFE CRACKERS
7/16/15	Launch party for Black Pages with new issues by Lisa Ruyter, Kate Levant, Rebecca M and Zin Taylor
7/16/15	Summer Screening Series: Geriatric Crimesolvers curated by Gary Cannone and Reb Morris
7/12/15	Book of Lies - Presented in Conjunction with The Box (2)
7/11/15	Book of Lies - Presented in Conjunction with The Box (1)
7/9/15	Summer Screening Series: Screening of L FOR LEISURE (14, 74 min) by Lev Kalman Whitney Horn followed by a discussion with the filmmakers and Sohrab Mohebbi
7/8/15	Summer Screening Series: MOOD SWING Day 2: PUNISHMENT PARK and SYMBIOPSYCHOTAXIPLASM presented by Stanya Kahn
7/7/15	Summer Screening Series: MOOD SWING Day 1: FUBAR and OUT OF THE BLUE presented by Stanya Kahn
6/28/15	SOME CLEANING A Choreographic Service by Adam Linder (1)
6/25/15	Summer Screening Series: Liliana Porter Video Works
6/20/15	Summer Screening Series: Stanya Kahn's DON'T GO BACK TO SLEEP (14, 74 min) followed by a discussion with Stanya Kahn and Frances Stark
6/19/15	Opening Reception of Shahryar Nashat's exhibition "Prosthetic Everyday"
6/18/15	Summer Screening Series: FUTURE DAYS: Sci Fi movies, Krautrock, and Trip Hop / presented by SAFE CRACKERS
6/13/15	Summer Screening Series: YOUR VACUUM SUCKS (15, 38 min) by Pieter Schoolwe and Alexandra Lerman with performance by Nate Young
6/7/15	Ooga Booga Warehouse Sale (2)
6/5/15	Ooga Booga Warehouse Sale (1)
5/29/15	Book launch for Gloria Sutton's "The Experience Machine"
5/29/15	Kids Day inspired by Kerry Tribe's exhibition "The Loste Note"

	On Discipline (LA) with Lex Brown, Jibade-Khalil Huffman, Dan Levenson, Sarah Mattes, and Carmen Winant
	Graham Lambkin performance as part of the opening reception for his exhibition "Marble on the Rot"
	Launch for Animal Shelter #4 and Mark Von Schlegell's "Sundogz" with a reading, discussion and a screening between Mark Von Schlegell and Chris Kraus
	Talking About Aphasia: A panel discussion organized in conjunction with Kerry Tribe's exhibition "The Loste Note"
	TATLO: A Meryenda Book Party presented by The Office of Culture and Design / Hardworking Goodlooking
	Openign Reception for Kerry Tribe's exhibition "The Loste Note"
	Screening and Discussion with Renée Green co-presented with the MAK Center
	A Night of Performance featuring Kerry Tribe "Critical Mass" & Ben Vida "Slipping Control"
	Opening reception for Katy Fischer and Ben Vida's exhibitions
	Charles Atlas Book Release and Conversation with Laurie Weeks and Screening
	Eric Wesley coloring event in conjunction with his exhibition "Some Work"
	Performance of Ben Vida's "Damaged Particulates" (3)
	Performance of Ben Vida's "Damaged Particulates" (2)
	Performance of Ben Vida's "Damaged Particulates" (1)
	Kath Bloom Performance and Record Release with Erin Durant
	Deborah Hay screening and discussion
	Burger Brunch and Book Party with Tamara Shopsin, Jason Fulford and Brooks Headley
	February 1: I.U.D. at Paramount Ranch presented by 356 Mission/Ooga Booga
	The Cats-in-Residence Social Hour
4	Opening Reception for The Cats-in-Residence Program
4	"She Said Boom" Screening and Performance by Sex Stains + DJ sets by Kate Mosher Hall, Seth Bogart, and Kevin Hegge
4	Kids Day inspired by the exhibition "Supports/Surfaces"
4	Maricón Collective presents: The Shhh (Alice Bag and Martin Sorrondeguy) Premier
	"Blondes in the Jungle" Screening and Discussion with Jay Chung and filmmaker Lev Kalman
	Sunday Sit: Mindfulness Meditation
	Reading with Jay Chung
	Pierluigi Billone's "1+1=1" performed by Samuel Dunscombe & Curt Miller
	Opening Reception for Jay Chung and Q Takeki Maeda's exhibition "Solutions to Compound Problems"
4	The Vanity East Opening Reception for Anna Helm and Lisa Lapinski's exhibitions "Uncle Xylophone"
4	Laura Owens: 12 Paintings Book Launch and Signing
4	Cookie Mueller in Film + presented by Bradford Nordeen of Dirty Looks
4	Supports / Surfaces Panel Discussion and opening reception
4	Sunday Sit: Mindfulness Meditation
4	Brooks Headley Fancy Desserts book launch and performance
4	Julien Ceccaldi Artist Talk and Zine Signing
	Mecca Vazie Andrews: Of Light and Dark Part III: The Matter of Compass
	Jesse Fleming and Lewis Pesacov: Meditations and Oscillations
4	The Fountain That Gushes and Gathers, by Shinzen Young and Jesse Fleming
4	Jonathan Horowitz "590 Dots" Completion Party with a performance by Black Dice
4	Oscar Tuazon: LIVE book launch + artist talk
4	Sunday Sit: Mindfulness Meditation
4	Ovahness 9: It's Your Time to Shine - Presented by REACHLA
4	The George Kuchar Reader - book launch and screening
4	Sunday Sit: Mindfulness Meditation
4	Changing of the Guard: Performance by Gracie De Vito
	Brian Calvin Book Launch / Discussion / Concert
	Sunday Sit: Mindfulness Meditation
	Sunday Sit: Mindfulness Meditation
	Jonathan Horowitz and Ali Subotnick in Conversation
	Book launch and Reading for "Robert Ashley: Yes, But Is It Edible?"
	Opening Reception for Jesse Fleming's exhibition "The Halftime Show"
	Thee Oh Sees and Jack Name in concert
	Cafe 356: Lunch by Jen Smith/Full Moon Pickles
	Sunday Sit: Mindfulness Meditation
	Oliver Payne's CHILL OUT Performance
	Sunday Sit: Mindfulness Meditation
	Hive Dwellers, Bouquet, and Dream Boys in concert
	NAAFI in Los Angeles
	Sunday Sit: Mindfulness Meditation
	Tehran vs. Tehrangeles: A Special Screening of MAXX
	Sunday Sit: Mindfulness Meditation
	Sunday Sit: Mindfulness Meditation
	Opening Reception for the exhibition "Another Cats Show" with performances by Odwalla88, Dean Spunt, and Bebe Whypz
	Hairy Who and the Chicago Imagists screening
	Sunday Sit: Mindfulness Meditation
	Alexis Taylor (Hot Chip) Special Solo Set with DJ set and visuals by Oliver Payne
	Sue Tompkins performance
	Sunday Sit: Mindfulness Meditation
	Cafe 356: Brunch prepared by Math Bass

6/28/14	Artist's Books and Cookies 3
6/22/14	Sunday Sit: Mindfulness Meditation
6/21/14	East of Borneo presents: Unforgetting LA #4 Wikipedia edit-a-thon
6/20/14	Screening of The Wooster Group's "Rumstick Road" with introduction by Shannon Ebner
6/11/14	Alex Katz exhibition walkthrough with Laura Owens and Kevin Salatino
6/8/14	Opening Reception of Trevor Shimizu's exhibition "Actor" at The Vanity East
6/4/14	Mark Verabioff Seminal tapes 1984 - 1992
5/31/14	Emily Sundblad - False True Love screening and performance
5/25/14	The Artist's House: From Workplace to Artwork by Kirsty Bell book launch and discussion
5/17/14	Ted Byrnes / Corey Fogel : Percussion Duo Live performance
5/11/14	Sunday Sit: Mindfulness Meditation led by Jesse Fleming
5/10/14	Desert Bus hosted by Oliver Payne
5/4/14	Michael Clark screening and performance at 356 Mission
4/27/14	Yuki Kimura: The Third Mirror at The Vanity East opening reception
4/26/14	Cadavere Telephone: X-TRA and Cadavere Quotidiano Launch Party
4/13/14	Opening Reception for Alex Katz exhibition
4/4/14	Advance Screening of Scott Reeder's "MOON DUST"
3/30/14	Book release for "Lee Lozano: Dropout Piece" by Sarah Lehrer-Graiwer
3/27/14	Oliver Payne talks about video games
3/14/14	Opening reception for Oliver Payne - Untitled (John Cage / Shadow of the Colossus)
2/26/14	Lucas Blalock book signing
2/20/14	William Leavitt record release & performance
2/9/14	Sunday Sit: Mindfulness Meditation led by Jesse Fleming
2/2/14	Breakfast at 356 - Pancakes by Shopsin's with a performance of Scott and Tyson Reeder's "Egg Fugue"
2/1/14	Paramount Ranch
1/30/14	LA Art Book Fair After Party - presented by Printed Matter, 356 Mission & Ooga Booga II
1/25/14	Scott Reeder exhibition opening
1/19/14	John Kaufman at The Vanity East exhibition opening
1/17/14	69 A/W 14 Collection Preview and Premiere
1/7/14	Club Lip Sync / Hosted by Ian Svenonius / With the California premiere of WHAT IS A GROUP?
12/14/13	Kids Day: Make a gift for mom and dad!
12/7/13	Under the Sign of [sic]: Sturtevant's Volte-Face book launch and discussion
11/30/13	Shimon Minamikawa at the Vanity East opening reception and discussion
11/23/13	The NSA Domestic Spying Program (2012) screening and discussion
11/19/13	N.A.A.F.I. + Friends in LA
11/17/13	Youth Art Workshop - Collage Drawing
11/9/13	neverhitsend opening + C.R.A.S.H. record release
11/3/13	Youth Art Workshop - T Shirt Factory
10/27/13	Anna Sew Hoy: Suppose and a Pair of Jeans book launch. Performance by L.A. Fog and panel discussion with Anna Sew Hoy, Trinie Dalton, Rita Gonzalez, Alex Klein, Mark Owens, Tanya Rubbak, and AL Steiner [Panel Discussion] [L.A. Fog]
10/20/13	K8 Hardy, How To: Untitled Runway Show book launch and freak out
10/20/13	Youth Art Workshop - COLLAGING with COLOR
10/16/13	Animal Shelter #3 launch and screening of Angel Diez AlvarezÕs film Le peine perdue de Jean Eustache (The Wasted Breath of Jean Eustache), 1997
10/6/13	Youth Art Workshop
9/27/13	Opening Reception for the exhibition "Sturtevant Finite / Infinite"
9/15/13	Cafe 356: Brunch by Math Bass
9/14/13	Joe Sola and Michael Webster present Shakey's in "Der Hintern in der Luft"
9/12/13	Barbara T. Smith, "Performance Audio 1969 - 1988" Record Launch & Screening
9/1/13	"Eric Palgon & Yshai Yudekovitz at the Vanity East" opening reception
8/25/13	Bidoun Magazine launch Los Angeles
8/24/13	"356 Sculptures" opening + performances
8/17/13	SASSAS Presents sound. at 356 S. Mission Rd. with Aaron Dilloway / Jason Lescalleet / John Wiese
8/15/13	De Porres Angelino East dinner
7/7/13	Ò12 Paintings by Laura OwensÓ closing party
7/2/13	A screening of 4 short films by Derek Boshier followed by an in conversation with Alex Kitnick
6/30/13	Artists Books and Cookies #2
6/7/13	"We Already See So Much" book launch with Euan MacDonald and Henri Lucas
6/1/13	Introduction to Basic Bookbinding lecture with Jennifer Phiffer
5/24/13	Dance performance by Flora Wiegmann with Alexa Wier
5/11/13	Northern New Mexico Dinner Party by Ken Ehrlich & Emily Joyce
4/27/13	Dinner cooked by Mina Stone
4/18/13	Rachel Kushner's "The Flamethrowers" dramatic reading & spaghetti dinner
4/14/13	Scrabble Sunday
4/5/13	"Mock-ups in Close-up: Architectural Models in Film 1919 to 2012" screening and discussion
3/16/13	Kids Day: Cookies and Painting
3/8/13	Clear Books by Asha Schechter release party + screening
3/3/13	Scrabble Sunday
2/22/13	Michael Webster: Nice Day For the Races
2/20/13	The New Dreamz (Rose Luardo and Andrew Jeffrey Wright) / Andre Hyland / Whitmer Thomas / Jessica Ciocci
2/17/13	Scrabble Sunday
1/20/13	"12 Paintings by Laura Owens & Ooga Booga #2" Grand Opening

I am organizing a series of karaoke events at my studio in the coming months. With the band
Pavement as a starting point, I invite you to select a song (or series of songs) that would not
normally be found in a standard karaoke songbook, and that you would want to sing Karaoke.

I am hoping to start with a small event of 10-20 people and then build it up over time, culminati
in a larger and more public event in 2013. Also, if you want to submit some extra songs that yo
are not sure you would sing, but that that you think would be easy for others to sing, please feel
free... Once you let me know which song(s), we'll find a high quality mp3, lower the vocal track
and sync the lyrics in a video. I am also hoping that you might want to submit a video or raw
footage th   too attache
to as word

Let me kr

thanks!!
Laura

Foreground: Karaoke video created for Pavement Karaoke with "Gold Soundz" by Pavement, 2013
Background: Email to friends, 2012

PAVEMENT KARAOKE

270 videos • 16 hours, 22 minutes   Edit Playlist

Shuffle All ⤨   •••

ABBA - Day Before You Came 🖵	5:46
ADAMS, RYAN - W|	3:41
THE AISLERS SET	2:50
ARIEL PINK - Symp|	4:41
ARMATRADING, JC|	3:23
ARMSTRONG, LOU|	2:22
AVENGERS - Ameri|	2:13
AZAELIA BANKS -	2:49
AZTEC CAMERA - We Could Send Letters 🖵	5:50
B-52's - 52 Girls 🖵	3:37
THE BAND - I Shall|	3:15
THE BAND- When		4:14
BARRETT, SYD - C|	3:25
BARRETT, SYD - W|	2:57
BAUHAUS -All We		3:55
BEACH BOYS - H.E|	2:36
BEACH BOYS - Hang Onto Your Ego 🖵	2:46
BEACH BOYS- Cabin Essence 🖵	3:33
BEAT HAPPENING - Our Secret 🖵	2:53
BEATLES - Happiness Is A Warm Gun 🖵	2:54

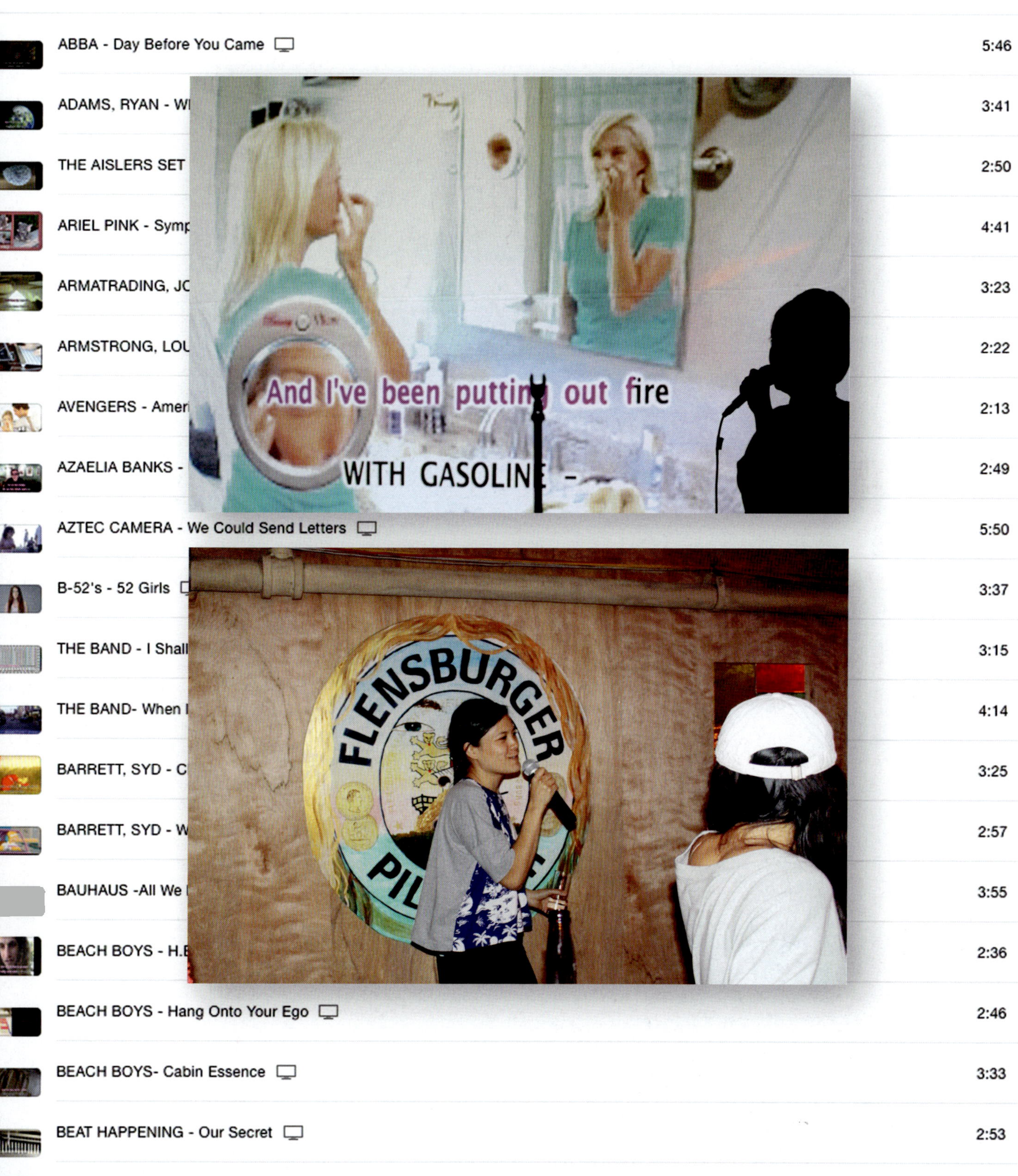

Foreground: Karaoke video created for Pavement Karaoke with "Gold Soundz" by Pavement, 2013; Wendy Yao performing at Pavement Karaoke, 356 S. Mission Rd., Los Angeles, 2013
Background: Playlist for Pavement Karaoke, 356 S. Mission Rd., Los Angeles, 2012–15

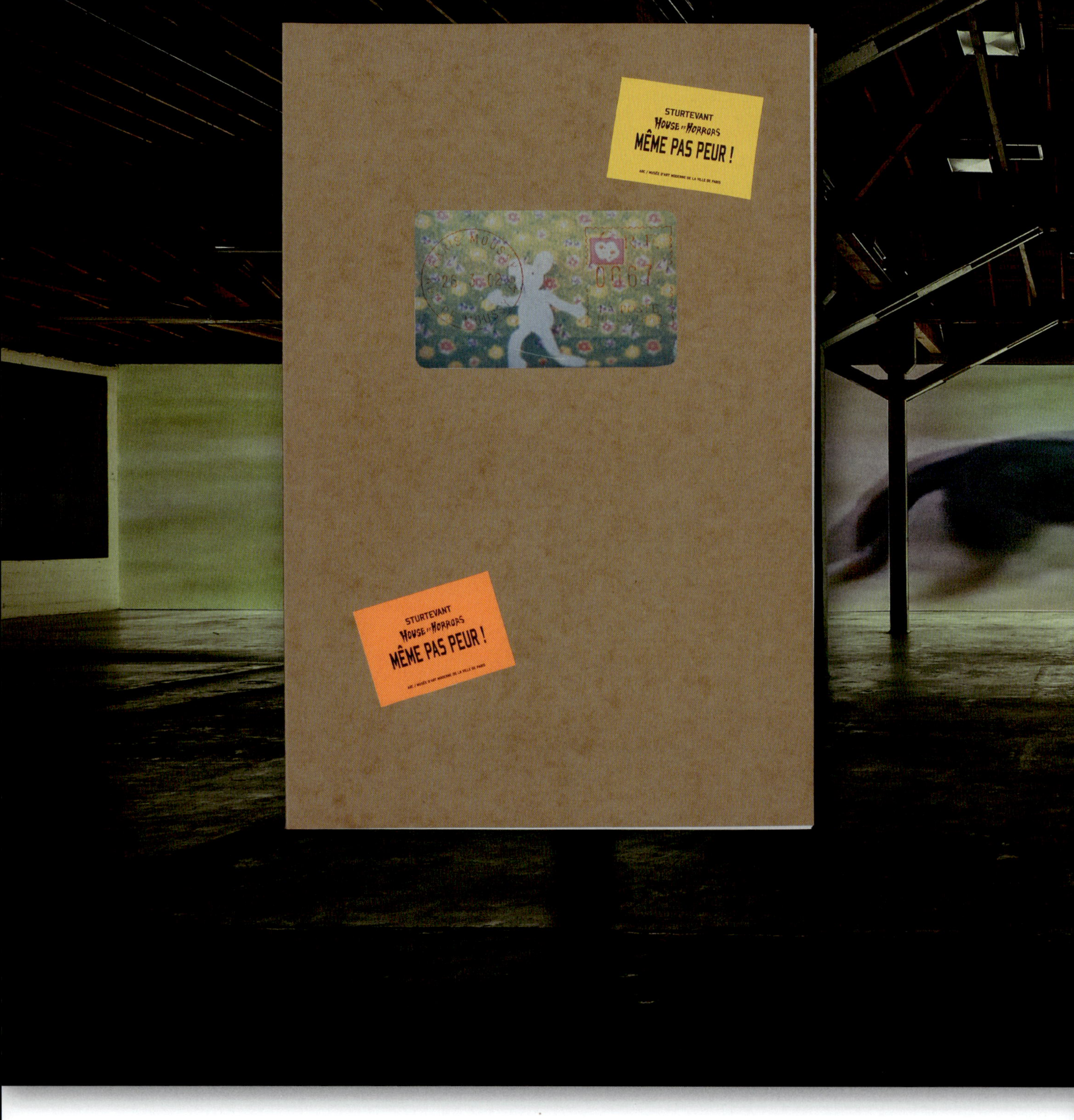

Foreground: Bruce Hainley, *Sturtevant: Selected Ephemera*, Ooga Booga and 356 S. Mission Rd., Los Angeles, 2013
Background: Installation view, *Sturtevant: Finite/Infinite*, 356 S. Mission Rd., Los Angeles, 2013, with Sturtevant, *Finite Infinite*, 2010, single-channel video projection, 0:09 min.

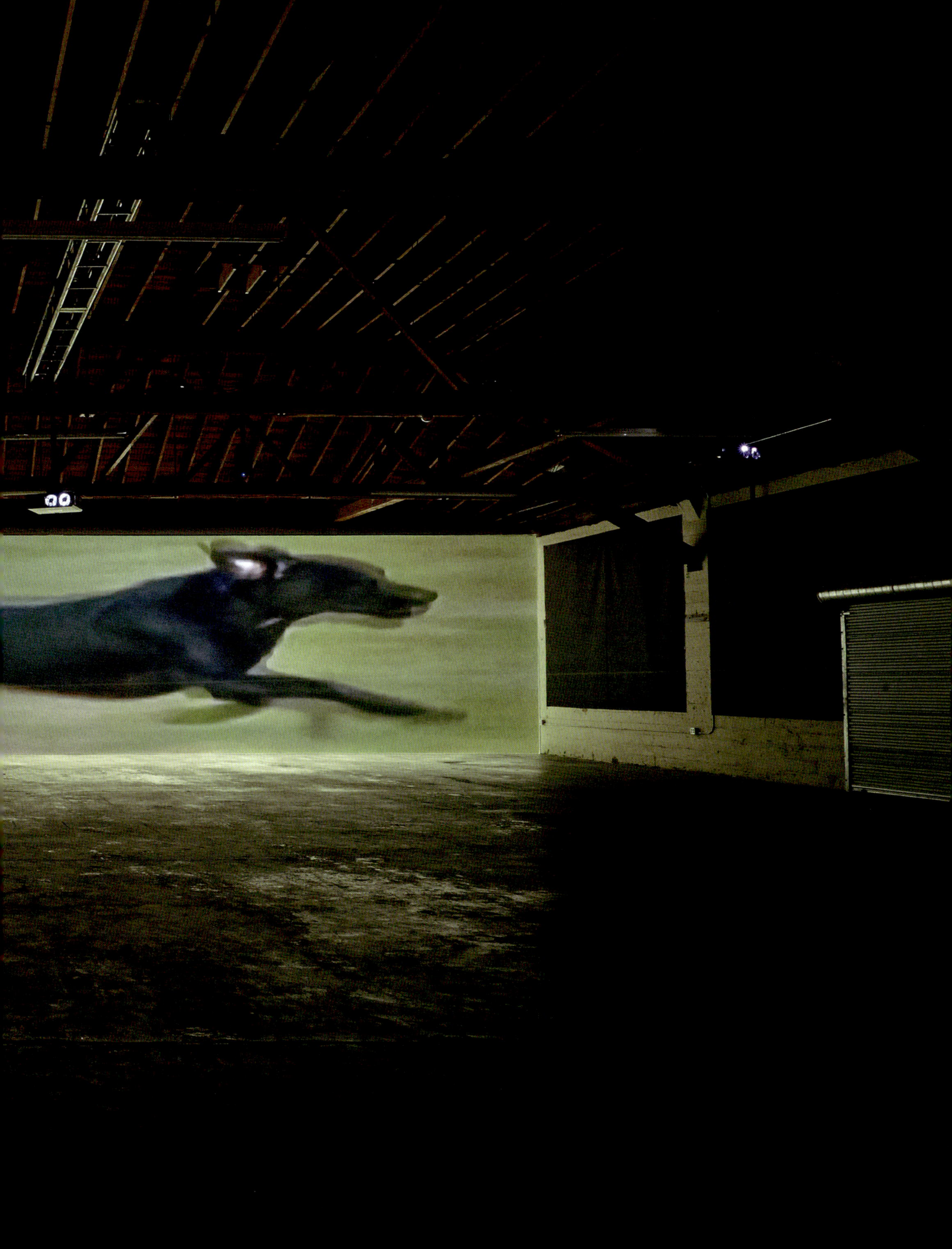

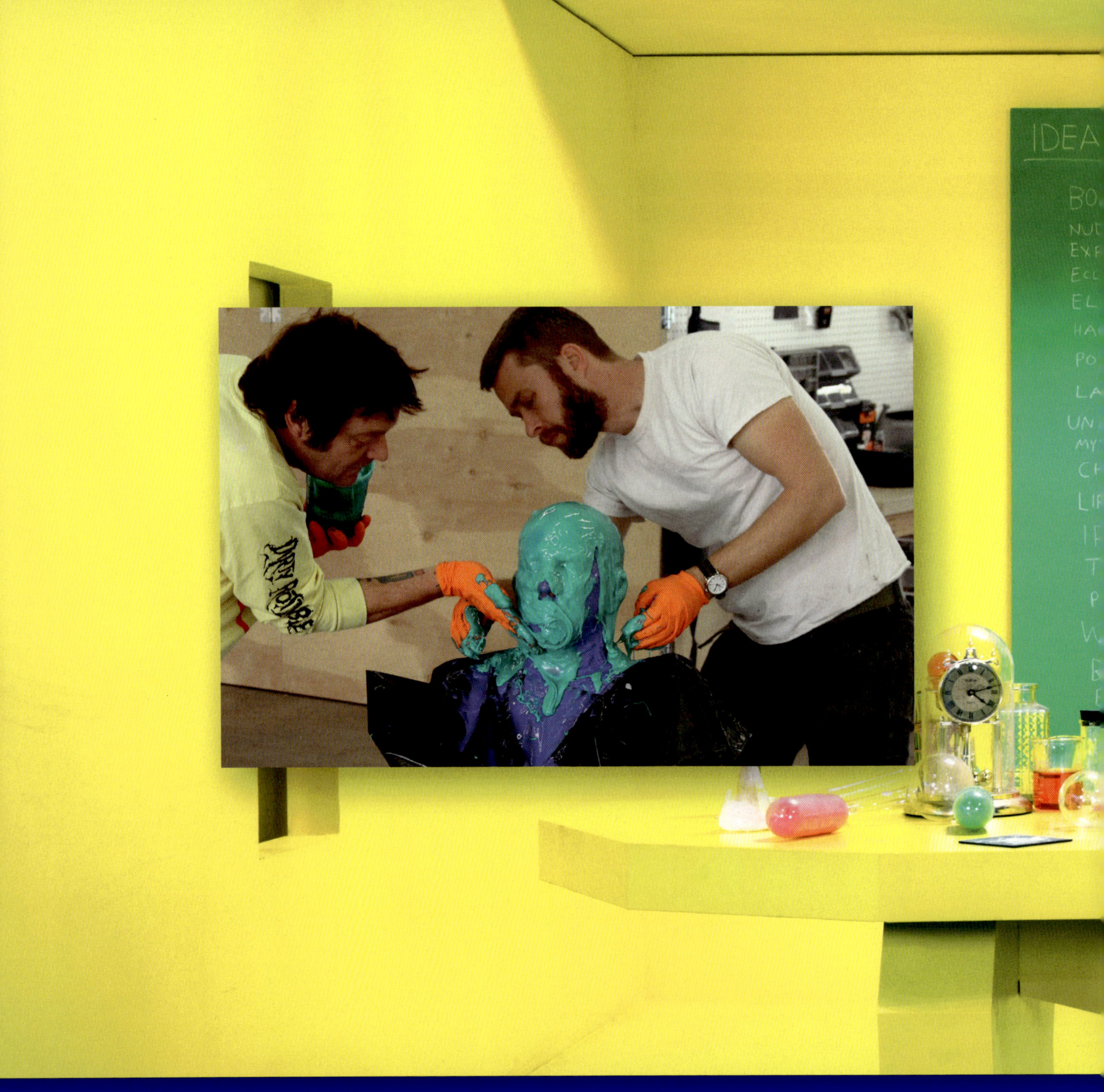

Michael Hayden: There's a scene in Scott Reeder's movie *Moon Dust* where his head explodes. We made a silicone mold of his face so that we could cast it and put explosives inside it. We did it in Laura's studio, where he was making paintings for his show at 356 while the film was being produced in the gallery space. He had a crew making props and costumes, but Laura's studio got drawn into it, and he came up here to make all the paintings. There was this cross-pollination between the film practice and the painting practice, and Laura was around and giving input most of the time that he was working. The other guy in the photo is an assistant at Paul McCarthy's studio who came in to help. He had a lot of experience making molds from live people. I had done it before but never from a live person. It's a very strange experience because you're basically giving someone a face massage. It's very intimate. I did not know Scott well at that point and I was running a brush along his eyes and nose and everything. You have to cover the entire face with a very smooth coat of silicone, without any bubbles. It was probably more strange for him. We made the molds in the studio and poured silicone of a few different thicknesses and colors into them. One of the makeup people for the movie helped paint the facial features on it and they made a wig for it before we rigged it and blew it up.

Foreground: Production photographs for Scott Reeder, *Moon Dust*, 2013. Clockwise from top left: Craig McIntyre, Scott Reeder, and
Michael Henry Hayden; Ian Svenonius, Tyson Reeder, and Scott Reeder; Michael Webster and Ross Caliendo
532 Background: Detail of *Moon Dust*, 2013

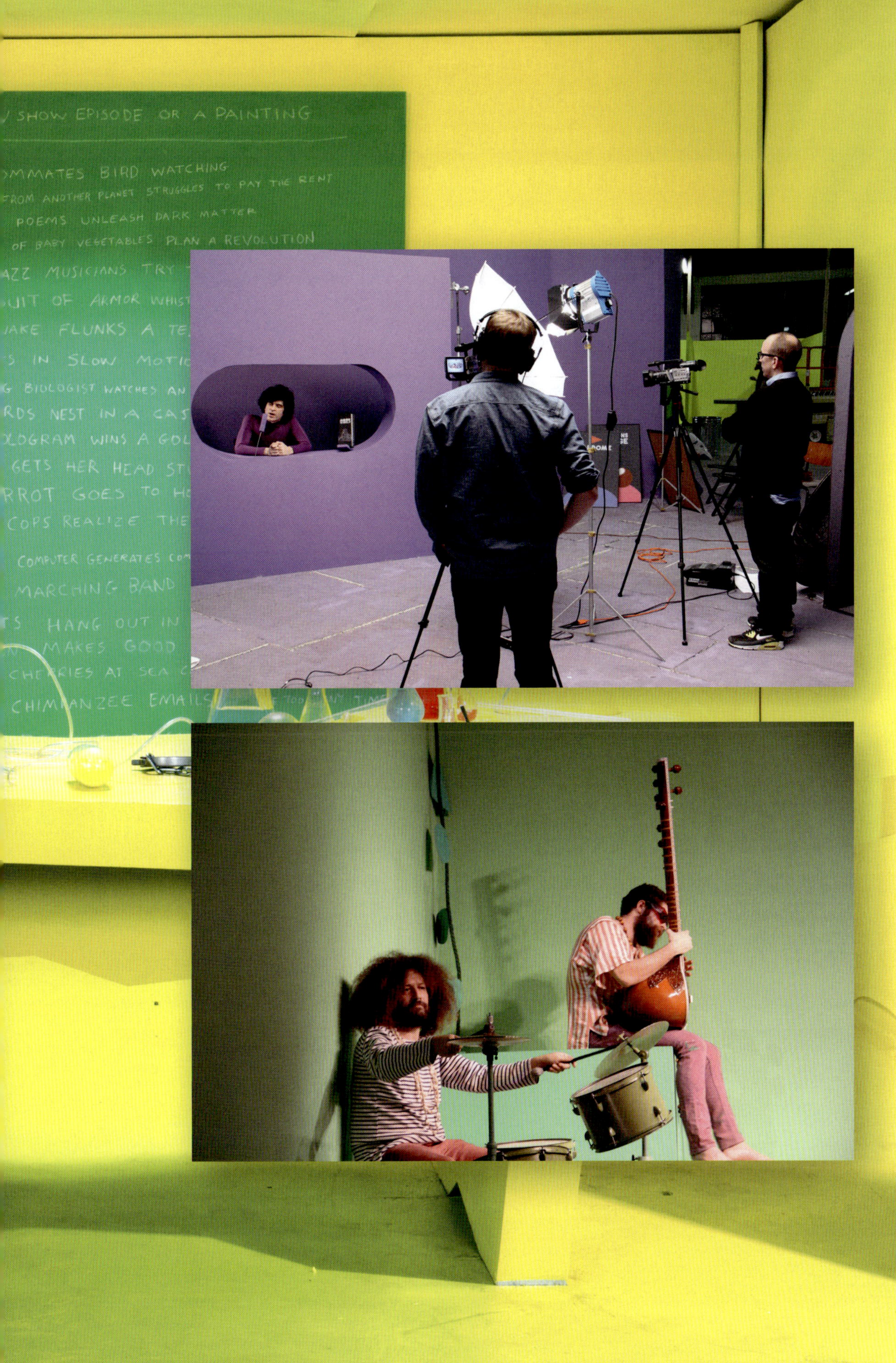

SHOW EPISODE OR A PAINTING
MMATES BIRD WATCHING
FROM ANOTHER PLANET STRUGGLES TO PAY THE RENT
POEMS UNLEASH DARK MATTER
OF BABY VEGETABLES PLAN A REVOLUTION
AZZ MUSICIANS TRY
UIT OF ARMOR WHIST
AKE FLUNKS A TE
S IN SLOW MOTIO
BIOLOGIST WATCHES AN
RDS NEST IN A CAS
LOGRAM WINS A GOL
GETS HER HEAD ST
RROT GOES TO HO
COPS REALIZE THE
COMPUTER GENERATES COM
MARCHING BAND
S HANG OUT IN
MAKES GOOD
CHERRIES AT SEA
CHIMPANZEE EMAILS

Rachel Kushner: "The Artist and Her Families" is the phrase that comes to mind when I think of Laura and 356, after Susanne Kippenberger's book about her brother, Martin Kippenberger, and the way he energized Cologne in the 1980s. An environment of makers and making and a continual pushing into every genre and domain was an unquestioned and unfettered drive for that legendary German artist. Maybe LA is Laura's Cologne, and its her 1980s now. She is constantly thinking about the city, other artists, community, and multiple forms of electric, inspired fun. And like Kippenberger, she can dance.

The idea of having a theatrical reading of a scene from my novel *The Flamethrowers* at 356 Mission was all Laura's idea. The scene takes place in the loft of two older and rather depressed artists, Stanley and Gloria Kastle. The loft I was thinking of was Rothko's old place on the Bowery, which was later occupied by the AbEx painter Michael Goldberg, who would tell me stories about punching people out in the navy. Having that reading of a scene that takes place on the Bowery, but in an old manufacturing warehouse in LA, was exactly right. Laura went into producer mode to make it happen. She was a visionary with very specific ideas for the casting, including Karen Adelman playing the unnamed narrator. Laura somehow knew that Karen would doctor the dialogue and that she'd telegraph exactly the right young-female-artist energy, and she did. Richard Prince considered playing his own alter ego, John Dogg, but could not make it. Alex Israel was John Dogg with full Warholian gusto, to pose a real oxymoron. He played it flat and affectless, in a black turtleneck and sunglasses. John Michael Higgins, who costarred in *Best in Show*, was Stanley. The actors sat at a long table surrounded by the audience. They ate spaghetti and drank wine as they performed. Afterward, spaghetti and red wine were served to everyone who came. I think there was enough food cooked for three hundred people.

    Rachel Kushner is a novelist who lives in Los Angeles.

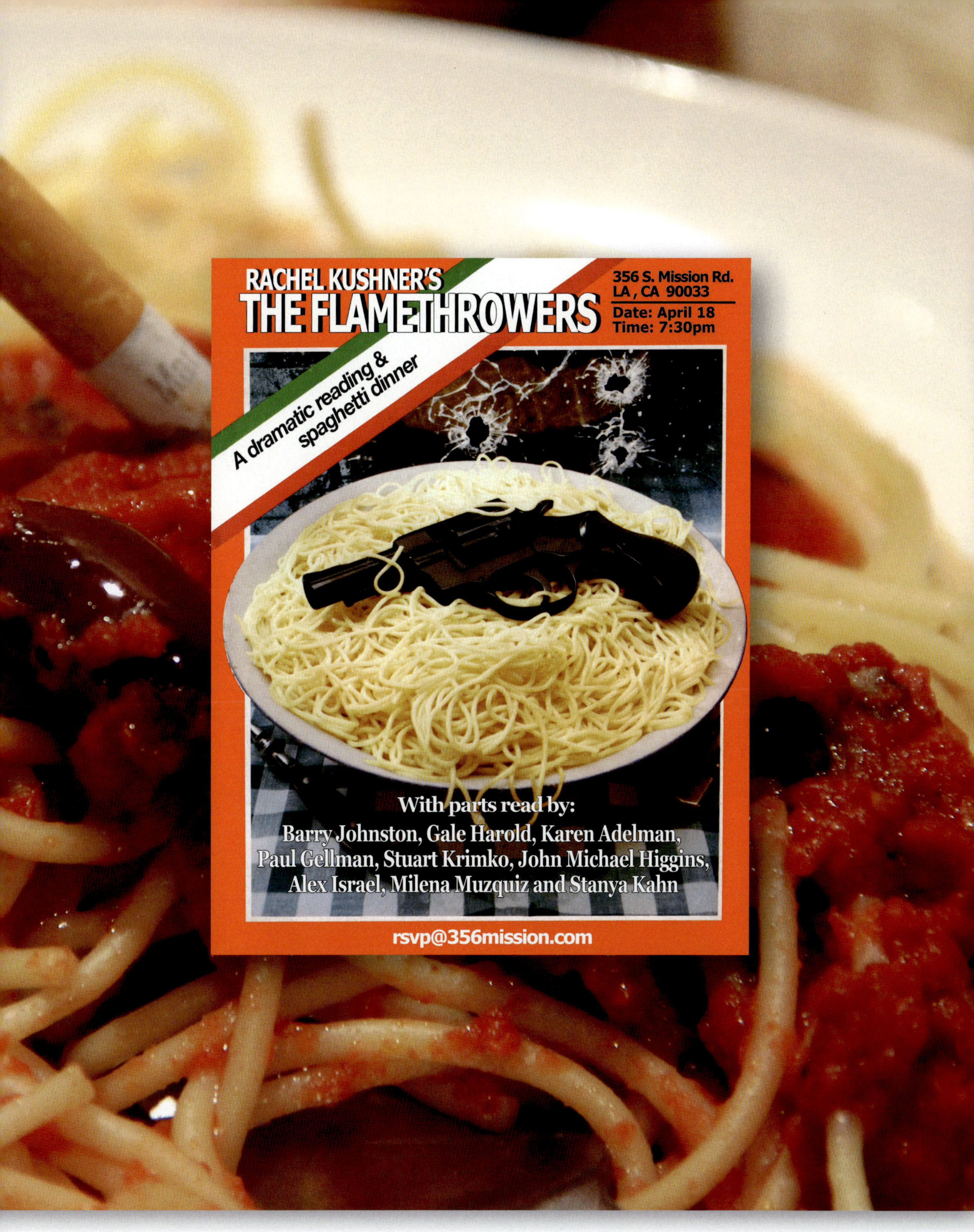

Foreground: Invitation, 356 S. Mission Rd., Los Angeles, 2013
Background: Event photograph, 356 S. Mission Rd., Los Angeles, 2013

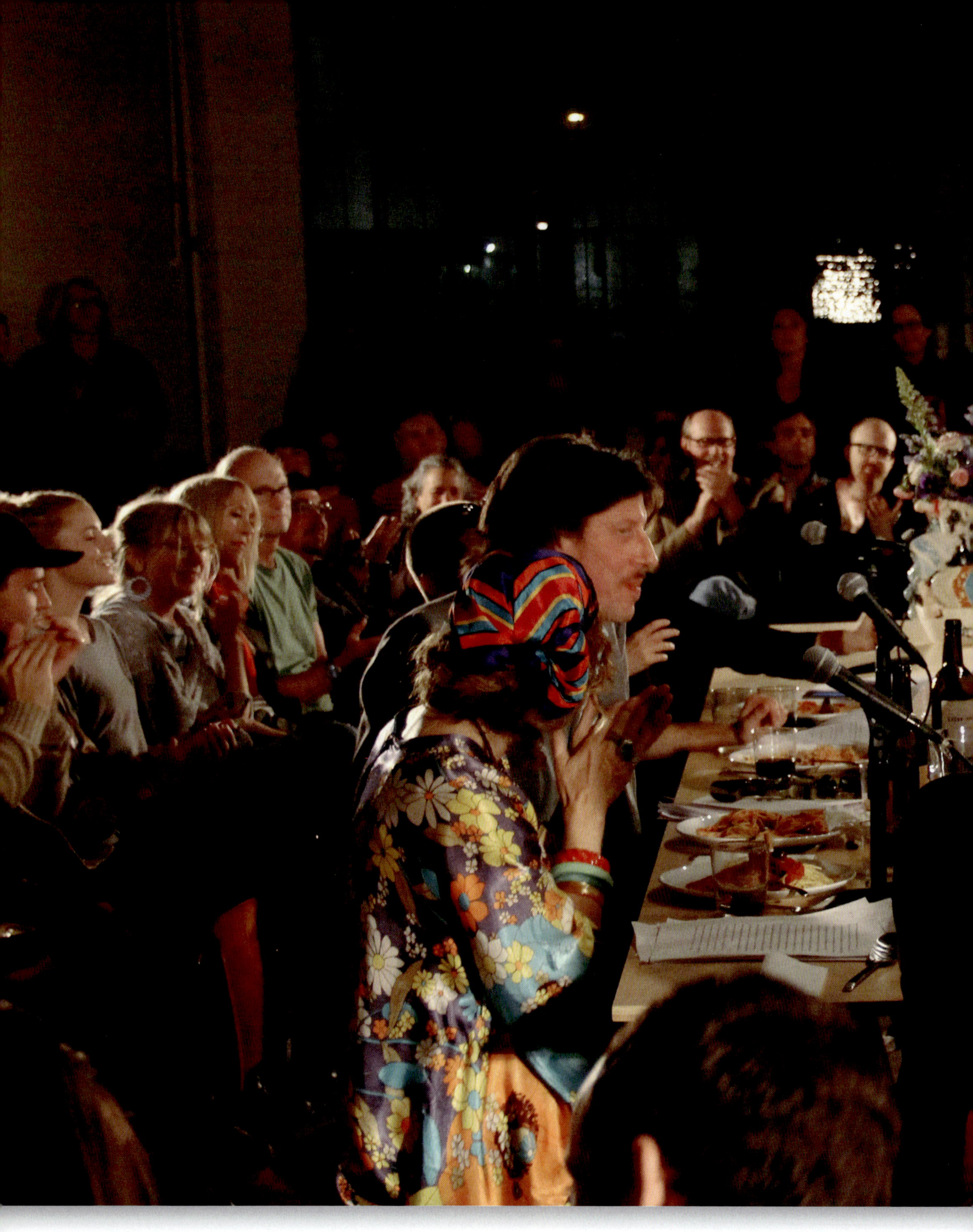

Rachel Kushner (standing) with performers (seated, clockwise from left) Stanya Kahn, Paul Gellman, Alex Israel, Milena Muzquiz, Karen Adelman, Gale Herold, John Michael Higgins, and (not visible) Barry Johnston, Stuart Krimko, 356 S. Mission Rd., Los Angeles, 2013

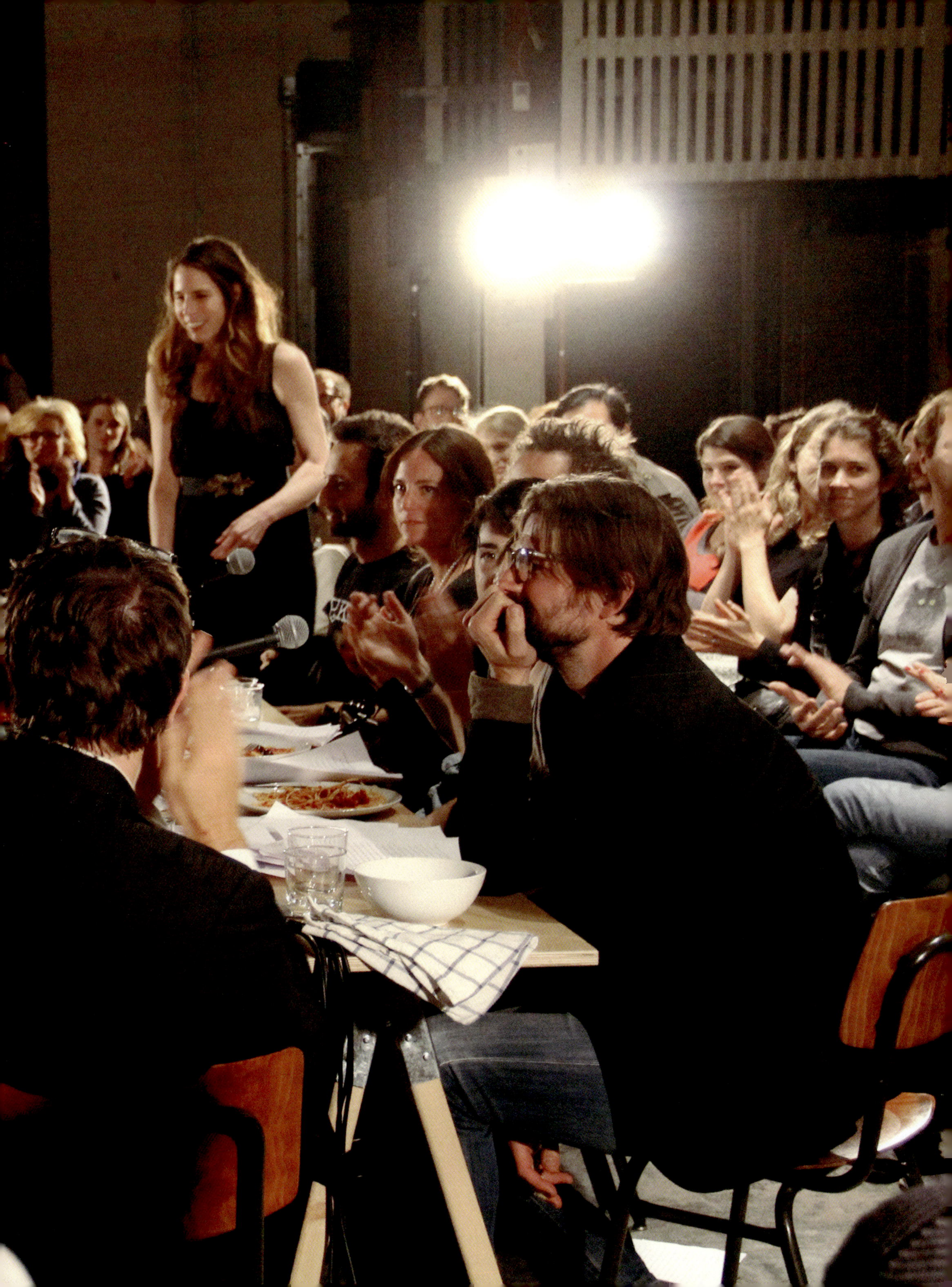

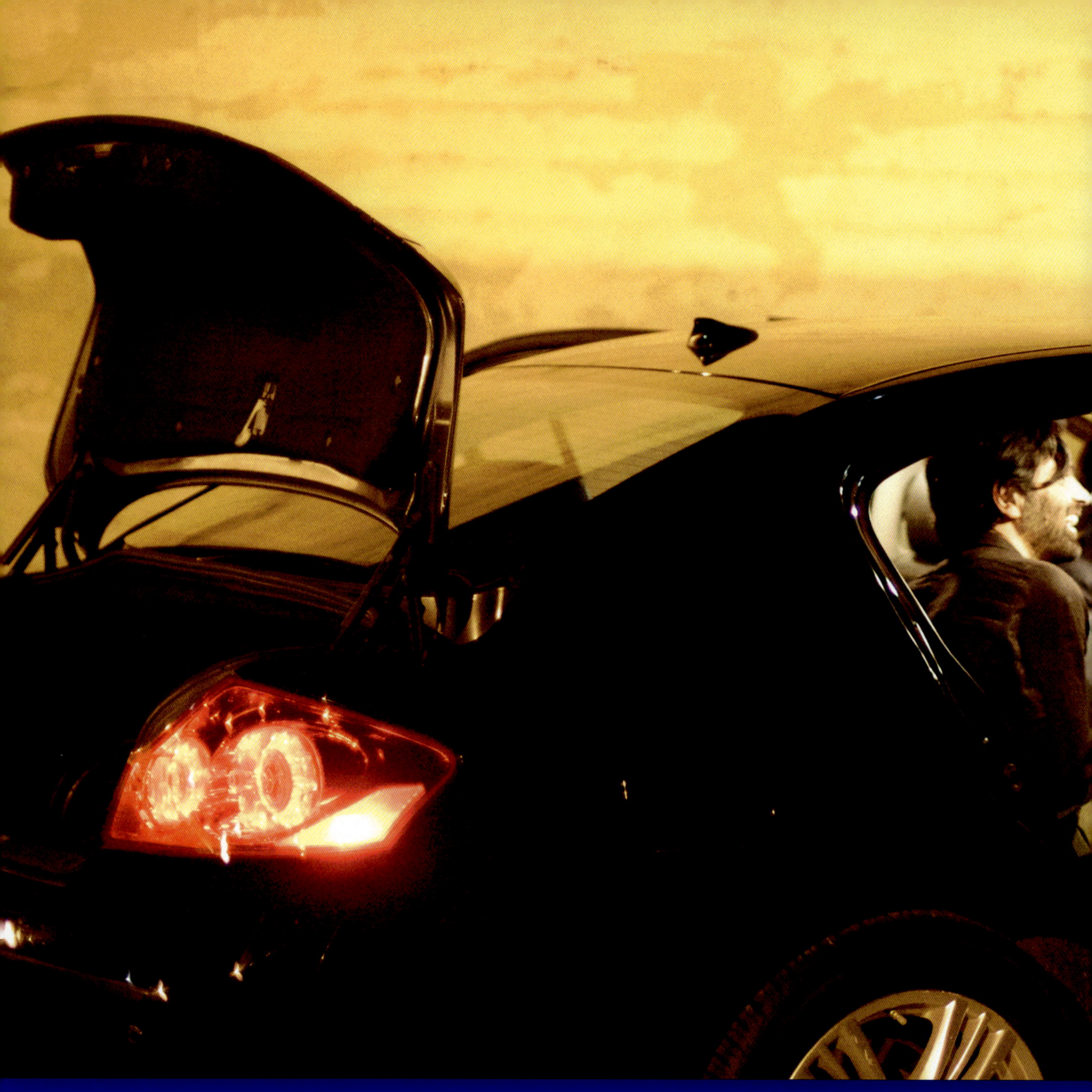

Alex Tuttle: Eric's idea was he wanted a white 2008 Infiniti to be clear coated. There were no restrictions on whether it was rented, borrowed, etc., it was just going to be "invisibly" adjusted. First, I realized that it's basically impossible to rent the specific car he was looking for. I finally found a place that had a black Infiniti a few years off and Eric agreed to this. Then I began talking to mechanics. Most told me, "You have to sand the car to clear coat it." So I went back to Eric and he kept repeating, "Just get the car clear coated, Alex. You can do this." There was a dealership in Irvine that told me they would do it without sanding, but when the mechanic saw it was a rental, he said no. I finally found a mechanic in the Valley who would do it. So I called the rental place and said we were using the car in a photo shoot, and I had to get it detailed and it was going to be returned much shinier but any scratches or dents would be more pronounced. They finally said okay. Eric was very happy even though he knew everything didn't go as planned. At the opening we put a rented subwoofer in the trunk and Oliver Payne made a New Order–centric mix to play. Throughout the night Eric kept asking me what actually happened and I just kept telling him I'd had the car clear coated.

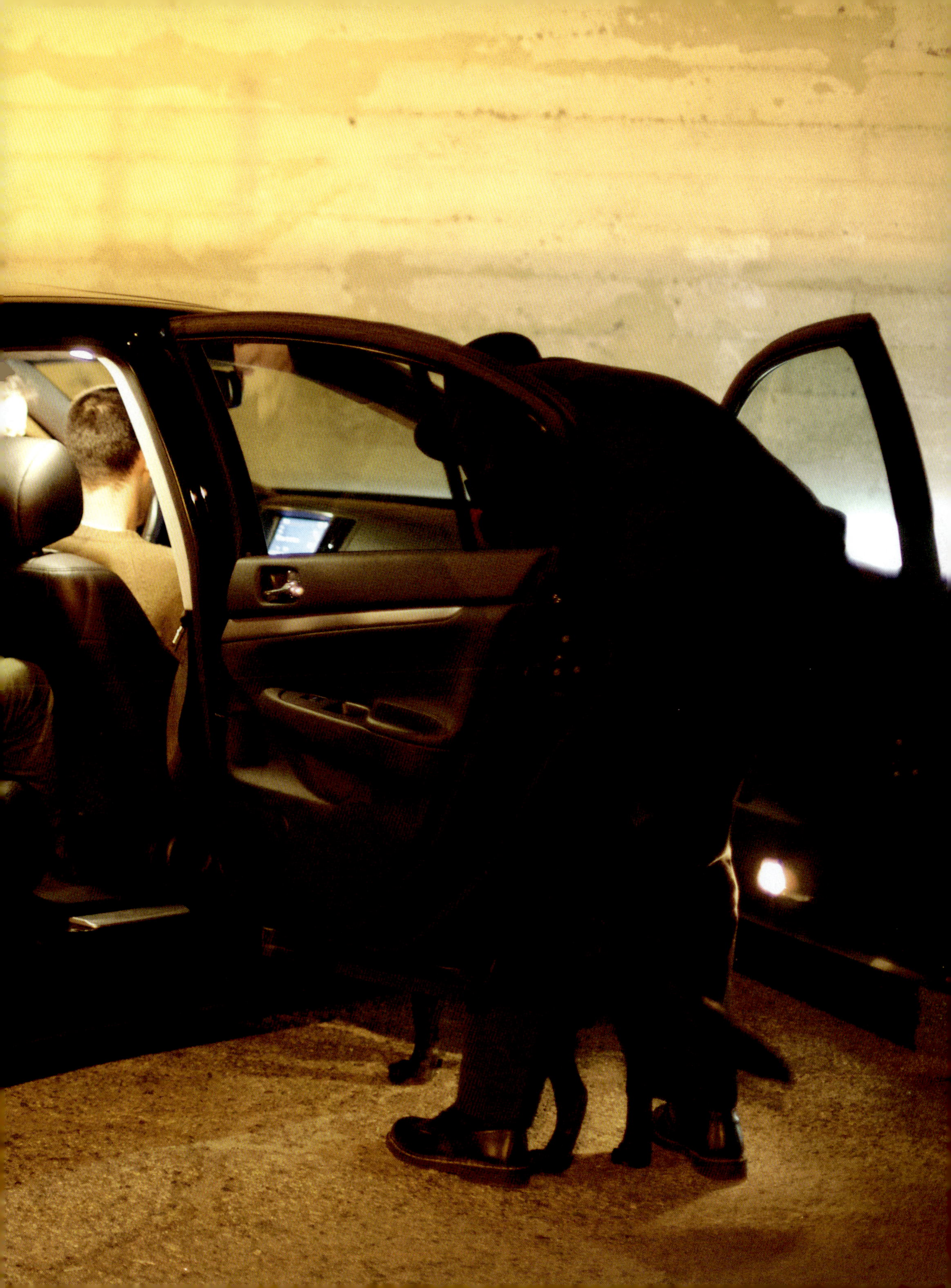

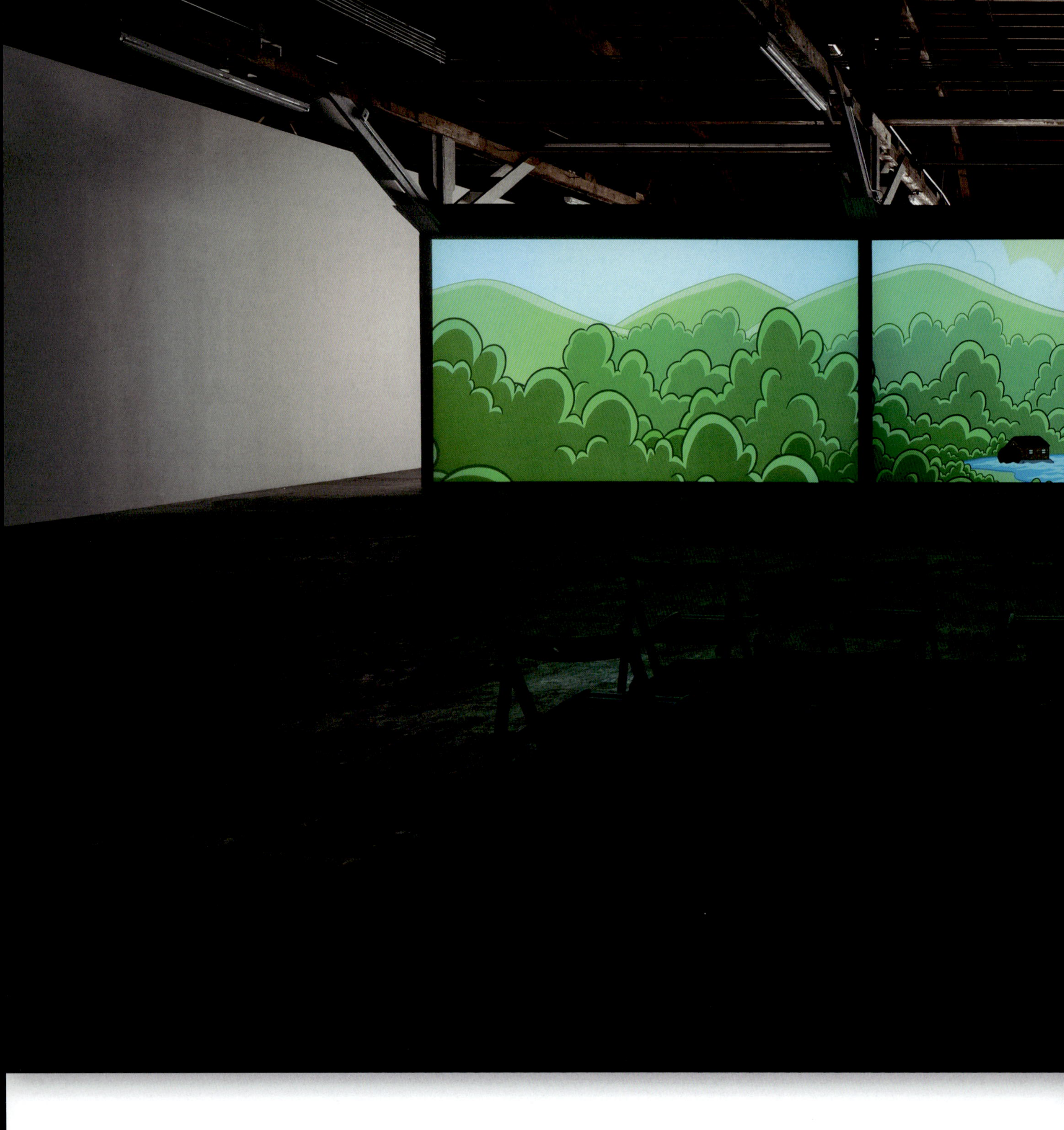

Installation view, *Kerry Tribe: The Loste Note*, 356 S. Mission Rd., Los Angeles, 2015, with Kerry Tribe, *The Aphasia Poetry Club*, 2015, three-channel video projection with sound, 28:27 min.

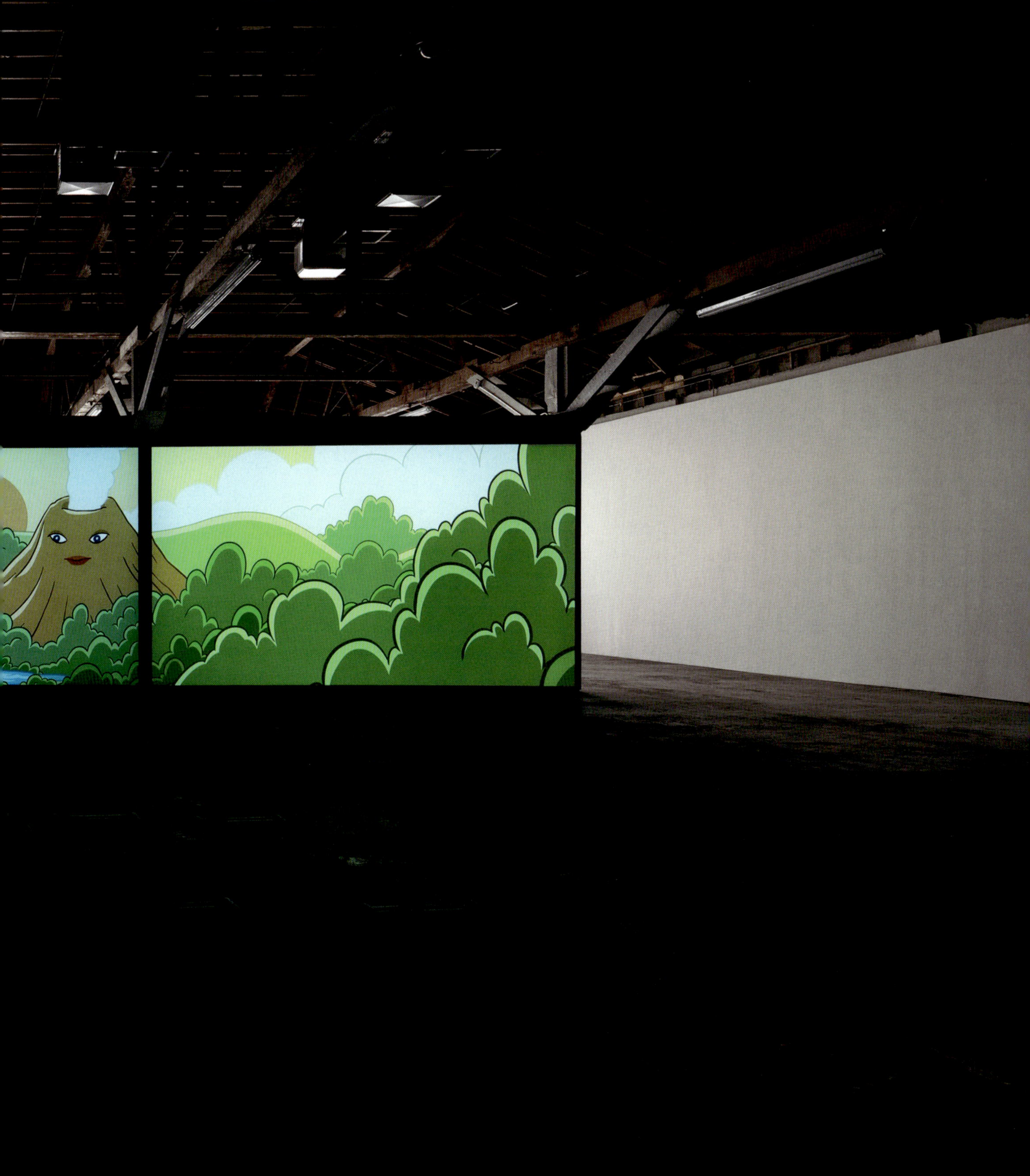

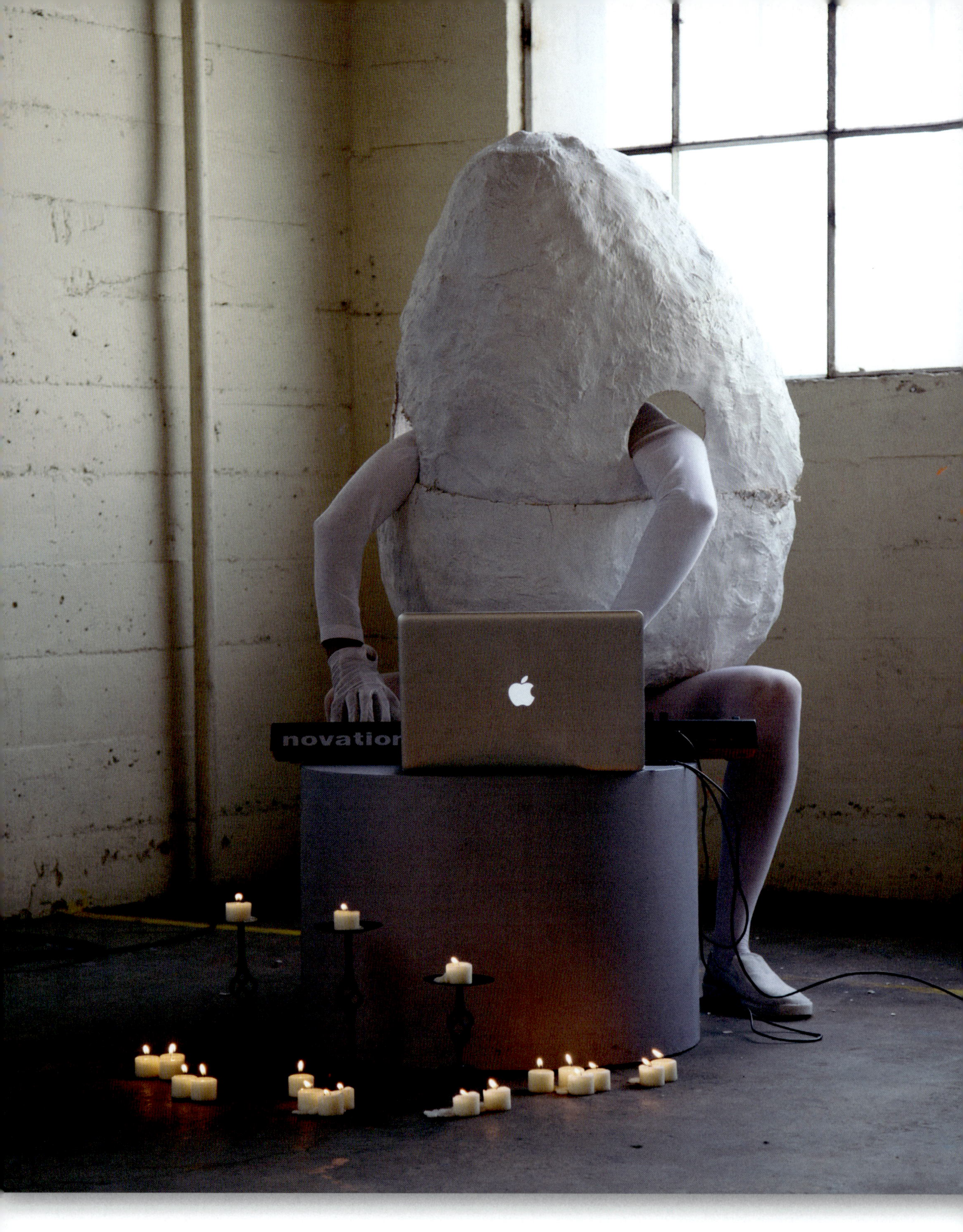

 Scott Reeder and Tyson Reeder, *Egg Fugue*, 356 S. Mission Rd., Los Angeles, 2014

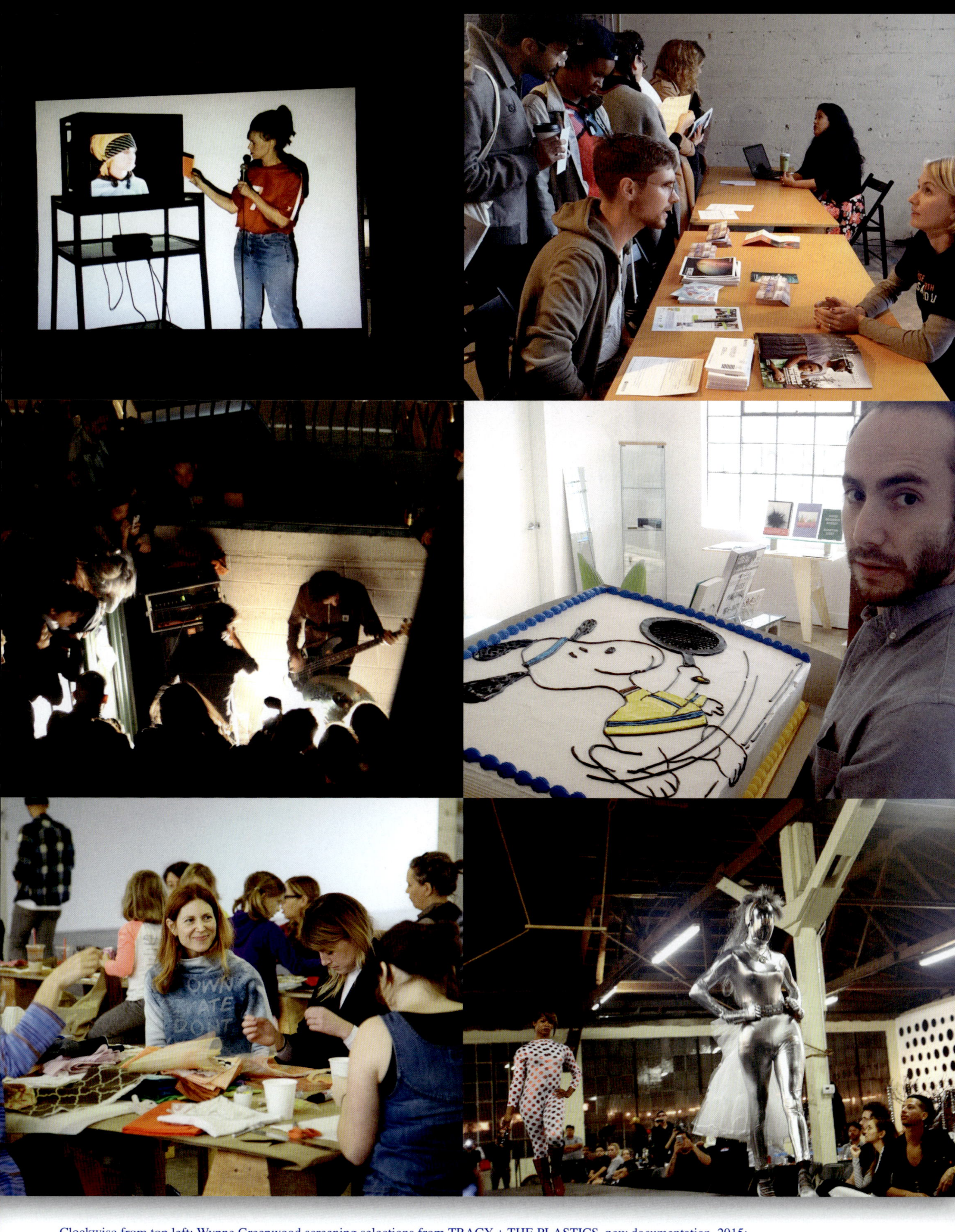

Clockwise from top left: Wynne Greenwood screening selections from TRACY + THE PLASTICS, new documentation, 2015; What's Now: an opportunity to meet with activists, nonprofits and community groups and mobilize our dismay, 2016; Asha Schechter, opening reception, *Twelve Paintings*, 2013; Ovahness Ball 10, 2015; RUN home quilting workshop: small quilts with Susan Cianciolo and Kiva Motnyk, 2016; C.R.A.S.H. album release party, 2013, 356 S. Mission Rd., Los Angeles

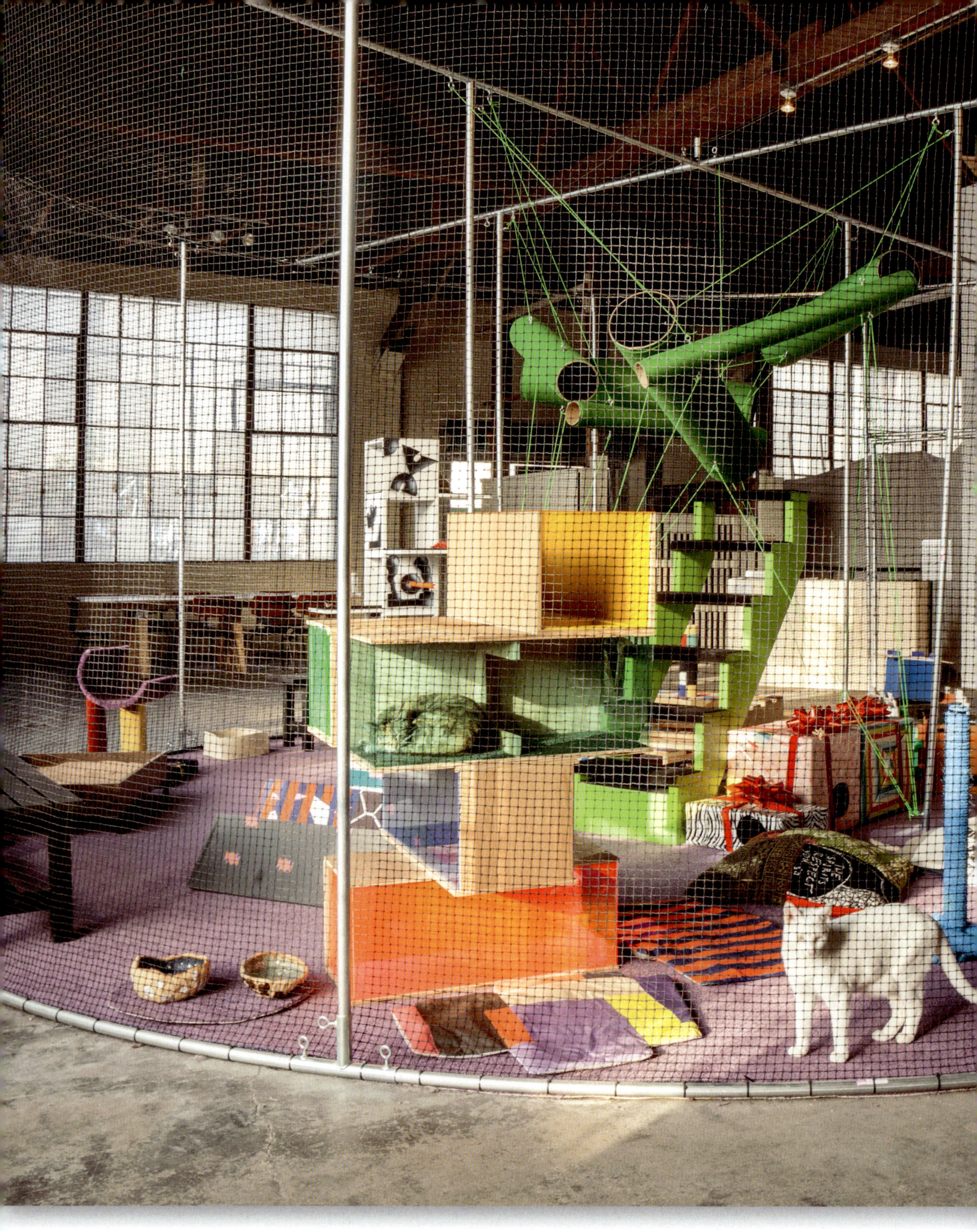

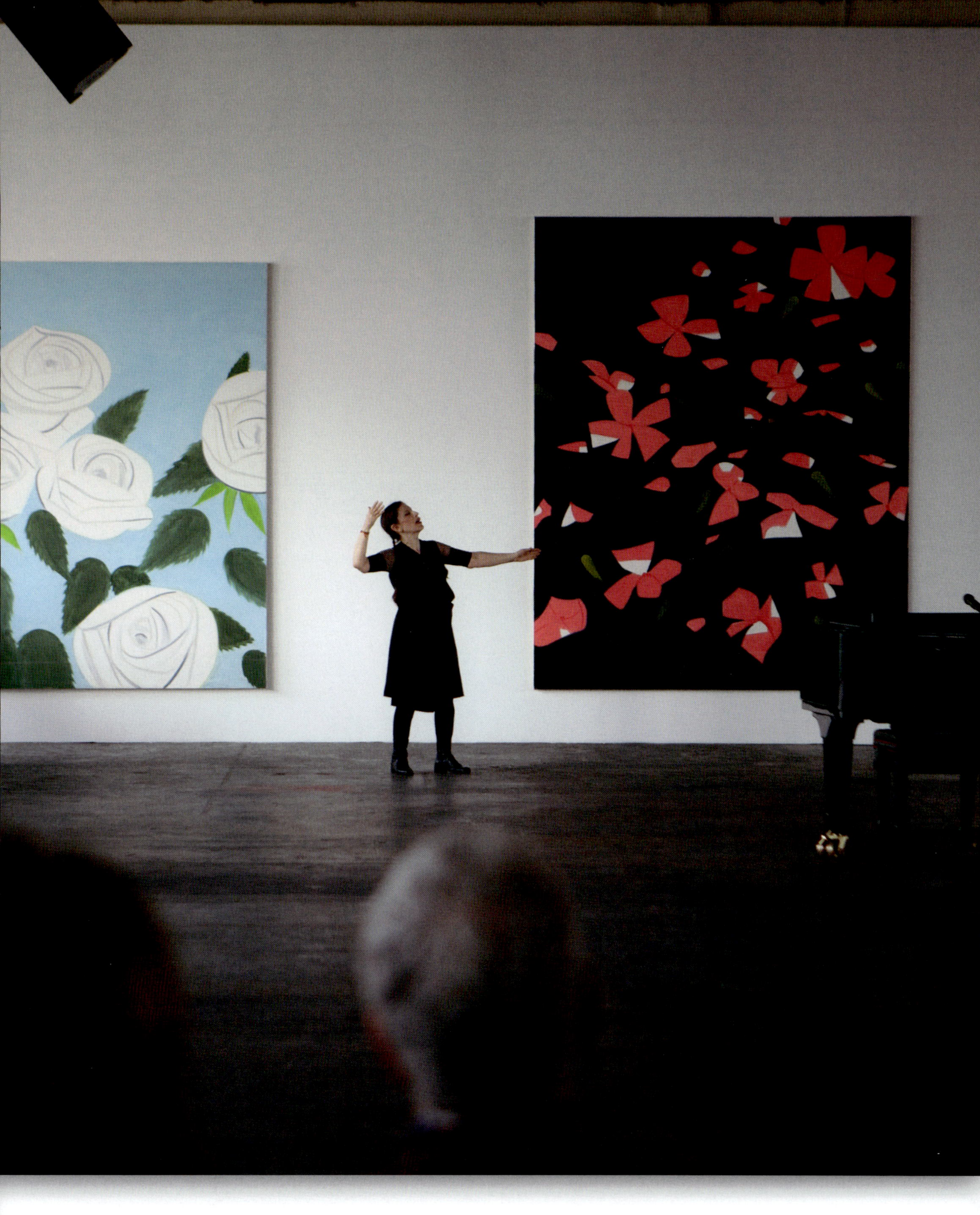

Meredith Monk with Alex Katz, *White Roses 9*, 2012, oil on linen, 108 × 216 in. (274.3 × 548.6 cm), and Alex Katz, *White Impatiens 4*, 2012, oil on linen, 120 × 96 in. (304.8 × 243.8 cm), 356 S. Mission Rd., Los Angeles, 2014

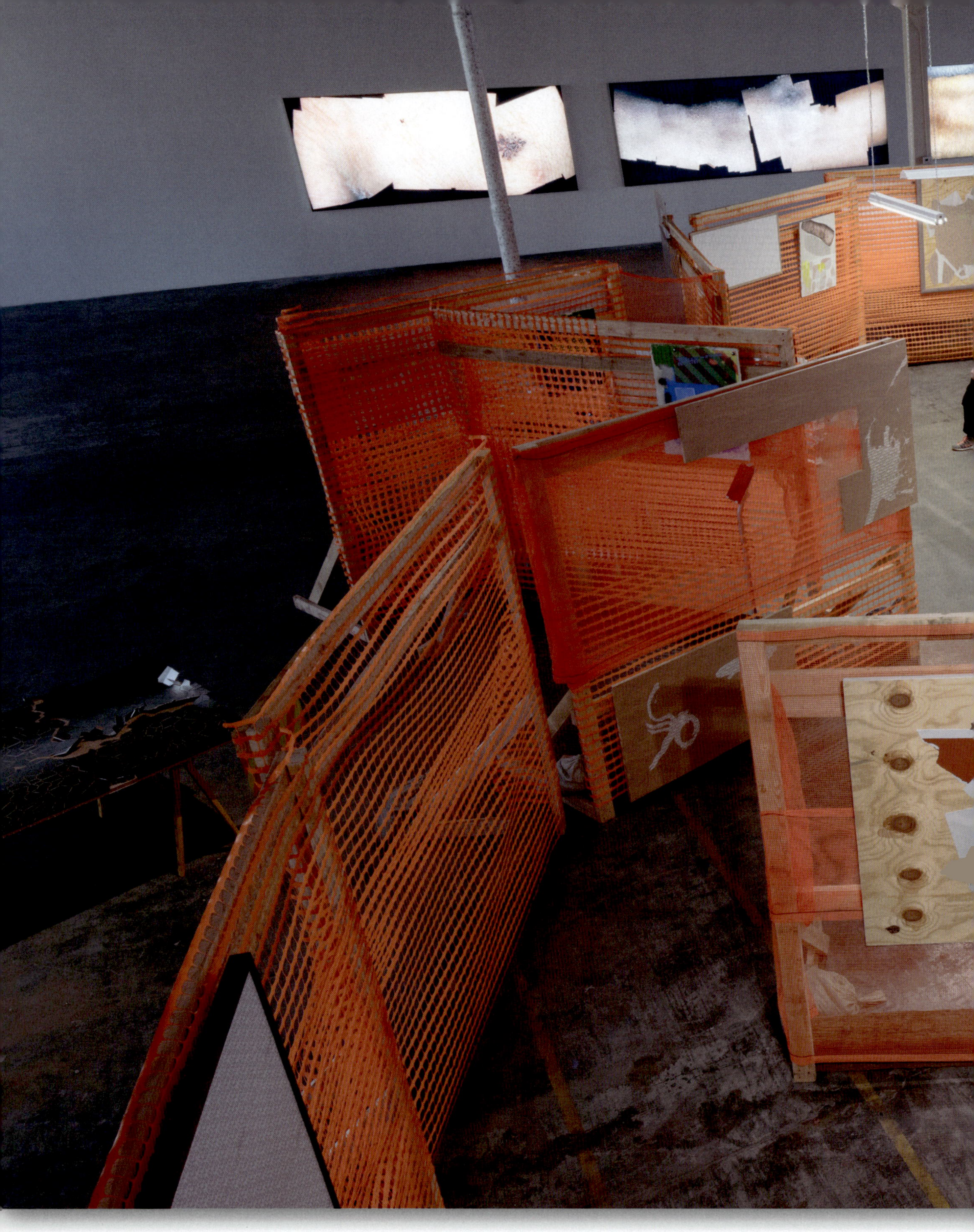

 Installation view, *Seth Price: Wrok Fmaily Freidns*, 356 S. Mission Rd., Los Angeles, 2016, with Cindy Conrad and Alix Ross

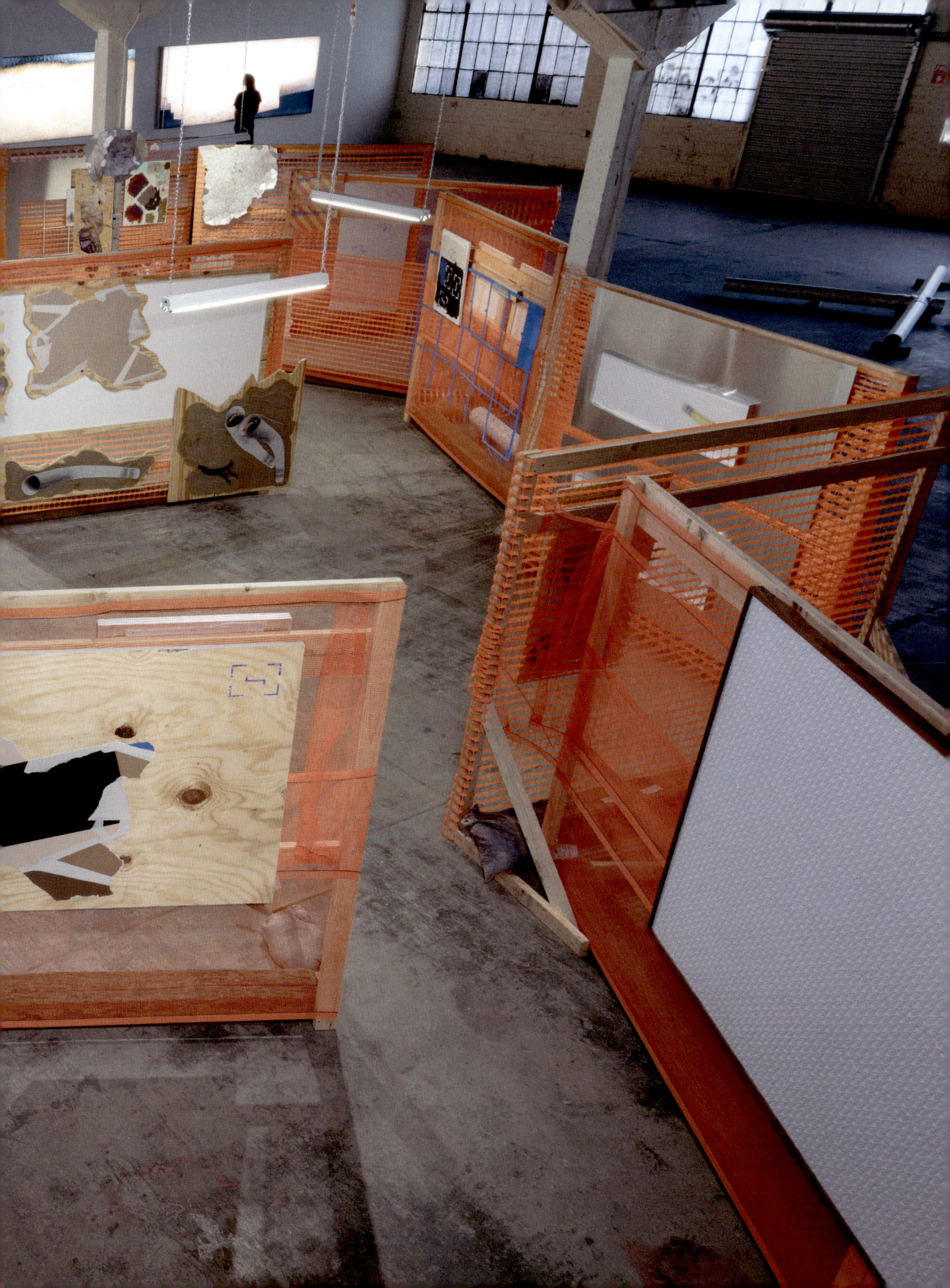

EXCERPT FROM *FUCK SETH PRICE*
SETH PRICE

He drifted through a thick and obscure world, observant but incapable of action. It took him a while to understand that he wasn't dreaming, but moving through the real world and actual life, only it was no longer his life, because his body and all of its doings were no longer under his control. He found himself carrying out strange and horrible acts: murder and abduction, most disturbingly, but also other furtive activities that he couldn't make sense of. Through all of this he was able only to watch, resigned to imprisonment in his physical machinery, his mind turning over slowly like an idle hard disk. This certainly afforded him plenty of time to figure out exactly where things had gone wrong, and he came to blame his obsession with "keeping up"—with technology, with the young, with the culture—a pursuit that had replaced even artistic production as his chief occupation, filling that vacuum that had opened up when he had more or less stopped making art.

It was easy to locate the moment of inspiration that had rejuvenated his painting career, making him rich but ultimately leading him to reject contemporary art. One day in the early 2000s, he'd been sitting in a new Italian restaurant, considering his supper. For decades now, he remarked to himself as he regarded a bowl of grated pecorino, Americans had possessed a sure idea of what Italian food was: what it tasted like, what it looked like, what it *meant*. For his parents' generation, and even within his own childhood, Italian food meant Italian-American food, an immigrant form, once alien but now ubiquitous, a way of putting dinner on the table, hardly a cuisine. Then the '80s happened, and everyone discovered real Italian food, food from Italy, and defiantly not Italian-American food, which consequently entered a kind of limbo. Spaghetti and meatballs: yes, everyone still liked it and cooked it, it still had its place, but that place was not a trendy restaurant.

Recently, however, which is to say in the early 2000s, shortly before he'd had his revelation, some notable chef had realized that spaghetti and meatballs was what people had wanted all along, and why shouldn't they have it? This chef understood that you could give diners what they wanted without abandoning culinary invention and the associated high prices. What you did was trundle out lowbrow recipes and thematize them, burnishing them for a new audience too young to remember why they'd been discarded in the first place. To use a mid-'90s term, the old recipes were upcycled. Originally this had implied the redemption of waste material through canny adaptation and was widely associated with environmentalism and Third World do-gooderism; no one had previously thought to apply the notion to the world of conceptual food service.

It was a runaway success. Customers were excited and relieved to plunge into the frisson of the old/new, and restaurants all over the city, and then internationally, adopted the formula. Soon came high-end tweakings of meat loaf, mac and cheese, donuts, PB&J sandwiches, chicken wings, and even Twinkies: all cherished comfort foods that no one had previously thought to rework as pricey lifestyle fare. It must have been the times, he mused, because something similar had also happened in the movie industry, which overwhelmingly pursued remakes of best-forgotten films, the crappier the better. We live in an era of expensive fetish food, he thought, but it's also an era in which poor, uneducated parents name their babies DeJohn because it sounds pungent yet sophisticated, unaware that these associations originated in a series of '80s television commercials for a style of mustard. But all this stuff—high and low, classic and contemporary, good and bad—was muddled and slippery, and everyone was equally clueless. When Grey Poupon actually rolled out a line called DeJawn's no one wanted it, not because it was marketed as "Da Street Mustard," but because it was widely considered too '80s.

548   Excerpted from *Fuck Seth Price* (New York: Leopard, 2015), 8–25. Price is a New York–based artist.

As he sat there devouring his *bucatini con le polpette*, he somehow made an associative leap and found himself wondering if abstract painting wasn't due for a spaghetti-and-meatballs recuperation. After all, it had enjoyed a history similar to that of Italian-American cuisine. Both had appeared early in the twentieth century and were widely received with suspicion and derision (all that garlic!); both enjoyed a midcentury, early-adopter hipster appeal that inevitably subsided, though not before preparing the ground for a broader mass appeal, which precipitated a fall from grace in the perception of elites, who came to see these phenomena as boring and outmoded. Artists continued to make abstract painting in large numbers, more than ever before, but, as with cooks of spaghetti and meatballs, they were amateur or otherwise removed from the real conversation, not cutting-edge professionals in sophisticated contexts.

Someone, he realized, needed to come along and devise a painterly abstraction that embodied cultural sophistication and "nowness." It had to look classically tasteful and refer to well-known historical byways, but it also had to be undergirded by utter contemporaneity, either of sensibility or production method. Upcycling was evolving as an idea and was perhaps itself being upcycled: in the '90s it had promised to help the developing world redeem its waste, at the turn of the century it grew to encompass the food consumption of a smaller set of First Worlders with extra time and money, and now it would take on an even more rarefied realm of cultural production available to only the wealthy few: fine art. But he knew this was the way of all culture, all trends: a continuous flow from top to bottom and back again, as in a trick fountain.

He went directly home after dinner and drew up a list of working methods and materials, which he would dutifully follow in the months to come. His new painting would be abstract, he decided; there was a broader audience for that since it matched all decors and lacked uncomfortable associations with real people, events, and political situations. Abstraction in and of itself was uninteresting, of course; the all-important twist here, the redeeming feature, would be the way in which this work was generated, which would expand in importance, endowing the abstraction with meaning. Here there was quite a bit of latitude. Most obviously the painting could be based on chance, which obliterated traditional notions of composition and looked kind of punk: accidental stains on canvas, for example; maybe the oil-pan drippings of a Foxconn machine as it produced iPhones. But then he wondered, did machines drip anymore? Did anything run on oil? Wasn't everything becoming electric? Maybe this avenue was far-fetched. Perhaps the work might play with the medium's material conventions: a "painting" that was in fact composed of vacuum-formed polystyrene: stretcher bars, canvas, markings, and all. Or it might be apparently abstract but actually full of charged referents that became clear only when you inspected the list of materials, e.g., "Coca-Cola spills on Nigerian mud cloth." It might also be computer-generated, e.g., it might consist of Photoshop manipulations printed out on canvas. Or you could hit all four possibilities at once: "Foxconn worker's accidental Coke spills on Nigerian mud cloth, scanned and randomly manipulated in Photoshop, printed on Belgian linen stretched over a vacuum-formed frame."

In truth, the production method hardly mattered, because whichever he chose, the results would look more or less the same: tepid compositions, hesitant and minimal in appearance, kind of pretty and kind of whatever, loaded with backstory. The main thing to remember, both in executing this work and in appreciating it on the wall, was to be *knowing*, just like the chefs who composed fancy renditions of red-sauce dishes, and the diners who paid top dollar, and the critics who wrote breezy acknowledgments.

The problem this solved was the persistent issue of taste in painting. In no arena of art-making did taste intrude so assertively and persistently as it did within the practice of painting. Unlike with installation art or conceptual art, where it was difficult to discern or comfortably judge the merits of a work without anxiety, with painting the problem of taste was always right on the surface, in the frame, so to speak. It was okay to point at a painting and assert "That's good" or "That's bad" without feeling like a complete idiot. You couldn't pull that off as easily when faced with a scrappy installation or a conceptual work composed of puns and feints. The problem was, while these artworks got to hover in the grace of doubt and inscrutability, there were far too many observers who were absolutely certain about their judgments as to what constituted good and bad painting, and the history of painting was therefore racked by cyclical surges of interest one way or another, now veering toward "bad" painting that indulged in tastelessness by way of excess, vulgarity, or prurience, now tacking back toward a more graphic, minimal style. Because fashions changed rapidly, a single painting might in twenty years traverse the spectrum of perceived value and then whip back again, and this variability made everyone nervous.

This new style he'd hit on, however, managed to finesse the taste problem by recourse to the old philosophical trick of playing *being* against *seeming*. In preparing the work, any number of methods or styles would do, so long as the result was "cool," insuring that the painting would seem classic and minimal, while emanating a vague awareness of rich historical struggle. To an observer it would *seem* tasteful, but in its apparent lack of concern for traditional skill or labor, its arguably cynical irreverence toward sincerity or depth, its dismissal of history, and its punk attitude, it would *be* tasteless.

Or perhaps it was the other way around? One couldn't really say, or rather one could, but only with a nagging feeling of insecurity. This instability was catnip to critics and journalists, and they wrote a lot about this new painting, bickering and bemoaning and celebrating. Collectors were thankful for those gusts of language in their sails as they blew through the auctions. Young artists and students were relieved to get back to doing what they'd secretly wanted to do all along, under the powerful sign of a new contemporaneity. In short, the entire art system latched on to this revived style, much as restaurant-goers had fallen for the reenchantment of chicken wings.

The style that gradually developed could be called *post-problem art*. It bore a clear if unacknowledged debt to the wonderful ad slogans of the period, like Staples' "That Was Easy" and Amazon's ". . . And You're Done." *Done!* An amazing word. Go ahead, have done with all the anguished historical debates over meaning and criticality and politics and taste. In a way, this development recapitulated some of Francis Fukayama's arguments in his essay "The End of History?," which suggested that the postwar phenomenon of Western liberal democracy and the capitalist market system had established a kind of plateau, from which one could survey the bloody slopes below. It certainly was true that the system Fukayama described was responsible for the floods of cash that coursed through the art system in the first fifteen years of the twenty-first century, a surge that raised all boats high above the oceanic currents of *issues*. For better or for worse, everyone was in agreement that the market was the only indicator that mattered now. This climate, in which artworks would certainly sell, and the fact of selling was sufficient verification of their quality, made it officially okay simply to "like" a painting. It was no longer necessary to deem a piece interesting, provocative, weird, or complex, and it was almost incomprehensible to hate something because you liked it, or like it because it unsettled you, or any of the other ambivalent and twisted ways that people wrestled with the intersection of feelings and aesthetics. You almost didn't need words any more: it was enough to say, "That painting is *awesome*," just as you'd say, "This spaghetti is *awesome*." Alternately you could use one of the other all-purpose terms of the era, like "nice," "crazy," "perfect," and "insane." This was a radical development, forgoing any more complicated relationship with art; it was a tremendous ironing-out process. Before you knew it, you'd spy a Malevich and declare, "That guy's a total badass." Or was it Marinetti who was the badass?

On the other hand, wasn't the goal of art not to sharpen your critical knives but to be a *fan*, to unquestioningly follow your unplumbed desires and inclinations, even if they tended toward things that weren't unambiguously cool or fun, and in this process begin to untangle yourself, to learn from your relationship with art all about experience and history and emotion?

He later realized, once he was showing his new work and making good money, that the particular genius of a *digitally* generated abstract artwork— and by this time he was applying his methods to sculpture as well as painting—lay not only in leveling aesthetic taste but also in managing to be both abstract and representational, thus neatly resolving another longstanding problem. Such a work was evidently abstract, since it portrayed nothing but an arrangement of computery markings or 3-D printed excrescences, but at the same time it could be seen as representational: it represented only itself; *it represented the digital process of abstraction*. This was a direct, materialist portrayal of our historical moment, when the alien productions of computers and their apparent meaninglessness threatened to redefine all traditional human values, including expression itself. If you said this work was *merely* abstract, weren't you by extension implying something similar about every other item or lifestyle concocted by digital means? By playing with these questions, his new work was capable of reconciling two opposed art-historical alternatives and synthesizing them into some weird, new, Janus-faced form that was capable of looking both backward and forward.

These new artworks aroused accusations of cynicism, and he admitted that he was inviting that conversation. But what was cynicism? He defined cynicism as proceeding in a way that you knew to be harmful or morally bankrupt, for reasons of greed or cowardice. This definition handily described the activity of most politicians, bureaucrats, and CEOs. The question was, what if you found such compromised behavior complex and compelling? What if you believed that exploring the world of perceived or actual cynicism was a powerful way to understand our contemporary moment? What if you *believed in not believing*? Executives or world leaders entertaining this question would rightly be classified as sociopaths, but in the world of art these questions were okay, because suffering wasn't directly involved and any apparent cynicism was likely to be banal and venal, i.e., cashing in by provoking your audience with facile or puerile gestures. He didn't feel that his work belonged in this category. If his paintings were provocative, it was because they drew out acute and omnipresent cultural toxins: anxieties about cynicism and selling out, feelings that had everything to do with how fucked-up it was to live under neoliberal free-market capitalism. He found this exhilarating; he *believed* in it. And this tangle of contradictions was the greatest thing about art: it always meant the opposite of what you thought it meant, or wanted it to mean. Abstract versus representational, old versus new, pure versus corrupt, tasteful versus tasteless: all artistic values and categories were inherently unstable and might suddenly swap places.

Recalling his breakthrough into digital art-making a decade earlier, he suspected that the moment he'd grasped the fact that digital art's genius was to reconcile all opposites was the start of his disenchantment with contemporary art, and with the digital more generally, which was a condition predicated on reconciliation, leveling, and synthesis. Representational painting was just as banal and outmoded as its old foe abstraction, so why was it interesting to gesture at both of them at once? Who gave a shit? From the point of view of the machine he'd set in motion, all these oppositions of taste and style were merely

marketing factors to be co-opted, the way Whole Foods might absorb a pair of rival local grocers only to preserve them as themed deli counters so as to snare all the old clientele. Either/or was irrelevant, save as a gimmick to capture market share. It was a deep irony that the mechanisms of digital culture were built on a binary fundament even as that culture sought to eradicate all opposition, contradiction, and friction on an ontological level, steadily reducing human variety to a kind of affirmative mush.

It was not a coincidence that his disenchantment with visual art occurred right around the time when making simplistic, often digitally formulated abstract paintings became suddenly passé, as was discussing them, critiquing them, even satirizing them. These paintings amounted to societal self-portraiture, and an age grows tired of its own face. Casting about for something to do, he found himself newly interested in writing, which, in comparison to art, offered delightfully fresh challenges. He recognized the peculiarity of this step: advanced painting since the Impressionists had jettisoned the aim of re-creating a recognizable, narrativized human world and had plunged into abstraction, whereas writing had remained in thrall to narrative and human psychology. Yes, there had been a modernist rupture in literature, and the achievements of Woolf, Joyce, and Beckett had been followed by generations of worthies, but the majority of serious literary fiction, and all mass product, went right on pursuing the realistic concerns of "adult literature," in distinction to the serious art world, where there was really no going back to representational realism. As MoMA's founding doctrine put it: "Modernism is the art that is essentially abstract." The field of contemporary art was activated by cataclysm and relentless progress, while contemporary literature remained relatively staid. This was because it was a mass form, he reasoned: who follows contemporary painting? The few. Who reads contemporary books? Everyone.

At this moment, however, he believed writing culture to be undergoing a tectonic shift and finally detaching itself from traditional narrative. No doubt this development was late in coming, trailing by a century visual art's own decisive mutations, but then again, for all that radical change, where was art now? Wallowing in hush money, patting itself on the back for having finally solved the evolutionary problem of how to be simultaneously good and bad, abstract and representational, popular and cutting edge, with the result that nothing was at stake but auction prices. Even much of the politically engaged work that positioned itself in opposition to "market art" was obsessed with finance, aiming its critical guns at Bitcoin, bank logos, credit-default swaps, and the mythical 1 percent. Ultimately, this neurotic relationship to the market was an impoverishment.

Writing, on the other hand, which had little connection to money and power, was only broadening its already considerable mass appeal, thanks to the proliferation of texting, tweeting, blogging, and so on, even as those same forces were emancipating writing from its long-standing narrative conventions. In fact, it was less apposite to say "Who reads? Everyone" than "Who writes? Everyone." Maybe this explained why writing was becoming at the same time more popular and more abstract. In short, writing was becoming just plain *weirder*.

In this situation, and in distinction to the problems of visual art, *everything* was at stake: "the Novel" of course, but also "the field of literature," "the book business," "the future of the word," and communication itself. And no one knew what it meant. You could feel the charge of that anxious energy, it was the motor thrumming behind many recent novels and columns and articles and blog posts. He imagined this to be a historical echo of the introduction of film, with all of that medium's looming ramifications for the image, and how odd that this contemporary upset concerned words!

He himself was not a writer, by any stretch. He'd tried it years ago, had even enjoyed success with some oddball critical essays that circulated in art-world contexts, but ultimately he'd dropped it. The problem with the art world was that you were *expected* to write uneven, eccentric, unresolved texts, it was like being a grad student in an "Experimental Writing" workshop. While many in the art world were wonderfully omnivorous, broad-minded readers, few were any good at writing, including most of the critics and curators, so it was easy to stand out. Most people didn't even bother with critiques of art-world writing, and for good reason: if people criticized you for being lazy or obscurantist, you could assert that you were being "artistic," that what you'd intended was less lucid rhetoric, more Delphic poesy. Writing these texts was like making films where everything was a dream sequence, and therefore immune to charges of illogic and sloppiness. At the same time, of course, nothing was at stake.

In the past couple of years, he'd started following a number of blogs, particularly those written by kids, "digital natives" whose brains were apparently wired differently. It had started as a meandering habit, a time waster, and had developed into something much more serious, in part because he'd stumbled on the fantastical and disturbing narrative of one boy, a preteen, if he was to be believed, who seemed to have gotten himself involved in something much larger than himself, or the auctions, or the credit crisis, or aesthetic taste, or art, or anything that anyone could have imagined.

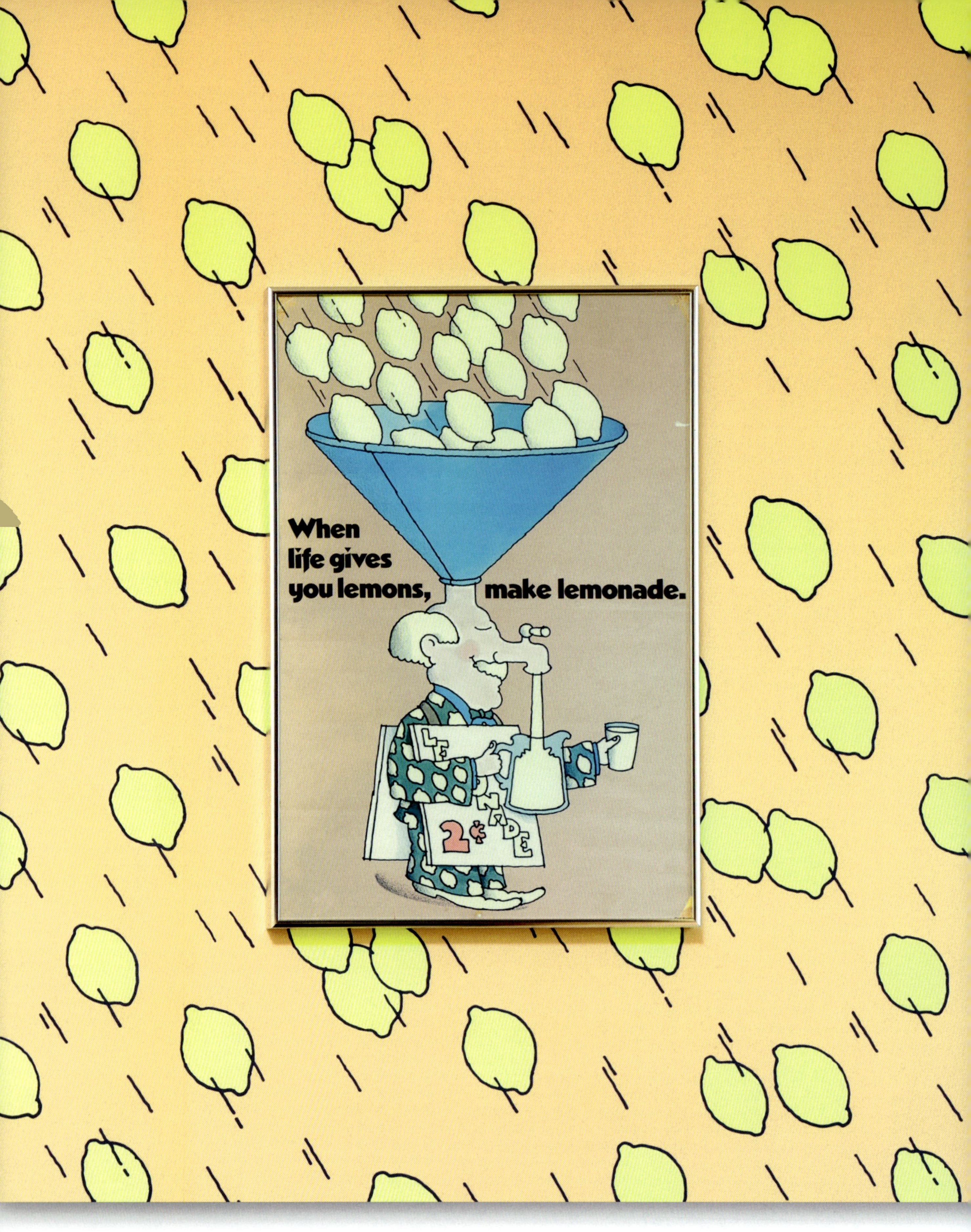

 Wallpaper by Owens with Argus posters, bathroom, Mission Rd. studio, Los Angeles, 2017

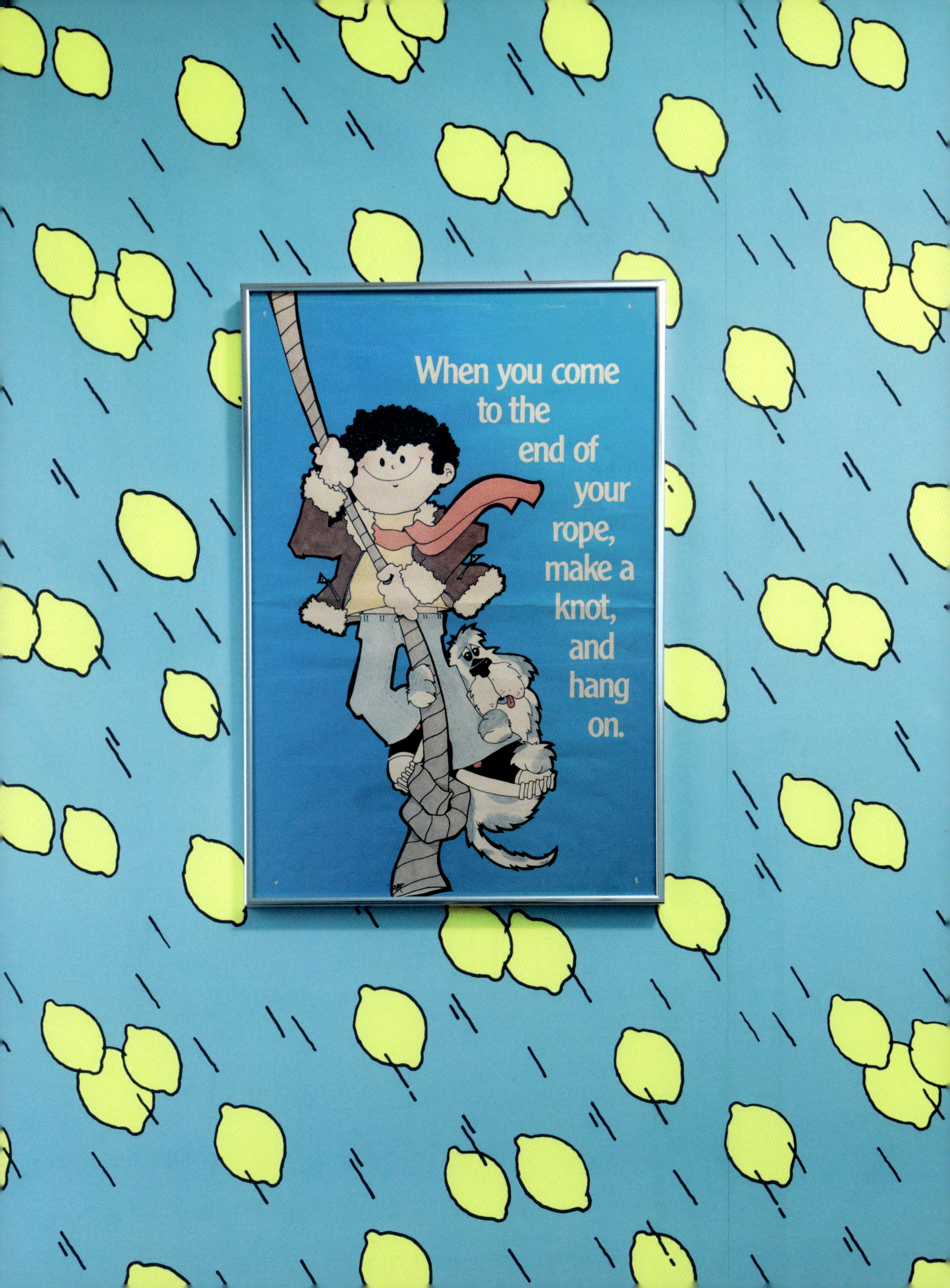

When you come
to the
end of
your
rope,
make a
knot,
and
hang
on.

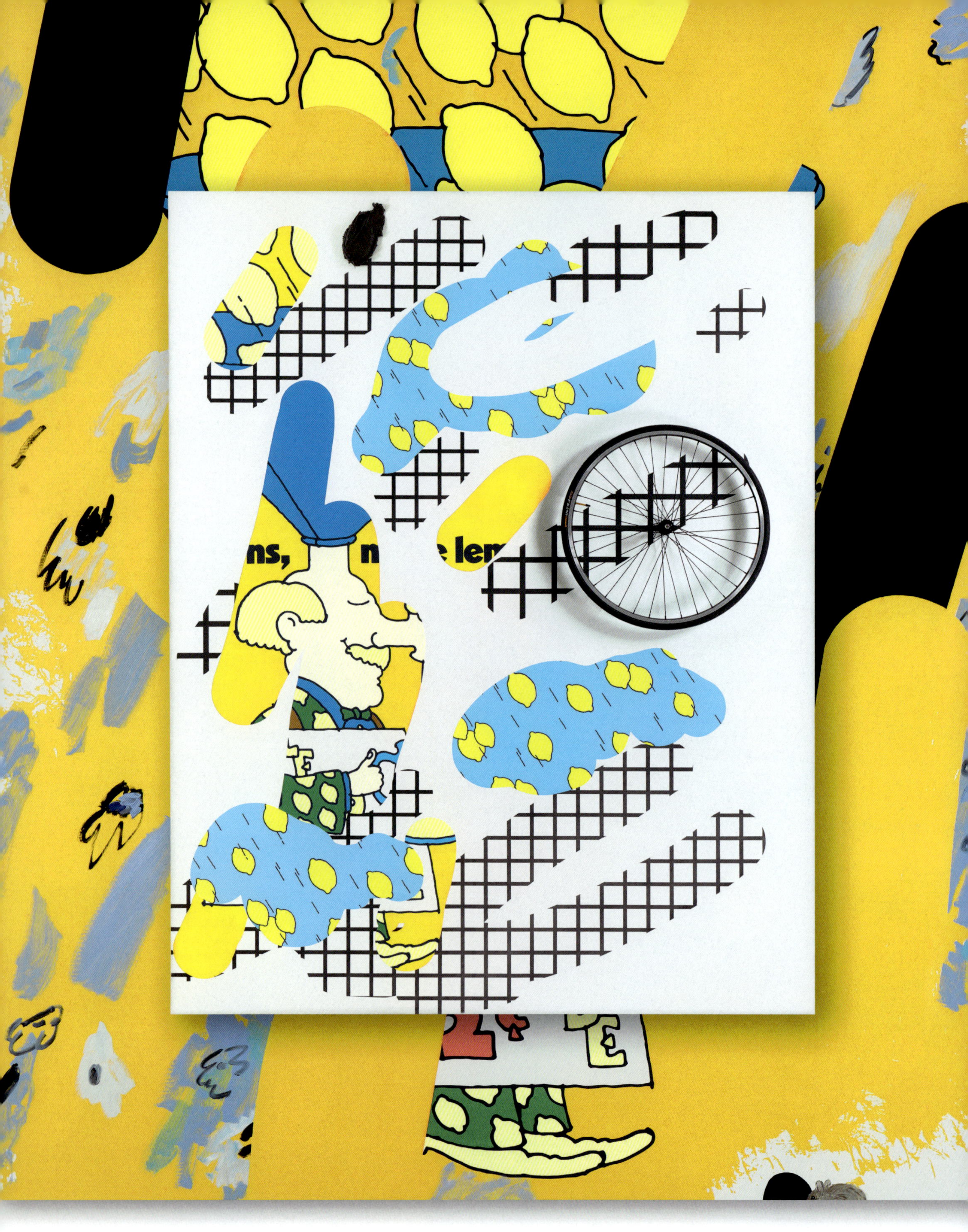

Foreground: *Untitled*, 2014, acrylic, oil, vinyl paint, silkscreen ink, charcoal, and wheel on linen, 108 × 84 in. (274.3 × 213.4 cm)
Background: Detail of *Untitled*, 2014, acrylic, oil, vinyl paint, silkscreen ink, charcoal, and paper on linen, 108 × 84 in. (274.3 × 213.4 cm)

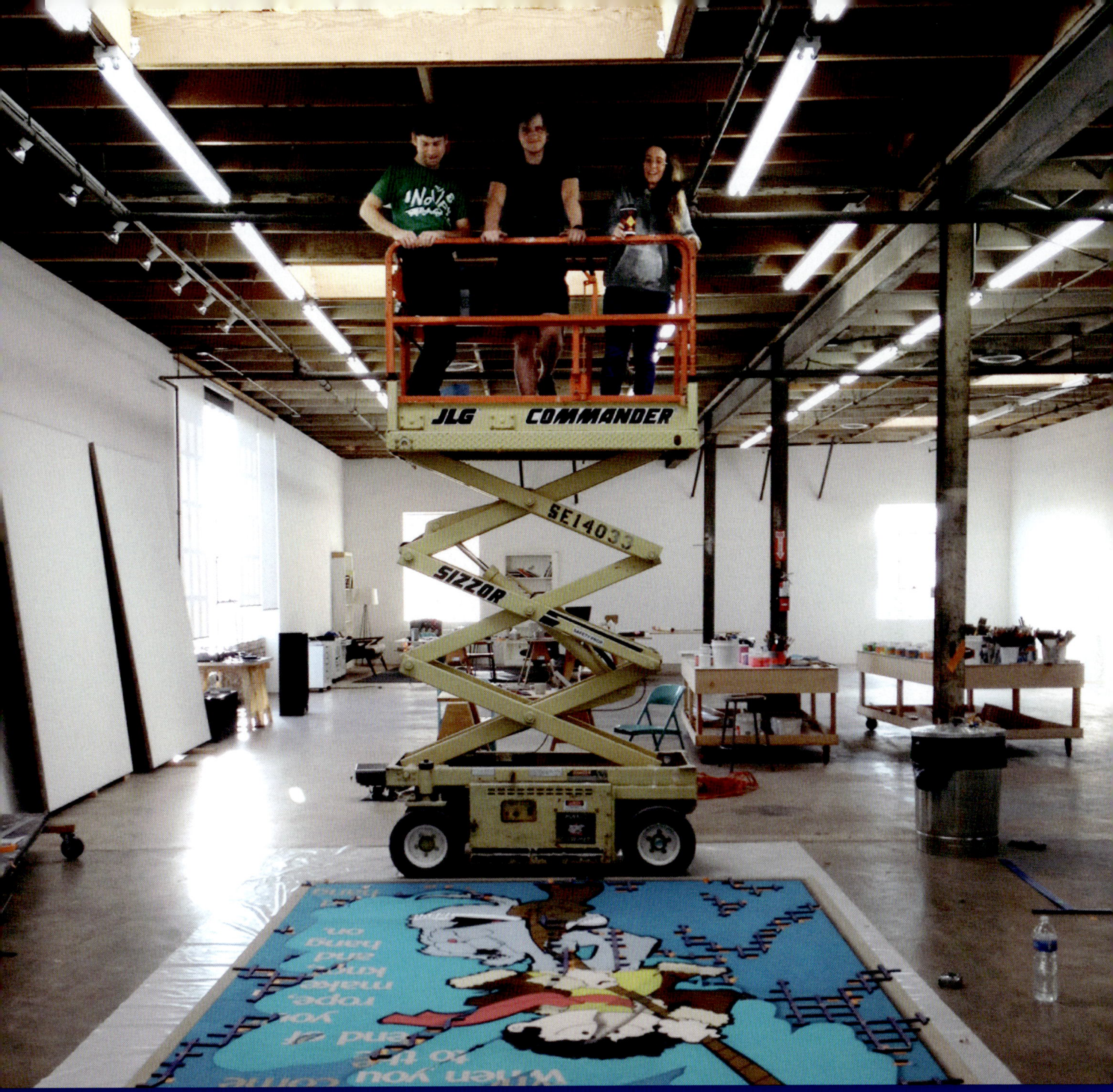

Kate Hall: The Whitney Biennial painting was the second project I worked on with Laura. We went from using four screens to about thirty. Screenprinting is essentially a grid-based process, but when you apply it to painting I think it's kind of like applying wabi-sabi to aesthetics, feelings, and narrative—i.e., the grid becomes imperfect. That happened a lot in this painting, where by chance there are little mistakes that create a feeling. Like in the top right corner it's not square. It was a mistake but Laura was responsive to it and said, "No, I want to leave it like that." It was a combination of making something on the computer and interacting with it—Laura uses chance and variables and materials to make stuff like that happen. The paintings inside the work are images from the biggest painting but with a twist: we'd take an abstraction and make it representational, or make it rain lemons on a sad dog. Through this you see the painting again but differently. The book is a wintergreen transfer with drawings, collage, and computer images. I remember looking at the finished painting with Laura and noticing that on the front it says, "When you come to the end of your rope, make a knot, and hang on." And then at the bottom it says "and hang" again, which seems spatially incorrect in relationship to everything else. I remember asking her about it and she was like, "You sometimes have to be a little fucked up."

John Seal, Andrew Cannon, and Owens with *Untitled*, 2014, ink, silkscreen ink, vinyl paint, acrylic, oil, pastel, paper, wood, solvent transfers, stickers, handmade paper, thread, board, and glue on linen and polyester, five parts: 138⅛ × 106½ × 2⅝ in. (350.8 × 270.5 × 6.7 cm) overall, Mission Rd. studio, Los Angeles, 2014

Stretcher Bars
138 x 104 x 1.5" - Alustretch
69 x 52 x 1.25" -Alustretch
34.5 x 26 x 1" -Alustretch
17.25 x 13 x .75" -Wood (made in studio)
8.625 x6.5 x .5" -Wood (made in studio)

Linen- Rosebrand medium weight artist's linen

Screens- 110 Mesh Count (16) 50x80 (2) 50x80 open screens (13) 40x30/30x24
Total: 31

138 x 104 x
Based on a
+The linen
+A gloss vir
+We lined u
    -It w
were made
+We taped
screens reg
+Ghost ima
TW extende
+Each indiv
by 1/3rd.
    -Jac
transparent
variegated t
    -Cut
successivel
weren't putt
laid too muc
Gorilla Duct
    -Sca
leaving a so
    -Shi

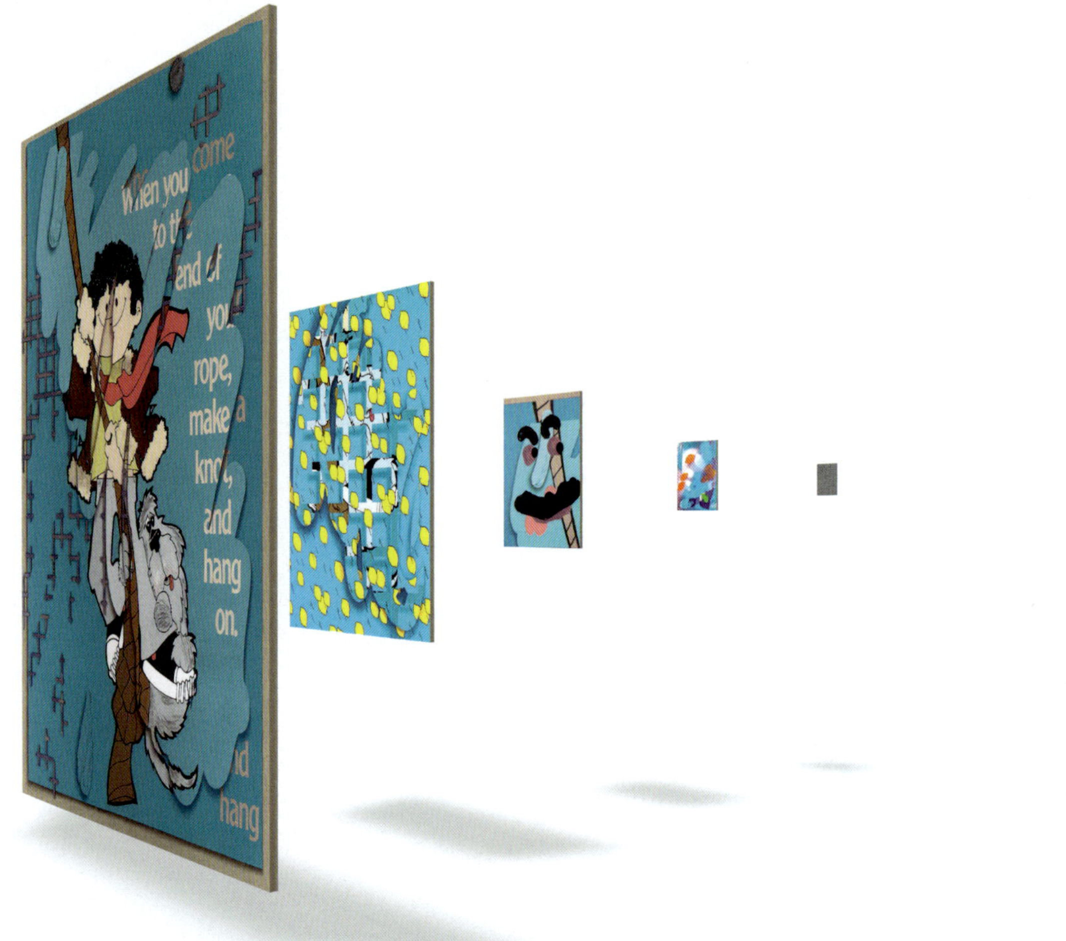

printed inconsistently to the rest of the shirt due to lack of ink being able to go through the screen. The vinyl mask is suspected to be the reason why the ink didn't reach this smaller surface area.
    -Rope: The rope was a Brown Flashe mix that was applied in four pulls. Each part of the rope was printed separately; bottom, middle, then top to insure perfect registration and printing of the paint.
    -Dog & Pants: A TW ink that was pulled four times yet the bottom part of the dog from his bum to his tail had a fade/gradient of ink that didn't lay consistently. Similarly to the shirt print, the issue was in close proximity to an edge of a vinyl mask.
    -Skin: The skin was a mixed Speedball ink that was pulled four times. It was printed in two parts; first the face and right hand, then the belly and left hand. The ink was consistent and

ad a smooth finish.

-Zippers, Hair & Pupils: A TW ink that was pulled four times. It was printed in three parts; air and pupils, right zipper, then the left zipper. The grey must be printed after the skin so the upils are grey and not skin colored when the black is applied on top.

-Tongue, Sneaker Detail & Pants Seam: Same Jantex pantone red as the scarf was sed and applied in two pulls. It was printed with a large screen but with small 3" squeegees for more concentrated print to insure detail.

-Shoes: White Flashe printed in two pulls.

-Dog Eyes: White Flashe printed in two pulls.

The entire boy image is then masked off with tape in extreme detail. All seams are layered to revent leakage and exposure to ink.

-Back

p left corner

he general

plied to ma

servoir for t

aving large

lls are don

ur times. O

e decision t

ask and the

fficulty of p

eeded more

th the large

The boy ma

-Text:

y in accord

arallel to the

line by two

verse sides

ottom and ir

-Final

lls. The pul

ison. It was

-Clear

nnection be

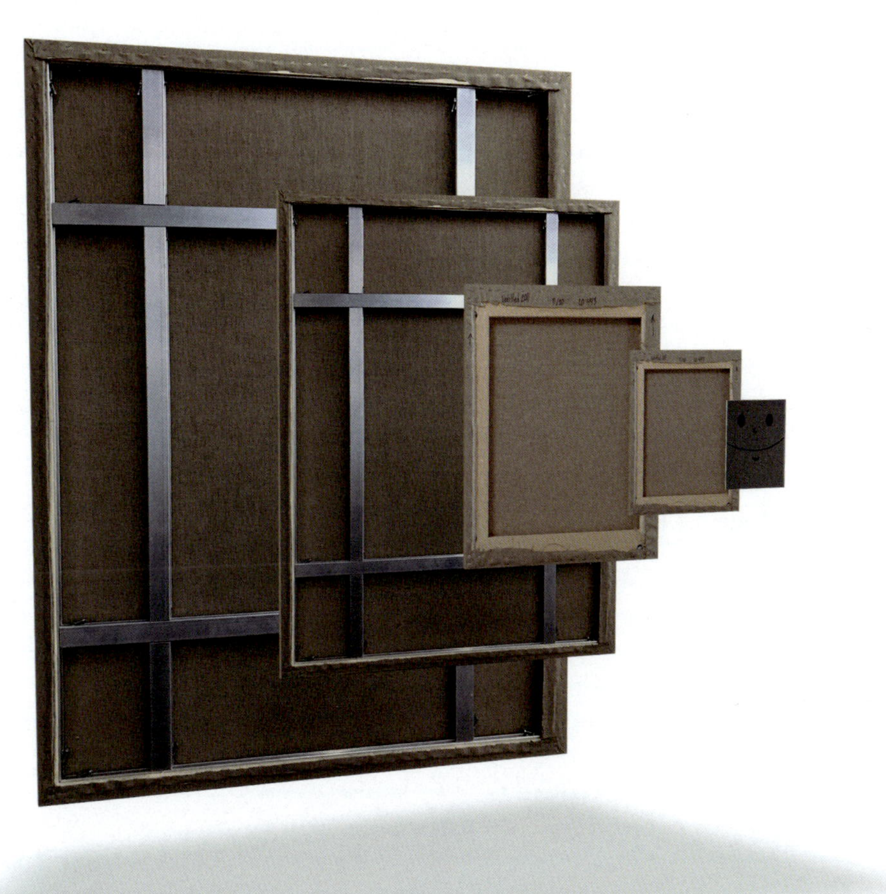

All vinyl is removed.

The background boy film is laid over the foreground mark until it aligned similar to the working e.

We taped off registration marks for the registration marks of the film.

The entire interior mark is then masked off and the background image is prepared to be inted.

All prior inks were then mixed to a darker shade.

Ghost image of full outline printed (a light transparent gray made of TW halftone black 5% and W extender base 95%)

Each individual color printed. The color screens were made to overlap the black (ghost image)

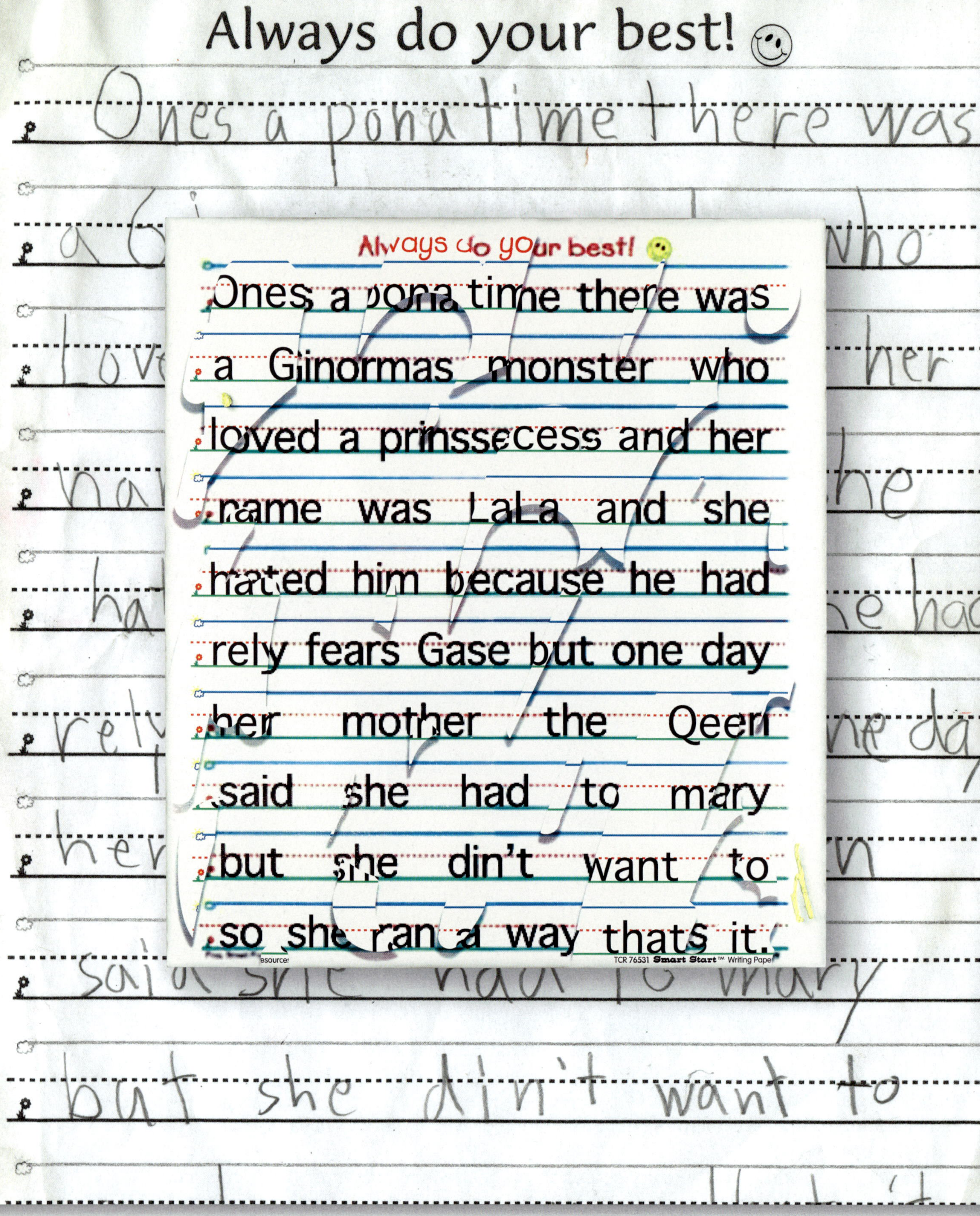

Always do your best!
Ones a pona time there was a Ginormas monster who loved a prinssecess and her name was LaLa and she hated him because he had rely fears Gase but one day her mother the Qeen said she had to mary but she din't want to so she ran a way thats it.

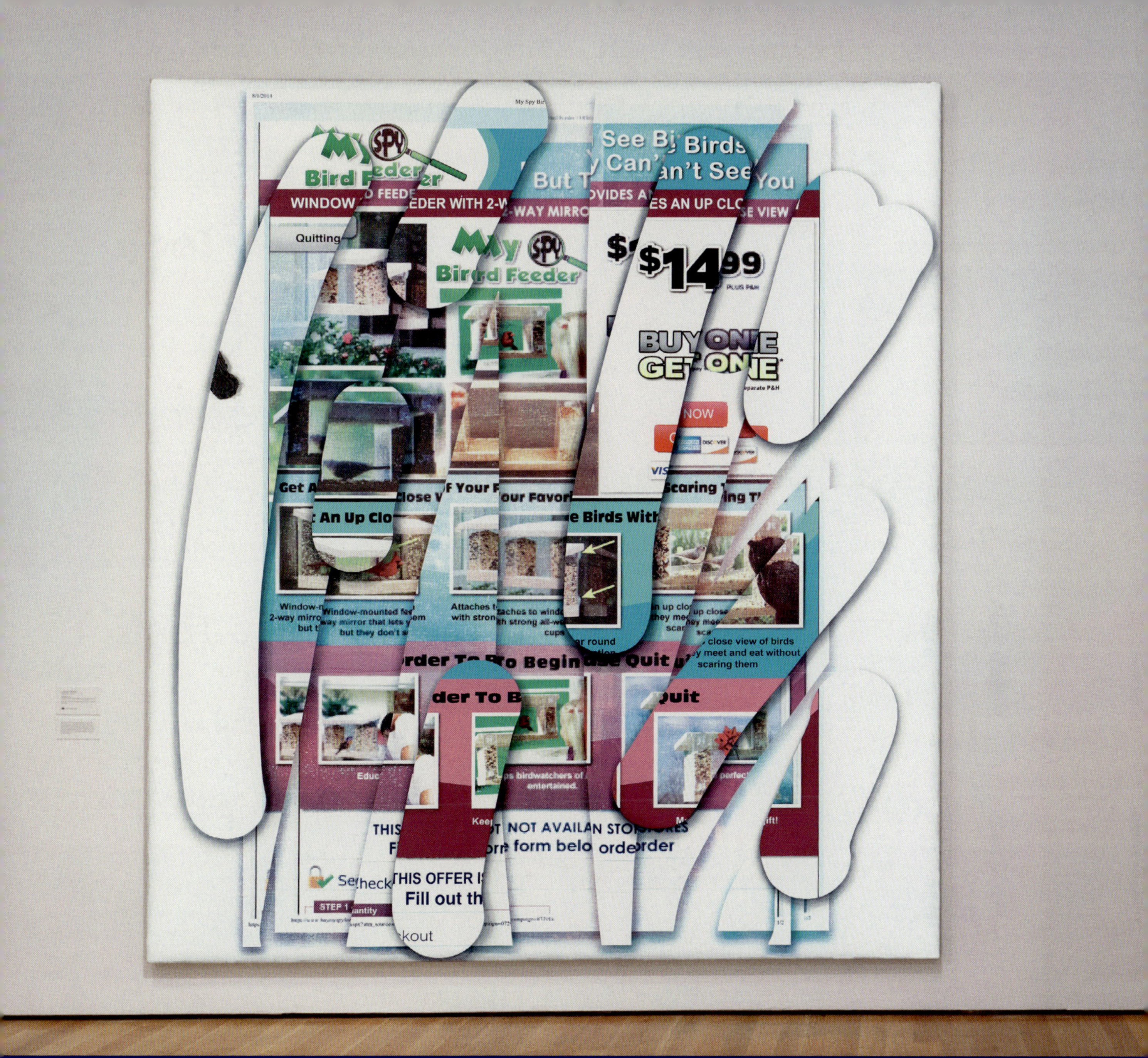

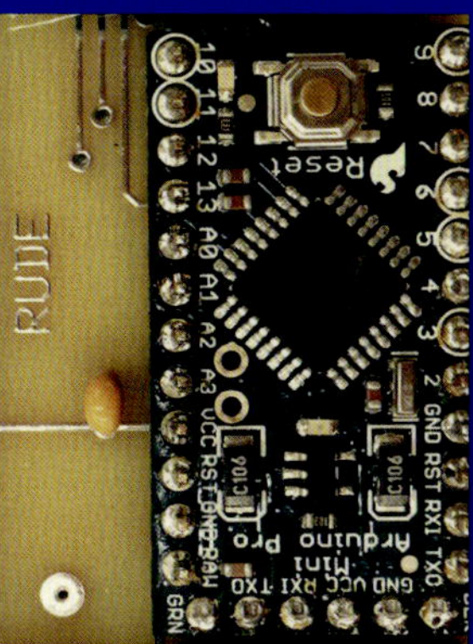

Andrew Cannon: Laura wanted sound to blast from this painting at scheduled intervals during the *Forever Now* show at MoMA. It was a secret to everyone, including the museum staff, so the sound system had to be built in a way that no one would discover it—even if they looked. We worked with a fabricator, Ben Dean of Pylon, that came up with an Arduino-controlled speaker that was small—about three inches tall and a foot long. It slid inside the hollow aluminum stretcher bars of the painting—you'd have had to unstretch the canvas and fully take apart the bars to get it out. The bulk of the device was mostly batteries, since it needed to run without a plug-in cord that would give it away. We joked about not being able to ship overseas, since it looked more like a pipe bomb than a radio. The idea was that sound would resonate against the metal bars and be amplified instead of muffled. We never heard it though. It was programmed to start playing after the install, for about five to ten seconds each day as determined by an algorithm that ensured it played only during open hours. The clips were from a pop song called "Rude" by MAGIC! I never really knew why that one specifically. We all weighed in on how often and how long it should play and perhaps made too safe a guess; rumors of it playing came back to the studio, but this was never confirmed.

Installation view, *The Forever Now: Contemporary Painting in an Atemporal World*, The Museum of Modern Art, New York, 2014, with *Untitled*, 2014, oil, vinyl paint, and silkscreen ink on linen, 137½ × 120 in. (349.3 × 304. 8 cm)
Inset: Image of breadboard from *Untitled*, 2014

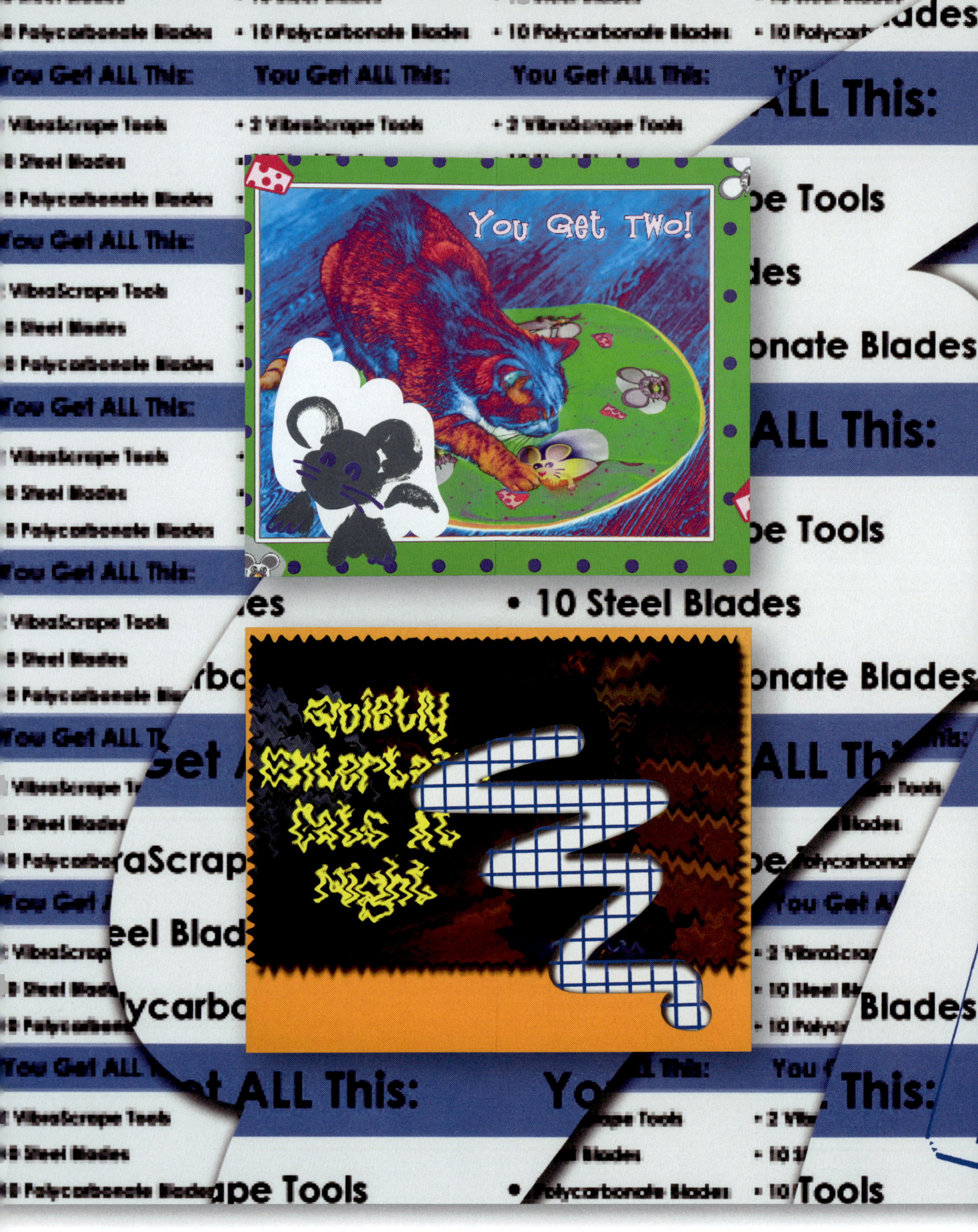

Foreground: Detail of *Twinkle Paws*, 2015, vinyl paint, wallpaper, and inkjet print on Japanese paper with parchment and book board, 16½ × 10 × 1¼ in. (41.9 × 25.4 × 3.2 cm)

Background: Detail of *Vibrascrape*, 2015, vinyl paint, wallpaper, and inkjet print on Japanese paper with parchment and book board, 16½ × 10 × 1¼ in. (41.9 × 25.4 × 3.2 cm)

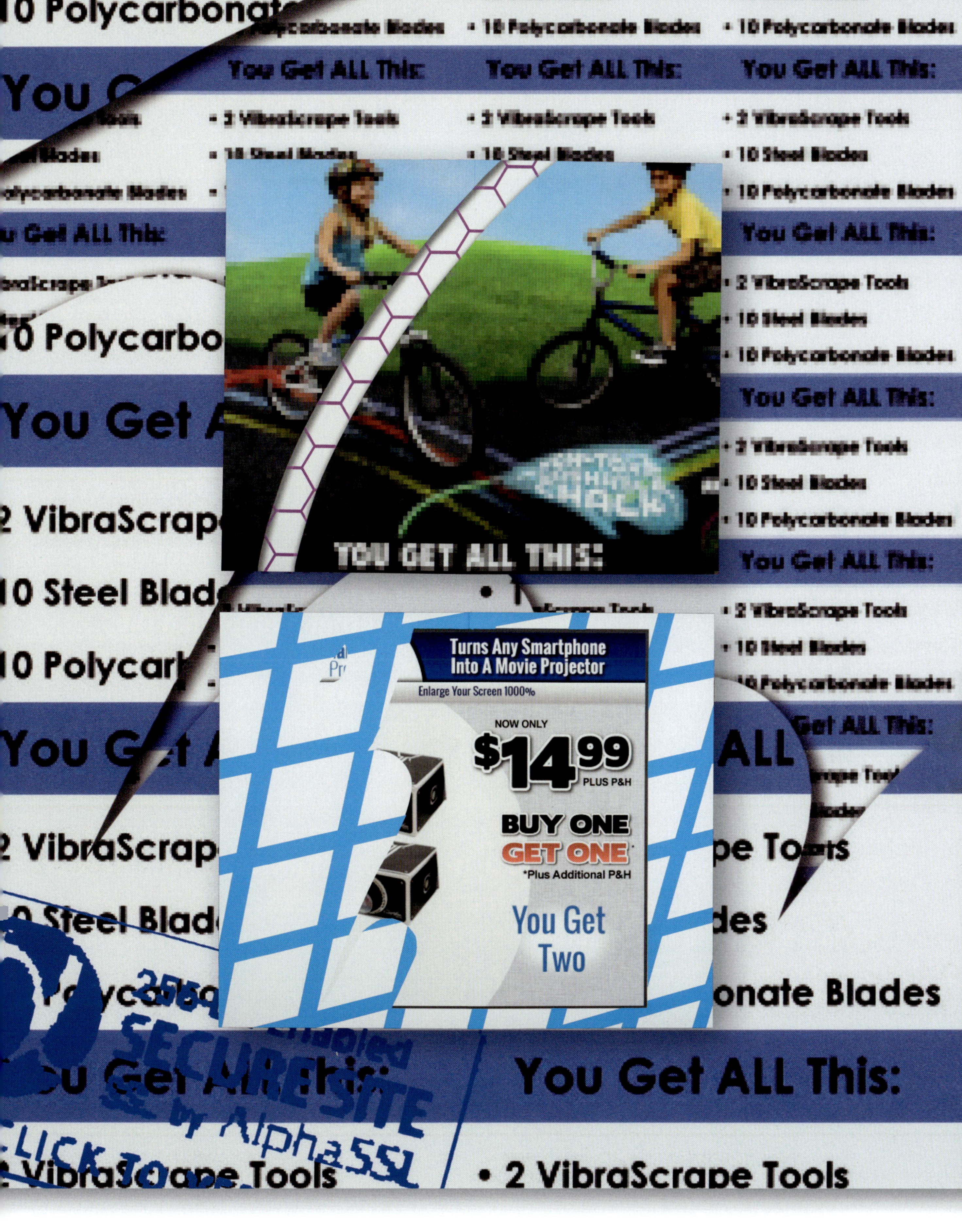

Foreground: Pages from *Rainbow Rider*, 2015, vinyl paint, wallpaper, and inkjet print on Japanese paper with parchment and book board, 16½ × 10 × 1¼ in. (41.9 × 25.4 × 3.2 cm), and *Smartphone Projector,* 2015, vinyl paint, wallpaper, and inkjet print on Japanese paper with parchment and book board, 16½ × 10 × 1¼ in. (41.9 × 25.4 × 3.2 cm)

Henry Bryan: I don't think my mom asked me if she could use my story for her painting. She told me later, after she had already started using it. I had been in a writing mood and was kind of bored, so I just wrote it. I was kind of into cats at that time and I like sci-fi a lot. Seeing my story on the painting I was pretty surprised, but I think it was cool. With the fruit drawings I was kind of bored again and I had these new markers that smelled like different things. One was like cherries, one smelled like licorice, and so on. So I just drew pictures of whatever the colors smelled like. I think my favorite smell was probably mint—or maybe grapes. I went to Germany for the show and I just waited in this other room while they were setting it up. I think I read a whole *Harry Potter* book. Or no, it was *The Hunger Games* that I read while I was there. That book was pretty good. While they were installing, a lot of times I would hear that sound of the clacking measuring tape. The images on the back of the paintings seemed kind of interesting; it was also interesting in a way that the story and the drawings have nothing to do with each other except that they were both created while I was bored. I think I went to the opening, I'm not sure. I probably did. If I did, I don't think it was very big and exciting because I don't remember it. It's pretty interesting having a mom who is an artist, but sometimes it's exhausting, like going to all the art galleries and stuff. I would probably describe this show as futuristic art. I don't know. Like if you've ever watched *The Hunger Games*, the police from the capital, they have white suits with these almost motorcycle helmets; it's that type of futuristic.

My mom's art is like science fiction—science fiction and in a way almost "Renaissancey."

 Henry Bryan lives in Los Angeles and is Owens's son. He is a fisherman, a sailor, and a seventh-grade student.

zel is pleased to
exhibition by Laura
in Petzel ng Friday, May 1st,
ce an exhi tist's first exhibition
Capitain P opening F w works. Large
announce a The Artist's dia paintings Laura
Owens ope es new various techniques
2015. The features ed media uses vari izes ranging from
matched m materializes rintmaking pictures.
Owens use s to printm re vividly alongside
and mater nces are vi 990s Lauras Owens
textiles to s. In 1990s ranslates into paint
References started and transl he (b. 1970 Euclid,
digitals. In ving. She (artist living in Los
in drawing. sis an artist teaches at Art
Ohio) is a College e of Design,
Angeles. na and runs runs the exhibition
Center C She te Mission with Gavin
Pasadena a 356 Missi Vendy Yao. She will
space 356 and Wendy ecession, Vienna in
Brown and t the Seces .
work at the ummer.
the summ

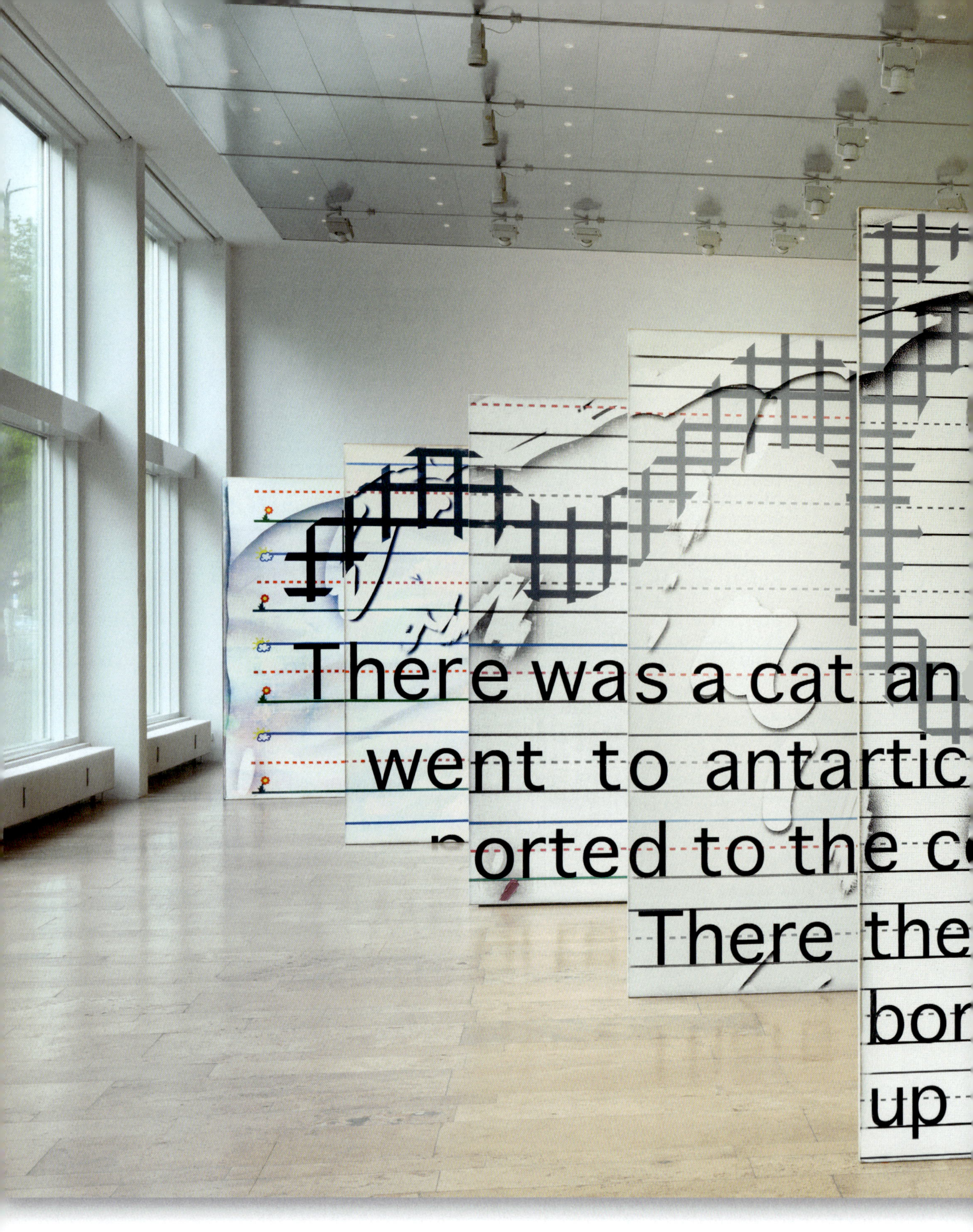

Installation view, Capitain Petzel, Berlin, 2015, with *Untitled*, 2015, acrylic, oil, and vinyl paint on linen, with powder-coated aluminum strainer, five panels: 108 × 84 in. (274.3 × 213.4 cm) each

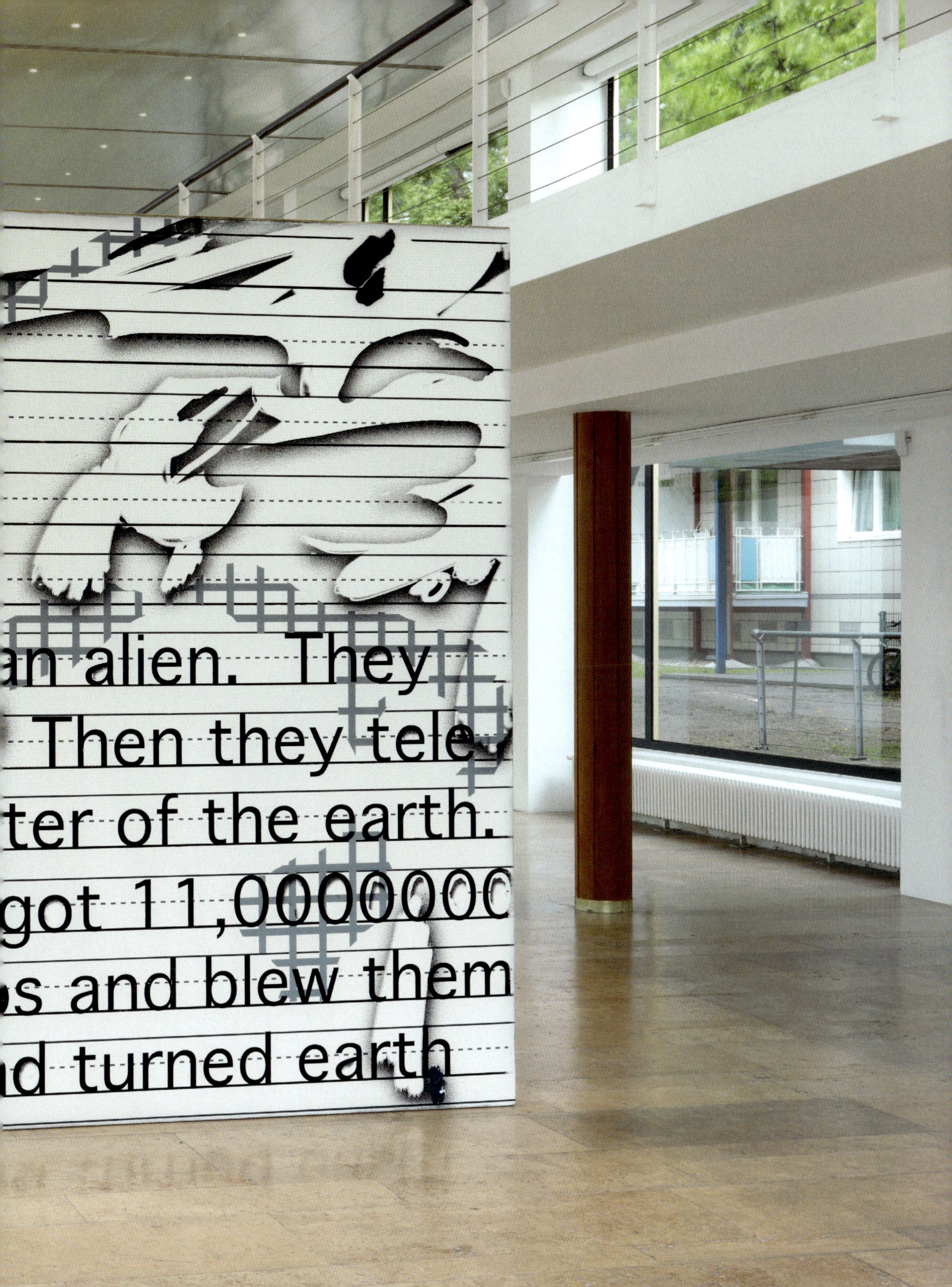
an alien. They
Then they tele
ter of the earth.
got 11,0000000
s and blew them
d turned earth

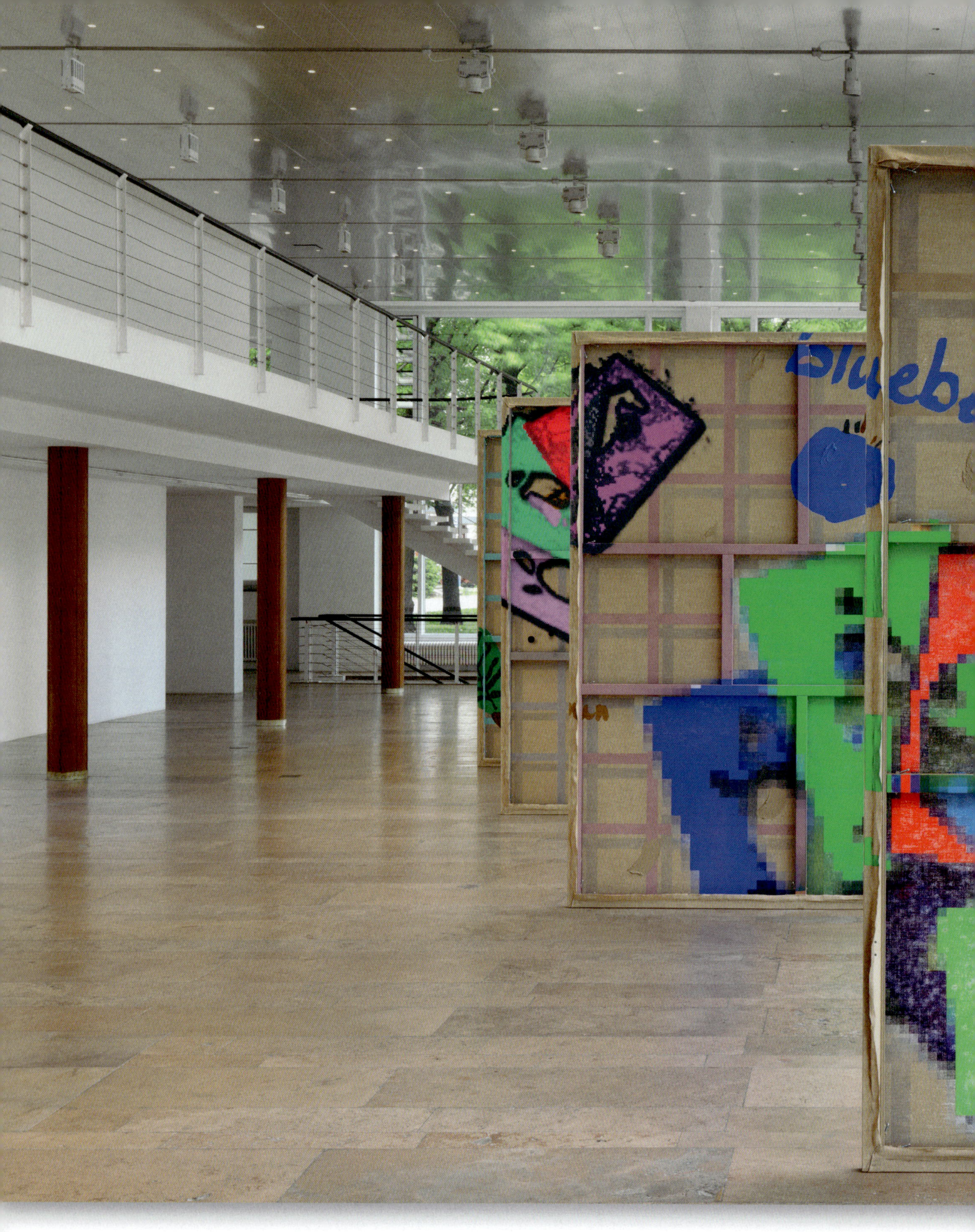

 Installation view, Capitain Petzel, Berlin, 2015, with *Untitled*, 2015 (see p. 566)

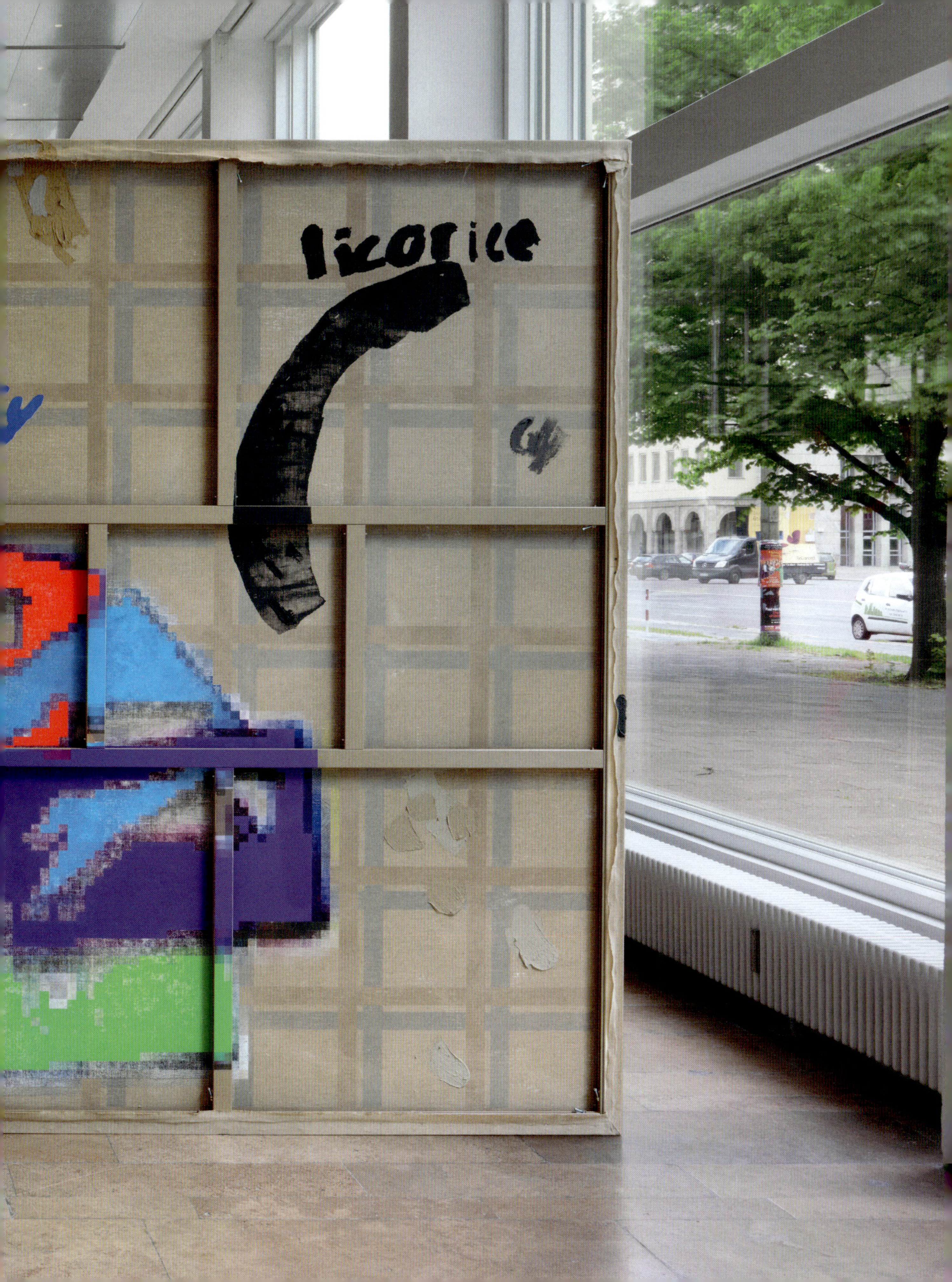

licorice

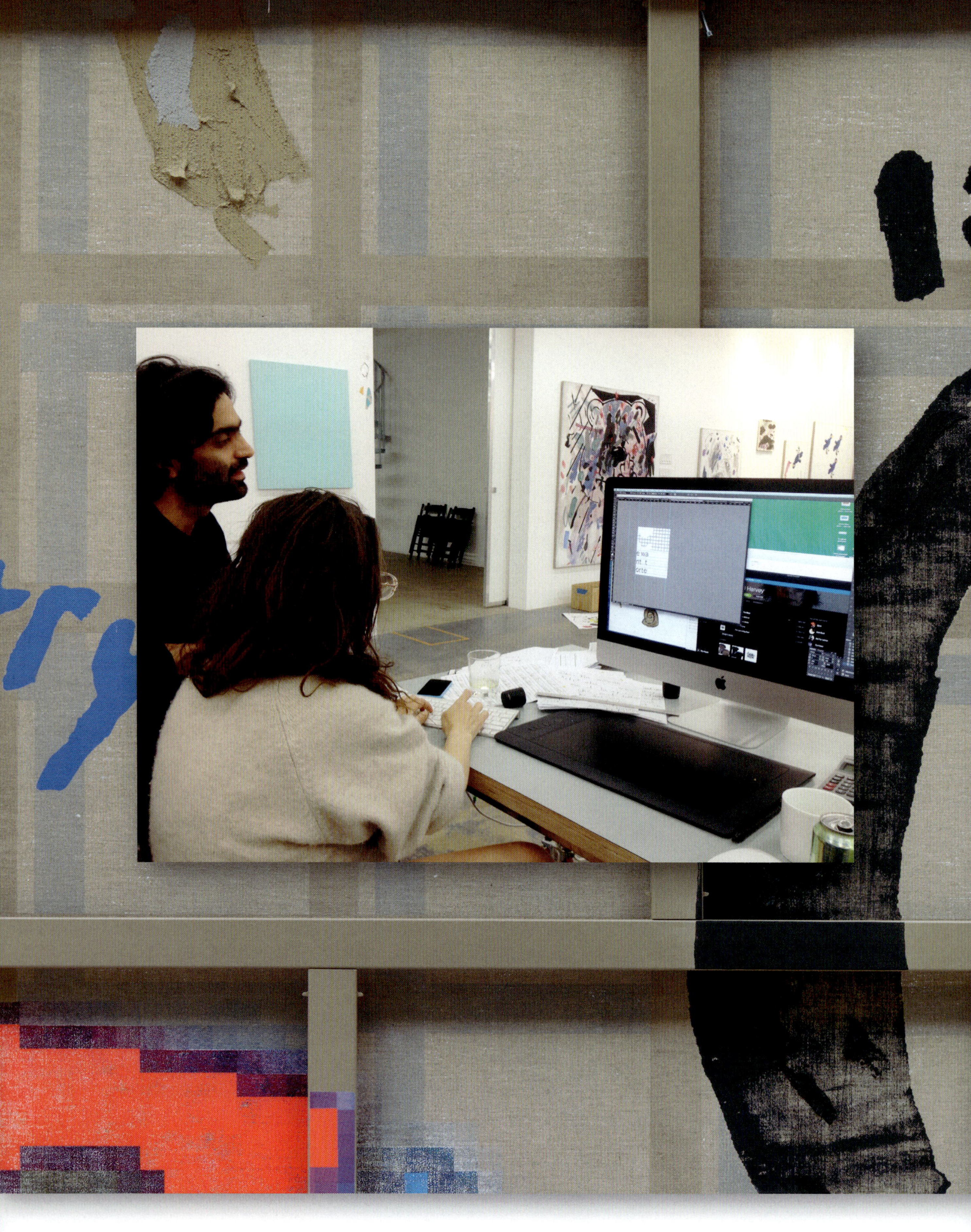

Foreground: Sohrab Mohebbi and Owens, Mission Rd. studio, Los Angeles, 2015
Background: Detail of *Untitled*, 2015 (see p. 566)

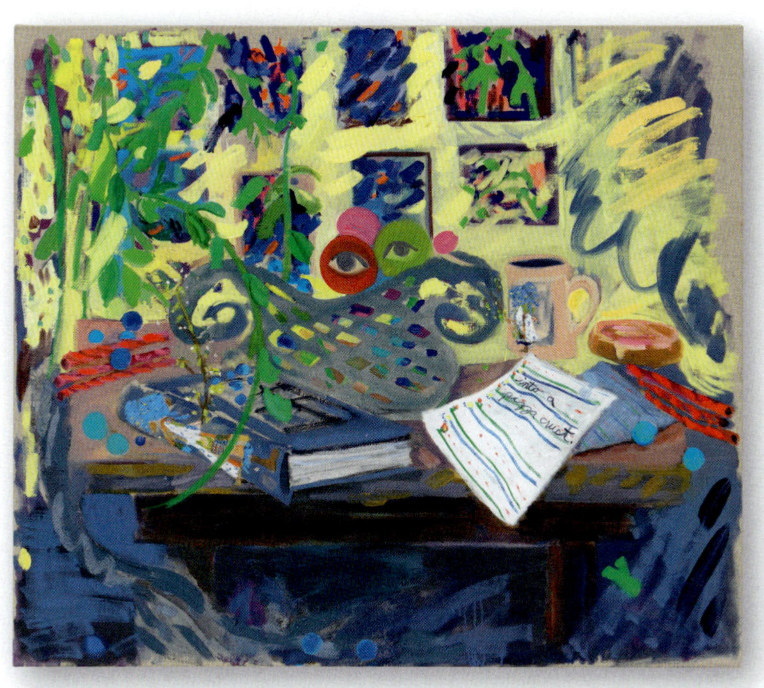

Untitled, 2015, oil and vinyl paint on linen, 38 × 42 in. (96.5 × 106.7 cm)

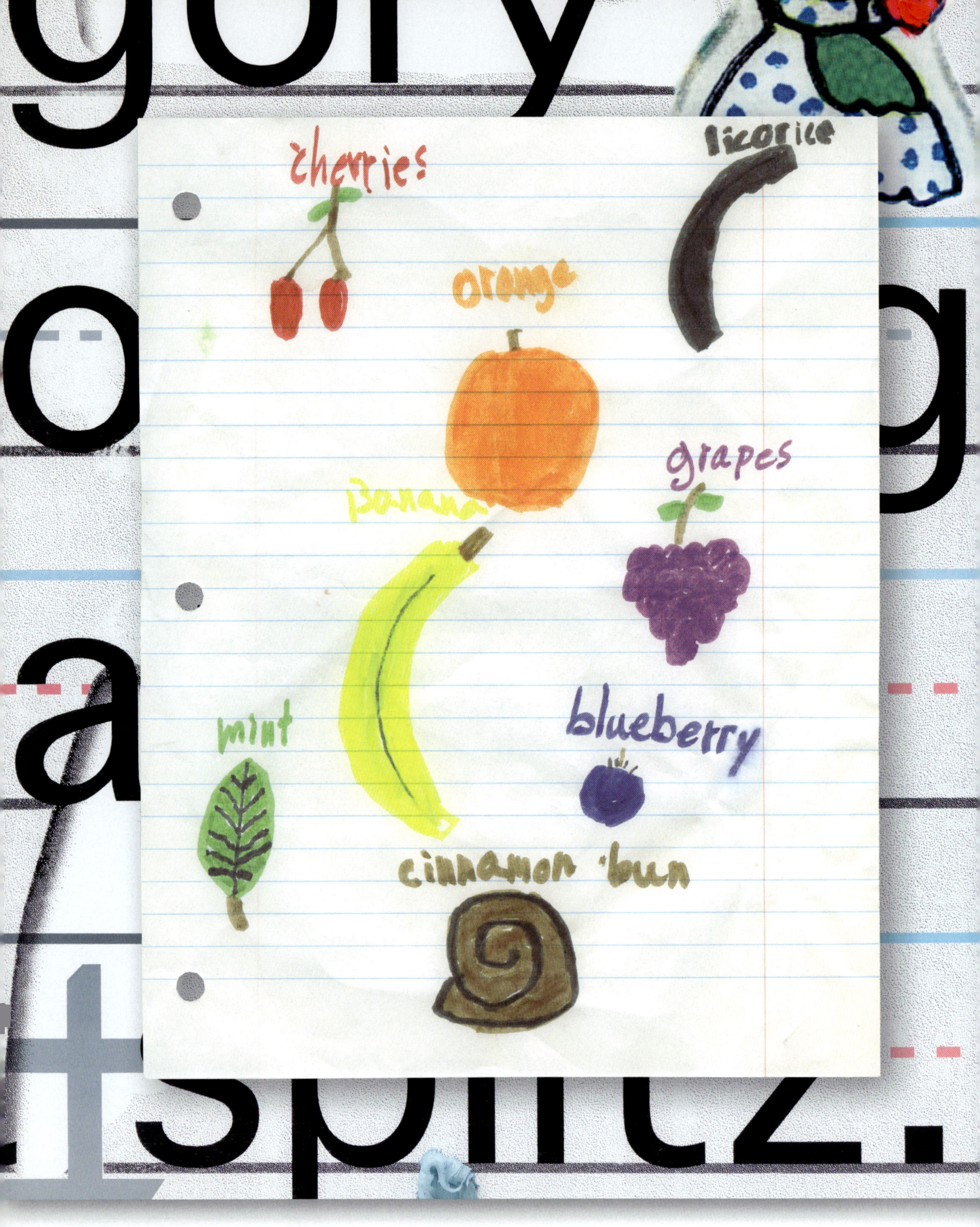

Foreground: Untitled drawing by Henry Bryan, 2014
Background: Detail of *Untitled*, 2015 (see p. 566)

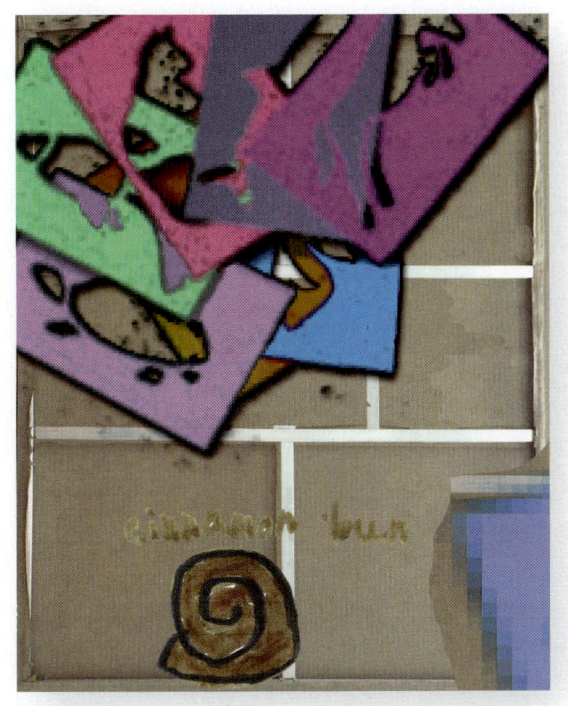
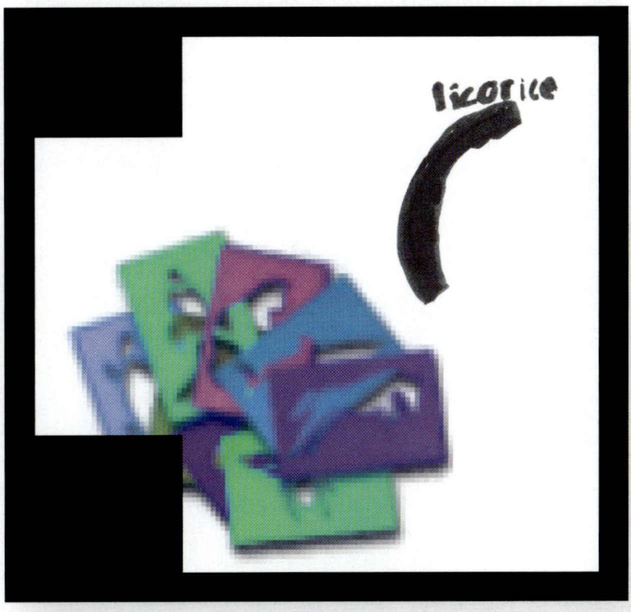
licorice
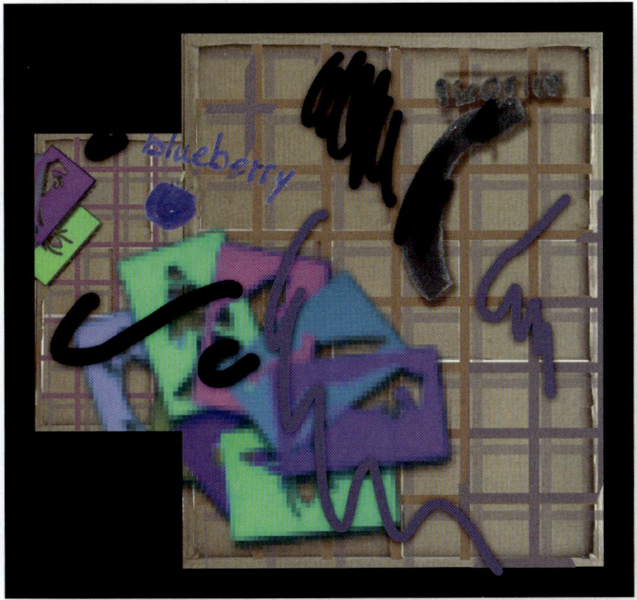
blueberry
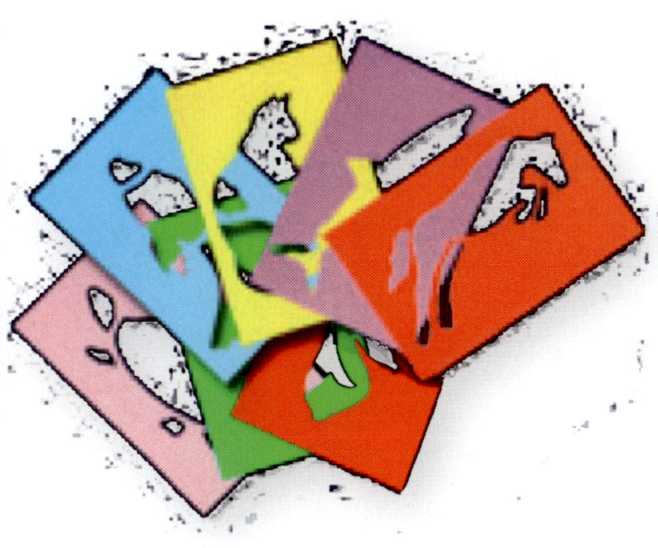

INSTALLATION MANUAL

Laura Owens
Untitled, 2015
Acrylic, oil, and Flashe on linen with powder coated aluminum strainer
Five-part work, each 108 x 84 inches
Inv# LO 555.1-5

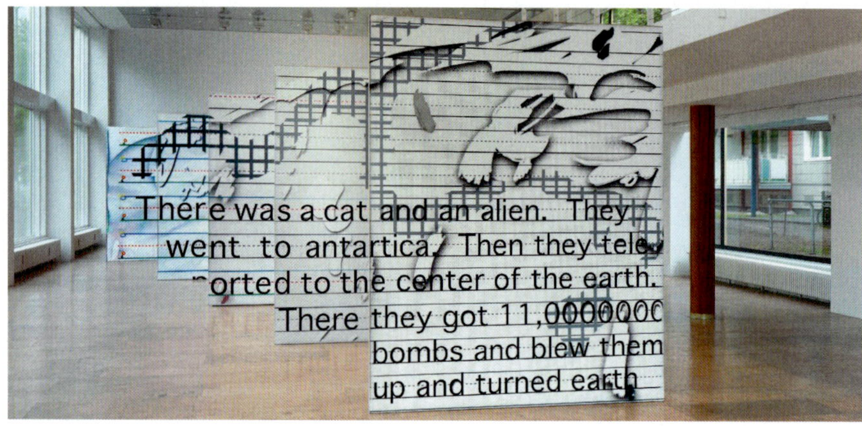

The following document contains install instructions for Laura Owens' five painting installation, "Untitled, 2015" (first installed at Capitain Petzel, Berlin). The installation consists of five paintings standing vertically, which viewed from the proper angles line up to create one large image.

The installation requires a minimum gallery size of 1068 x 295.25 inches (89 x 24.6 ft) with minimum 120 inch ceiling height (10 ft), and requires 5 holes drilled into the floor, each one 0.5" diameter and 8" deep. Each canvas is supported by a single rod, which is inserted into the bottom of the painting, and into the hole in the floor.

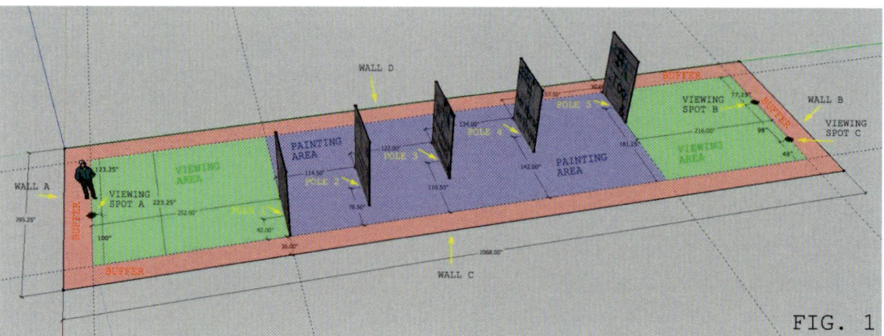

Foreground: Installation instructions, 2015
Background: Color chart, 2015

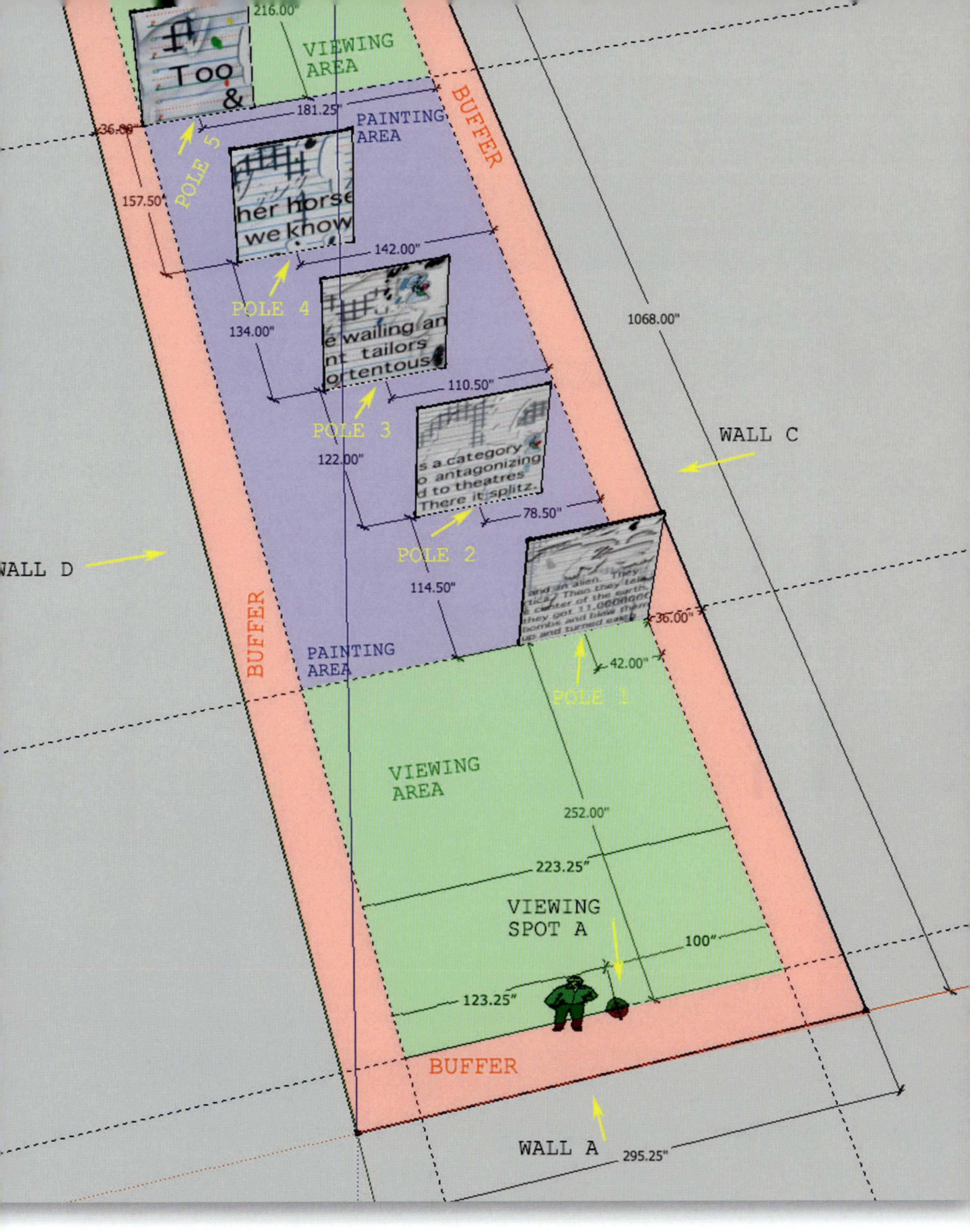

216.00"
VIEWING AREA
181.25"
PAINTING AREA
BUFFER
POLE 5
157.50"
her horse we know
142.00"
POLE 4
134.00"
1068.00"
e wailing an nt tailors ortentous
122.00"
POLE 3
110.50"
WALL C
s a category o antagonizing d to theatres There it splitz.
78.50"
POLE 2
114.50"
WALL D
BUFFER
36.00"
and an alien. They tica. Then they tele Custer of 11,000000 bombs, and blew ther up and turned eas
36.00"
42.00"
POLE 1
PAINTING AREA
VIEWING AREA
252.00"
223.25"
VIEWING SPOT A
100"
123.25"
BUFFER
WALL A
295.25"

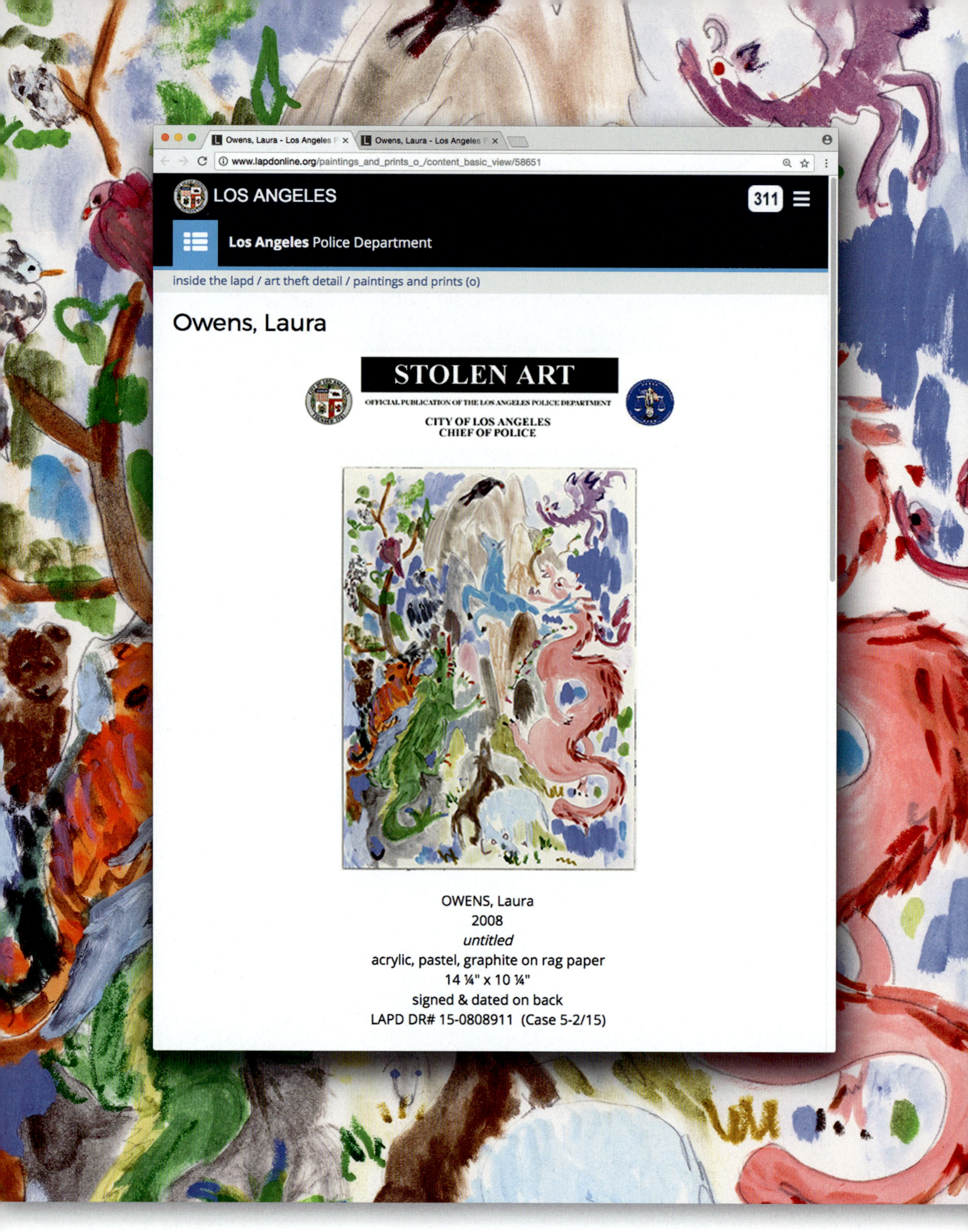

Foreground: Screenshot of lapdonline.org, 2010
Background: Detail of *Untitled*, 2008, acrylic, pastel, and graphite on paper, 14¼ × 10¼ in. (36.2 × 26 cm)

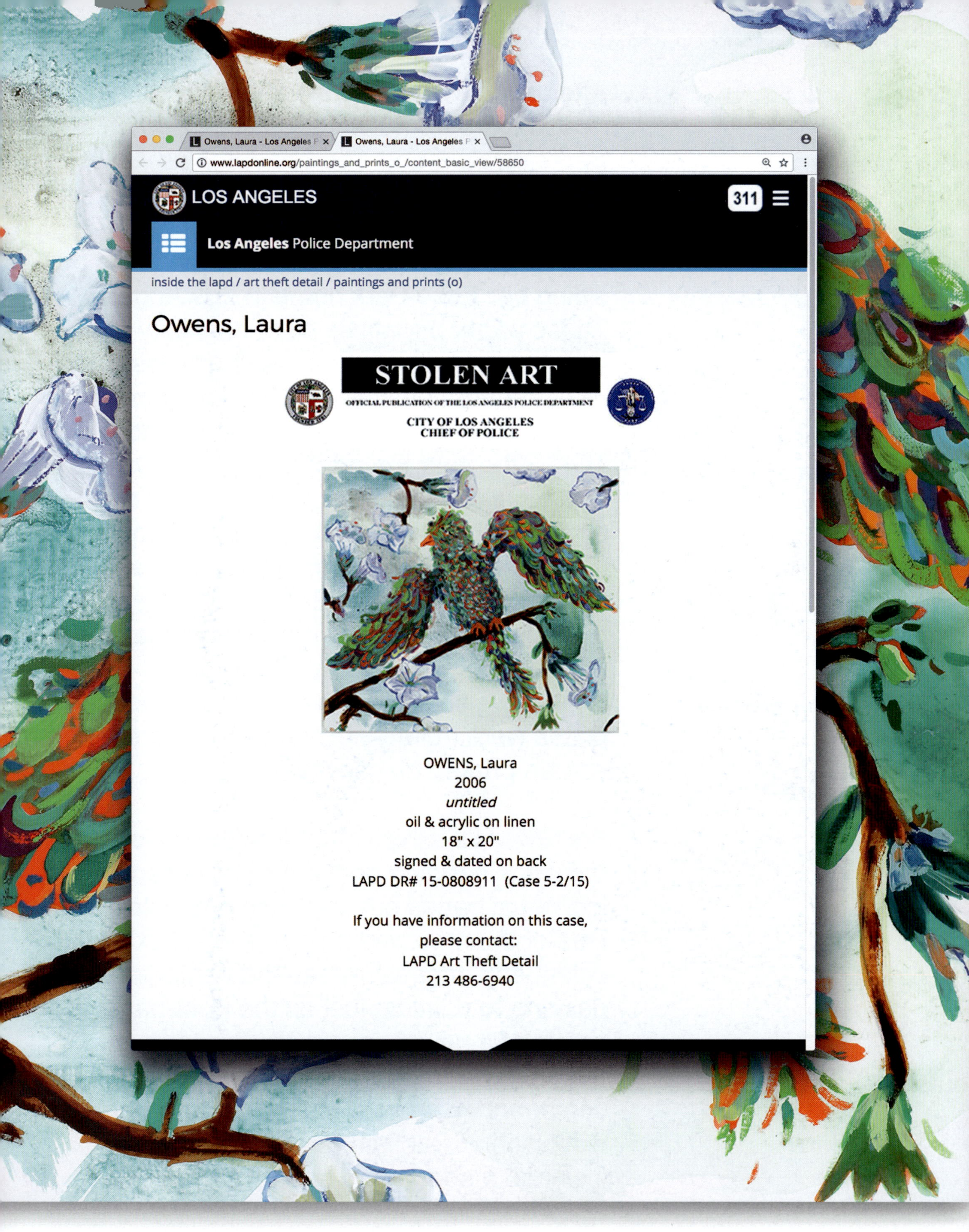

Foreground: Screenshot of lapdonline.org, 2010
Background: Detail of *Untitled*, 2006, oil and acrylic on linen, 18 × 20 in. (45.7 × 50.8 cm)

ecession

xhibitions

ecession

eethoven Frieze

isit & Service

vents

riends of the
ecession

upport

hop

ress

urrent

review

eview

rtists Index

eutsch

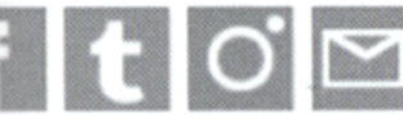

After working for several years with vintage newspapers from the 1960s such as *The Berkeley Barb* and *The Los Angeles Times*, Owens serendipitously found a set of newspaper stereotype plates that had been repurposed as flashing beneath the shingles siding her Echo Park home in Los Angeles. These paper negatives were originally made to cast the lead cylinders used on press, and all came from editions of *The Los Angeles Times* printed over a one-month period in 1942—the year the house was built. Owens was struck by the juxtaposition of world events in the months after Pearl Harbor alongside fait divers from a bygone era in her own neighborhood. To begin working with these images, she had rubber cast made of the original negative plates in order to make prints. The scans of the reprinted newspaper plates were edited in Photoshop before being screen-printed on canvas.

For Owens's exhibition at the Secession, the paintings hanging on the wall represent individual pages but comprise a constructed idea of the newspaper as a whole. Textures, colors and images repeat and continue from painting to painting just as the front-page article of a newspaper might continue on page 6. The artist began to work with compounded images of time following an exhibition at Capitain Petzel, Berlin, that included a short story spread across five

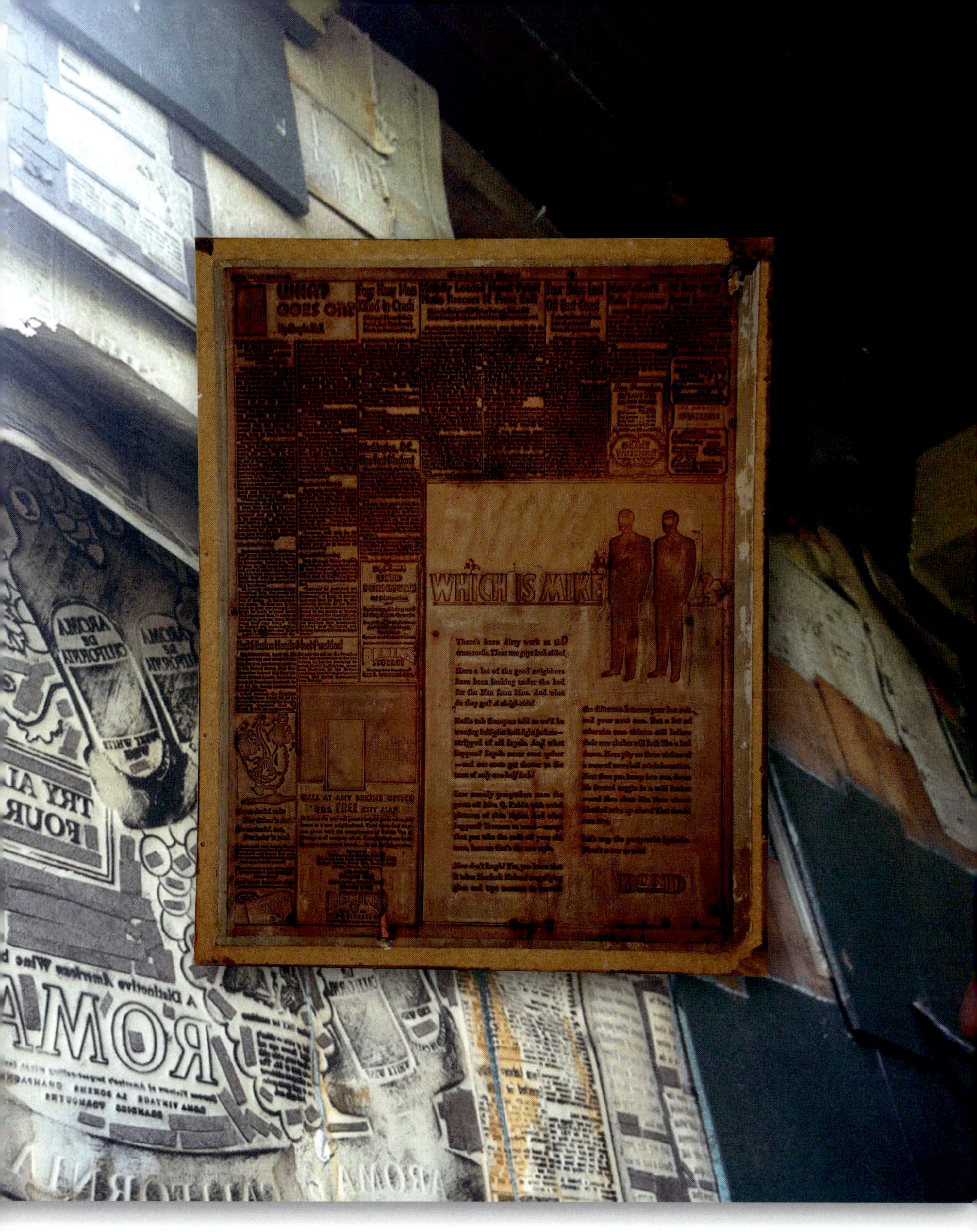

Foreground: Polyurethane mold of *Los Angeles Times* stereotype plate, 2015
Background: Newspaper stereotype plates found at Owens's home, Los Angeles, 2013

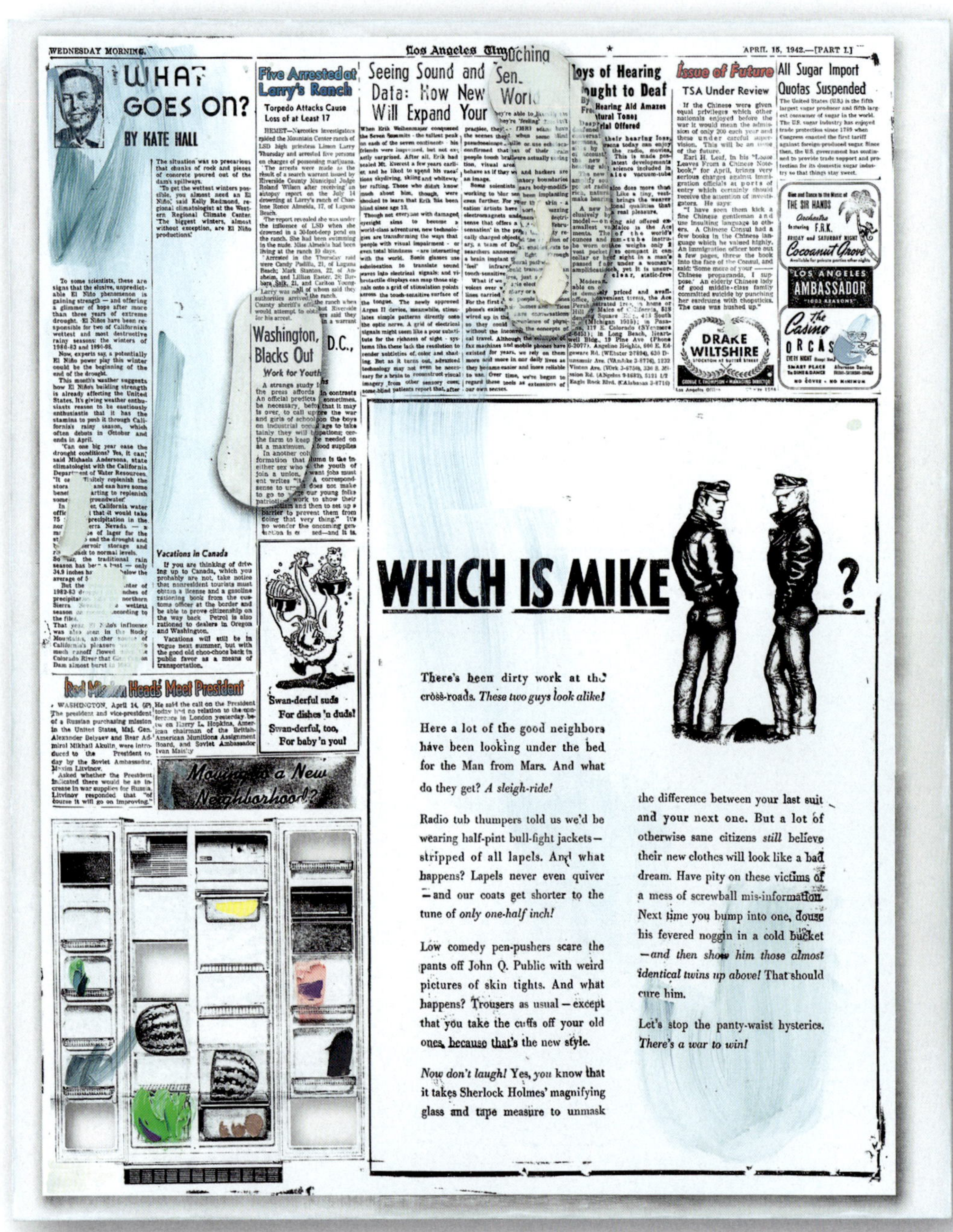

 Untitled, 2015, acrylic, oil, vinyl paint, and silkscreen inks on linen, 108 × 84 in. (274.3 × 213.4 cm)

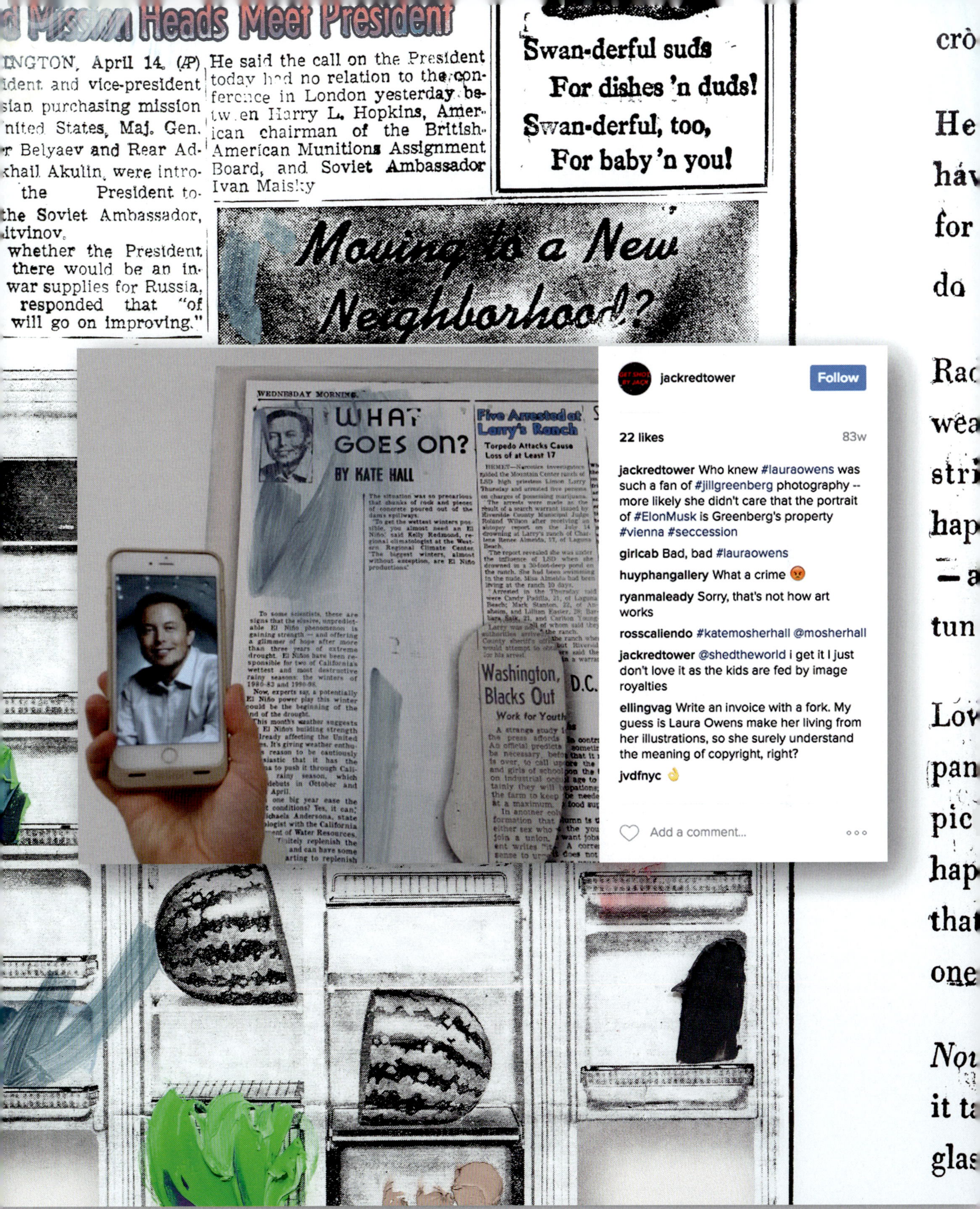

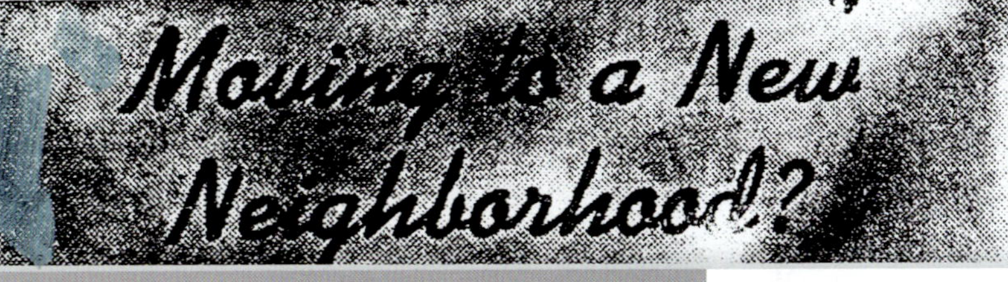

Foreground: Instagram post by Jill Greenberg, 2015
Background: Detail of *Untitled*, 2015 (see p. 580)

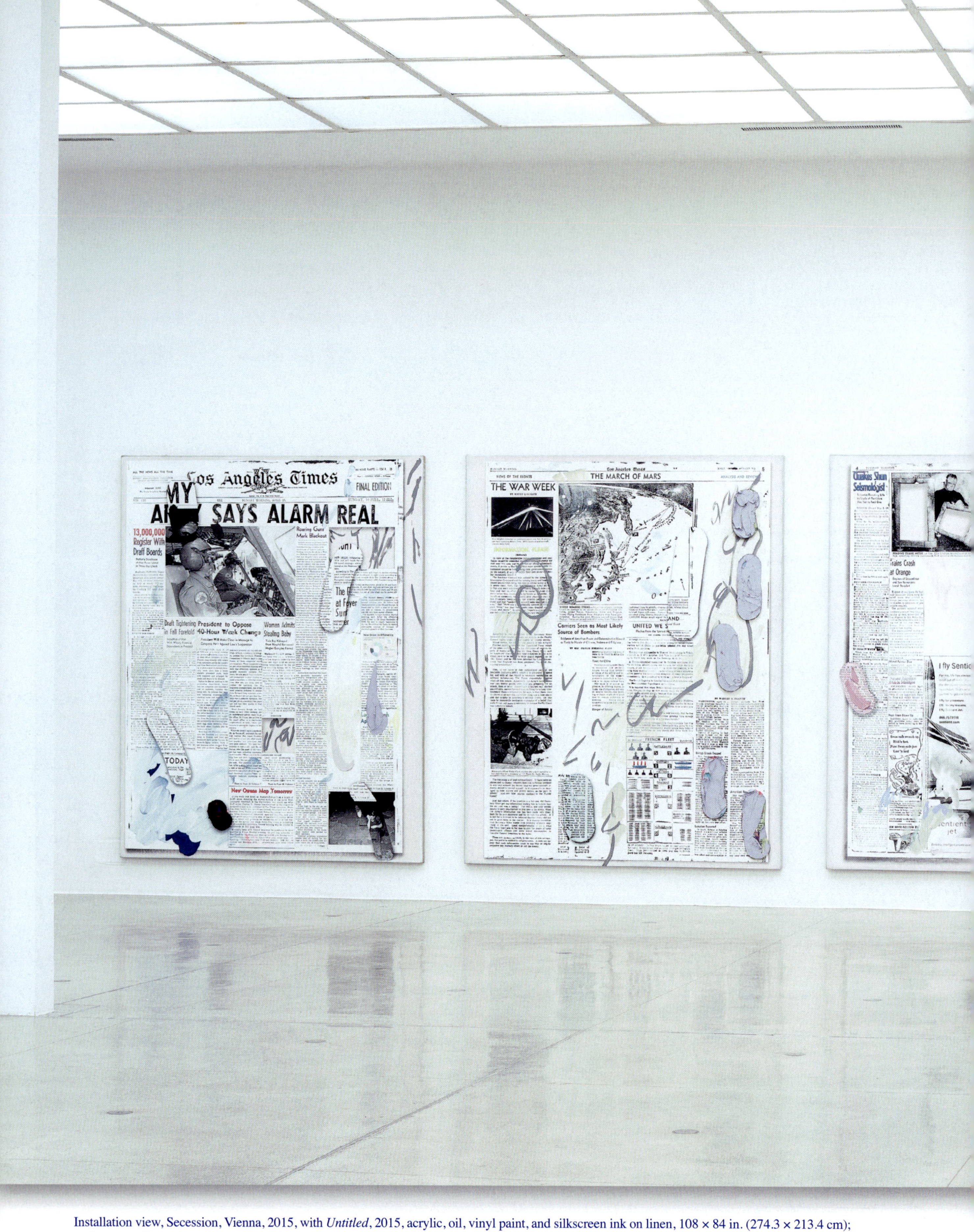

Installation view, Secession, Vienna, 2015, with *Untitled*, 2015, acrylic, oil, vinyl paint, and silkscreen ink on linen, 108 × 84 in. (274.3 × 213.4 cm); *Untitled*, 2015, acrylic, oil, vinyl paint, and silkscreen ink on linen, 108 × 84 in. (274.3 × 213.4 cm); *Untitled*, 2015, oil, silkscreen ink, vinyl paint, acrylic, and gesso on linen, 108 × 84 in. (274.3 × 213.4 cm); *Untitled*, 2015, acrylic, oil, vinyl paint, and silkscreen ink on linen, 108 × 84 in. (274.3 × 213.4 cm); and *Untitled*, 2015, acrylic, oil, vinyl paint, and silkscreen ink on linen, 108 × 84 in. (274.3 × 213.4 cm)

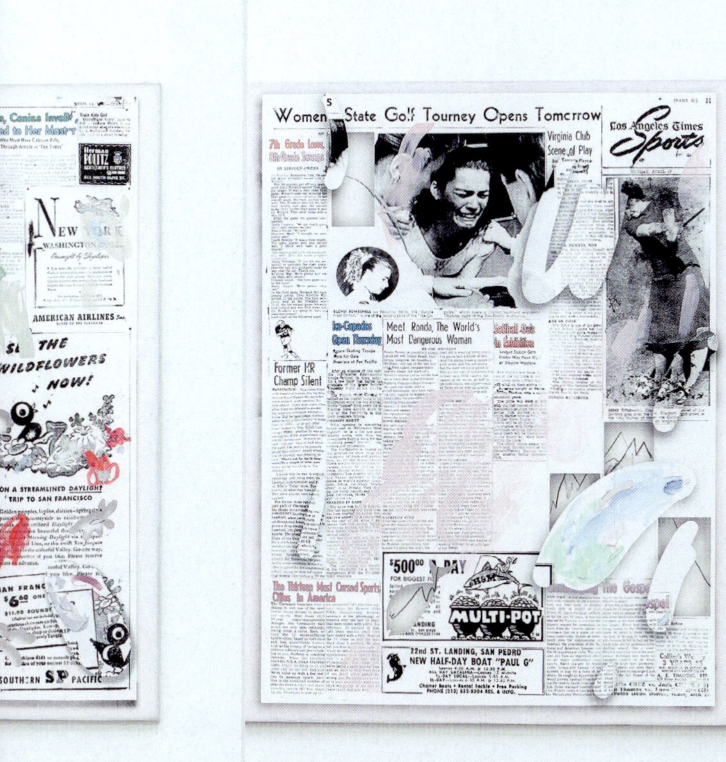

Women State Golf Tourney Opens Tomorrow
Los Angeles Times
Sports
7th Grade Loses, Fifth Grade Scores
Virginia Club Scene of Play
Meet Ronda, The World's Most Dangerous Woman
Former HR Champ Silent
$500.00 A DAY FOR BIGGEST FISH
MULTI-POT
22nd ST. LANDING, SAN PEDRO
NEW HALF-DAY BOAT "PAUL G"

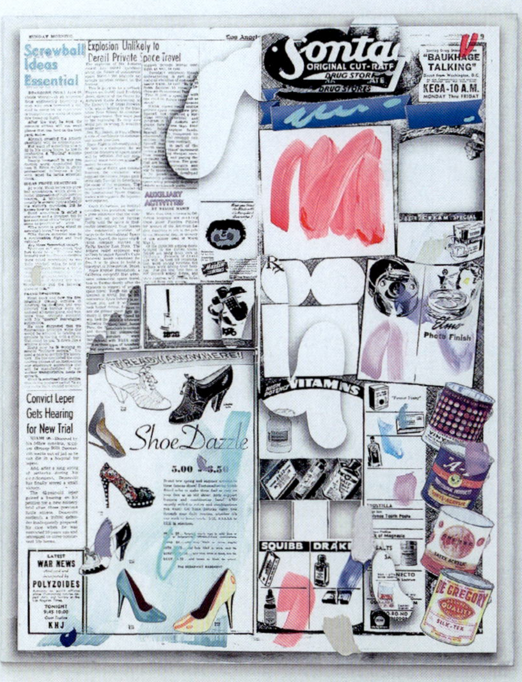

Screwball Ideas Essential
Explosion Unlikely to Derail Private Space Travel
Sontag
ORIGINAL CUT-RATE
DRUG STORE
"BAUKHOE TALKING"
KEGA-10 A.M.
MONDAY thru FRIDAY
Convict Leper Gets Hearing for New Trial
Shoe Dazzle
5.00   3.50
VITAMINS
Photo Finish
SQUIBB   DRAKE
WAR NEWS
POLYZOIDES
KHJ

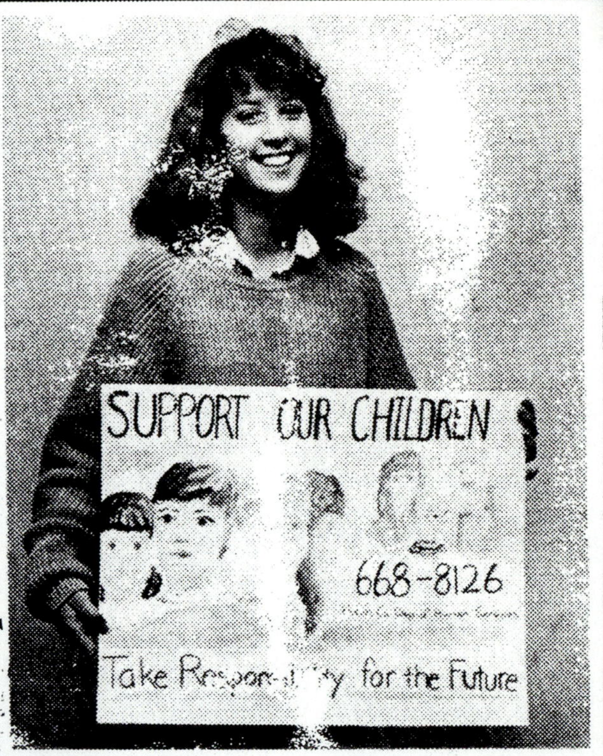

Foster Poster

NORWALK (Ohio) April 20. (AP) — Laura Owens, a junior at Norwalk High School, displays the poster she created that won first place in a contest sponsored by the Huron County Department of Human Services. The contest

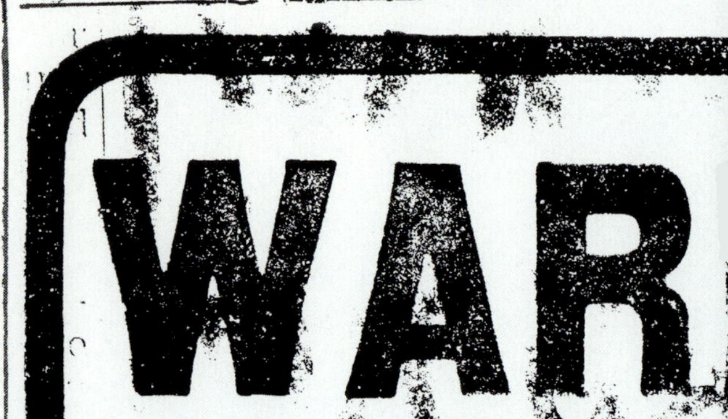

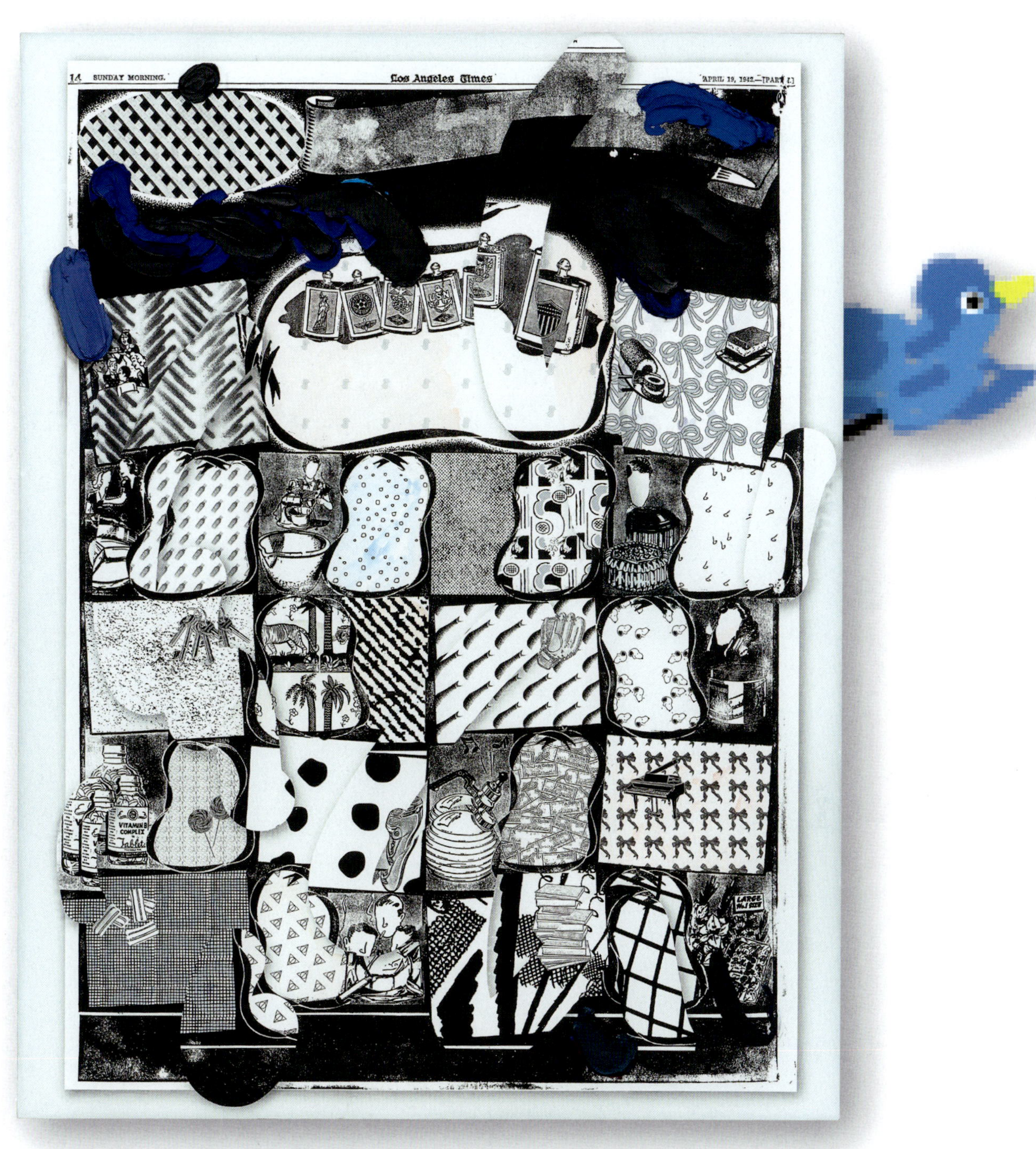

Untitled, 2015, acrylic, oil, vinyl paint, silkscreen ink, and charcoal on linen, 138 × 104 in. (350.5 × 264.2 cm)

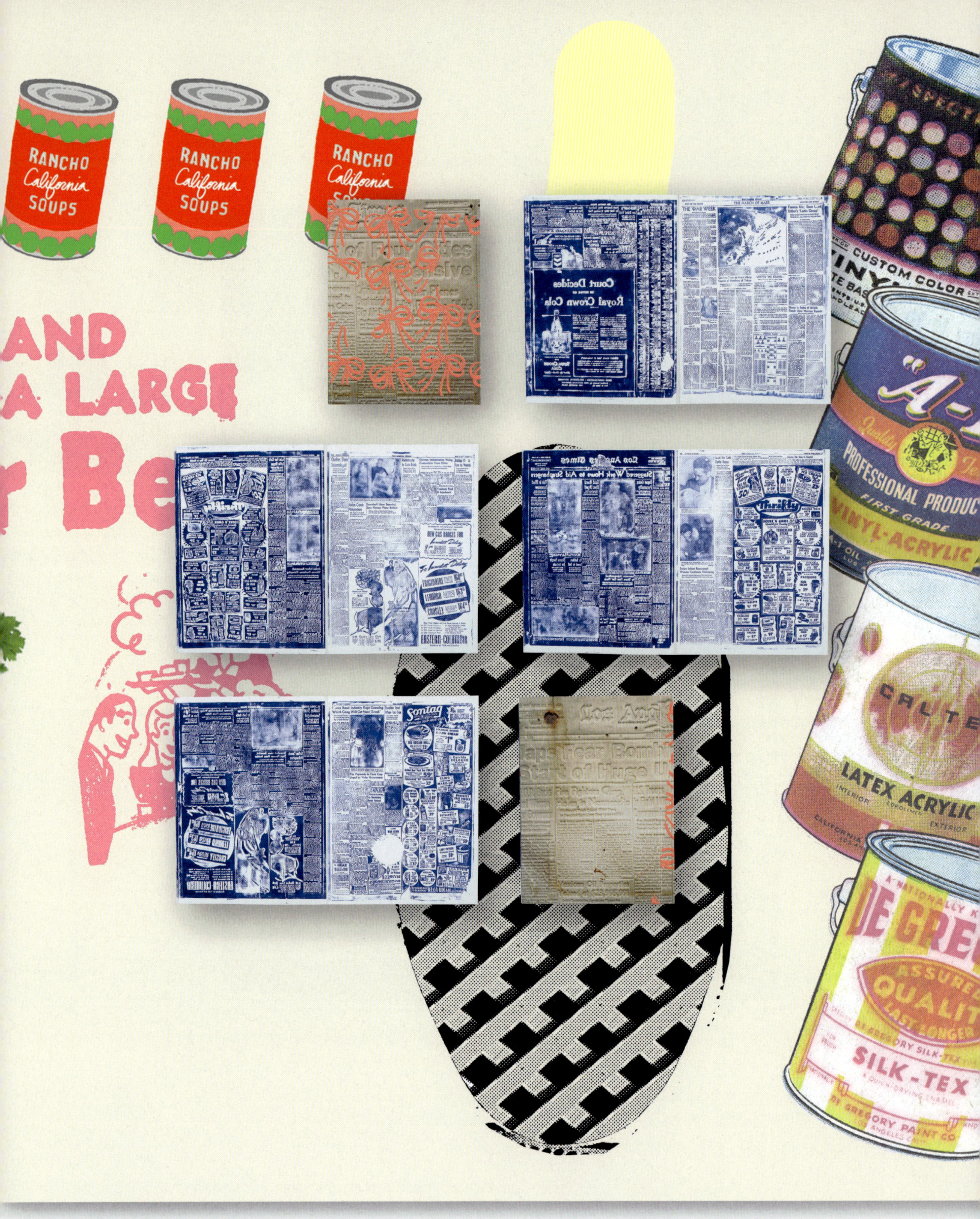

Foreground: Pages from *Untitled*, 2015, oil, vinyl paint, and inkjet print on Stonehenge paper, muslin, PVA, and book board, 24¼ × 17¾ × 1½ in. (61.6 × 45.1 × 3.81 cm)

 Background: Adobe CS6 file, 2015

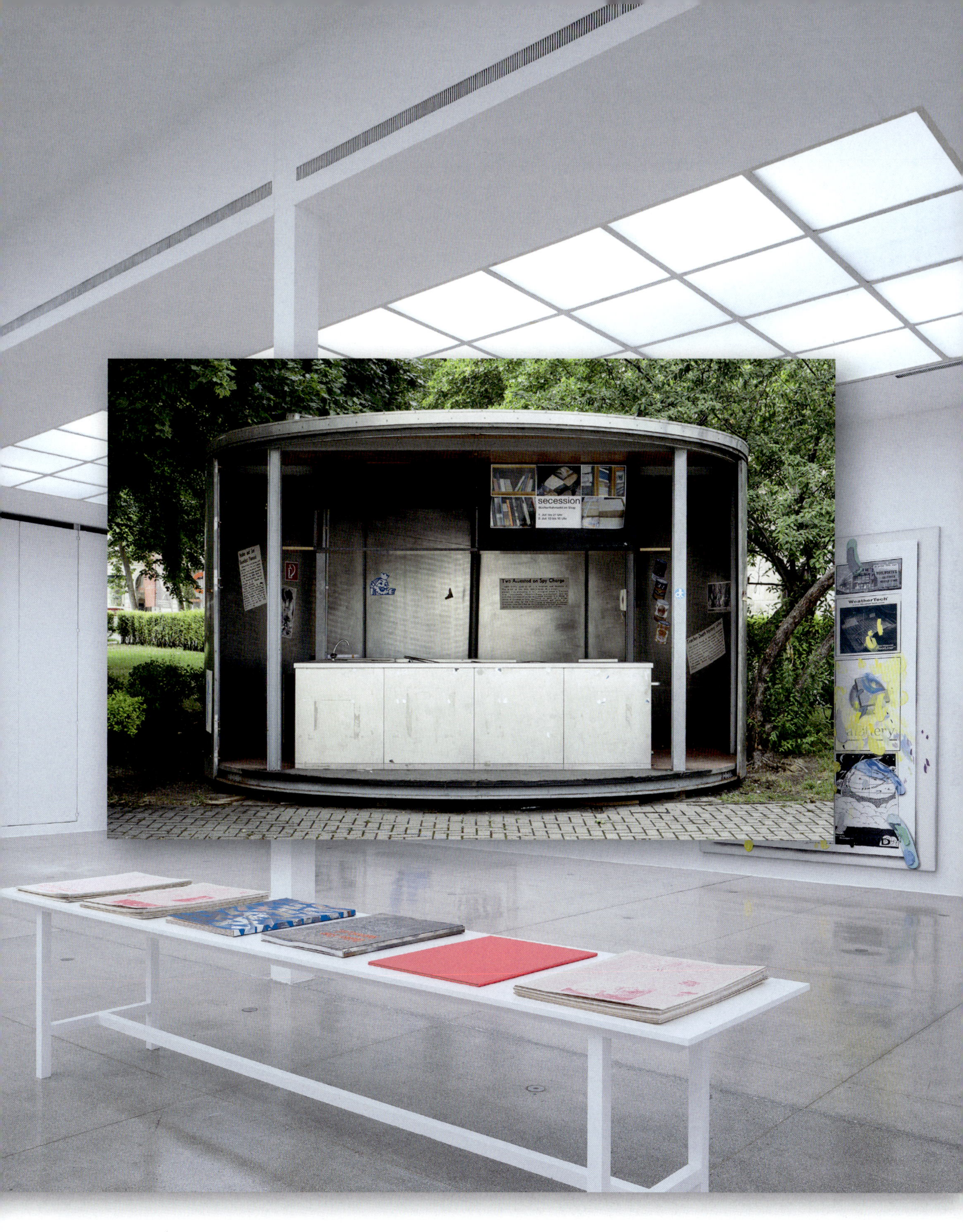

Foreground: Installation view, Secession, Vienna, 2015
Background: Installation view, Secession, Vienna, 2015, with *Untitled*, 2015, acrylic, oil, vinyl paint, silkscreen ink, and charcoal on linen,
    138 × 104 in. (350.5 × 264.2 cm)

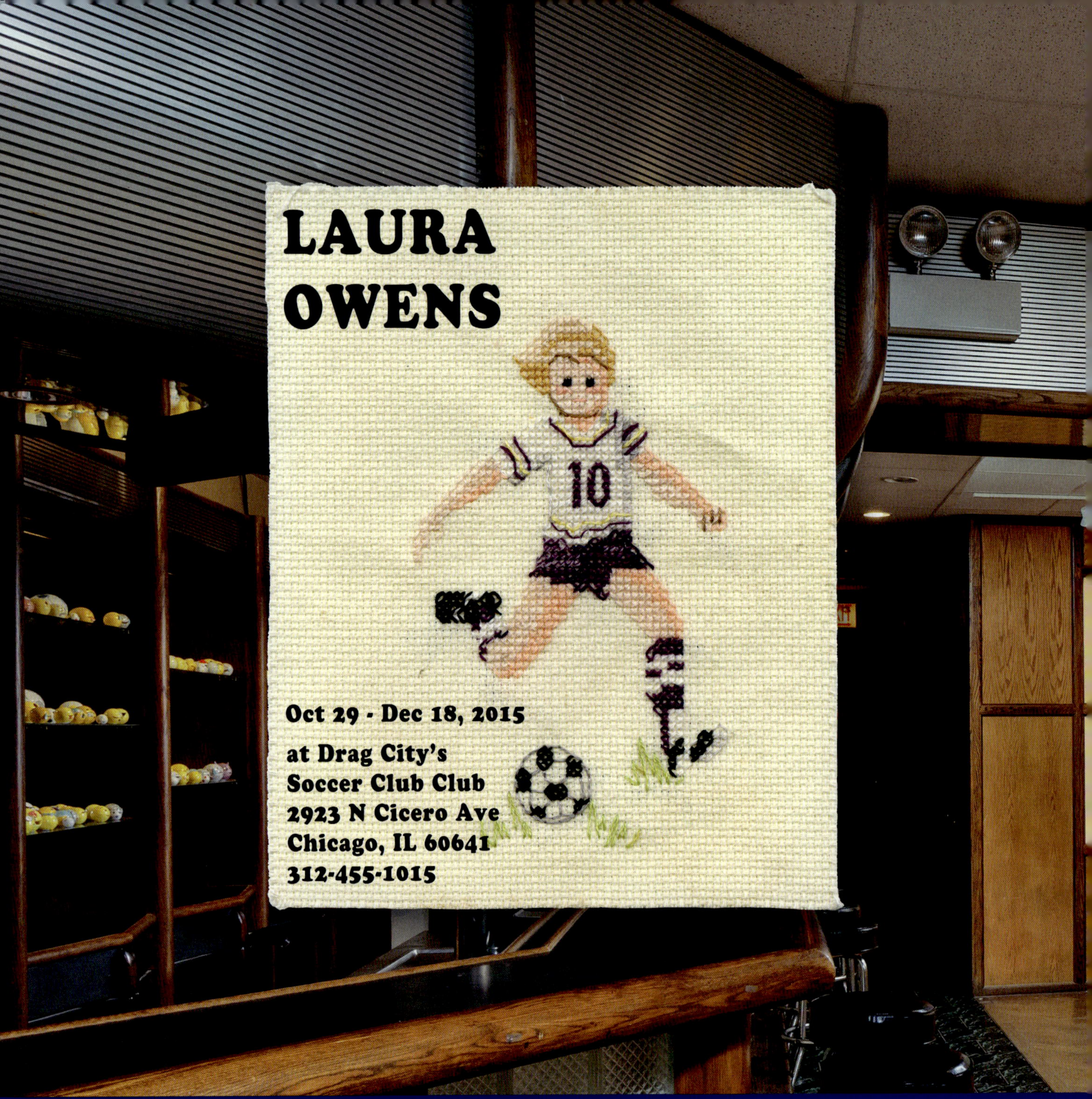

Amy Baumann: The first show I worked on with Laura was installed in a former Polish social club turned art space run by Drag City records. It's called Soccer Club Club. I didn't understand the name until I saw the tiled wall mural of a soccer player next to the DJ booth. The interior is super dark with a low drop ceiling and bad access for large artwork; it has a general funky basement bar feel. Laura had the idea to use the heavy wood molding in the interior as a framing device for works on paper, but the measurements of the panels were so inconsistent that we had to cut each drawing to size on-site, which was challenging as the works were mounted on museum board and still had wet paint on them. The show was anchored by a painting stretched exactly to the size of the wall that was perpendicular to a mirrored wall on the dance floor, creating a sort of Rorschach abstraction that revealed a soccer ball at its center. She made more than three hundred ceramic emoji and soccer ball sculptures that were installed on mirrored shelves behind the bar, and we sang karaoke at the opening. Someone bumped into a drawing and unknowingly left with green paint on their coat.

Foreground: Invitation, Soccer Club Club, Chicago, 2015
Background: Installation view, Soccer Club Club, Chicago, 2015, with *Untitled*, 2015; *Untitled*, 2015; *Untitled*, 2015; and *Untitled*, 2015, oil, vinyl paint, and silkscreen ink on Gampi Torinko paper, mounted on mat board, various dimensions

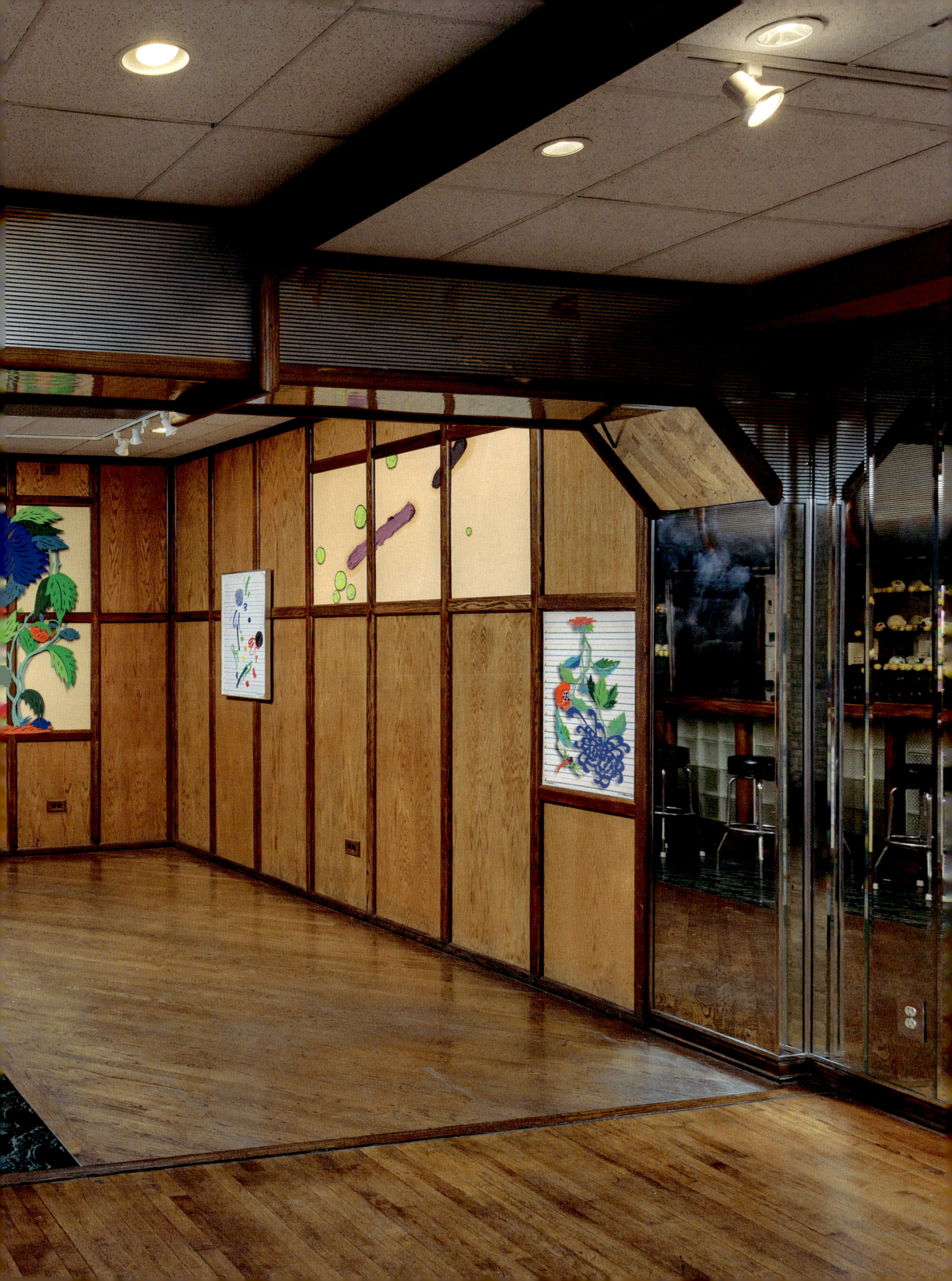

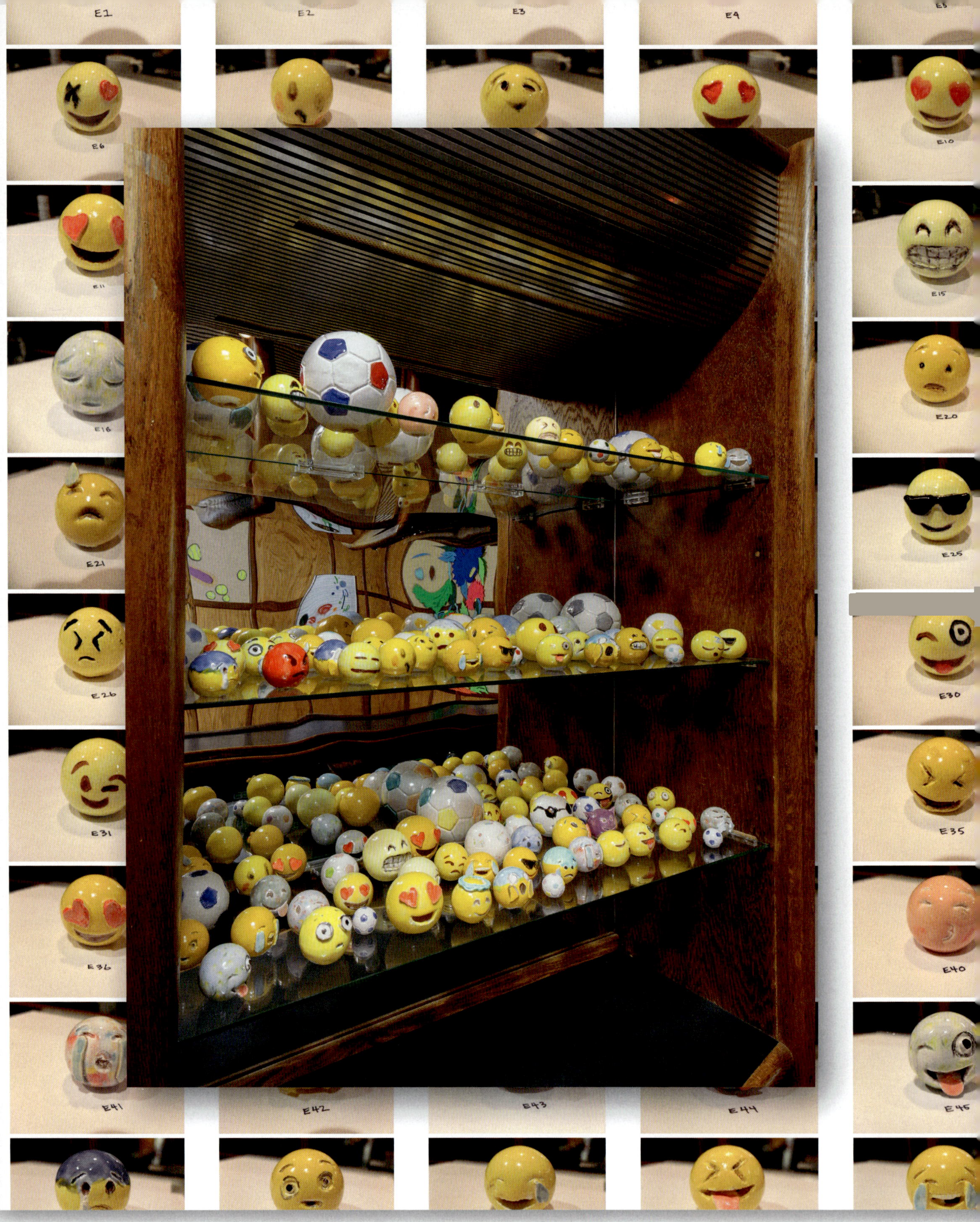

Foreground: Installation view, Soccer Club Club, Chicago, 2015, with *Untitled*, 2015, glazed porcelain, diameter: 3–5 in. (7.6–12.7 cm) each
Background: Digital contact sheet, 2015

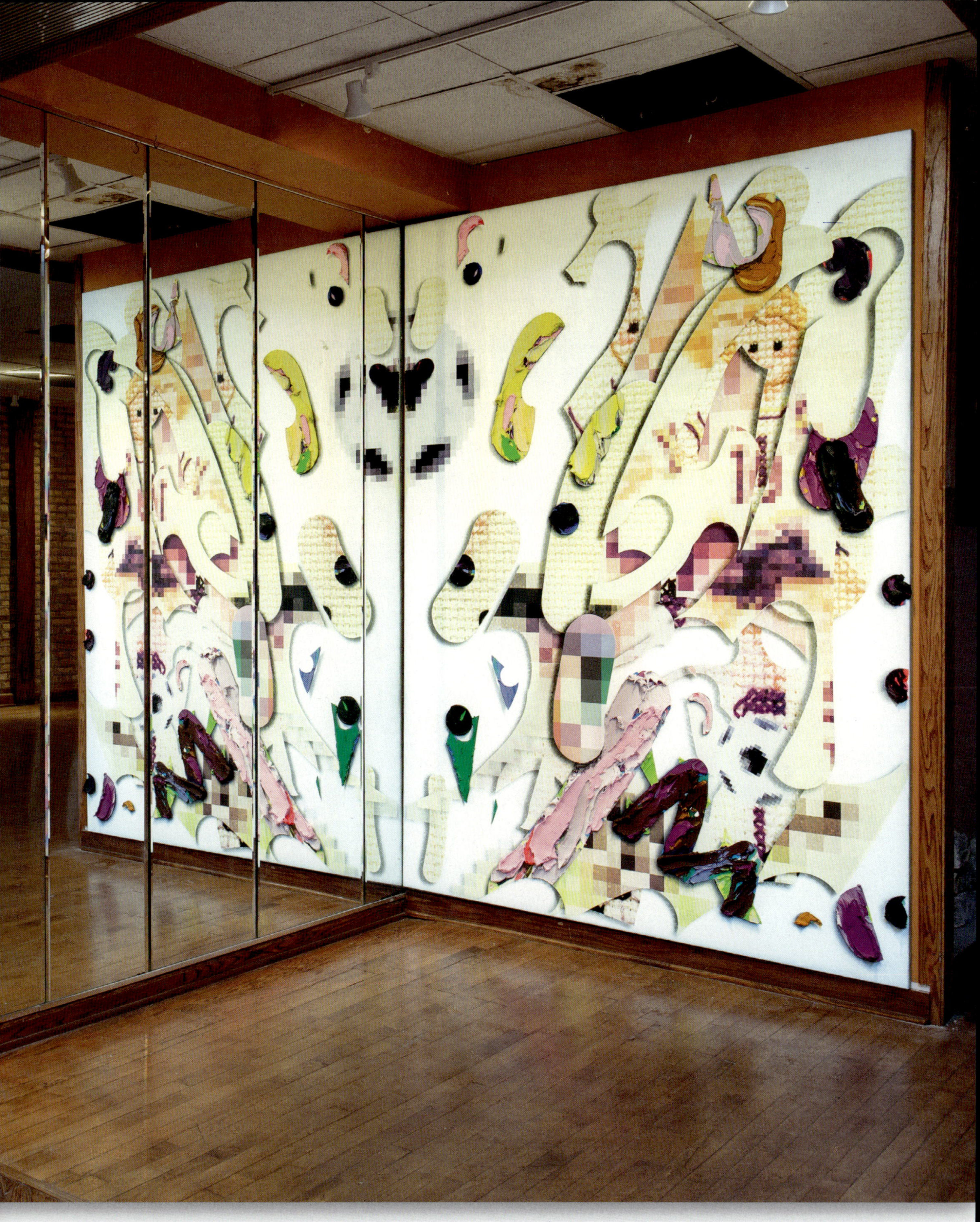

Installation view, Soccer Club Club, Chicago, 2015, with *Untitled*, 2015, oil, vinyl paint, and silkscreen ink on linen, 96 × 70 in. (243.8 × 177.8 cm)

David Berezin: The wallpaper for the Wattis show was site-specific to the quarter inch. It was a totally different way of thinking about the difference between a painting and a mural. We looked at history of wallpaper books, make-your-own wallpaper books, and pattern books; Laura wanted her wallpaper to be in that lineage rather than relating to sunset photomurals or something. She wanted it to be true wallpaper, which has a craftiness in it and an association with the Arts and Crafts movement and all these other things, whereas photomurals are very technological. Some of the images were motifs Laura had used before, some were new. The base pattern was from a scan of a crumpled piece of paper that was compressed and processed digitally. Laura had used that imagery before, but in this case it wasn't totally obvious what it was. When we started making it she thought it was too perfect and clean looking, so she got the idea to add charcoal. The base pattern was a black checkerboard in which some shapes were coated in clear medium that would get dusted with charcoal, which added a ton of inconsistency, dirtied up the process, and made it less predictable. At times the pattern got a drop shadow made of charcoal. Then the checkerboard sitting on top of the shadow would be printed with paint and have sand thrown on it. This gave it all more texture, which I think is what Laura liked. The wallpaper could have been digitally printed, and that would have been fairly easy to do, but I don't think she would have gotten what she wanted that way.

Making the wallpaper was very labor-intensive. We had to create three strips a day, so we had three teams printing. Each team was responsible for one strip at a time, and every strip required between twelve and eighteen five-by-seven-foot screens: one for the base, one for the shadow, another for each of the different images. After printing we had to clean each screen, coat it again, dry it, and then burn it. We used chemicals to remove the emulsion and the paint. The studio

     David Berezin is a Los Angeles–based artist who has worked in Owens's studio since 2015.

turned into a twenty-four-hour-a-day operation. We had a night crew doing the dirty work of reclaiming screens and getting the studio back into shape so that the printers could begin a new round the next morning. They went completely nocturnal—they would show up at eight at night and work until the sun rose. It's no exaggeration to say that the show would not have happened if they hadn't done that.

The installation was very complicated. We learned that wallpaper is not typically made to perfectly fit a specific site. It's a very inaccurate medium; it's messy, it stretches differently based on the temperature of the room. It was shocking to see the wallpaper hangers install our paper. There wasn't a repeating pattern, each strip was unique, but they were handling it like regular wallpaper and not like art. We had this model where every twenty feet there would be an architectural element, but it never lined up because the paper stretched way more than we expected. So we would have to cut the paper and paste it in place to make it line up. People who saw the show would not have noticed, it looked perfect. But there were countless problems during the installation. There was one point where a wallpaper hanger cut one of the columns in half. And I was like, "What are you doing? Oh my God!" because it had taken a whole twenty-four hours of work by multiple people to make that one strip. And he said, "It didn't fit, so I was going to paste it up a little bit." That's what wallpaper hangers typically do.

The other element was the sound. On the wallpaper, there were eight phone numbers, each paired with a line that said, "Text a question to." You could text any question, and it would get routed through custom computer hardware and software associated with the SIM card tied to the number you texted. The computer would choose from around a thousand responses that we had preprogrammed, which would be played from a speaker embedded in the wall behind the wallpaper where the phone number was written. I think Laura wanted to be able to have people talk to the paintings. I worked with a developer, Ben Dean, to invent the program. Half of the answers came from interviews where Laura and I asked who, what, where, when, why questions and some more complicated ones too. The other half came from sound clips, pieces of music, snippets of commercials, and text-to-speech software I wrote answers for. Like if someone said, "This show sucks; why did you make it?" my program gave us a way to respond directly. It became the voice of the paintings, but it also became an outlet for me to add a mildly sassy personality. We also included the answer: "That's the best question I've heard all day. You've won a prize. Go to the curator's office and ask for Leila and collect your prize." And there wasn't a prize. There was some back-and-forth with the institution too: the painting would say stuff about the Wattis. Or if someone said, "Why is this art?" one of the potential responses would be, "I don't know. Go ask Anthony Huberman," who was the curator of the show. It was super self-reflexive and playful; each painting was self-aware that it was a painting.

The show was called *Ten Paintings*, but you walked in and it was a wallpaper installation. There were no paintings in the gallery. Before we hung the wallpaper though, pieces of the drywall were removed, and in its place we installed inset panels. When the show came down, most of the wallpaper got torn down in a brutish way. But we carefully cut around the edges of each of the panels and pulled them out, so they could have a future exhibition life of their own. They weren't identified at the show—maybe if you were really observant you could tell where they were based on a little ripple in the paper or something. But if you texted the question "Where are the paintings?" all eight of the speakers would activate at different intervals and say the word "here." So it was like, "Here," "Here," "Here," "Here," bouncing around the room.

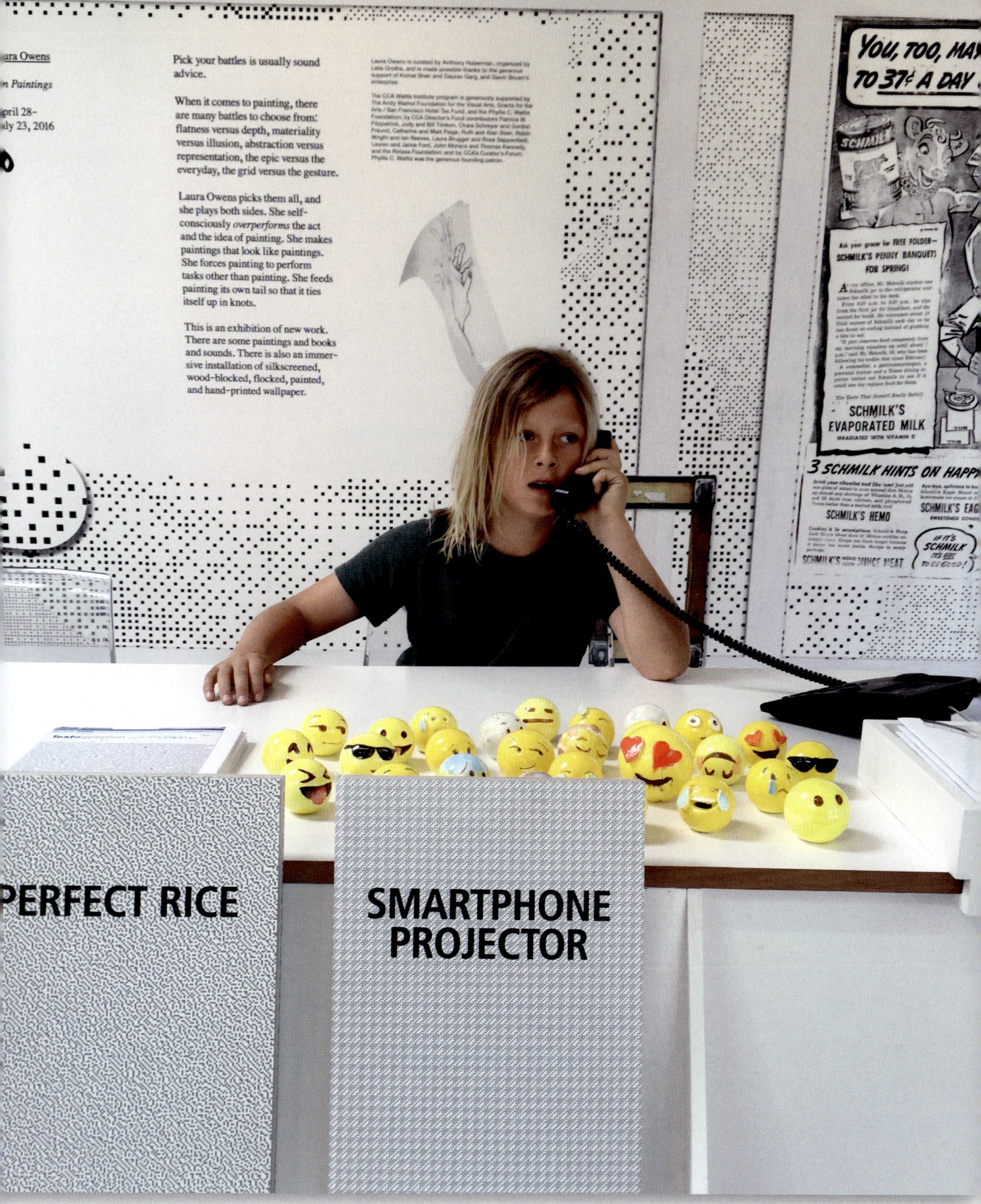

Henry Bryan, *Ten Paintings*, CCA Wattis Institute, San Francisco, 2016

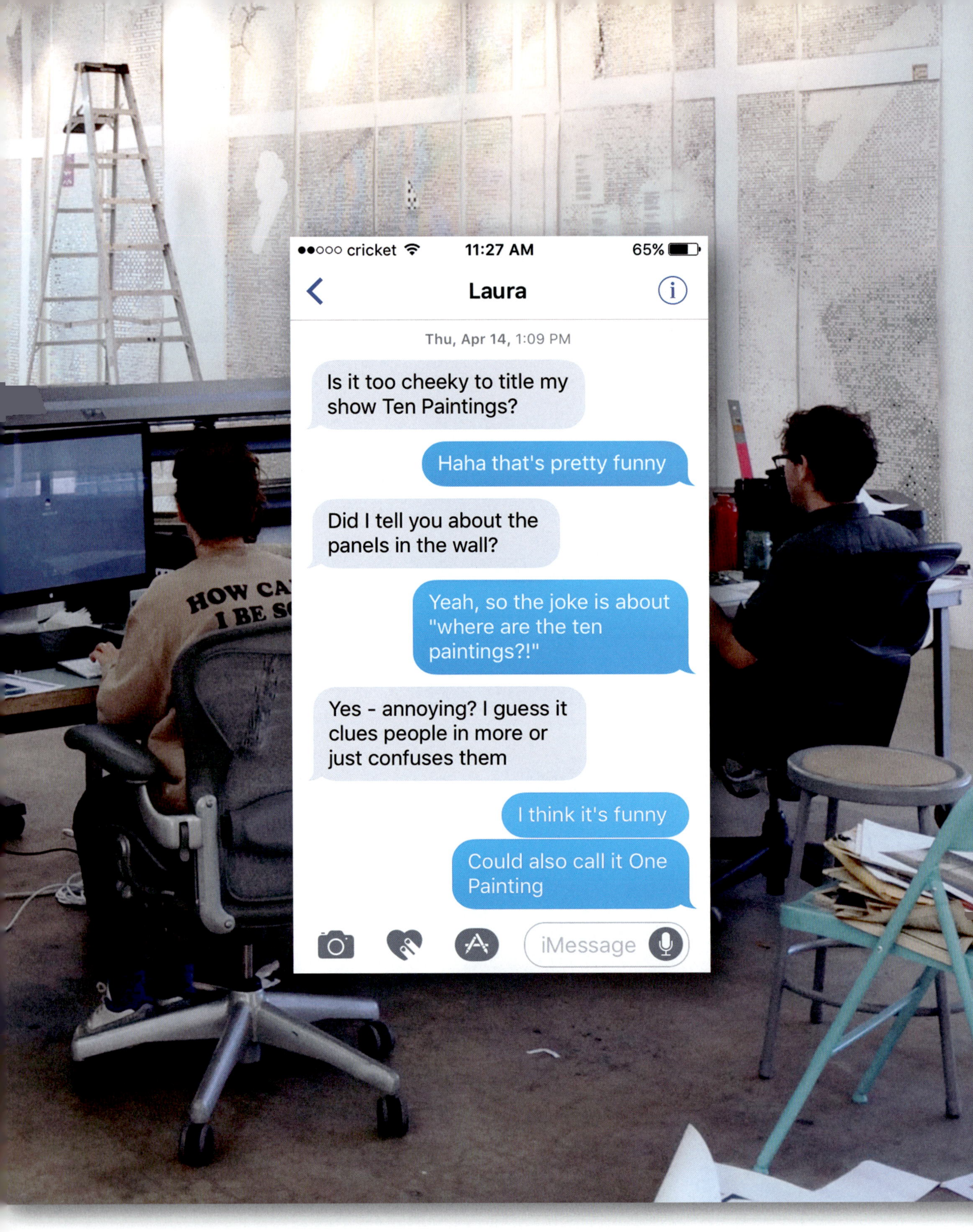

Foreground: Texts with Asha Schechter, 2016
Background: Owens and David Berezin, Mission Rd. studio, Los Angeles, 2016

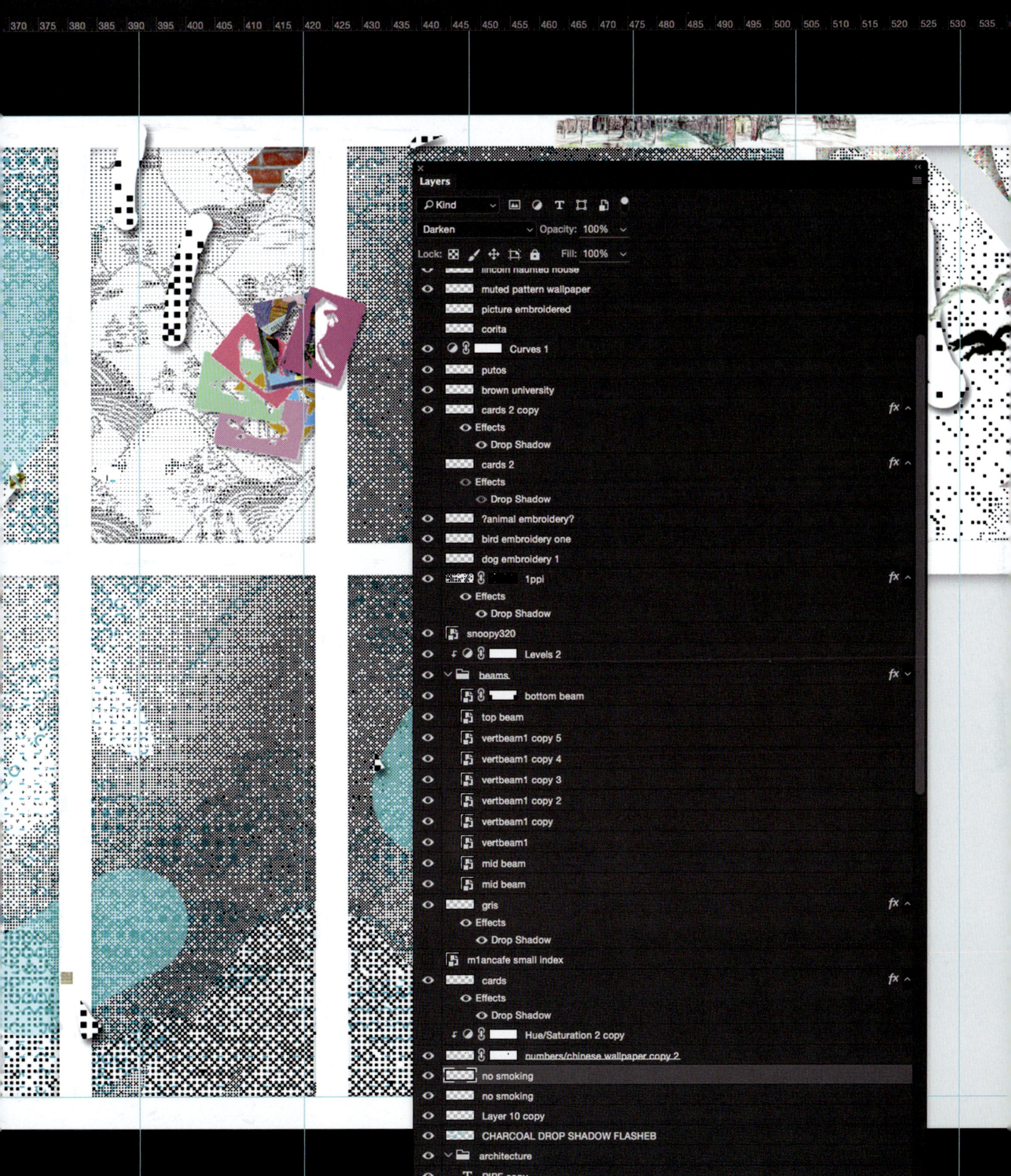

Adobe Photoshop CC 2015
370 375 380 385 390 395 400 405 410 415 420 425 430 435 440 445 450 455 460 465 470 475 480 485 490 495 500 505 510 515 520 525 530 535
Layers
Kind
Darken   Opacity: 100%
Lock: Fill: 100%
lincoln haunted house
muted pattern wallpaper
picture embroidered
corita
Curves 1
putos
brown university
cards 2 copy
Effects
Drop Shadow
cards 2
Effects
Drop Shadow
?animal embroidery?
bird embroidery one
dog embroidery 1
1ppi
Effects
Drop Shadow
snoopy320
Levels 2
beams
bottom beam
top beam
vertbeam1 copy 5
vertbeam1 copy 4
vertbeam1 copy 3
vertbeam1 copy 2
vertbeam1 copy
vertbeam1
mid beam
mid beam
gris
Effects
Drop Shadow
m1ancafe small index
cards
Effects
Drop Shadow
Hue/Saturation 2 copy
numbers/chinese wallpaper copy 2
no smoking
no smoking
Layer 10 copy
CHARCOAL DROP SHADOW FLASHEB
architecture
PIPE copy

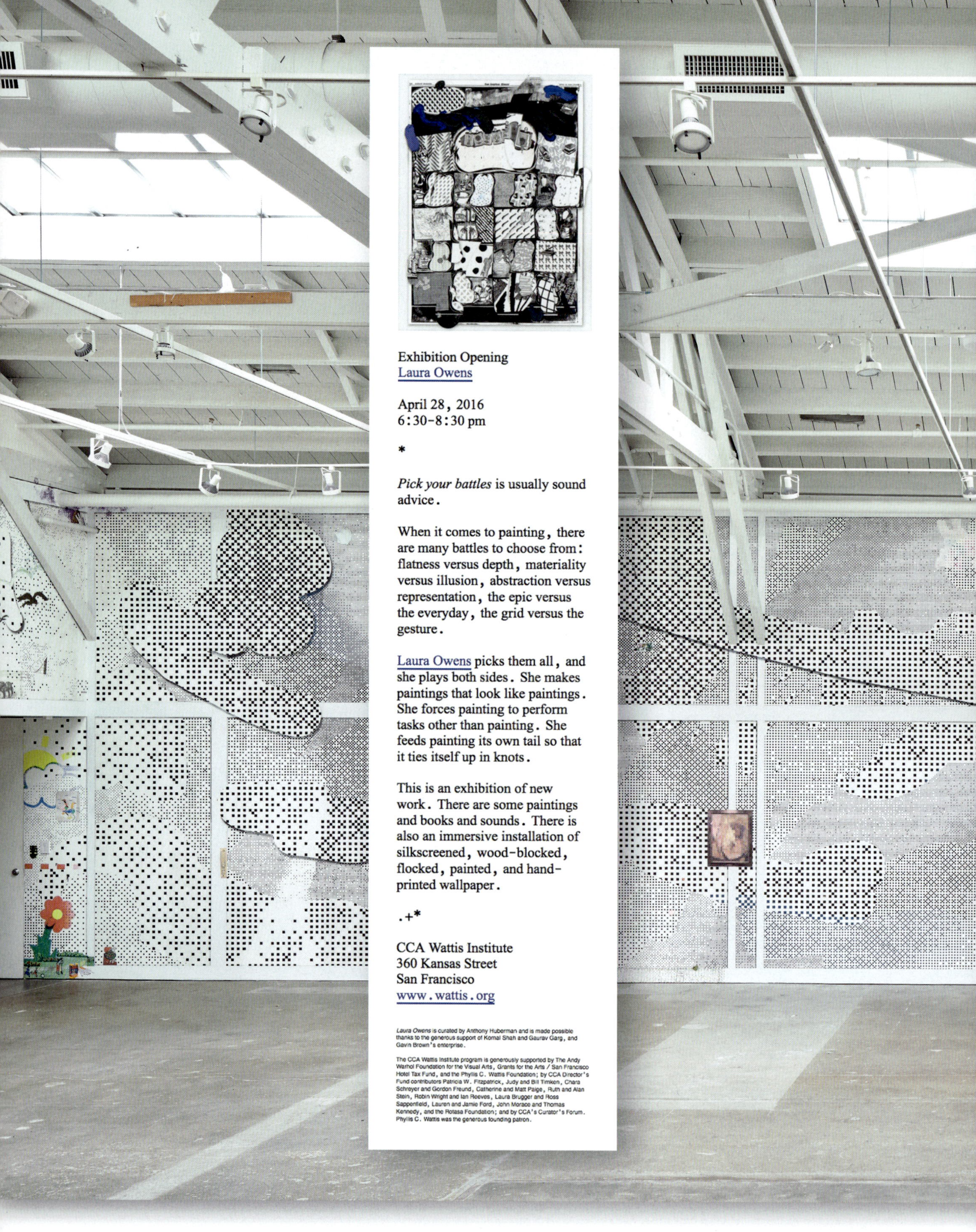

Foreground: Announcement, *Ten Paintings*, CCA Wattis Institute, San Francisco, 2016
Background: Installation view, CCA Wattis Institute, San Francisco, 2016

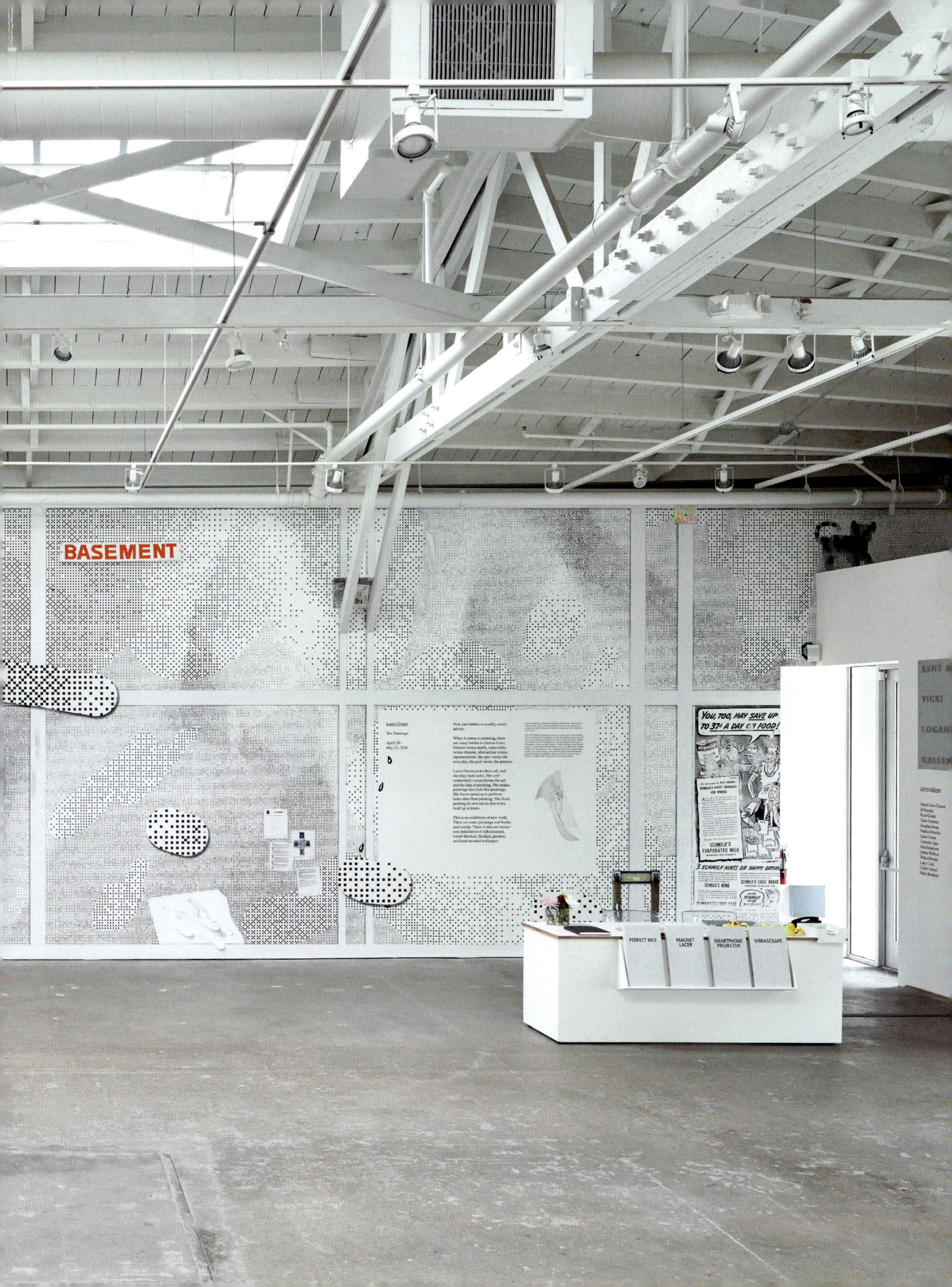

BASEMENT
PERFECT RICE
MAGNET LACER
SMARTPHONE PROJECTOR
VIBRASCRAPE
KENT &
VICKI
LOGAN
GALLERY
YOU, TOO, MAY SAVE UP TO 37¢ A DAY ON FOOD!
SCHMILK'S EVAPORATED MILK
3 SCHMILK HINTS ON HAPPY EATING

7 | 7:16 | "shipped: your amazon package with luxlady gaming mousepad image id: 33979466 vintage white ... will be delivered tue, jul 12. track at http://a.co/ckqls7i" | /012 y/colleen_better_luck_next_time.wav
7 | 7:31 | "sf dental house: rose is overdue for a visit with us. please call us at (415) 648-3500 to schedule an appointment." | /128 app/Developers.wav
7 | 8:12 | "shipped: your amazon package with mcgraw-hill education 5 teas practice tests, 2nd edition ... will be delivered tue, jun 21. track at http://a.co/106634s" | /012 y/nova_texting_stranger2.wav
1 | 10:23 | "how many people are in your walls?" | /030 how/asha_bad.wav
1 | 10:23 | "what color is god?" | /070 what/nova_i_dunno.wav
1 | 10:24 | "is he an artist or collector?" | /090 or /CV_latter.wav
1 | 10:36 | "play the song one dance by drake" | /012 y/colleen_how_often_think.wav
1 | 10:43 | "gentrification?" | /008 o/colleen_question_unanswerable.wav
5 | 10:47 | "do you love me?" | /979 love/colleen_def_break_up.wav
1 | 10:47 | "why am i sad?" | /040 why/elliot_because_earth_round.wav
1 | 10:47 | "why am i sad?" | /040 why/elliot_poor_structural_integrity.wav
5 | 10:47 | "give me a kiss" | /013 is/CV_woudlnt_count.wav
1 | 10:47 | "why do i hate my moth
1 | 10:47 | "why do i hate my moth
1 | 11:7 | "how late is the new mu
6 | 11:44 | "how am i to discern t   _was_really_good.wav
6 | 11:45 | "i would really hope t   just heard" | /013 is/
asha_seems_to_be_working.wav
6 | 11:46 | "i would agree with th   av
1 | 11:47 | "how much is hand pain
1 | 11:47 | "how much is hand pain
8 | 11:49 | "i have no materials f
1 | 11:50 | "what does tsa stand f
1 | 11:56 | "is art worth it?" | /
8 | 12:6 | "explain this show" | /
2 | 12:12 | "will trump win?" | /1
2 | 12:13 | "will trump resign" |
2 | 12:13 | "sanders" | /124 sande
1 | 12:16 | "how much are the emoj
5 | 12:20 | "did mom just fart?" |
5 | 12:21 | "are you sure" | /018
1 | 12:22 | "who was the third art   " at pat hearn?" | /
080 who/asha_trevor_shimizu.wav
1 | 12:25 | "what does intramural
1 | 12:38 | "why are you so checke
5 | 12:39 | "are babies welcome?"
5 | 12:39 | "do you like kids?" |
6 | 12:39 | "is it useless to purs   l3 is/
colleen_never.wav
6 | 12:41 | "steph curry" | /114 c
6 | 12:44 | "did laura owens reall   gibberish.wav
1 | 12:45 | "how much does this co
2 | 12:46 | "are kids annoying?" |
1 | 12:47 | "i am making a stateme
7 | 12:52 | "why are bay area resi
elliot_because_some_people.wav
1 | 12:55 | "why tarot?" | /040 wh
6 | 12:59 | "what is your interest
1 | 12:59 | "do you like rice?" | vav
1 | 12:59 | "do you like the whitn
1 | 13:0 | "do you like scott roth
6 | 13:0 | "what happened in 1991"
1 | 13:1 | "are you a vegetarian?"
6 | 13:14 | "have you joined a boo
1 | 13:22 | "why did you make this
1 | 13:23 | "why did you make this   ectrum Filterbank.mp3
6 | 13:28 | "are you siri?" | /018
1 | 13:29 | "did you know i was go   ever?" | /070 what/
1 | 13:29 | "what would it take to
CV_sign3.wav
1 | 13:30 | "do you like snoopy?"
1 | 13:33 | "jamie stevens" | /007
1 | 13:34 | "what's lorenza's shoe
1 | 13:35 | "what's daddy's horosc
1 | 13:35 | "sagittarius" | /103 sagittarius/elliot_sag.wav
1 | 13:37 | "do you like watching seinfeld?" | /097 hi/CV_wassup.wav
6 | 13:38 | "was iraq a mistake ?" | /013 is/nova_it_is_certain.wav
6 | 13:38 | "will you miss obama?" | /013 is/elliot_sometimes.wav
6 | 13:38 | "barack obama?" | /008 o/nova_stupid_question.wav
1 | 13:43 | "why does ego seem to win over harmony?" | /040 why/asha_my_sister.wav
6 | 13:39 | "do you know yasmine ?" | /014 do/nova_dont_count_on_it.wav
6 | 13:53 | "what's with the cat?" | /070 what/elliot_idonno_wish_you_luck.wav
6 | 13:53 | "does the cat have a name?" | /019 does/probably not.wav
6 | 13:54 | "does trump support artists?" | /973 sup/CV_wassup.wav
6 | 13:55 | "is this exhibit bullshit?" | /013 is/elliot_occasionally.wav
6 | 13:56 | "is red hair in?" | /013 is/maybe later.wav
3 | 14:0 | "does sabrina love this show?" | /979 love/Married With Children.wav
1 | 14:10 | "are the warriors winning tomorrow?" | /118 warriors/asha_lose_clippers.wav
1 | 14:11 | "why is grunder like this?" | /097 hi/33 Track 33.mp3

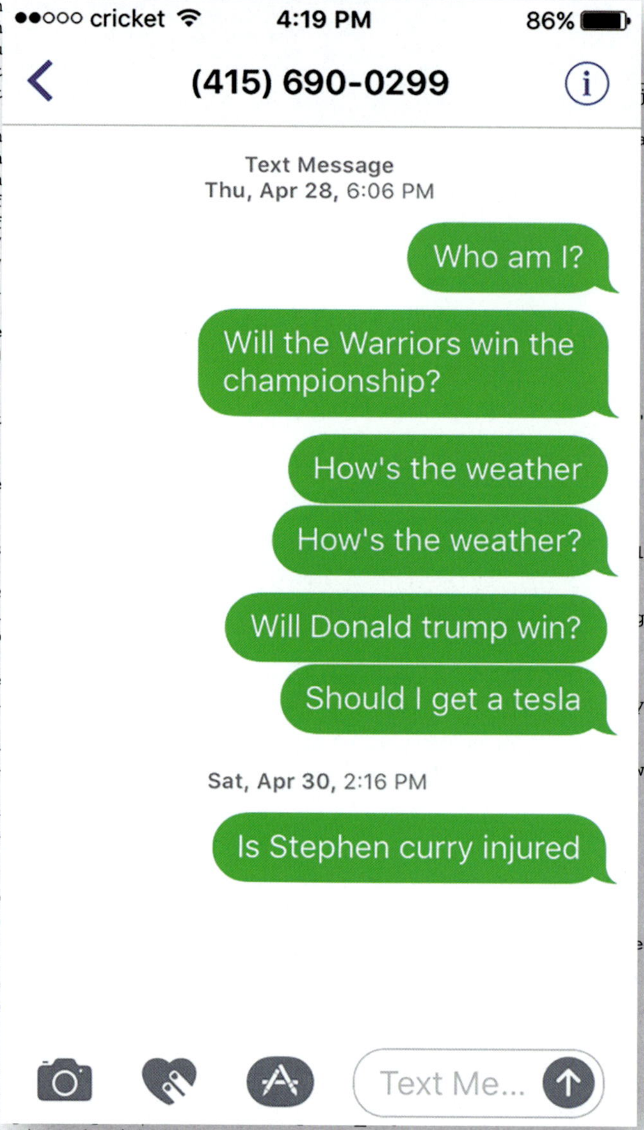

| 14:15 | "about your flaky skin" | /012 y/CV_actions.wav
| 14:15 | "was the most recent coup attempt in turkey a false flag perpetrated by erdogan to purge [d]issidents?" | /014 do/colleen_of_course.wav
| 14:26 | "do all dogs go to heaven" | /014 do/henry_yes.wav
| 14:30 | "why are the paintings talking?" | /040 why/colleen_because_doesnt_answer.wav
| 14:37 | "in three words, what is this show about ?" | /097 hi/cloud piano.mp3
| 14:37 | "will kim and kanye get a divorce?" | /012 y/CV_what_am_i.wav
| 14:46 | "who the fuck cares ?" | /080 who/asha_adam_maya.wav
| 14:39 | "hi!
| 14:40 | "trun
| 14:40 | "sanc
| 14:41 | "how
| 15:1 | "will
| 15:5 | "why
| 15:10 | "what
| 15:17 | "aga
| 15:17 | "aga
| 15:17 | "aga
| 15:17 | "aga
| 15:17 | "aga
| 15:17 | "aga
| 15:17 | "aga
| 15:17 | "aga
| 15:18 | "aga
| 15:18 | "aga
| 15:18 | "aga
| 15:18 | "aga
| 15:20 | "fli
| 15:26 | "can
| 15:29 | "how
| 15:29 | "sha
| 15:32 | "who
| 15:43 | "why
| 15:44 | "do
| 15:49 | "play
an, Bounty Kille
| 15:50 | "who
| 15:53 | "hei
| 15:53 | "can
| 15:53 | "how
| 15:54 | "say
| 15:55 | "what
| 15:56 | "who
| 15:56 | "who
| 15:58 | "what
| 15:58 | "cadr
| 16:8 | "what
| 16:10 | "how
| 16:10 | "fucl
| 16:16 | "does
| 16:17 | "what
| 16:17 | "what
| 16:18 | "will
| 16:18 | "will
| 16:25 | "how
| 16:25 | "pie
| 16:26 | "you
| 16:27 | "what
| 16:34 | "is
| 16:38 | ":)"
| 16:38 | ":)?
| 16:38 | ":(?
| 16:46 | "do
| 16:51 | "do
| 16:51 | "how
| 16:52 | "how
| 17:8 | "why
| 17:9 | "will
| 17:9 | "text
| 17:10 | "text
| 17:18 | "will
| 17:19 | "how
| 17:27 | "leb
| 17:28 | "mo
| 17:30 | "jor
| 17:37 | "will
| 17:37 | "where will my next job be?" | /984 job/colleen_def_wont_get_job.wav
| 17:38 | "i want a new job!" | /984 job/colleen_def_wont_get_job.wav
| 18:1 | "do you have a dog?" | /016 have/elliot_never.wav
| 18:1 | "are you angry?" | /018 are/CV_forget_it.wav
| 18:4 | "is being allergic to gluten a real thing?" | /013 is/CV_look_at_you.wav
| 18:30 | "what color are donkeys?" | /070 what/nova_i_dunno3.wav
18:30 | "did you eat fruit today?" | /017 did/henry_outlook_good.wav
18:30 | "do you like art?" | /014 do/nova_decidedly_so.wav

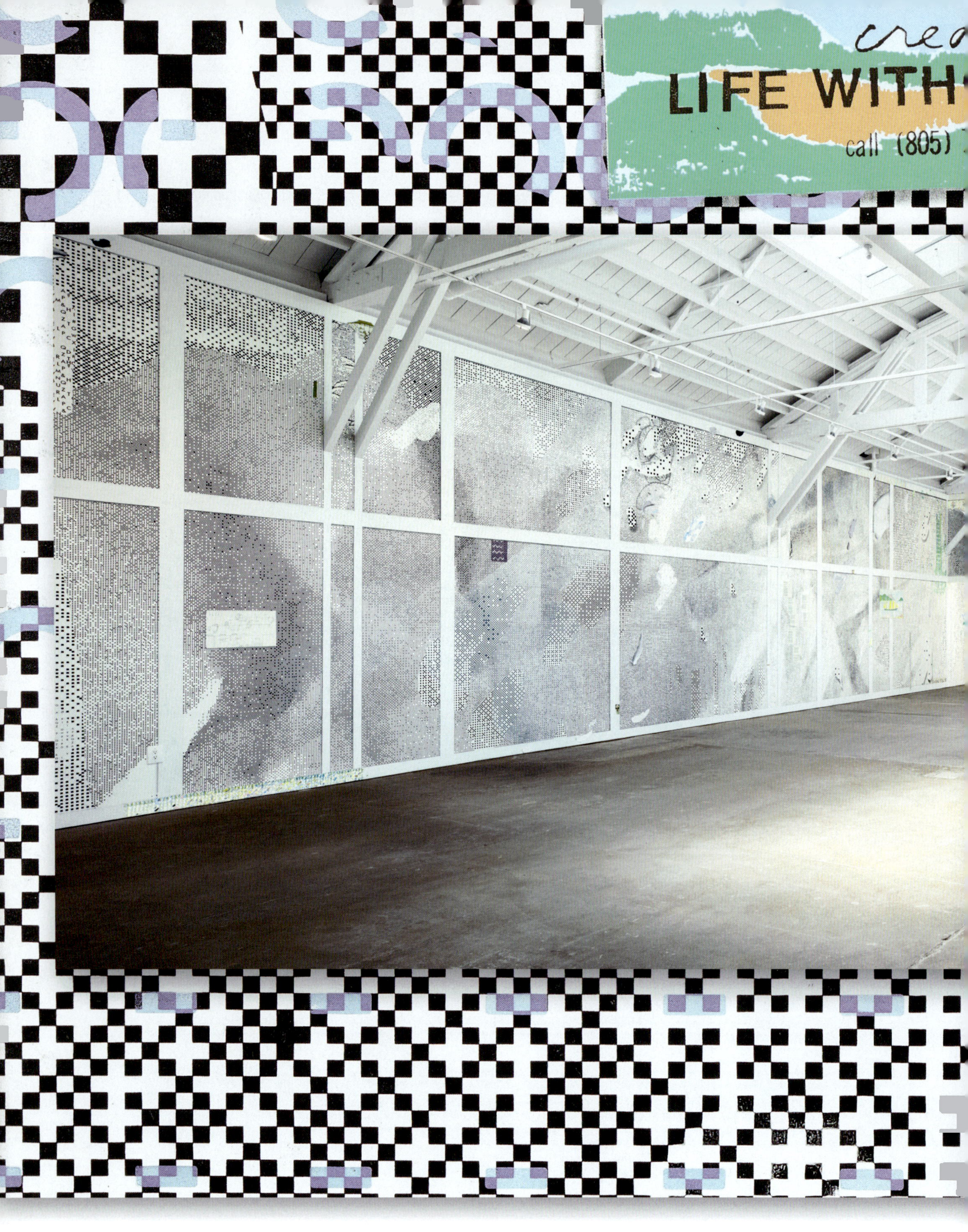

Foreground: Installation view, *Ten Paintings*, CCA Wattis Institute, San Francisco, 2016
Background: Detail, *Ten Paintings*, CCA Wattis Institute, San Francisco, 2016

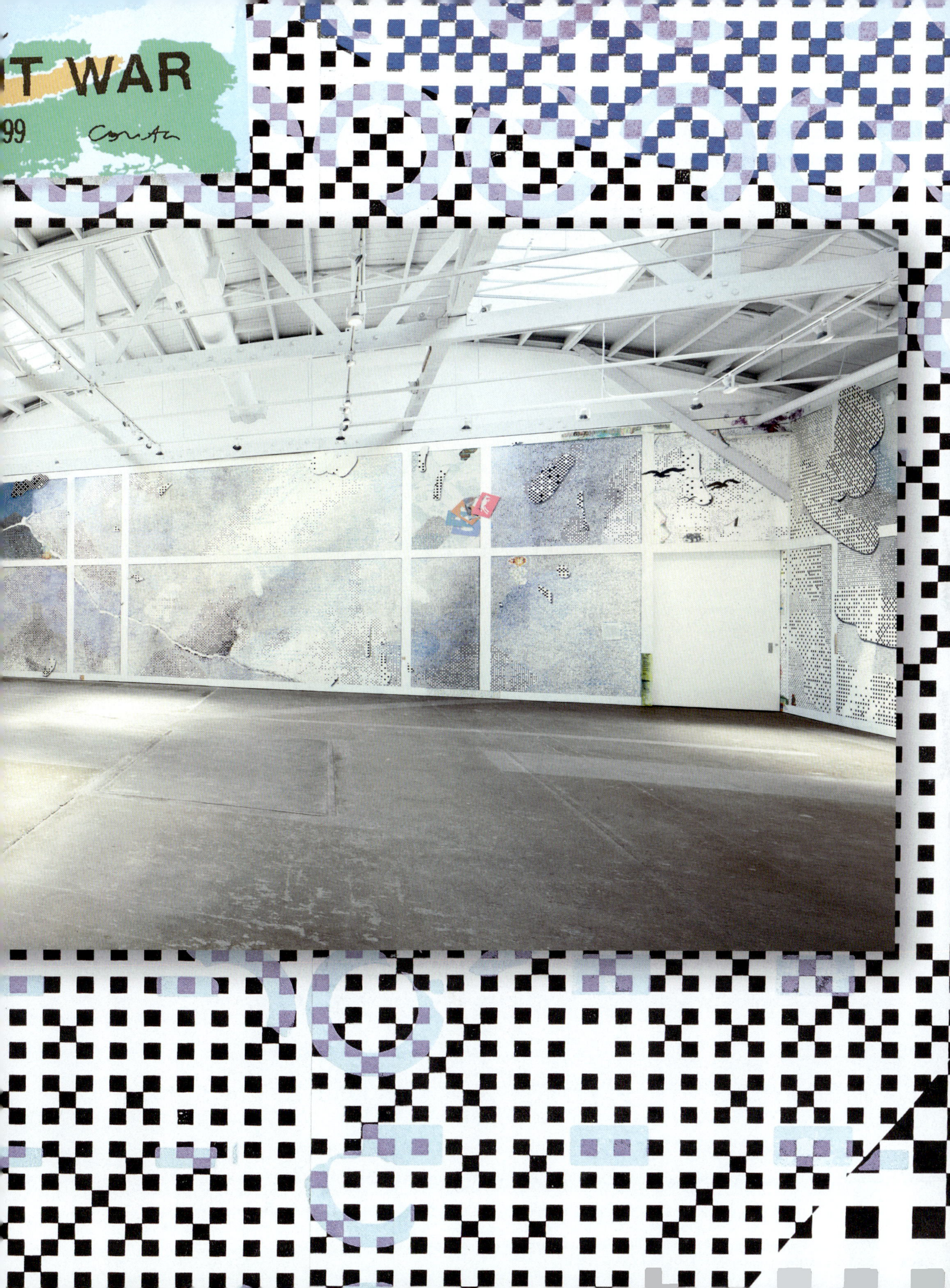
T WAR
99
Corita

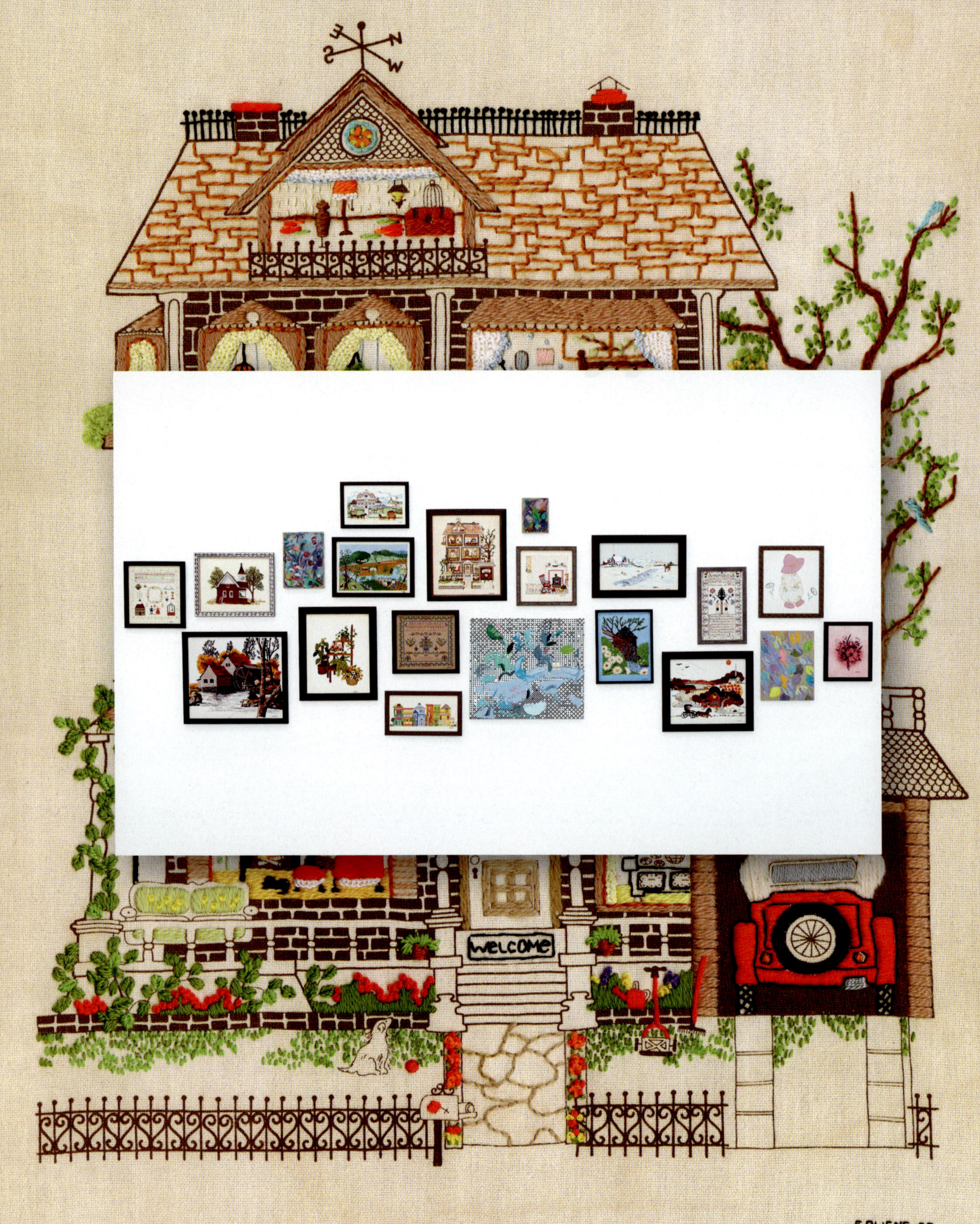

Foreground: Installation view, *Ten Paintings*, CCA Wattis Institute, San Francisco, 2016, with needlepoints by Eileen Owens, 1983, and (clockwise from top left) *Untitled*, 2016, oil, vinyl paint, and collage on linen; *Untitled*, 2016, oil and hair on linen; *Untitled*, 2016, oil and vinyl paint on linen; and *Untitled*, 2016, oil and silkscreen ink on linen, various dimensions

 Background: Detail of needlepoint by Eileen Owens, 1983

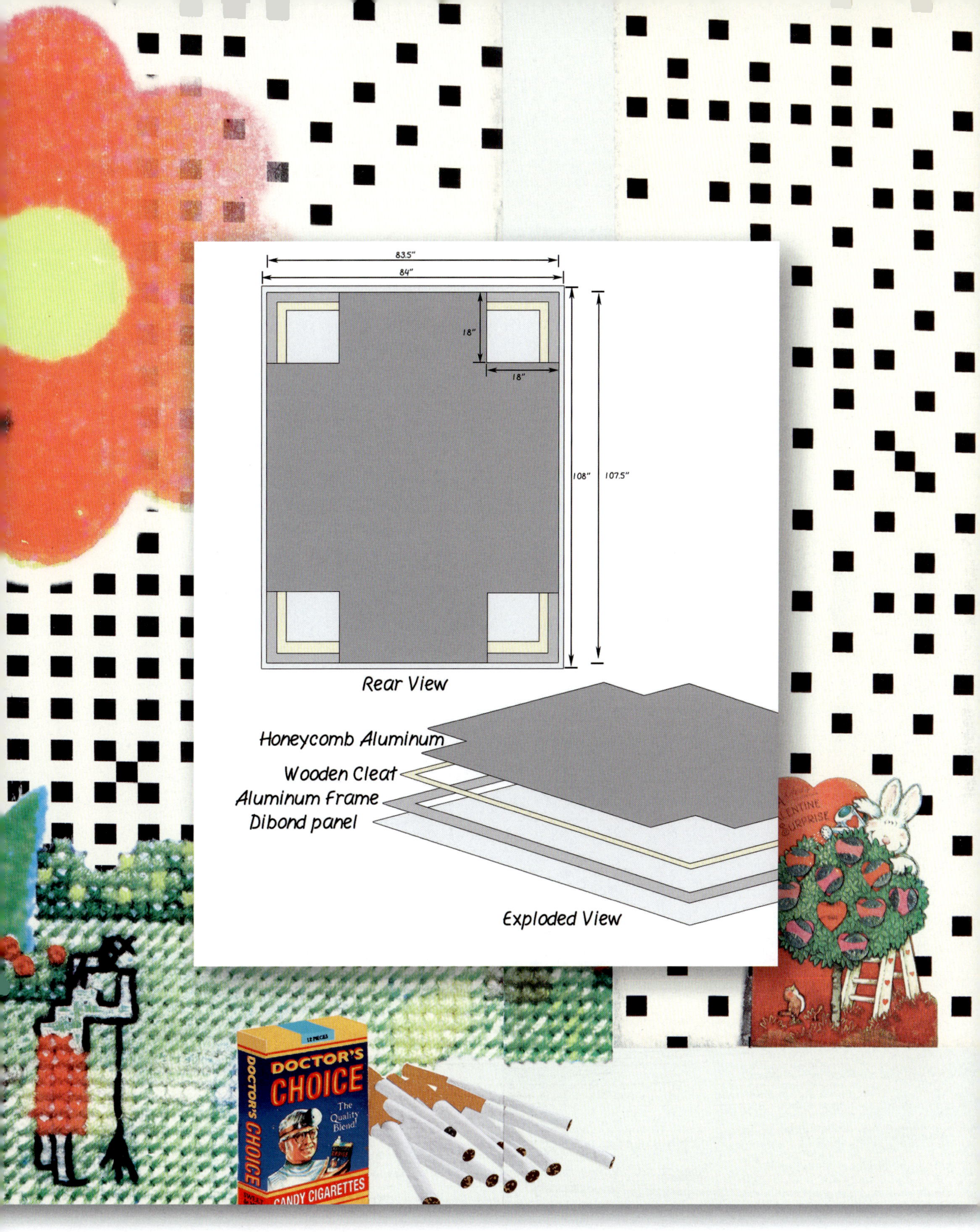

Foreground: Diagram for *Untitled*, 2016, wallpaper on aluminum composite, 108 × 84 in. (274.3 × 213.4 cm)
Background: Detail, *Ten Paintings*, CCA Wattis Institute, San Francisco, 2016

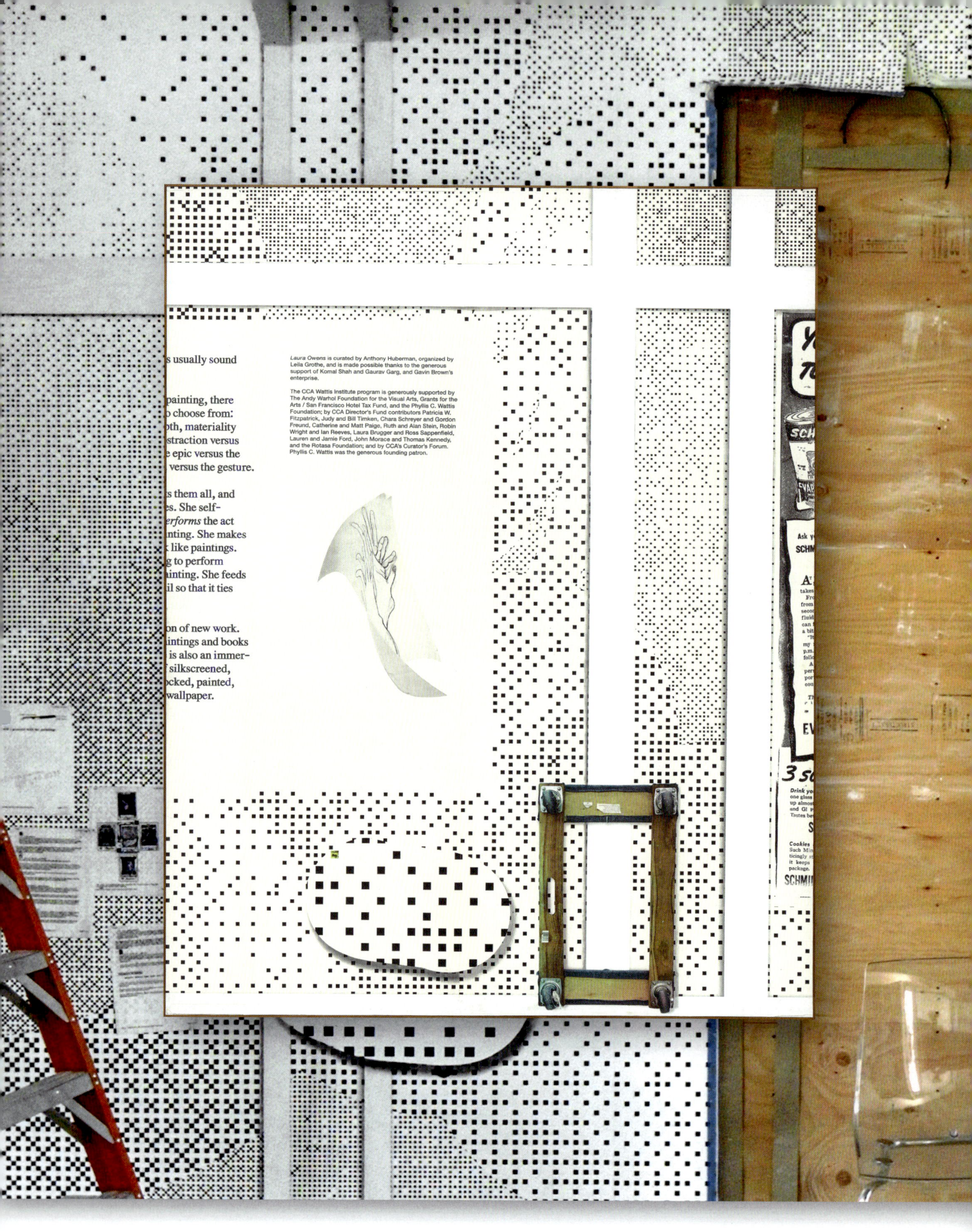

 Foreground: *Untitled*, 2016, wallpaper on aluminum composite, 108 × 84 in. (274.3 × 213.4 cm)
Background: Deinstallation, *Ten Paintings*, CCA Wattis Institute, San Francisco, 2016

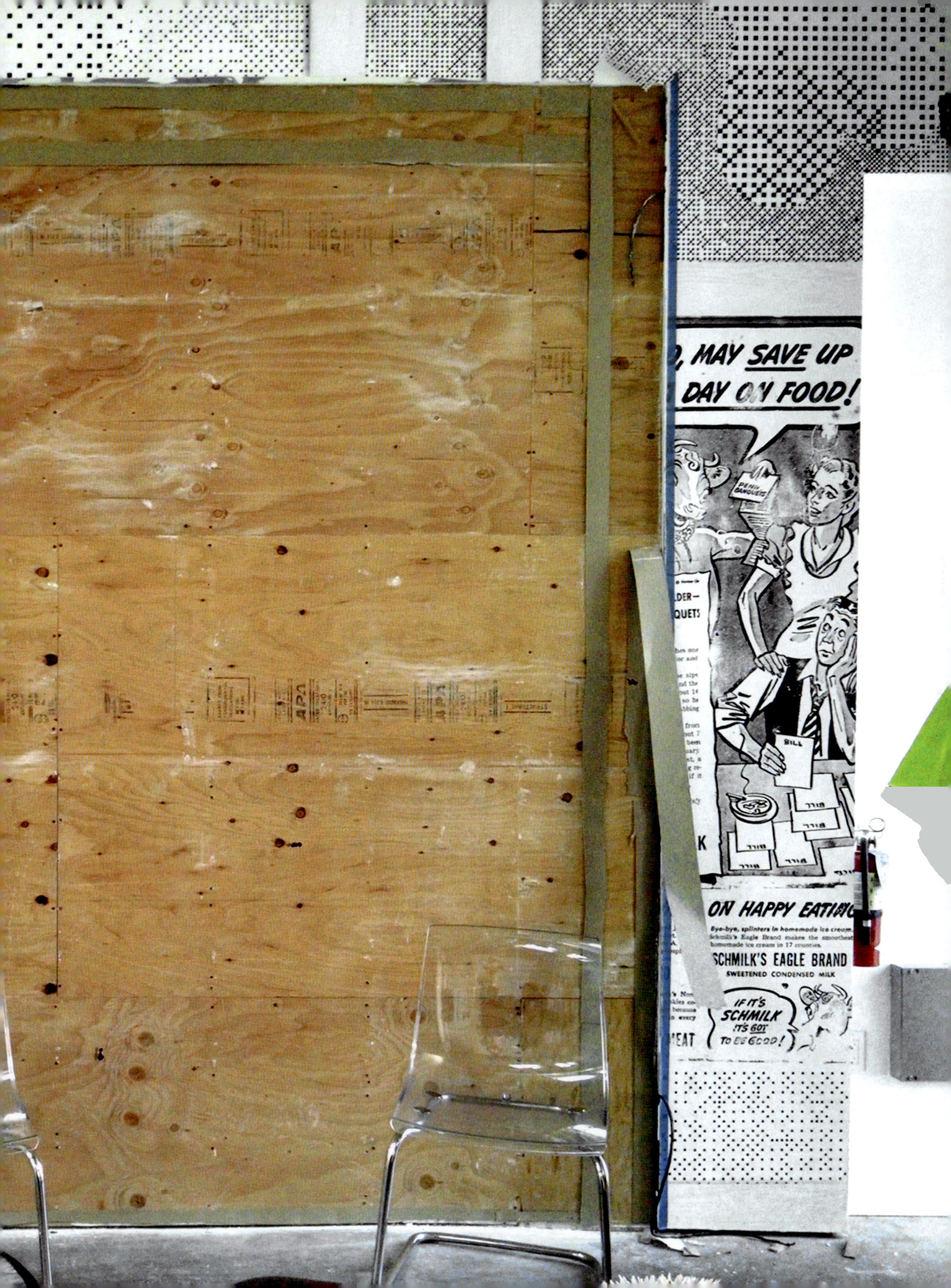

, MAY SAVE UP
DAY ON FOOD!
PENN
BANQUETS
BILL
BILL
BILL
BILL
BILL
BILL
ON HAPPY EATING
Bye-bye, splinters in homemade ice cream.
Schmilk's Eagle Brand makes the smoothest
homemade ice cream in 17 counties.
SCHMILK'S EAGLE BRAND
SWEETENED CONDENSED MILK
IF IT'S
SCHMILK
IT'S GOT
TO BE GOOD!
MEAT

WHO USED WALLPAPER AND WHERE?
GILL SAUNDERS

Any account of who used wallpapers, what they used, and where, is inevitably based on partial evidence. Wallpaper, by its very nature, is the most ephemeral feature of interior decoration, and this is compounded by the fact that it is often impossible to remove intact, and may well be obscured or obliterated by successive decorations. Naturally, unique or expensive wallpapers are the most likely to survive, and the use of wallpaper is more likely to be recorded in the houses of the wealthy and/or educated than in the homes of the lower classes. Though inventories, so valuable to furniture history, are of little use when studying wallpaper, there are many other sources: decorators' accounts and order books, letters, diaries, and the memoirs of travellers and visitors are all valuable sources of information about the usage of wallpaper and how it was regarded. The evidence for the decorating choices of the mass-market are more often found in the scornful and dismissive comments of those who saw themselves as arbiters of taste than in any record, textual or pictorial, by those who had chosen them. This does not really change until the twentieth century, when documentary photography, oral history and television began to record the lives of the many rather than the few.

The history of wallpaper, and especially its social history, is therefore full of holes, and seriously distorted by selective survival of material evidence and context. It has always been the poor relation of the decorative arts, often omitted entirely from histories of interior design, or mentioned only briefly in passing. The following account must be read with these provisos in mind. The focus is necessarily on British wallpaper and interiors, and there is no attempt at a comprehensive geographical coverage, although significant examples from France, the USA, China and Australia are represented or discussed.

From the evidence available it would seem that wallpaper was first used not in the grand houses of the aristocracy but in the town houses of the merchant class. Writing a brief account of wallpaper in 1699, John Houghton describes it as being available in "a great Variety, with curious Cuts [woodcuts] which are Cheap, and if kept from Wet, very lasting." He explains that these printed papers are designed to serve instead of hangings, by which he means tapestry and other textiles. These qualities—variety of pattern, durability. and cheapness—recommended wallpapers to a class of relatively wealthy but not aristocratic householders. Houghton specifically commends wallpaper as making "the houses of the more ordinary people look neat."[1]

However, the fashion for wallpaper was certainly given added impetus by its use in a royal residence. William Pyne, the historian of Kensington Palace, recorded that William Kent, the architect commissioned by George I to redecorate the place, had the King's Great Drawing Room papered, an unusual choice at the time. The result was greatly admired, and "the new art of paper-hanging, being both cheap and elegant, was generally adopted in preference to the old-style velvet flock hangings."[2] By 1752, the *Covent Garden Journal* could claim: "There is scarcely a modern house which has not one or more rooms lined with this furniture [i.e., wallpaper]."[3] In due course wallpapers became fashionable, elegant decorations, even preferred for grand houses in the first half of the nineteenth century.

Some of the earliest papers to survive on walls rather than as linings to chests, cupboards and deed boxes have been found in houses in areas such as Epsom, Surrey, and King's Lynn, Norfolk. Epsom was a spa town, and a number of wealthy merchants from London made their homes there. It has been suggested that wallpapers might have been manufactured in the area: Houghton makes specific reference to Ebbisham (Epsom) where, he says, paperhangings were known as "paper tapistry." King's Lynn, as a port and an important

Originally published in *Wallpaper in Interior Decoration* (New York: Watson-Guptill, 2002), 11–25, 151. Saunders is senior curator of prints at the Victoria and Albert Museum, London.

provincial trading centre, also had a population of well-to-do merchants and traders.

In France, it seems that wallpapers (both domino papers and *papiers de tapisserie*)[4] were first adopted by the less well-off and only later moved up the social scale as they improved in quality of design and manufacture. Jacques Savary de Bruslons wrote in the *Dictionnaire universel du commerce* (completed in 1713, published in 1723):

> This kind of paperhanging . . . had long been used only by country folk and the lower classes in Paris to decorate and, so to speak, "hang" certain parts of their huts, shops and rooms; but at the end of the 17th century [it] was raised to such a peak of perfection and attractiveness that, apart from the large consignments sent to foreign lands and to all the principal cities of the kingdom, there was not a house in Paris, however magnificent, that did not have somewhere, be it in a dressing room or an even more secret place, which was not hung with paper and quite pleasantly decorated.

The use of wallpapers was to an extent influenced by their price, which in turn was affected by taxes. In Great Britain from 1712, paperhangings were classed as luxury goods and subject to tax, which of course increased their cost. Duty was levied on all paper "Printed, Painted or stained in Great Britain to serve for Hangings and other Uses. . ." at 1d per square yard, raised to 1½d in 1714 and to 1¾d in 1787.[5] Duty was charged on imported paper from 1712 and raised to the same rate as English-made papers in 1773, but the Chinese papers were exempt until 1792. This tax was not abolished until 1836 (imports were taxed until 1861).

The definition of wallpaper as a luxury coincided with the development of more lavish and expensive papers, such as flocks, and the import of the hand-painted Chinese papers. Paperhangings of this kind were introduced into the houses of the nobility, and wallpaper enjoyed a new status as an elegant decoration in its own right rather than as a counterfeit or substitute for a more costly material. Cheaper, simpler papers were also produced—the ubiquitous "flower sprigs," diapers and stripes—and designs also mirrored changing architectural styles.

Certainly by the mid-eighteenth century wallpaper was widely used. The anonymous *General Description of All Trades* (London, 1747) refers to paperhangings, "the making and dealing of which has now become a considerable Branch of Trade."[6] Thomas Mortimer's *The Universal Director* (1763) includes the following under the heading "Paperhanging Manufacturers": ". . . for we annually export vast quantities of this admired article; and the home consumption is not less considerable, as it is not only a cheap, but an elegant part of furniture and saves the builders the expense of wainscotting: for which reason they have brought it into vogue, and most of the new houses lately erected are lined throughout with paper."[7]

The responsibility for furnishing the home and making decisions about decorating was in the eighteenth century a male preserve, in theory, if not in practice. Books illustrating architecture, furniture and suggestions for decorative schemes were specifically addressed to gentlemen—the subscribers to such works as Chippendale's *Gentleman and Cabinet-Maker's Director* (1754) were members of the nobility and gentry, as well as leading London artisans. Publications by Hepplewhite and Sheraton were addressed to the same audience. In practice, of course, women often initiated and managed decorative schemes. Several eighteenth-century trade cards show men and women choosing wallpapers together.

In the nineteenth-century home, decorating became the preserve of women, and this was recognised by the publishers of general interest periodicals and also by the writers of guides to home furnishing and interior decoration.

By the later nineteenth century wallpaper was widely used in Europe and America and was regarded as an essential element of interior decoration. The California architects Newsom and Newsom wrote in 1885: "The query 'What shall we do with our walls?' has long since been answered. . . . White walls unrelieved by any color are relics of barbarism and are almost a thing of the past. House-papering is now incorporated into building contracts and a house is considered incomplete without these adornments."[8] But by the 1920s leading architects were advocating white walls: Le Corbusier and others rejected the "decorative" in favour of the self-evidently functional. Writer Adolf Loos, praising the unornamented achievements in the other arts, such as music, declared that "whoever goes to Beethoven's Ninth Symphony and then sits down to design a wallpaper pattern is either a rogue or a degenerate."[9]

Since then wallpaper has moved in and out of fashion. Though it has continued to sell, the trade has declined considerably from the heights of the late nineteenth and early twentieth centuries, and its status has declined too, despite occasional revivals and the involvement of noted artists and designers.

Which Rooms?

Though conventions grew up about which patterns and colours were most appropriate for different rooms, the earliest makers and sellers of paperhangings rarely specified where their products should be hung. The Blue Paper Warehouse advertised "Figured Paper Hangings . . . for the hanging of rooms and staircases"; James Wheeley offered "Common Papers for Rooms"; and Matthew Darly made and sold papers in the "Modern, Gothic or Chinese Tastes for Town or Country," with specific mention only of staircases, ceilings and chimney boards. There are occasional exceptions: Zecheriah Mills of Hartford did specify in 1797 that he had "a great variety of small figures" which were best "for lower rooms and chambers [bedrooms]" and claimed that large figures were more suitable for halls.[10] Not until the later nineteenth century, with the proliferation of manuals of household management and the rise of self-appointed arbiters of taste in matters of domestic decoration, is there any prescriptive or proscriptive advice for those choosing to decorate with wallpapers. These authors are firm on the subject of where to hang large patterns, where to use dark papers (dining rooms, billiard rooms) and where to use lighter colours and simpler designs (bedrooms), when to avoid paper altogether, and how to effect an appropriate ambience through the agency of well-chosen colours and patterns.

However, certain conventions were quickly established—the most impressive and expressive papers were preferred for the more public rooms, those used for receiving and entertaining, while cheap papers and simple patterns sufficed for bedrooms and functional spaces. Records relating to the refurbishment of the Proprietary House in Perth Amboy, New Jersey, for the Royal Governor William Franklin and his wife between 1773 and 1775 show these considerations in practice: "a handsome *Yellow* paper" was wanted for the Drawing Room but in the Governor's Study or Office "A common *Green* paper will do, as a great Part of the Wall will be covered with Books, Maps, &c." The only room on the ground floor that "Needn't be papered" was the Housekeeper's Room.[11]

Though the eighteenth century had seen some differentiation of wallpaper designs according to the function of the rooms for which they were intended—the bedroom and the closet distinguished from the drawing room and the library, and decorated accordingly—and some styles and colours labelled as inherently "feminine" or "masculine," it was only in the nineteenth century that these distinctions were codified. This included the division of space—in the home and in public buildings—according to class, gender and age. Wallpapers were increasingly used in recognition of or to reinforce these distinctions—cheap simple patterns (often machine printed, from the 1850s) for servants' rooms, light feminine striped or floral designs in rooms used mainly by women (the morning room, the drawing room, boudoirs) and more assertive patterns in richer, darker colours for rooms associated with men's domestic lives and pastimes (the dining room, the smoking room, billiard room and library). And in due course children's living quarters (nursery and school-room) were distinguished by the use of specially designed wallpapers with pictorial motifs designed to educate and amuse.

Copious evidence of these conventions is to be found in the Cowtan archive: bold naturalistic florals or the ubiquitous white and gold patterns ordered for drawing rooms, rich flocks for the library and billiard room, imitation marbling for halls, passages and staircases, floral or tile-patterned sanitaries for bathrooms and sculleries.

Wallpapers in public buildings often refer either to the function of the room, or to the gender of the users. Pictorial patterns were often found in public spaces with specific functions or clienteles. In his short story, "Madame Tellier's Establishment" (which was a brothel) (1880–81), Maupassant relates that ". . . The 'Jupiter' drawing room, where the local tradesmen foregathered, had a blue wallpaper adorned with a bold design of Leda reclining with the Swan."[12] Though a scene from Greek mythology, this was a thoroughly risqué subject, with overtones of rape, and as such could only have been used in a room closed to respectable women. Though neither a 1902 American *Gibson Girls* wallpaper (illustrating the popular "beauty" of the day), nor the similar paper of semi-naked women were found in situ, the most likely use for both would have been in gentlemen's clubs.

A 1870s paper with Highland sporting scenes would have been an apt decoration for a club-house, gentlemen's games room, or a tourist hotel in Scotland. In 1933 the wallpaper hung in the Men's Smoking Room at the Radio City Music Hall, New York, was Nicotine by Donald Deskey

(b. 1894), a humorous design printed in shades of yellowish-brown showing pipes, cigars and tobacco leaves together with other motifs referring to predominantly male amusements— sailing, drinking and gambling.

Wallpapers have been used in theatres (the paper decorating the box at Ford's Theatre where Abraham Lincoln was shot was torn away in fragments by souvenir hunters, and has since been reproduced for a reconstruction of the original decoration), in cinemas, especially in their Art Deco heyday, in restaurants and in shops. A recent phenomenon has seen artists designing limited edition wallpapers for exhibitions and installations. One such paper— Sarah Lucas's *Tits in Space*, first produced for her exhibition *The Fag Show* at Sadie Coles HQ in London—has subsequently been used in the reception area of the British Council's visual arts department in Portland Place.

When selecting wallpapers, the aspect of the room was often taken into account. At Temple Newsam in the early nineteenth century, the north-facing attic rooms were hung with warm tones such as yellows, pinks and reds. When James Burton ordered papers from Cowtan & Son for St. Leonard's Hotel, St. Leonards-on-Sea, in 1829, he chose greens and blues for the south-facing rooms with sea views and mostly pinks and buffs for the sunless north-facing rooms. The papers for this "elegant but OECONOMICAL HOTEL"[13] are florals and stripes, much the same as those used in private houses at the same date. For the communal rooms, grander designs with deeper borders were chosen, and this again corresponds with the ordinary domestic practice of using more impressive patterns in reception rooms, and cheaper, simpler papers in private spaces.

It would seem that inns and hotels were often decorated with bolder patterns than might have been used in domestic settings, perhaps because the rooms were larger, and possibly because the oppressive tendencies of a dominant pattern would be of less account to a clientele merely passing through. In Charlotte Brontë's *Jane Eyre*, Jane describes "a room at the George Inn at Millcote, with such large figured papering on the walls as inn rooms have."[14] This is confirmed by real-life evidence where French panoramic papers have been found in inns and hotels, notably in Germany, and also in America (as remarked by travelers such as Harriet Martineau), and a bold

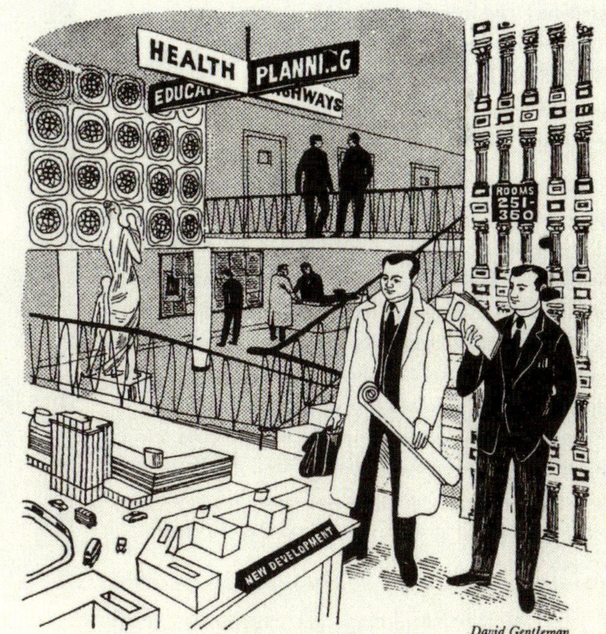

A SERVICE
FOR ARCHITECTS

ARCHITECTS CONCERNED
WITH THE SPECIFICATION OR DIRECTION
OF DECORATIVE SCHEMES
ARE INVITED TO USE THE FACILITIES
OFFERED BY OUR
ARCHITECTS' DEPARTMENT

Wallpaper of suitable design and colour lends character to the formal interior of civic buildings. Though the primary purpose of the ARCHITECTS' DEPARTMENT is to give advice on the use of wallpaper it is also able to deal with enquiries concerning the use and choice of paints and fabrics.

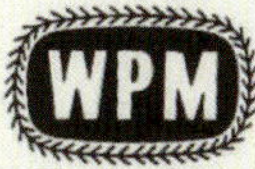

THE ARCHITECTS' DEPARTMENT
THE WALL PAPER MANUFACTURERS LIMITED
125 HIGH HOLBORN LONDON WC1
OR KING'S HOUSE KING STREET WEST MANCHESTER 3

Advertisement for the WPM's (Wall Paper Manufacturers Limited) Service for Architects, featuring a drawing by David Gentleman, 1955

Gothic "architecture" paper in the Ostrich Hotel at Swaffnam. Assertive graphic patterns were often recommended specifically for public buildings. An Art Deco diamond pattern produced by Sandersons in 1933, described as demonstrating dignity and strength, was intended for use in a living room. However, when a more elaborate version was issued in 1936 it was considered "too telling for domestic work, except on a staircase, but would often be just right for Hotel and Cinema work."[15]

The 1950s and 1960s saw manufacturers making a conscious effort to promote the use of wallpaper in a variety of civic and commercial buildings. Many of the papers in the *Palladio* ranges had large-scale patterns better suited to town halls, hotels, restaurants, shops, offices and corporate buildings than to the average house. An advertisement for the WPM's Service for Architects shows what appears to be a town hall interior with two large-scale wallpapers, one of which is clearly Robert Nicholson's *Columns*, produced for the first *Palladio* range in 1955. The advertising copy makes the point that "Wallpaper of a suitable design and colour lends character to the formal interior of civic building." Elsewhere, *Palladio* papers, many designed by artists, were recommended for use in a wide variety of post-war building types and interiors, including espresso bars, clinics, car showrooms, motels and local government buildings, as well as private houses.

From the sixteenth century to the present day, wallpaper has been a feature of domestic interiors and some public buildings in Western Europe and North America. Plain and gilded papers have been used in China, but in Africa and India wallpapers have rarely been used, despite the influence of the English colonisers. Accounts of life in India by eighteenth- and nineteenth-century travellers and expatriates often remark on the fact that the interiors of even quite grand houses were "bare" or "unadorned." Everett's *Observations on India* (1853) complains: "The splendour of the houses does not reach to their inside: we see nothing of English neatness. The rooms were full thrice the size we have been used to, lofty and gloomy, with bare whitewashed walls . . ."[16] Of course, the heat, humidity and insects made the use of wallpaper impractical, and even undesirable. There is only one known reference to the use of wallpaper in an Anglo-Indian interior, and that is a fictional example: Hartly House, Calcutta, was described as having a closet whose "walls are covered with pink paper from China, of the softest tint."[17]

Otherwise the bareness was relieved by painted decoration. Emily Eden, living in India with her brother George, the Governor-General, described the furnishing of her house in Simla in a letter of 1838:

We bought carpets and chandeliers, and wall shades . . . from Calcutta, and I have got a native painter in the house, and cut out patterns in paper, which he then paints in borders all around doors and windows, and it makes up for want of cornices, and breaks the eternal white walls of these houses. Altogether it is very like a cheerful middle-sized English country house, and extremely enjoyable.[18]

Nevertheless, a London firm, Allen, Cockshut & Co., produced a series of pictorial papers entitled *Hindoo Gods* for export to India around 1880. However it is thought that these were for use in religious festivals rather than as conventional domestic decoration. A paper from the 1870s, from an unknown English manufacturer, also has pseudo-Indian scenes, and was reputedly made for an Indian Rajah. And in 1865 Jeffrey & Co. printed a collection of designs by Owen Jones, including some lavishly gilded Moorish patterns, for the decoration of the Khedive's [Viceroy's] Palace in Cairo. But these are rare instances of attempts to translate a Western fashion for a largely unsuitable Eastern climate.

In Australia and New Zealand wallpaper use closely mirrored the tastes and fashions in England and America. Australia had no domestic wallpaper industry to speak of until after World War II. Instead papers were imported first from British manufacturers, and then, particularly from the 1920s when the British industry's output was hampered by post-war shortages of labour and materials from US companies.

Wallpaper and the Working-class Home
When the Council for Art and Industry produced a report on "The Working Class Home Its Furnishings and Equipment" in 1937, it set out a list of the essentials needed to furnish and decorate a home to an acceptable standard of comfort and cleanliness at the cheapest price. Carpets and curtains were considered to be basic necessities but no mention was made of wallpaper. This was surprising because wallpaper was available at very low cost and had long been regarded as a cheap and easy way to decorate a house and make it homely.

Even in rented housing (and for the working-class most properties were rented, from private landlords, and later from public authorities, or were tied houses) new tenants saw repapering as the best and cheapest way of making the place look clean and fresh, and of giving it the stamp of ownership, albeit temporary. By 1900 landlords in New York commonly redecorated a vacant apartment simply by replacing the wallpaper before renting it out again, according to a contemporary wallpaper trade journal.[19] Indeed, a view of a New York slum tenement (dated around 1896) shows a cheap wallpaper of a strong diaper pattern, damaged in places, but otherwise a bold counterpoint to the rest of the dingy furnishings.

There are plenty of references from the early years of the nineteenth century to the role of wallpaper as an affordable enhancement to modest or run-down accommodation. When Shelley went to London, following his expulsion from Oxford University in 1811, he found lodgings in a house on Poland Street. His friend and companion Thomas Hogg described Shelley's objection to the exterior of the house, but inside they found a back sitting room where "the walls . . . had lately been covered with trellised paper; in these days it was not common. There were trellises, vine leaves with their tendrils, and huge clusters of grapes, green and purple, all represented in lively colours. This was delightful," Shelley declared, "We must stay here; stay for ever!"[20] A "light wallpaper which lent an air of gaiety" had also improved the wretched ill-built hovel that was home to journeyman Agricol Perdiguier in Paris in the 1830s.[21]

Wallpaper was, of course, a cheap way of disguising or concealing faulty construction, such as cracks or uneven plastering, damp and other damage. The Rev. Whitwell Elwin included wallpaper in his schemes to improve the cottages of the labourers in his parish. He wrote to his friend Lady Emily Lytton that he had found a source of pretty printed wallpaper for only 2½d (1p) a roll. Apparently, many workers could not afford to buy wallpapers for themselves, even at this low price.[22] In 1850 the American architect Andrew Jackson Downing asserted that "The great advantage of papering the walls lies chiefly in the beauty of effect, and cheerful cottage-like expression, which may be produced at very little cost."[23]

Wallpapered walls represent a certain level of respectability, standards of living which support good character and morality. Moral decline of an individual, or their circumstances, is often mirrored in the deterioration of their living conditions. In *Clarissa* (1748–49), Richardson gives a minute description of the room in which the eponymous

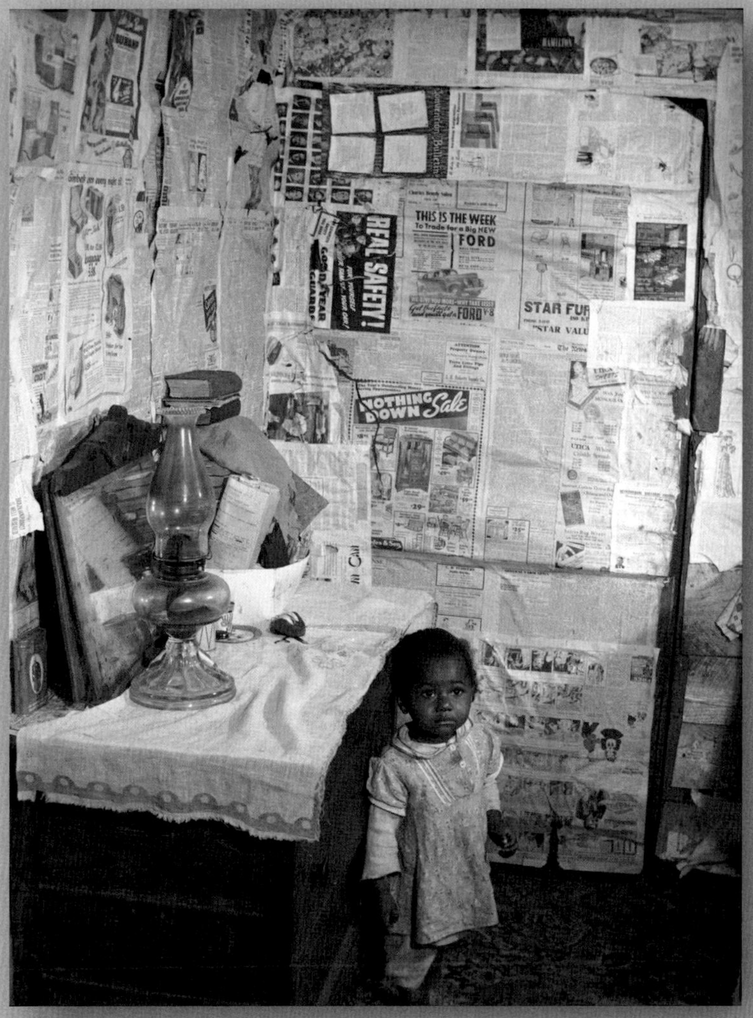

Interior of the one-room home of a farming family in the vicinity of Bonneau, South Carolina, 1941

heroine is imprisoned for debt. The room itself has lost its former respectable status, to the extent that it has no wallpaper, only fragments still attached to the heads of rusty tacks.

In cases of extreme poverty, it seems that a desire to decorate or pattern the walls could still stir the inhabitants. Mrs. Gaskell, in *Mary Barton*, describes John Barton's home, opening off a squalid slum courtyard but nevertheless neatly furnished, homely, and most importantly, clean: it has "a washy, but clean stencilled pattern on the walls."[24] In his *Notes sur l'Angleterre* (1861) Hippolyte Taine compares the typical English workman's cottage to that of the French peasant, and concludes that the former is better furnished and as such indicative of a more respectable character and way of life. In evidence he writes: Yet his little house is clean . . . there is often wallpaper, chairs of polished wood, little framed prints, always a Bible, sometimes some other volumes, devotional books, new novels, how to raise rabbits etc.; in short, more useful objects than in our very poor cottages."[25] And in her story "The Three Miss Kings," Ada Cambridge describes the characters' impoverished provincial home as "a poor setting . . . a long, low canvas-lined room papered with prints from the *Illustrated London News* . . . from the ceiling to the floor. . . ."[26] A decorated wall here represents a degree of feminine refinement achieved in financially straitened circumstances, but in a practical "making do" tradition.

Such strategies seem to have been commonplace in real life: Henry Mayhew, in his investigations into the lives of the London working classes, had found a home in which the wall over the fireplace was entirely "patched up to the ceiling with little square pictures of saints," and the other walls papered in four different patterns.[27] An 1898 American photograph of two former slaves in their log-cabin shows the walls densely papered with a variety of magazine pages, prints and advertisements in an idiosyncratic display that gives the small room an unmistakable air of homeliness.[28] This practice continued for many years in the homes of sharecroppers and black farmers in the American South and Midwest. Margaret Bourke-White recorded one such in 1937—a shabby interior entirely papered with sheets of newsprint, their advertisements for a consumer culture an ironic counterpoint to the poverty of the space they decorate. As Jack Delano's 1941 view of a similar scene makes clear, the use of newsprint is only incidentally decorative; its primary purpose is to conceal the rough, uneven boards from which the house is built, and to serve as insulation.

It was the introduction of machine printing which did more than anything else to make wallpapers generally affordable. By 1851 the anonymous author of *How to furnish a House and make it a Home* could write that "paperhangings are now so cheap that it is almost as little to paper a room as to whitewash or colour it. A papered room has a comfortable look which no ordinary material can impart . . ."[29] By the mid-century there were a number of manufacturers in England producing machine-printed papers at a price which placed them "within the reach of the working classes."[30] A roll of machine-printed wallpaper could be bought for as little as sixpence a roll; by 1890 a two-colour machine print cost as little as twopence a roll, whereas a hand-printed paper from Jeffrey & Co. might cost as much as 25s.

Many lower income households were furnished with old-fashioned pieces, family cast-offs, and things bought second-hand. Often the only aspect of their furnishings which such families could afford to replace or to have new was the wallpaper. A view of a working-class kitchen around 1935 shows old-fashioned ornaments and a Victorian washstand, but the room has been papered with a contemporary wallpaper and a frieze, in watered down versions of so-called "modernist" styles. Anecdotal evidence suggests that wallpapers in working-class homes were renewed regularly; the downstairs rooms would be papered every two years, and the bedrooms every four years or so.[31]

Several rooms of this kind were recorded by Bill Brandt in his series on the lives of Northumbrian coal mining communities. A 1937 scene of a miner at his bath shows an assertive "Modernist" pattern in stippled tones, almost certainly printed in the beige porridge-like colours typical of such designs. In another view of a miner at his evening meal the wallpaper is a mottled floral pattern, again typical of the period. Brandt's photographs were used by journals such as *Picture Post* to illustrate articles about social conditions for both rich and poor. In 1943 an anonymous bedroom with a modernist-style paper was used in a feature about the Beveridge Report, a proposal for a universal social insurance scheme intended to offer protection from absolute poverty through the introduction of family allowances and unemployment benefit. Brandt's photograph shows a dilapidated, barely furnished room; that it represents the lives of the deserving poor is suggested by the picture of Jesus above the bed, and by the wallpaper, which is relatively new and still clean and neat, though the mattresses and pillows are worn out, an unemptied chamber pot is in view and the floor flecked with litter.

Set against these contemporary styles were more traditional styles reminiscent of the mid-Victorian enthusiasm for bold florals and revival patterns. Edwin Smith photographed the interior of a cottage in Crewkerne, Somerset, in the late 1920s. The furniture is distinctly shabby, but the wallpaper is typical of the contemporary "cottage" style—a simple stripe enlivened by a vivid floral border pre-cut in festoon shape.

The fashion for wallpapers in middle-class homes underwent a gradual decline in the early twentieth century, but it remained popular in working-class homes throughout this period. In a review of the 1945 Wallpaper Exhibition at the

Suffolk Street Gallery, designed to raise the profile of good design and revive the market, H. Goodhart-Rendel noted that the class of people whose homes were featured in *Country Life* had more or less abandoned wallpaper. He goes on to observe that in fact:

> Wallpaper was still made and used in great quantities, but not in houses likely to be illustrated in art publications. Its patrons were undiscriminating but vastly numerous, and although we may regret the large amount of rubbish which they joyfully accepted, we should be grateful to them for refusing to be bounced by the more sophisticated people into unnatural puritanism. It was the patronage of people who had never heard of Shaw, or of Lutyens or of Voysey that kept wallpaper alive, of people with a natural healthy taste for the ornamental which no highbrow forms could quell.[32]

Notes

1 Both quoted in E. A. Entwisle, *A Literary History of Wallpaper* (London: B. T. Batsford, Ltd., 1960), 14.

2 Quoted in Alan Victor Sugden and John Ludlam Edmondson, *A History of English Wallpaper 1509–1914* (London: B. T. Batsford, Ltd., 1925), 45.

3 *Covent Garden Journal*, June 27, 1752. Quoted in Entwisle, 29.

4 *Domino* is a French term for single-sheet decorative papers, with various uses, which were precursors of wallpaper proper; *papiers de tapisserie* were patterned or pictorial papers, produced as single sheets to be joined in hanging, for wall decoration.

5 Quoted in Lesley Hoskins, ed., *The Papered Wall: History, Pattern, Technique* (New York: Harry N. Abrams, 1994), 25. The Act was 10 Anne c. 18. For a full account see H. Dagnall, *The Tax on Wallpaper: An Account of the Excise Duty on Stained Paper, 1712–1836* (Edgware, Middlesex: published by the author, 1990), the standard work in English on this subject.

6 Quoted in Entwisle, 24.

7 T. Mortimer, *The Universal Director: or the Nobleman and Gentleman's True Guide to the Masters and Professors of the Liberal and Polite Arts and Sciences* (London, 1763), 54. Quoted in Entwisle, 37.

8 Samuel and Joseph Newsom, *Picturesque California Homes*, no. 2 (San Francisco: S. and J. Newsom, 1885), 5.

9 Adolf Loos, "Ornament and crime" (1908), reprinted in *Adolf Loos*, ed. L. Münz and G. Künstler (New York: Praeger, 1966).

10 Quoted Catherine Lynn, *Wallpaper in America: From the Seventeenth Century to World War I* (New York: The Barra Foundation/Cooper-Hewitt Museum, 1980), 115.

11 John M. Dickey, *Research and Planning Studies for the Restoration of the Proprietary House, Perth Amboy, New Jersey* (Media, Pa.: unpublished report, July 1, 1973). Quoted in Hoskins, 118.

12 Guy de Maupassant, "Madame Tellier's Establishment," in *Selected Short Stories* (New York: Penguin, 1995), 210.

13 Contemporary advertisement quoted in Anthony Wells-Cole, *Historic Paper-Hangings from Temple Newsam and Other English Houses* (Leeds: Leeds City Art Galleries, 1983), 4.

14 Charlotte Brontë, *Jane Eyre* (1847; repr., New York: Penguin, 1987), 125.

15 See Christine Woods, *Sanderson 1860–1985*, exh. cat. (London: Arthur Sanderson and Sons, Ltd., 1985), cat. no. 92.

16 Everett, *Observations on India* (London, 1853), 22.

17 *Hartly House, Calcutta. A novel of the days of Warren Hastings*, ed. J. MacFarlane (1789; repr., London: 1908), 147.

18 Emily Eden, *Up the Country* (1866; repr., London: Virago, 1983), 128.

19 See *The Wall-Paper News and Interior Decorator* for December 1908.

20 Quoted in *A History of English Wallpaper*, 116.

21 Jacques Rancière, *La Nuit des prolétaires: Archives du rêve ouvrier* (Paris: Fayard, 1981); [*The Nights of Labour: The Workers' Dream in Nineteenth-Century France*, trans. John Drury (Philadelphia: Temple University Press, 1981), 30].

22 See Charlotte Gere, *Nineteenth Century Decoration: The Art of the Interior* (New York: Abrams, 1989), 53.

23 A. J. Downing, *The Architecture of Country Houses* (1850; repr., New York: Dover Publications, 1969), 369–70.

24 Mrs Gaskell, *Mary Barton* (1848; repr., New York: Penguin, 1996), 15.

25 Quoted in *Nineteenth Century Decoration*, 120.

26 *The Australian*, June 23, 1883.

27 Henry Mayhew, *London Labour and the London Poor* 1 (1851): 47.

28 Photo by Huestis Cook, Valentine Museum, Richmond, VA. Illustrated as fig. 9.14 in Myrna Kaye, *There's a Bed in the Piano: The Inside Story of the American Home* (Boston: Bulfinch Press, 1998).

29 *How to furnish a House and make it a Home* (London: Economic Library, 1851). Quoted in Entwisle, 97.

30 *Official Catalogue of the 1880 Melbourne International Exhibition* (Melbourne, 1882), 81.

31 Roberta De Joia, ed., *A Popular Art. British Wallpapers 1930–1960*, exh. cat. (London: The Silver Studio Collection at Middlesex Polytechnic, 1990), 9.

32 *The Architect & Building News*, June 1, 1945, 123.

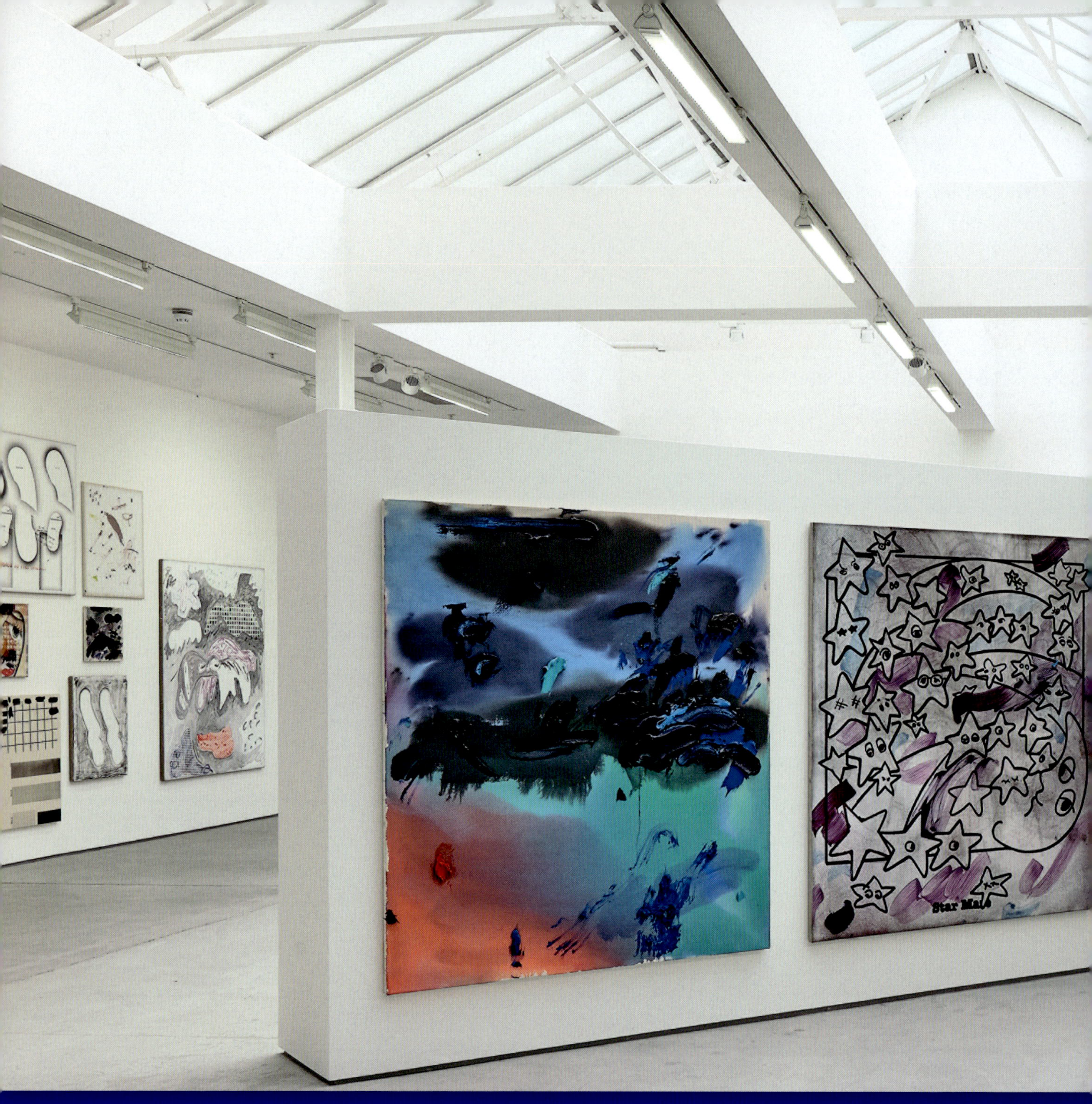

Sadie Coles: This show was an adrenaline rush because of course we didn't know what was coming or indeed whether anything would come. We had three or four days of the shippers going to the studio and the studio saying, "No, we're not ready." Laura gave us a very clear directive: "I want you to build three walls and the three walls can be in any position in the gallery, any size, but they have to be to this ratio." Martin, my head technician, figured it out. We made the decisions about scale and placement ourselves, which was a bit nerve-racking because we had no installation plan. One wall was very small, another was at a diagonal, and one was quite conventional, coming out at a right angle from one of the main walls. I was very nervous because I thought, "Maybe Laura's going to hate the diagonal." Our temporary architecture provided the gaps in a dense hang. Laura installed work on some of the walls, but most of the time she used them as blank space that helped organize this massive amount of material. It was a fantastic process, because it's the dream of any gallerist to be involved in such things. And the furious energy of that show was infectious.

Installation view, Sadie Coles HQ, London, 2016, with *Untitled*, 2016, oil and vinyl paint on canvas; *Untitled*, 2016, oil, vinyl paint, silkscreen ink, charcoal, and sand on linen; *Untitled*, 2016, oil, charcoal, and collage on linen; *Untitled*, 2016, oil and silkscreen ink on linen; *Untitled*, 2016 (see p. 619); and *Untitled*, 2016, acrylic, oil, wood, and collage on canvas, 69 × 60 in. (175.3 × 152.4 cm) each

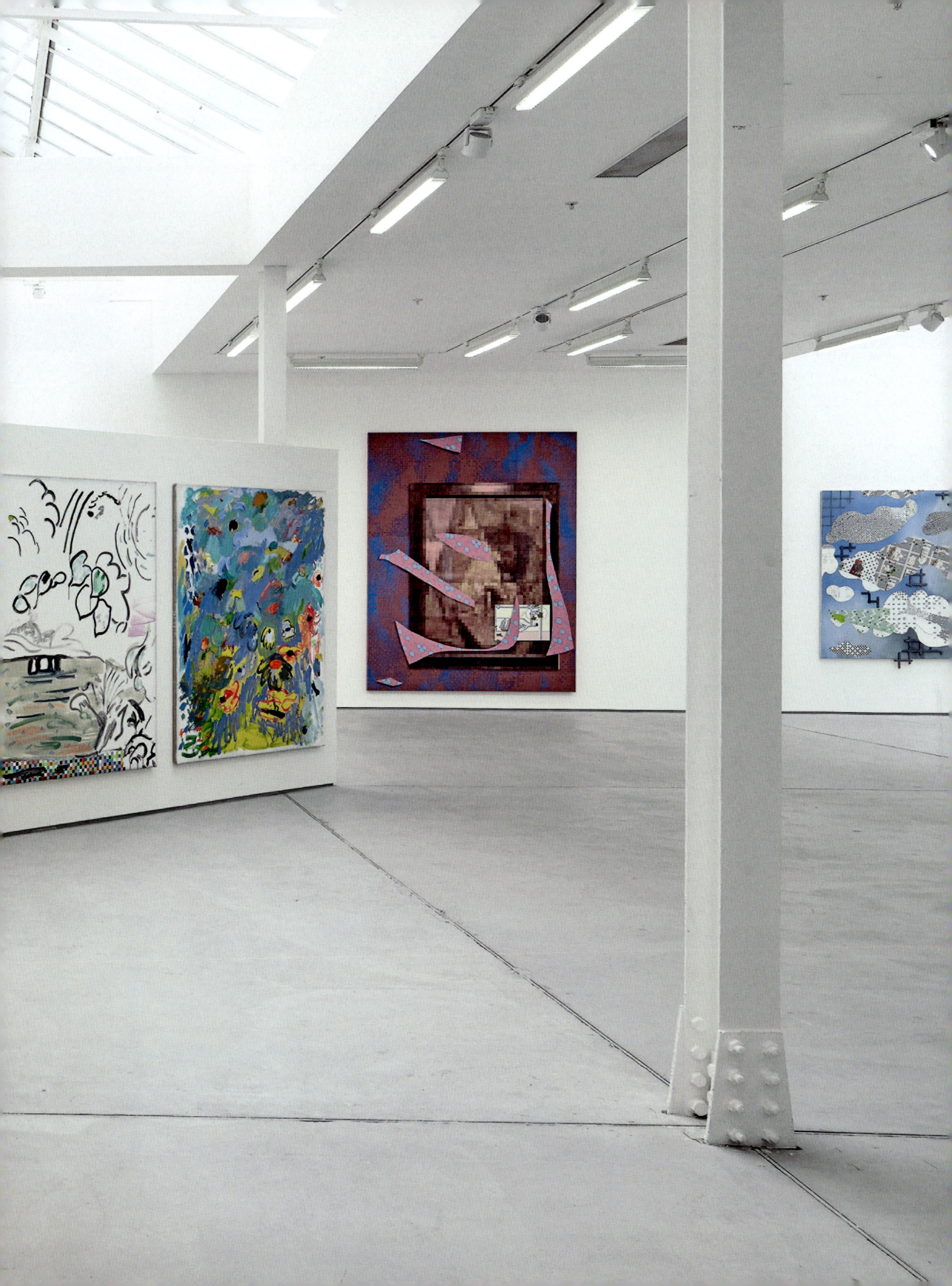

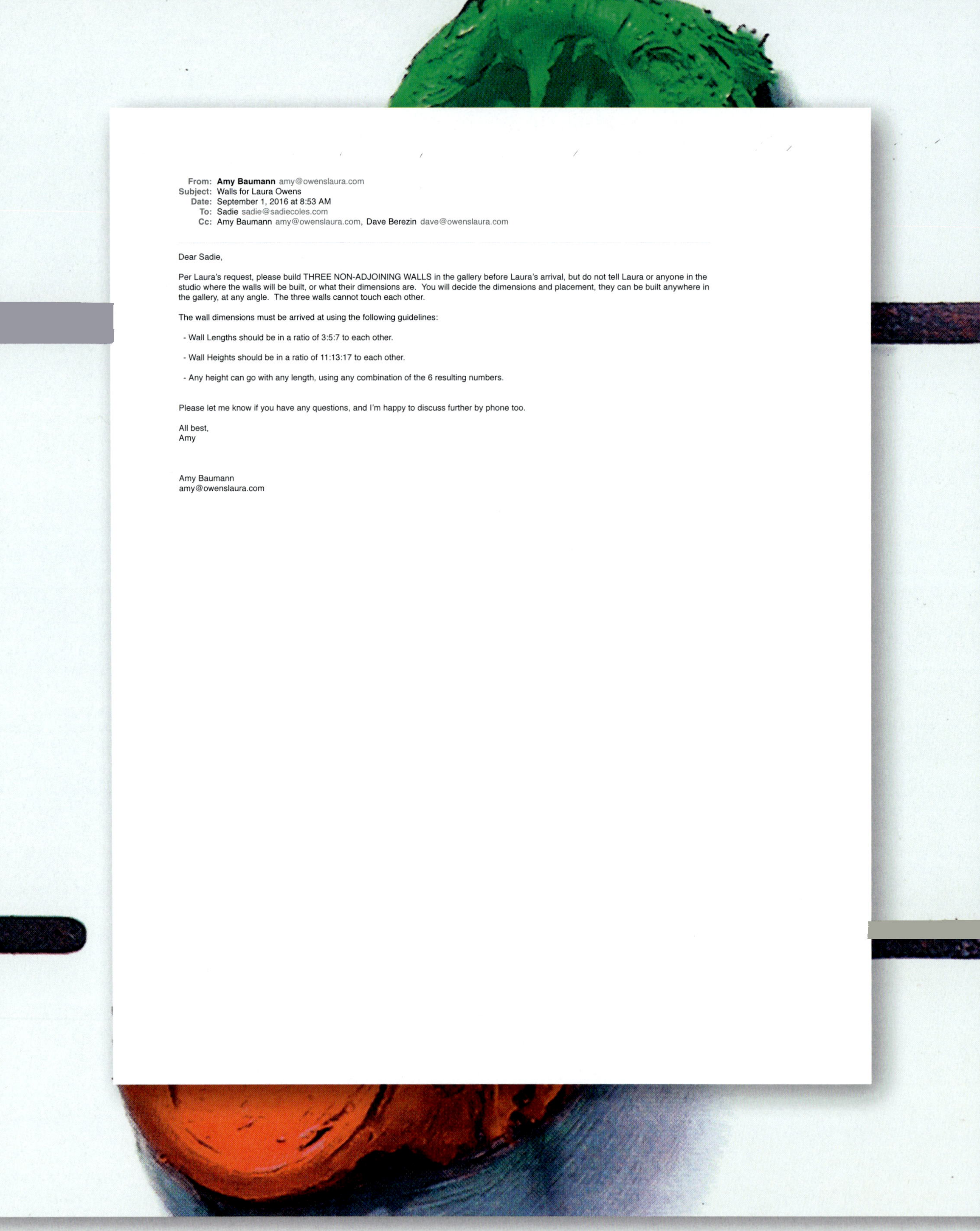

Foreground: Email from Amy Baumann to Sadie Coles, 2016
Background: Detail of *Untitled*, 2016, oil and silkscreen ink on linen, 20 × 18 in. (50.8 × 45.7 cm)

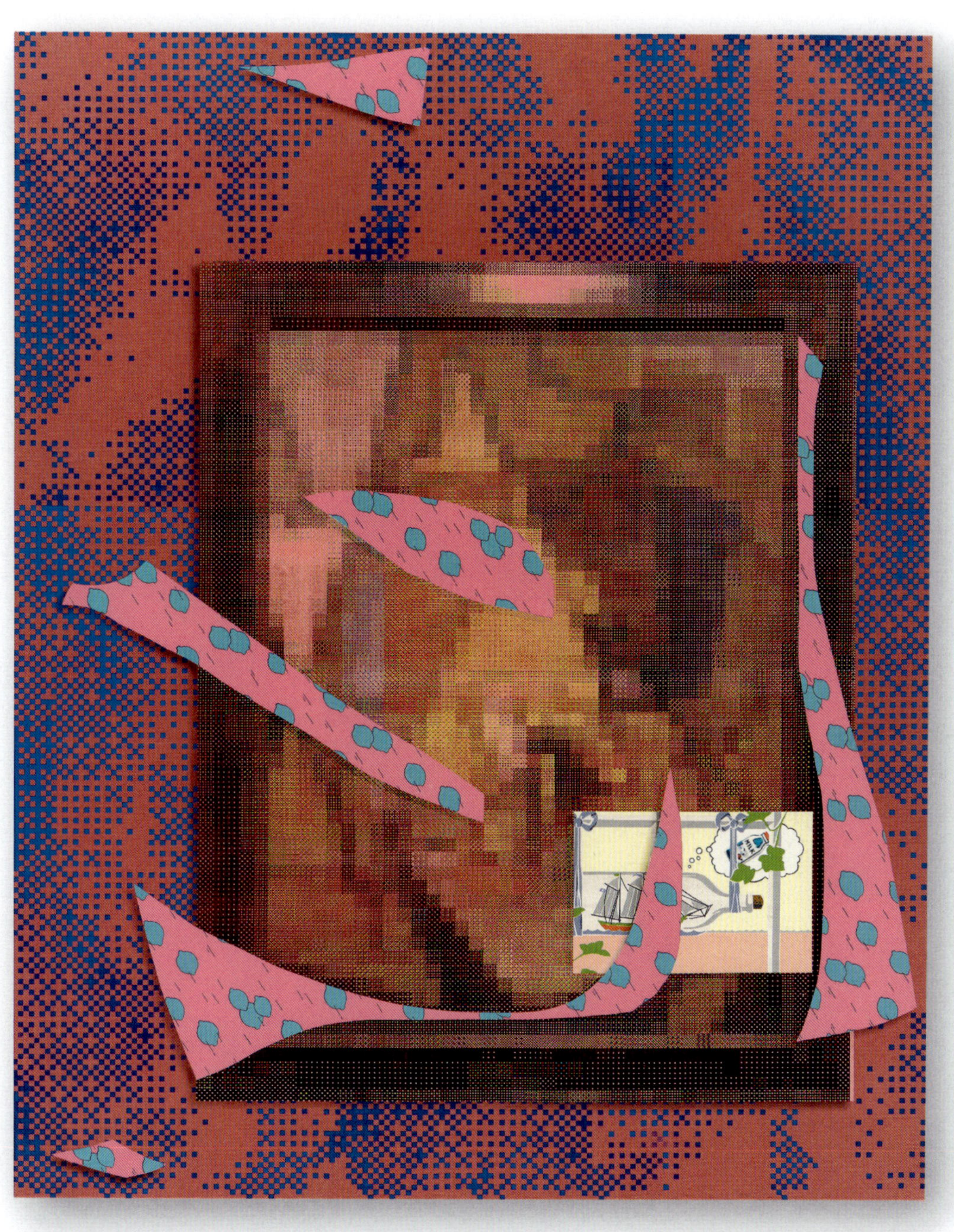

Untitled, 2016, vinyl paint and silkscreen ink on dyed linen, 108 × 84 in. (274.3 × 213.4 cm)

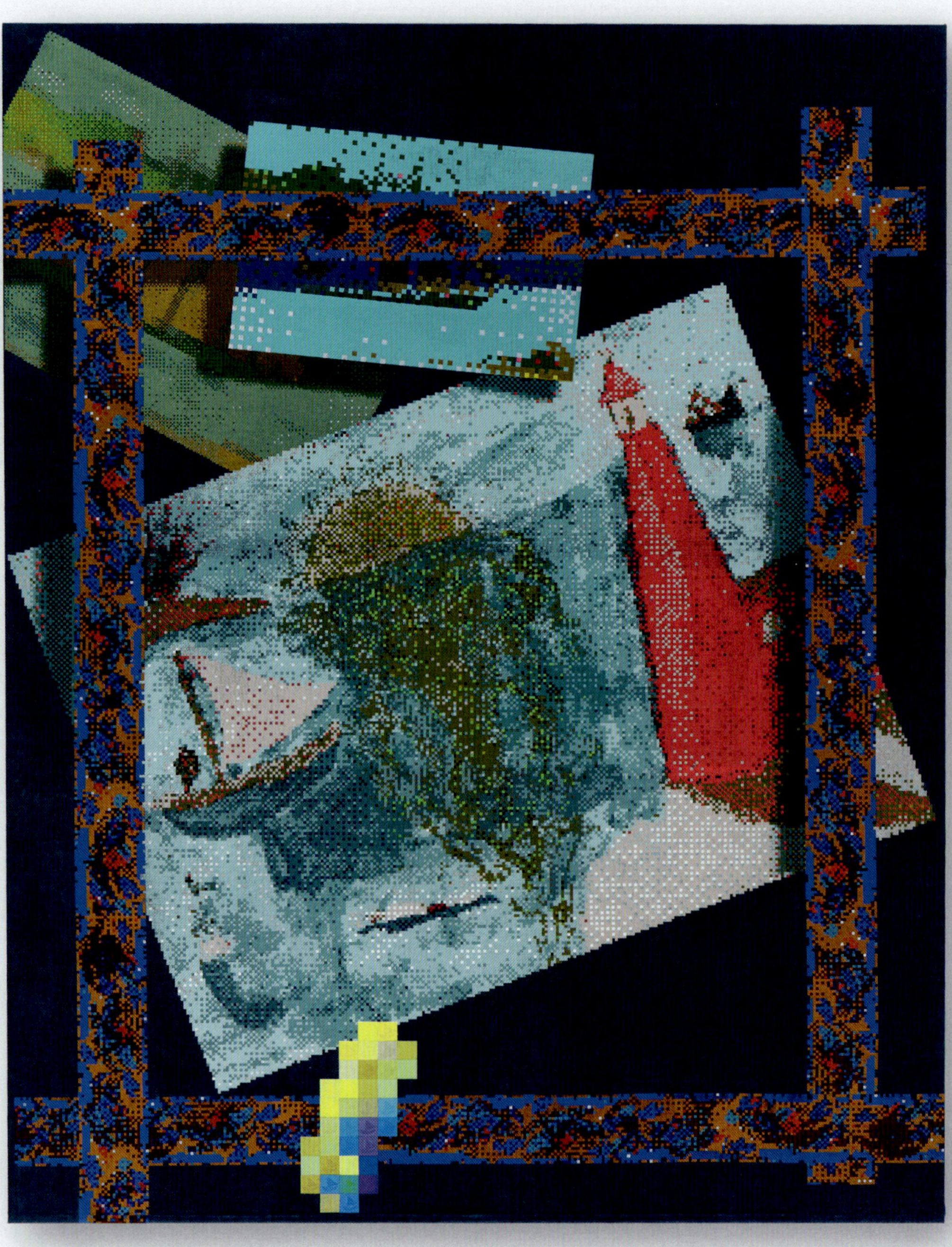

Foreground: *Untitled*, 2016, vinyl paint on dyed linen, 108 × 84 in. (274.3 × 213.4 cm)
Background: Screenshot of why11.com, 2016

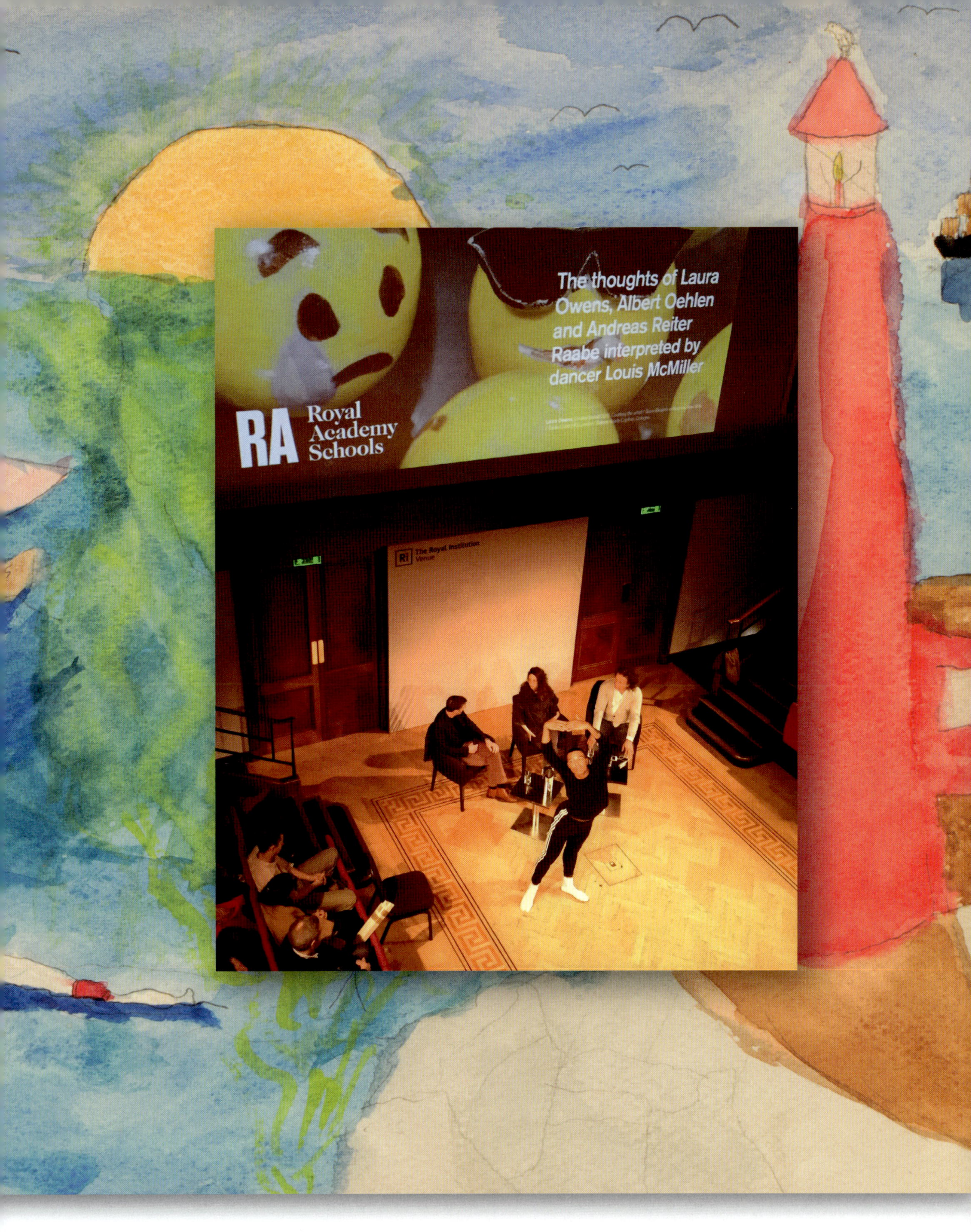

Foreground: Albert Oehlen, Owens, and Andreas Reiter Raabe with Louis McMiller (standing), "Thinking Out Loud: The Thoughts of Laura Owens, Albert Oehlen, and Andreas Reiter Raabe Interpreted by Dancer Louis McMiller," Royal Academy of Arts, London, 2016
Background: Detail of Lincoln Owens, *Untitled*, (ca. 1986), watercolor on paper, 11 × 15 in. (27.9 × 38.1 cm)

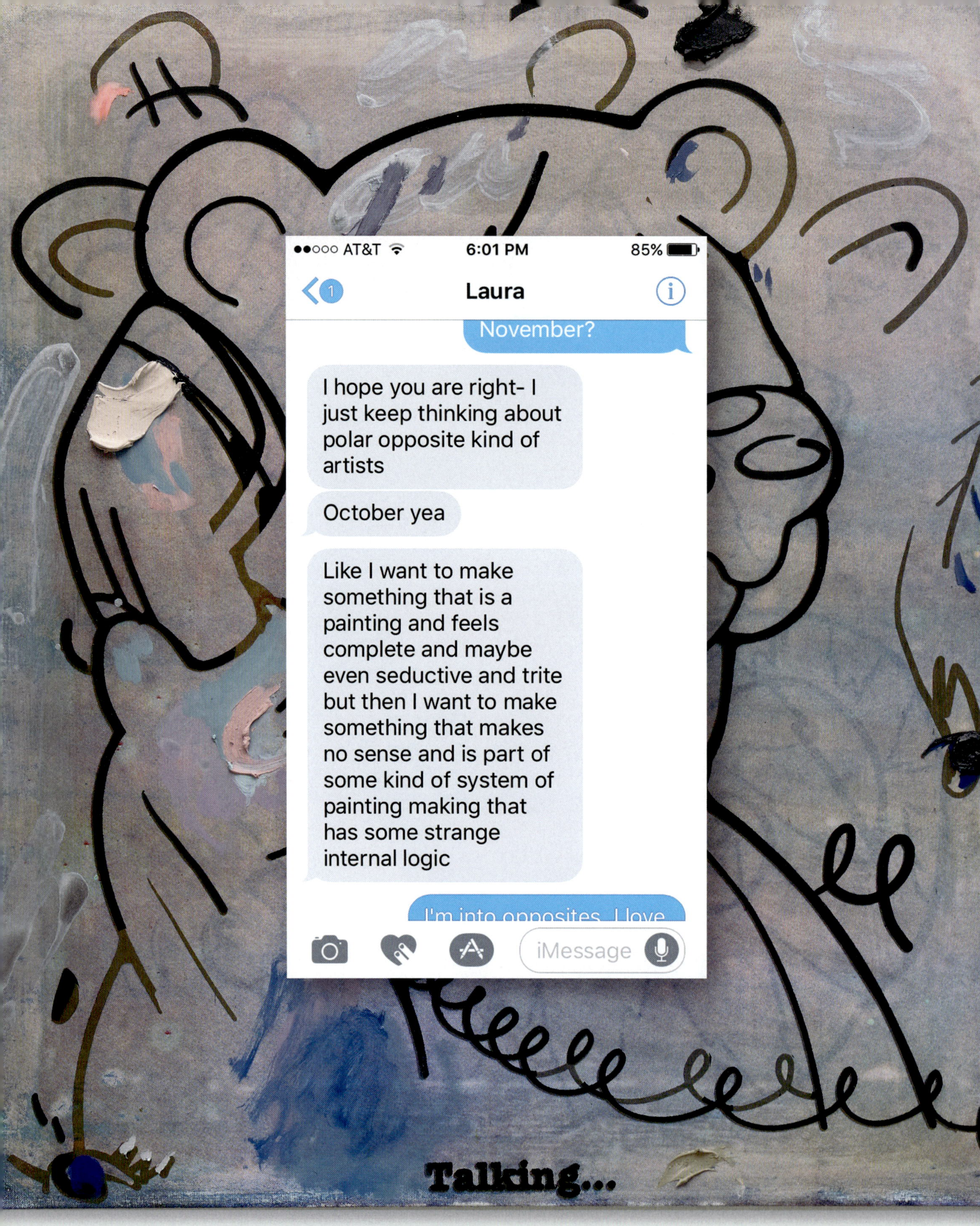

Foreground: Texts to Laeh Glenn, 2016
Background: *Untitled*, 2016, oil, vinyl paint, silkscreen ink, charcoal, and sand on linen, two panels: 32½ × 28 in. (82.6 × 71.1 cm) each

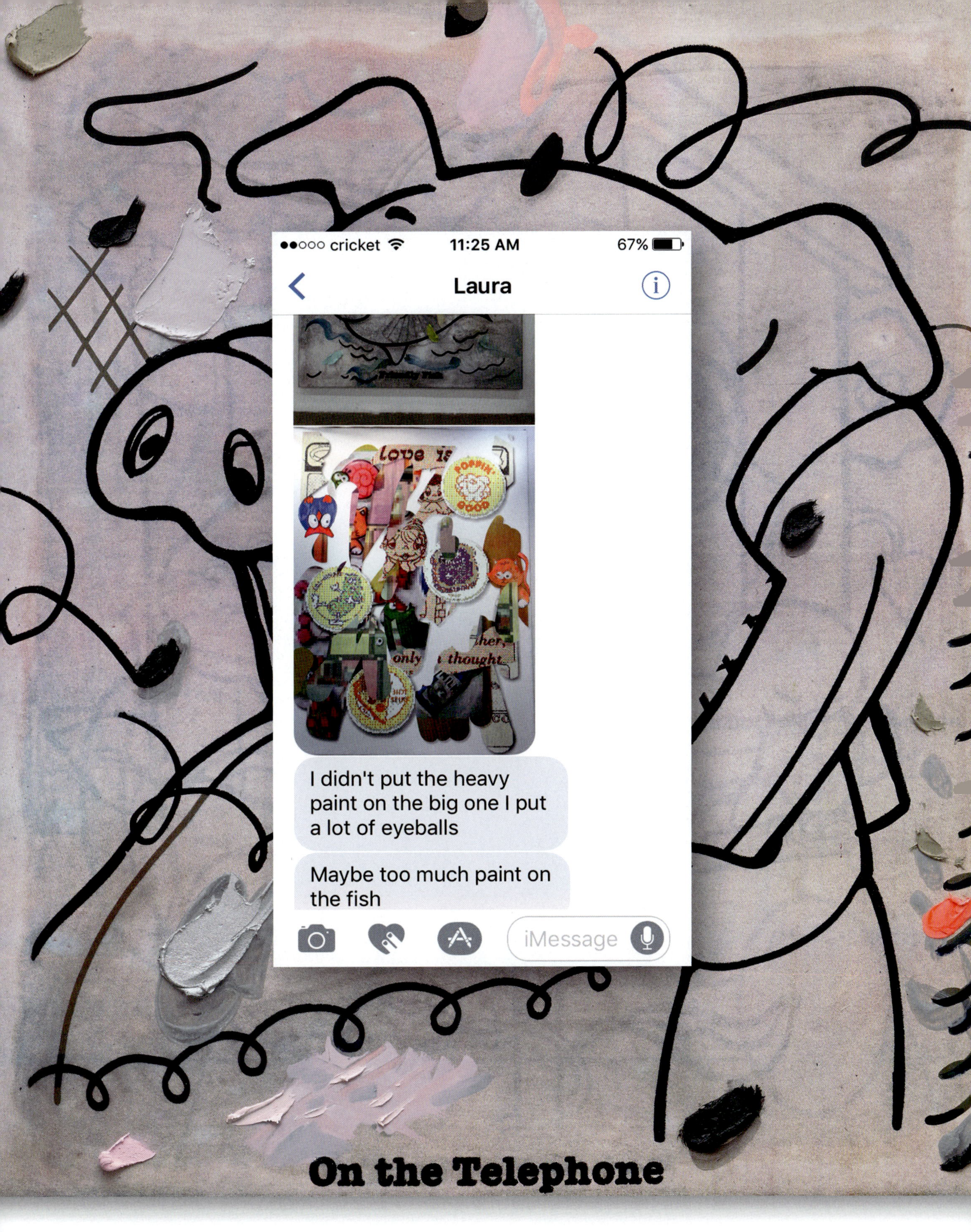
cricket
11:25 AM
67%
Laura
love is
POPPIN'
GOOD
her,
only   thought
I didn't put the heavy paint on the big one I put a lot of eyeballs
Maybe too much paint on the fish
iMessage
On the Telephone

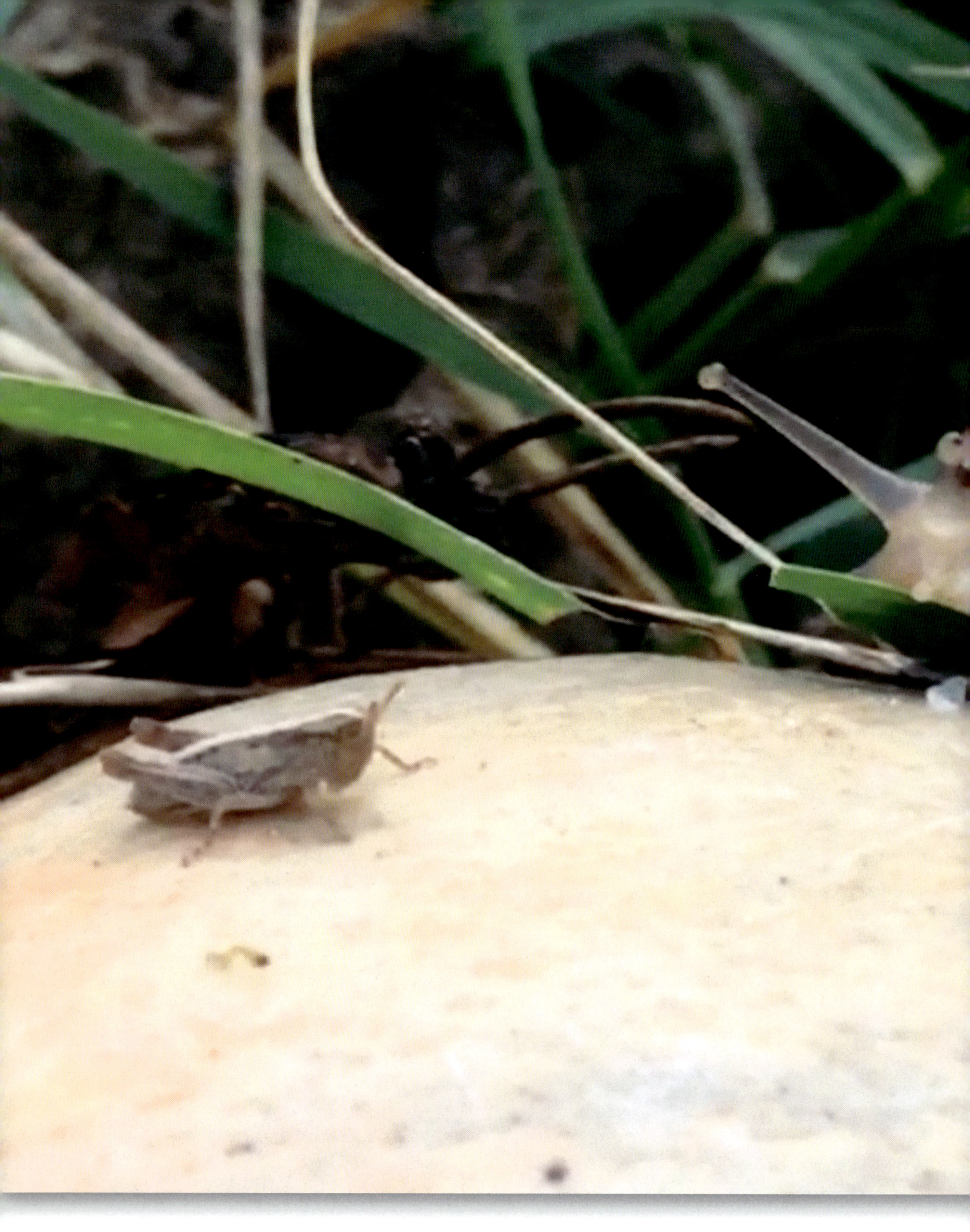

  Still from *Untitled*, 2016, single-channel video with sound, 0:20 min. loop

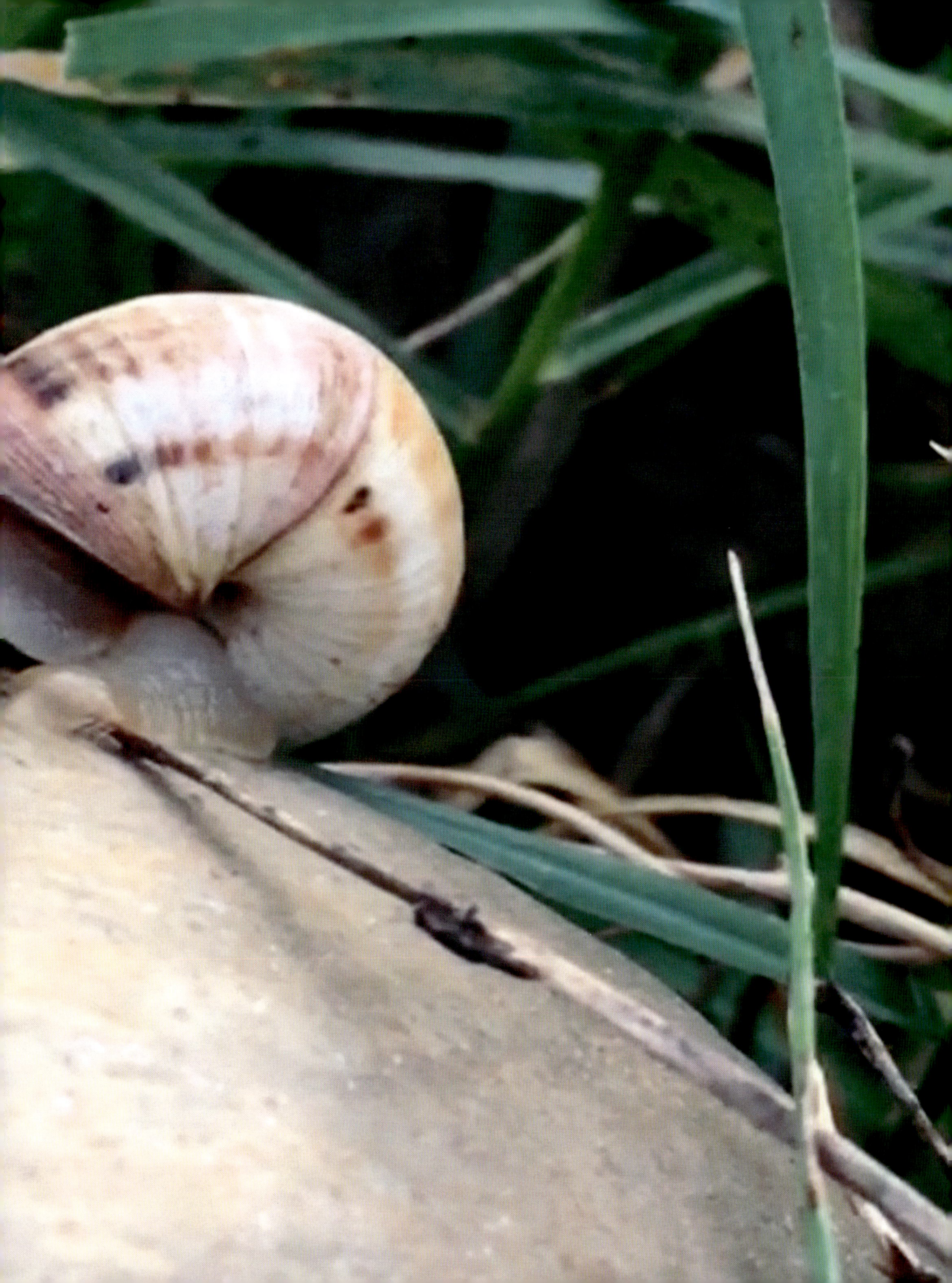

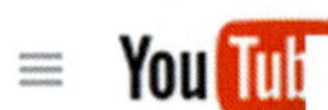

PIcabia

Hello
Thank you to Anne Umland and everyone at Moma for inviting me to talk on this panel.

I want to talk about Picabia as an idea   or another way of putting it
What do we mean when we say Picabia?
First I will back up and give some background on my own way of thinking, making art
When I first started working and showing and talking about my art I would explain to people that I was interested in starting a painting by asking What can a painting be? And it was important to me to be starting over every time with this question, knowing painting, laura owens painting can handle the effects of any stretching, abuse or perversity of this question, that the painting status as art is not fragile at all, to the contrary its indelible to a fault. More recently maybe the last 5-10 years I have found myself asking another question more and more
Where is the painting?
This comes out of continued thinking and talking about painting as an almost hyper arrived penultimate readymade, A painting can never not be art. Unlike contemporary art which status is always in flux of time and space(it needs the kunsthalle, the invitation, the website) its art status being specifically linked to context and discourse,-- Painting seems to never not be art even wether it is sitting on the shelf at the art supply store or in the dumpster. However because of this special status, weaker perhaps because of its portability or intrinsic mirror like links to capital, circulation etc, or stronger because of its imperviousness-- it is most importantly BOTH.
We are constantly reminded-- if it is working as art that Its location is not only with the auratic object but also always in the space around it, it is helping the institution become art institution, it is the gallery it supports, the lunch and the people attending the lunch, the talk about the painting or not. It resides in its own representations
And most importantly it FOR ME at this moment and in my thinking It is BETWEEN these spaces, the physical spaces, the object and the space of discourse.

BOTH
BETWEEN

So --- Picabia as an idea--
 And that is for many reasons, yes there was a person named Picabia that lived and died and had a life. And there are objects that exist that are collected and exchanged and exhibited with the name Picabia attached to them on the wall label.
But these objects, origin stories, anecdotes, biographical facts, writing , the shows curated around and about him and those that claim some influence or seek to link their art to him through written spoken admiration, conversations like the one we are having and will have. Basically all discourse and actions accumulated in the name of and around the idea of this artists become the idea of Picabia and the objects hanging upstairs may merely mark the occasion to rethink the positions he takes up . That the auratic object becomes an occasion to reingest and recirculate conventional ideas around his approach to making art, adding more, emphasizing different aspects maybe even repudiating past associations with the artist. It is our chance to reinvent or evaluate in contemporary terms what this idea may now mean.

I have asked this question for myself and other artists that I am looking at, by reframing an idea of painting- as then… Where is the painting, and perhaps like contemporary art -When is the painting?
Because the painting is both a firm and unbreakable container for the idea of art and also no longer where the art resides. It is a symbolic gesture for the discourse and thoughts it accumulates and produces. It is where its representations exist just as much as where the object lives in storage racks or museum. It is in my students idea of art --in class we talk about how many of our favorite artists works they have never seen.
I believe many of these idea begins to be firmly articulated in the early 20th century by Picabia and his peers
And so this is specifically a topic for Picabia because he does continue to make paitnings
But also Picabia has because of his sheer amount of time on the scene accumulated like a snowball rolling down the hill the most mass in regards to these ideas

What are these ideas that are Picabia—here are some

1)   Inconsistency as a value or a negation of consistency, image recognition and therefor value accumulation.

Foreground: Owens's remarks for Contemporary Perspectives on Francis Picabia, Museum of Modern Art, New York, 2017
Background: Screenshot of youtube.com, 2017

2) Pointing always to the How instead of the what –
This allows a democratic anything goes for type, image, visual content
Also inherently contains a strong ethic toward negating what is expected.
Hence pointing and Locating these expectations on the side of the viewer and reception, enunciating them.
Instead of authority the motive is one of the eternal student, the maker, the artist with less regard for appeasing or fulfilling a requirement.

3) Artists artist is brought up a lot --in the catalogue, I think this illuminates a bias and should be looked at—and regards to what I just brought up,should be replaced by another idea of " not working on behalf of an audience or expectation"
What we could learn if we don't hold this bias as Picabia to be viewed primarily by other artists- an influencer a teacher etc. Is that the goal of Picabia could be to alleviate the pressures of definitive recognition from the viewer.
It supposes that knowing or recognizing are simply fulfilling an idea based on past experience or faulty memory as a misrecognized authenticity. That instead pIcabia asks the audience should be awake and aware of their co participation in meaning production and fulfilling an experience of not knowing, play, heightened awareness of the space and a sensitivity to their own interaction.
Because they are uncomfortable.

Merlin Carpenter would be an artist who is adept at this sort of dislocation and interested in this exchange space between the viewer and the object(a show at overduin number of years ago where the press release stated Please Read and went on to tell you….)
In the introductory text I think Anne refers to putting the viewer in the hot seat—this is the same idea--
My question would be -- isn't this where the viewer always is?

And this then segues into another idea similar but different way of putting it,, predilection toward judgement on the part of the viewer, ideas of taste again in the catalogue "to state what is good or a bad picabia is entirely subjective"
I would take it further, and say it is a habitual ritual we perform as viewers to create ourselves as subjects.
And this is the idea of Picabia,
Again very much illuminated by Seth Price, in the book fuck seth price he sets this out completely.
It feels very much a paradox, and maybe that is a good word.
Because it is both Good and Bad art. The vichy paitnings are both ironic and not ironic. Sincere/insincere
Serious/ not serious.. I think of Mary Heilmann or Blinky Palermo.
Is Judgement a trap or a habit?
How is it both at the same time?
How is it both the paitning and the replica of the painting?

Back to inconsistency- and this idea of between—we see this most obviously when he does the show in Barcelona galerie dalmau-

I would say that this moment Picabia points to the space between- that it is this space between the paintings we need to find the paintings. And it is a multiplicity of betweens – between the image of the painting, the exhibition, the press release, the artists voice bio, the object – and this between that is first pointed to by picabia,

Peter fischli refers to Picabia as pre postmodern and I would go further and maybe say that Picabia indicates that postmodernism is born at the same time as modernism and they are like two sides of the same piece of paper. Both at the same time

========================

Modernisms inherent problem with renewing replenishing itself, avant gardist tendency, is at odds with accumulating value?

Painting is always art, you cannot take the art out of it= you can only attempt to negate and that in turns becomes another layer of art

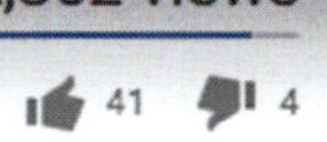

this panel explores key aspects of Picabia's wide-ranging body of work and its significance

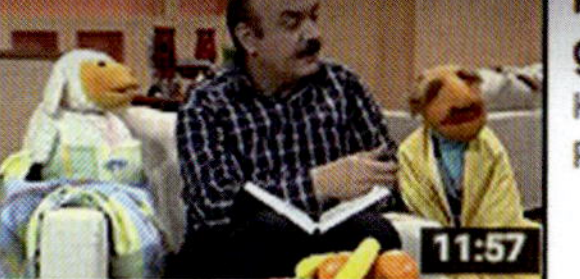

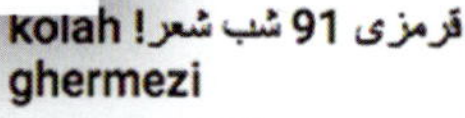

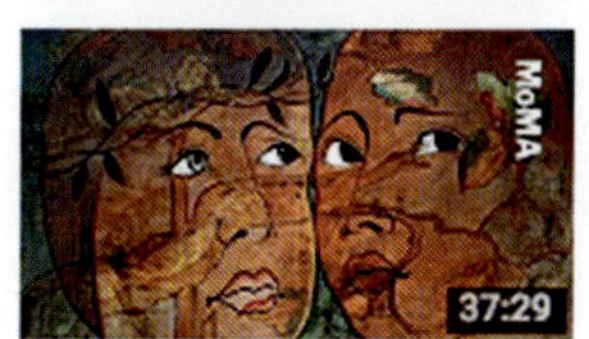

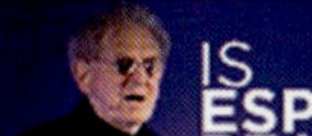

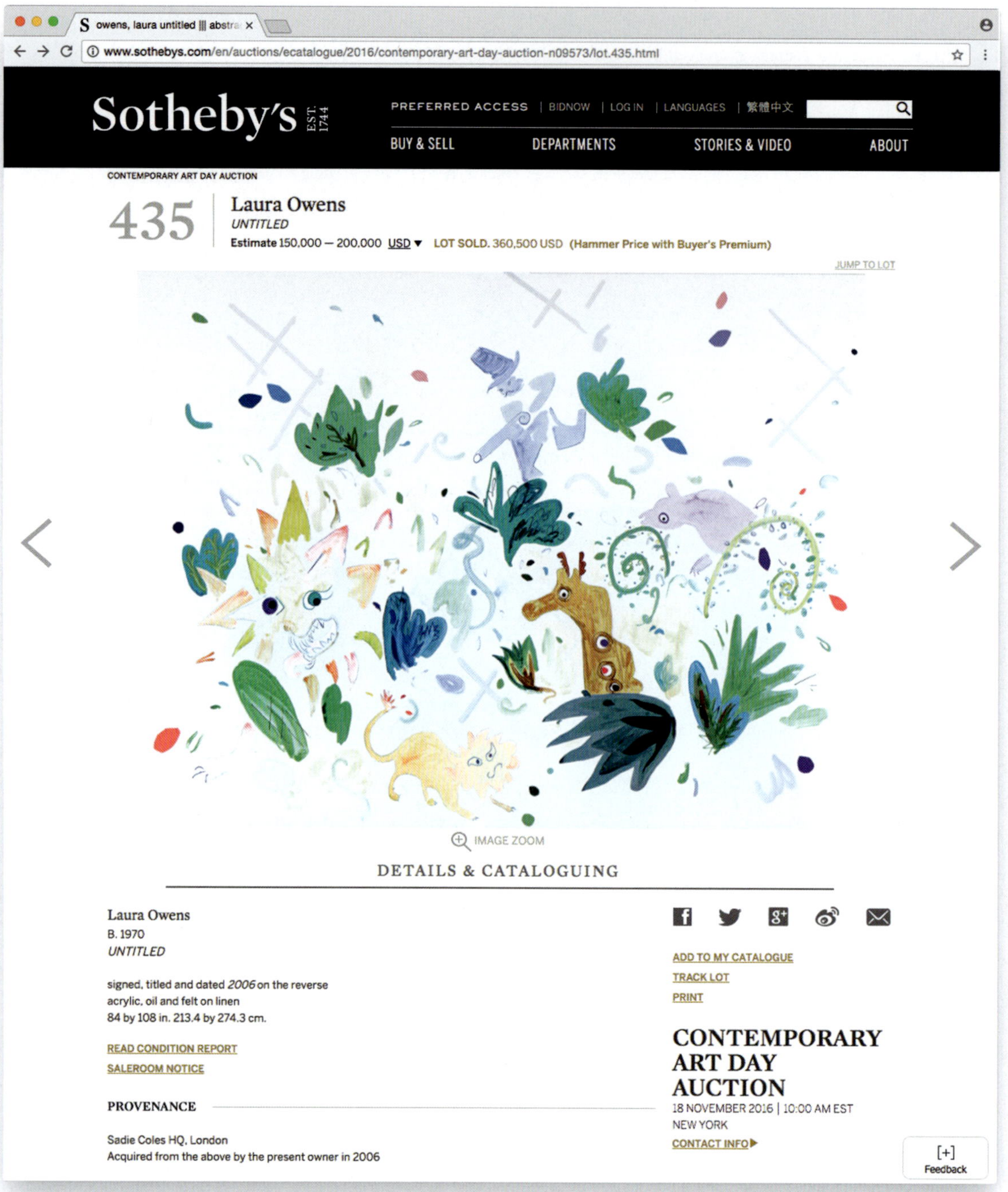

owens, laura untitled ||| abstra
www.sothebys.com/en/auctions/ecatalogue/2016/contemporary-art-day-auction-n09573/lot.435.html
Sotheby's EST. 1744
PREFERRED ACCESS | BIDNOW | LOG IN | LANGUAGES | 繁體中文
BUY & SELL   DEPARTMENTS   STORIES & VIDEO   ABOUT
CONTEMPORARY ART DAY AUCTION
435 | Laura Owens
UNTITLED
Estimate 150,000 — 200,000 USD ▼   LOT SOLD. 360,500 USD (Hammer Price with Buyer's Premium)
JUMP TO LOT
IMAGE ZOOM
DETAILS & CATALOGUING
Laura Owens
B. 1970
UNTITLED
signed, titled and dated 2006 on the reverse
acrylic, oil and felt on linen
84 by 108 in. 213.4 by 274.3 cm.
READ CONDITION REPORT
SALEROOM NOTICE
PROVENANCE
Sadie Coles HQ, London
Acquired from the above by the present owner in 2006
ADD TO MY CATALOGUE
TRACK LOT
PRINT
CONTEMPORARY
ART DAY
AUCTION
18 NOVEMBER 2016 | 10:00 AM EST
NEW YORK
CONTACT INFO ▶
[+]
Feedback

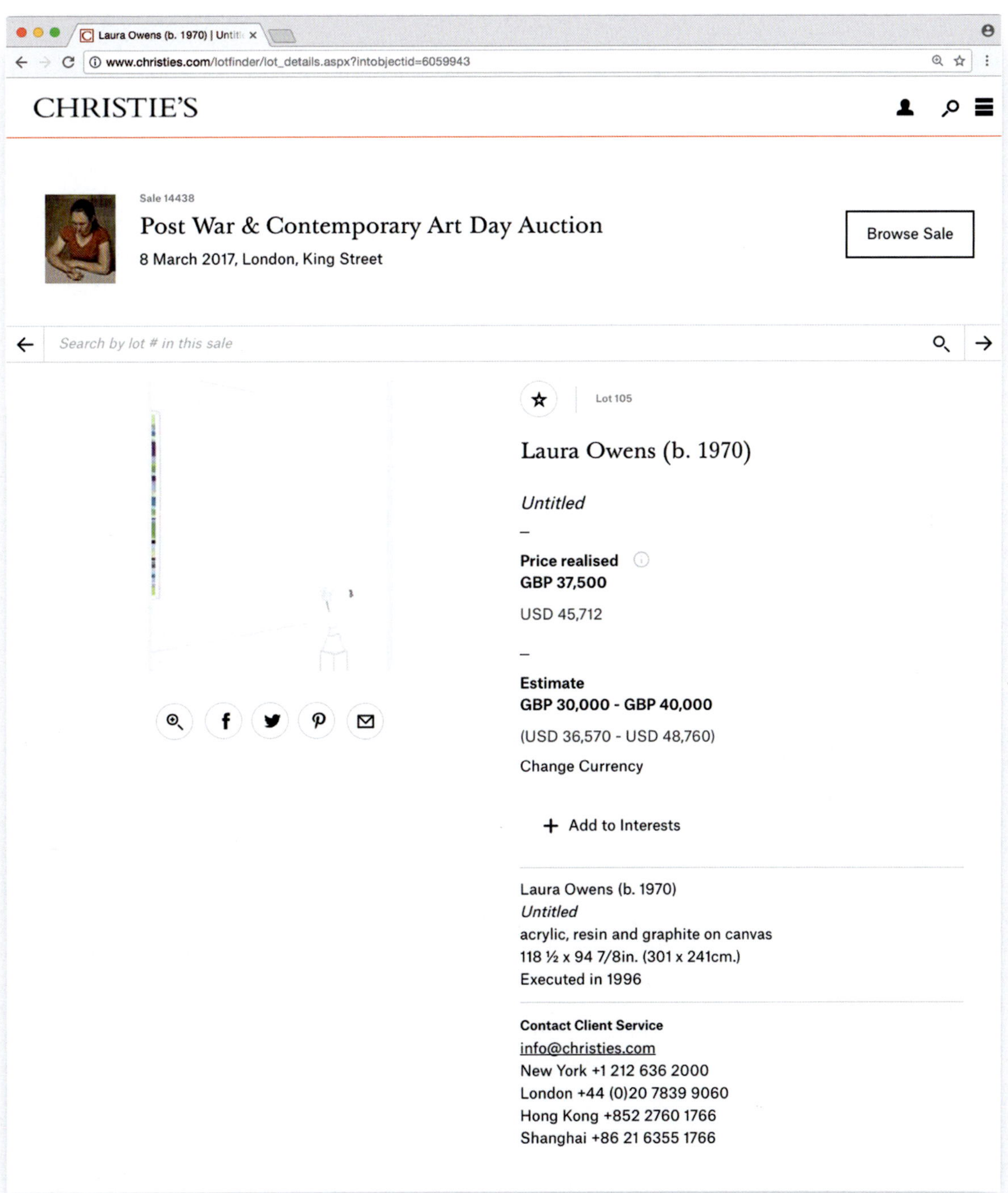

Laura Owens (b. 1970) | Untitl ×
www.christies.com/lotfinder/lot_details.aspx?intobjectid=6059943

CHRISTIE'S

Sale 14438
Post War & Contemporary Art Day Auction
8 March 2017, London, King Street

Browse Sale

Search by lot # in this sale

Lot 105

Laura Owens (b. 1970)

Untitled

—

Price realised
GBP 37,500

USD 45,712

—

Estimate
GBP 30,000 - GBP 40,000

(USD 36,570 - USD 48,760)

Change Currency

+ Add to Interests

Laura Owens (b. 1970)
Untitled
acrylic, resin and graphite on canvas
118 ½ x 94 7/8in. (301 x 241cm.)
Executed in 1996

Contact Client Service
info@christies.com
New York +1 212 636 2000
London +44 (0)20 7839 9060
Hong Kong +852 2760 1766
Shanghai +86 21 6355 1766

TALKING BACK
GAVIN DELAHUNTY

If you could ask one of Laura Owens's paintings a question, what would it be? "What is more important: form, color, surface, or ground?" "Do you feel instrumentalized?" "What is your favorite thing about being a painting?" "What are you hiding?" From April to July 2016 visitors to Owens's exhibition *Ten Paintings* at the CCA Wattis Institute had precisely this opportunity. Queries posed to the paintings via text message were answered through a network of speakers hidden in the gallery walls. This novel system communicates volumes about the conceptual foundations of Owens's work. Her paintings move beyond questions of content or medium specificity to speak to paradigm shifts in other fields—changes in how we communicate in the contemporary world, for instance. More than a resource for audience engagement, this clever, efficient means of enacting one-to-one conversation with an artwork tackles head-on the question of how a painting's "meaning" might be established. To facilitate retrieval of the works' knowledge, Owens and her team had to invent an index of terms, or keywords, that were stored on a custom computer concealed from view elsewhere in the gallery. In order for the question-and-answer system to run effectively they had to summarize the materiality, content, and narrative of each painting in anticipation of someone else's thoughts. The descriptive depth and vocabulary they attributed to each object in turn influenced the information received by its interrogators.

Requiring that the queries follow an all too familiar formula—who, what, when, where, why, in what way, by what means—the Wattis experiment delivered the sort of inquiry one might expect during a studio visit. The playful electronic exchanges between Owens and her audience that ensued also gave a nod to her creative process. For an exhibition at Sadie Coles HQ, London, in October 2016, she created an auxiliary website that was inserted into the gallery's website. why11.com provides a list of more than forty paintings, titled by number. Clicking on the title of a given work opens a link to its image, accompanied by an audio file. These files include an introduction by a text-to-speech automated voice that states, "Hello, I cannot wait to tell you more about these paintings . . . ," along with explanations by studio assistants of certain technical accomplishments, spoken inventories of the various materials used in the works, descriptions of formal experiments, and, more cryptically, several clips from George Harrison's *Wonderwall Music* (1968).

Clicking on the same link twice reveals that the audio is randomly generated and constantly changing, confounding the notion that a statement or sound might "explain" a particular painting. Offering no real direction as to where to begin or how to structure our selections, the site makes connections only to break them, thus performing, perplexing, and parodying the act of interpretation. Notably, *Wonderwall Music* seems to pop up with more frequency than the other audio files. Its nineteen songs are composed mostly of short musical vignettes, experimental arrangements that were designed to introduce Indian-style compositions and instruments that were largely unknown to the West at the time of the album's release by contrasting them with more familiar styles. Likewise, Owens's paintings are exemplary in their use of relational structures that arrange allusion, quotation, or virtual calque to make a new thing. The results are not logical, pivoting between this world and an otherworld. why11.com too is a procession of instinctive and arbitrary connections that parody the notion of a definitive interpretation while simultaneously resonating with the form and character of Owens's work. It is an attempt to move beyond the didactics on the wall telling you details such as her name and a given work's date of production or lender, and instead to imagine the origins of her syntax.

Owens's seemingly relentless push to abandon standardized interpretive formats and transfer

    Gavin Delahunty is Hoffman Family Senior Curator of Contemporary Art at the Dallas Museum of Art.

fresh meaning onto her paintings was arguably at its most anarchic in the audio guide she prepared to accompany her painted contribution to *The Forever Now: Contemporary Painting in an Atemporal World,* an exhibition presented at The Museum of Modern Art (MoMA), New York, from December 2014 to April 2015. Stripped of the high-tech tools used for why11.com or the Wattis experiment, the *Forever Now* recording is an unaccompanied monologue in which Owens expresses her thoughts aloud to the audience. It opens with a direct attack on the premise of the audio guide, challenging listeners to forego the apparatus altogether so that they might have a less mediated experience with the art on display and perhaps along the way strike up a conversation with another visitor and have a social interaction—something potentially real and valuable. As the recording progresses it delivers a number of rhetorical questions relating to the changing status of art and its institutions. Owens asks: "What constitutes a painting?" "Where is the painting?" "Is this a happy institution?" We might wonder whether this monologue is self-reflexive, or if Owens's questions are directed at her work. Perhaps the responses she gathered paved the way for the Wattis experiment, with its emphasis on encouraging every visitor to ask questions and generating a profusion of commentary. This strategy bypasses the authority of the artist and illustrates the ways in which paintings can comment on themselves and on the conditions of their production. This may not be that far away from Owens's beginnings, which is to say that perhaps it is an attempt to shift the emphasis of what is important and distinctive about a work of art from its physical appearance to the process of its making. An early painting, a more private group undertaking exhibited at Rosamund Felsen Gallery, underscores this point.

Untitled (1995, see p. 84) depicts numerous artworks suspended salon style on a distant green wall. It was a collaborative effort that took the surrealist parlor game Exquisite Corpse as its concept, with several of the paintings depicted within it having been created by invited artists who had dropped in and out of Owens's studio while it was being made. The paintings within the picture include colorful abstractions punctuated by flowers, sailboats, landscapes, figures, clocks, and calligraphic works. The painting could be understood as a basic inventory of Owens's pictorial language; the elements listed here would resurface and feature more and more prominently in her work to come. This multiuser exercise, with Owens acting as host connecting information back to the work, is an important early forerunner of the MoMA, why11.com, and Wattis projects, in which you press play on an audio guide, click on a link, or send a text message and receive a response from the artist.

Untitled is a dialogic work that involves a kind of call-and-response between Owens and visitors to her studio. In her more recent experiments that dialogue is extended to enable the viewer to verbally interact with her paintings. Rather than providing a definitive explanation, this interaction between audience and artwork often poses more questions than it answers. I am reminded of a 1946 cartoon by Ad Reinhardt in which a viewer points derisively at an abstract canvas, asking, "Ha ha, what does this represent?" *"What do you represent?"* the painting booms, startling its impudent interlocutor. Owens's talkative paintings in turn make us ponder the making of meaning in abstract art and the questions this process poses.

Scott Rothkopf: I first encountered Laura's work in 2001 at the Gardner Museum when I was just starting out in grad school. The exhibition made a big impression on me because it was the sort of thing I wasn't supposed to like but couldn't get out of my head. I bought the little catalogue in the gift shop and kept returning to the pictures of those interplanetary monkeys, not knowing quite what to make of them. After moving to New York in 2004 I saw Laura's towering, moody nocturne in the Whitney Biennial and began to follow her shows at Gavin Brown's. It was an odd period in her development to watch, since many people I respected thought she'd gone off the deep end into a sentimental morass of babies, knights, and lovers, often rendered in a super cloying palette. We met over the phone to do a brief interview for her 2006 Kunsthalle Zurich book. I tried to talk with her about manipulation of space and architecture in paintings of hers that I had never seen. I don't think it turned out very well.

Then in 2012 I saw *Pavement Karaoke* in London and it totally blew my mind. The bubble-gum colors and frosting impasto were unapologetically saccharine, but the variety of techniques and materials, along with the inventive screenprinting, seemed gutsy, assured, and urgent. At the time, critics and curators were talking a lot about contemporary approaches to abstract painting that mostly depended on all-over compositions with indirect mark making and slight pictorial incident, often resulting from chance. Laura's show seemed to take all this into account but also to thumb its nose at a way of thinking that had grown formulaic, chic, and overplayed in the market. Suddenly she had thrown a grenade into the conversation, refocusing a lot of people's thinking. The following year I was lucky to catch *Twelve Paintings* at 356 Mission; that's when things really gathered steam. Each new body of work after that added complexity yet clarity to the process, without ever seeming tricky or overeager. It was thrilling and rare to witness an artist rocketing along such an incendiary trajectory. Wherever I went, everyone from young art students to established painters like Julie Mehretu, Carroll Dunham, and even the octogenarian Alex Katz was talking about Laura's work.

In 2014 I was wrapping up the long process of curating Jeff Koons's Whitney retrospective, and as I considered speakers for an artists' panel on the show Laura unexpectedly came to mind. Although their art looks nothing alike, the technical demands of her painting, as well as her unembarrassed embrace of pop culture references and themes like love, made her work an apt if unintentional rejoinder to Jeff's. They also both operate outside the realm of conventional good taste. She gave an amazing, antagonistic talk about the show that left me feeling a little betrayed but weirdly hooked. I kept thinking that she was an artist I needed to work with, even though her paintings didn't quite match my aesthetic inclinations. She just felt totally necessary and like the perfect subject for the first midcareer survey in our new museum downtown. About six months later I finally overcame some lingering hesitation and mustered the nerve to invite Laura for a drink at her hotel when she was in town for the opening of *The Forever Now* at MoMA. We started making small talk but she was texting the whole time, and before I knew it the painters Jacqueline Humphries and Ryan Sullivan showed up, so I never got to ask her to do the show. It was like trying to make a move on someone who keeps deflecting by calling over friends. Now I realize that's just how Laura rolls—rarely alone, always multitasking. The next day I asked her to come over to my place and popped the question. She said yes.

We didn't really know each other at that point, but for the past two and a half years we've been in constant touch. A lot has happened over that time. She did her phenomenal Berlin and Wattis shows; the new Whitney opened; Trump got elected; and we both fell in love and attended each other's weddings. This seems both implausible and somehow fitting for an artist who's so emotionally present and aware. Laura and I are both headstrong control freaks, which has made for an intense if sometimes strained dialogue. She has very clear ideas about her work and how it's displayed, and she's not accustomed to being curated, whereas my style is pretty authorial. Until now, her survey shows have often mixed paintings from different bodies of work and presented them with little regard for the conditions of their genesis and initial display. Yet I've come to believe strongly that people need to sense the specific physical and referential relationships her paintings have to one another and to the spaces in which they are shown, as well as how they implicate all of us. The challenge is to animate this approach without descending into something hokey like period rooms.

Laura and I spent a lot of time looking at her paintings together across the country, and also just looking at other artists' work. Eventually I struck on the idea that the Whitney's open floor plan would allow us to build free-floating boxes or rooms of different sizes and heights related to the spaces for which her works were first made. One, for example, might approximate Sadie Coles's old gallery in London so that the paintings she showed there could once again function like the murals they originally were. Another would reunite for the first time Laura's beehive paintings and the Jorge Pardo bedroom sets they were made to accompany. Then we began to think of how bodies of work like the Clock and Alphabet paintings might encircle the exterior of the boxes or the perimeter of the gallery, engaging the container as a whole. At this point we still have no idea how any of this will work, but it feels like it's worth a shot. Curating, like painting, should be alive to contingency—the unpredictable interactions among artworks, a space, an imagined audience, and a larger world, to say nothing of those between Laura and me.

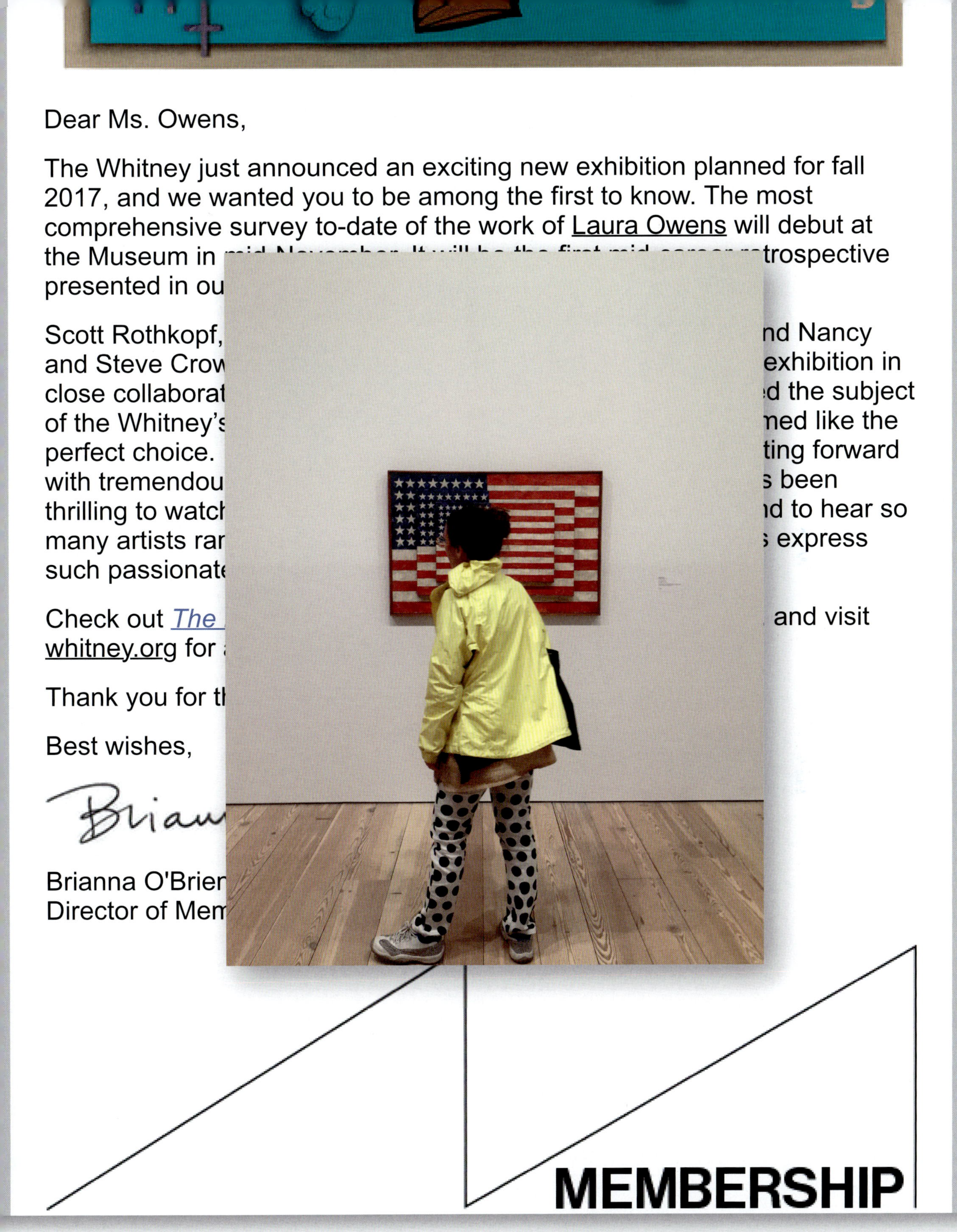

Dear Ms. Owens,

The Whitney just announced an exciting new exhibition planned for fall 2017, and we wanted you to be among the first to know. The most comprehensive survey to-date of the work of <u>Laura Owens</u> will debut at the Museum in mid-November. It will be the first mid-career retrospective presented in ou

Scott Rothkopf, and Nancy and Steve Crow exhibition in close collaborat the subject of the Whitney's ned like the perfect choice. ting forward with tremendou s been thrilling to watch d to hear so many artists rar s express such passionate

Check out <u>*The*</u> and visit <u>whitney.org</u> for

Thank you for th

Best wishes,

Brianna O'Brien
Director of Mem

MEMBERSHIP

Foreground: Owens with Jasper Johns, *Three Flags,* 1958, encaustic on canvas, 30⅝ × 45½ × 4⅝ in. (77.8 × 115.6 × 11.7 cm), Whitney Museum of American Art, New York, 2015
Background: Whitney Museum of American Art membership mailing, 2017

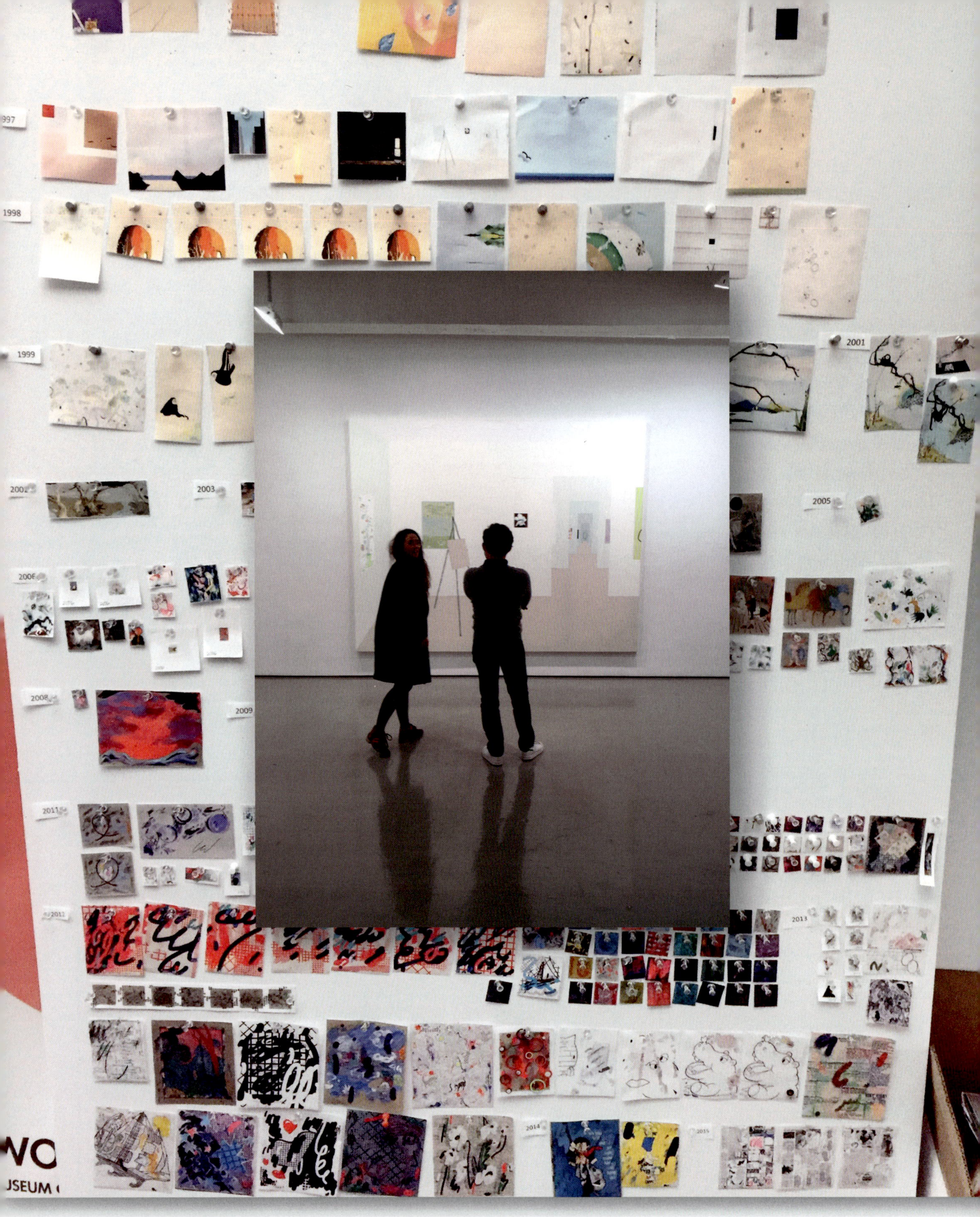

Foreground: Owens and Scott Rothkopf with *Untitled*, 1997 (see p. 175), Crozier Fine Arts, New Jersey, 2016
 Background: Exhibition research images, Whitney Museum of American Art, New York, 2016

Subject: RE: Whitney museum catalogue (TRYING AGAIN)

Dear Scott:

Laura's work is wonderful, and I'd be honored to do an essay for the book. Put me down for it. And we'll talk later.
   jg

From: Scott Rothkopf, Curatorial [S
Sent: Sunday, October 16, 2016 3:
To: Gold, Jonathan
Subject: Whitney museum catalog

Dear Jonathan (if I may),

I'm writing at the suggestion of La   ue of her survey
exhibition that I'm curating for the   ibition since the 2003
MoCA show and will include a broa   ill open in November
2017 and hopefully tour to an addi

In thinking about the book, we've   ring together essays on a
variety of subjects in and around h   vould be fascinating to
illuminate her various activities and   56 Mission, or even a
portfolio of her grandmother's nee   it painting and
contemporary art and life more bro   essarily all on Laura's
work per se), but in thinking about   k, we both immediately
agreed that you were at the top of

Now, you may be asking yourself v   interested in food, foodie
culture, eating, and hosting comm   f 356 Mission, where
she's tried to create a social space   ong with the email
misfire. That said, we're not lookin   ing to do with these
issues and how that might intersec   or beyond. Of course
you'd be welcome to mention her   just a huge fan of yours
and would love your voice in the b   certainly say that I would,
too.

I realize this is a somewhat vague   ough. I'd be happy to
talk further on the phone if that m   could even meet you in
person if you'd like. I'm thinking o   r a fee of $3,000 with a
deadline of January 2, 2017. Anot   was germane in this
context, though for reprinted texts

Thanks so much for taking the time to consider this request, and please let me know if you have any questions.

Best wishes,
Scott

--

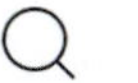
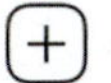
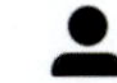

The following is the Instagram screenshot overlaid on the email:

Foreground: Instagram post by Scott Rothkopf, 2017
Background: Emails between Jonathan Gold and Scott Rothkopf, 2016

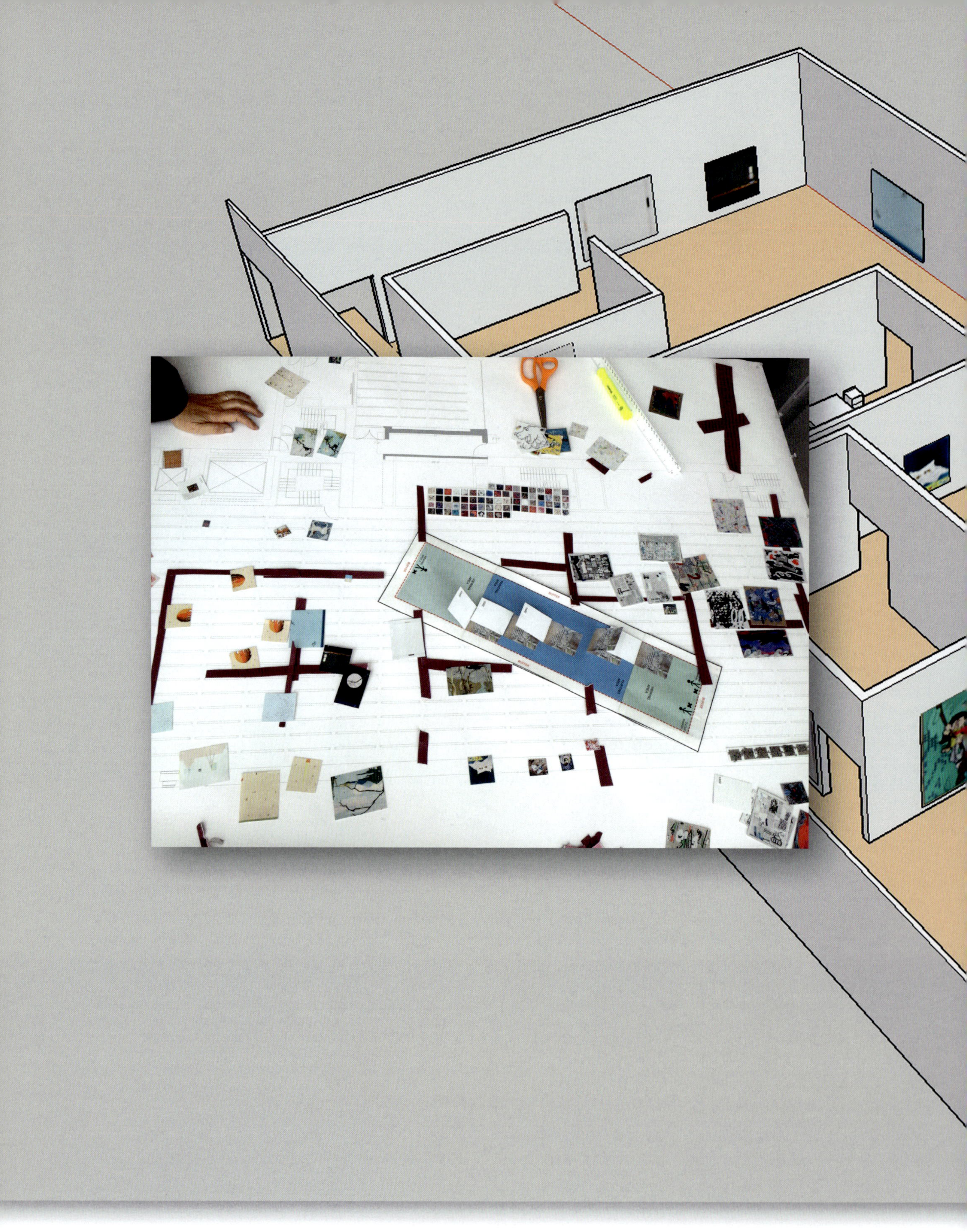

Foreground: Exhibition floor plan study, Whitney Museum of American Art, New York, 2016
Background: SketchUp file, 2017

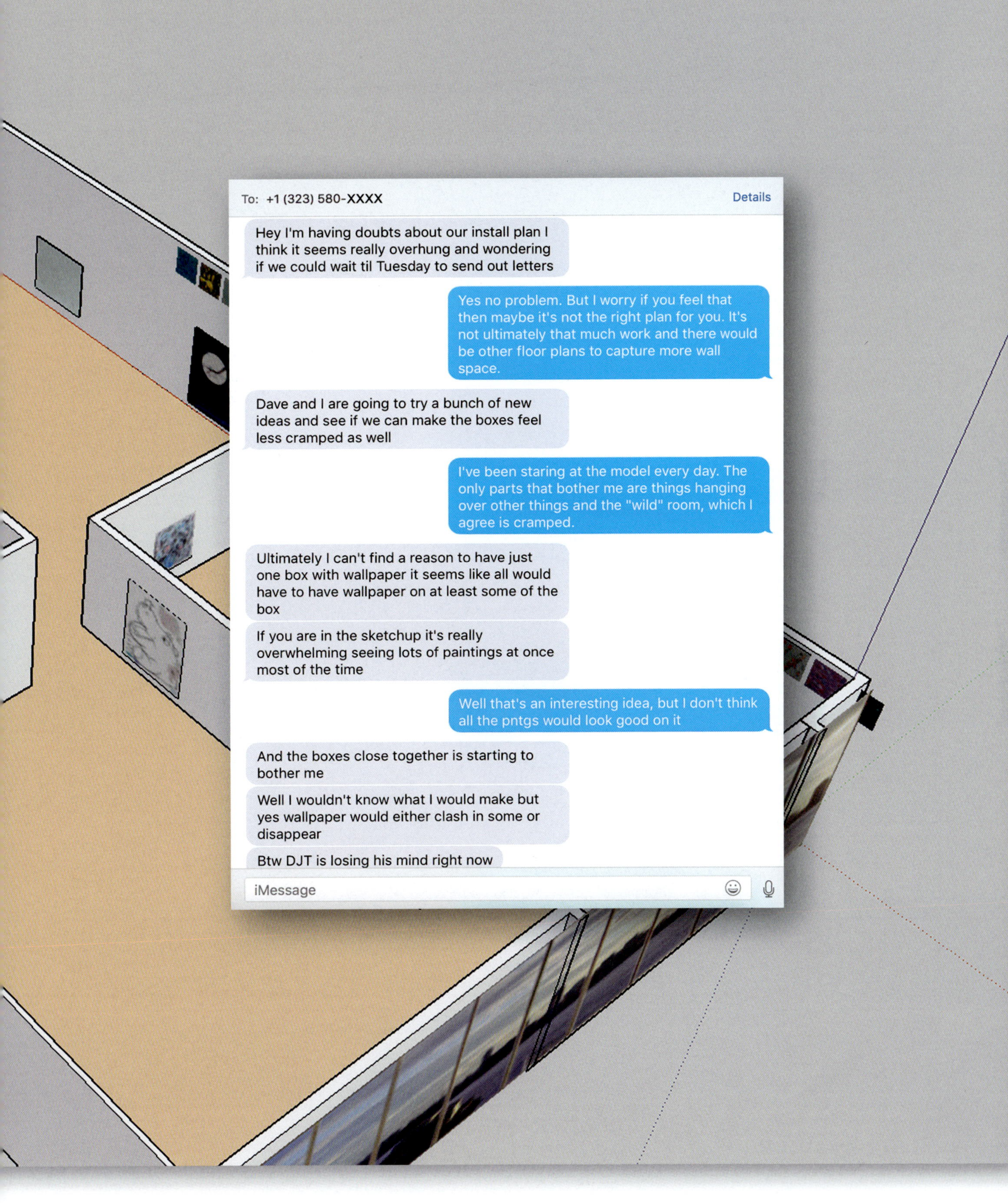

Foreground: Texts with Scott Rothkopf, 2017

	July 17	August 17	September 17	October 17	November 17

8TH FLOOR
Exhibitions

[Calder]
Curator: Sanders
20 or 21 weeks, Acct. Code: 7984

10/30/17 OR 11/6/17

11/10/17 OR 11/17/17

7TH FLOOR
Permanent Collection
(on continuous view with rotation)

Permanent Co[...]
Acct. Code: 7969

7TH FLOOR
Outdoor Gallery

6TH FLOOR
Permanent Collection
(on continuous view with rotation)

6TH FLOOR
Outdoor Gallery

[...oor Sculpture - Perm. Collection]

5TH FLOOR
Temporary Exhibitions

11/10/17 OR 11/17/17

11/3/17 — **Jimmie Durha[m]**
Organized by the H[...]
12[...]

5TH FLOOR
Outdoor Gallery
(M & O Roof)

[L...]

5TH FLOOR
Temporary Exhibitions
Gallery / Film & Video

11/3/17 — **Jimmie Durha[m]**
Organized by the H[...]
12[...]

3RD FLOOR
Theater Lobby

LOBBY GALLERY
Permanent Collection /
Temporary Exhibition

[Bunny Rogers]
Curators: Kross & Sherman

9/29/17

[Temporary Exhibition]

OFF-SITE

[Do-ho Suh: Title TBD]
95 Horatio Street Façade, Curator: Mitchell

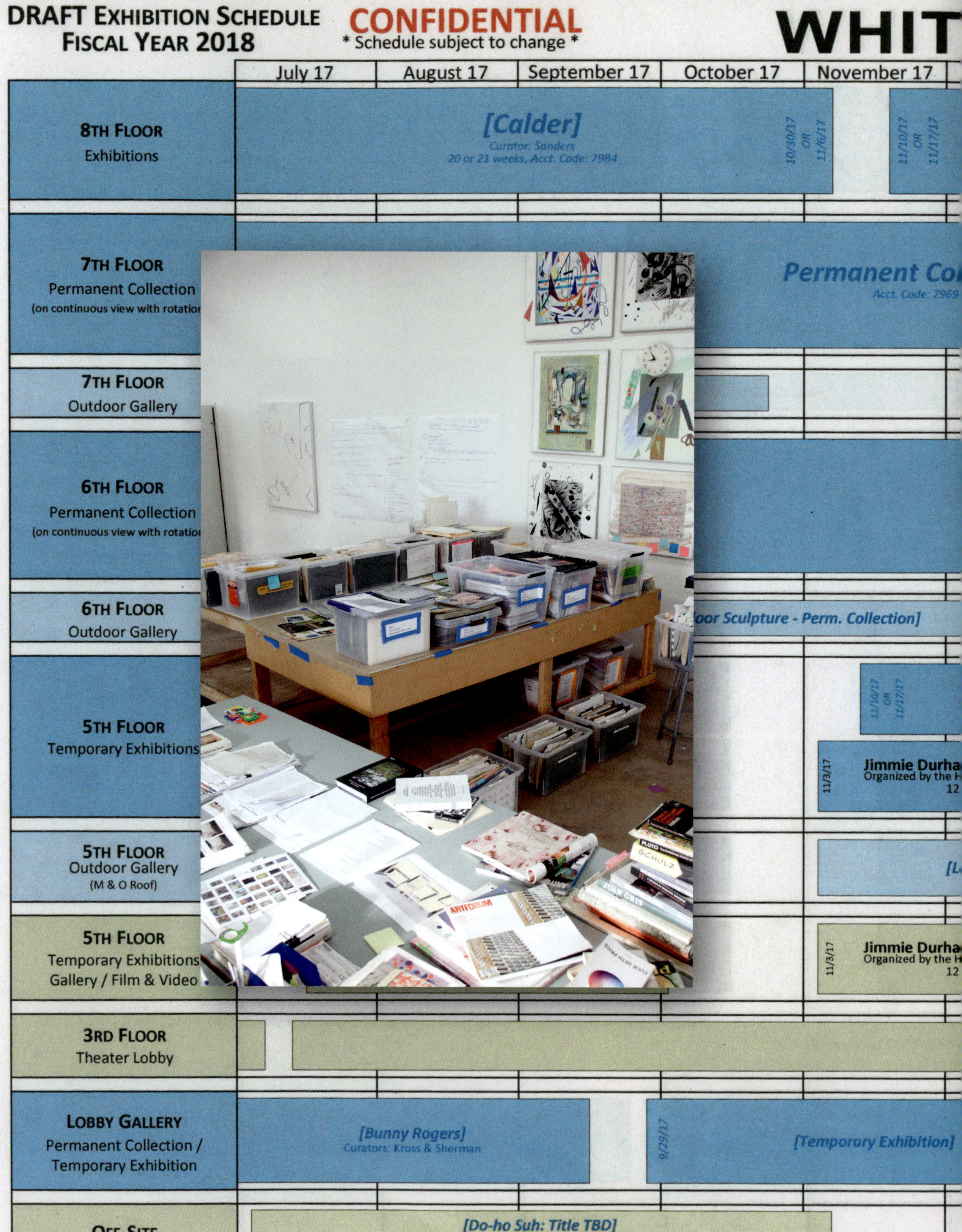

Foreground: Archival materials, Mission Rd. studio, Los Angeles, 2016
Background: Exhibition schedule draft, Whitney Museum of American Art, New York, 2016

ber 17	January 18	February 18	March 18	April 18	May 18	June 18

[Laura Owens]
Curator: Rothkopf
15 or 16 weeks, Acct. Code: 7976

3/4/18

[Temporary Exhibition]

Perma

[Laura Owens]
urator: Rothkopf
weeks, Acct. Code: 7976

e Center of the Wo
seum, Los Angeles / Suss
t. Code: 7975

le Project]

e Center of the Wo
seum, Los Angeles / Suss
t. Code: 7975

Permanent Col

[Temporary Exhibition]

[Temporary Exhibition]

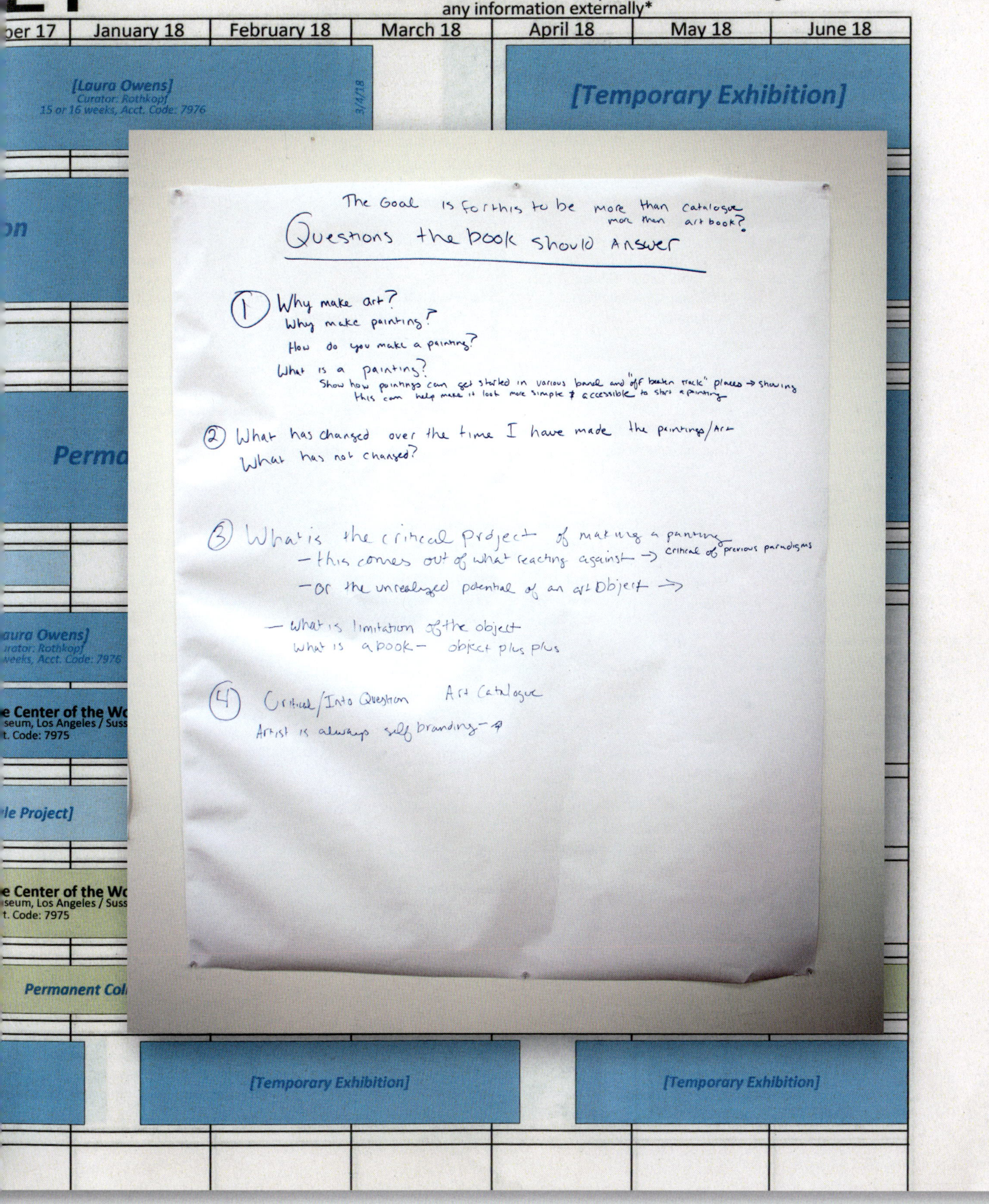

Foreground: Notes by Owens and Asha Schechter, Mission Rd. studio, Los Angeles, 2016

SELECTED BIBLIOGRAPHY

ARTIST'S PROJECTS

"A Project for *Open City* by Laura Owens." *Open City* 9 (Fall 1999): 145–52.

Untitled. Zurich: Nieves, 2006.

Ringier Annual Report 2013. Zurich: JRP | Ringier, 2014.

Artist Theater Program: Lava Plus Knives. Exh. cat. Paris: Lafayette Anticipation, Fondation d'enterprise Galeries Lafayette, 2015 (cover artwork).

Owens, Laura, and Asha Schechter. "DSKTP." *Kaleidoscope* 24 (Spring/Summer 2015): 226–35.

MONOGRAPHS

Morgan, Susan, and Henry Noltie. *New Work by Laura Owens (1999–2000) and John Hutton Balfour's Botanical Teaching Diagrams (1840–1879).* Exh. cat. Edinburgh: The Royal Botanic Garden Edinburgh, 2000. Published in association with California Institute of the Arts, Los Angeles; Sadie Coles HQ, London; and Gavin Brown's enterprise, New York.

Gross, Jennifer R., and Russell Ferguson. *New Work at the Isabella Stewart Gardner Museum.* Exh. cat. Boston: Isabella Stewart Gardner Museum, 2001.

Schimmel, Paul, and Thomas Lawson. Exh. cat. Los Angeles: The Museum of Contemporary Art, 2003.

Bell, Kirsty, and Haruko Kohno. Exh. cat. Tokyo: Shiseido Corporate Culture Department, 2005.

Exh. cat. Dublin: The Douglas Hyde Gallery, 2006.

Mengham, Rod, Gloria Sutton, Alex Katz, Elizabeth Peyton,

Christian Scheidemann, Mary Heilmann, Tomma Abts, and Scott Rothkopf. Exh. cat. Zurich: Kunsthalle Zurich, 2006.

Berg, Stephan, Stefan Gronert, and Sarah Lehrer-Graiwer. Exh. cat. Bonn, Germany: Kunstmuseum Bonn, 2011.

Clocks. New York: Karma, 2012.

Owens, Laura, Gavin Brown, Andrew Cannon, Corinna Durland, and Wendy Yao. *Twelve Paintings.* Exh. cat. Los Angeles: Ooga Booga, 2014.

Beshty, Walead, Gavin Brown, Trinie Dalton, Mark Godfrey, Suzanne Hudson, Rachel Kushner, Linda Norden, and Wendy Yao. *Laura Owens.* New York: Rizzoli, 2015.

BOOKS

1997
Project Painting. Exh. cat. New York: Basilico Fine Arts and Lehmann Maupin, 1997.

1998
Adams, Brooks, and Lisa Leibmann. *Young Americans 2: New American Art at the Saatchi Gallery.* Exh. cat. London: The Saatchi Gallery, 1998.

1999
Grynsztejn, Madeleine, ed. *Carnegie International 1999/2000.* Exh. cat. Pittsburgh: Carnegie Museum of Art, 1999.

Myers, Terry R. *Standing Still & Walking in Los Angeles.* Exh. cat. Beverly Hills, CA: Gagosian Gallery, 1999.

Nesbitt, Judith, and Francesco Bonami, eds. *Examining Pictures: Exhibiting Paintings.* Exh. cat. London: Whitechapel Art Gallery; Chicago: Museum of Contemporary Art, 1999.

Ohno, Megan, Prabha Viswanathan, and Alexandra Winokur. *The Perfect Life, Artifice in LA 1999.* Exh. cat. Durham, NC: Duke University Museum of Art, 1999.

Schuppli, Madeleine, ed. *Nach-Bild.* Exh. cat. Basel: Kunsthalle Basel, 1999.

2000
Balth, Carel. *The Beauty of Intimacy: Lens and Paper.* Exh. cat. The Hague: Gemeentemuseum The Hague, 2000.

Drawings 2000 at Barbara Gladstone Gallery. Exh. cat. New York: Barbara Gladstone Gallery, 2000.

Williams, Gilda, ed. *Fresh Cream: Contemporary Art in Culture.* London: Phaidon, 2000.

2001
Adams, Brooks. "'Raw Mineral Jaggedness': A Clyfford Still Legacy." In *Clyfford Still: Paintings 1944–1960,* edited by James T. Demetrion, 140–53. Exh. cat. Washington, DC: Hirshhorn Museum and Sculpture Garden, Smithsonian Institution, 2001.

Fogle, Douglas, ed. *Painting at the Edge of the World.* Exh. cat. Minneapolis: Walker Art Center, 2001.

Grosenick, Uta, ed. *Women Artists in the 20th and 21st Century.* Cologne: Taschen, 2001.

Schimmel, Paul, ed. *Public Offerings.* Exh. cat. Los Angeles: The Museum of Contemporary Art, Los Angeles, 2001.

Schumacher, Rainald, ed. *The Mystery of Painting.* Exh. cat. Munich: Kunstverlag Ingvild Goetz, 2001.

2002
Bossé, Laurence, Hans-Ulrich Obrist, and Julia Garimorth, eds.

Urgent Painting. Exh. cat. Paris: Éditions des musées de la Ville de Paris, 2002.

Bürgi, Bernhard Mendes, and Peter Pakesch, eds. *Painting on the Move.* Exh. cat. Basel: Kunstmuseum Basel and Kunsthalle Basel, 2002.

Cavepainting: Peter Doig, Chris Ofili, and Laura Owens. Exh. cat. Santa Monica: Santa Monica Museum of Art, 2002.

Grosenick, Uta, and Burkhard Riemschneider, eds. *Art Now.* Cologne: Taschen, 2002.

Hoptman, Laura. *Drawing Now: Eight Propositions.* Exh. cat. New York: The Museum of Modern Art, 2002.

Matsui, Midori. *Art in a New World.* Tokyo: Asahi Press, 2002.

Schwabsky, Barry, ed. *Vitamin P: New Perspectives in Painting.* London: Phaidon, 2002.

2003
Lütgens, Annelie, ed. *Painting Pictures: Painting and Media in the Digital Age.* Exh. cat. Wolfsburg, Germany: Kunstmuseum Wolfsburg, 2003.

2004
Contemporary Painting: Curated by Alex Katz. Exh. cat. Waterville, ME: Colby College Museum of Art, 2004.

Ferguson, Russell. *The Undiscovered Country.* Exh. cat. Los Angeles: Hammer Museum, University of California, Los Angeles, 2004.

Iles, Chrissie, Shamim M. Momin, and Debra Singer, eds. *Whitney Biennial.* Exh. cat. New York: Whitney Museum of American Art, 2004.

2005

25 Visuell: Deutsche Bank Art. Exh. cat. Berlin: Deutsche Guggenheim, 2005.

Dingwall, Kenneth, and John L. Moore. *Drawn to Cleveland.* Exh. cat. Cleveland: Museum of Contemporary Art Cleveland, 2005.

Falckenberg, Harald. *Goetz Meets Falckenberg.* Exh. cat. Hamburg: Sammlung Goetz, 2005.

Grachos, Louis, and Claire Schneider. *Extreme Abstraction.* Exh. cat. Buffalo, NY: Albright-Knox Art Gallery, 2005.

Hollein, Max, and Martina Weinhart, eds. *Ideal Worlds: New Romanticism in Contemporary Art.* Exh. cat. Frankfurt: Schirn Kunsthalle Frankfurt, 2005.

Hutchinson, John, ed. *Huts.* Exh. cat. Dublin: The Douglas Hyde Gallery, 2005.

Kraus, Chris, Jan Tumlir, and Jane McFadden. *LA Artland: Contemporary Art from Los Angeles.* London: Black Dog Publishing, 2005.

2006

Brown, Kathan. *Magical Secrets About Thinking Creatively: The Art of Etching and the Truth of Life.* San Francisco: Crown Point Press, 2006.

FOIL. Tokyo: Foil Gallery, 2006.

Grigoteit, Ariane. *All the Best: The Deutsche Bank Collection and Zaha Hadid.* Exh. cat. Frankfurt: Deutsche Bank Art, 2006.

Grigoteit, Ariane, Britta Färber, and Christina März, eds. *Blind Date. Zum ersten mal zu sehen: Die Neuankäufe für die Sammlung Deutsche Bank.* Exh. cat. Frankfurt: Deutsche Bank Art, 2006.

Nakanishi, Hiroyuki. *Essential Painting.* Exh. cat. Osaka: The National Museum of Art, Osaka, 2006.

Schlegel, Eva. *LA Women: Artists and Architects.* Vienna: Schlebrügge, 2006.

2007

Coetzee, Mark. *Red Eye: LA Artists from the Rubell Family Collection.* Exh. cat. Miami: Rubell Family Collection, 2007.

Cole-Cunningham, Ragan, ed. *Counterparts: Contemporary Painters and Their Influences.* Exh. cat. Virginia Beach: Contemporary Art Center of Virginia, 2007.

Geha, Katie, and Travis Nichols. *Poets on Painters.* Exh. cat. Wichita, KS: Ulrich Museum of Art, 2007.

Grigoteit, Ariane. *Affinities: Neuankäufe Sammlung Deutsche Bank.* Exh. cat. Frankfurt: Deutsche Bank Art, 2007.

Hoffmann, Jens. *Very Abstract and Hyper Figurative.* Exh. cat. London: Thomas Dane Gallery, 2007.

MoMA Contemporary Highlights: 250 Works since 1980. New York: The Museum of Modern Art, 2007.

Pinault, François. *Sequence 1: Painting and Sculpture in the François Pinault Collection.* Exh. cat. Venice: Palazzo Grassi, 2007.

Royal Academy Illustrated 2007: A Selection from the 239th Summer Exhibition. Exh. cat. London: Royal Academy of Arts, 2007.

2008

Biennale van de schilderkunst. Exh. cat. Deurle, Belgium: Museum Dhondt-Dhaenens, 2008.

Ruf, Beatrix, ed. *Blasted Allegories: Works from the Ringier Collection.* Exh. cat. Zurich: JRP | Ringier, 2008.

Schimmel, Paul, Ann Goldstein, and Rebecca Morse. *This Is Not to Be Looked At: Highlights from the Collection of the Museum of Contemporary Art, Los Angeles.* Exh. cat. Los Angeles: Museum of Contemporary Art, 2008.

Shore, Virginia, ed. *Landscapes of the Mind: Art Collection of the United States Embassy, Beijing.* Exh. cat. Washington, DC: United States Department of State Art in Embassies Program, 2008.

2009

Heinzelmann, Markus, ed. *Slow Paintings: Museum Morsbroich Leverkusen.* Exh. cat. Leverkusen, Germany: Museum Morsbroich, 2009.

Higa, Karin. *Living Flowers: Ikebana and Contemporary Art.* Exh. cat. Los Angeles: Japanese American National Museum, 2009.

2010

Art Tells the Times: Works by Women Artists. Exh. cat. Tokyo: Shiseido Corporate Culture Department, 2010.

Wehr, Anne. *At Home/Not at Home: Works from the Collection of Martin and Rebecca Eisenberg.* Exh. cat. Annandale-on-Hudson, NY: Center for Curatorial Studies, Bard College, 2010.

2011

Alexander, Darsie, ed. *The Spectacular of Vernacular.* Exh. cat. Minneapolis: Walker Art Center, 2011.

Craighill, Amara, ed. *Art Collection of the United States Consulate General, Karachi, Pakistan.* Exh. cat. Washington, DC: United States Department of State Art in Embassies Program, 2011.

Birnbaum, Daniel, Cornelia Butler, Suzanne Cotter, Bice Curiger, et al. *Defining Contemporary Art: 25 Years in 200 Pivotal Artworks.* New York: Phaidon, 2011.

Hoffmann, Jens, ed. *Painting Between the Lines.* Exh. cat. San Francisco: CCA Wattis Institute, 2011.

2012

Grachos, Louis, and Karen Lee Spaulding, eds. *Extreme Abstraction Revisited.* Buffalo, NY: Albright-Knox Art Gallery, 2012.

2013

Brodie, Judith, ed. *Yes, No, Maybe: Artists Working at Crown Point Press.* Exh. cat. Washington, DC: National Gallery of Art, 2013.

Harkawik, Peter, and Laura Owens, eds. *Made in Space Daily.* New York: Gavin Brown's enterprise and Venus Over Manhattan, 2013.

2014

Comer, Stuart, Anthony Elms, and Michelle Grabner. *Whitney Biennial.* Exh. cat. New York: Whitney Museum of American Art, 2014.

Hernando, Gladys-Katherina, and Adam D. Miller. *Death Ship: Tribute to H. C. Westermann.* Exh. cat. Los Angeles: The Pit, 2014.

Hoptman, Laura. *The Forever Now: Contemporary Painting in an Atemporal World.* Exh. cat. New York: The Museum of Modern Art, 2014.

2015

Macel, Christine, and Elisabeth Sussman. *Collected by Thea Westreich Wagner and Ethan Wagner.* Exh. cat. New York: Whitney Museum of American Art; Paris: Centre Pompidou, Musée national d'art moderne, 2015.

Miller, Dana, ed. *Whitney Museum of American Art: Handbook of the Collection.* New York: Whitney Museum of American Art, 2015.

Painting 2.0: Expression in the Information Age, Gesture and Spectacle, Eccentric Figuration, Social Networks. Exh. cat. Munich: Museum Brandhorst, 2015.

Pill, Katherine, Judith K. Brodsky, Susan Tallman, and Erika Greenberg Schneider. *Marks Made: Prints by American*

Women Artists from the 1960s to the Present. Exh. cat. St. Petersburg, FL: Museum of Fine Arts, St. Petersburg, 2015.

Roselione-Valadez, Juan. *NO MAN'S LAND: Women Artists from the Rubell Family Collection.* Exh. cat. Miami: Rubell Family Collection, 2015.

Schwartz, Alexandra. *Come as You Are: Art of the 1990s.* Exh. cat. Montclair, NJ: Montclair Art Museum, 2015.

Siegel, Katy, ed. *"The heroine Paint": After Frankenthaler.* New York: Gagosian Gallery, 2015.

Tumlir, Jan. *The Magic Circle: On the Beatles, Pop Art, Art-Rock and Records.* Eindhoven, The Netherlands: Onomatopee, 2015.

2016
Brinson, Katherine, and Susan Thompson. *The Hugo Boss Prize 2016.* New York: The Solomon R. Guggenheim Foundation, 2016.

Fine Young Cannibals. Exh. cat. New York: Friedrich Petzel Gallery, 2016.

Lehrer-Graiwer, Sarah, Jon Leon, Jonathan Richman, and Mark Roeder. *Can't Reach Me There.* Exh. cat. Minneapolis: Midway Contemporary Art, 2016.

Garait-Leavenworth, Nicolas, Gunnar B. Kvaran, and Thierry Raspail, eds. *Los Angeles—A Fiction.* Exh. cat. Oslo: Astrup Fearnley Museet, 2017. http://afmuseet.no/en/nettkataloger/katalog-los-angeles-a-fiction.

2017
Biesenbach, Klaus, and Peter Eleey, eds. *.com/cn.* Exh. cat. Hong Kong and Long Island City, NY: K11 Art Foundation and MoMA PS1, 2017.

ARTICLES AND EPHEMERA

1995
Weissman, Benjamin. "Openings: Laura Owens." *Artforum* 34, no. 3 (November 1995): 84–85.

Morgan, Charles. "Gorgeous Politics." *Las Vegas Weekly,* December 21, 1995.

1996
Smith, Roberta. "Screen." Review. *New York Times,* February 2, 1996.

Saltz, Jerry. "Review." *Time Out New York,* September 1996.

1997
Lawson, Thomas. *Hot Coffee.* Brochure. New York: Artists Space.

Schjeldahl, Peter. "La-la Band." Review. *Village Voice,* February 18, 1997.

Morris, Rebecca. "Programming Attitude: An Interview with Laura Owens." *Art Muscle* 11, no. 3 (February/March 1997):14–15.

Saltz, Jerry. "Regular, No Sugar." Review. *Time Out New York,* February 27–March 6, 1997, 40.

Smith, Roberta. "Art in Review: Laura Owens." Review. *New York Times,* April 18, 1997.

Carley, Michal Ann. "Palace." Review. *New Art Examiner* 24, no. 8 (May 1997): 49–50.

Schwendener, Martha. "Laura Owens." Review. *Time Out New York,* May 1–8, 1997, 37.

Auerbach, Lisa Anne. "Sharon Lockhart, Laura Owens and Frances Stark at Blum & Poe." Review. *LA Weekly,* June 27–July 3, 1997, 57.

Kandel, Susan. "Exploring Power of Three Among Friends." *Los Angeles Times,* July 4, 1997.

Owens, Laura. "On the *American Job*: Laura Owens Interviews Chris Smith." *New Art Examiner* 24, no. 10 (July/August 1997): 33–35.

Grabner, Michelle. "The Eagle Rock Show." Review. *X-Tra* 1, no. 3 (Fall 1997): 3–7, 10–11.

Schjeldahl, Peter. "Painting Rules." Review. *Village Voice,* September 30, 1997, 97.

Hainley, Bruce. "Sharon Lockhart, Laura Owens, Frances Stark." Review. *Artforum* 36, no. 3 (November 1997): 119–20.

Coomer, Martin. "Laura Owens." Review. *Time Out New York,* November 12–19, 1997, 56.

Intra, Giovanni. "Sharon Lockhart, Laura Owens, Frances Stark." Review. *Flash Art* 30, no. 197 (November/December 1997): 76.

1998
Owens, Laura. "Contemporary Studio: Interviews with Jorge Pardo, Monique Prieto, and Francis Stark." *Cakewalk* 1 (Spring/Summer 1998): 10–15.

Pagel, David. "Color Them Retro." *Los Angeles Times,* August 16, 1998.

Dorment, Richard. "A Brush with Young America." Review. *Daily Telegraph,* August 29, 1998.

Relyea, Lane. "Virtually Formal." *Artforum* 37, no. 1 (September 1998): 126–33, 173.

Ise, Claudine. "Showroom." Review. *Los Angeles Times,* September 18, 1998.

Pagel, David. "New Sophistication in Owens' Landscapes." Review. *Los Angeles Times,* October 23, 1998.

Smith, Roberta. "Laura Owens." Review. *New York Times,* November 6, 1998.

Liebmann, Lisa. "Best of 1998." *Artforum* 37, no. 4 (December 1998): 96–97.

Knight, Christopher. "Year in Review: A Wealth of Shows and Fund-Raising." *Los Angeles Times,* December 27, 1998.

1999
Avgikos, Jan. "Laura Owens." Review. *Artforum* 37, no. 5 (January 1999): 118–19.

Darling, Michael. "Laura Owens." Review. *Art Issue* 56 (January/February 1999): 43.

Frank, Peter. "Art Picks of the Week: Color Fields, Craig Kauffman, Jacob Hashimoto." *LA Weekly,* January 8–14, 1999, 103.

Princenthal, Nancy. "Laura Owens at Gavin Brown's Enterprise." *Art in America* 89, no. 2 (February 1999): 115.

Isermann, Jim. "Jim Isermann's Top Ten." *Artforum* 37, no. 8 (April 1999): 40.

Knight, Christopher. "Post-Boomers Spearhead the Boom." *Los Angeles Times,* April 4, 1999.

Jones, Kristen M. "Basel 1999: The Swiss Art Fair Turns 30." *Travel & Leisure* 29, no. 6 (May 1999): 132.

Tumlir, Jan, Jan Estep, and Yvette Brackman. "Laura Owens: Cross-Country Trilogy." *New Art Examiner* 26, no. 8 (May 1999): 44–47.

Maurer, Simon. "Alle gegen alle und all emit allen." Review. *Tages-Anzeiger* (Zurich), June 17, 1999.

Morgan, Susan. "A Thousand Words: Laura Owens Talks About Her New Work." *Artforum* 37, no. 10 (Summer 1999): 130–31.

Owens, Laura. "The Exchange of Ideas Among the Living." *Cakewalk* 3 (Fall 1999): 26–29.

Melrod, George. "Young at Art." *Los Angeles magazine* 44, no. 11 (November 1999): 98–105, 170.

Iannaccone, Carmine. "Entertainment Complex: Laura Owens." *Frieze* 49 (November/December 1999): 88–91.

Potter, Chris. "Far Away, So Close." *Pittsburgh City Paper,* November 3–10, 1999, 18–23.

Litt, Steven. "Exhibition of Today's Art a Triumph: Works at Carnegie Local and Global at Same Time." Review. *The Plain Dealer* (Cleveland), November 14, 1999.

Smith, Roberta. "Safe Among Seamless Shadows." Review. *New York Times*, November 17, 1999.

Pincus, Robert L. "World-Class Exhibition: Carnegie International Takes an Ambitious Look at Art of the Moment." Review. *San Diego Union-Tribune*, November 21, 1999.

Dannatt, Adrian. "Old Masters of Tomorrow." *Art Newspaper* 10, no. 98 (December 1999): 16.

Plagens, Peter, and Corie Brown. "Hollywood's Big Art Deal." *Newsweek*, December 6, 1999, 78–80.

Kent, Sarah. "Review." *Time Out New York,* 59.

Hot Spots: Los Angeles, Houston, Miami. Brochure. Greensboro, NC: Weatherspoon Art Gallery, the University of North Carolina at Greensboro, 1999.

2000
Siegel, Katy. "1999 Carnegie International: Carnegie Museum of Art, Pittsburgh." Review. *Artforum* 38, no. 5 (January 2000): 105–6.

Carrier, David. "Pittsburgh: Carnegie International." Review. *Burlington Magazine* 142, no. 1163 (February 2000): 128–29.

Farr, Louise. "Laura Owens." *W* magazine 29, no. 2 (February 2000): 102.

Fark, Bill. "North County Artists Featured in Museum Exhibition." *North County Times,* June 2, 2000.

———. "California Artists Show Diversity in Museum Show." *North County Times*, June 9, 2000.

Knight, Christopher. "Catching the 'Next Wave' of Painters." Review. *Los Angeles Times*, June 20, 2000.

Mottram, Jack. "A Natural Talent in All Its Glory." Review. *Sunday Herald* (Glasgow), June 25, 2000.

Sutherland, Giles. "Inverleith House, Royal Botanic Garden." *The Times* (London), June 28, 2000.

de Cruz, Gemma. "Eurovision." Review. *Flash Art* 33, no. 213 (Summer 2000): 69.

Pioselli, Alessandra. "Review." *Flash Art Italia* 223 (Summer 2000): 13.

Art on Paper 2000: The 36th Exhibition of Art on Paper. Brochure. Greensboro, NC: Weatherspoon Art Gallery, the University of North Carolina at Greensboro, 2000.

2001
Godfrey, Mark. "Laura Owens." Review. *Contemporary Visual Arts* 27 (January 2001): 64.

Muchnic, Suzanne. "Ascent of the Early Risers." Review. *Los Angeles Times*, April 1, 2001.

Wakefield, Neville. "Laura Owens." *Elle Decor* 12, no. 4 (June/July 2001): 48–51.

McQuaid, Cate. "Laura Owens Brings Zen to Her Bold Art." Review. *Boston Globe*, July 27, 2001.

Glueck, Grace. "Art Review: A Universe of Art, Centered in Boston." Review. *New York Times*, August 17, 2001.

Cutter, Kimberly. "East Side Story." *W* magazine 30, no. 9 (September 2001): 204–8.

Saltz, Jerry. "Babylon Now." *Village Voice*, September 18, 2001.

2002
Miller, Francine Koslow. "Laura Owens: Isabella Stewart Gardner Museum." Review. *Artforum* 40, no. 5 (January 2002): 144.

Allen, Helen. "NY Contemporary Sales: Top Drawer Fetches Top Prices." *Flash Art International* 34, no. 222 (January–February 2002): 37, 45.

Goodale, Gloria. "Artist Trio Shares a Simple Love of Painting." Review. *Christian Science Monitor*, February 15, 2002.

Knight, Christopher. "Bristling with Attitude." Review. *Los Angeles Times*, February 15, 2002.

Harvey, Doug. "Cavepainting." Review. *LA Weekly*, February 20, 2002.

Montagu, Jemima. "Urgent Painting." Review. *Frieze* 66 (April 2002): 88–89.

Pagel, David. "A Supersaturated Return to the Spirit of the Punk Era." Review. *Los Angeles Times*, May 10, 2002.

Ferguson, Russell. "Laura Owens Paints a Picture." *Parkett* 65 (September 2002): 58–64.

Thomson, Mungo. "From My Junkyard to Yours." *Parkett* 65 (September 2002): 82–87.

Weissman, Benjamin. "Monkey Man Killer." *Parkett* 65 (September 2002): 74–76.

Gute, Charles, Samuele Menin, and Michele Robecchi. "Focus Painting Part One: Contemporary Painting Today." *Flash Art* 34, no. 226 (October 2002): 84.

Smith, Roberta. "Retreat from the Wild Shores of Abstraction." Review. *New York Times*, October 18, 2002.

Schjeldahl, Peter. "The Drawing Board." *New Yorker*, November 4, 2002, 102–3.

2003
Rimanelli, David. "Preview: Laura Owens, Museum of Contemporary Art." *Artforum* 41, no. 5 (January 2003): 58.

Knight, Christopher. "Giving Girl Stuff a Good Name." Review. *Los Angeles Times*, March 24, 2003.

Greene, David A. "Class Reunion." *Modern Painters* 16, no. 1 (Spring 2003): 76–79.

Kazanjian, Dodie. "The Happy Painter." *Vogue* 193, no. 4 (April 2003): 242.

Kushner, Rachel. "Laura Owens." Interview. *The Believer* 1, no. 2 (May 2003): 78–87.

Singerman, Howard. "Laura Owens: Museum of Contemporary Art, Los Angeles." Review. *Artforum* 41, no. 9 (May 2003): 163.

Muller, Dave. "Top Ten." *Artforum* 41, no. 10 (Summer 2003): 67.

Weissman, Benjamin. "Laura Owens: MOCA, Los Angeles." Review. *Frieze* 76 (Summer 2003): 107–8.

Moreno, Gean. "Laura Owens: Never the Same Twice." Interview. *Flash Art* 36, no. 232 (October 2003): 94–96.

Auer, James. "Loving the Canvas." Review. *Milwaukee Journal Sentinel*, October 16, 2003.

Weissman, Benjamin. "Interview with Laura Owens." Interview. *Cakewalk* 5 (Winter 2003): 42–45.

2004
Owens, Laura. "A Painter's Vote." *ArtUS* 1 (January–February 2004): 38–39.

Pappalardo, Bethany Anne. "Laura Owens." Review. *Artforum.com,* March 2004. http://artforum.com/picks/id=6529.

Kimmelman, Michael. "Art Review: Touching All Bases At the Biennial." Review. *New York Times*, March 12, 2004.

Saltz, Jerry. "The OK Corral: Leaving Postmodernist and Post-minimalist Styles Behind and Breathing Fresh Air." Review. *Village Voice*, March 17–23, 2004.

Schjeldahl, Peter. "What's New: The Whitney Biennial." *New Yorker*, March 22, 2004, 100–101.

Sheets, Hilarie M. "Art: A Painter with Lots of Voices and No Comment." Review. *New York Times*, March 28, 2004.

Diez, Renato. "Alla Biennale del Whitney Torna La Pittura." *Arte* 368 (April 2004): 104–11.

Goodbody, Bridget L. "Laura Owens." Review. *Time Out New York*, April 1–8, 2004, 60.

Cotter, Holland. "Art in Review: Laura Owens." Review. *New York Times,* April 2, 2004.

Knight, Christopher. "Binary Days at the Biennial." Review. *Los Angeles Times*, April 11, 2004.

Feinstein, Roni. "An Unfettered Palette." Review. *Sun Sentinel* (Palm Beach, FL), April 27, 2004.

Casadio, Maruccia. "Dreamy." *Vogue Italia* 645 (May 2004): 230–32.

Dailey, Meghan. "Laura Owens bei Gavin Brown's enterprise." *Texte Zur Kunst* 54 (June 2004): 194–96.

Heartney, Eleanor. "The Well-Tempered Biennial." Review. *Art in America* 92, no. 6 (June/July 2004): 70–77.

Reylea, Lane. "Theory and Painting." *Flash Art* 37, no. 239 (November–December 2004): 63–65.

New Etchings. Newsletter. San Francisco: Crown Point Press, 2004.

2005
Julian Satterthwaite. "The Whimsical World of Laura Owens." *The Daily Yomiuri* (Tokyo), February 17, 2005.

Corkill, Edan. "In Sight/ Different Strokes: Soft Focus on Reality Links 'Loose' Women." Review. *Asahi Shimbun* (Tokyo), February 18, 2005.

Kyotara. "Deepest Fantasies. Laura Owens sona." *Barfout!* 115 (March 2005): 28–29.

Taguchi, Masami. "Creator's Voice." *MyLohas* (May 2005): 104–5.

Janku, Laura Richard. "Interim Print Report: Laura Owens." *Art on Paper* 9, no. 5 (May/June 2005): 35–36.

Huntington, Richard. "To the Extreme: The Albright-Knox Opens Its Entire Gallery to Abstract Exhibit That Pushes Boundaries of Size and Scope." Review. *Buffalo News*, July 15, 2005.

Smith, Roberta. "Art in Review: Desired Constellations." Review. *New York Times*, August 5, 2005.

Kaplan, Cheryl. "Friendly Place-Holders: A Conversation with Laura Owens." Interview. *db artmag*, December 12, 2005–January 17, 2006. http://www.db-artmag.com/archiv/2005/e/8/1/396.html.

2006
Johnson, Ken. "Art in Review: The Garden Party." Review. *New York Times*, April 21, 2006.

Owens, Laura. "*Untitled*, 2003." *McSweeney's Quarterly Concern* 20 (Summer 2006): 188.

Affentranger-Kirchrath, Angelika. "Nach dem Prinzip von Lust und Laune." *Neue Zürcher Zeitung*, June 24, 2006. https://www.nzz.ch/articleE8KZI-1.41796.

Mack, Gerhard. "Ausstellung." *NZZ am Sonntag*, July 2, 2006. https://www.nzz.ch/articleE8PN3-1.43885.

Schindler, Feli. "Heiterkeit aus dem Sunshine State." *Tager-Anzeiger,* July 4, 2006.

Teuwsen, Isabell. "Laura Owens: Luftig and leicht." *Schweizer Illustrierte,* July 10, 2006.

"Kunsthalle Zurich Presents Laura Owens." *Artdaily.com,* July 11, 2006. http://artdaily.com/news/16551/Kunsthalle-Zurich-Presents-Laura-Owens#.WMQ7CNIrKUk.

von Burg, Dominque. "Laura Owens's Gemälde und Studien: Mit unerschöpflicher Fabulierlust." *Zürichsee-Zietungen*, July 22, 2006.

von Burg, Dominque. "Laura Owens: Von der Suche nach der unbeshränkten Freiheit in der Kunst." *Kunst-Bulletin* 7/8 (July/August 2006): 44–46.

Smyth, Cherry. "Laura Owens." Review. *Modern Painters* (July/August 2006): 112.

O'Reilly, Sally. "Laura Owens." Review. *ArtReview* 2 (August 2006): 136.

Soutter, Lucy. "What Lies Beneath." *Frieze* 101 (September 2006): 176–79.

Ribas, João. "An Ecumenical Love of Painting." Review. *New York Sun*. December 14, 2006.

"Interview with Laura Owens and Elysia Borowy-Reeder." *The Wrong Times* (Winter 2006): 17–18.

Laura Owens. Brochure. London: Camden Arts Centre, 2006.

2007
"Laura Owens." Review. *New Yorker*, January 8, 2007, 14.

Griffin, Jonathan. "Very Abstract and Hyper Figurative." Review. *Frieze* 107 (May 2007): 157.

Gingeras, Alison, and Carlo Simula. "Sequence 1: Palazzo Grassi." *L'Uomo Vogue* 381 (May/June 2007): 188.

Rosenberg, Karen. "Needling More Than the Feminist Consciousness." Review. *New York Times,* December 28, 2007.

2008
McLaren, Malcolm. "For the Moment: Nibbles for Malcom McLaren." Review. *T: The New York Times Style Magazine,* June 5, 2008.

Cotter, Holland. "Art Makes Such Weird Bedfellows." Review. *New York Times,* July 25, 2008.

Collings, Matthew. "Put Downs and Suck Ups: Matthew Collings' Weekly Ventings on the Art World No 2: Get Sploshing—Laura Owens at Sadie Coles, London." Review. *Saatchi Art*, November 28, 2008. http://owenslaura.com/wp-content/uploads/2017/04/2008_SaatchiArtMagazine-1.pdf.

2009
Smith, Roberta. "Rewards and Clarity in a Show of Restraint." Review. *New York Times*, February 19, 2009.

Finkel, Jori. "Open the Store-room: Let's Put On a Show." *New York Times*, September 13, 2009.

Asfour, Nana. "Laura Owens, 'New Paintings.'" Review. *Time Out New York*, November 9, 2009. http://www.timeout.com/newyork/art/laura-owens-new-paintings.

Genocchio, Benjamin. "The Nature of Time, Ever Passing." Review. *New York Times*, November 20, 2009.

2010
Princenthal, Nancy. "Laura Owens: Gavin Brown." Review. *Art in America* 98, no. 1 (January 2010): 113.

Phillips, Brad. "Laura Owens Interview with Brad Phillips." Interview. *Hunter and Cook* 5 (Winter 2010): 18–22.

Byers, Dan, and Amanda Donnan. *Ordinary Madness: Pocket Guide*. Exhibition guide. Pittsburgh: Carnegie Museum of Art, 2010.

2011
Rivera, Laura. "Artist Laura Owens to Discuss Her Abstract Paintings Tonight for UCLA Hammer Museum's Lecture Series." *Daily Bruin*, February 3, 2011, 10.

Heiser, Jörg. "Laura Owens: Galerie Gisela Capitain." Review. *Frieze* 2 (Fall 2011).

Owens, Laura. "Lunch at the Landfill." In *The Lunch Break*

Times, ed. Sharon Lockhart (artist's book produced by the San Francisco Museum of Modern Art for the exhibition *Lunch Break,* October 11, 2011–January 16, 2012). http://openspace.sfmoma.org/2011/11/lbt7/.

Reiger, Christopher. "Painting Between the Lines @ CCA Wattis." *SquareCylinder.com,* November 29, 2011. http://www.squarecylinder.com/2011/11/painting-between-the-lines-cca-wattis/.

Owens, Laura. "Merlin Carpenter." *Artforum* 50, no. 4 (December 2011): 102.

Smolik, Noemi. "Alte Fragen neu gestellt" *Artblog Cologne,* December 11, 2011. http://www.artblogcologne.com/alte-fragen-neu-gestellt/.

Schumaker, Mary Louise. "Making a Scene: Milwaukee's Avant-Garde." *Journal Sentinel* (Milwaukee)*,* December 12, 2011. http://archive.jsonline.com/blogs/entertainment/135456663.html

New Etchings. Newsletter. San Francisco: Crown Point Press, 2011.

2012
Prince, Mark. "Laura Owens." Review. *Frieze* 144 (January/February 2012): 140.

Kazanjian, Dodie. "May Madness: A Guide to the New York Art Shows You Can't Miss This Spring." *Vogue.com,* April 28, 2012. http://www.vogue.com/article/may-madness-a-guide-to-the-new-york-art-shows-you-cant-miss-this-spring.

McCullough, Danielle. "OPEN NETWORK/PRINT IMPRINT." Review. *Whitehot Magazine,* May 2012. http://whitehotmagazine.com/articles/2012-open-network-print-imprint/2565.

"Modern Painters Magazine's Top Picks from Frieze New York." *Blouinartinfo.com,* May 5, 2012. http://www.blouinartinfo.com/news/story/803050/modern-painters-magazines-top-picks-from-frieze-new-york.

Huang, Yanyan. "Art Unlimited Artist Spotlight: Laura Owens at Art 43 Basel." *Haute Living,* June 16, 2012. http://hauteliving.com/2012/06/art-43-basel-art-unlimited-artist-spotlight-laura-owens/293264/.

Kherbek, William. "Laura Owens: Pavement Karaoke/Alphabet." Review. *PORT* magazine, October 14, 2012. http://www.port-magazine.com/art-photography/laura-owens-pavement-karaokealphabet/.

Russeth, Andrew. "Look at This! Laura Owens's 'Clocks' Book." Review. *Observer* (London), October 17, 2012.

Spears, Dorothy. "Gallery as Museum, Art Dealer as Curator." *New York Times,* October 28, 2012.

Myers, Holly. "Laura Owens." *Modern Painters* 24, no. 9 (November 2012): 46–47.

Stech, Fabian. "Laura Owens in Conversation with Fabian Stech." Interview. *Annual Magazine* 5 (December 2012): 217–19.

2013
Boucher, Brian. "The Brief: Laura Owens Opens in LA." *Art in America* 101, no. 1 (January 2013): 22.

Solway, Diane. "Solway Selects: Arts and Culture Editor Diane Solway's Must-Sees for January." *W* magazine 42, no. 1 (January 2013): 49.

van Arsdale, Joslin. "Laura Owens 12 Paintings." *The Art Reserve,* January 2013. http://theartreserve.com/blog/laura-owens-12-paintings.

"Optical Drive: Sarah Lehrer-Graiwer Talks with Laura Owens." Interview. *Artforum* 51, no. 7 (March 2013): 230–39.

Finkel, Jori. "Industrial Building Gives Artist Laura Owens Versatility." Review. *Los Angeles Times,* March 13, 2013.

Pagel, David. "Review: Laura Owens' Large-Scale Paintings an Immersive Experience." Review. *Los Angeles Times,* March 14, 2013.

Recinos, Eva. "A Sperm Mug, a Giant Tube Sculpture and More at Night Gallery." Review. *LA Weekly,* March 18, 2013. http://www.laweekly.com/arts/a-sperm-mug-a-giant-tube-sculpture-and-more-at-night-gallery-4185036.

Berardini, Andrew. "How Laura Owens's New Boyle Heights Exhibit Moves Painting Forward." Review. *LA Weekly,* March 21, 2013.

Drohojowska-Philp, Hunter. "The Night Gallery and Laura Owens: Art Talk." Review. *KCRW,* March 28, 2013.

Griffin, Jonathan. "Made in Space." Review. *Art Agenda,* March 28, 2013. http://www.art-agenda.com/reviews/%E2%80%9Cmade-in-space%E2%80%9D/.

Griffin, Jonathan. "Laura Owens: 356 South Mission Road, Los Angeles." Review. *Frieze* 154 (April 2013): 164.

Timberg, Scott. "Culture Jammers: Novelist Rachel Kushner and Painter Laura Owens Join Forces as They Both Gather New Acclaim." *Pasadena Magazine* 7, no. 4 (May/June 2013): 41.

Myers, Terry R. "12 Paintings by Laura Owens." Review. *The Brooklyn Rail,* May 3, 2013. http://www.brooklynrail.org/2013/05/artseen/12-paintings-by-laura-owens.

Wrightson, Erica Zora. "Laura Owens: Painting in Space." Review. *LA Weekly,* May 15, 2013.

Owens, Laura. " 'It's Spelled Motherfuckers.'—An Interview with Rachel Kushner." Interview. *The Believer,* May 24, 2013. http://logger.believermag.com/post/51246163032/its-spelled-motherfuckersan-interview-with.

Larkey, Molly. "To Live and Paint in LA: The Work of Laura Owens." Review. *Los Angeles, I'm Yours,* June 25, 2013. http://laimyours.com/46609/to-live-and-paint-in-la-the-work-of-laura-owens/.

Russeth, Andrew. " 'Made in Space' at Gavin Brown's Enterprise and Venus Over Manhattan." Review. *Observer* (London), July 23, 2013.

Colucci, Emily. "Fact or Fiction: Los Angeles Is Just New York Lying Down." *ArtParasites.com,* July 24, 2013. http://www.artparasites.com/fact-or-fiction-los-angeles-is-just-new-york-lying-down/.

Smith, Roberta. "Made in Space: Art in Review." Review. *New York Times,* August 1, 2013.

Cartwright, James. "Art: Laura Owens Creates Giant, Abstract Works like 1980s Album Art." *It's Nice That,* September 4, 2013. http://www.itsnicethat.com/articles/laura-owens.

Berens, Stephen, and Jan Tumlir. "A Room of Owens's Own: Laura Owens in Conversation with Jan Tumlir and Stephen Berens." Interview. *X-Tra* 16, no. 1 (Fall 2013): 80–91.

Groveman, Jessie. "Laura Owens: LA Artist with Larger Than Life Exhibit." *Lipstick & Politics,* September 27, 2013. https://www.lipstickandpolitics.com/fashion-culture/culture/laura-owens-la-artist-with-larger-than-life-exhibit.

Owens, Laura, and Glenn O'Brien. "Tragic Kingdom: Glenn O'Brien and Laura Owens on Paul McCarthy's *WS* at the Park Avenue Armory." Review. *Artforum* 52, no. 2 (October 2013): 115–16.

2014
The Machine Project: Field Guide to the Gamble House. Pamphlet. Pasadena, CA: Gamble House, 2014.

Reeder, Scott, and Laura Owens. "Scott Reeder and Laura Owens in Conversation." *356 Mission,* February 7, 2014. http://356mission.tumblr.com/post/81521890458/scott-reeder-and-laura-owens-in-conversation.

Kirsch, Corinna. "Coral: Laura Owens." *Art F City,* February 25, 2014. http://artfcity.com/2014/02/25/coral-laura-owens/.

Vogel, Carol. "State of Our Art, According to Whitney." Review. *New York Times,* February 27, 2014.

Berardini, Andrew. "The Empty-Handed Painter from Your Streets Is Drawing Crazy Patterns on Your Sheets: Lisa Williamson, Alex Olson, Laura Owens." *Mousse* 43 (April/May 2014): 204–7.

Godfrey, Mark. "Statements of Intent: Mark Godfrey on the Art of Jacqueline Humphries, Laura Owens, Amy Sillman, and Charline von Heyl." *Artforum* 52, no. 9 (May 2014): 294–303, 344.

Szewczyk, Monika. "Persian Rose Chartreuse Muse Vancouver Grey." Review. *Artforum* 52, no. 10 (Summer 2014): 375–76.

Weiskopf, Daniel A. "Painter's Painters: Gifts from Alex Katz." Review. *Artforum.com,* August 2014. https://www.artforum.com/picks/id=47672.

Owens, Laura. "Jeff Koons." *Artforum* 53, no. 1 (September 2014): 319, 398

"Laura Owens: 'Art Is The One Subject Without an Answer.'" *Lancia TrendVision,* September 3, 2014. http://trendvisions.lancia.it/en/article/laura-owens-art-is-the-one-subject-without-an-answer.

Fiduccia, Joanna. "The Shadow of the Virtual Sun." *Spike Art Quarterly* 41 (Fall 2014): 88–99.

Finkel, Jori. "Arts Scene in Downtown Los Angeles Grows Beyond the Broad." *The Art Newspaper* 24, no. 262 (November 2014): 7.

Burnham, Clint. "The Dreamscapes of Vienna's Sprawling 'Century of the Bed' Series." *Momus*, November 10, 2014. http://momus.ca/the-dreamscapes-of-viennas-sprawling-century-of-the-bed-series/.

Indrisek, Scott. "At MoMA, 17 Painting of Our 'Forever Now'." Review. *Blouinartinfo.com*, December 9, 2014. http://www.blouinartinfo.com/news/story/1067208/at-moma-17-painters-of-our-forever-now.

Solway, Diane. "Laura Owens: Brushes with Greatness." *W* magazine, December 11, 2014. http://www.wmagazine.com/culture/art-and-design/2014/12/laura-owens-artist/.

Farago, Jason. "The Forever Now Review: Calling Time on the Avant Garde." Review. *The Guardian* (London), December 12, 2014.

Saltz, Jerry. "'The Forever Now' Is MoMA's Market Moment." Review. *Vulture*, December 12, 2014. http://www.vulture.com/2014/12/momas-market-moment.html.

"Looking for a Few Good Tenants: LA's New Downtown Gallery Scene." *Huffington Post*, December 18, 2014. http://www.huffingtonpost.com/mutualart/las-new-downtown-gallery-scene_b_6346280.html.

Berens, Stephen, and Jan Tumlir. "Still Lifing: Conversation with Laura Owens." Interview. *X-Tra* 16, no. 2 (Winter 2014): 88–99.

2015

Schjeldahl, Peter. "Take Your Time: New Painting at the Museum of Modern Art." Review. *New Yorker,* January 5, 2015, 78–79.

Stromberg, Matt. "Why Do US and European Galleries Flock to Mexico City's Zona MACO?" *hyperallergic.com*, February 7, 2015. http://hyperallergic.com/180889/why-do-us-and-european-galleries-flock-to-mexico-citys-zona-maco/.

Griffin, Nora, Becky Brown, Dennis Kardon, Carrie Moyer, Raphael Rubinstein, and Jason Stopps. "Roundtable: 'The Forever Now' at MoMA." Review. *Artcritical*, February 9, 2015. http://www.artcritical.com/2015/02/09/a-critics-roundtable-on-the-forever-now/.

Indrisek, Scott. "'Come As You Are': A '90s Flashback in New Jersey." *Blouinartinfo.com*, February 10, 2015. http://www.blouinartinfo.com/news/story/1092804/come-as-you-are-a-90s-flashback-in-new-jersey.

Rosenberg, Karen. "Alt. History: 8 Groundbreaking Works That Show Why We Still Love the '90s." *Artspace.com*, February 14, 2015. http://www.artspace.com/magazine/interviews_features/exhibitions/1990s-art-at-the-montclair-art-museum-52616.

"Galleries—Downtown: Call and Response." Review. *New Yorker*, February 16, 2015, 10.

Farago, Jason. "Is Painting Dead?" *BBC Culture*, February 18, 2015. http://www.bbc.com/culture/story/20150217-is-painting-dead.

Salle, David. "Structure Rising: David Salle on 'The Forever Now' at MOMA." *Artnews.com,* February 23, 2015. http://www.artnews.com/2015/02/23/structure-rising-forever-now-at-moma/.

Tuchman, Phyllis. "Don't Shoot the Messenger." *The Brooklyn Rail,* March 5, 2015. http://www.brooklynrail.org/2015/03/artseen/dont-shoot-the-messenger.

Tarmy, James. "If You Only Go to Only One Gallery in LA, Go Here." Review. *Bloomberg*, March 30, 2015. http://www.bloomberg.com/news/articles/2015-03-30/365-s-mission-road-the-best-art-gallery-in-los-angeles-right-now.

Wise, Lloyd. "Call and Response: Gavin Brown's Enterprise." Review. *Artforum* 53, no. 8 (April 2015): 252.

Bell, Kirsty. "Gallery Weekend Berlin." Review. *Art Agenda*, May 4, 2015. http://www.art-agenda.com/reviews/gallery-weekend-berlin-3/.

Brown, Griselda Murray. "Berlin Gallery Weekend—review." *Financial Times* (London), May 5, 2015.

Buskirk, Martha. "Subversive Color at the Rose Art Museum." Review. *Hyperallergic*, May 30, 2015. http://hyperallergic.com/209292/subversive-color-at-the-rose-art-museum/.

Mak, Geoff. "Laura Owens." Review. *The Brooklyn Rail*. June 3, 2015. http://www.brooklynrail.org/2015/06/artseen/laura-owens.

Werneburg, Brigitte. "Laura Owens' malerisches Spiel mit der Wahrnehmung." *TAZ Lokal,* June 11, 2015, 15.

Della Corte, Vincenzo. "Laura Owens—Secession—Vienna." *Fisk Frisk Magazine*, July 8, 2015. https://fiskfrisk.com/2015/07/08/laura-owens-secession-vienna/.

Koerner von Gustorf, Oliver. "Süss, Süsser, Sauer." Interview. *Blau* 4 (September 2015): 58–65.

Prince, Mark. "Laura Owens: Capitain Petzel." Review. *Art in America* 103, no. 8 (September 2015): 161.

"Views–Berlin: Laura Owens, Capitain Petzel," *Spike 45* (Fall 2015): 178.

Bagley, Christopher. "Art and Commerce." *W* magazine, October 26, 2015. http://www.wmagazine.com/story/tony-salame-aishti-foundation.

Herbert, Martin. "Laura Owens: Capitain Petzel." Review. *Artforum* 54, no. 3 (November 2015): 318–19.

Saltz, Jerry. "Can a Show As Dreary As This One Be Good for the Whitney? Yes." *Nymag.com,* November 24, 2015. http://www.vulture.com/2015/11/can-a-show-this-boring-be-good-for-a-museum.html.

Mauser, Nicole. "Review: Laura Owens/Soccer Club Club." Review. *NewCity Art*, November 30, 2015. http://art.newcity.com/2015/11/30/review-laura-owenssoccer-club-club/.

Bennett, Lennie. "Review: Women Artists Shine in Print Show at Museum of Fine Arts, St. Petersburg." Review. *Tampa Bay Times* (Florida), December 2, 2015.

Wagley, Catherine G. "'The Only Thing I'm an Expert On Is My Own Work': Jordan Wolfson and Laura Owens in Conversation in Los Angeles." Interview. *ArtNews.com*, December 8, 2015. http://www.artnews.com/2015/12/08/the-only-thing-im-an-expert-on-is-my-own-work-jordan-wolfson-and-laura-owens-in-conversation-in-los-angeles/.

2016
Owens, Laura. "Seth Price and Laura Owens in Conversation." Interview. *356 Mission*, January 2016. http://356mission.tumblr.com/post/138501268495/seth-price-and-laura-owens-in-conversation.

Teicholz, Tom. "The Art of the Rubell Family Collection Miami." Review. *Forbes*, January 27, 2016. http://www.forbes.com/sites/tomteicholz/2016/01/27/the-art-of-the-rubell-family-collection-miami/#4d3823e650b8.

Bates, Rebecca. "Playing 'Would You Rather' with Laura Owens." Interview. *Paddle8*, February 5, 2016. https://paddle8.com/editorial/playing-would-you-rather-with-laura-owens/.

Binlot, Ann. "Print's Not Dead: This Year's Music-Themed LA Art Book Fair Hit All the Right Notes." Review. *Wallpaper*, February 29, 2016. http://www.wallpaper.com/art/this-years-music-themed-la-art-book-fair-hits-all-the-right-notes.

Malgré, Malerie, and Maria Muhle. "Malerei Malgré tout Maria Muhle on 'Painting 2.0' at Museum Brandhorst, Munich." Review. *Texte Zur Kunst* 101 (March 2016): 198–206.

Williams, Maxwell. "The Influx of International Galleries to LA Is More Complicated Than You Think." *Artsy*, March 9, 2016. https://www.artsy.net/article/artsy-editorial-can-los-angeles-actually-support-its-new-mega-galleries.

Hotchkiss, Sarah. "So Much More Than 'Ten Paintings' in Laura Owens Show at Wattis." Review. *KQED*, May 19, 2016. http://ww2.kqed.org/arts/2016/05/19/so-much-more-than-ten-paintings-in-laura-owens-show-at-wattis/.

Desmarais, Charles. "Laura Owens at CCA Wattis Institute a Pulse-Quickening Experience." Review. *SFGate*, May 20, 2016. http://www.sfgate.com/news/article/Laura-Owens-at-CCA-Wattis-Institute-a-7757510.php.

———. "Wallpaper Exhibition Compels and Conceals." Review. *San Francisco Chronicle*, May 21, 2016.

Thibault, Sarah. "Laura Owens, Ten Paintings: More Than Meets the Eye." Review. *SFAQ*, May 25, 2016. http://sfaq.us/2016/05/laura-owens-ten-paintings-more-than-meets-the-eye/.

La Rocco, Claudia. "Comin' Round the Mountain." Review. *Artforum.com*, June 2016. https://www.artforum.com/slant/id=61607.

Westin, Monica. "Laura Owens: The Wattis Institute for Contemporary Arts." Review. *Artforum.com*, June 2016. http://artforum.com/picks/id=60515.

Bankowsky, Jack. "Painting 2.0: Expression in the Information Age." Review. *Artforum* 54, no. 10 (Summer 2016): 384–87, 422.

Sienske, Michael. "Boom in the Bay." *Cultured* 21 (Summer 2016): 224–29.

Varadi, Keith J. "Laura Owens at the Wattis Institute (LA in SF)." Review. *Carla* 5 (2016): 48–51.

"Art: Fine Young Cannibals." Review. *New Yorker*, July 11 and 18, 2016, 15.

Geyer, Christina. "California's Most Important Painter Gets a Major Texas Moment." *PaperCity*, August 31, 2016. http://www.papercitymag.com/arts/california-most-important-painter-laura-owens-two-by-two-aids/.

Campbell, Andrianna. "Dash, Fragment, Bracket." *Even Magazine*, no. 5 (Fall 2016): 98–115.

Delahunty, Gavin. "Laura Owens in Conversation with Gavin Delahunty." *Whitewall* 43 (Fall 2016): 112–17.

La Rocco, Claudia. "Laura Owens." Review. *Bomb* 137 (Fall 2016): 158–59.

Godfrey, Mark. "Laura Owens." *Garage* 11 (Fall/Winter 2016): 224–29.

Smith, Paul Michael. "The Grid & the Jester: On the Trope of the Grid in Art." *The Seen* 3 (Fall/Winter 2016): 48–53.

Huberman, Anthony. "Laura Owens: In Conversation with Anthony Huberman." Interview. *LXAQ* 1, September 20, 2016. http://sfaq.us/2016/09/laura-owens-in-conversation-with-anthony-huberman/.

Wagley, Catherine. "The Female Cool School." *Carla* 6 (October 2016): 12–17.

Delahunty, Gavin. "A Stand for Medium and Materiality." *Patron Magazine* (October/November 2016): 63–65.

Vogel, Wendy. "Laura Owens: CCA Wattis Institute for Contemporary Arts." Review. *Modern Painters* (October/November 2016): 77.

Gat, Orin. "Critic's Guide: London." *Frieze.com*, October 3, 2016. https://frieze.com/article/critics-guide-london-1.

Breen, Matt. "Laura Owens." *Time Out London,* October 15, 2016. https://www.timeout.com/london/art/laura-owens.

Creswell, Joanna. "The Magic of Laura Owens' Radical Paintings," *AnOther.com,* October 27, 2016. http://www.anothermag.com/art-photography/9210/the-magic-of-laura-owens-radical-paintings.

Davies, Cassie. "Laura Owens." *Studio International,* November 27, 2016. http://www.studiointernational.com/index.php/laura-owens-review-sadie-coles-london.

Bankowsky, Jack. "Top Ten." *Artforum* 55, no. 4 (December 2016): 200–201.

Hatfull, Nicholas. "Laura Owens at Sadie Coles HQ, London." *Mousse Magazine* 56 (December 2016/January 2017): n.p.

Marten, Helen. "Fuzzy Logic." *Frieze.com,* December 12, 2016. https://frieze.com/article/fuzzy-logic.

Desmarais, Charles. "Top Ten Visual Arts Events of 2016." *San Francisco Chronicle*, December 23, 2016. http://www.sfchronicle.com/entertainment/article/Top-10-visual-arts-events-of-2016-10813668.php#photo-10065039.

Sharon Lockhart, Laura Owens, Frances Stark. Brochure. New York: The Artist's Institute at Hunter College, 2016.

Ten Paintings. Brochure. San Francisco: CCA Wattis Institute, 2016.

2017

Thorne, Harry. "Laura Owens."
Frieze 184 (January/February
2017): 148–49.

Kennedy, Randy. "Laura Owens
Retrospective Coming to the
Whitney." *New York Times*,
January 12, 2017.

Leese, Samantha Kuok,
".com/.cn." Review. *Artforum.
com,* March 2017. https://www
.artforum.com/picks/id=67206.

Russeth, Andrew. "A Florine
Stettheimer Painting Makes a
Rare Appearance at the Armory
Show." *Artnews.com,* March 1,
2017. http://www.artnews
.com/2017/03/01/a-florine-
stettheimer-painting-makes-a-
rare-appearance-at-the-armory-
show/.

Farago, Jason, and Martha
Schwendener. "What to See
at New York's Art Fairs This
Week." *New York Times,*
March 3, 2017.

Owens, Laura. "David Reed and
Laura Owens in Conversation."
Interview. *356 Mission*, April
2017. http://356mission.tumblr
.com/post/159131879345/
interview-with-david-reed-and-
laura-owens-on-the.

Barry, Tim. "*Vanishing
Points* Curated by Andrianna
Campbell." Review. *The Brooklyn Rail.* April 1, 2017. http://
brooklynrail.org/2017/04/
artseen/Vanishing-Points-
curated-by-Andrianna-
Campbell.

Diehl, Travis. "The Drop Shadow
of Doubt." *X-Tra* 19, no. 2
(Winter 2017): 49–63.

Compiled by Jessica Man

EXHIBITION HISTORY

SOLO EXHIBITIONS

1992
The End, Mint Gallery, California Institute of the Arts, Valencia, February 22–February 27.

1995
Rosamund Felsen Gallery, Santa Monica, October 14–November 11.

1997
Gavin Brown's enterprise, New York, April 5–May 10.

Sadie Coles HQ, London, October 22–November 22.

1998
ACME., Los Angeles, October 10–November 14.

Passerby at Gavin Brown's enterprise, New York, October 17–November 14.

Crown Center Gallery at Loyola University, Chicago, November 1–December 4.

1999
Galerie Gisela Capitain, Cologne, June 4–July 31.

Statements, Gavin Brown's enterprise, Art Basel, Basel, June 15–20.

Sadie Coles HQ, London, October 28–November 30.

Heaven and Hell, China Art Objects Galleries, Los Angeles, December 3, 1999–January 8, 2000.

2000
Studio Guenzani, Milan, April 19–June 10.

Inverleith House, The Royal Botanic Garden, Edinburgh, UK, June 17–July 30. Catalogue.

2001
ACME., Los Angeles, March 24–April 21.

New Work at the Isabella Stewart Gardner Museum, Isabella Stewart Gardner Museum, Boston, May 31–September 16. Catalogue.

2003
Museum of Contemporary Art, Los Angeles, March 16–June 22. Catalogue. Traveled to: Aspen Art Museum, Aspen, CO, August 2–September 28; Milwaukee Art Museum, October 18, 2003–January 18, 2004; Museum of Contemporary Art, North Miami, March 4–May 9, 2004.

General Store, Milwaukee, October 17–December 6.

2004
Gavin Brown's enterprise, New York, March 13–April 10.

The Fabric Workshop and Museum, Philadelphia, September 8–November 6.

Crown Point Press, San Francisco, September 17–November 6. Newsletter.

Galerie Gisela Capitain, Cologne, October 28–December 23.

2005
Shiseido Gallery, Tokyo, February 8–March 27. Catalogue.

2006
Sadie Coles HQ, London, April 27–May 27.

The Douglas Hyde Gallery, Dublin, June 7–July 22. Catalogue.

Kunsthalle Zurich, June 12–August 13. Catalogue. Traveled to: Camden Arts Centre, London, September 29–November 26; Kunsthalle Münster, Germany, January 20–April 22, 2007; Bonnefantenmuseum, Maastricht, the Netherlands, May 29–August 19, 2007.

Gavin Brown's enterprise, New York, November 30, 2006–January 13, 2007.

2007
Studio Guenzani, Milan, November 28, 2007–January 31, 2008.

2008
ACME., Los Angeles, February 16–March 15.

Gavin Brown's enterprise, New York, May 8–May 29.

Sadie Coles HQ, London, November 20, 2008–January 10, 2009.

2009
Gavin Brown's enterprise, New York, October 23–November 21.

2011
Crown Point Press, San Francisco, January 13–February 26. Newsletter.

Galerie Gisela Capitain, Cologne, April 14–June 25.

Kunstmuseum Bonn, Bonn, Germany, September 22, 2011–January 8, 2012. Catalogue.

2012
Clock Paintings, The Finley, Los Angeles, January 29–April 8.

Gavin Brown's enterprise, Galerie Giesela Capitain, and Sadie Coles HQ at Art Basel 43: Art Unlimited, Basel, June 14–17.

KARMA, New York, October 4.

Pavement Karaoke/Alphabet, Sadie Coles HQ, London, October 9–November 17.

2013
Twelve Paintings, 356 S. Mission Rd., Los Angeles, January 20–July 7. Catalogue.

Gavin Brown's enterprise at Foire Internationale d'Art Contemporain, Paris, October 24–27.

2015
Zona Maco México Arte Contemporáneo 2015, Mexico City, February 4–8.

Capitain Petzel, Berlin, May 1–August 22.

Secession, Vienna, July 2–August 30.

Soccer Club Club, Chicago, October 29–December 18.

2016
Ten Paintings, CCA Wattis Institute, San Francisco, April 28–July 23.

Sadie Coles HQ, London, October 5–December 17.

Artissima, Torino, November 3–6.

GROUP EXHIBITIONS

1992
LA Matter presents BY LOCATION: LEIMERT PARK, Crossroads Art Academy, Los Angeles, August 20–September 19.

ANTI (printed) MATTER & LA Matter, FAR Bazzar, Los Angeles, December 3–20.

1993
Childhood Fictions, Gallery D300, California Institute of the Arts, Valencia, October 25–October 29.

1994
Temporary, Temporary Contemporary (now The Geffen Contemporary) at MOCA, Los Angeles, April 15–17. Thesis show.

Playfield, Rio Hondo College Art Gallery, Whittier, CA, April 18–May 19.

LACE's 8th Annuale: Gorgeous Politics, Los Angeles

Contemporary Exhibitions, September 23–November 6. Traveled to Contemporary Arts Center, Las Vegas, December 9, 1994–January 14, 1995.

The Hot Crop, Claremont College, Claremont, CA.

Thanks Again, FOOD HOUSE, Santa Monica.

1995
Painting Invitational: Simrel Achenbach, Laura Owens, Ken Weaver, Regen Projects, Los Angeles, February 25–March 28.

Smells Like Vinyl, Roger Merians Gallery, New York, July 6–August 19, 1995.

TELL EVERYONE, Greene Naftali Gallery, New York, October 12–November 12.

From LA with Love, Galerie Praz-Delavallade, Paris, December 16, 1995–January 27, 1996.

1996
Screen: Painting on Television, Television on Painting, Friedrich Petzel Gallery, New York, January 19–February 24.

Studio 246, Künstlerhaus Bethanien, Berlin, April 26–28.

WUNDERBAR—DOPPELTES SPIEL MIT DEM SCHÖNEN, Kunstverein in Hamburg, Germany, May 24–August 11.

The Speed of Painting, Pat Hearn Gallery, New York, September 7–October 13.

Studio 246, Marc Foxx, Santa Monica, November 21–December 31.

1997
Hot Coffee, Artists Space, New York, January 18–March 15.

Palace, Beret International Gallery, Chicago, February 21–March 29, and Walker's Point Center for the Arts, February 22–March 30.

Sharon Lockhart, Laura Owens and Frances Stark, Blum & Poe, Santa Monica, June 7–July 12.

Restaged in 2016 at The Artist's Institute at Hunter College, New York.

The Eagle Rock Show, Eagle Rock Community Cultural Center, Los Angeles, August 30–September 26.

Project Painting, Basilico Fine Arts and Lehmann Maupin, New York, September 11–October 11. Catalogue.

Vertical Painting Show, PS1 Contemporary Art Center, Long Island City, NY, October 29, 1997–June 28, 1998.

The Prophecy of Pop, Contemporary Arts Center, New Orleans, December 6–February 8, 1998.

1998
I'm Still in Love with You, Women's 20th Century Club, Los Angeles, February 14–March 14.

Paintings Interested in Ideas of Architecture and Design, PØST, Los Angeles, February 28–March 28.

Exterminating Angel, Galerie Ghislaine Hussenot, Paris, March 7–May 2.

Laura Owens and Sharon Lockhart, Studio Guenzani, Milan, April 22–May 30.

Hello Out There, ACME., Los Angeles, May 23–June 20.

Visions, XXIX Rencontres Internationales de la Photographie, Arles, France, July 6–August 16.

Come and get it while you wait, Hollywood DMV at Cole, Los Angeles, July 13–31.

Jorge Pardo, Patrick Painter, Inc., Santa Monica, September 10–October 14.

Young Americans 2: New American Art at the Saatchi Gallery, The Saatchi Gallery, London, September 10–November 22. Catalogue.

Color Fields, Luckman Fine Arts Gallery, California State University, Los Angeles, November 14, 1998–January 10, 1999.

1999
Local Color, University of La Verne, La Verne, CA, March 22–April 22.

The Perfect Life, Artifice in LA 1999, Duke University Museum of Art, Durham, NC, April 9–June 6. Catalogue.

Examining Pictures, Exhibiting Paintings, Whitechapel Art Gallery, London, and the Museum of Contemporary Art Chicago, presented in London May 7–June 27 and in Chicago July 24–September 19. Catalogue. Traveled to Hammer Museum, University of California, Los Angeles, February 6–April 2, 2000.

Nach-Bild, Kunsthalle Basel, June 12–August 22. Catalogue.

Works on Paper, and Some Other Things, ACME., Los Angeles, July 9–August 7.

Hot Spots, Weatherspoon Art Gallery, The University of North Carolina at Greensboro, April 18–June 6. Traveled to Pittsburgh Center for the Arts, July 10–August 29.

Drawn to Nature, George's, Los Angeles, July 16–August 1.

Standing Still & Walking in Los Angeles, Gagosian Gallery, Beverly Hills, CA, August 13–September 18. Catalogue.

Pasadena Adjacent, Richard Heller Gallery, Santa Monica, October 16–November 13.

Carnegie International 1999/ 2000, Carnegie Museum of Art, Pittsburgh, November 6, 1999–March 26, 2000. Catalogue.

New Work: Painting Today, Recent Acquisitions, San Francisco Museum of Modern Art, December 17, 1999–March 28, 2000.

2000
Works on Paper from Los Angeles: J. Bishton, J. Bornstein, C. Finley, F. Gavviani, M. Grotjahn, J. Meadows, R. Neri, L. Owens, J. Pardo, J. Pastor, M. Prieto, F. Stark, P. White, Studio Guenzani, Milan, January 12–February 12.

On Canvas: Contemporary Painting from the Collection, Solomon R. Guggenheim Museum, New York, February 18–April 2.

The Next Wave: New Painting in Southern California, California Center for the Arts, Escondido, June 4–September 10.

Drawings 2000, Barbara Gladstone Gallery, New York, July–August, 2000. Catalogue.

Art on Paper 2000: The 36th Exhibition of Art on Paper, Weatherspoon Art Gallery, The University of North Carolina at Greensboro, November 19, 2000–January 14, 2001.

2001
Objective Color, Yale University Art Gallery, New Haven, CT, February 2–March 25.

Lens and Paper: The Beauty of Intimacy, Gemeentemuseum Den Haag, The Hague, the Netherlands, February 10–April 15. Catalogue. Traveled to: Staatliche Kunsthalle Baden-Baden, Germany, September 14–November 4; Kunstraum Innsbruck, Austria, November 24, 2001–January 12, 2002.

Painting at the Edge of the World, Walker Art Center, Minneapolis, February 10–May 6. Catalogue.

American Academy Invitational Exhibition of Painting and Sculpture, The American Academy of Arts and Letters, New York, March 5–April 1.

Public Offerings, Museum of Contemporary Art, Los Angeles, April 1–July 29. Catalogue.

Cal's Art: Sampling California Painting, University of North Texas Art Gallery, Denton, September 12–October 20.

Bastard (son of hot sauce), The Law Office, Chicago, September 21–October 19.

Accumulations, School of Art Gallery, Kent State University, Kent, OH, October 3–31.

Some Options in Abstraction, Carpenter Center for the Visual Arts, Harvard University, Cambridge, MA, October 15–November 11.

The Mystery of Painting, Sammlung Goetz, Munich, October 29, 2001–April 5, 2002. Catalogue.

Paintings, 5117 Eagle Rock Boulevard, Los Angeles.

2002

Urgent Painting, Musee d'Art Moderne de la Ville de Paris, January 17–March 3. Catalogue.

Cavepainting: Peter Doig, Chris Ofili, and Laura Owens, Santa Monica Museum of Art, February 8–March 31. Catalogue.

Strolling Through an Ancient Shrine and Garden, ACME., Los Angeles, April 27–May 25.

Painting on the Move, Kunstmuseum Basel and Museum fur Gegenwartskunst Basel (featuring Owens) and Kunsthalle Basel, May 26–September 8. Catalogue.

Drawing Now: Eight Propositions, The Museum of Modern Art, Queens, NY, October 17, 2002–January 6, 2003. Catalogue.

2003

Painting Pictures: Painting and Media in the Digital Age, Kunstmuseum Wolfsburg, Germany, March 1–June 29. Catalogue.

Inaugural Group Exhibition, Gavin Brown's enterprise, New York, September 20–October 4.

2004

Malerei, Galerie Rolf Hengesbach, Cologne, Germany, February 28–April 8.

Whitney Biennial, Whitney Museum of American Art, New York, March 11–May 30. Catalogue.

Drunk vs. Stoned, Passerby at Gavin Brown's enterprise, New York, April 22–May 31.

Painting's Edge: The Exhibition, Idyllwild Arts Campus, Idyllwild, CA, June 26–July 7.

Contemporary Painting: Curated by Alex Katz, Colby College Museum of Art, Waterville, ME, June 27–September 19. Catalogue.

Never Never Landscape, Atle Gerhardsen, Berlin, September 10–October 23.

The Undiscovered Country, Hammer Museum, University of California, Los Angeles, October 3, 2004–January 16, 2005. Catalogue.

Huts, The Douglas Hyde Gallery, Dublin, October 23–December 1. Catalogue.

The Four Color Pen Show, Locust Project, Miami, December 4–27.

2005

POST-MoDERN, Greene Naftali Gallery, New York, January 14–February 19.

25 Visuell: Deutsche Bank Art, Deutsche Guggenheim, Berlin, April 30–June 19. Catalogue.

Ideal Worlds: New Romanticism in Contemporary Art, Schirn Kunsthalle Frankfurt, May 12–August 28. Catalogue.

Old News, Los Angeles Contemporary Exhibitions, June 29–September 4.

Extreme Abstraction, Albright-Knox Art Gallery, Buffalo, NY, July 15–October 2. Catalogues (2005 and 2012).

Think Blue, Blum & Poe, Los Angeles, July 16–August 20.

plip, plip, plippity!, Richard Telles Fine Art, Los Angeles, September 10–October 8.

Drawn to Cleveland, Museum of Contemporary Art Cleveland, September 16–December 30. Catalogue.

Goetz meets Falckenberg, Sammlung Goetz, Munich, November 4, 2005–April 30, 2006. Catalogue.

After Cézanne, Museum of Contemporary Art, Los Angeles, November 20, 2005–May 19, 2006.

Recent Acquisitions, Museum of Contemporary Art, Los Angeles, November 20, 2005–January 9, 2006.

The Fluidity of Time: Selections from the MCA Collection, Museum of Contemporary Art Chicago, November 25, 2005–August 27, 2006.

Desired Constellations, Daniel Reich, New York.

2006

Hotel California, The Glendale College Art Gallery, Glendale, CA, February 4–March 18.

Opere su Carta: Margherita Manzelli, Aleksandra Mir, Laura Owens, Alessandro Pessoli, Danica Phelps, Studio Guenzani, Milan, February 15–March 18.

The Garden Party, Deitch Projects, New York, March 9–May 20.

Blind Date. Zum ersten mal zu sehen: Die Neuankäufe für die Sammlung Deutsche Bank, Galerie Kunstforum, Altes Haus, Seligenstadt, Germany, May 14–July 2. Catalogue.

The Art of Etching at Crown Point Press, Bobbie Greenfield Gallery, Santa Monica, July 15–August 19. Catalogue.

All the Best: The Deutsche Bank Collection and Zaha Hadid, Singapore Art Museum, September 1–November 20. Catalogue.

Essential Painting, The National Museum of Art, Osaka, October 3–December 24. Catalogue.

Red Eye: LA Artists from the Rubell Family Collection, Rubell Family Collection, Miami, December 4, 2006–May 31, 2007. Catalogue.

2007

Very Abstract and Hyper Figurative, Thomas Dane Gallery, London, March 15–April 14. Catalogue.

Poets on Painters, Ulrich Museum of Art at Wichita State University, KS, April 22–August 5. Catalogue.

Affinities: New Acquisitions from the Deutsche Bank Collection, Deutsche Guggenheim, Berlin, April 28–June 24. Catalogue.

Sequence 1: Painting and Sculpture in the François Pinault Collection, Palazzo Grassi, Venice, May 5–November 11. Catalogue.

2007 Royal Academy Summer Exhibition, Royal Academy of Arts, London, June 11–August 19. Catalogue.

Summer Show, Sadie Coles HQ, London, June 29–August 26.

Counterparts: Contemporary Painters and Their Influences, Contemporary Art Center of Virginia, Virginia Beach, June 29–September 23. Catalogue.

Legends Altered: Maps as Method and Medium, Carrie Secrist Gallery, Chicago, November 30, 2007–January 5, 2008.

2008

Collecting Collections: Highlights from the Permanent Collection of the Museum of Contemporary Art, Los Angeles, Museum of Contemporary Art, Los Angeles, February 9–May 19. Catalogue.

Tapestry, Karyn Lovegrove Gallery, Los Angeles, May 3–May 28.

Blasted Allegories: Werke aus der Sammlung Ringier, Kunstmuseum Luzern, Lucerne, Switzerland, May 16–August 3. Catalogue.

Living Flowers: Ikebana and Contemporary Art, Japanese American National Museum, Los Angeles, June 15–September 7. Catalogue.

Biennale of the Art of Painting: The Joy of Looking, Museum Dhondt-Dhaenens, Deurle, Belgium, and Roger Raveel Museum, Machelen-Zulte, Belgium, June 29–September 21 and June 29–October 5.

Landscapes of the Mind: Art Collection of the United States Embassy, Beijing, United States Embassy, Beijing. Commissioned work permanently installed in July 2008. Catalogue.

Painting Now and Forever: Part II, Greene Naftali Gallery and Matthew Marks Gallery, New York, July 3–August 15.

Pretty Ugly, Gavin Brown's enterprise and Maccarone, New York, July 10–August 29.

2009
The Still Life Show, Five Thirty Three, Los Angeles, and Milepost 5, Portland, OR, March 21–April 18.

BROODWORK: Creative Practice and Family Life, Center for the Arts Eagle Rock, Los Angeles, May 23–June 21.

Hello, Mrs. MacGruder, Benson Keyes Art, Southampton, NY, August 22–September 6.

Art Tells the Times, Works by Women Artists, Shiseido Gallery 90th Anniversary Exhibition, Shiseido Gallery, Tokyo, August 25–October 18. Catalogue.

Continuous Present, Yale University Art Gallery, New Haven, CT, October 6, 2009–January 10.

Collection: MOCA's First Thirty Years, Museum of Contemporary Art, Los Angeles, November 15, 2009–May 3, 2010.

15 Year Gallery Artist Group Exhibition, ACME., Los Angeles,

November 21—December 19, 2009.

Slow Paintings, Museum Morsbroich, Leverkusen, Germany, November 24, 2009–February 7, 2010. Catalogue.

2010
Hecate's Lab, Senior & Shopmaker Gallery, New York, June 17–August 16.

At Home/Not at Home: Works from the Collection of Martin and Rebecca Eisenberg, Hessel Museum of Art, Center for Curatorial Studies, Bard College, Annandale-on-Hudson, NY, September 26–December 19. Catalogue.

Ordinary Madness, Carnegie Museum of Art, Pittsburgh, October 15, 2010–January 9, 2011.

The Artist's Museum, Museum of Contemporary Art, Los Angeles, October 24, 2010–January 31, 2011.

Painting and Sculpture: Exhibition to Benefit the Foundation for Contemporary Arts, Lehmann Maupin, New York, December 9, 2010–January 9, 2011.

2011
The Spectacular of Vernacular, Walker Art Center, Minneapolis, January 29–May 8. Catalogue. Traveled to: Contemporary Arts Museum Houston, July 30–September 18; Montclair Art Museum, Montclair, NJ, October 7, 2011–January 1, 2012; Ackland Art Museum at the University of North Carolina at Chapel Hill, January 14–March 18, 2012.

A Painting Show, Harris Lieberman, New York, May 6–June 4.

The Boy Who Robbed You a Few Minutes Before Arriving at the Ball, Galerie Gisela Capitain, Cologne, July 2–September 3.

Painting Between the Lines, CCA Wattis Institute, San Francisco, October 4–December 17. Catalogue. Traveled to Williams

College Museum of Art, Williamstown, MA, February 16–June 9, 2013.

From Where You Just Arrived, Pepin Moore, Los Angeles, October 29–December 3.

Alex Zachary, New York, *Happy Holidays! Drawings!*, December 23–25.

The Cactus Painting Show, 3704 North Figueroa, Los Angeles, November 13.

Art Collection of the United States Consulate General, Karachi, Pakistan, Four works permanently installed in January 2011. Catalogue.

2012
Print Imprint, Cirrus Gallery and Actual Size, Los Angeles, March 10–May 5 and April 7–May 12.

Nudes Painting Show, 3704 North Figueroa, Los Angeles, March 25.

Pittura (1995–2009), Studio Guenzani, Milan, April 11–May 31.

Pure Perception: Kristin Baker, Laura Owens, Mai-Thu Perret, Amanda Ross-Ho, Galleria Monica De Cardenas, Milan, May 9–July 28.

Looking Back for the Future, Kunsthalle Zürich, June 10–17.

The Holodeck, PØST, Los Angeles, July 26.

Natural History, Carnegie Museum of Art, Pittsburgh, July 28–October 14.

Curatorial Exchange, Irvine Fine Arts Center, Irvine, CA, September 8–October 20.

Things, Words and Consequences, Moscow Museum of Modern Art, September 15–October 14.

2013
Small Gems: A Winter Group Show, Crown Point Press, San Francisco, January 19–March 9.

Wir Drei, Guggenheim Gallery, Chapman University, Orange, CA, January 30–March 2.

Finisce e Continua uno, Gesso Artspace, Vienna, March 19–May.

The Cat Show, White Columns, New York, June 14–July 27.

Highlights from the Venice Beach Biennial, Echo Park Film Center, Los Angeles, August 31.

Abstract—Nature: Selected Parkett Artists' Editions (1984–2013), Parkett Space, Zurich, August 31–November 30.

Yes, No, Maybe: Artists Working at Crown Point Press, National Gallery of Art, Washington, DC, September 1, 2013–January 5, 2014. Catalogue. Traveled to McNay Art Museum, San Antonio, TX, January 28–May 17, 2015.

Working Proofs: A Revelation, Crown Point Press, San Francisco, September 10–October 26.

2014
Capture the Rapture, CB1 Gallery, Los Angeles, February 9–March 16.

Whitney Biennial, Whitney Museum of American Art, New York, March 7–May 25. Catalogue.

Persian Rose Chartreuse Muse Vancouver Grey, Equinox Gallery, Vancouver, BC, March 22–April 19.

Loveless, Greene Naftali Gallery, New York, March 25–April 26.

Nature Study: A Group Exhibition, Crown Point Press, San Francisco, April 22–May 31.

Summer Choices: A Group Show, Crown Point Press, San Francisco, June 6–August 30.

Painter's Painters: Gifts from Alex Katz, High Museum of Art, Atlanta, June 14–November 2.

Joyride, Marlborough Broome Street, New York, June 25–August 3.

Another Cats Show, 356 S. Mission Rd., Los Angeles, August 16–September 14.

Variations: Conversations in and Around Abstract Painting, Los Angeles County Museum of Art, Los Angeles, August 24, 2014–March 22, 2015.

Cornucopia: Artists' Collaborations from 30 Years in One Room, Parkett Space, Zurich, August 29–December 20.

The Machine Project Field Guide to the Gamble House, Gamble House, Pasadena, CA, September 19–October 5.

The Good, The Bad and the Ugly (Part One), Gesso Artspace, Vienna, September 24–November 22.

Wake Up Early, Fear Death: Laura Owens, Caitlin Lonegan, Rebecca Morris, Galerie Nächst St. Stephan Rosemarie Schwarzwälder, Vienna, October 3–November 8.

Death Ship: Tribute to H. C. Westermann, The Pit, Glendale, CA, November 2–December 13. Catalogue.

The Forever Now: Contemporary Painting in an Atemporal World, The Museum of Modern Art, New York, December 14, 2014–April 5, 2015. Catalogue.

2015
Call and Response, Gavin Brown's enterprise, New York, January 24–February 28.

STAPLES (and Doodles), The Vanity Bakersfield, Bakersfield, CA, January 29–March 7.

Come as You Are: Art of the 1990s, Montclair Art Museum, Montclair, NJ, February 8–May 17. Catalogue. Traveled to: Telfair Museums, Savannah, GA, June 12–September 20; University of Michigan Museum of Art, Ann Arbor, October 17, 2015–January 31, 2016; Blanton Museum of Art, The University of Texas at Austin, February 21–May 15, 2016.

Pretty Raw: After and Around Helen Frankenthaler, The Rose Art Museum at Brandeis University, Waltham, MA, February 11–June 7.

Open Source: Art at the Eclipse of Capitalism, Galerie Max Hetzler, Berlin, March 12–April 18.

Making Traces: Painting After Technology, Tate Modern, London, April 1, 2015–May 1, 2016.

Printed Matters, Gesso Artspace, Vienna, April 10–May 15.

Project X Forum 2: FAR Bazzar, Foundation for Art Resources, 18th Street Arts Center, Santa Monica, April 15.

best students best teachers best schools, Michel Majerus, Albert Oehlen & Laura Owens, Michel Majerus Estate, Berlin, May 1, 2015–March 5, 2016.

Works on Paper, Greene Naftali Gallery, New York, May 15–June 20.

Storylines: Contemporary Art at the Guggenheim, Solomon R. Guggenheim Museum, New York, June 5–September 9.

Summer Choices, Crown Point Press, San Francisco, June 7–August 29.

Can't Reach Me There, Midway Contemporary Art, Minneapolis, July 30–October 3. Catalogue.

Marks Made: Prints by American Women Artists from the 1960s to the Present, Museum of Fine Arts, St. Petersburg, Florida, October 17, 2015–January 24, 2016. Catalogue.

Painting 2.0: Expression in the Information Age, Museum Brandhorst, Munich, November 14, 2015—April 30, 2016. Catalogue. Traveled to mumok Museum moderner Kunst Stiftung Ludwig Wien, Vienna, June 4–November 6, 2016.

Collected by Thea Westreich Wagner and Ethan Wagner, Whitney Museum of American Art, New York, November 20, 2015–March 6, 2016. Catalogue. Traveled to Centre Pompidou, Paris, as *La Collection Thea Westreich Wagner et Ethan Wagner*, June 10, 2016–March 27, 2017.

NO MAN'S LAND: Women Artists from the Rubell Family Collection, Rubell Family Collection, Miami, December 2, 2015–July 30, 2016. Catalogue. Traveled to National Museum of Women in the Arts, Washington, DC, September 30, 2016–January 8, 2017.

The World Is Made of Stories, Astrup Fearnley Museet, Oslo, December 4, 2015–September 30, 2017.

2016
Administrate: Jason Hirata, Garry Neill Kennedy, Laura Owens, Artspeak, Vancouver, BC, February 19–March 19.

L'Almanach 16, Le Consortium, Dijon, France, February 20–June 5.

Fine Young Cannibals, Friedrich Petzel Gallery, New York, June 24–August 5. Catalogue.

Apeirophobia/Aporia, Human Resources, Los Angeles, July 1–July 31.

Sharon Lockhart, Frances Stark, and Laura Owens, The Artist's Institute at Hunter College, New York, September 15—October 22. Reinstallation of a 1997 exhibition.

Los Angeles—A Fiction, Astrup Fearnley Museet, Oslo, September 22, 2016–January 22, 2017. Catalogue.

2017
Infected Foot, Greene Naftali Gallery, New York, January 17–February 25.

Depuis le temps, Galerie Mezzanin, Geneva, January 20–March 18.

Chapters: Book Arts in Southern California, Craft and Folk Art Museum, Los Angeles, January 29–May 7.

Tomorrow Will Still Be Ours, Gavin Brown's enterprise, New York, February 8–23.

Zeitgeist, Musée d'art moderne et contemporain, Geneva, February 22–May 7.

The Florine Stettheimer Collapsed Time Salon, presented by Jeffrey Deitch at The Armory Fair, New York, March 2–5.

.com/.cn, K11 Art Foundation Pop-Up Space, Sheung Wan, Hong Kong, March 21–April 30. Catalogue.

Vanishing Points, James Cohan Gallery, New York, March 23–April 22.

Compiled by Jessica Man

ACKNOWLEDGMENTS

This book and the exhibition it accompanies could only have been realized with the extraordinary efforts, good humor, and faith of many talented people. First among them is Adam D. Weinberg, the Whitney's Alice Pratt Brown Director, who has long made the dreams of artists and curators the guiding spirit of the Museum. I am always grateful for his unwavering support and sense of adventure, without which Laura Owens and I could never have pursued such an unconventional book and installation concept for the Whitney's first midcareer survey downtown.

Everyone on the Whitney's staff makes invaluable contributions to our exhibition program in a myriad of ways. The exhibition team for this considerable undertaking was adroitly led by Christy Putnam, associate director for exhibitions and collections management, with Maura Heffner, assistant director, exhibitions management. Numerous logistics and other details were expertly overseen by Seth Fogelman, senior registrar, exhibitions; Melanie Taylor, director, exhibition design; Mark Steigelman, director, exhibition design production; Anna Martin, exhibition designer and production coordinator; and Zabie Mustafa, associate exhibition designer. Related educational and public programs were organized with great creativity by Kathryn Potts, associate director, Helena Rubinstein Chair of Education; Anne Byrd, director of interpretation and research; Megan Heuer, director of public programs and public engagement; Heather Maxson, director of school, youth, and family programs; Sasha Wortzel, director of access and community programs; and Ellen Tepfer, manager of docent and teaching fellow programs. Carol Mancusi-Ungaro, Melva Bucksbaum Associate Director for Conservation and Research; Matthew Skopek, associate conservator; and Margo Delidow, assistant conservator, ensured the care and condition of the works on display.

Considerable fundraising and event planning were guided by Alexandra Wheeler, deputy director for advancement, along with her team members Stephanie Adams, director of individual and planned giving; Marilou Aquino, director of philanthropy; Eunice Lee, director of corporate partnerships; Morgan Arenson, senior officer, institutional relations; Ann Holcomb, senior officer, institutional relations; Brianna O'Brien Lowndes, director of membership and annual fund; and Gina Rogak, director of special events.

I am particularly indebted to the Museum's administration, including John S. Stanley, chief operating officer; I. D. Aruede, chief financial officer; Nicholas S. Holmes, general counsel; Jen Leventhal, chief of staff; Justin Romeo, executive coordinator, director's office; Rose O'Neill-Suspitsyna, manager of operations and trustee administration; and Lily Zhou, director's office and trustee office coordinator. Other colleagues who offered valuable expertise include Adrian Hardwicke, director of visitor experience; Sofie Andersen, director of digital media; Elyse Mallouk, senior manager, digital content; Sylvia Rupani-Smith, senior manager, digital content; Aliza Sena, digital producer; Stephen Soba, director of communications; Danielle Bias, senior communications manager; Zoe Jackson, director of marketing; Sarah Meller, senior marketing manager; Hilary Greenbaum, director of graphic design; Liz Plahn, graphic designer; Peter Scott, director of facilities; Lauri Freedman, retail product development manager; Farris Wahbeh, Benjamin and Irma Weiss Director of Research Resources; and Ivy Blackman, managing librarian.

One of the great pleasures and privileges of being a Whitney curator is benefitting from the generous insights of my colleagues: Donna De Salvo, deputy director for international initiatives and senior curator, who initially greenlighted this project; David Breslin, DeMartini Family Curator and Director of the Collection; Barbara Haskell, curator; David Kiehl, curator emeritus; Elisabeth Sussman, curator and Sondra Gilman Curator of Photography; Chrissie Iles, Anne and Joel Ehrenkranz Curator; Jay Sanders, former Engell Speyer Family Curator and Curator of Performance; Christiane Paul, adjunct curator of new media arts; Christopher Lew, Nancy and Fred Poses Associate Curator; Jane Panetta, associate curator; and Emily Russell, director of curatorial affairs. I am also particularly grateful to Laura Phipps, assistant curator, who contributed much to this project, and to Diana Matuszak, researcher; Micah Musheno, curatorial project assistant; and Anna Blum, curatorial project assistant, along with interns Harry Choi, Tabitha Piseno, Kerry Santullo, Colin Ross, Emma Holter, Nadia Gribkova, Seung Hee Kim, Alicia Schleifman, and Quinn Schoen. Above all, I am delighted to recognize the tireless efforts of Jessica Man, curatorial assistant, who attended to nearly every aspect of the exhibition and book, which would truly not have been possible without her good ideas, long hours, and poise under pressure.

Many people outside the Whitney aided this endeavor in innumerable ways, chief among them Laura's dealers, Gavin Brown, Gisela Capitain, and Sadie Coles. Each of them has been involved with her work for more than two decades, and their dedication is evidenced at many points throughout these pages. They also provided crucial financial

support to make this book exactly what Laura and I hoped
it might be. I am enormously grateful to our collaborating
tour partners: Agustín Arteaga, Eugene McDermott Director;
Gavin Delahunty, Hoffman Family Senior Curator of
Contemporary Art; and Katherine Brodbeck, Nancy and
Tim Hanley Assistant Curator of Contemporary Art at
the Dallas Museum of Art, and Philippe Vergne, director;
Helen Molesworth, chief curator; and Bennett Simpson,
senior curator at the Museum of Contemporary Art, Los
Angeles. Jorge Pardo has generously allowed us to include
his own works in reconstituting a collaborative exhibition
that he and Laura made in Los Angeles in 1998. Mecca
Vazie Andrews, along with Graham Lambkin, Oliver Payne,
Scott Reeder, and Ethan Swan, offered engaging and fresh
contributions to the Whitney's public programming.

I have been privileged to work on several remarkable
publications at the Whitney, but none has been the result of
such intense collaboration as the present volume. Tiffany
Malakooti and Asha Schechter offered their inspiration,
wisdom, and patience in its conception and execution,
and the result is as much a product of their vision as of
Laura's and mine. At the artist's studio our work was
greatly enhanced by the masterful orchestration of Amy
Baumann and the keen eye of David Berezin, as well as
the assistance of Ben Carlson and Katie Douglass. On
the Whitney side, I am most grateful to Beth Huseman,
director of publications, for her invaluable contributions
and never saying no even when she had every reason to
do so. She assembled a crackerjack team led by Elizabeth
Levy, with key input by Nerissa Dominguez Vales and
Amanda Glesmann, as well as Jacob Horn in the Museum's
publications department. Owens's work has been amply
illuminated by essayists Kirsty Bell, Gavin Delahunty, Bruce
Hainley, and Jenny Jaskey, as well as by the reminiscences
of Lisa Anne Auerbach, Amy Baumann, David Berezin,
Edgar Bryan, Henry Bryan, Andrew Cannon, Sadie Coles,
Corinna Durland, Laeh Glenn, Kate Hall, Michael Henry
Hayden, Mary Heilmann, Carol Hendrickson, Deborah Kass,
Rachel Kushner, Calvin Marcus, Chris Ofili, Eric Palgon,
Jorge Pardo, Jennifer Phiffer, Monique Prieto, Scott Reeder,
Paul Schimmel, Alex Slade, Ethan Swan, Mungo Thomson,
Kerry Tribe, Alex Tuttle, T. J. Wilcox, Jonas Wood, and
Wendy Yao. I am also grateful to those authors whose work
is reprinted in these pages: Diedrich Diederichsen, Jonathan
Gold, bell hooks, Sianne Ngai, the late Rozsika Parker, Seth
Price, Francine Prose, Gill Saunders, Frances Stark, and the
late David Foster Wallace.

Lastly, I owe my deepest thanks to Laura and her family.
Her children Henry and Nova Bryan kindly shared their
mother with me, and, as is clear from this book, have
made a huge impact on her work. Sohrab Mohebbi, her
husband, has been a great friend and confidante despite
my endless intrusions on Laura's time and his. And finally,

I am profoundly grateful to Laura, who is one of the most
extraordinary people I have ever known and serves as
an endless inspiration. There is, of course, her art, but
also her commitment to family and friends, students and
teachers, assistants and collaborators, the art community
and its audiences, the city of Los Angeles and the world
beyond. To call her a "multitasker" would be to deny her
the generosity and improbable grace with which she pulls it
all off and gives us so much. Her work and her life show us
what art can be and do.

ARTIST ACKNOWLEDGMENTS

I would like to humbly express my gratitude to the many people who have supported me throughout my life and career as an artist. For this project, I'm deeply indebted to the Whitney and Scott Rothkopf. It's been a great privilege to partner with a curator as dedicated to understanding my work and every detail of the history of my process as Scott. He not only served as the curator for the exhibition but as the editor of this book, turning an unwieldly mass of images and ephemera into a cohesive whole. It is hard to imagine another institution that would have thrown caution to the wind in order to allow an artist the time, space, and resources to experiment with a book that includes about a thousand images and spans almost seven hundred pages. I am deeply grateful to Adam D. Weinberg and the Whitney's staff for their dedication and support.

Tiffany Malakooti moved to LA and camped out in my studio in order to collaborate on this book. She sifted through an enormous amount of new, raw data that taxed all of our brains and found order and clarity in the chaos with her design of these pages. Through his insight and work with my extensive archive of materials, Asha Schechter created layers of meaning and multiple narratives in the book. He encouraged us to add the voices of friends to the book and conscientiously edited almost twenty interviews to make the oral histories as well as helped me to think through all my narrated captions, ultimately finding the words and pictures for our story. And thank you to Beth Huseman for guiding this process and allowing everything to congeal over time. Beth Levy oversaw countless details and kept things from veering off track and Amanda Glesmann took care of all the editing. Many thanks are also due to Jessica Man who provided essential help with the coordination and communication on all details of the book and the show. Nerissa Vales kept the standard of production very high and worked to find the best way to accommodate handmade covers made in my studio.

The place where all of this happens is an incubator of ideas, and I am very lucky that it is guided so thoughtfully and conscientiously by Amy Baumann. She managed to stave off and manage the laws of reality while we worked on this book for many months. Many thanks to Katie Douglass and Ben Carlson for their dedication to organizing digital files and an archive of thousands of scraps of what most people call trash—it was impressive. Thanks also go to Dave Berezin for organizing all image files on a server and color correcting them, while also making endless spreadsheets and to-do lists. Each of the covers for the book was made in the studio with great skill and care by Michael Henry Hayden, Ross Calendio, Cindy Conrad, Alix Ross, Kate Hall, Phil Davis, and Neal Uno. This process, which took tremendous effort and coordination, was shepherded by Dave and Amy.

Many thanks also go to Gavin Brown, Sadie Coles, and Gisela Capitain along with Pauline Daly, Marta Fontolan, and Sarah Moog, who supported this project and assisted in every way to supply content for the book and locate works for the exhibition.

Kirsty Bell, Gavin Delahunty, Bruce Hainley, and Jenny Jaskey all took the time to write meaningful new texts for this book and for that I am very grateful. A group of other authors or estates, including Diedrich Diederichsen, Jonathan Gold, bell hooks, Sianne Ngai, Rozsika Parker, Seth Price, Francine Prose, Gill Saunders, Frances Stark, and David Foster Wallace, kindly allowed us to reprint essays.

So much appreciation and gratitude goes to the many friends who not only contributed oral histories to this book but have also helped me in so many ways in my life and have been there along the way when I needed support. They include: Lisa Anne Auerbach, Edgar Bryan, Andrew Cannon, Corinna Durland, Laeh Glenn, Mary Heilmann, Deborah Kass, Rachel Kushner, Calvin Marcus, Chris Ofili, Eric Palgon, Jorge Pardo, Jennifer Phiffer, Monique Prieto, Scott Reeder, Paul Schimmel, Alex Slade, Frances Stark, Ethan Swan, Mungo Thomson, Kerry Tribe, Alex Tuttle, T. J. Wilcox, Jonas Wood, and Wendy Yao.

Additional thanks goes to all those friends and collaborators whose correspondence, notes, and images of themselves or their work appear in these pages. They include many mentioned elsewhere as well as the following: Karen Adelman, Matt Adelman, William Ahmanson, Melissa Altman, Leon Benn, Alexia Bernal, Timothy Blum, Cecily Brown, Julie Cart, Susan Cianciolo, John Currin, Kimberly Cutter, Ben Dean, Peter Doig, Graham Donk, Michael Dopp, Norman Dubrow, Katy Fischer, Marc Foxx, Charles Gaines, Paul Gellman, Ria German-Carter, Jeffrey Green, Renée Green, Liz Greene, Wynne Greenwood, Colleen Grennan, Uta Grosenick, Madeleine Grynsztejn, Elizabeth Hamilton, James Herman, Nick Herman, Roger Herman, Gale Herold, Charline von Heyl, John Michael Higgins, Jessica Jackson Hutchins, Alex Israel, Stefanie Jansen, Jasper Johns, Barry Johnston, Tony Just, Stanya Kahn, Alex Katz, Brad Killam, Martin Klosterfelde, David Korty, Thomas Krens, Stuart Krimko, Udomsak Krisanamis, Thomas Lawson, Steven D. Lavine, Ann Leese, Rick Levine, Rhonda Lieberman, Holger Liebs, Sharon Lockhart, Euan Macdonald, Craig McIntyre,

ADDITIONAL CONTRIBUTORS

Louis McMiller, Alex Meadows, Annette Messager, Dianna Molzan, Meredith Monk, Frank Moore, Nina Moore, Donald Morgan, Susan Morgan, Rebecca Morris, Kiva Motnyk, Jack Mottram, Dave Muller, Milena Muzquiz, Tim Neuger, Albert Oehlen, Justin Olerud, Eileen Owens, Lincoln Owens, Peter Pakesch, Kristin Parker, Elizabeth Peyton, Jeffrey Poe, Rob Pruitt, Andreas Reiter Raabe, Fiona Rae, Charles Ray, David Reed, Tyson Reeder, Lane Relyea, Burkhard Riemschneider, Ruth Root, Beatrix Ruf, Rainald Schumacher, John Seal, Daniela Short, Annette Sievert, Susan Smith, Randy Sommer, Josh Stone, Marion Boulton Stroud-Swingle, Elaine Sturtevant, Ali Subotnick, Ian Svenonius, Spencer Sweeney, Piotr Uklański, Monique van Genderen, Christy Walker, Mary Weatherford, Michael Webster, Benjamin Weissman, Eric Wesley, and Wallace Whitney.

Special thanks go to my family: Carol Hendrickson, Richard Hendrickson, Nova Bryan, and Henry Bryan. They all made contributions to this book, and they also provide so much love and support to me as an artist. My greatest love and deepest gratitude goes to my partner, Sohrab Mohebbi—without him this book would not have been possible.

Information about essay authors and oral history contributors appears with related texts elsewhere in this volume. The following list of individuals includes information about those who contributed short texts.

Lisa Anne Auerbach is a Los Angeles–based artist and writer and an associate professor of art at Pomona College in Claremont.

Amy Baumann has worked at Owens's studio since 2015.

Sadie Coles is the owner of Sadie Coles HQ in London.

Corinna Durland is a New York–based art dealer and was a director at Gavin Brown's enterprise in 2000–14.

Laeh Glenn is a Los Angeles–based artist.

Kate Hall is a Los Angeles–based artist and musician who has worked at Owens's studio since 2013.

Michael Henry Hayden is a Los Angeles–based artist who has worked at Owens's studio since 2013.

Mary Heilmann is a painter based in Bridgehampton and New York.

Jorge Pardo is an artist based in Mérida, Mexico.

Jennifer Phiffer is a bookbinder and the owner of Phiffer Books in Los Angeles.

Monique Prieto is a Los Angeles–based artist.

Kerry Tribe is a Los Angeles–based artist and filmmaker.

Alex Tuttle is a director at 356 Mission in Los Angeles.

Jonas Wood is a Los Angeles-based artist who worked at Owens's studio in 2003–5.

Wendy Yao is a Los Angeles–based publisher; the founder of the art, music, book, and clothing store Ooga Booga; and a co-founder and partner at 356 Mission.

Errol Coore
Brenna Cothran
Heather Cox
David Critides
Kenneth Cronan
Monica Crozier
Caroline David
Regine David
Amanda Davis
Monserrate DeLeon
Margo Delidow
Donna De Salvo
Larry DeBlasio
Pedro Del Corro
Anthony Desena
Lauren DiLoreto
Michelle Donnelly
John Donovan
Kelly Donovan
Marisa Donovan
Lisa Dowd
Anita Duquette
Kasim Earl
Erica Eaton
Nicolyna Enriquez
Cesar Espinoza
Alvin Eubanks
Katie Fallen
Reid Farrington
Katherine Flores
Seth Fogelman
Samuel Franks
Denis Frederick
Murlin Frederick
Lauri Freedman
Kyle Freeman
Annie French
Donald Garlington
Anthony Gennari
Ronnie George
Jennie Goldstein
Lucas Gonzalez
Alex Goodship
Hilary Greenbaum
Marcela Guerrero
Peter Guss
Stewart Hacker
Amanda Haggerty
Rita Hall
Adrian Hardwicke
Lola Harney
Tara Hart
Greta Hartenstein
Barbara Haskell
Maura Heffner
Dina Helal
Lawrence Hernandez

Jennifer Heslin
Megan Heuer
Rujeko Hockley
Ann Holcomb
Nicholas S. Holmes
Abigail Hoover
Jacob Horn
Ayyub Howard
Sarah Humphreville
Beth Huseman
Chrissie Iles
Gina Im
Carlos Jacobo
Zoe Jackson
Patricia James
Darnell Jenkins
Jesse Jenkins
Bailey Johnson
Vinnie Kanhai
Tracy Keenan
Chris Ketchie
David Kiehl
Thomas Killie
Elizabeth Knowlton
Elizabeth Kobert
Kathleen Koehler
Tom Kraft
Margaret Kross
Melinda Lang
Eunice Lee
Sang Soo Lee
Joseph Leib
Danielle Lencioni
Jen Leventhal
Christopher Lew
Ruth Lizardi
Kelley Loftus
Robert Lomblad
Kelly Long
Doug Madill
Elyse Mallouk
Claire Malloy
Erin Malone
Jessica Man
Carol Mancusi-Ungaro
Louis Manners
Joseph Marode
Anna Martin
Madison Martin
Heather Maxson
Patricia McGeean
Caitlin McKee
James McKnight
Michael McQuilkin
Sandra Meadows
Nicole Meily
Nicole Melanson

Sarah Meller
Bridget Mendoza
Conor Messinger
Graham Miles
David Miller
Lana Mione
Christie Mitchell
Matthew Moon
Lorryn Moore
Brancey Mora
Michael Moriah
Victor Moscoso
Lara Moynagh
Maggie Mugharbel
Sung Mun
Amelia Murcott
Rebecca Naegele
Eleonora Nagy
Daniel Nascimento
Ruben Negron
Randy Nelson
Tracey Newsome
Katy Newton
Carlos Noboa
Jaison O'Blenis
Brianna O'Brien Lowndes
Lindsay O'Connor
Kimie O'Neill
Rose O'Neill-Suspitsyna
Nelson Ortiz
Ahmed Osman
Eloise Owens
Nicky Ozir
Luis Padilla
Jane Panetta
Joseph Parise
Christiane Paul
Jessica Pepe
Natasha Pereira
Jason Phillips
Laura Phipps
Angelo Pikoulas
Elizabeth Plahn
Kathryn Potts
Eric Preiss
Eliza Proctor
Eric Pullet
Vincent Punch
Christy Putnam
Emma Quaytman
Julie Rega
Eduardo Restrepo-
    Castano
Gregory Reynolds
Omari Richards
Gene Riftin
Emanuel Riley

Felix Rivera
Manuel Rodriguez
Gina Rogak
Clara Rojas-Sebesta
Justin Romeo
Joshua Rosenblatt
Amy Roth
Scott Rothkopf
Sara Rubenson
Emily Russell
Isaiah Russell
Angelina Salerno
Laura Salomon
Leo Sanchez
Ximena Santiago
Galina Sapozhnikova
Lynn Schatz
Meryl Schwartz
Peter Scott
Michelle Sealey
David Selimoski
Aliza Sena
Jason Senquiz
Leslie Sheridan
Elisabeth Sherman
Adelina Simmonds
Dyeemah Simmons
Matt Skopek
Joel Snyder
Michele Snyder
Stephen Soba
Elizabeth Soland
Laura Solomon
Barbi Spieler
Carrie Springer
John S. Stanley
Mark Steigelman
Minerva Stella
Jennifer MacNair Stitt
Betty Stolpen
Emilie Sullivan
Denis Suspitsyn
Elisabeth Sussman
Daphne Takahashi
Jocelyn Tarbox
Melanie Taylor
Ellen Tepfer
Allie Tepper
Ashley Thimm
Latasha Thomas
Zoe Tippl
Ana Torres
Stacey Traunfeld
Sofia Trevino
Beth Turk
Lauren Turner
Matthew Vega

Ray Vega
Eric Vermilion
Billie Rae Vinson
Igor Vroublevsky
Farris Wahbeh
Rebecca Walsh
Jenyu Wang
Anteneque Webb
Adam D. Weinberg
Alexandra Wheeler
Clemence White
Ryan Witte
Andrew Wojtek
Sasha Wortzel
Madison Zalopany
Sefkia Zekiroski
Lily Zhou
Annmarie Zito
Nicolette Zorn

As of July 21, 2017

Monica De Cardenas, Milan/ Zuoz. Photograph by Andrea Rossetti. **473** Photograph by Laura Owens studio. **479** Courtesy the Norton Simon Foundation, Pasadena. **492–93** (foreground) Courtesy Laura Owens and Sadie Coles HQ, London. Photograph by Prudence Cuming Associates, London. **494–95** (background) Copyright © 1973 by Erica Wilson Kagan. Reprinted with the permission of Scribner, a division of Simon & Schuster, Inc. All rights reserved. **510** (foreground) Photograph by Fredrik Nilsen. **511** (foreground) Photograph by Fredrik Nilsen. **512** Photograph by Douglas M. Parker Studio. **513** Photograph by Douglas M. Parker Studio. **515** Photograph by Douglas M. Parker Studio. **516** Photograph by Charles Duprat. **517** (foreground) Photograph by Charles Duprat. **523** Photograph by Fredrik Nilsen. **532–33** (background) Photograph by Joshua White. **546–47** Photograph by Brica Wilcox. **554** Photograph by Fredrik Nilsen. **555** Photograph by Fredrik Nilsen. **556** (background) Photograph by Annik Wetter. **557** Photograph by Kate Hall. **561** (top) Digital image © The Museum of Modern Art, New York/Licensed by SCALA/Art Resource, New York. Photograph by John Wronn; (inset) Photograph by Laura Owens studio. **562–63** (foreground and background) Photographs by Jeff McLane. **566–67** Courtesy Capitain Petzel, Berlin. Photograph by Jens Ziehe. **568–69** Courtesy Capitain Petzel, Berlin. Photograph by Jens Ziehe. **570** (foreground) Photograph by Andrew Cannon; (background) Photograph by Jens Ziehe. **571** Photograph by Jens Ziehe. **572** (background) Photograph by Jens Ziehe. **580** Photograph by Jorit Aust. **581** (foreground) © Jill Greenberg; (background) Photograph by Jorit Aust.

582–83 Photograph by Jorit Aust. **584** Photograph by Jorit Aust. **585** Photograph by Jorit Aust. **586** (foreground) Photographs by Jorit Aust. **587** (foreground and background) Photographs by Jorit Aust. **588–89** (background) Photograph by Robert Chase Heishman. **590** (foreground) Photograph by Robert Chase Heishman. **591** Photograph by Robert Chase Heishman. **595** Photograph by Laura Owens. **596** (background) Photograph by Asha Schechter. **598–99** (background) Photograph by Tom Powel Imaging. **602–3** (foreground) Photograph by Johnna Arnold; (background) Photograph by Tom Powel Imaging. **604** (foreground) Photograph by Johnna Arnold; (background) Photograph by David Berezin. **605** (background) Photograph by Tom Powel Imaging. **606–7** (foreground) Photograph by Douglas M. Parker Studio; (background) Photograph by Calen Barca-Hall. **611** Courtesy the Whitworth Art Gallery, The University of Manchester. **613** Courtesy Library of Congress, Prints and Photographs Division, Washington, DC. Photograph by Jack Delano, March 1941. **616–17** Courtesy Laura Owens and Sadie Coles HQ, London. Photograph by Prudence Cuming Associates, London. **618** (background) Photograph by Prudence Cuming Associates, London. **619** Photograph by Prudence Cuming Associates, London. **620** (foreground) Photograph by Prudence Cuming Associates, London. **622–23** (background) Photograph by Prudence Cuming Associates, London. **640** (foreground) Photograph by David Berezin. **641** (foreground) Photograph by Asha Schechter. **Collateral image collection credits:** **64** (inset) Private collection. **86** (inset) Brooklyn Museum, gift of Mrs. Carll H. de Silver in

memory of her husband, 13.50. **90** (inset) Peter A. Juley & Son Collection, Smithsonian American Art Museum, Washington, DC. **95** Private collection, courtesy Galerie Max Hetzler, Berlin and Paris. **139** Van Gogh Museum, Amsterdam (Vincent van Gogh Foundation). **140** (top) Matthew Marks Gallery, New York and Los Angeles; (bottom) Collection of the Museum of Contemporary Art, Los Angeles. Installation view: *Felix Gonzalez-Torres: This Place*, Metropolitan Arts Centre, Belfast, Northern Ireland, October 30, 2015– January 24, 2016. Curated by Eoin Dara. **152** Courtesy the artist, neugerriemschneider, Berlin, and Gladstone Gallery, New York and Brussels. **153** Collection of Ellen and David Friedman, Los Angeles. **175** Collection of the artist. **283** Musée d'Orsay, Paris. **303** The Museum of Modern Art, New York; gift of Douglas S. Cramer Foundation. **304** National Gallery of Art, Washington, DC; gift of Anne and Joel Ehrenkranz, 2014.142.3. **342** (inset) The M. C. Escher Company–The Netherlands. **377** Courtesy of HathiTrust. **479** The Norton Simon Foundation, Pasadena. **611** The Whitworth Art Gallery, The University of Manchester. **613** Library of Congress, Prints and Photographs Division, Washington, DC. **Text and reprint credits: 22** Copyright © 1991 *Harper's Magazine*. All rights reserved. Reproduced from the December issue by special permission. **44** Republished with permission of Taylor and Francis Group LLC Books; permission conveyed through Copyright Clearance Center, Inc. **230** Reprinted by permission of the copyright owner, the Modern Language Association of America. **302** Copyright © 2003 by Francine Prose. All rights reserved. Reprinted with

permission of the Denise Shannon Literary Agency, Inc. **534** © Rachel Kushner. **608** Copyright © 2002 The Board of Trustees of the Victoria and Albert Museum, London. Reproduced by permission of the Victoria and Albert Museum. Gill Saunders asserts her moral rights to be identified as the author of this article.

Notes to the reader
With the exception of minor typographic and formatting corrections made for clarity and consistency, the texts of the previously published writings are presented without alteration. In selected cases, as noted in the works' titles, the texts have been excerpted by permission of the authors and/or publishers. Copyright notices appear on pages 662–63.

All works are by Laura Owens unless otherwise indicated.

This book was published on the occasion of the exhibition *Laura Owens*, organized by Scott Rothkopf, Deputy Director for Programs and Nancy and Steve Crown Family Chief Curator, Whitney Museum of American Art, New York.

Whitney Museum of American Art, New York
November 10, 2017–
February 4, 2018

Dallas Museum of Art
March 25–July 29, 2018

The Museum of Contemporary Art, Los Angeles
November 4, 2018–
March 25, 2019

Major support for *Laura Owens* is provided by The Andy Warhol Foundation for the Visual Arts and the Whitney's National Committee.

Significant support is provided by Nancy and Steve Crown; Candy and Michael Barasch; The Brown Foundation, Inc., of Houston; Mariel and Jack Cayre; Marcia Dunn and Jonathan Sobel; and Erin and Peter Friedland.

Generous support is provided by Fotene Demoulas and Tom Coté, Allison and Warren Kanders, Ashley Leeds and Christopher Harland, and anonymous donors.

Additional support is provided by Rebecca and Martin Eisenberg and Susan and Leonard Feinstein.

Generous endowment support is provided by Sueyun and Gene Locks, and Donna Perret Rosen and Benjamin M. Rosen.

Curatorial research and travel for this exhibition were funded by an endowment established by Rosina Lee Yue and Bert A. Lies, Jr., MD.

Significant support for the catalogue is provided by Galerie Gisela Capitain, Cologne; Gavin Brown's enterprise, New York; and Sadie Coles HQ, London.

Whitney Museum of American Art
99 Gansevoort Street
New York, NY 10014
whitney.org

Distributed by
Yale University Press
302 Temple Street
P.O. Box 209040
New Haven, CT 06520-9040
yalebooks.com/art

This publication was produced by the publications department at the Whitney Museum of American Art, New York (Beth A. Huseman, director of publications; Jennifer MacNair Stitt, editor; Beth Turk, editor; Anita Duquette, manager, rights and reproductions; and Jacob Horn, editorial coordinator) in collaboration with Laura Owens and her studio (Amy Baumann, David Berezin, Cindy Conrad, Katie Douglass, Kate Hall, Michael Henry Hayden, and Alix Ross).

Project manager: Elizabeth Levy
Editor: Amanda Glesmann
Photo editor: Asha Schechter
Oral history interviewer and editor: Asha Schechter
Designer: Tiffany Malakooti
Curatorial assistant: Jessica Man
Production: Nerissa Dominguez Vales and Sue Medlicott, The Production Department
Research: Anna Blum, Jacob Horn, Jessica Man, Diana Matuszak, and Micah Musheno
Typesetting: Julie Allred, BW&A Books, Inc.
Proofreader: Polly Watson

Printing and binding: Puritan Capital, Hollis, NH
Prepress: Altaimage, New York

Typeset in Arial and Times New Roman and printed on 70# Sappi Flo Gloss text

Printed and bound in the United States

Library of Congress Control Number: 2017025977
ISBN 978-0-300-23812-9

10 9 8 7 6 5 4 3 2

The first printing of this catalogue was published with the ISBN 978-0-300-22929-5 and featured a different cover.